Priests and Pastors

Felicity McNabb

Published by New Generation Publishing in 2022

Copyright © Felicity McNabb 2022

First Edition

The author asserts the moral right under the Copyright, Designs and Patents Act 1988 to be identified as the author of this work.

All Rights reserved. No part of this publication may be reproduced, stored in a retrieval system or transmitted, in any form or by any means without the prior consent of the author, nor be otherwise circulated in any form of binding or cover other than that which it is published and without a similar condition being imposed on the subsequent purchaser.

ISBN
    Paperback   978-1-80369-494-8
    Ebook   978-1-80369-495-5

www.newgeneration-publishing.com

 New Generation Publishing

Contents

1. FRENCH HISTORIC PRIESTS AND PASTORS II 1
2. NOUVEL FRENCH PRIESTS AND PASTORS.................. 4
   INTRODUCTION 10
   A STORY KNOWN INDIRECTLY 10
   PART ONE: OPPOSITE EACH OTHER, SIDE BY SIDE 26
   PART TWO: FACE TO FACE: MODELS AND COUNTER-MODELS 59
   PART THREE: CONTROVERSIES AND SERMONS......... 121
3. HISTORIC PRIESTS AND PASTORS 133
   DESCRIPTION OF WORK... 133
   PART ONE: OPPOSITE EACH OTHER, SIDE BY SIDE 155
   PART TWO: FACE TO FACE: MODELS AND COUNTER-MODELS 187
   PART THREE: CONTROVERSIES AND SERMONS......... 249
4. NEWEST FRENCH PRIESTS AND PASTORS.................. 261
5. NOUVEL FRENCH PRIESTS AND PASTORS.................. 317
6. NOVELLA PRIESTS AND PASTORS 323
7. NOVELLA PRIESTS AND PASTORS 420

1. FRENCH HISTORIC PRIESTS AND PASTORS II

It would be very suitable to establish trails of research by putting into correlation these restrained vocations and the number of apostates; unfortunately, we are tributaries of the sources which do not allow, in the territories studied, to issue conclusions. On the other hand, to become an apostate[1] implied, for the secular clergy, renouncing a benefice and/or a status.A simple formality for partisans of reformed ideas, a true obstacle for ecclesiastics to the "light" vocation and simply wishing to take a part of the conjugal theses of reformers.. Thus, the criminal files of the officialiities studied show this will not lead to lose one's position. On this matter, let us note that in 1614, Gilles Blaton, a priest in the town of Mons (Diocese of Cambrai), disturbed for the scandalous liaison that he had with his servant and penitent, replied to the promotor that he "has not left his state". Nor had he re-joined the Dutch, as he took one hundred thousand from his parish.

A second point, the men of the Church who wished to re-join the protestant movement and obtain a title of pastor underwent a type of "entrance exam" during which the old people of the consistories examined the certificates of good conduct that they could provide. When the witnesses were not promoters, these priests were sent back with a chaplain. In studying the deeds of the consistories kept in the national Archives, we find that there are 62% of habitual priests who make this request and their motivations are at 58% of material order. This same finding appears in the deeds of the Tournai consistory: among the requests made by ecclesiastics, 68% were habitual and out of the 68%, 41% see Protestantism more as a solution as a reply, as help. In order to illustrate this statistics, let us give the example of

---

[1]

an old habitual priest of the Tournai diocese. In 1607, Andre Fayt asked the members of the consistory to provide him with the means of learning "some honest vocation" as well as money. He cannot provide any certificate of good conduct and testimonies which were collected show a bawdy, debauched, person, a blasphemer, and a drunk who is then sent back with a fine of 2 ecus on account of "his bad habits" and the scandal that caused his wicked life"[2]. It is therefore obvious that the priests who have re-joined the protestant flocks have done so due to an extreme faith and not for matrimonial reasons, luxury and seduction being much less dangerous in the heart of a presbytery.

A conjugality influenced by the reformed ideas?

How did the spread of reformed ideas influence the position of southern Catholic clergy about marriage? If in "La correspondan[3]ce de Philippe II sur les affairs des Pays-Bas", we learn that in the States General of 1574, it is deplored that one "wanted priests and married clergy to hold the parish churches" to wish that the statistics of this influence are utopian as we only have scattered drawn from judicial procedures or local monographies. Nevertheless, in the light of these sources, it is possible to state that the rise of the Reformation is present, that it encourages some men of the Church to get married without thereby renouncing their office. On this matter, the example of a curate accused by the official of Cambrai in 1693 is revealing: after a promise of marriage, Guillaume Martin Genty and his friend, Laurent Thomas, took the road to Zuvol" a "Dutch town" (Zwolle, in fact in Overijssel) where, as in the rest of the United Provinces, the public Church is the Reformed church where everyone can get married, as is witnessed by the story of the wife stipulating that they would be married "in a place which passes for a church of their type, even though it may not be the church of the place". Having celebrated the marriage, Genty and his wife went back to

---

[2] AGR 1020 Great Council for Low countries Malines fol 56
[3] GACHARD L.P. "Grand conseil…Malines" registers fol 56

Cambrai where the married man of God continued his ministry, while fathering three children[4]. Analysis of most of the criminal files of officials studied enabled light to be shown on a period going from 1601 to 1789. In comparison, the study of the judjcial archives of the dioceses of Beauvais, Noyon, Chalons-en Champagne, Paris, Reims and Troyes has only inscribed one case[5] which means that 87.5% of married priests were such people in these dioceses, marked by reformed ideas and particularly near places where e marriage in the Calvinist public Church is allowed to everyone.

Finally, the depraved influence of the Reformation when, in examining a criminal file, we discover a priest regretting being unable to live conjugally and who witnesses, sometimes, to the official Nicolas Antoine, the priest of Soignies (Diocese of Cambrai) deploring the Catholic rigour, before concluding that he had to "leave the protestant lands in order to follow his vocation"[6]

---

[4] ADnorth 5G 516 Guillaume Martin Genty 1693.

[5] AD North Jean Dumenil 1711. Jean -Francois Poisier and Jean Dumenil

[6] AD North 5G 630 Nicolas Anthoine 1788.

2. NOUVEL FRENCH PRIESTS AND PASTORS

Translation Of "Priests And Pastors" Edited By Julien Leonard, Rennes University Press Isbn 978-2-7555-4905
Proposal From Felicity Mcnab
Title: "Priests And Pastors"
Subtitle: The Clergy In The Era Of Confessional Divisions Xvi-Xviith Centuries
florinda640@btinternet.com
TELEPHONE: 00441865841272 and 00447722387423
CV: attached

DESCRIPTION OF WORK

The confessional break which touched the Christian West in the 16th century permanently revolutionized the place of the clergy in societies and their influence on the faithful. The original principle of Lutheranism, then the Swiss reforms P of the universal priest was greatly relativized by setting up a progressive Protestant clergy, but it opened a breach that one can follow at the time of controversies and which continue to fix a fundamental difference between the two camps. However, the reciprocal and fundamental influences are observable in the areas of confessional co-existence; the spaces and frontiers can appear as privileged observatories to understand the reciprocal influences between the clergy, until in their way of interpreting and considering the pastoral ministry and forge their professional and social identities.

The training of clergy, their organization, their action, the oppositions to which they had to contend, their interactions, common points, even the sociability of their members are studied here through very diverse practices (preaching, conferences and controversies, studies, missions, institutional restriction, liturgical practices, suppression of deviation, or even definition of concurrent memories). These studies of the time plunge us into the process of definition of clerical identities which are certainly used against one another, but also, more subtly, in terms of the other and on common foundations.

TABLE OF CONTENTS
THANKS
ABBREVIATIONS

Julien Leonard – Introduction: the clergy at the time of confessional divisions, a story which is directly unknown. Reformation and Counter-Reformation co-existence practices. Edict of Nantes –training historiography – who are the "clergy"? Role of bishops – evangelical clergy.
Men of God and their influences. Discussions

PART ONE
IN FRONT OF THE OTHER, SIDE BY SIDE (1530-16)
ANNE BROGINI
CATHERINE BALLERIAUX

PART TWO
FACE TO FACE MODELS AND COUNTER-MODELS
LAURENT JALABERT - EMPIRE ARMIES
NICOLAS RICHARD - PROTESTANT INFLUENCES

Andreas Nijenhuis-Bescher
Claude Joly (1607-1700) inter-clerical travels in the 16th century

PART THREE
Controversies and sermons
Jeremie Fox – Don Quixote controversy
Clarisse Roche – sermon in, 17th century Vienna on co-existence
Stefano Siumiz – confrontation and sermons 16th and 17th centuries

Christabelle Thoun-Dieuaide
Sermons of Pierre du Moulin with Capuchins
Celine Borello – eloquent clerical contacts XVIIth century

PART FOUR
The French Laboratory
Philippe Moulis – Boulogne sur Mer XVI and XVIIth century
Sarah Dumortier Celibacy of clergy in west
Frederic Meyer - Franciscans in Burgundy, XVIth century
Frederic Meyer- Father Jacques Fodere
Estelle Martinazzo
Toulouse clergy v – Protestantism
Didier Boisson – Sancerre after the Edict of Nantes
Bruno Maes, Saumur Academy - 17th century orators

PART FIVE
CONSTITUTION OF CLERICAL IDENTITIES
Federico Zulani – is 16th century Italian Grisons
Nathalie Szczech – Calvin's Geneva 1540-1550
Genevieve Gross – The Geneva of Theodore de Beze
Irene Pasman-Labrune – Foreign pastors in France XVIIth century
Yves Krumenacker
Conclusions

INDEX

AUTHORS

Catherine Balleriaux – Doctor of religious history from the University of Auckland, New Zealand. Monograph: *Missionary Strategies in the New World 1610-1690*, Routledge, 2019.

Didier Boisson – Professor of Modern History, Angers University. *Les protestants de l'ancien colloque du Berry de la Revocation de l'Edict de Nantes (1679-1789* and *Les actes des synodes provinciaux*. Geneva, Droz, 2012.

Céline Borello – Modern History department at University of Haute-Alsace. *Les protestants de Provence au XVIIe* siècle"(2004) ."*Les oeuvres protestantes en Europe*(PUR, 2013).

Anne Brogini – Research master at University of Nice Sophia Antipolis. *Malte, frontiere de chrétienté 1530-1670* (Rome, 2006).

Sarah Dumortier – schoolteacher, Doctor at Lille University – ecclesiastical celibacy – religious history.

Jérémie Foa – alumnus of Ecole Normale Superieure de Fontenay-Saint-Cloud. *Le tombeau de la paix*.... Limoges, Pulim, 2015.

Genevieve Gross – Doctorate in Literature, Geneva University – francophone reformation. *Satire anticlericale au service de la Reforme"*. Paris, 2016.

Laurent Jalabert – Conference master at Lorraine University since 2008. *Catholiques et protestants sur la rive gauche du Rhin 1648-1789*, Brussels, 2009. Lutherans in Thirty Years War. *Dire et transmettre la foi* .... Paris, 2016.

Yves Krumenacker – Alumnus of École Normale Supérieure de Saint-Cloud (1977). Professor of Modern History at Lyons University, *Calvin: au-delà des légendes* Bayard, 2009.

Julien Leonard – Conference master, University of Lorraine – *Etre Pasteur au XVIIe siècle -Metz"* PUR, 2015. Thesis.

Bruno Maes – Conference master at Lorraine University. *Saint-Nicolas et les autres traditions*, 2011.*Dictionnaire de l'ancien regime*, 2004.

Estelle Martinazzo – Doctor of modern history. FRAMESMA – *Toulouse au Grand siècle 1590-1710*. Thesis.

Frédéric Meyer – Modern history professor, Savoy University (Chambery). *La foi des montagnes*.... (Annecy 2014)

Philippe Moulis – Doctor of Modern History, Artois University. Jansenism in Northern France. *Pierre de Langle et ses correspondents*. Paris, 2016.

Andreas Nijenhuis-Bescher. *Les voyages de Hollande – XVIIe siecle* and *L'abbaye de Saint-Maurice d'Agaune*, 2015. Editor of LODOCAT International.

Irene Plasman-Labrune – History alumna of Ecole Normale Superieure at Paris-Sorbonne Creteil 2015 "Favoriser, controller et exclure..age moderne (XV-XVIIe siècle).

Nicolas Richard – Doctor of History at Paris-Sorbonne and Charles de Prague. *"La clergéparoissial* due to appear in PUR.

Clarisse Roche – Doctor of History. La frontière incertaine…Vienne XVIe siècle". Thesis.

Stefano Simiz – Modern History professor, Lorraine University. Religious history: 16th, 17th and 18th centuries. *La parole publique en ville es Reformes*, Septentrion University Press, 2012. "La Renaissance en Europe…" 2015

Natalie Szczech, Conference master – French Polynesia University, 16th century Reformation *Calvin en polémique: une maieutique* Paris:Classiques Garnier, 2017

Christabelle Thouin-Dieuaide, Modern Literature, Limoges University. *Predication au XVIIe siècle.*

Federico Zuliani – bursary. "Georges et Pierre Regard" – Geneva University – *Rivista di Storia e Letteratura Religiosa.*

READERSHIP
This work will be of interest to all religious historians and particularly to those in religious colleges training for the priesthood in all denominations. It could be included in their history courses.

REVIEWERS
I would respectfully suggest that this work should be reviewed by Dr Diarmuid McCullough of Wycliffe Hall College in Oxford or his colleague Dr Atherton.

ABBREVIATIONS
AD   Departmental Archives
AEG   Archives of the State of Geneva

AGR	General Archives of the Kingdom of Belgium, Brussels
AM	Municipal Archives of the Inquisition of Malta, Malina (Malta)
AM	Municipal archives
AN	National Archives, Paris
AOM	Archives of the Order of Malta, Rabat (Malta)
ARSI	Romanum Societatis Iesu, Rome Archives
ASV	Archivio Segreto Vaticano, Vatican City
BM	Municipal library
BnF	National Library of France, Paris
ONB	Austrian National Library, Vienna
SHAG	Genevan Society of history and archaeology
SHD	Historic Society of La Defense Vincennes
SHPF	Society for the history of French Protestantism

INTRODUCTION

The clergy in the age of confessional divisions: for a comparative and decompartmentalised history

To devote a volume to the age of confessional divisions, to their contacts and the constitution of their identities, could seem to take up a beaten seam of historiography and to propose a balance sheet of research. For conservation reasons of sources and control of the proposed discussion by the communities, mainly in the areas marked by contacts and by coexistence, the pastors coming from various strands of Protestantism and Catholic clerks are directly at the root of the essence of our knowledge of new elements, studies of unknown cases, revised problems and viewpoints moved in relation to centres of interest in religious history of the latest decades, aiming to explain and emphasise certain reciprocal influences in the constitution of clerical identities, in a broad chronological perspective embracing both years of (re)construction after the bubbling of the Reformation, the affirmation of confessional identities, the "confessionalisation", without forbidding a look at the 18h century which, however was often seen as too late in this periodisation[7]. A typology of contacts between the clergy – and no doubt one would need a completely separate reflection on what these clergy were, for French historiography seems restive in using the plural – will enable research paths which a single volume obviously cannot claim to include, but rather favour and cause to develop.

A STORY KNOWN INDIRECTLY

The religious history of the time of confessional divisions was traditionally marked by the weight of its authors, often engaged themselves in a Church, aiming to underline the

---

[7] Büttgen, P And Duhamelle C. *Religion in Confession*. 2016

distinctive components. In this framework inbuilt at least until the 1960s, a form of apologetics fed into the historiography and was sure about pastors on the Protestant side and priests and bishops on the Catholic side as major actors, but always insisted on the discussion that they could develop for opposing the opposite side. From this perspective, contacts for the clergy are often limited to a study in terms of oppositions, conflicts and controversies. It is obviously not a question of throwing discredit on the history of those times today, for more recent works show at what point it is still possible to take out the elements required for our knowledge[8] and one will rely here on cases of head-on conflicts, even if that will be partly to show the reciprocal ambiguities and influences. But to restrain the contacts between the clergy to a single form seems to be very reductive. The historiographical turning point which saw the idea of "time of reforms" is an example, demolishing the traditional layout – "pre-Reformation – Reformation – Counter-Reformation" and scholars certainly relied on documents coming from the clergy and continued to study the clerical elite, but with a shifted perspective. The pastoral visits and synodal statutes are fundamental components of this historiographical renewal but one of the main aims was precisely the religious history of the Christian people, the laity as it was "lived"[9] [10]. However, the place of the clergy remains important, as witnessed by a great many passages of the monumental *Histoire du christianisme des origines a nos jours*[11]. Since

---

[8] See for example a historiographic point by Domnier,
B.*Histoire des controverses a l'epoque modern, une histoire des passion schriennes.* Bulletin dela shpp148-4 2002 pp.1055-1047.
[9]
[10] Delameau, J. *Histoire vecue du peuple chretien.* Toulouse, 1979.

the 1980s, the works of historians like Elizabeth Labrousse[12], Willem Frij[13]hoff,[14] or Robert Sauzet[15] have been taken up in broader syntheses[16]. In this sense, one of the more innovative aspects was to rely on[17] what Frijhoff qualified, for the Dutch case, of the "ecumenicity of daily life", which inspired a great many studies afterwards. Even if these founding works – for a long time doubtlessly unsurpassable – do not put the role of the clergy in the shadow and do not voluntarily hide their contacts, it is certain that the impression, perhaps simplistic, which comes from reading them is that the faithful co-existed while the "men of God" confronted each other and tried to discipline their flock. However, one should doubtlessly assess their double discussion, that is to say the discrepancy that can exist between their official vision of coexistence, that they generally condemn and in any case try to restrict as much as possible. and their practices, often difficult to see in the sources, of sociabilities, as I myself have been able to do with regard to the case of Metz in the 17th century[18]. In the Dutch case also, one re-assesses the debate between coexistence and confrontation, particularly in Utrecht where Bertrand Forclaz proposes developments in the role of the clergy without restricting oneself to the simple list of confrontations[19]. The fact is that the clergy oppose each other violently, especially through the bias of controversy. The list of publications and meetings makes one dizzy for the French case alone, under the regime of the Edict of

---

[12] """"Labrousse, E. *Conscience et conviction...* Paris. 1996.
[13]
[14] "Frijhoff, Willem. *Embodied belief...*, Hilversum, 2002.
[15] *Contre-Reform... e* Louvain, 1979.
[16] "Benedict, P.*Un roi, une loi, deux foi...* CUP, 1996.
[17] See Frijhoff, W. *Chretiente...* and Kaplan, B, *Divided by faith...*, Harvard 2007
[18] Leonard, J.*Les hommes de Dieu Chretiens et Societes – Documents et memoires* 2015, p.77.
[19] Forclaz, B.*Cathollliques au défi de la Réforme*. Paris 2014.

Nantes,[20] but this does not mean, on the contrary, that these contacts do not have as a result reciprocal influences in the constitution of clerical identities[21], were it not by rejection.

However, in some well-known areas, to study the clergy in a comparative view is a well-known completely pertinent step. The existence of converging disciplinary aims is already well known[22], even if the clerical action is different in the process of acculturation. Some works also show that on the field of training and instruction, common heritages going back to humanism bring Jesuits and Protestants together in France as Jean-Paul Pittion has shown[23], or abroad. Later the practices of learning are certainly settled in opposition on the field of history for example, little by little by the image of the "good pastor" in the Luthero-Calvinist world[24] which can be placed looking towards that of the "good priest" which emerges in the modern epoch[25]. Ian Green, on the English case, has already tried some connections in this field[26], but the years 1990 and 2000 are particularly marked by the works of Luise Schorn-Schutte which launch like a song the study of clergy in a resolutely comparative perspective[27] using a plural which still seems to inhibit francophone historiographic history;

---

[20] "Desgraves, L.*Repertoire des ouvrages...en France* Geneva 1984-1985. .

[21] Janse, W.*The formation of Clerical...identities*" Leyden, Brill 2006.

[22] Zinguer, I. *Les deux reformes chretiennes*. Leyden Brill.2004.

[23] Pittion, J.P.*Instruire et edifier...protestants...sous l'edit de Nantes*. Paris, 2011 pp. 19-45.

[24] Laplanche, F. *La controverse religieuse ...histoire* Paris, Crf 1995 pp. 373-404.

[25] Janse W. *The pastor bonus*... Leyden Brill, 2004.

[26] Bergin, J. *Between estate and profession.* London, Longman,1992.

[27] Schorn-Schutte L *The Christian clergy...Holy Roman Empire...Sixteenth century journal.* 1998 pp.717-731.

A point of historiographical controversy? What are "the clergy"?

The expression, used voluntarily, of "clergy" in the plural, can hinder and ask historiographical questions. It leaves an understanding – and this is in fact the aim – that there are Protestant clergy (in any case Lutheran and Reformed) and a Catholic clergy. One could even notice that the plural is usable and pertinent only for the Catholic world, in the measure where a study of the relations between the secular and the regular, and even between various internal categories to these great groups, can bring elements of reflection on the perspective which engages us here. The definition of the clergy and its members in the Catholic world is facilitated by the existence of a clear and recognised legal category, even if it is not always pertinent:– is a simple tonsured person really a clerk? But the idea of "clergy" for Protestants, whether it is general or for a special confession, may give rise to reserves and discussions. Its original reason for this is understandably the idea of the universal priest, developed by all the great reformers, which abolished the priesthood as a state of intercession between the faithful and God, but also in terms of a sacrifice and within the framework of the Mass. However, in order to struggle against some drifting towards the radicalisation of the universal priest, the same reformers and their successors have all insisted on the need for a pastoral body, formed, controlled and based on knowledge, which is only legitimate for interpreting the Scriptures, the unique foundation of the faith.

But the word "clergy" is not used in French, or very rarely and very marginally, to describe Lutheran or Calvinist pastors as a whole. The Protestants themselves are very prudent on questions of vocabulary; from the time of the reformers, they emphasise that the name given to the holders of different ministries is in the end rather indifferent, while explaining that the terms of bishops and priests were abandoned – in French at least – for practical reasons, especially to avoid confusion with ministries which had turned away from their original meaning as found with the Catholics. From Calvin's writing, the question is considered as secondary, not only because it is a point of ecclesiology and therefore not necessary for salvation, but also because the biblical passages are themselves rather vague on the words to use:

For the remainder, what I have named indifferently those who have the government of the Church, the Bishops, Pastors and Ministers: I have done it according to the use of Scripture, which takes all these words for one thing. For all those who are responsible for administering the word, they are called Bishops[28].

While Catholics try to deny as much as possible the title of "pastor" to preachers of Protestant doctrines, the most neutral term that the latter use is that of "minister". It is, according to its first sense, the one who serves. For most Protestants, the pastor was disputed in his own time; the famous Pierre du Moulin, defender of an episcopalian possibility, takes up a tradition which is already old, of assimilating between pastor, minister and bishop on the one hand, and elder and priest on the other hand, making it clear that the Catholics have completely distorted the words for bishop and priest and it is mostly for this reason that they have not deigned to give the name of "clergy" to Protestant pastors, even if Bossuet himself uses the name "clergy" for Protestant pastors in his sixth warning against Jurieu in 1691[29], but it is to mock them with irony. However, as the studies of Thierry Wanegffelen clearly show[30], it is truly a Protestant clergyman, not priestly however, which is constituted, without mentioning his name in order not to make the message of a universal priest unreadable, but

---

[28] Calvin, *Institution de la religion Chrétienne,* Geneva, Jean Crespin, 1560. p. 477

[29] Du Moulin, P. *De la vocation des pasteurs*, Geneva, Pierre Aubert, 1624.

[30] Bossuet, J.B, *Premier avertissement aux Protestants…* Paris, veuve Mabre-Cramoisy, 1689-1691 (part of sixth warning).

clearly defined by the ecclesiastical authorities in order not to lapse into the risk of total abolition of the clergy, as in certain Anabaptist communities and/or radicals. This clergy has academic foundations and takes its sources from the actual monopoly of the interpretation of biblical texts. This clericalization of Protestant parishes therefore fully legitimizes the use of the term "clergy", even if it remains rare in francophone historiography.

The idea of "Protestant clergy" and "clergies" in the plural and in a comparative perspective is relatively allowed among Anglo-Saxon historians, whose most recent works are those already quoted such as Luise Schorn-Schutte[31] but also with a sociologist like Celine Beraud who, in an article devoted to the clergy in the "Dictionnaire des faits religieux" does not forbid this comparatism[32]. Among French-speaking historians, the cases are rarer. One must certainly quote the important example of a part of the quoted "Histoire du christianisme", using this title in the plural[33]. But it is not insignificant to state that this editorial enterprise is presented explicitly as trans-confessional, even if a large part of its authors come from the disciplinary field of the study of Catholicism. At a low point, some works recognise the existence of this clergy by leaning on marks of anticlericalism[34]. But, generally, one may find more prudence among French-speaking historians of Protestantism, in spite of the already quoted distribution of the works of Thierry Wanegffelen[35]. From the 1970s, they had been preceded by the large thesis of State by Bernard

---

[31] See Wanegffelen, T. *Protestantism in France in XVII-XVIIIth centuries.*

[32] Baraud, C. *Clergy*. Azria, R .and Hervieu-Leger, D. *Dictionnaire des faits religieux,* Paris, PUF, 2010, pp. 152-157.

[33] Barrie-Curien, V and Venard, M. *The clergy*; *Le temps des confessions 1530-1560.*

[34] Krumenacker, Y."*L'Anticléricalisme intra-protestant (XVII-XVIII siecles.* Lyon, 2003.

[35] Ibid.

Vogler[36] and more recently a study by Veronique Castagnet on the Protestant clergy in Berne[37].But, in these two cases, it is a question of state clergy, who therefore belong to a rather special category. From this perspective, it is revealing that in a recent book comparing the German and French historiographies in some fields of religious history, the German historian, Manfred Jakubowski-Thiessen has used in his title the term "evangelical clergy" while the French Bernard Dompnier replies with an analysis of "people of the Church"[38] . But the latter expression may prove useful to the general extension of the clergy in some problems studied up to that point in relatively partitioned fields of study.

For a history of "men of God" and their reciprocal influences.

In Anglo-Saxon theory, the connection between anthropology and social history has already been considered in order to serve as a framework for a comparative study of clergy, with the idea of ending up with a "social biography" (Sozialbiographie) according to the historian Luise Schorn-Schutte[39]. Alphonse Dupront already referred in 1972 to a comparative study on this subject[40] but one must note that it is still only beginning. Thus, the thesis of Bruno Hūbsch, one of the rare works devoted to the subject, maintained in 1066, was only recently published, even if it is not interested

---

[36] Vogler, B. *Le clerge protestant rhenan au siècle de la reforme (1555-1619)*. Paris, 1976.

[37] Castagnet V. *Clerge protestant et clerge catholique face a...Bearne*Parlement(s)HS 6, 2010, pp. 29-43.

[38] Jakubowski-Tiessen, M. *Le clérge Evangéliqué dans les États territoriaux...*

[39] Schorn-Schutte L. *Das Predigtamtist nicht hose...Fruhen neuzeit*. Wiesbaden, 997[1997?] pp.-263-286.

[40] Dupront, A. *Vie et creation religieuse dans la France moderne:, XIV-XVIIIe siecle.* Gallimard, 1972 p 502.

in the clergy as such, but in theories of the ministry[41]. From this comparative perspective - which therefore that of this volume will be the most possible – one must detach oneself from some historiographic habits. Thus, the contributions proposed will not be confrontations between cases developed by historians of Catholicism and comparable cases studied by historians of Protestantism. A true speciality in the history of the clergy would no doubt be desirable, beyond confessional specialiities which surely have their legitimacy, but which lead to partitions risking perpetuation of the false image that one may have of relations between the clergy, especially from common sources. To study each clergyman from a confessional perspective certainly has its coherence that the sources organise and impose upon the historian, sometimes far from some realities which comparative research may relativise, by showing the existence of reciprocal influences on contact between the different clergy. If the latter term poses historiographical problems, as one has seen, one may also propose a comparative history of "men of God" to take up the title of a collective work in which Thierry Wanegffelen published one of his most convincing essays, and it is also the name of one of the axles of research of the team "Histoire des faits religieux" of the CRULI at the University of Lorraine. The idea that "people of the Church", this time in the plural, could also be called on in order to analyse the reciprocal relations and influences, including the constitution of clerical identities which are antagonistic a priori. In this decompartmentalization, one must also, doubtless, have an extensive definition of what the religious history must be, as Yves Krumenacker emphasises for pastors, with a statement which can be broadened to other areas and other clerical cases:

Thus, the opening of an overly strict history towards a vast cultural history must allow us to better understand the

---

[41] Hübsch B. "Le ministère de prêtres et des pasteurs…XVIIe siecle. Lyon 2010.

position that you the pastors can have in Protestant communities and, more broadly, in French society.

It is therefore in this renewed state of mind that researchers have offered their contributions. Chance has very happily made them come from authors at different times of their reflections or their works, giving at the same time an attraction of balance for sure, of research perspectives for others. A typology of contacts between the clergy in the constitution and consolidation of their identities will guide the reflections. We shall see particularly what the forms and the constitution of models are, usually in frontal opposition, but with inevitable exchanges and influences. From a very broad spatial perspective, we shall first of all observe what the attitudes are when the clergy find themselves confronting an alterity which is radical for all Christians whether it be in front of Muslims in Malta (Anne Brogini), or confronting native populations to evangelise in North America (Catherine Balleriaux). In these instances one can actually follow particular contacts, especially because they are geographically distant from centres of ecclesiastical decision. More classically, the models can also create forms which are sometimes less simple than what one may imagine: if in the 17th century it is a question of standing out, however, there remain areas of direct contact and influences, such as in the armies in the Germanic world, especially those of the Circles, with chaplains of different confessions (Laurent Jalabert). With the case of Claude Joly, a French canon who travelled to the United Provinces in the middle of the 17th century, one can notice the peculiarities of this state in relation to the confessional, but one must play the part of the religious dialogue of this canon with other men of God – a rare dialogue in this period – and which comes from sociability, properly proving that the cultural composts are close (Andreas Nijenhuis-Bescher). Earlier in the process of building confessional and therefore clerical identities, there are meeting areas, from which it is certain some elements will be drawn, as one may see by leaning towards the complex religious history of the Archdiocese of Prague at the end of the 16th century, where the clergy are, however, doubtless more often ignorant than influenced (Nicolas Richard),

We shall later see r a series of contributions more directly devoted to two central identities at the heart of the clergy: preaching and controversy. In these cases, it is more a question of being constituted in opposition, even if the work of Stefano Simiz shows exactly that there are points of reciprocal convergence and influences on the way of considering the sermon, and even in the manner of preaching. Already earlier, in the case of Vienna in the time of Maximilien II (1564-1576), reciprocal influences and a unique model, Christian and trans-confessional, are favoured in the field of preaching; however, this is in the specific context of the Ottoman threat and the conciliatory will of the sovereign (Clarisse Roche). But even in the case of controversy, the exchanges are more complex than they appear. Jérémie Foa has already analysed the controversy from the Wars of Religion as a means of constituting clergy who are only legitimate in explaining the dogma of both sides [42] the laity of the disputes reduced to simple passive spectators[43], and here he offers us the revealing case of Théophile Cassegrain. If at the end of the 16th century and the beginning of the 17th century a layman like Philippe Duplessis-Mornay was able to appear as a recognised theologian – including in opposition to professional theologians[44] – the pastoral monopoly is clearly affirmed afterwards. But the strictness of the confessional frontiers between the clergy does not mean that the influences disappear; on the contrary, the presence of Catholic controversies in the Protestant churches in France under the regime of the Edict of Nantes can considerably mark

---

[43] Foa, J. *Aujourd'hui, les disputes...* Septentrion University Press, 2012, p. 150.

[44] Daussy, H. *En debatant la religión...* 2004, pp. 93-103.

reformed preaching, as shown in the case of the famous Pierre du Moulin, who speaks from the pulpit before the Capuchins in 1640 (Christabelle-Thouin-Dieuaide). From a completely different perspective and in a radically different context, the French reformed preachers in the 18th century are still influenced by models of eloquence which are a priori out of their confessional field (Celine Borello).

A large part of attention will be concentrated on France, as much for practical as scientific reasons; in fact, it is a geographical area which knew, at different times in its history in the modern era, contrasting forms of confessional coexistence and therefore of contact between the clergy, both Catholic and Reformed. We shall therefore see that in sensitive areas, particularly on the political and confessional frontier, these "frontiers of Catholicity" that Pierre Chaunu brought to light[45], where contacts between the clergy depend on factors which are sometimes particular: in the north of the kingdom, in the dioceses of Boulogne-sur-Mer and Saint- Omer, it is the Franco-Spanish war or even the proximity of the English which generates reciprocal influences (Philippe Moulis). In a close area, Sarah Dumortier shows us that in the specific case (but actually emblematic of the celibacy of priests,) the clerical contacts play an equally important role in the definition of a stricter standard, and they are capable of replying to the challenge of the existence of a clergy of married men and that of the proximity of the United Kingdom. The world of regulars is also transformed by the proximity of pastors or "heretics" – but their divisions are sometimes stronger than the will to struggle together against them, as Frederic Meyer shows, from a memorial reconstruction of the Wars of Religion by the Franciscan observer Jacques-Fodere, who fought the Protestants, the Capuchins and the Recollets all at the same time. This internal differentiation from what one could describe as "Catholic clergy" in the plural against the

---

[45] Chaunu, P. *Jansénisme et frontière de catholicite* " Revue historique, 1962, p. 115.

Protestants is also observed between the secular and regulars, as in Toulouse in the 17th century, where the absence of Protestant clergy does not mean that controversy was absent from the definition of local clerical identities ((Estelle Martinasso). Cases of daily coexistence under the regime of the Edict of Nantes will also be developed, with contacts between pastors and Catholic ecclesiastics, either at Sancerre, which is known thanks to various synodal sources (Didier Boisson) or at Saumur (Bruno Maes), the latter case being particularly sensitised by the proximity of a reformed academy, training future pastors around an active centre of 17th century Calvinist theology, and a college of orators dynamised by the pilgrimage to Notre-Dame des Ardilliers.

A last part will be devoted to the various strategies of developing clerical identities, always from a comparative perspective and to research into reciprocal influences, as we will have seen already in the previous contributions. Through the example of the experience of pier Paolo Vergerio in Vicosoprano in the years 1549-1554, one sees a pastoral model which is still hesitating between the Zwinglian tendencies in preaching, heritages from Bullinger, that also Catholics, with the episcopate, which moreover places it in a certain proximity with Lutheranism (Federico Zuliani). The Genevan case will be particularly scrutinized by Nathalie Szczech and Genevieve Gross, who are interested in the first signs of development of a reformed pastoral responsibility in the years 1530-1560 and the definition of its contours of exercising discipline in the 1570s respectively, leading to the constitution of a true clergy, which is necessarily influenced by the proximity of the political and confessional frontier with France. This series of studies will be concluded by a reflection on an unrecognised subject, doubtless due to the discretion of actors and the rarity of sources, that of the presence in France, especially under the regime of the Edict of Nantes, of foreign reformed pastors whose relations with the royal power are rich in teaching about problems in which we are interested (Irene Plasman-Labrune).

Perspectives of discussions and research

As understood, the present volume will not have the pretention of brushing aside the whole of questionings within this field of research, and there are plenty of works to be undertaken or comparisons to make. At least five general questions which are not the subject of a specific contribution should be at the heart of reflections. One must firstly refine the chronology of the constitution of clerical identities and reciprocal influences that can be observed, the foaming of the boiling-up Reformation doubtless without tracks. But then there are two movements, already emphasised by researchers, which may seem contradictory from the perspective of the objectives of our reflections: in fact, if one looks properly, after the works of Thierry Wanegffelen, that depict a form of the clericalization of Protestant pastoral bodies, one may also interpret some developments linked to the application of decisions by the Council of Trent as a form of priestliness of the Catholic clergy, which would thereby maintain an ontological difference with the Protestants[46]. But one must not lose sight of the fact that if one reaches such modelling by studying standard texts, one must relativise them in daily life, inevitably difficult to see in the sources.

One must then question the spatial differentiations, on different scales, in the emergence of clerical identities. The urban world is naturally better known from the sources, but are there proximities between the clergy or privileged contacts in relation to the countryside? Bernard Moeller showed already in 1972 that a part of clerical identities could blossom in terms of bourgeois contexts[47]. Did the new worlds, by their distance from centres of authority, constitute a particular melting pot? The over-representation

---

[46] See for example BERAUD C."Clerge(s) art, cit.
[47] MOELLER B."Kleriker als Burger" Gottingen 1972 p 195.

of France in the cases that we shall study here must not allow us to forget national differences, or, on the contrary the existence of trans-frontal areas whose features would be comparable, such as the "Catholic Spine[48]" already defined by the works of Rene Taveneaux and today at the heart of a research programme financed by ANR[49].

Internal and external structures must also be specified. With the Catholics, contacts between regular clergy and the secular members, even between different regular orders, can play a basic role in re-structuring, and we shall see thiswith the contributions of Anne Brogini, Estelle Martinazzo and Frederic Meyer. Among the reformed churches there is a question of the definition of the limit between clergy and laity. In terms of perspectives, the pastors could in fact be considered as laity and, on the contrary, holders of other ministries, elders and deacons, could be seen as clerks. However,[50] a true limit is marked, which is seen by the fact that in French, "the minister" is the pastor. The other members of the consistory, elders and deacons, are in fact laity, even if some authors may qualify consistories and synods (where elders and deacons sit) as "collective clerks". The question could also be pertinent in Catholicism, where the hierarchy of the minor and major orders also poses the problem of adequation with social reality: who is socially seen as a member of the clergy? Have not the contacts between the clergy contributed to generate a type of "between ourselves", in each field, but also at a global level, which then gave rise to opposition on the part of the laity? Are the clerical figures and the identity of the clerks built independently, or in rejection of whatever is the status of

---

[48] Wanegffelen, T.*Le protestantisme en France* op.cit., p. 135.
[49] Meyer, F.*La Dorsale catholique*. Paris, Riveneuve, 2013, p. 321
[50] Wanegffelen T. *Le protestantisme en France XVIe -XVIIe siecles*. op.cit, p.135.

the laity? Is the aim to shake oneself off from them?[51] That would come back to ask "in fine" the question of anticlericalism and resistances to clerical acculturation, often close to the Catholics and Protestants, a question which was also dear to Thierry Wanegffelen, from a comparative perspective[52], and Nathalie Szczech shows for Geneva all the interest in leaning on this field. But one may also try to bring together the figures of the pastor and the priest when it is a question of controlling social conflicts[53].

Relations between the clergy and the ecclesiastical authorities are important in the constitution of coherent and shared identities, and often converge, necessarily influencing the birth of a solidarity connected with national texts or relations with the secular authorities, and Irene Plasman-Labrune shows this well. In fact, the next question to deal with is that of the relationship between power and influences in the circulation of models of clergy in the service of politics. Thus one could imagine some comparisons between existing works on the idea of the court clergy, for example those, while more than half a century distant, of Rudolf von Thadden on Brandeburg-Prussia and Benoist Pierre on France[54]. Obviously, all these questions are not exhaustive. The understood aim is that all these presented works give rise to reflections which will last a long time, between the contributors to this work and, let us hope, beyond.

---

[51] Domener B. "Laic", .Hervier-Leger and Azria, *Dictionnaire des faits religieux.* pp. 616-620.

[52] Wanegffelen, T. *L'anticlericalisme croyant...* "Annales de l'est", 2009, pp. 59-80.

[53] Bonzon, A. "Les cures mediateurs.." *Revue d'histoire de l'Eglise,* no.238,2011, p 35.

[54] von Thadden, R *Die Brandenburgisch...* Berlin,1959.

PART ONE

OPPOSITE EACH OTHER, SIDE BY SIDE

A regular clergyman on the Christian Frontier- The Order of Malta in the time of Reforms (1530-16)

Anne Brogini

Appearing towards 1070[55], transformed into a religious-military order in the context of the Crusades, the Hospitalers of Saint John of Jerusalem, better known by the name of the Order of Malta, are an international order made up from the Middle Ages from eight nations called "Languages" (France, Auvergne, Provence, Italy, Castile, Aragon, Germany, England) with more than 700 commanderies situated in Catholic Europe and an overseas convent which knew successive establishments, which were inherent to the military destiny of the order: Jerusalem, County of Tripoli, Cyprus, Rhodes, then Malta (1530-1798).

The religious history of the military orders constitutes a new construction [56] in European historiography, and its interest particularly keeps the specific problems in their conventual life, and in the manner in which the brothers manage to conciliate a monastic identity with their membership of the nobility and with their warring activities. The religious approach is also indissociable from charity and hospitality, which a number of them practice, and from a study of women in orders which are essentially masculine, but which accept sisters[57]. Apprehension of spirituality of the brothers presumes the study of the rules which govern them, forms of individual and collective devotion, pious

---

[55] Riley-Smith, J. *The Knights Hospitaller...c.1050-1309.* Palgrave Macmillan, 2012.

[57] [or De Avala Martinez?] Avala Martinez, C. *Practica religiosa e espiritualidad militar*. Palmela. GEOS,2012, pp. 135-138.

foundations and acts of charity, intellectual and religious education of novices, eventual pastoral responsibilities that the brothers take on in frontier lands where they are transplanted and religious teaching that they impose on societies placed under their authority[58]. It is interesting to project these interrogations onto the reality of the Order of Malta at the beginning of the modern era, when the Protestant and Catholic Reforms are breaking up, then restore Protestantism and on the suppression of the Language of England. The newly-found unity of the brothers going through a post-Tridentine religious renewal was the subject of a great many works,[59] which make it possible to seize in the best way the transformations of the convent, marked by a spiritual renewal based on stricter observance of the rule, on the foundation in the port of Malta of female monasteries, and on a renewal of hospitable practice which is close to what can be seen at the same time in the Italian peninsula[60].

The monastic order in a double crisis

The first half of the 16th century constitutes a difficult period for the Hospitallers of Saint John of Jerusalem, placed in a position of military defeat after the successive losses of Rhodes in 1522, which was taken away from them by the Sultan Suleiman, and by the capture of Tripoli in 1551, which had been given to them by Charles V in 1559, at the same tjme as Malta. Soiled by the cumulative loss of the nobility and the crusades, the knights lived sorrowfully through the separation from Muslim lands that their double eviction from Rhodes and Tripoli imposed on them: within

---

[58] De Avala Martinez C. *Espiritualidad y practica religiosa....*J.C. Ferreira Fernandes *As Ordens militares...* pp. 139-172.

[59] Venard, M.*Le temps des confessions" (1530-1620*) Paris, 1992.

[60] Henderson, J. *The Renaissance Hospital*. New Haven: Yale University Press, 2006.

thirty years, the Hospitllers found themselves separated from the Holy Land, but also expelled from Barbary, where in 1548 they had hoped to establish a convent in order to found there a Latin state in Africa in order to defend the frontier of Latin Christianity [61], according to the historic vocation of religious-military orders. These two defeats shook its identity as a religious-military order characterised by a mediaeval definition of nobility, which still prevailed in the early 16th century in France and generally in Europe, where nobility remained indissociable from warring virtues, from victory and from renown[62]. The losses of Rhodes and Tripoli reflect a general backing down of the Christian frontier in the Mediterranean in the middle of the 16th century, driven back towards the west and towards the north by the Turkish and barbaric pressure[63]. Added to the loss of the hospitaller role there is the warring stain, the geographical distance of the Levant making it difficult to practice the vow of aid to Christian pilgrims going towards the Holy Places.

The suppression

Threatened by an unfavourable Mediterranean context, the Order is also the victim of an internal crisis, following the example of Christianity which at the same time is receiving a double threat: external (Turkish pressure in the Balkans) and internal (the Protestant break). Migration towards the west and their facilities near the European bank face and connect the Hospitalers with Reformation ideals which are [64]stirring up Christianity, while the secularisation of the

---

[61] Brogini, A. and Ghazali, M. "Un enjeu espagnole in Mediterranée" – *Cahiers de la Mediterranee*, t . 70-1, 2005, pp. 9-43.

[62] Schalk, E. *"L'épé, et le sang. Une histoire du concept...* Seyssel, Champ Vappon, 1996, pp. 13-14.

[63] Brogini A. *L'Ordre de Saint-John de Jerusalem ...XVIe siecle* Fuess, A. and Heyberger, B. La frontiere méditerranéen ... Turnhout, Brepols, 2013, pp. 163-180.

[64] Le Gall, J.M. *Les moines au temps des Reformes* op. cit.

greater part of the assets of the Teutonics, after the conversion of their Grand Master to Lutheranism in 1525, is witness to the danger t[65]hat the new ideas represent for the Hospital[66]. Throughout the 1530s, several languages are affected in Malta by religious quarrels. The troubles broke out firstly in England, where duels and brawls for religious reasons broke out regularly[67].The Council of the Order is also affected by tensions from the turcopole (defender of the Order against attacks between 1537 and 1539[68]). Then in 1540, King Henry VIII confiscated the Order's assets in his kingdom and suppressed the same title as a large part of German and English nobility to the secularisation of the Church's lands, almost all the English brothers (23 out of 27) abandoned the convent to go back to their own country, in spite of a ban issued by the Council in 1451[69].

The suppression of the Language of England accelerated the spread of reformed ideas in the insular society and in the convent, weakly affecting German monks who were small in number, and more strongly the French. In 1536, a French servant of arms was deprived of his habit for having adhered to Luther's ideas, while in 1542, posters were put up on the door of the conventual church of Birgu[70] and the Bishop of Malta conducted an enquiry within the population to find the culprits and several of them were condemned for heresy in 1544[71]. In 1546, a French chaplain, Fra Francois Gesuald, preached reformed ideas in his turn and gathered the laity

---

[65]

[66]Josseband, P. *L'Ordre de Sainte-Marie des Teutoniques*. De Avala Martinez, C. *Le Gloire de la Croix"*.Paris, Menges, 2005, pp. 167-183.

[67] AOM, Liber Conciliorum 5, fol. 140 v 13 November, 1534.

[68] O'Malley, G. *The Knights Hospitaller of the English Language" 1460-1565*, Oxford, OUP 2005 pp. 215-216.

[69] AOM. LC. Fol. 12 January, 1541.

[70] Ibid.,fol. 51r, 13.12.1536.

[71] AOM, LC 87, fol. 43, 1.09.1544.

around him⁷². After being condemned to two years in prison in 1550⁷³, he started preaching again in the port, until his new sentence led to him losing his habit and being burnt at the stake for heresy in 1554⁷⁴. In the 1550s, careful of the broadness of the phenomenon, the Grand Master decreed that the number of clerks and laity who had adhered to the Reformation should be listed in an inventory⁷⁵ and the Council demanded severe control of entry into the galleries in the port area, so as to burn every Protestant work which might be on a ship⁷⁶. Grand Master Jean de la Valerte (1557-1568) hoped to be invested with an inquisitorial power within his order and with the harbour company but Pope Pius IV preferred to give the responsibility to the bishop in 1561 before setting up a court of the Roman Holy Office independent of the Order in Malta, in 1574,

The disappearance of the Language of England and the near totality of English brothers, enquiries conducted within the Hospital and exclusions from the convent pronounced against all French monks attracted by the Reformation until the 1560s, have two essential consequences for the Order. Firstly, its reunification around a presumed Catholic identity which is based especially on the loss of Tripoli in 1551, on a revival awakening in Spain in the holy war against Islam; then, the strengthening of its Mediterranean anchorage by the indisputable preponderance of the southern European nations. Of the two "Nordic" Languages which were already minorities before the 16th century, one was suppressed in 1540 and the other one, the Language of Germany, held little weight in the convent, both in the number of brothers and in terms of a political role. From the second half of the 16th century, the domination of the

---

[72] BM Aix-en-Provence ms1094 "Relations de l'inquisitori", undated.
[73] AOM, LC 88 March 1550.
[74] AOM, LC 52, 28.03.1554
[75] AOM, LC 4 May 1553
[76] AOM, LC 91, 16.03.1562

Italian, Spanish (Castile and Aragon) and French Languages therefore became considerable. This hegemony was based on their country and their members– although the French context was more ambiguous – and they were going to make an effort to apply themselves within the convent, by a wish for religious renewal and by an attached will for the Order of Malta to take root indefinitely in Mediterranean history.

The Order transformed by the Catholic Reformation

The wish for reform is broadly shared by the monastic orders of Christianity: the brothers aspire to it, without necessarily agreeing with each other on the manner of conducting the religious renewal[77]. In Malta, brothers and Languages make their aspirations go further with the Council through the bias of "lists" (suggestions made up of several carefully written pages) which reflect a thirst for renewal between the years 1570-1589.

In 1578, the Grand Master Jean de la Cassiere (1572-1581) witnessed the religious fervour of its author and a deep wish to return, within the convent, to a purified Catholic practice[78]. A reflection of the decisions of the Council of Trent, the programme of La Cassiere plans to insert the Order into a re-defined clerical model, within which monks, priests and bishops must master the dogma perfectly, in order to teach it to the faithful and laity in a better way. They are trained, within the framework of the establishment in the second half of the 16th century, of a re-defined Catholic education which hitherto was ruled by laws which were uniform in Europe, which are applied by everyone and only differ by the diversity of charismas and pedagogic practices which were suitable for each of the orders and congregations who were responsible for spreading knowledge[79]. La Cassiere thus offers to come

---

[77] Le Gall, J.M. *Renover l'Eglise catholique…* op..cit., p.66.
[78] ASV SS Malta,103, fol. 216r, 30.11.1578.
[79] Fragnito, G. "Gli ordini".op.cit., p 181 .

back to the "holy institution of the Collachium" which, in Rhodes, separates the knights and laity by walls. The Council of Trent has in fact debated monastic closing off, and within the area of discipline, revoked the "licentia extra standi" granted to monks, that is to say the faculty to live outside the convent in order to study or carry out an office near a lord's court or a private family; the obligation for religious closure was thus restored, and even more severely for monasteries[80]. Other lists insist on the need to teach chaplains and to no longer accept monks who do not know Latin and the rudiments of the Catholic religion[81], and to use military service to prevent the idleness of novices [82] and to fight their bad habits with spiritual exercises and a generally stricter management[83].

All these lists stick to decisions made by the Fathers of the Council of Trent, who were attached to improving the image of priests and their teaching and management duties. The "cura animarum" being the foundation of the Church, one must be certain of the good training of priests and regularity of their customs. On the model of a religious reform carried out in the Iberian and Italian peninsulas, by Archbishop Borromeo in Milan and by Bishop Gabriel Paleotti in Boulogne, provincial councils gathered in Europe, as in France where, from the end of the Wars of Religion, the episcopate becomes a powerful home of the Catholic Reformation in the campaigns[84].

Added to the wish of the brothers there is a manifest desire in the matter of the power to renew the convent. Between 1647 and 1650, 91 prescriptions were taken to

---

revue historique" 660 2011 p814-815.

[80] Zarri, G. "La clôture des religieuses et les rapports de genre…" Clio,Histoire no 26 297 p 38-39.

[81] AOM. Ruoli presentati ai Capitoli Generali 310 fol. 74r, 2.05.1612.

[82] Ibid., fol. 92v, 2.05.1612

[83] Ibid., fol.,107r, 2.05.1612.

[84] Brunet, S. *Les pretres de campagnes …XVIe siecle*. 234 2007 50

recall the five vows of the Hospitallers (obedience, chastity, poverty, hospitality, holy war). Obedience.is the subject of 60% of the magistral prescriptions in a century, followed by hospitality (17.5% of prescriptions), poverty, (12%), the holy war and chastity (5% each). The period following the closure of the Council of Trent (1560-1600) is the most concerned by the recall of monastic rules, with about sixty prescriptions, while the later period (1600-1650) is only the subject of about thirty prescriptions. Following the example of lavish laws taken by the religious powers and European politicians in the time of the Renaissance and the Catholic Reformation, in order to define the clothing codes and to ban ostentatious luxurious habits, social and sexual markers par excellence, prescriptions voted in by the Council and to recall the poverty of the brothers. Clothing in any colour other than black or a dark fabric is forbidden and all fabrics that are not cotton (velvet, silk, gold or silver thread)[85]. Accordingly, the noble knights were reluctant to abandon fashionable habits and in 1631, a knight complained to the Council that:

…the young nobles are wearing bright colours, and costly fabrics, habits trimmed with lace and embroidery and have hairstyles of such an extravagant and effeminate nature, that some of them are more like comedians or foreign actors than monks[86].

Food excesses were also condemned, linked less to greediness of the Knights than to the customs of an aristocratic life based on the maintenance of clients: the daily ration of wheat for the knights is thus fixed at six loaves[87]. Games of chance are the subject of the most merciless disapproval: not only is chance forbidden by the Church, but the possibility of financial gains goes against the usual abstention by monks. If in 1551, condemnation for having played cards or dice is "quarantined" (forty days'

---

[85] AOM LC 91, 4.4.1562. 14.02.1567.
[86] AOM Ruoli presentati ai Capitoli Generali 12.05.1631.
[87] AOM LC 92 fol. 100v, 26.12.1572

fasting, broken once a week by dry bread[88])[89] the sanction from that time is maximum, the brothers being liable to privation of the habit. Then, from the 1570s all amusements were prohibited; then in 1574, for having played ball in the streets of La Vallette, the knights are condemned to the loss of a year of seniority[90]; in 1582, hunting is forbidden around the harbour[91]; in 1588 the game of straw-mesh was banned, as it caused quarrels between brothers[92].

The rules relating to the vow of obedience are even stricter. In 1554 and 1577, the brothers are seen to recall their duty to eat in silence and to prove respect for obedience to the head (leader of the Language). It is forbidden to laugh, make jokes, mock another brother, to swear, to speak about "immoral or dishonest" things, to play with one's hands, with dice or cards[93]. The need to attend Mass is regularly emphasised: in 1551 a decree constrains the brothers to assemble in the church[94] at the time of Mass and in 1567 and 1568, to be attentive there, that is to say they are no longer to stroll around in the church while chatting, or play cards, or dice, even to play ball during the service[95].

Legislation on carrying arms is plentiful and raises the question for Knights of their double monastic and noble identity. Firstly, arms are forbidden at night, in 1551 and 1553, in order to fight against aggressions occurring between monks or meeting the laity[96]. They are then limited in number during the day, in the wake of the Council of Trent which, recalling the tradition of the Church, forbade

---

[88] AOM LC 97 fol. 114, 9.11.1587
[89] AOM LC 88 fol.107, 3.02.1551.
[90] AOM LC 94 fol. 18, 7.08.1574.
[91] AOM LC 96 fol. 86, 20.11.1582.
[92] AOM LC 89 fol. 105, 07.1554
[93] AOM LC fol. 18 5.07.1554.
[94] AOM LC 88 fol. 139, 22.12.1551.
[95] AOM LC 88 fol. 50, 30.12.1567.
[96] Gay, J.P. "La theologie morale dans le pre.." *Histoire economie et societe* 24-2 2005.

duels[97]. In 1562, Knights leaving on a journey only have one weapon, a sword and two arquebuses[98]. In 1568 the monks could no longer keep pistols, arquebuses and other firearms at home[99]. In1569 they no longer had the right to use white weapons[100]. Only the sword is authorised for it is a sign of the social status of the Knights; but in 1581, even if the Knights can carry their sword at their side, they forbidden to use it[101]. And from 1645, only the gesture of wearing a sheathed hand in the street could lead to losing four years of seniority in the Order[102].

These decrees favour a remarkable reduction in violence, after a great rise between 1530 and 1570, then stabilisation around one physical aggression per day for twenty years (1570-1590). The violence decreases to stabilise itself towards 1620 to a threshold which is identical to that of 1530 (fifty deeds per decade). A similar development is noted in Europe[103], linked to the effects of the Catholic Reformation, which strengthened the self-control of individuals, and a social development where the defence of the group fades out gradually before individual interests. By these sanctions, which restrict spontaneous noble reactions, in addition to religious instruction, which seeks to reform the customs of the brothers, the Catholic Reformation pushes the knights to reason from the end of the 16th century as members of an order which was religious rather than social. Beyond their family, and their parentage, it is the Hospital which becomes their reference group, the honour of which must be doubly defended: by monastic behaviour according to the renewal undertaken, as

---

[97] Ibid.,
[98] AOM LC 91 fol.74, 21.07.1562
[99] AOM LC 92 fol.67, 2.04.1568.
[100] Ibid., fol.117 12.01.1569.
[101] AOM LC 95 fol.2752, 9.08.1581.
[102] AOM LC 115 fol. 62, 23.07.1645.
[103] Nassiet, M. *La violence, une histoire sociale...* Seyssel, 2011.

a Christian militia taking a maritime path which enables masculine violence to be channelled.

For all that, the new austerity governing the convent between 1560 and 1566 does not create unanimity. Desertions from the convent were rising in the years 1560-1570, essentially connected to Protestantism and to the French Wars of Religion; then, after 1590, they suffered a new rise, at the time when the Catholic Reformation was expressed most strongly in the convent (1590-1610) before reducing and stabilising around forty desertions per decade.

An unexpected consequence of the Catholic Reformation, the desertions are a phenomenon which only affects Malta. The men of the Church become rarer in the French noble families of the 17th century[104], the Catholic Reformation re-establishing a way of life which was so exacting that it seems incompatible with the lack of religious vocation. For the Order of Malta, the stakes are important: it is about preserving its prestige beside European noble families and to continue to attract young people who expect to follow a military, even political career, and to receive regular income which presumes ownership of commanderies. Therefore, partially and officially strictly respecting the vows of poverty, chastity, and obedience, were difficult to reconcile with a noble state into which the Order cannot pass as it constitutes one of the pillars of its identity, the convent necessarily develops in the 17th century towards an austere life, where bending the rules is less severely condemned. In 1630, the novices receive official authorisation to re-create themselves by betting small sums of money in dice and card games[105]; in 1637, the Knights gain more popularity in the Inns[106], while

---

[104] Bourquin, L. *La noblesse du XVIIe siècle...* ""Dix-septieme siecle" n.249, 2010, p. 654.
[105] AOM LC110 fol.46 15.11.1630
[106] AOM LC fol.26, 2.04.1637. The Inns are large buildings where the brothers live and eat . Each Language has its own Inn (Auberge).

in 1641, a list of the prior of Messina is resigned to only tolerating the knights in future pinning up their cohabitation[107].

The Order renewed in the 17th century, between hospitality and crusade

From that time the Order of Malta goes from drawing away from its geographical situation on the frontier of Christianity and from its religious renewal to raise as never before the two remaining vows of hospitality and holy war, which attract the monks and appear definitively as the most necessarily for its survival and to the building of its famous image. The construction of a new city, La Valette, having become the residence of the convent in 1571, presumes the building from 1574 of a Sacred Infirmary, regularly managed and enlarged during the 17Ith and 18th centuries.[108]. The Infirmary contains a large room a hundred metres long where the patients' beds are lined up, as well as several other reserved rooms, one for incurables[109], the other for venereal diseases[110], and another for women[111]; on the ground floor, a herbarium, medical library and the rooms of the caring staff; in the basement, the kitchens, the lavatories and rooms for surgery and anatomy. In 1676, a school of anatomy and surgery was created in order to give better training for practicians serving the Order[112]. The students in the school, medical apprentices, barbers or surgeons, follow theoretical and practical training for ten years. The Hospitallers in modern times specialise in certain

---

[107] AOM. "Ruoli presentatati al Capitolo Generale" 311 fol. 87, 12.05.1631.
[108] Brogini, A. *Malte et l'oeuvre hospitalière de l'Ordre de Saint-Jean de Jerusalem…*
[109] AOM, Registres des Chapitres generaux, 291 fol.46r-46v, 1583.
[110] AOM,LC 99 fol.74r, 28.03.1596.
[111] AOM LC 109 fol.195, 1.06.1629.
[112] AOM"Libri Conciliorum Status (LCS) 262 fol. 65r, 19.12.1676.

branches of medicine and surgery such as kidney stones, benign tumours, cataracts, and all the treatments for venereal diseases.

If the infirmary is originally reserved for men, the Hospitallers renewing with their primitive history, from the time when two xenodochia (a term which described a hospital) coexisted in Jerusalem for each of the two sexes[113]. In the 17th century, images were spread of the Grand Master personally visiting the patients in the infirmary every Sunday after Mass, "making them read the Gospel, then tasting the bread and wine that is given to them, in order to prove to them that it is the best that can be found"[114].

Presented as a new Christ, the Grand Master communicates every Sunday with the patients, sharing bread and wine with them and reading from holy texts. Such a scene is also the subject of pictorial representation, like that carried out by the Italian painter in the service of the Order, Mattia Preti, at the time of the renovation of the conventual church of La Valette where the painter retraces the life of St John the Baptist in the 1660s. Beyond the many frescos of the vault, Preti creates a fresco above the front door of the church, which exalts the two Holy wars and hospitality vows. Grand Master Nicolas Cotoner, wearing the religious habit of the Hospitaliers (black robe with a white cross,) is represented simultaneously feeding a patient and with his powerful stick the picture of a galley, the symbol of the sea crusade.

Hospitality covers a wider reality than the medical care also showing help for the "poor people of Christ". This traditional charity is based on alms paid out regularly to the most deprived families, and on free care given to single women and to orphans gathered in the infirmary. Between

---

[113] Demurger, A. Les Hospitalers de Jérusalem à Rhodes (1050-1397). Paris, Talliender 2013.

[114] BM Aix-en-Provence ms 1094 "Relatione de l'isola de Malta non foliote".

the end of the 16th and the middle of the 17th century, however, thinkers, doctors and theologians examined in Europe a charity which was not merely based on alms and aid, but articulated around policy ideas, understood in the double sense of civic responsibility (submission to laws) and civility (good education), and regenerating work considered as an antidote to perverse idleness. Under the influence of actions led by Joao Ciudad ("John of God", 1495-1550), Camille de Lellis (1550-16140 and Vincent de Paul (1576-1660), the humanist theories of Juan Luis Vives ("De subventione pauperum 1526") or Perez de Herrera ("Discurso del amparo de los legitimos pobres y reduccion de los fingidos" 1598), the Order does not remain insensitive to the new ideas about aid to the poor and the resocialisation of the marginals.

Three decrees are issued in Malta during the first half of the 17th century, which reflect the development of behaviour towards poor and excluded people. In 1614, the Grand Master decreed a census of all beggars, d placing them in compulsory work, which appears to be more from punishment than a wish for education[115]. Thirty years later, in 1644, beggars were distinguished as either *honest ones" (invalids or those too old to work) and "dishonest ones" (authentic ones). The honest ones receive a papal bull authorising them to beg in the port, institutionalisation of mendicity accompanying the emergence of tolerance, even an acceptance of poverty. As for poor authentic ones, they are not only assigned to works of public utility, but placed in individual apprenticeships, in order to learn a skill that could ensure their subsistence in the near future[116]. In 1653 at last, the Hospitallers are interested in the children of beggars, who they take away from their parents in order to remove them from marginality. Put to work, these children aged from seven to eight years receive a monthly salary which is paid until they are f fifteen to sixteen years old, in

---

[115] AOM LC 105 fol. 38c, 31.01.1614.
[116] AOM LCS 257 fol. 179 v 189r, 25.09.1644.

order to serve as a dowry for girls at the marrying age, and with necessary funds to enter into an active life for the boys.[117]

About the poor or marginal women, the Order takes an interest at the end of the 16th century, to create, with the aid of the Inquisitor, a convent of Repentants taking together the old prostitutes of the port. Founded by the Knights in 1595 and placed in direct dependence on the Order of Malta. the convent adopts the rules of the Hospitaller nuns. In 1596, a letter from the Inquisitor to the pope reports that upon the death of each prostitute of the port, a part of their goods must be given to the convent, while those who are active are obliged to pay every month a sum intended for maintaining the convent and for the monks' daily life. Having become too old to operate, the prostitutes who have contributed to the financing of the convent see their future ensured: they can take the veil and live at the convent until the end of their lives[118]. In 1602, Pope Clement VIII acknowledged the official existence of the Convent for the Repentants, [119]which depended on the Order of Malta. Finally, in 1615, the Holy Office definitively fixed the "contribution imposed on the prostitutes", a fifth of the assets of dead prostitutes after having written a will was paid to the convent; if the latter died without a will, all of their assets went back to the convent of Repentance[120]. At this time however, the convent no longer depends on the Hospitallers who, from 1609, have placed it under the authority of the financial managers of La Vallette.

A second vow was exalted by the Order of Malta in the XVIIth century, the Holy War is exalted in its operation. Practised since Rhodes, the latter was [121]clothed with a

---

[117117] AOM LCS 259, fol. 71, 28.06.1653.

[118] ASV SS Malta 5, fol. 120r, 3.09.1596.

[119] AIM Corr.2, fol. 263 r, 29.12.1642

[120] AIM Corr .3, 111 r, 8.04.1645.

[121] Fontenay, M *La Méditerranée entre la Croix et le Croissant*. Paris, Classiques Garnier, 2010.

Crusader dimension after the truce between the Spaniards and the Ottomans, which ended in 1577 in the war of fleets and the great naval conflicts. Distinguished by piracy from the end of the 15th century, it became a codified and normalised act of war where privateers were mutually glorified: the activity was ennobled by its new actors, the Knights, who are comforted in their nobility by the size of the crusade covered with the race. In a similar hagiographical emotion, Hospitallers and speeches open these maritime operations to exaltation, raised up to the level of chivalrous deeds. Like the "classic" war beforehand, they become the expression of the nobility of the Knights of Malta and the means of maintaining the border between Islam and Christianity. An anonymous account of the 17th century in fact underlines that in taking great seizures, [122][the knights] freed a great many Christians from their miserable servitude[123].

A necessary tool for weakening the Infidels and strengthening Christianity by defending it with arms and in leading captured Christians back into its bosom, this activity hinges on holy work par excellence, which is the redemption of the captives. The latter doubly frees the Christians at the same time saving their bodies, freeing them from servitude, and their souls, preventing them from the temptation to deny their faith and become Muslims. It stirs up among the Hospitallers the wish to establish a Mount of Redemption in Malta in 1607, aimed at buying back the Maltese who were too poor to hope of[124] liberation and from an unbearable servitude as well as being deprived of all hope of freedom.

In fact, the Mount of Redemption of the Order is illustrated by its absence of activity in the 17Ith century, but its symbolic creation is evidence in everyone's eyes that the

---

[122]

[123] BM Aix-en-Provence, ms 1094 "Relations della Religione Geronolomitana of Malta".

[124] AOM LC 102 fol. 57, 13.06.1607.

Hospitallers continue to fulfil the mission for which they were created, that is to say the defence of Christianity with weapons in their hands, the Crusade recovering from the middle of the Middle Ages from large aims of struggle against all the dangers which threaten Catholicism from outside (infidels, pagans) or from inside (schismatics, heretics and all those who are opposed to the political interests of Rome)[125]. In the 16th and 17th centuries, the Order of Malta knew perfectly well how to gain from the double crisis that it met and put it back into the trouble on the outside (losses of Rhodes and Tripoli) and on the inside (Protestantism): It preferred renewal and revival of its damaged image. From the 17th century, the Hospitallers therefore present themselves to everyone and to themselves as monks who are strongly devoted to their sacred vows – especially to that of hospitality – and as perfect knights, the quintessence of pure European and Catholic nobility.

***

"He said, the French taught 'em, that the Lord Jesus Christ was of the French Nation"
Catholic and Calvinist Missions on the American frontier
Catherine Balleriaux

In 1676, the Reverend Cotton Mather was telling the story – popular in New England – of a Franciscan who, boasting of having converted thousands of Americans, wished however that a European friend "should send him the Book called the Bible, for he believed that such a book existed 'in Europe" which could be useful to him'[126]. This type of criticism was of Catholic methods of conversion (absence

---

[125] Josserand, P. "In servicio Dei et domini regis". De Ayala Martinez, C.

[126] Mather, I *A brief history of the wars with the Indians* London, Richard Chiswell 1676, p. 3.

of Bible translation, use of pictures), but mainly it was restricted to the verbal duel.

In 1722, after years of fighting with New France, Joseph Baxter, a Protestant minister was sent to the border of Maine, to try and win the converts of the Jesuit Sébastien Rasles to the reformed religion.

He addressed the very Savages; he asked the various questions about their debt; and in the replies that were given to him, he mocked the Sacraments, Purgatory, invocation of the Saints, the rosary, the Cross and its images, the lighting of our Churches, and all the practices of piety so piously observed in the Catholic religion[127].

In the border regions such as Maine, a great d to Boston. Two years later, after thirty years spent among the Wabanakis in Narrantsouac, many missionaries were competing directly for the souls of the Amerindians, who were more and more involved in these theological disputes. Rasles managed to keep his faithful flock, and Baxter returned to Boston. Rasles was killed by the English, who considered him as a "Fomentor and constant incendiary […] with the Indians so that they killed, burned and destroyed" [128].

Our study of the texts in fact shows that a significant change came about at the level of missionaries during the last quarter of the 17th century. In spite of the incendiary rhetoric often used by the Catholic and Protestant missionaries previously, the latter shared a great many ideals and used methods of conversion which were often similar, based on the principles of habituation, segregation and good example. These common features reflect belonging to missions for intense reform movements at the

---

[127] Rasles "Letter to his nephew Sebastian Rasles".
Narrantsuoak ,15.10.1722 . Thwaites, R.G. *The Jesuit Relations and Allied Documents ...1610-1791.* Cleveland, 1896, Burrows Company Vol. LXVII

[128] Dommer, W [Align with footnote]
Letter to Mons. Vaudreuil. Boston, NE, 19.01 1724.[align with above]

same time in Catholicism and Protestantism, fundamentally centred on a humanist vision of Christianity. The missions were fertile grounds for putting these ideas into practice, for they allowed the Erasmian ideal of reform of customs to be proven. A spirit of competition and debate between the confessions was omnipresent, but comparison of their methods shows fundamental common points in relation to their idea of conversion and their relations with the authorities and European settlers.

This idea evolved in a consequential manner throughout the end of the 17th and the beginning of the 18th century. The intercolonial wars, as well as the wishes of the French and English monarchies to strengthen their authority, had important repercussions on the missions. The missionary practices which were typical of the Reformation and the Counter-Reformation lost ground in favour of a policy which narrowly combined religious and national identities, and the missionaries had fewer independent opportunities with their neophytes where they could put their ideas into practice.

Relations between the clergy

From the beginnings of colonisation, the Puritans of Massachusetts saw their establishment as a possibility to create "a rampart against the kingdom of Anti Christ that the Jesuits worked to establish in these areas"[129]. The Jesuits were forbidden to stay in Massachusetts from 1647 and, according to law, had to be banished at the first proof, hung at the second[130].

The Jesuits were well aware of the animosity of the Puritans towards them. According to Giuseppe Bressant,

---

[129] Winthrop, J (attributed) "Reasons to be justifying the undertakers…" Winthrop, R.C. *Life and letters of John Winthrop governor of Massachusetts…*' Little, Brown, 1864 p. 309.

[130] Shurtleff ,N.B."Records of the Governor…" William White 185[date needs correcting]-1854, p. 123

working with the Hurons, the English trading with the Amerindians told them that the Jesuits were malicious people, harmful for the public good "and that their sole aim was to cause loss [of Indians] as quickly as possible"[131]. However, given their working strength and the extent of their missions in relation to the work carried out in New England, they expressed little care for their competition.

They could even sometimes acknowledge the greatest efforts of the Puritans to convert the Amerindians with the other colonies. Thierry Beschefer, in his account of 1683, mentions the baptism of several Indian Iroquoi prisoners, previously converted by John Eliot, the main missionary of Massachusetts. These Indians, Beschefer stated, had "been taught the main articles of our faith by some English people, very different from those from Orange and other American heretics[132]. The responsible priest, Francois Vaillant, it seems, found it no trouble to baptise them. As for the other Englishmen, according to Beschefer, several "of these heretics take no trouble for their health, saying that they only regard them as beasts, Heaven not being for that kind of people".

Even the most radical of the Calvinists acknowledged a certain merit in the Jesuit missions. Cotton Mather stated that the conversion of a single Indian by the Jesuits "is a greater production, than that of a thousand among them of which others boast elsewhere"[133]. He admitted, however, that in comparison with the Catholics, the Puritans must work harder on the conversion of Amerindians. And for that

---

[131] Dablon, C, "Letter to R.P. Pinette, 24.20.1674" Thwaites, R.G. *The Jesuit relations* vol .LIX p. 72.

[132] Bressani ,F.G. *Breve relatione... Macerata.* 19.07.1653

[133] Carre, E. *Echantillon de la doctrine...* Boston S Green, 1690.

reason, he claimed, the Jesuit missions had "prepared the way for something more sincere and healthy"[134].

Missionary approaches

Despite soteriological differences, the Catholic and Calvinist missionary practices shared the same gradual vision of conversion. Catholicism could be taught as a longterm habituation, a series of behaviours which, by their practice, would be internalised to the point of becoming second nature. The Jesuit Paul considered that the best way of gaining conversion would be to make the Indians sedentary and "having received the Law of Jesus Christ, one would make them take exercise and thus, little by little, they would become used to the way of truth and in a few years they would become a blessed people"[135]. Thanks to his free referee, the man would be capable.to some degree of distinguishing good from evil, even before the intervention of grace. By imitation and good example, the man could progressively internalise the precepts of Christianism.

In Calvinism, double predestination made the very idea of conversion problematical. In fact, that could only be granted to the elect by God alone. Nobody could obtain salvation by his own free will or cause it, and regeneration was also supposed to be as radical and sudden. All deeds before regeneration were considered as hypocrisies and conversion could only be conceived as a process[136] But, while grace could not be caused, it was also necessary to establish a Christian government which included regenerated and unregenerated people. Congregational ecclesiology needed the establishment of two alliances: one

---

[134] Haefeli, E. and Stanwood O, *Jesuits, Huguenots and the Apocalypse.* "Proceedings of the American Antiquarian society", vol. 116.

[135] On the importance of example see Herdt J.A., *Putting on virtue...vices*" University of Chicago Press, 2008, Ch, 5.

[136] Le Jeune P. *Relation de ce qui s'est passé en la Nouvelle France...1637.* Rouen, Jean le Boullenger, 1639, p. 102.

religious, the other political. The need for a form of community based on divine injunctions would require a process of education and habituation, at least external behaviour in accord with divine law. Putting into place Deuteronomic laws and the ten commandments, and the conscience that individuals would take their incapacity and follow it would also constitute an essential stage in the process of regeneration of the elect. The congregational community that John Eliot and the other Puritan leaders wanted to install among the Indians included not only the "Visible Saints", but also Indians who were converted, but not yet touched by grace[137].The latter could neither vote nor partake of the sacraments but nevertheless were members of the civil community[138]. Although a great many "Indians who pray" (Praying Indians) may not be called "saints" a ritual which was achieved by a confession of public faith before the congregation and required the approval of the latter, does not imply that many of them were not devoted Christians, hoping for salvation. In 1674, among the 1.100 converted Indians, only 119 were fully part of a congregation, but they all scrupulously followed the religious rituals and were an integral part of the civil community[139].

Conversion, for Calvinist missionaries as well as Catholic ones, was not only an act of faith, but also a process of transformation of the self, by means of the institution of civility, habits and controlling mechanisms which allowed the application of Christian morals and setting up an environment in which responsible Christians could convert others.

---

[137] Miller P."Preparation for salvation in 17th century New England," *Journal of the History of Ideas* vol. 4-3, pp.254-255.

[138] Gildrie, R.P. *The Profane, the Civil and the Ungodly.* 1679 Penn State University Press.

[139] Fisher. L.D. "Native Americans, Conversion.." Harvard Theological Review, vol. 102-1,2009 p. 1114

The idea of segregation was also a common subject in the first generation of Calvinist and Calvinist missionaries. The complaints about the bad example of settlers and even the persecutions suffered by the neophytes were omnipresent and systematically opened out on appeals on the separation of the two groups.

The Jesuits were particularly critical towards the French settlers. The sale of alcohol to the Indians was considered a crucial problem and associated with the greed of the merchants. The problem was so serious that, according to Father Chauchetière, "we all wish that [...] to see ourselves so far from the French: our dear savages that we no longer have such stumbling blocks[sic]"[140].

For this reason, the Jesuits preferred, contrary to the Recollets, segregation of their neophytes.[141] By combining a system of reserves and flying missions, and by trying to limit the trade on their reserves, the Jesuits tried to preserve their converts from the harmful influence of some settlers[142].

In Massachusets, John Eliot planned from the beginning to set up independent villages for his neophytes where they could create a civil and religious alliance amongst themselves, In complete autonomy[143]. Initially, nevertheless, he wanted to settle them near the English villages, for "if the Indians lived close to the English [...] he would not hold them in the heart of prayer, and they would not be ready to hear the divine word." But, very soon, a great many Puritans complained of the potential bad influence of the settlers who, according to Edward Winslow, "had put the stinking Christ and Christianism to

---

[140] Sagard, G. *Le grand voyage au pays des Hurons...* Paris, D. Moreau, 1632 p. 58 and pp. 239-240.

[141141141] Chauchetière C. *Lettre au r.b. Jean Chuchetiere. In Limoges*, Villemarie 07.08.1694.

[142] Sagard, G. *Le grand voyage au pays des Hurons...* Paris, D Moreau, 1632 p. 58, pp. 230-240.

[143]?? Iu

the nostrils of the poor infidels"[144]. Eliot quickly realised that cohabitation brought problems, [145]and complained of the settlers' greed for land throughout his career. He often regretted the introduction of setters to the lands of the "towns of prayer" (Praying towns,made "the profane Indians laugh at the "Indians who pray" and prayer. Therefore, Eliot decided to set up towns at some distance from the English[146]..

The idea of segregation illustrates the fact that Catholic missionaries as well as Calvinists consecrated their efforts to a non-national cause bu alsot to practically carrying out an ideal form of Christianism. Their work was destructive for many aspects of Amerindian societies, but they were also often, as pastors, the only defenders of what they considered to be the rights of Amerindians. They ceaselessly condemned European vices, greed, egoism and pride, which they considered as a threat to their missions. The missionaries, as a group with some specific interests, sometimes had more in common with the missionaries of an opposing confession than with their own settlers or colonial authorities.

The intense vision of Christianism that they shared was at its source at the same time as the competition of their interest in the work of their opposers. Their relations could sometimes even be cordial. In 1650, the Jesuit Gabriel Druillettes, head of the mission of Narrantsouac beside the Wabanakis of Maine, went on a diplomatic mission to New England to try to establish an alliance against the Mohawks, who were constantly threatening both New France and the missions of the Wabanakis. First of all he was welcomed by a Puritan of the Plymouth colony, John Winslow, who,

---

[144] Winslow, E. *Good news from New England*. London, Dawson and Eliot's Court Press, 1624, fol. A3

[145] Eliot, J. "Natik case drawn up in defence of poor Indians...Dedham", 1639-1673, vol. iv, pp. 255-261.

[146] Eliot, J. quoted in Winslow, E."*he glorious progress of the gospel...New England.*

according to Druillettes, stated to the Wabanakis present that he could stay with [147]him and "he knows he would treat him like his own brother among you and the life that he leads". According to Druillettes, Winslow had a special interest in converting the Amerindians, which made him kind to him. The Jesuit manifestly loved Winslow very much and was warmly welcomed by other eminent Puritans. William Gibbons received him and gave him the use of a private room to carry out the Catholic rites. He also spent a night at the home of John Eliot, who considered him "at the same time full of spirit, ingenious, and erudite"[148]. In Plymouth, John Bradford served him with fish, as it was a Friday. Druillettes also wrote a letter to the Governor of Massachusetts, John Winthrop, appealing to his "acknowledged affection and his particularly pious and religious sentiments towards the savages who are catechised in the Faith and in the Christian Profession".[149] Druillettes was particularly careful to separate the interests of the catechised from those of New France in his correspondence. In spite of his efforts and his welcome, the mission ended up as a failure, having been given the consequent financial investment that it extended.

Change of Policies

The relations of Druillettes' successor with the mission of Narrantsouac, Sebastien Rasles, were otherwise more extended with his English neighbours, as I have described above. It is true that in times of war, the Jesuits made up a particular threat for the New England colonies. which the

---

[147] Druillettes, G *Narre du voyage...Nouvelle Angleterre.* 1651.

[148] Eliot, J, "Letter to Richard Baxter, 20.06.1669." E.J.Powicke (ed) "some unpublished correspondence of Rev Richard Baxter and Rev John Eliot, Bulletin of John Rylands University Library, vol. 15-2, 1931, p. 455.

[149] Druillettes, G. *Epistola Patris Druillettes ad Jonnem Winthrop, Scutarium.* the Jesuit Relations.op.cit, vol XXXVI, p. 76.

French and English were well aware of. During the attack on Quebec, by Sir William Phipps, in 1690, the French were convinced that the English had a particular target, the Jesuits, therefore they wanted to make rosaries out of them for the soldiers' bandoliers and then break the rest[150].

According to Jacques -Rene de Brisay de Denonville, Governor General of New France, the English thought:

all our missionaries are like their most cruel enemies that they do not want to suffer with the savages who are at their door [...] when the interest in the Gospel would not encourage us to hold missionaries in all the savage villages [...]the interest of the civil government for the good of all must encourage us to deal with it and to always have some as the savage people can only be governed by missionaries who alone are capable of maintaining them in our interest and prevent them from rebelling every day against us[151].

The Count of Bellamont, governor of the provinces of New York, New Hampshire and Massachusetts. particularly feared the Jesuits. During a treaty with the Five Nations, he let them know that they could

give the King (William III) a better witness of their loyalty to him while in rejecting any type of correspondence with the papist priests and the Jesuits and by refusing imperatively to tolerate them in your country under any pretext whatever[152].

With the wars, the missions became associated with the political alliances, and the missionaries on the borders often complained of the attempts of the opposing group to "steal" their neophytes. In 1711, the Jesuit Joseph Germain lamented: "One of the great obstacles that we have in the propagation of the Faith and conversion of infidels are the

---

[150] Germain J. "Letter from Joseph Germain...1711". Thwaites, R.G. *The Jesuit relations...* op. cit. vol. LXVI, p. 193=2 191

[151151] de Brisay de Denonville, J.R.*Memoire de Monsieur de Denonville Marquis de Seignelay.* 4.05.1690".

[152] Coote, R. *His Excellency Richard Earl of Bellamont's Proposals to the Sachems...* Albany, 31.08.1700"

English"[153]. The Huguenot minister Jacques Laborie complained to Bellamont that a number of the faithful had left to join the Catholic mission in Narrantsouac. These people explained that they left, for "the religion of the Indians of Penikook was more beautiful than ours, that the French people gave them silver crosses to wear around their necks"[154].

The commentaries of the Amerindians which are found in the sources show that these people were well aware of the confessional divisions, and of the crucial role of religion in inter-colonial conflicts, and often associated religious and national allegiances.

During the first inter-colonial war (1690-1697). the Reverend Cotton Mather interrogated a sachem of New France imprisoned in Boston, Bommaseen. The latter, according to Mather, had asked him for advice, as he feared that the French had deceived him. He told him that they told him "that Jesus Christ was from the French Nation [...] that it was the English who killed him, and [.....] that all those who wished to return to his Favour must avenge the Quarrel with the English as much as they could"[155]. Mather, using a wine glass as a symbol of the Bible, explained that the French had poisoned him, to make him[156] mad and want to kill the English, and finally destroy them. The English, on the other hand, having translated the Bible into Algonquin, gave them direct access to the Divine Word, while the "papists" had deformed and altered all the articles of faith,

---

[153] Germain, J. "Lettre du P. Joseph Germain..." Thwaites R.G. *The Jesuit Relations,* p.202. See also Bigot, J. "Lettre a un pere de la compagnie de Jesus, 26.20.1699". Ibid., vol. LXV p.95.

[154] Laborie, J. "A New Oxford 17.08.1700."Baxter, J.P. ("Documentary History..op.cit vol. X, p.59-60.

[155] Mather, C. *Decennium Luctuosum. A history...of New England year 1688 to the year 1698.* Boston B Green 1699 p 127-128.

[156] Ibid., p. 130.

with "scandalous Ingredients of their own Invention"[157]. He confirmed to them that everything that the Jesuits had told them was only French Poison". The English often insisted on the fact that they had translated the Bible into Algonquin, perhaps to counterbalance the fact that few of them spoke the Indian languages, contrary to the Jesuits, who had become experts in that field[158].

In their criticisms as well as in their statements of fidelity, the Amerindians often insisted on the motivations of the missionaries, especially their economic interests. Rasles, in a letter to his brother, quotes a sachem who reproached the English who were trying to attract him for never having any interest in their conversion, but only for their diggers[159].These criticisms are doubtless exaggerated by the Jesuits. But one also finds them in the English documents. At the time of a negotiation with the Indians of the east of the English provinces, the English offered the services of missionaries "of the true religion", The latter, surprised that they should be offered anything of that type considering the previous lack of interest on the part of the English in their conversion, replied that if they were previously taught in their religion,

we would have adopted and detested the Religion that you offer us now, but as we are now taught by the French people, we have promised to be faithful to God in our religion, and we declare that we do not wish to abandon it.

With the arrival of the intercolonial wars, religious and national identities were more and more identified in the writings of missionaries. This tendency was strengthened by the colonial powers, wishing to consolidate their authority and knowing that the missionary work was essential for establishing alliances with Indian groups who

---

[157] Ibid., pp.129-130.
[158] Balleriaux C. *Reformation Strategies*.op. cit., pp. 150-159.
[159] Rasles, S. "Lettre a Monsieur son Frere Sebastian Rasles, Narrantsouak, 12.10.1723." R.G Thwaites, *The Jewish Relations* op. cit. vol LXVII, p.219.

could be useful to them in the conflict. In the 1720s, after decades of distant relations with the English, which ended by costing him his life, Father Rasles at Narrantsouac stated that these people:

persuaded with reason that in maintaining my Savages in their attachment to the Catholic faith I am more and more strengthening the connections that tie them to the French, they [160]have carried out all sorts of ruses and tricks in order to separate themselves from me.

The term "frenchified" was used more and more and associated with[161] the term "papified" in English texts. During the first intercolonial war, Cotton Mather spoke about his enemies as "half Indianised Frenchmen, and half-French Indians".

This tendency was actively encouraged by the colonial authorities, who insisted more and more on the need to assimilate the Amerindian populations into the colonies, on the premise that they had to become French or English and not only Christians.

In New France, there was a propensity to favour assimilation as soon as the colony was placed under royal administration, in 1663[162]. Colbert hoped in fact that by "mixing" the Amerindians with the French, and by teaching them the language, "by the succession of time, having only one law and one same master, thus they do nothing more than the same people and the same blood"[163].

In 1688, in his instructions to the new bursar Bouteroue, Colbert explained:

It has seemed up till now that the Jesuits' maxim was not to call the natural inhabitants of the country in community of life with the French, either by giving them land and common housing, either by educating their children and by

---

[160] Rasles, S. "Lettre a Monsieur son frere…" op.cit., p. 204.
[161] Mather, C. *Magnolia Christi*, op.cit p. 68.
[162] Phillips J. *Casco Bay, 7.06.1701.A memorial…Eastern Indians*
[163] Rasles ,S."Lettre a Monsieur son frere" op. cit p. 204

marriage. Their reason was that they believed they had to preserve the holiness of our religion more purely by keeping the converted savages in their ordinary way of life than by calling them among the French[164].

For Colbert, this principle of segregation[165] was far "from any good conduct, as much for religion as for the State". The growing authority of the court on colonial matters was accompanied by a "bodindian" tendency - to wish to consider [166]the Amerindians as obedient subjects, assimilated with the French in the service of absolute monarchy. The Jesuits maintained a great influence on the borders but were more and more encouraged to act as representatives of the government which was not produced without clashes, and they progressively lost their influence.

In New England, at the turn of the century, several circumstances also changed the conversion strategies of the Puritans. The war of Red Philip (1675-1678) as well as the inter-colonial wars, the revocation of the charter in 1684 and the death of the most active of the missionaries, John Eliot, in 1690, dealt a serious blow to the conversion work. The Glorious Revolution of 1688, on the accession to the throne of William III, seen as a fervent defenderr of Protestantism, as well as the repeated conflicts with France created a tendency among the inhabitants of New England to embrace, as Owen Stanwood suggested, "their identity as

---

[164] See :Baxter, J.P."Documentary history" op.cit.vol. V, p. 420.

[165] Like Jerome Lalemant has shown in his report of 146, the Fathers insisted on the fact that "for deeds of civility and policy [...]they were free to follow their ideas, provided that they do not go against God's laws". (Lalemant, J. *Relation ...Compagnie de Jesus...1645-1646*. Paris, S.Cramoisy, 1647, p.111.

[166] Havard, G. *"Les forcer à devenir Cytoyens" : Etat, Sauvages et citoyenneté en Nouvelle France (XVII-XVIIIe siècle)*. "Revue historique du droit francais et etranger" vol.76, 1998 pp. 75-92.

subjects of a powerful monarch"[167][168]The Earl of Bellamont systematically associated anti-Catholicism with loyalty to the King, and presented himself as a protector of Protestants. Successive governors insisted more and more on the required submission of the Amerindians, and the missionaries were considered essential for this task[169].

Perhaps as a result of this importance given to the intrinsic link between the English character, Protestantism, and a common submission to the English monarchs, here also the missionary strategies changed in favour of a new insistence [170]on anglicisation. Also, during the reign of King Philip, as Colonel Nathaniel Saltonstall noticed, "the impossibility of establishing a visible Distinction between our friends the Indian Christians, and our Enemies the Pagans became a vital problem"[171]. This tendency seems to be translated into new missionary strategies. In 1716, Cotton Mather, who had previously supported the Puritans' efforts to translate the Bible into Algonquin, held that:

The best thing that we could do for our Indians is to anglicise them in all possible ways; for the Language as well as the remainder. They can even keep their Language without a tint of other Savage tendencies […] Although some of their old men are rather strong in their "Indianism" (of which one must not be surprised) they sincerely wish that their people may be Anglicised as quickly as possible.

---

[167] "The English reformed…Glorious Revolution", Philadelphia, Univ. of Pennsylvania Press, 2011, p. 20.

[168] The answer of the House of Representatives, to His Excellency the Earl of Bellamont 's speech …Boston, Bartholomew Green and John Allen, 1699.

[169] Baxter, P. "Documentary history" op.cit. vol X, p. 223

[170] On the use of the term "franchiser" at the end of the 17th century see Havard, G. "Force them to become citizens", *French historical studies,* vol. 27-3,[27-30?] 2004 pp. 507-1018.

[171] Saltonstall, N. *Continuation of the State of New England…*London, D. Newman,1676 p. 7.

The missiologies of the 17ththth century had favoured the segregation of converted Indians and a slow and progressive habituation to the practice [172] of virtue and the Christian faith, to the combination of civility and faith, the latter without the need for "franciscanisation" or an "anglicisation" of the Amerindians.

In 1658, the Jesuit Paul Le Jeune compared the customs of different countries, and meditated on his experience with the Indians:

The world is full of variety and inconstancy, and one will never find solid firmness. If someone had climbed up a rather high tower, from which he can see, easily, all the Nations of the earth; he would have surely been prevented from saying which people are wrong, or those who are right: those who are mad, and those who are wise in variations, and in and in such strange colourings. Truly there is only God who is constant: he alone is unmovable; only he is invariable: it is to him that we must attach ourselves, in order to avoid change and inconstancy.

These conversion strategies were transformed progressively and ended by promoting the idea that in order to become a Christian, one had to become French or English, or adopt a European way of life. The radical vision of reform of the first missionaries was replaced by a much more instrumental conception of conversion in the colonies. The border regions were particularly significant for the development of missiological thought. In fact, the interactions in these regions made religion and nationality become progressively assimilated and the missionaries turned into – sometimes in spite of themselves – essential actors in the political strategies and negotiations in the inter-colonial wars. These changes exemplified the political, religious and intellectual interactions of the New World, and the way in which the missions among the Amerindians

---

[172] Le Jeune P, quoted in Ragueneau P. "Relation de ce qui' s'est passé...*Nouvelle France es annees 1657 et 1658.* Paris, S Cramoisy, 1659, p.121.

on the margins of the empire constituted the places where European thought was put into practice and crystallised. The comparative study of the missions makes it possible to assess the political and intellectual influences which determined the missiologies and how the development of religious principles influenced imperial practices.

PART TWO

FACE TO FACE: MODELS AND COUNTER-MODELS
FACE TO FACE: SIDE BY SIDE?

THE CHAPLAINS OF THE ARMIES OF THE EMPIRE BETWEEN CO-EXISTENCE, IGNORANCE AND CONFRONTATION (17th -18th century)

The question of chaplains of armies in the Empire has been researched over several years More particularly, the military field, in a real renewal of university research[173] was won by studies about the religious and the confessional. Now, in the history of the Holy Empire in the modern era, we know the importance of confessional questions, which have given way to numerous studies on various scales and to the development of the paradigm of confessionalisation. The territories, the towns, (less so the countryside) the institutions – like the imperial chamber of justice (Reichskammergericht) – have been scrubbed to one of the confessions. However, there is one institution, the army, which until the summer was fairly neglected by contemporary research. If one leaves aside the societal reluctance connected with the recent past in Germany, that can be understood in the light of the advance of research and above all of the territorial prism: a territory qualified – often falsely – as "Lutheran", as "reformed" or as Catholic could only have an army which was confessionally determined by the prince, or, at the very worst, have several holders of another religion, but without special religious rights.

Obviously, such an opinion is false, on account of the confessional structure of the territories of the Empire, which one can only tackle the reality by approaching the "terrain"

---

[173] See Prove, R. "Le nouvelle histoire …Allemagne", *Revue historique des armées,* no. 257, 2009 pp.14-36.

and on account of the structure of the armies of the Old Regime. If one leaves the Empire and one observes the composition of the French army, particularly after 1685, one sees "foreign" regiments, with Protestants and pastors. That asks the question straight away of coexistence between the confessions, but also clergymen in the heart of the army, something which has not, I believe, been tackled up to now. Thus the mosaic confessional with several scales of the Holy Empire is found in the Army of the Empire and the territorial armies; the pluri-confessionality implies an actual co-existence with right of confessions and clergymen. More precisely, there may be a supervised coexistence within each territorial army, as the very structure of the Empire army (Reichsarmee) requires contacts of confessions and clergymen. This is typically the case of armies called "Circles" (Kreise), purveyors of this Empire army as well as territorial armies used within the framework of a war led by the Empire.

It is essentially this double framework that we are going to use in order to observe, seize and measure the forms of contact between clergymen who could exist within the heart of these Empire armies, knowing that the context is obviously very different from that of France: confessional coexistence, especially after 1648 Is institutionalised and governed by the law of the Empire[174]. Within the military framework, coexistence can appear as necessity, in spite of rules issued by the Peace of Osnabrück (1648).

Thus, if we are going to evoke cases tied to territorial armies, we are also going to deal with the Circle armies in our report, which were accepted as a legal and institutional framework of coexistence. More precisely, it is reality faced with this standard desired or confessional balance which is going to be our guiding thread, In the background, it is also a matter of questioning the army's implication in the process of confessionalisation or "unconfessionalisation".

---

[174] For a synthesis in German, see Aretin,K.O, *Das alte Reich,1646-1806*, Stuttgart, Klett-Cotta,1997

More precisely, one could try to make out in what measure the army is a laboratory of experience for the spoiled confessional and therefore putting back the outline of the confessionalisation. The context of the reflection is double: on the one hand, of the myth of homogeneity and confessional homogenisation[175], a possible motor of a territorial confessional; on the other hand, that of the structural reality of the Empire armies which makes it possible to imagine, in the reality of daily life, an irreligious, but confessional in the whims of uniformisation[176].

Which armies for which chaplains?

The presence of chaplains in armies is not a completely new thing in the 17th century; still should one be precise on these terms: if one considers the only presence of clergymen and monks accompanying men of war, is the practice old? On the other hand, from the time when one defines the chaplain as a representative of an established and institutionalised structure, the chronology is complicated. In fact, the very essence of military chaplaincy – ecclesiastical institution, aimed for accompanying the soldier in a standardised religious practice during the course of a roving monk existence – is to be sought in the affirmation of confessional identities. If the German authors of the 18th century, like Georg Heinrich Goetze, affirm the antiquity of the institution[177], it is not a second reading of the past aimed at ennobling a fairly young creation. In the 16th century, the religious confrontations – at least in France – are accompanied by the presence of pastors and priests in the armies, in all cases theoretically since the order of Charles

---

[175] Straube, E. *Zum Herrscherideal im Jahrundedert...* no.32, 1969, pp.193-221.

[176] Prove, R. *Rationalisterungsdruck... Toleranz: Schilling In Spanungfeld/...* Berlin Zeitschrift ...Forsch 31003, pp. 53-69.

[177] The synthesis of the question...:Boniface, X. "L'aumônerie militaire francais" (1914-1962). Paris, 2001

IX in 1568[178].On the Empire side, one discovers this at the start of institutionalisation from the beginning of the 16th century. There are monks present, particularly after the reforms of Maximilian I, with a chaplain for every "Fähnlein" (about 500 men): these designated chaplains must take an oath, are subject to military discipline and must "exhort the men to live in an edifying manner"[179]. A vicar general for each Catholic army is named, perhaps from 1534[180], for example Anton Brus (1518-1589), "Feldkaplan" (military chaplain) from 1542 to 1545, [181]then vicar general of the army in 1554. In 1565, Leonhart Fronsperger produced the first dogmatic step with his *Geislichen Kriegundnung*, in which he indicates among other things that the ecclesiastic must:

in front of the captain, where the drum calls the soldiers, exhort officers and men to piety and rectitude, reprimand their vices by speaking and lead them by edifying speeches, to Christian behaviour and to conversion- business -which is agreeable to God.[182]

On the Protestant side, at a time of internal structuration of the confessions, the priority is not for armies; the armed interconfessional conflicts are moreover smaller and the essence of the energy of the Protestant confessions is turned towards the edification of the territorial Churches. However, the desire for religious accompaniment, also for questions of confessional identity, leads the Protestant princes to demand at the time of the Diet of Spire in 1542 that the Protestant soldiers should have their own pastors. In the end, one must see that the Empire armies are already

---

[179] ?

[180] Bielik, E *Geschichte K.U.K Militar-Seelsorge ... Vicariates*. Vienna selbuverla des Feld-Vicariates, 1901, p 18.

[181] Hanak, J. "Evangelische Militarcelborge in algen Osterreich...Verband." Kohnert, W. *Die evangelische Militareborge Vienna Jahrbuk ...Protestantism in Osterreich* 1974, pp. 6-8.

[182] Bielek F ."*Geschichte der K. U. K*, op.cit, p.45.

pluri-confessional in the 16th century[183]. The military authorities moreover are absolutely not looking for religious homogeneity ; the rules threaten severe penalties for those who generate quarrels for reasons of religion[184].

Things change partially with the 17th century and the Thirty Years War, of which it is known that the first decade can be seen [185]partly as a war of religion. It then becomes unthinkable to see pastors among the troops of the Catholic League and vice versa. On the other hand, Olivier Chaline has shown it well in the context of the war of Bohemia[186]. This reveals among other things the clearer emergence of a desire the faithful authorities of the soldier: up to counting on his engagement from then in the adverse troop, are there members of his confession that one rightly seeks to annihilate? Finally, one must imagine the viewpoint of belief in the true religion: "GottesKrieger - Gottes Siege". This adage in fact underlines the fact that for God to grant the victory, one must fight for the true faith. Maximilien of Bavaria engages his troops against the High-Palatinate on a Marian feast day and it is known that his banners are decorated with a picture of the Virgin. Thus, the question of confessional homogeneity is asked again, all the more as[187] the territorial prince is also invested in a religious duty for his subjects.

However, in spite of this reality that one may back up with other examples, one must not allow oneself to be

---

[183] Baumann, R.*Landsknechte...King.* Munich Beck,1994, p.194 sq.

[184] Kaiser, M.*Cuius exercitius, eius religio? Konfession...Kriegs.* "ArchiveReform",no. 91, 2000, pp.316-353.

[185] Burkhardt, J. "Religionskrieg". Muller, G. Theologische.Kriegs theologische.Berlin, New York de 1997, pp.681-687.

[186] La bataille de la Montagne Blanche (1620) Paris, Noesis, 2000.

[187] Reiff, M. *Von der Herrsch der Sachzwange...Heer (1628-1778).* Kaiser , M. and S. Kroll *Militar und Relgiositat,* op. Cit. Pp. 49-50.

deceived by quick reading; in spite of the desire for mono-confessional armies, the religious mixture still exists. In 1626, Tilly denies religious practice to its Lutheran troops in the town of Gottingen[188]. If one believes the Electoral Prince Ferdinand of Cologne, in a letter of 9 January 1628, he denounces the over-important share of Calvinism in the League [189]army to use it with safety against the United Provinces. Tilly, always needing soldiers, in 1632 suggests to Maximilien of Bavaria engaging some inhabitants of the High-Palatinate, or Calvinists, in the regiments: the Electoral Prince is very reticent but, practically. behind the appeals for confessional unity, the Protestant soldiers and officers are surely present in this Bavarian army of the League.[190] In August 1653, the Lutheran Andress Drost became colonel of the Bavarian army; in the following year, it is another Protestant,[191] Elias Lang, who becomes the head of a Bavarian regiment. Michael Kaiser has already emphasized one of the reasons for that: when Wallenstein put his army at the Emperor's service, the conditions attracted a great many officers of all confessions[192]. The reductions in the numbers of good officers "de facto" pushed Maximilien to put aside the idea of confessional unity of his troops[193] . Obviously, the military reality and need to have faith: the need in ken and for leaders of quality engages the prince to pass beyond the confession, particularly in recruiting soldiers among the prisoners. Oswald von Glaubitz, who served Christian IV of Denmark, is taken prisoner at the battle of Lutter am Barenberg. He went into the service of Maximilien of Bavaria and

---

[188] Kaiser, M, *Cuius exercitius,eius religio?* op.cit., p. 325.
[189] Ibid.
[190] For the Bavarian army, see Staudinger, K. *Geschichte des kurbayerischen...Maria (1651-1679)* Munich, Jl Buchhandlung The 1951.
[191] Kaiser, M. *Cuius exercitius, eius religio?*. p.331
[192] Kaiser, C. "Die bayerische...Krieges 1635-1648. Munster Aschendorff, 1997
[193] Kaiser, M. *Cuius exercitius, eius religio?* op..cit., p. 332.

remained faithful to him. In 1645, he was even named "Oberstwachtmeister"[194]. In the same way, strategic interests pushed the princes to play confessions. When Munich is occupied by the Swedish, in 1632, the commander of the named garrison is Colonel Jakup Hepburn, a Catholic.[195] Even in the army of Christian of Brunswick, who also showed a strong Lutheran identity, as is shown in the "Pfaffentaler," struck in 1622 with the inscription "Gotte Freund,der Pfaffen Freund", there were Catholic soldiers in 1623[196].

What is true for the pluri-confessionality of the armies of this war, is also true for the territorial armies after 1648. Let us go back to the Bavarian army. The recruitment of the Bavarian army does not rest on a single state which counts perhaps 800,000 inhabitants in 1700. In peacetime, recruitment is essentially Bavarian, except the officers (a number of Austrians, Frenchmen, Italians), but with the war, the ranks had to be opened to neighbouring territories, both Catholic and Protestant. The Bavarian recruiters did not hesitate to go to Souab in Francony in order to find volunteers [197], Catholic or not. Moreover, confessional belonging is put in brackets in the very process of soldiers' inscription. In the recruitment instruction of Ferdinand Marie of 17 April 1657, it is written that the new soldiers must only "be described by the baptism and, place of birth, as well as the judiciary or lordship on which the place depends"[198]. An instruction of April 1702 only requires the surname and first name, profession, place of origin, state of health and celibacy. During a large part of the 18th century, confession only appears rarely on registration lists of troops. Therefore, one finds a great many Protestants in Catholic Bavaria. One example – in 1685, the Latour armoured

---

[194] Ibid., p.352.
[195] Ibid., p. 337.
[196] Ibid., p.341.
[197] Reiff, M. "Von Herrschaft der Sachrzange." Op. cit., p.55.
[198] Ibid., p.361 and p. 370.

regiment is almost decimated. In summer, a new regiment is raised with almost exclusively Lutheran officers and cavalry. In 1685, in the regiment of 790 soldiers identified in the eleven companies of the Truchess regiment, there are 60.2 % Catholics, 32% Lutherans and 7.8% Calvinists[199]. This state of affairs is sometimes associated with confessional difficulties, more so in peacetime in the garrison among the Catholic population, where, it is the clergy of the place of the garrison who fulfil the duty. Among the chaplains, there are Jesuits, Benedictines, Carmelites and Augustines but no pastors. There have been exceptions, like the Truchsess Regiment, which had three chaplains, one Catholic, one Lutheran and one Calvinist. When there are concerns, as in 1742 and 1745, it is the civilian population which complains about the Protestant religion[200]. In order to avoid any recrimination, an order is given to send back the two pastors, but the Protestant soldiers, [201]of one regiment or another, could go to the Protestant neighbourhood for communion. One finds, moreover, that border practices are identified in the framework of territorial and confessional intertwined communities of the Empire.

In order to try to give all the keys of the spiritual framework in the Empire years, one must also consider the case of the armies of the Circles. The Souab one is particularly interesting due to its composition. IN 17000.one sees two bishops, two abbot princes, thirteen lay princes including the Duke of Wurtemberg, the Margrave of Baden-Baden, twenty-eight counts and lords (and two with the title the Elector Prince of Bavaria) as well as thirty-one Empire towns (Augsburg, Reutligen, etc.) of which two-thirds are Lutheran. Two-thirds of the territory of the

---

[199] Ibid., p.56.
[200] Ibid., p. 63.
[201] Jalabert, C. "Catholics and Protestants", op. cit.

Circle are around 55% Catholic[202]. At the heart of the Circle, in order to avoid any concerns, there is application of the joint law, from the "trio in partes"[203] which one finds also in the operation of the Circle army. The joint rule is imposed on the management of the army – where the important posts are occupied alternatively -and in the composition of the army. In 1673, the decision is taken to raise two infantry regiments and two of the cavalry, either each time one Catholic and one Lutheran, effectively with the same weight, [204] If the tendency is for regrouping, the scale of the regiment or of the company, of members of a same confession, nothing prevents the presence of soldiers of another confession in the same unity. In 1760, the regiment of dragoons of the Circle of Souab is made up of nine officers (five Lutherans and four Catholics), with the exception of a Calvinist member of the cavalry[205].

It is in the armies, whether they are territorial, Empire or Circle, that the chaplains must dissolve. The very composition of the armies pushes the military chaplains to be in contact with colleagues, but also with the members of the clergy of their confession crossed in their taste with the movement of units, at the time of campaigns and times of garrison.

One has understood that the very composition of the armies is a mirror of the territorial and confessional reality of the Empire. The rules of confessional coexistence are applied thus, up to a certain point, in the armies, with differences according to whether one is in a Circle army, of the Empire or in a territorial army.

---

[202] Storm, P.C."Der Schulische Kreis …Zeit ton", 1648 bis 1732, Berlin Duncker & Humblot, 1974,. Pp. 51, 55-56.

[203] Heckel, M. *Itio in partes. Zur Religionverfassung…Nation Paritat*[Spanish} 49 1963 pp. 261-420.

[204] Storm P.C. *Der schulbische de Kreis als Feldbere…* op. cit., p. 307.

[205] Passman, M. *Bikonfessionnelle Streitkräfte: Das belspiel…Reichkreises (1648-1803)* Kaiser, M. and S Kroll, S. *Militar und Religiositat…* p 33-48 here -.p 35.

In some Circle armies, coexistence was "de facto", inscribed into the operating rules and confessional questions had to be a potential cause of dysfunction. Reading the historians of the Circles,[206] it seems that the conflicts between the confessions at the heart of the Souab Circle army were rare and could in no way be general. The Circle regiment is a legal circumscription and also a military parish (militar kirchengemeinde)[207]. More precisely, it is even a double parish in the framework institutionalized bi-confessionality of unity, with no connection with the religion of the colonel of the regiment[208]. In this respect the surrender of the Circle in 1730, which rests a great deal on that of 1664, is clear: the seventh point indicates that "the chaplains of both confessions must be protected in the exercise of their duties and maintained in their administration"[209]. Concretely, in each major state of a Circle regiment, there must be a Catholic and a Lutheran chaplain. The Lutheran pastor is called by the consistory of the Church of Wurtemberg, installed in Stuttgart, after an inspection: as for, the priest, he is designated by the Bishop of Constance[210]. It is up to the commander of the unit to have the equality of law in the exercise of the religion. When the Duke of Wurtemberg raises three regiments, it is specified in writing that:

No difference in religion must be made, Catholics as well as Protestants must be accepted, also a Catholic chaplain and two Lutherans for these three regiments.
The case of territorial armies is different: the chaplain of a religion other than that of the prince depends upon the goodwill of the latter, but nothing is simple. From the peace

---

[206] Storm, P.C. *Der Schulbische* ... op.cit.
[207] Ibid., p. 299.
[208] Ibid.,p 370.
[209] Landesacive, spire, E3/2090 fol. 421/424, agreement between the Souab circle and the Duke of Wurtemberg, 11.02.1693.
[210] Ibid., p 389

of 1648 and recognized frameworks there emanates a yoke which is partly anchored in the territory, but also in the men. The soldiers are roving monks and they are called to cross the territories of another confession. The Empire rule wants the 'Lutheran" regiment, for example, served by the princely authority, to enjoy the free practice of the religion with the idea that "the regiment carries with it his jurisdiction in all the territories"[211]. From that time, even in a Catholic territory, worship must be celebrated with full honours before the troops, after a call by beating drums (Trommelschlag). This also means that the Catholic soldiers in such a regiment, if there is only one Lutheran chaplain, take over his spiritual jurisdiction, for example for marriage. The inverse is also true. One may guess that this rule may create difficulties with the Catholic clergy when one crosses into a Catholic country. If the regiment serves the Emperor of a Catholic power, it goes in the other direction,: the Lutheran chaplain does not fully bring his ecclesiastical jurisdiction and must conform either to his granted capitulation, or to the freedom of conscience recognized by the peace of 1648. The men are not called by the drum but orally warned by the sub-officers of the place; divine service cannot take place before the troops and very rarely in a Catholic church, the Catholic princes being very restrictive on conditions of practising other religions on their territories, particularly on Hapsburg lands. It is certainly not for nothing that Philipp[212]Christoph Fischer is called to a caution for celebrating holy communion. On 6 May 1664, he was installed as chaplain for the Souab Circle within the framework of the rising against the Turks, but in order to avoid useless tension, he is enjoined at the time of crossing Catholic territories not to seek to use the churches,

---

[211] Kolb, C.*Feldprediger in Alt Wurtemberg Blatter ...Kirchengeschichte,»* 9, 1905,pp. 70-8.5
[212]212?

but only private halls or then quite simply stay in the open air[213].

There we go into a war context and service of a territorial army at the heart of the imperial army. The rules for confessional coexistence must be rubbed up against the reality which is sometimes something else. It is what can be seen at Freibourg im-Brisgau twice over, in 1699[214]. That was in 1735. In 1733, an agreement was reached between the Duke of Wurtemberg, Charles Alexander and the Emperor to provide the latter with 4000 infantry and 1000 cavaliers. Pastor Zenneck was integrated into the regiment of the inheriting Prince Frederic, in position in Fribourg in 1735. The divine Sunday service took place during a certain time without any problems in a room belonging to a senior officer, without any drum-calling, as "a priori" the rule desired in a Catholic land. However, on the complaint from the priests of Fribourg, the commander of the garrison notified the pastor that this worship was forbidden according to the imperial orders, as there was no clear specification regarding free Protestant worship following the surrender.

In Fribourg, an emissary was sent to the Stuttgart consistory, then it was the chaplain Zenneck who pleaded the case in February 1736. On 1st June, the Duke of Wurtemberg stated in a letter to the commander of the garrison that the current surrender was identical to that of 1713 which confirmed the free practice of worship for its troops in Hungary, in Italy and in Sicily, even in consecrated chapels. Fifteen days after receipt, the situation has not changed and the affair goes up to the "Kriegsrat" in Vienna. Behind what seems to be an infringement of the rule, there is something else: from January 1736, Zenneck required the consistory to insist that the Lutheran soldiers confronted the holy sacrament. The inheriting prince gave an order of military respect – the presentation of weapons –but not

---

[213] Ibid., p. 75.
[214] See Plassman, M. *Krug und Defension* ... op. cit. p. 14.

kneeling or uncovering oneself. Moreover, in order to avoid quarrels, Charles Alexander even advised his men to go into in passing the "Venerabile". The Lutherans' problems are therefore the fruit of a Catholic reply which is taken as an insult to the Holy Sacrament: refusal to kneel. After Pastor Zenneck's departure, nothing is ruled. His successor, Brastburger, is confronted with the same refusal by Tillier the commander who,when he authorises Lutheran worship, in return demands the absence of singing! The service without canticles is obviously unthinkable. Brastburger also forbids access to the "lazarett" (infirmary) with the pretext that in order to receive holy communion, the patient must go to the barracks, then come back to the infirmary; for the "rest" the Catholic clergyman is enough. The complaints to Vienna are useless and at the beginning of 1738, things are unchanged, and even get worse with the question of participation of the Wurtemberg troops at Corpus Christi, under the pretext that they belong to a Catholic commander, in the same way as the restriction on attending Mass. In 1740 a letter from the consistory concerning new complaints with the commander and the Vienna court remain without consequence[215]. This affair, which remains without a real solution, is not an isolated case in the 18th century[216].

Behind the practice of worship there are other potential problems between chaplains and priests. In fact, evidence allows it to be understood that Lutheran soldiers, even before being married, create babies with women who follow the regiment, and that they sometimes leave them unbaptised or then go to see the priests to have the Catholic child baptised and have a letter of paternal recognition.[217] In the same way, mixed couples can give rise to discords between chaplains, if there is no respect for the Empire rules

---

[215] Plassman, M, *Bikonfessionnelle Streitkräfte...* op.cCit.,p. 40.
[216] Kolb, C. *Feldprediger in Alt Wurtemberg,* p. 99-107.
[217] Ibid., p 97.

(the father's religion to the son, that of the mother to the daughter).

Another example shows the inherent problems in the Empire army. The practice of spiritual jurisdiction and free worship can give rise to tensions between authorities and clergy as well as between members of the clergy, in spite of the published rules. In 1712, the Capuchins of Weilderstadt officiate with the Badoo troops in a garrison in Calais. We are just before Easter and about one thousand Catholic troops are divided into four groups so as to be able to confess. The news comes to the Duke of Wurtemberg and an order is sent in order to forbid such a practice on his land. In reply, the General Wachtmeister of Vauchoir writes that he himself wanted to use the services of a Capuchin, but he gave it up out of respect for the order; however, one must not fail to say that such a practice took place in quarters in Bietigheim, [218]Besigheim and Markgröningen. One would guess that the application of this measure would depend largely on the context and individuals, and that sometimes what is tolerated at one time may no longer be at another time. In 1760, the abbot of the monks of Marechtal lets the Lutheran chaplain Vaihinger know that he can neither celebrate worship nor visit the patients at Munderkingen, which depends on the abbey. The prelate himself moves to inform the ecclesiastics and the mayor of the little town, and a deputation brings the order in his own hands to the pastor. The latter has the constitution, his experience and his respect for the rules assessed both in Catholic and Protestant territories, but nothing is done. Then he addresses Colonel Honold in Ulm, who takes it up to the imperial minister von Ramswag, who informs the mayor of Munderkingen that Catholics and Protestants must have free practice of their worship under the direction of the Circle chaplains. One sees that pressure can be exerted beyond the rules. Moreover, this same Vaihinger, while he serves in 1758 at Buschtirad (Bohemian states), undergoes taunts from

---

[218] On

Catholics and even a visit from two Catholics from Prague, "like two soldiers", so that he prefers to keep his distance[219]. In 1759, another Lutheran chaplain, Mieg, finds himself prevented from reaching the infirmary by Catholics – men and women armed with batons. On his return he meets the priest who had beforehand notified him of access being forbidden and indicates to him that he is going to take his complaint to the commander, Baron von [220]Order.

One sees, through these examples, that the chaplains had to compromise with territorial realities, with a taste for movements, also contacts with ecclesiastics in the places visited, which moreover are not necessarily bad. In the Royal-German Regiment, the Lutheran pastor Josef Fuoss holds the position of chaplain from 1768 to 1776. The major state of the regiment was then completely Lutheran and he is in charge of the men, who are half Lutheran and half Calvinist. That does not seem to be a problem with his four reformed colleagues in other regiments, at the time of the campaign in Sardinia. If one of them is sent back, that is on the order of the king, seemingly as a mark of caution[221] in respect of the Catholic chaplain. Johann Ludwig Hocker is a (Lutheran) chaplain at the very beginning of the 18th century and takes part in the War of Spanish Succession in Colonel Schmertau's regiment. When he reached Arnheim, Hocker holds a note offering him permission to use the French church and he stays with a baker and not with a pastor; however, he is apparently in contact with a Lutheran pastor – Mr Manne – the Calvinist pastor, Mr D'Outrein, without our knowing more about him[222]. In the autumn of 1701, he goes to Dusseldorf and preaches in the Lutheran church and receives from the Jesuits "two richly decorated

---

[219] Ibid., p 98
[220] ?
[221] Kolb, C.*Feldprediger...*" pp. 24-25.
[222] Mr Johann Ludwig Hocken (…)…Johann Jacob Enderes, 1749, p. 26.

globes".[223] While he is in Cologne, he officiates in private homes: he even baptises a soldier's child, whose godfather is a Catholic innkeeper. On this occasion, a monk – "Ein Prediger- monch" – whose preaching he had already heard, leads him into a separate room and pleasantly chats with him over some good wine. He is also in contact with another monk who brings him to his convent – "S. Thomas Aquinatis" to show him a schoolroom[224]. One may guess that he is also in contact with other priests and reformed pastors, even if the details are sometimes missing. At the beginning of 1702, on the date of the siege of Kaiserswerth, nine soldiers of a Palatine regiment were condemned to hang: one Calvinist, two Catholics and six Lutherans. He looked after the latter and took care of the Lutherans but not only: of an Englishman. At the hospital there were a great many wounded people.[225]

A Jesuit father is also present, but because he does not speak French, it is Hocker who converses with him. A reformed chaplain of an Anhalt regiment calls to him to celebrate holy communion with the Lutheran soldiers of the regiment; an incident took place but it was not due to any of the pastors, only [226]inebriated soldiers.

Models in contacts? Duties and images of chaplains

Up to now we have essentially seen the contacts that the military chaplains could have with external representatives of religions, whether they be clergy themselves or leaders of the territorial Church, like the Duke of Wurtemberg. It is more delicate to glimpse fairly the relations of the chaplains among them. In fact, there are codes and rules which enable us to glimpse between them, while knowing that it is about safeguards from deviations which the princely and military

---

[223] Ibid., p 28 "kostbare globi".
[224] ?
[225] Ibid., p 39
[226] Ibid, p. 47.

authorities do not wish to see emerging at the heart of their units.

The rules and instructions intended for the chaplains enable us to glimpse in fact what must be, from the normal viewpoint, relations and behaviours of the men of God in respect of one another. The principle is simple: it is a question of preventing the chaplains themselves from sowing trouble. That is why. for example, Eberhard Ludwig of Wurtemberg demands fidelity from ecclesiastics to the fundamental laws of the Circle[227]. Some chaplains, however, can meanwhile reveal themselves as authors of problems due to their animosity in relation to their colleagues and to cause veritable little wars[228], even if one can read elsewhere that a cordial agreement is in force. That is why, in the Circle of Souab, a text of 6 July 1757 forbids raising any religious question between chaplains. In order to preserve the symbolic and real balance, steps are taken such as controlling preaching in front of troops on the right wing, which has primacy in the army. In order to prevent trouble among the chaplains, on one occasion it is the pastor, another time the priest, who officiates in this place, whatever the public may be. However, this is not always carried out without conflict: in May1758, the Lutheran chaplain preaches twice in front of the right wing where there is an exclusively Catholic regiment of Bade-Durlach and, making it worse, he refuses to give the place away. Moreover this system of rotation is also a source of quarrelling among chaplains[229]; but is this for confessional reasons and/or a question of prestige?

However, to look closely at rules of territorial armies, one does not see appearing – or seldom – the question of the relationship between chaplains of different confessions: the Brandebourg rules of 1646 and 1673 indicate nothing for

---

[227] Generallandesarchiv, Karlsruhe 46/3818, letter to Ludwig Wukgekn von Baden. 8.04.1699.
[228] Plassman, M.*Bikonfessionnelle Streitkräfte...* op. cit. p. 42
[229] Ibid., p. 41.

example as to these possible relationships. It is more in the instructions given to chaplains that one finds this aspect. They are in direct relation with the rules issued, but, chronologically, they can precede them, as matrixes of what these relationships should be. On 2 July 1658, an instruction is given to Michael Heinemann, chaplain of Duke Ulrich of Wurtemberg, Lieutenant General of the King of France. On eight points, two are concerned directly with interconfessional relations. Heinemann thus has a mission to prevent "Jesuits, monks, priests as former pastors, reformed clergy" from approaching the Duke and always to prevent him from the latter with fidelity. In the same way, at the time of these contacts with these other servants of God, he must be discreet in his discussions and not allow these "chaplains" to touch on the Lutherans' money.[230]

It is therefore on another wavelength that one can determine these relationships, which occur because one is waiting for chaplains and the image that the latter send out. Whatever the confession and also the military rank, the wait in respect of religion and its representatives is identical[231].

All the princes expect a contribution to discipline from the chaplain, for the health of the men and also the maintenance of a religious identity. In fact, the army, a separate world from society, could be a vehicle of a confessionalisation: from that time, with the first identity being that of the soldier and not Catholic or Protestant. At least during the Thirty Years War., confessional difference does not seem to have been a special reason for quarrels between soldiers[232]. If one considers this proposition likely, one understands better the States' interest in setting up an institutionalised chaplaincy, certainly aimed at moralising

---

[230] Kolb, C. *Feldprediger in Alr-Wurtemberg*. Op. cit. p.75.
[231] A rule coming from the Souab Circle of 2.05.1687 stating "Alldien aber…Kriegraison…Gottlichem…Caplan und Feld-Prediger .."(quoted according to Storm, C. *Der Schulbiache Fedherr*…op cit. p.359, note 74).
[232] Kapser, C. *DiebayerischeKriegorganisation*" op.cit. p. 68.

and disciplining the soldiers, but also keeping them in a living faith and in a confessional identity, while a number of soldiers, during the Thirty Years War, seem to be religiously indifferent after the first years of fighting. How many soldiers were there, like this Ackermann, a Lutheran who formerly served under the order of Mansfield and Christian of Brunswick, and who took part in the siege and massacre of a great many co-religionists at Magdeberg in 1631? Among the first efforts, one may pick up a rule decreed by Christian IV of Denmark for his troops working in the empire where the soldier's duties are mentioned, the obligation to attend the Sunday sermon under the leadership of pastors whose names are not known, nor the terms of recruitment. It is with Gustavus Adolphus of Sweden, accompanied by Jacob Fabricius, King's chaplain, also senior of the army chaplains, which is held precisely as one chaplain per regiment.

That is why the image of the pastor and priest in the regiment must be exemplary, otherwise it is the very image of his religion which is damaged. Thus, all the military rules raise the question of alcohol for the chaplains, which is at the same time a reality and a means intended to throw disgrace on the other confession. Pastor Moser of Magdeberg left an account in which he particularly states that, on 28 October 1630, he had to have the Catholic chaplain Fredrich Schenck to stay in his home,[233] whom he denounces due to drink: "That is very painful for me. He often brings guests home in the evening, especially all sorts of monks and priests, and that is done at the cost of my beer". In 1631, he complains about another Catholic chaplain, who also devotes himself to drink and who is a "gottloser bube", a godless tearaway[234]. Obviously, one must take this feature prudently, but one knows whatever the confession, that the abuse of drink is denounced among the chaplains, and the rules are intended to stop this practice.

---

[233] Winter, R."*Moser...Magdeburg*" r.1874, p.27.
[234] Ibid., p 31.

In the case of Brandebourg in 1656, paragraph V says clearly: ...no pastor, when he must celebrate divine service, must be drunk, or in such case he must be taken away from the camp[235],

Paragraph VI states about him that:
...a pastor who, outside the times of his services, followed a bad downward path, and did not adapt his life to his teaching, such a pastor, if he does not mend his ways after receiving three warnings to have to change his behaviour, must not be tolerated in our camp.

The same ruling, renewed in 1673, indicates the same points *ne varietur*. The young failure then goes before the consistory and can be sent away. With different structures for Catholic chaplains, again we find the same ambitions to limit the abuses of the men of God. The latter are really true. Officers and representatives of the Churches complain, at least in the 17thth century, of the bad conduct of a number of chaplains, all mainly due to drink. These deviant behaviours may come from the mediocre pay or from a lack of preparation and maturity, from which derive the authorities' efforts to better control the training of applicants.

The question of the image that one gives to the men and to other confessions is certainly present. Some of them are anxious about the quality and frequency of worship. When the rules insist so much on the duty to hold regular services or masses, it is sure that this is in order to teach the soldiers but also, in the case of mixed armies, to give a positive image of one's own religion. One must, however, apprehend the soldiers' world for what it is: a separate society where the porosity of types of military behaviour makes soldiers reticent souls, for many of them, not to God, but to religious practice, while superstitious practices have some success. In a 1762 report for the Wurtemberg troops,

---

[235] ..Churfulriches...Brandenburgefechet Oder... Berlin Christof Runge, 1656

one may read that "atheism and naturalism" are making progress, that "often it happens for a whole month", in spite of efforts, for divine service to be held while the Catholic chaplains regularly hold their own, even in a Protestant territory, without for all that leading the Protestants to Catholicism[236]. This is not an isolated case, but also exists elsewhere, as pointed out by [237]Albert Babeau for the French army. The army is certainly not a place of peacefulness, but of co-existence for the chaplains and soldiers, and indifference everywhere for the latter.

To deal with military chaplains, here within the framework of the Holy Empire, calls for taking a double reality into account, in order not to imagine contacts between clergymen outside a very pregnant context. On the one hand, their presence at the heart of armies and units remains subject at the same time to the regulatory and confessional framework of the Empire, but also, in some cases, the proper will of the territorial lord. On the other hand, they intervene in a military framework which, in spite of the efforts of civil and religious authorities, tends to form a very special societal entity in which religion is not really the first preoccupation of the men: works of piety must not deceive the present reader. The contacts between chaplains and also between chaplains and local clergymen cannot therefore only be seen with this background and cannot only be considered in terms of opposition and competition. In fact, even if there had been individual oppositions between chaplains, do these problems[238] arise in respect of both confessional and personal questions? It is difficult to give a firm answer. On the other hand, real oppositions met by

---

[236] Kolb, C. *Feldprediger in Alt-Wurtemberg* art.cit.p. 80.

"[237] Babeau, A. "*La vie militaire sous l'ancien Régime*", Firmin-Didot,1890 p220 sq,

[238] A systematic article in, J.L. "Document, history in ecclesiastical study…modernes". "Recherches.. ..religieuse" t 92-4 2004, pp. 597-635 Paris institut d'Etudes Augustiniennes 1999.

these chaplains during their travels often rely on territorial law and Empire law, which obviously does not exclude confessional rejection. However, latent or actual opposition does not prevent a connection between individuals and practices. The considerations as regards the men of God are identical, in the same way that the uncertain roving monk's life, which is free, could lead one to another question: is there a community of chaplains? Or, more precisely, is a chaplain also a pastor or priest? Finally, a great many things are still to be questioned beyond some enlightenment given here, in order to apprehend these chaplains in contact. Among them, the reality of relationships between Catholic and Protestant chaplains in the face of a common enemy, certainly France, but especially the Turk, the true enemy of the faith, made it possible to sound out, to qualify and hierarchise these contacts.

***

Protestant influences or general ignorance?
Some Catholic parishes of the Archdiocese of Prague visited by Mgr Berka of Duba in 1594
NICOLAS RICHARD

It is fairly well known, from the studies of Jean-Louis Quantin, that doctrinal studies greatly contributed to the progress of learning. The contacts, intellectual and controversial, between theologians of different obediences, gave a shot in the arm to patristic studies and to the rise of the critical method[239]. Outside the Republic of Letters, did contacts between Catholics and non-Catholics have the same type of effect as the critical method[240]? Or, to express

---

[239] Good example: Quantin, J.L. "Les Jésuites de l'érudition anglicane" *Dix-septieme siècle* no.237, 2007, pp. 167-195.

[240] On the political idea of friendship, it is true in diplomacy: Haan, B. *Ll'amitié entre princes...Religion (1500-1570)* Paris PUE 2011 eso pm1-3 pp. 167-195.

it more neutrally, what were the consequences of situations where the clergy were in close contact?

If there was a kingdom in the 16th century where the clergy were in close contact, it was Bohemia. Elsewhere, in France, Poland or Hungary, the fact that a law forced the clergy to co-exist was a new thing or something in the future. In Bohemia, this lasted from the middle of the 15th century. The country lived under the so-called "double legal faith" ("legalni dvojveri"). This made Catholics and Hussites, later called Utraquists, coexist. This regime created a kingdom of two peoples ("stadt dvojiho lidu"), where the unity of the country was strengthened by an ideology of friendship between the members of the two parts[241], a friendship which nostalgically emphasises the[242] memorialists of the time of the Thirty Years War, when the system hailed splinters[243].

This framework not only organised the coexistence of the two types of clergy. It also made the necessary contacts. The parishes of the old archdiocese of Prague were shared between two consistories, the Catholic (from on high, based at the cathedral) and the Utraquist (from below, meeting at Notre-Dame of Tyn). The second, without a bishop who could ordain candidates to the ministry, had not abandoned, in spite of its criticism of Rome's bad habits, the need for sacramental ordination by a bishop holding the apostolic succession (although Luther had advised the opposite from 1523)[244]. He founded, beyond his canonical legitimacy of

---

[241] ?

[242] The Hussite Jan Rokycana (1396-1471) chosen as Archbishop by the Diet of Bohemia (1435) never recognised that Rome left the seat open.
[Is this footnote 237?]E.g. that of the defenestration in 1628 of Vilém Slavata (1572-1652) JIRECEJ=K H, "Pameti …slavery to 1608 to 1629". Prague, Kober 186601868, p 40 sq

[244] E.g., Krarup, M. *Ordination in Wittemberg,* Tubingen Siebek, 2007, pp. 57-66,

the vacancy of the Prague siege from the 1420s. With the restoration of the Roman Catholic archbishopric in Prague in 1562, he was in fact forced to recognise "de jure", while refusing his authority "de facto et grosso modo". As for the Catholics, from 1564 they enjoyed the result of taking communion with the faithful "sub utraque", in order to facilitate unity of the Utraquists with Rome. For all that, saying that the two priesthoods were in contact, better, intertwined, passages moreover being continuous with the jurisdiction of one consistory to that of another.

What were the concrete religious consequences of these contacts, of this intertwining of the two priesthoods? This is not a new question. But it is usually asked the other way round. Historians talk about the parish situation in Bohemia at the end of the 16th century. They observed what we will call abuses, and in a large number. Now, among them, some of these, such as cohabitation, are legal in ecclesiastical disciplines coming from the Reformation. Then, their explanation is easily found: these abuses come from the intertwining of the priesthoods[245]. What we [246]shall try to work out here is the soundness of the minority in this syllogism: is it a question of reciprocal influences? And therefore more broadly: what are the actual consequences of this intertwining of the priesthoods?

To reply exhaustively to these questions goes beyond the scope of one article. We concentrate our attention on one example, from a document which is precious due to its rarity[247], an inspection of the parishes of Brandys and Labem in 1594, by the Archbishop of Prague, Mgr Berka de

---

[245] E.g. analysis by Winter, Z. *Zivot cirkevni* Prague Orta 1894, p. 631.
[246] Brandes am der elbe 25km NE from Prague
[247] Narodni archive, Prague, vol. 8 41 /2 18 4.07.1594 Brandys and Labem..occupation of benefices.

Duba[248] . The <u>study of this text will enable one for the second time, to see the true nature</u> of these contacts between priesthoods and to determine their reciprocal influence and its limits.

Administration of the royal region of Brandys nad Labem north-east of Prague - this great lordship had been from the beginnings of the reign of the Emperor Rodolphe II (1576-1612) the favourite summer residence of the sovereign. It was therefore not surprising that the Archbishop was there. In good Tridentine prelacy, he gained fro his presence in order to inspect his clergy.

There was something more: Rodolphe II had conceded his right of collature on the parishes of his estates[249]. This meant that the Chamber of Bohemia, the administration in charge of the estate, left to the Archbishop the right to present the priests of these parishes. This grant "ad hominem" de facto brought the parishes of the royal estate under the jurisdiction of the Catholic consistory. It was therefore Catholic priests, at least *de jure*", that Berka had called that day, and that he decreed to come in, after being informed with the "l'heitman" on possible complaints against them – there were none.

The Archbishop began with a sermon where he explained that the sovereign had given him their benefices. He stated that there was no senior member among them, and decreed to those who received the holy oils from the Notre Dame de Tyn church, that is from the utraquat, that in future they should receive them from the cathedral, in other words from himself. Six priests were then examined in turn and their replies were an eloquent picture of the diversity of practices in Bohemia. The first, the priest of Brandys, Jean

---

[248] On Berka (Dube) (1551-1606) historic literature is poor; see Eberhard, W. "Berka und Leipa"; Chaline, O. *Les princes eveques en Boheme – 1550-1650*.

[249] His predecessor Martin Medek (1581-1590) had received it 10.09.1581. Rozpravy Ceske Akademie 46 Alois wiesner, 1912 p. 328) also? Incomplete

Cleska (in Czech: Cejca) was undoubtedly Catholic. Born in a region which was partly faithful to Rome ("Stedre"), he had been ordained by Archbishop Anton Brus of Mohelnice (1561-1580) and had always stayed under his jurisdiction. He was not cohabiting and recited his breviary. The rite that he practised on the other hand was low orthodox: he chanted the gospel and epistle in Czech and maintained the practice of dry masses, he celebrated the feast of Jan Hus, gave communion to the faithful without prior confession, ruling out the local custom. He was also accused of a typically Hussite practice, that of having given communion to a baby. He defended himself, claiming that the host that he had given was not consecrated. While that may have been true, the scandal remained. We should pause for a moment to consider this practice. What did it mean? It is difficult to resolve. Analogies are possible: thus, in the archdeaconry of Longuyon (diocese of Treves) in the years 1627-1628, a great many priests gave hosts which were simply blessed to children at Easter and to women at the time of their menstruation[250][251]. The faithful did not know they had received a sacramental, and not a sacrament. It is not obvious – at Brandys, the added difficulty is that the host was even blessed. Five years after Berka's visit, the commentary of Saint Thomas of Suarez appeared in Rome. He discussed the possibility of giving an un-consecrated host in communion to a sinner, in order[252] to avoid sacrilege and scandal at the same time. If he rejected this solution, having studied the different cases, it was not insoluble; having it was not without having been discussed it at length,

---

[250] The index of Kaiser by Carriere, V. *Revue de...l'Église de France* r. 1569, 1929, p. 496 – the faithful thought they received consecrated hosts.

[251] Kaiser, J B. "*Die Archdiakonat Longuyon ... Visitations 1628-1629.* Colmar 1928-1929 III, pp. 17-18 IV, p. 76, p.157.

[252][252] Suárez, F.J. "Commentarium...Sacramentis", Venice, Franscechi 1590. t III pp. 820-821. Professor at Alcala.

while pointing out that some authors admitted it[253]. In what measure did the practice correspond to these theories? In this type of matter, the question collides with an almost insoluble problem of sources (as the usage that some present Orientals would make of blessed but un-consecrated eucharistic bread, in order to give communion to the faithful while avoiding debasement, with what seems to be disputed pastoral effects).

But let us go on to the next parish. The priest of Chotetŏv, Kean Makarius, ordained by Mgr Brun in1573, gave communion to his parishioners from both groups, also without prior confession. However, he said he had "kept processions, in the Catholic manner" in his subsidiary of Slivno, in the Kosarky estate which belonged, not to the sovereign, but to the Kolovrat family. He recited his hours. His itinerary was not without sudden changes. Born in Litoměřice, he had been a cantor, was ordained, then had kept his distance towards the Catholic discipline. A pastor from Frankfurt-on-Main had married himself and his wife. At the time of his visit, his wife was dead. Moreover, he had spent some time under the jurisdiction of the Utraquist consistory.

The third person to be examined was the priest of Kostelec nad Labem (lbekosteletz), Etienne Benedicti, a Hungarian ordained in Presbourg, which had always been under the jurisdiction of the Utraquist consistory. However, this Benedicti was a curious heretic: he recited his breviary and had neither wife nor child. He refused communion of small children in spite of their parents' wishes. He also demanded an intervention of the Archbishop against the faithful of the Moravian Brothers who lived in his parish under the direction of an old woman. The Archbishop ordered him to come under his obedience and to keep his parish, but from that time to refuse communion without prior confession.

---

[253] Skybova, A. *Le ordinationi dei sacerdoti...scolo*. Graciotti, S, "*talia...europeo*, Florence: Olschki 1999, p. 51565.

Although he was Silesian, the priest of Předměřice nad Jizerou was called Jean Moravus. He had been ordained in Vienna and had spent five years under the jurisdiction of the Utraquist consistory, kept the chastity of his state and recited his hours when he could. If he gave communion to his faithful people "sub utraque" and without prior confession, he had a personal interpretation of the ban on giving communion to small children required by the consistory from below the archbishop; he neglected it here, in the face of the well-settled custom, but did not always respect it outside his parish.

The priest of Dřevčice, Andre Passecky, from Bohemia, a sexagenarian, had passed,[254] under the jurisdiction of the Church of Tyn, as soon as he was ordained in Venice. His parish took communion "sub utraque" and celebrated the annual feast of Jan Hus. Was he, however, an Utraquist himself? He certainly recited his hours, but he justified himself by the infidelity of his servants of the obligation where he was found to have taken a wife, evoking examples of the Old Testament and clerks of the consistory. That did not prevent him from being obedient to Berka and to promise not to give communion to small children in future.

The priest of Svémyslice for two years, Jean Xenomenes, was a Polish Catholic, ordained in Krakov, who recited the Prague breviary. His maid was of canonical age. He certainly gave communion to his faithful people "sub utraque" but he had, he said, brought many of them back to practising confession, which had cost him unfriendliness from someof the parishioners, who were going to receive the sacraments from the previous priest, in Dřevčice. But even the orthodoxy of Xenomenes was not without a hitch: he gave communion to children at puberty. Such a practice was curious and difficult to interpret. It does not seem to correspond with the folklore of purification

---

[254] Graciotti, S. *Italia Boemia...europeo*, Florence, Olschki,1999, pp. 51-65.

which did not require the presence of the new-born baby[255]. It could be the influence of countries which had been through the Reformation, when they had maintained the ceremony of purification -although the rite of Svémyslice was not Protestant at all[256]. In the same way, the natural link that one could make with the Utraquist need for communion for small children is largely illusory: reformers in Prague did not connect this practice at the time of purification[257]. On the other hand, the relationship between purification (on average, according to doctors and folklorists, forty days after giving birth) and oriental baptism (which was also forty days after birth) without possible exception – is obvious. Also in Moravia, moreover, Cardinal Dietrichstein, Bishop of the neighbouring diocese of Olomouc, was confronted at the beginning of the next decade by one of his priests, who was not Polish, but originally from the Balkans, [258]who followed the original rite. His only reaction was to find out whether he was united or not.

Berka did not take this trouble. After interrogation, he decreed to his priests – "gravissimis verbis": to live a chaste and exemplary life, not to give communion to children, to restore (rursus pristino usus restituerent) sacramental confession, not to introduce "new" feasts – in other words, those of Jan Hus – and to disperse the conventicles of the Brothers. The next day the priests promised to obey him,

---

[255] van Gennep, A., *Manuel du folklore francais* contemporain, 1943, Picard 1972ed t 1

[256] If Luther, then English Puritans, denounced purification as a papist superstition, the ceremony was maintained in the English churches and those of the Empire; see *Oxford History of the Reformation* OUP, 1996. Vol. 1, p.331-332.

[257] One cannot omit an influence of the Hussites' old need as the Hussites of the Brandys area accepted this practice.

[258] Oriental discipline was then to give communion to children after baptism up to Maronite synod of 1596; see Heyberger, R, *Chrtiens du proche orient catholique*……Rome: BEFAR 1994 p.236.christianisme boheme"

announced their profession of faith from the Council of Trent and from the Archbishop they received absolution for their faults. Berka was able to inspect the parish church of Brandys and have inscriptions that were insulting to the work of Jan Hus removed.

Clergymen in contact or ignorant clerks?

One may ask a question: these parishes that the Archbishop inspected, could one describe them as Catholic? It is not clear whether the historian's response would be the same as that of the Archbishop – even if it is not really probable that the historian was right[259]. One would be tempted to reason thus: if a population is hostile to the Roman church and its priest is of doubtful orthodoxy, who practises "sui generis" rites or those tasting of heresy, or he obeys an excommunicated hierarchy, then one hesitates to consider that parish as Catholic.

There is a type of paradox. The questions of the enquiry seek to determine which priests have (or do not have) heretical practices. The conclusion itself places them all on the same level. Berka grants them all, after reciting the "Credo" of Pius IV, absolution for their mistakes. Such an act had a very strong value. It did not mean anything other than the fact the Archbishop gave up requiring a recantation or at least the specific oath that Rome demanded from Utraquists returning to the Church[260].This meant that the priests had not been heretics. From the canonical viewpoint, it was certainly wisdom. The fidelity of these priests to Berka was not forcibly acquired by him for a long time. In any case, the Archbishop protected them from the complex legal consequences of recanting. Recanting is in fact the most irrefutable formal proof of a heresy, because it is a declaration of heresy "a posteriori" and therefore is at risk

---

[259] Parma, T. *Frantick Kardinal moravske cirkve,* Brno Matice Moravska, 2011, pp. 318-319.

[260] Aries, P. *Religions populaires et reformes…* Paris: Cerf, 1975, p 77.

of creating relapses[261]. How could one do that, however, so that the priests could escape recanting? All these priests had been validly ordained. Those who had passed under the jurisdiction of the Utraquist consistory were therefore apostates. In addition, a clergyman passed to heresy is "a priori" even more than a faithful member, a "notorious" heretic or "denounced as such". One could not therefore suffer "communication" (even the simple "communication foris") with them[262].

The texts do not give the reasons that the Archbishop had for acting in this way. The most likely reason is that he used a possibility that recalled for example the Jesuit Francisco Toledo. Speaking of peasants, he thought that it was possible to find errors there against the faith, without them being heretics themselves. There could be a belief of good faith in heretic doctrines preached by their bishop and ; ideas against the Scriptures (that they did not know) without there being a sin or a heresy. Toledo used pertinacity above all on the scholars. About "rustic and ignorant people", the Jesuit went so far as to write:

If one of them held something against the apostolic traditions or a definition of the Pope, he would not for all that be tenacious ("pertinax"); for he himself is not held to know that it is a question of a rule of faith [which excuses him from sin)] he does not know that it is about things against the Church (which keeps him from heresy).

Manifestly, Mgr Berka exploited it with his priests. He did not consider them as heretical priests from Utraquist parishes returning to the bosom of the Church, no, but as ignorant Catholic priests at the head of an uneducated flock.

---

[261] Participation with heretics at sacraments, in acts of worship or legal life, is banned: the decree "Ad vivanda" scandal (21.07.1418 agreement of Boulogne) ruled on methods of defence.

[262] Toletus, F.J. "*Instructio sacerdotum* [1564]. Rouen, M de Preauls, 1619, pp. 594-595 lib IV cap iii 4 "Quod si teneat aliquid …contra ecclesiam"

And after all, he had jurisdiction to decree what was Catholic and what was not, a power that the historian does not have. The nature of this ignorance was problematic. In order that it should dispense with fault against the doctrine, it was necessary for it not to be vincible, crass or supine, but truly invincible, being the only thing that truly excuses violation of the law, as [263]Suárez noted. From the pastoral point of view, thanks to this solution, therefore there was not, at least in theory, sacrilege or "communication in sacris". Was it therefore a question of clergymen in contact, or of a single clergyman, the Catholic clergyman of the archdiocese? It is sure that a Mgr Berka, anxious to enlarge as much as possible the arch of the Church outside which there was no salvation, saw in all these priests Catholic but ignorant priests, which led them to heretical behaviours without falling into heresy.

So much, therefore, for the nature of these contacts between clergymen. What were the consequences of it?

Reciprocal influences

Although they were all Catholics, each of these priests had a very special career, with contact with non-Catholics. And their parishes, although Catholic, knew a form of worship and ecclesiastical discipline which seemed to be very marked by the influences of the other confessions. However, was it a matter of influences? In the conclusion of this volume, Yves Krumenacker is on his guard against "essentialising" research of the influences between clergymen of different confessions. That is fair. The ideal purity that the reformers were seeking never actually came into the order of the facts. And the confessions, even separated from the old trunk of the mediaeval Catholic church, were broadly heirs. The historiography, looking for influences, forgot this. Nonetheless, the problem of Bohemia remains. There, the division of the parishes into

---

[263] Suáez F.J. *Disputionnum de censuris in communi ... divi Thomas.* Opera omnia, Mayence 1618, t. XVIII p. 32 sq.

two camps dated from a century and a half. However, this vagueness, this mixture of practices, was maintained. How could one interpret it? In what way was it tied to the intertwining of the two types of clergyman?

The question of priestly celibacy seems to provide a school case. On the difference of the two consistories, Luther did not advocate it. It seems that his influence was obvious in the case of Makarius, a priest married by a pastor. It was the analysis of the Praguian consistories at the time that the marriage of priests was a sign of the penetration of Lutheranism. However, if it is well known that clerical cohabitation in the Catholic clergy in the century of the Reformation was much less developed at the time and it was still written down sometimes[264]. There was an old background of justification of priestly cohabitation which had no need of Luther in order to exist. Not that it was a question of a theological position opposed to the pseudo-invention of priestly celibacy at the Council of Latran (which leaves out the canons fixed at the Council of Elvire (and the fifth century and their reiteration up to 1139): it was rather the sociological justification of cohabitation. The priest of Dřevčice provided a good example: he claimed to be married without being able to be satisfied with his female servants in the example of patriarchs and some of his superiors. As for Makarius, the fact that he was married in Frankfurt, this Protestant land where his union had legal power, showed that he belonged to a world where the decree "Tamesi" demanding the presence of his own clergyman had still not become customary. Besides, on him, the Lutheran influence was not obvious. It was however a risk that the consistories were not wrong to safeguard.

---

[264] See the interesting connections brought by Hubert Jedin on affirmation of Reformationslibell sent by Ferdinand1 to Council of Trent : "servens...matrimonii cupido...matitus"; "Concilium Tridentini..." Fribourg-en-Brisgau Herder t.XIII pp. 677-678, 6-7.

This report of a visit shows what interested Berka: to enquire into certain key practices between Catholics and heretics. Whatever he thought of them, all the abuses that he found were not reducible to these current models. Thus, the dry Masses of Brandys, in the absence of confession everywhere, were mediaeval Catholic survivals. The communion of an infant with an unconsecrated host was an abuse which was found elsewhere in Europe, and one which some doctors, as witnessed by Suárez, tolerated. As for communion given to babies at the time of purification by the Polish priest, this was nothing else, it seems to us, than a practice of the Greek Orthodox Church which must have been known in Poland!

From that time, the true cultural consequences of contacts among the confessions were particularly connected with the intertwining of Catholics and Utraquists. The influence was not one- way: better maintenance of processions "in the Catholic manner" in parishes that were faithful to Rome, brought the utraquists durably to these types of ceremonies, that they had regrettably [265] seen supressed. In another direction, chanting readings in Czech at Mass by the priest of Brandys bore witness to the attraction of Hussite church music. There was also communion for infants, which the only one to refuse was paradoxically the most "Utraquist" of all our priests, and the celebration of the feast of Jan Hus, in parishes that were officially Catholic.

But at what point could one talk about the matter of a consequence of contacts between clergymen? The problem was that of pressure on the faithful. They were not content to let their unhappiness be known or to vote with their feet, as at Svémyslice: in Brandys, after the visit, the members of the town council took on the priest for failing to celebrate the feast of Jan Hus and had the inscriptions blotted out. This was important: in 1587, there was a riot by Protestants

---

[265] See Jedin, H at Council of Trent: (*Concilium tridentini...*) Fribourg -en-Brisgau 1937 t. XIII pp. 677-678, no.6-7.

and the Czech Brothers against the Catholics[266]. In 1595, the complaint went to the Diet and the priest, faithful to Berka, preferred to leave. [267]. The town council again demanded that his successor Valentin Zavadsky leave, by requests that were also repeated in vin with the Archbishop[268]. Both in Brandys and in other parishes, the basis of the argument was the same: rather than belonging to one or another religious party, the communities preferred to cancel local traditions or customs in order to challenge their priests or require them to give communion to infants. The language used was that of political privilege, not of the religious rite.

The visit of 1594 also had political consequences. The Chamber of Bohemia had acknowledged its errors in the choice of some priests – the worst, that of Chotětov, defender of the marriage of priests, had been expelled. But at the same time, the Chamber was not ready to acknowledge[269] the Archbishop's right of patronage that the sovereign had given to him. The Vice-Chancellor Krystof Zelinsky, a member of the Unity of Brothers, notoriously hostile to Catholics, developed a fairly special legal[270] argument by granting the right of presentation in his parishes, did not grant the Archbishop the choice of the priest to invest. He thought that Berka had to give the parishes, which he held from the king, the patronage of Utraquist priests, if that was the local custom. But Zelinsky only wanted to see a lay person as the Archbishop, a

---

[266] Winter, Z. *Zivot cirkevni...* " op.cit. p. 214.

[267] S L. 16.01.1595, Cejka to Berka, Palacky, F. op.cit. t IX no. 9.

[268] Palacky, F. *Snemy ceske...* op.cit X 179, 18.07.1601. See Narodni Archive Prague Archbishops APA I 3284 C 103/1 2002 fol. 88-97, fol. 99 1597.

[269] Borovicka, J "Pad Zelinskeho...Cechach v letech 1597-1599"; Cesky Casopis Historicky 28, 1922 o 277-304;

[270] Palacky, F. et al. *Snemy ceske...* op.cit. IX11 Brandys, 22.01.1595. S.Redfester "heitman" at Berka.

particular type of committed lord, deprived as of usufruct of his temporary right. He refused to consider him as a Catholic prelate chosen by the Emperor, in other words, the owner of a jurisdiction in the parishes in which he invested the priests.

In this configuration, one must go back a little way to the effect of narrow contacts between the clergymen in Bohemia in the 16th century. Most of what Berka brought up such as abuses or errors were not an influence of neighbouring and adverse confessions, between local communities and the Archbishop or between the Archbishop and political authorities, the master-word of these polemics being the defence of traditions, in other words privileges, and not considerations of doctrine. In other terms, there were a great many contacts, although less than it seemed – but in this muddle of power, could one still talk about a clergyman, that is to say, of an autonomous order?

The example presented is not different from what is known elsewhere in other Catholic parishes in Bohemia[271]. One can therefore without too much extrapolation draw general conclusions from it.

In the Europe of contacts between clergymen, Bohemia has a special place, which in our view can only be compared with the mixed chapters of Empire[272]: Catholic and non-Catholic clergymen co-existed there in a unique hierarchical structure. Such a situation ruled until 1609 where the letter of his Majesty Rudolf II, establishing freedom of worship, suppressed the guarantees.

From this situation a remarkable confessional haziness in the parishes was born, of which this visit is a good example. It is not a question of a mediaeval heritage, of a

---

[271] Cf 3.03.1585 M.Strakonicky, Narodni Archive, Prague APA 1 2901 C 73 cart 721.

[272] Nottarp, H. *Zur communication...heretics*, t.1933, pp. 107-125. Odenthal, A. *Die ordinatio...* Munster Aschendorfff 2005.

delay of confessionalisation, but of a modern phenomenon, partly born from a policy of union of the Tridentine papacy. But this haziness does not make the studied parishes the place where clergymen of different confessions operated. Here, they are, to the great astonishment of the historian, Catholic, the ignorance of the clergymen seeming to excuse them from heresy.

Did the Catholic clergy undergo the influence of that of the other confessions? The appearances were deceptive; the influences are very much less than seemed at the very beginning, one must conclude after an examination.

What about the clergymen in contact in Bohemia of the end of the 16th century? Certainly, even if the question is expressed in voluntarily anachronistic terms, which do not exactly come within the framework of the era; they are more complex than one would have thought at the beginning. Which is not a supplementary sign of the interest in the proposed problem.

Claude Joly (1607-1700) on a journey
A man of the Church and his inter-clerical contacts
In a pluri-religious Europe
In the middle of the XVIIth century
Andreas NIJENHUIS-BESCHER

"saw there Monsieur Manasseh Ben Israel, a very famous doctor among those through his writings. I came to know him by means of his book called "Conciliator" which took place in Paris –
Voyage de Hollande, Claude Joly (1607-1700).

The Congress of Westphalia is an important marker in the history of Europe. This first peace conference on the European scale ended up, in terms of tedious discussions[273]

---

[273] In the town of Munster, an Empire garrison is made neutral by temporary suspension of its duties towards the Empire from May 1643. Osnabrück is guaranteed neutrality.

(1645-1648) in a new political and religious balance. In future, the issue of the main European conflicts is negotiated in a diplomatic congress, in the same area, which became the political crossroads of Europe[274].

On a social level, the 1648 treaties took on the religious coexistence at the very heart of Christianity. In spite of the resurgence, in the second half of the 17th century, of the religious dimension of the battles, confessional diversity is admitted as fact. As a result, once the religious alteration was accepted, peaceful exchanges can be conceived between the ecclesiastics of different sides. The polemics of the time of the colloquiums and tractarian struggles surely hoped that with their strong "truth" could overcome the "horrible obstinance" of the persistent opposite camp.

The conditions of an inter-confessional communication are above all united in the States where a religious coexistence without spatial segregation existed, such as France under the regime of the Edict of Nantes (1598), and the United Provinces thanks to the freedom of conscience granted by the Union of Utrecht (1579)[275]. The Parisian ecclesiastic Claude Joly (1607-1700) confirms the treaty of union between the situations of French and Dutch religious coexistence, by multiplying the inter-clerical and interconfessional contacts from Munster, where he stays from July 1646 to March1647, during the diplomatic congress.

With an educational and recreational aim (or perhaps simply in order to elude boredom?) Canon Joly made several excursions into the outskirts of the Rhenish town, particularly to Osnabrück and to Cologne. He also goes

---

[274] After the 1648 treaties of Munster and Osnabrück, the diplomatic congresses at Aix-la-Chapelle (1668 and 1748) Nimwegen (1697), Ryswick (1697) and Utrecht (1713-1715) punctuate the modern European story.

[275] Kaplan, B. *Divided by Faith... Modern Europe*. Cambridge (MA) Harvard University Press, 2007 Saupin, G. *Naissance... temps modernes,* Rennes PUR, 1998.

three times to the nearby United Provinces for a long period of thirty days. The "Voyage" made to Munster in Westphalia, and other nearby places, in 1646 and 1647 offers several examples of contacts, both literary and physical, between clergymen, particularly of a meeting with the Amsterdam rabbi Menasseh Ben Israel[276]. This chapter explores the methods of inter-confessional relations and, beyond that, the question of the position held by clergymen in the society of the mid-17th century.

The journey, a favourable context for inter-confessional contacts

Coming from a Picardian family, Claude Joly is a Canon of the Catholic Chapter of Notre Dame de Paris when he is called to follow his former pupil Anne-Genevieve de Bourbon-Conde, Duchess of Longueville (1619-1679) by travelling. The latter prepares in June 1646 to join her husband, Henri II of Orleans, Duke of Longueville (1595-1664) in Munster. The Duke of Longueville represents France "in this august Assembly of the Plenipotentiaries of Christianity, of which all of Europe awaits its salvation!"[277].

A letter signed in May 1646 by the Secretary of State Henri-Auguste de Lomenie de Brienne (1595-1666) on behalf of the very young enjoint Louis XIV invites "our dear and beloved Monsieur Joly, Canon of the Church of our Beautiful town of Paris" to accompany the Duchess of Longueville with [278]"our first Plenipotentiary for the general Peace Treaties in Munster" with "Misters of Avaux and Servien"[279]. The imposing cortege of "three carriages above those of Madame the Princess"[280] is put in motion on

---

[276] Thanks to the length of his stay, Claude Joly also meets famous scholars at Leyden and Utrecht.

[277] Joly, C. *Voyage...* op.cit. p IV (letter)

[278] Ibid., p. XVIII (letter with royal mark).

[279] Ibid., p. 77. Abel Servien (1595-1659) and Claude de Mesnes, Count of Avaux (1595-1650).

[280] Ibid., p. 1

"Wednesday 20th day of [281] June 1646, at three and a quarter hours after noon". The journey proceeds without any trouble.

By coming back from Munster, as in going there, both foreign towns and in those in France, where all the companies receive them with drums beating and signs on show, and they fired the cannon when she arrived, and when she left[282].

The group made its "entry into the Town with fifteen carriages, each of them pulled by six horses "[283] into Munster on "Monday 23rd July"[284]. The Canon then stayed in Munster until 27th March 1647, that is for eight months. "Madame de Longueville had become fat in Munster and not wishing to give birth, she decided to return to France. Thus, Claude Joly returned to his chapter on 2 May 1647, after a journey lasting nearly a year."

Aged around forty-four years, the publisher had not undertaken another journey beforehand. The genesis of his "Voyage", published almost a quarter of a century after these events, at the same time reflects the spirit of curiosity of its author and the custom of travellers [285] to put into writing that which he did not judge, for the relief of his memory"[286]. In fact, Joly states:

As we had the pleasure of going for a walk, it being in the long summer days, and Madame and Mademoiselle de Longueville, with whom we were going out, only taking one outing per day, and sometimes staying two and three days in the best towns, I had plenty of time [287] to look around the places we passed through.

---

[281] Ibid., p. 76.
[282] Hardly so, when a Spanish "Captain" asked Madame de Longueville for her passport, p 63.
[283] Ibid., p 77
[284] Ibid., p262. On return, Madame de Longueville gave birth to Marie Gabrielle (1647-1650).
[285] Ibid.,
[286] Ibid., p. XI (preface) "Not at all" at that time (in some way).
[287] Ibid., p. X-XI (preface).

Adopting a posture of modesty that he enjoyed ("I, who was nothing"[288]) Joly tells us that "Monsieur Godefroy, Historiographer of the King[289] encourages him to keep a diary of the journey. He follows the advice of "this old man":

…having stayed some time in Munster, we went to Holland: and on returning to Osnabrugh, then to Cologne, and to some other nearby places we came back to France through the Low Countries. And I took care to continue my little remarks.

The "Voyage fait a Munster" later reflects the notes taken in action during the trip.

The meticulous care with which Claude Joly mentions details enables us to reconstruct precisely the production of his journal. For several decades, the text "put in an orderly way in the form of a Diary, according to the dates that I had marked on my notebook"[290] circulates in manuscript form. The growing fashion for travel tales from the middle of the 17th century, could have encouraged its publication. As the interest in the Low Countries and the United Provinces during the 1660s and 1670s grew, although they were becoming more and more warlike, it doubtless stimulated the demand for chorographic works covering these countries. Having "even learnt that some people had taken a copy"[291] the Canon decides to undertake its publication in order to give "these Memoirs to the public"[292]. The traveller prides himself on his position as an ecclesiastic, signing "M. Joly, Canon of Paris"[293]. "Dedicated, on account of the mutual friendship which has brought us together so happily

---

[288] Ibid., p 263. Joly asks for permission "for me, who was nothing, to go to Brussels and Anvers" Ibid., pp. 263-264).
[289] Ibid., p. XI (preface) about Théodore Godefroy (1589-1649).
[290] Ibid.
[291] Ibid., p. XIV "Monsieur Ogier Predicateur"; "Antoine d'Herouval" 1606-1689), privileged readers of his manuscript.
[292] Ibid., p. XIII
[293] Ibid.. p. XV.

for twenty-four years²⁹⁴" to Francois Ogier (1597-1670) a priest that he met in Munster, the work is "Acheve d'imprimer pour la premiere fois le 4 Decembre 1669"²⁹⁵".

The appearance of the "Voyage fait a Munster en Westphalie, et autres lieux voisins en 1646 et 1647" took place on the eve of the war with Holland (1672-1678) when the seven united ²⁹⁶Provinces" of the Low Countries became long-term enemies of Louis XIV, having been historic allies of the "Gallic Hercules"²⁹⁷. This change of diplomatic paradigm doubtless explains the updating of 1672, the only re-edition of the work. Holland appears in the title, whose dates are entrenched, and a map of the region replaces the boundary parts of the first edition. The body of the text, nevertheless, remains unchanged²⁹⁸.

(MAP)
Caption

The 1672 edition of *Voyage de Claude Joly* includes a "Nouvelle Carte d'allemagne Corrigé" inserted near the title page to "update" the report in the context of the war with Holland (1672-1678). BM Dieppe (MT P 1899 Fonds Cas).

Making up part of the Longueville custom, Canon Joly holds a privileged place in order to observe the operation of the Westphalia congress. Belonging to a prestigious house fully opens up opportunities to meet people of various

---

²⁹⁴ Ibid., p. IX
²⁹⁵ Ibid., p. XII – privilege date of 30.11.1668 and registration on 11.11.1669. p XX.
²⁹⁶ Ibid., p. 95. Knowing of his diplomatic presence, Joly describes Guelde, Holland, Zeeland, Utrecht, Frisia, Overjissel and Groningen.
²⁹⁷ Ire For diplomatic ties in France-United Provinces, see Nijenhuis, A. "L'hercule français....Temps Modernes" *Deshima pays du nord* no. 8, pp. 57-74,
²⁹⁸ Joly, C.*Les voyages de Munster, ...et de Cologne*.Paris, Pierre Prome, 1672. Brunet, J C. *Manuel de libraire ...livres*. Paris, Silvestre, 1842.

views. Thus, in 1646 he attends a meeting with "the army of Mr Marechal of Turenne"[299] near Wesel, a strategic Rhenish town occupied then by the Republic. In fact, the French army "crossed the Rhine on the Vezel bridge" and "Mr de Turenne wanted to see their Highnesses in battle with all the luggage, carriages and horses, on which there was a quantity of women, even some who seemed conditioned, with their children[300]". Finally, "Mr Turenne having come to take leave of their Highnesses, all their soldiers saluted with a wonderful noise: 'terribilis ut castrorum acies ordinata'[301]" A formidable army in battle, with weapons, luggage and women, according to the custom of the time.

In September of the same year, Joly accompanied the Duke of Longueville to Osnabrück, where negotiations between Sweden and the German Empire took place, in order to "therefore at the same time put affairs into a state of peace to all Christianity [..] and he was pleased that I should travel with him"[302]. The Canon stayed for ten days in the town as a guest of the Swedish plenipotentiaries, led by the Count of Oxenstiern, whose residence he visited. The Swedish plenipotentiaries who were at war with the Emperor "did not stay in Munster, because being Protestants (Lutherans) they did not want to use the mediation of the Nuncio"[303].

On the difference between generals or diplomats, observed from a distance, the ecclesiastic Joly held close

---

[299] Joly, C. *Voyage...* op.cit. p. 75.

[300] Ibid., During the Fronde, Turenne was very close to Madame de Longueville. See Joly, C. *L'histoire de la prison... de M. le Prince.* Paris, A. Courbe, 1651. See also Joly, C. *Traite des restitutions des grands...* Amsterdam: Elzevir, 1665.

[301] Ibid., p 76.

[302] Ibid. Joly is at Osnabrück from 18 to 28 September 1646. France and Spain only made peace in 1659, with the Treaty of the Pyrenees,

[303] Ibid., p. 174. The Republic of Venice acted as mediator in Osnabrück.

links with the pontifical mediator in Munster. "Le Voyage" clearly states his role in the congress:

There still lives in this town [of Cologne] a Nuncio of the Pope, who has spiritual administration of all the towns of the Rhine and of the rest of Germany, which is a country of obedience, and where there is nothing like France or the Liberties. It was therefore Mr Chigi who was responsible for the Nuncio: but who lived in Munster in order to moderate peace between the Christian Princes, as we have said[304].

This is about Fabio Chigi (1500-1667), who was installed in the Franciscan monastery with his retinue. The success of the Congress of Westphalia would contribute to "raising up from [in April 1655] the Sovereign Pontificate, in which he died two years ago, where [Joly] judged from that time that he could succeed one day"[305]. The Parisian Canon and the future Pope Alexander VII had occasion to visit Munster, so that two churchmen were present at the time of departure:,Two or three days before our departure from Munster [in March 1647] I went to visit the Nuncio to take leave of him and receive his orders. He welcomed me warmly: and the next day he sent me to a guest house of one of his churchmen, called Mr (Theodorus) Severus, who was of Dutch nationality, and spoke good French. In order to pay me compliments, he gave me a personal gift of a book containing the life of a Saint of his family[306].

The "Dutch by nationality" churchman Severus was perhaps active in the Dutch Mission, created the day after the Twelve-Year Truce (1609-1621) when hostilities were resumed between the United Provinces and the Spanish Low Countries. The "Missio Hollandica" tried to keep the Catholic Church in the Republic, compensating by

---

[304] Ibid., p 227. "The land of obedience" to the Pope. "Liberties" under temporal power.

[305] Ibid., p 93.

[306] Ibid., p.264.Vita B. Ioannis Christi. Augustini" Anvers enricus Aertssens 1641.

clandestine activity for the suppression of the church organisation by the Dutch temporal authorities.

A Tridentine breath re-animated Catholicism in the United Provinces at this time of strong "concurrence" between the confessions:

Also, Mr Severus brought me this gift [on behalf of the Nuncio] and had literature, of which [I read] a Latin translation of which Matthias Martinez of the town of Middlebourg, wrote the Introduction[307] to the devout life of Mr de Sales, of which Mr Severus had already given to me previously.

The Borromean Catholicism of the Bishop of Geneva, Francois de Sales (1567-1622), in "exile" in Annecy, and his work of religious re-conquest in the Savoy Chablais, at the gates of Geneva the Calvinist epicentre, surely stimulated by analogy the imaginary Dutch missionary. Is there a chance that Francois de Sales was beatified (1662) then canonised (1655) under the pontificate of Alexander XVII, in other words the Nuncio Fabio Chigi, the representative of the "Missio Hollandica", visited by Joly[308]?

An inter-confessional curiosity

The multiple contacts of Claude Joly with the Westphalian Catholic clergy did not in any way go against his curiosity. Appointed by the canonical library of Notre Dame of Paris, Joly uses his long stay in the Rhineland and the "Voyage de Hollande" to acquire a large number of books. The amount of books intended for the Parisian chapter being difficult to transport, the Canon gained logistic support from Longueville:

---

[307] Ibid., pp. 265-266. *L'introduction ..Francois de Sales (1567-1622)* 1608.

[308] The Sovereign Pontiff is the superior of the Missio Hollandica, seconded by the Nuncio in Brussels. Vicars of the Mission were represented by the Nuncio in Cologne.

During my long stay in Munster, some bookshops from outside came (for in the town, there were only two or three) among which I found some fairly good books and I bought some of them, which with those I brought from Leyden, filled a box which I was lucky to have brought to Paris with the luggage of my Princesses[309].

Also, with the apostolic Nuncio in Cologne, he "engaged in a large traffic of books. I bought some unbound ones that the Bookshop is sending to reach me in Paris"[310].

The order from the chapterhouse of Notre Dame de Paris witnessed by books "in blank", in other words books without binding, to bind in the colours of his own library, makes one presume a preponderance of religious themes. Nevertheless, the curiosity of the ecclesiastical librarian embraces a number of fields. At Osnabrück, he buys at the "only bookshop" which was also a bindery "in the whole town" a "Cosmographie de Sebastien Munster en latin, qui etait peut-etre le meilleur de ses livres"[311]. He is a good bibliophile: "I bought it, it seems to be well-worn, although he sold it to me at a high price"[312]. "La cosmographie" by the Protestant scholar Sebastien Munster (1488-1552) dating from the middle of the 16th century, is symbolic of "the inertia" of the geographical references of travellers in those countries up to the middle of the 16th century. In the absence of more recent chorographies, Munster's work remained a reference for a century. In spite of the dispersion of his library in the French Revolution, a trace survives of the collection made up over more than a half-century by Claude Joly. A "Catalogue" from the middle of the 18th

---

[309] Joly, C *Voyage...* op. cit. p. 269. The Princesses bought porcelain and spices. The friendly printer gave Madame de Longueville a box of books for Claude Joly.

[310] Ibid., p. 244. The Dutch publishers usurped the publishing place in Cologne for customs reasons.

[311] Ibid., p. 183.

[312] Ibid. He details the two reasons for the price of the book on p. 184: its rarity and appeal to foreigners."

century gives a very interesting view of the composition of the "library" and makes it possible to identify some editions gleaned by the Canon during his travels[313].

In Amsterdam, the Parisian is extremely interested in the works on geography, going:

...o see the Blaeu printing works, which are held to be the most beautiful in the whole of Europe [...]. For it is he who printed the Great Atlas, and almost all the beautiful, illustrated maps that we have [314]there: there are also all sorts of characters [mobile] and even Oriental languages, which he has cast in his works.

Of course, about Joan Blaeu (1596-1673), he states: "I bought from him a box unbound books that he sent to me in Paris, with porcelains that Madame de Longueville bought"[315].

Of the United Provinces, the Canon reports "a good amount of books that he had bought, most of them in Leyden[316][...] [317]the main place for Letters, and the first Academy in the whole of Holland", like the Elzevirs whose boutique he visited, not printing there [...] "all sorts of Catholic books as easily as Amsterdam, where there is great freedom for that"[318]. In fact, the practice of the Catholic Religion is not allowed as freely as elsewhere, on account

---

[313] The "Catalogue des livres...l'Eglise de Paris" p. 85 mentions the 1572 edition of Munster, S. *Cosmographia Universals, Basle: Description des pays Bas* by Louis Guichardin (1521-1582),

[314] Joly, C. *Voyage...* op. cit. p. 116, The atlas series is Blaeu, J. *Le theatre du monde. Blaeu 1635-1654.* 5 vol. "Catalogue...l'Eglise de Paris" op.cit. p. 85.

[315] Joly, C. *Voyage...* op. cit. pp. 116-117.

[316] Ibid., p. 173.

[317] Ibid. /312- Ibid

of the residence taken there by their Doctors of Theology, who are zealous in their Religion, as we are in our own[319]."

The curiosity of the book-loving Canon is decidedly eclectic.

Among the titles mentioned exactly inside the "box" filled by the Canon, there are also controversial works. Crossing the Low Countries on the return journey to Paris, he made a few purchases in the university town of Louvain:

There I bought some unbound books, and among others what Jansenius had written on the Old and New Testament in two volumes and several small books [320] dealing with time differences on the question of grace, which the bookshop sent after […] to Paris.

When the traveller published his report in 1670, these works of Cornelius Jansen (1585-1638) had appeared in the index for a long time. The Jansenist quarrel lasted in France until the 18th century, with a strong political presence, and as a result the subject is therefore sensitive. Also, on the difference in other bibliographical references of the "Voyage", Joly describes the Jansenist works in an allusive manner. Is our rebellious ecclesiastic afraid of censorship?

The theological readings of the Parisian also cover Protestantism, even Judaism. The ecclesiastic has a passion, through reading, for Anne-Marie de Schurman (1607-1678), "an excellent lady"[321] of her age, whom he met in Utrecht in September 1646 during the excursion to the Republic. [322] Beyond a discussion led by Joly "and the ecclesiastic Canon whom I was with [323] together with the Calvinist scholar" on predestination[324], the Canon

---

[319] Ibid.
[320] The meeting, and that of Jean Le Laboureur, with the scholar is described by Nijenhuis A. Forclaz, B. (ed).
L'experience....moderne, Neuchatel, Alphil Presses, Universitaires de Suisse, 2013, pp. 157-187.
[321] Joly, C. *Voyage...* op.cit. p.151.
[322] Ibid.,p 153. About a chaplain called Aubert.
[323] Ibid.
[324] Ibid.

continued the exchange through reading. In particular, "She had written and from that time had some works published, which I found in Utrecht, and bought[325], on theological and learned subjects." In a substantial historiographical reasoning, spread over fifteen pages, Joly deals with the question, "If several young girls can, and should, be instructed in letters"[326]. To conclude, he quotes Erasmus, and replies in the affirmative[327]. The "wonder of our century"[328].

The idea of creating a dialogue, including an inter-confessional one, by handing over books is formulated explicitly by Claude Joly. He recalls a literary contact prior to a physical meeting with "Mr Manasseh Ben Israel a very famous Doctor [...] from his writing. I came to know him by means of his book called "Conciliator" that I had read in Paris"[329]. In the margin of the story there are the references "Mr S. Manasseh Ben Israel" and a precise reference to the "Conciliator" 'Sivede Convenienentia locorum scripturesque pugnare inter sevidentur' Editum Amstelodami an.1633, In quarto[330] "The "Conciliator", a

Latin translation by Dionysius Vossius (1612-1642) with the same title, "ductoris impensis" by the young Rabbi in Spanish, aims at conciliating passages which are apparently contradictory of the Word [331].

---

[325] "Ibid. The work explores the question of knowing why Christ used a medical device (rather than his word alone) to heal the blind man (ink) (Jn 9 1-41) (Jean Maire), Shurman, A.M. "Beverovici responsis" (Jean Maire) d (1639).

[326] Joly C. *Voyage* ..op. cit. p154. He quotes Shurman, A.M., "Amica...capacítate", Paris, 1638.

[327] Ibid.,pp. 157-159 "Car comme ...l'integrite des moeurs". Joly published a new translation of Erasmus: "*Codicille d'or...Claude Joly*. Amsterdam:Elzevir, 1665.

[328] Ibid., p. 167.

[329] Ibid., p.187.

[330] Ibid., p. 108-109.

[331] Ibid. Joly refers to Ben Israel, M. *Conciliator ...videntur*. Amsterdam, Auctoris impensis, 1652.

Thus prepared beforehand by reading, the Catholic ecclesiastic can "make his acquaintance" in speaking, and open up the theological discussion with Rabbi Menasseh Ben Israel (1604-1657) at the time of his "Voyage de Hollande".

In August 1646, "after staying some time in Munster, Monsieur de Longueville persuaded Madame his wife and Mademoiselle his daughter to go and travel around Holland"[332]. Once again, the Canon is travelling. The trip lasts a little more than three weeks, from 21st August to 12 September 1646. The length of the stay is well above the average[333], and the quality of the company certainly opened doors.

At the end of the month of August 1646, "Madame de Longueville, whom one knows very well, although she wanted to travel incognito, and not to be declared at all[334], spent four days in Amsterdam. Completely "incognito" on this journey, the company probably stayed in a completely new house of the "Doelens", the quarter general of the militia of the Amsterdam bourgeoisie, as the guest house of the town, at the point of being confused with the "Maison de Ville, otherwise called the Doulle"[335] by Jean Le Laboureur (1623-1679). This young Frenchman, of whom Joly quotes the "Voyage de Pologne"[336], stayed in Amsterdam some months before that, in December 1645, in very similar conditions, as part of a French diplomatic group.

In the main town of the Republic, Claude Joly has the chance to meet, Rabbi Menasseh Israel two days later. It is

---

[332] Ibid.,.p. 99

[333] Most French travellers at the time stayed about a week in the United Provinces, travelling also with French nobility, staying eighteen days in the Republic. Nijenhuis, A. *Voyages de Hollande...XVIIe siècle*. Frijhoff, W. Amsterdam: Vrije Universiteit, 2012, p. 34.

[334] Joly, C. *Voyage* ..op.cit. p. 106.

[335] Le Laboureur, J. Histoire…Maréchal de Guébriant.. Paris: Veuve Jean Camusat, 1647, p. 67

[336] Joly, C. *Voyage* ... op.cit. p. 152.

at the Rabbi's home that the most important discussion, necessarily theological, took place:

I was going to see him the next morning 28 [August] at his home with Mr Courtin, now the State Councillor, who was Councillor in the Rouen Parliament who had travelled with us out of curiosity, from some other honest people[337].

The Rabbi's home in the Breestraat, not far from Rembrandt's home, was manifestly full of French people who were curious to find the religious leader of a confession which was formally missing from France from the end of the 14th century.

The only details of the dialogue reported by Joly are about "these very important matters of Faith"[338]. In fact, "we asked him various questions, among others Chapter 7 of Isaiah. Ecce virgo concipiet pariet filium" [339]. The Rabbi replied according to the text, "ordinaire des Juifs sur ce lieu important de l'Ecriture Sainte, disant que c'est un nom d'age, et non pas de l'Etat virginal"[340]. Menasseh Ben Israel argued effectively that the word...[almah a young girl or young wife] which is in the Hebrew text, does not correctly mean "virgo" but "puella" [young girl] or adolescentula [child][341].

The discussion on Marian virginity gives way to eight pages of philological and theological developments, mobilising the Greek, Latin and Hebrew languages[342].

It is possible that the Jews who came later (Christ), and who remained in their blindness with a horrible obstinacy have done their best to suppress the true meaning of Scripture, which could serve to the enlightenment of the

---

[337] Ibid., p. 109. Honore Courtin (12-1703), assistant to the plenipotentiary of Avaux.
[338] Ibid., p.116.
[339] Ibid., p. 109. Is,7.14, "Bible of Jerusalem...Emmanuel."
[340] Ibid.
[341] Ibid.
[342] For a restoration of the dialogue, see Nijenhuis, A. *The Canon, the philology*. op. Cit.

Faith of Jesus Christ, (and that, in spite of that) the truth […] so strong[343].

The inter-religious colloquium does not seem to lead to a theological connection. Coming back to more cordiality, Joly closes the debate by describing it as an incidental question[344].

Notwithstanding the persistent differences, "the intelligent curiosity"[345] of Canon Joly and the "honest people" accompanying him engage the inter-confessional dialogue, in his studies as on his travels.

The interest extends to places of worship. The description of churches, including those "diverted" from Catholic worship, unavoidable places in visiting all the towns, is a "leitmotif" of the description of the journey[346]. Of the different towns visited, Joly's "Voyage" draws up a confessional geography. In February he picks out the Jewish quarter in Cologne:

On the other side of the town towards Germany, there is a small fake town, where there are the Jews and a synagogue: from where they are not allowed to go into the town without having asked for permission, and paid a certain fee[347].

In the same way, the description emphasises that in the Rhineland diocese, only the Catholic rite is authorised: "For Protestants, Lutherans and Calvinists, they have no freedom to practise their religion. Therefore their meetings take place in a place called Mulheim, at half a league below Cologne"[348].

---

[343] Ibid..

[344] Joly, C. *Voyage* ... op. cit., p 113.N

[345] Ibid., p. 116.

[346] Samaran, C. Les archives…de Notre-Dame: *Revue d'histoire de l'Église de France*. Vol. 50 147 (194, p.107)

[347] For a view of Calvinists in the United Provinces, see Nijenhuis, A.*Appartenance...Catholiques* (100-1650)

[348] "Le faux-bourg est Deutz" – Joly, C. *Voyage,* op.cit.pp. 46-7.

For Amsterdam, the description also draws up a balance of the confessional co-existence, as seen by the traveller:

The practice of any type of Religion is allowed in Amsterdam, except Catholicism, whose practice however it houses so publicly, that those who profess it, of whom there is a great number, do not hide it at all[349].

Stricto sensu throughout the existence of the Republic meant only the freedom of conscience defined by Article XIII of the Union of Utrecht in January 1579, and not freedom of worship[350]. However, on the eve of the conclusion of the triumphant peace of Westphalia, the climate of tolerance in Amsterdam is confounded by foreign observers' codified regime of co-existence, as in France (again) at this time[351].

The height of religious curiosity: "Even the Jews have a very beautiful synagogue, which our Princesses wanted to see, and we with them[352]. As a large number of buildings in this great town of Amsterdam are growing every day, and another new quarter was being built while we were there[353], the synagogue is completely new." Hardly dissembling, behind an elegant façade, Talmud Total (Study of the Torah) was set up in October 1639, for the 5400 Hebrew New Year[354]. It came from the merger of three pre-existing communities. The synagogue was presided over by Menasseh Ben Israel.

Born into a Spanish Christian family in 1604 in Portugal (Madeira) during the personal union of the Lusitanian kingdom with Spain, Manod Dias Soeiro reached the United

---

[349] Ibid., pp.107-108.

[350] See Frijhoff, W. *Confessional coexistence....United Provinces*. Delumeau, J. *Histoire... chretien.* Toulouse 2, pp. 229-257. M. MONGE *Des religieux...XVII-XVIII siècles*" Rennes, PUR, 2010, pp. 55-80.

[351] Le Laboureur, J.*Histoire de voyage...* op. cit. P.71. "Ville d'Amsterdam 1645".

[352] Joly, C. *Voyage..* p. 108.

[353] Ibid., p 122.

[354] AGT J.F. VAN Synagogue...(La Haye Staatsuigevei) 1974,

Provinces via La Rochelle. Since the town of Amsterdam from the end of the 16th century allowed "new Iberian Christians" to take on the Jewish confession, his family embraced Judaism. While using his Christian name in the civil sphere, Dias Soeiro invents a religious name affiliating him with the tribe of Manasseh, son of Joseph, a son of Israe,: Menasseh Ben Yossef Ben Israel, sometimes abridged into "MB'Y". He attains the position of rabbi when very young in 1622 and remains the figurehead of the Jews called "Portuguese" in Amsterdam until his death in 1657.

The visit by Madame de Longueville and her group took place on Monday 27 August 1646, the day after her arrival in Amsterdam at dusk. Then Joly explores the town "by the amount of candles which shine through windows on this canal, surrounded by high and beautiful buildings: which was delightful to see"[355]. Welcomed by Mr Manasseh Ben Israel the Doctor famous for his writings[356], the company discovered the place: "It is a long, high room, around which there are galleries for placing the women apart"[357]. The French people attend an enactment of divine service revived with the vocabulary which is familiar to the Canon:

At the end of the high part there are the tables of Moses in Hebrew on the altar (the temple or arch) :at the side there is a cupboard in which there was enclosed the Pentateuch, in other words the five books of Moses that they call the Law, which they have taken by one of their cantors, the "hazzan", who carries it towards the low part of the Synagogue on a type of step or tribune (the rebab) where he sings some verses in Hebrew; and then all the Jews together start to sing also in Hebrew blessings to their Highnesses.

---

[355] ?

[356] Ibid., p. 108 *Catalogue des livres ...l'Eglise de Paris*. Amsterdam Sumptibus auctoris, 1635. Hebrew Publisher 1627.

[357] Joly, C.*Voyage*... op.cit. p. 108.

During the intellectual route of Joly the traveller and of his companions, places of worship of his companions are an object of "curiosity[358]", under the same category as places of "Letters"[359] ". Thus, "On the same day, 27th, I went to see the printing works of Blaeu" [360]", already described.

Temporary clergy and authorities
Even if the visit of a French princess and her retinue to a place of worship of another confession does not imply any theological agreement, the event is highly symbolic. Some years before, the "Highnesses" were preceded at the synagogue by other high personalities. In 1642 the governor Frederic-Henri d'Orange (1584-1647), the main political figure of the Republic, is welcomed by Menasseh Ben Israel at the Talmud Torah synagogue. Crowned with his success in the Twenty-four Years War, the governor is a personality of European range. The "grand general" of the franco-netherlandish troops is, for example "deferred to as his Highness the Prince of Orange"[361] at the beginning of the French operation in the Thirty Years War in 1635.

The Prince of Orange is accompanied by Henriette-Marie (1609-1660) the sister of Louis XIII (1601-1643) and Queen Consort of England. They bring their respective children, recently married, William of Nassau (1626-1650) and Henriette-Marie Stuart (1631-1660), the Princess Royal, daughter of the King of England and wife of the young Prince of Orange[362].

---

[358] Ibid., p. 135.
[359] Joly often uses the term "curiosity". Ibid., p. 150, p. 168, p. 347.
[360] Ibid., p. 116.
[361] Parival, J. N. *Les delices de la Hollande...l'an de grace 1660.* Leyde Gerf Stecoren 160, pp. 32-343. Ibid., p. III "Sy hebben...Breda" Convents of Nuns are gone. Jalabert, L. "Le soldat fase au clerc". Rennes, PUR.
[362] Joly, C. *Voyage...* op.cit. p. 141. Madame de Longueville meets Princess Marie Henriette Stuart in May 1641. Ibid., p 141.

The ceremony of this "entry" is no doubt similar to that which was undertaken by Claude Joly in honour of the notable guests. They were preceded by a brief sermon given by Menasseh Ben Israel. In order to perpetuate the words spoken in Latin on Thursday 22 May 1642, monograms inscribe the queen for reasons of protocol, the Rabbi then speaks to the governor "the invincible and great hero"[363]. Drawing a parallel between the entry of Alexander the Great into Jerusalem (in 332 BC) and the arrival of Frederic-Henri in the "powerful town of Amsterdam"[364], he thanks his guests for honouring the synagogue with their presence.

Described as "Exiles"[365] "as they had no property, the "Portuguese"[366] that he represents are placed explicitly under the protection of the governor. Drawing again on old history and the Jewish people, the speech compares the revolt of the Jews led by Mattathias (165 BC) against the Seleucids and that of "Your Father Guillaume (who) also liberated Hollande from the cruel Tyranny of the Spaniards"[367] The founder of Israel before Herod and William of Orange, whom the Dutch hold as their liberator from the Spanish tyranny"[368] and therefore of the Republic[369], have points in common with Ben Israel. Describing their successor Frederic-Henri as protector of the country, even as his conqueror, "as Grooloo, Bois-le-Duc, Wesel, Maastricht, Breda (and what can I already anticipate?)"[370], the Rabbi states that his people, certainly

---

[363] IIbid p 1 ".Onover…..held".
[364] Ibid., p. 1 "Dese machrige …Stadt" Alexander the Great in Jerusalem.
[365] IIbid., p. 11 "Portugysen"
[366] Ibid.
[367] Ibid., p 111. "Vvader Wilhelm …Spanjaerden vry ghemeckt."
[368] Joly C. "voyage…op.cit p 142
[369] Ben Israel, M. "Menasseh Ben Israel…" op.cit. p 11, "Gemerne beste"
[370] Ibid.

"not numerous in that Republic"[371] "have found refuge in your heart"[372].

The sermon congratulates itself on this rescue: "We live, we are protected, and like others, we enjoy freedom[373] defended by your sword"[374]. Arguing for the loyalty of the Jews, Ben Israel indicates: "We no longer hold for Castile or Portugal, but for Holland, for our Country"[375]. As a result, he concludes:

It is not surprising that we pray every day for MM the States-General, for Your Highness, and also for the Nobles and Junior Regents of this famous town, since your Salvation depends on ours.

This stirring sermon of allegiance[376] ("since we longer respect the Spanish or Portuguese king, by MM, the States, but you, for our Lords") places the religion under the protection, even the guardianship, of the temporary authorities of the Republic. The latter are spread out from the magistrate to the governor and the States General. Ant "Country" whether it be the Republic the Jews live there up to 1796 as a foreign "nation", without civil rights and whose freedoms come from the goodwill of the local authorities within the confederal structure of the United Provinces. In 1657, however, the Estates General place the Dutch Jews under their protection, like "the true subjects of this State" but only if they are confronted with problems of a stranger[377].

The visit of the governor, his son and successor, persons of the royal line and other "very noble Gentlemen of great

---

[371] Ben Israel, M. "Menasseh Ben Israel .." op.cit. V :Wy…zijn"
[372] Ibid., p II-III. "Als tot…h. Arfebben"
[373] Ibid., p II-III "Nu leven vryheyt."
[374] Ibid., "Door…worden"
[375] Ibid., p. IV. "Vvant…voor anse Vaterlant."
[376] Ibid., p. IV-V. "Wy…Herren".
[377] Nijenhuis, W, "Ecclesia reformata…of his state." Leyde 1994, vol.2, p 134.

renown"[378] to Menasseh's synagogue is emblematic. In fact, it takes note of religious co-existence in the United Provinces and indicates dispassionate relations between the temporary authorities and religious groups. The influence of Frederick Henri, more conciliating than his predecessor Maurice of Orange (1557-1625) and the political and military context which was favourable to the United Provinces no doubt created a good climate. The event opens the way for other international visits, like that of Madame de Longueville and her group or, in 1669, of the Grand Duke of Tuscany, Cosmo III of Medici (1639-1723)[379].

The work of Canon Claude Joly also questions the place of the clergy in society. Implicitly, religious co-existence is accepted by Joly, through inter-clerical contacts, even conviviality, as at the end of [380] *Voyage de Hollande*:

In Steinfort, I was given my lodgings with Madame de Longueville's chaplain and the Minister who was good humoured and wanted us to drink beer before going to bed, to his health. But later he told us he would give us wine to drink to the health of her Highness, Madame.

One may imagine the charming picture of Canon Joly and Chaplain Aubert drinking in Germany at the end of the Thirty Years War, to the health of a pastor who was not austere.

The context of the Congress of Westphalia, responsible for establishing "peace between the Christian Princes"[381] is also favourable to reflection. The "opening letter to Monsieur Ogier" contains Joly's convictions as to the

---

[378] Ben Israel, M. "Menasseh Ben Israel Vvelkomst..." op. cit. P. I "Seere dele Herren".
[379] "The Grand Duke ...Livourne. Calafat, G. (1590-1630) *Des religions dans la ville.*
[380] Joly, C. *Voyage...* op. cit. P. 171-172. "Steinfort...de la Republique."
[381] Ibid., p 227

finality of the peace "whose salvation was awaited by the whole of Europe"[382].

The letter takes the form of homage to Francois Ogier, dedicatee of the "Voyage". Describing this priest as[383] "Evangelist of the Peace", Joly refers to a "panegyric to S. Louis" sermon[384] delivered before French diplomats on 25th August 1646 in Munster, in the Church of the Franciscans, taking in other words with the apostolic Nuncio. Taking up the framework of the sermon, of which his library holds a copy, Joly resumes its essential points, looking at "exhorting them to promote this great work of the General Peace, at the same time as the Saviour hanging on the Cross, gave it to all men".

In eulogising the "Christian policy of the great Saint Louis" [Louis IX 1226-1270][385], the text goes back to Louis XIV, working nominally via his diplomats for the "General Peace". The latter must invite:

These dear children to an agreement with a perfect union, which saves the blood of their subjects, and which can give them the means of overturning the Mosques of Mahomet, and to re-establish the true worship of God in Greece and in Asia[386].

Ogier had ended his exhortation:

There you will find laurels which do not turn red from the blood of your brothers. The victories which will not be wept by the eyes of Christians: churches or Altars will not be overturned: on the contrary, you will re-establish the true worship of God which was abolished by the impiety of Mahomet[…] and after having reigned happily on earth, you will come to reign more happily with me in Heaven,

---

[382] Ibid., p IV (Letter)
[383] Ibid.
[384] Ogier, F . *Actions ....Eglise de Paris*. op. cit. p 36, 1665.
[385] Ibid.
[386] Ibid., pV-VI (Letter)

and enjoy the Crown of glory and immortality that Jesus Christ promised to his Elect[387]. So be it.

The plan to bring "peace to all Christianity"[388] certainly accepts the religious diversity of Europe. but with the superior finality of uniting this in a struggle against the "Turk"[389]. Written in the 1660s, the letter resonates with the battle of Saint-Gothard where in August 1664, allied European troops win a victory over the Ottoman army. The French participation in this success is cleverly carried out to glorify[390] Louis XIV. Ogier's prophecy, formulated in 1646 and relayed by Joly, is not however realised. At the time of the appearance of the "Voyage", the "Christian princes" again entered a cycle of conflicts, where the revocation of the Edict of Nantes re-introduces an irreversible religious dimension.

Towards a pluri-confessional Christianity

Throughout his long life, Canon Joly could observe the vicissitudes of the Great Century in the religious field. Born under the reign of Henry IV, he was a Canon in the chapter of Notre-Dame de Paris under Louis XIII and Louis XIV. Making up a part of the people of Longueville, the chance was offered to him to join the French plenipotentiary at the Diplomatic Congress of Munster, where at that time a general European peace was being negotiated.

Living in Westphalia in 1646 and 1647, at the time of criss-crossing the roads of France, of the Empire, of the United Provinces and the Low Countries, he was able to observe and compare the conditions of religious co-existence in these parts of Europe. During these journeys, the Parisian Canon multiplies inter-clerical contacts. His condition as a churchman and his membership of the circle of the Plenipotentiary opened a great many doors to him.

---

[387] Ogier F.J "Actions publiques ...) op.cit p 31-32
[388] Joly C. "Voyage..." op.cit p 176.
[389] Linon-Chipon, S *Turcs....siecles*" Paris, PUPS 10009.
[390] Coligny-Saligny, J. "Memoirs.." 1841, p. 100.

Also, he visited priests (Francois Ogier and the "Dutchman" Severus) and the Nuncio of the future pope, Fabio Chigi. Beyond his own "camp" he shows a great inter-religious curiosity, as much by his reading as by meetings. The most noteworthy exchange in the "Voyage" took place in Amsterdam, in August 1646, with Rabbi Menasseh Ben Israel.

These intellectual meetings and theological debates reveal pragmatic acceptance of the confessional diversity at the heart of "Christianity". The peace of Westphalia confirms *de jure* in 1648 the future of a pluri-religious Europe. In relieving his friend, the preacher Ogier, Joly conceives a feeling of belonging to one Europe, where "an agreement of a perfect union" would prevent fratricidal religious wars. The way would thus be open to the re-establishment of the "true worship of God in Greece and in Asia" to the detriment of the Ottomans. To sum up, a "just war" between a pluri-religious Europe and the unbelievers.

Beyond these considerations of "Christian politics" the cultural majority also became an object of curiosity, even entertainment. In order to stave off the boredom of the long stay in Germany[391], any amusement is welcome. Thus, after the visit in 1646 by the Dutch elephant of the Hansken[392] a curious person proposed to distract the French with the Armenian rite. In March 1647:

A certain prelate called Thomas Antiochenus, because he was from Antioch, who called himself the Patriot of the Armenians, said Mass in the presence of Monsieur de Longueville and our Princesses, who had the curiosity to see the ceremonies[393].

---

[391] "In Germany, ..trouble eating" – Joly, C. *Voyage* op.cit. p. 255

[392] Joly, C. *Voyage* pp. 190-204.

[393] Ibid., p 259.

That interested Canon Joly at the highest point: "As the thing was new, I went very close to the Altar"[394]. He observes with his usual precision his Armenian colleague:

The Mass that he celebrated was in the Samaritan language, which we were told by his Assistant and Interpreter. I saw the Missal, but I did not[395] recognise anything, the letters not being Hebrew, Greek, or Latin. I did not find the ceremonies very different from our own.

Alas! Doubtless, it was an impostor, transforming Joly's interconfessional curiosity[396] and consorts into a lucrative attraction:

This Patriarch had passed his titles to Monsieur the Nuncio, who had testified to be fully content. Nevertheless someone told me since then that he had been deceived and that it was acknowledged that he was a rogue[397].

And Joly concludes; "Whatever he may be, he was recommended to the generosity of Monsieur de Longueville, who gave him one hundred large coins".

***

---

[394] Ibid.
[395] Ibid.
[396] ?
[397] Ibid p., 26.

PART THREE

CONTROVERSIES AND SERMONS

Don Quixote controversialist
The disputes of Théophile Cassegrain
(end16th - beginning 17th century)
Jérémie Foa

Théophile Cassegrain has not passed into posterity. At the great displeasure, doubtless, of the main person interested who put all his heart into competing with his most illustrious colleagues, Philippe Duplessis-Mornay or Daniel Chamier. Pastor of the large town of Pont-de-Veyle in Burgundy at the end of the sixteenth century, Cassegrain was a tireless fighter for the faith, ceaselessly preaching and fighting, always hoping for a great spread of his word: the desire to convince by the love of God? The need to please and to be known by self-respect? Great is the temptation to psychologise this story without researching more general causes of it. The search for glory and the building of a reputation are always difficult to measure when one is talking about men of God, which everything pushes to conceal these problems.

One may accompany this pastor for the eight years which follow the establishment of the Edict of Nantes in Burgundy (1598-1605), a period during which he showed flawless activism, going into controversy willingly and inviting into the dispute the most famous doctors of the Church: Jacques Davy Duperron and Francis de Sales. What pushed this "humble pastor" from Bresse to provoke the most beautiful jewels of the Catholicism of the time? What was the point of all this controversial, dissymmetrical activity? Was Cassegrain seeking to convince of the supremacy of his theology or of his superiority as a theologian? Did he increase his local foundation by defying men whose fame was already international? Did he not on the contrary weaken his credibility by showing his weak "sense of reality", in other words his lack of "sense of equivalence" as much as the likelihood of a real meeting between members of clergy of [398]social and geographical origins who were so far away was extremely weak? Cassegrain's windmills are his giant enemies.

However, for the happiness of the historian, by committing these slips, if that is what they were -, Cassegrain restricted his enemies by explaining codes which were often implied in contact between reputation or notoriety, equivalence of diploma and social standing, capacity of influence, (local, provincial, national or international). By infringing the "rules of grammar of the argument", Cassegrain brought this to make his enemies bring to light the "unconscious academic" of the controversies which this article plans to analyse and in particular the grammars of the inter-clerical contact[399].

The exile of Théophile Cassegrain

Not much is known about Théophile Cassegrain. But whoever takes the trouble to collect his traces, dispersed in a myriad of sources, comes, in spite of everything, to rebuild a talking portrait. Doubtless the most credible of his biographers is Father Louis Jacob de Saint-Charles (1608-1670), of the order of Carmel, a recognised bibliophile from Chalon-sur-Saône and author of a work on the "Famous people from Chalon". He states that Cassegrain's birth was in 1556 in Etampes and he died in Chalon at the age of ninety years[400]. This Etampan origin is testified by several

---

[398] For an investigation into Don Quixote, Schutz, A. "Don Quixote and the problem of reality" *Societies* 89 2005 p 9-27.

[399] See Christin, O. "Actes...sociales", no. 144, 2000, pp. 53-61. Kappler, E. *Les conferences ..France XVIIe siècle* . Paris: Honore Champion, 2011.

[400] JACOB DE SAINT-CHARLES L. "De claris ...libri III" Paris Cramoisy 1652 p 100.

Latin poems, signed "theophilim Quatigranum Tempensis"[401]. The notability of the Cassegrains among the municipal and ecclesiastical elite is confirmed in Etampes. His father, Claude Cassegrain, a certified lawyer and Lieutenant general of the administration of Etampes was at the birth of Théophile.. He was a man of letters, whose reputation as a humanist led him to preface a Latin poem for recording the customs of the administration of Etampes[402]. As was typical in the case of royal officers and lawyers who were educated at the turn of [403]the 1560s, Claude Cassegrain wais a Protestant. An arrest of the Paris parliament condemned him to hanging with tens of other Huguenots, in November 1562 for "rebellion, felony and the crime of Lèse-Majesté".

Etampes was in fact taken then occupied by Conde's troops from 13 November 1562, and it is likely that Cassegrain's father took part in these events[404]. There is a sudden new direction in the history of a family which was hitherto well-settled who must probably now leave the town. At the time, Théophile was six. Also, he was not converted, but belonged to the first generation of "baptised Huguenots", as his vetero-testamentary first name indicates. A child of civil wars, born of the last troubles, Cassegrain is shaken about on the exile roads and soon undergoes the sufferings that minority confessional choices bring. He knows that lives fall down to reach a religious frontier which was however guarded; he lived through the trials that God keeps for his elect. Precociously, he suffered intolerance, violent religious confrontation, banishment,

---

[401] Ad Iona…Tempensis J.JACMOTIUS "Ioannis…Lyrica" Geneva Stoer1591 p 9.

[402] …Arret du parlement…"Memoirs de Conde …l'histoire de France" London C.de Bose-G.Darres IV 1743 p 122-123.

[404] Fleureau, B. *Antiquites…l'histoire generale de France*. Paris, J B Coignard, 1683.

hatred of neighbours. That does not prevent him from wishing to convert others, again and again.

When one goes back to his journey, in 1579 Cassegrain has become a pastor in Cormaillon, in Auxois[405]. The position is not prestigious, that is understood, but Cassegrain is only twenty-three years old and Burgundy is his adopted country. From 1581 to1583 he served several small churches in Burgundy: he is found at Nuits-Saint-Georges in February 1583[406] and at Cormaillon in May of the same year[407]. It is there that the family is settled and where in 1586 his first son was born. Married, as is the duty of pastors, Cassegrain loses his first wife, Avoye Chicheret, on an unknown date, but before 1590, because the poet Pierre Pouo publishes an "epitaph" in honour of her death[408]. Two children were born of this first bed: Anne and Salomon, a vetero-testamentary first name marking a strong confessional identity. Cassegrain is everything but a Nicodemite. Like a number of his colleagues, he makes it his duty to make his home a model of piety and to pass on his vocation to his son, without so much as creating a dynasty of pastors studying theology[409]. Cassegrain remarries in November 1590 [410]to Louise Goulart, who gives birth to Suzanne, baptised in Geneva in December 1591. Here again, the vetero-testamentary first name shows confessional name. "This "family investment" is visible enough and known for being mocked by his enemies, who noticed how gifted Cassegrain must be in economy "he who

---

[405] 28.0.1579…Cassegrain appointed Minister in Cormaillon. See Christin, O., univ. Lumiere -Lyon, 1999, p. 32.

[406] Geneva Library, ms.fr.409. See Dufour, A. *Correspondance deTheodore de Beze*. Geneva Droz v 2 2002, p. 14, note 3.

[407] Letter to Theodore de Beze May 1583. *Correspondance de Theodore de Beze*. op. cit. v 24 p 153—154.

[408] See Poupo, P. "La Muse Chretienne". Mantero, A. Textes modernes, Paris, 1997, p. 255

[409] Salomon Casssegrain, "Professor of Theology" ,Cormaillon, died 22.03.1637.

[410] Poupo, P " op.cit. p. 553. *La Muse Chretienne.*

is a minister, [411]father of a family, all together". In the eyes of his Catholic opponents, this family detail aggravates the local implantation of Cassegrain, his impossible nomadism, which they compare with their life of celibacy spent on mission glued to their country. Cassegrain is not "worthwhile" nor exchangeable on all the religious markets of the kingdom, in the difference of its interchangeable Catholic theologians, all doctors, who spend their lives moving around and are valuable in their competence in all the churches in the country. In1583, Cassegrain refuses the seat of Tremilly in Champagne, as it's too far away[412]. His Catholic enemies never fail to recall that there are those who were moved towards the pastor, not the reverse. For them, Cassegrain is only a "local candidate" who is literally rooted to the spot. Keeping one's distance, everything is already there.

After the birth of his third child, Cassegrain preached in Burgundy at the end of the year 1591: at Saint-Jean-de-Losne, between 24 December 1591 and 7 February 1592, at the request of Captain Saint-Matthew, then again in Geneva until October 1592[413]. His track is lost for a few years. He serves the Church of Pont-de-Veyle at least between January 1596 and the end of November 1601,[414] Vosne-Romanee in 1601, Pont-de-Vaux in 1603, finishing at Chalon-sur-Saône from 1609 to 1634. Very active between 1580 and1605, he disappears from the public scene after that date, even if one finds him again in 1620 as a deputy of the Church of Chalon at the national Synod at Ales[415].This

---

[411] François Humblot. "La dispute…Cassegrain ministre". Lyon. Pillechotte1587, p. 293 .

[412] Citron, S. and Junod, M. C .*Registres …Pasteurs de Geneve*. Geneva, Droz. v 6, 1980 pp. 89-94.

[413] Archives Pont-de-Veyle. "Les protestants…XVIe siecle", 1975, p. 12

[414] "Compagnie des pasteurs 08.10.1601". Cassegrain serves Dijon as "VIP"."Registres …" op.cit. v 8, 1986, p. 100

[415] Aymon, J.*Tous les synodes...de France*. La Haye, Charles Delo, 110, v.I,I p. 252.

eclipse is probably explained by the blindness of the pastor, who died in 1637 then "blind for fifteen years", that is from 1622. But already in a pamphlet from 1618, regarding a dispute from 1603, one of his enemies, the Capuchin Marcellin de Pont de Beauvois described Cassegrain as "an old Rabbi who is blind in his body, and even more so in spirit"[416]. It is thus likely that his sight was declining from the decade of 1610, the Judeophobic critic referring to the image of a man who was prematurely old through study and reading. For a Catholic tractarian, the eye disease is a divine surprise, a visible mark of the heretic: by a type of law of an eye for an eye, blindness came to punish the one who sinned and throughout his life remained obstinately blinded to the light of God[417]. This disease marks the second exile of Theophile Cassegrain, reduced to silence and anonymity, stripped of his glory of yesteryear.

Cormaillon-Geneva, return journey

At the beginning of the 1580s, Cassegrain enjoyed a solid reputation at the heart of the Burgundy churches, which extend progressively to Geneva. In 1583, Simon Goulart warmly recommends him to take his succession at the Church of Tremilly. It is true that Goulart is very bored and hopes to shorten his exile by nominating a volunteer to replace him. Cassegrain's local fame however enables him to refuse this poisoned chalice. He says he is installed with the faithful of Is-sur-Tille.

Cassegrain is then invited to complete his education in Geneva from the years 1583-1584. He stays there until towards the beginning of 1592, while coming back to preach regularly in France[418]. On the banks of the Leman, he

---

[416] Marcellin duu Pont De Beauvoisin. *La piperie des ministres* ...Grenoble: Lyon, Loys Muguet, 1618.

[417] Crouzet, D. *Les guerriers de Dieu...religion.* Seyssel Champ Vallon, 1990, v. 1, p.284.

[418] Fatio, O. and Labarthe, O. *Registres de la compagnie...* op.cit. v 3, 1969, p. 83.

preached, baptised and made friends with the learned Protestants, particularly the humanists, Hellenic circles and Hebrewists, and particularly the French scholars, who had emigrated with the Edict of Nemours (1585). The works that he prefaced, those that are dedicated to him and the poems in his honour indicate his growing fame. Verses from the poet Pierre Poupo are dedicated to him, especially praising his virtuosity in ancient languages[419]. Thesonnet LIX from the first book of *La Muse Chretienne* published in 1590, celebrates Cassegrain's linguistic talents, which Poupo considers matchless[420]. With Isaac Casaubon, Cassegrain gives Latin poems for the edition of poetry of his friend pastor Jean Jacquemot in 1591[421]. This insistence of the sources on recalling Cassegrain's talents in ancient languages (Greek, Hebrew and Syriac) earns him an appearance in the list of great Hebrewists, published some years later by Paul Colomies[422]. The contrast with the speech of his enemies is so much more striking: on many occasions the junior Francois Humblot, who argues against Cassegrain in 1598, writes that his opponent "does not understand Hebrew at all[423]". Poor theologian? How can one believe that such a great scholar preached in such a small town?

A downgraded Protestantism

As regards the growing reputation of his remarkable erudition, everything leads one to believe that Théophile Cassegrain felt downgraded in these small Burgundian or Bressan churches which limited his horizon. In order to

---

[419] Bellenger, Y and Ester, R. *Pierre Poupo (1552-1590): un poète protestant ...* Paris, Klincksieck, 1992.

[420] Poupo, P *La Muse Chretienne*. op.cit. p. 255.

[421] Jacquemot, J. "Joannis ...lyrica". Geneva, Stoer, 1591.

[422] Colomies, P. *Gallia orientalis ...vitae*. La Haye, A Vlacq, 1665, p 273.

[423] Francois Humblot, *La dispute solennelle*. op.cit. p. 12.

understand him, we must go back a little way on the thread of his story.

At the beginning of the wars of religion, La Bresse is not French, but Savoyard from 1559. The Duke of Savoy then happily welcomes onto his lands the French reformed people who were chased out by the civil wars and cyclic persecutions in 1562, 1568 or 1572, less from the size of his heart than for keeping in reserve a potential for destabilisation of his powerful neighbour. Thus, when the Catholics take back Mâcon during the first civil war (August 1562) hundreds of Huguenots flee towards La Bresse and spread out into its small towns, especially at Pont-de-Veyle and Thoissey, but also Montluel, Bages and Bourg-en- Bresse[424].Prudently, the Duke of Savoy insisted that these fugitives should not travel in troops of more than twenty-five cavalry. The Protestants are therefore straight away condemned to dispersal, but they acclimatise poorly in these smaller and less prestigious towns than those that they left and which they see from a distance like a forbidden Eldorado. Small Protestant centres take root on the edge of important towns: at Vosnes for the district of Nuits; in Volnay, for that of Beaune; at Is-sur-Tille for the district of Dijon; at Saint-Jean-de-Losne for the district of Auxonne; at Pont-de-Veyle for Bresse and some adherents of Mâcon. So many peripheral place names which will come back in the adventures of Théophile Cassegrain. All these towns are one day called "little Geneva" but it is the word "little" which must draw attention. These exiles form herds scattered from an "urban Protestantism" made up of exiled city-dwellers in the country or in large towns, but who always have the town character in their minds. This peri-urbanity or end-of-century French Protestantism is still very unknown, although the certainty of its urban implantation is well established. However, a number of great cities closed their doors to reformed people at that time.

---

[424] AM MACON EE 49 .See Turrel ,D. *Bourg-en-Bresse...historique...* 1986, pp. 170-171.

On the publication of the Treaty of Lyon (17 January 1601), Bresse, Buey and Pays de Gex passed over to France. From being simply tolerated, Bressan Protestantism became legal. But it had to comply with the strict articles of the Edict of Nantes; all preaching is thus forbidden in Dijon and four places nearby; which restricts the pastors from living there if they wish to make their celebrations regularly [425]. The united past of Dijon thus comes to swell the Protestant presence in the small surrounding towns. All of that contributes to depriving the Huguenots of a "capital" (Paris not being in the least of restrictions) if one adapts the problem which was developed by Pierre Bourdieu in another context:

The major capital is, without playing on words, at least in the case of France, the place of the capital, in other words the place of a physical space where the positive poles of all the fields are concentrated and most of the agents who have these dominant positions: it can only therefore be considered enough in the relation to the province (and the "provincial") which is nothing but privation (all relative) of the major [426] capital and the capital.

After Dijon, the league members of Lyon obtained from Henry IV a rule that Huguenots could not celebrate, preach sermons or baptise in the town or its suburbs (24 May 1594): it is known that at that time several reformed Lyon people are restricted to going to Pont-le-Veyle. At this time they made contact with Pastor Cassegrain, who baptised their children[427].

Measuring the frustrations of this group of exiled citizens, of their consciousness of downgrading, especially geographically, but also socially and culturally and their unhappiness in the town, also gives the means of widening

---

[425] Barbiche, B . *L'édit de Nantes* 1562-1598. Sorbonne.fr.

[426] Bourdieu, P. "Effets de lieu: *La misere du Monde.*» Paris: Seuil, 1993 p. 29-249-262.

[427] Puyroche, A. "Le chateau …XVIe siècle". Bulletin SHPF, 1890, pp. 278-283.

their circle of recognition. There is no doubt that they did not consider with their eyes open the capacity of their minister to export himself, that they praised his ability to cross, even fictitiously, through discussion and books, thanks to the power of "fame", distances that had forced them to take with the "home country". This consciousness of not being in one's place, not to be judged by one's true value showed up in all the words and gestures of Cassegrain – his enemies themselves made light of it and tried to coax the minister by his Achilles heel. One of his opponents, the minister Gaspard Dinet would have assured him "that he well knew that he was not treated according to his merits: that if he ruled with them he would be with people of honour; and that as regards facilities, he could easily have a better appointment"[428]. There, perhaps, something was delivered from the subconscious of Cassegrain as a crystallisation of the frustrations of a number of his co-religionists: was he really treated according to his merits? Where would he be if he were a Roman Catholic? It is with this feeling of failure that he must in future consider provocations in the dispute started by Pastor Cassegrain.

The quarter-hour of fame of Theophile Cassegrain
In 1597, Théophile Cassegrain is well known in Geneva and in the intellectual reformed circles. Locally, his notoriety is even stronger: "I am too well known here", he writes to the Company of Pastors in Geneva. But what is this "local" who is confined? Can he be satisfied, he, the exile who already dreams of national glory? Must the glory of God suffer these barriers that are too human? Whereas, returning from Geneva, he is the pastor in Pont-de-Veyle, in June 1597 Cassegrain knew his quarter-hour of fame and committed the act bearing his name in the whole of France: he wrote a "universal challenge" by which he provoked all the doctors of the Catholic Church into a dispute. He alone against the

---

[428] Cassegrain, T.*Advertissement sur le libelle…Humblot minime*", Geneva, Etienne Gamonet, 1600, p. 12.

Roman world. His fame then extended on a national scale. Twenty years later, his enemies will still remember Cassegrain publishing "superb challenges against all the doctors of the Roman Church"[429]. Signed at Pont-de-Veyle in June 1597, the challenge is also launched in geography, fired between the indexicality of a toponomy ("Pont-de-Veyle") and zeal for the universal ("all theologians"):

"Cartel of Theophile Cassegrain, Minister"

To all theologians of the Roman Church,

I have always thought that there was nothing more beneficial, and less difficult, to lead men to the knowledge of truth than a soft and peaceful conference, either in full voice or in writing. For thus opening up to one another, doubts are proposed and resolved and if one of the parties is persistent in his mistake, that person is easily convinced by the only opposition of the principles, and necessary and impossible conclusions; especially in theology rightly called to Science and the sciences, and rich in very sure and very infallible maxims. Leaving If there is someone between the learned and expert Theologians of the Roman Church, who watches me do this honour of conferring on me the following Theses or a part of them, or others of his choice, I protest against God and men to examine his themes and in all good conscience with the intention of embracing them with all my heart and to acknowledge as very worthy of the Doctor of truth, if I find them acceptable: and also to refute them without any disguise, if I consider them unworthy. The thing that makes me implore this as he loves the honour of God and the salvation of poor souls, if he is not disdainful of a work which is so necessary, so suitable to his proion: but for him to be released with dignity and he brings a modest spirit to it, and warmed up, with reasons that are stronger than numerous, without a show, embarrassment, and affected language in order to give myself a chance to reply more openly and analytically, so that one can handle a serious and solid Conference.

---

[429] Marcellin De Pont De Beauvoisin, *La piperie...* op. cit. p. 15.

Cassegrain's audience

⁴³⁰ See for example BAXTER J.P. "Documentary history" op.cit. vol V p 420. See particularly POINARD
⁴³¹R. "L'aumonerie d'ancien regime" (1568-17)95) Paris, L'harmattan 2012.

" ⁴³⁰ policies,see HAVARD G.and VIX\ C."Histoire de l'Amerique francais", Paris Flarion 2008p 100-107 and 162-163.

Ibid, p.337.

⁴³¹ One must understand the dialogue –"Interrogatus an duo Sacrauno diehabeg Ridit Non, usque ad S" - see Carthusian liturgy.2 the

3. HISTORIC PRIESTS AND PASTORS

TRANSLATION OF "PRIESTS AND PASTORS" EDITED BY JULIEN LEONARD, RENNES UNIVERSITY PRESS ISBN 978-2-7555-4905
PROPOSAL FROM FELICITY MCNAB
TITLE: "PRIESTS AND PASTORS"
SUBTITLE: THE CLERGY IN THE ERA OF CONFESSIONAL DIVISIONS XVI-XVIIth CENTURIES
florinda640@btinternet.com
TELEPHONE: 00441865841272 and 00447722387423
CV: attached

DESCRIPTION OF WORK

The confessional break which touched the Christian West in the 16th century permanently revolutionized the place of the clergy in societies and their influence on the faithful. The original principle of Lutheranism, then the Swiss reforms P of the universal priest was greatly relativized by setting up a progressive Protestant clergy, but it opened a breach that one can follow at the time of controversies and which continue to fix a fundamental difference between the two camps. However, the reciprocal and fundamental influences are observable in the areas of confessional co-existence; the spaces and frontiers can appear as privileged observatories to understand the reciprocal influences between the clergy. until in their way of interpreting and considering the pastoral ministry and forge their professional and social identities.

The training of clergy, their organization, their action, the oppositions to which they had to contend, their interactions, common points, even the sociability of their members are studied here through very diverse practices (preaching, conferences and controversies, studies, missions, institutional restriction, liturgical practices, suppression of deviation, or even definition of concurrent memories). These studies of the time plunge us into the process of definition of clerical identities which are certainly used against one another, but also, more subtly, in terms of the other and on common foundations.

TABLE OF CONTENTS

THANKS

ABBREVIATIONS

Julien Leonard – Introduction: the clergy at the time of confessional divisions, a story which is directly unknown. Reformation and Counter-Reformation co-existence practices. Edict of Nantes –training historiography – who are the "clergy"? Role of bishops – evangelical clergy. Men of God and their influences. Discussions

PART ONE
IN FRONT OF THE OTHER, SIDE BY SIDE (1530-16)
ANNE BROGINI
CATHERINE BALLERIAUX

PART TWO
FACE TO FACE MODELS AND COUNTER-MODELS
LAURENT JALABERT - EMPIRE ARMIES
NICOLAS RICHARD - PROTESTANT INFLUENCES

Andreas Nijenhuis-Bescher
Claude Joly (1607-1700) inter-clerical travels in the 16th century

PART THREE
Controversies and sermons
Jeremie Fox – Don Quixote controversy

Clarisse Roche – sermon in, 17h century Vienna on co-existence
Stefano Siumiz – confrontation and sermons 16th and 17th centuries
Christabelle Thoun-Dieuaide
Sermons of Pierre du Moulin with Capuchins
Celine Borello – eloquent clerical contacts XVIIth century

PART FOUR
The French Laboratory
Philippe Moulis – Boulogne sur Mer XVI and XVIIth century
Sarah Dumortier Celibacy of clergy in west
Frederic Meyer - Franciscans in Burgundy, XVIth century
Frederic Meyer- Father Jacques Fodere
Estelle Martinazzo
Toulouse clergy v – Protestantism
Didier Boisson – Sancerre after the Edict of Nantes
Bruno Maes, Saumur Academy - 17thth century orators

PART FIVE
CONSTITUTION OF CLERICAL IDENTITIES
Federico Zulani – is 16th century Italian Grisons
Nathalie Szczech – Calvin's Geneva 1540-1550
Genevieve Gross – The Geneva of Theodore de Beze
Irene Pasman-Labrune – Foreign pastors in France XVIIth century
Yves Krumenacker

Conclusions

INDEX

AUTHORS
Catherine Balleriaux – Doctor of religious history from the University of Auckland, New Zealand. Monograph: *Missionary Strategies in the New World 1610-1690*, Routledge, 2019.

Didier Boisson – Professor of Modern History, Angers University. *Les protestants de l'ancien colloque du Berry de la Revocation de l'Edict de Nantes (1679-1789* and *Les actes des synodes provinciaux*. Geneva, Droz, 2012.

Céline Borello – Modern History department at University of Haute-Alsace. *Les protestants de Provence au XVIIe siècle"* (2004). *"Les oeuvres protestantes en Europe*(PUR, 2013).

Anne Brogini – Research master at University of Nice Sophia Antipolis. *Malte, frontiere de chrétienté 1530-1670* (Rome, 2006).

Sarah Dumortier – schoolteacher, Doctor at Lille University – ecclesiastical celibacy – religious history.

Jérémie Foa – alumnus of Ecole Normale Superieure de Fontenay-Saint-Cloud. *Le tombeau de la paix....* Limoges, Pulim, 2015.

Genevieve Gross – Doctorate in Literature, Geneva University – francophone reformation. *Satire anticlericale au service de la Reforme"*. Paris, 2016.

Laurent Jalabert – Conference master at Lorraine University since 2008. *Catholiques et protestants sur la rive gauche du Rhin 1648-1789*, Brussels, 2009. Lutherans in Thirty Years War. *Dire et transmettre la foi ....* Paris, 2016.

Yves Krumenacker – Alumnus of École Normale Supérieure de Saint -Cloud (1977). Professor of Modern History at Lyons University, *Calvin: au-delà des légendes* Bayard, 2009.

Julien Leonard – Conference master, University of Lorraine – *Etre Pasteur au XVIIe siècle -Metz"* PUR, 2015. Thesis.

Bruno Maes – Conference master at Lorraine University. *Saint-Nicolas et les autres traditions*, 2011.*Dictionnaire de l'ancien regime*, 2004.

Estelle Martinazzo – Doctor of modern history. FRAMESMA – *Toulouse au Grand siècle 1590-1710*. Thesis.

Frédéric Meyer – Modern history professor, Savoy University (Chambery). *La foi des montagnes....* (Annecy 2014)

Philippe Moulis – Doctor of Modern History, Artois University. Jansenism in Northern France. *Pierre de Langle et ses correspondents*. Paris, 2016.

Andreas Nijenhuis-Bescher. *Les voyages de Hollande – XVIIe siecle* and *L'abbaye de Saint-Maurice d'Agaune*, 2015. Editor of LODOCAT International.

Irene Plasman-Labrune – History alumna of Ecole Normale Superieure at Paris-Sorbonne Creteil 2015 "Favoriser, controller et exclure..age moderne (XV-XVIIe siècle).

Nicolas Richard – Doctor of History at Paris-Sorbonne and Charles de Prague. "*La clergéparoissial* due to appear in PUR.

Clarisse Roche – Doctor of History. La frontière incertaine…Vienne XVIe siècle". Thesis.

Stefano Simiz – Modern History professor, Lorraine University. Religious history: 16th, 17th and 18th centuries. *La parole publique en ville es Reformes*, Septentrion University Press, 2012. "La Renaissance en Europe…" 2015

Natalie Szczech, Conference master – French Polynesia University, 16th century Reformation *Calvin en polémique: une maieutique* Paris:Classiques Garnier, 2017

Christabelle Thouin-Dieuaide, Modern Literature, Limoges University. *Predication au XVIIe siècle*.

Federico Zuliani – bursary. "Georges et Pierre Regard" – Geneva University – *Rivista di Storia e Letteratura Religiosa.*

READERSHIP

This work will be of interest to all religious historians and particularly to those in religious colleges training for the priesthood in all denominations. It could be included in their history courses.

REVIEWERS

I would respectfully suggest that this work should be reviewed by Dr Diarmuid McCullough of Wycliffe Hall College in Oxford or his colleague Dr Atherton.

ABBREVIATIONS

AD	Departmental Archives
AEG	Archives of the State of Geneva
AGR	General Archives of the Kingdom of Belgium, Brussels
AM	Municipal Archives of the Inquisition of Malta, Malina (Malta)
AM	Municipal archives
AN	National Archives, Paris
AOM	Archives of the Order of Malta, Rabat (Malta)
ARSI	Romanum Societatis Iesu, Rome Archives
ASV	Archivio Segreto Vaticano, Vatican City
BM	Municipal library
BnF	National Library of France, Paris
ONB	Austrian National Library, Vienna
SHAG	Genevan Society of history and archaeology
SHD	Historic Society of La Defense Vincennes
SHPF	Society for the history of French Protestantism

INTRODUCTION
The clergy in the age of confessional divisions: for a comparative and decompartmentalised history

To devote a volume to the age of confessional divisions, to their contacts and the constitution of their identities, could seem to take up a beaten seam of historiography and to propose a balance sheet of research. For conservation reasons of sources and control of the proposed discussion by the communities, mainly in the areas marked by contacts and by coexistence, the pastors coming from various strands of Protestantism and Catholic clerks are directly at the root of the essence of our knowledge of new elements, studies of unknown cases, revised problems and viewpoints moved in relation to centres of interest in religious history of the latest decades, aiming to explain and emphasise certain reciprocal influences in the constitution of clerical identities, in a broad chronological perspective embracing both years of (re)construction after the bubbling of the Reformation, the affirmation of confessional identities, the "confessionalisation", without forbidding a look at the 18h century which, however was often seen as too late in this periodisation[432]. A typology of contacts between the clergy – and no doubt one would need a completely separate reflection on what these clergy were, for French historiography seems restive in using the plural – will enable research paths which a single volume obviously cannot claim to include, but rather favour and cause to develop.

A STORY KNOWN INDIRECTLY

The religious history of the time of confessional divisions was traditionally marked by the weight of its authors, often engaged themselves in a Church, aiming to underline the distinctive components. In this framework inbuilt at least until the 1960s, a form of apologetics fed into the historiography and was sure about pastors on the Protestant

---

[432] Büttgen, P And Duhamelle C. *Religion in Confession*. 2016

side and priests and bishops on the Catholic side as major actors, but always insisted on the discussion that they could develop for opposing he opposite side. From this perspective, contacts for the clergy are often limited to a study in terms of oppositions, conflicts and controversies. It is obviously not a question of throwing discredit on the history of those times today, for more recent works show at what point it is still possible to take out the elements required for our knowledge[433] and one will rely here on cases of head-on conflicts, even if that will be partly to show the reciprocal ambiguities and influences. But to restrain the contacts between the clergy to a single form seems to be very reductive. The historiographical turning point which saw the idea of "time of reforms" is an example, demolishing the traditional layout – "pre-Reformation – Reformation – Counter-Reformation" and scholars certainly relied on documents coming from the clergy and continued to study the clerical elite, but with a shifted perspective. The pastoral visits and synodal statutes are fundamental components of this historiographical renewal but one of the main aims was precisely the religious history of the Christian people, the laity as it was "lived"[434] [435]. However, the place of the clergy remains important, as witnessed by a great many passages of the monumental *Histoire du christianisme des origines a nos jours*[436]. Since the 1980s, the works of historians like Elizabeth

---

[433] See for example a historiographic point by Domnier, B.*Histoire des controverses a l'epoque modern, une histoire des passion schriennes.* Bulletin dela shpp148-4 2002 pp.1055-1047.

[434]

[435] Delameau, J. *Histoire vecue du peuple chretien* .Toulouse, 1979.

Labrousse[437], Willem Frij[438]hoff,[439] or Robert Sauzet[440] have been taken up in broader syntheses[441]. In this sense, one of the more innovative aspects was to rely on[442] what Frijhoff qualified, for the Dutch case, of the "ecumenicity of daily life", which inspired a great many studies afterwards. Even if these founding works – for a long time doubtlessly unsurpassable – do not put the role of the clergy in the shadow and do not voluntarily hide their contacts, it is certain that the impression, perhaps simplistic, which comes from reading them is that the faithful co-existed while the "men of God" confronted each other and tried to discipline their flock. However, one should doubtlessly assess their double discussion, that is to say the discrepancy that can exist between their official vision of coexistence, that they generally condemn and in any case try to restrict as much as possible. and their practices, often difficult to see in the sources, of sociabilities, as I myself have been able to do with regard to the case of Metz in the17th century[443] . In the Dutch case also, one re-assesses the debate between coexistence and confrontation, particularly in Utrecht where Bertrand Forclaz proposes developments in the role of the clergy without restricting oneself to the simple list of confrontations[444]. The fact is that the clergy oppose each other violently, especially through the bias of controversy. The list of publications and meetings makes one dizzy for the French case alone, under the regime of the

---

[437] """" Labrousse, E. *Conscience et conviction...* Paris. 1996.
[438]
[439] "Frijhoff, Willem. *Embodied belief...*, Hilversum, 2002.
[440] *Contre-Reform... e* Louvain, 1979.
[441] "Benedict, P.*Un roi, une loi, deux foi...* CUP, 1996.
[442] See Frijhoff, W. *Chretiente...* and Kaplan, B, *Divided by faith...*, Harvard 2007
[443] Leonard, J .*Les hommes de Dieu Chretiens et Societes – Documents et memoires* 2015, p.77.
[444] Forclaz, B.*Catholliques au défi de la Réforme*. Paris 2014.

Edict of Nantes,[445] but this does not mean, on the contrary, that these contacts do not have as a result reciprocal influences in the constitution of clerical identities[446], were it not by rejection.

However, in some well-known areas, to study the clergy in a comparative view is a well-known completely pertinent step. The existence of converging disciplinary aims is already well known[447], even if the clerical action is different in the process of acculturation. Some works also show that on the field of training and instruction, common heritages going back to humanism bring Jesuits and Protestants together in France as Jean-Paul Pittion has shown[448], or abroad. Later the practices of learning are certainly settled in opposition on the field of history for example, little by little by the image of the "good pastor" in the Luthero-Calvinist world[449] which can be placed looking towards that of the "good priest" which emerges in the modern epoch[450]. Ian Green, on the English case, has already tried some connections in this field[451], but the years 1990 and 2000 are particularly marked by the works of Luise Schorn-Schutte which launch like a song the study of clergy in a resolutely comparative perspective[452] using a plural which still seems to inhibit francophone historiographic history;

---

[445] "Desgraves, L.*Repertoire des ouvrages...en France* Geneva 1984-1985. .

[446] Janse, W.*The formation of Clerical...identities*" Leyden, Brill 2006.

[447] Zinguer, I. *Les deux reformes chretiennes*. Leyden Brill.2004.

[448] Pittion, J.P.*Instruire et edifier...protestants...sous l'edit de Nantes*. Paris, 2011 pp. 19-45.

[449] Laplanche, F. *La controverse religieuse ...histoire* Paris, Crf 1995 pp. 373-404.

[450] Janse W. *The pastor bonus…* Leyden Brill, 2004.

[451] Bergin, J. *Between estate and profession.* London, Longman,1992.

[452] Schorn-Schutte L *The Christian clergy...Holy Roman Empire...Sixteenth century journal.* 1998 pp.717-731.

A point of historiographical controversy? What are "the clergy"?

The expression, used voluntarily, of "clergy" in the plural, can hinder and ask historiographical questions. It leaves an understanding – and this is in fact the aim – that there are Protestant clergy (in any case Lutheran and Reformed) and a Catholic clergy. One could even notice that the plural is usable and pertinent only for the Catholic world, in the measure where a study of the relations between the secular and the regular, and even between various internal categories to these great groups, can bring elements of reflection on the perspective which engages us here. The definition of the clergy and its members in the Catholic world is facilitated by the existence of a clear and recognised legal category, even if it is not always pertinent:– is a simple tonsured person really a clerk? But the idea of "clergy" for Protestants, whether it is general or for a special confession, may give rise to reserves and discussions. Its original reason for this is understandably the idea of the universal priest, developed by all the great reformers, which abolished the priesthood as a state of intercession between the faithful and God, but also in terms of a sacrifice and within the framework of the Mass. However, in order to struggle against some drifting towards the radicalisation of the universal priest, the same reformers and their successors have all insisted on the need for a pastoral body, formed, controlled and based on knowledge, which is only legitimate for interpreting the Scriptures, the unique foundation of the faith.

But the word "clergy" is not used in French, or very rarely and very marginally, to describe Lutheran or Calvinist pastors as a whole. The Protestants themselves are very prudent on questions of vocabulary; from the time of the reformers, they emphasise that the name given to the holders of different ministries is in the end rather indifferent, while explaining that the terms of bishops and priests were abandoned – in French at least – for practical reasons, especially to avoid confusion with ministries which had turned away from their original meaning as found with the Catholics. From Calvin's writing, the question is considered as secondary, not only because it is a point of ecclesiology and therefore not necessary for salvation, but also because the biblical passages are themselves rather vague on the words to use:

For the remainder, what I have named indifferently those who have the government of the Church, the Bishops, Pastors and Ministers: I have done it according to the use of Scripture, which takes all these words for one thing. For all those who are responsible for administering the word, they are called Bishops[453].

While Catholics try to deny as much as possible the title of "pastor" to preachers of Protestant doctrines, the most neutral term that the latter use is that of "minister". It is, according to its first sense, the one who serves. For most Protestants, the pastor was disputed in his own time; the famous Pierre du Moulin, defender of an episcopalian possibility, takes up a tradition which is already old, of assimilating between pastor, minister and bishop on the one hand, and elder and priest on the other hand, making it clear that the Catholics have completely distorted the words for bishop and priest and it is mostly for this reason that they have not deigned to give the name of "clergy" to Protestant pastors, even if Bossuet himself uses the name "clergy" for Protestant pastors in his sixth warning against Jurieu in 1691[454], but it is to mock them with irony. However, as the studies of Thierry Wanegffelen clearly show[455], it is truly a Protestant clergyman, not priestly however, which is constituted, without mentioning his name in order not to make the message of a universal priest unreadable, but

---

[453] Calvin, *Institution de la religion Chrétienne,* Geneva, Jean Crespin, 1560. p. 477

[454] Du Moulin, P. *De la vocation des pasteurs*, Geneva, Pierre Aubert, 1624.

[455] Bossuet, J.B, *Premier avertissement aux Protestants…* Paris, veuve Mabre-Cramoisy, 1689-1691 (part of sixth warning).

clearly defined by the ecclesiastical authorities in order not to lapse into the risk of total abolition of the clergy, as in certain Anabaptist communities and/or radicals. This clergy has academic foundations and takes its sources from the actual monopoly of the interpretation of biblical texts. This clericalization of Protestant parishes therefore fully legitimizes the use of the term "clergy", even if it remains rare in francophone historiography.

The idea of "Protestant clergy" and "clergies" in the plural and in a comparative perspective is relatively allowed among Anglo-Saxon historians, whose most recent works are those already quoted such as Luise Schorn-Schutte[456] but also with a sociologist like Celine Beraud who, in an article devoted to the clergy in the "Dictionnaire des faits religieux" does not forbid this comparatism[457]. Among French-speaking historians, the cases are rarer. One must certainly quote the important example of a part of the quoted "Histoire du christianisme", using this title in the plural[458]. But it is not insignificant to state that this editorial enterprise is presented explicitly as trans-confessional, even if a large part of its authors come from the disciplinary field of the study of Catholicism. At a low point, some works recognise the existence of this clergy by leaning on marks of anticlericalism[459]. But, generally, one may find more prudence among French-speaking historians of Protestantism, in spite of the already quoted distribution of the works of Thierry Wanegffelen[460]. From the 1970s, they had been preceded by the large thesis of State by Bernard

---

[456] See Wanegffelen, T. *Protestantism in France in XVII-XVIIIth centuries.*

[457] Baraud, C. *Clergy*. Azria, R .and .Hervieu-Leger, D. *Dictionnaire des faits religieux,* Paris, PUF, 2010, pp. 152-157.

[458] Barrie-Curien, V and Venard, M. *The clergy*; *Le temps des confessions 1530-1560.*

[459] Krumenacker, Y."*L'Anticléricalisme intra-protestant (XVII-XVIII siecles*. Lyon, 2003.

[460] Ibid.

Vogler[461] and more recently a study by Veronique Castagnet on the Protestant clergy in Berne[462]. But, in these two cases, it is a question of state clergy, who therefore belong to a rather special category. From this perspective, it is revealing that in a recent book comparing the German and French historiographies in some fields of religious history, the German historian, Manfred Jakubowski-Thiessen has used in his title the term "evangelical clergy" while the French Bernard Dompnier replies with an analysis of "people of the Church"[463]. But the latter expression may prove useful to the general extension of the clergy in some problems studied up to that point in relatively partitioned fields of study.

For a history of "men of God" and their reciprocal influences.

In Anglo-Saxon theory, the connection between anthropology and social history has already been considered in order to serve as a framework for a comparative study of clergy, with the idea of ending up with a "social biography" (Sozialbiographie) according to the historian Luise Schorn-Schutte[464]. Alphonse Dupront already referred in 1972 to a comparative study on this subject[465] but one must note that it is still only beginning. Thus, the thesis of Bruno Hūbsch, one of the rare works devoted to the subject, maintained in 1066, was only recently published, even if it is not interested

---

[461] Vogler, B. *Le clerge protestant rhenan au siècle de la reforme (1555-1619)*. Paris, 1976.

[462] Castagnet V. *Clerge protestant et clerge catholique face a...Bearne*Parlement(s)HS 6, 2010, pp. 29-43.

[463] Jakubowski-Tiessen, M. *Le clérge Evangéliqué dans les États territoriaux...*

[464] Schorn-Schutte L. *Das Predigtamtist nicht hose...Fruhen neuzeit.* Wiesbaden, 997[1997?] pp.-263-286.

[465] Dupront, A. *Vie et creation religieuse dans la France moderne:, XIV-XVIIIe siecle.* Gallimard, 1972 p 502.

in the clergy as such, but in theories of the ministry[466]. From this comparative perspective - which therefore that of this volume will be the most possible – one must detach oneself from some historiographic habits. Thus, the contributions proposed will not be confrontations between cases developed by historians of Catholicism and comparable cases studied by historians of Protestantism. A true speciality in the history of the clergy would no doubt be desirable, beyond confessional specialities which surely have their legitimacy, but which lead to partitions risking perpetuation of the false image that one may have of relations between the clergy, especially from common sources. To study each clergyman from a confessional perspective certainly has its coherence that the sources organise and impose upon the historian, sometimes far from some realities which comparative research may relativise, by showing the existence of reciprocal influences on contact between the different clergy. If the latter term poses historiographical problems, as one has seen, one may also propose a comparative history of "men of God" to take up the title of a collective work in which Thierry Wanegffelen published one of his most convincing essays, and it is also the name of one of the axles of research of the team "Histoire des faits religieux" of the CRULI at the University of Lorraine. The idea that "people of the Church", this time in the plural, could also be called on in order to analyse the reciprocal relations and influences, including the constitution of clerical identities which are antagonistic a priori. In this decompartmentalization, one must also, doubtless, have an extensive definition of what the religious history must be, as Yves Krumenacker emphasises for pastors, with a statement which can be broadened to other areas and other clerical cases:

Thus, the opening of an overly strict history towards a vast cultural history must allow us to better understand the

---

[466] Hübsch B. "Le ministère de prêtres et des pasteurs…XVIIe siecle. Lyon 2010.

position that you the pastors can have in Protestant communities and, more broadly, in French society.

It is therefore in this renewed state of mind that researchers have offered their contributions. Chance has very happily made them come from authors at different times of their reflections or their works, giving at the same time an attraction of balance for sure, of research perspectives for others. A typology of contacts between the clergy in the constitution and consolidation of their identities will guide the reflections. We shall see particularly what the forms and the constitution of models are, usually in frontal opposition, but with inevitable exchanges and influences. From a very broad spatial perspective, we shall first of all observe what the attitudes are when the clergy find themselves confronting an alterity which is radical for all Christians whether it be in front of Muslims in Malta (Anne Brogini), or confronting native populations to evangelise in North America (Catherine Balleriaux). In these instances one can actually follow particular contacts, especially because they are geographically distant from centres of ecclesiastical decision. More classically, the models can also create forms which are sometimes less simple than what one may imagine: if in the 17th century it is a question of standing out, however, there remain areas of direct contact and influences, such as in the armies in the Germanic world, especially those of the Circles, with chaplains of different confessions (Laurent Jalabert). With the case of Claude Joly, a French canon who travelled to the United Provinces in the middle of the 17th century, one can notice the peculiarities of this state in relation to the confessional, but one must play the part of the religious dialogue of this canon with other men of God – a rare dialogue in this period – and which comes from sociability, properly proving that the cultural composts are close (Andreas Nijenhuis-Bescher). Earlier in the process of building confessional and therefore clerical identities, there are meeting areas, from which it is certain some elements will be drawn, as one may see by leaning towards the complex religious history of the Archdiocese of Prague at the end of the 16th century, where the clergy are, however, doubtless more often ignorant than influenced (Nicolas Richard),

We shall later see r a series of contributions more directly devoted to two central identities at the heart of the clergy: preaching and controversy. In these cases, it is more a question of being constituted in opposition, even if the work of Stefano Simiz shows exactly that there are points of reciprocal convergence and influences on the way of considering the sermon, and even in the manner of preaching. Already earlier, in the case of Vienna in the time of Maximilien II (1564-1576), reciprocal influences and a unique model, Christian and trans-confessional, are favoured in the field of preaching; however, this is in the specific context of the Ottoman threat and the conciliatory will of the sovereign (Clarisse Roche). But even in the case of controversy, the exchanges are more complex than they appear. Jérémie Foa has already analysed the controversy from the Wars of Religion as a means of constituting clergy who are only legitimate in explaining the dogma of both sides [467] the laity of the disputes reduced to simple passive spectators[468], and here he offers us the revealing case of Théophile Cassegrain. If at the end of the 16th century and the beginning of the 17th century a layman like Philippe Duplessis-Mornay was able to appear as a recognised theologian – including in opposition to professional theologians[469] – the pastoral monopoly is clearly affirmed afterwards. But the strictness of the confessional frontiers between the clergy does not mean that the influences disappear; on the contrary, the presence of Catholic controversies in the Protestant churches in France under the regime of the Edict of Nantes can considerably mark

---

[468] Foa, J. *Aujourd'hui, les disputes…* Septentrion University Press, 2012, p. 150.

[469] Daussy, H. *En debatant la religión…* 2004, pp. 93-103.

reformed preaching, as shown in the case of the famous Pierre du Moulin, who speaks from the pulpit before the Capuchins in 1640 (Christabelle-Thouin-Dieuaide). From a completely different perspective and in a radically different context, the French reformed preachers in the 18th century are still influenced by models of eloquence which are a priori out of their confessional field (Celine Borello).

A large part of attention will be concentrated on France, as much for practical as scientific reasons; in fact, it is a geographical area which knew, at different times in its history in the modern era, contrasting forms of confessional coexistence and therefore of contact between the clergy, both Catholic and Reformed. We shall therefore see that in sensitive areas, particularly on the political and confessional frontier, these "frontiers of Catholicity" that Pierre Chaunu brought to light[470], where contacts between the clergy depend on factors which are sometimes particular: in the north of the kingdom, in the dioceses of Boulogne-sur-Mer and Saint- Omer, it is the Franco-Spanish war or even the proximity of the English which generates reciprocal influences (Philippe Moulis). In a close area, Sarah Dumortier shows us that in the specific case (but actually emblematic of the celibacy of priests,) the clerical contacts play an equally important role in the definition of a stricter standard, and they are capable of replying to the challenge of the existence of a clergy of married men and that of the proximity of the United Kingdom. The world of regulars is also transformed by the proximity of pastors or "heretics" – but their divisions are sometimes stronger than the will to struggle together against them, as Frederic Meyer shows, from a memorial reconstruction of the Wars of Religion by the Franciscan observer Jacques-Fodere, who fought the Protestants, the Capuchins and the Recollets all at the same time. This internal differentiation from what one could describe as "Catholic clergy" in the plural against the

---

[470] Chaunu, P. *Jansénisme et frontière de catholicite* " Revue historique, 1962, p. 115.

Protestants is also observed between the secular and regulars, as in Toulouse in the 17th century, where the absence of Protestant clergy does not mean that controversy was absent from the definition of local clerical identities ((Estelle Martinasso). Cases of daily coexistence under the regime of the Edict of Nantes will also be developed, with contacts between pastors and Catholic ecclesiastics, either at Sancerre, which is known thanks to various synodal sources (Didier Boisson) or at Saumur (Bruno Maes), the latter case being particularly sensitised by the proximity of a reformed academy, training future pastors around an active centre of 17th century Calvinist theology, and a college of orators dynamised by the pilgrimage to Notre-Dame des Ardilliers.

A last part will be devoted to the various strategies of developing clerical identities, always from a comparative perspective and to research into reciprocal influences, as we will have seen already in the previous contributions. Through the example of the experience of pier Paolo Vergerio in Vicosoprano in the years 1549-1554, one sees a pastoral model which is still hesitating between the Zwinglian tendencies in preaching, heritages from Bullinger, that also Catholics, with the episcopate, which moreover places it in a certain proximity with Lutheranism (Federico Zuliani). The Genevan case will be particularly scrutinized by Nathalie Szczech and Genevieve Gross, who are interested in the first signs of development of a reformed pastoral responsibility in the years 1530-1560 and the definition of its contours of exercising discipline in the 1570s respectively, leading to the constitution of a true clergy, which is necessarily influenced by the proximity of the political and confessional frontier with France. This series of studies will be concluded by a reflection on an unrecognised subject, doubtless due to the discretion of actors and the rarity of sources, that of the presence in France, especially under the regime of the Edict of Nantes, of foreign reformed pastors whose relations with the royal power are rich in teaching about problems in which we are interested (Irene Plasman-Labrune).

Perspectives of discussions and research
As understood, the present volume will not have the pretention of brushing aside the whole of questionings within this field of research, and there are plenty of works to be undertaken or comparisons to make. At least five general questions which are not the subject of a specific contribution should be at the heart of reflections. One must firstly refine the chronology of the constitution of clerical identities and reciprocal influences that can be observed, the foaming of the boiling-up Reformation doubtless without tracks. But then there are two movements, already emphasised by researchers, which may seem contradictory from the perspective of the objectives of our reflections: in fact, if one looks properly, after the works of Thierry Wanegffelen, that depict a form of the clericalization of Protestant pastoral bodies, one may also interpret some developments linked to the application of decisions by the Council of Trent as a form of priestliness of the Catholic clergy, which would thereby maintain an ontological difference with the Protestants[471]. But one must not lose sight of the fact that if one reaches such modelling by studying standard texts, one must relativise them in daily life, inevitably difficult to see in the sources.

One must then question the spatial differentiations, on different scales, in the emergence of clerical identities. The urban world is naturally better known from the sources, but are there proximities between the clergy or privileged contacts in relation to the countryside? Bernard Moeller showed already in 1972 that a part of clerical identities could blossom in terms of bourgeois contexts[472]. Did the new worlds, by their distance from centres of authority, constitute a particular melting pot? The over-representation

---

[471] See for example BERAUD C."Clerge(s) art, cit.
[472] MOELLER B."Kleriker als Burger" Gottingen 1972 p 195.

of France in the cases that we shall study here must not allow us to forget national differences, or, on the contrary the existence of trans-frontal areas whose features would be comparable, such as the "Catholic Spine[473]" already defined by the works of Rene Taveneaux and today at the heart of a research programme financed by ANR[474].

Internal and external structures must also be specified. With the Catholics, contacts between regular clergy and the secular members, even between different regular orders, can play a basic role in re-structuring, and we shall see thiswith the contributions of Anne Brogini, Estelle Martinazzo and Frederic Meyer. Among the reformed churches there is a question of the definition of the limit between clergy and laity. In terms of perspectives, the pastors could in fact be considered as laity and, on the contrary, holders of other ministries, elders and deacons, could be seen as clerks. However,[475] a true limit is marked, which is seen by the fact that in French, "the minister" is the pastor. The other members of the consistory, elders and deacons, are in fact laity, even if some authors may qualify consistories and synods (where elders and deacons sit) as "collective clerks". The question could also be pertinent in Catholicism, where the hierarchy of the minor and major orders also poses the problem of adequation with social reality: who is socially seen as a member of the clergy? Have not the contacts between the clergy contributed to generate a type of "between ourselves", in each field, but also at a global level, which then gave rise to opposition on the part of the laity? Are the clerical figures and the identity of the clerks built independently, or in rejection of whatever is the status of

---

[473] Wanegffelen, T.*Le protestantisme en France* op.cit., p. 135.
[474] Meyer, F.*La Dorsale catholique*. Paris, Riveneuve, 2013, p. 321
[475] Wanegffelen T. *Le protestantisme en France XVIe -XVIIe siecles*. op.cit, p.135.

the laity? Is the aim to shake oneself off from them?[476] That would come back to ask "in fine" the question of anticlericalism and resistances to clerical acculturation, often close to the Catholics and Protestants, a question which was also dear to Thierry Wanegffelen, from a comparative perspective[477], and Nathalie Szczech shows for Geneva all the interest in leaning on this field. But one may also try to bring together the figures of the pastor and the priest when it is a question of controlling social conflicts[478].

Relations between the clergy and the ecclesiastical authorities are important in the constitution of coherent and shared identities, and often converge, necessarily influencing the birth of a solidarity connected with national texts or relations with the secular authorities, and Irene Plasman-Labrune shows this well. In fact, the next question to deal with is that of the relationship between power and influences in the circulation of models of clergy in the service of politics. Thus one could imagine some comparisons between existing works on the idea of the court clergy, for example those, while more than half a century distant, of Rudolf von Thadden on Brandeburg-Prussia and Benoist Pierre on France[479]. Obviously, all these questions are not exhaustive. The understood aim is that all these presented works give rise to reflections which will last a long time, between the contributors to this work and, let us hope, beyond.

---

[476] Domener B. "Laic", .Hervier-Leger and Azria, *Dictionnaire des faits religieux.* pp. 616-620.

[477] Wanegffelen, T. *L'anticlericalisme croyant...*. "Annales de l'est", 2009, pp. 59-80.

[478] Bonzon, A. "Les cures mediateurs.." *Revue d'histoire de l'Eglise,* no.238,2011, p 35.

[479] von Thadden, R *Die Brandenburgisch...* Berlin,1959.

PART ONE

OPPOSITE EACH OTHER, SIDE BY SIDE

A regular clergyman on the Christian Frontier- The Order of Malta in the time of Reforms
(1530-160)
Anne Brogini

Appearing towards 1070[480], transformed into a religious-military order in the context of the Crusades, the Hospitalers of Saint John of Jerusalem, better known by the name of the Order of Malta, are an international order made up from the Middle Ages from eight nations called "Languages" (France, Auvergne, Provence, Italy, Castile, Aragon, Germany, England) with more than 700 commanderies situated in Catholic Europe and an overseas convent which knew successive establishments, which were inherent to the military destiny of the order: Jerusalem, County of Tripoli, Cyprus, Rhodes, then Malta (1530-1798).

The religious history of the military orders constitutes a new construction [481] in European historiography, and its interest particularly keeps the specific problems in their conventual life, and in the manner in which the brothers manage to conciliate a monastic identity with their membership of the nobility and with their warring activities. The religious approach is also indissociable from charity and hospitality, which a number of them practice, and from a study of women in orders which are essentially masculine, but which accept sisters[482]. Apprehension of spirituality of

---

[480] Riley-Smith, J. *The Knights Hospitaller...c.1050-1309.* Palgrave Macmillan, 2012.

[482] [or De Avala Martinez?] Avala Martinez, C. *Practica religiosa e espiritualidad militar*. Palmela. GEOS,2012, pp. 135-138.

the brothers presumes the study of the rules which govern them, forms of individual and collective devotion, pious foundations and acts of charity, intellectual and religious education of novices, eventual pastoral responsibilities that the brothers take on in frontier lands where they are transplanted and religious teaching that they impose on societies placed under their authority[483]. It is interesting to project these interrogations onto the reality of the Order of Malta at the beginning of the modern era, when the Protestant and Catholic Reforms are breaking up, then restore Protestantism and on the suppression of the Language of England. The newly-found unity of the brothers going through a post-Tridentine religious renewal was the subject of a great many works,[484] which make it possible to seize in the best way the transformations of the convent, marked by a spiritual renewal based on stricter observance of the rule, on the foundation in the port of Malta of female monasteries, and on a renewal of hospitable practice which is close to what can be seen at the same time in the Italian peninsula[485].

The monastic order in a double crisis
The first half of the 16th century constitutes a difficult period for the Hospitallers of Saint John of Jerusalem, placed in a position of military defeat after the successive losses of Rhodes in 1522, which was taken away from them by the Sultan Suleiman, and by the capture of Tripoli in 1551, which had been given to them by Charles V in 1559, at the same tjme as Malta. Soiled by the cumulative loss of the nobility and the crusades, the knights lived sorrowfully

---

[483] De Avala Martinez C. *Espiritualidad y practica religiosa*....J.C. Ferreira Fernandes *As Ordens militares...* pp. 139-172.

[484] Venard, M.*Le temps des confessions" (1530-1620)* Paris, 1992.

[485] Henderson, J. *The Renaissance Hospital*. New Haven: Yale University Press, 2006.

through the separation from Muslim lands that their double eviction from Rhodes and Tripoli imposed on them: within thirty years, the Hospitllers found themselves separated from the Holy Land, but also expelled from Barbary, where in 1548 they had hoped to establish a convent in order to found there a Latin state in Africa in order to defend the frontier of Latin Christianity [486], according to the historic vocation of religious-military orders. These two defeats shook its identity as a religious-military order characterised by a mediaeval definition of nobility, which still prevailed in the early 16th century in France and generally in Europe, where nobility remained indissociable from warring virtues, from victory and from renown[487]. The losses of Rhodes and Tripoli reflect a general backing down of the Christian frontier in the Mediterranean in the middle of the 16th century, driven back towards the west and towards the north by the Turkish and barbaric pressure[488]. Added to the loss of the hospitaller role there is the warring stain, the geographical distance of the Levant making it difficult to practice the vow of aid to Christian pilgrims going towards the Holy Places.

The suppression

Threatened by an unfavourable Mediterranean context, the Order is also the victim of an internal crisis, following the example of Christianity which at the same time is receiving a double threat: external (Turkish pressure in the Balkans) and internal (the Protestant break). Migration towards the west and their facilities near the European bank face and

---

[486] Brogini, A. and Ghazali, M. "Un enjeu espagnole in Mediterranée" – *Cahiers de la Mediterranee*, t . 70-1, 2005, pp. 9-43.

[487] Schalk, E. "*L'épé, et le sang. Une histoire du concept...* Seyssel, Champ Vappon, 1996, pp. 13-14.

[488] Brogini A. *L'Ordre de Saint-John de Jerusalem ...XVIe siecle* Fuess, A. and Heyberger, B. La frontiere méditerranéen ... Turnhout, Brepols, 2013, pp. 163-180.

connect the Hospitalers with Reformation ideals which are [489]stirring up Christianity, while the secularisation of the greater part of the assets of the Teutonics, after the conversion of their Grand Master to Lutheranism in 1525, is witness to the danger t[490]hat the new ideas represent for the Hospital[491]. Throughout the 1530s, several languages are affected in Malta by religious quarrels. The troubles broke out firstly in England, where duels and brawls for religious reasons broke out regularly[492].The Council of the Order is also affected by tensions from the turcopole (defender of the Order against attacks between 1537 and 1539[493]). Then in 1540, King Henry VIII confiscated the Order's assets in his kingdom and suppressed the same title as a large part of German and English nobility to the secularisation of the Church's lands, almost all the English brothers (23 out of 27) abandoned the convent to go back to their own country, in spite of a ban issued by the Council in 1451[494].

The suppression of the Language of England accelerated the spread of reformed ideas in the insular society and in the convent, weakly affecting German monks who were small in number, and more strongly the French. In 1536, a French servant of arms was deprived of his habit for having adhered to Luther's ideas, while in 1542, posters were put up on the door of the conventual church of Birgu[495] and the Bishop of Malta conducted an enquiry within the population to find the culprits and several of them were condemned for heresy

---

[489] Le Gall, J.M. *Les moines au temps des Reformes* op. cit.
[490]

[491] Josseband, P. *L'Ordre de Sainte-Marie des Teutoniques*. De Avala Martinez, C. *Le Gloire de la Croix"*.Paris, Menges, 2005, pp. 167-183.

[492] AOM, Liber Conciliorum 5, fol. 140 v 13 November, 1534.

[493] O'Malley, G. *The Knights Hospitaller of the English Language" 1460-1565*, Oxford, OUP 2005 pp. 215-216.

[494] AOM. LC. Fol. 12 January, 1541.

[495] Ibid.,fol. 51r, 13.12.1536.

in 1544[496]. In 1546, a French chaplain, Fra Francois Gesuald, preached reformed ideas in his turn and gathered the laity around him[497]. After being condemned to two years in prison in 1550[498], he started preaching again in the port, until his new sentence led to him losing his habit and being burnt at the stake for heresy in 1554[499]. In the 1550s, careful of the broadness of the phenomenon, the Grand Master decreed that the number of clerks and laity who had adhered to the Reformation should be listed in an inventory[500] and the Council demanded severe control of entry into the galleries in the port area, so as to burn every Protestant work which might be on a ship[501]. Grand Master Jean de la Valerte (1557-1568) hoped to be invested with an inquisitorial power within his order and with the harbour company but Pope Pius IV preferred to give the responsibility to the bishop in 1561 before setting up a court of the Roman Holy Office independent of the Order in Malta, in 1574,

The disappearance of the Language of England and the near totality of English brothers, enquiries conducted within the Hospital and exclusions from the convent pronounced against all French monks attracted by the Reformation until the 1560s, have two essential consequences for the Order. Firstly, its reunification around a presumed Catholic identity which is based especially on the loss of Tripoli in 1551, on a revival awakening in Spain in the holy war against Islam; then, the strengthening of its Mediterranean anchorage by the indisputable preponderance of the southern European nations. Of the two "Nordic" Languages which were already minorities before the 16th century, one

---

[496] AOM, LC 87, fol. 43, 1.09.1544.
[497] BM Aix-en-Provence ms1094 "Relations de l'inquisitori", undated.
[498] AOM, LC 88 March 1550.
[499] AOM, LC 52, 28.03.1554
[500] AOM, LC 4 May 1553
[501] AOM, LC 91, 16.03.1562

was suppressed in 1540 and the other one, the Language of Germany, held little weight in the convent, both in the number of brothers and in terms of a political role. From the second half of the 16th century, the domination of the Italian, Spanish (Castile and Aragon) and French Languages therefore became considerable. This hegemony was based on their country and their members– although the French context was more ambiguous – and they were going to make an effort to apply themselves within the convent, by a wish for religious renewal and by an attached will for the Order of Malta to take root indefinitely in Mediterranean history.

The Order transformed by the Catholic Reformation
The wish for reform is broadly shared by the monastic orders of Christianity: the brothers aspire to it, without necessarily agreeing with each other on the manner of conducting the religious renewal[502]. In Malta, brothers and Languages make their aspirations go further with the Council through the bias of "lists" (suggestions made up of several carefully written pages) which reflect a thirst for renewal between the years 1570-1589.

In 1578, the Grand Master Jean de la Cassiere (1572-1581) witnessed the religious fervour of its author and a deep wish to return, within the convent, to a purified Catholic practice[503]. A reflection of the decisions of the Council of Trent, the programme of La Cassiere plans to insert the Order into a re-defined clerical model, within which monks, priests and bishops must master the dogma perfectly, in order to teach it to the faithful and laity in a better way. They are trained, within the framework of the establishment in the second half of the 16th century, of a re-defined Catholic education which hitherto was ruled by laws which were uniform in Europe, which are applied by everyone and only differ by the diversity of charismas and

---

[502] Le Gall, J.M. *Renover l'Eglise catholique…* op..cit., p.66.
[503] ASV SS Malta,103, fol. 216r, 30.11.1578.

pedagogic practices which were suitable for each of the orders and congregations who were responsible for spreading knowledge[504]. La Cassiere thus offers to come back to the "holy institution of the Collachium" which, in Rhodes, separates the knights and laity by walls. The Council of Trent has in fact debated monastic closing off, and within the area of discipline, revoked the "licentia extra standi" granted to monks, that is to say the faculty to live outside the convent in order to study or carry out an office near a lord's court or a private family; the obligation for religious closure was thus restored, and even more severely for monasteries[505]. Other lists insist on the need to teach chaplains and to no longer accept monks who do not know Latin and the rudiments of the Catholic religion[506], and to use military service to prevent the idleness of novices [507] and to fight their bad habits with spiritual exercises and a generally stricter management[508].

All these lists stick to decisions made by the Fathers of the Council of Trent, who were attached to improving the image of priests and their teaching and management duties. The "cura animarum" being the foundation of the Church, one must be certain of the good training of priests and regularity of their customs. On the model of a religious reform carried out in the Iberian and Italian peninsulas, by Archbishop Borromeo in Milan and by Bishop Gabriel Paleotti in Boulogne, provincial councils gathered in Europe, as in France where, from the end of the Wars of

---

[504] Fragnito, G. "Gli ordini".op.cit., p 181.
revue historique" 660 2011 p814-815.
[505] Zarri, G. "La clôture des religieuses et les rapports de genre…" Clio,Histoire no 26 297 p 38-39.
[506] AOM. Ruoli presentati ai Capitoli Generali 310 fol. 74r, 2.05.1612.
[507] Ibid., fol. 92v, 2.05.1612
[508] Ibid., fol.,107r, 2.05.1612.

Religion, the episcopate becomes a powerful home of the Catholic Reformation in the campaigns[509].

Added to the wish of the brothers there is a manifest desire in the matter of the power to renew the convent. Between 1647 and 1650, 91 prescriptions were taken to recall the five vows of the Hospitallers (obedience, chastity, poverty, hospitality, holy war). Obedience.is the subject of 60% of the magistral prescriptions in a century, followed by hospitality (17.5% of prescriptions), poverty, (12%), the holy war and chastity (5% each). The period following the closure of the Council of Trent (1560-1600) is the most concerned by the recall of monastic rules, with about sixty prescriptions, while the later period (1600-1650) is only the subject of about thirty prescriptions. Following the example of lavish laws taken by the religious powers and European politicians in the time of the Renaissance and the Catholic Reformation, in order to define the clothing codes and to ban ostentatious luxurious habits, social and sexual markers par excellence, prescriptions voted in by the Council and to recall the poverty of the brothers. Clothing in any colour other than black or a dark fabric is forbidden and all fabrics that are not cotton (velvet, silk, gold or silver thread)[510]. Accordingly, the noble knights were reluctant to abandon fashionable habits and in 1631, a knight complained to the Council that:

…the young nobles are wearing bright colours, and costly fabrics, habits trimmed with lace and embroidery and have hairstyles of such an extravagant and effeminate nature, that some of them are more like comedians or foreign actors than monks[511].

Food excesses were also condemned, linked less to greediness of the Knights than to the customs of an aristocratic life based on the maintenance of clients: the

---

[509] Brunet, S. *Les pretres de campagnes ...XVIe siecle*. 234 2007 50

[510] AOM LC 91, 4.4.1562. 14.02.1567.

[511] AOM Ruoli presentati ai Capitoli Generali 12.05.1631.

daily ration of wheat for the knights is thus fixed at six loaves[512]. Games of chance are the subject of the most merciless disapproval: not only is chance forbidden by the Church, but the possibility of financial gains goes against the usual abstention by monks. If in 1551, condemnation for having played cards or dice is "quarantined" (forty days' fasting, broken once a week by dry bread[513])[514] the sanction from that time is maximum, the brothers being liable to privation of the habit. Then, from the 1570s all amusements were prohibited; then in 1574, for having played ball in the streets of La Vallette, the knights are condemned to the loss of a year of seniority[515]; in 1582, hunting is forbidden around the harbour[516]; in 1588 the game of straw-mesh was banned, as it caused quarrels between brothers[517].

The rules relating to the vow of obedience are even stricter. In 1554 and 1577, the brothers are seen to recall their duty to eat in silence and to prove respect for obedience to the head (leader of the Language). It is forbidden to laugh, make jokes, mock another brother, to swear, to speak about "immoral or dishonest" things, to play with one's hands, with dice or cards[518]. The need to attend Mass is regularly emphasised: in 1551 a decree constrains the brothers to assemble in the church[519] at the time of Mass and in 1567 and 1568, to be attentive there, that is to say they are no longer to stroll around in the church while chatting, or play cards, or dice, even to play ball during the service[520].

Legislation on carrying arms is plentiful and raises the question for Knights of their double monastic and noble

---

[512] AOM LC 92 fol. 100v, 26.12.1572
[513] AOM LC 97 fol. 114, 9.11.1587
[514] AOM LC 88 fol.107, 3.02.1551.
[515] AOM LC 94 fol. 18, 7.08.1574.
[516] AOM LC 96 fol. 86, 20.11.1582.
[517] AOM LC 89 fol. 105, 07.1554
[518] AOM LC fol. 18 5.07.1554.
[519] AOM LC 88 fol. 139, 22.12.1551.
[520] AOM LC 88 fol. 50, 30.12.1567.

identity. Firstly, arms are forbidden at night, in 1551 and 1553, in order to fight against aggressions occurring between monks or meeting the laity[521]. They are then limited in number during the day, in the wake of the Council of Trent which, recalling the tradition of the Church, forbade duels[522]. In 1562, Knights leaving on a journey only have one weapon, a sword and two arquebuses[523]. In 1568 the monks could no longer keep pistols, arquebuses and other firearms at home[524]. In1569 they no longer had the right to use white weapons[525]. Only the sword is authorised for it is a sign of the social status of the Knights; but in 1581, evenif the Knights can carry their sword at their side, they forbidden to use it[526]. And from 1645, only the gesture of wearing a sheathed hand in the street could lead to losing four years of seniority in the Order[527].

These decrees favour a remarkable reduction in violence, after a great rise between 1530 and 1570, then stabilisation around one physical aggression per day for twenty years (1570-1590). The violence decreases to stabilise itself towards 1620 to a threshold which is identical to that of 1530 (fifty deeds per decade). A similar development is noted in Europe[528], linked to the effects of the Catholic Reformation, which strengthened the self-control of individuals, and a social development where the defence of the group fades out gradually before individual interests. By these sanctions, which restrict spontaneous noble reactions, in addition to religious instruction, which seeks to reform the customs of the brothers, the Catholic Reformation pushes the knights to reason from the end of

---

[521] Gay, J.P. "La theologie morale dans le pre.." *Histoire economie et societe* 24-2 2005.

[522] Ibid.,

[523] AOM LC 91 fol.74, 21.07.1562

[524] AOM LC 92 fol.67, 2.04.1568.

[525] Ibid., fol.117 12.01.1569.

[526] AOM LC 95 fol.2752, 9.08.1581.

[527] AOM LC 115 fol. 62, 23.07.1645.

[528] Nassiet, M. *La violence, une histoire sociale...* Seyssel, 2011.

the 16th century as members of an order which was religious rather than social. Beyond their family, and their parentage, it is the Hospital which becomes their reference group, the honour of which must be doubly defended: by monastic behaviour according to the renewal undertaken, as a Christian militia taking a maritime path which enables masculine violence to be channelled.

For all that, the new austerity governing the convent between 1560 and 1566 does not create unanimity. Desertions from the convent were rising in the years 1560-1570, essentially connected to Protestantism and to the French Wars of Religion; then, after 1590, they suffered a new rise, at the time when the Catholic Reformation was expressed most strongly in the convent (1590-1610) before reducing and stabilising around forty desertions per decade.

An unexpected consequence of the Catholic Reformation, the desertions are a phenomenon which only affects Malta. The men of the Church become rarer in the French noble families of the 17th century[529], the Catholic Reformation re-establishing a way of life which was so exacting that it seems incompatible with the lack of religious vocation. For the Order of Malta, the stakes are important: it is about preserving its prestige beside European noble families and to continue to attract young people who expect to follow a military, even political career, and to receive regular income which presumes ownership of commanderies. Therefore, partially and officially strictly respecting the vows of poverty, chastity, and obedience, were difficult to reconcile with a noble state into which the Order cannot pass as it constitutes one of the pillars of its identity, the convent necessarily develops in the 17th century towards an austere life, where bending the rules is less severely condemned. In 1630, the novices receive official authorisation to re-create themselves by

---

[529] Bourquin, L. *La noblesse du XVIIe siècle...* "*"Dix-septieme siecle" n.249, 2010, p. 654.

betting small sums of money in dice and card games[530]; in 1637, the Knights gain more popularity in the Inns[531], while in 1641, a list of the prior of Messina is resigned to only tolerating the knights in future pinning up their cohabitation[532].

The Order renewed in the 17th century, between hospitality and crusade

From that time the Order of Malta goes from drawing away from its geographical situation on the frontier of Christianity and from its religious renewal to raise as never before the two remaining vows of hospitality and holy war, which attract the monks and appear definitively as the most necessarily for its survival and to the building of its famous image. The construction of a new city, La Valette, having become the residence of the convent in 1571, presumes the building from 1574 of a Sacred Infirmary, regularly managed and enlarged during the 17Ith and 18th centuries.[533].The Infirmary contains a large room a hundred metres long where the patients' beds are lined up, as well as several other reserved rooms, one for incurables[534], the other for venereal diseases[535], and another for women[536]; on the ground floor, a herbarium, medical library and the rooms of the caring staff; in the basement, the kitchens, the lavatories and rooms for surgery and anatomy. In 1676, a school of anatomy and surgery was created in order to give

---

[530] AOM LC110 fol.46 15.11.1630
[531] AOM LC fol.26, 2.04.1637. The Inns are large buildings where the brothers live and eat . Each Language has its own Inn (Auberge).
[532] AOM. "Ruoli presentatati al Capitolo Generale" 311 fol. 87, 12.05.1631.
[533] Brogini, A. *Malte et l'oeuvre hospitalière de l'Ordre de Saint-Jean de Jerusalem...*
[534] AOM, Registres des Chapitres generaux, 291 fol.46r-46v, 1583.
[535] AOM,LC 99 fol.74r, 28.03.1596.
[536] AOM LC 109 fol.195, 1.06.1629.

better training for practicians serving the Order[537]. The students in the school, medical apprentices, barbers or surgeons, follow theoretical and practical training for ten years. The Hospitallers in modern times specialise in certain branches of medicine and surgery such as kidney stones, benign tumours, cataracts, and all the treatments for venereal diseases.

If the infirmary is originally reserved for men, the Hospitallers renewing with their primitive history, from the time when two xenodochia (a term which described a hospital) coexisted in Jerusalem for each of the two sexes[538]. In the 17th century, images were spread of the Grand Master personally visiting the patients in the infirmary every Sunday after Mass, , "making them read the Gospel, then tasting the bread and wine that is given to them, in order to prove to them that it is the best that can be found"[539].

Presented as a new Christ, the Grand Master communicates every Sunday with the patients, sharing bread and wine with them and reading from holy texts. Such a scene is also the subject of pictorial representation, like that carried out by the Italian painter in the service of the Order, Mattia Preti, at the time of the renovation of the conventual church of La Valette where the painter retraces the life of St John the Baptist in the 1660s. Beyond the many frescos of the vault, Preti creates a fresco above the front door of the church, which exalts the two Holy wars and hospitality vows. Grand Master Nicolas Cotoner, wearing the religious habit of the Hospitaliers (black robe with a white cross,) is represented simultaneously feeding a patient

---

[537] AOM"Libri Conciliorum Status (LCS) 262 fol. 65r, 19.12.1676.
[538] Demurger, A. Les Hospitalers de Jérusalem à Rhodes (1050-1397). Paris, Talliender 2013.
[539] BM Aix-en-Provence ms 1094 "Relatione de l'isola de Malta non foliote".

and with his powerful stick the picture of a galley, the symbol of the sea crusade.

Hospitality covers a wider reality than the medical care also showing help for the "poor people of Christ". This traditional charity is based on alms paid out regularly to the most deprived families, and on free care given to single women and to orphans gathered in the infirmary. Between the end of the 16th and the middle of the 17th century, however, thinkers, doctors and theologians examined in Europe a charity which was not merely based on alms and aid, but articulated around policy ideas, understood in the double sense of civic responsibility (submission to laws) and civility (good education), and regenerating work considered as an antidote to perverse idleness. Under the influence of actions led by Joao Ciudad ("John of God", 1495-1550), Camille de Lellis (1550-16140 and Vincent de Paul (1576-1660), the humanist theories of Juan Luis Vives ("De subventione pauperum 1526") or Perez de Herrera ("Discurso del amparo de los legitimos pobres y reduccion de los fingidos" 1598), the Order does not remain insensitive to the new ideas about aid to the poor and the resocialisation of the marginals.

Three decrees are issued in Malta during the first half of the 17th century, which reflect the development of behaviour towards poor and excluded people. In 1614, the Grand Master decreed a census of all beggars, d placing them in compulsory work, which appears to bebe more from punishment than a wish for education[540]. Thirty years later, in 1644, beggars were distinguished as either *honest ones" (invalids or those too old to work) and "dishonest ones" (authentic ones). The honest ones receive a papal bull authorising them to beg in the port, institutionalisation of mendicity accompanying the emergence of tolerance, even an acceptance of poverty. As for poor authentic ones, they are not only assigned to works of public utility, but placed in individual apprenticeships, in order to learn a skill that

---

[540] AOM LC 105 fol. 38c, 31.01.1614.

could ensure their subsistence in the near future[541]. In 1653 at last, the Hospitallers are interested in the children of beggars, who they take away from their parents in order to remove them from marginality. Put to work, these children aged from seven to eight years receive a monthly salary which is paid until they are f fifteen to sixteen years old, in order to serve as a dowry for girls at the marrying age, and with necessary funds to enter into an active life for the boys.[542]

About the poor or marginal women, the Order takes an interest at the end of the 16th century, to create, with the aid of the Inquisitor, a convent of Repentants taking together the old prostitutes of the port. Founded by the Knights in 1595 and placed in direct dependence on the Order of Malta. the convent adopts the rules of the Hospitaller nuns. In 1596, a letter from the Inquisitor to the pope reports that upon the death of each prostitute of the port, a part of their goods must be given to the convent, while those who are active are obliged to pay every month a sum intended for maintaining the convent and for the monks' daily life. Having become too old to operate, the prostitutes who have contributed to the financing of the convent see their future ensured: they can take the veil and live at the convent until the end of their lives[543]. In 1602, Pope Clement VIII acknowledged the official existence of the Convent for the Repentants, [544]which depended on the Order of Malta. Finally, in 1615, the Holy Office definitively fixed the "contribution imposed on the prostitutes", a fifth of the assets of dead prostitutes after having written a will was paid to the convent; if the latter died without a will, all of their assets went back to the convent of Repentance[545]. At this time however, the convent no longer depends on the

---

[541] AOM LCS 257 fol. 179 v 189r, 25.09.1644.

[542542] AOM LCS 259, fol. 71, 28.06.1653.

[543] ASV SS Malta 5, fol. 120r, 3.09.1596.

[544] AIM Corr.2, fol. 263 r, 29.12.1642

[545] AIM Corr .3, 111 r, 8.04.1645.

Hospitallers who, from 1609, have placed it under the authority of the financial managers of La Vallette.

A second vow was exalted by the Order of Malta in the XVIIth century, the Holy War is exalted in its operation. Practised since Rhodes, the latter was [546]clothed with a Crusader dimension after the truce between the Spaniards and the Ottomans, which ended in 1577 in the war of fleets and the great naval conflicts. Distinguished by piracy from the end of the 15th century, it became a codified and normalised act of war where privateers were mutually glorified: the activity was ennobled by its new actors, the Knights, who are comforted in their nobility by the size of the crusade covered with the race. In a similar hagiographical emotion, Hospitallers and speeches open these maritime operations to exaltation, raised up to the level of chivalrous deeds. Like the "classic" war beforehand, they become the expression of the nobility of the Knights of Malta and the means of maintaining the border between Islam and Christianity. An anonymous account of the 17th century in fact underlines that in taking great seizures, [547][the knights] freed a great many Christians from their miserable servitude[548].

A necessary tool for weakening the Infidels and strengthening Christianity by defending it with arms and in leading captured Christians back into its bosom, this activity hinges on holy work par excellence, which is the redemption of the captives. The latter doubly frees the Christians at the same time saving their bodies, freeing them from servitude, and their souls, preventing them from the temptation to deny their faith and become Muslims. It stirs up among the Hospitallers the wish to establish a Mount of Redemption in Malta in 1607, aimed at buying back the

---

[546] Fontenay, M *La Méditerranée entre la Croix et le Croissant*. Paris, Classiques Garnier, 2010.

[547]

[548] BM Aix-en-Provence, ms 1094 "Relations della Religione Geronolomitana of Malta".

Maltese who were too poor to hope of[549] liberation and from an unbearable servitude as well as being deprived of all hope of freedom.

In fact ,the Mount of Redemption of the Order is illustrated by its absence of activity in the 17Ith century, but its symbolic creation is evidence in everyone's eyes that the Hospitallers continue to fulfil the mission for which they were created, that is to say the defence of Christianity with weapons in their hands, the Crusade recovering from the middle of the Middle Ages from large aims of struggle against all the dangers which threaten Catholicism from outside (infidels, pagans) or from inside (schismatics, heretics and all those who are opposed to the political interests of Rome)[550] . In the 16th and 17th centuries, the Order of Malta knew perfectly well how to gain from the double crisis that it met and put it back into the trouble on the outside (losses of Rhodes and Tripoli) and on the inside (Protestantism): It preferred renewal and revival of its damaged image. From the 17th century, the Hospitallers therefore present themselves to everyone and to themselves as monks who are strongly devoted to their sacred vows – especially to that of hospitality – and as perfect knights, the quintessence of pure European and Catholic nobility.

"He said, the French taught 'em, that the Lord Jesus Christ was of the French Nation"
Catholic and Calvinist Missions on the American frontier
Catherine Balleriaux

In 1676, the Reverend Cotton Mather was telling the story – popular in New England – of a Franciscan who, boasting of having converted thousands of Americans, wished however that a European friend "should send him the Book called the Bible, for he believed that such a book existed 'in

---

[549] AOM LC 102 fol. 57, 13.06.1607.
[550] Josserand, P. "In servicio Dei et domini regis". De Ayala Martinez, C.

Europe" which could be useful to him'[551]. This type of criticism was of Catholic methods of conversion (absence of Bible translation, use of pictures), but mainly it was restricted to the verbal duel.

In 1722, after years of fighting with New France, Joseph Baxter, a Protestant minster was sent to the border of Maine, to try and win the converts of the Jesuit Sébastien Rasles to the reformed religion.

He addressed the very Savages; he asked the various questions about their debt; and in the replies that were given to him, he mocked the Sacraments, Purgatory, invocation of the Saints, the rosary, the Cross and its images, the lighting of our Churches, and all the practices of piety so piously observed in the Catholic religion[552].

In the border regions such as Maine, a great d to Boston. Two years later, after thirty years spent among the Wabanakis in Narrantsouac, many missionaries were competing directly for the souls of the Amerindians, who were more and more involved in these theological disputes. Rasles managed to keep his faithful flock, and Baxter returned to Boston. Rasles was killed by the English, who considered him as a "Fomentor and constant incendiary […] with the Indians so that they killed, burned and destroyed" [553].

Our study of the texts in fact shows that a significant change came about at the level of missionaries during the last quarter of the 17th century. In spite of the incendiary rhetoric often used by the Catholic and Protestant missionaries previously, the latter shared a great many

---

[551] Mather, I *A brief history of the wars with the Indians* London, Richard Chiswell 1676, p. 3.

[552] Rasles "Letter to his nephew Sebastian Rasles". Narrantsuoak ,15.10.1722. Thwaites, R.G. *The Jesuit Relations and Allied Documents ...1610-1791.* Cleveland, 1896, Burrows Company Vol. LXVII

[553] Dommer, W [Align with footnote]
Letter to Mons. Vaudreuil. Boston, NE, 19.01 1724.[align with above]

ideals and used methods of conversion which were often similar, based on the principles of habituation, segregation and good example. These common features reflect belonging to missions for intense reform movements at the same time in Catholicism and Protestantism, fundamentally centred on a humanist vision of Christianity. The missions were fertile grounds for putting these ideas into practice, for they allowed the Erasmian ideal of reform of customs to be proven. A spirit of competition and debate between the confessions was omnipresent, but comparison of their methods shows fundamental common points in relation to their idea of conversion and their relations with the authorities and European settlers.

This idea evolved in a consequential manner throughout the end of the 17th and the beginning of the 18th century. The intercolonial wars, as well as the wishes of the French and English monarchies to strengthen their authority, had important repercussions on the missions. The missionary practices which were typical of the Reformation and the Counter-Reformation lost ground in favour of a policy which narrowly combined religious and national identities, and the missionaries had fewer independent opportunities with their neophytes where they could put their ideas into practice.

Relations between the clergy

From the beginnings of colonisation, the Puritans of Massachusetts saw their establishment as a possibility to create "a rampart against the kingdom of Anti Christ that the Jesuits worked to establish in these areas"[554]. The Jesuits were forbidden to stay in Massachusetts from 1647

---

[554] Winthrop, J (attributed) "Reasons to be justifying the undertakers…" Winthrop, R.C. *Life and letters of John Winthrop governor of Massachusetts...*' Little, Brown, 1864 p. 309.

and, according to law, had to be banished at the first proof, hung at the second[555].

The Jesuits were well aware of the animosity of the Puritans towards them. According to Giuseppe Bressant, working with the Hurons, the English trading with the Amerindians told them that the Jesuits were malicious people, harmful for the public good "and that their sole aim was to cause loss [of Indians] as quickly as possible"[556]. However, given their working strength and the extent of their missions in relation to the work carried out in New England, they expressed little care for their competition.

They could even sometimes acknowledge the greatest efforts of the Puritans to convert the Amerindians with the other colonies. Thierry Beschefer, in his account of 1683, mentions the baptism of several Indian Iroquoi prisoners, previously converted by John Eliot, the main missionary of Massachusetts. These Indians, Beschefer stated, had "been taught the main articles of our faith by some English people, very different from those from Orange and other American heretics[557]. The responsible priest, Francois Vaillant, it seems, found it no trouble to baptise them. As for the other Englishmen, according to Beschefer, several "of these heretics take no trouble for their health, saying that they only regard them as beasts, Heaven not being for that kind of people".

Even the most radical of the Calvinists acknowledged a certain merit in the Jesuit missions. Cotton Mather stated that the conversion of a single Indian by the Jesuits "is a greater production, than that of a thousand among them of which others boast elsewhere"[558]. He admitted, however,

---

[555] Shurtleff ,N.B."Records of the Governor…" William White 185[date needs correcting]-1854, p. 123

[556] Dablon, C, "Letter to R.P. Pinette, 24.20.1674" Thwaites, R.G. *The Jesuit relations* vol .LIX p. 72.

[557] Bressani ,F.G. *Breve relatione… Macerata.* 19.07.1653

[558] Carre, E. *Echantillon de la doctrine…*Boston S Green, 1690.

that in comparison with the Catholics, the Puritans must work harder on the conversion of Amerindians. And for that reason, he claimed, the Jesuit missions had "prepared the way for something more sincere and healthy"[559].

Missionary approaches

Despite soteriological differences, the Catholic and Calvinist missionary practices shared the same gradual vision of conversion. Catholicism could be taught as a longterm habituation, a series of behaviours which, by their practice, would be internalised to the point of becoming second nature. The Jesuit Paul considered that the best way of gaining conversion would be to make the Indians sedentary and "having received the Law of Jesus Christ, one would make them take exercise and thus, little by little, they would become used to the way of truth and in a few years they would become a blessed people"[560]. Thanks to his free referee, the man would be capable.to some degree of distinguishing good from evil, even before the intervention of grace. By imitation and good example, the man could progressively internalise the precepts of Christianism.

In Calvinism, double predestination made the very idea of conversion problematical. In fact, that could only be granted to the elect by God alone. Nobody could obtain salvation by his own free will or cause it, and regeneration was also supposed to be as radical and sudden. All deeds before regeneration were considered as hypocrisies and conversion could only be conceived as a process[561] But, while grace could not be caused, it was also necessary to establish a Christian government which included

---

[559] Haefeli, E. and Stanwood O, *Jesuits, Huguenots and the Apocalypse.* "Proceedings of the American Antiquarian society", vol. 116.

[560] On the importance of example see Herdt J.A., *Putting on virtue...vices*" University of Chicago Press, 2008, Ch, 5.

[561] Le Jeune P. *Relation de ce qui s'est passé en la Nouvelle France...1637*. Rouen, Jean le Boullenger, 1639, p. 102.

regenerated and unregenerated people. Congregational ecclesiology needed the establishment of two alliances: one religious, the other political. The need for a form of community based on divine injunctions would require a process of education and habituation, at least external behaviour in accord with divine law. Putting into place Deuteronomic laws and the ten commandments, and the conscience that individuals would take their incapacity and follow it would also constitute an essential stage in the process of regeneration of the elect. The congregational community that John Eliot and the other Puritan leaders wanted to install among the Indians included not only the "Visible Saints", but also Indians who were converted, but not yet touched by grace[562].The latter could neither vote nor partake of the sacraments but nevertheless were members of the civil community[563]. Although a great many "Indians who pray" (Praying Indians) may not be called "saints" a ritual which was achieved by a confession of public faith before the congregation and required the approval of the latter, does not imply that many of them were not devoted Christians, hoping for salvation. In 1674, among the 1.100 converted Indians, only 119 were fully part of a congregation, but they all scrupulously followed the religious rituals and were an integral part of the civil community[564].

Conversion, for Calvinist missionaries as well as Catholic ones, was not only
an act of faith, but also a process of transformation of the self, by means of the institution of civility, habits and controlling mechanisms which allowed the application of

---

[562] Miller P."Preparation for salvation in 17th century New England," *Journal of the History of Ideas* vol. 4-3, pp.254-255.

[563] Gildrie, R.P. *The Profane, the Civil and the Ungodly*. 1679 Penn State University Press.

[564] Fisher. L.D. "Native Americans, Conversion." Harvard Theological Review, vol. 102-1,2009 p. 1114

Christian morals and setting up an environment in which responsible Christians could convert others.

The idea of segregation was also a common subject in the first generation of Calvinist and Calvinist missionaries. The complaints about the bad example of settlers and even the persecutions suffered by the neophytes were omnipresent and systematically opened out on appeals on the separation of the two groups.

The Jesuits were particularly critical towards the French settlers. The sale of alcohol to the Indians was considered a crucial problem and associated with the greed of the merchants. The problem was so serious that, according to Father Chauchetière, "we all wish that […] to see ourselves so far from the French: our dear savages that we no longer have such stumbling blocks[sic]"[565].

For this reason, the Jesuits preferred, contrary to the Recollets, segregation of their neophytes.[566] By combining a system of reserves and flying missions, and by trying to limit the trade on their reserves, the Jesuits tried to preserve their converts from the harmful influence of some settlers[567].

In Massachusets, John Eliot planned from the beginning to set up independent villages for his neophytes where they could create a civil and religious alliance amongst themselves, In complete autonomy[568]. Initially, nevertheless, he wanted to settle them near the English villages, for "if the Indians lived close to the English […] he would not hold them in the heart of prayer, and they would not be ready to hear the divine word." But, very soon,

---

[565] Sagard, G. *Le grand voyage au pays des Hurons…* Paris, D. Moreau, 1632 p. 58 and pp. 239-240.

[566566566] Chauchetière C. *Lettre au r.b. Jean Chuchetiere. In Limoges*, Villemarie 07.08.1694.

[567] Sagard, G. *Le grand voyage au pays des Hurons…* Paris, D Moreau, 1632 p. 58, pp. 230-240.

[568] ?? Iu

a great many Puritans complained of the potential bad influence of the settlers who, according to Edward Winslow, "had put the stinking Christ and Christianism to the nostrils of the poor infidels"[569]. Eliot quickly realised that cohabitation brought problems, [570]and complained of the settlers' greed for land throughout his career. He often regretted the introduction of setters to the lands of the "towns of prayer" (Praying towns, made "the profane Indians laugh at the "Indians who pray" and prayer. Therefore, Eliot decided to set up towns at some distance from the English[571]..

The idea of segregation illustrates the fact that Catholic missionaries as well as Calvinists consecrated their efforts to a non-national cause but also to practically carrying out an ideal form of Christianism. Their work was destructive for many aspects of Amerindian societies, but they were also often, as pastors, the only defenders of what they considered to be the rights of Amerindians. They ceaselessly condemned European vices, greed, egoism and pride, which they considered as a threat to their missions. The missionaries, as a group with some specific interests, sometimes had more in common with the missionaries of an opposing confession than with their own settlers or colonial authorities.

The intense vision of Christianism that they shared was at its source at the same time as the competition of their interest in the work of their opposers. Their relations could sometimes even be cordial. In 1650, the Jesuit Gabriel Druillettes, head of the mission of Narrantsouac beside the Wabanakis of Maine, went on a diplomatic mission to New England to try to establish an alliance against the Mohawks,

---

[569] Winslow, E. *Good news from New England*. London, Dawson and Eliot's Court Press, 1624, fol. A3

[570] Eliot, J. "Natik case drawn up in defence of poor Indians…Dedham", 1639-1673, vol. iv, pp. 255-261.

[571] Eliot, J. quoted in Winslow, E."*he glorious progress of the gospel…New England.*

who were constantly threatening both New France and the missions of the Wabanakis. First of all he was welcomed by a Puritan of the Plymouth colony, John Winslow, who, according to Druillettes, stated to the Wabanakis present that he could stay with [572]him and "he knows he would treat him like his own brother among you and the life that he leads". According to Druillettes, Winslow had a special interest in converting the Amerindians, which made him kind to him. The Jesuit manifestly loved Winslow very much and was warmly welcomed by other eminent Puritans. William Gibbons received him and gave him the use of a private room to carry out the Catholic rites. He also spent a night at the home of John Eliot, who considered him "at the same time full of spirit, ingenious, and erudite"[573]. In Plymouth, John Bradford served him with fish, as it was a Friday. Druillettes also wrote a letter to the Governor of Massachusetts, John Winthrop, appealing to his "acknowledged affection and his particularly pious and religious sentiments towards the savages who are catechised in the Faith and in the Christian Profession".[574] Druillettes was particularly careful to separate the interests of the catechised from those of New France in his correspondence. In spite of his efforts and his welcome, the mission ended up as a failure, having been given the consequent financial investment that it extended.

Change of Policies

The relations of Druillettes' successor with the mission of Narrantsouac, Sebastien Rasles, were otherwise more

---

[572] Druillettes, G *Narre du voyage...Nouvelle Angleterre.* 1651.

[573] Eliot ,J, "Letter to Richard Baxter, 20.06.1669." E.J.Powicke (ed) "some unpublished correspondence of Rev Richard Baxter and Rev John Eliot, Bulletin of John Rylands University Library, vol. 15-2, 1931, p. 455.

[574] Druillettes, G. *Epistola Patris Druillettes ad Jonnem Winthrop, Scutarium.* the Jesuit Relations.op.cit, vol XXXVI, p. 76.

extended with his English neighbours, as I have described above. It is true that in times of war, the Jesuits made up a particular threat for the New England colonies. which the French and English were well aware of. During the attack on Quebec, by Sir William Phipps, in 1690, the French were convinced that the English had a particular target, the Jesuits, therefore they wanted to make rosaries out of them for the soldiers' bandoliers and then break the rest[575].

According to Jacques -Rene de Brisay de Denonville, Governor General of New France, the English thought:

all our missionaries are like their most cruel enemies that they do not want to suffer with the savages who are at their door [...] when the interest in the Gospel would not encourage us to hold missionaries in all the savage villages [...]the interest of the civil government for the good of all must encourage us to deal with it and to always have some as the savage people can only be governed by missionaries who alone are capable of maintaining them in our interest and prevent them from rebelling every day against us[576].

The Count of Bellamont, governor of the provinces of New York, New Hampshire and Massachusetts. particularly feared the Jesuits. During a treaty with the Five Nations, he let them know that they could

give the King (William III) a better witness of their loyalty to him while in rejecting any type of correspondence with the papist priests and the Jesuits and by refusing imperatively to tolerate them in your country under any pretext whatever[577].

With the wars, the missions became associated with the political alliances, and the missionaries on the borders often complained of the attempts of the opposing group to "steal"

---

[575] Germain J. "Letter from Joseph Germain...1711". Thwaites, R.G. *The Jesuit relations...* op. cit. vol. LXVI, p. 193=2 191

[576][576] de Brisay de Denonville, J.R.*Memoire de Monsieur de Denonville Marquis de Seignelay.* 4.05.1690".

[577] Coote, R. *His Excellency Richard Earl of Bellamont's Proposals to the Sachems...* Albany, 31.08.1700"

their neophytes. In 1711, the Jesuit Joseph Germain lamented: "One of the great obstacles that we have in the propagation of the Faith and conversion of infidels are the English"[578]. The Huguenot minister Jacques Laborie complained to Bellamont that a number of the faithful had left to join the Catholic mission in Narrantsouac. These people explained that they left, for "the religion of the Indians of Penikook was more beautiful than ours, that the French people gave them silver crosses to wear around their necks"[579].

The commentaries of the Amerindians which are found in the sources show that these people were well aware of the confessional divisions, and of the crucial role of religion in inter-colonial conflicts, and often associated religious and national allegiances.

During the first inter-colonial war (1690-1697). the Reverend Cotton Mather interrogated a sachem of New France imprisoned in Boston, Bommaseen. The latter, according to Mather, had asked him for advice, as he feared that the French had deceived him. He told him that they told him "that Jesus Christ was from the French Nation […] that it was the English who killed him, and […..] that all those who wished to return to his Favour must avenge the Quarrel with the English as much as they could"[580]. Mather, using a wine glass as a symbol of the Bible, explained that the French had poisoned him, to make him[581] mad and want to kill the English, and finally destroy them. The English, on the other hand, having translated the Bible into Algonquin,

---

[578] Germain, J. "Lettre du P. Joseph Germain…" Thwaites R.G. *The Jesuit Relations,* p.202. See also Bigot, J. "Lettre a un pere de la compagnie de Jesus, 26.20.1699". Ibid., vol. LXV p.95.

[579] Laborie, J. "A New Oxford 17.08.1700."Baxter, J.P. ("Documentary History..op.cit vol. X, p.59-60.

[580] Mather, C. *Decennium Luctuosum. A history… of New England year 1688 to the year 1698.* Boston B Green 1699 p 127-128.

[581] Ibid., p. 130.

gave them direct access to the Divine Word, while the "papists" had deformed and altered all the articles of faith, with "scandalous Ingredients of their own Invention"[582]. He confirmed to them that everything that the Jesuits had told them was only French Poison". The English often insisted on the fact that they had translated the Bible into Algonquin, perhaps to counterbalance the fact that few of them spoke the Indian languages, contrary to the Jesuits, who had become experts in that field[583].

In their criticisms as well as in their statements of fidelity, the Amerindians often insisted on the motivations of the missionaries, especially their economic interests. Rasles, in a letter to his brother, quotes a sachem who reproached the English who were trying to attract him for never having any interest in their conversion, but only for their diggers[584].These criticisms are doubtless exaggerated by the Jesuits. But one also finds them in the English documents. At the time of a negotiation with the Indians of the east of the English provinces, the English offered the services of missionaries "of the true religion", The latter, surprised that they should be offered anything of that type considering the previous lack of interest on the part of the English in their conversion, replied that if they were previously taught in their religion, we would have adopted and detested the Religion that you offer us now, but as we are now taught by the French people, we have promised to be faithful to God in our religion, and we declare that we do not wish to abandon it.

With the arrival of the intercolonial wars, religious and national identities were more and more identified in the writings of missionaries. This tendency was strengthened by the colonial powers, wishing to consolidate their

---

[582] Ibid., pp.129-130.

[583] Balleriaux C. *Reformation Strategies*.op. cit., pp. 150-159.

[584] Rasles, S. "Lettre a Monsieur son Frere Sebastian Rasles, Narrantsouak, 12.10.1723." R.G Thwaites, *The Jewish Relations* op. cit. vol LXVII, p.219.

authority and knowing that the missionary work was essential for establishing alliances with Indian groups who could be useful to them in the conflict. In the 1720s, after decades of distant relations with the English, which ended by costing him his life, Father Rasles at Narrantsouac stated that these people:

persuaded with reason that in maintaining my Savages in their attachment to the Catholic faith I am more and more strengthening the connections that tie them to the French, they [585] have carried out all sorts of ruses and tricks in order to separate themselves from me.

The term "frenchified" was used more and more and associated with[586] the term "papified" in English texts. During the first intercolonial war, Cotton Mather spoke about his enemies as "half Indianised Frenchmen, and half-French Indians".

This tendency was actively encouraged by the colonial authorities, who insisted more and more on the need to assimilate the Amerindian populations into the colonies, on the premise that they had to become French or English and not only Christians.

In New France, there was a propensity to favour assimilation as soon as the colony was placed under royal administration, in 1663[587]. Colbert hoped in fact that by "mixing" the Amerindians with the French, and by teaching them the language, "by the succession of time, having only one law and one same master, thus they do nothing more than the same people and the same blood"[588].

In 1688, in his instructions to the new bursar Bouteroue, Colbert explained:

It has seemed up till now that the Jesuits' maxim was not to call the natural inhabitants of the country in community

---

[585] Rasles, S. "Lettre a Monsieur son frere…" op.cit., p. 204.
[586] Mather, C. *Magnolia Christi*, op.cit p. 68.
[587] Phillips J. *Casco Bay, 7.06.1701.A memorial…Eastern Indians*
[588] Rasles ,S."Lettre a Monsieur son frere" op. cit p. 204

of life with the French, either by giving them land and common housing, either by educating their children and by marriage. Their reason was that they believed they had to preserve the holiness of our religion more purely by keeping the converted savages in their ordinary way of life than by calling them among the French[589].

For Colbert, this principle of segregation[590] was far "from any good conduct, as much for religion as for the State". The growing authority of the court on colonial matters was accompanied by a "bodindian" tendency - to wish to consider [591]the Amerindians as obedient subjects, assimilated with the French in the service of absolute monarchy. The Jesuits maintained a great influence on the borders but were more and more encouraged to act as representatives of the government which was not produced without clashes, and they progressively lost their influence.

In New England, at the turn of the century, several circumstances also changed the conversion strategies of the Puritans. The war of Red Philip (1675-1678) as well as the inter-colonial wars, the revocation of the charter in 1684 and the death of the most active of the missionaries, John Eliot, in 1690, dealt a serious blow to the conversion work. The Glorious Revolution of 1688, on the accession to the throne of William III, seen as a fervent defender of Protestantism, as well as the repeated conflicts with France created a tendency among the inhabitants of New England to embrace, as Owen Stanwood suggested, "their identity as

---

[589] See :Baxter, J.P."Documentary history" op.cit.vol. V, p. 420.

[590] Like Jerome Lalemant has shown in his report of 146, the Fathers insisted on the fact that "for deeds of civility and policy […]they were free to follow their ideas, provided that they do not go against God's laws". (Lalemant, J. *Relation …Compagnie de Jesus…1645-1646*. Paris, S.Cramoisy, 1647, p.111.

[591] Havard, G. *"Les forcer à devenir Cytoyens" : Etat, Sauvages et citoyenneté en Nouvelle France (XVII-XVIIIe siècle)*. "Revue historique du droit francais et etranger" vol.76, 1998 pp. 75-92.

subjects of a powerful monarch"[592][593] The Earl of Bellamont systematically associated anti-Catholicism with loyalty to the King, and presented himself as a protector of Protestants. Successive governors insisted more and more on the required submission of the Amerindians, and the missionaries were considered essential for this task[594].

Perhaps as a result of this importance given to the intrinsic link between the English character, Protestantism, and a common submission to the English monarchs, here also the missionary strategies changed in favour of a new insistence [595] on anglicisation. Also, during the reign of King Philip, as Colonel Nathaniel Saltonstall noticed, "the impossibility of establishing a visible Distinction between our friends the Indian Christians, and our Enemies the Pagans became a vital problem"[596]. This tendency seems to be translated into new missionary strategies. In 1716, Cotton Mather, who had previously supported the Puritans' efforts to translate the Bible into Algonquin, held that:

The best thing that we could do for our Indians is to anglicise them in all possible ways; for the Language as well as the remainder. They can even keep their Language without a tint of other Savage tendencies [...] Although some of their old men are rather strong in their "Indianism" (of which one must not be surprised) they sincerely wish that their people may be Anglicised as quickly as possible.

---

[592] "The English reformed...Glorious Revolution", Philadelphia, Univ. of Pennsylvania Press, 2011, p. 20.

[593] The answer of the House of Representatives, to His Excellency the Earl of Bellamont 's speech ...Boston, Bartholomew Green and John Allen, 1699.

[594] Baxter, P. "Documentary history" op.cit. vol X, p. 223

[595] On the use of the term "franchiser" at the end of the 17th century see Havard, G. "Force them to become citizens", *French historical studies,* vol. 27-3,[27-30?] 2004 pp. 507-1018.

[596] Saltonstall, N. *Continuation of the State of New England...* London, D. Newman,1676 p. 7.

The missiologies of the 17thth century had favoured the segregation of converted Indians and a slow and progressive habituation to the practice [597] of virtue and the Christian faith, to the combination of civility and faith, the latter without the need for "franciscanisation" or an "anglicisation" of the Amerindians.

In 1658, the Jesuit Paul Le Jeune compared the customs of different countries, and meditated on his experience with the Indians:

The world is full of variety and inconstancy, and one will never find solid firmness. If someone had climbed up a rather high tower, from which he can see, easily, all the Nations of the earth; he would have surely been prevented from saying which people are wrong, or those who are right: those who are mad, and those who are wise in variations, and in and in such strange colourings. Truly there is only God who is constant: he alone is unmovable; only he is invariable: it is to him that we must attach ourselves, in order to avoid change and inconstancy.

These conversion strategies were transformed progressively and ended by promoting the idea that in order to become a Christian, one had to become French or English, or adopt a European way of life. The radical vision of reform of the first missionaries was replaced by a much more instrumental conception of conversion in the colonies. The border regions were particularly significant for the development of missiological thought. In fact, the interactions in these regions made religion and nationality become progressively assimilated and the missionaries turned into – sometimes in spite of themselves – essential actors in the political strategies and negotiations in the inter-colonial wars. These changes exemplified the political, religious and intellectual interactions of the New World, and the way in which the missions among the Amerindians

---

[597] Le Jeune P, quoted in Ragueneau P. "Relation de ce qui' s'est passé...*Nouvelle France es annees 1657 et 1658*. Paris, S Cramoisy, 1659, p.121.

on the margins of the empire constituted the places where European thought was put into practice and crystallised. The comparative study of the missions makes it possible to assess the political and intellectual influences which determined the missiologies and how the development of religious principles influenced imperial practices.

PART TWO

FACE TO FACE: MODELS AND COUNTER-MODELS
FACE TO FACE: SIDE BY SIDE?
THE CHAPLAINS OF THE ARMIES OF THE EMPIRE BETWEEN CO-EXISTENCE, IGNORANCE AND CONFRONTATION
(17th -18th century)

The question of chaplains of armies in the Empire has been researched over several years More particularly, the military field, in a real renewal of university research[598] was won by studies about the religious and the confessional. Now, in the history of the Holy Empire in the modern era, we know the importance of confessional questions, which have given way to numerous studies on various scales and to the development of the paradigm of confessionalisation. The territories, the towns, (less so the countryside) the institutions – like the imperial chamber of justice (Reichskammergericht) – have been scrubbed to one of the confessions. However, there is one institution, the army, which until the summer was fairly neglected by contemporary research. If one leaves aside the societal reluctance connected with the recent past in Germany, that can be understood in the light of the advance of research and

---

[598] See Prove, R. "Le nouvelle histoire …Allemagne", *Revue historique des armées,* no. 257, 2009 pp.14-36.

above all of the territorial prism: a territory qualified – often falsely – as "Lutheran", as "reformed" or as Catholic could only have an army which was confessionally determined by the prince, or, at the very worst, have several holders of another religion, but without special religious rights.

Obviously, such an opinion is false, on account of the confessional structure of the territories of the Empire, which one can only tackle the reality by approaching the "terrain" and on account of the structure of the armies of the Old Regime. If one leaves the Empire and one observes the composition of the French army, particularly after 1685, one sees "foreign" regiments, with Protestants and pastors. That asks the question straight away of coexistence between the confessions, but also clergymen in the heart of the army, something which has not, I believe, been tackled up to now. Thus the mosaic confessional with several scales of the Holy Empire is found in the Army of the Empire and the territorial armies; the pluri-confessionality implies an actual co-existence with right of confessions and clergymen. More precisely, there may be a supervised coexistence within each territorial army, as the very structure of the Empire army (Reichsarmee) requires contacts of confessions and clergymen. This is typically the case of armies called "Circles" (Kreise), purveyors of this Empire armyas well as territorial armies used within the framework of a war led by the Empire.

It is essentially this double framework that we are going to use in order to observe, seize and measure the forms of contact between clergymen who could exist within the heart of these Empire armies, knowing that the context is obviously very different from that of France: confessional coexistence, especially after 1648 Is institutionalised and governed by the law of the Empire[599]. Within the military framework, coexistence can appear as necessity, in spite of rules issued by the Peace of Osnabrück (1648).

---

[599] For a synthesis in German, see Aretin,K.O, *Das alte Reich,1646-1806*, Stuttgart, Klett-Cotta,1997

Thus, if we are going to evoke cases tied to territorial armies, we are also going to deal with the Circle armies in our report, which were accepted as a legal and institutional framework of coexistence. More precisely, it is reality faced with this standard desired or confessional balance which is going to be our guiding thread, In the background, it is also a matter of questioning the army's implication in the process of confessionalisation or "unconfessionalisation". More precisely, one could try to make out in what measure the army is a laboratory of experience for the spoiled confessional and therefore putting back the outline of the confessionalisation. The context of the reflection is double: on the one hand, of the myth of homogeneity and confessional homogenisation[600], a possible motor of a territorial confessional; on the other hand, that of the structural reality of the Empire armies which makes it possible to imagine, in the reality of daily life, an irreligious, but confessional in the whims of uniformisation[601].

Which armies for which chaplains?

The presence of chaplains in armies is not a completely new thing in the 17th century; still should one be precise on these terms: if one considers the only presence of clergymen and monks accompanying men of war, is the practice old? On the other hand, from the time when one defines the chaplain as a representative of an established and institutionalised structure, the chronology is complicated. In fact, the very essence of military chaplaincy – ecclesiastical institution, aimed for accompanying the soldier in a standardised religious practice during the course of a roving monk existence – is to be sought in the affirmation of confessional identities. If the German authors of the 18th century, like

---

[600] Straube, E. *Zum Herrscherideal im Jahrundedert...* no.32, 1969, pp.193-221.

[601] Prove, R. *Rationalisterungsdruck...Toleranz: Schilling In Spanungfeld/...* Berlin Zeitschrift ...Forsch 31003, pp. 53-69.

Georg Heinrich Goetze, affirm the antiquity of the institution[602], it is not a second reading of the past aimed at ennobling a fairly young creation. In the 16th century, the religious confrontations – at least in France – are accompanied by the presence of pastors and priests in the armies, in all cases theoretically since the order of Charles IX in 1568[603].On the Empire side, one discovers this at the start of institutionalisation from the beginning of the 16th century. There are monks present, particularly after the reforms of Maximilian I, with a chaplain for every "Fähnlein" (about 500 men): these designated chaplains must take an oath, are subject to military discipline and must "exhort the men to live in an edifying manner"[604]. A vicar general for each Catholic army is named, perhaps from 1534[605], for example Anton Brus (1518-1589), "Feldkaplan" (military chaplain) from 1542 to 1545, [606]then vicar general of the army in 1554. In 1565, Leonhart Fronsperger produced the first dogmatic step with his *Geislichen Kriegundnung*, in which he indicates among other things that the ecclesiastic must:

in front of the captain, where the drum calls the soldiers, exhort officers and men to piety and rectitude, reprimand their vices by speaking and lead them by edifying speeches, to Christian behaviour and to conversion- business -which is agreeable to God.[607]

On the Protestant side, at a time of internal structuration of the confessions, the priority is not for armies; the armed

---

[602] The synthesis of the question…:Boniface, X. "L'aumônerie militaire francais" (1914-1962). Paris, 2001

[604] ?

[605] Bielik, E *Geschichte K.U.K Militar-Seelsorge …Vicariates*. Vienna selbuverla des Feld-Vicariates, 1901, p 18.

[606] Hanak, J. "Evangelische Militarcelborge in algen Osterreich…Verband." Kohnert, W. *Die evangelische Militareborge Vienna Jahrbuk …Protestantism in Osterreich* 1974, pp. 6-8.

[607] Bielek F ."*Geschichte der K. U. K*, op.cit, p.45.

interconfessional conflicts are moreover smaller and the essence of the energy of the Protestant confessions is turned towards the edification of the territorial Churches. However, the desire for religious accompaniment, also for questions of confessional identity, leads the Protestant princes to demand at the time of the Diet of Spire in 1542 that the Protestant soldiers should have their own pastors. In the end, one must see that the Empire armies are already pluri-confessional in the 16th century[608]. The military authorities moreover are absolutely not looking for religious homogeneity; the rules threaten severe penalties for those who generate quarrels for reasons of religion[609].

Things change partially with the 17th century and the Thirty Years War, of which it is known that the first decade can be seen [610]partly as a war of religion. It then becomes unthinkable to see pastors among the troops of the Catholic League and vice versa. On the other hand, Olivier Chaline has shown it well in the context of the war of Bohemia[611]. This revealsamong other things the clearer emergence of a desire the faithful authorities of the soldier: up to counting on his engagement from then in the adverse troop, are there members of his confession that one rightly seeks to annihilate? Finally, one must imagine the viewpoint of belief in the true religion: "GottesKrieger - Gottes Siege". This adage in fact underlines the fact that for God to grant the victory, one must fight for the true faith. Maximilien of Bavaria engages his troops against the High-Palatinate on a Marian feast day and it is known that his banners are

---

[608] Baumann, R.*Landsknechte...King.* Munich Beck,1994, p.194 sq.
[609] Kaiser, M.*Cuius exercitius, eius religio? Konfession...Kriegs.* "ArchiveReform",no. 91, 2000, pp.316-353.
[610] Burkhardt, J. "Religionskrieg". Muller, G. Theologische.Kriegs theologische.Berlin, New York de 1997, pp.681-687.

[611] La bataille de la Montagne Blanche (1620) Paris, Noesis, 2000.

decorated with a picture of the Virgin. Thus, the question of confessional homogeneity is asked again, all the more as[612] the territorial prince is also invested in a religious duty for his subjects.

However, in spite of this reality that one may back up with other examples, one must not allow oneself to be deceived by quick reading; in spite of the desire for mono-confessional armies, the religious mixture still exists. In 1626, Tilly denies religious practice to its Lutheran troops in the town of Gottingen[613]. If one believes the Electoral Prince Ferdinand of Cologne, in a letter of 9 January 1628, he denounces the over-important share of Calvinism in the League [614]army to use it with safety against the United Provinces. Tilly, always needing soldiers, in 1632 suggests to Maximilien of Bavaria engaging some inhabitants of the High-Palatinate, or Calvinists, in the regiments: the Electoral Prince is very reticent but, practically. behind the appeals for confessional unity, the Protestant soldiers and officers are surely present in this Bavarian army of the League.[615] In August 1653, the Lutheran Andress Drost became colonel of the Bavarian army; in the following year, it is another Protestant,[616] Elias Lang, who becomes the head of a Bavarian regiment. Michael Kaiser has already emphasized one of the reasons for that: when Wallenstein put his army at the Emperor's service, the conditions attracted a great many officers of all confessions[617]. The reductions in the numbers of good officers "de facto"

---

[612] Reiff, M. *Von der Herrsch der Sachzwange...Heer (1628-1778)*. Kaiser, M. and S. Kroll *Militar und Relgiositat,* op. Cit. Pp. 49-50.

[613] Kaiser, M, *Cuius exercitius,eius religio?* op.cit., p. 325.

[614] Ibid.

[615] For the Bavarian army, see Staudinger, K. *Geshichte des kurbayerischen...Maria (1651-1679)* Munich, Jl Buchhandlung The 1951.

[616] Kaiser, M. *Cuius exercitius, eius religio?*. p.331

[617] Kaiser, C. "Die bayerische...Krieges 1635-1648. Munster Aschendorff, 1997

pushed Maximilien to put aside the idea of confessional unity of his troops[618] . Obviously, the military reality and need to have faith: the need in ken and for leaders of quality engages the prince to pass beyond the confession, particularly in recruiting soldiers among the prisoners. Oswald von Glaubitz, who served Christian IV of Denmark, is taken prisoner at the battle of Lutter am Barenberg. He went into the service of Maximilien of Bavaria and remained faithful to him. In 1645, he was even named "Oberstwachtmeister"[619]. In the same way, strategic interests pushed the princes to play confessions. When Munich is occupied by the Swedish, in 1632, the commander of the named garrison is Colonel Jakup Hepburn, a Catholic.[620] Even in the army of Christian of Brunswick, who also showed a strong Lutheran identity, as is shown in the "Pfaffentaler," struck in 1622 with the inscription "Gotte Freund,der Pfaffen Freund", there were Catholic soldiers in 1623[621] .

What is true for the pluri-confessionality of the armies of this war, is also true for the territorial armies after 1648. Let us go back to the Bavarian army. The recruitment of the Bavarian army does not rest on a single state which counts perhaps 800,000 inhabitants in 1700. In peacetime, recruitment is essentially Bavarian, except the officers (a number of Austrians, Frenchmen, Italians), but with the war, the ranks had to be opened to neighbouring territories, both Catholic and Protestant. The Bavarian recruiters did not hesitate to go to Souab in Francony in order to find volunteers [622], Catholic or not. Moreover, confessional belonging is put in brackets in the very process of soldiers' inscription. In the recruitment instruction of Ferdinand Marie of 17 April 1657, it is written that the new soldiers

---

[618] Kaiser, M. *Cuius exercitius, eius religio?* op..cit., p. 332.

[619] Ibid., p.352.

[620] Ibid., p. 337.

[621] Ibid., p.341.

[622] Reiff, M. "Von Herrschaft der Sachrzange." Op. cit., p.55.

must only "be described by the baptism and, place of birth, as well as the judiciary or lordship on which the place depends"[623]. An instruction of April 1702 only requires the surname and first name, profession, place of origin, state of health and celibacy. During a large part of the 18th century, confession only appears rarely on registration lists of troops. Therefore, one finds a great many Protestants in Catholic Bavaria. One example – in 1685, the Latour armoured regiment is almost decimated. In summer, a new regiment is raised with almost exclusively Lutheran officers and cavalry. In 1685, in the regiment of 790 soldiers identified in the eleven companies of the Truchess regiment, there are 60.2 % Catholics, 32% Lutherans and 7.8% Calvinists[624]. This state of affairs is sometimes associated with confessional difficulties, more so in peacetime in the garrison among the Catholic population, where, it is the clergy of the place of the garrison who fulfil the duty. Among the chaplains, there are Jesuits, Benedictines, Carmelites and Augustines but no pastors. There have been exceptions, like the Truchsess Regiment, which had three chaplains, one Catholic, one Lutheran and one Calvinist. When there are concerns, as in 1742 and 1745, it is the civilian population which complains about the Protestant religion[625]. In order to avoid any recrimination, an order is given to send back the two pastors, but the Protestant soldiers, [626]of one regiment or another, could go to the Protestant neighbourhood for communion. One finds, moreover, that border practices are identified in the framework of territorial and confessional intertwined communities of the Empire.

In order to try to give all the keys of the spiritual framework in the Empire years, one must also consider the case of the armies of the Circles. The Souab one is

---

[623] Ibid., p.361and p. 370.
[624] Ibid., p.56.
[625] Ibid., p. 63.
[626] Jalabert, C. "Catholics and Protestants", op. cit.

particularly interesting due to its composition. IN 17000.one sees two bishops, two abbot princes, thirteen lay princes including the Duke of Wurtemberg, the Margrave of Baden-Baden, twenty-eight counts and lords (and two with the title the Elector Prince of Bavaria) as well as thirty-one Empire towns (Augsburg, Reutligen, etc.) of which two-thirds are Lutheran. Two-thirds of the territory of the Circle are around 55% Catholic[627]. At the heart of the Circle, in order to avoid any concerns, there is application of the joint law, from the "trio in partes"[628] which one finds also in the operation of the Circle army. The joint rule is imposed on the management of the army – where the important posts are occupied alternatively -and in the composition of the army. In 1673, the decision is taken to raise two infantry regiments and two of the cavalry, either each time one Catholic and one Lutheran, effectively with the same weight, [629] If the tendency is for regrouping, the scale of the regiment or of the company, of members of a same confession, nothing prevents the presence of soldiers of another confession in the same unity. In 1760, the regiment of dragoons of the Circle of Souab is made up of nine officers (five Lutherans and four Catholics), with the exception of a Calvinist member of the cavalry[630].

It is in the armies, whether they are territorial, Empire or Circle, that the chaplains must dissolve. The very composition of the armies pushes the military chaplains to be in contact with colleagues, but also with the members of the clergy of their confession crossed in their taste with the

---

[627] Storm, P.C."Der Schulische Kreis …Zeit ton", 1648 bis 1732, Berlin Duncker & Humblot, 1974,. Pp. 51, 55-56.

[628] Heckel, M. *Itio in partes. Zur Religionverfassung…Nation Paritat*[Spanish} 49 1963 pp. 261-420.

[629] Storm P.C. *Der schulbische de Kreis als Feldbere…* op. cit., p. 307.

[630] Passman, M. *Bikonfessionnelle Streitkräfte: Das belspiel…Reichkreises (1648-1803)* Kaiser, M. and S Kroll, S. *Militar und Religiositat...* p 33-48 here -.p 35.

movement of units, at the time of campaigns and times of garrison.

One has understood that the very composition of the armies is a mirror of the territorial and confessional reality of the Empire. The rules of confessional coexistence are applied thus, up to a certain point, in the armies, with differences according to whether one is in a Circle army, of the Empire or in a territorial army.

In some Circle armies, coexistence was "de facto", inscribed into the operating rules and confessional questions had to be a potential cause of dysfunction. Reading the historians of the Circles,[631] it seems that the conflicts between the confessions at the heart of the Souab Circle army were rare and could in no way be general. The Circle regiment is a legal circumscription and also a military parish (militar kirchengemeinde)[632]. More precisely, it is even a double parish in the framework institutionalized bi-confessionality of unity, with no connection with the religion of the colonel of the regiment[633]. In this respect the surrender of the Circle in 1730, which rests a great deal on that of 1664, is clear: the seventh point indicates that "the chaplains of both confessions must be protected in the exercise of their duties and maintained in their administration"[634]. Concretely, in each major state of a Circle regiment, there must be a Catholic and a Lutheran chaplain. The Lutheran pastor is called by the consistory of the Church of Wurtemberg, installed in Stuttgart, after an inspection: as for, the priest, he is designated by the Bishop of Constance[635]. It is up to the commander of the unit to have the equality of law in the exercise of the religion.

---

[631] Storm, P.C. *Der Schulbische* ... op.cit.
[632] Ibid., p. 299.
[633] Ibid.,p 370.
[634] Landesacive, spire, E3/2090 fol. 421/424, agreement between the Souab circle and the Duke of Wurtemberg, 11.02.1693.
[635] Ibid., p 389

When the Duke of Wurtemberg raises three regiments, it is specified in writing that:

No difference in religion must be made, Catholics as well as Protestants must be accepted, also a Catholic chaplain and two Lutherans for these three regiments.

The case of territorial armies is different: the chaplain of a religion other than that of the prince depends upon the goodwill of the latter, but nothing is simple. From the peace of 1648 and recognized frameworks there emanates a yoke which is partly anchored in the territory, but also in the men. The soldiers are roving monks and they are called to cross the territories of another confession. The Empire rule wants the 'Lutheran" regiment, for example, served by the princely authority, to enjoy the free practice of the religion with the idea that "the regiment carries with it his jurisdiction in all the territories"[636]. From that time, even in a Catholic territory, worship must be celebrated with full honours before the troops, after a call by beating drums (Trommelschlag). This also means that the Catholic soldiers in such a regiment, if there is only one Lutheran chaplain, take over his spiritual jurisdiction, for example for marriage. The inverse is also true. One may guess that this rule may create difficulties with the Catholic clergy when one crosses into a Catholic country. If the regiment serves the Emperor of a Catholic power, it goes in the other direction,: the Lutheran chaplain does not fully bring his ecclesiastical jurisdiction and must conform either to his granted capitulation, or to the freedom of conscience recognized by the peace of 1648. The men are not called by the drum but orally warned by the sub-officers of the place; divine service cannot take place before the troops and very rarely in a Catholic church, the Catholic princes being very restrictive on conditions of practising other religions on their territories, particularly on Hapsburg lands. It is

---

[636] Kolb, C.*Feldprediger in Alt Wurtemberg Blatter ...Kirchengeschichte,»* 9, 1905,pp. 70-8.5

certainly not for nothing that Philipp[637]Christoph Fischer is called to a caution for celebrating holy communion. On 6 May 1664, he was installed as chaplain for the Souab Circle within the framework of the rising against the Turks, but in order to avoid useless tension, he is enjoined at the time of crossing Catholic territories not to seek to use the churches, but only private halls or then quite simply stay in the open air[638].

There we go into a war context and service of a territorial army at the heart of the imperial army. The rules for confessional coexistence must be rubbed up against the reality which is sometimes something else. It is what can be seen at Freibourg im-Brisgau twice over, in 1699[639]. That was in 1735. In 1733, an agreement was reached between the Duke of Wurtemberg, Charles Alexander and the Emperor to provide the latter with 4000 infantry and 1000 cavaliers. Pastor Zenneck was integrated into the regiment of the inheriting Prince Frederic, in position in Fribourg in 1735. The divine Sunday service took place during a certain time without any problems in a room belonging to a senior officer, without any drum-calling, as "a priori" the rule desired in a Catholic land. However, on the complaint from the priests of Fribourg, the commander of the garrison notified the pastor that this worship was forbidden according to the imperial orders, as there was no clear specification regarding free Protestant worship following the surrender.

In Fribourg, an emissary was sent to the Stuttgart consistory, then it was the chaplain Zenneck who pleaded the case in February 1736. On 1st June, the Duke of Wurtemberg stated in a letter to the commander of the garrison that the current surrender was identical to that of 1713 which confirmed the free practice of worship for its troops in Hungary, in Italy and in Sicily, even in consecrated

---

[637637?]

[638] Ibid., p. 75.

[639] See Plassman, M. *Krug und Defension* ... op. cit. p. 14.

chapels. Fifteen days after receipt, the situation has not changed and the affair goes up to the "Kriegsrat" in Vienna. Behind what seems to be an infringement of the rule, there is something else: from January 1736, Zenneck required the consistory to insist that the Lutheran soldiers confronted the holy sacrament. The inheriting prince gave an order of military respect – the presentation of weapons –but not kneeling or uncovering oneself. Moreover, in order to avoid quarrels, Charles Alexander even advised his men to go into in passing the "Venerabile". The Lutherans' problems are therefore the fruit of a Catholic reply which is taken as an insult to the Holy Sacrament: refusal to kneel. After Pastor Zenneck's departure, nothing is ruled. His successor, Brastburger, is confronted with the same refusal by Tillier the commander who, when he authorises Lutheran worship, in return demands the absence of singing! The service without canticles is obviously unthinkable. Brastburger also forbids access to the "lazarett" (infirmary) with the pretext that in order to receive holy communion, the patient must go to the barracks, then come back to the infirmary; for the "rest" the Catholic clergyman is enough. The complaints to Vienna are useless and at the beginning of 1738, things are unchanged, and even get worse with the question of participation of the Wurtemberg troops at Corpus Christi, under the pretext that they belong to a Catholic commander, in the same way as the restriction on attending Mass. In 1740 a letter from the consistory concerning new complaints with the commander and the Vienna court remain without consequence[640]. This affair, which remains without a real solution, is not an isolated case in the 18th century[641].

Behind the practice of worship there are other potential problems between chaplains and priests. In fact, evidence allows it to be understood that Lutheran soldiers, even before being married, create babies with women who follow

---

[640] Plassman, M, *Bikonfessionnelle Streitkräfte…* op.cCit.,p. 40.
[641] Kolb, C. *Feldprediger in Alt Wurtemberg,* p. 99-107.

the regiment, and that they sometimes leave them unbaptised or then go to see the priests to have the Catholic child baptised and have a letter of paternal recognition.[642] In the same way, mixed couples can give rise to discords between chaplains, if there is no respect for the Empire rules (the father's religion to the son, that of the mother to the daughter).

Another example shows the inherent problems in the Empire army. The practice of spiritual jurisdiction and free worship can give rise to tensions between authorities and clergy as well as between members of the clergy, in spite of the published rules. In 1712, the Capuchins of Weilderstadt officiate with the Badoo troops in a garrison in Calais. We are just before Easter and about one thousand Catholic troops are divided into four groups so as to be able to confess. The news comes to the Duke of Wurtemberg and an order is sent in order to forbid such a practice on his land. In reply, the General Wachtmeister of Vauchoir writes that he himself wanted to use the services of a Capuchin, but he gave it up out of respect for the order; however, one must not fail to say that such a practice took place in quarters in Bietigheim, [643]Besigheim and Markgröningen. One would guess that the application of this measure would depend largely on the context and individuals, and that sometimes what is tolerated at one time may no longer be at another time. In 1760, the abbot of the monks of Marechtal lets the Lutheran chaplain Vaihinger know that he can neither celebrate worship nor visit the patients at Munderkingen, which depends on the abbey. The prelate himself moves to inform the ecclesiastics and the mayor of the little town, and a deputation brings the order in his own hands to the pastor. The latter has the constitution, his experience and his respect for the rules assessed both in Catholic and Protestant territories, but nothing is done. Then he addresses Colonel Honold in Ulm, who takes it up to the imperial minister von

---

[642] Ibid., p 97.
[643] On

Ramswag, who informs the mayor of Munderkingen that Catholics and Protestants must have free practice of their worship under the direction of the Circle chaplains. One sees that pressure can be exerted beyond the rules. Moreover, this same Vaihinger, while he serves in 1758 at Buschtirad (Bohemian states), undergoes taunts from Catholics and even a visit from two Catholics from Prague, "like two soldiers", so that he prefers to keep his distance[644]. In 1759, another Lutheran chaplain, Mieg, finds himself prevented from reaching the infirmary by Catholics – men and women armed with batons. On his return he meets the priest who had beforehand notified him of access being forbidden and indicates to him that he is going to take his complaint to the commander, Baron von [645]Order.

One sees, through these examples, that the chaplains had to compromise with territorial realities, with a taste for movements, also contacts with ecclesiastics in the places visited, which moreover are not necessarily bad. In the Royal-German Regiment, the Lutheran pastor Josef Fuoss holds the position of chaplain from 1768 to 1776. The major state of the regiment was then completely Lutheran and he is in charge of the men, who are half Lutheran and half Calvinist. That does not seem to be a problem with his four reformed colleagues in other regiments, at the time of the campaign in Sardinia. If one of them is sent back, that is on the order of the king, seemingly as a mark of caution[646] in respect of the Catholic chaplain. Johann Ludwig Hocker is a (Lutheran) chaplain at the very beginning of the 18th century and takes part in the War of Spanish Succession in Colonel Schmertau's regiment. When he reached Arnheim, Hocker holds a note offering him permission to use the French church and he stays with a baker and not with a pastor; however, he is apparently in contact with a Lutheran pastor – Mr Manne – the Calvinist pastor, Mr D'Outrein,

---

[644] Ibid., p 98
[645] ?
[646] Kolb, C.*Feldprediger...*" pp. 24-25.

without our knowing more about him[647]. In the autumn of 1701, he goes to Dusseldorf and preaches in the Lutheran church and receives from the Jesuits "two richly decorated globes".[648] While he is in Cologne, he officiates in private homes: he even baptises a soldier's child, whose godfather is a Catholic innkeeper. On this occasion, a monk – "Ein Prediger- monch" – whose preaching he had already heard, leads him into a separate room and pleasantly chats with him over some good wine. He is also in contact with another monk who brings him to his convent – "S. Thomas Aquinatis" to show him a schoolroom[649]. One may guess that he is also in contact with other priests and reformed pastors, even if the details are sometimes missing. At the beginning of 1702, on the date of the siege of Kaiserswerth, nine soldiers of a Palatine regiment were condemned to hang: one Calvinist, two Catholics and six Lutherans. He looked after the latter and took care of the Lutherans but not only: of an Englishman. At the hospital there were a great many wounded people.[650]

A Jesuit father is also present, but because he does not speak French, it is Hocker who converses with him. A reformed chaplain of an Anhalt regiment calls to him to celebrate holy communion with the Lutheran soldiers of the regiment; an incident took place but it was not due to any of the pastors, only [651]inebriated soldiers.

Models in contacts? Duties and images of chaplains

Up to now we have essentially seen the contacts that the military chaplains could have with external representatives of religions, whether they be clergy themselves or leaders of the territorial Church, like the Duke of Wurtemberg. It is

---

[647] Mr Johann Ludwig Hocken (…)…Johann Jacob Enderes, 1749, p. 26.
[648] Ibid., p 28 "kostbare globi".
[649] ?
[650] Ibid., p 39
[651] Ibid, p. 47.

more delicate to glimpse fairly the relations of the chaplains among them. In fact, there are codes and rules which enable us to glimpse between them, while knowing that it is about safeguards from deviations which the princely and military authorities do not wish to see emerging at the heart of their units.

The rules and instructions intended for the chaplains enable us to glimpse in fact what must be, from the normal viewpoint, relations and behaviours of the men of God in respect of one another. The principle is simple: it is a question of preventing the chaplains themselves from sowing trouble. That is why. for example, Eberhard Ludwig of Wurtemberg demands fidelity from ecclesiastics to the fundamental laws of the Circle[652]. Some chaplains, however, can meanwhile reveal themselves as authors of problems due to their animosity in relation to their colleagues and to cause veritable little wars[653], even if one can read elsewhere that a cordial agreement is in force. That is why, in the Circle of Souab, a text of 6 July 1757 forbids raising any religious question between chaplains. In order to preserve the symbolic and real balance, steps are taken such as controlling preaching in front of troops on the right wing, which has primacy in the army. In order to prevent trouble among the chaplains, on one occasion it is the pastor, another time the priest, who officiates in this place, whatever the public may be. However, this is not always carried out without conflict: in May1758, the Lutheran chaplain preaches twice in front of the right wing where there is an exclusively Catholic regiment of Bade-Durlach and, making it worse, he refuses to give the place away. Moreover this system of rotation is also a source of quarrelling among chaplains[654]; but is this for confessional reasons and/or a question of prestige?

---

[652] Generallandesarchiv, Karlsruhe 46/3818, letter to Ludwig Wukgekn von Baden. 8.04.1699.
[653] Plassman, M.*Bikonfessionnelle Streitkräfte*... op. cit. p. 42
[654] Ibid., p. 41.

However, to look closely at rules of territorial armies, one does not see appearing – or seldom – the question of the relationship between chaplains of different confessions: the Brandebourg rules of 1646 and 1673 indicate nothing for example as to these possible relationships. It is more in the instructions given to chaplains that one finds this aspect. They are in direct relation with the rules issued, but, chronologically, they can precede them, as matrixes of what these relationships should be. On 2 July 1658, an instruction is given to Michael Heinemann, chaplain of Duke Ulrich of Wurtemberg, Lieutenant General of the King of France. On eight points, two are concerned directly with interconfessional relations. Heinemann thus has a mission to prevent "Jesuits, monks, priests as former pastors, reformed clergy" from approaching the Duke and always to prevent him from the latter with fidelity. In the same way, at the time of these contacts with these other servants of God, he must be discreet in his discussions and not allow these "chaplains" to touch on the Lutherans' money.[655]

It is therefore on another wavelength that one can determine these relationships, which occur because one is waiting for chaplains and the image that the latter send out. Whatever the confession and also the military rank, the wait in respect of religion and its representatives is identical[656].

All the princes expect a contribution to discipline from the chaplain, for the health of the men and also the maintenance of a religious identity. In fact, the army, a separate world from society, could be a vehicle of a confessionalisation: from that time, with the first identity being that of the soldier and not Catholic or Protestant. At least during the Thirty Years War., confessional difference does not seem to have been a special reason for quarrels

---

[655] Kolb, C. *Feldprediger in Alr-Wurtemberg.* Op. cit. p.75.
[656] A rule coming from the Souab Circle of 2.05.1687 stating "Alldien aber…Kriegraison…Gottlichem…Caplan und Feld-Prediger .."(quoted according to Storm, C. *Der Schulbiache Fedherr*…op cit. p.359, note 74).

between soldiers[657]. If one considers this proposition likely, one understands better the States' interest in setting up an institutionalised chaplaincy, certainly aimed at moralising and disciplining the soldiers, but also keeping them in a living faith and in a confessional identity, while a number of soldiers, during the Thirty Years War, seem to be religiously indifferent after the first years of fighting. How many soldiers were there, like this Ackermann, a Lutheran who formerly served under the order of Mansfield and Christian of Brunswick, and who took part in the siege and massacre of a great many co-religionists at Magdeberg in 1631? Among the first efforts, one may pick up a rule decreed by Christian IV of Denmark for his troops working in the empire where the soldier's duties are mentioned, the obligation to attend the Sunday sermon under the leadership of pastors whose names are not known, nor the terms of recruitment. It is with Gustavus Adolphus of Sweden, accompanied by Jacob Fabricius, King's chaplain, also senior of the army chaplains, which is held precisely as one chaplain per regiment.

That is why the image of the pastor and priest in the regiment must be exemplary, otherwise it is the very image of his religion which is damaged. Thus, all the military rules raise the question of alcohol for the chaplains, which is at the same time a reality and a means intended to throw disgrace on the other confession. Pastor Moser of Magdeberg left an account in which he particularly states that, on 28 October 1630, he had to have the Catholic chaplain Fredrich Schenck to stay in his home,[658] whom he denounces due to drink: "That is very painful for me. He often brings guests home in the evening, especially all sorts of monks and priests, and that is done at the cost of my beer". In 1631, he complains about another Catholic chaplain, who also devotes himself to drink and who is a "gottloser bube", a godless tearaway[659]. Obviously, one

---

[657] Kapser, C. *DiebayerischeKriegorganisation*" op.cit. p. 68.
[658] Winter, R."*Moser...Magdeburg*" r.1874, p.27.
[659] Ibid., p 31.

must take this feature prudently, but one knows whatever the confession, that the abuse of drink is denounced among the chaplains, and the rules are intended to stop this practice. In the case of Brandebourg in1656, paragraph V says clearly: ...no pastor, when he must celebrate divine service, must be drunk, or in such case he must be taken away from the camp[660],

Paragraph VI states about him that:

...a pastor who, outside the times of his services, followed a bad downward path, and did not adapt his life to his teaching, such a pastor, if he does not mend his ways after receiving three warnings to have to change his behaviour, must not be tolerated in our camp.

The same ruling, renewed in 1673, indicates the same points *ne varietur*. The young failure then goes before the consistory and can be sent away. With different structures for Catholic chaplains, again we find the same ambitions to limit the abuses of the men of God. The latter are really true. Officers and representatives of the Churches complain, at least in the 17thth century, of the bad conduct of a number of chaplains, all mainly due to drink. These deviant behaviours may come from the mediocre pay or from a lack of preparation and maturity, from which derive the authorities' efforts to better control the training of applicants.

The question of the image that one gives to the men and to other confessions is certainly present. Some of them are anxious about the quality and frequency of worship. When the rules insist so much on the duty to hold regular services or masses, it is sure that this is in order to teach the soldiers but also, in the case of mixed armies, to give a positive image of one's own religion. One must, however, apprehend the soldiers' world for what it is: a separate society where the porosity of types of military behaviour makes soldiers reticent souls, for many of them, not to God, but to religious practice, while superstitious practices have some success. In a 1762 report for the Wurtemberg troops,

---

[660] ..Churfulriches...Brandenburgefechet Oder... Berlin Christof Runge, 1656

one may read that "atheism and naturalism" are making progress, that "often it happens for a whole month", in spite of efforts, for divine service to be held while the Catholic chaplains regularly hold their own, even in a Protestant territory, without for all that leading the Protestants to Catholicism[661]. This is not an isolated case, but also exists elsewhere, as pointed out by [662]Albert Babeau for the French army. The army is certainly not a place of peacefulness, but of co-existence for the chaplains and soldiers, and indifference everywhere for the latter.

To deal with military chaplains, here within the framework of the Holy Empire, calls for taking a double reality into account, in order not to imagine contacts between clergymen outside a very pregnant context. On the one hand, their presence at the heart of armies and units remains subject at the same time to the regulatory and confessional framework of the Empire, but also, in some cases, the proper will of the territorial lord. On the other hand, they intervene in a military framework which, in spite of the efforts of civil and religious authorities, tends to form a very special societal entity in which religion is not really the first preoccupation of the men: works of piety must not deceive the present reader. The contacts between chaplains and also between chaplains and local clergymen cannot therefore only be seen with this background and cannot only be considered in terms of opposition and competition. In fact, even if there had been individual oppositions between chaplains, do these problems[663] arise in respect of both confessional and personal questions? It is difficult to give a firm answer. On the other hand, real oppositions met by

---

[661] Kolb, C. *Feldprediger in Alt-Wurtemberg* art.cit.p. 80.

[662] Babeau, A. "*La vie militaire sous l'ancien Régime*", Firmin-Didot,1890 p220 sq,

[663] A systematic article in , J.L. "Document, history in ecclesiastical study…modernes". "Recherches.. ..religieuse" t 92-4 2004, pp. 597-635 Paris institut d'Etudes Augustiniennes 1999.

these chaplains during their travels often rely on territorial law and Empire law, which obviously does not exclude confessional rejection. However, latent or actual opposition does not prevent a connection between individuals and practices. The considerations as regards the men of God are identical, in the same way that the uncertain roving monk's life, which is free, could lead one to another question: is there a community of chaplains? Or, more precisely, is a chaplain also a pastor or priest? Finally, a great many things are still to be questioned beyond some enlightenment given here, in order to apprehend these chaplains in contact. Among them, the reality of relationships between Catholic and Protestant chaplains in the face of a common enemy, certainly France, but especially the Turk, the true enemy of the faith, made it possible to sound out, to qualify and hierarchise these contacts.

***

Protestant influences or general ignorance?
Some Catholic parishes of the Archdiocese of Prague
visited by Mgr Berka of Duba in 1594
NICOLAS RICHARD

It is fairly well known, from the studies of Jean-Louis Quantin, that doctrinal studies greatly contributed to the progress of learning. The contacts, intellectual and controversial, between theologians of different obediences, gave a shot in the arm to patristic studies and to the rise of the critical method[664]. Outside the Republic of Letters, did contacts between Catholics and non-Catholics have the same type of effect as the critical method[665]? Or, to express

---

[664] Good example: Quantin, J.L. "Les Jésuites de l'érudition anglicane" *Dix-septieme siècle* no.237, 2007, pp. 167-195.

[665] On the political idea of friendship, it is true in diplomacy: Haan, B. *Ll'amitié entre princes...Religion (1500-1570)* Paris PUE 2011 eso pm1-3 pp. 167-195.

it more neutrally, what were the consequences of situations where the clergy were in close contact?

If there was a kingdom in the 16th century where the clergy were in close contact, it was Bohemia. Elsewhere, in France, Poland or Hungary, the fact that a law forced the clergy to co-exist was a new thing or something in the future. In Bohemia, this lasted from the middle of the 15th century. The country lived under the so-called "double legal faith" ("legalni dvojveri"). This made Catholics and Hussites, later called Utraquists, coexist. This regime created a kingdom of two peoples ("stadt dvojiho lidu"), where the unity of the country was strengthened by an ideology of friendship between the members of the two parts[666], a friendship which nostalgically emphasises the[667] memorialists of the time of the Thirty Years War, when the system hailed splinters[668].

This framework not only organised the coexistence of the two types of clergy. It also made the necessary contacts. The parishes of the old archdiocese of Prague were shared between two consistories, the Catholic (from on high, based at the cathedral) and the Utraquist (from below, meeting at Notre-Dame of Tyn). The second, without a bishop who could ordain candidates to the ministry, had not abandoned, in spite of its criticism of Rome's bad habits, the need for sacramental ordination by a bishop holding the apostolic succession (although Luther had advised the opposite from 1523)[669]. He founded, beyond his canonical legitimacy of the vacancy of the Prague siege from the 1420s. With the

---

[666]?

[667] The Hussite Jan Rokycana (1396-1471) chosen as Archbishop by the Diet of Bohemia (1435) never recognised that Rome left the seat open.

[Is this footnote 237?]E.g. that of the defenestration in 1628 of Vilém Slavata (1572-1652) JIRECEJ=K H, "Pameti …slavery to 1608 to 1629". Prague, Kober 186601868, p 40 sq

[669] E.g., Krarup, M. *Ordination in Wittemberg,* Tubingen Siebek, 2007, pp. 57-66,

restoration of the Roman Catholic archbishopric in Prague in 1562, he was in fact forced to recognise "de jure", while refusing his authority "de facto et grosso modo". As for the Catholics, from 1564 they enjoyed the result of taking communion with the faithful "sub utraque", in order to facilitate unity of the Utraquists with Rome. For all that, saying that the two priesthoods were in contact, better, intertwined, passages moreover being continuous with the jurisdiction of one consistory to that of another.

What were the concrete religious consequences of these contacts, of this intertwining of the two priesthoods? This is not a new question. But it is usually asked the other way round. Historians talk about the parish situation in Bohemia at the end of the 16th century. They observed what we will call abuses, and in a large number. Now, among them, some of these, such as cohabitation, are legal in ecclesiastical disciplines coming from the Reformation. Then, their explanation is easily found: these abuses come from the intertwining of the priesthoods[670]. What we [671]shall try to work out here is the soundness of the minority in this syllogism: is it a question of reciprocal influences? And therefore more broadly: what are the actual consequences of this intertwining of the priesthoods?

To reply exhaustively to these questions goes beyond the scope of one article. We concentrate our attention on one example, from a document which is precious due to its rarity[672], an inspection of the parishes of Brandys and Labem in 1594, by the Archbishop of Prague, Mgr Berka de Duba[673]. The <u>study of this text will enable one for the</u>

---

[670] E.g. analysis by Winter, Z. *Zivot cirkevni* Prague Orta 1894, p. 631.
[671] Brandes am der elbe 25km NE from Prague
[672] Narodni archive, Prague, vol. 8 41 /2 18 4.07.1594 Brandys and Labem..occupation of benefices.
[673] On Berka (Dube) (1551-1606) historic literature is poor; see Eberhard, W. "Berka und Leipa"; Chaline, O. *Les princes eveques en Boheme – 1550-1650*.

second time, to see the true nature of these contacts between priesthoods and to determine their reciprocal influence and its limits.

Administration of the royal region of Brandys nad Labem north-east of Prague - this great lordship had been from the beginnings of the reign of the Emperor Rodolphe II (1576-1612) the favourite summer residence of the sovereign. It was therefore not surprising that the Archbishop was there. In good Tridentine prelacy, he gained fro his presence in order to inspect his clergy.

There was something more: Rodolphe II had conceded his right of collature on the parishes of his estates[674]. This meant that the Chamber of Bohemia, the administration in charge of the estate, left to the Archbishop the right to present the priests of these parishes. This grant "ad hominem" de facto brought the parishes of the royal estate under the jurisdiction of the Catholic consistory. It was therefore Catholic priests, at least *de jure*", that Berka had called that day, and that he decreed to come in, after being informed with the "l'heitman" on possible complaints against them – there were none.

The Archbishop began with a sermon where he explained that the sovereign had given him their benefices. He stated that there was no senior member among them, and decreed to those who received the holy oils from the Notre Dame de Tyn church, that is from the utraquat, that in future they should receive them from the cathedral, in other words from himself. Six priests were then examined in turn and their replies were an eloquent picture of the diversity of practices in Bohemia. The first, the priest of Brandys, Jean Cleska (in Czech: Cejca) was undoubtedly Catholic. Born in a region which was partly faithful to Rome ("Stedre"), he had been ordained by Archbishop Anton Brus of Mohelnice (1561-1580) and had always stayed under his jurisdiction.

---

[674] His predecessor Martin Medek (1581-1590) had received it 10.09.1581. Rozpravy Ceske Akademie 46 Alois wiesner, 1912 p. 328) also ? Incomplete

He was not cohabiting and recited his breviary. The rite that he practised on the other hand was low orthodox: he chanted the gospel and epistle in Czech and maintained the practice of dry masses, he celebrated the feast of Jan Hus, gave communion to the faithful without prior confession, ruling out the local custom. He was also accused of a typically Hussite practice, that of having given communion to a baby. He defended himself, claiming that the host that he had given was not consecrated. While that may have been true, the scandal remained. We should pause for a moment to consider this practice. What did it mean? It is difficult to resolve. Analogies are possible: thus, in the archdeaconry of Longuyon (diocese of Treves) in the years 1627-1628, a great many priests gave hosts which were simply blessed to children at Easter and to women at the time of their menstruation[675676]. The faithful did not know they had received a sacramental, and not a sacrament. It is not obvious – at Brandys, the added difficulty is that the host was even blessed. Five years after Berka's visit, the commentary of Saint Thomas of Suarez appeared in Rome. He discussed the possibility of giving an un-consecrated host in communion to a sinner, in order[677] to avoid sacrilege and scandal at the same time. If he rejected this solution, having studied the different cases, it was not insoluble; having it was not without having been discussed it at length, while pointing out that some authors admitted it[678]. In what measure did the practice correspond to these theories? In this type of matter, the question collides with an almost insoluble problem of sources (as the usage that some present

---

[675] The index of Kaiser by Carriere, V. *Revue de...l'Église de France* r. 1569, 1929, p. 496 – the faithful thought they received consecrated hosts.

[676] Kaiser, J B. *"Die Archdiakonat Longuyon ...Visitations 1628-1629.* Colmar 1928-1929 III, pp. 17-18 IV, p. 76, p.157.

[677677] Suárez, F.J. "Commentarium…Sacramentis", Venice, Franscechi 1590. t III pp. 820-821.Professor at Alcala.

[678] Skybova, A. *Le ordinationi dei sacerdoti...scolo*. Graciotti, S, "*talia...europeo*, Florence: Olschki 1999, p. 51565.

Orientals would make of blessed but un-consecrated eucharistic bread, in order to give communion to the faithful while avoiding debasement, with what seems to be disputed pastoral effects).

But let us go on to the next parish. The priest of Chotetŏv, Kean Makarius, ordained by Mgr Brun in1573, gave communion to his parishioners from both groups, also without prior confession. However, he said he had "kept processions, in the Catholic manner" in his subsidiary of Slivno, in the Kosarky estate which belonged, not to the sovereign, but to the Kolovrat family. He recited his hours. His itinerary was not without sudden changes. Born in Litoměřice, he had been a cantor, was ordained, then had kept his distance towards the Catholic discipline. A pastor from Frankfurt-on-Main had married himself and his wife. At the time of his visit, his wife was dead. Moreover, he had spent some time under the jurisdiction of the Utraquist consistory.

The third person to be examined was the priest of Kostelec nad Labem (lbekosteletz), Etienne Benedicti, a Hungarian ordained in Presbourg, which had always been under the jurisdiction of the Utraquist consistory. However, this Benedicti was a curious heretic: he recited his breviary and had neither wife nor child. He refused communion of small children in spite of their parents' wishes. He also demanded an intervention of the Archbishop against the faithful of the Moravian Brothers who lived in his parish under the direction of an old woman. The Archbishop ordered him to come under his obedience and to keep his parish, but from that time to refuse communion without prior confession.

Although he was Silesian, the priest of Předměřice nad Jizerou was called Jean Moravus. He had been ordained in Vienna and had spent five years under the jurisdiction of the Utraquist consistory, kept the chastity of his state and recited his hours when he could. If he gave communion to his faithful people "sub utraque" and without prior confession, he had a personal interpretation of the ban on giving communion to small children required by the consistory from below the archbishop; he neglected it here, in the face of the well-settled custom, but did not always respect it outside his parish.

The priest of Dřevčice, Andre Passecky, from Bohemia, a sexagenarian, had passed,[679] under the jurisdiction of the Church of Tyn, as soon as he was ordained in Venice. His parish took communion "sub utraque" and celebrated the annual feast of Jan Hus. Was he, however, an Utraquist himself? He certainly recited his hours, but he justified himself by the infidelity of his servants of the obligation where he was found to have taken a wife, evoking examples of the Old Testament and clerks of the consistory. That did not prevent him from being obedient to Berka and to promise not to give communion to small children in future.

The priest of Svémyslice for two years, Jean Xenomenes, was a Polish Catholic, ordained in Krakov, who recited the Prague breviary. His maid was of canonical age. He certainly gave communion to his faithful people "sub utraque" but he had, he said, brought many of them back to practising confession, which had cost him unfriendliness from someof the parishioners, who were going to receive the sacraments from the previous priest, in Dřevčice. But even the orthodoxy of Xenomenes was not without a hitch: he gave communion to children at puberty. Such a practice was curious and difficult to interpret. It does not seem to correspond with the folklore of purification which did not require the presence of the new-born baby[680]. It could be the influence of countries which had been through the Reformation, when they had maintained the ceremony of purification -although the rite of Svémyslice

---

[679] Graciotti, S. *Italia Boemia...europeo*, Florence, Olschki,1999, pp. 51-65.

[680] van Gennep, A., *Manuel du folklore francais* contemporain, 1943, Picard 1972ed t 1

was not Protestant at all[681]. In the same way, the natural link that one could make with the Utraquist need for communion for small children is largely illusory: reformers in Prague did not connect this practice at the time of purification[682]. On the other hand, the relationship between purification (on average, according to doctors and folklorists, forty days after giving birth) and oriental baptism (which was also forty days after birth) without possible exception – is obvious. Also in Moravia, moreover, Cardinal Dietrichstein, Bishop of the neighbouring diocese of Olomouc, was confronted at the beginning of the next decade by one of his priests, who was not Polish, but originally from the Balkans, [683]who followed the original rite. His only reaction was to find out whether he was united or not.

Berka did not take this trouble. After interrogation, he decreed to his priests – "gravissimis verbis": to live a chaste and exemplary life, not to give communion to children, to restore (rursus pristino usus restituerent) sacramental confession, not to introduce "new" feasts – in other words, those of Jan Hus – and to disperse the conventicles of the Brothers. The next day the priests promised to obey him, announced their profession of faith from the Council of Trent and from the Archbishop they received absolution for their faults. Berka was able to inspect the parish church of Brandys and have inscriptions that were insulting to the work of Jan Hus removed.

---

[681] If Luther, then English Puritans, denounced purification as a papist superstition, the ceremony was maintained in the English churches and those of the Empire; see *Oxford History of the Reformation* OUP, 1996. Vol. 1, p.331-332.

[682] One cannot omit an influence of the Hussites' old need as the Hussites of the Brandys area accepted this practice.

[683] Oriental discipline was then to give communion to children after baptism up to Maronite synod of 1596; see Heyberger, R, *Chrtiens du proche orient catholique...*...Rome: BEFAR 1994 p.236.christianisme boheme"

Clergymen in contact or ignorant clerks?

One may ask a question: these parishes that the Archbishop inspected, could one describe them as Catholic? It is not clear whether the historian's response would be the same as that of the Archbishop – even if it is not really probable that the historian was right[684]. One would be tempted to reason thus: if a population is hostile to the Roman church and its priest is of doubtful orthodoxy, who practises "sui generis" rites or those tasting of heresy, or he obeys an excommunicated hierarchy, then one hesitates to consider that parish as Catholic.

There is a type of paradox. The questions of the enquiry seek to determine which priests have (or do not have) heretical practices. The conclusion itself places them all on the same level. Berka grants them all, after reciting the "Credo" of Pius IV, absolution for their mistakes. Such an act had a very strong value. It did not mean anything other than the fact the Archbishop gave up requiring a recantation or at least the specific oath that Rome demanded from Utraquists returning to the Church[685].This meant that the priests had not been heretics. From the canonical viewpoint, it was certainly wisdom. The fidelity of these priests to Berka was not forcibly acquired by him for a long time. In any case, the Archbishop protected them from the complex legal consequences of recanting. Recanting is in fact the most irrefutable formal proof of a heresy, because it is a declaration of heresy "a posteriori" and therefore is at risk of creating relapses[686]. How could one do that, however, so that the priests could escape recanting? All these priests had

---

[684] Parma, T. *Frantick Kardinal moravske cirkve,* Brno Matice Moravska, 2011, pp. 318-319.

[685] Aries, P. *Religions populaires et reformes…* Paris: Cerf, 1975, p 77.

[686] Participation with heretics at sacraments, in acts of worship or legal life, is banned: the decree "Ad vivanda" scandal (21.07.1418 agreement of Boulogne) ruled on methods of defence.

been validly ordained. Those who had passed under the jurisdiction of the Utraquist consistory were therefore apostates. In addition, a clergyman passed to heresy is "a priori" even more than a faithful member, a "notorious" heretic or "denounced as such". One could not therefore suffer "communication" (even the simple "communication foris") with them[687].

The texts do not give the reasons that the Archbishop had for acting in this way. The most likely reason is that he used a possibility that recalled for example the Jesuit Francisco Toledo. Speaking of peasants, he thought that it was possible to find errors there against the faith, without them being heretics themselves. There could be a belief of good faith in heretic doctrines preached by their bishop and ; ideas against the Scriptures (that they did not know) without there being a sin or a heresy. Toledo used pertinacity above all on the scholars. About "rustic and ignorant people", the Jesuit went so far as to write:

If one of them held something against the apostolic traditions or a definition of the Pope, he would not for all that be tenacious ("pertinax"); for he himself is not held to know that it is a question of a rule of faith [which excuses him from sin)] he does not know that it is about things against the Church (which keeps him from heresy).

Manifestly, Mgr Berka exploited it with his priests. He did not consider them as heretical priests from Utraquist parishes returning to the bosom of the Church, no, but as ignorant Catholic priests at the head of an uneducated flock. And after all, he had jurisdiction to decree what was Catholic and what was not, a power that the historian does not have. The nature of this ignorance was problematic. In order that it should dispense with fault against the doctrine, it was necessary for it not to be vincible, crass or supine, but truly invincible, being the only thing that truly excuses

---

[687] Toletus, F.J. "*Instructio sacerdotum* [1564]. Rouen, M de Preauls, 1619, pp. 594-595 lib IV cap iii 4 "Quod si teneat aliquid …contra ecclesiam"

violation of the law, as [688]Suárez noted. From the pastoral point of view, thanks to this solution, therefore there was not, at least in theory, sacrilege or "communication in sacris". Was it therefore a question of clergymen in contact, or of a single clergyman, the Catholic clergyman of the archdiocese? It is sure that a Mgr Berka, anxious to enlarge as much as possible the arch of the Church outside which there was no salvation, saw in all these priests Catholic but ignorant priests, which led them to heretical behaviours without falling into heresy.

So much, therefore, for the nature of these contacts between clergymen. What were the consequences of it?

Reciprocal influences
Although they were all Catholics, each of these priests had a very special career, with contact with non-Catholics. And their parishes, although Catholic, knew a form of worship and ecclesiastical discipline which seemed to be very marked by the influences of the other confessions. However, was it a matter of influences? In the conclusion of this volume, Yves Krumenacker is on his guard against "essentialising" research of the influences between clergymen of different confessions. That is fair. The ideal purity that the reformers were seeking never actually came into the order of the facts. And the confessions, even separated from the old trunk of the mediaeval Catholic church, were broadly heirs. The historiography, looking for influences, forgot this. Nonetheless, the problem of Bohemia remains. There, the division of the parishes into two camps dated from a century and a half. However, this vagueness, this mixture of practices, was maintained. How could one interpret it? In what way was it tied to the intertwining of the two types of clergyman?

The question of priestly celibacy seems to provide a school case. On the difference of the two consistories,

---

[688] Suáez F.J. *Disputionnum de censuris in communi …divi Thomas.* Opera omnia, Mayence 1618, t. XVIII p. 32 sq.

Luther did not advocate it. It seems that his influence was obvious in the case of Makarius, a priest married by a pastor. It was the analysis of the Praguian consistories at the time that the marriage of priests was a sign of the penetration of Lutheranism. However, if it is well known that clerical cohabitation in the Catholic clergy in the century of the Reformation was much less developed at the time and it was still written down sometimes[689]. There was an old background of justification of priestly cohabitation which had no need of Luther in order to exist. Not that it was a question of a theological position opposed to the pseudo-invention of priestly celibacy at the Council of Latran (which leaves out the canons fixed at the Council of Elvire (and the fifth century and their reiteration up to 1139): it was rather the sociological justification of cohabitation. The priest of Dřevčice provided a good example: he claimed to be married without being able to be satisfied with his female servants in the example of patriarchs and some of his superiors. As for Makarius, the fact that he was married in Frankfurt, this Protestant land where his union had legal power, showed that he belonged to a world where the decree "Tamesi" demanding the presence of his own clergyman had still not become customary. Besides, on him, the Lutheran influence was not obvious. It was however a risk that the consistories were not wrong to safeguard.

This report of a visit shows what interested Berka: to enquire into certain key practices between Catholics and heretics. Whatever he thought of them, all the abuses that he found were not reducible to these current models. Thus, the dry Masses of Brandys, in the absence of confession everywhere, were mediaeval Catholic survivals. The

---

[689] See the interesting connections brought by Hubert Jedin on affirmation of Reformationslibell sent by Ferdinand1 to Council of Trent : "servens…matrimonii cupido…matitus"; "Concilium Tridentini…" Fribourg-en-Brisgau Herder t.XIII pp. 677-678, 6-7.

communion of an infant with an unconsecrated host was an abuse which was found elsewhere in Europe, and one which some doctors, as witnessed by Suárez, tolerated. As for communion given to babies at the time of purification by the Polish priest, this was nothing else, it seems to us, than a practice of the Greek Orthodox Church which must have been known in Poland!

From that time, the true cultural consequences of contacts among the confessions were particularly connected with the intertwining of Catholics and Utraquists. The influence was not one- way: better maintenance of processions "in the Catholic manner" in parishes that were faithful to Rome, brought the utraquists durably to these types of ceremonies, that they had regrettably [690] seen supressed. In another direction, chanting readings in Czech at Mass by the priest of Brandys bore witness to the attraction of Hussite church music. There was also communion for infants, which the only one to refuse was paradoxically the most "Utraquist" of all our priests, and the celebration of the feast of Jan Hus, in parishes that were officially Catholic.

But at what point could one talk about the matter of a consequence of contacts between clergymen? The problem was that of pressure on the faithful. They were not content to let their unhappiness be known or to vote with their feet, as at Svémyslice: in Brandys, after the visit, the members of the town council took on the priest for failing to celebrate the feast of Jan Hus and had the inscriptions blotted out. This was important: in 1587, there was a riot by Protestants and the Czech Brothers against the Catholics[691]. In 1595, the complaint went to the Diet and the priest, faithful to Berka, preferred to leave. [692]. The town council again

---

[690] See Jedin, H at Council of Trent: (*Concilium tridentini...*) Fribourg -en-Brisgau 1937 t. XIII pp. 677-678, no.6-7.

[691] Winter, Z. *Zivot cirkevni...* " op.cit. p. 214.

[692] S L. 16.01.1595, Cejka to Berka, Palacky, F. op.cit. t IX no. 9.

demanded that his successor Valentin Zavadsky leave, by requests that were also repeated in vin with the Archbishop[693]. Both in Brandys and in other parishes, the basis of the argument was the same: rather than belonging to one or another religious party, the communities preferred to cancel local traditions or customs in order to challenge their priests or require them to give communion to infants. The language used was that of political privilege, not of the religious rite.

The visit of 1594 also had political consequences. The Chamber of Bohemia had acknowledged its errors in the choice of some priests – the worst, that of Chotětov, defender of the marriage of priests, had been expelled. But at the same time, the Chamber was not ready to acknowledge[694] the Archbishop's right of patronage that the sovereign had given to him. The Vice-Chancellor Krystof Zelinsky, a member of the Unity of Brothers, notoriously hostile to Catholics, developed a fairly special legal[695] argument by granting the right of presentation in his parishes, did not grant the Archbishop the choice of the priest to invest. He thought that Berka had to give the parishes, which he held from the king, the patronage of Utraquist priests, if that was the local custom. But Zelinsky only wanted to see a lay person as the Archbishop, a particular type of committed lord, deprived as of usufruct of his temporary right. He refused to consider him as a Catholic prelate chosen by the Emperor, in other words, the owner of a jurisdiction in the parishes in which he invested the priests.

---

[693] Palacky, F. *Snemy ceske...* op.cit X 179, 18.07.1601. See Narodni Archive Prague Archbishops APA I 3284 C 103/1 2002 fol. 88-97, fol. 99 1597.

[694] Borovicka, J "Pad Zelinskeho...Cechach v letech 1597-1599"; Cesky Casopis Historicky 28, 1922 o 277-304;

[695] Palacky, F. et al. *Snemy ceske...* op.cit. IX11 Brandys, 22.01.1595. S.Redfester "heitman" at Berka.

In this configuration, one must go back a little way to the effect of narrow contacts between the clergymen in Bohemia in the 16th century. Most of what Berka brought up such as abuses or errors were not an influence of neighbouring and adverse confessions, between local communities and the Archbishop or between the Archbishop and political authorities, the master-word of these polemics being the defence of traditions, in other words privileges, and not considerations of doctrine. In other terms, there were a great many contacts, although less than it seemed – but in this muddle of power, could one still talk about a clergyman, that is to say, of an autonomous order?

The example presented is not different from what is known elsewhere in other Catholic parishes in Bohemia[696]. One can therefore without too much extrapolation draw general conclusions from it.

In the Europe of contacts between clergymen, Bohemia has a special place, which in our view can only be compared with the mixed chapters of Empire[697]: Catholic and non-Catholic clergymen co-existed there in a unique hierarchical structure. Such a situation ruled until 1609 where the letter of his Majesty Rudolf II, establishing freedom of worship, suppressed the guarantees.

From this situation a remarkable confessional haziness in the parishes was born, of which this visit is a good example. It is not a question of a mediaeval heritage, of a delay of confessionalisation, but of a modern phenomenon, partly born from a policy of union of the Tridentine papacy. But this haziness does not make the studied parishes the place where clergymen of different confessions operated. Here, they are, to the great astonishment of the historian,

---

[696] Cf 3.03.1585 M.Strakonicky, Narodni Archive, Prague APA 1 2901 C 73 cart 721.

[697] Nottarp, H. *Zur communication...heretics*, t.1933, pp. 107-125. Odenthal, A. *Die ordinatio...* Munster Aschendorfff 2005.

Catholic, the ignorance of the clergymen seeming to excuse them from heresy.

Did the Catholic clergy undergo the influence of that of the other confessions? The appearances were deceptive; the influences are very much less than seemed at the very beginning, one must conclude after an examination.

What about the clergymen in contact in Bohemia of the end of the 16th century? Certainly, even if the question is expressed in voluntarily anachronistic terms, which do not exactly come within the framework of the era; they are more complex than one would have thought at the beginning. Which is not a supplementary sign of the interest in the proposed problem.

Claude Joly (1607-1700) on a journey
A man of the Church and his inter-clerical contacts
In a pluri-religious Europe
In the middle of the XVIIth century
Andreas NIJENHUIS-BESCHER

"saw there Monsieur Manasseh Ben Israel, a very famous doctor among those through his writings. I came to know him by means of his book called "Conciliator" which took place in Paris –
Voyage de Hollande, Claude Joly (1607-1700).

The Congress of Westphalia is an important marker in the history of Europe. This first peace conference on the European scale ended up, in terms of tedious discussions[698] (1645-1648) in a new political and religious balance. In future, the issue of the main European conflicts is negotiated

---

[698] In the town of Munster, an Empire garrison is made neutral by temporary suspension of its duties towards the Empire from May 1643. Osnabrück is guaranteed neutrality.

in a diplomatic congress, in the same area, which became the political crossroads of Europe[699].

On a social level, the 1648 treaties took on the religious coexistence at the very heart of Christianity. In spite of the resurgence, in the second half of the 17th century, of the religious dimension of the battles, confessional diversity is admitted as fact. As a result, once the religious alteration was accepted, peaceful exchanges can be conceived between the ecclesiastics of different sides. The polemics of the time of the colloquiums and tractarian struggles surely hoped that with their strong "truth" could overcome the "horrible obstinance" of the persistent opposite camp.

The conditions of an inter-confessional communication are above all united in the States where a religious coexistence without spatial segregation existed, such as France under the regime of the Edict of Nantes (1598), and the United Provinces thanks to the freedom of conscience granted by the Union of Utrecht (1579)[700]. The Parisian ecclesiastic Claude Joly (1607-1700) confirms the treaty of union between the situations of French and Dutch religious coexistence, by multiplying the inter-clerical and interconfessional contacts from Munster, where he stays from July 1646 to March1647, during the diplomatic congress.

With an educational and recreational aim (or perhaps simply in order to elude boredom?) Canon Joly made several excursions into the outskirts of the Rhenish town, particularly to Osnabrück and to Cologne. He also goes three times to the nearby United Provinces for a long period of thirty days. The "Voyage" made to Munster in

---

[699] After the 1648 treaties of Munster and Osnabrück, the diplomatic congresses at Aix-la-Chapelle (1668 and 1748) Nimwegen (1697), Ryswick (1697) and Utrecht (1713-1715) punctuate the modern European story.

[700] Kaplan, B. *Divided by Faith...Modern Europe*. Cambridge (MA) Harvard University Press, 2007 Saupin, G. *Naissance...temps modernes,* Rennes PUR, 1998.

Westphalia, and other nearby places, in 1646 and 1647 offers several examples of contacts, both literary and physical, between clergymen, particularly of a meeting with the Amsterdam rabbi Menasseh Ben Israel[701]. This chapter explores the methods of inter-confessional relations and, beyond that, the question of the position held by clergymen in the society of the mid-17th century.

The journey, a favourable context for inter-confessional contacts

Coming from a Picardian family, Claude Joly is a Canon of the Catholic Chapter of Notre Dame de Paris when he is called to follow his former pupil Anne-Genevieve de Bourbon-Conde, Duchess of Longueville (1619-1679) by travelling. The latter prepares in June 1646 to join her husband, Henri II of Orleans, Duke of Longueville (1595-1664) in Munster. The Duke of Longueville represents France "in this august Assembly of the Plenipotentiaries of Christianity, of which all of Europe awaits its salvation!"[702].

A letter signed in May 1646 by the Secretary of State Henri-Auguste de Lomenie de Brienne (1595-1666) on behalf of the very young enjoint Louis XIV invites "our dear and beloved Monsieur Joly, Canon of the Church of our Beautiful town of Paris" to accompany the Duchess of Longueville with [703]"our first Plenipotentiary for the general Peace Treaties in Munster" with "Misters of Avaux and Servien"[704]. The imposing cortege of "three carriages above those of Madame the Princess"[705] is put in motion on "Wednesday 20th day of [706]June 1646, at three and a quarter

---

[701] Thanks to the length of his stay, Claude Joly also meets famous scholars at Leyden and Utrecht.

[702] Joly, C. *Voyage...* op.cit. p IV (letter)

[703] Ibid., p. XVIII (letter with royal mark).

[704] Ibid., p. 77. Abel Servien (1595-1659) and Claude de Mesnes, Count of Avaux (1595-1650).

[705] Ibid., p. 1

[706] Ibid., p. 76.

hours after noon". The journey proceeds without any trouble.

By coming back from Munster, as in going there, both foreign towns and in those in France, where all the companies receive them with drums beating and signs on show, and they fired the cannon when she arrived, and when she left[707].

The group made its "entry into the Town with fifteen carriages, each of them pulled by six horses "[708] into Munster on "Monday 23rd July"[709]. The Canon then stayed in Munster until 27th March 1647, that is for eight months. "Madame de Longueville had become fat in Munster and not wishing to give birth, she decided to return to France. Thus, Claude Joly returned to his chapter on 2 May 1647, after a journey lasting nearly a year."

Aged around forty-four years, the publisher had not undertaken another journey beforehand. The genesis of his "Voyage", published almost a quarter of a century after these events, at the same time reflects the spirit of curiosity of its author and the custom of travellers [710]to put into writing that which he did not judge, for the relief of his memory"[711]. In fact, Joly states:

As we had the pleasure of going for a walk, it being in the long summer days, and Madame and Mademoiselle de Longueville, with whom we were going out, only taking one outing per day, and sometimes staying two and three days in the best towns, I had plenty of time [712]to look around the places we passed through.

---

[707] Hardly so, when a Spanish "Captain" asked Madame de Longueville for her passport, p 63.

[708] Ibid., p 77

[709] Ibid., p262. On return, Madame de Longueville gave birth to Marie Gabrielle (1647-1650).

[710] Ibid.,

[711] Ibid., p. XI (preface) "Not at all" at that time (in some way).

[712] Ibid., p. X-XI (preface).

Adopting a posture of modesty that he enjoyed ("I, who was nothing"[713]) Joly tells us that "Monsieur Godefroy, Historiographer of the King[714] encourages him to keep a diary of the journey. He follows the advice of "this old man":

…having stayed some time in Munster, we went to Holland: and on returning to Osnabrugh, then to Cologne, and to some other nearby places we came back to France through the Low Countries. And I took care to continue my little remarks.

The "Voyage fait a Munster" later reflects the notes taken in action during the trip.

The meticulous care with which Claude Joly mentions details enables us to reconstruct precisely the production of his journal. For several decades, the text "put in an orderly way in the form of a Diary, according to the dates that I had marked on my notebook"[715] circulates in manuscript form. The growing fashion for travel tales from the middle of the 17th century, could have encouraged its publication. As the interest in the Low Countries and the United Provinces during the 1660s and 1670s grew, although they were becoming more and more warlike, it doubtless stimulated the demand for chorographic works covering these countries. Having "even learnt that some people had taken a copy"[716] the Canon decides to undertake its publication in order to give "these Memoirs to the public"[717]. The traveller prides himself on his position as an ecclesiastic, signing "M. Joly, Canon of Paris"[718]. "Dedicated, on account of the mutual friendship which has brought us together so happily

---

[713] Ibid., p 263. Joly asks for permission "for me, who was nothing, to go to Brussels and Anvers" Ibid., pp. 263-264).

[714] Ibid., p. XI (preface) about Théodore Godefroy (1589-1649).

[715] Ibid.

[716] Ibid., p. XIV "Monsieur Ogier Predicateur"; "Antoine d'Herouval" 1606-1689), privileged readers of his manuscript.

[717] Ibid., p. XIII

[718] Ibid.. p. XV.

for twenty-four years[719]" to Francois Ogier (1597-1670) a priest that he met in Munster, the work is "Acheve d'imprimer pour la premiere fois le 4 Decembre 1669"[720].

The appearance of the "Voyage fait a Munster en Westphalie, et autres lieux voisins en 1646 et 1647" took place on the eve of the war with Holland (1672-1678) when the seven united [721]Provinces" of the Low Countries became long-term enemies of Louis XIV, having been historic allies of the "Gallic Hercules"[722]. This change of diplomatic paradigm doubtless explains the updating of 1672, the only re-edition of the work. Holland appears in the title, whose dates are entrenched, and a map of the region replaces the boundary parts of the first edition. The body of the text, nevertheless, remains unchanged[723].

(MAP)
Caption

The 1672 edition of *Voyage de Claude Joly* includes a "Nouvelle Carte d'allemagne Corrigé" inserted near the title page to "update" the report in the context of the war with Holland (1672-1678). BM Dieppe (MT P 1899 Fonds Cas).

Making up part of the Longueville custom, Canon Joly holds a privileged place in order to observe the operation of the Westphalia congress. Belonging to a prestigious house fully opens up opportunities to meet people of various

---

[719] Ibid., p. IX

[720] Ibid., p. XII – privilege date of 30.11.1668 and registration on 11.11.1669. p XX.

[721] Ibid., p. 95. Knowing of his diplomatic presence, Joly describes Guelde, Holland, Zeeland, Utrecht, Frisia, Overjissel and Groningen.

[722] Ire For diplomatic ties in France-United Provinces, see Nijenhuis, A. "L'hercule français....Temps Modernes" *Deshima pays du nord* no. 8, pp. 57-74,

[723] Joly, C.*Les voyages de Munster, ...et de Cologne.*Paris, Pierre Prome, 1672. Brunet, J C. *Manuel de libraire ...livres*. Paris, Silvestre, 1842.

views. Thus, in 1646 he attends a meeting with "the army of Mr Marechal of Turenne"[724] near Wesel, a strategic Rhenish town occupied then by the Republic. In fact, the French army "crossed the Rhine on the Vezel bridge" and "Mr de Turenne wanted to see their Highnesses in battle with all the luggage, carriages and horses, on which there was a quantity of women, even some who seemed conditioned, with their children[725]". Finally, "Mr Turenne having come to take leave of their Highnesses, all their soldiers saluted with a wonderful noise: 'terribilis ut castrorum acies ordinata'[726]". A formidable army in battle, with weapons, luggage and women, according to the custom of the time.

In September of the same year, Joly accompanied the Duke of Longueville to Osnabrück, where negotiations between Sweden and the German Empire took place, in order to "therefore at the same time put affairs into a state of peace to all Christianity [..] and he was pleased that I should travel with him"[727]. The Canon stayed for ten days in the town as a guest of the Swedish plenipotentiaries, led by the Count of Oxenstiern, whose residence he visited. The Swedish plenipotentiaries who were at war with the Emperor "did not stay in Munster, because being Protestants (Lutherans) they did not want to use the mediation of the Nuncio"[728].

On the difference between generals or diplomats, observed from a distance, the ecclesiastic Joly held close

---

[724] Joly, C. *Voyage…* op.cit. p. 75.

[725] Ibid., During the Fronde, Turenne was very close to Madame de Longueville. See Joly, C. *L'histoire de la prison… de M. le Prince.* Paris, A. Courbe, 1651. See also Joly, C. *Traite des restitutions des grands…* Amsterdam: Elzevir, 1665.

[726] Ibid., p 76.

[727] Ibid. Joly is at Osnabrück from 18 to 28 September 1646. France and Spain only made peace in 1659, with the Treaty of the Pyrenees,

[728] Ibid., p. 174. The Republic of Venice acted as mediator in Osnabrück.

links with the pontifical mediator in Munster. "Le Voyage" clearly states his role in the congress:

There still lives in this town [of Cologne] a Nuncio of the Pope, who has spiritual administration of all the towns of the Rhine and of the rest of Germany, which is a country of obedience, and where there is nothing like France or the Liberties. It was therefore Mr Chigi who was responsible for the Nuncio: but who lived in Munster in order to moderate peace between the Christian Princes, as we have said[729].

This is about Fabio Chigi (1500-1667), who was installed in the Franciscan monastery with his retinue. The success of the Congress of Westphalia would contribute to "raising up from [in April 1655] the Sovereign Pontificate, in which he died two years ago, where [Joly] judged from that time that he could succeed one day"[730]. The Parisian Canon and the future Pope Alexander VII had occasion to visit Munster, so that two churchmen were present at the time of departure:,Two or three days before our departure from Munster [in March 1647] I went to visit the Nuncio to take leave of him and receive his orders. He welcomed me warmly: and the next day he sent me to a guest house of one of his churchmen, called Mr (Theodorus) Severus, who was of Dutch nationality, and spoke good French. In order to pay me compliments, he gave me a personal gift of a book containing the life of a Saint of his family[731].

The "Dutch by nationality" churchman Severus was perhaps active in the Dutch Mission, created the day after the Twelve-Year Truce (1609-1621) when hostilities were resumed between the United Provinces and the Spanish Low Countries. The "Missio Hollandica" tried to keep the Catholic Church in the Republic, compensating by

---

[729] Ibid., p 227. "The land of obedience" to the Pope. "Liberties" under temporal power.

[730] Ibid., p 93.

[731] Ibid., p.264.Vita B. Ioannis Christi..Augustini" Anvers enricus Aertssens 1641.

clandestine activity for the suppression of the church organisation by the Dutch temporal authorities.

A Tridentine breath re-animated Catholicism in the United Provinces at this time of strong "concurrence" between the confessions:

Also, Mr Severus brought me this gift [on behalf of the Nuncio] and had literature, of which [I read] a Latin translation of which Matthias Martinez of the town of Middlebourg, wrote the Introduction[732] to the devout life of Mr de Sales, of which Mr Severus had already given to me previously.

The Borromean Catholicism of the Bishop of Geneva, Francois de Sales (1567-1622), in "exile" in Annecy, and his work of religious re-conquest in the Savoy Chablais, at the gates of Geneva the Calvinist epicentre, surely stimulated by analogy the imaginary Dutch missionary. Is there a chance that Francois de Sales was beatified (1662) then canonised (1655) under the pontificate of Alexander XVII, in other words the Nuncio Fabio Chigi, the representative of the "Missio Hollandica", visited by Joly[733]?

An inter-confessional curiosity

The multiple contacts of Claude Joly with the Westphalian Catholic clergy did not in any way go against his curiosity. Appointed by the canonical library of Notre Dame of Paris, Joly uses his long stay in the Rhineland and the "Voyage de Hollande" to acquire a large number of books. The amount of books intended for the Parisian chapter being difficult to transport, the Canon gained logistic support from Longueville:

---

[732] Ibid., pp. 265-266. *L'introduction ..Francois de Sales (1567-1622)* 1608.

[733] The Sovereign Pontiff is the superior of the Missio Hollandica, seconded by the Nuncio in Brussels. Vicars of the Mission were represented by the Nuncio in Cologne.

During my long stay in Munster, some bookshops from outside came (for in the town, there were only two or three) among which I found some fairly good books and I bought some of them, which with those I brought from Leyden, filled a box which I was lucky to have brought to Paris with the luggage of my Princesses[734].

Also, with the apostolic Nuncio in Cologne, he "engaged in a large traffic of books. I bought some unbound ones that the Bookshop is sending to reach me in Paris"[735].

The order from the chapterhouse of Notre Dame de Paris witnessed by books "in blank", in other words books without binding, to bind in the colours of his own library, makes one presume a preponderance of religious themes. Nevertheless, the curiosity of the ecclesiastical librarian embraces a number of fields. At Osnabrück, he buys at the "only bookshop" which was also a bindery "in the whole town" a "Cosmographie de Sebastien Munster en latin, qui etait peut-etre le meilleur de ses livres"[736]. He is a good bibliophile: "I bought it, it seems to be well-worn, although he sold it to me at a high price"[737]. "La cosmographie" by the Protestant scholar Sebastien Munster (1488-1552) dating from the middle of the 16th century, is symbolic of "the inertia" of the geographical references of travellers in those countries up to the middle of the 16th century. In the absence of more recent chorographies, Munster's work remained a reference for a century. In spite of the dispersion of his library in the French Revolution, a trace survives of the collection made up over more than a half-century by Claude Joly. A "Catalogue" from the middle of the 18th

---

[734] Joly, C *Voyage...* op. cit. p. 269. The Princesses bought porcelain and spices. The friendly printer gave Madame de Longueville a box of books for Claude Joly.

[735] Ibid., p. 244. The Dutch publishers usurped the publishing place in Cologne for customs reasons.

[736] Ibid., p. 183.

[737] Ibid. He details the tworeasons for the price of the book on p. 184: its rarity and appeal to foreigners."

century gives a very interesting view of the composition of the "library" and makes it possible to identify some editions gleaned by the Canon during his travels[738].

In Amsterdam, the Parisian is extremely interested in the works on geography, going:

...o see the Blaeu printing works, which are held to be the most beautiful in the whole of Europe [...]. For it is he who printed the Great Atlas, and almost all the beautiful, illustrated maps that we have [739]there: there are also all sorts of characters [mobile] and even Oriental languages, which he has cast in his works.

Of course, about Joan Blaeu (1596-1673), he states: "I bought from him a box unbound books that he sent to me in Paris, with porcelains that Madame de Longueville bought"[740].

Of the United Provinces, the Canon reports "a good amount of books that he had bought, most of them in Leyden[741][...] [742]the main place for Letters, and the first Academy in the whole of Holland", like the Elzevirs whose boutique he visited, not printing there [...] "all sorts of Catholic books as easily as Amsterdam, where there is great freedom for that"[743]. In fact,

the practice of the Catholic Religion is not allowed as freely as elsewhere, on account of the residence taken there

---

[738] The "Catalogue des livres...l'Eglise de Paris" p. 85 mentions the 1572 edition of Munster, S. *Cosmographia Universals, Basle: Description des pays Bas* by Louis Guichardin (1521-1582),

[739] Joly, C. *Voyage...* op. cit. p. 116, The atlas series is Blaeu, J. *Le theatre du monde. Blaeu 1635-1654.* 5 vol. "Catalogue...l'Eglise de Paris" op.cit. p. 85.

[740] Joly, C. *Voyage...* op. cit. pp. 116-117.

[741] Ibid., p. 173.

[742] Ibid. /312- Ibid

by their Doctors of Theology, who are zealous in their Religion, as we are in our own[744]."

The curiosity of the book-loving Canon is decidedly eclectic.

Among the titles mentioned exactly inside the "box" filled by the Canon, there are also controversial works. Crossing the Low Countries on the return journey to Paris, he made a few purchases in the university town of Louvain:

There I bought some unbound books, and among others what Jansenius had written on the Old and New Testament in two volumes and several small books [745] dealing with time differences on the question of grace, which the bookshop sent after […] to Paris.

When the traveller published his report in 1670, these works of Cornelius Jansen (1585-1638) had appeared in the index for a long time. The Jansenist quarrel lasted in France until the 18th century, with a strong political presence, and as a result the subject is therefore sensitive. Also, on the difference in other bibliographical references of the "Voyage", Joly describes the Jansenist works in an allusive manner. Is our rebellious ecclesiastic afraid of censorship?

The theological readings of the Parisian also cover Protestantism, even Judaism. The ecclesiastic has a passion, through reading, for Anne-Marie de Schurman (1607-1678), "an excellent lady"[746] of her age, whom he met in Utrecht in September 1646 during the excursion to the Republic. [747] Beyond a discussion led by Joly "and the ecclesiastic Canon whom I was with [748] together with the Calvinist scholar" on predestination[749], the Canon

---

[744] Ibid.
[745] The meeting, and that of Jean Le Laboureur, with the scholar is described by Nijenhuis A. Forclaz, B. (ed).
L'experience....moderne, Neuchatel, Alphil Presses, Universitaires de Suisse, 2013, pp. 157-187.
[746] Joly, C. *Voyage...* op.cit. p.151.
[747] Ibid.,p 153. About a chaplain called Aubert.
[748] Ibid.
[749] Ibid.

continued the exchange through reading. In particular, "She had written and from that time had some works published, which I found in Utrecht, and bought[750], on theological and learned subjects." In a substantial historiographical reasoning, spread over fifteen pages, Joly deals with the question, "If several young girls can, and should, be instructed in letters"[751]. To conclude, he quotes Erasmus, and replies in the affirmative[752]. The "wonder of our century"[753].

The idea of creating a dialogue, including an inter-confessional one, by handing over books is formulated explicitly by Claude Joly. He recalls a literary contact prior to a physical meeting with "Mr Manasseh Ben Israel a very famous Doctor [...] from his writing. I came to know him by means of his book called "Conciliator" that I had read in Paris"[754]. In the margin of the story there are the references "Mr S. Manasseh Ben Israel" and a precise reference to the "Conciliator" 'Sivede Convenienentia locorum scripturesque pugnare inter sevidentur' Editum Amstelodami an.1633, In quarto[755] "The "Conciliator", a Latin translation by Dionysius Vossius (1612-1642) with the same title, "ductoris impensis" by the young Rabbi in Spanish, aims at conciliating passages which are apparently contradictory of the Word [756].

---

[750] "Ibid. The work explores the question of knowing why Christ used a medical device (rather than his word alone) to heal the blind man (ink) (Jn 9 1-41) (Jean Maire), Shurman, A.M. "Beverovici responsis" (Jean Maire) d (1639).

[751] Joly C. *Voyage* ..op. cit. p154. He quotes Shurman, A.M., "Amica...capacítate", Paris, 1638.

[752] Ibid.,pp. 157-159 "Car comme ...l'integrite des moeurs". Joly published a new translation of Erasmus: "*Codicille d'or...Claude Joly*. Amsterdam:Elzevir, 1665.

[753] Ibid., p. 167.

[754] Ibid., p.187.

[755] Ibid., p. 108-109.

[756] Ibid. Joly refers to Ben Israel, M. *Conciliator ...videntur*. Amsterdam, Auctoris impensis, 1652.

Thus prepared beforehand by reading, the Catholic ecclesiastic can "make his acquaintance" in speaking, and open up the theological discussion with Rabbi Menasseh Ben Israel (1604-1657) at the time of his "Voyage de Hollande".

In August 1646, "after staying some time in Munster, Monsieur de Longueville persuaded Madame his wife and Mademoiselle his daughter to go and travel around Holland"[757]. Once again, the Canon is travelling. The trip lasts a little more than three weeks, from 21st August to 12 September 1646. The length of the stay is well above the average[758], and the quality of the company certainly opened doors.

At the end of the month of August 1646, "Madame de Longueville, whom one knows very well, although she wanted to travel incognito, and not to be declared at all[759], spent four days in Amsterdam. Completely "incognito" on this journey, the company probably stayed in a completely new house of the "Doelens", the quarter general of the militia of the Amsterdam bourgeoisie, as the guest house of the town, at the point of being confused with the "Maison de Ville, otherwise called the Doulle"[760] by Jean Le Laboureur(1623-1679). This young Frenchman, of whom Joly quotes the "Voyage de Pologne"[761], stayed in Amsterdam some months before that, in December 1645, in very similar conditions, as part of a French diplomatic group.

---

[757]Ibid.,.p. 99

[758] Most French travellers at the time stayed about a week in the United Provinces, travelling also with French nobility, staying eighteen days in the Republic. Nijenhuis, A. *Voyages de Hollande...XVIIe siècle*. Frijhoff, W. Amsterdam: Vrije Universiteit, 2012, p. 34.

[759] Joly, C. *Voyage* ..op.cit. p. 106.

[760] Le Laboureur, J. Histoire...Maréchal de Guébriant.. Paris: Veuve Jean Camusat, 1647, p. 67

[761] Joly, C. *Voyage* ... op.cit. p. 152.

In the main town of the Republic, Claude Joly has the chance to meet, Rabbi Menasseh Israel two days later. It is at the Rabbi's home that the most important discussion, necessarily theological, took place:

I was going to see him the next morning 28 [August] at his home with Mr Courtin, now the State Councillor, who was Councillor in the Rouen Parliament who had travelled with us out of curiosity, from some other honest people[762].

The Rabbi's home in the Breestraat, not far from Rembrandt's home, was manifestly full of French people who were curious to find the religious leader of a confession which was formally missing from France from the end of the 14th century.

The only details of the dialogue reported by Joly are about "these very important matters of Faith"[763]. In fact, "we asked him various questions, among others Chapter 7 of Isaiah. Ecce virgo concipiet pariet filium" [764]. The Rabbi replied according to the text, "ordinaire des Juifs sur ce lieu important de l'Ecriture Sainte, disant que c'est un nom d'age, et non pas de l'Etat virginal"[765] . Menasseh Ben Israel argued effectively that the word...[almah a young girl or young wife] which is in the Hebrew text, does not correctly mean "virgo" but "puella" [young girl] or adolescentula [child][766].

The discussion on Marian virginity gives way to eight pages of philological and theological developments, mobilising the Greek, Latin and Hebrew languages[767].

It is possible that the Jews who came later (Christ), and who remained in their blindness with a horrible obstinacy

---

[762] Ibid., p. 109. Honore Courtin (12-1703), assistant to the plenipotentiary of Avaux.
[763] Ibid., p.116.
[764] Ibid., p. 109. Is,7.14, "Bible of Jerusalem...Emmanuel."
[765] Ibid.
[766] Ibid.
[767] For a restoration of the dialogue, see Nijenhuis, A. *The Canon, the philology*. op. Cit.

have done their best to suppress the true meaning of Scripture, which could serve to the enlightenment of the Faith of Jesus Christ, (and that, in spite of that) the truth [...] so strong[768].

The inter-religious colloquium does not seem to lead to a theological connection. Coming back to more cordiality, Joly closes the debate by describing it as an incidental question[769].

Notwithstanding the persistent differences, "the intelligent curiosity"[770] of Canon Joly and the "honest people" accompanying him engage the inter-confessional dialogue, in his studies as on his travels.

The interest extends to places of worship. The description of churches, including those "diverted" from Catholic worship, unavoidable places in visiting all the towns, is a "leitmotif" of the description of the journey[771]. Of the different towns visited, Joly's "Voyage" draws up a confessional geography. In February he picks out the Jewish quarter in Cologne:

On the other side of the town towards Germany, there is a small fake town, where there are the Jews and a synagogue: from where they are not allowed to go into the town without having asked for permission, and paid a certain fee[772].

In the same way, the description emphasises that in the Rhineland diocese, only the Catholic rite is authorised: "For Protestants, Lutherans and Calvinists, they have no freedom to practise their religion. Therefore their meetings take

---

[768] Ibid..
[769] Joly, C. *Voyage* ... op. cit., p 113.N
[770] Ibid., p. 116.
[771] Samaran, C. Les archives...de Notre-Dame: *Revue d'histoire de l'Église de France*. Vol. 50 147 (194, p.107)
[772] For a view of Calvinists in the United Provinces, see Nijenhuis, A.*Appartenance...Catholiques* (100-1650)

place in a place called Mulheim, at half a league below Cologne"[773].

For Amsterdam, the description also draws up a balance of the confessional co-existence, as seen by the traveller:

The practice of any type of Religion is allowed in Amsterdam, except Catholicism, whose practice however it houses so publicly, that those who profess it, of whom there is a great number, do not hide it at all[774].

Stricto sensu throughout the existence of the Republic meant only the freedom of conscience defined by Article XIII of the Union of Utrecht in January 1579, and not freedom of worship[775]. However, on the eve of the conclusion of the triumphant peace of Westphalia, the climate of tolerance in Amsterdam is confounded by foreign observers' codified regime of co-existence, as in France (again) at this time[776].

The height of religious curiosity: "Even the Jews have a very beautiful synagogue, which our Princesses wanted to see, and we with them[777]. As a large number of buildings in this great town of Amsterdam are growing every day, and another new quarter was being built while we were there[778], the synagogue is completely new." Hardly dissembling, behind an elegant façade, Talmud Total (Study of the Torah) was set up in October 1639, for the 5400 Hebrew New Year[779]. It came from the merger of three pre-existing communities. The synagogue was presided over by Menasseh Ben Israel.

---

[773] "Le faux-bourg est Deutz" – Joly, C. *Voyage,* op.cit.pp. 46-7.
[774] Ibid., pp.107-108.
[775] See Frijhoff, W. *Confessional coexistence....United Provinces.* Delumeau, J. *Histoire...chretien.* Toulouse 2, pp. 229-257. M. MONGE *Des religieux...XVII-XVIII siècles*" Rennes, PUR, 2010, pp. 55-80.
[776] Le Laboureur, J.*Histoire de voyage...*op. cit. P.71. "Ville d'Amsterdam 1645".
[777] Joly, C. *Voyage..* p. 108.
[778] Ibid., p 122.
[779] AGT J.F. VAN Synagogue...(La Haye Staatsuigevei) 1974,

Born into a Spanish Christian family in 1604 in Portugal (Madeira) during the personal union of the Lusitanian kingdom with Spain, Manod Dias Soeiro reached the United Provinces via La Rochelle. Since the town of Amsterdam from the end of the 16th century allowed "new Iberian Christians" to take on the Jewish confession, his family embraced Judaism. While using his Christian name in the civil sphere, Dias Soeiro invents a religious name affiliating him with the tribe of Manasseh, son of Joseph, a son of Israe,: Menasseh Ben Yossef Ben Israel, sometimes abridged into "MB'Y". He attains the position of rabbi when very young in 1622 and remains the figurehead of the Jews called "Portuguese" in Amsterdam until his death in 1657.

The visit by Madame de Longueville and her group took place on Monday 27 August 1646, the day after her arrival in Amsterdam at dusk. Then Joly explores the town "by the amount of candles which shine through windows on this canal, surrounded by high and beautiful buildings: which was delightful to see"[780]. Welcomed by Mr Manasseh Ben Israel the Doctor famous for his writings[781], the company discovered the place: "It is a long, high room, around which there are galleries for placing the women apart"[782]. The French people attend an enactment of divine service revived with the vocabulary which is familiar to the Canon:

At the end of the high part there are the tables of Moses in Hebrew on the altar (the temple or arch) :at the side there is a cupboard in which there was enclosed the Pentateuch, in other words the five books of Moses that they call the Law, which they have taken by one of their cantors, the "hazzan", who carries it towards the low part of the Synagogue on a type of step or tribune (the rebab) where he

---

[780] ?

[781] Ibid., p. 108 *Catalogue des livres ...l'Eglise de Paris*. Amsterdam Sumptibus auctoris, 1635. Hebrew Publisher 1627.

[782] Joly, C.*Voyage*... op.cit. p. 108.

sings some verses in Hebrew; and then all the Jews together start to sing also in Hebrew blessings to their Highnesses.

During the intellectual route of Joly the traveller and of his companions, places of worship of his companions are an object of "curiosity[783]", under the same category as places of "Letters"[784] ". Thus, "On the same day, 27th, I went to see the printing works of Blaeu" [785]", already described.

Temporary clergy and authorities
Even if the visit of a French princess and her retinue to a place of worship of another confession does not imply any theological agreement, the event is highly symbolic. Some years before, the "Highnesses" were preceded at the synagogue by other high personalities. In 1642 the governor Frederic-Henri d'Orange (1584-1647), the main political figure of the Republic, is welcomed by Menasseh Ben Israel at the Talmud Torah synagogue. Crowned with his success in the Twenty-four Years War, the governor is a personality of European range. The "grand general" of the franco-netherlandish troops is, for example "deferred to as his Highness the Prince of Orange"[786] at the beginning of the French operation in the Thirty Years War in 1635.

The Prince of Orange is accompanied by Henriette-Marie (1609-1660) the sister of Louis XIII (1601-1643) and Queen Consort of England. They bring their respective children, recently married, William of Nassau (1626-1650) and Henriette-Marie Stuart (1631-1660), the Princess

---

[783] Ibid., p. 135.
[784] Joly often uses the term "curiosity". Ibid., p. 150, p. 168, p. 347.
[785] Ibid., p. 116.
[786] Parival, J. N. *Les delices de la Hollande...l'an de grace 1660*. Leyde Gerf Stecoren 160, pp. 32-343. Ibid., p. III "Sy hebben...Breda" Convents of Nuns are gone. Jalabert, L. "Le soldat fase au clerc". Rennes, PUR.

Royal, daughter of the King of England and wife of the young Prince of Orange[787].

The ceremony of this "entry" is no doubt similar to that which was undertaken by Claude Joly in honour of the notable guests. They were preceded by a brief sermon given by Menasseh Ben Israel. In order to perpetuate the words spoken in Latin on Thursday 22 May 1642, monograms inscribe the queen for reasons of protocol, the Rabbi then speaks to the governor "the invincible and great hero"[788]. Drawing a parallel between the entry of Alexander the Great into Jerusalem (in 332 BC) and the arrival of Frederic-Henri in the "powerful town of Amsterdam"[789], he thanks his guests for honouring the synagogue with their presence.

Described as "Exiles"[790] "as they had no property, the "Portuguese"[791] that he represents are placed explicitly under the protection of the governor. Drawing again on old history and the Jewish people, the speech compares the revolt of the Jews led by Mattathias (165 BC) against the Seleucids and that of "Your Father Guillaume (who) also liberated Hollande from the cruel Tyranny of the Spaniards"[792] The founder of Israel before Herod and William of Orange, whom the Dutch hold as their liberator from the Spanish tyranny"[793] and therefore of the Republic[794], have points in common with Ben Israel. Describing their successor Frederic-Henri as protector of the country, even as his conqueror, "as Grooloo, Bois-le-

---

[787] Joly, C. *Voyage...* op.cit. p. 141. Madame de Longueville meets Princess Marie Henriette Stuart in May 1641. Ibid., p 141.
[788] IIbid p 1 ".Onover…..held".
[789] Ibid., p. 1 "Dese machrige …Stadt" Alexander the Great in Jerusalem.
[790] IIbid., p. 11 "Portugysen"
[791] Ibid.
[792] Ibid., p 111. "Vvader Wilhelm …Spanjaerden vry ghemeckt."
[793] Joly C. "voyage…op.cit p 142
[794] Ben Israel, M. "Menasseh Ben Israel…" op.cit. p 11,""Gemerne beste"

Duc, Wesel, Maastricht, Breda (and what can I already anticipate?)"[795], the Rabbi states that his people, certainly "not numerous in that Republic"[796] "have found refuge in your heart"[797].

The sermon congratulates itself on this rescue: "We live, we are protected, and like others, we enjoy freedom[798] defended by your sword"[799]. Arguing for the loyalty of the Jews, Ben Israel indicates: "We no longer hold for Castile or Portugal, but for Holland, for our Country"[800]. As a result, he concludes:

It is not surprising that we pray every day for MM the States-General, for Your Highness, and also for the Nobles and Junior Regents of this famous town, since your Salvation depends on ours.

This stirring sermon of allegiance[801] ("since we longer respect the Spanish or Portuguese king, by MM, the States, but you, for our Lords") places the religion under the protection, even the guardianship, of the temporary authorities of the Republic. The latter are spread out from the magistrate to the governor and the States General. Ant "Country" whether it be the Republic the Jews live there up to 1796 as a foreign "nation", without civil rights and whose freedoms come from the goodwill of the local authorities within the confederal structure of the United Provinces. In 1657, however, the Estates General place the Dutch Jews under their protection, like "the true subjects of this State" but only if they are confronted with problems of a stranger[802].

---

[795] Ibid.
[796] Ben Israel, M. "Menasseh Ben Israel .." op.cit. V :Wy…zijn"
[797] Ibid., p II-III. "Als tot…h. Arfebben"
[798] Ibid., p II-III "Nu leven vryheyt."
[799] Ibid., "Door…worden"
[800] Ibid., p. IV. "Vvant…voor anse Vaterlant."
[801] Ibid., p. IV-V. "Wy…Herren".
[802] Nijenhuis, W, "Ecclesia reformata…of his state." Leyde 1994, vol.2, p 134.

The visit of the governor, his son and successor, persons of the royal line and other "very noble Gentlemen of great renown"[803] to Menasseh's synagogue is emblematic. In fact, it takes note of religious co-existence in the United Provinces and indicates dispassionate relations between the temporary authorities and religious groups. The influence of Frederick Henri, more conciliating than his predecessor Maurice of Orange (1557-1625) and the political and military context which was favourable to the United Provinces no doubt created a good climate. The event opens the way for other international visits, like that of Madame de Longueville and her group or, in 1669, of the Grand Duke of Tuscany, Cosmo III of Medici (1639-1723)[804].

The work of Canon Claude Joly also questions the place of the clergy in society. Implicitly, religious co-existence is accepted by Joly, through inter-clerical contacts, even conviviality, as at the end of [805] *Voyage de Hollande*:

In Steinfort, I was given my lodgings with Madame de Longueville's chaplain and the Minister who was good humoured and wanted us to drink beer before going to bed, to his health. But later he told us he would give us wine to drink to the health of her Highness, Madame.

One may imagine the charming picture of Canon Joly and Chaplain Aubert drinking in Germany at the end of the Thirty Years War, to the health of a pastor who was not austere.

The context of the Congress of Westphalia, responsible for establishing "peace between the Christian Princes"[806] is also favourable to reflection. The "opening letter to Monsieur Ogier" contains Joly's convictions as to the

---

[803] Ben Israel, M. "Menasseh Ben Israel Vvelkomst..." op. cit. P. I "Seere dele Herren".

[804] "The Grand Duke ...Livourne. Calafat, G. (1590-1630) *Des religions dans la ville.*

[805] Joly, C. *Voyage...* op. cit. P. 171-172. "Steinfort...de la Republique."

[806] Ibid., p 227

finality of the peace "whose salvation was awaited by the whole of Europe"[807].

The letter takes the form of homage to Francois Ogier, dedicatee of the "Voyage". Describing this priest as[808] "Evangelist of the Peace", Joly refers to a "panegyric to S. Louis" sermon[809] delivered before French diplomats on 25th August 1646 in Munster, in the Church of the Franciscans, taking in other words with the apostolic Nuncio. Taking up the framework of the sermon, of which his library holds a copy, Joly resumes its essential points, looking at "exhorting them to promote this great work of the General Peace, at the same time as the Saviour hanging on the Cross, gave it to all men".

In eulogising the "Christian policy of the great Saint Louis" [Louis IX 1226-1270][810], the text goes back to Louis XIV, working nominally via his diplomats for the "General Peace". The latter must invite:

These dear children to an agreement with a perfect union, which saves the blood of their subjects, and which can give them the means of overturning the Mosques of Mahomet, and to re-establish the true worship of God in Greece and in Asia[811].

Ogier had ended his exhortation:

There you will find laurels which do not turn red from the blood of your brothers. The victories which will not be wept by the eyes of Christians: churches or Altars will not be overturned: on the contrary you will re-establish the true worship of God which was abolished by the impiety of Mahomet[…] and after having reigned happily on earth, you will come to reign more happily with me in Heaven,

---

[807] Ibid., p IV (Letter)
[808] Ibid.
[809] Ogier, F . *Actions ....Eglise de Paris*. op. cit. p 36, 1665.
[810] Ibid.
[811] Ibid., pV-VI (Letter)

and enjoy the Crown of glory and immortality that Jesus Christ promised to his Elect[812]. So be it.

The plan to bring "peace to all Christianity"[813] certainly accepts the religious diversity of Europe. but with the superior finality of uniting this in a struggle against the "Turk"[814]. Written in the 1660s, the letter resonates with the battle of Saint-Gothard where in August 1664, allied European troops win a victory over the Ottoman army. The French participation in this success is cleverly carried out to glorify[815] Louis XIV. Ogier's prophecy, formulated in 1646 and relayed by Joly, is not however realised. At the time of the appearance of the "Voyage", the "Christian princes" again entered a cycle of conflicts, where the revocation of the Edict of Nantes re-introduces an irreversible religious dimension.

Towards a pluri-confessional Christianity
Throughout his long life, Canon Joly could observe the vicissitudes of the Great Century in the religious field. Born under the reign of Henry IV, he was a Canon in the chapter of Notre-Dame de Paris under Louis XIII and Louis XIV. Making up a part of the people of Longueville, the chance was offered to him to join the French plenipotentiary at the Diplomatic Congress of Munster, where at that time a general European peace was being negotiated.

Living in Westphalia in 1646 and 1647, at the time of criss-crossing the roads of France, of the Empire, of the United Provinces and the Low Countries, he was able to observe and compare the conditions of religious co-existence in these parts of Europe. During these journeys, the Parisian Canon multiplies inter-clerical contacts. His condition as a churchman and his membership of the circle of the Plenipotentiary opened a great many doors to him.

---

[812] Ogier F.J "Actions publiques …) op.cit p 31-32
[813] Joly C. "Voyage…" op.cit p 176.
[814] Linon-Chipon, S *Turcs....siecles*" Paris, PUPS 10009.
[815] Coligny-Saligny, J. "Memoirs.." 1841, p. 100.

Also, he visited priests (Francois Ogier and the "Dutchman" Severus) and the Nuncio of the future pope, Fabio Chigi. Beyond his own "camp" he shows a great inter-religious curiosity, as much by his reading as by meetings. The most noteworthy exchange in the "Voyage" took place in Amsterdam, in August 1646, with Rabbi Menasseh Ben Israel.

These intellectual meetings and theological debates reveal pragmatic acceptance of the confessional diversity at the heart of "Christianity". The peace of Westphalia confirms *de jure* in 1648 the future of a pluri-religious Europe. In relieving his friend, the preacher Ogier, Joly conceives a feeling of belonging to one Europe, where "an agreement of a perfect union" would prevent fratricidal religious wars. The way would thus be open to the re-establishment of the "true worship of God in Greece and in Asia" to the detriment of the Ottomans. To sum up, a "just war" between a pluri-religious Europe and the unbelievers.

Beyond these considerations of "Christian politics" the cultural majority also became an object of curiosity, even entertainment. In order to stave off the boredom of the long stay in Germany[816], any amusement is welcome. Thus, after the visit in 1646 by the Dutch elephant of the Hansken[817] a curious person proposed to distract the French with the Armenian rite. In March 1647:

A certain prelate called Thomas Antiochenus, because he was from Antioch, who called himself the Patriot of the Armenians, said Mass in the presence of Monsieur de Longueville and our Princesses, who had the curiosity to see the ceremonies[818].

---

[816] "In Germany, ..trouble eating" – Joly, C. *Voyage* op.cit. p. 255

[817] Joly, C. *Voyage* pp. 190-204.

[818] Ibid., p 259.

That interested Canon Joly at the highest point: "As the thing was new, I went very close to the Altar"[819]. He observes with his usual precision his Armenian colleague:

The Mass that he celebrated was in the Samaritan language, which we were told by his Assistant and Interpreter. I saw the Missal, but I did not[820] recognise anything, the letters not being Hebrew, Greek, or Latin. I did not find the ceremonies very different from our own.

Alas! Doubtless, it was an impostor, transforming Joly's interconfessional curiosity[821] and consorts into a lucrative attraction:

This Patriarch had passed his titles to Monsieur the Nuncio, who had testified to be fully content. Nevertheless someone told me since then that he had been deceived and that it was acknowledged that he was a rogue[822].

And Joly concludes; "Whatever he may be, he was recommended to the generosity of Monsieur de Longueville, who gave him one hundred large coins".

...

---

[819] Ibid.
[820] Ibid.
[821] ?
[822] Ibid p., 26.

PART THREE

CONTROVERSIES AND SERMONS

Don Quixote controversialist
The disputes of Théophile Cassegrain
(end16th - beginning 17th century)
Jérémie Foa

Théophile Cassegrain has not passed into posterity. At the great displeasure, doubtless, of the main person interested who put all his heart into competing with his most illustrious colleagues, Philippe Duplessis-Mornay or Daniel Chamier. Pastor of the large town of Pont-de-Veyle in Burgundy at the end of the sixteenth century, Cassegrain was a tireless fighter for the faith, ceaselessly preaching and fighting, always hoping for a great spread of his word: the desire to convince by the love of God? The need to please and to be known by self-respect? Great is the temptation to psychologise this story without researching more general causes of it. The search for glory and the building of a reputation are always difficult to measure when one is talking about men of God, which everything pushes to conceal these problems.

One may accompany this pastor for the eight years which follow the establishment of the Edict of Nantes in Burgundy (1598-1605), a period during which he showed flawless activism, going into controversy willingly and inviting into the dispute the most famous doctors of the Church: Jacques Davy Duperron and Francis de Sales. What pushed this "humble pastor" from Bresse to provoke the most beautiful jewels of the Catholicism of the time? What was the point of all this controversial, dissymmetrical activity? Was Cassegrain seeking to convince of the supremacy of his theology or of his superiority as a theologian? Did he increase his local foundation by defying men whose fame was already international? Did he not on the contrary weaken his credibility by showing his weak "sense of reality", in other words his lack of "sense of equivalence" as much as the likelihood of a real meeting between members of clergy of [823]social and geographical origins who were so far away was extremely weak? Cassegrain's windmills are his giant enemies.

However, for the happiness of the historian, by committing these slips, if that is what they were -, Cassegrain restricted his enemies by explaining codes which were often implied in contact between reputation or notoriety, equivalence of diploma and social standing, capacity of influence, (local, provincial, national or international). By infringing the "rules of grammar of the argument", Cassegrain brought this to make his enemies bring to light the "unconscious academic" of the controversies which this article plans to analyse and in particular the grammars of the inter-clerical contact[824].

The exile of Théophile <u>Cassegrain</u>

Not much is known about Théophile Cassegrain. But whoever takes the trouble to collect his traces, dispersed in a myriad of sources, comes, in spite of everything, to rebuild a talking portrait. Doubtless the most credible of his biographers is Father Louis Jacob de Saint-Charles (1608-1670), of the order of Carmel, a recognised bibliophile from Chalon-sur-Saône and author of a work on the "Famous people from Chalon". He states that Cassegrain's birth was in 1556 in Etampes and he died in Chalon at the age of ninety years[825]. This Etampan origin is testified by several Latin poems, signed "theophilim

---

[823] For an investigation into Don Quixote, Schutz, A. "Don Quixote and the problem of reality" *Societies* 89 2005 p 9-27.
[824] See Christin, O. "Actes…sociales", no. 144, 2000, pp. 53-61. Kappler, E. *Les conferences ..France XVIIe siècle* . Paris: Honore Champion, 2011.
[825] JACOB DE SAINT-CHARLES L. "De claris …libri III" Paris Cramoisy 1652 p 100.

Quatigranum Tempensis"[826]. The notability of the Cassegrains among the municipal and ecclesiastical elite is confirmed in Etampes. His father, Claude Cassegrain, a certified lawyer and Lieutenant general of the administration of Etampes was at the birth of Théophile.. He was a man of letters, whose reputation as a humanist led him to preface a Latin poem for recording the customs of the administration of Etampes[827]. As was typical in the case of royal officers and lawyers who were educated at the turn of [828]the 1560s, Claude Cassegrain wais a Protestant. An arrest of the Paris parliament condemned him to hanging with tens of other Huguenots, in November 1562 for "rebellion, felony and the crime of Lèse-Majesté".

Etampes was in fact taken then occupied by Conde's troops from 13 November 1562, and it is likely that Cassegrain's father took part in these events[829]. There is a sudden new direction in the history of a family which was hitherto well-settled who must probably now leave the town. At the time, Théophile was six. Also, he was not converted, but belonged to the first generation of "baptised Huguenots", as his vetero-testamentary first name indicates. A child of civil wars, born of the last troubles, Cassegrain is shaken about on the exile roads and soon undergoes the sufferings that minority confessional choices bring. He knows that lives fall down to reach a religious frontier which was however guarded; he lived through the trials that God keeps for his elect. Precociously, he suffered intolerance, violent religious confrontation, banishment, hatred of neighbours. That does not prevent him from wishing to convert others, again and again.

---

[826] Ad Iona…Tempensis J.JACMOTIUS "Ioannis…Lyrica" Geneva Stoer1591 p 9.

[827] …Arret du parlement…"Memoirs de Conde …l'histoire de France" London C.de Bose-G.Darres IV 1743 p 122-123.

[829] Fleureau, B. *Antiquites…l'histoire generale de France*. Paris, J B Coignard, 1683.

When one goes back to his journey, in 1579 Cassegrain has become a pastor in Cormaillon, in Auxois[830]. The position is not prestigious, that is understood, but Cassegrain is only twenty-three years old and Burgundy is his adopted country. From 1581 to1583 he served several small churches in Burgundy: he is found at Nuits-Saint-Georges in February 1583[831] and at Cormaillon in May of the same year[832]. It is there that the family is settled and where in 1586 his first son was born. Married, as is the duty of pastors, Cassegrain loses his first wife, Avoye Chicheret, on an unknown date, but before 1590, because the poet Pierre Pouo publishes an "epitaph" in honour of her death[833]. Two children were born of this first bed: Anne and Salomon, a vetero-testamentary first name marking a strong confessional identity. Cassegrain is everything but a Nicodemite. Like a number of his colleagues, he makes it his duty to make his home a model of piety and to pass on his vocation to his son, without so much as creating a dynasty of pastors studying theology[834]. Cassegrain remarries in November 1590 [835]to Louise Goulart, who gives birth to Suzanne, baptised in Geneva in December 1591. Here again, the vetero-testamentary first name shows confessional name. "This "family investment" is visible enough and known for being mocked by his enemies, who noticed how gifted Cassegrain must be in economy "he who

---

[830] 28.0.1579…Cassegrain appointed Minister in Cormaillon. See Christin, O., univ. Lumiere -Lyon, 1999, p. 32.

[831] Geneva Library, ms.fr.409. See Dufour, A. *Correspondance deTheodore de Beze*. Geneva Droz v 2 2002, p. 14, note 3.

[832] Letter to Theodore de Beze May 1583. *Correspondance de Theodore de Beze*. op. cit. v 24 p 153—154.

[833] See Poupo, P. "La Muse Chretienne". Mantero, A. Textes modernes, Paris, 1997, p. 255

[834] Salomon Casssegrain, "Professor of Theology" ,Cormaillon, died 22.03.1637.

[835] Poupo, P " op.cit. p. 553. *La Muse Chretienne.*

is a minister, [836]father of a family, all together". In the eyes of his Catholic opponents, this family detail aggravates the local implantation of Cassegrain, his impossible nomadism, which they compare with their life of celibacy spent on mission glued to their country. Cassegrain is not "worthwhile" nor exchangeable on all the religious markets of the kingdom, in the difference of its interchangeable Catholic theologians, all doctors, who spend their lives moving around and are valuable in their competence in all the churches in the country. In1583, Cassegrain refuses the seat of Tremilly in Champagne, as it's too far away[837]. His Catholic enemies never fail to recall that there are those who were moved towards the pastor, not the reverse. For them, Cassegrain is only a "local candidate" who is literally rooted to the spot. Keeping one's distance, everything is already there.

After the birth of his third child, Cassegrain preached in Burgundy at the end of the year 1591: at Saint-Jean-de-Losne, between 24 December 1591 and 7 February 1592, at the request of Captain Saint-Matthew, then again in Geneva until October 1592[838]. His track is lost for a few years. He serves the Church of Pont-de-Veyle at least between January 1596 and the end of November 1601,[839] Vosne-Romanee in 1601, Pont-de-Vaux in 1603, finishing at Chalon-sur-Saône from 1609 to 1634. Very active between 1580 and1605, he disappears from the public scene after that date, even if one finds him again in 1620 as a deputy of the Church of Chalon at the national Synod at Ales[840].This

---

[836] François Humblot. "La dispute…Cassegrain ministre". Lyon. Pillechotte1587, p. 293 .

[837] Citron, S. and Junod, M. C .*Registres …Pasteurs de Geneve*. Geneva, Droz. v 6, 1980 pp. 89-94.

[838] Archives Pont-de-Veyle. "Les protestants…XVIe siecle", 1975, p. 12

[839] "Compagnie des pasteurs 08.10.1601". Cassegrain serves Dijon as "VIP"."Registres …" op.cit. v 8, 1986, p. 100

[840] Aymon, J.*Tous les synodes...de France*. La Haye, Charles Delo, 110, v.I,I p. 252.

eclipse is probably explained by the blindness of the pastor, who died in 1637 then "blind for fifteen years", that is from 1622. But already in a pamphlet from 1618, regarding a dispute from 1603, one of his enemies, the Capuchin Marcellin de Pont de Beauvois described Cassegrain as "an old Rabbi who is blind in his body, and even more so in spirit"[841]. It is thus likely that his sight was declining from the decade of 1610, the Judeophobic critic referring to the image of a man who was prematurely old through study and reading. For a Catholic tractarian, the eye disease is a divine surprise, a visible mark of the heretic: by a type of law of an eye for an eye, blindness came to punish the one who sinned and throughout his life remained obstinately blinded to the light of God[842]. This disease marks the second exile of Theophile Cassegrain, reduced to silence and anonymity, stripped of his glory of yesteryear.

Cormaillon-Geneva, return journey
At the beginning of the 1580s, Cassegrain enjoyed a solid reputation at the heart of the Burgundy churches, which extend progressively to Geneva. In 1583, Simon Goulart warmly recommends him to take his succession at the Church of Tremilly. It is true that Goulart is very bored and hopes to shorten his exile by nominating a volunteer to replace him. Cassegrain's local fame however enables him to refuse this poisoned chalice. He says he is installed with the faithful of Is-sur-Tille.

Cassegrain is then invited to complete his education in Geneva from the years 1583-1584. He stays there until towards the beginning of 1592, while coming back to preach regularly in France[843]. On the banks of the Leman, he

---

[841] Marcellin duu Pont De Beauvoisin. *La piperie des ministres* ...Grenoble: Lyon, Loys Muguet, 1618.

[842] Crouzet, D. *Les guerriers de Dieu...religion.* Seyssel Champ Vallon, 1990, v. 1, p.284.

[843] Fatio, O. and Labarthe, O. *Registres de la compagnie...* op.cit. v 3, 1969, p. 83.

preached, baptised and made friends with the learned Protestants, particularly the humanists, Hellenic circles and Hebrewists, and particularly the French scholars, who had emigrated with the Edict of Nemours (1585). The works that he prefaced, those that are dedicated to him and the poems in his honour indicate his growing fame. Verses from the poet Pierre Poupo are dedicated to him, especially praising his virtuosity in ancient languages[844]. Thesonnet LIX from the first book of *La Muse Chretienne* published in 1590, celebrates Cassegrain's linguistic talents, which Poupo considers matchless[845]. With Isaac Casaubon, Cassegrain gives Latin poems for the edition of poetry of his friend pastor Jean Jacquemot in 1591[846].This insistence of the sources on recalling Cassegrain's talents in ancient languages (Greek, Hebrew and Syriac) earns him an appearance in the list of great Hebrewists, published some years later by Paul Colomies[847]. The contrast with the speech of his enemies is so much more striking: on many occasions the junior Francois Humblot, who argues against Cassegrain in 1598, writes that his opponent "does not understand Hebrew at all[848]". Poor theologian? How can one believe that such a great scholar preached in such a small town?

A downgraded Protestantism

As regards the growing reputation of his remarkable erudition, everything leads one to believe that Théophile Cassegrain felt downgraded in these small Burgundian or Bressan churches which limited his horizon. In order to

---

[844] Bellenger, Y and Ester, R. *Pierre Poupo (1552-1590): un poète protestant ...* Paris, Klincksieck, 1992.

[845] Poupo, P *La Muse Chretienne*. op.cit. p. 255.

[846] Jacquemot, J. "Joannis ...lyrica". Geneva, Stoer, 1591.

[847] Colomies, P. *Gallia orientalis ...vitae.* La Haye,A Vlacq, 1665, p 273.

[848] Francois Humblot, *La dispute solennelle.* op.cit. p. 12.

understand him, we must go back a little way on the thread of his story.

At the beginning of the wars of religion, La Bresse is not French, but Savoyard from 1559. The Duke of Savoy then happily welcomes onto his lands the French reformed people who were chased out by the civil wars and cyclic persecutions in 1562, 1568 or 1572, less from the size of his heart than for keeping in reserve a potential for destabilisation of his powerful neighbour. Thus, when the Catholics take back Mâcon during the first civil war (August 1562) hundreds of Huguenots flee towards La Bresse and spread out into its small towns, especially at Pont-de-Veyle and Thoissey, but also Montluel, Bages and Bourg-en- Bresse[849].Prudently, the Duke of Savoy insisted that these fugitives should not travel in troops of more than twenty-five cavalry. The Protestants are therefore straight away condemned to dispersal, but they acclimatise poorly in these smaller and less prestigious towns than those that they left and which they see from a distance like a forbidden Eldorado. Small Protestant centres take root on the edge of important towns: at Vosnes for the district of Nuits; in Volnay, for that of Beaune; at Is-sur-Tille for the district of Dijon; at Saint-Jean-de-Losne for the district of Auxonne; at Pont-de-Veyle for Bresse and some adherents of Mâcon. So many peripheral place names which will come back in the adventures of Théophile Cassegrain. All these towns are one day called "little Geneva" but it is the word "little" which must draw attention. These exiles form herds scattered from an "urban Protestantism" made up of exiled city-dwellers in the country or in large towns, but who always have the town character in their minds. This peri-urbanity or end-of-century French Protestantism is still very unknown, although the certainty of its urban implantation is well established. However, a number of great cities closed their doors to reformed people at that time.

---

[849] AM MACON EE 49 .See Turrel ,D. *Bourg-en-Bresse...historique...* 1986, pp. 170-171.

On the publication of the Treaty of Lyon (17 January 1601), Bresse, Buey and Pays de Gex passed over to France. From being simply tolerated, Bressan Protestantism became legal. But it had to comply with the strict articles of the Edict of Nantes; all preaching is thus forbidden in Dijon and four places nearby; which restricts the pastors from living there if they wish to make their celebrations regularly [850]. The united past of Dijon thus comes to swell the Protestant presence in the small surrounding towns. All of that contributes to depriving the Huguenots of a "capital" (Paris not being in the least of restrictions) if one adapts the problem which was developed by Pierre Bourdieu in another context:

The major capital is, without playing on words, at least in the case of France, the place of the capital, in other words the place of a physical space where the positive poles of all the fields are concentrated and most of the agents who have these dominant positions: it can only therefore be considered enough in the relation to the province (and the "provincial") which is nothing but privation (all relative) of the major [851] capital and the capital.

After Dijon, the league members of Lyon obtained from Henry IV a rule that Huguenots could not celebrate, preach sermons or baptise in the town or its suburbs (24 May 1594): it is known that at that time several reformed Lyon people are restricted to going to Pont-le-Veyle. At this time they made contact with Pastor Cassegrain, who baptised their children[852].

Measuring the frustrations of this group of exiled citizens, of their consciousness of downgrading, especially geographically, but also socially and culturally and their unhappiness in the town, also gives the means of widening

---

[850] Barbiche, B . *L'édit de Nantes* 1562-1598. Sorbonne.fr.

[851] Bourdieu, P. "Effets de lieu: *La misere du Monde.*» Paris: Seuil, 1993 p. 29-249-262.

[852] Puyroche, A. "Le chateau …XVIe siècle". Bulletin SHPF, 1890, pp. 278-283.

their circle of recognition. There is no doubt that they did not consider with their eyes open the capacity of their minister to export himself, that they praised his ability to cross, even fictitiously, through discussion and books, thanks to the power of "fame", distances that had forced them to take with the "home country". This consciousness of not being in one's place, not to be judged by one's true value showed up in all the words and gestures of Cassegrain – his enemies themselves made light of it and tried to coax the minister by his Achilles heel. One of his opponents, the minister Gaspard Dinet would have assured him "that he well knew that he was not treated according to his merits: that if he ruled with them he would be with people of honour; and that as regards facilities, he could easily have a better appointment"[853]. There, perhaps, something was delivered from the subconscious of Cassegrain as a crystallisation of the frustrations of a number of his co-religionists: was he really treated according to his merits? Where would he be if he were a Roman Catholic? It is with this feeling of failure that he must in future consider provocations in the dispute started by Pastor Cassegrain.

The quarter-hour of fame of Theophile Cassegrain

In 1597, Théophile Cassegrain is well known in Geneva and in the intellectual reformed circles. Locally, his notoriety is even stronger: "I am too well known here", he writes to the Company of Pastors in Geneva. But what is this "local" who is confined? Can he be satisfied, he, the exile who already dreams of national glory? Must the glory of God suffer these barriers that are too human? Whereas, returning from Geneva, he is the pastor in Pont-de-Veyle, in June 1597 Cassegrain knew his quarter-hour of fame and committed the act bearing his name in the whole of France: he wrote a "universal challenge" by which he provoked all the doctors of the Catholic Church into a dispute. He alone against the

---

[853] Cassegrain, T.*Advertissement sur le libelle...Humblot minime*", Geneva, Etienne Gamonet, 1600, p. 12.

Roman world. His fame then extended on a national scale. Twenty years later, his enemies will still remember Cassegrain publishing "superb challenges against all the doctors of the Roman Church"[854]. Signed at Pont-de-Veyle in June 1597, the challenge is also launched in geography, fired between the indexicality of a toponomy ("Pont-de-Veyle") and zeal for the universal ("all theologians"):

"Cartel of Theophile Cassegrain, Minister"

To all theologians of the Roman Church,

    I have always thought that there was nothing more beneficial, and less difficult, to lead men to the knowledge of truth than a soft and peaceful conference, either in full voice or in writing. For thus opening up to one another, doubts are proposed and resolved and if one of the parties is persistent in his mistake, that person is easily convinced by the only opposition of the principles, and necessary and impossible conclusions; especially in theology rightly called to Science and the sciences, and rich in very sure and very infallible maxims. Leaving If there is someone between the learned and expert Theologians of the Roman Church, who watches me do this honour of conferring on me the following Theses or a part of them, or others of his choice, I protest against God and men to examine his themes and in all good conscience with the intention of embracing them with all my heart and to acknowledge as very worthy of the Doctor of truth, if I find them acceptable; and also to refute them without any disguise, if I consider them unworthy. The thing that makes me implore this as he loves the honour of God and the salvation of poor souls, if he is not disdainful of a work which is so necessary, so suitable to his proion: but for him to be released with dignity and he brings a modest spirit to it, and warmed up, with reasons that are stronger than numerous, without a show, embarrassment, and affected language in order to give myself a chance to reply more openly and analytically, so that one can handle a serious and solid Conference.

---

[854] Marcellin De Pont De Beauvoisin, *La piperie*… op. cit. p. 15.

Cassegrain's audience

⁸⁵⁵ See for example BAXTER J.P. "Documentary history" op.cit. vol V p 420. See particularly POINARD
⁸⁵⁶R. "L'aumonerie d'ancien regime"(1568-17)95)Paris, L'harmattan 2012.
857

" [855] [855] policies,see HAVARD G.and VIX\ C."Histoire de l'Amerique francais", Paris Flarion 2008p 100-107 and 162-163. Ibid, p.337.

[856] One must understand the dialogue –"Interrogatus an duo Sacrauno diehabeg Ridit Non, usque ad S" - see Carthusian liturgy.2 the
857

4. NEWEST FRENCH PRIESTS AND PASTORS

31.08.21
P. 229 of French text

In Fodere's book, 24% of the men's houses and 53% of the women's houses are quoted without known patronage, which shows the limits of his work and the failures of the memory of his Order.

In spite of his capacity for verbosity, a great many of his notices are badly researched. For example, his knowledge of the very old convent of Vienne, founded around 1212 and re-founded in [858] 1260 on the other side of the Rhône (at Sainte-Colombe) is very thin. He does not know its name any more. He only remembers the names of the founders, and some anecdotes like the loss of the special relic consisting of the habit of a monk who died in the odour of sanctity, Michel de Peruse, at the time when the town was sacked by the Calvinists in 1566[859]. About the convent of Nozeroy, in the Franche-Comté (Diocese of Besançon) he tells us that it was founded on a lordship of the Chalon-Oranges in 1460 by Prince Louis who had to be pardoned for having mistreated a Franciscan convent in the Kingdom of Naples during the Italian wars[860]. But he admits that he knows neither the name nor the date of the consecration of the church. However, he went there in 1583 and had then questioned its old caretaker.

It is even worse in Auvergne, for the house of Vic-le-Comte:

I do not have to acknowledge the fault if the town of Vic-le-Comte remains blank here, and if I go ahead silently, so

---

[858] Ibid., p. 884.
[859] Ibid., p. 356.
[860] Ibid., pp. 814-924.

that I have never been able to obtain the slightest instruction from so many people with whom I made enquiries and because we have to be content with what I could learn about our convent in this place.

However, he knows some things about this house. He remembers the names of the first brothers (of the family of La Bulle), the foundation of the convent in 1473, its consecration in 1484 and by whom, the beauty of the convent and its surrounding rivers. But the difficulties of the time emptied the convent of its brothers (it had only eight) and its memories.

It is the same, at the Mâcon convent [861], but its reasons are slightly different. Fodere is sorry, of course, that the convent's archives were lost during the troubles of the years 1562 and 1567. He assures us that he is a serious historian, saying that in 1583-1584 and in 1586-1587, when he preached at Advent and Lent, he had gone to consult the archives of the Dominicans, but that was only a small thing and as he says "I must be content with what I was able to take out of its hair"[862]. Thus, he does not know the founders of the convent, though he thinks that it cannot be more recent than that of the Dominicans, because in the urban processions the two orders march at the same level, therefore they are of a comparable age. At this point of his reasoning he accuses other actors, the Protestants, of being responsible for this memorial theft. Mâcon was a Conventual Franciscan foundation, which was reformed by the Observants in 1503 at the same time as eight other houses. But when they abandoned the convents, the Conventuals left for Bourg en-Bresse with the archives, which he has therefore been unable to consult.

Fodere is not regularly tender with the other branches of the Franciscan Order, whose complex vicissitudes of the Observance are contemporary with the Protestant crisis. For a great many houses, if he cannot give all the required

---

[861] Ibid., p. 406
[862] Ibid., p 416.

information, it is because according to him the Conventuals had seized or destroyed archives while reluctantly abandoning the convents to the Observants at the beginning of the 16th century. That means also that he does not imagine going to the convents of the Conventuals or even to write to them in order to gather information as he did, we have seen, with the Dominicans. At the beginning of the 16th century, even before the "heresy" ,the struggle is bitter between the new observants and the old : the general Franciscan Conventual is described by Fodere in his historical essay as the "sworn enemy" of the first ones, the brothers of La Bulle, "jealous, seeing the observants so well favoured... hatching them all their journeys and annoying them under the bad offices as they could, bribing the brothers of .the observance underhand[863]".One would vainly search under one's pen with whatever fraternal indulgence in the name of Saint Francis. The era exacerbated the brotherly resentment.

Then at the end of the 16th century, the rise of a reformed branch of the Observance, the Recollects, from Spain and Portugal, again lost several convents to the observing Franciscans. In 1603, Henry IV had required the Friars Minor to yield one or two convents per Diocese to the Recollects[864]. In Burgundy, they had to leave, after the decisions of the General observing the Franciscan chapter of Aracoeli of 1612, their house of Romans, that they had renovated after the Wars of Religion, and the direction of the Poor Clares of Montbrison. Fodere considers the attitude of the Recollects "scandalous" in this affair and contrary to Franciscan unity. The Friars Minor refused to yield the convent of Vienne. Or more precisely, the Archbishop, the secular and regular clergy and the

---

[863] Meyer, F. *Pauvreté et assistance...*" Saint-Etienne, CERCOR, Travaux et recherches IX, 1997, pp. 33-35.

[864] Bayle, P. *Eitique generale...Maimbourg*, Ville-Franche (Amsterdam)p. le Blanc A.Wolfgang, 3 ed. 1684 v 1 np 2290230.

significant people of the town were against it, preferring to remain faithful to the Observants. At least that is what Fodere says[865].

We know Fodere's free speech. For him, the "newcomers" have brought great trouble and caused great disorder in the Order of Saint Francis among French convents, "having made their efforts to send away the Observant fathers from several convents". While religious peace and the protection of the princes allowed Catholic reconquest, the Recollects

have drawn them into an argument and litigation before secular magistrates, raising among full audiences the imperfections of cloisters, denigrated, detracted and slandered in [866]any company, against all divine, ecclesiastical and human rights of their brothers of religion and wish to introduce a high struggle[867].

Having failed in Vienne, they brought their efforts to the second Franciscan convent in Lyon, Notre-Dame-des-Anges, in Pierre-Seize. The affair went up as far as the King. The Recollects were agitating "still with knocked up weapons" [sic]. Fodere can only pray to God:

to enlighten the Recollect fathers to leave the Order of Saint Francis in peace, that they build convents without trying to send away their people, their brothers of religion and that it may please God also to inspire our lords in council and parliament to keep things in the state that the elders have established[868]

Three convents have not been replaced after the wars of Religion (Bevret, Tournon and Morges) to which there should be added the Hermitage of Val d'Aude (between Chaumont and Châteauvillain), but three others had to be yielded on the order of the General of the Recollects

---

[865] Fodere, J. *Narration...* op.cit. book 1, pp. 359-359.
[866] ?
[867] Ibid., pp. 974-975.
[868] Ibid., p. 98.

(Bourg-Saint-Andre, La-Cote-Saint-Andre and Romans)[869]. Briefly, what the Protestants have not done, the Recollects have done. Fodere finishes his enormous book [870]with this disillusioned and bitter notation. He is more courteous with the Capuchins, another Franciscan reformation, born in Italy this time, whom he calls "the good Capuchin fathers" who threatened the Observants less directly, and had become very popular. Thus Monducon has now, according to him, two beautiful "protected" convents of the Franciscan Order, that of[871][872] the Capuchins and that of the Friars Minor. It is true that the Capuchins had become an independent Order in 1609 and that they demanded nothing from the Observants.

Protestant missions, the Wars of Religion, competition with other regulars, vicissitudes of the Franciscan observance: the times are very hard for the Friars Minor and the Order is in disarray. The religious (as political) frontier is particularly harmful to memory. From here comes Fodere's will to rebuild a history which is the most exact possible, up to the details of history observing a province over a long time since the foundations of the 13th century, an indication of legitimacy until the 17th century, an element of security also for the new generations of Franciscans. The Franciscans love to write of the traditions. As Fodere writes about the small hermitage of Provencheres (Diocese of Besancon), founded at the end of the 15th century at the place called "La Fontaine Saint-Antoine" it was dedicated to Notre-Dame "in order to preserve the old memory of the place"[873] . One must notice about the monastery of the Poot Clares of Seure (Franche-Comte) that the name of the town was spelt with a single "r" but the use

---

[869] Ibid., p. 1017.
[870]?
[871] Ibid., p 695
Ibid.
[872] Ibid..
[873] Ibid., p 919.

of the two was imposed in the way of the Lorraines who put two where only one is needed. Thus the convent of Chalon-sur-Saône on which he found a large amount of information, is described at length, with an unaccustomed precision on the dedication of the chapels and the themes of the pictures. It is a question of being unable to forget any more, and what happens afterwards, his book will lead to faith. It is an attitude which is known to the regulars, but especially inside the Franciscan family, among the Observants who are known as "better historians than the others since they are going to draw on the sources which is their reason for distinguishing themselves" as Jacques Dalarun[874].

But one feels all the same with Fodere's depressive effects, perhaps inherent in different situations of clergy on the border, as can be seen in the testimonies of Franciscan missionaries sent to Rome to the Congregation of the Propagation of the Faith[875]. He has, often in delicate situations, misjudged who are his real enemies and allies, and his aggression against the Franciscan brothers, but also the Catholic significant people here or there taken in the lack of compromise, makes him accuse other actors. What remained of the documents of the Mâcon convent, "a small punt after such a great shipwreck" [sic] disappeared effectively after the attacks by Protestants in 1562 and 1566-1567, the "first and second troubles" as he liked to say. But the Conventual Church was indeed a victim of the Calvinist iconoclasm, with brother Jean Bossu of the Beaune convent savagely tortured and assassinated in 1567. Fodere admits that the two beggar convents of the town, the Dominican and the Franciscan, were not destroyed by the Protestants, but on the order of the Catholic managers after

---

[874] Dalarun, J. "Conclusion" in Bouter, N. *Ecrire son histoire: Les communautés...passé*". PU Saint-Etienne, CERCOR 2005, p. 680.

[875] Meyer, F. "Rome et les protestants...XVIIe siècle".
Melanges de l'Ecole ...Mediterranee, vol. 109-2 pp. 853-879.

the repossession of the town in 1568, in order to use the fortifications and avoid a "new revolt" [sic] of the population. The furniture and the conventual objects were stolen by Catholic individuals. Within even two years, there was no longer a Franciscan presence in Mâcon. This example shows us how much the return of the Catholic clergy into a town brought back the Protestants not inevitably by themselves. A type of rejection of religious questions had affected the inhabitants, perhaps also the attitude of the Franciscans. Perhaps the attachment of the inhabitants to Calvinism was sincere. Fodere recognises the talent of a Genevan minister, a certain "Raymond" (Chauvet?) who came to preach, convert and teach, singing Mâcon's psalms[876]. When two Franciscans appeared in 1569, they:

received a great welcome from the inhabitants, because the greatest part of them was still cooled down on religion, on account of the heresy which was so fashionable a few years earlier, the remainder being necessary by the sack that they had suffered by all means to the two said invasions of their town.

The religious frontier remained a living scourge. On the other hand, the memory remained very close in Fodere's mind so that he remembers the help given to his Order by the canons of the Saint Vincent church, and the patient rebuilding of the Franciscan church by their own means. The gifts from the Catholics were repeated in 1583. The unfinished church, however, was dedicated to Saint Bonaventure and consecrated by Mgr Gaspard Dinet, in 1608[877].

***

The historic reflections of Jacques Fodere, but also his style and disenchanted resentment, show us that the dominant

---

[876] ?

[877] Ibid., p. 431-432.

discussion with the Franciscans (at least that which has come down to us) is a story which is often triumphant about heroic missionaries in the border area. He delivers to us, for example, the story of Father Charles of Geneva in the Alps towards 1650[878] to cause rage. It is not the only feeling of the Order before the Protestant presence at the beginning of the 17th century. The price to be paid for the events of the end of the previous century was very dear for the Franciscans. The border appears to us to be very broad, confused, associated with suffering at that time and above all like an area of combat and destruction. Fodere is interested in putting the emphasis on one moment, the years 1580-1620, which for the Franciscan order were particularly difficult. His reply was sensitive and the consequences were long-lasting for the Order. The contact with the new structures of Protestantism, also with the new orders of the regulars and Catholicism have deeply destabilised an order however powerful as that of the Friars Minor. What to think then of the effect that this period had on the more modest orders? On the other hand, one will note how much the "Henrician peace" from 1598 allowed the Catholic forces to rebound, but on other bases.

***

Contacts, confrontations or unequal combat?
The Toulouse clergy in the face of Protestantism
Estelle MARTINAZZO

The intolerance of the Toulousians, as mystical as it was mythical, was an identical actor between the 16th and 17th centuries, with as many paroxysms as the Vanini and Calais cases. Thus, Pierre Bayle writes of Toulouse that it was "without contradiction one of the most superstitious in

---

[878] dE Geneve, C. *Les trophées...XVIIe siecle* F. Tisserand, Lausanne Suisse Romande, 1976 3 vol.

Europe [...]. Its hatred for the Hug[879]uenots is the strangest in the world." The philosopher, however, shows the porosity of the contacts between the two confessions. Born a Protestant in 1647 at Carla, in the heart of the Foix country, he recants at Toulouse in 1669 at the Jesuit college before returning into the Protestant faith one year later. He testifies also in his writings of the violence between religious communities in the Toulousian south. Everything begins in 1562, at the time of the episode of the Deliverance, while the Protestants, on the point of taking the town, are chased by the Catholics, armed by the parliament of Toulouse[880].This Pentecost day then became a sign of Divine Providence, commemorated every year by a procession gathering laymen and clerks, relics and saints. Toulouse therefore lived an identical destiny to other towns of the kingdom, like Verdun[881]. In fact, in October 1572, the Toulousian Saint-Bartholomew's Day again made two or three hundred extra Huguenot victims[882]. Then, throughout the 17th century, the violence remained extreme. Among other examples, in 1622, the crowd persevered with sword swipes on the body of a Calvinist condemned to death, dragged him through the streets before burning him, for he had not renounced his "heresy" at the foot of the gallows.

At the heart of the "Huguenot growth", Toulouse became in favour of this deliverance, and saw itself as a symbol of the Catholic citadel, that of orthodoxy, of refuge, a town that one would like to take, but which remains impregnable, ringed by the Protestant communities[883].In

---

[879] ?

[880] Taillefer, M. *Vivre à Toulouse...régime.* Paris, Perrin, 2000, p. 128.

[881] Simiz, S. "La memoire catholique ...1562", *Annale de l'Est* no. 1, 2009, pp. 123-139.

[882] Brunet, S. *"De l'Espagnol dedans le ventre" :Les catholiques du Sud-Ouest...Réforme* (1540-1589). Honore Champion, 2017.

[883] J. Garrisson counts 800 churches where ....documentation is incomplete.

fact, from 1567, the Protestants controlled Montauban, Castres, Mazamet, Lavaur, Puylaurens and[884] Revel. In the south, they also hold a number of places in the Foix country. From that citadel, the Protestants are apparently excluded, but they remain, however, invisible. They have strongholds, of which some are strategic, in their hands, like Carman, L'Isle-Jourdain and Mas-Grenier. A community of a thousand souls remains therefore in the borders of the religious diocese, even though they are in constant regression until the revocation of the Edict of Nantes. To be at the same time both a Protestant and a Toulousian is therefore a difficult state. These communities have, until now, remained in the shadows, for they are mainly presented from the angle of the Wars of Religion and material destruction; moreover, the documents are not plentiful enough in order for anyone to study them from the inside[885]. In works on the history of the Toulousian South, the Protestant question has therefore often been treated in a secondary manner, studied with the theme of material destruction. Thus, the works of Jean Lestrade are keen to show the role of Protestants in the destructions at the end of the 16th century, but do not enable a statement to be made about the reformed communities in the diocese[886]. The works of Urbain de Robert-Labarthe and Camille Rabaud study the punctual and political aspects of the Wars of Religion[887]. Finally, the articles by the pastor Romane-Musculus bring elements that cannot be ignored on the conversions.

---

[884] Garrisson J. *Protestants du Midi, 1559-1598 ...* Toulouse, Privat, 1991, p. 65.

[885] Ibid., p. 35.

[886] Lestrade, J. *Les Huguenots ... Toulouse*, Toulouse: Berthoumieu, 1939.

[887] Robert-Labarthe. U. *Histoire... comté de Foix 1789*. Rabaud, C.*Histoire... Lauragis..Nantes* Paris: Sandoz et Fischbacher, 1983.

Toulouse builds itself up during the 17th century as an active centre for propagation of the Catholic Reformation, radiating across a vast territory. The Catholic superabundance contributed to the colouring of these southern Catholics, and towards this uniting and converging city with a great many clergy who came from the broad South-West. There, in the Toulousian region, the Catholics and their clergy – whether they are secular or regular – are in contact with Protestants, but without any face-to-face meeting. In this century of Catholic reconquest, Protestantism is denounced and the literature constantly evokes the metaphor of combat. Different methods are used, jointly by the Church and by the Parliament, to eradicate Protestantism within the limits of the diocese, but also beyond. Why describe the combat as unequal? Because, in the controversy, the Protestants are seen as better armed – intellectually speaking – but the combat is doubtless won by the Catholic Church, not from its own resources and its fish-hooks, but thanks to the help of royal policy. Unequal combat also, for the Church is going to try to bring back Protestants into its bosom, but again the clergy are unequally armed and unequally active. This constantly leads to questioning on the efficiency of the interior missions. Did they not see above all to convert the Catholic populations who were also as suspicious at the level of dogma as the Huguenots, invisible in the eyes of the Ordinary?

A battle in writing? The controversy, a militant literature

The controversy is a "total weapon", insofar as it serves the conversion of the adversary by demonstrating that he is in error[888]. Also, it looks forward to strengthening the confessional identity of each camp. More than ninety works of controversy, of propaganda or theological conferences,

---

[888] Dompnier, B. *Le venin de ll'hérésie...siècle*. Paris: Le Centurion, 1985, p. 169.

as well as stories of conversions were published in Toulouse between 1600 and 1685[889]. The controversies aim at everything as much as individual conversion and the ruin of theses and adverse positions. Their publication in Toulouse enables one to reflect on a chronology of contacts and confrontations between religious communities. Between 1600 and 1685, theological controversy is particularly absent, especially around the Peace of Alès (1629), then between 1645 and 1654, where no work was published in Toulouse. On the other hand, at this time, in Montauban the controversy bursts out around the Jean de Labadie affair (1610-1651). This former Jesuit, authorised by Charles de Montchal, Archbishop from 1628 to 1651, who particularly gave him the management of Terrtiarieds, recanted the Catholic faith in Montauban. An excellent preacher, he would have raised a riot at the time of the burial of a woman, who, having become Protestant at the time of her marriage, became Catholic again at her death[890]. The written controversy therefore bursts out about her, in one camp as in the other, for over ten works were published, between 1650 and 1660, in Montauban, on this affair[891].

Among these numerous works, the conferences are a minority class, with only eight listed titles, exclusively up to 1620, and only one after that date. At that time, it seemed to be necessary for the Catholic authorities to give out a religious instruction which was contradictory to chosen Protestant laymen in order to convert them to the Catholic religion. The controversies naturally do not take place in Toulouse, but in certain towns that were relatively near, such as Castres or l'Isle-Jourdain. They oppose almost exclusively ministers to regulars, Capuchins, Jesuits and

---

[889] Desgraves, L. *Repertoire...France* (1598-1685). Geneva: Droz, 1984-1985. 2 vol.

[890] Bremond, H. *Histoire ...nos jours*, Paris: A. Colin, 1968 t. XI, pp. 175-174.

[891] E.g. de Labadie, J. *Déclaration...l'Eglise reformee*. Montauban: Philippe Braconnier. 1650.

sometimes Dominicans. These monks are better armed intellectually than the secular clergy in front of the pastors who were trained at the Academy[892].The ritual at these conferences is fairly well controlled. They all begin with a challenge and are organised to obtain the conversion of a hesitant person. According to the studied works, the attacker, almost always a Catholic, offers theses f[893]or the debate. The discipline of the reformed churches in France forbids in theory that a pastor is at the initiative. If this debate is accepted, the conference can last for several hours, even several days. Most often it ends by the exhaustion of the arguments. A report is then signed and the debate is continued by a publication, sometimes spread out over several years[894].

Thus, in 1596, in l'Isle-Jourdain, at a theological conference, Michel Berauld, a pastor and professor at the Academy of Montauban, puts an argument to the Jesuit Pierre de Sapetz [895]. The Toulousians considered the town of L'Isle-Jourdain, situated about fifty kilometres from their city, as a dangerous Protestant bastion, such as Montauban and the Foix country could be[896]. This feeling increased the fantasy more, for the population was Catholic in majority, but in the imagination, it was connected to the fact that Henry of Navarre had become the Count of L'Isle-Jourdain in 1572. Actually, he was only interested in this county from a distance but was attached, indirectly, to transforming the city into a reformed bastion. In 1580, the collegiate was destroyed and the religious orders found refuge in Toulouse. The town knew religious coexistence from that date and

---

[892] Martin, P. *Une religion des livres (1640-1850)*. Paris: Cerf, 2003.

[893] D'Huisseau, I. *La discipline ...gouvernes*. Geneva-Saumur, Desbordes 1667, pp. 243-244.

[894] Dompnier, B Le venin de l'hérésie, op. cit. p. 176.

[895] Bibliotheque de Geneve, *Les conferences...XVIe siècle*. Paris: Honore Champion, 201 pp. 280-281.

[896] Lestrade, J. *Les Huguenots...rurales*. op. cit.

became, between 1598 and 1622, a place of Protestant safety. In this politico-religious context, Cardinal de Joyeuse, Archbishop of Toulouse from 1588 to 1605, sent Sapetz to organise his conferences[897]. The first theological dispute led by Pastor Berauld then raises the question of "expiatory sacrifice that one claims to make in the Mass". In the second part, the Jesuit in his turn questions the pastor on "the evidence and sufficiency of Holy Scripture" and of "participation in the flesh of Jesus Christ". The consequences and methods of this conference are not better known, but the best controversists were sent to the south of France to contradict the Protestants. Father Sebastien Michaelis, a Toulousian and excellent orator, joins in an oratory sparring match in front of the pastor of Montpellier, Jean Gigord[898]. A preaching brother of the province of Occitane in 1589, Michaelis is called by the cathedral chapter of Montpellier to talk to the Huguenot theologians. In 1596, he preaches there and leads public conferences in front of Gigord and other ministers about the eucharist, Later, he becomes the prior of the Toulouse convent in 1599 and has his works published, in 1600 and 1604, in the city of Toulouse.

In the continuity of these conferences, the stories of conversions, individual or collective, have been fairly broadly spread out. They have an impact which is much more important when it is about an influential person such as a minister or a lord. Between 1618 and 1621, the conversions are particularly numerous on account of events which shook the south of France. In the titles the "conversion" is very often qualified as "happy"[899] and

---

[897] Cahier, J. and Grandjean, M *Regustres ...Geneve*. Geneva: Droz, v. 7, 1984, p. 315.

[898] Archimbaud, J. *Sébastien Michaelis...Occitane (1594-1647)*, ed. Montagnes, B. Home Instituto storico domenicano, 1984.

[899] "L'heureuse Conversion...Cure De Montoire," Toulouse, P. d'Estay, 1640, Limoges.

famous preachers, such as Etienne Molinier were also of this type.[900] The latter, a priest and vicar of Saubens, Chaplain of Notre-Dame de Garaison, was keen, through his numerous works, to spread Marian worship[901]. He also preached in a great many places in the kingdom, describing himself as a "vagabond from diocese to diocese"[902]. He describes the conversion himself of Madame de Fontrailles, the wife of a Huguenot governor as well as his daughter in 1618. This took place after a controversy in Lectoure which was against Father Alesandre Regourd, a Jesuit of Toulouse, and the pastors Sylvius de Layrac, Albade Tonneins and Chamier de Montauban. It seems that the debate was aimed particularly at the saints and confession, but also the Marian form of worship. The Jesuit father triumphed over all his enemies. He won over Sylvius who "changed his mind with his small shame and retired with a disastrous flight, only wishing to act by letters and writings". Alba himself was "so confused and out of the subject that for any conclusion he had to be arrested on the slope of his deviation". During these oratory joustings, the governor's wife was a witness of several conversions which would have taken place at Father Regourd's sermons. As for Daniel Chamier, he was obliged to abandon the territory and, as during the war, "the one who remains master of the field is the conqueror, the one who leaves it is conque[903]red". Father Francois Garasse also describes the Lectoure incident, [904]awarding the victory to Regourd[905].

---

[900] Molinier, E. *Les oeuvres méslees de feu M.E.de Molinier, ...amis* Toulouse: A. Colomiez, pp. 97-137.

[901] Molinier, E."*Histoire de Notre-Dame de Grace...Languedoc.* Toulouse: A. Colomiez, 1644 *Le Lys du Val de Garaison* Toulouse: R. Colomiez, 1630.

[902] Molinier, E. *Les oeuvres meslees...* op. cit. p. 393.

[903] Molinier, E. *Histoire de Notre Dame de Grace...* Toulouse: A. Colomiez, 1644.

[904] Molinier, E. *Les oeuvre méslees..."* op. cit. p. 393.

[905] Molinier, E. "Advis sur le triomphe ...Mitauban", *Les oeuvres méslees...* op. cit. p. 139.

Moreover, the pastor published *Jesuitomania* in 1618 inn Montauban "" seven or eight weeks after these meetings[906]. The Jesuits handed themselves over then to invectives against him, particularly in a book entitled *Les Désespoirs de Chamier* [907]. This work takes us through the history of the conference and was described as a memoir "as large as this minister's stomach". The attacks deal with the mistakes made by the reformed people, especially in their Latin translations, with the example of the word "tabula":

Of Minister Chamier seeing the stoutness,
Which is so long, but wider than a lance,
I wonder if he is well fed,
And if he drags as he walks a large rotten stomach,
For the moment, don't wait for a large pig from a pigsty,
Of a man who everywhere speaks and makes a LONG TABLE[908]

Thus, Etienne Molinier can conclude, as for himself, in a less combative and ironic manner, that conversion is the true victory. In fact, Madame de Fontrailles vows to go to the Notre-Dame de Garaison Chapel in the Pyrenees to make her profession of faith publicly in the presence of the Jesuit Father and the assistant] Bishop of Lectoure. This recantation would have taken place in the presence of five hundred people in the chapel. In fact, in the militant literature, it is always a question of combat:

If the assault is violent, is the rampart invincible? If the Molinier sword is sharp, the shield is impenetrable. How many heretics, from the beginning, have been forced to turn it over, and using this plan all their forces have done nothing but show their weakness? They have vanished and the

---

[906] Chamier, D. *La Jesuitomanie,* Montauban: D. Haultin, 1618.

[907] de Sainte-Foy, T. (Regourd, A.j.) *Les désespoirs de Chamier,…celebres difficultes* Cahors, J. Dalvy and C. Rousseau, 1618.

[908] Quoted in Joly, P.L. *Remarques critiques…Bayle.* Paris: E. Gameau, 1759, v. 1, p. 277, "Chamier".

Church remains, they are lying down and the Church is standing up[909].

These works of controversy are almost exclusively the work of the regular clergy and had considerable publicity, especially if they led to conversions. The theological and doctrinal works on the other hand consist of a great many pamphlets, essays or other theological tracts. If twenty-seven different authors were noted among the sources published in Toulouse, they have as a common point personalities who were well-known in the region. Many of them are members of the regular clergy. For example, Father Gilles Camart (1571-1623) entered the Order of the Minors in 1589. A Professor of his order, he dedicates himself at first to preaching around Saumur in order to convince the Calvinists. Having become a provincial of Aquitaine, he was led to preach sermons on the Holy Sacrament, in 1606, in Castres, in which he refutes the argumentation of the minister Jean Josio. He would then be inspired, in his sermons, by a "Discours poétique à messieurs de la Religion prétendue réformée", a work which is impossible to find today, by the Toulousian Alexandre Filiere, in the form of poetry. Thanks to the allegory of impossible love, the author evokes the separation of the two bodies of the Church. The unsatisfied nymph then invokes the gods: "Act, [she says to them) to make our two bodies reduced to one body". Her prayer was, by a miracle, granted; she symbolises […] But alas! This is heresy with its obstinate wickedness that could re-unite the two bodies of the Church. The author adds in fact:

Thus the Church seems loving/called heretic and too scornful to my eyes   This heresy with its obstinate wIckedness reduced to embrace it by a saint Hyménée[910]

There are other versified texts, such as "Les quatrains de la muse Chrétienne", appearing in Toulouse in 1635 and doubtless written by a Jesuit, whose name remains

---

[909] Molinier, E. *Les oeuves méslees…* op. cit. p. 133.
[910] Bremond, H. *Histoire litteraire ...* op. cit. v 1. I p. 202.

unknown. The work is designed as a reply to the "Bouclier de la foy" by the famous Pierre du Moulin, a Protestant minister. A part of the text is in fact entitled "The crucifix of the Huguenots"[911]. The famous Father Jean Lejeune, or "blind father", a missionary of the Oratory also wrote controversies that he applies in his missions where he meets "heretics".[912] He also preached in Toulouse between 1640 and 1646, then in 1659; in the strength of the Jansenist dispute, his sermons particularly aim to show, thanks to scripture, that the Catholics are in "the true faith". Finally they have a pedagogic vocation which serves to instruct the Catholics or the Huguenots in the mysteries of the faith[913]. The hagiographic stories given by Father Gabriel Ruben especially his funeral oration, , insist on the importance of the missions that he managed on account of penitence, which was at the same time linked to his handicap, but also to his oratory methods. A wandering missionary, he is, however, recalled and assigned to residence by the bishop of Limoges.

Among the controversists, the Jesuits win over all the other religious congregations. Studying the shelves of the Beziers library also shows the importance of these Jesuit authorsthat one finds in Toulouse, such as Louis Richeome, Pierre Coton, Alexandre Regourd, but also many other theologians, such as the apostate minister Jeremie Ferrier[914]. However, according to the facts, do the Catholic Church and its clergy really fight? There is certainly a myth of a clash, connected with the spread of this mystical and spiritual

---

[911] Les quatrains de la muse Chrétienne, Toulouse, A. Coplomiz, 1635. The work, dedicated to M. Sevin de Mansancal, was approved by Charles de Montchal.

[912] Father Lejeune died in Limoges in 1672. He was the originator of the General Hospital in Toulouse. B. Hours (dir) Universite Jean Moulin, Lyon 3 2013 v. 2, pp. 622-626.

[913] Lejeune, J. "Le Missionaire de l'Oratoire…excitent" Toulouse: J. Boude, 1669, p. 1037.

[914] Fouilleron, J. *Tradition….XVIIIe siècle*.

literature, for in the Toulousian reality, the clash is not the model.

Varied contacts between the clergy

In the Toulousian Catholic sources in the top rank of which are the pastoral visits, there is a very small mention of Huguenots, for the Protestant question is always treated secondarily. These pastoral series, extremely rich for the period, began in 1596, before being continued into the middle of the 17th century, then finally into the 1690s[915]. The visits are accompanied by "secret relations" at the end of the 16th century, where the priests were asked to list all the abuses of their parish and the presence of "heretics", in replying to a questionnaire sent to the Archbishop in a sealed envelope. These replies unfortunately have almost never[916] been preserved. Similarly, in 1625 and then in 1640, a quick question at the end of the visit, enables one to know if there are "heretics" in a parish. But these last sections are, once again, rarely filled in. The priority is to rebuild the churches and to reform the clergy before thinking of converting possible heretics, of often invisible increase. One must therefore wait until the 18th century for the pastoral visits to grant a more marked interest in the existence of new converts in the parishes. Of Protestant ministers, it is never a question in the sources.

The lower clergy are in the category which is most concerned in daily life by the Protestant problem, because of the scattered communities subsisting in the countryside around Toulouse. As an example, near Carman, [917]a reformed community was implanted in Auriac, without a consistory. The small town is sacked again and again by the religionaries, then by the league members and the Duke of Joyeuse. The priest states in his report of 1617 that "heretics

---

[915] AD Haute-Garonne 2MI 967. Parish accounts.
[916] AD Haute-Garonne IG 489. 16 parishes visited (September-October 1615)
[917] AD h

are buried pell-mell" with the Catholics[918]. In Bourg-Saint-Bernard the Protestants had asked the Toulouse parliament to build a place of worship from 1562. In the same way, around Mas-Grenier, Protestants lived scattered throughout the neighbourhoods of Grenade-sur-Garonne, Verdun-sur-Garonne and Beaumont de Lomagne. In fact, a diffused rural Protestantism subsisted, which was difficult to investigate in the absence of sources. If the pastoral visits make the "heretics" appear punctually, as at Noumerens, Toutens or Caragoudes, we have only a few pieces of information on the contacts that the families had with the Catholic clergy. However, we see the rector of the parish of Aussonne confronted, around 1615, by a parishioner who is trying to indoctrinate sick people in order to convert them "in extremis" to Calvinism. She makes herself pass for Catholic and also is confessed by the priest. The sermon of this Huguenot is composed of simple arguments, which the rector reports to Jean de Rudele, vicar general (1616-162)). Thus, when she meets a woman praying before a cross with her children, she speaks to them by way of altercation:

Do you kiss this cross and this image thinking this is an image of Our Lord? God [….]is not on earth: but only in heaven and this image […] is only a piece of stone […] And what do you think when you go to church? Do you think that God is there? Oh, you are very mistaken, for he is not there[919].

One can measure in these words all the weight of the dispute about images and the vicar general advises the priest to use, in a fairly vague manner, persuasion while staying moderate. The priest of Ramonville-Saint-Agne also confronts a group of "heretics". The vicar general "enjoins the rector to try to put them back into the way of salvation", without any other detail [920]. The priests of the parishes,

---

[918] AD Haute-Garonne 2MI 803. Auriac pastoral visit, 1617.

[919] Lestrade, L. *Les Huguenots dans les paroisses rurales…* op. cit. pp. 143-144.

[920] AD Haute-Garonne 1G. Saint-Agne secret procedure, 1615.

badly trained and often infrequent residents, especially at the beginning of the 17th century, leaving their pastoral work to their vicars, are therefore helpless in the face of the Protestants, through lack of training, but also because they are still impregnated by village solidarities. They feel obliged to witness the presence of Huguenots in their parishes, but only obtain, on behalf of their hierarchy, few concrete replies in return.

However, the idea of converting the Huguenots is not absent from the preoccupations of the Toulousian Catholic Church. It grew in the last third of the 17th century, thanks to the action of certain personalities of the episcopal chancellorship. Thus, Joseph Morel (1676-1704) vicar general of the Archbishop Colbert de Villacerf (1687-1710) appears, around the Revocation, as one of the most active participants in the struggle against the Protestants. Vicar general from 1676, Morel entered the Oratory in 1650, before being ordained as a priest in 1658. He became the Superior of the Oratory in 1669. As vicar general, he travelled around the Diocese in order to suppress the abuses of the clergy. He published a code, named by his contemporaries as the "Morel code", then he worked on the conversion of the Protestants. For him, the privileged action of the Church is situated in the Word and he writes thus in 1685:

The town of Carmain (Caraman) has always been one of the most obstinate [...] for several years when we have applied ourselves to convert the inhabitants of this town, as much as we have. The Archbishop has been there in person and we have preached there in public, being unable to attract them into the church to listen to us[921].

In Mas-Grenier the Archbishop and his vicars preached in person a number of times over several years, but all in vain. Joseph Morel moves also, with the theological canon, the dean and official ushers to L'Isle-Jourdain in 1683-1684, coming to this same title meaning the pastoral

---

[921] AN TT 272 104

warnings to the clergy of France about the future of the temple[922]. They were received by Pastor Molinier, four elders of the church and six inhabitants of the claimed reformed religion. Morel advances traditional arguments according to which the Catholic Church is one and indivisible, and that Louis XIV is at the same time the new Constantine and the new Theodosis, for he also is seeking the re-unification of all Christians. This metaphor is common to that of the writings of Bossuet after the Revocation. For they wished to be the holders of the only true and unique doctrine, only the Catholics can acquire interest, in any case they think so, also adhesion and therefore the conversion of Protestants, including their ministers, which will make them aware of their mistake quite naturally. The pastor's reply aims at showing that his flock, who are obedient to the king, have told him:

that they want freedom of conscience which they have until now here [...] that[923] they conform perfectly to the word of God and that they wanted to live and die in this faith that they profess.

In the face of the pastoral warning of the clergy assembly that the vicar general and his acolytes have come to present, the reformed minister and the members of the consistory stand firmly in their positions. An external aid is therefore required. In Mas-Grenier, the vicar generals come in their turn to preach in the surroundings of the Revocation. Until 1621, in this place of safety, the Protestants were in the order of 6 to 800 but are not more than 220 in the 1680s. In August 1685 at the time of the great Dragonnade, the vicar general describes the situation. He evokes the need and the will of the Protestants to be instructed by the Catholic clergy. He then writes:

They came to the church in order to listen to the sermons that we gave to them and after they were instructed, they

---

[922] Boisson, D. *Un affrontement religieux... consistories*. Rennes: PUR, pp. 215-226.
[923] AN TT 246 46.

recanted and then we preached to them four times a day; several new converts attended all the sermons and had so much taste that they discussed among themselves to ask for a preacher for Advent and Lent (in) Mas[924].

In fact, the Protestant houses in Mas had been occupied by retired missionaries and fifty-four families had then recanted from 23 August in front of the priest, without the sacred word having played the slightest part in that.

Archbishop Colbert de Villacerf had also appealed to missionaries, Capuchins and Jesuits, who he maintained without a royal subsidy, in order to teach the doctrine to the new converts on the day after the Revocation. However, these missions certainly acted less to convert the Protestants or to teach new Catholics than to educate the rural populations in their group. These missions mostly did not work in the whole of the diocese of Toulouse. Thus, the Dominicans dedicated themselves strongly to the apostolate towards the Huguenots of the South. In the same way, the Capuchins organised a great many missions. Great preachers, such as Father Thomas of Turin, the founder of the Toulouse convent, Pierre Barthélemy of Saint-Julia or even Benin of Toulouse, described as a "great theologian and [925]sublime preacher", were all involved. One must not omit the great mission organised by Father Honore of Cannes, which is finished by the erection [926]of a giant cross in the Saint-Cyprien in Toulouse in 1678. The aim of this mission was to bring back all the populations to the true faith as proof that these lands were essentially papist; the missions of the interior were aimed at everyone, Catholics as much as Protestants. However, in fact, it seems that rather few ecclesiastics were scraping along with the Protestant problem. Moreover, there was no establishment in Toulouse

---

[924] AN TTT 272 104.

[925] Douais, C. *Capucins et Huguenots…Louis XIV*. Lyon: Vitte Et Perrussel, 1888, p. 9.

[926] AD Haute-Garonne 122H 14. "Memorabilia…Sive Tolose", fol. 200.

of the Compagnie de la Propagation de la Foi. This absence is explained by the activity of devout militarism in the heart of the pink town, of which Gabriel de Ciron is the most outstanding symbol. Having become a priest in 1640, close to Nicolas Pavillon, at first he played an active part by putting an end to the disorders caused by the doctrine of the former Jesuit Jean de Labadie. He is also very close to the training of the clergy in taking part in the seminary of Caraman from 1653 to 1662, and creating an ephemeral seminary in high science from 1651 to 1659. Sensitised to the problem of converting the Protestants, in the end he created the seminary for new converts in 1653, in order to obtain Catholic instruction for children born into Protestantism. His hagiographer, the Father of Mas, describes him coming back from the Cevennes in 1658 and writing that "Languedoc never saw a more beautiful sight than Monsieur de Ciron coming back from the Cevennes or any other similar place. He was walking with a group of children converted from heresy"[927].

This house of new converts, situated in Saint-Pierre-des-Cuisines de Toulouse, welcomed 236 young boys between 1655 and 1662. They were there to be taught or "to receive instructions required for the Catholic faith". Some of them had already been converted before they arrived, others were already there. These boys came from the forty-two dioceses of the South, going from Bayonne to La Rochelle and to Poitou, then up to Nîmes and Viviers[928]. If most of them came from areas close to Toulouse, a great many of them also came from places that were much further away like Meude, proof of the great fame of the house created by Gabriel de Ciron. This geographical distribution, which was based on the limits of the resilience of the Toulouse parliament, is understood thanks to the method of recruitment. This is the case of Francois de Rességuier,

---

[927] Father Pierre du Mas(165-1703) doctrinaire…Chateau de Monestrol, fol. 192.
[928] AM Toulouse GG 838,

received as counsellor to the Toulouse Parliament, then appointed counsellor to the Chamber of the Edict of Castres in 1661-1662[929]. This member of the brotherhood of black penitents put his five daughters with the Carmelites, and in the matter of conversions provided a particular zeal. In fact, the institution housed five protestants who were converted in Castres. In the heart of the Counter-Reformation, the role of the parliamentary elite constituting the devout Toulousian group therefore deserves to be emphasised.. However, the majority of Protestants were brought to Toulouse by priests and in the first place by bishops and their vicars general. The Bishop of Montauban, Pierre de Bertier (1652-1674) and his vicar general were very active[930]. Pierre de Bertier, who was a canon and archdeacon of the metropolitan Church of Toulouse, is the younger son of the President of Enquiries Jean de Bertier and a nephew of the Bishop. Together with his vicar, General Dagan, between 1658 and 1661 he made several Protestants recant, before bringing them to, Toulouse. Alain de Solminihac, Bishop of Cahors (1636-1659) had three sons of the same family sent to him, then his successor Nicolas Sevin (1660-1678) recommends several other boys to Gabriel de Ciron. As regards conversion, the example of these reforming bishops shows the importance of these networks and their efficiency in the matter of the anti-Protestant struggle.

The stay of new converts was generally very short, ranging from a few days to some weeks, with a fairly concise general instruction. After this short stay, for example, some were placed in the service of the Bishop of Rieux, Jean-Louis de Bertier (1620-1662). Thus, thanks to the activity of the clergy, Toulouse became an important

---

[929] de Beauregard, A. *Parlement de Toulouse ... histoire de l'art*. Bruand, Y. Universite de Toulouse 2, 2001. p Capot, S. *La Chambre de l'Édit de Castres ... Nantes*. Paris Ecole nationale des chartes, 1998, p. 406.

[930] Contrasty, J. "Histoire…Évêques.Toulouse: Sistac, 1936.

centre of conversions, in spite of the late interest in this mission.

In spite of the controversy of the 12th century and the supposed role of the Church and its clergy in conversions, the Toulousian laboratory shows that most of the Catholic clergy did not seek contact with the Protestants, especially during missions, and even less often with their reformed opposite numbers. These missions from the interior were more aimed at educating the Catholic populations even more than in the Toulouse area; the Protestant was an invisible enemy. It is the same in the Pyrenees, studied by Serge Brunet, where the Jesuits were only interested in the reformed communities from a distance[931]. Must one see there a semi-failure of the pastoral effort, such as that shown by Frederic Meyer in Languedoc[932]? Certainly. The contacts between the clergy and across them the issue of conversions, show clearly the efficiency of the royal policy, relayed by the active participation by devout people in the missionary epoch. Thus, the Catholic Reformation can be seen as a weapon of the Counter-Reformation. If the Church has not absolutely sought contact with the Protestants, its action was aimed to improve the intellectual condition of its clergy, in order to be able a second time to struggle against this invisible enemy. This is where its great success resides.

***

The face-to-face pastors-priests
In Sancerre under the regime of the Edict of Néantes
Didier BOISSON

---

[931] Forcaud, J. *Relation ...Pyrénées (1635-1649.)* Brunet, S. *Le Jesuite Jean Forcaud...montagne*
Paris, CTHS, 2008.
[932] Meyer, F. "Rome ...Languedoc....XVIIe siècle".*Mélanges de l'École française...Méditerranée* v. 109-2,1997, p. 879.

From the 16th century, especially with the siege of the strong p[933]lace in 1573, the town of Sancerre has been one of the symbols of the Calvinist presence in the northern half of France. If the reformed community was studied by Yves Gueneau in his thesis on Protestants of the province of Orleans-Berry under the regime of the Edict of Nantes, the relations between Catholics and reformed people, especially between priests and pastors, have not been tackled while the two communities co-existed[934].

Situated on a hill some kilometres from the left bank of the Loire, the town of Sancerre and its surroundings make up, according to Roger Dion, "a picture that no riverside site, [935]between Roanne and Nantes, can equal in grandeur". The demographic weight of reformed people is very low: in the Bourges election, to which Sancerre belongs, it is around 2% of the total population. In the town of Sancerre itself, it is different: the reformed community is a minority from the 1640s and towards 1680, out of the 2,400 Sancerrans, the reformed people are around 1,000. There were some 200 deaths of reformed people in the decade preceding the Revocation of the Edict of Nantes, to which one can add 100 deaths throughout the neighbouring villages. But it is a diminished community which must face the Edict of Fontainebleau. In fact, the number of reformed baptisms is around eighty-five in the years 110-1620 but only four in the 1670s.[936] This demographic reduction is partly compensated by the socio-professional differences between Catholics and Protestants. If the weight of the rural and semi-rural people is predominant with the Catholics (58%) this is not so with the reformed people (20% of

---

[933] de Léry, J. *Histoire memorable...assiegeants*, Geneva, 1574.

[934] Gueneau, Y. *Les protestants du Centre ...1598-1685*, these doctorate Sauzet, R. Universite Rabelais, Tours, 1982.

[935] Dion, R. *Le Val de Loire* Tours: Arrault et Cie, 1934, p. 138.

[936] The demograhic data mainly rely on Benedict, P. *La population réformée française de 1600-1685,* no 6, 197, pp. 1433-1465.

professionals). On the other hand, the latter are proportionately more numerous among the artisans (37% on one side, 20% on the other hand) and particularly among the nobility, especially with wine merchants or wood dealers, officers, to whom the pastors can be added[937].

These pastors must confront priests who wish to put an end to the existence of a reformed minority. In a small town like Sancerre, by leaning on Protestant sources (the provincial or Catholic synod's cases against the pastors) the interest is in wondering whether the clergy of Sancerre can alone rival the reformed pastors.

What are the forces that are present in the two professions? They are not as unbalanced as one might have thought. The reformed church has one to two pastors under the regime of the Edict of Nantes, and if one puts aside the 1641-1651 decade, in the course of which, on the order of the Prince of Condé, lord of the area, the minister must interrupt his activity.[938] In fact in 1598, the case of Sancerre was regulated by Article 5 of the details of the Edict of Nantes:

As for Sancerre, the said exercise continued as it is at present, except to establish it in the said town, making consent appear by the lord of the place, - this will be provided by the commissionaires that His Majesty will deputise for the execution of the Edict.

This article therefore adds a restrictive condition – the agreement of the lord – to the planned arrangements.[939] On the eve of the revocation of the Edict of Nantes, there are two of them. This pastoral body of Sancerre is dominated by five names: Adam Dorival and Paul Alard in the first half of the 16th century and Jacques Gantois, his son Pierre, and Jean le Fèvre after 1650.

---

[937] Gueneau, Y. *Les Protestants du Centre...* op. cit. pp. 132-133.

[938] Poupard, V. *Homme de la ville de Sancerre* Paris: Berton, 1777, pp. 391-392.

[939] See Gueneau, Y. *Les protestants du Centre...* op. cit. p. 59.

Adam Dorival, minister of Sancerre from 1594 to 1613, operates a certain influence on the Churches of the Orleanais-Berry province if one refers to his role at the time in the provincial synods held during this period or to the fact that he was delegated from his province to several national synods and political assemblies. Thus, he represents the province of Orleanais-Berry at the time of the national synods of Saumur in June 1596 and of Jargeau in May 1601; he was moderator at the time of the provincial synods in 1601, 1602, 1604,1607 and in March 1611 [940]. Paul Alard, originally from La Rochelle, was probably pastor of Corbigny; Etienne de Monsangland, who was with the Company of Pastors in Geneva[941], was in post until 1647.

The Gantois are Sedanais and form a dynasty of pastors in the 17century with Eusebe Gantois, minister of Sedan, his son Jacques who became the pastor of Sancerre in 1637, before going back to Sedan between 1641 when reformed worship was forbidden in Sancerre; he returned to Sancerre in 1651 and [942]stayed. His son Pierre, born in 1644, succeeded him in the same year until 1667, having pursued his studies in Geneva; he married a lady from Sancerre, Rachel Renouard, whose sister was married to Pastor d'Henichemont, Daniel de Fougeres, who manages this parish between 1659 and 1685; in 1695 he returned to the Refuge. In the end, the last pastor is Jean le Fevre who operates in Sancerre from 1674 and whose origins are unknown[943].

Thus there is a difference in recruitment of other pastors in the province; the ministers of Sancerre did not all come from the Church in which they practised or even from the

---

[940] Haag, E. *La France protestante...* Paris: Chebullier, v. 4, 1853, pp. 303-304.

[941] Fornerod, N., Boros, P. and Campagnolo, M. *Registres...* Geneve: Droz v. 13, 2001, p. 154.

[942] Nots, H. *Les pasteurs français au Refuge... 1680-1710.*

[943] Ibid.,p 49. Declared in1685 in Rotterdam, refugee in Leeuwarden – went to England in 1692.

synodal province of Orleanais-Berry – with the exception of Adam Dorival – but their personalities and the Church that they served make them influential and respected ministers. They received the active support of the provincial synods of Orleanais-Berry. For example, the latter set the rules for the controversy between pastors and priests. The synod of 1602 held at Châtillon-sur-Loing states that as regards disputes and conferences with those of the Roman church, having noticed that several people engage the pastors under various pretexts, the company exhorts all persons of whatever quality, and also the consistories, not to engage a pastor lightly[944].

Two years later, at the time of the provincial synod of Châtillon-sur-Loire, in order to remedy and so that one could reply promptly to the writings of the enemies of piety without awaiting the time for the assembly of synods and colloquiums, which makes the delayed writings unfruitful, the synod names a pastor accused by a symposium of replying to an essay on Catholic controversy[945]. However, we do not know how these different recommendations are applied by the pastors of Sancerre.

However, the Catholic Church has more strengths, in spite of the current Wars of Religion when they were chased from the town until the siege of 1573, the Saint-Jean church was transformed into a temple and the others mostly ruined. After the capitulation of the town, Catholic worship is re-established and the usurped ecclesiastical goods must in theory be restituted. During the following two decades, no priest succeeds in durably re-establishing Catholic worship and the Archbishop of Bourges, on whom Sancerre depends, does not obtain any restitution of goods. To the great displeasure of Abbot Poupard, Etienne Jacquelin becomes priest of the parish, a former priest who had apostasised at the time of the siege, but also sold the titles

---

[944] BnF fr.15829 fol 95.
[945] Ibid., fol.100 v.

of the parish before returning to the Catholic Church[946]. The situation changes in 1596 with the nomination of Durand Fargent as priest; the latter remains for almost a half century at the head of the parish, profiting from the peace signed in 1598. During the first decades under the regime of the Edict of Nantes, the priest ionly helped by a vicar. Thus, in this town at the beginning of the 17th century there are no converts, those in existence in the previous century having been chased out and destroyed at the time of the passing of inhabitants of the city to the Protestant Reformation: this was especially the case for the Benedictine convent of Saint-Martin which depended on that of Bonne-Nouvelle d'Orleans. However, the priest of Sancerre gained from the support, from 1630, of the Ermites of the Order of Saint-Augustin, who were under its supervision. In fact, accordIng to the agreement approved by Louis XIII: "The said fathers will only be able to administer any sacrament, or preach sermons, both during the time of Advent and Lent, outside those times, without leave, licence and permission; also they will not be allowed to receive the sacrament at the feasts of Christmas and Easter, without the licence and permission of Monsieur the priest and to the detriment of his rights"[947].

The priest finally obtains the support of the brotherhood of the Holy Sacrament, the only brotherhood re-established in the 17th century by the intervention of the priest, initiated on 11 June 1664. Nuns are only installed in Sancerre in 1686: there are – unsurprisingly – nuns from Notre-Dame de la Miséricorde responsible for instructing new converts: they settled in the house which was[948] formerly occupied by Pierre Gantois, the former minister.

It is thus striking to note that the Catholic Church, and especially the Archbishop of Bourges, did not truly give himself the means of a reconquest in this land which was

---

[946] Poupard, V. *Histore de la ville de Sancerre,*. p. 325.
[947] Ibid., pp. 379-380.
[948] Ibid.

partially hostile. This is also the case, under the regime of the Edict of Nantes, of the other two main reformed communities of the diocese, that is Châtillon-sur-Loire, a town close to Bourges, and Asnières-les-Bourges, a village situated outside the ramparts of Bourges, but dependent on a parish in the town, the Saint-Privé parish.[949] For the Catholic Church, help can only come from the manorial and royal power [950], but also priests outside the city, especially that of the missionaries. The events which occurred in Sancerre in the years preceding the revocation of the Edict of Nantes reveal the tensions between the Catholic clergy and the reformed pastors.

During the years 1684-1685, as in so many other reformed communities, the Church of Sancerre is shaken by a whole mixture of affairs involving opposing ministers and priests, from Sancerre or elsewhere.

On 17 April 1684, two reformed children, Noel Laurent, twelve years old, and Etienne Corsange, eight years old, took refuge in the house of the agency of Sancerre and asked to be converted to Catholicism. The younger one added "that for more than a year he had a plan that at bedtime sleeping with the said Laurent, he had asked him if he also wanted to become a Catholic because he wanted to go there the next day; he promised him while holding his hand." Upon announcing these acts more than two hundred people had gathered in groups in front of the house of the agent where the father of the young Corsange and other members of the community "in order to enter forcibly by striking violently" tried to recover the two children. In the absence of her husband, the wife of the agent intervened to say "that they were with God and the King and that having declared that they wished to recant from the RPR, it was no longer

---

[949] Boisson, D. *Les protestants de l'ancien...Ancien Regime (1670-1789.)* Paris: Honore Champion, 2000, p.581.

[950] See Gueneau, Y. *Les protestants du Centre*. In 1621 Sancerre lost its Protestant garrison.

up to the father to be responsible for their behaviour"[951]. These conversions are possible on account of the declaration of 17 June 1681 which authorises the children of reformed parents to convert from the age of seven years[952]. The troubles lasted all night long, the agent's house being subjected to stone-throwing "against the doors and windows", the rioters "spat out several insults and seditious words saying that the house should be burned, that the agent's wife was a prostitute, that she had a brothel." The priest intervened on the morning of the next day, asking Father Dieudonne of Saint-Albert, a white friar preacher, to carry out the recantation of the two children. This took place on 20 April, also in the presence of an Augustinian monk. On the same day, in a letter to the bursar of Bourges, the agent wrote: "a sovereign authority is needed in order to suppress them and make examples" and states that no Catholic came to defend himself and his wife, "for it is known that these people are only looking for a quarrel, being the stronger ones. I have even been warned that they have a large amount of weapons in their homes"[953]. These two conversions were so much more interesting as it seems that few reformed people were converted in the years preceding the revocation of the Edict of Nantes – only nineteen have been named[954].

On 29 April 1684, the bursar of Bourges launched a notice against the two ministers of Sancerre, Gantois and Le Fèvre, following depositions from five witnesses, among whom were Gabriel Grosson, a priest and vicar of Sancerre, and Father Ebriat, an Augustinian monk, one of those installed recently in the role. The latter had attended a reformed service of worship on 19 and 23 March and they

---

[951] AN IT 265.

[952] Pilatte, R. *Edits, declarations... (166-1751)* Paris: Fischbacher, 1885, p. 88.

[953] AN TT 265.

[954] Boisson, D.*Les protestants de l'ancien ...Berry*. op. cit. p. 132.

reproached the pastor Le Fevre for saying words against the king: "Monsieur Le Fèvre said in his sermon that their church can speak like the persecuted primitive Church as it has become the hatred of men who only breathe blood and carnage." He even stated that "there were people who only sought to lose the ministers of the true Gospel so that having lost them, one easily lost all their brothers"[955]. In fact, the declaration of 22 May 1683 enabled this presence.

…as it is useful for the Catholic Religion that the people who were knowledgeable in this matter used to go to the said temples, in order to hear there what the ministers said in their sermons, in order to be able to refute them if necessary, but also to prevent them by their presence from advancing anything contrary to the respect for the Catholic Religion, apostolic and Roman, and prejudicial to the state.[956]

In another sermon, he is accused by Le Fèvre, who preached on the Gospel of Matthew when Jesus chased the merchants from the Temple, of having spoken these words: "The vendors' tables are today taken down in the church because grave, Heaven, is sold for the burying and ringing of bells…" On Easter Sunday, 22 April, a short time after the riot, he made " …his exhortation to dispose his people to celebrate the Supper". He points out to them the pitiable state that the Israelites suffered under Pharaoh's persecution without being charged, without office, without empire, and that however God had taken them away by the victories that they had won by his servants Joshua and the others[957].

Other sermons by pastors are criticised by the priest or any other priest attending the sermons. On 19 March, even before the rebellion, Pierre Gantois stated that "any war that takes us for fatal, which it may be, we will support it vigorously because the interest of our consciences is

---

[955] AN TT 265. See also Boisson, D, *Les protestants…Berry.* op.cit. pp. 138-139.

[956] Pilatte, L.R. *Edits, declarations…*" op.cit, pp. 137-139.

[957] AN TT 265.

nothing other than that of our religion to which we are obliged, and that we would not know how to behave against the good of our consciences." In other [958]words, an appeal to the resistance and freedom of conscience. In another sermon, always in the presence of some priest who carefully notes his statements, he said:

that one must never make peace with the Roman Catholics, that one could have with the Lutherans, but although the Roman Catholics offer to live in peace with the Reformed people, it is impossible for us to live in peace with them, having taken us away from their communion by the anathema that they have fulminated against us.[959]

These sermons are after the confrontation which occurred – during the year 1683, but on an unknown date – between the pastors of Sancerre and the representative of the Archbishop of Bourges, at the time of the reading of the Pastoral warning written by the extraordinary meeting of the clergy in 1682. In fact, this text must have been read in front of the consistories. In the province of Orleanais-Berry, it is first of all at the end of the month of January 1683 in Orleans before the Superintendent Bazin de Bezons; the latter in September was in La Charité-sur-Loire, a community situated in this same general area. These visits give way to a moderate discussion from the superintendent, then to a more offensive one from the Bishop or his representative, and finally to a reply from one of the pastors of the reformed Church. The pastor of Sancerre who made the reply was probably inspired by the texts of the pastors who had previously been able to be published, especially Jean Claude, pastor in Charenton, and Claude Pajon, pastor in Orleans. This exchange, imposed by the King, probably gave the tone to the controversies and denunciations sparked off by the sermons of pastors during the year 1684.

However, beyond these questions of the conversion of two children and sermons, this same year 1684 is marked

---

[958] Ibid.
[959] Ibid.

by other conflicts confronting Catholic clergy and reformed pastors. First of all, Jeanne Desfilles and Etienne Dijon were considered as apostates and the minister Pierre Gantois is accused by the priest of Sancerre of having received the two apostates: the priest even states that the minister "is currently in Sancerre without any suspicion[960]". The case of Jeanne Desfilles has disturbed the communities of Gien, Sancerre and La Charité-sur-Loire. In fact, she would been born of Catholic parents and in 1681, while it was still forbidden to convert to Calvinism, "she went to the sermon at eight o'clock and only came out at four o'clock in the afternoon, being in the middle of two ministers of the said place who were with her. Four Catholic witnesses stated this truth, who called her an apostate"[961]. Then she left Sancerre in order to find refuge with the reformed people of Given, then La Charité-sur-Loire. Then, in December 1684, following a request from the priest of Sancerre, the situation of the temple is contested, which is "only forty steps" from the town and "was placed by usurpation, being sure that it is not at the same place where it was at the time of the Edict of Nantes"; as this new position is "by their private authority". Thus, in spite of all these offences, the pastors of the Sancerre community do not seem to be treated in the same way as other neighbouring churches.

In numerous reformed churches, such accusations made by the clergy would have led to justice quickly closing down the temple and condemning the pastors to exile. The example of Châtillon-sur-Loire is significant in this respect. This other church in Berry has many points in common with that of Sancerre, as much demographically as sociologically, also weak Catholic supervision. The pastor, Bompart, is thus accused by the priest that he attended sermons "for having compared the present time to the reigns

---

[960] AN TT 265.
[961] AN TT 240
AN TT 265 5.12.1684 letter sent to Dey de Serancourt superintendent of the generality of Bourges.

of the Emperors who persecuted the Church". However, he succeeded in being proved innocent by showing that the three witnesses presented by the priest had never even come into the temple[962]. However, the affair which puts an end to the temple of Châtillon-sur-Loire is the conversion of Marie Courault, the wife of Philippe de Jaucourt, who is accused of being relapsed. By an order of the Paris parliament of 9 February 1684, the two protagonists are condemned to banishment, Marie Courault from the kingdom, the pastor from the competence of the Paris parliament for a period of nine years; the temple must be destroyed[963]. In Saumur, a mission was organised between 7 July and 9 August 1684 by Father Honore of Cannes. The Bishop of Angers, Henri Arnauld, obtained a ruling that the temple would be closed during that period. However, the reformed people went bagainst this ban and gathered there and a baptism was celebrated. Nothing more is needed for two orders of the council on 8 January 1685 to supress the Academy and on 15 June the practice of Protestant worship in the town, also ordering the destruction of the temple[964].

Now, in Sancerre, there is nothing of this, or at least the sanctions taken are not so definitive. On 26 May 1684, after all the sermons previously mentioned, an order of the Council of State of the King forbade the two pastors to practise their ministry for six months only. The reformed worship can resume on Christmas Day 1684. In August 1684, the superintendent of Bourges, however, opened up a notice on meeting them because he was making "a defence for those who would have been ministers in the places where the practice of the RPR would have been forbidden

---

[962] Fueneau, Y. *Les protestants du Centre...* op.cit. p 208.

[963] Boisson, D. *Les protestants de l'ancien colloque...* op. cit. pp. 115-116. (AN O 28 fol. 36).

[964] Boisson, D. *Actes des synodes provinciaux... (1594-1683)*. Geneva: Droz, 2012, p. 35. Landais, H. *Histoire de Saumur.* Toulouse: Privat, 1997.

or to make their[965] home there. The decree of 17 May 1683 condemns pastors who were in breach to a fine of 3,000 pounds and to be deprived "forever of the operation of their ministry in the whole kingdom." The decree states:

His Majesty having made defences to all ministers and disposers of the RPR to stay or come to live in future in places where the practice of the said Religion would have been forbidden, those who were ministers in the said places in order to avoid the execution of this decree are going to settle in the neighbourhood and so close that they are there as often as they made their residence there and by this means make the said decree almost useless.

Again, this offence does not seem to have any consequences for whether the Sancerre temple is open until the revocation of the Edict of Nantes. Elements of explanation can be brought from the history of Sancerre and relations between priests and pastors from the middle of the 16th century. Therefore we must pause on the publication in the 17th and 18th centuries of two works by Catholic authors who knew the history of this town very well, Gaspard Thaumas de la Thaumassière and Father Poupard.

Gaspard Thomas de la Thamassière, a lawyer from Bourges, but of Sancerre origin, in 1690 published his *Histoire du Berry*. In this erudite work, he hardly alludes at all to the existence of reformed people in the town of Sancerre. He finishes his masterpiece by not describing the passing of the town to Calvinism, the Wars of Religion and the siege of 1573, or the Edict of Nantes. It is when he describes the Count of Sancerre, Henri de Conde, that he deals with this question in a few words:

The heretics considered it in its birth as support and experience on their part; however, when they had recognised their mistakes, they have never had a greater scourge and more irreconcilable enemy, being able to eradicate heresy, and taken away the freedom of public operation, of their claimed Religion in the extent of all lands

---

[965] AN TT 265.

and made it possible to completely banish them from the whole of the county of Sancerre, whose town had been a refuge from the time of the birth of Calvin's heresy[966].

According to him there was a rampart against Calvinism in Sancerre, and one must look for it in the person of the Count and not in any place with the local clergy in the locality or with Berry, which is never mentioned.

Father Poupard, a century later, published his *Histoire de la ville de Sancerre* (1777). "Protestantism in Sancerre and the relations between Catholics and reformed people held an important place"[967]. In a work of 412 pages, the first 100 pages of the book are dedicated to the history of the Counts of Sancerre. In Book II Father Poupard deals with "Sieges of the town of Sancerre", mainly describing his predecessor Thaumas de la Thaumassière. Father Poupard describes in more than 200 pages in Book III the "ecclesiastical part" (eighty pages) and finally in the last book, the "natural part". He shows that the reformed identity of the Sancerre community was built on an unbalanced relationship between priests and pastors. It is even more interesting that its author is himself a priest who must one century after the revocation of the Edict of Nantes co-exist with an important reformed minority which has never disappeared, and henceforth from the 1770s thus openly declare the Catholic Church's inability to bring them back into its bosom[968]. He especially insists on the importance of the Siege of Sancerre in 1573 in the formation of the reformed identity, by placing the inscription of the primordial of pastors who were sheltering in the town, among whom was Jean de Léry, who returned to Sancerre having escaped the massacre of Huguenots in La Charité-

---

[966] de la Thaumassière, T. *Histoire de Berry...* Bourges, Toulouse, 1689 v. 11, p. 286.
[967] Poupard, V.*Histoire de la ville de Sancerre.* op. cit.
[968] Boisson, D. *Les protestants de l'ancien...Berry...*" op. cit. pp. 401-405.The renewal of the reformed community of Sancerre in the 1770s.

sur-Loire, where he had just been nominated as pastor[969]. Thus, for example, to describe the Siege of Sancerre, Father Poupard writes:

In this terrible situation, in the middle of such a general and deplorable calamity, the ministers, the main authors of the rebellion who had every place to fear the King's anger should not fall upon them, behaved in Sancerre as their brothers did in La Rochelle. They made out of their own danger that of all the others and took time for a prayer that they said every evening in the church of Saint John, in order to exhort the people to patience and to encourage those who were disturbed[970].

A study of the relationship between Catholic clergy and reformed pastors shows at Sancerre a powerful connection which is not, contrary to what one likes to think in the reformed communities of the north of France, to the detriment of the religious minority. If Calvinism is maintained in this town, it is above all due to the weakness of the Catholic clergy, as much by its presence than by the means used to reconquer in the 17th century, but also in the 18th century, the people of Sancerre who had passed over to the Protestant reformation. Only civil – and military – power is in a position to fight against the reformed community: this was the case at the time of the siege of 1573, in the years 1618-1621, then between 1641 and 1651, and finally with the Edict of Fontainebleau. The writings of Father Poupard in this respect are revealing of the failure of the clergy and therefore of his own failure.

***

Orators and professors of the Academy of Saumur: a Republic of Letters in the 17th century

---

[969] de Léry J. *Histoire memorable...* op. cit.
[970] Poupard, V. *Histoire de la ville de Sancerre* op.cit. pp. 225-226.

In memory of Francois Laplanche and his friendly guidance through the archives of Saumur.

Between 1619 and 1685, the town of Saumur was on a confessional border, an ideal place for studying relations between Catholic and Protestant clergy. There two institutions face each other, the reformed Academy and the Orators. The Academy effectively opens its doors in 1607, thanks to Philippe Duplessis-Mornay. The Oratory is present in three places: the pilgrimage from Notre-Dame des Ardilliers which is given to it in 1619, the College in 1624, and the School of Theology in 1630. The two heads of the two Churches, Calvinist and Catholic.

An essential question is to wonder which logic will win in the thread of the century, that of a disinterested connection among the professors who are seeking truth beyond the confessions, or that of the defence of the collective identity of the group to which they belong and which looks at the other with suspicion.

Firstly, the context and the two institutions will be presented as they are often seen by historiography, which takes things in blocks, and insists on rejecting the other one, while showing that the relations are courteous. Then, this presentation will be nuanced, for it depends on the epochs – the years 1640-1660 are calmer that those preceding the revocation of the Edict of Nantes – and the people, for the bishop of Angers, for example, finds the Orators too open towards the Calvinists. In the end, the common points will be shown, which enable one to say that one may at some moments talk about the "Republic of Letters".[971]

Saumur, a confessional border

A confessional border was created in 1589 when King Henry III granted Saumur to Philippe Duplessis-Mornay, governor of the town from 15 April of that year. It remained

---

[971] The term is particularly used by Kleinstuber, J.A. *La Republique des Lettres a SaumurTanneguy Le Fèvre.* Lebrun, F. *Saumur capitale ...siècle*. Fontevraud, 1991, p 9196.

in the hands of a Protestant garrison until 1621, when Louis XIII's soldiers took it back. The map drawn by Samuel Mours shows the actual communes counting Protestants towards 1650-1685 and clearly shows that one is on a confessional border, a space of co-existence[972]. It is the same with the map of Protestant strongholdsin the Centre-West towards 1620, which shows Saumur, for every person coming from Paris, as the head of this area, whose main town would be La Rochelle.

In cultural practices[973],the segregation in Saumur between the Catholic and Protestant communities is often present. One only counts four mixed marriages for the whole century. Until 1675, changes in confession remain exceptional. But the son of Mark Duncan, married to a Catholic, for example, had some of his children baptised in the temple and others in the church. Professionally, the confessional differentiation depends on careers: it is total in printing but not in medicine where the wife of Duplessis-Mornay appeals to a Catholic doctor and Orators consult Mark Duncan.[974] There is no socio-spatial segregation in the area, no Protestant quarter, and some Catholics [975] lived in the Rue du Temple. On the other hand, the Fenet quarter, where the sanctuary of the Ardilliers is found, is occupied by the Catholics[976]. But it is the rise of absolutism and the spread of the Catholic Reformation that are essential for understanding the deep forces which made the situation develop.

---

[972] Mours S. *Les églises reformees en France*. Paris, Libraire protestante, 1958, p. 196.

[973] Soulan, N. *Catholiques et protestants de Saumur…*

[974] Mark Duncan (1581-1640) was a Scottish philosopher and doctor. Gentleman to James I, he came to Saumur and was called to the Academy.

[975] The Fenet quarter is often mentioned in Cron, E. and Bureau, A. *Saumur: Urbanism…* Nantes 303 Cahiers du patrimoine, 2010.

The Protestants created an academy for training future pastors and the education of the youth. This institution was created in 1593, and effectively opened its doors in 1607. It was visited by a floating population that is found in the registers of baptisms, marriages and burials, especially as godparents. The students are more and more numerous, and 200 of them are counted in the third quarter of the 17th century. Two-thirds of them are French (Anjou, Maine, Touraine) and a third come from abroad (United Provinces, England, Scotland, Holy Empire, Switzerland). They mixed a stable Protestant population which was highly educated (clockmakers, goldsmiths, writers,printers, merchants) which declined at the end of the 17th century and dropped from 1300 to 700 individuals[977] The outreach of the Academy made it a European capital of Protestantism, whose study continued up to today[978]. Its success explains, among other things, its focus for the Oratorians in 1619.

The teaching body of the Academy consists of seven chairs: three in theology, one in philosophy, one in Hebrew – for a time taken by Alpron, a Jew converted to Protestantism – one in Greek, and one in mathematics. This teaching institution trains, among others, "proposers", students in their last year in theology who, in order to become pastors, then sit an exam before a provincial synod or a colloquium. Equipped with their certificates from the Academy and being already doctors of theology in the latter, the candidates for pastorship underwent an interrogation on logic and one on ancient languages before the church institutions. The Academy is administered by a council made up of the rector and professors, pastors of Saumur,

---

[977] Lebrun, F. *Saumur au XVII siècle*. Launay, M. *La Tolérance*, Rennes; PUR, 1999, p. 42.

[978] The last reference is from the 21 March 2015 meeting of Group for History of Protestantism 9GRHP).

and the principal of the Protestant College[979]. In fact, this college is part of the Academy[980], and it knew great success: the regents and professors are paid by the King and the Protestants welcomed the children of Catholics, hoping that they would change their religion. The professors of the Academy are eminent people: Bomar teaches there, but moves on (1615-1618) and the theological sensitivity of the Academy is particularly marked by the Scotsman John Cameron, accused by his enemies of professing in the grace of ideas that were close to those of Arminius, then by Moise Amyraut.

Why did the royal power choose the Oratorians, rather than another Congregation which was more famous such as the Jesuits, whose distant origins go back to Paris in 1534? The reason is certainly the recent character of this association of priests, still unknown, installed in France from only 1611, by Cardinal de Bérulle, a friend of Marie de Medici. In 1614, King Louis XIII gives them the pilgrimage of Ardilliers, that they effectively took charge of in 1619 in order to obtain funds intended for maintaining a college, which opened its doors in 1624. However, a great many Protestants were opposed to the installation of a Catholic congregation of any nature. In 1629, the professor of. the Academy vigorously attacked the Roman church, calling it "Babylon" [981].His famous friend Moise Amyraut, for his part, wrote that the College of the Oratory is "a fort that the Roman church opposes in the place of weapons that the Protestants have established in this town[982]". However, the peaceful climate which was later installed would

---

[979] Pittion, J.P *Instruire et edifier*" Sheridan, G. and Prest, V. (eds.) *Les Huguenots...moderne*. Paris: Honore Champion, 2011, pp. 19-45.

[980] Maillard, J. *L'Oratoire de Saumur...XVII siècle*. Lebrun, F. *Saumur capitale...* op.cit. p. 128.

[981] Batterel, L. *Memoires domestiques ...Oratoire*. Paris: Picard et Fils, 1904. v 3, p. 479.

[982] Maillard, J. *L'Oratoire de Saumur et les protestants.* art.cit., p. 196.

perhaps have been more difficult to establish with the Jesuits[983].

The main centre of the congregation is the sanctuary of Notre-Dame des Ardilliers. On 8 August 1614, Louis XIII signed the letters patent giving the chapel to the Oratory. In 1619 the Oratorians took possession of the premises, and Marie de Medici in that year witnessed a miracle, an event which spread the fame of the sanct[984]uary far and wide. The map of declared miracles, which occur from 1594 to 1713, states that the chapel quickly became a national sanctuary, where the Marian identity of the Catholics is forged in order to be spread widely by prodigies[985]. These graces are propagated in a small book, *L'histoire de l'origine de l'image et de la chapelle de Notre-Dame-des-Ardilliers*[986]. This anonymous work, made simply in order to be sold cheaply, decorated with a simple wood engraving placed on the title page, is endlessly increased with new miracles, until the last edition in 1713. This book, which reflects a modest intellectual level, is a weapon against the Protestants, especially by the marvellous style in which the pilgrims continued to live.

The legendary writer describes that in the olden times, a snake was killed by Saint Florent, the patron saint of Saumur, on the site of the sanctuary of the Ardilliers. This text continues by presenting the invention of the Pietà in 1545, the statue moving to show the place where she wanted to be honoured.

Then the journeys of great people and kings come in, which show by their position that one is on a national

---

[983] *Histoire d'in miracle advenu…* Paris: Michel Sonnius, 1619.
[984] Maes, B. *Le Roi, la Vierge et la nation…Revolution/* Paris: Publisud, 2002. Balzamo, N. *Les miracles …surnaturel.* Paris: Les Belles Lettres, 2014.
[985] *L'Histoire de l'origine de l'image…vierge.* Saumur: Francis Ernou, 1681. (1634)
[986] *L'histoire de l'origine…Sainte Verge.* Saumur: Francis Ernou, 1682 (1634)

pilgrimage on a border of Catholicity. Then there is a description of brotherhoods, recantation of Protestants, and especially the miracles which make up three-quarters of the book[987].

The second centre is the Oratorians' College. Its history is little known due to lack of documents. On 7 August 1624, the contract is signed between the municipality and the management of the Oratory[988]. The Oratorians take over this establishment which includes six classes of humanities and two courses of philosophy[989]. In 1664, 300 students are found there, with the sixth in the philosophy class[990]. However, there is a staff shortage and it has only – outside the Oratorians – one principal and one regent[991].

Finally, the third centre is the school of theology, a seminary for future priests from the Oratory, which opened its doors in 1630, under the second Superior General of the congregation, Charles de Condren[992]. It is thus that the young Louis Thomassin reaches Saumur, at the same time as Charles Lecointe. It is the second institution [993]in France after that of Paris. In 1640, the Oratorians had sixty-three rooms in Ardilliers, fifty-four for the students. In 1649, the works were finished. Thus the two sides were presented: on the one side college and academy for the Protestants, on the other side pilgrimage, college and the school of theology for the Oratorians. Relations between them were courteous, but what lies hidden behind this amiability?

---

[987] Maes, B. *Les conditipns de voyage...l'Ancien Regime.*
Boisson, D. *Annales e Bretagne...Ouest.* V. 121-3, 2014, pp. 79-96.
[988] Maillard, J. *L'oratoire de Saumur et les protestants....* op..cit. p. 128.
[989] Lebrun, F. *Saumur au XVIIth siècle.* op. cit., p. 45.
[990] Maillard, J. *"L'oratoire de Saumur... "*op. cit., p. 132.
[991] Ibid., p 128
[992] Ibid.
[993] Lebrun, F. *Saumur au XVIe siècle...* op. cit., p. 45.

Tensions depending on circumstances

The Bishop of Angers is the first of the people against a good understanding between Catholics and Protestants. Mgr Henri Arnauld was the brother of the Great Arnauld and the Abbess of Port-Royal-des-Champs, Mother Angelique. A scrupulous bishop of the Counter-Reformation, he resides and visits his parishes.[994] He goes on a pilgrimage to Saumur every year, on foot, in penitence, since he was dedicated, to make amends to Jesus Christ and the Virgin for the outrages that heresy confronts him with in this town. Contrary to what most Oratorians think, holding the conversion of hearts in first place, the bishop thinks that God can also act on the body[995]. On 1 April 1659 he forbade his diocesans in Saumur to send their children to the Protestant college under penalty of excommunication He uses all his toolsof persuasion, but also recourse to legal procedure, a short time before the revocation of the Edict of Nantes, for the closure of the Academy and the temple. In Saumur, his intermediaries in the population are the secular clergy and the Dominicans but from the Oratorians he had little or no support. On 2 June 1668 the "miracle of Les Ulmes", the name of a small parish two leagues from Saumur, comes to comfort his mission in this meaning. This time, it is no longer the Virgin Mary who acts as intermediary, but Jesus himself, present in the Holy Sacrament, at the time when the Protestants were gathering in Saumur for a provincial synod. During the procession of the Holy Sacrament the priests show the silver host-holder to the faithful, who for a quarter of an hour see the image of Christ in the host. The Bishop leads an enquiry and comes to Les Ulmes on 20 June. He acknowledges the miracle and

---

[994] Bonnot, I. *Hérétique ou saint?...Angers au XVIIe siècle*. Paris: Nouvelles Editions, Latines 194.

[995] The Marie Le Brun miracle. Récit de guérison, 1616." François Ernou, 1675. AM Saumur II C 10).

has his letter of witness[996] printed in order to spread it among the faithful.

The sanctuary of Ardillis is the place in Saumur where most of the recantations take place, especially from the 1670s. In the records of the Oratory within the municipal archives of Saumur there is found a "Ritus absolvendi ab heresie"[997].Altogether, twenty-seven ceremonies took place in the chapel. One finds those of two elder brothers of the Saumur professor Louis Cappel, that of Jean des Ardilliers, in the hands of Jean Morin, delegated by the Bishop of Angers, and that of Louis Cappel du Tilloy before Henri Arnauld on 8 March 160, in the chapel of the Oratory of Angers.

Louis XIII and Louis XIV used the Oratorians to strengthen the Protestant area of the Centre-West in the kingdom, for it was a badly managed area, far away from the capital. The act of withdrawing the Ardilliers to communal administrators, in 1614, to grant this sanctuary to the Oratorians of Cardinal de Bérulle, adds to the unification of the kingdom. This Society of the Oratory created in France, which was based on the model of the Congregation of the Oratory founded in 1575 in Rome by Philippe Neri, at his seat in Paris, makes Protestantism recede, and unifies the country around Tridentine Catholicism, the King's religion. In letters of August 1614, by which Louis XIII returns Notre-Dame-des-Ardilliers to the Oratorians, the latter declares himself "founder of the said house and church of Notre-Dame-des-Ardilliers" and asks them to pray to God for prosperity, for repose and tranquillity of his kingdom[p].

Pilgrimage is a means of the Protestant Centre-West becoming more intimate with the King, especially as the abbesses of monasteries close to Fontevraud have belonged to the Bourbon family since the 15th century. The concern

---

[996] Lebrun, F. *Saumur au XVIIe siècle* op.cit., pp. 44-45.
[997] AM Saumur, *L'histoire de l'origine*. op. cit., pp. 28-30 (chap. 10)

for unification is manifested, among others, by the disappearances of the strongholds that the Edict of Nantes created for the Protestants. This ruin of the Huguenots created by the Edict of Nantes, one of the three aims that Richelieu presented in his *Testament politique* appears in his absolutist programme. In 1621 Duplessis-Mornay must give the young King the keys of the Protestant stronghold. After the end of the siege of La Rochelle in 1628, the Peace of Ales in 1629 ended the Huguenot party.[998] The royal pilgrimages will have been short in the Ardilliers, of Marie de Medici unp to the 1660's, but the magnificent classical monument of the Ardilliers continues to keep this presence of the Sovereign until the Revolution.

Once the Huguenots were eliminated by his father in 1629, Louis XIV, as soon as he ascended the throne, wanted to have the power to limit the freedom left to the Protestants. His representatives, such as Voysin de la Noiraye, superintendent of Tours from 1666 to 1671, show a strong anti-Calvinist zeal. He forbade the creation of a third chair of theology in the Academy, and sought to drive away foreign teachers. From 1671, he declares himself favourable to the suppression of reformed worship in Saumur and proposes that the Protestant college and its library be given to the Oratorians.

The peak of this rivalry –which we will talk about again later – takes place at about the time of the revocation of the Edict of Nantes, in 1685. But the "mission" in the sanctuary of the Ardilliers is not ended, since in 1695 Louis XIV has an inscription placed in bronze letters inside the dome of the chapel, to celebrate his victory over the Protestants including those of the kingdom and those abroad who belonged to the League of Augsburg:

In the year 1695, the piety of the Great King for the Virgin Mary Mother of God, Louis XIV, King of France

---

[998] Hubac, J. *La paix d'Ales….1629*. Paris: Les Editions de Paris – Max Chaleil, 2010.

and Navarre, destroyed heresy throughout his kingdom, and sent away the troublemakers by land and by sea[999]

Examples of judiciary oppositions are the proof. In 1680, on the occasion of the funeral of the Rector of the Saumur Academy, who was also the Professor of Theology, his body was carried by six proposers towards the cemetery of Bilanges, towards five o'clock in the evening. Now the reformed people could at this time only bury their dead at daybreak or at nightfall, and the cortège was restricted to five people. An enquiry is urgently held. In 1684, the Capuchin Honore de Cannes came to take part in a mission to Saumur[1000] at the request of Mgr Henri Arnauld, and a witness saw twenty-four to twenty-six people gathered and another witness twenty-eight or twenty-nine.[1001] He obtained a ban on Protestant religious services for five weeks. The vicar can touch the hearts of heretics who attend his sermons voluntarily where he always mixes in some features of controversies, but, strangely, without any fruit[1002]. In January 1685, ten months before the Edict of Fontainebleau, two decrees of the King's council suppress the Academy and order the demolition of the temple[1003]. On this occasion the head of the garrison of the town sent soldiers to limit violent scenes carried out by the Catholics at the time of the destruction of the church. [1004] The small cemetery which surrounds it is attacked, and shrouds were gored with lead.

---

[999] POP MDCXCV. "Deiparae Virginis …profllagavit."

[1000] On Father Honore de Cannes, see Maes, B. *Missions et grands sanctuaires…siecles*. Sorbel, C. and Meyer, F. Chambery Institut d'Etudes savoisimes, 2001, pp. 177-186.

[1001] Lebrun, F. *Saumur au XVIIe siècle…* op.cit., p 46.

[1002] Chambery Institut d'Etudes savoisiennes 2001, pp. 177-186. Father Honore de Cannes, see Maes, B. *Missions …XVIII siecles*. C. SORREL and E. MEYER

[1003] Ibid,.p.41.

[1004] AM Saumur records of the Oratory, iii A.3 d. *En foy..les miracles*. Brother Francois Bareire of the Oratory of Jesus.

The series of baroque miracles, conserved in writing after an enquiry, is another argument against the reformed people. It reveals the glory of God and his mother against the Protestant negations, and begins the year when Henry IV is the sacred King of France. The need to declare the miracles, as described in *L'histoire de l'origine*, therefore begins in 1598 (where fourteen prodigies are recorded) and ends in 1713. The Oratorians are installed in the Ardilliers in 1619, but one must wait until 1634 for the first edition of *L'histoire de l'origine* – that is, fifteen years later. One may question the causes of this discrepancy. The Oratorian Bareyre, who took part in the writing of this work, in ex-voto of a cured illness, is not a particularly brilliant person, and states in his declaration that he had to ask his superiors several times for authoris[1005]ation. Now, this book, *L'histoire de l'origine*, mediocre in terms of its shape and its base, also was no longer re-edited until 1713. The Oratorians do not like the baroque sensibility, for they come from the French school of spirituality, created by their founder, Bérulle. The beginning of the text of the unexpected event of 1676, describing the miracle of Marie Le Brun, is revealing of their state of mind:

Now that the church is so well established and that the faith has happily succeeded to error and infidelity, the works of all divine power [the physical miracles] are no longer necessary[1006].

However, they obey their bishop Henri Arnauld, who asks them to describe the miracle as a report on an unexpected event. The Oratorians prefer to talk about the healing of hearts, graces which remain secret between three people: God, the person who gains from it, and the confessor.

[1005] Am Saumur, Declaration of a miracle...Baryere
[1006] ?

A "Republic of Letters" in Saumur in the 17th century?

[1007]There is a good understanding in Saumur between some Catholic andProtestant circles. The contacts between the two confessions are important not only in the diocese of Angers, but in the group of regions of the West. The directors show a good example. Religious dualism is accepted. In the 1620s Duplessis-Mornay has good relations with the magistrate Jean Bourneau and his family. The town is consecrated to Notre-Dame-des-Ardilliers at the time of the flood of the Loire in 1615, and there are few acts of intolerance. The governor Urbain de Maillé-Brézé, brother-in-law of Cardinal de Richelieu, has good relations with Moise Amyraut. In the years 1639-1680, Julien Avril, magistrate and mayor, a strongly pious Catholic and a powerful man, is satisfied with the Protestant presence in the Academy. He attends the orals for theses of Protestants and hands out prizes. He allows the installation of Jean-Robert Chouet, although he was born in Geneva.[1008]. Elie Bracken Hoffer, an Alsatian Lutheran traveller passing through Saumur in the years 1643-1644, notes in his journal:

The Huguenots are here in a good position, however without ringing bells. They have their temple in the town and it is very beautiful. Their burials, their baptisms take place in full daylight; there are sermons on Sunday and Wednesday. However, without ringing bells or other means of summoning....[1009]

This respect is manifested by the erudite circle of Tanneguy Le Fèvre. This old Catholic, the pupil of the Jesuits in their college of La Fleche, was converted to Potestantism, then became regent of Saumur in 1651. A great Hellenist, he holds a large correspondence with the

---

[1007] ?

[1008] Maillard, J.*L'Oratoire de Saumur et les protestants...* op.cit., p 129.

[1009] Brackenhoffer, E. *Voyage en France 1643-1644.* trans. H. Lehr ,Strasbourg: Berger-Levrault, 1928, p. 212.

scholars [1010] of his time. The Protestants attend the sermons of the Oratorians in the churches. In 1662 and 1663, a great many reformed people, especially Tannneguy Le Fèvre, are going to listen to the sermons of the Oratorian [1011] Mascaron at Saint-Pierre, in spite of the ban by pastors.

The conferences of church history given by the oratorian Louis Thomassin in the Ardilliers School of Theology, from 16343 to 1654, are followed by the Protestants[1012], perhaps for purposes of controversy and conversion, but also for reasons of curiosity. Similarly, the orals of theses, at Ardilliers and at the Academy, are followed by two public sessions, where sometimes, attendees can ask each other questions and express their feelings. Even if it is contrary to the spirit of the time and the very lively hostility of the Catholic clerks, including Jansenists, towards reformed people, the professors put forward their points of convergence, rather than what separates them. They are all impregnated with the thinking of Saint Augustine. The contacts are fully witnessed for thirty years, from 1643 to 1674, and these high-calibre intellectuals do not hide the mutual respect that they have for each other.

In 1674 the Protestant Pierre de Villemandy, with several people "of the Religion" attended the theses held by the students of Father Andre Martin, as they usually did. Pierre de Villemandy too[1013]k the word to say "that there was no difference between his feelings on Justification and those of Father Martin." That provokes an offensive from the Jansenists and Angevin anti-Cartesians against the fathers of the Oratory.

[1010] Lebrun, E. *Saumur au XVIIe siecle…* op.cit., p 197.

[1011] Maillard, J. *L'Oratoire de Saumur et les protestants…* op. cit., p 153.

[1012] Clair, P. *Louis Thomassin (1619-1695)*. Paris PUE, 1964. *L'oratoire de France….siecle*. Paris Douniniol, 1866, p. 450 and p. 452.24-27 Berraud A.

[1013] AN M230, quoted by Maillard,J. *L'oratoire de Saumur…*.

The climate of Saumur seems, in some ways, peaceful at the beginning of the third section of
the 17th century, between the professors of the Academy and the oratorians. In 1667, a letter written by Jean-Robert Chouet , a young professor at the academy, reports:

Imagine, I ask you, that I am in one of the most delightful places and one of the most polished in Europe, on account of various people, and of Religion and Roman Catholics, that I am in a town which is very convenient for people of my profession, with whom I can discuss philosophy, that I am near Paris, which is certainly the source of people of letters, and that thus I am informed of an infinity of things which look at the sciences, that perhaps I would not know if I was somewhere else.

In 1670, Isaac d'Huisseau, the pastor of Saumur from 1630 who became a prominent "confession de foi" professor in the Academy, published a book entitled *La reunion du christianisme ou la manière de rejoindre tous les chretiens sous une meme confession de foi*. This local irenism, fed by the action of some people, found a reciprocal tolerance on the "adiaphora", these questions were considered on-fundamental, on [1014]rites and especially discipline. But d'Huisseau's book is condemned by both the consistory of Saumur and the provincial synod of Anjou [1015].

"The positive anthropology" of Saumur (F. Laplanche) is due firstly to the personality of Philippe Duplessis-Mornay, a humanist of the Renaissance as much as a convinced reformed person[1016],who wishes to bring the "papists" back to the Gospel by the Word. This governor of

---

[1014] Maillard, J. *L'Oratoire de Saumur et les protestants...* op.cit., p. 131.

[1015] Stauffer, R. *L'Affaire d'Huisseau:Une controverse au sujet de la reunion...(1670-1671)*. Paris: PUE, 1969.

[1016] Laplanche, F. *La doctrine saumuroise...religieuse*. Lebrun, F. *Saumur, capitale européenne...* op. cit., p 43.

a Protestant stronghold, a friend of Henry IV, wanted to make Saumur an intellectual island of the French Reformation. For him, reasoning by the Word or the pen could lead the Catholics to the truth[1017]. Hostile to verbal violence, he refuses to take part in the quarrels between Gomar and Arminius on predestination. He replies to a pastor who was wom over to Arminianism:

Thank the Lord, we hold ourselves under the terms of Scripture, without searching for something else, in order to tie ourselves in a common effort against idolatry, superstition and Roman tyranny! It is my view to deal soberly with these doctrines and the people who treat them prudently, provided that for their part they proceed religiously there[1018].

Duplessis-Mornay refuses to take an entrenched position on the quarrels on predestination which stir up his co-religionaries since Arminius, a professor in Leyde, held against his colleague Francois Gomar that, contrary to Calvin's affirmations, God had not wished for the fall of Adam, and that grace was open to everyone. Duplessis-Mornay appeals to Gomar, who taught at Saumur Academy from 1615-1618, and asks the Scotsman John Cameron to succeed him, the one who responds to Arminianism by a path founded on a much more posi[1019]tive anthropology, possibly inherited from Erasmian humanism.

A second reason for Saumurian irenicism is the theology of Amyraut, a professor at the Academy of Saumur from 1626 to 1664.[1020]. He becomes famous for the manner,

---

[1017] Ibid. Lebrun, F.*Saumur, capitale européenne...* op.cit. pp. 113-124.

[1018] Quoted in Lebrun, F., *Saumur au XVIIe siècle...* op. cit., p 43.

[1019] , F. *L'ecriture, le sacre et l'histoire...siècle* Amsterdam APA-HUP 1986; Muller, R.A., *Divine Covenants, Absolute and Conditional...*

[1020] On "L'Ecole de Saumur" Laplanche, F. *Orthodoxie et predication...universelle* Paris: PUF 1965: Armstrong, B.G.

which was new according to his enemies such as Andre River or Pierre Du Moulin, of presenting universal grace in Calvinism. In 1634 in Saumur he published *Un brief traitéde la predestination* which had a great impact. He also elaborates on other treatises that François Laplanche calls "the political theology of Saumur", marked by a rejection of violence, and by the distinction between secular and ecclesiastical power. Amyraut is alarmed by the execution of King Charles Stuart the First in 1649, and advocates loyalty to the King. With such masters, the Academy knew great success and saw its number of students increase, at least until the end of the 1590s.

A third reason lies in the Oratorians' spirituality. These people, after Bérulle, share the Augustinian doctrine of grace and freedom. And this thought of grace facilitates their good relations with the Academy, but the actual tolerance which exists among them does not rely on a political theology which is comparable with that of Amyraut, who refuses to represent it by political power.

Calvinism ...seventeenth century France
Madison,University of Wisconsin Press.

5. NOUVEL FRENCH PRIESTS AND PASTORS

Pilgrimage is a means of attaching more intimately the Protest Centre-West to the king, all he more because the abbesses of the monastery near Fontevraud belonged to the family of Bourbon from the XVth century. Concern for unification is manifest, among others, through the disappearance of strong places given by the Edict of Nantes to the protestants. This[1021] ruin of the "protestant party, one of Richelieu's three aims presented in his "Testament politique", appears in his absolutist programme. In 1621, Duplessis-Mornay must give the young king the keys of the strong protestant place. After the end of the siege of La Rochelle in 1628, the peace of Ales in 1629 ended the Huguenot party. The royal pilgrimages would have been short in the Ardilliers, from Marie de Medici until the 1660'sbut the magnificent classical monument of the Ardilliers continues to keep this presence of the sovereign until the Revolution.

Once the "Huguenot party" was eliminated by his father in 1629, Louis XIV wanted from his accession to power to restrict the freedom left to the protestants. His representatives, such as Voysin de la Noiraye, superintendent of Tours from 1666 to 1671, show a keen anti-Calvinist zeal. He forbids the creation of a third Chair of theology in the Academy, and seeks to expel the foreign teachers. From 1671, he declares himself favourable to the suppression of reformed worship in Saumur, and suggests that the Protestant college and its library should be given to the Oratorians.

The peak of this rivalry which we will talk about later – took place at the time of the revocation of the Edict of Nantes, in 1685. But the "mission" of the sanctuary of the

---

[1021] HUBAC J. "La paix d'Ales…Huguenot (1629) Paris Les Editions de Paris- Max Chaleil 2010.

Ardilliers is not finished, since in 1695 Louis XIV had an inscription placed in bronze inside the dome of the chapel, to celebrate his victory over the protestants, for both those of the kingdom and those from outside belonging to the League of Augsburg:

"In the year 1695, the piety of the Great King to the Virgin Mother of God, Louis XIV, King of France and Navarre, destroyed the heresy in all his kingdom, and chased the wrongdoers by land and by sea".[1022]

Examples of judiciarised oppositions are proof of this. In 1679, on the occasion of the funeral of the rector of the academy of Saumur who was also the professor of theology, his body was carried by six proposes towards the cemetery of Bilanges, towards six hours in the evening. Now the reformed people at that time could only bury their dead at daybreak or nightfall and the cortege was limited to five people. An enquiry was set up: a [1023] witness saw 24 to 26 people and another saw 28 or 29, In 1684 the Capuchin Honore de Cannes came to take part in a mission in Saumur[1024] at the request of Mgr Henri Arnauld, and he obtained a ban on religious services of protestants for five weeks. The vicar general Joseph Grande notes in his memoirs that he did all that he could to touch the hearts of heretics who came willingly to his sermons where he always mixed in some feature of controversies, but strangely, without any fruit. In January 1685 ten months before the Edict of Fontainebleau, two decrees from the King's council supressed the academy and ordered the destruction of the temple. The small temple surrounding it was and some brass shrouds were gutted.

[1022] POPMDCXCV "Deparae VIRGINIS Ludovicus XIV Dei Gratia Franc et Navare.

[1023] LEBRUN F. "Saumur au XVIIe siècle" art.cit.p 46.

[1024] On Father Honore de Cannes see MAES B "Missions et grands sanctuaires. …XVIIIe siecles" C.SORREL Chambery Institut d'etudes savoiennes 2091 p 177-186.

The series of baroque miracles, recorded in writing after an enquiry had another argument against the reformed people. It revealed the glory of God and His mother against the protestants and began in the year that Henry IV is the sacred King of France. The need to declare miracles, as it appears in "L'Histoire de l'origine" therefore begins in 1594 (where 14 miracles were recorded) and ends in 1713. The Oratorians settled in the Ardilliers in 1619, but one must wait for 1634 to see the first edition of "ll'Histoire de 'l'origine", that is fifteen years later. One may question the cause of this gap. The Oratorian Bareyre, who took part in the writing of this work, in ex-voto of a healed illness, is not a particularly brilliant person, and states in his declaration that he had to ask several times for the authorisation from his superiors[1025]. Now, this book of "L'histoire de l'origine" mediocre in terms of its shape and source, has been endlessly re0edited until in 1713 the Oratorians did not like its baroque sensitivity, for they come from the French School of spirituality, incarnated by their founder Berulle. The beginning of the text of the casual document of 1676, describing the miracle of Marie Le Brun, is revealing of their state of mind:

"Now that the Church is well established, that the faith has happily succeeded error, and infidelity, the works of the divine Almighty [the physical miracles] are no longer necessary[1026]".

However, they obey their bishop Henri Arnauld, who asks them to describe the miracle in a casual document. The Oratorians prefer to speak about the healing of hearts, graces which remain a secret between three people: God, the beneficiary, and the confessor.

A "Republic of Letters" in Saumur of the XVIIth century?

[1025] AM Saumur archive of the oratory III A 3 declaration of a miracle of Faher Francois Bareyre

[1026] AM Saumur archive of the Oratory IIIA 3, "Recit de la guerison…" op. vit.

There is a good understanding in Saumur between some Catholic and Protestant groups. The contacts between the two confessions are important, not only in the diocese of Angers, but for the whole of the region of the West. The directors show a good example. Religious dualism is well accepted. Duplessis-Mornay has good relations in the years 1620 with the magistrate Jean II Bonneau and the family of the Bourneaus. The town is consecrated to Notre Dame des Ardilliers at the time of the flood of the Loire in 1615, and there were few actions of intolerance. The governor Urbain de Maille-Breze, brother in law of Richelieu, had good relations with Moise Amyraut. In the years 1639-1680, Julien Avril, magistrate and mayor, a very strong Catholic and a powerful man, is satisfied with the Protestant presence and with the academy. He attends orals for theses by protestants and prize-givings. He allows the installation of Jan-Robert Chouet, even though he was born in Geneva[1027] Elie Brackenhoffer, an Alsatian Lutheran traveller, going to Saumur in the years 143-1644, notes in his journal:

"The Huguenots are here in a good position. They have their temple in the town and it is very beautiful. Their interments, their baptisms take place in daylight, they preach on Sundays and Wednesdays, however without bell-ringing or other means of convocation.[1028]

This respect is manifested by the erudite circle of Tinneguy le Fevre. This former Catholic is the pupil of the Jesuits [1029] a great Hellenist, he carries on a great network of correspondence with the erudite people of his time. The protestants attend his sermons for the Oratorians in the churches. In 1663, with a great many reformed people, especially Tanneguy le Fevre, go to listen to the sermons of

---

[102710271027] MAILLARD J. "L'Oratoire de Saumur et ls protestants..." art.cit. 129.
[1028] BRACKENHOFFER E. "Voyage en France" 1643-1644 trad. H.LEHR Strasbourg Berger-Levrault 1025 p 212.
[1029] LEBRUN F. "Saumur au XVIIe siècle..."art.cit. p 197.

the Oratorian Mascaron Saint-Pierre, in spite of the ban on pastors[1030].

The conferences on church history, given by the oratorians Louis Thomassin in the school of theology to the Ardilliers, from 1643 to 1654, are followed by the protestants[1031], maybe for purposes of controversy and conversion, but also for reasons of curiosity. In the same way, the orals of theses, with the Ardillliers and the academy, are followed by both publics. Sometimes, some and others of them ask questions and express their feelings. The time of aggressive controversies is over. Even if it is contrary to the spirit of the time and the very lively hostility of the Catholic clergy including Jansenists, against the reformed people, the professors put their points of convergence forward, rather than that which separates them. They are all impregnated with the mind of Saint Augustine. The contacts are fully witnessed for thirty years, from 1643 to 1674, and these high calibre individuals do not hide the mutual respect that they have. In 1674, the protestant Pierre de Villemandy, with several "people of the Religion", as they usually do, attended the theses heard by the students of Father Andre Martin[1032]. Pierre de Villemandy spoke to say "that there was no difference between his feelings on Justification and those of Father Martin"[1033] This causes an offensive to the Jansenists and Angevin anti-Cartesians against the fathers of the Oratory.

The climate of Saumur seems in some ways, irenic at the beginning of the third part of the XVIIth century, between the professors of the academy and the oratorians, A letter

---

[1030] MAILLARD J. "L'Oratoie de Saumur et les protestants"…art.cit.p 133.

[1031] MAILLARD J. "The oratory of Saumur and the protestants…" art.cit. p 133.

[1032] CLAIR E. "Louis Thomassin (1619-1695) Paris PUF 1964 p 24-27

[1033] BORGEAUD C. "Histoire de l;universite de Geneve….(1559-1798) Geneva Georg. 1900 p 415.

written by Jean-Robert Chouet in 1667, a young professor at the academy, wrote:

"Imagine, I ask you that I am in a town that is one of the most agreeable places and one of the politest in Europe, very convenient for my profession, on account of various people, and of the Religion and Roman Catholic, with whom I can confer in philosophy, that I am near Paris, which is certainly the source of people of letters and that thus I am informed about an infinity of things regarding the sciences and that I would know nothing about them if I were not here". [1034]

In 1670, Isaac d'Huisseau, pastor of Saumur from 1630 who became a professor in the academy, published a book entitled "La reunion de Christianisme de la manière de rejoindre tous les chretiens sous une meme confession de foi". This locali irenism, fed by the activity of some people founds a reciprocal tolerance on the "adiaphora",[1035] these questions considered not fundamental, on the rites and on discipline in particular. But d'Huisseau's book is condemned by the consistory of Saumur and by the provincial synod of Anjou.

The "positive anthropology" of Saumur (F Laplanche) is due firstly to[1036] the personality of Philippe Duplessis-Mornay, a humanist of the Renaissance as much as a convinced reformed person who wants to bring back the "papists" to the Gospel through the word. This governor of a strong place, friend of Henry IV, wanted to make Saumur an intellectual island of the French Reformation. For him, reasoning by the[1037] word or the pen could lead the Catholics to the truth.

[1034] STAUFFER R. "L'affaire d'Huisseau...chretiens (1670-1671) Pairs PUF 1969,

[1035] MAILLARD J. "'Oratoire de Saumur et les protestants",art.cit p 131.

[1036] DAUSSY H. "lLes Huguenots et le roi:...Duplessis-Mornay (1572-1600) Geneva Droz 20002.

[1037] LAPLANCHE F."Ladoctrine saumuroise...reliigeuse"
F.LEBRUN "Saumur capitale... op.cit. p 113-124.

6. NOVELLA PRIESTS AND PASTORS

P 274 PRIESTS AND PASTORS

Finally, the fourth reason which comes near Catholics and protestants, is the idea of Descartes, a former pupil of the Jesuits in La Fleche college. In 1664, the Genevan Jean-Robert Chouet reports that the Catholics, who made up the audience at the time of the examination for candidates for a professor's chair, had strongly applauded his ability to win a difficult competition.

There was truly a "Republic of Letters" in Saumur in the XVIIth century, between the professors in Saumur and those of the School of Theology, especially from 1650 from 1650 to 1675. Both religious reforms have the same causes, their oppositions have been insisted upon too much. True research into the truth was the same among a great many members of a professional body. But it is another logic which has carried it away, that of people outside Saumur, who acted for the unity of the kingdom around the King's religion. It is made up of pilgrims, of the Bishop of Angers, but particularly of the court and Louis XIV, who instrumentalised the Catholic religion against the benevolence and freedom advocated by the professors, who imposed the revocation of the Edict of Nantes in 1685.

***

[1038]

[1039] AN TT 266 "Relation succinct et faible de la reception…octobre 1655"

The Constitution of Clerical identities.
Father Paolo Vergerio:
Minister or Bishop of Vicosoprano?
Pastoral models and ecclesiastics who were concurrent in the Italian-speaking Grisons
(1549-1553)
Federico Zuliani

This contribution dwells on a particular feature – and relatively unknown by historians – of the four years that Father Paolo Vergerio spent as a reformed pastor in Vicosoprano, a small village in the Grisons[1040]. It is a matter of finding out If he was then changed into a Minister or into a Bishop. Having briefly presented the years as minister of Vergerio, who leaned on the use of the term "bishop" when he talks about himself, then on the role of bishops at that time, and finally how much he is presented in the writings of Vergerio written at that time, and finally on his pastoral approach. The hypothesis of leaving, based on a first analysis of sources, is that Vergerio, who was a Catholic Bishop before his flight to Italy, was also acting as a bishop during his activity as a reformed minister in Vicosoprano. Therefore one must see if such an attitude was simply the fact of Vergerio's experience, or if it was based on another interpretation, protestant, of this role.

This study is integrated into a greater framework. In fact I want to present some results which, even though partial, could throw light on his particular problem and, more generally. Could enrich a wider discussion on the episcopal models which were present in a space like the Grisons where several pastoral and episcopal models which were present in a space like the Gtisons, where several pastoral and ecclesiastical traditions -Catholic, Zwinglian and Calvinist – meet each other, often in open opposition ,some

---

[1040]. Translated from English by JULIEN LEONARD.Thanks to Stefano SIMIZ for his previous help in translating passages into Italian.

in relation to the others[1041] These models, it will be seen, cannot be limited to a simple dichotomy between Catholics and protestants, but were formed by different influences and by bitter struggles, including at the heart of the two officially recognised confessional denominations. These different models are particularly well known as regards Catholicism (torn in this area by various competitors between the dioceses of Come, Coire and Milan). They should be studied more on the protestant side which was also torn between the models which were difficultly conciliable with the Churches of Zurich and Geneva, but also touched by external influences, such as Lutheranism and Anabaptism.

Vergerio in the Grisons

Father Paolo Vergerio was born in Capodistria, a town on the border with Venice.[1042] He died in 1565, in Tubingen[1043]. In the 1539's and at the beginning of the 1540's, he was the pontifical nuncio at the imperial court in Vienna and became famous in Italy and in Europe as a fervent defender of the need for a general council. From 1535to 1549, he occupied the main episcopal seat of his native town, where he stayed for four years. But in 1548, a process of the Holy Office[1044] for heresy opened against him in Padua[1045], and at the beginning of 1549, he left Italy to settle finally in Vicosoprano, a small village in an Italian-speaking areas of the Grisons, where he was elected minister of the local reformed Church. Vergerio lived until 1553 when, in the summer of that year, he accepted the offer

---

[1041][1041] See research in Dipartimenti di Studi Stoici (Milan) "Pastor "LODOCAT – (ANR "Pastoral models".

[1042] Now Koper, in Slovenia.

[1043]

[1044] FERRAI L.A. "Il processo di Pier Paolo Vergerio" L.A.FERRAI, Studo stprici {adua, Fratelli Drucker 1892 p 88-173., and

SIXT C.H."Petrus Paulus Vergerio …monographie" Brunswick Schwetschke und Sohn,1855

of Duke Christophe de Wurtemberg to become his counsellor and settled in Germany[1046]. From his flight from Italy until his death, Vergerio was a celebrity in the whole of Europe for his indefatigable work as writer and editor of protestant books and pamphlets, both in Italian and in Latin [1047].

Thanks particularly to an anonymous text published between the end of December 1549 and the beginning of January 1550 (and which was not until very recently attributed to him) we can certainly put forward the opinion that Vergerio's departure from Italy was not to settle in the Alps[1048]. On the contrary he was [1049]heading for Germany. As with a great many Italians, before and after him[1050]. Vergerio returned to the Grisons due to their proximity to Italy [1051]and their accessibility both to Milan and the lands of Serenissism. The Grisons, for a great number of Italian protestants, constituted a natural first stage for a longer journey which from there leads hem towards Swiss, French, even English and Polish towns[1052]. The however, are not then a territory like the others, especially on account of their unequalled ecclesiastical situation.

The Graubunden, literally "Grey Leagues" in the Grisons or Grisonists, in fact constituted a confederation of

---

[1046] KAUSLER E.H. VON and SCHOTT T. "Briefwechel …Vergerius" Tubingen E. Laupp 1875.

[1047] PIERCE RA Pier Paolo Gergerio": Propaandistu Rome Edizioni fdi Storia e Letteratura 2003 Gottingen Vandenhoeck & Rupreacht 1993.

[1048] VERGERIO P.P. "del battesimo…grisoni" ZULIANI F. !Quaderni ..Storia" no. 35 2014 p 29-60.

[1049] CALVIN J. "Johannis Calvini…omnia" Brunswick CA. Schwetschke vol 13 88

[1050] CALVIN J, "Johannnis Calvini opera…omnia" G.BAUM Brunswick v 13 1888 col. 448 Gribaldi to Calvin 15.11.1549

[1051] ROTONDO A."Esuli Iraliani in Valtellina nel Cinquecento" Revista storica italiana no 88,1976 p 756-791 .

[1052] CHUECH E.C. "I reormaoi italiani" Flrence La Nuova Italia 1935 2 vols Milan Il Saggiatore

three republics or cantons. While very strongly tied to the Confederation pf the thirteen cantons, and particularly to Zurich[1053]. By economic connections and treaties of defensive alliance, these leagues were not less fiercely independent. From 1526, by virtue of the promulgation of the Articles of Ilanz,, the Catholic and reformed confessions were both recognised as legal and enjoyed an equivalent status[1054]. All the men and all the women, at the same time among the citizens and among the subjects, were thus free to choose their religious confession among these two options) Anabaptism, on the other side, was still illegal). Even if The Grauer Bund (Grey League) and the Zehngerichtebund (League of the Ten Jurisdictions) were mainly in German and romance, some valleys in the Gotteshausbund (League of Maison-Dieu) were peopled with Italian speakers[1055]. One mainly found there local populations or immigrants from Italy[1056]. Vicosoprano, the village where Vergerio settled after his election as minister, was the economic and administrative capital of the Val Bregaglia, one of the valleys where the great majority of the local population had converted to Protestantism.

In the small booklet mentioned from 1549-1550, Vergerio describes to his former faithful flock of Istria the reasons for his sudden decision not to continue his journey towards Germany, but to stay in the Grisons. What made him change his plans, was the discovery that these Churches share "this same purity and simplicity" of the apostolic Church[1057]. In spite of his initial optimism and favourable bias, Vergerio however quickly realised the reality of his

---

[1053] SCHIESS T. "Die Beziehungen …Jarhundert"" no. 27 1902,p 29-194.

[1054] LIVER P. "DieIlanze Artikl "Jahrsbericht der …Graubunden no. 59 p 1-136.

[1055] HEAD R.C. "Early Modern Democracy in the Grisons…Canton" 1470-1620 Cambridge CUP 2002.

[1056] CAMENISCH E. "Geschichte der Reformation…Bormio, Coire Bicshofberger 1950.

[1057] VERGERIO P.P. "Del battesimo et de fumi…" fol. A2r

new church. He had not come to a new Jerusalem, he had not fallen into an apostolic church of the first century. To his great surprise, at Vicosoprano "new antichrists, many wolves in sheeps' clothing, a great many false brothers" not only among t[1058]he Catholics, but also his reformed faithful people and the members of his Church.

That became particularly clear if one relies on some catechisms that Vergerio published in Switzerland[1059]. One of the texts is particularly significant in this sense, especially when one reads the two editions, which include from one to the other very revealing changes. In 1549, some months after his arrival. and when he still intends to go to Germany, Vergerio published his "Instruttione christiana"[1060]. It is a very general catechism, not addressing any Church in particular, and intended for circulation in Italy. In the following year, the text is published again under the title, this time, of "Uno brieve, et semplice modo per informare le fanciulli, nella religione Christiana. Fatto per uso Chiesa di Vicosoprano et de gl'altri luochi di valle Bregaglia". As this title shows, the new edition is more specifically intended by Vergerio for the new church of Vicosoprano. The additions which were brought in show very clearly everything that was not expected to be found among the faithful flock, and which he deplores: among other things, fornication, perseverance in some Catholic practic[1061]es and beliefs, a general rebel attitude towards the ecclesiastical authorities.

[1058] Zentralbibliothek Zurich ms F 40 fol 563v Pier Paolo Vergerio to Rudolf Gwalther Vicosoprano 13.09.1550 "multi sunt Antichristi".

[1059] CAVASSA S. "Quell oche Giesu Christo…Evangelio" METODI E RICERCHE N.S. NO. 18 1998 P 3-22/

[1060] ZULIANA F. "Un catechismo perduro …Vergerio" "Bibliotheque d'Humanism et Renaissance" v 75-3 2013 p 463-497.

[1061] Zentralbibliohek Zurich ms F. fol. 562 r letter from Vergerio to Gwalther,Basle,26.07.1551 "fuor ddi pericolic della Retia".

At the beginning of the year 1550, Vergerio is already not more comfortable in the heart of his community. In the following year the problems persist: in July 1551, Vergerio thus presses Rudolf Gwalther to help him, by his letters of recommendation, to find a new position in the Bernese lands "far from the dangers of the Rhetia"[1062]. During these years, he also studies the possibility of settling in England[1063]. Through Bonifacius Amerbach, he contacts Christophe de Wurtemberg[1064]. Finally, at the end of 1553 he leaves his charge and tries to become the reformed minister in Sondrio, in the nearby Valteline, although he was warned of an epidemic of the plague. He spent a part of this year in Chiavenna, a Lombardian town which was then, like its neighbour Sondrio, under the authority of the Leagues of Grisons. At that time, violent polemics burst out[1065] between him and Agostino Mainardi, the minister of Chiavenna. The main point of the dispute is a new catechism that Vergerio had published. Mainardi goes as far as writing to Bullinger in Zurich to prevent the risk of a reprint of the text. The later in fact present a Lutheran position of the eucharistic doctrine, but this is not the only problem at play, as will be seen more precisely[1066].

A Bishop in the Grisons

If one leans towards the years that Vergerio spent in the Grisons, two elements are particularly striking: the people

---

[1062] SOWERBY T.A. "Renaissance und Reform
...England..Morison" c.1513-1556 Oxford OUP 2010 p 216.
[1063] CHURCH F.C. "I riformatori italiani
2 op.cit. p 334-337.
[1064] ARMAND HUGON A. "Agostino Mainardo...inItalia" Torre Pellice Societa di Sudi Valdesi Rome Instituto dell Enciclopedia Italiana vol LXVII 2006 p 585-590. (1553)
[1065] ZULIANA F. "I contrasti tra e mAINARDO circa un catechism riformato per la Valtellina (153) "Rivista di Storia della Chiese in Italia" 2015 p 49-78,
[1066] SCHIESS T. "Bullingers Korespndent..." op. cit. vol 1 p 145 letter from Mainardo to Bullinger Chiavenna 15.05.1549.

continue to address him by calling him a bishop, and he maintained this usage. It is in a certain surprising manner that one can find out that several Protestants - including the protestants who were sincerely convinced that he was no longer a Catholic, but had embraced Protestantism addressed Vergerio as bishop. For example, that is the case of fervent protestants such as Agostino Mainardi[1067], Baldassare Altiere[1068]., or even Johannes Comander[1069], the list being doubtless somewhat longer. Moreover, one must emphasise that when Vergerio matriculated in the University of Basle in 1550, no doubt in order to move into the bourgeoisie of the city or in a teaching position, he was registered as "reverendus dominus episcopus Justinopolitanus"[1070]. Vergerio is not the only Italian bishop of the XVIth century having embraced the ideas of the Protestant Reformation or being considered as a heretic [1071]by the Roman authorities. However, he is the only one to have left Italy. This particularity could suggest that the representatives of Vergerio used this title, in addressing him, either because they did not know want to do in this case, uniquely by courtesy. However, when Celio Curione wrote to Bullinger in January 1550 asking himself "What should be said about our Vergerio who lately wore the mask of a bishop, and now he is really a bishop of the Church of

---

[1067] Ibid p 475 letter ti Altieri to Bullinbger, Poschiavo 5 August 1549.

[1068] ARBENZ E. and WARTMANN H. "die Vadianishe …S Gallen" Saint-Gall Huber & co. vol 6 p 802 letter from Comander to Joachim Vadian, Coire 6.06.1549.

[1069] BUSINO g. "italiani all'Universita di Basiliea dal 1460 al 1601""'Bibliotheque d'Humanisme et Renaissance" v 20-3, 1958 p 524.

[1070] Vittore Soranzo and Jacopo Nacchianti are among the most famous cases but the list could be longe e.g. Giovanni Batista Vergerio Bishop of Pola andbrother of Pier aolo

[1071] Qupted in BIASIORI L. "L'uomo scaltro" Celio Secondo Curione Pietro Paolo Vergerio "Bibliotheque d'humanisme et Renaissance v 72-2 2010 p 394.

Christ, his sincere servant and a man who should be venerated in every way"[1072], the expression "now really a bishop of the Church of Christ" can with difficulty be considered as simply honorary.

When one turns towards public works, one realises also that on several occasions Vergerio calls himself a bishop even if, in spite of his excessive activity, several of his works are anonymous. In 1549 for example he signed the pamphlet Oratione de perseguitati et fuorusciti per lo evangelio et per Giesu" in this manner: "Vergerio, by the grace of God Bishop of Christ"[1073]. It is in some way surprising to find out that several protestants – including protestants who are sincerely convinced that he was no longer a Catholic, and

had embraced Protestantism, addressing himself in Vergerio as a bishop. This is the case for example of fervent pastors such as Agostino Mainardi[1074], Baldassare Altiere[1075], or even Johannes Comander[1076], the list doubtless was much longer. Also, one must emphasise that when Vergerio matriculated in the University of Basle in 1550, no doubt in order to enter the bourgeoisie of the city or a teaching position, he is registered as "reverendus

---

[1072] CAVAZZA S. "Pier Paolo Vergerio nei Grigioni..." art.cit.p 42 "Vergerio per la Dio gratia vescovo di Christo"

[1073] [CALVIM J.J. Apologia dello Illustre Giacobo di Burgundia ...rende conto della sua fede [Geneva][Jean Girard] 1550 VERGERIO P.P. Dodici trattatelli ...dall'Italia [Basle] Giacomo Parco] 1550

[1074] SCHIESS T. Bullingers Korrespondence...op.cit.vol 1 p 145 letter from Mainardo to Bullinger Chiavenna 15.05.1549.

[1075] Ibid.p 475 letter from Altieri to Bullinger Poschiavo 3.08.1549.

[1076] ARBENZ E. and WARTMANN H "Die Vadianische...St. Gallen", St Gall Huber & co vol 6 1908 letter from Comander to Joachim Vadian..Coire 6.06.1549.

dominus episcopus Justinopolitanus"[1077]. Vergerio is not the only Italian bishop of the XVIth century having embraced the ideas of the protestant Reformation or being considered as a heretic by the Roman authorities. However he is the only one to have left Italy[1078].

This particularity could suggest that the speaking to Vergerio used this title, in addressing him either because they did not know what to do in such a case, or uniquely by courtesy. However, when Celio Secondo Curione wrote to Bullinger in January 1550 asking "What to say about our [1079]Vergerio who formerly wore the mask of a Bishop, and is a true Bishop of the Church of Christ" can with difficulty be considered as simply honorary now such a Bishop of the Church of Christ, his sincere servant and a man who should be venerated in every way", the expression "now truly bishop of the church of Christ" can with difficulty be considered as purely honorary"

When one turns towards his public works, one realises that on some occasions, Vergerio calls himself a bishop, even of in spite of his exessive activity, several of his works are anonymous. In 1549 for example, he signs the pamphlet "Oratione de perseguitati et fuor[1080]usciti per lo evangelio et per Giesu Christo" in this way: Vergerui, by the grace of God bishop of Christ. On the title page on a translation by Calvin into Italian, as well as in his "Dici Trattaelli" and his "Otto Defensioni" published in 1440, Vergerio is "Bishop

---

[1077107710177] BUSINO G. "Italiani all'Universita di Basilea dal 1460 to 1601" Bubliotheque d'Humanisme et Renaissance v 20-3 1958 p 524i

[1078] Vittore Soranzo and Jacopo Nacchianti are among the most famous cases the list is long.

[1079]

[1080] CAVAZZA Si. "Pier Paolo Vergerio nei Grigioni…" art.cit. p 42 "Vergerio …Christo".

of Capodistria[1081]. Two years later[1082]er, in his treatise against his old friend Friedrich Nausea, he presents himself as "Bishop Vergerio" while the next year, in publishing a translation of the confession of faith of German princes, he signs again "your Vergerio Bishop of Christ by the grace of Gd£[1083]

Contrary to the correspondence, these treatises constitute "public" documents. The use of the term "vescovo", bishop, is therefore deliberate and cannot be considered as a simple language mistake or an old habit. In order to understand the reasons which guided these precise choices, it is essential to analyse what are Vergerio's ideas about episcopacy.

Vergerio and the episcopacy

If one focuses on the works of Vergerio, it appears clearly that, during his Swiss years, his reflection on the episcopacy is really placed at the heart of his theological and pastoral thought. The interest for this theme is however rather older. The previously quoted small anonymous book from 1549-1550 is finished by a long passage on the figure of the bishop. Vergerio advances that several functions attributed to the bishop are not apostolic, especially the consecration of the holy water for baptism and the sacrament of confirmation, of which he here denies the apostolic origin. The most interesting part in this passage - the Italian protestants and his faithful people remaining in Istria- and he emphasises: "You want a simple priest to baptise, but does not confirm, and you reserve this enterprise of greater value in the hands of a bishop and that

---

[108110811081] [CALVIN J.] "Apologia dello Illustre…Carlo V Imperatore della sua fide [Geneva] Jean sua fiede 1550.

[1082] VERGERIO P.P. Risposta del vescovo di …Concilio" Poschiavo [dolphin Landolfi] 1552.,

[1083] Confessione della
, Tiningrn [ulrich Morhatt] 1553 fol (L9) "il vostro Vergerio vescovo di Christo Deo gratia"pia dopttrina…Concilio de Trento

is enough[1084].". Vergerio's critics show that the group that he had led to avoid denial, at least up to that time, the very existence of bishops, and even thought that the consecrated bishops had the legitimate authority to celebrate certain ceremonies. The Istrian peninsula was then perhaps the only Italian region where Lutheranism, and not Calvinism, was able to take root, and now moreover after the 1540's[1085]. It therefore seems probable that such an interpretation was the consequence of this local Lutheran influence. In fact the Lutherans did not deny the apostolic nature of the [1086]episcopal functions and, in certain Lutheran areas, the episcopacy was never abolished.

The reflections and considerations about the episcopacy are dispersed into several works of Vergerio during the years 1549-1553.Without being able to claim exhaustivity here, two books seem particularly to arise from this subject. [1087]They are "Al serenissimo re d'Inghilterrra Eduardo Sesto, de portamento di Papa Giulio III (November 1550)[1088]and the "Rispsta ad un libro del Nausea" (1552). One must emphasise that the two works were written in two years, at a time when one can decently suppose that Vergerio precisely knows the specific religious situation of the Italian-speaking Italian Besides, the second work explicitly goes back to the first one[1089], which makes them a type of diptyque.

[1084] [VERGERIO P.P.] "Del batteismo et de fiumi …op.vit.fol.a5r.

[1085] CAPONETTO S. "La Reforma protestante nell'italia…Cinquecento", Turin, Claudiana 1997 p 65-68.

[1086] KLAUS W. "Episcopacy" H.J. HILLEBRAND "The Oxford Encyclopaedia of the Reformation" New York – Oxford OUP 1996 vol 2 p 51-54.

[1087] See above, =and see JEDIN H. "Die Deutschen an Truenter Jibzuk 1551-52 Historische Zeitschrif no. 188 1959 p -16

[1088] VERGERIO P,P, Al serenissimo re a Inghilterra …Giulio III [Dolphin Landolfi] 1550.

[1089] VERGERIO P.P. "Risposta…" op. cit. p XXXIII.

Writing to Edward VI of England about the Council of Trent, Vergerio explains that there are two types of bishop: those who "were elected by the popes, or at least confirmed and anointed, and mitred[1090]" and those who "were so by the consensus of the city, elected by the people, and have not received any anointing other than that of the Holy Spirit"[1091].

While the first are sunken into superstitions and idolatry through and through[1092], the second "have neither mitre nor sandals and are poor,and take care to preach the pure doctrine of the Gospel and to oppose contrary elements[1093]. Those who belong to the second group are "the true bishops"; they are "learned and pious"[1094], and however, they do not sit on the council. In fact, if they had appeared at Trent, they "would not have been received to the council" and hey would have undergone the same joke as that played to on Jerome of Prague and to Jan Hus at the Council of Constance[1095].Aiming at refuting the Catholic positions on the possibility of welcoming the laity into the Council[1096]. Vergerio leans on the history of the ancient church. He emphasises that it is not true, as the Catholics claim, that in the ancient times "only the bishops" had "decisive voices", because others were found who had them, who were not bishops[1097]. But Vergerio strongly underlines another point. Along the following lines, we can in fact read that "the ministers of the churches of Germany, England and Swiss

---

[1090] VERGERIO P.P. "Al serenissimo re..." op. cit. "furono da Papi eletti...et mitrato".

[1091] Ibic,fol Dijr- Dijv "Furono del consent della citta...spirio santo".

[1092] Ibid.fol.Dijr "Finoogli occhi immerse"

[1093] Ibid fol Dijv "Non usano mitre...contraire"

[1094] Ibid. "I veri Vescovi,

[1095] Ibid. "Non saranno...costantinense si fece"

[1096] See above, note 51.

[1097] [VERGERIO P.P. "Al serenissimo re..." op.it folmEv "Soli o vescovi...Vescovi".

cantons, can decide[1098], because they are bishops, and bishops such as those of the ancient councils, [1099]and especially those who were in Nicea, Constantinople, Ephesus and Chalcedonia. They can therefore be called bishop, ministers of the Church, preachers of the Wprd of Gods, since he "vescovi" who attended the ancient councils "were pastors of the people"[1100].At that time, in fact

"There were not [...] any bishops like our modern papists [papei] who wear mitres. Pastoral clothing, sandals or even shoes, who bless the oils, who polish the stones, and baptise the bells, who, once the churches were left in the hands of mercenaries, run all day long behind the Cardinals, and for adoring the popes living un delight, in so many vices and so many abominations[1101].

The main distinguishing point according to Vergerio "I veri Vescovi" of the old times and the papist bishops of his time, is that the first ones themselves ordinarily elected the bishops and ministers, and those who were not elected by the welcome of citizens and confirmed by neighbouring bishops were not known or regarded as legitimate bishops and ministers[1102].

The Catholic bishops of his time, as a result, "are not bishops" or rather "are only bishops in name"[1103]. In a polemic manner, Vergerio addresses the Roman bishops directly and asks them: "How can you not be ashamed to consider yourselves as the successors of the Apostles?"[1104]"

When he leans over what he wrote to Bishop Nausea two years later, one realises that, in the interval, Vergerio has not changed his position. On the contrary, his ideas on the question have become strong convictions. The tone is

---

[1098] Ibid, "I minisrire...op.cit. fol.E v "soli I vescovi...dexidere"
[1099] Ibid. "I"sono Vescovi ...nel Cancedonese".
[1100] Ibid."Furono pastori de ministry ..parole di Dio".
[1101] Ibid Non vi erano [...] Vescovi simili...abominarioni".
[1102] Ibid.fol.Eijr "[n] gli antichi et meglior tempo...approvati"
[1103] Ibid. fol. Eijv "Non sono Vescovi sed no di nome"
[1104] IIbid. Fol. [Eiv]v "Come non..gli Apostoli/?"

rough, as often happens with Vergerio, and even defamatory. The Roman Catholic bishops are "small bishops"[1105], "mitred creatures"[1106], "papist bishops" or "popes" "[1107]. In one place, Vergerio asks:

"Are they nothing but masks? Or bishops only in name? Who elected them? Certainly not the cities nor the peoples according to the commandment of their laws, but the tyranny of a Roman bishop [...] What doctrine do they follow? What life do they have? A life consecrated to guiding the souls? Or do they teach the Gospel? When do they administer the sacraments according to the order of Christ? Thus therefore if they are not legitimately elected, if they do not have all the other qualities that I i have described, if they depend upon a false leader, I say that they [1108]are not bishops, that they are not judges, that they are not on the Council.

In this work, Vergerio does not explain in detail either the foundations of the idea that he expresses, since he has already done so in "one of the long letters to the very Christian King of England "£[1109], nor the reasons for which the protestant bishops are "legitimate bishops and ministers[1110]. However he explains that "we are not either cardinals, nor patriarchs, nor abbots, nor provosts, nor archbishops, nor bishops, I mean papist bishops, and consecrators with your oils "but (thanks be to God) we are bishops and pastors and consecrators of his spirit"[1111].

One may therefore resume that for Vergerio, "I veri Vescovi" must be poor, live in the middle of their flock and, even more important, preach the Gospel and administer the

---

[1105] VERGERIO P.P. "Risposta..." op.cit. p VII "Vescovetti".
[1106] Ibid. p XVIII "Creature mitrate"
[1107] Ibid p XLII "Vescovi supersitiosi".
[1108] IBID p LIX "Sono esso altro...concilio"
[1109] Ibid. p XXXIII "Una mia lunga epistola...d' Inghiltterra"
[1110] Ibid. "Vescovi, et ministry legitimi"
[1111] Ibid " p XXXII "Noi non siamo ne cardinali...suo spirito unti"

sacraments. At the highest level of his requirements, the "veri vescovi" must be elected by their own community. The analysis really seems to explain what Vergerio thinks when, in his works, he calls himself "vescovo". He does so not because he was consecrated several years before as Bishop of Capodistria by the Pope, ten years after his nomination, as he describes himself in one of his writings[1112], but because the church of Vicosoprano elected him as minister, Vergerio knows that this treatise will be read by the Catholic controversists aiming to find angles of attack against him. For this reason, it is particularly important to note that, speaking about the "vescovi, et ministri legitimi" he writes "noi" "we", therefore including himself: in the same order of ideas, in the title of his book, he calls himself "vescovo Vergerio".

This specific instruction of the bishop [1113] as an expression of a precise Christian community one finds a supplementary confirmation in the fact that, after the beginning of 1553, when he abandoned his charge as minister of Vicosoprano, Vergerio also abandoned the title of bisho[1114]p. In 1554, he adopted instead the Paulinian formulation of "server of Christ[1115], "servo di Jesu Christo, "servo di Christo"[1116] or even "Servus Jesu Christi" When in 1555 a new edition of his "Oratione de perseguitati ...evangelio (1549) by the grace of God Bishop of Christ" is withdrawn. According to Vergerio's own criteria, at that time he is no longer a bishop.

[1112] VERGERIO P.P. "Retrattione {Tubingen] [I;roch Morhai] 1556 fol A4rv.

[1113]

[1114] ATAN [VERGERIO P.P. "Fra Leandro Bolognese [Tubingen] [Ulrich Morhart] 1554 fol.A1v

[1115][1115] "Paul, serviteur du Christ Jesus,apotre par vocation ...il signe "servitor " not "servo", declined "servo di Jesu Christo

[1116][1116] VERGERIO P.P. "Retrattatione" op.cit.
]D4]r.VERGERIO P.P. "De idolo luretano [Tibingen] [Ulrich Morhat] fol.Aiijv.

.

One must emphasise that Vergerio's ideas on the episcopacy are not unique among the Italian protestants in the Grisons. For example, even his main example, Mainardo, in his "Anatomia della Messa" or the same time (1552) states that the "office" of bishops is "to teach people and preach to them", and that since the contemporary Catholic bishops "have abandoned him and still let things be done by others", such clerks have shown that "they are not bishops, assuredly they are not, other than by name". In fact, if t[1117]hey were true bishops, they would not be ashamed to do their work "

Behaving as a bishop and its consequences

Now that we have seen what Vergerio had in mind by calling himself a bishop, it remains to analyse whether he behave, during his ministry, as a bishop. Here, however, I do not understand "bishop" in the meaning that Vergerio gives to this word, but in the more traditional meaning of a pastor who oversees an ecclesiastical district and deals with it as a whole. When one leans more in detail on Vergerio's activity as a minister, it appears that he does not restrict himself to the only congregation that elected him, but he oversees several other communities ad, even more important, he claims a form of authority on all the other Reformed Churches of the Val Bregaglia (up to December 1552) and Valteline (from January 1553) [1118]. For example, he is in close contact with several ministers, preaches sermons in Casaccia[1119], and in Bondo[1120]; he takes part in

---

[1117] ANTONIO DI ADAMO [MAINARDO A.] "Annatomia della messa 1552 fol.A5rv.

[1118] Rosius a Porta spoken, for Vergerio, of a "episcopales […] spiritus" see ROSIUS A PORTA P. D. "Historia Reformationis…" op.cit. vol 1,book 2, p 154..

[1119] Zentralbibliothek Zurich ms.F 40 fol 557 rv, letter from Vergerio to Gwalther, Vicosoprano, 15 May 1551.

[1120] (ZONCA G.) "Della statue et imagini" s.l.1553 fol.A3rv/ It must be noted that Vergerio acts in opposition with the ecclesiastical tradition of the region. Vicosoprano is richest town in the region. See NOSCHELE.R . "Die

the abolition of the mass in Samedan[1121] and in Souz[1122], both in Engadine. He is implicated in the propagation of the Reformation in the Val Malenco[1123]. He also, very probably, tries to uniformise the liturgies of the different communities of the Val Bregaglia, even of all the Italian-speaking Grisons[1124]. Beyond that, in some public [1125]works, Vergerio continues to act as if he were the spokesman of the whole Val Bregaglia. This is for example the case of "La terra di Vico Soprano",Pope Giulio III said, and even more explicitly in his Orarione che dovea…passare", both in 1552. There, he addresses his reader with these words: "Let us consider that all the members and brothers of other Reformed Churches speak with you through my mouth"[1126]. In fact. Already, his "Brieve, et semplice modo per informare lii Fanciulli (1550)" [1127]states, in its title that the catechism is not only designed by Vergerio's Church, but also for "the other places in the valley of Bregaglia"[1128]

Vergerio acts in the same way when he leaves going to Valteline at the beginning of 1553. Before that date, he was busy with local communities, although that was forbidden by the law:

Gotteshauser der Schweis…" vol 1,bisthum Chur Zurich Orell, Fussli & co 1864 p 116-117.

[1121] CAMPELL U. "Historia Rhaetica ed. PLATTNER P. basle Adolf Geering vol 2 p 116-117

[1122] SCHIESS T "Bullinges Korrespondenz…" op. cit.vol 1 p 259-260 letter from Vergerio to Bullinger 22.08.1552.

[1123] Ibid. p 167 letter from Giovanni Beccaria in Bullinger Coire 5 June 1550.

[1124] [VERGEROP P.P.] "Oratione che doveaesser…passae" [Poschiavo] [dolph Landofi [152] fol,.Alir"

[1125] ATANASIO [VERGERIIO P.P,.] "Delle commissioni…Grisoni [Tubingen] 1554 Ulrich morhart]] fol A6r

[1126] ZULIANA F. "Un caechismo perduto…" art,cit. p 479-380. This subject will soon be the themef of a specific article.

"It is true that during the prohibition we could however sometimes go there and, in some private homes, he preached Jesus Christ, as in secret and among some people".

Some months later "after abandoning the ministry of Vicosoprnano" he goes to Valteline and describes his activity, thus; "I settled myself in order to live, preach, expose books and give Communion and everything [1129]that, summing up, I knew and could do[1130]. It is still the case when he publishes in1553, "Fondamento della religione christiana per uso della Valtelina[1131]. As the title suggest, Vergerio is not addressing only one Church, but the whole of Valteline. Then on account of the fierce opposition of Mainardo - who recalls Bullinger: "we have our catechisms"[1132]". Vergerio publishes the work by stating that it is aimed uniquely at the Churches who recognise his authority: Fondamento della religione christiana per uso di quella parte di Valtelina, dove ministra Athnasio (Athanasio, or Atanasio, is his notorious pen name[1133]. Mainardo,however[1134], is not fully satisfied, for what he contests is that Vergerio can claiim such an authority?"

Vergerio must face fairly strong local opposition. We have already seen the mention of Antechrist" "wolves" and "false brothers" in his community, but it is rather on account

---

[1129]

[1130] Ibid fol [A6] v "Lasciato il ministerio di Vicosuproano...otea".

[1131] Ibis. 1554 fol.A6r. "Lasciato il miniserio...et tra pochi"...et potea"

[1132] SCHIESS T. "Bllingers Korrespondenz..." op.cit.vol/1 p 319 letter frpmMainardo to Bulliger Chiavenna 3 September 1553, "(h)abemus nostros catechismos".

[1133113311331133] [VERGERIO P.P.] Fondamento della Religione Chrisinnnnama...Athanasio (Tubngrn [Ulrich Morart 1553.

[1134] SCHIESS T. "Bullinger Korespondenz op.cit vol.1, p 318
(a) Vergerio se nolleministrum evangeli...vult obtrudedre?
CANTIMORI D. "Eretici italiani...op.cit. ROTONDO A .
"Esuli italiani " art.cit Coire, Archivio di Stato e aibliotecaCantonale dei rigioni 1978.

of his catechism "in the usage of Valtelline" and for his action there, that in the end he must leave the area. However, he benefits greatly from a great many supports: ministers who invite him to preach, or who accept his presence among the faithful flock. For him, as for many other protestant ministers, but also, laymen the main problem is to find an effective means of converting those who have remained Catholic and at the same time to strengthen the Churches which are already reformed. secretly. I think that this aspect of Vergerio's activity can be explained, by the fact that this area is at the crossroads of different ecclesiastical and pastoral models.

Concurrent pastoral models

To begin, one must state that Vergerio's strong convictions are without doubt. For him, as for many other protestants, ministers and laity, the main problem is to find an effective means for converting those who remained Catholics and strengthen the Churches that were already reformed. One must also state that the Italian-speaking Grisons are an area that knows a strong presence of "sectarians", antitrinitarians and Anabaptists, who for several reasons (and particularly because only Catholic and reformed confessions are legal) often join the local reformed communities. As a result, a great part of Vergerio's activity and other ministers is devoted to the strengthening of the ecclesiastical discipline. However, the means of attaining this goal are the subject of debates.

Unfortunately, the current knowledge on the composition of the Italian Churches of the Grisons and their inner life is much too superficial. No doubt the question would deserve a systematic study in the future. It would be particularly interesting to lean on their composition of a prosopographic point of view.[1135] They consist of local populations, but also of emigrants freshly arrived,

---

[1135] FIRPO M "PREFAZIONE".A.PASTORE "Nella Valtellina del tardo conquecento. Fede, cultura,sociea, " Rome Viella 2015 p

"religionis causa". In spite of their common faith and language, these two groups doubtless partook of few things and evolved in very different contexts. As regards Vergerio, it sems possible to state that his activity took root in a Catholic terrain. He was a bishop and, for four years, from 1541 to 1544, [1136]he tried to reform his own diocese according to methods which were close to those introduced in the Grisons, (sermons against idols, spread of "good books", work in proximity with his clergy etc,) doubtless he tried to copy in this way the success of his previous experience and to put his own skill at the service of his new Church".

More interesting still would be the hypothesis according to which the model created by Vergerio could be known and adaptable for others. I think this is particularly the case for emigrant Catholic clerks. For them- who in Italy were under the authority of bishops or abbots – the model of a more centralised control must seem relatively familiar and it is easy to adapt to it. That could explain why, among Vergerio's supports, one finds several reformed ministers who were clerks in Italy, as for example Guido Zonca or Pietro Perisotto, but also the Calvinist theologian Celso Martinengo (later minister of the Italian Church in Geneva) who recently fled Italy and who, during the few months that he spent in the Grisons, helped Vergerio in his pastoral duties in Vicosoprano[1137]. There are also those men who invited Vergerio to preach or ask him for help when iit happens to them that they had to fight against a Catholic opposition. Now a great many local protestants are recent converts and have problems in completely breaking

---

[1136] JACOBSON SCHUTTE A. "Pier Paolo Vergerio e la reforma…" op.it. p 242-202.

[1137] SCHIESS T. "Bullingers Korrespondenz …" op.cit. vol 1 p 239-240, letter from Vergerio to Bulllinger Vicosoprano 27.02.1552 at the time of Martinengo leaving

contacts with their old Catholic life[1138]. That could probably help to explain Vergerio's success. in Valteline..

At that time however, two other traditions are pregnant in the region: one more ancient, that of Zurich (via Coire)[1139] and the other more recent, that of Geneva. Contrary to the Catholic, these two models have a strong legitimacy among the protestants. Some years before, the two churches had established the famous "Consensus Tigurinus (1549)". A study of the implantation of the "Consensus" Italian-speaking Rhetie remains to be written and would be very useful. In fact, the region is one of the co-existence of very rare cases where reformed models coming from these two traditions, up to the same Churches. Although that rests on non-exhaustive witness of the sources, one may reasonably maintain that the original inhabitants of the area are closer to the Zurichan model. They are members completely separate from the Leagues, they recognise the authority of the general Diet, and are in commercial relations with German Switzerland where they often know the language. On the contrary, a significant share of the Italian immigrants – without including the sectarians" – is closer to Geneva, and the influence of the Genevan church in Italy at that time is well known[1140].

During the years where Vergerio is in the Grisons, the area is touched by a massive

immigration from Italy, a consequence of inquisitorial activity[1141] The influence, in the local churches, of these

---

[1138] ZULIANI F. "Un catechismo perduto e ritrovato…art.cit.p 468-471.

[1139] BONOBRAND C. "Lerelazzioni culturali …Swizzera tedesca" Archivio Lombardo s.9 no. 5-6 p 39-45 TAPLIN "The Italian Reformers…Church 1540-1629," Ashgate 2005

[1140] FELICI L "Giovanni Calvino e l'Italia" TurinClaudiana 2012

[1141] See for example tlhe letters from Vergerio to Gwalther (Zentralbibliohek Zurich ms. F 40 fol, 363 1,Vicosoprano 13.09.1550) and to Bullinger (Shiess T " op.cit vol 1 p 184 p 191 Vicosoprano 15 or 20.12.1550 nd 13.02/1551).

immigrants attracted by the Genevan model remains unknown. In a situation where the ministers are elected and revoked by the local communities, the weight of their presence must bot especially be under-estimated. One may obviously say that the pro-Genevan Italian laity do not show great sympathy for episcopalian solutions. On the contrary, they promote a Presbyterian model, which, in fact begins to come forth in these years. By way of opposition, the Zurichan approach is very different. For examp[e, one must emphasise that the name of "antistes" de facto attracted several figures of the episcopacy[1142]. It is not by chance that Bullinger continues to be called "episcopus" in his correspondence[1143]. From the Zurichan point of view, Vergerio's name of bishop and his episcopalian approach probably do not constitute a problem in itself. Vergerio's activity could in this sense be encouraged. It is for this reason that I think, contrary to other historians, that at the beginning of 1551 and at least for a brief moment, Vergerio was chosen by the authorities of Coire, narrowly linked to Zurich, as "visitor designated for the preachers" in order to reconcile Camillo Renato[1144]. These faithful people near Zurich probably constitute a significant share of the community of Vicosoprano, which elected him on leaving, and they could therefore have found his actions legitimate.

What seems very interesting to me, is that, in the letters which I have found, Vergerio never mentions the presence

---

[1142] BALTISCHWEILER W. "Die Institutionen der evangelisch-reformierren ...Entwitwicklung" Zurich Schulthess & Co 1905.

[1143] For IItalians using this name in referring to Bujllinger, see for example the letters from Renato, Mainardo and Bartolomeo Paravicini. The name, however, is also systematically used by the reformed clergy of Coire,as with Johannes Blasius,Johannes Comander eand Philippus Gallicuis (Ibid passim).

[1144] RENATO C. "Opere, documenti e testimonianze" ROTONDO a. Florence, Chicago, Sansoni Newberry Library 1068 p 233-241...Vergerio.

of Presbyterians In Vicosoprano. Does he simply ignore them? Or are they not really present in Vicosoprano? It is sure that, for these reformed people who believe in the validity of the Presbyterian model, this specific aspect of Vergerio's pastoral approach may be considered as unacceptable.

Reform of the ecclesiastical discipline and Pastoral assertion in Calvin's Geneva (years 1540-1550)
Nathalie Szczech

"A minister must not talk other than about the Gospel and, as for the rest of the appointed things, he must not get mixed up in them[1145].

It is in these terms that Jacques Gruet expressed his opposition to the changes that the pastoral minister knew in Geneva, during the 1540's. This secretary, condemned for "atheism" by the civil authorities and executed on 26j July 1547, here formalises his fierce rejection of the extension of the pastoral prerogatives beyond preaching and administration of the sacraments. Far from being only an isolated attack, Gruet's words translate as a more general incomprehension and the refusal, by an important part of the Genevan population, of the expansion of pastoral expertise, in the years following Calvin's [1146]return to Geneva. This complex face to face among the ministers and the Genevan faithful flock, and the anticlerical reactions that he introduced enable one to question an essential problem of the birth years of the Reformation: that of the definition of

---

[1145] Theme of Jacques Gruet addressed to his judges. Criminal case [PC]quoted in BERRIOT F . "Un process d'atheisme a Geneve:l'affaire Gruet (1547-1550"Bulletin de la SHPF vol 125-4 1979 p 577-592 p 583.

[1146] On this climate of opposition, reported by Calvin, see, for example,CALVINJ. "Des scandales" FATIO Geneva,Droz, 1984 p 17-8 p 82 p 194 and no.379;

the contours of the pastoral mission, from the legitimacy of the foundations of the authority if ministers and of the constitution of a specifically reformed clerical identity.

On 21 May 1536, the General Council of Geneva officially chose the Reformation, after several years of silent penetration of Lutheran ideas, sermons, then public debates[1147]. This rupture however did not constitute a point of outcome, since everything remained to build in order to establish Geneva in the new faith and to root the Gospel in hearts and practices. How did pastors and the pastorate re-invent themselves in the bosom of a protestant world in formation? The mass was abolished, images broken and the clerks, mostly, were exiled, but how was the separation with a neighbouring Catholicism, in time as in space, built?

This study proposes to tackle these questions through the problem which underlines the ecclesiastical discipline, that is to say institutionalisation, with the creation of the consistory and by applying evangelical precepts[1148] of an unpublished reformed practice of fraternal correction, in which the pastors take the most active part, seeking to ensure the orthodoxy and orthopraxy of the faithful flock, to close obstinate sinners access to the sacrament of communion and to work for progressive sanctification of the community. This aspect of the pastoral mission, which covers examination, admonitions, even excommunications, and reconciliation of repentant sinners, seems in fact like an essential motor of the process of clericalisation which moves the Genevan Reformation in Calvin's time[1149]. It

---

[1147] See NAEF H. "Les origins de la Reforme a Geneve", Geneva, Librairie A. Jlien 1936 vol 2 (repub. 1968).

[1148] Mt, 18, 15-20 is the reference text for evoking fraternal correction. Verses 17-18 justify the institutionalisation of the discipline.

[1149] On this idea, see WANEGFFELEN T "Un clericalism reforme. Le Protestantism francais entre principe du sacerdoce universel et theologie …(XVI-XVII siecles)" conference du "Reformation Studies Colloquium Birmingham (2004)

puts an important problem before the ministers of positioning in relation to the Catholic past and to the legacy of the first reformers and constitutes, as a result, the intrigue of anticlericalism which touched Geneva in the years 1542-15555, but also became the dynamic principal of forming, in the ordeal, of a pastoral body and culture.

The study of the registers of the consistory, more particularly in the years 1542-1555, fed by an analysis of the registers of the Company of pastors, of surveys in the registers of the Council and criminal cases, as well as in the correspondence of Genevan ministers, at the top class of which Calvin, enables one to understand how a reformed ecclesiastical discipline is imposed, which will soon become an essential "brand" of the Reformed Church[1150]. The Genevan consistorial sources are known and have already been studied fir the XVIth century, social[1151], political[1152], or anthropolpgical[1153] issues. Their critical edition, currently in process[1154] enables one to survey them freshly and to use them more easily in order to tackle the fabric of a pastoral authority and a clerical identity.

The creation of the Geneva consistory and the organisation of an unpublished disciplinary procedure

In September 1541, the civil authorities recalled Calvin to Geneva and gave him a task to reorganise a Church which was racked by disorder. Strengthened by the support of the faction which was then in power and in a context of urgency, the reformer could quickly have his proposals for

---

[1150] On discipline as a third" brand" of the "true" Church, see GROSSE C."Les rituels de la cene..Geneva (XVI-XVII siecles) Geneva Droz 2008 p 340-342.

[1151] One dreams of the works of Raymond a. Mentzer and Robert M. Kingdon and gus oyouks.

[1152] NAOHY W.G. "Calvin and the Consolidation of the Genevan Reformation", Manchester, Manchester University Press 1994.

[1153] FROSSE C."Les rituels de la Cene…" op,cit.

[1154] KINGDON R.M. (Then WANDEL L.P "Registres du Conseil de Geneve au temps de Calvin", Geneva,,Droz 1996

reforms adopted by the Councils. Ecclesiastical Decrees were thus voted in from the month of November 1541, in order to control the order of the Church, from then on structured around four ministries[1155].Calvin came to have the principle of an ecclesiastical discipline approved, institutionalised in a new court, the consistory[1156]. Assembled every Thursday in the old cloister of the canons of Saint-Pierre cathedral, the pastors and a dozen old people, placed under the authority of a manager, are charged to guarantee respect for the doctrine, to safeguard the morality of the Genevans and to punish sins committed against the law or charity[1157]. Informed by their own observations, rumour or informing, they intervene in the name of the Church, when private correction has failed, and they set out to [1158]reconstitute the facts by the interrogation of the sinner and possible witnesses[1159]. The sessions were sanctioned, mostly, by very ritualised warnings, often pronounced by Calvin, and by pedagogic prescriptions, such as attendance at sermons or sessions on the catechism. If the accused party is considered obstinate or if the actions are considered as particularly serious, the procedure to lead to excommunication or to complexify themselves par sending back the deviant person before the Small Council, which has full authority to take on other sanctions. By spreading the stain of the error, a source of divine anger, by

---

[1155] AEG. "Reistres du conseil de Geneve" RC35, 20.11.1541 fol.405 reproduced in KINGDON R.M.and BERIER J.F. "Registres de la compagnie des Pasteurs de Geneve au temps de Calvin" Geneva Droz t.l.p 1-13.

[1156] KINGDON R.M.and BWEFIER J.C. "Registres de la Compagmir…" op.cit. t t.l. p 2 p 6-7 p 12-13.

[1157] See the list of sins evoked in CALVIN J. "Institution de la religion chretienne" [159] J D BENOIT Paeis Vrin 1957-1963 book IV Chap XII.

[1158]

[1159] CALVIN J. "Institution…" op.cit. book IV chap XII 2 and commentaries by GROSSE C. "Les rituels de la Cene…" op.cit/p346-347.

preserving the community from sin and by inviting the faithful flock to penitence by example of the sanction, the ecclesiastical discipline which is thus organised must enable the Church to present itself as a healthy body, moulded in the image of Christ, with which it aspires to be united.

The creation of a court which is specifically dedicated to this mission, and particularly the role of activity that it gains by relation to civil justice determining where the pastors operate, mark a rupture in the recent history of the city and make Geneva in the years 1540-1550 an unpublished case. The departure of the Prince-Bishop in 1534 and the adoption of the Reformation in 1536 have led to putting back into effect the mediaeval system of ecclesiastical discipline, broadly criticised by the humanists, then by the first reformers [1160] and have widened the responsibilities of the Magistrate. While at the turn of the XVth and XVIth centuries, supervision of beliefs and customs was organised in a permanent overlap of the episcopal and communal justices, the Small council takes it fully in charge from that time, whether it is a question of office in the past, or to [1161]have the divine prescriptions respected, the action of the councillors extending, for example, to matrimonial cases which up to then the official took in charge[1162]. Breaking with the old system considered as abusive.[1163] And dissolving the principle of a priest as the only clergyman, the Magistrate thus takes the responsibility for the public morality and the respect for the precepts of the new faith,

---

[1160] DENIS P. "Remplacer la confession: absolutions…XVIe siècle" GROUPE DE LA BUSSIERE "Pratiques de la confession. Des Peres du desert ….histoire" paris Cerf 1983 p 165-176.

[1161]

[1162] NAEF H. "Les origines de la Reforme a Geneve" op.cit.vol.p 219-236Mbaud h. "Le diocese de Geneve-Annecy" Paris Beauchesne 1985 p 80- 81.

[1163] See, for example, FEBVE L. "Un abus et son climat social;..Franche-Comte" L.FEBVRE "Au Coeur religieux XVIe siècle" Paris SEVPEN 1957 p 301-337.

the pastors no longer intervening on disciplinary questions except in consultation, even not at all.

This initial organisation is inspired from elaborate models by the first Swiss reformers. In Zurich, under the inspiration of Zwingli, discipline is in fact ensured, from 1525, by a matrimonial court, the "Ehegericht", made up of four members of the municipal Magistrate and two pastors. This institution controls difficulties which come from marriages, but it soon also deals with other problems coming from general supervision of the faithful flock. It sends back disobedient members before the civil authorities[1164]. The civil authorities, whose representatives are in the majority are in h bosom of the institution and before whom the accused parties can be provided with an appeal, seized the exercise of the discipline, in a gesture determined to break with the old practices of ecclesiastical justice. Under the Zwinglian influence, the State of Berne adopted a similar organisation and put in place, from 1528, a "Chorgericht" progressively reduced in the different parishes of the area, in charge of matrimonial cases, but more broadly responsible for the doctrinal and moral supervision of the faithful flock – doctrinal deviations, sorcery, disrespect for Sunday, dancing, drunkenness, bawdiness, adultery are the reasons for the most common appearance[1165]. It is a civil institution, in the bosom of which the pastors do not have a dominant position and which leaves the responsibility for sanctions to the Magistrate .This model is imposed in the lands that Berne progressively conquered from the XIVth century[1166], in

---

[1164] KOHLER W. "Zurcher Ehegericht und Genfer…" Leipzig M. Heinsuis Nachfolge 1932-1942 2 vol

[1165] SCHMIDT H.R. "Durf und Religion. Reformierte …Fruhen Neuzeit" Stuttgart – iene – NEW Yori Gustav Verlag 1995 Saint Gall (1526)

[1166] MATZINGER-PISTER R. "L'introductio des Consistoires dans le pays de Vaud" D.TOSADORIGO and N, STAREMBERG "Sous l'oeil du consistoire…op. cit" p 113-123 .

spite of the exchanges with Berne, in 1540, about creating an institution which could specifically take responsibility for questions of discipline[1167], and in spite of the creation, on paper, of a consultative consistory in 1541[1168] this is a Zwinglian model of continuity and leaves the responsibility for supervising the faith and customs to the Genevan civil authorities. During the first years of the Reformation, the Genevan pastors are only considered, at best, as collaborators, whose daily presence with the faithful flock can enlighten the decisions of the magistrates in the matter of discipline.

The principle of a discipline is ensured by the ministers is not however abandoned by all the reformers, in spite of their wish to break with the practices of the Roman clergy and to establish the pastoral ministry on reformed foundations. Influenced by the ideas of Olampiad and Bucer and by his contacts with the Baslian and Strasbourgian clergy in the second half of the 1530's, it is Calvin who goes further in the reflection on the usage of discipline, who defends his full belonging to the pastoral mission and conquers a space of autonomous exercise for the consistory, in front of the new civil authorities until in [1169]1555. Inspired, like Oecolampade and Bucer, by the example of the independent primitive church of the secular authorities, Calvin thinks that discipline can only be exercised by an autonomous ecclesiastical instance[1170]. His argument, which was drawn up at the turn of the years

---

[1167] AEWG Registres du Conseil de Geneve RC 34 fol21 dfol 27 fol 376.

[1168] Ibid RC 35 fol145r and fol 154r commented by GROSSE C."Les rituels de la cene" op.cit p 352-355.

[1169] On the conflict between the consistory …see GROSSE C. "L'excommunicarion de Philibert …Reforme genevoise (1547-15555)" MANETSCH S.M "Calvin's company of Pastors…"Oxford University Press 2013 chap 7.

[1170] MCKEE E.A. "Calvin, Discipline and Exeesis …sixteenth century" I. BACKUS and F.HIGMAN "Theorie et pratique de l'exegese" Geneva Droz 1990 p 319-327.

1550-1540 and states in the "Institution" of 1543, defends the exercise of discipline by a council formed from ministers and old people,[1171] and using the power of codes in the name of the whole Church. Discipline and excommunication are considered as instruments that God gives to pastors and old school people, responsible for supervising the sanctification of the social body.

An enlargement of the disciplinary practices for recasting the social body

This unpublished Calvinist positioning is not so clear in the Decrees of 1541, which appear like a vague compromise between temporal and spiritual authorities. The translation of Calvin's ideas in the daily pastoral activity enables them to be described through practice, but also makes a misunderstanding grow up which, hidden in 1541, is rapidly revealed and becomes worse up to the [1172]political crisis which the city declares in 1555. It is the question of the respective prerogatives of the pastors. of civil authorities and the faithful flock themselves which is bitterly fought, when it is a question of concreting founding principles, such as the rejection of "papist" abuses, the universal priest or the collaboration of the spiritual and temporal swords, on which all or nearly all seemed to agree in the middle of the 1530's. From 1542, the disciplinary activity grows and in fact tackles everything that waw known up till then in Geneva, the ecclesiastical Decrees only prescribing in imprecise terms that "the old school people must admonish" every faithful person who "neglects to conform with the

---

[1171] On the historical constitution of this doctrine, see HOPEL "The Christian Policy of John Calvin, Cambridge, CUP 1985 p 58-60.

[1172] On 16 May 1555, after a large riot, the faction of the Children of Geneva fiercely opposing, for ten years, Calvin and his French pastors surrounding him, is defeated. The politico-religious scene is then left free for the defenders of the reforming Calvinian ideal – see NAPHY W.C. "Calvin and the Consolidatgion…" op.cit.

church so much that one can see a [1173]noteworthy scorn for the communion of the faithful" or which appears contemptuous of the ecclesiastical order

The consistory, heir of the officialdom and the Swiss matrimonial courts which have replaced it. Is ensured in fact, most often, by the matrimonial promises and lead, in this case, the number if actions for broken engagements, adulteries or other regrouped sexual offences in the registers, under the term of "bawdiness[1174]. To the escapades od the famous Francois Favre, the patriarch of a great Genevan family, several times charged with bawdiness, the determination of the consistory replies in reforming what is considered as a life of debauchery which is incompatible with the plan for sanctification of the social body[1175]. This famous case, and the cases of hundreds of other "bawdy people" today forgotten, give testimony to the considerable effort made by the ministries to limit the sexual relations without a promise of marriage and the illegitimate births which may follow, to punish more broadly the cases of fornication and adultery and to thus restrict the sexuality of the Geneva within the strict frameworks of marriage established by God. This enterprise of control of sexual morality is not, at first, the disciplinary action most contested by the faithful people, insofar as this type of control is accepted, even though the authorities were pressed, from the turn of the XVth and XVIth centuries, to

---

[1173] KINGDON R.M. and BERGIER J.F. Registre d la Compagnie…" op.cit. v.1 p 1-12.

[11741174] The cases of bawdiness and intra-familial quarrels arising from it represent more than half of the cases of volume 3 *147-1548) see KINGDON R.M. Registres d Consistoire op.cit. v 3 2004 p x.

[1175] KINGDON R.M/" Registres du Consistoire…" op. cit. v 2 2001 p 84(3.12.1545)in.272 p 146-148 9Feb 146) 8.04.146) v 3 p 20-21 (3.02.1547) p 37-38 (3.03.1547)

suppress debauchery[1176]. Thus do the members of the consistory follow practices in place in Geneva before the Reformation and the models of other Swiss cities, which have institutionalised this matrimonial control from the end of the 1520's, can it only be to comfort their legitimacy to intervene in this way.

The control of orthodoxy of the faithful flock and the struggle against ignorance and the persistence of [1177] Catholic practices of piety, which occupied a major place in the activity of the consistory, particularly in 1542 and 1543[1178] are not however the most badly received dispositions. By representing the faithful flocks attend the neighbouring Catholic villages to go to Mass, to take communion, get married or have their children baptised, while suppressing the Latin prayers to the Virgin and to the saints, fasting and celebration, the pastors and old-school people in fact prolonged the inaugural gesture of reversal of the altar and destruction of images, which marked the entrance of the community into its new story. If they did not succeed in removing all trace of Catholicism[1179].at least they only stirred up a passive resistance of the inhabitants and so much more that on questions of faith, their attitude is patient and broadly more pedagogic than repressive. Mirroring the control of souls, pastors and old school people intend also to channel people during the time of worship and more particularly the sermon. Movements and untimely

---

[1176] On the reinforcement of the policy on customs on the eve of the Reformation, see NAEF H. "Les origins de la Refprme a Geneve" op. cit/v 1 p228-235.

[1178] KINGDON R.M "L'usage quantitative des registres …Geneve" P.CHAREYRE P.and R.A. MENTZER "Lla mesure religeuse calvini europeen XVI-XVIIIe siecles" Bulletin de ka SHPF v 153-4 2997 0 585-592

[1179] In 1536, for example 29 people were condermned for Catholic practices in ANNECY: REGISTRES DU CONSISTOIRE 11 FOL FOLM60 V 924.09.1556)

activities[1180] must be stopped, silence and immobility were imposed, to promote listening, impregnation of the soul by the Word and the action of the Holy Spirit, in connection with the or the specifics of the reformed liturgy, which places the Word which was read, or chanted, prayed or taught in the centre of the service and minimises gestures outside the sacramental time. Movements and restlessness[1181] noise and restless interruptions[1182], laughing and grimacing[1183] are thus revealed in the consistory and give rise to reprimands and sanctions, to the point that as Jean Vuilliemoz, Lieutenant of Genthod, his minister "can only stir the pot [1184]".

But discipline regulates matrimonial problems and the control of orthodoxy and the attitude of the faithful flock in the space of the temple, in order to touch, from the 1540's, all aspects of daily life, and to move from the street to family intimacy. In fact it is a question of reforming the social body completely according to a principle of unity[1185], which is translated, without the consistory always managing is purposes, however by a work of appeasement of conflicts, an enterprise of smoothing over social practices and struggling against the traditions and signs of communal belonging. Relations in the bosom of the families, areas or professional communities are thus observed, aiming to pacify the interpersonal violence which endanger communion[1186]. Even more, the members of the consistory intend progressively to unify the city under the banner of

---

[1180]1180

[1181] For example, AEG Registres du Conseil a Geneve RC 41 fol.41 fol 59v (29.03.15460

[1182] For example, KINGDON R.M. "Registres du Consistoire..." RC fol 41 fol 59v 929.03.1546)(

[1183] AEG For example KINGDON R.M. "Registres du consistoire..." op. cit v 4 p 45 (12.O4.1548)

[1184] Ibid p 109 M (908.1548)

[1185] CALVIN J. "Institution..." op. cit book IV chap XVII 40.

[1186] See GROSSE C. "Les rituels de la Cene..." op.cit.p 511-565.

the Gospel, by reforming the rites of passage, by moralising the spaces and traditional leisure or in fighting similar signs. The choice of first names in baptism, which do not have to be biblical, became, for example, a knot of the consistorial activity between 1546 and the middle of the 1530's[1187]. By refusing traditional first names, such as Claude, Gaspard or Balthasar, the pastors put off the tradition which allows the godfather to give his first name to the child and fight against a usage which up to then cemented the solidarities in the heart of the city. In a similar momentum, the consistory supervises the activities of bands of young people, tracks the games, songs and dances or tries to moralise the traditional places for socialising which are the steam rooms[1188], Calvin supports for example, forbidding punctured shoes. By representing the struggle against this ostentatious dress style, he sanctions what, according to him is a manifestation of pride, but he plans especially to reform the traditions of young members of military companies which, according to him, who willingly wear this clothing as a sign of recognition[1189]. It is thus about containing particularisms, to teach a stirring youth and to incorporate it into the community of the faithful flock, in order to unify the social body into the image of Christ.

Persuaded that all immorality remains unpunished constitutes an attack in God's honour and restricts the advancement of the Gospel, it is with a strong zeal that the consistory and, more particularly, the pastors struggle day after day to apply a reformed normal standard. If this

---

[1187] See NAPHY W.G "Baptism, Church Riots…Geneva", Sixteenth century journal v. 26 1995 p 86-97.

[1188] The pastors obtain from the Council on 29.04.1546, the closing of taverns, R.M "Registres du consistoire…op.cit v 2 p 157 Sauelander vII p 478. See GROSSE C. "Les rituels de la cene" op.cit. p 337-339 .

[1189] See he letter from Calvin to the faithful people of France 24.97.1547 CALVIN J, "Johannis Calvini opera…" op.cit v 10 1879 col 561-562 quoted in KINGDON R,M "Registres du Consistoire" op.cit. v 2 158.

disciplinary activity crosses political and social problematics, it is in the much broader framework of a view of the world and a history of salvation that one must consider its inclusion in the frameworks of pastoral mission, which are fixed in these founding years.

A pastoral body tested by ecclesiastical discipline

They are these interventions in gestures, daily times and spaces and the rewriting of the social body which are the most virulently contested in the years 1545-1555, a growing part of the Genevan population questioning the legitimacy of the consistory, but most particularly the expansion of the pastors' prerogatives, lived like an intrusion. Nicolas Gentil, chateau owner of Jussy, thus refuses to be interviewed by the consistory and explained that "he [does not hold the pastors for ministers except when they are in the [1190]pulpit].". In a time when, hardly a few years after the official passage of Geneva to the Reformation, the authority of ministers remains to be built and their mission to be limited, a misunderstanding was dug in the middle of the 1540's to the middle of the 1550's and fed an anticlerical criticism which is more and more visible and violent.

This contest is precociously translated by a passive resistance of the Genevans, who refuse to join the convocations of the court[1191], or are disobedient in obeying the consistory[1192]. Explicit and pronounced contests, in a first time, in the closed hearing of the court, take over. Thus in 1542, Andre Piard states before the members that Calvin

---

[1190] AEG Registres du Conseil de Geneve RC 44 fol 126 bis (7,06.1549

[1191] See, for example, KINGDON R.M. "Registres du Conseil".. op. cit. v1 1996 p 209 922.04.1546)

[1192] AEG "Registres du Conseil de Geneve RC35 fol 442 (23.12.15410

is not his superior and he does not intend to obey him[1193]. Called on 3 February 1550, Francois Favre states that the consistory is "a new jurisdiction to restrict people"[1194] He refuses to address the pastors during his interrogation and only talks to the manager who presides over the meeting. In a gradual outbreak of verbal violence, the ministers are soon publicly taken aside. In 1550, the saddler is thus accused of having hurled, in his shop, violent words towards the ministers, who, according to him, "have better deserved to be taken to Plant Pallais than a great many people who were taken there"[1195]. The exasperation of some faithful people, who no longer tolerate the repeated reprimands of the pastors clearly showed in the registers of the consistory, in the example of the themes of Guillaume Du Bois, persuaded that Calvin's repeated reprimands are proof that the Reformer shows upon meeting him. [1196].

Genevan anticlericalism manifests itself as much by words as by gestures. Calvin and his colleagues thus complain to the Council about loud jokes, such as young people who, at night, come to ring the doorbell at night at their door in Rue des Chanoines[1197] about provocations such as those of Gaspard Favre, seen while playing skittles with friends, at the time of worship at Easter 1546[1198], or found playing tennis noisily in front of St Peter's during a lesson

---

[1193] KINGDON R.M. "Registres du Consistoire…" op.cit/ v 1 p 102 (17.08/1542).

[1194] Ibid v 3 p 14 (3.02.1547).

[1195] Ibid v 5 2010 p 14 (27.02.1550) Plainpalais was the place where those who were condemned to capital punishment were executed.

[1196] Report of the consistory to the Council AEG" PC 1t series, no 437 (30.12.1546) reproduced in KINGDON R.M. "Registres du Consistoire…" op.cit v 2 p 379.

[1197] AEG "Recistres du Conseil de Geneve RC 44 fol.141 v (25.0.1549) quoted in KINGDON R.M. "Registres du Consistoire…" op. cit/v 4 p 218.

[1198] AEG "Registres du Conseil de Geneve", RC 41 fol.82 fol.84 fol.87 926,17,30 April and 6 May 1546.

by Calvin in 1551[1199]. The contesting gestures also invade the temples, key spaces of sanctification. The repeated absence of faithful people from the sermon is scandalous[1200], while play in their presence: Jean-Philibert Bonna, entering and leaving the temple. As if acting a joke, "came to accompany the [1201]children who are brought for baptism, then retires from the sermon, then comes back at the end, a scandalous thing and a mockery". In a society of precedence, these incivilities become sharp weapons, which wound the honour of the pastors and are lived, doubling at the pace that the tensions are becoming intensified, physical violence: the temples are thus the theatre of repeated troubles, which could go to a brawl at the time of baptisms[1202], and the registers even record the cases of aggression to pastors[1203].

The number and intensity of these anticlerical reactions invite one to emphasise the rupture in which the activity pf the consistory leads Geneva at the beginning of the 1540's. For the aim of the members of this new institution is not reduced to supervise and punish in order to guarantee social peace, nor to control and punish to counteract the accession of a faction to power, but to work for the sanctification of the Genevan community, such as "eyes", "ears", "nose" and "mouth" of a social body which must be made only for the

---

[1199] Ibid. RC 45 fol 233 (25.03.1551).

[1200] See, for example, KINGDON R. M. "Registres du Consistoire…" op. cit. "Registres du Consistoire" op. cit v 6 2012 p 72.

[1201] Ibid p 178 (1,10 1551) and AEG Registres du Conseil de Geneve RC 46 fol. 68 v 69 (5.10.1551).

[1202] Ibid. See, for example, AEG, "Registres du Conseil de Geneve "RC 41, fol.238 (9 November 1546).

[1203] See, for example. AEG "Registres du Conseil de Geneve" RC 31. Fol. 238 (9.11.1546) KINGDON R.M. "Registres du conseil de Geneve" RC 44 fol.171 v quoted in "Registres du Conseil de Geneve" fol.221 v 4 p 222(29.07.1549) AEG "Registres du Conseil de Geneve RC 45 fol.221 (12.03.1551).

glory of God[1204]. Discipline, as necessary as the nerves in a body[1205], thus became a spiritual issue and not only social and political. In a break with the neighbouring Swiss examples and with the recent history of the city, the ministers opposed this imperative of collective sanctification to the imagination and to Genevan traditions and do not hesitate to break the balance between the necessary exclusion of the sinner in or[1206]der to preserve the social order and the desire to maintain the cohesion of the latter. This unpublished positioning, which is not afraid of breaking up hierarchies, solidarities and traditional balances, is resented as an illegitimate symbolic violence by a number of Genevans, anxious to establish the changes in the community structure that they know. It is thus symptomatic that Jacques Gruet emphasises, during interrogations that he suffered in July 1542, the shock that for him constituted the humiliating spectacle of the powerful merchant Francois Favre, acknowledged to be capable of bawdiness and obliged by the Council, at the request of the consistory, to shout "mercy, kneeling" and thus to soil his honour.

This determined engagement in the re-foundation of the community brings about setting apart and affirmation of the group of pastors in reaction to that of the laity, favouring a process of clericalization. For if a clerical identity comes uncontestably from the authority given to the pastors to assemble, to judge, to sanction within the framework of the consistory, this identity is also forged in the discussions of the opponents who consider the pastors as a group, as a

---

[1204] See VIRET P. "Instruction Chretienne …l'Evangile" Geneva Jean Rivey, 1564 v 2 p 360-363; ID "Response aux questions…Ropitel, Lyon, C. Senneton 1565 p 87 passages quoted by ZEMON DAVIS N. "The sacred …sixteenth century Lyon" "Past and Present v 90 p 64-65.

[1205] CALVIN J, "Institution …" op. cit. book IV chap. XVII 1

[1206] BERRIOT I. "Un process d'atheisme a Geneve…" art.cit. p 580.

separate group, even as a group of clerks. In the consistory, some Genevans thus identify the pastors with former priests, have the impression of living a return to Catholicism and to be deprived of the gains of the Reformation. The case of "the Marrechauda of Russin", accused of having said "that the preachers were more wicked than the priests" is, in this case, eloquent[1207]. The resolute engagement of the pastors in the disciplinary action therefore contributes to isolate them and a reaction among the Genevans of a Catholic memory which is still alive.

Beyond the stigmatising words of the faithful flock, who outwardly create a group pastoral identity, the increasing violence that the ministers try give rise to mutuality and a common imagination, which come to reduplicate the efficient factors of cohesion, such as the French origin which is almost exclusive to the Genevan pastors, the literate culture that they share and the constant exchanges that they carry out, thanks especially to the weekly meetings of the little group[1208]. The pastors, who share the responsibility for the three churches of the city and a dozen of rural parishes, then form a true company, whose members are united by a similar ideal of sanctification of the community and fed by a similar fighting imagination, which gives sense and legitimates the enterprise of discipline. Going broadly outside the political or social issues, the engagement of pastors in this project, of which they are the movers, and the Genevan resistances with which they are confronted are in fact considered as the tragic manifestations of a dramatic tension between Good

---

[1207] Thanks to the eviction of old elements, to the recruitment of new pastors and the control of French pastors, Calvin finds himself in 1546 at the head of a group exclusively made up of French pastors, with the exception of Jacques Bernard, relegated into a rural parish NAPHY W.G. "Calvin and the consolidation…" p 53-75. MANETSCH S.M. "Calvin's company of Pastors" op.cit.chap 2.

[1208] WANDEL L.P. "Registres du Consistoire…" op.cit. v 8 2014 p 227 (21.12.1553).

and Evil, as the signs of a holy struggle which is intensified until 1555 and the fall of the Children of Geneva[1209]. The attacks experienced in Geneva are understood as characteristic proof of a time of advancement of the Gospel and are lived as an update of the troubles of holy history, which feed the faith of the group in itself and in its project. Far from running away from the fight and even entertaining it by an enterprise which is always more passionate about purification[1210]. Calvin and his colleagues find there the confirmation of their view of the world, the legitimation of their action and forge a common culture there. The process of clericalization is thus fed paradoxically in Geneva from the anticlericalism of the faithful flock.

***

During the years 1540-1560.Geneva become the laboratory of reformed disciplinary practices, qui aim not only to anchor the new faith in hearts, but also to re-found the society, which had to become a purified body and fashioned in the image of Jesus Christ. Ecclesiastical discipline was invented in confrontation and was imposed, from a high struggle in 1555, as a kingpin of the pastors' mission: the latter are no longer only ministers of the Word, but are installed in a posture of guardians, whose vocation is to supervise respect for the honour of God and the integrity of the community. A melting-pot of political and major social renewals, the years 1545-1555 therefore also mark the birth of a true Genevan pastoral body, soldered by preaching, administration of the sacraments and care of the faithful flock, but also by the practice of ecclesiastical discipline

---

[1209] See. For example, the letter to Blaurer of 19.11.1552, CALVIN J. "Johannis Calvini opera..." op. cit. v 14 1888 col.412.

[1210] On this tension which is willingly conducted in the town, particularly between March and May 1555, aww CROUZET D. "Calvin, parallel live" Paris Fayard p 287-302.

included like a necessary combat. This invention was not any evidence, to the extent where discipline, especially in the most advanced form of excommunication, took Geneva away from the other Swiss churches and paradoxically caused the resurgence of a Catholic memory which had to be erased.

Pastors who became bourgeois
Limits and consequences of a new model of incorporation of actors into the
Ministry in the Geneva of Theodore de Beze
Reflections around the removals
Of Nicolas Colladon and Jean le Gagneux (1571)
Genevieve

GROSS

On 3 December 1571, on the issue of a procedure planned between the ecclesiastical authorities and magistrates who had begun four months earlier, the Small Council of Geneva pronounced, in his absence, the removal of pastor Jean Le Gagneux. By this sentence, Le Gagneux was removed from his pastoral ministry practiced in the town from 1562, but also from his temporary position as a teacher of theology, in 1571 helping Theodore de Beze and Nicolas Colladon in this parish in the heart of the Academy of Geneva, of which he was rector since 1568[1211] Upon reading the deed of condemnation, we are facing a second offending minister having more than three times gained from the "sweetness

---

[1211] AEG, REPORTS OF MEETINGS OF THE Small Council, RC66, 3.12.1571, fol. 148r.There is a contemporary manuscript kept separate from this deed, kept in the French section of the Geneva library (ms.fr. 73-77)/On Nicolas Le Gagneux, see KINGDON R.M. "Geneva and the consolidation of French Protestant Movement 1564-1572.." Geneva, Droz, 1967, p 23.

and mildness" of the magistrates, after having "notoriously [between 1564 and 1571] abused the liberty of the ministry in order to serve his special passions" and led sermons on the great scandal of the honour of the Lord, neglecting the advice of his brothers" as if he had been promised and allowed in such a case according to God and reason[1212]". In September 1571, if Le Gagneux again described his disobedience to the body of ministers, of his affairs voluntarily cut off from the town, leaving it in the wake of his trouble instead of asking for it according to his duty and his oath[1213]". While trying to defend himself in letters, sent several days later from Lyon to the Genevan authorities, he became and remained blamed for "true desertion of his ministry" and will be accused of perjury […] committed against his duty and oath as minister as a middle-class person"

A few months earlier, in February 1571, Pastor Nicolas Colladon, then secretary of the Company of pastors, had also left the consistory of the Lordship, leaving the town at the heart of wrangles that his last sermon had caused[1214]". Leaving for Nyon, a Church under the jurisdiction of Bern, he signs thus at the time of one his conflicts with the Council and the ministers a passing of the border, by a period of leave far from being formally required and authorised by the corcumstances guaranteed by his ministry. It was on the insistence of his brothers, friends and parents, that he decided several days later to come back to the own.

There, before the Council, he justifies himself for this absence, saying he wanted "a change of air […] for the great trouble that was in my heart "and" not to become distracted from his duty". He thus unravelled an accusation of desertion of the own and abandoning his ministerial duties,

---

[1212] Report of the Smalll Council, RC 66, 3.12.1571 fl. 148r.
[1213] Ibid. fol,148v.
[1214] On Nicolas Colladon, refer ti the literature quoted in FATIO O. and LABARTHE O. "Registres de la Compagmie" op. cit. v3 p VIII-XII.

pleading that he had followed and transformed himself in the period of reflection, granted by the ministers and magistrates a week earlier, in order to gain from it willingly. He then submits to censure, confesses and again joins the group of his brothers. However, with a new series of sermons against the institution of the exchange[1215], he signs at the end of August 1571, in an institutional document for the case which is widely kept by historiography, his manifest disobedience to the ministers and magistrates. He became an author, in full exercise of his pastoral duties, of an attack against the temporal and ecclesiastical authorities of the town. Removed in September, he thus ended his pastoral career in Geneva[1216]

A border crossed: between lectures from the authorities and questioning the strength of the connection. The issues of the Colladon and Le Gagneux affairs

By his transgression of the political and confessional border of September 1571, Le Gagneux is shown, for the authorities, in a consciously reflected strategy, that which was adopted by a minister seeking to protect himself from judiciary and disciplinary cases about his actions. The town and Church of Geneva seem to be thus short-circuited in the resolution of the case and in spite of the decision of the Company of Pastors to wan the consistory of Lyon and the conference of Beaujolais in activating the network of the Churches of France and thus to lead the fleeing minister to acknowledge his mistake[1217]. Another consequence will come to be added to this crossing of the border and will act as a second brake, which will not be expressed more

---

[1215] MONTER E.W. "Le change public a Geneve 156801581" "Melangs d'histoire economique…anniversaire" Geneva Tribune de Geneve 1963 v 1 p 265-290.

[1216] MANETSCH S.M/ "Calvin's cpmpany of Pastprs …Recormed Church 1536-1609 New York, Oxford University Press 2913 p 64; KINGDON R.M. "Geneva and the consolidation…"op. cit. p 17-29.

[1217] FATIO O.and LABARTHE O. "Registres de la Compagnie…" op.cit.p 43 p 51.

uniquely in the geographical and political space, but will be henceforth described in the promise of a new institutional association.

In fact, in March 1572, after having literally stayed at the gates of the town and come to the Pont d'Arve – the natural border between Catholic Savoy and the town of Geneva – a requirement for safe-conduct, Le Gagneux finally decided to go into the town, where he was heard and held prisoner. It happened then [1218] in Berne, between March and April, the rumour then the news of the election of Le Gagneux in Lausanne, accompanied by a condition "sine qua non" to his engagement, that of the rule of the disagreement[1219]. Now. Less than a month later, on 1st May, Berne asks to shorten the length of the detention of Le Gagneux so that the pastor could finally take up his position[1220].. The ministers of Geneva think at the time and again later, according to their own terms, to have their hands tied b Berne, certainly consider themselves under the eye of heir confessional and political partner from the signature in 1566 of the "Confession helvetique posterieure" and the perpetual treaty of "combourgeoisie" in 1559[1221].Some weeks earlier, on 18 April, the magistrates had, according to them, renounced sending to the Bernese an account of the proceedings followed and interrogations carried out until then with the accused minister. Retracting from its first intentions, the town of Geneva however proposed and validated in the heart of the Small Council, the town of Geneva finally considers that such a letter is no longer suitable and that "it could seem to them that that could be

---

[1218] Ibid. p 60 AEG Report of the meetings of the small Council RC 67 4.04.1572 fol.51r.

[1220] AEG Reports of the meetings of the Small Council RC 67 1st MY 1572 FOL. 69V.

[1221 1221] FATIO and LABARTHE O. "Registres de la Compagnie…" op.cit. v 3 p 37.

done in order to disgrace them", planning among others through this bias and its fear of appearing passionate and obstinate in respect of Le Gagneux, to seek to take away from him any possibility of practicing elsewhere[1222]

Not only is the pastoral and humane value of the minister Le Gagneux found at that time in the centre of the disagreements, but with that there are surely also the credit of a reformation, of its outlook, as at las the place that Berne and Geneva could occupy in their enterprise to install and defend a true Church. As common as this leap could nevertheless marked by an argument in disciplinary practices and the ecclesiastical concept of Berne and Geneva, having led earlier, in 1588.an important wave of withdrawals. At that date, the Church's academy of Lausanne was deprived of several reformed personalities, professors and pastors of whom Calvin's city will benefit. In 1571, Berne and more particularly the Church of Lausanne gain for themselves and for at least a time, two former Genevan ministers, Nicolas Colladon and Jean le Gagneux. These cases point to a phenomenon which is far from being new in the space of the French-speaking Reformation and even more in Roman Switzerland, that of the transfer of staff and competition between Geneva and Berne, where the ministers withdrawn in one of these churches follow their career in the other[1223].

As we stop, in presenting these clerical conflicts, even more as we cross the border than to the more frequent policy of the sermons, we have sought to emphasise two processes of separation and acquisition of external support adopted by the ministers Le Gagneux and Colladon accused or at least suspected of being, by their sermons, an instrument of

---

[1222] AEG 2Reports of the meetings of the Small council RC67 8.04.1572 fol 60v. NPHY W.G. "Calvin and the consolidation…" Manchester Manchester University press 1994 p 53-83.

[1223] NAPHY W.G. "Calvin and the consolidation…Reformation" Manchester, Manchester University Press 1994 p 53-83.

dissent in the heart of the Company. To follow the deeds of the condemnations, these two pastors are in fact distinct from the rest of the body preferring, in the exercise of their duty of enlightenment, to put forward their particular opinion and interpretation. Manifestly breaking up equality through this bias and before acting among the members of this college, they tried to take authority not only on the Word that they have to preach, but also over their brothers, elected like them to the ministry and exercising their vocation under Christ's presence and the inspiration of the Holy Spirit With their public criticisms and complaints upon meeting the Magistrate, they would come to weaken the orientation and the christian validity of the sovereign authority, an approving authority and guarantor of their installation to the ministry. With them one ma also predict the existence of a disagreement between the temporal and ecclesiastical instances of the town, thus leaving open an eventual alliance between unhappy subjects and these protesting pastors, with the possibility of breaking the social balance. What is understood here, in an institutional reading of the cases, is [1224]the description of "clerical and democratic opposition" used by Eugene Choisy in his analysis of these ecclesiastical conflicts".

For our part, without denying this interpretation, we consider that this latter would serve more as a marker in the enunciation of definitions of the ministry and understanding the clergy who seek to defend between 1564 and 1571, through these conflicts, the Company of Pastors and the Magistrates. The idea of the clergy would then become plural, nor it was different after the perspective of the State or the Church, on ideas which are however far from disagreeing. This plurality of definitions would find an extra branch , that coming from the same framework of the regulation of the disagreement on consistorial or civil procedures leading to withdrawal. In front of institutional instances and their idea in the manners of exercising its

---

[1224] CHOISY E. "L'Etat chretien…" op.cit. p 49 p 58

responsibilities and prerogatives, the perception arises called to fail, that outline and try to defend the pastors accused of non-submission.

From that time, if these ecclesiastical conflicts plainly brought obedience into discussion, according to us, in the strength of the link, less visible in the new institutional affiliation acquired by the accused ministers that increasingly presents inside a Church body and at own which is weakened in its borders, of a city put into an enclave [1225] and finding itself at its gates. In fact, the treaty of Lausanne in 1564 and its application in 1567 by the return to Savoy of lands conquered in 1536 by Berne, Geneva moves towards its political isolation. From then, the town has no longer direct access, through land at least.to its ally and sole protector, Berne, a situation which will remain unchanged until the Treaty of Soleure in 1579[1226]. "Leaving the Genevan area and cross the border would more come to symbolise among these eminent actors in the ministry the need to break up or at and resented as being restraining. Crossing the border would, according to us, show an execution of the break by an instrumentalised use of the political and/or confessional border. Colladon and Le Gagneux would seek by this bias to distance itself from a group of connections, acting between the ministers themselves, at the heart of this unity of equal parties being guided under the presidency of Christ which is the Company of pastors. But they would also try to distance themselves from present connections, and doubtless even more active, between the pastors and the magistrates. The time is then in the gradual seizure of power by the Small Council on the Church by strengthening he judicial

---

[1225] Ibid ;GUICHONNET P. "Histoire de Geneve" Toulouse – Lausanne Privat 2986 p 151.
[1226] IBIID, P 99 225.GUICHONNET P "Histoire de Geneve" Toulouse – Lausanne Privat Payot 1986 p 151.

apparatus[1227] of the State to the detriment of an exercise of discipline, of the community towards the community, according to the prerogatives of the consistory.

Under this angle, the strength of the connection can first of all be questioned in its institutional dimension of election and the practice of a pastor, most often a French one, assigned and named to the ministry of enlightenment in Geneva, a town which was also engaged in duties and an effort to evangelise France to which from 1555, its Church and its academy contributed. In this perspective in front of this intrinsic border which defined the Genevan clergy, it should be emphasised and appreciated in its consequences a feature which was common with the former pastors Le Gagneux and Colladon, that of having been freely made bourgeois people between 1557 and 1562, in recognition of their ministry.[1228] Now, this process of naturalisation is accompanied among other things by a duty, if it is not settlement, at least of residence. It also includes economic and political rights and a first opening to the decision-making scene. With the citizen, the bourgeois person in fact forms the general council, an assembly uniting the Genevan electoral body which designates the main magistrates. He can from henceforth present himself and have himself elected to the Council of the Two Hundred, a Chamber founded in 1526 by the Bernese model, adopting the laws on the proposal of the Small Council[1229].

From then, in what measure these two sections of the Bourgeois statute, that of a territoriorial anchorage was in future capable of being ruled and controlled by the

---

[1227] GROSSEC. "There was too much harshness over there" Ecclesiastical discipline in Geneva in the time of Theodore de Beze". I.BACKUS "Theodore de Beze (1519-1605) Geneva,Droz 2007 55-69.

[1228] COVELLE A.L. ""Le livre des Bourgeois del 'ancienne…Geneve" Geneva j.Jullien 1897 p 257 (22.07.1557) p 272 (28.08.1563).

[1229] ROTH-LICHNER B. "De la bouche…Ancien regime" Geneva,Doz 1997 p 530-532.

sovereign authorities like that of a participation in the economic and political life of the town by its privileges, whether or not they have an impact on the minister. This change in the statute is accompanied by determining consequences on pastoral and missionary activity as on the definition of a priest, or more precisely on varied expressions, from the State or from the Church, in their idea of a clerical body that the time of Calvin's death and in front of the challenges of a confessional identified and spatial defence of Geneva and the reformed Church in general that is why the question of repercussion of this new condition of the minister must also be asked at the simple level of pastoral practice in Geneva, and comes from that time to touch more specifically the relations between the Church and the State. The pastor in fact operates, following his oath and his prerogatives, an office turned towards the teaching of everybody, including magistrates. His pastoral duty is led by the requirement to preserve a united social body, harmonious, for purged by the discipline and mutual correction between the minister brothers themselves as on the scale of the community of the faithful people. This practice of reprehension may also touch each and every especially, without any distinction. Finally, he interaction between the two instances is not done uniquely in the duty edification and admonishment of the corporal body. It is also written in the political space and intervenes at the heart of the decision taken by the Small Council – seat of the court as the executive and legislative power of the town – in front of the consultative authority that the magistrates granted to the Company in laying down new decrees, treaties or rulings in law cases. In this perspective, one must consider this participation in the power of the pastors in strengthening which could be caused by their access to the bourgeoisie and the eventual consequences that such a statute would have on its space of activity, or more exactly on the practice of the "freedom of the ministry", of which Le Gagneux and Colladon are suspected, then accused of having several times abused, leading with sermons against the honour of the Lord.

A new model of incorporation:
Attaching pastors by making them bourgeois people of Geneva

The double swearing-in of bourgeois people and the minister of Le Gagneux and Colladon, originally pastors respectively of Tours and Bourges, is written firstly in a form of radical incorporation other than that proposed by Calvin and his Company between 1541 and 1555. In fact, until in 1555, the Company of pastors is inserted and implanted in Geneva thanks to a conscious use of its marginalisation, subject as it is, by the French origin of its members, to attacks orchestrated by family and clan solidarities with a broadly xenophobic nature, aiming to weaken and reject the plan for ecclesial renewal brought in by Calvin[1230]. At this time, Calvin moreover cultivates, against this so-called opposition of the "Children of Geneva", his position as a member of an ostracised body, because he was foreign. He is exposed in the pulpit until the paroxysm of the communiity rupture in a verbal violence fed by the imagination of the holy struggle. The request and free acceptance by the bourgeoisie in January 1556 of four ministers who were elected and assigned to the town of between 1545 and 1548, all of French origin, also mark the beginning of a more systematic access by the actors of the Genevan ministry to this privilege which was for a long time protected by the landed stock and citizens of Geneva[1231].

[1230] SZCZECH N. "Fortus Francis" Tensions and xenophobia in Calvin's Geneva (1546-1555). A.ROUILLET, O.SPINA and N. SZCZECH "Trouver sa place" Madrid Casa de Velazquez 2011 p 117-134.

[1231] Made bourgeois on 14 January 155, it is about Francois Bourgoin,of Raymond Chauvet,Jean Fabri and Jean de St-Andre. KINGDON R.M "Registres de la Compagnie…Calvin" Geneva Droz op. cit p 248.

After being assured of the support thanks to the massive accession in February and April 1555 of immigrants into the bourgeoisie and four years after the defeat in May 1555 of the "Children of Geneva", Calvin finally followed his colleagues and goes into the bourgeoisie. In December 1559, however he faces the authorities asking him to join the bourgeoisie and even regretting his slowness to do so, Justifying his reserves to his care to have sought to "avoid the suspicions to which some people are inclined, he approved the initiative of the Magistrate and replies here even more to the wishes of the Small Council to join them[1232].

This action is significant, for on the same day in December 1559, four professors and resigned ministers of the academy and the Church in Lausanne present themselves with Calvin before the Small Council. According to them, they are formulating a similar request, that of being received as bourgeois of Geneva. With this bias and thanking the Genevan authorities already for "other good things they have done". Pierre Viret, Antoine Le Chevalier, Jean Raymond Merlin and Jean Tagaut asked the Council to "receive them and accept them [1233] to the number of bourgeois so as to have greater opportunity to be devoted to this Republic" they all receive and sign here one of these other transfers of succeeding pastoral people between Geneva and Berne. This reception into the bourgeoisie, which was also valid for Theodore de Beze in April 1559, seems, even more, to mark a transition[1234]. A faster incorporation confronts Calvin's slow affiliation, or claimed as such, by conserving his foreign status or as a simple inhabitant, or claimed as such which he was able to

---

[1232] 1232 AEG. "Proces-verbaux des seances du Petit Conseil RC 55 25.12.15559 fol 163r COVELLE A.L. "Le livre des bourgeois…" op. cit. p 265-266 (25.12.1559)

[1233] Ibid.

[1234] COVELLE A.L. (le livre des bourgeois…op.cit. p 264 (17.04.15

instrumentalise, using this experience and personal reality lor purposes of implantation, shared for a long time by his ministerial brothers. The new arrivals, also in their majority being French immigrants, appear more engaged in a collaboration which would come to be inscribed in a will to strengthen the political and confessional connections in Geneva by participation, thanks to their bourgeois status, to economic privileges and extensive political rights.

On the Magistrate's side, accession to the bourgeoisie would resound as a reply to the intrinsic nature of this pastoral body in a town and a Church which was in contact by their geographical situation as by their evangelising aspirations. It would also respond to the challenge shared by the town and the Church in the aftermath of Calvin's death to hold "firm to make its ministers ready and not to have a break" according to the same terms of the Company of pastors at the time of the extension of leave given to Le Gagneux in 1565 to settle his family affairs[1235]. I It is in this same sense of holding the pastoral people in Geneva that the sovereign authorities asked the minister Charles Perrot, for who they authorise a holiday in France, not to "listen to anyone un order to be turned away from coming[1236]". Again in this same perspective, they asked Antoine le Chevalier, a bourgeois and professor from 1559 at the Academy of Geneva, "to weigh up the consequence of this school and keeping it in balance against the need to offer the glory of God for its special gain", He must finally consider and confront "his duty and obligation that he has to the town as the vocation and the bourgeoisie to serve this town and church according to the grace that God has given "in front of the promise made to his native town, Caen, to come there and preach the Evangel, in front of the management of his

---

[1235] AEG "Proces-verbaux des seances du Petit conseil RC 060 27.12.156 folm137r.

[1236] Ibid 26.05.1565 fol,v 58r   Proces-verbaux des seances du petit Conseil RC 59 4.07.1564 FIL 67 4.12.FOL.149R.

assets which required, at risk of losing everything, his imperative presence.[1237].

Finally yielding to the Genevans' complaints, LD Chevalier "agreed to stay there on condition that they (the ministers] relieve him from the Church …and the gentlemen also and that there may be some regard for what will be unhappy for his well-being[1238]".

From that time, entry into the bourgeoisie surely allowed that affiliation to a particular Church, foreseen and defended by the reformer of Geneva in his "Institution de la religion chrestienne" so as to give order[1239]. The documented research * in papers left by Calvin of the terms of loans and leaves granted to the minister Nicolas Des Gallars, engaged between 1560 and 1568 London and Orleans before returning towards Geneva in 1568, towards "the church to which he is primarily attracted" his election to the ministry having been given in 1544, would illustrate this[1240]. Across this case, the expression of a priority link given to Geneva is made. After two years spent in the town serving the college, the authorities ensure Des Gallars before his fears of being blamed with the Church of Orleans. In fact, Geneva again wants to employ him in the ministry, however, as the magistrates maintain to Des Gallars "as to the Church of Orleans, it has no opportunity to be unhappy about it, considering that he was always held to be bourgeois and that being sent back by God to Geneva he

---

[1238] AEG Proces-verbaux des seances du Petit conseil RC 60, 12.03.1565 fol 25v

[1239] CALVIN J. "Institution de la religion chrestienne" ed. J-D BENOIT Paris Vrin 1957-1963 book IV chap III 6-7.

[1240] AEG" Proces-verbaux des seances du Petit Conseil" RC 65 26.09.1570 folm147v RC 66 11.01/1571 fol 4r.

was held by the Lord without those of the said church having [1241] given him help a thousand times[1242]".

Moreover, with a minister who had become bourgeois, Geneva could be ensured in a pastoral body which had become likely to be of a variable dimension, able to extend and therefore to allow its members to practice elsewhere, in short or long term, in order to acquire support and protects while being able, if required, to be strong in himself. That is what can be understood by the long absence of leave granted to Gilles Chausse and to Paul Baduel, both bourgeois from Geneva, sent respectively to Lyon and to Auvergne[1243]. Facing their departure, these two pastors from Geneva asked "to be held at the level of you bourgeois", they were assured this would be so, under the promise and condition to be recalled "when it would seem […] to the gentlemen whom they must remember that they are "primarily obliged, to come back as a member of this church without the Churches of Lyon and Auvergne being able to prevent them[1244].By the status of bourgeois granted to its ministers, Geneva thus built a solid platform and, if necessary, closed upon itself in the defence of its confessional identity, a form of rampart where the sword of the word is conjugated to carrying arms, then required for taking an oath of any new bourgeois person having to be, for the defence of the town "supplied and matched with arms", a connection which is also strengthened in his obligation, common to the bourgeois person and to the minister, to live in Geneva," in time of need" and "not to

---

[1242] AEG "Proces-verbaux des seances du Petit Conseil RC 22.1.1571 fol 11r

[1243] Giolles Chausse is accepted freely o the bourgeoisie on 10.12.1562:COVELLE A.L. "Le livre des bourgeois" op.cit p 274.Paul Baduel son of Claude professor in the Academy of Geneva was received for" 16 crowns" bourgeois on 9.05.1555 ibid p 343.

[1244] AEG "Peoces-verbaux des seances du Petit Conseil" RC 61 24.05.1506 fol 44r RC 65 11.12.1570 fol 181r.

abandon it" authorising him officially to able to live elsewhere but doing so never without a licence[1245]Incorporation of pastors and relationship to obedience:

Before the Magistrate, before the Company

Now, this incorporation into the bourgeoisie would also mark a stronger connection of obedience to the magistrates, expressing itself through taking an oath aimed towards loyalty owed to the town, especially legible in a role of punctual counsellor who is called to be, in times of crisis, the bourgeois, through his participation in the Council. He is then held in secret of the discussions and in secret with the decision. More generally, he must not work to safeguard "franchises, edicts and decrees of the city[1246]". Under this angle, this swearing would come to further consolidate "the good example of obedience" which promises to be the pastor at the time of his swearing [1247]the oath at the ministry of the Word, "by which he becomes subject and obedient to the laws and to the Magistrate". He then swears to "keep and maintain the honour and benefit of the Seignory[1248]. However, if the elected minister promises and swears "to be subject to the policy and the statutes of the City" he places a limit to his obedience. Now it is the pastoral office and its practice that come to mark out the contours of the submission of the new pastor in the temporal framework. In fact, the allegiance to the Magistrate of the pastoral body is made "without prejudicing the freedom that we must have

---

[1245][1245] Reformulated on 24.1.1538 after theown moved into the Reformation see introduction to EG "Proces-verbaux des seances du Petit conseil RC 72 6.01.1577-3.01.1578

[1246] AEG "Proces-verbaux des seances du Petit Conseil" RC 72.
[1247]

[1248] PEISTERER E. "Le catechisme de l'eglise de Geneve (1542) Es ordonnances ecclesiastiques de l'Eglise de Geneve" 1561 W.NIESEL Bekenntmisschriften …reformierten Kirche" Munich 1938 v 1 p 45 19, 1,.18

to teach according to God and do the things that are from our duty[1249]. Between 1565 and 1571, this question of freedom left to the position of the pastor is found clearly and constantly at the centre of tensions between the Small Council and the company. On the occasion of collective sermons or of dues to isolated members of the Genevan clergy, it must oblige the pastors to define and redefine their area of activity, for the handling of the Word of God generates a true conflict between these two instances, in its dimension of mutual and community public censure, capable at the time to come to revert to possible abuses which were present with the Magistrate. The confrontation is developed between December 1564 and February 1571, and is established n a process of ruling on preaching, at the heart of which the withdrawal affairs of Le Gagneux and Colladon are placed.

In front of ministers who, in order to protect their bothers Colladon and Le Gagneux, in two cases emphasise the complexity of handling a forthright Word of God, which is neither "pleasing for everyone" nor Easily received" for one only has to omit or change a word which will overturn the intention of the speaker" which is stated again in a principle laid down in 1564 following the withdrawal of Jean Raymond Merlin[1250]. In fact if the pastors came to see or perceive an abuse on the part of the Magistrate, they had too let him know "kindly and discreetly. Then they had to resort to the Council, going to them while acting thus, in this closed area, to inform the magistrates of their complaints[1251]. They pushed finally, in the case of a confirmed abuse, the authorities to amend it and correct it.

In exercising discretion, the magistrates take care to prevent any unjustified scandal caused by a revelation or

---

[1249] Ibid l. 21-22.

[1250] AEG "Proces-verbaux des seances du Petit Conseil" RC 66 6.02.1571 fol 23v 26.01.1571 fol 14r.

[1251] AEG "Proces-verbaux des seances du Petit Conseil" RC 60 4.12.1564 Fol 151R rc62 12.02.1567

dissemination from the pulpit and, with that, the risk of passing in the eyes of the faithful flock, respective subjects, for bad leaders. Through this bias, they keep the union between Church and State intact and defend it openly. No doubt the very terms of the minister's oath as exactly laid down and consolidated are seen, according to which the pastor undertakes to correct, in the framework of the consistory as a the time of his responsibility for enlightenment and therefore of preaching about [1252]"those who have fallen" nevertheless having to commit vengeance, without giving room for hate or favour", but working much more "for people to stay in peace and union under the government of the Seignory". In this perspective, and facing the comprehension of the magistrates of the social cohesion, the pastor would act as essential agent to the connection and to the exercise of power, becoming a mediator placed between the authorities and the subjects. In February 1571, the will for affiliation of the minister to preserving the social unity and read more again at the time of an umpteenth[1253] request from the Small Council to the pastors where, one by one, they are exhorted on pain of being "rebels and disobedient to their superior magistrates" to subscribe to this clause of discretion in the public correction of the magistrates[1254]. On that date, Collladon is away for Nyon, without duly approved leave and without consenting to this measure. Coming back several days later to Geneva, on the prayer of his brothers, he joins in and confesses to having been blind, a state of blindness and straying from which God by grace took him away. Seven months later, he goes up into the pulpit "under the shadow of some abuses that he said he had overcome [...] publicly and without any meeting against" the state and a decree of change drawn up

---

[1252] PETSTERER E. "Le Catechisme..." art.ci. p 45 17-18 l.9 l.12.

[1253]

[1254] AEG "Proces-verbaux des seances..." RC 66 8.02.1571 FOL. 24V.

about three years ago by the small and great council after the change drawn up on the advice of the ministers of the word of God with whoever was there[1255]. This gesture is described as "intolerable and contravening the oath of a good and faithful bourgeois as much as a minister" and causes Theodore de Beze that one of the two, himself or that of Colladon, would be a false prophet[1256].

A perjurer and propagator of false doctrines are two acccusations come to us at the heart of the process of decision=taking, as much in the consultative charge that recurs sometimes and on appeal of the authorities the company in its resulting enactment by the Small council of a new decree, here there was change[1257]. At the time of a minister becoming bourgeois, they emphasise not only the effects of narrowing that this statute could cause on the pastor and his area of activity, but would also indicate the dynamic and tensions which were present even inside the ecclesial body. Through the remark of Theodore le Beze and the resistance expressed by Collladon, the collegial practice is revealed in the differentiated value given to the final resolution which the whole of the Company by the voice of its moderator will propose to the Magistrate. Three years earlier it is therefore on the change that these pastors, on the request of the magistrates. Now, in September 1571, Colladon makes a claim in the name of is pastoral duty and his conscience, the right to retract an arrangement to which he had previously subscribed to, but which, according to him, showed it to be obsolete, because it was badly applied, unadapted and inadequate for the present circumstances[1258]. The actual methods of his application even make the institution of exchange contrary to the first intentions. For Beze and the rest of the Company, Colladon here doubts the truth and therefore the inspired value of the collegial advice,

---

[1255] Ibid 28.09.1571 fol 120
[1256] Ibid fol 120v 27.08.1571 fol 104.
[1257] Ibid 26.01.1571 fol. 15v.
[1258] Ibid 27.08.1571 fol. 104.

becoming, in his act of autonomy and authority, an agent to schisms. He has left to the "devil" his entrances within the heart of this college of equals, renouncing the principle present in chapter 14 of this first Epistle, to the Corinthians – the minds of the prophets are submitted to the prophets - which the pastors recall already in 1564 in front of recourse to the special conscience of the pastor Merlin who then was interrogated and blamed for wishing by his sermons to place himself above his brothers and even claimed to want a Church "managed by himself alone"[1259] With his position, Colladon thus faces a first narrowing, that of a Company afifirming itself as a body of doctrine, charging from that time its resolutions coming from a conscience operated collectively in a perpetual dimension which would finally turn into a form of infallibility. By obedience to the Company pr by conviction, he nevertheless participated three years earlier, in the institution by the Small Council of a decree, which must be respected as bourgeois of Geneva and following his oat

***

From that time, with Colladon the risk is expressed that a servant of the Word of God, however marginal and contestable it may be, becomes even more a bade example of obedience and a bad citizen, swearing that he is in his double promise as a pastor and a bourgeois to defend the honour of the Signory so as to respect and safeguard the decrees and laws of the town. More than manifesting themselves thus by heir repeated speeches, he and Le Gagneux stir up and give rise to a counter-power by an alliance with the subjects. By the use of the pulpit, the place of activating their resistance, they incarnate altogether some fear for the authorities, which is precisely of hat limit of obedience to th Magistrate to which and following their own

---

[1259] AEG "Proces-verbaux des seances du Petit Conseil, RC 59, 28.10.154 fol. 127r 31.10.1564 fol 13.

minister's oath, the pastors can claim in the name of the freedom of the ministry. From this, the tightenings that the Magistrate tries to operate on his clerical body by negotiation and regulation of a space of words, of teaching and correction of the ministers carried out in respect of them. Resentment by some pastors as a stricture of the ministerial space of activity, the process would only have been emphasised by the more systematic access to the bourgeoisie of the actors of the Genevan ministry thanks to the resonances and effects of reinforcement of the connection that the oath of the bourgeois gives to the oath of a minister. This dynamic, if it has, according to us, created this tissue of restrictions pushing Colladon and Le Gagneux to cross the border without legitimate authorisation, would have better served the construction of a Company as an instance gifted with a single and unique conscience, being built as a guardian of the Truth, where the practice of the authority would rest on the body completely, Through this bias, Beze would be forced not only to limit the institution of a particular and charismatic figure within the Company, but would also try to prevent its possible collection by the Magistrate in his decision-taking and would from seek that time to safeguard the independence of the Church. Also it would be much less the personality of Beze alone which would have marked the development of the Genevan church, by its spirit of conciliation in front of the authorities, than the conscious use of an enterprise of control of the pastors, emanating from the magistrates, which would serve the construction and the assertion of a clergy as a body of theologians.

***

Foreign clerks to foreign pastors
The building of a category in XVIIth century France:
Individuals, Churches and royal power
IRENE PLASMAN-LABRUNE

Dealing with foreign pastors. not under the angle of a social impossibility - the number and nature of available sources do no allow one to establish with certainty that an individual is a foreigner – but under the political angle, through the negative construction of a category, implies being situated at the crossing of the issue of control, internally in the ecclesiastical institutions and that of assuming relations with the political authority. Civil and political belonging of Church people tends in fact to take on a growing importance[1260], "a portiori" when the question of allegiance becomes central at the beginning of the XVIIth centtury[1261]

Not many of them, the foreign pastors represent in France of the XVIIth century an embedded exception in the one which constitutes the reformed minority under the regime of the Edict of Nantes. Doubly a minority, they are as a result in the connection of the confessional and national divisions. This exceptional situation is made brutally clear when the royal power in 1623 imposes in 1623 the exclusion of foreigners to the pastorship. Being identified until then in a punctual manner, through the institutionalisation of the Refprmation in the kingdom, the foreign pastors, taken for a target by the royal power and by the clergy, from that time form a negative category. Their exclusion constitutes one of the early elements of t[1262]he repressive devices which were progressively put in place in front of reforms throughout the XVIIth century.

The exclusion of foreigners to the pastorship can apparently go back to that of foreigners to the access to the benefices of the kingdom, begun in the XVth century and re-started in the second half of the XVIth century. But,

---

[1260] See the contribution of Genevieve Gross in this volume.

[1261] DE FRANCESCHI S.H/ "La crise theologico-politique ....prisme francais (1607-1627" Rome, BEFAR 2010c.

[1262] DOMPNIER B. "Le venin de l'heresie....Image...XVIIe siècle" Paris Le Centurion 1985. LABRIYSSE e. "Une foi, une loi, un roi?...Nantes" Paris Geneva Payot – Labor et Fides 1985.

while the exclusion of foreigners from the benefices came from a face-to-face between the royal power and the papacy for control, notably financial, of the French church, the exclusion of foreign pastors reveals more the issue of allegiance and sees the confessional claims of the clergy being taken back by the royal power.

Crossing the sources produced by the reformed people themselves, particularly at the time of the national synods, with those coming from the royal power and the Catholic clergy across the meetings of the clergy, enables one to study here through the exclusion of foreign pastors the conflictual process by which a standard of political order is imposed, outside its own field, in the ecclesiastical space. In other words, as the foreign pastors become, in favour of confessional combat, the support of the assertion of the royal authority through the double construction of the kingdom as a national space and as a confessional space .After a first part summing up the second part of the XVIth century, the second part of this contribution will precisely deal with the construction of foreign pastors as a negative category on the periphery of the royal power, before analysing in the last part its repossession by the royal power.

Foreign pastors? The promotion of a question and its limits in the second half of the XVIth century

If the control of mobility has always constituted for the Church a disciplinary issue of importance, it is in the framework defined by the first councils (especially Canon XCI of the Council of Nicea in 325 and Canon XX of the Council of Chalcedony in 451) that is, that of the Diocese: from this point of view, the Council of Trent does not innovate[1263]. The national or political framework never forms a pertinent space from the canonical point of view[1264].

[1263] ALBERIGO G. "Les conciles ecumeniques)" Paris Cerf 1994 v 1 p 51 and p. 219.
[1264] LAPRAT R. "Incapaxirt...des urbains" R. NAZ "Dictionnaire...canonique" Paris Ltouzy et Ane, v 1 col 1322-1380.

At most, is it admitted that the pastoral needs can possibly justify the recourse to a discrimination based on the linguistic criterion: created by Gregory XI in 1373, the rule "De Idiomate" taken from hose of the Apostolic Chancellorship, acknowledges the need to confer benefices with the charge for souls to clerks who were capable of preaching and teaching in the language of the place[1265]. This stability of the canonical framework has not however prevented Charles VII from banning in 131, at the time of a conflict with the papacy, on access by foreigners to the benefices of the kingdom[1266].

If the association between foreigner and heretic is a fact which was already observed in the Middle Ages[1267], the repression which is quickly practised in the Kingdom of France against the supporters of the Reformation confirms, even emphasises, that assimilation, fed by transnational circulations that stirs up Protestantism in the European area[1268] In fact, insofar as the French national feeling is broadly constructed, Colette Beaune has shown,[1269] on the religious excellence of the kingdom, any form of divergence seems like a double rejection, of the community of faith that the King and his subjects create , as a result, a rejection of the royal authority.

Because it brings about a growing recourse to exile, repression feeds and reinforces this assimilation of the heretic toa foreigner. Even if it is first of all considered on the style of temporary refuge, and that a great many individual and family continuities exist. Failing to be

---

[1265] Ibid col. 1340.
[1266] ISAMBERT F.A. "Recueiil general..1789" Paris Pion 1829 v XVI (1610-1643 p 783 sq.
[1267] BOZOKY E. "The cathars…exils" C. GAUVARD "L'etranger au Moyen Age" Paris Publications de la Sorbonne 2000 p 107-118.
[1268] MONTER E.W. "Judging…Reformation…Parlements" Cambridge M.A. Harvard University Press 1999.
[1269] BEAUNE C. "Naissance de la nation France" Paris Gallimard 1985.

unique[1270], the role of Geneva is considered essential on this point. Having in fact become a refuge in front of the per[1271]persecutions, the city of Leman also becomes a potential fish tank for the communities of the kingdom, as is shown by sending pastors to the kingdom from 1555[1272]. If these pastors are French in the majority, sending them is however considered by the royal power as a foreign interference, and a letter from Charles IX in 1562 calls for the Council of the town to stop this circulation and the recall of the pastors sent into the kingdom[1273]. It is doubtless for this reason that Article XIII of the declaration of 14 December 1563 stipulates that "the only people received to preach in future will be French people and our subjects[1274]. Unpublished, this putting forward of the national criterion by the royal power against the reformed people appears however to be a "hapax".

The national argument is however widely used in the political polemic of the second half of the XVIth century, whether it be by the royal power itself in order to re-establish the unity of the kingdom against the Council of Trent, or by the reformed people against the Guise family[1275]. The States General of 1576 constitute the peak of a xenophobia which, essentially directed against the

---

[1270] BENEDICT P. "Refuge churches and Exile…Reformation" P. BENEDICT, S.SEIDEL MENCI and A.TALLON "La Reforme… Italie ..contrastes" Rome, BEFAR 2007 p 535-552.

[1271] KINGDON R.M. "Geneva and the coming…France" Geneva Droz 2007 p 8. See also WILCOX P "l'envoi de pastors…" lists made up by Colladon (1561-1562) "Bulletin de la SHPF v 139-3 1993 p 37-37t.

[1274] FONTANON A "Les Edicts et ordonnances…sur icelles" Paris J. Du Puys 1589 v IV p 278 Paris 14.1.1563. The article also forbids ministers from preaching rebellion.

[1275] Speech by Michel deL'Hopital in Poissy; "La France et le concile de Trente"(1518-1563) Rome BEFAR 1993 p 302

Italians[1276] does not spare the Catholic clergy. On the other hand, the presence of foreign pastors does not seem to have attracted enough attention to become a point of crystallisation of the action of the royal power in front of reformed people at the time of civil wars. Contrary to other measures, the exclusion of foreigners from preaching of 1563is not in fact taken up later in the edicts nor in later declarations. The available data on the presence of foreign pastors, not plentiful in France, does not enable one to establish certainly whether the measure of 1563 was known and applied outside the expulsion in 1565 of a friend of Calvin, Pierre Viret, from the strategic town of Lyon[1277], The pastors probably remain so much more easily in the background that the nobility plays in an essential role and the confrontations were military confrontations.

Even while the national mobilisation was widely used in the service of the legitimisation of Henri de Navarre as the successor of Henry III, [1278] the national criterion nis not mobilised in the area of reformed people. Significantly, the first particular article of the Edict of Nantes extends its benefice to the non-regnicols[1279]. The case of the children of exiles is also described: contrary to an idea of national belonging based upon birth in the kingdom, the children of exiles at the time of troubles are also acknowledged as regnicols[1280]. The national criterion therefore appears at the

---

[1276] DUBOST J. J. "La France italienne" Paris aubier 1993 chap II "La haine" p 307 sq HELLER H. "Anti-Italianism...France" Toronto University of Toronto Press 2003.

[1277] BARNAUD B. "Ledit dr Nantes et ses antecedants (1562-1598) elec.sorbonne,fr/editsdeoacification) 2602/2016.

[1278] YARDENI M. "Dix annees de patriotism: 158-1594" M.YARDENI "Enuetes sur l'"identite de la "Nation France" Seyssel Champ Vallon 2004 0 308-317.

[1279] BARBICHE B. "Edit de Nantes et ses antecedents 1562-1598" [http:elec.enc.sorbonne, fr/editsdeoacification] consulted on 26/02/2016.

[1280] Ibid, art, 70 of the general rules of the Edict of Nantes.

beginning of the XVIIth century in the relations of the royal power and the reformed people as lacking n pertinence, and that while it constitutes at the same time an essential issue in the relations between the royal power and the religious orders, especially the Jesuits.

The foreign pastors, targets of the construction of a confessional issue

If national belonging of pastors does not visibly constitute an issue for the royal power off Henry IV, it seems however as an object of preoccupation in the internal sources of the reformed Churches that constitute the deeds of the national synods[1281]. In 1607 the national synod of La Rochelle predicts in fact that the deputies in the court will help the foreign pastors to obtain letters of naturalisation for them[1282]. If the measure is presented as relating to all the foreign pastors, one may wonder, failing more precise elements, if it is not essentially connected with the arrival in the kingdom of pastors expelled by James 1st's desire to introduce bishops into Scotland, some pastors who were judged and banished took up residence in France. Among them one finds in particular John Welsh, the nephew of John Knox.[1283]. The aim of the measure more remains ambiguous. In the measure where the letters of naturality are essentially for the purpose to discovering the incapacities which strike the foreigners in a successful manner, obtaining those in order to create a strategy of a family taking root than looking for a possible legitimation by royal power. If he synod, an ecclesiastical authority with

---

[1281] AYMON J. "Tus les synods…de France" La Haye Charle Delo 1710 2 vol.

[1282] Ibid v 1 p347 national synod of La Rochelle (1607) "Matieres concernant les deputes en cour" art.IV.

[1283] LEFEVRE DELA BODERIE A. "Ambassades dem. De la Boderie…"…Louis XIII…1611" P.D.BURTIN s.l.n 1750 v 1 letter to Puisieux 2.12.…1606.

doctrinal and disciplinary preoccupations, seems on this occasion to take into consideration a criterion which to him is in an external principle, this precaution does not seem to have concrete results in the letters of naturality effectively granted. No individual identified as a pastor appears for the following years in removals carried out.

The brutal death of Henry IV at the same time fragilises the royal power, opening up a period of regency, and the position of reformed people, dependent on the King. It is in this context that the meeting of the States General in 1614 is the theatre of an initiative of the clergy aiming precisely to make from the national criterion a tool at the service of the confessional fight[1284]. Stating these "contraventions" to the edict and denouncing the foundation of teaching institutions, colleges and academies, by the reformed people, the journal of the clergy claims in fact that the only foreigners who were authorised to "dogmatise regulate and teach in the kingdom are" Catholics ,the reformed people being only able to have recourse[1285] to individuals who were originally from the kingdom The clergy tries thus to place at the service of a claim of religious essence, the return to Catholic unity, a political claim which shows the prerogative of the royal power, the foreigners having in fact from the Middle Ages constituted a privileged support for the assertion of [1286]the royal authority. The clergy returns also against the reformed people the argument of national belonging to the holders of teaching positions used by the royal power against the Jesuits[1287]

[1284] On the attitude of the clergy, see DOMPNIER B. "le venin dl'heresie…" op.cit.

[1285] LALOURCE (son) and DUVAL "Recueil des cahiers Etats generaux" Paris barrios l;aine 1789 v IV p 145 art.CCC=XCB.

[1286] 'QLTEROCHE B. De l'etranger a la seignurie….XV siecle" Paris LDJ 2002.

[1287] Nelson e. "The Jesuits and the Monarch"…op.cit.

By using an argument of political order which implicitly is out of its order in the religious field assimilates the protestants with a foreign threat, the clergy on return legitimises the action of the royal power our of its order in the religious and ecclesiastical field. The fact that this claim, formulated very generally, only applies uniquely to the pastors shows that the construction of the category of pastors as the main target has not yet been achieved.

While the claims of the clergy at the time of the States General have remained without a sequel, it is outside the framework of the confessional confrontation, even inside a reformed community, that the national argument is again mobilised, but this time against a particular pastor. During the years 1625-1616, in a context of military confrontations between the reformed people and the royal power, an internal conflict in the local protestant community is brought before the Bordeaux parliament and, on this occasion, the national argument is again mobilised against the pastors, Cameron and Primerose, who are found to be Scottish[1288]. The use of the national argument by their enemy, a lawyer member of the consistory, thus offers opportunely a contest which is first of all disciplinary in a political and legal justification. This unpublished case paradoxically presents many analogies with the instrumentalisation of the national argument in internal conflicts of the religious orders. Recourse to this argument is facilitated by the competition which locally opposes the Bordeaux Parliament in the Chamber of the benefice of the Edict of Castres for the contentious parties implying [1289]the reformed people. To deny the benefit of the Edict of Nantes to foreigners thus enables the parliament to assert its authority against that of the Chamber of the Edict, while contributing to the construction of a restrictive

---

[1288] AYMON j. "Tous les synodes..." op. cit. v1 p29 national synod of La Rochelle (1607) "Matieres particulieres" art.IX it

[1289] DOMPNIER J.E. "Le venin del 'heresie"...op.cit.

interpretation of the Edict of Nantes. Placed at the service of the hierarchisation of the institutions at the time of an internal conflict (a phenomenon which one finds in the conflicts that the religious orders may know), the national argument sees its pertinence and its validity reinforced at the time when it is moreover also used in contesting the authority of Marie de Medici[1290].

The intervention of the Bordeaux Parliament is not limited as far as this episode: it plays a second time a motoring role by transforming this time the appearance of particular individuals in general exclusion. The registration of the Peace of Montpellier, signed on 18 October 1622, offers the Bordeaux Parliament a new opportunity to restrict the application of the Edict of Nantes. While the Peace of Montpellier confirms the Edict of Nantes, while forbidding political assemblies and by taking away from the reformed people eighty places of safety, the Parliament adds to it on 26 November 1622 the ban imposed on foreign ministers to preach in its area:

Nevertheless, according to the laws of the State, those who are not natives will not in future be received to preach, or dogmatise in this area.

Nor similarly without infringing or prejudicing the commissions awarded, towards the demolition of fortifications, walls, doorways or houses, etc.

Its [1291] resumption by the "Mercure francais" gives this decision, of local range at the outset, a much wider impact: "This confirmation does not need interpretation, on wishes to take away ever y subject to fall into new troubles"[1292]. That contributes to taking one of the parameters of a "legal war" against reformed people which broadly began as a

---

[1290] DUBOST j.F. "Marrie de Medici La reine devoilee" Paris Payot 2009

[1291] ISAMBERT F.A. "Recueil general…" op. cit. V XVI p XVIp 144.

[1292] "Le Mercure francais …Navarre Louis XIII v IX 1623 p 436.

peripheral guerrilla war. None of these episodes is mentioned, directly or indirectly, in the deeds of t[1293]he national synods, even while Cameron, was nominated at Saumur, is an eminent figure[1294]. If the synod of Vitre (1617) had recommended the recruitment of pastors into the kingdom[1295], it was probably more by the worry of orthodoxy and internal control in the perspective of seeing the national conformity guaranteeing political loyalty.

From the peripheries to the centre, the exclusion of foreign pastors to the service of the royal offensive against the reformed people

If the royal power ends by intervening, it is only in a second time, Then management, ecclesiastical, of the reformed Churches through the figure of theatre of direct intervention of the royal power in the internal commissioner[1296], the national synod of Charenton (1623) is the occasion of an expansion, this time in the whole of the kingdom, of the Bordeaux ban. In 1623, there are doubts weighing on the reality of their allegiance towards the royal authority which justify the ban to resort to foreign pastors. Essentially, this mobilisation of the question of allegiance against the reformed people is the product of a true transfer from an issue which was initially drawn up as a tool against the Jesuits and against the Roman authority in service to the monarchy[1297]. In this return to the initiative of royal power, the question of national belonging, taken as a sign of weak loyalty, represents the first stage of a more general and more

---

[1293] AYMON J. "Tous les synodes…op. it v II P 205
NATIONAL SYNOD OF Ales (120) "/Matieres generales" art VIII. the synod of Vitre (1617) ref ecolier a Geneve.

[1295] "…Louis XIII" v IX 1623 p 436. Le Mercure francais

[1296] AYMON K. "Tous les synods…" op.cit.v II p 205 national synod of Ales (1620) "Matieres generales" art.VIII.

[1297] NELSON E."The Jesuits and the M onarchy…" op. cit. and DE FRNCESCHI S.H. "La crise theologico-politique…" op.cit.

systematic view of the loyalty of the reformed people[1298]. In assimilating foreign status and disloyalty, real or supposed, the royal commissioner's speech in front of the synod contributes moreover to the formation of assimilation between birth and loyalty. r Birth appears from that time as the criterion of loyalty making in fact "a contrario" loyalty the necessary corollary of birth in the kingdom.

Announced in the commissioner's speech in front of the synod, the exclusion of foreigners from the pastorate is not however formalised legally. More than faith, it reveals then the specific relationship uniting the king with the privileged bodies which the reformed people establish under the regime of the Edict of Nantes. If this exclusion has an obvious symbolic responsibility, it is equally likely to increase the difficulties that some communities know in the matter of recruitment[1299]. Trying to open a dialogue space, even of negotiation, the synod deputies respond to this "innovation" in evaluating the loyalty of the incriminated pastors so that the prejudice that some Churches would suffer, meeting the wish for peace given to the king. Especially, they use the argument of the foreign presence in the heart of the Catholic clergy to claim the right for them also to have recourse to foreigners as pastors[1300]. The failure of this argument, which does not even receive a response, shows the derogatory dimension, not equivalent, which characterises the status of reformed people to foreign pastors in the kingdom in relation to the Catholic standard. The question of recourse to foreign pastors is thus a revelation of the ambiguities which make of the privilege which the Edict is, a possible case of gossip. Failing to succeed in bringing power back on the principle of

---

[1298] KRETZER H. "Calvinisme und fransosische ...Jureiu" Berlin Duncker & Humblot 1975

[1299] MOURS S. "Le Protestantisme en France au XVIIIth siècle" Paris Librairie protstante1967 p 100 et seq.

[1300] AYMON J. "Tous les synodes..." op. cit v II p 262 national synod of Charenton (1632).

exclusion, the synod however does obtain a respite for foreign pastors who were in post at the time: the latter remain tolerated, except for the famous Cameron and Primerose. This special treatment is assumed as a mystery independent of their origin, "not because of their birth, but for reasons which affect his service"[1301] ". The exclusion of foreign pastors is integrated into a wider group of measures aimed at breaking the links which unite reformed French people with their foreign co-religionaries. If the range of this international network is no longer in the XVIIth century of the same scale as that of a Duplessis-Mornay. The very existence of these links does not become less problematic and compromises the reformed French people in the eyes of power as that of Catholic opinion[1302]. In 1618, the representatives named by the reformed Churches of France are also seen to be forbidden to attend the synod of Dordrecht, the participation in a gathering situated abroad being considered against the laws of the kingdom[1303]. On the occasion of the synod of 1623, it is the reception of the deeds of Dordrecht by the Churches of the kingdom which was challenged insofar as these canons are considered foreign[1304]. Taken as targets in the framework of these measures, the foreign pastors also suffer the attacks which affect all of their brothers, the destruction of the group and the withdrawal of its noble supports leaving the latter in the first line.

In 1627, a declaration trying to unify the miscellaneous arrangements made against the pastors shows that from that

---

[1301] Ibid p 268.No element of justification is brought in

[1302] GREENGRASS M. "The French Pastorate: confessional identity…Huguenot minority 1559-1685" C.S. DIXON and L.SCHORN [SHUTTE "The Protestant clergy…Europe" New York Palgrave Macmillan 2003 p 176 -195.

[1303] PANNIER J. "L'eglise reformee de Paris…XIII" Paris Honore Champion 1022 p 668 supporting items no. XV.

[1304] AYMON J. "Tous les synodes…" op. cit. v II p261 national synod of Charenton (1623).

time they are the main targets[1305]. The perimeter of the exclusion of foreign pastors is stated clearly on this occasion. The lasting criterion is that of birth in the kingdom, which also allows the exclusion from that time of individuals born of refugee parents who were abroad during the troubles, however recognised as French by the Edict of Nantes as, in principle, by the law of the Parliament of Paris (Mabile decree 1576). A consecration which, in reverse, indicates the concrete problems which were met, the content of the declaration of 1627, and with it the exclusion of foreigners from the pastorate, is taken up in the framework of the great prescription prepared by the Guardian of the seal. Michel de Marillac. Ultimately called "Code Michau"[1306], this prescription of reformation is registered on 15 January 1629, between the surrender of La Rochelle (28 October (1629) and the Edict of Nimes (July 1629). Although the question of the reformed people was not covered on its own, it gives place, in the title of the reform of justice, to a great many articles about their legal privileges.

From devout inspiration, the text allows a real dread of contacts with foreign people[1307], especially factors of moral corruption. In spite of this general preoccupation, the contrast is striking and from a confessional point of view. While the foreign pastors are covered again, there is no measure relating to the Catholic clergy[1308]: the last general arrangements covering foreigners in the heart of the clergy

---

[1305] ISAMBERT F.A. "Recuel general…" op.cit.v XVI p 201 "Declaration du roi Louis XIII …Sa Majeste"

[1306] KADLEC L. "Le "Code Michau" : the reformation according to the Guardian of the Seal Michel de Marillac, "Les Dossiers de Grihl (on line) special no. "La vie de Michel de Marillac and the political experiences of the Guardian of the Seal"! consulted 26/02/2016.

[1307] ISAMBERT F.A. "Recueil general…" op.cit. v XVI p 275 art.175.

[1308] Ibid, p 86 Loudon Peace art.8.

in fact go back to 1616[1309]. Emphasising this discrepancy allows the scope of travel to be measured, even of coming and going, which took place during the 1620's: the national argument which was drawn up and used by the royal power in order to establish his control on the French Church, and more particularly to establish the legitimacy of Henry IV, is from that time turned against the reformed people through their pastors. The reconstruction of the unity of the kingdom on a national base has, during the 1620's, a clear confessional colour. A decade of direct confrontation between the royal power and the reformed people, these 1620's are also years of crystallisation of suspicion of disloyalty in respect of them.

But far from cutting of their speech, and the acknowledgement of the wish to exclude foreigners from the pastorate, and therefore the control [1310] of the reformed communities, does not pre-judge the reality of its application. It is especially right to question the conditions of carrying out this exclusion. On this complex question, insofar as it is asked for the main thing at the local level, different points can be emphasised.

The first thing is that the 1630's are effectively the theatre of a concrete offensive, which reflect not only the deeds of the assemblies of the clergy, but also the correspondence of Andre Rivet, a French pastor installed as Professor in the United Provinces[1311]. Challenged as foreigners in different places in the kingdom, several pastors found themselves in Paris in order to carry out their challenge. It is particularly about Sharp, Professor in Die, then Le Faucheur, Rousssele and Chauve, in Languedoc. As well as Mestrezat and Delincourt in Paris. To these prestigious names are added those of Chanterton, Hametm, Home. This local dimension enables an emphasis to be placed on the importance of coming-and-going between the

---

1310

[1311] BU Leyde BPL.301.

centre of power and the peripheries in the application of a measure, as well as the importance of local intermediaries, as the clergy here, better also to be able to locally identify possible objectors. Made possible by the conjunction of the action of the clergy and the royal power, particularly through the parliaments, this offensive does not spare, on the contrary, some of the most visible figures among the pastors officiating in the kingdom. The diversity of individual status of different pastors who are challenged (some are natives of Scotland, others from Geneva or from Neuchatel. Delincourt is a native of Sedan (independent until 1642), on the one hand, and the refusal of the royal power to concede the slightest exception (the 1623 engagement about foreign pastors who were already in their makes a long appointment , on the other hand, suggests that these pastors are, to their defending body, the laboratory of a vision which was always more restrictive of the definition of national affiliation through the challenge of collective exceptions which were traditionally recognised, especially for the Scots and for the Genevans. This challenge has however a time of advance on reality to the extent that some pastors, like Mestrat or Le Faucheur, born in Geneva, could pursue their career. In the immediate moment, this offensive against foreign pastors, was possible compensation in order to make (in the eyes of the devout) the choice of the struggle against Spain acceptable, shows in any case that the Code Michau was at least partially applied, contrary to a widespread idea.

After the offensive of the 1630s, the question of foreign pastors sems to reveal more of the war of the see: it appears on the list of griefs expressed at each national synod by the royal power against the reformed people. While the line of defence followed during the synods had been to try to obtain and guarantee exceptions to this exclusion, the synod of 1645 in Charenton capitulated by affirming to conform strictly to this exclusion and abandoned "de facto" the struggle for the exceptions. The foreign pastors seem to have paid the expenses, at least in the mind of the moderator of the synod, for the wish to preserve the possibility of studying abroad, which was also threatened[1312] The national standard, of political The essence, is from that time passing [1313]to impose itself inside the ecclesiastical field[1314]. The mistrust of the French reformed people against the British Independents who disembarked into the maritime provinces also bears witness to this,

While the principle of exclusion can in future seem to be acquired in theory, the obstinance shown by assemblies of the clergy to claim the application and to denounce the contravenants during the years 1660-1670 reveal its limits On. the continuous reduction of the perimeter of the exceptions (case of the Genevans, children born abroad) there is added a phenomenon of amplification, with a ban on access to the pastorate to individuals who have studied abroad[1315].It is the simple contact with the foreigner which henceforth constitutes a central issue. Failing to disappear completely, the question of foreign pastors throws light on new targets, reflections of the retractation of space for reformed people. The conflict between confessional imperatives and diplomatic imperatives however meanwhile protects this situation for some of the latter. The Edict of Fontainebleau adds nothing to an exclusion whose construction is broadly previous: not more than the texts which immediately precede it, it does not mention foreign pastors

Directly henceforth, the challenge of the reformed people does not require any longer to pass through the bias of contracts, real or supposed, with the foreigner. A royal declaration of 1st July 186 foresees on the other hand the

---

[131213121312] AYMON J. "Tous les synodes…" op.cit.v II P 642 National Synod of Charenton(1645).

[1313] Ibid, p 678.

[1315] DE CARBON DE MONTPEZAT J. "Proces-verbal de l'assemblee generale…1655 et 1656" Paris A. Vitre 1655 p 537.

death sentence for pastors, French or foreign, who entered the kingdom without royal authority, article IV however authorising the presence of foreign ministers, but confined in the framework of embassies[1316]. Having disappeared with the Edict of Nantes, the question of foreign pastors only appears in a limited manner, through the problem of the attractiveness that the chapels of embassies are liable to exert on new converts.

***

A minority inside a minority, passed unseen at the same time individually and collectively until the beginning of the XVIIth century, the foreign pastors benefit in their defending body from a disproportionate attention during that time. Targets of an instrumentalization by the clergy of the national argument in the service of the confessional combat, the form the involuntary support of the construction of a national standard which progressively assimilates the imperative of the community of faith. In this process, the foreign pastors, the foreign pastors but also indirectly the reformed people as a whole, come to incarnate the conflict of allegiance initially discovered against the Jesuits. Decisively, this phenomenon of transfer of one clergyman to the other does not work so much on the method of analogy or of symmetry. While the bans which strike the foreign clerks can bel lifted into the framework of a specific arrangement, leave to hold benefices[1317]. This fund resumed, nearly wo centuries later, by the Concord of 1891 and the organic articles of 1802.a mental asymmetry is

---

[1316] PILATTE L.R. "Edits, declarations…Reformee (1662-1751)" Paris Fischbacher 1885 p 292,

[13171317131713171317]DUBOST J.F."Les etrangers en France XVI siècle 1709…archives nationales" Paris Archives narionales.

See ARDURA B. "Le concordat entre Pie VII et Bonaparte 15.07. 1801 Bicentenaire …reconciliation Paris Cerf 2001 p 8=72-89.

strong enough to be resumed, nearly two centuries later, by [1318]the Concord of 1801 and the organic articles of 1802.

Conclusions
Yves KRUMENACKER

For a long time, he historic study of monks was an ecclesiastical story, confessional and national. If it is still the case in a certain number of countries, it is not the same in a number of others[1319]. In France, religious history has taken over ecclesiastical history from the 1960's, with an interest brought to Christian people and not only any longer only to the gre[1320]at personalities, institutions and dogma, and the search for a ""popular religion" which would nor any longer be simply the product of teaching which is more or less well understood. The last decades of the XXth century have also produced a "non-[1321]confessional history of Christianism" dealing conjointly with the different Christian Churches. The very great majority of historians of religious people are not at the moment more like clerks, but staff of universities or members of the CNRS, less and less engaged in Churches, often even outside these Churches. In this development, groups which are more or less informal have played an important role, the first place

---

[1318] Art. XXXIII of section IV "Des cures du titre II"Des ministers du concordat de 1801 "Aucun etranger ne p[ourra etre employe ..sans la permission du Gouvernement."

[1319] See the contrasting balnces, for contemporary histoire in DURAND J.D. "Le monde de l'histoire religieuse Essais d'historiographie" Lyon Chrretiens et Societes 2012.

[1320132013201320] Among the most resounding books of the present day, after pioneering studies of LE BRAS G,"Etudes de socioogiereligieuse" Paris PUF 1955-1956 32 vo.

[1321] MAYEUR J.M. PIETRI C. VAUCHEZ A.and VENADM "Histoire du Christianism des origines a nos jours" Paris Deslee-fayard 1990-2001 14 vol

the group of la Bussiere[1322], founded in 1958 and of which some members are original or took part in the symposium of Nancy on clergy in contact of which this volume gathers the deeds.

The latter seems to me to be significant of a double development which is even more recent. Firstly, the internationalisation of French research on Christianity. In spite of brilliant exceptions, a great many researchers stay confined to the French space and pass rather al little to vast European enquiries[1323], and the symposiums which confront the different spaces are certainly not numerous. The other development consists in the re-appropriation by historians of subjects which were either reserved to the clerks[1324] or abandoned because they were tied too much to traditional history, like the parish[1325] or, exactly, the clergy. And it is the crossing of these two new tendencies which makes the richness of the preceding pages.

One must still accept the use of the term "clergy" for all the Christian confessions. The introduction to this volume is well explained, and there is nothing to be added there. One must simply state exactly that one considers the clergy as a body of clergy and that one carefully distinguishes this notion from that of a priest, rejected by the protestants. However, the ambiguity is that the clergy, of all confessions, claim a power of mediation. It is clear for the Catholics, but it is no less true in the reformed tradition: Calvin makes the pastors ambassadors of God, to the point that one cannot know him as the Saviour but through them; in the "Catechism of Heidelberg", it is preaching, reserved

---

[1322] FLIPPI B. "le Groupe de l a Bussiiere"" Revue d'histoire de l'Eglise de France v 86 no 217 2000 p 755-745.

[1323] One must quote, among others, Jean Delumeau with his research the fear and sentiment of safety or, in Nancy, the work of Louis Chatellier.

[1324] One may think about MARTIN P. "Le theatre divin…XXe siècle" Paris CNRS 2010.

[1325] BONZON A. GUIGNET and VENARD M ."La paroisse urbaine. A nos jours" Paris Cerf 2014.

to the pastors, which is the true ministry of keys, opening the kingdom of the skies.

Comparing: through time, the places and the confessions

AS J. Leonard recalls in the introduction, the study of clergy in a systematic perspective was put forward in the 1990's by Luise Schorn—Schutte. It is an aspect of the problem, partially treated in this volume but which does not form the heart; for to compare the clergy does by force presuppose that the latter had contacts between them. In there, there are differences of method: the comparatism studies the clergy of diverse Churches in various times and places, in order to see clearly what separates them and what brings them near. The historian may well deduce the existence of logics which are not purely confessional or on the contrary developments which ae only explained by ecclesiastical choices. This work is very precious in the way that it enables blind points to be revealed, the particularities which are proper to a specific clergy, or to give evidence of comparable developments.

This method enables a great many lessons to be drawn that several of the contributions to this volume have strengthened.

- The historiography has adopted the idea of social disciplinarisation, introduced by Gerhard Oestreich, developed by the Italians and Wolfgang Reinhard in that of confessionalisation[1326].The more the studies are developed in different Churches, the more it seems obvious that a parallel process is at work with very similar objectives, even if the means sometimes diverge.

- A growing clericalisation is at work. It is to be distinguished from the priestly creation and the process of mediation, described above. But it is clear that, from each

---

[1326] OESTREICH G."Geis und Gestalt…States" Berlin Duncker7 Humblot 1969.

side of the confessional border, the clergy are seeking to be distinguished from the faithful members and to have authority over them. The "good "Catholic" priest[1327] of the model protestant pastor"[1328] are the archetypes of his clerks. The controversies, analysed here by J.Foa, are a good means of showing that only the clergy have the necessary abilities to argue, and that therefore they are the only ones to have the right to do it. In the same way access to the pulpit is more and more reserved for the clerks. In the Calvinist type of Church, in opposition to the Bernese model the pastors [1329] seize discipline, and in almost making a third mark of the Church; N. Szcech shows it precisely for Geneva and G.Gross explains how the company of Pastors in Geneva was gradually transformed into a Church body. Among French protestants, the deacons are quickly excluded from administering the sacraments and only the pastors can distribute communion in two types.

-The place of [1330] clergy in the population, in the culture, in politics is not appreciably different from one confession to the other. There are court clergy in Brandenburg or in Saxony, State prelates in France as in England[1331]. In another

---

[1327] KRUMENACKER Y."Du pretre tridentin au "bon pretre". D.PISTER "L'image du pretre dans la literature Classique 9XVII-XVIIIe siecles Bern,Peter Lang 2001 p 121-139.

[1328] LEONARD J. "Etre Pasteur au XVIIe siècle. Le ministere de Paul Fery a Met (1612-1659) Rennes PUR 2915.

[1329] GROSSE C. "La coupe et le pain de la discorde:…xviiie siècle" Paris Honore Champion 2000 p 33—35e.

[1330] THADDEN R. VON" Die brandenburgisch-preufischen Hofprediger…Brandenburg Preusseb" Berlin De Gruter 1959 SOMMER W. SOMMER W, "Die lutherischen…Sachsen, Stuttgart, Franz Verlag 2006; PIERRE B

[13311331] MICHON C. "La Crosse et le Sceptre. Les prelats…HENRI VIII" Paris Tallandier 2008

ROUSSEL B. "Ensevelir hnnetement les corps" "Funeral corteges and Huguenot culture" R.A.MENTZER and A. SPICER "society and Culture in the HUGUENOT WORLD" 1559-185 CAMBRIDGE CUP2001 p 194-208.

domain, one sees that everywhere, in spite of clericalisation, the clergy must sometimes submit to the pressure of the populations: the protestants hold on to their pastors solemnising burials even more than what is allowed by the discipline of the Churches and. As N Richard shows, in Bohemia, the priests are asked to maintain traditions which are not always Catholic.

The social origin of the clergy is relatively well known: mostly coming from the bourgeoisie, the only noteworthy exception being the bishops, rather coming from the aristocracy. The tendency, well studied in France, of a certain depreciation of the Catholic clerical status in the XVIIth century to the benefit of legal studies, is found in the Protestantism of the Desert, due to secrecy, and doubtless in other European countries This challenge to the clerical status is doubtless also explained by a certain increase in literacy in theology[1332], by radical pietism. However, throughout the modern period, belonging to the clergy is a factor of social rising, including within the heart of this unknown clergy whjch is military chaplaincy, presented here by L. Jalabert, for chaplains can be easily be noticed by the nobility.

- Similarities exist also when one examines the material conditions of preaching, an activity which is promoted by the protestants as by the Catholics. Doubtless they are explained largely by the inherent restrictions in preaching (one must be heard and understood) as well as by a common heritage. The question of sacred eloquence is asked in all confessions, and everywhere libraries are set up for the use of preachers. However S. Simiz can note some differences, especially in the décor and C. Borelo insists on the bodily postures and gestures that are imitated or, on the contrary, they are avoided.

[1332] GAY J P and .STIKER -METAL C.O. "Les metamorphoses de la theologie" Paris Honore Champion 2012.

- However it would not be necessary, on reading these different points, to conclude a total resemblance between the clergy. Obviously differences exist. One of the most striking is perhaps the very strong engagement of the Catholic clergy In external missions, while there is until the XVIIIth century, a certain protestant missionary abstention. But, even in his area, one must remain prudent, for C.Balleriaux has shown us great similarities between he Jesuit and puritan missions on America, about whjch one may ask if they are explained by the contacts between the missionaries, by observance of the practices of the other, by the fact that the processes of conversion are not infinite, or that the proposed models of Christianity are finally fairly close.

- Geography and chronology of contacts
  If a certain number of contributions to this volume have enabled the possibility of affirming and comparing the clergy, most of them however depend on real contacts.

On which period should studying these contacts dwell? This volume opens up the XVIth, XVIIth and XVIIh centuries; it is the confessional age (1555-1648) come out, as the whole of the so-called modern period which is viewed. But, in doing so, one makes the frameworks of the confessional period come out (1555-1648) as it has been defined by the theorists of confessionalisation, while the act of viewing the different clergy comes strongly from this issue. Before 1555, the question is to discover whether one can really talk about confessions face to face. There is a doctrinal concept ruling in protestant Istria, where F. Zulliani has shown us that confirmation was accepted, in the same way as the existence of bishops. In fact, even at this date, where there were different ecclesiological models in competition, one also sees,

without one of them having gone back; it seems To be the case in Bohemia still in 1594 (N.Richard) the case in the beginnings of the Reformation in France[1333]. That asks the whole question of the "faithful flock between two pulpits" as Thierry Wanegffelen[1334] called them, as well as passing into the Reformation in Protestantism, that is that the conscious taking of an irremediable separation, at least on human view. Is it possible, for this period, to speak of Conergy in contact/ However, from their birth, the confessions are formed by differentiation: in Calvin's Geneva, the consistory draws up an ecclesiastical discipline allowing a break with the ancient practices of piety proposed by the Catholic clergy; it is therefore, even before the confessional era, by contact with what is not wanted any more than the confessional construction. But, in so doing, the consistory serves the clericalisation of the pastoral body thus paradoxically bringing the pastors and the priests close together (N. SCZECH). As for after 1648, historiography has a tendency to consider that confessionalisation in Europe is prolonged more and more from a distance, even until the XXth century sometimes[1335]; and for America, it is only after the second half of the XVIIth century that the construction of the State is linked to religion (C. Balleriaux).

[1333] See also the MORELY model;: DENIS P.and ROTT J ."Jean Morely…dans l'Eglise" Geneva Droz 1993

[1334] See particularly the model of Morely:,DENIS P and ROTT J "Jean Morely (1524-1594) "Utopia..dans l'Eglise " Geneva Droz 1993

[1335] BLASCHKE O. "Konfessionem im Konflikt. Deitschland…Zeitaler" Gottingen Vandenhoeck and Ruprecht 2002.

During this period, beside the contacts between Catholics and Protestants, one must note the existence of contacts with members of other religions. In Amsterdam, a canon can meet a rabbi (A. Nijenhuis-Bescher); it is also the case in Metz, where pastor Ferry seeks o exchange with the great rabbi Joseph Levy[1336]. In the New World, he discovery of pagan populations opens up a competition for converting the Indians (/c. Balleriaux). As for Islam, analysed in Malta by A. Brogini, it enables the defence of Christianity to define the identity of the Order of Malta; an order which renews itself, which surmounts the crisis due to Protestantism by a purely Catholic identity. In the spirit of the Council of Trent. Inversely, In the Vienna of Maximilian II studied by Roche, it is a transconfessional identity which is imposed in front of the Turkish threat. The difference is doubtless explained by different relations of power. But, in these two cases, it is always the other one who allows one to forge an identity.

The most frequent cases are however contacts between Catholic and Protestant clergy. They are, by the power of things, numerous in multi-confessional territories. These territories are to be taken in the wide sense, including armies, because they often mix with men of different confessions, also even during the wars of Religion in France, with Swiss and German troops, partially protestant, on the side of the King of France[1337], and during the Thirty Years War as L. Jalabert describes to us. <u>He also reminds us that it was arranged, after 1648, that there should be Catholic and Protestant chaplains in the same army, like that of the Circle of Souabe. But the most numerous contacts are obviously in the most pluri- confessional States like Bohemian, France, the United Provinces, Hungary, the</u>

[1336] LEONARD J. "Etre Pasteur au XVIIe ssiec…" op. cit. p. 151.

[1337] The last work to consult in this aspect is that of DAUSSY H."Le Paris Huguenot .Chronique d'ine disillusion (1557-1572) Geneva Droz 2014.

Grisons. A whole range of attitudes is found here, analysed in several contributions; adaptation of sermons in the presence of opponents (C. Thouin-Dieuaide), controversies (J.Foa) spiritual literature (E. Martinazzo) etc. but without however minimising their contacts in France should not be exaggerated: in France, the reformed synods ask to avoid controversies, the zones with strong protestant implantation, such as Languedoc in some corners of the Berry (D. Boisson) in reality saw few Catholic ecclesiastics, or not many. As for the missions, it is known that they cover the protestants less than converting the Catholics to a better practice of their religion[1338]. The clergy of the various confessions seek to establish the impenetrable frontiers between them as Keith Luria has shown[1339]. In spite of that, they knew each other, read each other, copied each other in their sermons, as S..Simiz and C.Borello have shown very well. However, the close presence of the clergy of another confession, doubtless had the result of a certain emulation: it is necessary to have enlightening pastors. In a great many texts, sermons, synod decisions, ecclesiastical decrees, the proximity of the other one is often evoked in order to push to:a better Catholic in Malta when the Turk threatens, a better Protestant in France when the Catholic attacks become more pressing, etc.

Paradoxically, one may also speak about contacts in territories which are in theory mono-confessional, even if these contacts are sometimes indirect. It is especially wars which put clerks of different religions in place. Thus Lutheran armies, with a Lutheran chaplain, can be found in

---

[1338] KRUMENACKER Y. "La mission dans l'Oratoire de France au XVIIe siècle" C.SORRELANS F. MEYER "Les missions interieures …siècle" Chambery Institut d'etudes savoisiennes 2001 p 73-86.

[1339] LURIA K.P. Sacred Boundaries,,,op. cit: \ID "Les fronieres du sacre" "Chreiens et sociees (xvi-XXI siecles) no 15 2009 p 7-28 [http://chretienssociees.revues.or/562] consulted 27/0/2016.

a Catholic territory, and inversely. That can cause complaints against worship in the armies – but one finds sometimes also very peaceful relations (L. Jalabert). Outside these particular cases, direct relationships are rare. But it is known that in the dioceses of Boulogne and Saint-Omer where the emphasis is placed on the training of clergy (P. Moulis); one can read oneself, or fight by books. It is especially the case of "frontiers of Catholicity" among the "Catholic Backbone", whose neighbouring countries are Protestant[1340] The religious orders are often very well implanted there, such as garrison towns intended for preventing the enemy confessional invasion, and Catholicism, whether it be papist or Gallican, especially anti-protestant in the XVIth century; it is therefore an intimate knowledge, but old on the other hand. One must question the memory of Protestantism, as was done for the wars of Religion[1341]. The problem is also raised in the Empire where, in principle, each territory has the religion of its prince, even if the peace of Augsburg of 1555 planned some rare exceptions. In reality, it is known that most of the States were not completely homogeneous; but that does not mean the co-existence of two clergymen

Conflicts or pacified relationships?

One comes to see it by evoking the types of contact and their geography. They can take place also in conflicts which are resolved in very peaceful relationships. The case of

---

[1340] On rhese ideas, advanced y Pierre Chaunu and Rene Taveneaux, see DEREGNAUCOURT G., KRUMENACKER Y, MARTIN P. and MEYER F. "Dorsal catholique, Jansenisme, Devotions…historiographique" Paris, Riveneuve, 2014.

[1341] BERCHTOLD J, and FRAGONARD M-M. "La memoire des guerres de Religion, La concurrence des guerres historiques (XVI-XVIIIe siecles" Geneva,Droz 2007; SOTTOCASA V."Memoires affrontees…Languedoc" Rennes PUR 2004.

military chaplains on the lands of the adverse confession shows very well that, according to the place and times, situations that are completely different, exist.

It must also be understood on what one calls conflict. The controversies, well known for the XVIIth century, less studied for the XVIth century but seen by J. Foa,are in this category vey ambiguous. They appear in time of peace, arms are banished there; but all the same there are confrontations where there is a conqueror and a conquered person, each often proclaiming also to be the conqueror! In the same way, in Holland the relationships between priests or pastors and rabbis, which were generally cordial, give way to writings which were often very closed off, even polemic.

Most of the works presented here show that the context is important in the intensification of the conflicts. In fact, these seem to be more frequent when, in the difference of confession, a national difference is added and the nations differ; thus, the wars between France and England contributed to harden relationships between French Jesuits and Puritan pastors, even in the New World. It is the same, inside the same country, when the political context refuses confessional co-existence,as is the case in France in the 1680's.But before that, the difference in nationality is invoked in order to exclude foreign pastors. (I,Plasman-Labrune). One must not forget a number of other factors, hardly seen here as they are already well known, such as the role of the clergy in refusing a peaceful co-existence, provocations made sometimes in sermons or protestant synods, denunciations of actions against the law or the partisan interpretation that one makes of the law, rivalry between priests and pastors to be beside dying people, etc.[1342]

[1342] For an essay on typology, KRUMENACKER Y. "La co-existence confessionnelle aux XVIIe-XVIIIe siecles. Quelques problemes de methode "Y. KRUMENACKER and D.BOISSON "La co-existence…France modern" Lyon

Conflicts or pacified relationships?

One comes away from seeing it by evoking the types of contact and their geography,
 They can give way also to conflicts which are resolved in very peaceful relationships, The case of military chaplains on lands of adverse confession shows very well that, according to the places and the times, cpmpletely different situations exist.
 It must also be understood on what is called conflict. Controversies, well known for the XVIIth century, less studied for the XVIth century, but seen here by J. Foa, are very ambiguous in his area. They appear in times of peace, weapons are banished there; but all; the same there are confrontations where there is a conqueror and a conquered person, each of them also proclaiming often to be the conqueror! All the same, in Holland, relationships between priests or pastors and rabbis, generally cordial, give way to written relationships which are often very close, even polemic.
 Most of the works presented here show that the context is important in the intensification of conflicts. These seem in fact to be more frequent when, on the difference in confession, a national difference is added and the nations confront each other; thus, the wars between France and England contributed to harden relationships between French Jesuits and puritan pastors, even in the New World It is the same, inside one country, when the political context refuses confessional co-existence, as is the case in the 1680's. It is at this time that the conflicts in Sancerre are multiplied (D. Boisson). But well before, the difference in nationality is invoked to exclude foreign pastors (I.Plasman-labrune). One must not forget a number of ot other factors, not often seen here but well known, as the role of the clergy in refusing peaceful co-existence, the

---

Chretiens e Societes – Documents et memoire2009 p 107-125.

provocations sometimes made in sermons or protestant synods, denunciations of actions opposed to the law or partisan interpretation that is carried on within the law, rivalries between priests and pastors to be beside the dying, etc.

But, inversely, this volume has brought to light a great many cordial relationships between the clergy, in certain precise cases:

- When common interests are at issue: when it is a case of struggling against some Indians, Jesuits and Americans, pastors learn how to understand each other; to struggle against lack of belief, in the XVIIIth century, a common front of apologists from different camps appeared; theological convergences allow confessional "adversaries" to read each other and to appreciate each other, as is the case in Saumur (B. Maes)
- When there is a need to maintain a balance – that is the case in the armies, for the leader must take care for a certain neutrality in order not to create divisions in the troops; it is also seen in German towns with confessional parity or precise rules are drawn up in order to enable a common life; in the Vienna of Maximilian II, the existence of a court which is confessionally diverse imposes a certain restraint, it is forbidden to talk about "heretics", that is in spite of the Jesuits' resistance and "flacians" (C. Roche). That asks the question of legal bi-confessionality, which favorises the confrontation by word to the detriment of weapons, for one may ask whether the rules laid down really enable the maintenance of peace or whether they only congeal latent conflicts
- When the issue is not the conversion of the other one: In the United Provinces, Canon Joly can peacefully talk about wise and profane questions with. Cllaude Saumaise, and he can even discuss theology with Anne-Marie de Schurman – as it is about a scholarly conversation it is not a question of trying to convert.

One observes the same phenomenon in inter-confessional correspondence from the Republic of Letters, where the cordial relations between scholars of two confessions reach out to each other when it is about converting the other one[1343]. In the elite circle of Saumur, B. Maes shows that even doctrinal convergences ae emphasised; it is true that this sociability is limited to the professors, excluding the pastors and priests.I It is doubtles also what explains the interest of protestants in Catholic sermons and eloquent treatises. or reading Le Faucheur by Catholics: in both these cases, it is the technical aspect which matters and which enables a positive view to be sent out, not the depth of the works.

- - When it is essentially a question of sociability: the examples do not fail good relationships in elite people, in provincial academies in the XVIIth century as on the eve pf the Revolution. To take only one example, the Archbishop of Lyon, Malvin de Montazet, on 1784 offered a banquet in honour of the King of Sweden, on his way to Lyon and invited the reformed pastor of the town, Frossard- whose sermons he admired and which he wanted to pass on[1344].
- These cordial relationships made the differences between the clergy much looser. While there is even a will for confessionalisation which should on the contrary reinforce them harden them. There is a good example of the manner wjhose process of confessional construction and the imposition of a discipline seeking to sanctify society by building a

---

[1343] MOREAO Y. "Parcours, itineraires, rizome: applications,…Lettres" "Les Carnets du larhra no. 2 2014 p 147-168 here p. 152-153.

[1344] BLANC R . "Un pastor au temps des Lumieres…Frossard (1754-1830) Paris Honore Champion 2000 p 42 and p 52.

distinct confessional identity in reality blurs identity, for the process is the same in all confessions.
- However one must not go too far in this direction, for indomitable particularities remain. One of them is marriage, The importance of concubinage of clerks at the beginning of the XVIth century.is known. The reaffirmation of ecclesiastical celibacy by the Catholic reformation has appeared. In reaction to Protestantism, less as [1345]a restraint than as a means of accompanying the new ecclesiastic ideal, which explains its relative success. Inversely, the marriage of pastors very quickly became almost systematic; for most of the clerks who passed to the Protestant Reformation an identifying marker for the priest. However, has S. Dumortier has shown, ecclesiastical marriages, in the North, until the XVIIth century, bear witness of the influence of protestantism in this area. And it is known that at the end of the XVIIIth century, a great many pleas in favour of the marriage of priests are based on Protestant writings.[1346]
- By way of conclusion:
- may one speak of oppositions or influences?
- He clergy in contact disagree, but they can also have good relationships and hey even sometimes seem to influence. That is at least the impression which comes out of the texts of this volume. But is the language used appropriate? Can one really speak about opposition among the clergy or reciprocal influences? To think that the Catholic clergy is against the Lutheran, or Calvinist, clergy, is that not to enlarge the feature?

[1345] DOI A. "Un oggetto sconsiderabile ...politica" Celibato del clero a criticailluminista in Europa nel XVIIIsiecle, thesis of history doctorate. E. BRAMBILLA and C. PEYRARD Universita degli Sudi (Milan and University of aix-Marseille 2013.

[1346]

- The future Cardinal de Berulle, after the introduction of the reformed Carmelites into France, had to undergo opposition from the Carmes and some bishops, even more than the pastors, anti-protestant as he was. In the following decades, it was particularly Jansenism which divided the Catholic clergy, while the reformed pastors fought between partisans and enemies ot the theology of Saumur. As F. Meyer has shown, the division between the different branches of the Franciscan family is often stronger than opposition to the protestants. On the Lutheran side, the Philippists and gnesio-Lutherans deeply disagreed, before pietism sowed trouble. That is useless to follow up, these examples pietism began the trouble. Quarrels, in the United Provinces, between Armenian and Gomarists are even more serious. And what is there to say about confrontations in England between the various Protestant confessions? These examples show clearly that it is not possible to speak about a Catholic clergy, or Lutheran, Calvinist or Anglican clergy.
- The risk, to identify too quickly the clergy of one well determined confession, is to essentialise the religious phenomena. A re-reading of the example, developed in this volume by N.Richard, of the Archdiocese of Prague, is from this point of view very enlightening. A quick view of the priests of Bohemia in 1594 seems to show Hussite, Lutheran, even orthodox influences through practices such as communion in two kids, absence of prior confession or at the time of childbirth, readings in Czech,the feast of Jan Hus, etc. However, one quickly realises that the influences are difficult to establish with certainty, for they are mixed with relationships of power, with attachment to traditions, to the attraction to some practices, etc. Thus, Catholics can love the readings and songs in the common languages without ceasing to feel so

Catholic, as the Protestants can take part in processions or Catholic feasts
- (the same phenomenon is noted in the United Provinces, in France and numerous German areas). Is it not going a little quickly to assimilate a sensitivity,,a conservatism or the taste for novelty, social pressures, confessions? These are not only the doctrines described in confessions of faith, according to the use which is spreading in the modern epoch, but also badly controlled beliefs, practices and traditions which can evolve partially independently from one and the other.
- The religious phenomena are the result of complex alchemies, that one cannot reduce to very undefined bodies of doctrine. To analyse the results of contacts between clergy requires being very careful about the different elements which are at play. Social conventions, common sensitivities or well-anchored prejudices, a great many other phenomena that one would spontaneously describe as "religious" must be taken into account. That must remind us that clergy in contact are only matters of confrontation of doctrines brought in by ecclesiastics, but also affairs of men situated in very precise contexts. There is no doubt that what explains the extreme diversity and complexity of situations analysed in his work. The historian, whose task is not only to describe, but especially to understand, tries very hard to classify, to typologies obstinacy to allow oneself to be enclosed inside a single category., but reality resists in its infinite variety and in its obstinacy not to allow one to be enclosed inside a single category.

As a conclusion, may one speak of oppositions or influences?

Clergy in contact fight each other, but they can also have good relationships and the sometimes appear to be influenced. That is at least the impression whjch comes from the texts of this volume. But is the language used appropriate? May one speak about opposition between the clergy or reciprocal influences? To think that the Catholic clergy is against the Lutheran, or Calvinist clergy, is it not to enlarge the fearture?

The future Cardinal de Berulle, after the introduction of the reformed Carmelites in France, had to undergo opposition from the Carmes and some bishops, more than pastors, completely anti-protestant that he was. In the following decades, it is especially Jansenism which divides the Catholic clergy, while the reformed pastors fight among partisans and enemies of the theology of Saumur. As F. Meyer has shown, the division between the different branches of the Franciscan family is often stronger than the opposition to protestants. On the Lutheran side, the Philipists and the gnesio-Lutherans argue deeply, before pietism sows trouble. Quarrels, in the United Provinces, between Armenians and Gomarists are even more serious. And what to say about confrontations in England between the various Protestant confessions? Useless to follow up, these examples show very well that it is not possible to speak of a Catholic clergyman, or a Lutheran, Calvinst or Anglican clergyman.

The risk, to identify too quickly the clergy of a well determined confession, is to make the religious phenomena essential. A re-reading of he example, developed in this volume by N. Richard, of the Archdiocese of Prague, is from this point of view very enlightening. A rapid view of the priests of Bohemia in 1594 seems to show Hussite, Lutheran, even Orthodox influences, through practices such as communion in two kinds, the absence of prior confession, communion of infants or at the time of childbirth, readings in Czech, the feast of Jan Hus, etc. However, one quickly realises that the influences are difficult to establish with certainty, for the become mixed with relationships of power, attachment to traditions, to the attraction for certain practices etc. Thus, Catholics may love the readings and songs in the common language without ceasing at all to feel themselves Catholic, just as the protestants can take part in processions or in Catholic feasts (the same phenomenon is noted in the united Provinces, in France and in a number of German regions). Is it not to go a little slower than to assimilate a sensibility, a conservatism or the taste for novelties, social pressures, confessions?

These are not only doctrines exposed in confessions of faith, according to the usage which is spreading in the modern age, but also badly controlled beliefs, practices. Traditions, which can evolve partially independently from one another.

Religious phenomena are the result of complex alchemies, which cannot be reduced to very undefined bodies of doctrine. To analyse the consequences of contacts between clergy requires being very attentive to the different elements coming into play. Social conventions, strategies of co-existence, of survival or conquest, intellectual affinities, common sensibilities or strongly anchored prejudices, a great many other phenomena which would not spontaneously be described as religious" are to be taken into account. That mut remind us that the clergy in contact only affairs of confrontation of doctrines brought by ecclesiastics, but also the affairs of men situated in exact contexts. That is doubtless what explains the extreme diversity and complexity of situations analysed in this work.

[1347]7. NOVELLA PRIESTS AND PASTORS

P 274 PRIESTS AND PASTORS

Finally, the fourth reason which comes near Catholics and protestants, is the idea of Descartes, a former pupil of the Jesuits in La Fleche college. In 1664, the Genevan Jean-Robert Chouet reports that the Catholics, who made up the audience at the time of the examination for candidates for a [1348]professor's chair, had strongly applauded his ability to win a difficult competition.

There was truly a "Republic of Letters" in Saumur in the XVIIth century, between the professors in Saumur and those of the School of Theology, especially from 1650 from 1650 to 1675. Both religious reforms have the same causes, their oppositions have been insisted upon too much. True research into the truth was the same among a great many members of a professional body. But it is another logic which has carried it away, that of people outside Saumur, who acted for the unity of the kingdom around the King's religion. It is made up of pilgrims, of the Bishop of Angers, but particularly of the court and Louis XIV, who instrumentalised the Catholic religion against the benevolence and freedom advocated by the professors, who imposed the revocation of the Edict of Nantes in 1685.

***

The Constitution of Clerical identities.
Father Paolo Vergerio:
Minister or Bishop of Vicosoprano?

[1347]

[1348] AN TT 266 "Relation succinct et faible de la reception…octobre 1655"

Pastoral models and ecclesiastics who were concurrent in
the Italian-speaking Grisons
(1549-1553)
Federico Zuliani

This contribution dwells on a particular feature – and relatively unknown by historians – of the four years that Father Paolo Vergerio spent as a reformed pastor in Vicosoprano, a small village in the Grisons[1349]. It is a matter of finding out If he was then changed into a Minister or into a Bishop. Having briefly presented the years as minister of Vergerio, who leaned on the use of the term "bishop" when he talks about himself, then on the role of bishops at that time, and finally how much he is presented in the writings of Vergerio written at that time, and finally on his pastoral approach. The hypothesis of leaving, based on a first analysis of sources, is that Vergerio, who was a Catholic Bishop before his flight to Italy, was also acting as a bishop during his activity as a reformed minister in Vicosoprano. Therefore one must see if such an attitude was simply the fact of Vergerio's experience, or if it was based on another interpretation, protestant, of this role.

This study is integrated into a greater framework. In fact I want to present some results which, even though partial, could throw light on his particular problem and, more generally. Could enrich a wider discussion on the episcopal models which were present in a space like the Grisons where several pastoral and episcopal models which were present in a space like the Gtisons, where several pastoral and ecclesiastical traditions -Catholic, Zwinglian and Calvinist – meet each other, often in open opposition ,some in relation to the others[1350] These models, it will be seen,

---

[1349] . Translated from English by JULIEN LEONARD.Thanks to Stefano SIMIZ for his previous help in translating passages into Italian.

[13501350] See research in Dipartimenti di Studi Stoici (Milan) "Pastor "LODOCAT – (ANR "Pastoral models".

cannot be limited to a simple dichotomy between Catholics and protestants, but were formed by different influences and by bitter struggles, including at the heart of the two officially recognised confessional denominations. These different models are particularly well known as regards Catholicism (torn in this area by various competitors between the dioceses of Come, Coire and Milan). They should be studied more on the protestant side which was also torn between the models which were difficultly conciliable with the Churches of Zurich and Geneva, but also touched by external influences, such as Lutheranism and Anabaptism.

Vergerio in the Grisons

Father Paolo Vergerio was born in Capodistria, a town on the border with Venice.[1351] He died in 1565, in Tubingen[1352]. In the 1539's and at the beginning of the 1540's, he was the pontifical nuncio at the imperial court in Vienna and became famous in Italy and in Europe as a fervent defender of the need for a general council. From 1535to 1549, he occupied the main episcopal seat of his native town, where he stayed for four years. But in 1548, a process of the Holy Office[1353] for heresy opened against him in Padua[1354], and at the beginning of 1549, he left Italy to settle finally in Vicosoprano, a small village in an Italian-speaking areas of the Grisons, where he was elected minister of the local reformed Church. Vergerio lived until 1553 when, in the summer of that year, he accepted the offer of Duke Christophe de Wurtemberg to become his

---

[1351] Now Koper, in Slovenia.

[1352]

[1353] FERRAI L.A. "Il processo di Pier Paolo Vergerio"
L.A.FERRAI, Studo stprici {adua, Fratelli Drucker 1892 p 88-173., and
SIXT C.H."Petrus Paulus Vergerio ...monographie" Brunswick Schwetschke und Sohn,1855

counsellor and settled in Germany[1355]. From his flight from Italy until his death, Vergerio was a celebrity in the whole of Europe for his indefatigable work as writer and editor of protestant books and pamphlets, both in Italian and in Latin[1356].

Thanks particularly to an anonymous text published between the end of December 1549 and the beginning of January 1550 (and which was not until very recently attributed to him) we can certainly put forward the opinion that Vergerio's departure from Italy was not to settle in the Alps[1357]. On the contrary he was [1358]heading for Germany. As with a great many Italians, before and after him[1359]. Vergerio returned to the Grisons due to their proximity to Italy [1360]and their accessibility both to Milan and the lands of Serenissim. The Grisons, for a great number of Italian protestants, constituted a natural first stage for a longer journey which from there leads hem towards Swiss, French, even English and Polish towns[1361]. The however, are not then a territory like the others, especially on account of their unequalled ecclesiastical situation.

The Graubunden, literally "Grey Leagues" in the Grisons or Grisonists, in fact constituted a confederation of three republics or cantons. While very strongly tied to the

---

[1355] KAUSLER E.H. VON and SCHOTT T. "Briefwechel …Vergerius" Tubingen E. Laupp 1875.

[1356] PIERCE RA Pier Paolo Gergerio": Propaandistu Rome Edizioni fdi Storia e Letteratura 2003 Gottingen Vandenhoeck & Rupreacht 1993.

[1357] VERGERIO P.P. "del battesimo…grisoni" ZULIANI F. !Quaderni ..Storia" no. 35 2014 p 29-60.

[1358] CALVIN J. "Johannis Calvini…omnia" Brunswick CA. Schwetschke vol 13 88

[1359] CALVIN J, "Johannnis Calvini opera…omnia" G.BAUM Brunswick v 13 1888 col. 448 Gribaldi to Calvin 15.11.1549

[1360] ROTONDO A."Esuli Iraliani in Valtellina nel Cinquecento" Revista storica italiana no 88,1976 p 756-791 .

[1361] CHUECH E.C. "I reormaoi italiani" Flrence La Nuova Italia 1935 2 vols Milan Il Saggiatore

Confederation pf the thirteen cantons, and particularly to Zurich[1362]. By economic connections and treaties of defensive alliance, these leagues were not less fiercely independent. From 1526, by virtue of the promulgation of the Articles of Ilanz, the Catholic and reformed confessions were both recognised as legal and enjoyed an equivalent status[1363]. All the men and all the women, at the same time among the citizens and among the subjects, were thus free to choose their religious confession among these two options) Anabaptism, on the other side, was still illegal). Even if The Grauer Bund (Grey League) and the Zehngerichtebund (League of the Ten Jurisdictions) were mainly in German and romance, some valleys in the Gotteshausbund (League of Maison-Dieu) were peopled with Italian speakers[1364]. One mainly found there local populations or immigrants from Italy[1365]. Vicosoprano, the village where Vergerio settled after his election as minister, was the economic and administrative capital of the Val Bregaglia, one of the valleys where the great majority of the local population had converted to Protestantism.

In the small booklet mentioned from 1549-1550, Vergerio describes to his former faithful flock of Istria the reasons for his sudden decision not to continue his journey towards Germany, but to stay in the Grisons. What made him change his plans, was the discovery that these Churches share "this same purity and simplicity" of the apostolic Church[1366]. In spite of his initial optimism and favourable bias, Vergerio however quickly realised the reality of his new church. He had not come to a new Jerusalem, he had

---

[1362] SCHIESS T. "Die Beziehungen ...Jarhundert"" no. 27 1902,p 29-194.

[1363] LIVER P. "DieIlanze Artikl "Jahrshericht der ...Graubunden no. 59 p 1-136.

[1364] HEAD R.C. "Early Modern Democracy in the Grisons...Canton" 1470-1620 Cambridge CUP 2002.

[1365] CAMENISCH E. "Geschichte der Reformation...Bormio, Coire Bicshofberger 1950.

[1366] VERGERIO P.P. "Del battesimo et de fumi…" fol. A2r

not fallen into an apostolic church of the first century. To his great surprise, at Vicosoprano "new antichrists, many wolves in sheeps' clothing, a great many false brothers" not only among t[1367]he Catholics, but also his reformed faithful people and the members of his Church.

That became particularly clear if one relies on some catechisms that Vergerio published in Switzerland[1368]. One of the texts is particularly significant in this sense, especially when one reads the two editions, which include from one to the other very revealing changes. In 1549, some months after his arrival. and when he still intends to go to Germany, Vergerio published his "Instruttione christiana"[1369]. It is a very general catechism, not addressing any Church in particular, and intended for circulation in Italy. In the following year, the text is published again under the title, this time, of "Uno brieve, et semplice modo per informare le fanciulli, nella religione Christiana. Fatto per uso Chiesa di Vicosoprano et de gl'altri luochi di valle Bregaglia". As this title shows, the new edition is more specifically intended by Vergerio for the new church of Vicosoprano. The additions which were brought in show very clearly everything that was not expected to be found among the faithful flock, and which he deplores: among other things, fornication, perseverance in some Catholic practic[1370]es and beliefs, a general rebel attitude towards the ecclesiastical authorities.

At the beginning of the year 1550, Vergerio is already not more comfortable in the heart of his community. In the

---

[1367] Zentralbibliothek Zurich ms F 40 fol 563v Pier Paolo Vergerio to Rudolf Gwalther Vicosoprano 13.09.1550 "multi sunt Antichristi".

[1368] CAVASSA S. "Quell oche Giesu Christo…Evangelio" METODI E RICERCHE N.S. NO. 18 1998 P 3-22/

[1369] ZULIANA F. "Un catechismo perduro …Vergerio" "Bibliotheque d'Humanism et Renaissance" v 75-3 2013 p 463-497.

[1370] Zentralbibliohek Zurich ms F. fol. 562 r letter from Vergerio to Gwalther,Basle,26.07.1551 "fuor ddi pericolic della Retia".

following year the problems persist: in July 1551, Vergerio thus presses Rudolf Gwalther to help him, by his letters of recommendation, to find a new position in the Bernese lands "far from the dangers of the Rhetia"[1371]. During these years, he also studies the possibility of settling in England[1372]. Through Bonifacius Amerbach, he contacts Christophe de Wurtemberg[1373]. Finally, at the end of 1553 he leaves his charge and tries to become the reformed minister in Sondrio, in the nearby Valteline, although he was warned of an epidemic of the plague. He spent a part of this year in Chiavenna, a Lombardian town which was then, like its neighbour Sondrio, under the authority of the Leagues of Grisons. At that time, violent polemics burst out[1374] between him and Agostino Mainardi, the minister of Chiavenna. The main point of the dispute is a new catechism that Vergerio had published. Mainardi goes as far as writing to Bullinger in Zurich to prevent the risk of a reprint of the text. The later in fact present a Lutheran position of the eucharistic doctrine, but this is not the only problem at play, as will be seen more precisely[1375].

A Bishop in the Grisons

If one leans towards the years that Vergerio spent in the Grisons, two elements are particularly striking: the people continue to address him by calling him a bishop, and he

---

[1371] SOWERBY T.A. "Renaissance und Reform
…England..Morison" c.1513-1556 Oxford OUP 2010 p 216.
[1372] CHURCH F.C. "I riformatori italiani
2 op.cit. p 334-337.
[1373] ARMAND HUGON A. "Agostino Mainardo…inItalia"
Torre Pellice Societa di Sudi Valdesi Rome Instituto dell Enciclopedia Italiana vol LXVII 2006 p 585-590. (1553)
[1374] ZULIANA F. "I contrasti tra e mAINARDO circa un catechism riformato per la Valtellina (153) "Rivista di Storia della Chiese in Italia" 2015 p 49-78,
[1375] SCHIESS T. "Bullingers Korespndent…" op. cit. vol 1 p 145 letter from Mainardo to Bullinger Chiavenna 15.05.1549.

maintained this usage. It is in a certain surprising manner that one can find out that several Protestants - including the protestants who were sincerely convinced that he was no longer a Catholic, but had embraced Protestantism addressed Vergerio as bishop. For example, that is the case of fervent protestants such as Agostino Mainardi[1376], Baldassare Altiere[1377]., or even Johannes Comander[1378], the list being doubtless somewhat longer. Moreover, one must emphasise that when Vergerio matriculated in the University of Basle in 1550, no doubt in order to move into the bourgeoisie of the city or in a teaching position, he was registered as "reverendus dominus episcopus Justinopolitanus"[1379]. Vergerio is not the only Italian bishop of the XVIth century having embraced the ideas of the Protestant Reformation or being considered as a heretic [1380]by the Roman authorities. However, he is the only one to have left Italy. This particularity could suggest that the representatives of Vergerio used this title, in addressing him, either because they did not know want to do in this case, uniquely by courtesy. However, when Celio Curione wrote to Bullinger in January 1550 asking himself "What should be said about our Vergerio who lately wore the mask of a bishop, and now he is really a bishop of the Church of Christ, his sincere servant and a man who should be

---

[1376] Ibid p 475 letter ti Altieri to Bullinbger, Poschiavo 5 August 1549.

[1377] ARBENZ E. and WARTMANN H. "die Vadianishe …S Gallen" Saint-Gall Huber & co. vol 6 p 802 letter from Comander to Joachim Vadian, Coire 6.06.1549.

[1378][1378] BUSINO g. "italiani all'Universita di Basiliea dal 1460 al 1601""Bibliotheque d'Humanisme et Renaissance" v 20-3, 1958 p 524.

[1379] Vittore Soranzo and Jacopo Nacchianti are among the most famous cases but the list could be longe e.g. Giovanni Batista Vergerio Bishop of Pola andbrother of Pier aolo

[1380] Qupted in BIASIORI L. "L'uomo scaltro" Celio Secondo Curione Pietro Paolo Vergerio "Bibliotheque d'humanisme et Renaissance v 72-2 2010 p 394.

venerated in every way"[1381], the expression "now really a bishop of the Church of Christ" can with difficulty be considered as simply honorary.

When one turns towards public works, one realises also that on several occasions Vergerio calls himself a bishop even if, in spite of his excessive activity, several of his works are anonymous. In 1549 for example he signed the pamphlet Oratione de perseguitati et fuorusciti per lo evangelio et per Giesu" in this manner: "Vergerio, by the grace of God Bishop of Christ"[1382]. It is in some way surprising to find out that several protestants – including protestants who are sincerely convinced that he was no longer a Catholic, and

had embraced Protestantism, addressing himself in Vergerio as a bishop. This is the case for example of fervent pastors such as Agostino Mainardi[1383], Baldassare Altiere[1384], or even Johannes Comander[1385], the list doubtless was much longer. Also, one must emphasise that when Vergerio matriculated in the University of Basle in 1550, no doubt in order to enter the bourgeoisie of the city or a teaching position, he is registered as "reverendus

---

[1381] m[13811381] CAVAZZA S. "Pier Paolo Vergerio nei Grigioni..." art.cit.p 42 "Vergerio per la Dio gratia vescovo di Christo"

[1382] [CALVIM J.J. Apologia dello Illustre Giacobo di Burgundia ...rende conto della sua fede [Geneva][Jean Girard] 1550 VERGERIO P.P. Dodici trattatelli ...dall'Italia [Basle] Giacomo Parco] 1550

[1383] SCHIESS T. Bullingers Korrespondence...op.cit.vol 1 p 145 letter from Mainardo to Bullinger Chiavenna 15.05.1549.

[1384] Ibid.p 475 letter from Altieri to Bullinger Poschiavo 3.08.1549.

[1385] ARBENZ E. and WARTMANN H "Die Vadianische...St. Gallen", St Gall Huber & co vol 6 1908 letter from Comander to Joachim Vadian..Coire 6.06.1549.

dominus episcopus Justinopolitanus"[1386]. Vergerio is not the only Italian bishop of the XVIth century having embraced the ideas of the protestant Reformation or being considered as a heretic by the Roman authorities. However he is the only one to have left Italy[1387].

This particularity could suggest that the speaking to Vergerio used this title, in addressing him either because they did not know what to do in such a case, or uniquely by courtesy. However, when Celio Secondo Curione wrote to Bullinger in January 1550 asking "What to say about our [1388]Vergerio who formerly wore the mask of a Bishop, and is a true Bishop of the Church of Christ" can with difficulty be considered as simply honorary now such a Bishop of the Church of Christ, his sincere servant and a man who should be venerated in every way", the expression "now truly bishop of the church of Christ" can with difficulty be considered as purely honorary"

When one turns towards his public works, one realises that on some occasions, Vergerio calls himself a bishop, even of in spite of his exessive activity,several of his works are anonymous.In 1549 for example, he signs the pamphlet "Oratione de perseguitati et fuor[1389]usciti per lo evangelio et per Giesu Christo" in this way: Vergerui, by the grace of God bishop of Christ. On the title page on a translation by Calvin into Italian, as well as inhis"Dici Trattaelli" and his "Otto Defensioni" published in 1440, Vergerio is "Bishop

---

[1386][1386][1386] BUSINO G. "Italiani all'Universita di Basilea dal 1460 to 1601" Bubliotheque d'Humanisme et Renaissance v 20-3 1958 p 524i

[1387] Vittore Soranzo and Jacopo Nacchianti are among the most famous cases the list is long.

[1388]

[1389] CAVAZZA Si. "Pier Paolo Vergerio nei Grigioni…" art.cit. p 42 "Vergerio …Christo".

of Capodistria[1390]. Two years lat[1391]er, in his treatise against his old friend Friedrich Nausea, he presents himsl as "Bishop Vergerio" while the next year, in publishing a translation of the confession of faith of German princes, he signs again "your Vergerio Bishop of Christ by the grace of Gd£[1392]

Contrary to the correspondence, these treatises constitute "public" documents. The use of the term "vescovo", bishop, is therefore deliberate and cannot be considered as a simple language mistake or an old habit. In order to understand the reasons which guided these precise choices, it is essential to analyse what are Vergerio's ideas about episcopacy.

Vergerio and the episcopacy

If one focuses on the works of Vergerio, it appears clearly that, during his Swiss years, his reflection on the episcopacy is really placed at the heart of his theological and pastoral thought. The interest for this theme is however rather older. The previously quoted small anonymous book from 1549-1550 is finished by a long passage on the figure of the bishop. Vergerio advances that several functions attributed to the bishop are not apostolic, especially the consecration of the holy water for baptism and the sacrament of confirmation, of which he here denies the apostolic origin. The most interesting part in this passage - the Italian protestants and his faithful people remaining in Istria- and he emphasises: "You want a simple priest to baptise, but does not confirm, and you reserve this enterprise of greater

---

[139013901390] [CALVIN J.] "Apologia dello Illustre…Carlo V Imperatore della sua fide [Geneva] Jean sua fiede 1550.

[1391] VERGERIO P.P. Risposta del vescovo di …Concilio" Poschiavo [dolphin Landolfi] 1552.,

[1392] Confessione della
Tiningrn [ulrich Morhatt] 1553 fol (L9) "il vostro Vergerio vescovo di Christo Deo gratia"pia dopttrina…Concilio de Trento

value in the hands of a bishop and that is enough[1393].". Vergerio's critics show that the group that he had led to avoid denial, at least up to that time, the very existence of bishops, and even thought that the consecrated bishops had the legitimate authority to celebrate certain ceremonies. The Istrian peninsula was then perhaps the only Italian region where Lutheranism, and not Calvinism, was ab le to take root, and now moreover after the 1540's[1394]. It therefore seems probable that such an interpretation was the consequence of this local Lutheran influence. In fact the Lutherans did not deny the apostolic nature of the [1395]episcopal functions and, in certain Lutheran areas, the episcopacy was never abolished.

The reflections and considerations about the episcopacy are dispersed into several works of Vergerio during the years 1549-1553.Without being able to claim exhaustivity here, two books seem particularly to arise from this subject. [1396]They are "Al serenissimo re d'Inghilterrra Eduardo Sesto, de portamento di Papa Giulio III (November 1550)[1397]and the "Rispsta ad un libro del Nausea" (1552). One must emphasise that the two works were written in two years, at a time when one can decently suppose that Vergerio precisely knows the specific religious situation of the Italian-speaking Italian Besides, the second work explicitly goes back to the first one[1398], which makes them a type of diptyque.

[1393] [VERGERIO P.P.] "Del batteismo et de fiumi …op.vit.fol.a5r.

[1394] CAPONETTO S. "La Reforma protestante nell'italia…Cinquecento", Turin, Claudiana 1997 p 65-68.

[1395] KLAUS W. "Episcopacy" H.J. HILLEBRAND "The Oxford Encyclopaedia of the Reformation" New York – Oxford OUP 1996 vol 2 p 51-54.

[1396] See above, =and see JEDIN H. "Die Deutschen an Truenter Jibzuk 1551-52 Historische Zeitschrif no. 188 1959 p -16

[1397] VERGERIO P,P, Al serenissimo re a Inghilterra …Giulio III [Dolphin Landolfi] 1550.

[1398] VERGERIO P.P. "Risposta…" op. cit. p XXXIII.

Writing to Edward VI of England about the Council of Trent, Vergerio explains that there are two types of bishop: those who "were elected by the popes, or at least confirmed and anointed, and mitred[1399]" and those who "were so by the consensus of the city, elected by the people, and have not received any anointing other than that of the Holy Spirit"[1400].

While the first are sunken into superstitions and idolatry through and through[1401], the second "have neither mitre nor sandals and are poor,and take care to preach the pure doctrine of the Gospel and to oppose contrary elements[1402]. Those who belong to the second group are "the true bishops"; they are "learned and pious"[1403], and however, they do not sit on the council. In fact, if they had appeared at Trent, they "would not have been received to the council" and hey would have undergone the same joke as that played to on Jerome of Prague and to Jan Hus at the Council of Constance[1404].Aiming at refuting the Catholic positions on the possibility of welcoming the laity into the Council[1405]. Vergerio leans on the history of the ancient church. He emphasises that it is not true, as the Catholics claim, that in the ancient times "only the bishops" had "decisive voices", because others were found who had them, who were not bishops[1406]. But Vergerio strongly underlines another point. Along the following lines, we can in fact read that "the ministers of the churches of Germany, England and Swiss

---

[1399] VERGERIO P.P. "Al serenissimo re…" op. cit. "furono da Papi eletti…et mitrato".

[1400] Ibic,fol Dijr- Dijv "Furono del consent della citta…spirio santo".

[1401] Ibid.fol.Dijr "Finoogli occhi immerse"

[1402] Ibid fol Dijv "Non usano mitre…contraire"

[1403] Ibid. "I veri Vescovi,

[1404] Ibid. "Non saranno…costantinense si fece"

[1405] See above, note 51.

[1406] [VERGERIO P.P. "Al serenissimo re…" op.it folmEv "Soli o vescovi…Vescovi".

cantons, can decide[1407], because they are bishops, and bishops such as those of the ancient councils, [1408]and especially those who were in Nicea, Constantinople, Ephesus and Chalcedonia. They can therefore be called bishop, ministers of the Church, preachers of the Wprd of Gods, since he "vescovi" who attended the ancient councils "were pastors of the people"[1409].At that time, in fact

"There were not [...] any bishops like our modern papists [papei] who wear mitres. Pastoral clothing, sandals or even shoes, who bless the oils, who polish the stones, and baptise the bells, who, once the churches were left in the hands of mercenaries, run all day long behind the Cardinals, and for adoring the popes living un delight, in so many vices and so many abominations[1410].

The main distinguishing point according to Vergerio "I veri Vescovi" of the old times and the papist bishops of his time, is that the first ones themselves ordinarily elected the bishops and ministers, and those who were not elected by the welcome of citizens and confirmed by neighbouring bishops were not known or regarded as legitimate bishops and ministers[1411].

The Catholic bishops of his time, as a result, "are not bishops" or rather "are only bishops in name"[1412]. In a polemic manner, Vergerio addresses the Roman bishops directly and asks them: "How can you not be ashamed to consider yourselves as the successors of the Apostles?"[1413]"

When he leans over what he wrote to Bishop Nausea two years later, one realises that, in the interval, Vergerio has not changed his position. On the contrary, his ideas on the question have become strong convictions. The tone is

---

[1407] Ibid, "I minisrire…op.cit. fol.E v "soli I vescovi…dexidere"
[1408] Ibid. "I"sono Vescovi …nel Cancedonese".
[1409] Ibid."Furono pastori de ministry ..parole di Dio".
[1410] Ibid Non vi erano [...] Vescovi simili…abominarioni".
[1411] Ibid.fol.Eijr "[n] gli antichi et meglior tempo…approvati"
[1412] Ibid. fol. Eijv "Non sono Vescovi sed no di nome"
[1413] IIbid. Fol. [Eiv]v "Come non..gli Apostoli/?"

rough, as often happens with Vergerio, and even defamatory. The Roman Catholic bishops are "small bishops"[1414], "mitred creatures"[1415], "papist bishops" or "popes" "[1416]. In one place, Vergerio asks:

"Are they nothing but masks? Or bishops only in name? Who elected them? Certainly not the cities nor the peoples according to the commandment of their laws, but the tyranny of a Roman bishop [...] What doctrine do they follow? What life do they have? A life consecrated to guiding the souls? Or do they teach the Gospel? When do they administer the sacraments according to the order of Christ? Thus therefore if they are not legitimately elected, if they do not have all the other qualities that I i have described, if they depend upon a false leader, I say that they [1417] are not bishops, that they are not judges, that they are not on the Council.

In this work, Vergerio does not explain in detail either the foundations of the idea that he expresses, since he has already done so in "one of the long letters to the very Christian King of England "£[1418], nor the reasons for which the protestant bishops are "legitimate bishops and ministers[1419]. However he explains that "we are not either cardinals, nor patriarchs, nor abbots, nor provosts, nor archbishops, nor bishops, I mean papist bishops, and consecrators with your oils "but (thanks be to God) we are bishops and pastors and consecrators of his spirit"[1420].

One may therefore resume that for Vergerio, "I veri Vescovi" must be poor, live in the middle of their flock and, even more important, preach the Gospel and administer the

---

[1414] VERGERIO P.P. "Risposta..." op.cit. p VII "Vescovetti".
[1415] Ibid. p XVIII "Creature mitrate"
[1416] Ibid p XLII "Vescovi supersitiosi".
[1417] IBID p LIX "Sono esso altro...concilio"
[1418] Ibid. p XXXIII "Una mia lunga epistola...d' Inghiltterra"
[1419] Ibid. "Vescovi, et ministry legitimi"
[1420] Ibid " p XXXII "Noi non siamo ne cardinali...suo spirito unti"

sacraments. At the highest level of his requirements, the "veri vescovi" must be elected by their own community. The analysis really seems to explain what Vergerio thinks when, in his works, he calls himself "vescovo". He does so not because he was consecrated several years before as Bishop of Capodistria by the Pope, ten years after his nomination, as he describes himself in one of his writings[1421], but because the church of Vicosoprano elected him as minister, Vergerio knows that this treatise will be read by the Catholic controversists aiming to find angles of attack against him. For this reason, it is particularly important to note that, speaking about the "vescovi, et ministri legitimi" he writes "noi" "we", therefore including himself: in the same order of ideas, in the title of his book, he calls himself "vescovo Vergerio".

This specific instruction of the bishop [1422]as an expression of a precise Christian community one finds a supplementary confirmation in the fact that, after the beginning of 1553, when he abandoned his charge as minister of Vicosoprano, Vergerio also abandoned the title of bisho[1423]p. In 1554, he adopted instead the Paulinian formulation of "server of Christ[1424], "servo di Jesu Christo, "servo di Christo"[1425] or even "Servus Jesu Christi" When in 1555 a new edition of his "Oratione de perseguitati …evangelio (1549) by the grace of God Bishop of Christ" is withdrawn. According to Vergerio's own criteria, at that time he is no longer a bishop.

[1421] VERGERIO P.P. "Retrattione {Tubingen] [I;roch Morhai] 1556 fol A4rv.

[1422]

[1423] ATAN [VERGERIO P.P. "Fra Leandro Bolognese [Tubingen] [Ulrich Morhart] 1554 fol.A1v

[1424]1424 "Paul, serviteur du Christ Jesus,apotre par vocation …il signe "servitor " not "servo", declined "servo di Jesu Christo

[1425]1425 VERGERIO P.P. "Retrattatione" op.cit.
]D4]r.VERGERIO P.P. "De idolo luretano [Tibingen] [Ulrich Morhat] fol.Aiijv.

One must emphasise that Vergerio's ideas on the episcopacy are not unique among the Italian protestants in the Grisons. For example, even his main example, Mainardo, in his "Anatomia della Messa" or the same time (1552) states that the "office" of bishops is "to teach people and preach to them", and that since the contemporary Catholic bishops "have abandoned him and still let things be done by others", such clerks have shown that "they are not bishops, assuredly they are not, other than by name". In fact, if t[1426]hey were true bishops, they would not be ashamed to do their work "

Behaving as a bishop and its consequences
Now that we have seen what Vergerio had in mind by calling himself a bishop, it remains to analyse whether he behave, during his ministry, as a bishop. Here, however, I do not understand "bishop" in the meaning that Vergerio gives to this word, but in the more traditional meaning of a pastor who oversees an ecclesiastical district and deals with it as a whole. When one leans more in detail on Vergerio's activity as a minister, it appears that he does not restrict himself to the only congregation that elected him, but he oversees several other communities ad, even more important, he claims a form of authority on all the other Reformed Churches of the Val Bregaglia (up to December 1552) and Valteline (from January 1553) [1427]. For example, he is in close contact with several ministers, preaches sermons in Casaccia[1428], and in Bondo[1429]; he takes part in

---

[1426] ANTONIO DI ADAMO [MAINARDO A.] "Annatomia della messa 1552 fol.A5rv.

[1427] Rosius a Porta spoken, for Vergerio, of a "episcopales […] spiritus" see ROSIUS A PORTA P. D. "Historia Reformationis…" op.cit. vol 1,book 2, p 154..

[1428] Zentralbibliothek Zurich ms.F 40 fol 557 rv, letter from Vergerio to Gwalther, Vicosoprano, 15 May 1551.

[1429] (ZONCA G.) "Della statue et imagini" s.l.1553 fol.A3rv/ It must be noted that Vergerio acts in opposition with the ecclesiastical tradition of the region. Vicosoprano is richest

the abolition of the mass in Samedan[1430] and in Souz[1431], both in Engadine. He is implicated in the propagation of the Reformation in the Val Malenco[1432]. He also, very probably, tries to uniformise the liturgies of the different communities of the Val Bregaglia, even of all the Italian-speaking Grisons[1433]. Beyond that, in some public [1434]works, Vergerio continues to act as if he were the spokesman of the whole Val Bregaglia. This is for example the case of "La terra di Vico Soprano",Pope Giulio III said, and even more explicitly in his Orarione che dovea…passare", both in 1552. There, he addresses his reader with these words: "Let us consider that all the members and brothers of other Reformed Churches speak with you through my mouth"[1435]. In fact. Already, his "Brieve, et semplice modo per informare lii Fanciulli (1550)" [1436]states, in its title that the catechism is not only designed by Vergerio's Church, but also for "the other places in the valley of Bregaglia"[1437]

Vergerio acts in the same way when he leaves going to Valteline at the beginning of 1553. Before that date, he was

---

town in the region. See NOSCHELE.R . "Die Gotteshauser der Schweis…" vol 1, bisthum Chur Zurich Orell, Fussli & co 1864 p 116-117.

[1430] CAMPELL U. "Historia Rhaetica ed. PLATTNER P. basle Adolf Geering vol 2 p 116-117

[1431] SCHIESS T "Bullinges Korrespondenz…" op. cit.vol 1 p 259-260 letter from Vergerio to Bullinger 22.08.1552.

[1432] Ibid. p 167 letter from Giovanni Beccaria in Bullinger Coire 5 June 1550.

[1433] [VERGEROP P.P.] "Oratione che doveaesser…passae" [Poschiavo] [dolph Landofi [152] fol,.Alir"

[1434]ATANASIO [VERGERIIO P.P,.] "Delle commissioni…Grisoni [Tubingen] 1554 Ulrich morhart]] fol A6r

[1435] ZULIANA F. "Un caechismo perduto…" art,cit. p 479-380. This subject will soon be the themef of a specific article.

busy with local communities, although that was forbidden by the law:
"It is true that during the prohibition we could however sometimes go there and, in some private homes, he preached Jesus Christ, as in secret and among some people". Some months later "after abandoning the ministry of Vicosoprnano" he goes to Valteline and describes his activity, thus; 'I settled myself in order to live, preach, expose books and give Communion and everything [1438]that, summing up, I knew and could do[1439]. It is still the case when he publishes in1553, "Fondamento della religione christiana per uso della Valtelina[1440]. As the title suggest, Vergerio is not addressing only one Church, but the whole of Valteline. Then on account of the fierce opposition of Mainardo - who recalls Bullinger: "we have our catechisms"[1441]". Vergerio publishes the work by stating that it is aimed uniquely at the Churches who recognise his authority: Fondamento della religione christiana per uso di quella parte di Valtelina, dove ministra Athnasio (Athanasio, or Atanasio, is his notorious pen name[1442]. Mainardo,however[1443], is not fully satisfied, for what he contests is that Vergerio can claiim such an authority?"

[1438]

[1439] Ibid fol [A6] v "Lasciato il ministerio di Vicosuproano…otea".

[1440] Ibis. 1554 fol.A6r. "Lasciato il miniserio…et tra pochi"…et potea"

[1441] SCHIESS T. "Bllingers Korrespondenz…" op.cit.vol/1 p 319 letter frpmMainardo to Bulliger Chiavenna 3 September 1553, "(h)abemus nostros catechismos".

[1442144214421442] [VERGERIO P.P.] Fondamento della Religione Chrisinnnnama…Athanasio (Tubngrn [Ulrich Morart 1553.

[1443] SCHIESS T. "Bullinger Korespondenz op.cit vol.1, p 318
(a) Vergerio se nolleministrum evangeli…vult obtrudedre?
CANTIMORI D. "Eretici italiani…op.cit. ROTONDO A .
"Esuli italiani " art.cit Coire, Archivio di Stato e aibliotecaCantonale dei rigioni 1978.

Vergerio must face fairly strong local opposition. We have already seen the mention of Antechrist" "wolves" and "false brothers" in his community, but it is rather on account of his catechism "in the usage of Valtelline" and for his action there, that in the end he must leave the area. However, he benefits greatly from a great many supports: ministers who invite him to preach, or who accept his presence among the faithful flock. For him, as for many other protestant ministers, but also, laymen the main problem is to find an effective means of converting those who have remained Catholic and at the same time to strengthen the Churches which are already reformed. secretly. I think that this aspect of Vergerio's activity can be explained, by the fact that this area is at the crossroads of different ecclesiastical and pastoral models.

Concurrent pastoral models
To begin, one must state that Vergerio's strong convictions are without doubt. For him, as for many other protestants, ministers and laity, the main problem is to find an effective means for converting those who remained Catholics and strengthen the Churches that were already reformed. One must also state that the Italian-speaking Grisons are an area that knows a strong presence of "sectarians", antitrinitarians and Anabaptists, who for several reasons (and particularly because only Catholic and reformed confessions are legal) often join the local reformed communities. As a result, a great part of Vergerio's activity and other ministers is devoted to the strengthening of the ecclesiastical discipline. However, the means of attaining this goal are the subject of debates.

Unfortunately, the current knowledge on the composition of the Italian Churches of the Grisons and their inner life is much too superficial. No doubt the question would deserve a systematic study in the future. It would be particularly interesting to lean on their composition of a prosopographic point of view.[1444] They consist of local populations, but also of emigrants freshly arrived, "religionis causa". In spite of their common faith and language, these two groups doubtless partook of few things and evolved in very different contexts. As regards Vergerio, it sems possible to state that his activity took root in a Catholic terrain. He was a bishop and, for four years, from 1541 to 1544, [1445]he tried to reform his own diocese according to methods which were close to those introduced in the Grisons, (sermons against idols, spread of "good books", work in proximity with his clergy etc,) doubtless he tried to copy in this way the success of his previous experience and to put his own skill at the service of his new Church".

More interesting still would be the hypothesis according to which the model created by Vergerio could be known and adaptable for others. I think this is particularly the case for emigrant Catholic clerks. For them- who in Italy were under the authority of bishops or abbots – the model of a more centralised control must seem relatively familiar and it is easy to adapt to it. That could explain why, among Vergerio's supports, one finds several reformed ministers who were clerks in Italy, as for example Guido Zonca or Pietro Perisotto, but also the Calvinist theologian Celso Martinengo (later minister of the Italian Church in Geneva) who recently fled Italy and who, during the few months that he spent in the Grisons, helped Vergerio in his pastoral duties in Vicosoprano[1446]. There are also those men who invited Vergerio to preach or ask him for help when iit

---

[1444] FIRPO M "PREFAZIONE".A.PASTORE "Nella Valtellina del tardo conquecento. Fede, cultura,sociea, " Rome Viella 2015 p

[1445] JACOBSON SCHUTTE A. "Pier Paolo Vergerio e la reforma…" op.it. p 242-202.

[1446] SCHIESS T. "Bullingers Korrespondenz …" op.cit. vol 1 p 239-240,letter from Vergerio to Bulllinger Vicosoprano 27.02.1552 at the time of Martinengo leaving

happens to them that they had to fight against a Catholic opposition. Now a great many local protestants are recent converts and have problems in completely breaking contacts with their old Catholic life[1447]. That could probably help to explain Vergerio's success. in Valteline..

At that time however, two other traditions are pregnant in the region: one more ancient, that of Zurich (via Coire)[1448] and the other more recent, that of Geneva. Contrary to the Catholic, these two models have a strong legitimacy among the protestants. Some years before, the two churches had established the famous "Consensus Tigurinus (1549)". A study of the implantation of the "Consensus" Italian-speaking Rhetie remains to be written and would be very useful. In fact, the region is one of the co-existence of very rare cases where reformed models coming from these two traditions, up to the same Churches. Although that rests on non-exhaustive witness of the sources, one may reasonably maintain that the original inhabitants of the area are closer to the Zurichan model. They are members completely separate from the Leagues, they recognise the authority of the general Diet, and are in commercial relations with German Switzerland where they often know the language. On the contrary, a significant share of the Italian immigrants – without including the sectarians" – is closer to Geneva, and the influence of the Genevan church in Italy at that time is well known[1449].

During the years where Vergerio is in the Grisons, the area is touched by a massive immigration from Italy, a consequence of inquisitorial activity[1450] The influence, in

---

[1447] ZULIANI F. "Un catechismo perduto e ritrovato…art.cit.p 468-471.

[1448] BONOBRAND C. "Lerelazzioni culturali …Swizzera tedesca" Archivio Lombardo s.9 no. 5-6 p 39-45 TAPLIN "The Italian Reformers…Church 1540-1629," Ashgate 2005

[1449] FELICI L "Giovanni Calvino e l'Italia" TurinClaudiana 2012

[1450] See for example tlhe letters from Vergerio to Gwalther (Zentralbibliohek Zurich ms. F 40 fol, 363 1,Vicosoprano

the local churches, of these immigrants attracted by the Genevan model remains unknown. In a situation where the ministers are elected and revoked by the local communities, the weight of their presence must bot especially be underestimated. One may obviously say that the pro-Genevan Italian laity do not show great sympathy for episcopalian solutions. On the contrary, they promote a Presbyterian model, which, in fact begins to come forth in these years. By way of opposition, the Zurichan approach is very different. For examp[e, one must emphasise that the name of "antistes" de facto attracted several figures of the episcopacy[1451]. It is not by chance that Bullinger continues to be called "episcopus" in his correspondence[1452]. From the Zurichan point of view, Vergerio's name of bishop and his episcopalian approach probably do not constitute a problem in itself. Vergerio's activity could in this sense be encouraged. It is for this reason that I think, contrary to other historians, that at the beginning of 1551 and at least for a brief moment, Vergerio was chosen by the authorities of Coire, narrowly linked to Zurich, as "visitor designated for the preachers" in order to reconcile Camillo Renato[1453]. These faithful people near Zurich probably constitute a significant share of the community of Vicosoprano, which

---

13.09.1550) and to Bullinger (Shiess T " op.cit vol 1 p 184 p 191 Vicosoprano 15 or 20.12.1550 nd 13.02/1551).

[1451] BALTISCHWEILER W. "Die Institutionen der evangelisch-reformierren …Entwitwicklung" Zurich Schulthess & Co 1905.

[1452] For IItalians using this name in referring to Bujllinger, see for example the letters from Renato, Mainardo and Bartolomeo Paravicini. The name, however, is also systematically used by the reformed clergy of Coire,as with Johannes Blasius,Johannes Comander eand Philippus Gallicuis (Ibid passim).

[1453] RENATO C. "Opere, documenti e testimonianze" ROTONDO a. Florence, Chicago, Sansoni Newberry Library 1068 p 233-241…Vergerio.

elected him on leaving, and they could therefore have found his actions legitimate.

What seems very interesting to me, is that, in the letters which I have found, Vergerio never mentions the presence of Presbyterians In Vicosoprano. Does he simply ignore them? Or are they not really present in Vicosoprano? It is sure that, for these reformed people who believe in the validity of the Presbyterian model, this specific aspect of Vergerio's pastoral approach may be considered as unacceptable.

Reform of the ecclesiastical discipline and Pastoral assertion in Calvin's Geneva (years 1540-1550)
Nathalie Szczech

"A minister must not talk other than about the Gospel and, as for the rest of the appointed things, he must not get mixed up in them[1454].

It is in these terms that Jacques Gruet expressed his opposition to the changes that the pastoral minister knew in Geneva, during the 1540's. This secretary, condemned for "atheism" by the civil authorities and executed on 26j July 1547, here formalises his fierce rejection of the extension of the pastoral prerogatives beyond preaching and administration of the sacraments. Far from being only an isolated attack, Gruet's words translate as a more general incomprehension and the refusal, by an important part of the Genevan population, of the expansion of pastoral expertise,

---

[1454] Theme of Jacques Gruet addressed to his judges. Criminal case [PC]quoted in BERRIOT F . "Un process d'atheisme a Geneve:l'affaire Gruet (1547-1550"Bulletin de la SHPF vol 125-4 1979 p 577-592 p 583.

in the years following Calvin's [1455]return to Geneva. This complex face to face among the ministers and the Genevan faithful flock, and the anticlerical reactions that he introduced enable one to question an essential problem of the birth years of the Reformation: that of the definition of the contours of the pastoral mission, from the legitimacy of the foundations of the authority if ministers and of the constitution of a specifically reformed clerical identity.

On 21 May 1536, the General Council of Geneva officially chose the Reformation, after several years of silent penetration of Lutheran ideas, sermons, then public debates[1456]. This rupture however did not constitute a point of outcome, since everything remained to build in order to establish Geneva in the new faith and to root the Gospel in hearts and practices. How did pastors and the pastorate re-invent themselves in the bosom of a protestant world in formation? The mass was abolished, images broken and the clerks, mostly, were exiled, but how was the separation with a neighbouring Catholicism, in time as in space, built?

This study proposes to tackle these questions through the problem which underlines the ecclesiastical discipline, that is to say institutionalisation, with the creation of the consistory and by applying evangelical precepts[1457]of an unpublished reformed practice of fraternal correction, in which the pastors take the most active part, seeking to ensure the orthodoxy and orthopraxy of the faithful flock, to close obstinate sinners access to the sacrament of communion and to work for progressive sanctification of the community. This aspect of the pastoral mission, which

---

[1455] On this climate of opposition, reported by Calvin, see, for example,CALVINJ. "Des scandales" FATIO Geneva,Droz, 1984 p 17-8 p 82 p 194 and no.379;

[1456][1456] See NAEF H. "Les origins de la Reforme a Geneve", Geneva,Librairie A. Jlien 1936 vol 2 (repub. 1968).

[1457] Mt, 18, 15-20 is the reference text for evoking fraternal correction. Verses 17-18 justify the institutionalisation of the discipline.

covers examination, admonitions, even excommunications, and reconciliation of repentant sinners, seems in fact like an essential motor of the process of clericalisation which moves the Genevan Reformation in Calvin's time[1458]. It puts an important problem before the ministers of positioning in relation to the Catholic past and to the legacy of the first reformers and constitutes, as a result, the intrigue of anticlericalism which touched Geneva i in the years 1542-15555, but also became the dynamic principal of forming, in the ordeal, of a pastoral body and culture.

The study of the registers of the consistory, more particularly in the years 1542-1555, fed by an analysis of the registers of the Company of pastors, of surveys in the registers of the Council and criminal cases, as well as in the correspondence of Genevan ministers, at the top class of which Calvin, enables one to understand how a reformed ecclesiastical discipline is imposed, which will soon become an essential " brand" of the Reformed Church[1459]. The Genevan consistorial sources are known and have already been studied fir the XVIth century, social[1460], political[1461], or anthropolpgical[1462] issues. Their critical edition, currently in process[1463] enables one to survey them

---

[1458] On this idea, see WANEGFFELEN T "Un clericalism reforme. Le Protestantism francais entre principe du sacerdoce universel et theologie …(XVI-XVII siecles)" conference du "Reformation Studies Colloquium Birmingham (2004)

[1459] On discipline as a third" brand" of the "true" Church, see GROSSE C."Les rituels de la cene..Geneva (XVI-XVII siecles) Geneva Droz 2008 p 340-342.

[1460] One dreams of the works of Raymond a. Mentzer and Robert M. Kingdon and gus oyouks.

[1461] NAOHY W.G. "Calvin and the Consolidation of the Genevan Reformation", Manchester, Manchester University Press 1994.

[1462] FROSSE C."Les rituels de la Cene…" op,cit.

[1463] KINGDON R.M. (Then WANDEL L.P "Registres du Conseil de Geneve au temps de Calvin", Geneva,,Droz 1996

freshly and to use them more easily in order to tackle the fabric of a pastoral authority and a clerical identity.

The creation of the Geneva consistory and the organisation of an unpublished disciplinary procedure

In September 1541, the civil authorities recalled Calvin to Geneva and gave him a task to reorganise a Church which was racked by disorder. Strengthened by the support of the faction which was then in power and in a context of urgency, the reformer could quickly have his proposals for reforms adopted by the Councils. Ecclesiastical Decrees were thus voted in from the month of November 1541, in order to control the order of the Church, from then on structured around four ministries[1464]. Calvin came to have the principle of an ecclesiastical discipline approved, institutionalised in a new court, the consistory[1465]. Assembled every Thursday in the old cloister of the canons of Saint-Pierre cathedral, the pastors and a dozen old people, placed under the authority of a manager, are charged to guarantee respect for the doctrine, to safeguard the morality of the Genevans and to punish sins committed against the law or charity[1466]. Informed by their own observations, rumour or informing, they intervene in the name of the Church, when private correction has failed, and they set out to [1467]reconstitute the facts by the interrogation of the sinner and possible witnesses[1468]. The sessions were

---

[1464] AEG. "Reistres du conseil de Geneve" RC35, 20.11.1541 fol.405 reproduced in KINGDON R.M.and BERIER J.F. "Registres de la compagnie des Pasteurs de Geneve au temps de Calvin" Geneva Droz t.l.p 1-13.

[1465] KINGDON R.M.and BWEFIER J.C. "Registres de la Compagmir..." op.cit. t t.l. p 2 p 6-7 p 12-13.

[1466] See the list of sins evoked in CALVIN J. "Institution de la religion chretienne" [159] J D BENOIT Paeis Vrin 1957-1963 book IV Chap XII.

[1467]

[1468] CALVIN J. "Institution..." op.cit. book IV chap XII 2 and commentaries by GROSSE C. "Les rituels de la Cene..." op.cit/p346-347.

sanctioned, mostly, by very ritualised warnings, often pronounced by Calvin, and by pedagogic prescriptions, such as attendance at sermons or sessions on the catechism. If the accused party is considered obstinate or if the actions are considered as particularly serious, the procedure to lead to excommunication or to complexify themselves par sending back the deviant person before the Small Council, which has full authority to take on other sanctions. By spreading the stain of the error, a source of divine anger, by preserving the community from sin and by inviting the faithful flock to penitence by example of the sanction, the ecclesiastical discipline which is thus organised must enable the Church to present itself as a healthy body, moulded in the image of Christ, with which it aspires to be united.

The creation of a court which is specifically dedicated to this mission, and particularly the role of activity that it gains by relation to civil justice determining where the pastors operate, mark a rupture in the recent history of the city and make Geneva in the years 1540-1550 an unpublished case. The departure of the Prince-Bishop in1534 and the adoption of the Reformation in 1536 have led to putting back into effect the mediaeval system of ecclesiastical discipline, broadly criticised by the humanists, then by the first reformers [1469] and have widened the responsibilities of the Magistrate. While at the turn of the XVth and XVIth centuries, supervision of beliefs and customs was organised in a permanent overlap of the episcopal and communal justices, the Small council takes it fully in charge from that time, whether it is a question of office in the past, or to [1470]have the divine prescriptions respected, the action of the councillors extending, for example, to matrimonial cases

---

[1469] DENIS P. "Remplacer la confession: absolutions…XVIe siècle" GROUPE DE LA BUSSIERE "Pratiques de la confession. Des Peres du desert ….histoire" paris Cerf 1983 p 165-176.
[1470]

which up to then the official took in charge[1471]. Breaking with the old system considered as abusive.[1472] And dissolving the principle of a priest as the only clergyman, the Magistrate thus takes the responsibility for the public morality and the respect for the precepts of the new faith, the pastors no longer intervening on disciplinary questions except in consultation, even not at all.

This initial organisation is inspired from elaborate models by the first Swiss reformers. In Zurich, under the inspiration of Zwingli, discipline is in fact ensured, from 1525, by a matrimonial court, the "Ehegericht", made up of four members of the municipal Magistrate and two pastors. This institution controls difficulties which come from marriages, but it soon also deals with other problems coming from general supervision of the faithful flock. It sends back disobedient members before the civil authorities[1473]. The civil authorities, whose representatives are in the majority are in h bosom of the institution and before whom the accused parties can be provided with an appeal, seized the exercise of the discipline, in a gesture determined to break with the old practices of ecclesiastical justice. Under the Zwinglian influence, the State of Berne adopted a similar organisation and put in place, from 1528, a "Chorgericht" progressively reduced in the different parishes of the area, in charge of matrimonial cases, but more broadly responsible for the doctrinal and moral supervision of the faithful flock – doctrinal deviations, sorcery, disrespect for Sunday, dancing, drunkenness, bawdiness, adultery are the reasons for the most common

---

[1471] NAEF H. "Les origines de la Reforme a Geneve" op.cit.vol.p 219-236Mbaud h. "Le diocese de Geneve-Annecy" Paris Beauchesne 1985 p 80- 81.

[1472] See, for example, FEBVE L. "Un abus et son climat social;..Franche-Comte" L.FEBVRE "Au Coeur religieux XVIe siècle" Paris SEVPEN 1957 p 301-337.

[1473] KOHLER W. "Zurcher Ehegericht und Genfer…" Leipzig M. Heinsuis Nachfolge 1932-1942 2 vol

appearance[1474]. It is a civil institution, in the bosom of which the pastors do not have a dominant position and which leaves the responsibility for sanctions to the Magistrate .This model is imposed in the lands that Berne progressively conquered from the XIVth century[1475], in spite of the exchanges with Berne, in 1540, about creating an institution which could specifically take responsibility for questions of discipline[1476], and in spite of the creation, on paper, of a consultative consistory in 1541[1477] this is a Zwinglian model of continuity and leaves the responsibility for supervising the faith and customs to the Genevan civil authorities. During the first years of the Reformation, the Genevan pastors are only considered, at best, as collaborators, whose daily presence with the faithful flock can enlighten the decisions of the magistrates in the matter of discipline.

The principle of a discipline is ensured by the ministers is not however abandoned by all the reformers, in spite of their wish to break with the practices of the Roman clergy and to establish the pastoral ministry on reformed foundations. Influenced by the ideas of Olampiad and Bucer and by his contacts with the Baslian and Strasbourgian clergy in the second half of the 1530's, it is Calvin who goes further in the reflection on the usage of discipline, who defends his full belonging to the pastoral mission and conquers a space of autonomous exercise for the consistory, in front of the new civil authorities until in

---

[1474] SCHMIDT H.R. "Durf und Religion. Reformierte …Fruhen Neuzeit" Stuttgart – iene – NEW Yori Gustav Verlag 1995 Saint Gall (1526)

[1475] MATZINGER-PISTER R. "L'introductio des Consistoires dans le pays de Vaud "D.TOSADORIGO and N, STAREMBERG "Sous l'oeil du consistoire…op. cit" p 113-123 .

[1476] AEWG Registres du Conseil de Geneve RC 34 fol21 dfol 27 fol 376.

[1477] Ibid RC 35 fol145r and fol 154r commented by GROSSE C."Les rituels de la cene" op.cit p 352-355.

[1478]1555. Inspired, like Oecolampade and Bucer, by the example of the independent primitive church of the secular authorities, Calvin thinks that discipline can only be exercised by an autonomous ecclesiastical instance[1479]. His argument, which was drawn up at the turn of the years 1550-1540 and states in the "Institution" of 1543, defends the exercise of discipline by a council formed from ministers and old people,[1480] and using the power of codes in the name of the whole Church. Discipline and excommunication are considered as instruments that God gives to pastors and old school people, responsible for supervising the sanctification of the social body.

An enlargement of the disciplinary practices for recasting the social body

This unpublished Calvinist positioning is not so clear in the Decrees of 1541, which appear like a vague compromise between temporal and spiritual authorities. The translation of Calvin's ideas in the daily pastoral activity enables them to be described through practice, but also makes a misunderstanding grow up which, hidden in 1541, is rapidly revealed and becomes worse up to the [1481]political crisis which the city declares in 1555. It is the question of the

---

[1478] On the conflict between the consistory …see GROSSE C. "L'excommunicarion de Philibert …Reforme genevoise (1547-15555)" MANETSCH S.M "Calvin's company of Pastors…"Oxford University Press 2013 chap 7.

[1479] MCKEE E.A. "Calvin, Discipline and Exeesis …sixteenth century" I. BACKUS and F.HIGMAN "Theorie et pratique de l'exegese" Geneva Droz 1990 p 319-327.

[1480] On the historical constitution of this doctrine, see HOPEL "The Christian Policy of John Calvin, Cambridge, CUP 1985 p 58-60.

[1481] On 16 May 1555, after a large riot, the faction of the Children of Geneva fiercely opposing, for ten years, Calvin and his French pastors surrounding him,is defeated. The politico-religious scene is then left free for the defenders of the reforming Calvinian ideal – see NAPHY W.C. "Calvin and the Consolidatgion…" op.cit.

respective prerogatives of the pastors. of civil authorities and the faithful flock themselves which is bitterly fought, when it is a question of concreting founding principles, such as the rejection of "papist" abuses, the universal priest or the collaboration of the spiritual and temporal swords, on which all or nearly all seemed to agree in the middle of the 1530's. From 1542, the disciplinary activity grows and in fact tackles everything that waw known up till then in Geneva, the ecclesiastical Decrees only prescribing in imprecise terms that "the old school people must admonish" every faithful person who "neglects to conform with the church so much that one can see a [1482]noteworthy scorn for the communion of the faithful" or which appears contemptuous of the ecclesiastical order

The consistory, heir of the officialdom and the Swiss matrimonial courts which have replaced it. Is ensured in fact, most often, by the matrimonial promises and lead, in this case, the number if actions for broken engagements, adulteries or other regrouped sexual offences in the registers, under the term of "bawdiness[1483]. To the escapades od the famous Francois Favre, the patriarch of a great Genevan family, several times charged with bawdiness, the determination of the consistory replies in reforming what is considered as a life of debauchery which is incompatible with the plan for sanctification of the social body[1484]. This famous case, and the cases of hundreds of other "bawdy people" today forgotten, give testimony to the considerable effort made by the ministries to limit the sexual relations without a promise of marriage and the

---

[1482] KINGDON R.M. and BERGIER J.F. Registre d la Compagnie…" op.cit. v.1 p 1-12.

[14831483] The cases of bawdiness and intra-familial quarrels arising from it represent more than half of the cases of volume 3 *147-1548) see KINGDON R.M. Registres d Consistoire op.cit. v 3 2004 p x.

[1484] KINGDON R.M/" Registres du Consistoire…" op. cit. v 2 2001 p 84(3.12.1545)in.272 p 146-148 9Feb 146) 8.04.146) v 3 p 20-21 (3.02.1547) p 37-38 (3.03.1547)

illegitimate births which may follow, to punish more broadly the cases of fornication and adultery and to thus restrict the sexuality of the Geneva within the strict frameworks of marriage established by God. This enterprise of control of sexual morality is not, at first, the disciplinary action most contested by the faithful people, insofar as this type of control is accepted, even though the authorities were pressed, from the turn of the XVth and XVIth centuries, to suppress debauchery[1485]. Thus do the members of the consistory follow practices in place in Geneva before the Reformation and the models of other Swiss cities, which have institutionalised this matrimonial control from the end of the 1520's, can it only be to comfort their legitimacy to intervene in this way.

The control of orthodoxy of the faithful flock and the struggle against ignorance and the persistence of [1486] Catholic practices of piety, which occupied a major place in the activity of the consistory, particularly in 1542 and 1543[1487] are not however the most badly received dispositions. By representing the faithful flocks attend the neighbouring Catholic villages to go to Mass, to take communion, get married or have their children baptised, while suppressing the Latin prayers to the Virgin and to the saints, fasting and celebration, the pastors and old-school people in fact prolonged the inaugural gesture of reversal of the altar and destruction of images, which marked the entrance of the community into its new story. If they did

---

[1485] On the reinforcement of the policy on customs on the eve of the Reformation, see NAEF H. "Les origins de la Refprme a Geneve" op. cit/v 1 p228-235.

[1487] KINGDON R.M "L'usage quantitative des registres …Geneve" P.CHAREYRE P.and R.A. MENTZER "Lla mesure religeuse calvini europeen XVI-XVIIIe siecles" Bulletin de ka SHPF v 153-4 2997 0 585-592

not succeed in removing all trace of Catholicism[1488].at least they only stirred up a passive resistance of the inhabitants and so much more that on questions of faith, their attitude is patient and broadly more pedagogic than repressive. Mirroring the control of souls, pastors and old school people intend also to channel people during the time of worship and more particularly the sermon. Movements and untimely activities[1489] must be stopped, silence and immobility were imposed, to promote listening, impregnation of the soul by the Word and the action of the Holy Spirit, in connection with the or the specifics of the reformed liturgy, which places the Word which was read, or chanted, prayed or taught in the centre of the service and minimises gestures outside the sacramental time. Movements and restlessness[1490] noise and restless interruptions[1491], laughing and grimacing[1492] are thus revealed in the consistory and give rise to reprimands and sanctions, to the point that as Jean Vuilliemoz, Lieutenant of Genthod, his minister "can only stir the pot [1493]".

But discipline regulates matrimonial problems and the control of orthodoxy and the attitude of the faithful flock in the space of the temple, in order to touch, from the 1540's, all aspects of daily life, and to move from the street to family intimacy. In fact it is a question of reforming the social body completely according to a principle of unity[1494], which is translated, without the consistory always managing

---

[1488] In 1536, for example 29 people were condermned for Catholic practices in ANNECY: REGISTRES DU CONSISTOIRE 11 FOL FOLM60 V 924.09.1556)

[1489]

[1490] For example, AEG Registres du Conseil a Geneve RC 41 fol.41 fol 59v (29.03.15460

[1491] For example, KINGDON R.M. "Registres du Consistoire…" RC fol 41 fol 59v 929.03.1546)(

[1492] AEG For example KINGDON R.M. "Registres du consistoire…" op. cit v 4 p 45 (12.O4.1548)

[1493] Ibid p 109 M (908.1548)

[1494] CALVIN J. "Institution…" op. cit book IV chap XVII 40.

is purposes, however by a work of appeasement of conflicts, an enterprise of smoothing over social practices and struggling against the traditions and signs of communal belonging. Relations in the bosom of the families, areas or professional communities are thus observed, aiming to pacify the interpersonal violence which endanger communion[1495]. Even more, the members of the consistory intend progressively to unify the city under the banner of the Gospel, by reforming the rites of passage, by moralising the spaces and traditional leisure or in fighting similar signs. The choice of first names in baptism, which do not have to be biblical, became, for example, a knot of the consistorial activity between 1546 and the middle of the 1530's[1496]. By refusing traditional first names, such as Claude, Gaspard or Balthasar, the pastors put off the tradition which allows the godfather to give his first name to the child and fight against a usage which up to then cemented the solidarities in the heart of the city. In a similar momentum, the consistory supervises the activities of bands of young people, tracks the games, songs and dances or tries to moralise the traditional places for socialising which are the steam rooms[1497], Calvin supports for example, forbidding punctured shoes. By representing the struggle against this ostentatious dress style, he sanctions what, according to him is a manifestation of pride, but he plans especially to reform the traditions of young members of military companies which, according to him, who willingly wear this clothing as a sign of recognition[1498]. It is thus about containing

---

[1495] See GROSSE C. "Les rituels de la Cene…" op.cit.p 511-565.

[1496] See NAPHY W.G "Baptism, Church Riots…Geneva", Sixteenth century journal v. 26 1995 p 86-97.

[1497] The pastors obtain from the Council on 29.04.1546, the closing of taverns, R.M "Registres du consistoire…op.cit v 2 p 157 Sauelander vII p 478. See GROSSE C. "Les rituels de la cene" op.cit. p 337-339.

[1498] See he letter from Calvin to the faithful people of France 24.97.1547 CALVIN J, "Johannis Calvini opera…" op.cit v

particularisms, to teach a stirring youth and to incorporate it into the community of the faithful flock, in order to unify the social body into the image of Christ.

Persuaded that all immorality remains unpunished constitutes an attack in God's honour and restricts the advancement of the Gospel, it is with a strong zeal that the consistory and, more particularly, the pastors struggle day after day to apply a reformed normal standard. If this disciplinary activity crosses political and social problematics, it is in the much broader framework of a view of the world and a history of salvation that one must consider its inclusion in the frameworks of pastoral mission, which are fixed in these founding years.

A pastoral body tested by ecclesiastical discipline

They are these interventions in gestures, daily times and spaces and the rewriting of the social body which are the most virulently contested in the years 1545-1555, a growing part of the Genevan population questioning the legitimacy of the consistory, but most particularly the expansion of the pastors' prerogatives, lived like an intrusion. Nicolas Gentil, chateau owner of Jussy, thus refuses to be interviewed by the consistory and explained that "he [does not hold the pastors for ministers except when they are in the [1499]pulpit].". In a time when, hardly a few years after the official passage of Geneva to the Reformation, the authority of ministers remains to be built and their mission to be limited, a misunderstanding was dug in the middle of the 1540's to the middle of the 1550's and fed an anticlerical criticism which is more and more visible and violent.

This contest is precociously translated by a passive resistance of the Genevans, who refuse to join the

---

10 1879 col 561-562 quoted in KINGDON R,M "Registres du Consistoire" op.cit. v 2 158.

[1499] AEG Registres du Conseil de Geneve RC 44 fol 126 bis (7,06.1549

convocations of the court[1500], or are disobedient in obeying the consistory[1501]. Explicit and pronounced contests, in a first time, in the closed hearing of the court, take over. Thus in 1542, Andre Piard states before the members that Calvin is not his superior and he does not intend to obey him[1502]. Called on 3 February 1550, Francois Favre states that the consistory is "a new jurisdiction to restrict people"[1503] He refuses to address the pastors during his interrogation and only talks to the manager who presides over the meeting. In a gradual outbreak of verbal violence, the ministers are soon publicly taken aside. In 1550, the saddler is thus accused of having hurled, in his shop, violent words towards the ministers, who, according to him, "have better deserved to be taken to Plant Pallais than a great many people who were taken there"[1504]. The exasperation of some faithful people, who no longer tolerate the repeated reprimands of the pastors clearly showed in the registers of the consistory, in the example of the themes of Guillaume Du Bois, persuaded that Calvin's repeated reprimands are proof that the Reformer shows upon meeting him. [1505].

Genevan anticlericalism manifests itself as much by words as by gestures. Calvin and his colleagues thus complain to the Council about loud jokes, such as young people who, at night, come to ring the doorbell at night at

---

[1500] See, for example, KINGDON R.M. "Registres du Conseil". op. cit. v1 1996 p 209 922.04.1546)

[1501] AEG "Registres du Conseil de Geneve RC35 fol 442 (23.12.15410

[1502] KINGDON R.M. "Registres du Consistoire…" op.cit/ v 1 p 102 (17.08/1542).

[1503] Ibid v 3 p 14 (3.02.1547).

[1504] Ibid v 5 2010 p 14 (27.02.1550) Plainpalais was the place where those who were condemned to capital punishment were executed.

[1505] Report of the consistory to the Council AEG" PC 1t series, no 437 (30.12.1546) reproduced in KINGDON R.M. "Registres du Consistoire…" op.cit v 2 p 379.

their door in Rue des Chanoines[1506] about provocations such as those of Gaspard Favre, seen while playing skittles with friends, at the time of worship at Easter 1546[1507], or found playing tennis noisily in front of St Peter's during a lesson by Calvin in 1551[1508]. The contesting gestures also invade the temples , key spaces of sanctification. The repeated absence of faithful people from the sermon is scandalous[1509], while play in their presence: Jean-Philibert Bonna, entering and leaving the temple. As if acting a joke, "came to accompany the [1510]children who are brought for baptism, then retires from the sermon, then comes back at the end, a scandalous thing and a mockery". In a society of precedence, these incivilities become sharp weapons, which wound the honour of the pastors and are lived, doubling at the pace that the tensions are becoming intensified, physical violence: the temples are thus the theatre of repeated troubles, which could go to a brawl at the time of baptisms[1511], and the registers even record the cases of aggression to pastors[1512].

[1506] AEG "Recistres du Conseil de Geneve RC 44 fol.141 v (25.0.1549) quoted in KINGDON R.M. "Registres du Consistoire…" op. cit/v 4 p 218.

[1507] AEG "Registres du Conseil de Geneve", RC 41 fol.82 fol.84 fol.87 926,17,30 April and 6 May 1546.

[1508] Ibid. RC 45 fol 233 (25.03.1551).

[1509] See, for example, KINGDON R. M. "Registres du Consistoire…" op. cit. "Registres du Consistoire" op. cit v 6 2012 p 72.

[1510] Ibid p 178 (1,10 1551) and AEG Registres du Conseil de Geneve RC 46 fol. 68 v 69 (5.10.1551).

[1511] Ibid. See, for example, AEG, "Registres du Conseil de Geneve "RC 41, fol.238 (9 November 1546).

[1512] See, for example. AEG "Registres du Conseil de Geneve" RC 31. Fol. 238 (9.11.1546) KINGDON R.M. "Registres du conseil de Geneve" RC 44 fol.171 v quoted in "Registres du Conseil de Geneve" fol.221 v 4 p 222(29.07.1549) AEG "Registres du Conseil de Geneve RC 45 fol.221 (12.03.1551).

The number and intensity of these anticlerical reactions invite one to emphasise the rupture in which the activity pf the consistory leads Geneva at the beginning of the 1540's. For the aim of the members of this new institution is not reduced to supervise and punish in order to guarantee social peace, nor to control and punish to counteract the accession of a faction to power, but to work for the sanctification of the Genevan community, such as "eyes", "ears", "nose" and "mouth" of a social body which must be made only for the glory of God[1513]. Discipline, as necessary as the nerves in a body[1514], thus became a spiritual issue and not only social and political. In a break with the neighbouring Swiss examples and with the recent history of the city, the ministers opposed this imperative of collective sanctification to the imagination and to Genevan traditions and do not hesitate to break the balance between the necessary exclusion of the sinner in or[1515]der to preserve the social order and the desire to maintain the cohesion of the latter. This unpublished positioning, which is not afraid of breaking up hierarchies, solidarities and traditional balances, is resented as an illegitimate symbolic violence by a number of Genevans, anxious to establish the changes in the community structure that they know. It is thus symptomatic that Jacques Gruet emphasises, during interrogations that he suffered in July 1542, the shock that for him constituted the humiliating spectacle of the powerful merchant Francois Favre, acknowledged to be capable of bawdiness and obliged by the Council, at the

---

[1513] See VIRET P. "Instruction Chretienne …l'Evangile" Geneva Jean Rivey, 1564 v 2 p 360-363; ID "Response aux questions…Ropitel, Lyon, C. Senneton 1565 p 87 passages quoted by ZEMON DAVIS N. "The sacred …sixteenth century Lyon" "Past and Present v 90 p 64-65.
[1514] CALVIN J, "Institution …" op. cit. book IV chap. XVII 1
[1515] BERRIOT I. "Un process d'atheisme a Geneve…" art.cit. p 580.

request of the consistory, to shout "mercy, kneeling" and thus to soil his honour.

This determined engagement in the re-foundation of the community brings about setting apart and affirmation of the group of pastors in reaction to that of the laity, favouring a process of clericalization. For if a clerical identity comes uncontestably from the authority given to the pastors to assemble, to judge, to sanction within the framework of the consistory, this identity is also forged in the discussions of the opponents who consider the pastors as a group, as a separate group, even as a group of clerks. In the consistory, some Genevans thus identify the pastors with former priests, have the impression of living a return to Catholicism and to be deprived of the gains of the Reformation. The case of "the Marrechauda of Russin", accused of having said "that the preachers were more wicked than the priests" is, in this case, eloquent[1516]. The resolute engagement of the pastors in the disciplinary action therefore contributes to isolate them and a reaction among the Genevans of a Catholic memory which is still alive.

Beyond the stigmatising words of the faithful flock, who outwardly create a group pastoral identity, the increasing violence that the ministers try give rise to mutuality and a common imagination, which come to reduplicate the efficient factors of cohesion, such as the French origin which is almost exclusive to the Genevan pastors, the literate culture that they share and the constant exchanges that they carry out, thanks especially to the weekly meetings of the little group[1517]. The pastors, who share the

---

[1516] Thanks to the eviction of old elements, to the recruitment of new pastors and the control of French pastors, Calvin finds himself in 1546 at the head of a group exclusively made up of French pastors, with the exception of Jacques Bernard, relegated into a rural parish NAPHY W.G. "Calvin and the consolidation…" p 53-75.MANETSCH S.M. "Calvin's company of Pastors" op.cit.chap 2.

[1517] WANDEL L.P. "Registres du Consistoire…" op.cit. v 8 2014 p 227 (21.12.1553).

responsibility for the three churches of the city and a dozen of rural parishes, then form a true company, whose members are united by a similar ideal of sanctification of the community and fed by a similar fighting imagination, which gives sense and legitimates the enterprise of discipline. Going broadly outside the political or social issues, the engagement of pastors in this project, of which they are the movers, and the Genevan resistances with which they are confronted are in fact considered as the tragic manifestations of a dramatic tension between Good and Evil, as the signs of a holy struggle which is intensified until 1555 and the fall of the Children of Geneva[1518]. The attacks experienced in Geneva are understood as characteristic proof of a time of advancement of the Gospel and are lived as an update of the troubles of holy history, which feed the faith of the group in itself and in its project. Far from running away from the fight and even entertaining it by an enterprise which is always more passionate about purification[1519]. Calvin and his colleagues find there the confirmation of their view of the world, the legitimation of their action and forge a common culture there. The process of clericalization is thus fed paradoxically in Geneva from the anticlericalism of the faithful flock.

***

During the years 1540-1560.Geneva become the laboratory of reformed disciplinary practices, qui aim not only to anchor the new faith in hearts, but also to re-found the society, which had to become a purified body and fashioned in the image of Jesus Christ. Ecclesiastical discipline was

---

[1518] See. For example, the letter to Blaurer of 19.11.1552, CALVIN J. "Johannis Calvini opera..." op. cit. v 14 1888 col.412.

[1519] On this tension which is willingly conducted in the town, particularly between March and May 1555, aww CROUZET D. "Calvin, parallel live" Paris Fayard p 287-302.

invented in confrontation and was imposed, from a high struggle in 1555, as a kingpin of the pastors' mission: the latter are no longer only ministers of the Word, but are installed in a posture of guardians, whose vocation is to supervise respect for the honour of God and the integrity of the community. A melting-pot of political and major social renewals, the years 1545-1555 therefore also mark the birth of a true Genevan pastoral body, soldered by preaching, administration of the sacraments and care of the faithful flock, but also by the practice of ecclesiastical discipline included like a necessary combat. This invention was not any evidence, to the extent where discipline, especially in the most advanced form of excommunication, took Geneva away from the other Swiss churches and paradoxically caused the resurgence of a Catholic memory which had to be erased.

Pastors who became bourgeois
Limits and consequences of a new model of incorporation of actors into the
Ministry in the Geneva of Theodore de Beze
Reflections around the removals
Of Nicolas Colladon and Jean le Gagneux (1571)
Genevieve

GROSS

On 3 December 1571, on the issue of a procedure planned between the ecclesiastical authorities and magistrates who had begun four months earlier, the Small Council of Geneva pronounced, in his absence, the removal of pastor Jean Le Gagneux. By this sentence, Le Gagneux was removed from his pastoral ministry practiced in the town from 1562, but also from his temporary position as a teacher of theology, in 1571 helping Theodore de Beze and Nicolas Colladon in this parish in the heart of the Academy of Geneva, of which he was rector since 1568[1520] Upon reading the deed of condemnation, we are facing a second offending minister having more than three times gained from the "sweetness and mildness" of the magistrates, after having "notoriously [between 1564 and 1571] abused the liberty of the ministry in order to serve his special passions" and led sermons on the great scandal of the honour of the Lord, neglecting the advice of his brothers" as if he had been promised and allowed in such a case according to God and reason[1521]". In September 1571, if Le Gagneux again described his disobedience to the body of ministers, of his affairs

---

[1520] AEG, REPORTS OF MEETINGS OF THE Small Council, RC66, 3.12.1571, fol. 148r. There is a contemporary manuscript kept separate from this deed, kept in the French section of the Geneva library (ms.fr. 73-77)/On Nicolas Le Gagneux, see KINGDON R.M. "Geneva and the consolidation of French Protestant Movement 1564-1572.." Geneva, Droz, 1967, p 23.

[1521] Report of the Smalll Council, RC 66, 3.12.1571 fl. 148r.

voluntarily cut off from the town, leaving it in the wake of his trouble instead of asking for it according to his duty and his oath[1522]". While trying to defend himself in letters, sent several days later from Lyon to the Genevan authorities, he became and remained blamed for "true desertion of his ministry" and will be accused of perjury [...] committed against his duty and oath as minister as a middle-class person"

A few months earlier, in February 1571, Pastor Nicolas Colladon, then secretary of the Company of pastors, had also left the consistory of the Lordship, leaving the town at the heart of wrangles that his last sermon had caused[1523]". Leaving for Nyon, a Church under the jurisdiction of Bern, he signs thus at the time of one his conflicts with the Council and the ministers a passing of the border, by a period of leave far from being formally required and authorised by the corcumstances guaranteed by his ministry. It was on the insistence of his brothers, friends and parents, that he decided several days later to come back to the own.

There, before the Council, he justifies himself for this absence, saying he wanted "a change of air [...] for the great trouble that was in my heart "and" not to become distracted from his duty". He thus unravelled an accusation of desertion of the own and abandoning his ministerial duties, pleading that he had followed and transformed himself in the period of reflection, granted by the ministers and magistrates a week earlier, in order to gain from it willingly. He then submits to censure, confesses and again joins the group of his brothers. However, with a new series of sermons against the institution of the exchange[1524], he signs

---

[1522] Ibid. fol,148v.

[1523] On Nicolas Colladon, refer ti the literature quoted in FATIO O. and LABARTHE O. "Registres de la Compagmie" op. cit. v3 p VIII-XII.

[1524] MONTER E.W. "Le change public a Geneve 156801581" "Melangs d'histoire economique...anniversaire" Geneva Tribune de Geneve 1963 v 1 p 265-290.

at the end of August 1571, in an institutional document for the case which is widely kept by historiography, his manifest disobedience to the ministers and magistrates. He became an author, in full exercise of his pastoral duties, of an attack against the temporal and ecclesiastical authorities of the town. Removed in September, he thus ended his pastoral career in Geneva[1525]

A border crossed: between lectures from the authorities and questioning the strength of the connection. The issues of the Colladon and Le Gagneux affairs

By his transgression of the political and confessional border of September 1571, Le Gagneux is shown, for the authorities, in a consciously reflected strategy, that which was adopted by a minister seeking to protect himself from judiciary and disciplinary cases about his actions. The town and Church of Geneva seem to be thus short-circuited in the resolution of the case and in spite of the decision of the Company of Pastors to wan the consistory of Lyon and the conference of Beaujolais in activating the network of the Churches of France and thus to lead the fleeing minister to acknowledge his mistake[1526]. Another consequence will come to be added to this crossing of the border and will act as a second brake, which will not be expressed more uniquely in the geographical and political space, but will be henceforth described in the promise of a new institutional association.

In fact, in March 1572, after having literally stayed at the gates of the town and come to the Pont d'Arve – the natural border between Catholic Savoy and the town of Geneva – a requirement for safe-conduct, Le Gagneux

---

[1525] MANETSCH S.M/ "Calvin's cpmpany of Pastprs …Recormed Church 1536-1609 New York, Oxford University Press 2913 p 64; KINGDON R.M. "Geneva and the consolidation…" op. cit. p 17-29.

[1526] FATIO O.and LABARTHE O. "Registres de la Compagnie…" op.cit.p 43 p 51.

finally decided to go into the town, where he was heard and held prisoner. It happened then [1527] in Berne, between March and April, the rumour then the news of the election of Le Gagneux in Lausanne, accompanied by a condition "sine qua non" to his engagement, that of the rule of the disagreement[1528]. Now. Less than a month later, on 1st May, Berne asks to shorten the length of the detention of Le Gagneux so that the pastor could finally take up his position[1529].. The ministers of Geneva think at the time and again later, according to their own terms, to have their hands tied b Berne, certainly consider themselves under the eye of heir confessional and political partner from the signature in 1566 of the "Confession helvetique posterieure" and the perpetual treaty of "combourgeoisie" in 1559[1530].Some weeks earlier, on 18 April, the magistrates had, according to them, renounced sending to the Bernese an account of the proceedings followed and interrogations carried out until then with the accused minister. Retracting from its first intentions, the town of Geneva however proposed and validated in the heart of the Small Council, the town of Geneva finally considers that such a letter is no longer suitable and that "it could seem to them that that could be done in order to disgrace them", planning among others through this bias and its fear of appearing passionate and obstinate in respect of Le Gagneux, to seek to take away from him any possibility of practicing elsewhere[1531]

[1527] Ibid. p 60 AEG Report of the meetings of the small Council RC 67 4.04.1572 fol.51r.

[1529] AEG Reports of the meetings of the Small Council RC 67 1st MY 1572 FOL. 69V.

[15301530] FATIO and LABARTHE O. "Registres de la Compagnie…" op.cit. v 3 p 37.

[1531] AEG 2Reports of the meetings of the Small council RC67 8.04.1572 fol 60v.

NPHY W.G. "Calvin and the consolidation…" Manchester Manchester University press 1994 p 53-83.

Not only is the pastoral and humane value of the minister Le Gagneux found at that time in the centre of the disagreements, but with that there are surely also the credit of a reformation, of its outlook, as at las the place that Berne and Geneva could occupy in their enterprise to install and defend a true Church. As common as this leap could nevertheless marked by an argument in disciplinary practices and the ecclesiastical concept of Berne and Geneva, having led earlier, in 1588.an important wave of withdrawals. At that date, the Church's academy of Lausanne was deprived of several reformed personalities, professors and pastors of whom Calvin's city will benefit. In 1571, Berne and more particularly the Church of Lausanne gain for themselves and for at least a time, two former Genevan ministers, Nicolas Colladon and Jean le Gagneux. These cases point to a phenomenon which is far from being new in the space of the French-speaking Reformation and even more in Roman Switzerland, that of the transfer of staff and competition between Geneva and Berne, where the ministers withdrawn in one of these churches follow their career in the other[1532].

As we stop, in presenting these clerical conflicts, even more as we cross the border than to the more frequent policy of the sermons, we have sought to emphasise two processes of separation and acquisition of external support adopted by the ministers Le Gagneux and Colladon accused or at least suspected of being, by their sermons, an instrument of dissent in the heart of the Company. To follow the deeds of the condemnations, these two pastors are in fact distinct from the rest of the body preferring, in the exercise of their duty of enlightenment, to put forward their particular opinion and interpretation. Manifestly breaking up equality through this bias and before acting among the members of this college, they tried to take authority not only on the Word that they have to preach, but also over their brothers,

---

[1532] NAPHY W.G. "Calvin and the consolidation…Reformation" Manchester, Manchester University Press 1994 p 53-83.

elected like them to the ministry and exercising their vocation under Christ's presence and the inspiration of the Holy Spirit With their public criticisms and complaints upon meeting the Magistrate, they would come to weaken the orientation and the christian validity of the sovereign authority, an approving authority and guarantor of their installation to the ministry. With them one ma also predict the existence of a disagreement between the temporal and ecclesiastical instances of the town, thus leaving open an eventual alliance between unhappy subjects and these protesting pastors, with the possibility of breaking the social balance. What is understood here, in an institutional reading of the cases, is [1533]the description of "clerical and democratic opposition" used by Eugene Choisy in his analysis of these ecclesiastical conflicts".

For our part, without denying this interpretation, we consider that this latter would serve more as a marker in the enunciation of definitions of the ministry and understanding the clergy who seek to defend between 1564 and 1571, through these conflicts, the Company of Pastors and the Magistrates. The idea of the clergy would then become plural, nor it was different after the perspective of the State or the Church, on ideas which are however far from disagreeing. This plurality of definitions would find an extra branch, that coming from the same framework of the regulation of the disagreement on consistorial or civil procedures leading to withdrawal. In front of institutional instances and their idea in the manners of exercising its responsibilities and prerogatives, the perception arises called to fail, that outline and try to defend the pastors accused of non-submission.

From that time, if these ecclesiastical conflicts plainly brought obedience into discussion, according to us, in the strength of the link, less visible in the new institutional affiliation acquired by the accused ministers that increasingly presents inside a Church body and at own

---

[1533] CHOISY E. "L'Etat chretien…" op.cit. p 49 p 58

which is weakened in its borders, of a city put into an enclave [1534] and finding itself at its gates. In fact, the treaty of Lausanne in 1564 and its application in 1567 by the return to Savoy of lands conquered in 1536 by Berne, Geneva moves towards its political isolation. From then, the town has no longer direct access, through land at least.to its ally and sole protector, Berne, a situation which will remain unchanged until the Treaty of Soleure in 1579[1535]. "Leaving the Genevan area and cross the border would more come to symbolise among these eminent actors in the ministry the need to break up or at and resented as being restraining. Crossing the border would, according to us, show an execution of the break by an instrumentalised use of the political and/or confessional border. Colladon and Le Gagneux would seek by this bias to distance itself from a group of connections, acting between the ministers themselves, at the heart of this unity of equal parties being guided under the presidency of Christ which is the Company of pastors. But they would also try to distance themselves from present connections, and doubtless even more active, between the pastors and the magistrates. The time is then in the gradual seizure of power by the Small Council on the Church by strengthening he judicial apparatus[1536] of the State to the detriment of an exercise of discipline, of the community towards the community, according to the prerogatives of the consistory.

Under this angle, the strength of the connection can first of all be questioned in its institutional dimension of election and the practice of a pastor, most often a French one,

---

[1534] Ibid ;GUICHONNET P. "Histoire de Geneve" Toulouse – Lausanne Privat 2986 p 151.

[1535] IBIID, P 99 225.GUICHONNET P "Histoire de Geneve" Toulouse – Lausanne Privat Payot 1986 p 151.

[1536] GROSSEC. " There was too much harshness over there" Ecclesiastical discipline in Geneva in the time of Theodore de Beze". I.BACKUS "Theodore de Beze (1519-1605) Geneva,Droz 2007 55-69.

assigned and named to the ministry of enlightenment in Geneva, a town which was also engaged in duties and an effort to evangelise France to which from 1555, its Church and its academy contributed. In this perspective in front of this intrinsic border which defined the Genevan clergy, it should be emphasised and appreciated in its consequences a feature which was common with the former pastors Le Gagneux and Colladon, that of having been freely made bourgeois people between 1557 and 1562, in recognition of their ministry.[1537] Now, this process of naturalisation is accompanied among other things by a duty, if it is not settlement, at least of residence. It also includes economic and political rights and a first opening to the decision-making scene. With the citizen, the bourgeois person in fact forms the general council, an assembly uniting the Genevan electoral body which designates the main magistrates. He can from henceforth present himself and have himself elected to the Council of the Two Hundred, a Chamber founded in 1526 by the Bernese model, adopting the laws on the proposal of the Small Council[1538].

From then, in what measure these two sections of the Bourgeois statute, that of a territoriorial anchorage was in future capable of being ruled and controlled by the sovereign authorities like that of a participation in the economic and political life of the town by its privileges, whether or not they have an impact on the minister. This change in the statute is accompanied by determining consequences on pastoral and missionary activity as on the definition of a priest, or more precisely on varied expressions, from the State or from the Church, in their idea of a clerical body that the time of Calvin's death and in front of the challenges of a confessional identified and spatial

---

[1537] COVELLE A.L. ""Le livre des Bourgeois del 'ancienne...Geneve" Geneva j.Jullien 1897 p 257 (22.07.1557) p 272 (28.08.1563).

[1538] ROTH-LICHNER B. "De la bouche...Ancien regime" Geneva,Doz 1997 p 530-532.

defence of Geneva and the reformed Church in general. that is why the question of repercussion of this new condition of the minister must also be asked at the simple level of pastoral practice in Geneva, and comes from that time to touch more specifically the relations between the Church and the State. The pastor in fact operates, following his oath and his prerogatives, an office turned towards the teaching of everybody, including magistrates. His pastoral duty is led by the requirement to preserve a united social body, harmonious, for purged by the discipline and mutual correction between the minister brothers themselves as on the scale of the community of the faithful people. This practice of reprehension may also touch each and every especially, without any distinction. Finally, he interaction between the two instances is not done uniquely in the duty edification and admonishment of the corporal body. It is also written in the political space and intervenes at the heart of the decision taken by the Small Council – seat of the court as the executive and legislative power of the town – in front of the consultative authority that the magistrates granted to the Company in laying down new decrees, treaties or rulings in law cases. In this perspective, one must consider this participation in the power of the pastors in strengthening which could be caused by their access to the bourgeoisie and the eventual consequences that such a statute would have on its space of activity, or more exactly on the practice of the "freedom of the ministry", of which Le Gagneux and Colladon are suspected, then accused of having several times abused, leading with sermons against the honour of the Lord.

A new model of incorporation:
Attaching pastors by making them bourgeois people of Geneva

The double swearing-in of bourgeois people and the minister of Le Gagneux and Colladon, originally pastors respectively of Tours and Bourges, is written firstly in a form of radical incorporation other than that proposed by

Calvin and his Company between 1541 and 1555. In fact, until in 1555, the Company of pastors is inserted and implanted in Geneva thanks to a conscious use of its marginalisation, subject as it is, by the French origin of its members, to attacks orchestrated by family and clan solidarities with a broadly xenophobic nature, aiming to weaken and reject the plan for ecclesial renewal brought in by Calvin[1539]. At this time, Calvin moreover cultivates, against this so-called opposition of the "Children of Geneva", his position as a member of an ostracised body, because he was foreign. He is exposed in the pulpit until the paroxysm of the communiity rupture in a verbal violence fed by the imagination of the holy struggle. The request and free acceptance by the bourgeoisie in January 1556 of four ministers who were elected and assigned to the town of between 1545 and 1548, all of French origin, also mark the beginning of a more systematic access by the actors of the Genevan ministry to this privilege which was for a long time protected by the landed stock and citizens of Geneva[1540]. After being assured of the support thanks to the massive accession in February and April 1555 of immigrants into the bourgeoisie and four years after the defeat in May 1555 of the "Children of Geneva", Calvin finally followed his colleagues and goes into the bourgeoisie. In December 1559, however he faces the authorities asking him to join the bourgeoisie and even regretting his slowness to do so,. Justifying his reserves to his care to have sought to "avoid the suspicions to which some people are inclined, he approved the initiative of the Magistrate and replies here

---

[1539] SZCZECH N. "Fortus Francis" Tensions and xenophobia in Calvin's Geneva (1546-1555). A.ROUILLET, O.SPINA and N. SZCZECH "Trouver sa place" Madrid Casa de Velazquez 2011 p 117-134.

[1540] Made bourgeois on 14 January 155, it is about Francois Bourgoin,of Raymond Chauvet,Jean Fabri and Jean de St-Andre. KINGDON R.M "Registres de la Compagnie...Calvin" Geneva Droz op. cit p 248.

even more to the wishes of the Small Council to join them[1541].

This action is significant, for on the same day in December 1559, four professors and resigned ministers of the academy and the Church in Lausanne present themselves with Calvin before the Small Council. According to them, they are formulating a similar request, that of being received as bourgeois of Geneva. With this bias and thanking the Genevan authorities already for "other good things they have done". Pierre Viret, Antoine Le Chevalier, Jean Raymond Merlin and Jean Tagaut asked the Council to "receive them and accept them [1542]to the number of bourgeois so as to have greater opportunity to be devoted to this Republic" they all receive and sign here one of these other transfers of succeeding pastoral people between Geneva and Berne. This reception into the bourgeoisie, which was also valid for Theodore de Beze in April 1559, seems, even more, to mark a transition[1543]. A faster incorporation confronts Calvin's slow affiliation, or claimed as such, by conserving his foreign status or as a simple inhabitant, or claimed as such which he was able to instrumentalise, using this experience and personal reality lor purposes of implantation, shared for a long time by his ministerial brothers. The new arrivals, also in their majority being French immigrants, appear more engaged in a collaboration which would come to be inscribed in a will to strengthen the political and confessional connections in Geneva by participation, thanks to their bourgeois status, to economic privileges and extensive political rights.

On the Magistrate's side, accession to the bourgeoisie would resound as a reply to the intrinsic nature of this

---

[1541] AEG. "Proces-verbaux des seances du Petit Conseil RC 55 25.12.15559 fol 163r COVELLE A.L. "Le livre des bourgeois…" op. cit. p 265-266 (25.12.1559)

[1542] Ibid.

[1543] COVELLE A.L. (le livre des bourgeois…op.cit. p 264 (17.04.15

pastoral body in a town and a Church which was in contact by their geographical situation as by their evangelising aspirations. It would also respond to the challenge shared by the town and the Church in the aftermath of Calvin's death to hold "firm to make its ministers ready and not to have a break" according to the same terms of the Company of pastors at the time of the extension of leave given to Le Gagneux in 1565 to settle his family affairs[1544]. I It is in this same sense of holding the pastoral people in Geneva that the sovereign authorities asked the minister Charles Perrot, for who they authorise a holiday in France, not to "listen to anyone un order to be turned away from coming[1545]".Again in this same perspective, they asked Antoine le Chevalier, a bourgeois and professor from 1559 at the Academy of Geneva, "to weigh up the consequence of this school and keeping it in balance against the need to offer the glory of God for its special gain", He must finally consider and confront "his duty and obligation that he has to the town as the vocation and the bourgeoisie to serve this town and church according to the grace that God has given "in front of the promise made to his native town, Caen, to come there and preach the Evangel, in front of the management of his assets which required, at risk of losing everything, his imperative presence.[1546].

Finally yielding to the Genevans' complaints, LD Chevalier "agreed to stay there on condition that they (the ministers] relieve him from the Church ...and the gentlemen also and that there may be some regard for what will be unhappy for his well-being[1547]".

[1544] AEG "Proces-verbaux des seances du Petit conseil RC 060 27.12.156 folm137r.

[1545] Ibid 26.05.1565 fol,v 58r   Proces-verbaux des seances du petit Conseil RC 59 4.07.1564 FIL 67 4.12.FOL.149R.

[1547] AEG Proces-verbaux des seances du Petit conseil RC 60, 12.03.1565 fol 25v

From that time, entry into the bourgeoisie surely allowed that affiliation to a particular Church, foreseen and defended by the reformer of Geneva in his "Institution de la religion chrestienne" so as to give order[1548]. The documented research * in papers left by Calvin of the terms of loans and leaves granted to the minister Nicolas Des Gallars, engaged between 1560 and 1568 London and Orleans before returning towards Geneva in 1568, towards "the church to which he is primarily attracted" his election to the ministry having been given in 1544, would illustrate this[1549]. Across this case, the expression of a priority link given to Geneva is made. After two years spent in the town serving the college, the authorities ensure Des Gallars before his fears of being blamed with the Church of Orleans. In fact, Geneva again wants to employ him in the ministry, however, as the magistrates maintain to Des Gallars "as to the Church of Orleans, it has no opportunity to be unhappy about it, considering that he was always held to be bourgeois and that being sent back by God to Geneva he was held by the Lord without those of the said church having [1550]given him help a thousand times[1551]".

Moreover, with a minister who had become bourgeois, Geneva could be ensured in a pastoral body which had become likely to be of a variable dimension, able to extend and therefore to allow its members to practice elsewhere, in short or long term, in order to acquire support and protects while being able, if required, to be strong in himself. That is what can be understood by the long absence of leave granted to Gilles Chausse and to Paul Baduel, both bourgeois from Geneva, sent respectively to Lyon and to

---

[1548] CALVIN J. "Institution de la religion chrestienne" ed. J-D BENOIT Paris Vrin 1957-1963 book IV chap III 6-7.

[1549] AEG" Proces-verbaux des seances du Petit Conseil" RC 65 26.09.1570 folm147v RC 66 11.01/1571 fol 4r.

[1551] AEG "Proces-verbaux des seances du Petit Conseil RC 22.1.1571 fol 11r

Auvergne[1552]. Facing their departure, these two pastors from Geneva asked "to be held at the level of you bourgeois", they were assured this would be so, under the promise and condition to be recalled "when it would seem [...] to the gentlemen whom they must remember that they are "primarily obliged, to come back as a member of this church without the Churches of Lyon and Auvergne being able to prevent them[1553]. By the status of bourgeois granted to its ministers, Geneva thus built a solid platform and, if necessary, closed upon itself in the defence of its confessional identity, a form of rampart where the sword of the word is conjugated to carrying arms, then required for taking an oath of any new bourgeois person having to be, for the defence of the town "supplied and matched with arms", a connection which is also strengthened in his obligation, common to the bourgeois person and to the minister, to live in Geneva," in time of need" and "not to abandon it" authorising him officially to able to live elsewhere but doing so never without a licence[1554]Incorporation of pastors and relationship to obedience:

Before the Magistrate, before the Company
Now, this incorporation into the bourgeoisie would also mark a stronger connection of obedience to the magistrates, expressing itself through taking an oath aimed towards loyalty owed to the town, especially legible in a role of punctual counsellor who is called to be, in times of crisis,

---

[1552] Giolles Chausse is accepted freely o the bourgeoisie on 10.12.1562:COVELLE A.L. "Le livre des bourgeois" op.cit p 274.Paul Baduel son of Claude professor in the Academy of Geneva was received for" 16 crowns" bourgeois on 9.05.1555 ibid p 343.

[1553] AEG "Peoces-verbaux des seances du Petit Conseil" RC 61 24.05.1506 fol 44r RC 65 11.12.1570 fol 181r.

[1554] Reformulated on 24.1.1538 after theown moved into the Reformation see introduction to EG "Proces-verbaux des seances du Petit conseil RC 72 6.01.1577-3.01.1578

the bourgeois, through his participation in the Council. He is then held in secret of the discussions and in secret with the decision. More generally, he must not work to safeguard "franchises, edicts and decrees of the city[1555]". Under this angle, this swearing would come to further consolidate "the good example of obedience" which promises to be the pastor at the time of his swearing [1556]the oath at the ministry of the Word, "by which he becomes subject and obedient to the laws and to the Magistrate". He then swears to "keep and maintain the honour and benefit of the Seignory[1557]. However, if the elected minister promises and swears "to be subject to the policy and the statutes of the City" he places a limit to his obedience. Now it is the pastoral office and its practice that come to mark out the contours of the submission of the new pastor in the temporal framework. In fact, the allegiance to the Magistrate of the pastoral body is made "without prejudicing the freedom that we must have to teach according to God and do the things that are from our duty[1558]. Between 1565 and 1571, this question of freedom left to the position of the pastor is found clearly and constantly at the centre of tensions between the Small Council and the company. On the occasion of collective sermons or of dues to isolated members of the Genevan clergy, it must oblige the pastors to define and redefine their area of activity, for the handling of the Word of God generates a true conflict between these two instances, in its dimension of mutual and community public censure, capable at the time to come to revert to possible abuses which were present with the Magistrate. The confrontation is developed between December 1564 and February 1571,

---

[1555] AEG "Proces-verbaux des seances du Petit Conseil" RC 72.
[1556]

[1557] PEISTERER E. "Le catechisme de l'eglise de Geneve (1542) Es ordonnances ecclesiastiques de l'Eglise de Geneve" 1561 W.NIESEL Bekenntmisschriften …reformierten Kirche" Munich 1938 v 1 p 45 19, l,.18

[1558] Ibid l. 21-22.

and is established in a process of ruling on preaching, at the heart of which the withdrawal affairs of Le Gagneux and Colladon are placed.

In front of ministers who, in order to protect their bothers Colladon and Le Gagneux, in two cases emphasise the complexity of handling a forthright Word of God, which is neither "pleasing for everyone" nor Easily received" for one only has to omit or change a word which will overturn the intention of the speaker" which is stated again in a principle laid down in 1564 following the withdrawal of Jean Raymond Merlin[1559]. In fact if the pastors came to see or perceive an abuse on the part of the Magistrate, they had too let him know "kindly and discreetly. Then they had to resort to the Council, going to them while acting thus, in this closed area, to inform the magistrates of their complaints[1560]. They pushed finally, in the case of a confirmed abuse, the authorities to amend it and correct it.

In exercising discretion, the magistrates take care to prevent any unjustified scandal caused by a revelation or dissemination from the pulpit and, with that, the risk of passing in the eyes of the faithful flock, respective subjects, for bad leaders. Through this bias, they keep the union between Church and State intact and defend it openly. No doubt the very terms of the minister's oath as exactly laid down and consolidated are seen, according to which the pastor undertakes to correct, in the framework of the consistory as a the time of his responsibility for enlightenment and therefore of preaching about [1561]"those who have fallen" nevertheless having to commit vengeance, without giving room for hate or favour", but working much more "for people to stay in peace and union under the

---

[1559] AEG "Proces-verbaux des seances du Petit Conseil" RC 66 6.02.1571 fol 23v 26.01.1571 fol 14r.

[1560] AEG "Proces-verbaux des seances du Petit Conseil" RC 60 4.12.1564 Fol 151R rc62 12.02.1567

[1561] PETSTERER E. "Le Catechisme…" art.ci. p 45 17-18 l.9 l.12.

government of the Seignory". In this perspective, and facing the comprehension of the magistrates of the social cohesion, the pastor would act as essential agent to the connection and to the exercise of power, becoming a mediator placed between the authorities and the subjects. In February 1571, the will for affiliation of the minister to preserving the social unity and read more again at the time of an umpteenth[1562] request from the Small Council to the pastors where, one by one, they are exhorted on pain of being "rebels and disobedient to their superior magistrates" to subscribe to this clause of discretion in the public correction of the magistrates[1563]. On that date, Collladon is away for Nyon, without duly approved leave and without consenting to this measure. Coming back several days later to Geneva, on the prayer of his brothers, he joins in and confesses to having been blind, a state of blindness and straying from which God by grace took him away. Seven months later, he goes up into the pulpit "under the shadow of some abuses that he said he had overcome […] publicly and without any meeting against" the state and a decree of change drawn up about three years ago by the small and great council after the change drawn up on the advice of the ministers of the word of God with whoever was there[1564]. This gesture is described as "intolerable and contravening the oath of a good and faithful bourgeois as much as a minister" and causes Theodore de Beze that one of the two, himself or that of Colladon, would be a false prophet[1565].

A perjurer and propagator of false doctrines are two acccusations come to us at the heart of the process of decision=taking, as much in the consultative charge that recurs sometimes and on appeal of the authorities the company in its resulting enactment by the Small council of

---

[1562]

[1563] AEG "Proces-verbaux des seances…" RC 66 8.02.1571 FOL. 24V.

[1564] Ibid 28.09.1571 fol 120

[1565] Ibid fol 120v 27.08.1571 fol 104.

a new decree, here there was change[1566]. At the time of a minister becoming bourgeois, they emphasise not only the effects of narrowing that this statute could cause on the pastor and his area of activity, but would also indicate the dynamic and tensions which were present even inside the ecclesial body. Through the remark of Theodore le Beze and the resistance expressed by Collladon, the collegial practice is revealed in the differentiated value given to the final resolution which the whole of the Company by the voice of its moderator will propose to the Magistrate. Three years earlier it is therefore on the change that these pastors, on the request of the magistrates. Now, in September 1571, Colladon makes a claim in the name of is pastoral duty and his conscience, the right to retract an arrangement to which he had previously subscribed to, but which, according to him, showed it to be obsolete, because it was badly applied, unadapted and inadequate for the present circumstances[1567]. The actual methods of his application even make the institution of exchange contrary to the first intentions. For Beze and the rest of the Company, Colladon here doubts the truth and therefore the inspired value of the collegial advice, becoming, in his act of autonomy and authority, an agent to schisms. He has left to the "devil" his entrances within the heart of this college of equals, renouncing the principle present in chapter 14 of this first Epistle, to the Corinthians – the minds of the prophets are submitted to the prophets - which the pastors recall already in 1564 in front of recourse to the special conscience of the pastor Merlin who then was interrogated and blamed for wishing by his sermons to place himself above his brothers and even claimed to want a Church "managed by himself alone"[1568] With his position, Colladon thus faces a first narrowing, that of a Company afifirming itself as a body of doctrine, charging from that

---

[1566] Ibid 26.01.1571 fol. 15v.
[1567] Ibid 27.08.1571 fol. 104.
[1568] AEG "Proces-verbaux des seances du Petit Conseil, RC 59, 28.10.154 fol. 127r 31.10.1564 fol 13.

time its resolutions coming from a conscience operated collectively in a perpetual dimension which would finally turn into a form of infallibility. By obedience to the Company pr by conviction, he nevertheless participated three years earlier, in the institution by the Small Council of a decree, which must be respected as bourgeois of Geneva and following his oat

***

From that time, with Colladon the risk is expressed that a servant of the Word of God, however marginal and contestable it may be, becomes even more a bade example of obedience and a bad citizen, swearing that he is in his double promise as a pastor and a bourgeois to defend the honour of the Signory so as to respect and safeguard the decrees and laws of the town. More than manifesting themselves thus by heir repeated speeches, he and Le Gagneux stir up and give rise to a counter-power by an alliance with the subjects. By the use of the pulpit, the place of activating their resistance, they incarnate altogether some fear for the authorities, which is precisely of hat limit of obedience to th Magistrate to which and following their own minister's oath, the pastors can claim in the name of the freedom of the ministry. From this, the tightenings that the Magistrate tries to operate on his clerical body by negotiation and regulation of a space of words, of teaching and correction of the ministers carried out in respect of them. Resentment by some pastors as a stricture of the ministerial space of activity, the process would only have been emphasised by the more systematic access to the bourgeoisie of the actors of the Genevan ministry thanks to the resonances and effects of reinforcement of the connection that the oath of the bourgeois gives to the oath of a minister. This dynamic, if it has, according to us, created this tissue of restrictions pushing Colladon and Le Gagneux to cross the border without legitimate authorisation, would have better served the construction of a Company as an instance gifted with a single and unique conscience, being built as a guardian of the Truth, where the practice of the authority would rest on the body completely, Through this bias, Beze would be forced not only to limit the institution of a particular and charismatic figure within the Company, but would also try to prevent its possible collection by the Magistrate in his decision-taking and would from seek that time to safeguard the independence of the Church. Also it would be much less the personality of Beze alone which would have marked the development of the Genevan church, by its spirit of conciliation in front of the authorities, than the conscious use of an enterprise of control of the pastors, emanating from the magistrates, which would serve the construction and the assertion of a clergy as a body of theologians.

***

Foreign clerks to foreign pastors
The building of a category in XVIIth century France:
Individuals, Churches and royal power
    IRENE PLASMAN-LABRUNE

Dealing with foreign pastors. not under the angle of a social impossibility - the number and nature of available sources do not allow one to establish with certainty that an individual is a foreigner – but under the political angle, through the negative construction of a category, implies being situated at the crossing of the issue of control, internally in the ecclesiastical institutions and that of assuming relations with the political authority. Civil and political belonging of Church people tends in fact to take on a growing importance[1569], "a portiori" when the question of

---

[1569] See the contribution of Genevieve Gross in this volume.

allegiance becomes central at the beginning of the XVIIth century[1570]

Not many of them, the foreign pastors represent in France of the XVIIth century an embedded exception in the one which constitutes the reformed minority under the regime of the Edict of Nantes. Doubly a minority, they are as a result in the connection of the confessional and national divisions. This exceptional situation is made brutally clear when the royal power in 1623 imposes in 1623 the exclusion of foreigners to the pastorship. Being identified until then in a punctual manner, through the institutionalisation of the Reformation in the kingdom, the foreign pastors, taken for a target by the royal power and by the clergy, from that time form a negative category. Their exclusion constitutes one of the early elements of t[1571]he repressive devices which were progressively put in place in front of reforms throughout the XVIIth century.

The exclusion of foreigners to the pastorship can apparently go back to that of foreigners to the access to the benefices of the kingdom, begun in the XVth century and re-started in the second half of the XVIth century. But, while the exclusion of foreigners from the benefices came from a face-to-face between the royal power and the papacy for control, notably financial, of the French church, the exclusion of foreign pastors reveals more the issue of allegiance and sees the confessional claims of the clergy being taken back by the royal power.

Crossing the sources produced by the reformed people themselves, particularly at the time of the national synods, with those coming from the royal power and the Catholic clergy across the meetings of the clergy, enables one to

---

[1570] DE FRANCESCHI S.H/ "La crise theologico-politique ….prisme francais (1607-1627" Rome, BEFAR 2010c.

[1571] DOMPNIER B. "Le venin de l'heresie….Image…XVIIe siècle" Paris Le Centurion 1985. LABRIYSSE e. "Une foi, une loi, un roi?...Nantes" Paris Geneva Payot – Labor et Fides 1985.

study here through the exclusion of foreign pastors the conflictual process by which a standard of political order is imposed, outside its own field, in the ecclesiastical space. In other words, as the foreign pastors become, in favour of confessional combat, the support of the assertion of the royal authority through the double construction of the kingdom as a national space and as a confessional space .After a first part summing up the second part of the XVIth century, the second part of this contribution will precisely deal with the construction of foreign pastors as a negative category on the periphery of the royal power, before analysing in the last part its repossession by the royal power.

Foreign pastors? The promotion of a question and its limits in the second half of the XVIth century

If the control of mobility has always constituted for the Church a disciplinary issue of importance, it is in the framework defined by the first councils (especially Canon XCI of the Council of Nicea in 325 and Canon XX of the Council of Chalcedony in 451) that is, that of the Diocese: from this point of view, the Council of Trent does not innovate[1572]. The national or political framework never forms a pertinent space from the canonical point of view[1573]. At most, is it admitted that the pastoral needs can possibly justify the recourse to a discrimination based on the linguistic criterion: created by Gregory XI in 1373, the rule "De Idiomate" taken from hose of the Apostolic Chancelllorship, acknowledges the need to confer benefices with the charge for souls to clerks who were capable of preaching and teaching in the language of the place[1574]. This stability of the canonical framework has not however

---

[1572] ALBERIGO G. "Les conciles ecumeniques)" Paris Cerf 1994 v 1 p 51 and p. 219.

[1573] LAPRAT R. "Incapaxirt…des urbains" R. NAZ "Dictionnaire…canonique" Paris Ltouzy et Ane, v 1 col 1322-1380.

[1574] Ibid col. 1340.

prevented Charles VII from banning in 131, at the time of a conflict with the papacy, on access by foreigners to the benefices of the kingdom[1575].

If the association between foreigner and heretic is a fact which was already observed in the Middle Ages[1576], the repression which is quickly practised in the Kingdom of France against the supporters of the Reformation confirms, even emphasises, that assimilation, fed by transnational circulations that stirs up Protestantism in the European area[1577] In fact, insofar as the French national feeling is broadly constructed, Colette Beaune has shown,[1578] on the religious excellence of the kingdom, any form of divergence seems like a double rejection, of the community of faith that the King and his subjects create , as a result, a rejection of the royal authority.

Because it brings about a growing recourse to exile, repression feeds and reinforces this assimilation of the heretic toa foreigner. Even if it is first of all considered on the style of temporary refuge, and that a great many individual and family continuities exist. Failing to be unique[1579], the role of Geneva is considered essential on this point. Having in fact become a refuge in front of the

---

[1575] ISAMBERT F.A. "Recueiil general..1789" Paris Pion 1829 v XVI (1610-1643 p 783 sq.

[1576] BOZOKY E. "The cathars...exils" C. GAUVARD "L'etranger au Moyen Age" Paris Publications de la Sorbonne 2000 p 107-118.

[1577] MONTER E.W. "Judging...Reformation...Parlements" Cambridge M.A. Harvard University Press 1999.

[1578] BEAUNE C. "Naissance de la nation France" Paris Gallimard 1985.

[1579] BENEDICT P. "Refuge churches and Exile...Reformation" P. BENEDICT, S.SEIDEL MENCI and A.TALLON "La Reforme... Italie ..contrastes" Rome, BEFAR 2007 p 535-552.

per[1580] persecutions, the city of Leman also becomes a potential fish tank for the communities of the kingdom, as is shown by sending pastors to the kingdom from 1555[1581]. If these pastors are French in the majority, sending them is however considered by the royal power as a foreign interference, and a letter from Charles IX in 1562 calls for the Council of the town to stop this circulation and the recall of the pastors sent into the kingdom[1582]. It is doubtless for this reason that Article XIII of the declaration of 14 December 1563 stipulates that "the only people received to preach in future will be French people and our subjects[1583]. Unpublished, this putting forward of the national criterion by the royal power against the reformed people appears however to be a "hapax".

The national argument is however widely used in the political polemic of the second half of the XVIth century, whether it be by the royal power itself in order to re-establish the unity of the kingdom against the Council of Trent, or by the reformed people against the Guise family[1584]. The States General of 1576 constitute the peak of a xenophobia which, essentially directed against the Italians[1585] does not spare the Catholic clergy. On the other hand, the presence of foreign pastors does not seem to have

---

[1580] KINGDON R.M. "Geneva and the coming…France" Geneva Droz 2007 p 8. See also WILCOX P "l'envoi de pastors…" lists made up by Colladon (1561-1562) "Bulletin de la SHPF v 139-3 1993 p 37-37t.

[1583] FONTANON A "Les Edicts et ordonnances…sur icelles" Paris J. Du Puys 1589 v IV p 278 Paris 14.1.1563. The article also forbids ministers from preaching rebellion.

[1584] Speech by Michel deL'Hopital in Poissy; "La France et le concile de Trente"(1518-1563) Rome BEFAR 1993 p 302

[1585] DUBOST J. J. "La France italienne" Paris aubier 1993 chap II "La haine" p 307 sq HELLER H. "Anti-Italianism…France" Toronto University of Toronto Press 2003.

attracted enough attention to become a point of crystallisation of the action of the royal power in front of reformed people at the time of civil wars. Contrary to other measures, the exclusion of foreigners from preaching of 1563is not in fact taken up later in the edicts nor in later declarations. The available data on the presence of foreign pastors, not plentiful in France, does not enable one to establish certainly whether the measure of 1563 was known and applied outside the expulsion in 1565 of a friend of Calvin, Pierre Viret, from the strategic town of Lyon[1586], The pastors probably remain so much more easily in the background that the nobility plays in an essential role and the confrontations were military confrontations.

Even while the national mobilisation was widely used in the service of the legitimisation of Henri de Navarre as the successor of Henry III, [1587] the national criterion nis not mobilised in the area of reformed people. Significantly, the first particular article of the Edict of Nantes extends its benefice to the non-regnicols[1588]. The case of the children of exiles is also described: contrary to an idea of national belonging based upon birth in the kingdom, the children of exiles at the time of troubles are also acknowledged as regnicols[1589]. The national criterion therefore appears at the beginning of the XVIIth century in the relations of the royal power and the reformed people as lacking n pertinence, and that while it constitutes at the same time an essential issue in he relations between the royal power and the religious orders, especially the Jesuits.

[1586] BARNAUD B. "Ledit dr Nantes et ses antecedants (1562-1598) elec.sorbonne,fr/editsdeoacification) 2602/2016.

[1587] YARDENI M. "Dix annees de patriotism: 158-1594" M.YARDENI "Enuetes sur l'′identite de la "Nation France" Seyssel Champ Vallon 2004 0 308-317.

[1588] BARBICHE B. "Edit de Nantes et ses antecedents 1562-1598" [http:elec.enc.sorbonne, fr/editsdeoacification] consulted on 26/02/2016.

[1589] Ibid, art, 70 of the general rules of the Edict of Nantes.

The foreign pastors, targets of the construction of a confessional issue

If national belonging of pastors does not visibly constitute an issue for the royal power off Henry IV, it seems however as an object of preoccupation in the internal sources of the reformed Churches that constitute the deeds of the national synods[1590]. In 1607 the national synod of La Rochelle predicts in fact that the deputies in the court will help the foreign pastors to obtain letters of naturalisation for them[1591]. If the measure is presented as relating to all the foreign pastors, one may wonder, failing more precise elements, if it is not essentially connected with the arrival in the kingdom of pastors expelled by James 1st's desire to introduce bishops into Scotland, some pastors who were judged and banished took up residence in France. Among them one finds in particular John Welsh, the nephew of John Knox.[1592]. The aim of the measure more remains ambiguous. In the measure where the letters of naturality are essentially for the purpose to discovering the incapacities which strike the foreigners in a successful manner, obtaining those in order to create a strategy of a family taking root than looking for a possible legitimation by royal power. If he synod, an ecclesiastical authority with doctrinal and disciplinary preoccupations, seems on this occasion to take into consideration a criterion which to him is in an external principle, this precaution does not seem to have concrete results in the letters of naturality effectively granted. No individual identified as a pastor appears for the following years in removals carried out.

[1590] AYMON J. "Tus les synods…de France" La Haye Charle Delo 1710 2 vol.

[1591] Ibid v 1 p347 national synod of La Rochelle (1607) "Matieres concernant les deputes en cour" art.IV.

[1592] LEFEVRE DELA BODERIE A. "Ambassades dem. De la Boderie…"…Louis XIII…1611" P.D.BURTIN s.l.n 1750 v 1 letter to Puisieux 2.12.…1606.

The brutal death of Henry IV at the same time fragilises the royal power, opening up a period of regency, and the position of reformed people, dependent on the King. It is in this context that the meeting of the States General in 1614 is the theatre of an initiative of the clergy aiming precisely to make from the national criterion a tool at the service of the confessional fight[1593]. Stating these "contraventions" to the edict and denouncing the foundation of teaching institutions, colleges and academies, by the reformed people, the journal of the clergy claims in fact that the only foreigners who were authorised to "dogmatise regulate and teach in the kingdom are" Catholics ,the reformed people being only able to have recourse[1594] to individuals who were originally from the kingdom The clergy tries thus to place at the service of a claim of religious essence, the return to Catholic unity, a political claim which shows the prerogative of the royal power, the foreigners having in fact from the Middle Ages constituted a privileged support for the assertion of [1595]the royal authority. The clergy returns also against the reformed people the argument of national belonging to the holders of teaching positions used by the royal power against the Jesuits[1596]

By using an argument of political order which implicitly is out of its order in the religious field assimilates the protestants with a foreign threat, the clergy on return legitimises the action of the royal power our of its order in the religious and ecclesiastical field. The fact that this claim, formulated very generally, only applies uniquely to

---

[1593] On the attitude of the clergy, see DOMPNIER B. "le venin dl'heresie..." op.cit.

[1594] LALOURCE (son) and DUVAL "Recueil des cahiers Etats generaux" Paris barrios l;aine 1789 v IV p 145 art.CCC=XCB.

[1595] 'QLTEROCHE B. De l'etranger a la seignurie....XV siecle" Paris LDJ 2002.

[1596] Nelson e. "The Jesuits and the Monarch"...op.cit.

the pastors shows that the construction of the category of pastors as the main target has not yet been achieved.

While the claims of the clergy at the time of the States General have remained without a sequel, it is outside the framework of the confessional confrontation, even inside a reformed community, that the national argument is again mobilised, but this time against a particular pastor. During the years 1625-1616, in a context of military confrontations between the reformed people and the royal power, an internal conflict in the local protestant community is brought before the Bordeaux parliament and, on this occasion, the national argument is again mobilised against the pastors, Cameron and Primerose, who are found to be Scottish[1597]. The use of the national argument by their enemy, a lawyer member of the consistory, thus offers opportunely a contest which is first of all disciplinary in a political and legal justification. This unpublished case paradoxically presents many analogies with the instrumentalisation of the national argument in internal conflicts of the religious orders. Recourse to this argument is facilitated by the competition which locally opposes the Bordeaux Parliament in the Chamber of the benefice of the Edict of Castres for the contentious parties implying [1598]the reformed people. To deny the benefit of the Edict of Nantes to foreigners thus enables the parliament to assert its authority against that of the Chamber of the Edict, while contributing to the construction of a restrictive interpretation of the Edict of Nantes. Placed at the service of the hierarchisation of the institutions at the time of an internal conflict (a phenomenon which one finds in the conflicts that the religious orders may know), the national argument sees its pertinence and its validity reinforced at

---

[1597] AYMON j. "Tous les synodes…" op. cit. v1 p29 national synod of La Rochelle (1607) "Matieres particulieres" art.IX it

[1598] DOMPNIER J.E. "Le venin del 'heresie"…op.cit.

the time when it is moreover also used in contesting the authority of Marie de Medici[1599].

The intervention of the Bordeaux Parliament is not limited as far as this episode: it plays a second time a motoring role by transforming this time the appearance of particular individuals in general exclusion. The registration of the Peace of Montpellier, signed on 18 October 1622, offers the Bordeaux Parliament a new opportunity to restrict the application of the Edict of Nantes. While the Peace of Montpellier confirms the Edict of Nantes, while forbidding political assemblies and by taking away from the reformed people eighty places of safety, the Parliament adds to it on 26 November 1622 the ban imposed on foreign ministers to preach in its area:

Nevertheless, according to the laws of the State, those who are not natives will not in future be received to preach, or dogmatise in this area.

Nor similarly without infringing or prejudicing the commissions awarded, towards the demolition of fortifications, walls, doorways or houses, etc.

Its [1600] resumption by the "Mercure francais" gives this decision, of local range at the outset, a much wider impact: "This confirmation does not need interpretation, on wishes to take away ever y subject to fall into new troubles"[1601]. That contributes to taking one of the parameters of a "legal war" against reformed people which broadly began as a peripheral guerrilla war. None of these episodes is mentioned, directly or indirectly, in the deeds of t[1602]he national synods, even while Cameron, was nominated at

---

[1599] DUBOST j.F. "Marrie de Medici La reine devoilee" Paris Payot 2009

[1600] ISAMBERT F.A. "Recueil general..." op. cit. V XVI p XVIp 144.

[1601] "Le Mercure francais ...Navarre Louis XIII v IX 1623 p 436.

[1602] AYMON J. "Tous les synodes...op. it v II P 205
NATIONAL SYNOD OF Ales (120) "/Matieres generales" art VIII. the synod of Vitre (1617) ref ecolier a Geneve.

Saumur, is an eminent figure[1603]. If the synod of Vitre (1617) had recommended the recruitment of pastors into the kingdom[1604], it was probably more by the worry of orthodoxy and internal control in the perspective of seeing the national conformity guaranteeing political loyalty.

From the peripheries to the centre, the exclusion of foreign pastors to the service of the royal offensive against the reformed people

If the royal power ends by intervening, it is only in a second time, then management, ecclesiastical, of the reformed Churches through the figure of theatre of direct intervention of the royal power in the internal commissioner[1605], the national synod of Charenton (1623) is the occasion of an expansion, this time in the whole of he kingdom, of the Bordeaux ban. In 1623, there are doubts weighing on the reality of their allegiance towards the royal authority which justify the ban to resort to foreign pastors. Essentially, this mobilisation of the question of allegiance against the reformed people is the product of a true transfer from an issue which was initially drawn up as a tool against the Jesuits and against the Roman authority in service to the monarchy[1606]. In this return to the initiative of royal power, the question of national belonging, taken as a sign of weak loyalty, represents the first stage of a more general and more systematic view of the loyalty of the reformed people[1607]. In assimilating foreign status and disloyalty, real or supposed, the royal commissioner's speech in front of the synod contributes moreover to the formation of assimilation between birth and loyalty. r Birth appears from that time as

---

[1604] "…Louis XIII" v IX 1623 p 436. Le Mercure francais

[1605] AYMON K. "Tous les synods…" op.cit.v II p 205 national synod of Ales (1620) "Matieres generales" art.VIII.

[1606] NELSON E."The Jesuits and the M onarchy…" op. cit. and DE FRNCESCHI S.H. "La crise theologico-politique…" op.cit.

[1607] KRETZER H. "Calvinisme und fransosische …Jureiu" Berlin Duncker & Humblot 1975

the criterion of loyalty making in fact "a contrario" loyalty the necessary corollary of birth in the kingdom.

Announced in the commissioner's speech in front of the synod, the exclusion of foreigners from the pastorate is not however formalised legally. More than faith, it reveals then the specific relationship uniting the king with the privileged bodies which the reformed people establish under the regime of the Edict of Nantes. If this exclusion has an obvious symbolic responsibility, it is equally likely to increase the difficulties that some communities know in the matter of recruitment[1608]. Trying to open a dialogue space, even of negotiation, the synod deputies respond to this "innovation" in evaluating the loyalty of the incriminated pastors so that the prejudice that some Churches would suffer, meeting the wish for peace given to the king. Especially, they use the argument of the foreign presence in the heart of the Catholic clergy to claim the right for them also to have recourse to foreigners as pastors[1609]. The failure of this argument, which does not even receive a response, shows the derogatory dimension, not equivalent, which characterises the status of reformed people to foreign pastors in the kingdom in relation to the Catholic standard. The question of recourse to foreign pastors is thus a revelation of the ambiguities which make of the privilege which the Edict is, a possible case of gossip. Failing to succeed in bringing power back on the principle of exclusion, the synod however does obtain a respite for foreign pastors who were in post at the time: the latter remain tolerated, except for the famous Cameron and Primerose. This special treatment is assumed as a mystery independent of their origin, "not because of their birth, but for reasons which affect his service"[1610] ". The exclusion of

---

[1608] MOURS S. "Le Protestantisme en France au XVIIIth siècle" Paris Librairie protstante1967 p 100 et seq.

[1609] AYMON J. "Tous les synodes…" op. cit v II p 262 national synod of Charenton (1632).

[1610] Ibid p 268.No element of justification is brought in

foreign pastors is integrated into a wider group of measures aimed at breaking the links which unite reformed French people with their foreign co-religionaries. If the range of this international network is no longer in the XVIIth century of the same scale as that of a Duplessis-Mornay. The very existence of these links does not become less problematic and compromises the reformed French people in the eyes of power as that of Catholic opinion[1611]. In 1618, the representatives named by the reformed Churches of France are also seen to be forbidden to attend the synod of Dordrecht, the participation in a gathering situated abroad being considered against the laws of the kingdom[1612]. On the occasion of the synod of 1623, it is the reception of the deeds of Dordrecht by the Churches of the kingdom which was challenged insofar as these canons are considered foreign[1613]. Taken as targets in the framework of these measures, the foreign pastors also suffer the attacks which affect all of their brothers, the destruction of the group and the withdrawal of its noble supports leaving the latter in the first line.

In 1627, a declaration trying to unify the miscellaneous arrangements made against the pastors shows that from that time they are the main targets[1614]. The perimeter of the exclusion of foreign pastors is stated clearly on this occasion. The lasting criterion is that of birth in the kingdom, which also allows the exclusion from that time of individuals born of refugee parents who were abroad during the troubles, however recognised as French by the Edict of

---

[1611] GREENGRASS M. "The French Pastorate: confessional identity…Huguenot minority 1559-1685" C.S. DIXON and L.SCHORN[SHUTTE "The Protestant clergy…Europe" New York Palgrave Macmillan 2003 p 176 -195.

[1612] PANNIER J. "L'eglise reformee de Paris…XIII" Paris Honore Champion 1022 p 668 supporting items no. XV.

[1613] AYMON J. "Tous les synodes…" op. cit. v II p261 national synod of Charenton (1623).

[1614] ISAMBERT F.A. "Recuel general…" op.cit.v XVI p 201 "Declaration du roi Louis XIII …Sa Majeste"

Nantes as, in principle, by the law of the Parliament of Paris (Mabile decree 1576). A consecration which, in reverse, indicates the concrete problems which were met, the content of the declaration of 1627, and with it the exclusion of foreigners from the pastorate, is taken up in the framework of the great prescription prepared by the Guardian of the seal. Michel de Marillac. Ultimately called "Code Michau"[1615], this prescription of reformation is registered on 15 January 1629, between the surrender of La Rochelle (28 October (1629) and the Edict of Nimes (July 1629). Although the question of the reformed people was not covered on its own, it gives place, in the title of the reform of justice, to a great many articles about their legal privileges.

From devout inspiration, the text allows a real dread of contacts with foreign people[1616], especially factors of moral corruption. In spite of this general preoccupation, the contrast is striking and from a confessional point of view. While the foreign pastors are covered again, there is no measure relating to the Catholic clergy[1617]: the last general arrangements covering foreigners in the heart of the clergy in fact go back to 1616[1618]. Emphasising this discrepancy allows the scope of travel to be measured, even of coming and going, which took place during the 1620's: the national argument which was drawn up and used by the royal power in order to establish his control on the French Church, and more particularly to establish the legitimacy of Henry IV, is from that time turned against the reformed people through their pastors. The reconstruction of the unity of the

---

[1615] KADLEC L. "Le "Code Michau" : the reformation according to the Guardian of the Seal Michel de Marillac, "Les Dossiers de Grihl (on line) special no. "La vie de Michel de Marillac and the political experiences of the Guardian of the Seal"! consulted 26/02/2016.

[1616] ISAMBERT F.A. "Recueil general..." op.cit. v XVI p 275 art.175.

[1617] Ibid, p 86 Loudon Peace art.8.

kingdom on a national base has, during the 1620's, a clear confessional colour. A decade of direct confrontation between the royal power and the reformed people, these 1620's are also years of crystallisation of suspicion of disloyalty in respect of them.

But far from cutting of their speech, and the acknowledgement of the wish to exclude foreigners from the pastorate, and therefore the control [1619] of the reformed communities, does not pre-judge the reality of its application. It is especially right to question the conditions of carrying out this exclusion. On this complex question, insofar as it is asked for the main thing at the local level, different points can be emphasised.

The first thing is that the 1630's are effectively the theatre of a concrete offensive, which reflect not only the deeds of the assemblies of the clergy, but also the correspondence of Andre Rivet, a French pastor installed as Professor in the United Provinces[1620]. Challenged as foreigners in different places in the kingdom, several pastors found themselves in Paris in order to carry out their challenge. It is particularly about Sharp, Professor in Die, then Le Faucheur, Rousssele and Chauve, in Languedoc. As well as Mestrezat and Delincourt in Paris. To these prestigious names are added those of Chanterton, Hametm, Home. This local dimension enables an emphasis to be placed on the importance of coming-and-going between the centre of power and the peripheries in the application of a measure, as well as the importance of local intermediaries, as the clergy here, better also to be able to locally identify possible objectors. Made possible by the conjunction of the action of the clergy and the royal power, particularly through the parliaments, this offensive does not spare, on the contrary, some of the most visible figures among the pastors officiating in the kingdom. The diversity of individual status of different pastors who are challenged

---

[1619]

[1620] BU Leyde BPL.301.

(some are natives of Scotland, others from Geneva or from Neuchatel. Delincourt is a native of Sedan (independent until 1642), on the one hand, and the refusal of the royal power to concede the slightest exception (the 1623 engagement about foreign pastors who were already in their makes a long appointment , on the other hand, suggests that these pastors are, to their defending body, the laboratory of a vision which was always more restrictive of the definition of national affiliation through the challenge of collective exceptions which were traditionally recognised, especially for the Scots and for the Genevans. This challenge has however a time of advance on reality to the extent that some pastors, like Mestrat or Le Faucheur, born in Geneva, could pursue their career. In the immediate moment, this offensive against foreign pastors, was possible compensation in order to make (in the eyes of the devout) the choice of the struggle against Spain acceptable, shows in any case that the Code Michau was at least partially applied, contrary to a widespread idea.

After the offensive of the 1630s, the question of foreign pastors sems to reveal more of the war of the see: it appears on the list of griefs expressed at each national synod by the royal power against the reformed people. While the line of defence followed during the synods had been to try to obtain and guarantee exceptions to this exclusion, the synod of 1645 in Charenton capitulated by affirming to conform strictly to this exclusion and abandoned "de facto" the struggle for the exceptions. The foreign pastors seem to have paid the expenses, at least in the mind of the moderator of the synod, for the wish to preserve the possibility of studying abroad, which was also threatened[1621] The national standard, of political The essence, is from that time passing [1622]to impose itself inside the ecclesiastical field[1623]. The

---

[1621,1621,1621] AYMON J. "Tous les synodes…" op.cit.v II P 642
National Synod of Charenton(1645).
[1622] Ibid, p 678.

mistrust of the French reformed people against the British Independents who disembarked into the maritime provinces also bears witness to this,

While the principle of exclusion can in future seem to be acquired in theory, the obstinance shown by assemblies of the clergy to claim the application and to denounce the contravenants during the years 1660-1670 reveal its limits On the continuous reduction of the perimeter of the exceptions (case of the Genevans , children born abroad) there is added a phenomenon of amplification, with a ban on access to the pastorate to individuals who have studied abroad[1624].It is the simple contact with the foreigner which henceforth constitutes a central issue. Failing to disappear completely, the question of foreign pastors throws light on new targets, reflections of the retractation of space for reformed people. The conflict between confessional imperatives and diplomatic imperatives however meanwhile protects this situation for some of the latter. The Edict of Fontainebleau adds nothing to an exclusion whose construction is broadly previous: not more than the texts which immediately precede it, it does not mention foreign pastors

Directly henceforth, the challenge of the reformed people does not require any longer to pass through the bias of contracts, real or supposed, with the foreigner. A royal declaration of 1st July 186 foresees on the other hand the death sentence for pastors, French or foreign, who entered the kingdom without royal authority, article IV however authorising the presence of foreign ministers, but confined in the framework of embassies[1625]. Having disappeared with the Edict of Nantes, the question of foreign pastors only appears in a limited manner, through the problem of the

---

[1624] DE CARBON DE MONTPEZAT J. "Proces-verbal de l'assemblee generale…1655 et 1656" Paris A. Vitre 1655 p 537.

[1625] PILATTE L.R. "Edits, declarations…Reformee (1662-1751)" Paris Fischbacher 1885 p 292,

attractiveness that the chapels of embassies are liable to exert on new converts.

***

A minority inside a minority, passed unseen at the same time individually and collectively until the beginning of the XVIIth century, the foreign pastors benefit in their defending body from a disproportionate attention during that time. Targets of an instrumentalization by the clergy of the national argument in the service of the confessional combat, the form the involuntary support of the construction of a national standard which progressively assimilates the imperative of the community of faith. In this process, the foreign pastors, the foreign pastors but also indirectly the reformed people as a whole, come to incarnate the conflict of allegiance initially discovered against the Jesuits. Decisively, this phenomenon of transfer of one clergyman to the other does not work so much on the method of analogy or of symmetry. While the bans which strike the foreign clerks can be1 lifted into the framework of a specific arrangement, leave to hold benefices[1626]. This fund resumed, nearly wo centuries later, by the Concord of 1891 and the organic articles of 1802.a mental asymmetry is strong enough to be resumed, nearly two centuries later, by [1627]the Concord of 1801 and the organic articles of 1802.

[1626162616261626162616261626] DUBOST J.F."Les etrangers en France XVI siècle 1709...archives nationales" Paris Archives narionales.
See ARDURA B. "Le concordat entre Pie VII et Bonaparte 15.07. 1801 Bicentenaire ...reconciliation Paris Cerf 2001 p 8=72-89.

[1627] Art. XXXIII of section IV "Des cures du titre II"Des ministers du concordat de 1801 "Aucun etranger ne p[ourra etre employe ..sans la permission du Gouvernement."

Conclusions
Yves KRUMENACKER

For a long time, he historic study of monks was an ecclesiastical story, confessional and national. If it is still the case in a certain number of countries, it is not the same in a number of others[1628]. In France, religious history has taken over ecclesiastical history from the 1960's, with an interest brought to Christian people and not only any longer only to the gre[1629]at personalities, institutions and dogma, and the search for a ""popular religion" which would nor any longer be simply the product of teaching which is more or less well understood. The last decades of the XXth century have also produced a "non-[1630]confessional history of Christianism" dealing conjointly with the different Christian Churches. The very great majority of historians of religious people are not at the moment more like clerks, but staff of universities or members of the CNRS, less and less engaged in Churches, often even outside these Churches. In this development, groups which are more or less informal have played an important role, the first place the group of la Bussiere[1631], founded in 1958 and of which some members are original or took part in the symposium of Nancy on clergy in contact of which this volume gathers the deeds.

The latter seems to me to be significant of a double development which is even more recent. Firstly, the

---

[1628] See the contrasting balnces, for contemporary histoire in DURAND J.D. "Le monde de l'histoire religieuse Essais d'historiographie" Lyon Chrretiens et Societes 2012.

[1629162916291629] Among the most resounding books of the present day, after pioneering studies of LE BRAS G,"Etudes de socioogiereligieuse" Paris PUF 1955-1956 32 vo.

[1630] MAYEUR J.M. PIETRI C. VAUCHEZ A.and VENADM "Histoire du Christianism des origines a nos jours" Paris Deslee-fayard 1990-2001 14 vol

[1631] FLIPPI B. "le Groupe de l a Bussiiere"" Revue d'histoire de l'Eglise de France v 86 no 217 2000 p 755-745.

internationalisation of French research on Christianity. In spite of brilliant exceptions, a great many researchers stay confined to the French space and pass rather al little to vast European enquiries[1632], and the symposiums which confront the different spaces are certainly not numerous. The other development consists in the re-appropriation by historians of subjects which were either reserved to the clerks[1633] or abandoned because hey were tied too much to traditional history, like the parish[1634] or, exactly, the clergy. And it is the crossing of these two new tendencies which makes the richness of the preceding pages.

One must still accept the use of the term "clergy" for all the Christian confessions. The introduction to this volume is well explained, and there is nothing to be added there. One must simply state exactly that one considers the clergy as a body of clergy and that one carefully distinguishes this notion from that of a priest, rejected by the protestants. However, the ambiguity is that the clergy, of all confessions, claim a power of mediation. It is clear for the Catholics, but it is no less true in the reformed tradition: Calvin makes the pastors ambassadors of God, to the point that one cannot know him as the Saviour but through them; in the "Catechism of Heidelberg", it is preaching, reserved to the pastors, which is the true ministry of keys, opening the kingdom of the skies.

Comparing: through time, the places and the confessions

AS J. Leonard recalls in the introduction, the study of clergy in a systematic perspective was put forward in the 1990's by Luise Schorn—Schutte. It is an aspect of the problem, partially treated in this volume but which does not

---

[1632] One must quote, among others, Jean Delumeau with his research the fear and sentiment of safety or, in Nancy, the work of Louis Chatellier.

[1633] One may think about MARTIN P. "Le theatre divin…XXe siècle" Paris CNRS 2010.

[1634] BONZON A. GUIGNET and VENARD M . "La paroisse urbaine. A nos jours" Paris Cerf 2014.

form the heart; for to compare the clergy does by force presuppose that the latter had contacts between them. In there, there are differences of method: the comparatism studies the clergy of diverse Churches in various times and places, in order to see clearly what separates them and what brings them near. The historian may well deduce the existence of logics which are not purely confessional or on the contrary developments which ae only explained by ecclesiastical choices. This work is very precious in the way that it enables blind points to be revealed, the particularities which are proper to a specific clergy, or to give evidence of comparable developments.

This method enables a great many lessons to be drawn that several of the contributions to this volume have strengthened.

- The historiography has adopted the idea of social disciplinarisation, introduced by Gerhard Oestreich, developed by the Italians and Wolfgang Reinhard in that of confessionalisation[1635].The more the studies are developed in different Churches, the more it seems obvious that a parallel process is at work with very similar objectives, even if the means sometimes diverge.
- A growing clericalisation is at work. It is to be distinguished from the priestly creation and the process of mediation, described above. But it is clear that, from each side of the confessional border, the clergy are seeking to be distinguished from the faithful members and to have authority over them. The "good "Catholic" priest[1636] of the model

---

[1635] OESTREICH G."Geis und Gestalt…States" Berlin Duncker7 Humblot 1969.

[1636] KRUMENACKER Y."Du pretre tridentin au "bon pretre". D.PISTER "L'image du pretre dans la literature Classique 9XVII-XVIIIe siecles Bern,Peter Lang 2001 p 121-139.

protestant pastor"1637are the archetypes of his clerks.The controversies, analysed here by J.Foa, are a good means of showing that only the clergy have the necessary abilities to argue, and that therefore they are the only ones to have the right to do it. In the same way access to the pulpit is more and more reserved for the clerks. In the Calvinist type of Church, in opposition to the Bernese model the pastors 1638seize discipline, and in almost making a third mark of the Church; N. Szcech shows it precisely for Geneva and G.Gross explains how the company of Pastors in Geneva was gradually transformed into a Church body. Among French protestants, the deacons are quickly excluded from administering the sacraments and only the pastors can distribute communion in two types.

- The place of 1639clergy in the population, in the culture, in politics is not appreciably different from one confession to the other. There are court clergy in Brandenburg or in Saxony, State prelates in France as in England1640.In another domain, one sees that everywhere, in spite of clericalisation, the clergy must sometimes submit to the pressure of the populations: the protestants hold on to their pastors

---

[1637] LEONARD J. "Etre Pasteur au XVIIe siècle. Le ministere de Paul Fery a Met (1612-1659) Rennes PUR 2915.

[1638] GROSSE C. "La coupe et le pain de la discorde:…xviiie siècle" Paris Honore Champion 2000 p 33—35e.

[1639] THADDEN R. VON" Die brandenburgisch-preufischen Hofprediger…Brandenburg Preusseb" Berlin De Gruter 1959 SOMMER W. SOMMER W, "Die lutherischen…Sachsen, Stuttgart, Franz Verlag 2006; PIERRE B

[1640]1640 MICHON C. "La Crosse et le Sceptre. Les prelats…HENRI VIII" Paris Tallandier 2008

ROUSSEL B. "Ensevelir hnnetement les corps" "Funeral corteges and Huguenot culture" R.A.MENTZER and A. SPICER "society and Culture in the HUGUENOT WORLD" 1559-185 CAMBRIDGE CUP2001 p 194-208.

solemnising burials even more than what is allowed by the discipline of the Churches and. As N Richard shows, in Bohemia, the priests are asked to maintain traditions which are not always Catholic.

The social origin of the clergy is relatively well known: mostly coming from the bourgeoisie, the only noteworthy exception being the bishops, rather coming from the aristocracy. The tendency, well studied in France, of a certain depreciation of the Catholic clerical status in the XVIIth century to the benefit of legal studies, is found in the Protestantism of the Desert, due to secrecy, and doubtless in other European countries This challenge to the clerical status is doubtless also explained by a certain increase in literacy in theology[1641], by radical pietism. However, throughout the modern period, belonging to the clergy is a factor of social rising, including within the heart of this unknown clergy whjch is military chaplaincy, presented here by L. Jalabert, for chaplains can be easily be noticed by the nobility.
- Similarities exist also when one examines the material conditions of preaching, an activity which is promoted by the protestants as by the Catholics. Doubtless they are explained largely by the inherent restrictions in preaching (one must be heard and understood) as well as by a common heritage. The question of sacred eloquence is asked in all confessions, and everywhere libraries are set up for the use of preachers. However S. Simiz can note some differences, especially in the décor and C. Borelo insists on the bodily postures and gestures that are imitated or, on the contrary, they are avoided.
- However it would not be necessary, on reading these different points, to conclude a total resemblance

---

[1641] GAY J P and .STIKER -METAL C.O. "Les metamorphoses de la theologie" Paris Honore Champion 2012.

between the clergy. Obviously differences exist. One of the most striking is perhaps the very strong engagement of the Catholic clergy In external missions, while there is until the XVIIIth century, a certain protestant missionary abstention. But, even in his area, one must remain prudent, for C.Balleriaux has shown us great similarities between he Jesuit and puritan missions on America, about whjch one may ask if they are explained by the contacts between the missionaries, by observance of the practices of the other, by the fact that the processes of conversion are not infinite, or that the proposed models of Christianity are finally fairly close.
- Geography and chronology of contacts
If a certain number of contributions to this volume have enabled the possibility of affirming and comparing the clergy, most of them however depend on real contacts.

On which period should studying these contacts dwell? This volume opens up the XVIth, XVIIth and XVIIh centuries; it is the confessional age (1555-1648) come out, as the whole of the so-called modern period which is viewed. But, in doing so, one makes the frameworks of the confessional period come out (1555-1648) as it has been defined by the theorists of confessionalisation, while the act of viewing the different clergy comes strongly from this issue. Before 1555, the question is to discover whether one can really talk about confessions face to face. There is a doctrinal concept ruling in protestant Istria, where F. Zulliani has shown us that confirmation was accepted, in the same way as the existence of bishops. In fact, even at this date, where there were different ecclesiological models in competition, one also sees, without one of them having gone back; it seems To be the case in Bohemia still in 1594 (N.Richard) the case in the beginnings of the Reformation in France[1642]. That asks the whole question of the "faithful flock between two pulpits" as Thierry Wanegffelen[1643] called them, as well as passing into the Reformation in Protestantism, that is that the conscious taking of an irremediable separation, at least on human view. Is it possible, for this period, to speak of Conergy in contact/ However, from their birth, the confessions are formed by differentiation: in Calvin's Geneva, the consistory draws up an ecclesiastical discipline allowing a break with the ancient practices of piety proposed by the Catholic clergy; it is therefore, even before the confessional era, by contact with what is not wanted any more than the confessional construction. But, in so doing, the consistory serves the clericalisation of the pastoral body thus paradoxically bringing the pastors and the priests close together (N. SCZECH). As for after 1648, historiography has a tendency to consider that confessionalisation in Europe is prolonged more and more from a distance, even until the XXth century sometimes[1644]; and for America, it is only after the second half of the XVIIth century that the construction of the State is linked to religion (C. Balleriaux).

During this period, beside the contacts between Catholics and Protestants, one must note the existence of contacts with members of other religions. In Amsterdam, a canon can meet a rabbi (A. Nijenhuis-Bescher); it is also the case in Metz, where pastor Ferry seeks o exchange with the great rabbi Joseph Levy[1645]. In the New World, he discovery of pagan populations opens up a competition for

---

[1642] See also the MORELY model;: DENIS P.and ROTT J ."Jean Morely…dans l'Eglise" Geneva Droz 1993

[1643] See particularly the model of Morely:,DENIS P and ROTT J "Jean Morely (1524-1594) "Utopia..dans l'Eglise " Geneva Droz 1993

[1644] BLASCHKE O. "Konfessionem im Konflikt. Deitschland…Zeitaler" Gottingen Vandenhoeck and Ruprecht 2002.

[1645] LEONARD J. "Etre Pasteur au XVIIe ssiec…" op. cit. p. 151.

converting the Indians (/c. Balleriaux). As for Islam, analysed in Malta by A. Brogini, it enables the defence of Christianity to define the identity of the Order of Malta; an order which renews itself, which surmounts the crisis due to Protestantism by a purely Catholic identity. In the spirit of the Council of Trent. Inversely, In the Vienna of Maximilian II studied by Roche, it is a transconfessional identity which is imposed in front of the Turkish threat. The difference is doubtless explained by different relations of power. But, in these two cases, it is always the other one who allows one to forge an identity.

The most frequent cases are however contacts between Catholic and Protestant clergy. They are, by the power of things, numerous in multi-confessional territories. These territories are to be taken in the wide sense, including armies, because they often mix with men of different confessions, also even during the wars of Religion in France, with Swiss and German troops, partially protestant, on the side of the King of France[1646], and during the Thirty Years War as L. Jalabert describes to us. He also reminds us that it was arranged, after 1648, that there should be Catholic and Protestant chaplains in the same army, like that of the Circle of Souabe. But the most numerous contacts are obviously in the most pluri- confessional States like Bohemian, France, the United Provinces, Hungary, the Grisons. A whole range of attitudes is found here, analysed in several contributions; adaptation of sermons in the presence of opponents (C. Thouin-Dieuaide), controversies (J.Foa) spiritual literature (E. Martinazzo) etc. but without however minimising their contacts in France should not be exaggerated: in France, the reformed synods ask to avoid controversies, the zones with strong protestant implantation, such as Languedoc in some corners of the Berry (D. Boisson) in reality saw few Catholic ecclesiastics,

---

[1646] The last work to consult in this aspect is that of DAUSSY H."Le Paris Huguenot .Chronique d'ine disillusion (1557-1572) Geneva Droz 2014.

or not many. As for the missions, it is known that they cover the protestants less than converting the Catholics to a better practice of their religion[1647]. The clergy of the various confessions seek to establish the impenetrable frontiers between them as Keith Luria has shown[1648]. In spite of that, they knew each other, read each other, copied each other in their sermons, as S. Simiz and C.Borello have shown very well. However, the close presence of the clergy of another confession, doubtless had the result of a certain emulation: it is necessary to have enlightening pastors. In a great many texts, sermons, synod decisions, ecclesiastical decrees, the proximity of the other one is often evoked in order to push to:a better Catholic in Malta when the Turk threatens, a better Protestant in France when the Catholic attacks become more pressing, etc.

Paradoxically, one may also speak about contacts in territories which are in theory mono-confessional, even if these contacts are sometimes indirect. It is especially wars which put clerks of different religions in place. Thus Lutheran armies, with a Lutheran chaplain, can be found in a Catholic territory, and inversely. That can cause complaints against worship in the armies – but one finds sometimes also very peaceful relations (L. Jalabert). Outside these particular cases, direct relationships are rare. But it is known that in the dioceses of Boulogne and Saint-Omer where the emphasis is placed on he training of clergy (P. Moulis); one can read oneself, or fight by books. It is especially the case of "frontiers of Catholicity" among the "Catholic Backbone", whose neighbouring countries are

---

[1647] KRUMENACKER Y. "La mission dans l'Oratoire de France au XVIIe siècle" C.SORRELANS F. MEYER "Les missions interieures …siècle" Chambery Institut d'etudes savoisiennes 2001 p 73-86.

[1648] LURIA K.P. Sacred Boundaries,,,op. cit: \ID "Les fronieres du sacre" "Chreiens et sociees (xvi-XXI siecles) no 15 2009 p 7-28 [http://chretienssociees.revues.or/562] consulted 27/0/2016.

Protestant[1649] The religious orders are often very well implanted there, such as garrison towns intended for preventing the enemy confessional invasion, and Catholicism, whether it be papist or Gallican, especially anti-protestant in the XVIth century; it is therefore an intimate knowledge, but old on the other hand. One must question the memory of Protestantism, as was done for the wars of Religion[1650]. The problem is also raised in the Empire where, in principle, each territory has the religion of its prince, even if the peace of Augsburg of 1555 planned some rare exceptions. In reality, it is known that most of the States were not completely homogeneous; but that does not mean the co-existence of two clergymen

Conflicts or pacified relationships?
One comes to see it by evoking the types of contact and their geography. They can take place also in conflicts which are resolved in very peaceful relationships. The case of military chaplains on the lands of the adverse confession shows very well that, according to the place and times, situations that are completely different, exist.

It must also be understood on what one calls conflict. The controversies, well known for the XVIIth century, less studied for the XVIth century but seen by J. Foa,are in this category vey ambiguous. They appear in time of peace, arms are banished there; but all the same there are confrontations where there is a conqueror and a conquered person, each often proclaiming also to be the conqueror! In

---

[1649] On rhese ideas, advanced y Pierre Chaunu and Rene Taveneaux, see DEREGNAUCOURT G., KRUMENACKER Y, MARTIN P. and MEYER F. "Dorsal catholique, Jansenisme, Devotions…historiographique" Paris, Riveneuve, 2014.

[1650] BERCHTOLD J, and FRAGONARD M-M. "La memoire des guerres de Religion, La concurrence des guerres historiques (XVI-XVIIIe siecles" Geneva,Droz 2007; SOTTOCASA V."Memoires affrontees…Languedoc" Rennes PUR 2004.

the same way, in Holland the relationships between priests or pastors and rabbis, which were generally cordial, give way to writings which were often very closed off, even polemic.

Most of the works presented here show that the context is important in the intensification of the conflicts. In fact, these seem to be more frequent when, in the difference of confession, a national difference is added and the nations differ; thus, the wars between France and England contributed to harden relationships between French Jesuits and Puritan pastors, even in the New World. It is the same, inside the same country, when the political context refuses confessional co-existence,as is the case in France in the 1680's.But before that, the difference in nationality is invoked in order to exclude foreign pastors. (I,Plasman-Labrune). One must not forget a number of other factors, hardly seen here as they are already well known, such as the role of the clergy in refusing a peaceful co-existence, provocations made sometimes in sermons or protestant synods, denunciations of actions against the law or the partisan interpretation that one makes of the law, rivalry between priests and pastors to be beside dying people, etc.[1651]

Conflicts or pacified relationships?
One comes away from seeing it by evoking the types of contact and their geography,

They can give way also to conflicts which are resolved in very peaceful relationships, The case of military chaplains on lands of adverse confession shows very well

---

[1651] For an essay on typology, KRUMENACKER Y. "La co-existence confessionnelle aux XVIIe-XVIIIe siecles. Quelques problemes de methode "Y. KRUMENACKER and D.BOISSON "La co-existence…France modern" Lyon Chretiens e Societes – Documents et memoire2009 p 107-125.

that, according to the places and the times, cpmpletely different situations exist..

It must also be understood on what is called conflict. Controversies, well known for the XVIIth century, less studied for the XVIth century, but seen here by J. Foa, are very ambiguous in his area. They appear in times of peace, weapons are banished there; but all; the same there are confrontations where there is a conqueror and a conquered person, each of them also proclaiming often to be the conqueror! All the same, in Holland, relationships between priests or pastors and rabbis, generally cordial, give way to written relationships which are often very close, even polemic.

Most of the works presented here show that the context is important in the intensification of conflicts. These seem in fact to be more frequent when, on the difference in confession, a national difference is added and the nations confront each other; thus, the wars between France and England contributed to harden relationships between French Jesuits and puritan pastors, even in the New World It is the same, inside one country, when the political context refuses confessional co-existence, as is the case in the 1680's. It is at this time that the conflicts in Sancerre are multiplied (D. Boisson). But well before, the difference in nationality is invoked to exclude foreign pastors (I.Plasman-labrune). One must not forget a number of ot other factors, not often seen here but well known, as the role of the clergy in refusing peaceful co-existence, the provocations sometimes made in sermons or protestant synods, denunciations of actions opposed to the law or partisan interpretation that is carried on within the law, rivalries between priests and pastors to be beside the dying, etc.

But, inversely, this volume has brought to light a great many cordial relationships between the clergy, in certain precise cases:
- When common interests are at issue: when it is a case of struggling against some Indians, Jesuits and

Americans, pastors learn how to understand each other; to struggle against lack of belief, in the XVIIIth century, a common front of apologists from different camps appeared; theological convergences allow confessional "adversaries" to read each other and to appreciate each other, as is the case in Saumur (B. Maes)

- When there is a need to maintain a balance – that is the case in the armies, for the leader must take care for a certain neutrality in order not to create divisions in the troops; it is also seen in German towns with confessional parity or precise rules are drawn up in order to enable a common life; in the Vienna of Maximilian II, the existence of a court which is confessionally diverse imposes a certain restraint, it is forbidden to talk about "heretics", that is in spite of the Jesuits' resistance and "flacians" (C. Roche). That asks the question of legal bi-confessionality, which favorises the confrontation by word to the detriment of weapons, for one may ask whether the rules laid down really enable the maintenance of peace or whether they only congeal latent conflicts
- When the issue is not the conversion of the other one: In the United Provinces, Canon Joly can peacefully talk about wise and profane questions with. Cllaude Saumaise, and he can even discuss theology with Anne-Marie de Schurman – as it is about a scholarly conversation it is not a question of trying to convert. One observes the same phenomenon in inter-confessional correspondence from the Republic of Letters, where the cordial relations between scholars of two confessions reach out to each other when it is about converting the other one[1652]. In the elite circle of Saumur, B. Maes shows that even doctrinal

---

[1652] MOREAO Y. "Parcours, itineraires, rizome: applications,…Lettres" "Les Carnets du larhra no. 2 2014 p 147-168 here p. 152-153.

convergences ae emphasised; it is true that this sociability is limited to the professors, excluding the pastors and priests. It is doubtless also what explains the interest of protestants in Catholic sermons and eloquent treatises. or reading Le Faucheur by Catholics: in both these cases, it is the technical aspect which matters and which enables a positive view to be sent out, not the depth of the works.

- - When it is essentially a question of sociability: the examples do not fail good relationships in elite people, in provincial academies in the XVIIth century as on the eve pf the Revolution. To take only one example, the Archbishop of Lyon, Malvin de Montazet, on 1784 offered a banquet in honour of the King of Sweden, on his way to Lyon and invited the reformed pastor of the town, Frossard- whose sermons he admired and which he wanted to pass on[1653].
- These cordial relationships made the differences between the clergy much looser. While there is even a will for confessionalisation which should on the contrary reinforce them harden them. There is a good example of the manner wjhose process of confessional construction and the imposition of a discipline seeking to sanctify society by building a distinct confessional identity in reality blurs identity, for the process is the same in all confessions.
- However one must not go too far in this direction, for indomitable particularities remain. One of them is marriage, The importance of concubinage of clerks at the beginning of the XVIth century.is known. The reaffirmation of ecclesiastical celibacy by the Catholic reformation has appeared. In reaction to

---

[1653] BLANC R . "Un pastor au temps des Lumieres…Frossard (1754-1830) Paris Honore Champion 2000 p 42 and p 52.

Protestantism, less as [1654]a restraint than as a means of accompanying the new ecclesiastic ideal, which explains its relative success. Inversely, the marriage of pastors very quickly became almost systematic; for most of the clerks who passed to the Protestant Reformation an identifying marker for the priest. However, has S. Dumortier has shown, ecclesiastical marriages, in the North, until the XVIIth century, bear witness of the influence of protestantism in this area. And it is known that at the end of the XVIIIth century, a great many pleas in favour of the marriage of priests are based on Protestant writings.[1655]

- By way of conclusion:
- may one speak of oppositions or influences?
- He clergy in contact disagree, but they can also have good relationships and hey even sometimes seem to influence. That is at least the impression which comes out of the texts of this volume. But is the language used appropriate? Can one really speak about opposition among the clergy or reciprocal influences? To think that the Catholic clergy is against the Lutheran, or Calvinist, clergy, is that not to enlarge   the feature?
- The future Cardinal de Berulle, after the introduction of the reformed Carmelites into France, had to undergo opposition from the Carmes and some bishops, even more than the pastors, anti-protestant as he was. In the following decades, it was particularly Jansenism which divided the Catholic clergy, while the reformed pastors fought between partisans and enemies ot the theology of Saumur. As

---

[1654] DOI A. "Un oggetto sconsiderabile ...politica" Celibato del clero a criticailluminista in Europa nel XVIIIsiecle, thesis of history doctorate. E. BRAMBILLA and C. PEYRARD Universita degli Sudi (Milan and University of aix-Marseille 2013.

[1655]

F. Meyer has shown, the division between the different branches of the Franciscan family is often stronger than opposition to the protestants. On the Lutheran side, the Philippists and gnesio-Lutherans deeply disagreed, before pietism sowed trouble. That is useless to follow up, these examples pietism began the trouble. Quarrels, in the United Provinces, between Armenian and Gomarists are even more serious. And what is there to say about confrontations in England between the various Protestant confessions? These examples show clearly that it is not possible to speak about a Catholic clergy, or Lutheran, Calvinist or Anglican clergy.
- The risk, to identify too quickly the clergy of one well determined confession, is to essentialise the religious phenomena. A re-reading of the example, developed in this volume by N.Richard, of the Archdiocese of Prague, is from this point of view very enlightening. A quick view of the priests of Bohemia in 1594 seems to show Hussite, Lutheran, even orthodox influences through practices such as communion in two kids, absence of prior confession or at the time of childbirth, readings in Czech, the feast of Jan Hus, etc. However, one quickly realises that the influences are difficult to establish with certainty, for they are mixed with relationships of power, with attachment to traditions, to the attraction to some practices, etc. Thus, Catholics can love the readings and songs in the common languages without ceasing to feel so Catholic, as the Protestants can take part in processions or Catholic feasts
- (the same phenomenon is noted in the United Provinces, in France and numerous German areas). Is it not going a little quickly to assimilate a sensitivity, a conservatism or the taste for novelty, social pressures, confessions? These are not only the doctrines described in confessions of faith, according to the use which is spreading in the modern epoch,

but also badly controlled beliefs, practices and traditions which can evolve partially independently from one and the other.
- The religious phenomena are the result of complex alchemies, that one cannot reduce to very undefined bodies of doctrine. To analyse the results of contacts between clergy requires being very careful about the different elements which are at play. Social conventions, common sensitivities or well-anchored prejudices, a great many other phenomena that one would spontaneously describe as "religious" must be taken into account. That must remind us that clergy in contact are only matters of confrontation of doctrines brought in by ecclesiastics, but also affairs of men situated in very precise contexts. There is no doubt that what explains the extreme diversity and complexity of situations analysed in his work. The historian, whose task is not only to describe, but especially to understand, tries very hard to classify, to typologies obstinacy to allow oneself to be enclosed inside a single category., but reality resists in its infinite variety and in its obstinacy not to allow one to be enclosed inside a single category.

As a conclusion, may one speak of oppositions or influences?

Clergy in contact fight each other, but they can also have good relationships and the sometimes appear to be influenced. That is at least the impression which comes from the texts of this volume. But is the language used appropriate? May one speak about opposition between the clergy or reciprocal influences? To think that the Catholic clergy is against the Lutheran, or Calvinist clergy, is it not to enlarge the feature?

The future Cardinal de Berulle, after the introduction of the reformed Carmelites in France, had to undergo opposition from the Carmes and some bishops, more than pastors, completely anti-protestant that he was. In the following decades, it is especially Jansenism which divides the Catholic clergy, while the reformed pastors fight among partisans and enemies of the theology of Saumur. As F. Meyer has shown, the division between the different branches of the Franciscan family is often stronger than the opposition to protestants. On the Lutheran side, the Philipists and the gnesio-Lutherans argue deeply, before pietism sows trouble. Quarrels, in the United Provinces, between Armenians and Gomarists are even more serious. And what to say about confrontations in England between the various Protestant confessions? Useless to follow up, these examples show very well that it is not possible to speak of a Catholic clergyman, or a Lutheran, Calvinst or Anglican clergyman.

The risk, to identify too quickly the clergy of a well determined confession, is to make the religious phenomena essential. A re-reading of he example, developed in this volume by N.Richard, of the Archdiocese of Prague, is from this point of view very enlightening. A rapid view of the priests of Bohemia in 1594 seems to show Hussite, Lutheran, even Orthodox influences, through practices such as communion in two kinds, the absence of prior confession, communion of infants or at the time of childbirth, readings in Czech, the feast of Jan Hus, etc. However, one quickly realises that the influences are difficult to establish with certainty, for the become mixed with relationships of power, attachment to traditions, to the attraction for certain practices etc. Thus, Catholics may love the readings and songs in the common language without ceasing at all to feel themselves Catholic, just as the protestants can take part in processions or in Catholic feasts (the same phenomenon is noted in the united Provinces, in France and in a number of German regions). Is it not to go a little slower than to assimilate a sensibility, a conservatism or the taste for novelties, social pressures, confessions?

These are not only doctrines exposed in confessions of faith, according to the usage which is spreading in the modern age, but also badly controlled beliefs, practices. Traditions, which can evolve partially independently from one another.

Religious phenomena are the result of complex alchemies, which cannot be reduced to very undefined bodies of doctrine. To analyse the consequences of contacts between clergy requires being very attentive to the different elements coming into play. Social conventions, strategies of co-existence, of survival or conquest, intellectual affinities, common sensibilities or strongly anchored prejudices, a great many other phenomena which would not spontaneously be described as religious" are to be taken into account. That mut remind us that the clergy in contact only affairs of confrontation of doctrines brought by ecclesiastics, but also the affairs of men situated in exact contexts. That is doubtless what explains the extreme diversity and complexity of situations analysed in this work.

Ingram Content Group UK Ltd.
Milton Keynes UK
UKHW022145180423
420354UK00011B/123

TWO LANDS ON ONE SOIL
Ulster Politics before Home Rule

UNDERSTANDING CONFLICT...
AND FINDING WAYS OUT OF IT

In 1988 Frank Wright, together with Roel Kaptein, Duncan Morrow and Derick Wilson established a charitable community relations project called "Understanding Conflict . . . and Finding Ways Out of it". This project offered training, study materials and research to a wide range of groups involved in seeking ways forward together, especially in Northern Ireland and linked the Corrymeela Community, the Centre for the Study of Conflict, University of Ulster, Queen's University Belfast, and the University of Limerick (1989-95). In 1995 a new programme "Future Ways" took this work further within the University of Ulster.

Two Lands on One Soil is an initial contribution from Understanding Conflict to the work of the Cultural Traditions Programme of the Northern Ireland Community Relations Council.

ALSO BY FRANK WRIGHT

Northern Ireland: A Comparative Analysis
(Gill and Macmillan).

"Finding Ways to Go . . ." A discussion paper about Community
Relations in Northern Ireland
Kaptein, Morrow, Wilson and Wright.

"Integrated Education and New Beginnings in Northern Ireland".
Examines relationships between education and traditions from 1831
(Corrymeela Press).

TWO LANDS ON ONE SOIL

Ulster Politics before Home Rule

Frank Wright

GILL & MACMILLAN

Gill & Macmillan Ltd
Goldenbridge
Dublin 8
with associated companies throughout the world
© The estate of the late Frank Wright 1996
0 7171 2179 8
Index compiled by Helen Litton
Print origination by Typeform Repro, Dublin
Printed by Mackays of Chatham plc, Kent

All rights reserved. No part of this publication may be copied,
reproduced or transmitted in any form or by any means,
without permission of the publishers.

A catalogue record is available for this
book from the British Library.

1 3 5 4 2

CONTENTS

List of maps and diagrams	vii
Preface	ix
CHAPTER ONE Introduction: The Settlement Legacy	1
CHAPTER TWO The Decay of the Colonial Settlement Structure	23
CHAPTER THREE Ulster, O'Connell and the Whigs	47
CHAPTER FOUR Onset of Rural Crisis in Pre-Famine Ulster	70
CHAPTER FIVE The Famine in Ulster	104
CHAPTER SIX Ulster Politics in 1848	135
CHAPTER SEVEN 1848–1852: The League of North and South— the Tenant League	165
CHAPTER EIGHT The Decline of the Old Whigs	208
CHAPTER NINE Violence and the Law	241
CHAPTER TEN Belfast 1868—Expectations of Democracy	284
CHAPTER ELEVEN Belfast 1869–1874—Democracy and Disillusion	333
CHAPTER TWELVE The Region Beyond Belfast	383

CHAPTER THIRTEEN
The Land War and the Climax of Liberalism—
the Land League   432

CHAPTER FOURTEEN
Militant Pan-Protestantism and Conservatism—
the Formation of Unionism   476

CHAPTER FIFTEEN
Conclusions   510

NOTES   524

INDEX   566

MAPS AND DIAGRAMS

Page

xi   1. Ulster, showing places and parishes named in the text

16   2. Catholics in rural Ulster, 1861

57   3. Ulster, showing numbers of Orange lodges, 1835

76   4. Rural weavers, 1841

80   5. Quality of rural housing

108   6. Oat prices at Belfast markets

113   7. Rural weavers, 1851

117   8. Reduction in population by Baronies, 1841–51

119   9. Population employed on public works (road building), April 1847

120   10. Poor Law Union boundaries

125   11. Maximum dependence upon the soup kitchens established under the 1847 Temporary Relief Act

127   12. Proportion of 1841 population being relieved by the Poor Law, July 1848

129   13. Poor rate collected by Poor Law Union (pence on £ valuation), October 1847 – September 1848

130.   14. Percentage of farms over 30 acres in 1847

131   15. Percentage reduction in numbers of 1–5 acre farms between 1847 and 1855

249   16. West Belfast, 1864–72, naming streets and ward boundaries mentioned in text

386 17. Populations of Baronies, 1872, as percentages of 1851 population

391 18. Irish speakers by Baronies, 1851

393 19. Catholic pupils at Model Schools up to 1870

499 20. County Down by-election, May 1884. Electorate in each polling district; Catholic percentage in electorate; Percentage turnout; Liberal vote

PREFACE

At a particularly tense moment in the province a few years ago, paramilitary slogans appeared on a wall in the street where Frank Wright lived in Belfast. He took a paint brush and painted them out, to the approbation of his neighbours, which was what pleased him most about the episode. However, the main focus of Frank's efforts was cross-community dialogue. He saw it as contributing at an individual level to trust across the sectarian divide. He devoted a lot of time to the Corrymeela community for Christian reconciliation because of the opportunity it gave him to take part in and to facilitate cross-community meetings. For a time Frank lived in a cottage near Ballycastle basically so that he could be close to Corrymeela. But for all his personal commitment and engagement with such cross-community endeavour, he did not lose his sense of proportion about what it could achieve. He saw it as important because he saw individuals as important, not because he imagined that it could solve the Northern Ireland problem.

Frank Wright died peacefully in Oxford in 1993, the city where he was born and educated, in the care of his devoted parents. His tragic death at the age of 44 represented the loss of a brilliant colleague, a gifted and devoted teacher, and a man whose friendship enriched the lives of many. That it should have occurred so soon after the value of his work had been recognised in his appointment to the new Chair of Peace Studies at Limerick University was particularly poignant.

Professor Wright studied Philosophy, Politics and Economics at Trinity College, Oxford, in the heady days of the late 1960s, winning the Gibbs Prize for Politics in 1969, and graduating with First Class Honours in 1970. After postgraduate research in Belfast and Oxford, he became a lecturer in the Politics Department at Queen's University, Belfast. His first publication in 1973, *Protestant Ideology and Politics in Ulster*, continues to be widely cited as a penetrating understanding of the structure and continuity of ideas. Thereafter, along with his colleague Adrian Guelke, he pioneered an approach towards Northern Ireland which studied it, not as a unique and anomalous social and political problem, but through parallels with other deeply divided societies forged by history on the frontiers between different cultures and communities. The main offshoot of this was his difficult, but widely respected book, *Northern Ireland—A Comparative Perspective*

(1988). With his understanding of ethnic relations, Frank at this time became one of the few external observers to anticipate the calamity about to overwhelm Yugoslavia, and to appreciate the latent violence which underlay the fragile veneer of order and tranquillity in the region. He discovered a deep affection for the country, and became active in the work for peace there. His special concern, however, remained Northern Ireland, on which he wrote extensively. In 1989 he completed his doctorate, a detailed and sophisticated study of the emergence of the nationalist-unionist divide, which is now published as the core of the text of this book.

Frank and I worked together on a paper, "Agrarian Opposition in Ulster 1848–87", which appeared in Sam Clark and Jim Donnelly (eds), *Irish Peasants: Violence and Political Unrest*, Madison 1983. I quickly realised then that he had an incredible knowledge of the public intercommunal discourse of nineteenth-century Ulster. His historical work is stressed by the intensity of ethnic conflict. *Two Lands on One Soil* clearly sees the colonial structures arising from the original Plantations as being both of enduring and crucial importance. Wright saw Northern Ireland as belonging to a group of 'frontier societies', including Prussian Poland, French Algeria, The Balkans, the southern states of the United States. Inevitably, those obsessed with the very specific nature of Northern Ireland's political history within the UK's parliamentary polity were uncomfortable with the comparative focus—for so many in both communities, compassions with others sometimes are simply intended not to advance knowledge but to provide a 'philosophical guarantee' for pre-given positions. Frank never fell into this trap. He had too sure a grasp of the complications and intractability of the conflict. In a reference to one of Frank's more contemporary analyses, the late Professor John Whyte elegantly summarised Frank's position:

> 'Frank Wright, in a brilliant article, examined two competing claims—that British withdrawal is essential because otherwise the two sides will never have the incentive to work out a compromise and that British withdrawal would be disastrous because it would lead to civil war. He suggested that the peculiar malignancy of the Northern Ireland situation is that the two claims are true at the same time.'

Paul Bew

1. Ulster, showing places named in the text

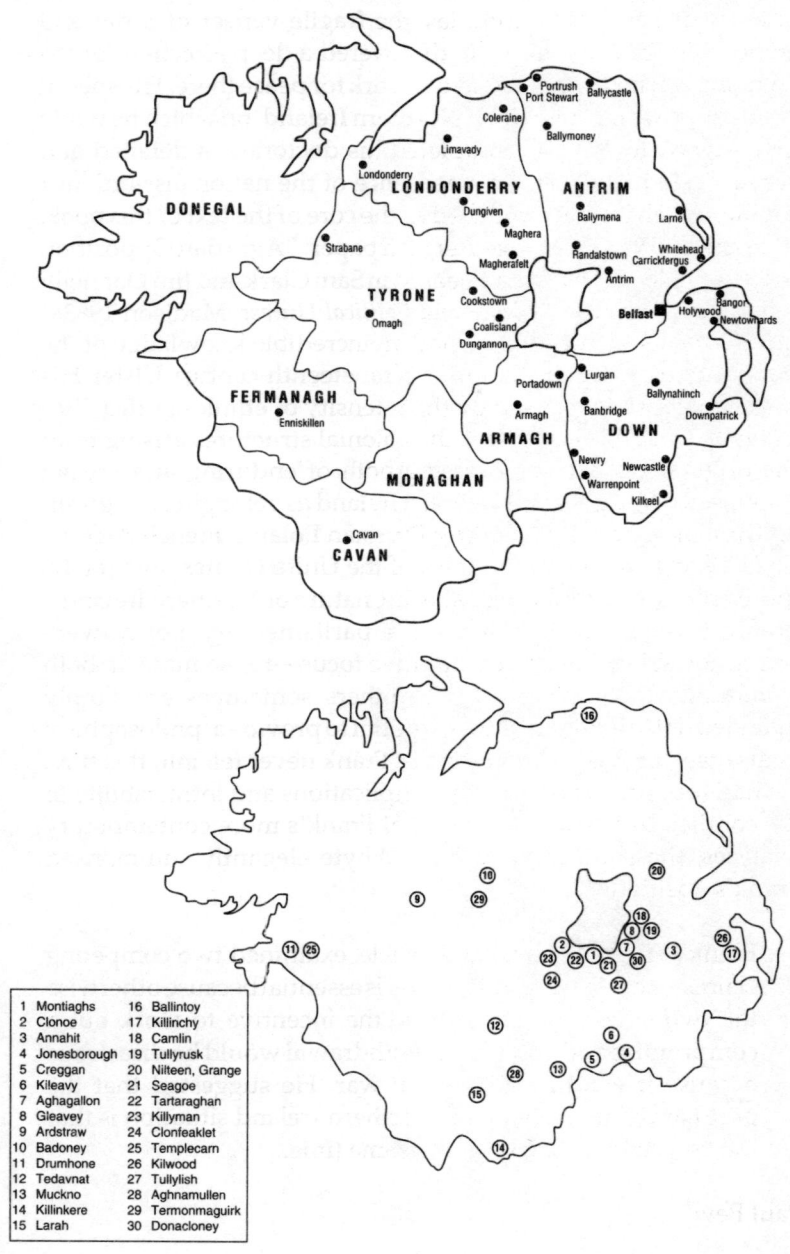

1. Introduction: The Settlement Legacy

Ulster Unionists opposing the Home Rule Bills of 1886, 1893 and 1912 used to say that their society had been permanently under siege since its plantation or colonial origins in the 17th century. This continual sense of siege has been recognized by historians as the central reality of northern Protestant society.[1] From this perspective, the most significant historical periods were the occasions of major sectarian confrontations, on the one hand, and the seemingly aberrant 1790s on the other. The confrontations are important because they explain and validate the Protestant fears or sense of siege. The 1790s, by contrast, are important because many Presbyterians supported the United Irishmen. Then they opposed British power in alliance with Catholics. As this is the opposite kind of behaviour to what the continuity thesis suggests Protestants habitually exhibited, this period needs to be explained.

In the interpretations of David Miller[2] and A. T. Q. Stewart,[3] the Protestant population is shown to have had a continuous preoccupation with the Catholics in their midst and uncertainty about how far they could rely upon British power to support them. Societies which are formed by colonial settlement are usually unable to shake free of the relationship set up between themselves and the dispossessed natives, so long as the native population remains a presence of any magnitude. So at one level this "Protestant fears" interpretation, far from introducing a note of peculiarity into the understanding of the North of Ireland, actually helps to place it in the wider context of colonial settlement studies. They are, in effect, showing how different religious identities became the labels by which the descendants of settlers and descendants of natives came to identify each other in the North of Ireland.

Peter Gibbon criticises some of the continuity theses for setting up something like a Jungian folk myth and losing sight of the material realities which underlie Protestant politics.[4] In place of the Protestant fears, he attempts to discern a pattern of class interests. But his treatment of the United Irishmen and Orangeism ends up talking about Protestant classes. He invokes traditional explanations when he speaks about the way different groups understood the penal laws.[5] Gibbon has correctly objected to free-floating ideologies which seem to exist regardless of any changes in the material conditions of the society, but he has found the wrong remedy. Sectarian relationships were a reality and they were anchored in the relationships of different sectarian groups to state power and to each other. Nothing is gained by tossing this out and attempting to insert a far more flimsy set of class relationships in their stead. So while the opening bars of Gibbon's Marxist criticisms of traditional interpretations of Ulster history are correct, his remedy is inappropriate.

For me, continuity theses themselves are not a problem, so long as it is the continuity in the relationship between Protestant and Catholic that is being stressed. What seems to me deficient in the accounts of Stewart and Miller (and indeed in my own early writing on the subject)[6] is that they sometimes abstract the Protestant fears from the relationship with the Catholics who are being feared. They do not see any system in the Catholic response to being feared. The whole in fact becomes a circular relationship. Once the reciprocal aspect of the relationship is grasped, then we are looking at a circle of fear and distrust. What this means is that to understand this society, we must first abandon all assumptions about social tranquillity which come naturally to people who live in societies with normal judicial order.[7] Otherwise the human reality of life in this society is certain to be misunderstood. The Stewart and Miller theses are very important, because they familiarize their readers with a sense of encirclement experienced by Protestants in the North of Ireland; but they lose sight of the reciprocal element in the relationship. The missing element in Stewart's and Miller's histories of the North of Ireland are the northern Catholics. To omit them is not only to omit them, but also to make the story of liberalism in the North only partly intelligible. In short, failure to look at the sectarian relationship as a relationship weakens the credibility of what are otherwise the best interpretations of Ulster history.

My thesis asserts the primacy of the deterrence relationship between the sectarian subsocieties. In doing so it places the experience of the North of Ireland alongside that of other older European colonial settlements.[8] The economic inequalities between Protestant and Catholic in the North of Ireland were substantial in the 19th century, but on their own quite insufficient to explain the primacy of the sectarian relationship. That could be explained only by looking at the threatened force or deterrence relationships between sectarian subsocieties, and the way these were woven round their relationships with state power. In the 19th century when modern states were coming to monopolize the use of legitimate force, the ongoing sectarian relationship in the North of Ireland compromised this severely, and with momentous consequences. It is a central part of my story to look at the way in which any possibility of normal liberal order was aborted in the North of Ireland, although many knew that it was the only possibility of a better future.

I shall begin by outlining how I understand the primacy of the deterrence relationship. I want to look at what people tried to do within the political space they found they had. The sectarian split was all pervasive and made the society vulnerable to things happening outside it. A. T. Q. Stewart's analogy between the sectarian division and the San Andreas fault-line is a good one. I want to show that many of the better hopes that are about today were also there in the past. But they have been forgotten, because in the long run they failed. Instead, we remember the things that contributed to fearful preoccupations with the sectarian division. We remember what is important to us, and the important things we learn in school are things with echoes outside school.

It is often said that part of the trouble in Northern Ireland today is that we will not forget our history. For me the real difficulty is that our versions of history are in fact ways of explaining our feelings and especially our fears in everyday life.⁹ By contrast, history in societies enjoying normal order does not feel as though it is about relationships which matter today. Proposals are sometimes made for "re-education" in Northern Ireland. New histories will take root beyond academic settings only if they grow out of new relationships which give them meaning. If we explore our histories together with people whose experience is of the opposite side of the deterrence relationships, then new history may eventually flourish.

It is often and quite rightly said that the sectarian conflict in the North of Ireland has a life of its own.¹⁰ But what exactly does that mean? To make clear what it means we need to look at how people in most parts of the West today are insulated from feuds and conflicts that have a life of their own. Universally accepted law and order systems halt the spread of many kinds of fears and reasons for violence that would otherwise lead to potentially endless spirals of revenge and chaos.¹¹ In a "normal" society, if someone breaks the law and attacks someone else, the "Law" criminalizes the attacker. Nearly everyone in the society is content that the "Law" has done this. The criminal is isolated. No one, except perhaps his immediate friends and family, is interested in any reasons or justifications he may have for what he did. And when the "Law" punishes him, that is the end of the matter. The person he attacked is expected to be content and not to look for any further vengeance. If the crime is a rare kind of occurrence, then the victim may be able to live without the fear of its repetition. Before the crime no one in the society had an acceptable reason for private acts of violence; and the same is true afterwards. There are no feuds or chains of reasons for violence. Without having to think about it, people talk of the state using force and criminals using violence. When offenders are criminalized (which is the same thing as isolating them from any public sympathy), everyone else, including their victims, remains in the same relation to the "Law". A difference is clearly established between criminals and law-abiding citizens. So in any court case, the only things that matter are the circumstances immediately connected with it. The law treats each case as having a clear beginning and an end. If the law became less interested in what people had actually done, and more in why they did what they did, the distinction between the lawbreaker and everyone else would crumble. Once we start to ask "why", the "reasons" begin to mitigate the crime.

In the North of Ireland, there has never been "normal" order like this in which everyone could be regarded as an individual citizen before the law. Capt. B. Warburton told the 1852 Select Committee on Outrages: "I have often observed at the assizes that people feel perfectly satisfied, when they see the jury sworn, as to the result of the trial beforehand", and Edward Golding, J.P., from Castleblaney, said: "I do not think they look upon trial by jury in Ireland so much as the administration of justice, as that it is rather a lottery."[12] Everyone knows that people are different. We could argue about what the difference is, Catholic v. Protestant, Nationalist v. Unionist; and we could argue about which "side" a few doubtful people belonged to; but the legacy of the settlement is that there are "sides" and there have been "sides" since the plantation. Nor do most people feel entirely secure. Certainly Unionists who are defending their position have a permanent anxiety. The story of the Apprentice Boys of Derry and the marching of the Orange Order (which we will see was once explicitly concerned with patrolling Catholics) were undertaken out of anxious defensiveness. Peace was never taken for granted and deterrence does not gradually melt into trust despite there being periods without overt violence. Nationalists who were being deterred knew they were not trusted and experienced actions taken to deter them as a humiliation, a provocation or a threat. The support of most Catholics for the Fenian amnesty movement was a statement of alienation from the system of power which treated them as a threat. It did not usually mean support for Fenianism itself, as we shall see in Chapters 9–11. The reaction of those who are being deterred is at least resentful, if not hostile. That gives those who are deterring them more reasons for doing it. And so it goes on.

In a deterrence relationship, all incidents of violence or humiliation between members of opposed communities are seen to have a meaning for the whole attacked community. For an incident to be an exception to this rule people have to be convinced that this particular case, unlike most others, really had only private significance. Such exceptions prove the general rule that an attack upon one member of a group becomes an attack on the group. We will see throughout this story, time and again, that people are often attacked for who they are and not for anything they have done themselves. This is not merely a characteristic of the present troubles; it has been true for much of our history. If someone is attacked, the first thing we need to know, if we want to understand it, is of what religion the attacker and the victim were. We will see how people were almost invariably interested in the reasons for violence, though they did not usually agree with it. Violence would spread from one incident in a chain reaction. If people know that an attack upon some person is an attack upon a whole group of people, of whom that person is only a representative, it has a massive effect. This is quite unlike an isolated murder in a normal society. It isn't necessary for people to agree with violence; they only have to understand what is happening and to be frightened by it. This is how each act of violence somehow involves everybody. It is either an attack on us; or something done by our side to them, in which case we understand it in some way. We may give reasons for it, which somehow take away from our sense of outrage at it; or, alternatively, it may even make us especially ashamed, because we feel somehow responsible for it. But in whatever way these attacks are different, they are different none the less, depending on how we relate to the perpetrators and the victims.

The more violence escalates, the more threatened we are by violence directed against those who are like us; and the more sympathy/understanding we are liable to feel about those of our side who respond. I will demonstrate this point at some length in the story of the 1864 Belfast riots. However much we dislike the violence done by our own people to the others, the other side's violence becomes more dangerous to us; and we can even end up being protected from it by the people on our side who provoked it in the first place. At this point our identities are being shaped by the different directions from which we expect danger.

Fear spreads reasons for itself. Once the cycle is under way, some acts of violence done by our side are seen by us as self-defence, reprisal, pre-emptive strike or deterring actions. And we fear "them"—the violent people on the other side or indeed anyone on the other side whom we don't know and who might be a threat. When some of "them" are known to be dangerous to us and we treat all of them as strangers, then we fear that the one we meet might be one of the worst of them. There is already the temptation to judge them by what we fear they could be like. And just as the most dangerous on their side become the most important for us, so we can be judged by how our worst affect them.

Throughout this story we shall see time and again how in this society people tend to judge "them" by their worst representatives. This is not just bigotry; it is sometimes pessimistic common sense. It means that people are made different from each other by the quarter from whom they expect violence and humiliation.

Differences like this do not just go away after a period of communal disturbance. The way things work during times of tranquillity is based on the outcome of the last outbreak of violence. Much of the time the differences seem to be hidden. In order to keep relationships polite and civil, any conversation is kept well away from subjects that might touch these kinds of difference. But avoiding any communication means that the division remains alive and well, because the differences anxiously concealed in this way do not change.

Finally, fear is not only what divides us, it is also what unites us. We need to shelter with our own. Anxiety to be accepted by our side means sharing or at least pretending to share the fear of the other side. Then what the militant elements on our side do may provoke the "other" side to attack us. All of us are put in a position where we may be held responsible by the "other" side for things done by the most aggressive forces on our own side. And because they claim to be defending us, our militants may attack us as traitors if we criticize or oppose them. The words of two leaders of militant Orangeism during the "Invasion of Ulster" in 1883 succinctly pinpoint this discomfort for Protestant Liberals.[13] Rev. J. D. Crawford said: "Orangeism had done more to preserve order and good government in Ireland than at least some governments had done. Unfortunately however the men who lived under its shade were often amongst the first to denounce it." And E. S. W. Cobain, Grand Master of Belfast, referring to a time when the Orange institution was regarded as an organization, the outcome of which was merely to revive bitter memories, and as a mere exasperating symbol of bygone triumphs which should be allowed to slumber on the pages of history, he asked "where now was the appropriate application of taunts?" Many Protestant Liberals had indeed denounced Orangeism and on some occasions acted against it. But faced with the reality of nationalism, now embracing most of the northern Catholic population, they found themselves living under the shade of Orangeism. In a society of communal deterrence, the militant elements in each community have an influence in excess of their numbers. This influence grows as fears spread out and multiply.

We must now trace the connections between the deterrence relationship and the colonial settlement origin of the society. We must explain how the ideological themes of colonial settlement could become more important, even after the colonial socio-economic inequality had decayed.

Towards the end of our period the themes of colonial settlement legacy were expounded much more loudly than they had been for forty years before. By 1883 political contest in the Ulster border area had already been reduced to a sectarian headcount. After the Nationalist victory in the Sligo by-election in 1883, the Belfast *Newsletter*, the principal organ of northern conservatism, had this to say to the leaders of Sligo conservatism:[14]

"The Protestant yeomen of Sligo, for the most part descended from Cromwell's veterans, are weakened and humiliated in a county for which they have done so much. 230 years ago the disbanded Ironsides settled among a people ignorant, superstitious and semi-barbarous claiming protection from the moon for their cattle and trying to eke out a miserable existence. Large districts of the county were given over to the Protector's heroes, whose industry turned wastes and bogs into well tilled fields and rich pasture . . . and they should have been taken care of by men who had power in the country. Away they went, however, one after another; and now they are fighting in the colonies the battle they might be fighting at home. The results of the polling on Saturday testify to the decreasing number of the Protestant yeomanry of Sligo . . . The Conservative candidate may rest assured an absentee landlord will never sit in the House of Commons as one of the members of Sligo. He must come to the country and make himself familiar with the Protestant yeomen of the county . . . letting them have their farms at moderate rents and avoiding harshness on gale days. His nominal income might be lower, but his real income is sure to be higher, and not a word would be said about 'ounces of lead' or 'hold the harvest' when rent payments are to be made. . . . The hint is intended for all landlords . . . Constitutional clubs are excellent things in their way and there is room for them in Ireland. But what is their value without constitutional yeomen in the counties?"

Advice of this kind to Irish Protestant landlords was not something the *Newsletter* had given much of previously. And as far as Sligo with a 10 per cent Protestant population was concerned, the sermon about conserving Protestants in the area had come rather late. But the editorial gives a useful starting point for surveying the dynamics of colonial settlement both in general and in the North of Ireland in particular. The emphasis on the need for interdependence between Protestants was not unusual. But the specific criticisms of landlords were unusual for the *Newsletter*. The suggestion that maintaining a Protestant population, strong enough to overawe (Catholic) rebellion, required some economic sacrifice from landlords was new. So was the hint that if they did not do it voluntarily they would face political challenge from Protestant activists.

Two aspects of this will be emphasised. First there is an economic factor contributing to popular settler antagonism against the native people, which affects any society created by colonial settlement. So long as the native population is prepared to endure a subsistence level significantly below whatever the settlers will endure, normal economic forces tend to displace the settlers. When native labour is cheaper, the natives will tend to fill up all the economic spaces in the society that are opened to them; and it will be in the interests of owners of land and capital to open those spaces to them.[15] Taking the long view of the Cromwellian settlers in Sligo, this may be part of their story. It may indeed be that they emigrated for the reasons the *Newsletter* was implying.

Another question about this editorial is why the *Newsletter*, the landlord organ for decades, should be raising this line of attack in the 1880s. Similar concerns about the displacement of settler descendants by native descendants, with the connivance of big property, were also manifest in Prussian Poland and Austrian Bohemia in the late 19th century.[16] There have been many periods in these societies' histories when settler descendants have felt insecure about their position. Often this has been conceived in terms of struggling to hold on to a space that is threatened by natives. So democratization in the second half of the 19th century tended to heighten the concern about holding ground against the native descendants for two reasons. To begin with, the relative balances of numbers became a matter of greater importance when they affected the outcomes of elections. In the North of Ireland in the 1840s, when power was monopolised by an exclusively Protestant elite, orators could talk confidently about "Protestant Ulster" in a way that they could not in the 1880s. But equally, concerns of this kind had little impact while landlords were politically unassailable. Democratization facilitated popular challenges from settler descendants, who could denounce them for putting their economic interests before those of the settlement as a whole.

If the North of Ireland had still had the economic characteristics of a recently settled colony—if there had still been significant differences between Protestant and Catholic subsistence levels as in more recently established settler colonies—then no mere appeals to owners of land and capital would have had any impact. Employers and landlords would have taken on Catholic employees and tenants wherever possible and they would have been prevented from doing so only by legal restrictions that preserved spaces for Protestants. If this had been the case, then meeting the *Newsletter*'s criticisms would have required the restoration of a tougher version of the penal laws, adapted in the manner of modern apartheid to counteract free market forces. It was only because differences in the subsistence levels had become residual and the colonial economic structure had decayed that informal mechanisms could be devised to discriminate in favour of Protestants. In the North of Ireland we shall see that there were no signs of the settler displacement effect operating from after the Famine of the 1840s. Once this economic determinant of antagonism had become residual, it did not mean that antagonisms generated in earlier periods would necessarily fade. But it did mean that there was now an opportunity for workplace solidarity between workers of all denominations on a basis of equal pay for equal work; and that antagonism might fade. Or it might mean that conflict over places and spaces simply became more reciprocal and equal. In this case the decay of the economic substance of colonization might leave behind a more unlimited battle between two sectarian blocs that were actually becoming more and more alike. In fact this possibility is the origin of national conflict pure and simple.[17]

Working-class Protestant attacks upon the economically dominant classes for their supposed part in the displacement of Protestants signified both a challenge to their political leadership of the pan-Protestant bloc and an intention to demand preferential economic treatment as a right, not as a thing given by others on their behalf. What was happening was that plebeian Protestant activists were beginning to claim a place in the overall pan-Protestant politics of the period. The *Newsletter* was coming to terms with plebeian pan-Protestant challenges, which would be integrated eventually into Ulster unionism.

The really central legacy of the colonial settlement process was not so much the economic inequality it gave rise to, as the relationship of fear and distrust between the descendants of settlers and natives. Once a control system had been created, liberty for those who had been held down by it meant making sure that the system's controlling intent was clearly broken. But from the standpoint of the settler descendants, native power to do this did not spell justice so much as threat. The capacity of the settlement to take roots in spite of the weakness of the penal laws depended on the relatively low levels of inequality between the settler and native. But so long as the penal law was an instrument of control, it ensured an antagonism in the relationship between settler and native descendants.

From the time of the plantation around 1610 to the second decade after the Williamite Revolution of 1690, the greater part of the expansion of the Protestant settlement had been brought about in the aftermath of war and devastation. The original confiscation of the lands of the earls, the Cromwellian and Williamite confiscations had augmented Protestant land ownership. Each had also been the occasion for the start of another wave of Protestant tenant farming immigration.[18] In what way were the extensions of land ownership and increase in settlement population connected? It could be argued that the terms of the original undertaking leases and later penal legislation against Catholics are the fundamental link. But if that is the case, then Protestant immigration to the North of Ireland would have been made possible by debarring Catholics from the space the immigrants occupied. On the face of it, the evidence is rather the other way about: that the devastation of war created shortages of labour which, through the medium of low rents, acted as a magnet to secure Protestant immigration.[19] The Londonderry companies—after the pacification and early formative works had been undertaken—readily took on Catholic tenants from whom they charged higher rents than they were allowed to charge incoming Protestants.[20]

In the early phases of a mass settlement, its security, the introduction of new techniques of husbandry, and the creation of novel forms of physical infrastructure require the mass influx of settler population. The interests of state, of settlement entrepreneurs, of settlers themselves, are interdependent. All saw the defeated natives as a threat. This is in sharp contrast to an orthodox colonization which draws the ruling groups of an indigenous society into subordinate alliance with the colonizing power, and which intends to exploit native labour. Orthodox colonization could not operate by treating all strata of native society as enemies of the new order as mass colonial settlement does. The more dense the settlement presence, the less use does the society have for the native, even as a source of servile labour. Expulsion or eradication seem to be his fate initially; but while such ruthlessness is possible in the course of defeating native opposition, it is rarely sustained. Tranquillity creates the problem or opportunity of the defeated native who acquiesces.

The determination to "Protestantize" Ireland was manifested in the early stages of the plantation project by the flight of the earls when they appreciated what was happening; and the effort to dominate the Irish parliament by the creation of Protestant boroughs. But then shifts of emphasis in the plantation policy became inextricably bound up with the conflicts between the Stuarts and the rising English gentry in parliament. And in Ireland Wentworth set out to "bow and govern the native by the planter, and the planter by the native", to secure from Ireland revenues outside the control of the English parliament, and a base for military preparations against it.[21] State policy toward the settlement was rarely consistent, even though the latter Stuarts made few efforts to undermine the Cromwellian land settlement after their restoration in 1660.[22] The significance of the Williamite victory of 1690 lay in the consolidation of an Anglican landlord veto over English policy in Ireland, at least in so far as it affected their property rights and the exclusion of Catholics and Presbyterians from state patronage and institutions of local control (grand juries, borough corporations, etc.). It put an end to any prospect that rebellious forces in Ireland would be encouraged by parties in conflict in Britain.[23]

The Williamite victory in 1690 is celebrated as the securing of the Protestant ascendancy. In fact the security it created for the Anglican landlord elite enabled the landlords to loosen their ties to the mass of the Protestant population. The penal laws, rather than being a 17th-century version of apartheid and creating a secure economic space for the Protestant masses, became protective of elite positions only. With Protestant land ownership secure and the politico-administrative structure reckoned able to control and overawe the Catholics, Catholic labour could be distinguished from Protestant labour by its submissiveness and exploitability. Protestant tenants who spoke of their "rights" became more dispensable than hitherto. Throughout the 18th century, the wave of Protestant immigration reversed itself. R. J. Dickson's account of this emigration of Ulster Presbyterians to America leaves us in little doubt that here we see the operation of the settler displacement effect.[24] As the low rent leases granted to immigrants in the immediate aftermath of the Williamite wars expired, rent levels were raised fairly rapidly throughout most of the rest of the century.[25] And though there must be some doubt as to the precise implication of their emigration, i.e. whether emigration functioned to arrest subdivision of Presbyterian family farms, or whether they were ousted by Catholics prepared to pay higher rents, yet the fact that the vast bulk of the emigrants were Protestants (not Catholics) is not open to serious dispute. Just how secure the landlords felt about any possible threat from Catholics is shown by how little concerned they were at the scale of the Presbyterian exodus. By the 1770s, sections of state power worried about the Protestant emigration, precisely because it weakened the garrison presence.[26] Far from supporting them, the penal laws excluded Presbyterians from borough corporations and obliged them, like the Catholics, to pay tithes to uphold a Church opposed to their own. Being speakers of English and Protestants, they were keenly sought by promoters of American colonies.

The decay of any Protestant interdependence affected the development of penal law in relation to the borough corporations. The corporations, which were generally self-selecting, had trusteeship over corporate property and the right/duty of admitting (Protestant) freemen to boroughs.[27] The freedom of a borough involved the right to vote in borough elections and the right to conduct crafts and occupations within the borough, and it exempted its holder from tolls. In Derry a 1709 byelaw stated that no person without freedom of the city "except Protestant weavers of the hempen or flaxen manufacturers in this kingdom" shall use any craft or occupation for gain until admitted to the freedom.[28] In 1735 a fraternity existed to keep out non-freeman traders, which gave up its efforts in the 1790s. As a general rule the corporations restricted the creation of freemen, thus depriving any but themselves of elective rights, and making a fiction of freemen's special economic status. In 1747 the Ponsonby influence secured the passage of the Newtown Act to allow non-residents to become members of corporations whenever there was "a want for Protestant inhabitants". This Act was used liberally to create non-resident corporations and, in some boroughs, the alienation of corporate property to corporate members reduced those bodies to the role of nominators of members of parliament.[29] The consistent picture that emerges is the increasing irrelevance of the freeman status.

As a protection of the Protestant masses from the competitive effects of Catholic poverty the penal laws became nearly, if not totally, useless. An interesting exception proves the rule. In Belturbet, Co. Cavan, the corporation kept hold of some common land which was periodically redistributed to "poor inhabitants deserving assistance", and in the 1830s it was still employing this resource for pan-Protestant purposes.[30] Maureen Wall has observed that the decay of much of the penal law depended not only on the clash between dominant interest groups' economic interests and its restrictions, but also on the fact that in large areas it was simply unenforceable.[31] In places like Belturbet on the outer edge of Ulster, settlement had been sufficiently disruptive to leave visible day-to-day evidence of the historic fact of native removal; but the native removal had never been carried far enough to create security amongst the mainly Anglican settlers. It would be in just such areas that one would have expected the penal law to survive longest.

Even if the direct effects in favour of the mass of Protestants were limited, the penal laws none the less had a drastic effect upon Catholic society. If most Catholics also remained unaffected directly, the decimation of their social leadership was to be of lasting significance. Designed ostensibly to undermine Catholicism, the penal laws left the faith of the masses untouched but demoralized, and decimated the land owning and professional sections of Catholic society. In this way Catholicity became ever more clearly the hallmark of the excluded mass of the population. Irish Catholics showed little or no tendency to support the terminal outbreaks of Jacobite rebellion. 1745 produced almost no echo in Ireland and this was one of the factors that encouraged Protestants to allow the penal laws to decay.[32] But even as they decayed, they still affected any who aspired to high positions. Assimilation meant discarding Catholicism—apostasy from the stigmatized religion. The Sovereign of Armagh in the 1780s, Thomas McCann, is an example of a 'Catholic' by birth, whose route to advancement involved conversion to Anglicanism.[33] Penal law shaped the directions taken by those Catholics who did secure distinction. It obstructed avenues to professional education and to investment in fixed immovable assets, such as bleach greens. In this way it closed off Catholic involvement in the more highly capitalized and important departments of the northern linen trade. Significantly, the first of the penal laws to be repealed was the limitation on the length of leases that Catholics could take on land to be reclaimed from bog and waste, which

2. Catholics in rural Ulster, 1861

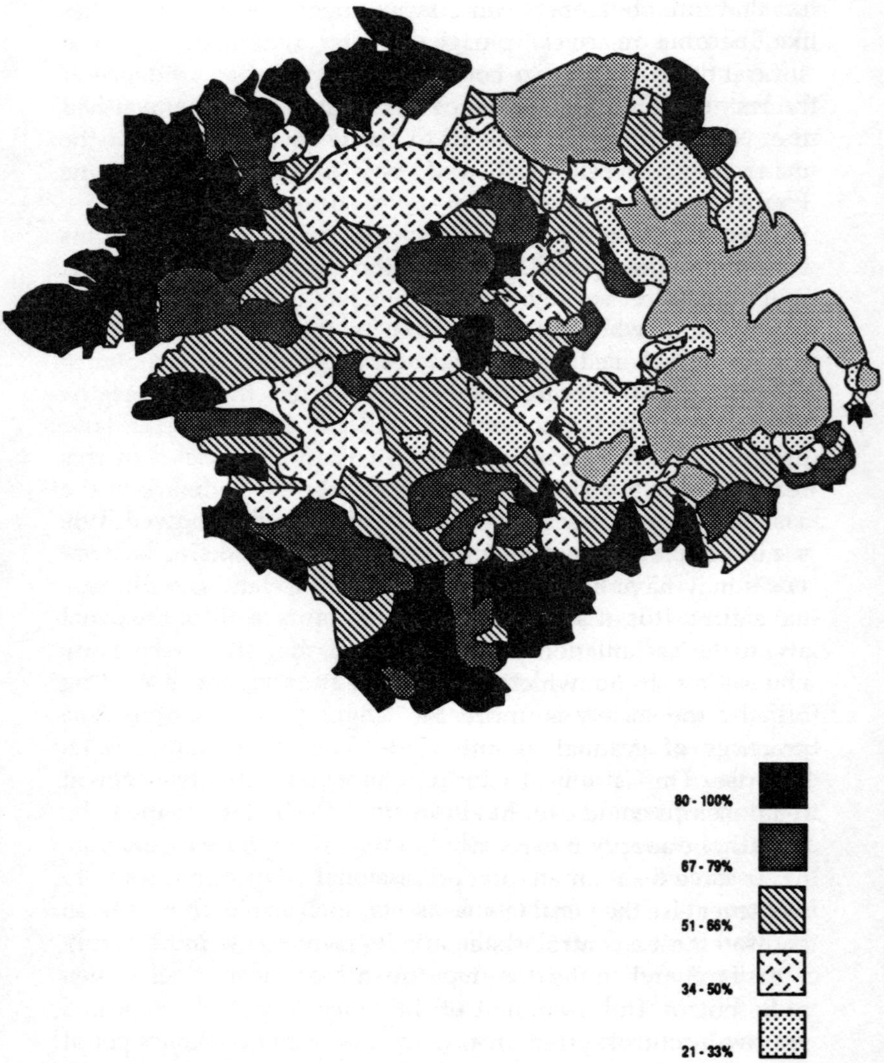

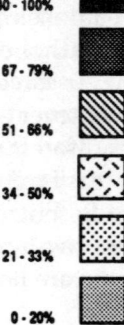

80 - 100%
67 - 79%
51 - 66%
34 - 50%
21 - 33%
0 - 20%

indicates into which cracks in the system Catholics who had managed to accumulate anything were finding their way.[34]

There is a tendency to imagine that as the penal laws fell into disuse, it was no longer accurate to talk of denominational subsocieties. There are some seeking to locate the origins of renewed sectarian division in the 1830s, who imply that before that time relations between different religious denominations had become relatively pluralistic.[35] In defence of this view several types of evidence could be given. First, in the early 19th century there is ample evidence that schools were very mixed in the North.[36] Second, the linen industry was eroding the differences between Irish (Catholic), Scottish (Presbyterian) and English (Anglican) cultures.[37] Third, there is clear evidence of widespread Protestant initiative in the relaxation of the penal laws before their repeal.[38] But we should not infer from this that religion had ceased to be important. We saw earlier how there were periods when elite concern with sustaining the settlement presence slackened because native society appeared powerless for any purpose "threatening" or otherwise. But I also showed how vulnerable the society was to polarization. Quite small groups may be able to disturb a process in which sectarian realities seem to be just fading away. This happens when ad hoc assimilation processes cross some kind of rubicon. As we shall see in Chapter 2, the trigger for the Armagh disturbances of the 1780s may have been landlords permitting Catholic tenants to have guns. It is at such a point that any slumbering hesitations about the assimilation process will articulate themselves and may set off a feud, which ends up affecting everyone. And just because the society is unprepared, having grown used to the practices of gradual assimilation, hidden forces take it by surprise. This is why it is idealistic to imagine that sectarian relationships could ever have just withered away.

Catholic adaption to formal equality, however it came, could never have been an adaptation of a legion of individuals. For whatever else the penal law was intended to achieve, it was first and foremost a control system. The removal of control systems is easy only when the dominant society can control the process of decontrol. This seeming paradox means that the initiative to remove a control system from a victim group is taken by people who are not part of it. The Irish Volunteers' part in the repeal of the penal laws up to 1782 was something like this. The whole process is conceived as doing justice to a victim, though it is not the victim who defines what justice is. Victims do not define; they are expected to be grateful. When the victim cannot be made to accept others' definition of his suffering and can organize himself, the process of readjustment becomes much more painful for the dominant group which is controlling him before. Arguably it becomes more and more difficult to remove the control the longer it is left, because the sufferer toughens his expectations to reflect his experience of disappointment.

There are always risks attached to removing any social control mechanism, because the forces unleashed by its removal cannot be clearly anticipated. The tendency in any society where this is being done is to attempt to take precautions to minimize those risks. The importance of Wolfe Tone's writing is that he addresses himself at length to this problem.[39] Precisely because he himself was not prepared to hide behind the control system that had secured Catholic subordination, what is significant is the nature of his argument to others about why they should not do so either. We set Tone up as the hidden current of much that follows. We shall see that the more powerful Catholic Ireland becomes during our period, the more difficult it becomes to follow Tone's prescriptions. The compact which Tone dreamed of making with the Catholics in the 1790s would have included more and more non-negotiable items as the next century progressed. And, most important, by the 1830s the Catholics had experienced success of their own despite very widespread Protestant opposition.

In Chapter 3 we shall see how the first major moves towards equality for northern Catholics were inaugurated by central government in spite of opposition from dominant powers in the North. Central government intervention in law and order and education came about because of the new power of pan-Catholicism in the rest of the island. That is why by the 1830s pan-Catholicism already had a substantial basis in the North which was no mere matter of sentiment. After the crushing of the 1798 Rebellion and the Act of Union, local order in the frontier districts of Ulster was often kept by local magistrates using the Orangemen and yeomen as patrolmen of Catholic areas. The introduction of a centralized police and magistracy produced a considerable improvement in the security of northern Catholics. Likewise the Second Reformation, a drive to thwart Catholic emancipation and to intensify efforts to convert Catholics to Protestantism, alerted Catholics to the need for an education system free of conversionist intent. The national education system was a particular advantage to Catholics in the North. Conservatives in Ulster attempted to resist the Whig government's effort to centralize police and judicial functions and free them of dependence upon local forces; and they opposed the spread of the national education system. The vital point for northern Catholic experience was that the two major advances toward practical equality—a reduction in the partiality of the magisterial and police system, and access to education free of conversionist intent—were inaugurated from outside the province in opposition to the dominant political forces within it. The advance of northern Catholic society depended on pan-Catholicism in the rest of the island. At the same time we shall see how local clerical leadership was necessary to make use of these Whig reforms.

Even if the lesson of pan-Catholicism for Catholics was to trust to the strength of Catholic Ireland as a whole, there was a very substantial body of Protestants in the North who supported the Whigs' reforms of the 1830s. In Belfast the Whigs had some power which they did not generally have elsewhere. Their economic interests were built around industrial Belfast, which grew rapidly in the years after the Union and contrasted sharply with the underdevelopment of the greater part of Ireland. Pan-Protestant and pan-Catholic politics were mutually reinforcing; and between the two the space for the Whigs was shrinking. Ultimately, the credibility of the northern Whigs' position depended upon whether Whig governments could create a framework in which people felt safer about abandoning sectarian "pan" politics.

We have seen that this society was very vulnerable to polarization and that it is therefore unrealistic to expect any major transformation of it to occur by stealth. Although the northern Protestant Liberals were not always aware of it, the limits to polarizing tendencies often depended upon Catholic clerical leadership preventing response to pan-Protestant actions. This in its turn depended upon how actively the central government law and order apparatus intervened in sectarian confrontations. We have seen how in the circumstance of polarization, each society is liable to be represented by its most aggressive tendencies. Settler ideology, which expresses those most aggressive tendencies, has everywhere the same function to emphasise the danger posed by the native. In this society settler fear and distrust has always been expressed in Protestant theological attacks upon Catholicism. Throughout this story we shall come across Protestant religious leaders, such as Drew, Hanna, Johnston, and Kane, whose message was that Catholic self-organization is an ontological threat to Protestants.[40] In this particular situation we shall see how Protestant theological ideas are progressively deformed as they are torn from their traditional place. Where they had once been about the relationship of the believer to God, their transformation into settlement ideology depends upon them becoming a preoccupation with the sins, ignorance, unsavable nature etc. of the papists and popery. Religious concepts were used to affirm ideas about relationships between Protestants and Catholics which were basically typical of colonial situations: (i) the continuous and total enmity of Catholics and Catholicism to Protestants and Protestantism; (ii) the unity of purpose of all political manifestations of all forms of Catholic self-organization, outward appearances notwithstanding; (iii) the justification of the Protestant society in Ireland as an absolute; (iv) the need for pan-Protestant solidarity to counter Catholic self-organization; and (v) the affirmation of the timeless and inevitable continuity of the conflict between Protestant and Catholic.

I have developed the central themes sketched out in this introduction around the narrative of political life in Ulster between the collapse of O'Connell's challenge to Peel in 1843 and the Home Rule Bill of 1886. After 1830 the balance of powers within Ireland shifts drastically. From then onwards no northern Protestant could think about the future of Ireland without first thinking of O'Connell's movement. The primary axis in Irish politics was then between the British government and the leadership of Irish Catholic society. The pan-Catholic organization throughout the whole island also strengthened the northern Catholics, who became less and less like victims as they laid the infrastructure of their own subsociety. The less like victims they became, the greater became the difficulties with which northern liberalism had to deal, because now Catholics began to define law and order and education issues in their own way. This period is a lot less romantic than the United Irish period, because it was only after O'Connell's rise that Protestant society had to face the full consequences of the penal era. Catholic distrust and suspicion of things British and Protestant may have seemed unreasonable to many Protestants, as the education controversies suggest; but given the penal experience, they were very understandable.

The reason for starting around 1843 is that after O'Connell's setback and the move of Peel away from the traditional Conservative hostility towards Catholicism in Ireland, there seemed to be new spaces opening up politically. The Famine and the story of the Tenant League of the North and South are a good point to start the narrative of the democratization process. Most of the story is about the trials and tribulations of the various kinds of Liberalism. They are of hopeful beginnings and eventual disappointments. To span the sectarian division all political co-operation had to begin by finding an immediate community of interest. Often these lasted for a time, but without creating a tradition or an accepted way of operating together. In only one instance did Liberalism manage to redefine a situation that seemed already to be defined by contending sectarian forces. That was in 1880–81 when it reshaped the impending confrontation during the Land War. For me the importance of these episodes is to look at occasions in the past when people of the two traditions have worked and hoped together.

It was not only Liberalism which offered new possibilities. For a while it was not clear what might become of the Independent Orange movement. This sprang to life in 1868 with the election of William Johnston of Ballykilbeg as MP for Belfast. For a while it seemed a possible vehicle for working-class organization in politics. Even if it can be argued that in the end this was an unlikely road to less sectarian politics, it seemed hopeful to many at the time. Exploring how and why it seemed to be so will help to show something of the constraints within which politics was being conducted. The collapse of these hopes after the 1872 riots will also help us to understand why the preservation of "peace" in Belfast eventually led people to accept elite leadership and to lose faith in popular political organization.

Once Nationalism and Orangeism confronted each other directly on the ground during the nationalist "Invasion of Ulster" from 1883, both camps were aiming to demonstrate territorial supremacy. The leadership of the Conservative bloc shifted away from the industrial and commercial business elite towards those landlords who had taken the lead in the Orange counter-demonstration movement. And at their shoulders loomed more militant Protestant activists of the kind who had previously been kept on the margins by the Conservative leadership. It is a tragedy of this society that men such as Hanna have ended up as statues. So I conclude this introduction with a dedication to George McMullan about whom a little will be said in Chapter 9.

2. The Decay of the Colonial Settlement Structure

In the last three decades before the Act of Union in 1801, the decay of the colonial settlement structure proceeded rapidly. What happened in north Armagh, and came to a climax in the expulsion of Catholics after the formation of the Orange Order, established the pattern of the sectarian polarizing process. What happened in the solidly Presbyterian districts in mid-Antrim and north-east Down, where the United Irish rising took place in the North, showed how Protestants and Catholics could unite politically at a time when the opportunities for this were greatest.

The United Irishmen were unique in many ways. But to let them illuminate the much less exciting later period of Ulster history or to learn anything from them today, we have to shed our preoccupation with what made them unique. If we confine ourselves to the obvious differences between the United Irishmen and the Orangemen, then the United Irishmen will remain unique and separated from everything that came after them. They opposed British power in alliance with Catholics, while the Orangemen upheld British power against Catholics. Throughout the 19th century nearly all classes of northern Protestants who articulated any political opinion supported the Union with Britain in some way or other, while Catholic Ireland, including the northern Catholics, came to support some kind of nationalism. But this, on its own, does not mean that the Orange tradition eclipsed the United Irish tradition. I want to identify these two traditions as two ways in which Protestants related to Catholics, rather than as two opposed sets of positions on the question of the Union with Britain.

If we look upon the United Irishmen as part of a succession of Irish separatists, a great deal of intellectual and emotional energy can be expended in showing that they were not really like later separatists. In this kind of rivalry it is even possible to construct a view that makes the United Irishmen, rather than the early Orangemen, the forefathers of the Union with Britain. Thus Archibald Hamilton Rowan, the United Irish leader in 1799, said that he saw in the Union "the downfall of one of the most corrupt assemblies, I believe, ever existed".[1] This was at a time when the Orange Order was the most active opponent of the Union and when the yeomen considered withdrawing their services if it passed.[2] Disputing which future constitutional option is the proper heir of the United Irish tradition will tend to drive out the fundamental point which is about the different ways of approaching relationships between Protestant and Catholic. That was once what distinguished Orangeism from the United Irishmen.

First, let us pinpoint what aspect of colonial development the 1770–1800 period in Ireland corresponds to in the wider picture. In the last chapter I showed that once a colonial society seems to be stabilized and the native population quieted, solidarity amongst settlers decays. But this decay process does not necessarily promote any settler-native solidarity. Commonly it generates a paternalistic relationship between sections of the ruling classes and the natives. But when it does that it generates displacement effects, and can be expected to provoke plebeian settler opposition to the natives and to the landlords (or employer classes) at the same time. So, although the withering away of the penal law regime might seem to have heralded a better state of settler-native relationships, it was never a probability that it would wither away without a major crisis. In any situation like this some plebeian settlers regard the decontrol process as something motivated by the self-interest of upper-class settlers. They themselves sense that they must lose from this. When they challenge the decontrol process, they force the ruling groups either to take even more unambiguous steps towards removing the control system; or else to retreat and to refurbish some aspects of their coercive relationship with the natives. The instability and the polarizing possibility arise from the reaction of the natives to this. The moment the natives show signs of organizing themselves, in other words, not remaining within the bounds of the paternalistic relationship with the ruling groups, all the comfortable assumptions about how the withering away process has been working are threatened. In short, the plebeian settler challenge puts a stop to the withering away process and makes everything explicit, including its risks. The dominant classes at this point are in danger of losing control over native and plebeian settler alike. Unless there is some structure they can lean upon to bolster their control from outside their immediate situation, they are nearly sure to restore control by working out a new relationship with the plebeian settlers. All moves at this stage are fraught with hazard, but this is the least hazardous for them and for most settlers within the zone in which the polarization is occurring. Settler anxiety to reimpose some kind of control, and natives' resentment of the renewed effort to control them, feed each other and become polarizing. The core of the polarization process is that the settlers' fear of the natives makes them unwilling, afraid or powerless to restrain the worst things done by militant settlers in their name. When this happens, all structure, legality and so on is thrown to the winds. There is a strong prospect of cyclical violence growing. Then, more or less whatever the mass of settlers may think or do has little effect upon the shape of the overall polarization. Something like this happened in County Armagh in the 1790s.

How do alternative responses to the withering of the control system cut across this polarizing process? The polarization we have just outlined tends to spread. What stops it? For settlers not to be caught up in the polarization, they need to be free of the fear of it. This is only partly a question of choice. It is more a question of having the necessary space. Obviously they must not see themselves as locked in a struggle for space, with natives threatening to displace them; they must not fear the natives' reaction against other settlers' aggression towards them; and they must not feel at risk from the native anger; and if all these conditions are fulfilled, they have some space in which to break the polarizing process. They need both some distance from the polarizing process and some empathy with the situation of the native, even though they themselves have not shared the natives' experience. The United Irishmen, taken as a whole, had elements of both. The mass of the United Irishmen were some distance from the polarizing process. When eventually Orange violence came to their districts, they were also the target of it; so they also had reasons of their own for opposing the control system, because they were then on the receiving end of it. A considerable part, including their leadership, also empathized with the native Catholic experience which they did not directly share themselves. In this sense at least 1798 was not two separate and accidentally related risings.

In a settlement society where the barriers of fear and distrust remain alive and are hidden only by consideration or politeness, there are few ways in which settler-native solidarity is generated automatically. The patterns of life experience are different even for people in the same workplace. The solidarity that is worth anything, and overcomes fears, requires each to empathize at least a little with the other's experience. It is for me particularly notable that some of the United Irish leaders involved themselves in giving legal assistance to Catholics being harassed in north Armagh, before they became committed to the insurrection and before the same treatment was meted out to the United Irish districts.[3] There was enough space so that the Presbyterians of mid-Antrim were not drawn into the polarization in the way that Presbyterian minorities in mid-Armagh almost certainly were. But there was also enough awareness of what the Armagh Catholics were experiencing so that mid-Antrim Presbyterian sympathy went further than merely having the same enemy for the moment. Everything in a settlement society that tends to break up the legacy of fear and antagonism depends upon these kinds of developments. In no society is empathy a normal or routine thing. In settlement societies gulfs of experience remain between native and settler. The native society, as it grows stronger and faces disappointments, gradually learns to trust primarily its own resources and not allies within the settler community. And as the native society becomes more and more self-organized and able to define what it means by ending control over it, the less easily can empathetic settlers join with them, except as isolated individuals. The story of the United Irishmen brings out possibilities which existed once and then reappeared only in more diminished forms. In later years the kinds of hopes held out by Tone of working out a compact grew more and more unrealizable. But the "small print" of the "Argument on behalf of the Catholics" runs like a thread through our history until the polarization engulfs the whole relationship between Britain, unionism and nationalism in the 1880s.

During the ten years before the Act of Union, the Anglican landlord class was obliged to accept that its security depended upon British military might. Britain was therefore able to impose upon it the Act of Union which abolished the separate legislature of Ireland.[4] The major changes that led up to this had begun with the rise of the Irish Volunteers in the late 1770s. The Volunteers were a popular Protestant movement intent upon securing a voice in the governing of Ireland; they were stronger in Ulster than elsewhere because that was where the Protestant middle classes were strongest. They were encouraged by the American revolt in which many of their emigrant families participated; this also had the further effect of reducing the British garrison in Ireland and provided them with the pretext to "defend" Ireland against French invasions. They were initially encouraged by a section of the northern landlords in order to strengthen their hand in bargaining with England for greater autonomy for the Irish parliament. But after this was secured in 1782–83, the movement's demands for parliamentary reform were obstructed by the combined power of the landlords and the English government. Because they did not link their demand for reform with any demand for the inclusion of Catholics within it, they could not call upon any Catholic support and so their challenge failed.[5] The decision not to support the Catholic claims was not unanimous and in fact there were parts of the North where the Volunteers not only supported them, but enrolled Catholic members. As they disintegrated as a national movement, their successors evolved in very different ways in different parts of the North. Both the Orange Order and the United Irishmen grew out of the twilight years of the Volunteers.

The Volunteers' mobilization in 1777–78 was not the first popular movement whose appearance threatened existing patterns of authority. But the previous ones had made no serious political pretences and did not contain socially prestigious strata. What is significant about the Volunteers is that they were the armed might of the northern Protestant middle classes, and even if they were under landlord leadership, the relationship was clearly two-way. The growth of transatlantic markets and the removal of 1759 English restrictions on exports of provisions had encouraged a transition from tillage to grazing. The Oak Boys and the Hearts of Steel had appeared in opposition to different manifestations of intensified commercialization.[6] The former had attempted to stop the exaction of unpaid labour from tillage farmers in central Ulster, and to reduce the county cess (the tax imposed by the landlord-dominated grand jury for road construction). And the latter had appeared in south Antrim to oppose the efforts of landlords to impose large charges for the renewal of leases, a development which led to the granting of new leases to Belfast merchants and "even some Papists" who would pay them. Both movements appealed to the powers that be to hear their grievances and attempted to reassure them that they had no anti-government or Jacobite objectives. The then Lord Lieutenant Townshend was actually sympathetic and saw the landlords as the guilty party, but was obliged to respond to landlord calls for vigorous prosecution after the Hearts of Steel liberated two cattle houghers from the Belfast barracks in 1772.[7] The incident reveals how little weight landlords then attached to Protestant demands for recognition of mutual obligation. The years that followed saw the peak of migration from Ulster.[8] The upward pressure on rents at a time of high food prices and a slump in the linen industry created a mass exodus to America on the eve of the War of Independence. The Hearts of Oak and Steel had opposed the consequences of the switch from tillage to livestock, but the main precipitant of the Volunteer mobilization was the English embargo on exports of provisions which it was supposed would adversely affect livestock farmers and cattle merchants.[9] The presence in the Volunteer leadership of figures who had called loudly for the suppression of the Hearts of Steel lends strength to the supposition that the landlord leadership saw them not merely as a political asset but also as a means of bolstering their local control.[10] The price the landlords had to pay for this was to make some concessions to the rather democratic flavour of the Volunteer command structure.[11] It is reasonable to presume that the landlords became in some degree dependent on the Volunteers to maintain order against more plebeian disorder, and that they filled a role which did not just vanish when the Volunteer movement went into decline nationally after 1784.

What had changed the North so much in the later part of the 18th century was the rise of the domestic linen industry. It was this transformation to which landlords' traditional methods of keeping social control were unequal. It created both a substantial middle class and a mass of weavers. The domestic production of brown (unbleached) linen by smallholders— taking the process from flax cultivation and preparation, through spinning to the weaving of linen cloth—maximized the quantity of productive labour time that could be employed by the family of a smallholder on a limited acreage of land.[12] From the standpoint of the landlords, it was a source of vastly increased rentable capacity. It was also one of the few areas of productive activity that was not subject to periodic commercial restrictions by English power. At its high point in 1810, the linen industry was diffused throughout most areas of Ulster and beyond.[13] In some areas such as north Armagh it virtually displaced tillage farming altogether, while in others where relatively large-scale farming remained, as in much of County Antrim, weaving became a counter-seasonal supplement to agricultural labourer earnings. Depending upon distances from brown linen markets, labourers might sell their webs directly or be organized as employees of "farmers" who became small-scale manufacturers. The closer one approached the centres of the linen districts, the more thoroughly was farming, properly speaking, eradicated. The total monetarization of journeymen weaver incomes expressed both a degree of freedom and a source of insecurity—high wages in periods of high demand, punctuated by periods of unemployment. It was upon this section of the population that the displacement effect might work in its most volatile and subjective ways: they were the people who were least susceptible to control by landowners on account of the very looseness of their connection with the land.

Peter Gibbon has argued that the reasons for the appearance of the United Irish movement in Antrim and Down, and of the Orange Order in County Armagh, can be found in the class structure of each area.[14] I believe that this approach ignores far more obvious differences between the two areas which have to do with their sectarian composition. The importance of the weaving centres is that their existence explains why there were new problems of social control. Since I wrote this work first, David Miller has published his article, "The Armagh Troubles 1784–1795".[15] In that article he argues that efforts to explain these troubles have not so far taken sufficiently seriously the need to explain the breakdown of authority that occurred at this time. And after exploring three contemporary accounts which implied "breakdown" theses, he concludes that the troubles are seen to begin "with events leading up to the first occasion on which the observer found them impinging on his own life". His focal point is how the landlords (and others) found that the traditional ways in which they had kept control had broken down. Significantly his approach would also fit the United Irish experience. Jeremy Hope, the weaver leader of the Templepatrick United Irishmen, lamented the growth of speculative activity and his ideas were restorationist. He was originally a United man only to further the programme of the Volunteers. For him and indeed for Henry Munro, the Lisburn draper and master of a Freemason lodge, the decisive shift towards insurrection was caused by witnessing the law being set at nought by yeomen terrorism against their neighbours.[16] Hope would have preferred to settle for small-scale self-defensive action against Orangemen and yeomen. These United men most surely experienced a "breakdown" of social order in the shape of a lawless law. It will be clear from what I have said so far about deterrence relationships, that there are always volcanic possibilities lurking within them. Most crises will therefore be explicable in terms of the breakdown in the balance of deterrence, and most observers will first notice it when their fears are engaged; and that depends upon whom they have most reason to fear.

In dealing with the 1790s, there are some fundamentals which seem to me to stand out above all details. The first point, which can be seen very easily from the maps of Presbyterian and Catholic populations, is that the 1798 Rebellion had its two epicentres in the areas where the Presbyterian population was over 75 per cent of the total. (I shall call these areas Presbyteria from now on.) By contrast, the area where Orangeism began was both heavily Anglican and contained a large Catholic population. When we remember that in the period before the railroads a fifteen mile return journey took a day, these differences between the two types of district were very real.[17] What happened in one might not have much effect on another. This kind of distance would eventually be eroded by easier transport. But in the 1790s the polarizing effect of the conflict in Armagh upon events in Presbyteria was indirect.

The second kind of difference between the experience of the two districts had to do with the looseness of the central government's presence. It was no quirk which made the United Irishmen in County Antrim decide to capture Antrim on the day the grand jury was meeting. To do so would have been to capture a big part of the "government" of the time and place.[18] In mid-Antrim the ruling class was Anglican and just about everyone else was Presbyterian; the penal law was experienced as an anti-Presbyterian device. A revolt in County Antrim at this time had no horizon beyond the county. The more real central government eventually became, the more questions about government became bound up with the relationship between one region and another, and with the relationships of the people of different regions.

Gibbon sees farmers and weavers in Antrim respecting each other's spaces, being able to co-operate and so on. It is curious that a Marxist should find this a more fertile ground for solidarity than the situation in Armagh, where he describes the proletarianized weavers as "homogenized".[19] To make this explanation seem valid he clearly cannot have the weavers in mid-Antrim outbidding farmers for their holdings, although it is far from clear why they would not be doing that. In fact, in his effort to construct a picture of the two localities in terms of the different farmer-weaver relationships, he has to smuggle the obvious argument through the back door.[20] It does indeed become clear how a farmer and a weaver in Ballyclare could accept each other and be in solidarity with each other if both were Presbyterians, using the reading club together, sharing a common dislike of the Anglican squire and the grand jury.[21]

I shall now look at the two areas separately. County Armagh contained within itself (indeed, into a much later period) enormous regional variations. The flat northern part of the county was the centre of the linen industry and, in particular, the seat of the fine linen (cambric and damask) productions. Further south, below Armagh city and Markethill, the land rises into mountains, beyond which it falls away towards Crossmaglen and Forkhill. The northern part of the county is heavily populated with Anglicans; its minority were Catholics. In fact the only other parts of Ireland with equally high Anglican populations are the adjacent areas of south-west Antrim, around towards Glenavy and Derriaghy—which are an extension of north Armagh in most respects—and County Fermanagh to which weaving had not spread in this period, and never did very much. In a couple of parishes around the shore of Lough Neagh there were Catholic majority areas. These existed in the marshy areas around the whole of Lough Neagh, where natives had taken refuge during the Plantations. There were very few Presbyterians. In the middle of the county, from Armagh southwards, the Presbyterians were far more numerous. The most Protestant parish in County Armagh was Mullabrack (Markethill) which contained roughly equal numbers of Anglicans and Presbyterians. Finally, into and beyond the mountains, the Catholics became more numerous, until the solidly Catholic parishes of Creggan (Crossmaglen), Forkhill and Jonesborough. In this period the linen industry had spread through most of the county, excluding these southern, very Gaelic parishes.

Armagh city with a Catholic population of about 40 per cent of the total in 1770, was very much a "Protestant" place.[22] The Catholics were disproportionately concentrated in the servant and labourer strata. And perhaps reflecting the impact of the penal laws in earlier times in such places, the Roman Catholic primate did not reside there. Yet Catholic merchants there were, and it appears that the Volunteer company had enrolled some of them,[23] suggesting that the Armagh section had favoured linking Catholic emancipation with parliamentary reform, and that the penal laws were rather loosely enforced in that district. It is a reasonable conjecture that, as the middle classes of this district had a very large Anglican element (unaffected by the penal laws) the Volunteers were an easier ally for the landlords than they were in County Antrim. A publican who wrote a pamphlet about the sectarian disturbances in the area between

1786 and 1791 opens his story by speaking of weavers who were in the habit of gathering in large groups for entertainment (contests, fights, etc.) and who had access to considerable quantities of cash "before they knew its real value". Such groups were not assembled for any political reason, and disputes and conflicts that arose out of their activities could be resolved by the intervention of people like Byrne, the publican. What moved him to write was the outbreak of a new species of disturbance that defied the existing social control.

By 1783, the penal economic disabilities had been largely repealed. There remained, however, prohibitions on Catholic voting and arms-bearing, together with certain restrictions on religious organization (notably of religious orders), and teaching. Questions of religious moment appear to have crept into the activities of the "Fleets", as the weaver groups were called in 1784, but they took a decisive turn when the leader of one such body delivered the following speech to his assembled men in 1785. "There are many Papists in the place where [his informant] lives, who have taken the oath of allegiance, having got long leases, and of course they must have arms to shoot the sparrows from their grain. And even the perfidious Volunteers have taken them into their ranks." At that time it does not seem as though the law permitted Catholics to have weapons at all, but it does appear that landlords in this area had permitted them to do so, subject to their taking the oath. At all events, this particular "fleet", which had been engaged in "secular" looting on previous occasions, now turned its attention to Catholics in particular.

The period was one in which the linen industry was undergoing rapid expansion. Exports climbed from 15 million yards in 1781 to 26 million in 1785 and 45 million in 1792.[24] Weaving was rapidly expanding in this period, so that the destruction of looms which was associated with the seizure of arms cannot be supposed to have been on account of Protestant weavers experiencing depressing effects of Catholic competition. At this point Catholics were becoming more involved, as weaving spread out from its original location and perhaps as more weavers moved into the central zone. It is probable that the new relationships between landlords and Catholic weaver-tenants, and between the established middle class and some aspirant Catholic members, were seen by some of these weavers as a betrayal. Once they raised the issue, in whatever way, it became an explicit test of how far assimilation had gone.

Initially the response of the Volunteers, the landlords and the Armagh traders was to oppose the Protestant Peep O'Day Boys' activities. When an effort was made to stir up a "No Popery" sentiment in Armagh at the time of the first Catholic High Mass, "a great treat in this county", it had little reverberation. The inhabitants of the city were horrified by Peep O'Day attacks on prominent Catholic members of the Volunteers, while that body vowed to protect Catholics, and some landlords provided weapons to Catholics for self-protection. But the Peep O'Day activities were sufficiently effective to encourage some of Lord Charlemont's tenants to give up their leases and leave the district; and the light sentences received by some Peep O'Day Boys followed by acquittals of others encouraged the Catholics to organize for self-defence. The lines were by no means precisely drawn, and some rural Protestants joined the Defenders "For any Protestant who seemed averse to their [Peep O'Day] actions at this period, was looked upon as a little better than a Papist." But they became more sharply drawn when the hitherto mixed "Bawnfleet" displaced its Catholic leader and elected an ex-Oakboy as its leader. He turned it into a Peep O'Day unit.

To begin with, it was clear to the Protestant middle class that the Catholics were victims. But when they began to organize themselves, they organized a boycott of traders they considered to be Peep O'Day sympathizers. This did not go down well in Armagh city. The paternalistic relationship began to crack. Byrne said of the boycott that it was the worst sort of revenge to take, "by turning their best friends against them, they have got both the rich and the poor for their enemies". In 1788 he reports the growing prevalence of the sentiment: "we'll deal with none but our own sort", and reflecting the growing sectarian self-organization, the habit of talking of rioters as "Scotch" and "Irish", and the circulation of rumours of massacres. The growing scale of Catholic self-organization was shown in the 1788 march of the Defenders through Charlemont, close to the small and solidly Catholic pocket of Blackwatertown. This triumphalism alarmed the elite, who decided they now had to do something. Lord Charlemont and the grand jury passed a resolution against all assemblies of papists with arms and against all who tried to disarm them. In the eyes of the ruling powers the idea was to separate out the part of the Peep O'Day Boys that could be disciplined and used to refurbish the semi-defunct Volunteers. The new Volunteers would then be used to put down the Defenders and the residual Peep O'Day Boys. Later that year, for the first time, some Peep O'Day were convicted in the courts, but the Defenders saw the raising of the new companies as "a sure omen of their own destruction". They were "panic stricken with hearing the roll call drum in adjacent villages". Sure enough the battle of Drumbee in November 1788 between the inhabitants of a Catholic townland and a company of new Volunteers who passed through it drew new lines of conflict between the forces of local order and the Catholics.

It will be clear that this new antagonism grew up at precisely the time when the cultural differences between the Protestants and Catholics were being eroded. William Grieg's report on the Gosford estate in mid-Armagh, where weaving was widely diffused, states that nowhere else that he knew were the differences between the Scottish and English on the one hand, and the native Irish on the other, so few.[25] Wherever the linen trade penetrated, it brought with it the English language of the market and began the undermining of Irish in the previously remoter Catholic market. It was the fact that Catholics were seeking assimilation which triggered the crisis. To begin with, their political methods were very modern and constitutional. Mountains and marshland (such as the Mointaghs and Clonoe parishes), to which Catholics had been earlier displaced, were economically marginal in a farming context, but became less so in the era of the linen industry. In 1789, some sixty Catholics came to Armagh from the Mointaghs to swear the oath of allegiance. But the Armagh court criers demanded of them 4s. 4d. per man, so they returned with their mission to be included as citizens thwarted by the local apparatus of the state which had provided a formal mechanism for their assimilation.

After 1789 clashes between Defenders and Volunteers became increasingly common sequels to clashes between Peep O'Day and Defenders, and after one such, Byrne was moved to comment: "I am sorry to have to say it that a few of the townspeople [of Armagh] on that occasion forfeited their character of neutrality, that they are so famed for." The Defenders' strategy of attempting to surround and besiege Peep O'Day assailants until magistrates arrived all too commonly turned to shoot-outs, after which Defenders as well as Peep O'Days would be arrested. At the assizes, he said, "The oath of a papist was looked on no more than a fly blow." Landlords' and urban dwellers' sympathy for the Catholics appears to have declined. The problem, seen from where they stood, turned from being a question of Catholics experiencing persecution from Peep O'Day Boys into one of Catholic organizations going about with guns and causing trouble for the legal Volunteers and the magistrates. Unlike the Catholics they were not so mindful of the fact that the early Peep O'Days and the new Volunteers had overlapping membership. To the Catholics it was a source of fear and alarm. If Protestants had been asked to explain why they found the existence of the Defenders disturbing, they might have found many fears to give utterance to; but in 1791 an incident occurred which was to give them substance and by which this period has been remembered.

In 1791 Peep O'Day activity spread southwards. An attack on the parish priest of Forkhill was followed by an outrage which is rarely omitted from any account of the period. In this largely Catholic and Gaelic area, more or less untouched by the linen industry, the relationship between language, religion and class was much sharper than it was in the core of the province. The will of a Protestant landlord made provision for Anglican children at the age of 25 to be given £5, a loom, and "a small holding in preference to other tenants who may offer". A schoolmaster who, it was said, refused to teach Catholic children prayers in Irish as his predecessor had done, was tortured and had his tongue cut out. This was alleged to be a reprisal for the "banishing of Papists from the lands of Mr. Jackson [a reference to the will]", the exclusion of the favoured schoolmaster, the attack on the Forkhill parish priest and the executions in 1790 of some Defender leaders. That the outrage "revived fears of a 1641 massacre" is scarcely surprising. It occurred in an area where settlement realities were reproduced in their more or less racial integrity and was a clear manifestation of enmity towards anything Saxon or Protestant. This was Catholic self-organization taken to the conclusions anticipated in fearful Protestant expectations.

What had happened in Armagh demonstrated a pattern. First, plebeian Protestant action against Catholics had not been sufficiently effectively curbed to avoid Catholic disenchantment with the law. Second, the Catholic self-organization appeared and defined the problem its own way. It made its own efforts to discourage Peep O'Day activity against themselves (boycotting, surrounding and besieging of aggressors, triumphal procession). Third, the secondary response of the local elite was to exert control along the line of least resistance, by co-opting the disciplinable sections of the Peep O'Day Boys into a new Volunteer corps and preventing Catholic assembly with arms. And this was against a background in which conviction of Protestants by Protestant juries became difficult, local petty officials interfered with the practical implementation of the post-penal law, and confrontation increasingly became Volunteers versus Catholics. When Peep O'Day activity spread southwards into the area where "Protestant" and "Catholic" corresponded to sharply visible distinctions of race and class, the Forkhill outrage took on "1641" characteristics—a conflict of races. At each turn the question moved one step further from a matter of doing justice to those in "victim status". It became increasingly one of having to choose between Catholic self-organization, with all that entailed, and defending the current balance by relying on the very forces within the Protestant community which provoked Catholic anger in the first place.

The all too obvious trigger for the disturbances was the quantum jump in status accorded to Catholics by permitting them to hold weapons. A society that lives in fear of native self-organization does not arm natives. To do so is to say, by a symbolic action, something very definite about the redundancy of "Protestant interdependence" as an organizing principle. One then might argue that "ultimately" the plebeian Protestant counteraction was really concerned with defending their own economic interests. If so, then what is interesting is that so long as the issue was seen in this limited way, the plebeian wreckers could not enlist much Protestant middle-class sympathy for their cause. To get Protestants as a whole united, it was necessary for the issues to stop being particular ones. It was necessary for Protestants in general to start seeing Catholic self-organization as a threat. Then the abstract rights of Catholics were submerged under the consideration: what kind of social forces would be unleashed by Defenders who had fought their way to victory over the opposition of the Orangemen? The Freemasons, who in this period often represented the same political tendencies as the Volunteers, had this to say of developments in Aughnacloy, Co. Tyrone, near the Armagh border, in 1795: "We have with regret for a considerable time past beheld the internal peace of this kingdom greatly annoyed, the lives and properties of His Majesty's subjects destroyed by a bunch of fanatics who call themselves 'Defenders' and we are sorry that it has spread even to this neighbourhood."[26] They resolved to help the magistrates put down all unlawful combinations. The Defenders had become a straightforward threat. Their origins in conflicts with the Peep O'Day Boys—who were about to become Orangemen, and shortly to become yeomen defending society against the Defenders—had become ancient history to the Aughnacloy Freemasons. The renewed conflict in north Armagh in 1795, which led to the expulsion of many Catholics from the area and the establishment of Orangeism, spread the Defender organization into ever widening areas.[27] The incorporation of the Orangemen into the yeomanry in 1796 completed the circle. First local power, and then state power felt obliged to incorporate expulsionist forces into the forces of the law, which became more and more lawless.

The Volunteers of Antrim and north Down were overwhelmingly Presbyterians in solidly Presbyterian areas, for whom the penal laws were a device for upholding Anglican landlordism. Presbyterians were excluded from state offices, from certain professions, and from borough corporations. Presbyterians were not, however, subject to the general economic disabilities that weighed upon the Catholics. The linen trade in particular gave birth to a large middle class of bleachers and merchants, together with the Presbyterian clergy. In days when the Churches were responsible for many aspects of daily life, subsequently taken over by organs of civil

THE DECAY OF THE COLONIAL SETTLEMENT STRUCTURE 39

government, the main impact of the penal laws (the Test Act) for these districts was to throw into sharp relief the unrepresentative character of local governing institutions. The Presbyterian mass of the population was required, besides supporting their own ministers, to pay tithes to the Anglican clergy. The Presbyterian merchants and bleachers were debarred from the corporations of boroughs in their districts (such as Carrickfergus, Coleraine, Belfast, Bangor and Newtownards).[28] There was virtually a fully developed society, complete with all social classes, but technically excluded from political power.

Unlike the Catholics, they had votes in county elections (and in the borough of Carrickfergus) which meant that there was a substantial minority in the Irish parliament beholden to them. In the 1776 elections, shortly after the outbreak of the American War of Independence, challenges were mounted by small landlords, backed up by a mass revolt against territorial control. Popular candidates were pledged to independence of territorial influences and opposition to "the unconstitutional influences of Peers or the increasing power of the Crown". At a victory parade for the victorious candidates in Ballymena, 20,000 assembled. "All the leaders of the procession wore orange and blue cockades—the emblems of liberty in that day—and four hundred Freemasons formed the rere guard."[29] These county elections from 1776 to 1790 were real political contests of a kind that could not happen elsewhere. In 1780 the Test Act was repealed and, while this removed the specific barriers against Presbyterians, it served to show that the real mechanism of exclusion—such as the grand juries and the borough corporations—had to be directly reformed.

In these districts there was considerable continuity in the development of the Volunteers into the United Irishmen. If there was a major break it was not so much at the point where the United Irishmen were formed, as in 1793, when it became plain both that the government would not accept parliamentary reform and that it was intent upon treating reform pressures that persisted as a pro-French treason.[30] In 1790 it was possible for Lord Castlereagh to be the popular candidate in County Down on an advanced reform pledge, and until about 1793 many who joined the United Irishmen were hardly distinguishable from Whigs. The United Irishmen were seen as the logical development from the experience of the early 1780s. The Volunteer effort for parliamentary reform of 1783 had failed because it omitted the Catholics who, forming the vast mass of the population, secured it an indifferent reception. There could be no serious independence without reform that did not include them. All this is in the resolutions of the Belfast branch of the United Irishmen of 1791:

> "First, resolved, that the weight of English influence in the Government of this country is so great, as to require a cordial union among ALL THE PEOPLE OF IRELAND, to maintain that balance which is essential to the preservation of our liberties and the extension of our commerce.
>
> Second. That the sole constitutional mode by which this influence can be opposed, is by the complete and radical reform of the representation of the people in Parliament.
>
> Third. That no reform is practicable, efficacious or just, which shall not include Irishmen of every religious persuasion." [31]

Many might have retreated from the logic that the Catholics had to be included if there was to be a reform, but none of these sentiments were in themselves revolutionary, even though they were to become so. In the beginning the United Irishmen had very socially distinguished leaders, many of whom were on good social terms with their political adversaries.[32] So long as the plan of action was to proceed by normal political channels, a large all-class section of Presbyterian society might move together. Including the Catholics seemed possible on their terms, and anyway, there were very few Catholics indeed in Presbyteria.[33]

In 1793 Britain went to war with France. Pitt was concerned to conciliate pressures for relief of the Catholics, while at the same time suppressing all forms of popular agitation; hence the Catholic Relief Act and the Convention Act. The military riot in Belfast served notice that all sympathy for things French would be treated as subversion.[34] British policy wobbled somewhat in 1794–95 when it appeared that under the Viceroy, Lord Fitzwilliam, a final Catholic Relief Act would admit Catholics to the parliament and that the ultra-Protestant managers in the Castle administration would be sacked. But after Fitzwilliam resigned and Lord Clare's allies were restored to office, the policy of the government towards all kinds of reform pressures became more and more arbitrary and severe. We have already noted the circumstances of the birth of the Orange Order in County Armagh in 1795. In 1796 an Insurrection Act provided for Draconian powers which were used against both United Irish and Defender districts. The militia established by central government in 1793 was now supplemented by the yeomanry recruited by landlord-magistrates.[35]

The effects of these developments cast the United Irishmen in a very different light from the one in which they first appeared. It is notable how amongst the leaders of the United movement who stayed with the movement, a very strong concern developed with the need for French intervention. The reckoning seems to have been that with 20,000 French troops the outcome would be settled without much fight,[36] the horrors of war (and the dangerous side-shows that might take place within such a war) would be avoided, and possibly a large part of the dominant classes would have come to terms quickly. If this was the spirit of many of the leaders who seemed to stay with the plan for a rising, we can conjecture why many others abandoned it altogether and attempted to make their peace with the authorities. Did this indicate any movement away from the United Irish objectives on the part of those who either remained neutral or helped to put the rebellion down? The Rasharkin Freemasons in 1793 passed a resolution to form themselves into a Volunteer corps to assist the civil magistrates. And though they declared their attachment to the constitution "at the same time we wish for a fair and equal representation of all the people in Parliament, which would of course bring about the redress of all real grievances and which we hope to achieve by legal and constitutional means".[37] In the final analysis, just as in Armagh—although to a lesser degree and under less compelling immediate circumstances—sections of the Liberal middle class who favoured the constitutional demands of the United Irishmen supported the state in putting down a rebellion whose ostensible aims they may have supported, but whose wider implications they feared.

In the end a very big part of the insurrection seems to have been a response to the yeomanry terror which swept over suspect districts, using torture to extract denunciations. Henry Joy McCracken had once run a calico-printing works in Glenavy, which was affected by the growth of Orangeism. He gave an attorney's bond for expenses to prosecute an Armagh magistrate after the destruction of the houses of Catholics in Armagh. It was through this work that he made contact with the Defenders and persuaded some of them to abandon their Jacobitism in favour of the United Irishmen's post-1795 republicanism.[38]

It is often said that the Presbyterian rebels weren't very interested in the alliance with the Catholics. James Dickey, the Ballymena leader, is reported to have said before he was hanged, that if they had won they would then have had to take on the Catholics.[39] It was widely reported—indeed Protestants from the Newtownards district have told me about it in recent years—that Catholics left the battlefield on the eve of the encounter at Ballynahinch, declaring that the Presbyterians wanted to set up a Presbyterian state.[40] In fact Dr Maddyn said he had investigated it and found that it was not true.[41] But the interesting thing about these stories is that they create a picture of a United rising that really had very little to do with the Catholics, and which was anyway seen as a mistake later. These kinds of stories do have their legitimate purpose. They dispose of the romantic rubbish about how the 1798 Republicans were 1916 rebels a little over a hundred years before their time; and how the United Irishmen had none of the concerns about religion having anything to do with politics that their grandchildren are supposed to have credulously fallen into. As there was a Covenanter minister involved in the rebellion, the suggestion that some of its participants may have had ideas about founding a "Presbyterian state" would not have been absurd.[42] Finally, I quoted at the beginning of the chapter the words of one prominent United Irishman who thought that parliamentary reform and Catholic emancipation would be easier to obtain within the context of the impending Union of Britain and Ireland, which he therefore supported. There are then plenty of reasons for thinking—actually for knowing—that the rising cannot have had the same significance for

Presbyterian and for Catholic, even apart from the fact that it did not actually occur in a mixed district. But this point is very far from the claim that the United Irish rebelled on the same side as the Catholics only because they did not know what fire they were playing with. In this version the 1798 participants were victims of collective error which they subsequently recognized after the reports of what happened to the Protestants at Wexford bridge and the barn of Scullabogue in the southern rising.[43] To say this is to say that when they looked at the Catholics in their neighbourhoods, who were quite numerically insignificant and powerless, or even when they looked at the more numerous Catholics being driven from north Armagh, their vision should have passed through these self-evident victims and seen instead fanatics like those who committed the atrocities in Wexford. The important point is that in the actual situation they were in, they were not frightened enough to do this. That is something that ought not to be forgotten or historically annihilated. It may be said that the risks attached to being tolerant of Catholics in Ballyclare were not as great as they were in Newton Hamilton, but in that case it is no moral judgment on Newton Hamilton to say "Thank God for Ballyclare." The fatal tip-over point where a space becomes highly vulnerable to polarization is when the mass of people within it are sufficiently fearful of the other side that they will do nothing to inhibit their "own" worst, as seems to have happened in Armagh. The arguments that the Presbyterians saw the error of their ways after Wexford is part of the arsenal of fear that makes such things happen. To accept such interpretations is to accept uncritically the claims of later political actors who wanted to destroy the very idea that there might be any unity of purpose between Protestant and Catholic in Ireland, when the actual basis for such political co-operation had substantially weakened. Serious understanding requires not only an exposition of the nature of settlers' colonial fears, but also attention to their limits.

I will conclude by suggesting that once we see the United Irishmen from this angle, some of the small print in the "Argument on Behalf of the Catholics of Ireland" by Theobald Wolfe Tone becomes more interesting and significant. It has been objected that Tone had never met a Catholic until he was

18 and didn't understand what they were like. It is objected that by 1796 he had become a separatist and that this casts doubt on how seriously we should treat his 1791 work. The idea that he is not really very relevant and may not have represented the opinions of the Presbyterians of Ballymena very accurately goes together with the vision of 1798 as an aberration, or of the insurrectionists coming only from areas where there were so few Catholics that they did not understand the implications of their actions.

In fact Tone addresses a very real dilemma for Protestants that has remained since he wrote. Tone was historically situated in a position in which this dilemma had more chance of a clean resolution than at any other time. We need, in other words, not only to grasp the nature of his vantage point but also the need for that vantage point. In the resolution of the Belfast United Irishmen of 1791 it was stated that no reform would be "practicable" which did not include the Catholics. Of Tone's 23 pages, 18 are concerned with "the case of the Catholics in the view of expediency". The central thrust of his pamphlet is concerned with why Protestants must take the risk of including Catholics in their programme. He goes through the absurdity of the doctrine that Catholics keep no faith with heretics (pointing out that if they set oaths at such a low discount, they could have bodily evaded the penal laws), observing the failure of Irish Catholics to support the Jacobites, and the fact that many Catholics now have a vested interest in the land ownership arrangements, which would stand in the way of the "restoration of the forfeited estates". I shall quote him at length on three subjects: first the power of the Pope, second the danger of giving liberty to the "ignorant", and finally the necessity of compact.

"I do believe the Pope has now more power in Ireland than in some Catholic countries, or than he perhaps ought to have here. But I confess I look on his power with little apprehension, because I cannot see to what evil purpose it could be exerted; and with less apprehension, as every liberal extension of property or franchise to Catholics will tend to diminish it. Persecution will keep alive the foolish bigotry and superstition of any sect, as the experience of 5,000 years has demonstrated. Persecution bound the Irish

Papist to his Priest, and the Priest to the Pope; the bond of union is drawn tighter by oppression: relaxation will undo it.[44]

It will be said that the Catholics are ignorant and therefore incapable of liberty . . . but what is the common sense or justice of the argument? We plunge them by law, and continue them by statute, in gross ignorance, and then we make the incapacity we have created an argument for their exclusion from the common rights of man! We plead our crime in justification of itself.[45]

The liberation of the Catholics will be a work of compact and like all other compacts, subject to stipulations. It will be for the wisdom and moderation of both sides to concede somewhat: allowance must be made on the one hand for the difficult sacrifice of parting with power, obtained in injustice, and long held by force; on the other hand, there may be something to be pardoned in men condemned to ignorance by the law of the land, and whose minds have for a century been irritated by injuries, and inflamed by open insults, or still more offensive connivance and toleration."[46]

Tone is often read as though he thought the self-organized mass of the Catholic population was "no threat" any longer to Protestants in Ireland. Seen in this way he becomes a naive idealist; or alternatively he is used as a moral stick with which to beat those who do not share this supposed idealism. But a closer inspection reveals that he is actually saying something rather different underneath the rhetoric of the former point. He is saying that if Protestants do not take the risk of coming to grips with the problem of Catholic liberty it will continue to haunt them. His later actions show that the safeguarding effect of a property franchise was not something that preyed on his mind very much. It was intended here to illustrate the kind of arrangement that might arise out of a work of compact. He clearly foresaw difficulties in the work of compact. But empathy with the position of the Catholics was the only way of dissolving the fears of Catholics, which otherwise trapped Protestants in pleading "crime in justification of itself". We might also add an implicit theme that time is not on the side of the compact. There is never a "right time", as his remarks about

Catholic ignorance show. "Pleading crime in justification of itself" means seeking protection from the anger and resentment of those whose oppression one may have done nothing more to preserve than fail to recognize it in the past.

It is true that there are circumstances in which the injunction not to fear Catholic self-organization is idealistic. We have already seen what happened in Armagh in the same period. But the problems involved in coming to terms with Catholic self-organization are not uniform as to place and time, in any more than a very general sense. The enduring spirit of Tone's 1791 message therefore is not exhausted by demands for moral heroism in crisis conjunctures. It is a demand for empathy with Catholic experience and a recognition that successful compact is necessarily just that—a synthesis of different objectives. It is a warning: "And if ye injure us, shall we not revenge?" If the liberties of the Catholic are denied by Protestants, "Let Administration proceed to play upon the terrors of the Protestants, the hopes of the Catholics, and balancing one party by the other, plunder and laugh at, and defy both."[47]

3. Ulster, O'Connell and the Whigs

The Act of Union abolished the Irish parliament and incorporated its representation in the parliament of the United Kingdom of Great Britain and Ireland. Pitt wanted to incorporate Ireland within the British commercial system, and to remove a potential source of weakness in foreign affairs. Lord Clare and the managers of the Castle, who wished to preserve what remained of the Protestant ascendancy, saw that there was no alternative to the Union after the 1793 Catholic Relief Act had enfranchised the Catholic 40 shilling freeholders and the 1798 Rebellion had been put down only with British military support. Although Lord Castlereagh and Pitt wanted to complete Catholic emancipation as part of the process of the Union, and although not only the Catholic clergy but also some of the United Irishmen supported the Union in the expectation that this would follow, yet in fact Britain depended upon the influence of Lord Clare and his allies to secure the Union. It was therefore conducted in such a manner that it seemed to shore up the Protestant ascendancy.[1] The structure of Anglican landlord control in the counties and the influence of the ascendancy factions in the central administration at Dublin Castle remained.

The big changes that occurred were not so much in 1801 as during the O'Connellite mobilizations of the 1820s and during the Whig governments of the 1830s. The O'Connell mobilization touched the outer edges of Ulster (especially during the Monaghan election of 1826). The changes brought about during the Whig decade and especially from 1835 to 1839, however, affected the whole of Ulster very considerably. In the fields of law and order and of education the changes enabled Catholic society in the North to build itself up. Pan-Catholicism—the interdependence of Catholics for political, social and other purposes—was strengthened in several ways. First, these changes were a product of O'Connell's mobilizations and the Whigs' alliance with him. Both were aspects of the new-found power of Catholic Ireland. Second, to realize the potential advantages from the Whigs' reforms, it was necessary for Catholic society to become cohesive, hence the premium on clerical leadership. Third, both of these things meant that northern Protestant Liberals were no longer able to presume that they led the anti-ascendancy bloc. They often had to face the fact that conflict between O'Connell and the Conservatives would define the issues, and that they themselves would then have to choose sides.

The fact that Catholic emancipation had to be extracted from Britain by a mass movement has been looked upon as a tragedy.[2] Had Britain granted it in response to earlier pressures from Grattan and the Whigs, it is possible that the relationship between religion and national antagonism would have been weaker. At all events because the British government held firm against Catholic emancipation, it ensured that the modern Irish nation was defined by religion and not, say, by language. I have argued elsewhere that in ethnic frontier areas, which were products of earlier and decayed colonization, settler-native divisions reappear as national divisions in the 19th century.[3] The new national conflicts begin revolving around educational systems and relationships to the law. As we shall see in the next chapter the Irish language, especially in Ulster, was being eroded by the linen industry. The language of the market place—English—chipped it away. But very little British coercion was involved in this process, so it did not provoke Irish society into fighting against it. The contrast with the contention over the rights of Catholicism could not be starker. So what is unusual about 19th-century national conflict in Ireland is that religion became the dividing line instead of language. How many Catholics might have been effectively assimilated to the British population in Ireland if language had eventually become the mark of nationality cannot be guessed.

The important point, in considering the change in the meaning of being Irish from 1798 to 1830, is that changes from geographic to cultural senses of nationhood were the norm of this period (or slightly later in other parts of Europe). In 1798, being Irish had meant living in the place called Ireland. It was a fact about which institutional jurisdiction you lived under and therefore an almost geographical statement. The rise of culture-based (which is to say education system-based) nationalisms changed the meaning of nationality into something like the belonging together of a people with the same educational culture. This point resolves some of the alleged problems about why the United Irishmen of 1798 were so opposed to Repeal of the Union, when O'Connell called for it in 1840. The rise of O'Connell had changed the meaning of being Irish. This would have been obvious if his movement had been built around the defence of the Irish language, rather than the rights of the Catholic religion. But because the change of meaning was not clear-cut, the word Irish developed two meanings corresponding to two different political senses.

In the 19th century nation came, as a general rule, to have to do with language. In fact it was not so much the language itself that mattered, as the Irish case showed. It was the struggle over education systems which suddenly began to take on much greater significance when education ceased to be restricted to a narrow elite.[4] National groups grew around education systems which they built to stop education from syphoning off their people into the dominant culture. People began to identify their nation in terms of whatever cultural attribute was stigmatized by the dominant nation. When the Second Reformation (see below) proposed to use the existing educational system to decatholicize the Catholics who were being educated within it, a Catholic educational system became a need if Catholic society was to be able to respect itself. As far as many were concerned, Catholic and Irish must have seemed interchangeable, because Protestant, English and planter seemed interchangeable to them. The United Irishman William Macneven said at his inquisition by Lord Clare in August 1798: "In his language the Irish peasant has but one name for Protestant and Englishman, and confounds them; he calls them both by the same name of Sasanagh; his conversation is less against a religionist than against a foe; his prejudice is the effect of the ignorance he is kept in, and the treatment he receives."[5] By the 1820s, we shall see how the Irish as a dominated group built up a religious rather than linguistic personality. Thus the meaning of the term Irish began to mean Catholic, and the confrontation over emancipation made it so. But a matching change of meaning did not occur for Protestants. The terms English or Scottish were never used by them except hyphenated with Irish. Protestants continued to think of themselves as Irish, because for them it remained a geographical association and not a cultural badge. If language had become the dividing point, then they might very well have begun to call themselves English, Scottish or British. This partly explains why the United Irishmen of 1798 could be so "anti-Irish" in the 1830s and 1840s. It also explains why criticism of O'Connell for his sectarianism fundamentally miscarries. In fact he built up Catholic society in Ireland in the way that linguistic nationalists most often built their societies—in opposition to some of the people living in the same territory as themselves.

By 1840 the political centre of gravity of Ireland had shifted. With the rise of O'Connell and the practical enfranchisement of Catholic Ireland, the importance of the North declined and the primary political axis was between his movement and the British state. He was about to turn to mass action for the repeal of the Union, abandoning his previous alliance with Whig governments to secure reform. The northern Whigs were the heirs of the liberal Volunteers and the 1791 United Irishmen. O'Connell's new direction threatened to magnify their difficulties and differences with him. The practical effect of his visit to Belfast to promote repeal of the Union was to demonstrate to any who did not know it already that virtually all sections of the dominant landlord and capitalist classes, virtually all sections of Protestant political opinion and clerical leadership, and a very large part of the mass Protestant population could, forty-two years after the 1798 Rebellion, be mobilized to defend the Union.

Furthermore, the leadership of this pro-Union opposition was taken by those who expressed it in its most absolute and unconditional form. Speakers linked the commercial prosperity of Belfast and the "North", rather loosely defined, to the condition of Ireland under the Union, and served up contrasts between Protestantism and popery, liberty and enslavement, North and South. Rev. Dr Henry Cooke, whose challenge to public debate O'Connell had refused, would declare that the challenge was issued "in the name of the Word of God and of His truth, in the name of our common and concentrated Protestantism". And as though to close a chapter: "I tell you, Mr. O'Connell, the unhappy men and women who fell victims at Scullabogue barn and Wexford Bridge [in 1798] have been the political saviours of their country. [*Loud cheering.*] Though they perished, they live. They live in our remembrance—their deaths opened the political eyes of the many thousands of Ulster."[6] In other words, 1798 was a mistake, and in 1840 his cheering Protestant audience thought of it as such.

For the Liberal Protestant leadership in Belfast, the occasion was a cause of considerable embarrassment. Many were descendants of United Irishmen (at least of 1791 vintage), and had supported Catholic emancipation and the Whig-O'Connell alliance between 1835 and 1839. They were, for the greater part, opposed to the repeal of the Union, though they would certainly not have expressed their opposition in the terms Cooke employed, being opponents of Protestant ascendancy. But recently tensions had arisen between these leaders and sections of the local Catholic leadership over the question of allocating a quota of civic offices to Catholics. The Belfast Conservative MP Emerson Tennent observed that O'Connell was driving Liberal Protestants to become Conservatives or repealers, and that Belfast was the only place where Liberal Protestants and Roman Catholics were still in alliance.[7]

During the later 1830s, O'Connell and his largely clerically organized movement had provided English governments with some order. The introduction of national education gave Catholics access to state funds to erect formally non-denominational schools, and undermined the monopoly of the largely Anglican-endowed school system. The introduction of the constabulary and stipendiary magistrates reduced the "law and order" functions of local landlords and retainers. The tithe commutation removed a major irritant and reduced the Anglican clergy to dependants of landlords. The Municipal

Corporations Act struck down exclusively Protestant town governing councils. The Orange Order was officially discountenanced and, for a period at least, Catholics received patronage from the Castle administration.[8] Taken overall, the direction of governing strategy moved toward accommodation with the responsible and/or influential leadership of Catholic Ireland. But it was an accommodation which involved not so much handing over control as centralizing it in the hands of the Castle and employing it to bargain with such leaders. In the long run, this must have increased the power of clerical leadership over Catholic society.

Ulster's position was that it was the part of Ireland where these kinds of developments, rather than restoring some order where there was little previously, actually confronted a landlord-dominated order that retained some vitality. The Whigs' reforms had different implications in the North than in the South. The dominant Conservative political forces in the North were in a position to create a counter-mobilization. The northern Whigs opposed the Conservatives and contributed very much to making the reforms a reality. But as the Whig-O'Connell alliance began to break up, O'Connell moved back to his earlier position of opposition to the Union. The alignment with the Whigs had opened the institutional space for the advancement of Catholic middle-class and clerical claims, but the basis of his movement was mass popular Catholic mobilization. The revival of the repeal demand may have been intended both to revive the mass involvement and to deter the Conservatives from attempting to reverse the Whig reforms.[9] But it exposed a growing sectionalism between "North" and "South".

Once the Union had become a political fact, all democratization in Britain and Ireland was inseparably bound together. The Whigs soon became resigned to being a minority pincered between the Conservative successors of the Anglican ascendancy and the rising O'Connell. Their existence depended upon some kind of link between democratizing forces in Britain and in Ireland. In a century that was to witness the gradual democratization of institutions and the political process generally, the presence of Ireland within the UK national framework was to pose long-term problems. The development of democracy by successive adaptions of a non-revolutionary nature is always a question of calculated risks taken by sections of the dominant classes. Extending the political arena can provoke irresolvable tensions. But the rewards for successfully taking the risks are that potentially revolutionary forces are incorporated in relatively manageable alliances, which extend the popular legitimacy of government. But in districts or regions with colonial legacies, such risks are likely to be greatest. The local ruling groups and a substantial part of the settler-descendants are likely to be amongst the keenest opponents of all democratizing tendencies in the nation as a whole, and important components of all reactionary blocs. Democratization raises the political importance of the native-descendants' numbers.

For metropolitan power there are various possible solutions to this problem. The first is to accept loss of control of the area in question altogether, if that is one of the consequences of democratization in the metropolis. The second (described above) is to extend bureaucratic control over it as a counterweight to the new forces unleashed by democratic reform. The third is to permit the continuation of a "peculiar" regime where special institutional devices are allowed to stay to ensure that the settler-descendants do not lose control over the contested area. And the fourth is that the contested area contributes towards the continuation of reactionary dominance throughout the nation and arresting change in the metropolis itself. Of these options the only one acceptable to the Whigs, confronted with the reality of O'Connell's movements, was the second. Up to 1829, Ireland's relationship to Britain was close to the fourth paradigm. During the 1830s it moved towards the second. Thereafter it oscillated round the second notwithstanding pressures to move toward the first (nationalism) and the third (conservatism).

The continuation of war had effects upon the methods chosen to put down the 1798 Rebellion and on the coercive agencies used to retain local control afterwards. The 1796 mobilization of the Orangemen as yeomen, although only a secondary component of the total military strength, was to have lasting consequences,[10] for they remained a local presence in many districts of the North after 1798, especially in southern

Ulster. This was not so elsewhere. In the Glens of Antrim the 1798 yeomen were a mixed body.[11] But in areas where the conflict between Orangemen and defenderism in 1795 had crystallized, this tendency was dominant. In subsequent years, the yeomanry were frequently found participating in Orange processions. In 1815 a detachment sent out to stop a collision between Catholics and Orangemen in Lurgan, helped the latter to drive out the former. And in the light of later developments, the implications of an Orange-yeomanry march in Crossmaglen in the same period should be obvious.[12] In fact, their nominal officers, the local landlord-magistrates, were quite aware of the dilemma posed by their existence. The landowners in the Portadown weaving district were confronted after 1800 by the existence of a Protestant combination for "limiting their rents and preventing any stranger from taking lands in the neighbourhood".[13] A leader of this combination, Saunders Bell, was wanted for murder in 1806, but could not be apprehended for three years as the yeoman corps of which he was a member refused to take him in. In 1809 he was caught, tried, and sentenced to hang. There then followed a split amongst the landlords as to whether to seek clemency on the ground of danger from the yeomen if he was hanged, or to proceed with his execution in Portadown to set an example and give a check to popular Protestant expulsionist forces. The fact that there was this hesitation speaks volumes about how local control in the area depended upon Orange support. This was to be re-emphasised in the late 1820s when the pan-Catholic mobilization for Catholic emancipation reached the North and was given a further push during the first repeal and anti-tithe conflicts, during which sections of the northern landlord class attempted to mount a full-scale popular opposition to O'Connell and the Irish policy of the Whigs.

The ambivalent relationships between landlords, the yeomanry and the Orange Order meant that the exercise of justice in sectarian cases tended to be exceedingly partial. This statement is of course a generalization to which there are notable exceptions. John Hancock—Lord Lurgan's agent—for example, attempting to keep an even-handed justice in the Lurgan area, was incidentally burned in effigy for his pains.[14] The magistrates of Cavan County as a whole fairly systematically disavowed any dependence upon Orangeism with consequences we shall deal with in the next chapter. In the early 1830s, in the high period of opposition to the Whigs, there are definite indications that sections of the landlord class and magistracy encouraged Orangeism and regarded its activities as supportive of the social system.

Randall Kernan, a Catholic barrister from Enniskillen, declared: "Every Protestant young man in Fermanagh is an Orangeman: and all with a few exceptions able to carry arms is a yeoman . . . the high sheriff generally and the sub sheriff always are both Orangemen. And I conceive that for the last 30 years there has been no jury consisting of other persons than Orangemen."[15] And as Judge Fletcher put it: "'I am a loyal man', says the witness: that is, 'gentlemen of the petty jury, believe me, let me sware what I will.' When he swares he is a loyal man, he means 'gentlemen of the jury, forget your oaths and acquit the Orangemen.'"[16] The most unequivocal of magisterial Orangemen, Colonel Blacker, is reported to have said, in answer to a request to admonish Orangemen to obey the law: "It was a law made by the Whigs and they had made many laws as well as it, which ought not to be obeyed."[17]

The importance of the 1836 Constabulary Bill, the parliamentary select committee inquiry into the Orange Order, and the beginning of the purge of Orange magistrates (such as Colonel Blacker in 1833) was that in the North they were a very definite attempt to break the ruling assumption that order was something preserved by Orangemen and yeomen patrolling Catholics. The stipendiary magistrates as central government officials, and the constabulary as a force wholly under their instruction, could be employed to put down Orange processions, rather than merely deal with the outcome of collisions to which such processions gave rise. The reforms did not touch the jury system, but they did create the possibility of putting down sectarian assemblies generally and preventing collisions which brought cases to the courts in the first place. So for Catholics these reforms offered a major opportunity. So long as Catholics could be prevented from getting involved in confrontation with Orangemen, and matters not taken before the juries, it was possible for the stipendiary magistrates to treat Orange demonstrations as challenges to the law, which they were. If Catholics collided with Orange processions, then the stipendiaries got caught up in the middle of conflict, arresting both parties, and then finding the courts settle the matter to the advantage of the Orangemen. So for Catholics to make these reforms work in practice, it was vital that they did nothing to justify the pan-Protestant accusation that all Catholic organisation was a threat to order. Here clerical discipline acquired a vital force. If Catholic priests could keep control of their flocks, it left the constabulary and the stipendiaries to deal with the Orangemen. Later on we shall have cause to comment at length on the importance of relationships between the magistracy and the Catholic priests in maintaining order. The major achievement of Thomas Drummond,[18] the Under Secretary at the Castle in the 1836-39 period, was creating a situation in which the pan-Protestant basis of order in the North could be replaced by a more "neutral" one. In so far as the achievement was lasting, it eventually made possible accommodation between magistrate/landlords and the Catholic clergy, an accommodation which was tacitly underwritten by the mediating agency in the Castle. After the 1830s Catholic self-organization had to be accepted as fact. Drummond's reforms created the framework in which people of influence had to understand that tranquillity depended upon accommodation with the Catholic clerical and middle-class leadership to secure anything like social peace.

Democratization in spirit, whatever the institutional changes that may happen, needs social and political space. The social order in the Ulster frontier districts in the aftermath of 1798 hinged upon the interdependence between dominant landlords and the yeomanry/Orange Order, patrolling the threat posed to itself by defenderism/ribbonism. The coercive force of this set of relationships denied a space for democratic middle-class challenge. Sometimes individual Whigs like John Hancock became important pivotal figures in the process that had to precede any kind of tentative sense of acceptance between the sectarian subgroups. There was somewhat more space for effective group action by Whigs in some of the boroughs away from the southern frontier. In many of the frontier districts of Ulster the sectarian conflict often meant that confrontations between popular forces and the established order were more or

3. Ulster, showing numbers of Orange lodges, 1835

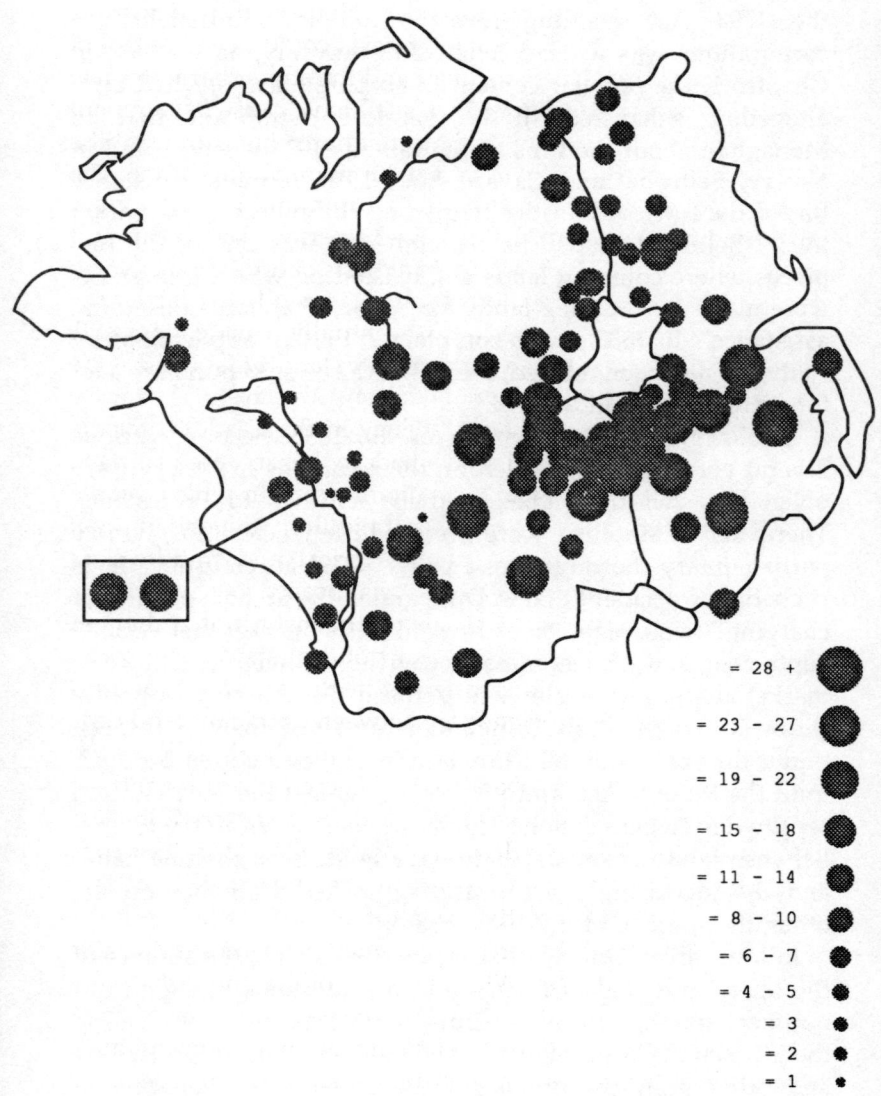

less subsumed within sectarian confrontation. This left very little space for non-sectarian Whig opposition to the ascendancy. The landlords and their retainers would use whatever institutional assets (e.g. corporations) they had to keep control, and the most effective direct action against them would be pan-Catholic, rather than Whig. Nearly everywhere the 1793 Act granting formal Catholic admissibility to corporations was a dead letter. And anyway, as we saw in Chapter 1, the popular content of corporate activity had been altogether exhausted. It is therefore significant that in Monaghan about the time of the famous 1826 election, and in Newry, Belturbet and Cavan about 1830, farmers' resistance forced the town authorities to give up the collection of market tolls.[19] Belturbet, it will be remembered, was one of the few places where common lands still existed on which free grants were made for building lands for "poor inhabitants deserving assistance". In 1833 it was complained that all applications by Catholics had been refused, including the offer to purchase a lot for a Roman Catholic chapel.[20]

In Newry, in the aftermath of the 1835 election, various Liberal voters who had lived on the commons in Newry were obliged to sell the rights in their holdings to Protestants. Thereafter Catholics were refused tenancies in Newry parliamentary borough to ensure political control.[21] It is probably no accident that in Dungannon the archaic practice of charging "tongueage" on cattle sold in the market (between 29 September and 25 December) survived, as well as the usual market charges. A dealer who refused the charge was bodily thrown out of the stalls. Dungannon remained, in every respect, under the control of the Knox family. It was a closed borough until the Reform Act, and petitioners against the 1841 election result were (where they had no leases) evicted from the town.[22] Between landowners and patronage holders on the one hand, and the increasingly vigorously organized Catholics on the other, the space left for Whigs shrank.

In some areas, principally County Fermanagh, the absence of the linen trade and of non-Anglican Protestants in significant numbers simplified the problems of local control. Anticipating the Municipal Corporations Act of 1840, the Earl of Enniskillen and other grandees organized the wholescale alienation of

Enniskillen's corporate property, making the town virtually useless as an asset for independent middle-class opposition to landed power. The commissioners enquiring into corporations in 1833 found "to a degree nothing similar to which we met in any of the other places we visited, a strong sense of apprehension of offending the Patron by coming forward to give evidence in an open court, singularly coupled with a disposition to acknowledge his private virtues".[23] It was in fact in County Fermanagh that the Orange Order was both most thoroughly under landlord control and most universal amongst the (largely Anglican) Protestant population. The patron, Lord Enniskillen, was for a long time its grand master. And there was a continuity in the internal structure of Orangeism in this area quite unlike the sharp discontinuities experienced in areas to the east. It was not substantially broken till the 1880s.

Only in areas where Catholic self-organization was weaker and where a large proportion of the population was Presbyterian was the opposition to the Conservatives more clearly Liberal or Whiggish. The symptom of this was that strictly local issues were leading to divisions of a more secular kind. In some areas of inner Ulster, especially the overwhelmingly Presbyterian areas where the 1798 Rising had taken place, the density of Orange lodges in the 1830s was very low. Larne and Carrickfergus were virtually free of them. And in the 1830s in the Route (Dervock, Stranocum, Ballymoney, Armoy) Freemasons were more in evidence than Orangemen.[24] In Coleraine, a town entirely dominated by the Beresford interest, an effort to move the corn market from the centre of the town caused protest from traders in the Diamond, objections from the Irish Society, and general opposition to the expenditure involved. In the 1832 election, various members of the yeomanry of 1797, who had been made freemen in recognition of their services, used their rights as voters to support Alderman Copeland against Sir John Beresford. The clerk of the markets, who was also the Orange district master and the organizer of the "gun clubs", led a mob into the town to attack the houses of Copeland's supporters.[25] Pan-Protestant strategy might be employed in areas where there were virtually no Catholics, and certainly no significant Catholic self-organization, to maintain control over Protestant opponents of patronage. In so far as reform was a central national question in 1832, this seemingly very local and peculiar case was actually an example of Protestant middle-class participation in what was the central national political current. The case of Coleraine intersects with developments along the Ulster frontier only in the sense that a pan-Protestant system of patronage was the enemy. The case of Derry showed "normal" Whig reform pressures intersecting with Catholic opposition to pan-Protestantism. The victory of Sir Richard Ferguson eclipsed the "slamming of the gates" ceremony in 1832, and temporarily put on one side the growing practice of territorial marching confrontations that characterized frontier politics.

Derry in the early 19th century had been a more or less closed borough run by a corporation, which had largely excluded local trading and commercial interests.[26] It contrived by a series of private acts of parliament to extend its juridiction and borrowing powers to build a bridge across the Foyle, loading quays, a piped water system, and the new Corporation Hall. Yet its income derived from such sources was rarely applied to the repayment of outstanding debt or the repair of its own property. In 1814 the bridge was destroyed by ice and floods. Its MP was Sir George Hill, who had organized the Londonderry yeomanry and had been responsible for the detection of his college colleague Wolfe Tone amongst a group of French officers captured after the landing at Lough Swilly.[27] In 1817 Sir George became the Vice-Treasurer for Ireland and secured a treasury minute releasing the corporation of its obligations to pay an instalment of a government advance. It permitted favoured inhabitants to buy annuities in a manner that verged upon the corrupt. It provided salaried posts for bell ringers and funds to the "Bottle and Glass Society". It accepted loans from members of the common council on lucrative terms. And the members of the common council patronized the annual "slamming of the gates" celebrations (commemorating the beginning of the seige of Derry by King James's forces in 1689). Its methods caused increasing alarm within the Irish Society, who were the ultimate landowners of the city, and the unofficial chamber of commerce, representing city traders. And the bread and circuses approach to maintaining support of Protestant freemen was generally reckoned to be irresponsible. In 1830 Sir

George became Governor of St Vincent's Islands. The whole edifice collapsed in 1831, following efforts by the Irish Society to compel the corporation to fulfil its financial obligations. Creditors took action to secure the execution of bonds, and much corporate property had to be sold, leaving it with a derisory income. In 1832 Sir Robert Ferguson, a Whig, was elected MP in the first contested election since the 1780s. The municipal corporation's commissioners in 1833 found £151,000 unaccounted for in the corporate accounts. In this case the Protestant ascendancy regime had narrowed its base of support sufficiently severely to become vulnerable to overthrow by conventional middle-class, commercial and professional interests the moment the Reform Bill widened the electorate.

In the next chapter I will fill in the implications of the sectarian and law and order conflicts as they affected different areas. We must now turn to the controversy over the national education system which carried the politicization of religious identity into the core areas of inner Ulster. The national education system was a paradigm example of the extension of state responsibility in a manner that reflected peculiarly Irish conditions.[28] Antedating the extension of state responsibility for primary education in Britain by forty years, it reflected the institutional bankruptcy of the Anglican landlord order as a local ruling class in much of the island. Its impact in Ulster was affected not only by this directly political question, but also by its interaction with the evangelical revival within the Presbyterian Church.

During the 1820s much of the opposition to Catholic emancipation had been linked to a campaign to undermine Catholicism altogether. The so-called "Second Reformation", in its more grandiose conceptions, envisaged the liquidation of Catholicism by religious conversion;[29] it intended to resolve a national political problem by religious means as the penal laws had purported to do in the previous century. The immediate effect of the Second Reformation was to accentuate suspicion of Protestant proselytizing intent by the existing educational agencies. There is considerable evidence that before 1820, schools in parts of Ulster were "mixed", both in the sense that pupils were drawn from Catholic and non-Catholic sources, and that frequently teachers would be found in charge of schools, the majority of whose pupils were of the opposite denomination to that of the teacher.[30] But while such arrangements could flourish then (and would in many areas do so in future), they were jeopardized by the climate of controversy in the 1820s. The issue that faced the hierarchy in Ireland as a whole was the provision of a basic education system which it could be sure could not be used in the way in which the Second Reformationists proposed to use the schools over which they had some influence. Indeed, taking the long run, the problem was that many schools were in effect "legal" hedge-schools, and if the mainly Anglican-endowed schools were able to offer a higher quality utilitarian education, there was a distinct possibility that the embryonic Catholic middle class would be detached from the mass of the Catholic population. Before the emancipation controversy, the education system may have tended to draw educated Catholics away from the body of their coreligionists; but if that was true, it was happening as a seemingly natural consequence of the educated separating themselves off from the poverty of their origins. The Second Reformation raised this unwelcome possibility into a matter of deliberate policy, expressing a Protestant concern to prevent the growth of an educated Catholic middle class that was organized separately. The anxiety promoted the overtly sectarian policy and, in its turn, provoked that narrow and distrustful Catholic response. From this point on, Catholic suspicions of proselytizing intent fused religious and political defensiveness into one. This defensiveness baffled many later Protestant Liberals who never felt able to accept it, and seemed to treat it as an attack upon themselves. But to say this is only to talk in a particular case about the dilemmas faced in other national conflicts over educational questions.[31]

The Whigs, on coming to power in 1830, recognized the necessity of providing a system that would meet Catholic aspirations, and the impossibility of relying upon the existing Protestant-connected educational agencies like the Kildare Place Society. They hoped to create an educational system which would service all denominations in Ireland. Central funding would be the principal attraction, and the rules would be designed to promote interdenominational co-operation at local level.[32] The system would have to overcome several difficulties. First, the existing providers of education—the Anglican-endowed bodies and their Conservative landlord supporters—would oppose such an intrusion on their domain. Second, any system of rules designed to secure inter-denominational co-operation would necessarily touch not just the question of equality between members of different faiths, but the far more difficult question of the equal status of the faiths themselves. This was going to force Protestant supporters of equality of rights for Catholics to cope with an equality of status for Catholicism, as for their denomination of Protestantism. Any change of this kind was going to have a particularly dramatic effect in areas where Catholics had previously been a powerless minority of citizens, to be treated as individuals with individual rights. So the most severe shocks were to be experienced in the very areas of Presbyterian dominance where the United Irishmen had been so strong thirty years before.

There has been a tendency with some writers to view the rise of Dr Henry Cooke to leadership of the Synod of Ulster as a triumph of anti-Catholic intolerance over the Presbyterian liberalism of Dr Henry Montgomery.[33] Thus the exclusion of Montgomery and the Remonstrants in 1829, the Presbyterian vote against the national education system in 1834, and the adoption of unqualified subscription to the Westminster Confession of Faith (which includes the proposition that the Pope is Antichrist) in 1835–36, are seen as progress towards a militant anti-Catholicism. Indeed, some writers have even linked Henry Cooke and the notorious Rev. Hugh Hanna who will feature at length later in our story. The biography of Dr Cooke by Rev. R. Finlay Holmes requires us to reinterpret this earlier period substantially.[34]

Presbyterianism in both Ulster and Scotland experienced a resurgence of evangelical fervour in the early 19th century. The theological liberalism of the late 18th century—partially a response to embryonic bourgeois conceptions of individual freedom and the supremacy of the rational intellect—had already led to the schism of the Secession Churches. But whereas Secession in Scotland was a protest against lay patronage, its spread in Ulster was an unmixed orthodox opposition to theological liberalism. Taking the long run, the development of extended influence of the state in most spheres of local government and educational provision, together with the growth of towns and cities, would undermine the pre-eminent role of the Churches in society. But in the early 19th century the evangelical revival within the mainline Presbyterian Churches sought amongst other things to reassert the centrality of the Church both institutionally and in the life of believers. In this respect it had a very different political impact in the Church of Scotland and in the Synod of Ulster, because they had different relationships to state and landed power. The Church of Scotland was formally attached to the civic order and the institution of patronage enshrined the dominance of the lairds and corporations over the Church. The Synod of Ulster had no such formal civic function, and appointments of ministers were confirmed by "two-thirds men and money", a system which gave disproportionate influence to the growing middle class in commerce and linen manufacture. Holmes observes that the "new-light" theological liberals were overwhelmingly found east of the River Bann[35] and tended to include the wealthy and those of rank (but one should note middle-class rank, rather than land ownership, which was generally linked to Anglicanism). In Scotland, where the evangelical revival eventually collided with landlord-patron dominance, it acquired a politically "progressive" flavour. In Ulster it collided with the politico-religious liberalism of the Whig Presbyterian established middle class, the Volunteers and the pre-1793 United Irishmen. As this group was becoming more and more identified with standing up for pro-Catholic and Whig reforming causes in the 1830s, the evangelical revival here acquired a "regressive" flavour.

The Liberal politics of the United Irish period were carried forward in the context of the Union, including widespread support for Catholic emancipation, parliamentary reform, free trade and the general policy of the Whigs. Many of the leading personalities in the Northern Banking Company were Liberals, and at its foundation banquet we find Rev. Henry Montgomery toasted as a guest of honour, and himself proposing a toast to "the Linen Trade with J. S. Ferguson as Chairman of it in this Country".[36] Before the creation of the Belfast Corporation in 1840, the Whigs dominated its principal local governing institutions, the police commissioners, harbour commissioners and the Belfast Charitable Society (which acted as water commissioners). The powers of the corporation were minimal and the landlord, the Marquis of Donegall, sufficiently financially embarrassed to have to grant perpetuity leases on his property which freed it from his personal control. As the main centre of the northern linen and cotton trades, and increasingly the major port, Belfast remained the area of the North most effectively freed of landlord or patron control.

We shall see that correlations between religious and political opinions are not always reliable, and that no genuine religious phenomenon ever has a straightforward political implication. Political implications were acquired situationally. The evangelical revival of the 1820s and 1830s had many advocates who were political Liberals. The important point we must bring out here is how evangelical revival interacted with the new political problem of the 1830s, which was to recognize the Roman Catholic faith as a branch of the Christian Church like any other Protestant denomination, and entitled to the same kind of respect within the framework of the national education system.

What is most striking about the rise of Dr Cooke is the way in which he managed to splinter the various groups of his opponents in the Synod of Ulster. The victory over the Remonstrants, for example, involved isolating a small group who were not prepared to subscribe to the Trinitarian Shorter Catechism.[37] It was scarcely a mark of political intolerance to consider such subscription a legitimate test of religious orthodoxy; but the effect of the crisis was to ensure the departure from the Synod of Ulster of a group of ministers who were articulate opponents of Cooke on a wide range of questions. And it was the thus "purified" synod that then had to face the national education question.

The National Board provided for two-thirds of the building costs and (after 1834) the running costs of schools that would be under local management. To begin with, attempts were made to encourage applications jointly sanctioned by members of different denominations in a locality in preference to those which emanated from one denomination only.[38] The design was to provide for united secular instruction with careful safeguards against proselytism: ministers of the different denominations would have *ex officio* visitor status (with rights of entry during school hours);[38] at specified times of religious instruction, all children would be withdrawn to the charge of their respective clergy;[39] and existing schools could come under the scheme and receive running costs subject to acceptance of such rules.[40] The difficulties in regard to Presbyterian relations with the board arose from the *ex officio* status accorded to Roman Catholic priests (especially at hitherto Presbyterian schools joining the board system), the "restriction" on the use of the Bible in school hours, and the duty to send Catholic children to their priests at the times of religious instruction.[41] All of these issues touched the recognition of the legitimate status of a Catholic priest as the spiritual guardian of Catholic children, the state's assumption of the authority to "regulate" Bible study, and the repudiation of the "duty" to spread the gospel to Catholic children. Consideration of the terms of the supposed compromise of 1834, and the actual compromise as it affected the non-vested schools in 1839 (those existing schools brought into connection with the board and subject after 1839 to a loosened regulation), indicates what the issue boiled down to in essence. The acceptable settlement involved open hours for Bible classes, no visitorial rights for Catholic priests, and no obligation to send away children during instruction—although they had a right to leave if their parents wanted them to do so at such times.[42] It is significant that many of the Presbyterian ministers who were keen for a settlement on this basis were political Liberals and shared Dr Thomas Chalmers' anxieties about the way in which the political opposition to national education was developing.[43] And if even the supporters of Cooke's position at the synod meeting in Derry in 1834 included political Liberals, then the fact that his resolution was passed by a small majority (and depended upon the votes of elders against a hostile majority of ministers) indicates that Cooke cannot be regarded as "representing" Presbyterian feeling, if by that is understood more than that there was serious religious misgiving about the design of the national education system. Cooke did not carry a general Presbyterian blessing (nor did he claim it) for his appearance at the October

1834 meeting at Hillsborough or for his identification with the Conservatives.[44]

How then can we characterize his influence generally? He claimed consistently that he had engaged in political life because politics had concerned itself with religious questions.[45] In the Irish context, where the primary task of any government seeking to conciliate was to come to grips with the legacy of the penal era, politics was necessarily concerned with religio-institutional questions. If Catholics sought to achieve recognition as citizens, the touchstone of success or failure would be whether their religion was accepted as having status (at least) comparable to other religions. It was impossible to resolve this issue without at some stage confronting the question of the relationship between different denominational faiths, and that is what the national education system had to do. Cooke's demand for an "open Bible" was in effect a demand for no let or hindrance, beyond that which was compatible with a minimal recognition of the rights of private judgment, to evangelize all children in schools, including all Catholic children who didn't actually object to being so evangelized. Any opponent of Cooke's position who took the task of evangelicalism seriously would find it difficult to justify secular compromises, without declaring explicitly why they were necessary—namely, to take account of Catholic fears of proselytism. In short, just as he had isolated those who were prepared to declare their opposition to a Trinitarian test, he now attempted to isolate those amongst the orthodox body who felt that the secular compromises involved in participation in national education were legitimate. They were put in the awkward position of having to argue that they were not compromising articles of faith. And they had to do so against a background in which Anglican landlord conservatism was employing its political and institutional resources to link opposition to national "Godless" education to a generalized opposition to the Whig government and all its works. Cooke may not have made explicit anti-Catholicism the centre-piece of his rhetoric—indeed if he had done so, the width of his support might have been reduced—but he took up a position which guaranteed the support of anti-Catholicism and which could only be effectively opposed in the political and religious context of 1834 by those who were prepared to argue the rights of Catholic clergy to some kind of guardian status over their flocks. Having disposed of those most likely to do this in 1829, his task thereafter was somewhat easier.

The relationship of Cooke to explicit and undiluted anti-Catholicism can best be gauged by the defence he offered for excessive zeal for righteousness displayed by two Presbyterian ministers in the Ahoghill/Portglenone district who in 1833–34 toured the countryside with mobs vandalizing schools that had been placed under the National Board. The very fact that any extenuating circumstance could be pleaded at all for such antics indicates how far the duty to the "open Bible" could be stretched.[46] The relationship between this kind of hoodlum activity, and the theological premises from which it might seek its justification, could only be sustained by representing opponents of the "open Bible" as agents of an absolute enemy. The letter "P" for popery was scrawled on the doors of such schools. In a climate in which the dominant political forces were legitimizing a generalized opposition to popery, anything less than a total repudiation of such activity had a partial legitimizing effect. Certainly the direct action of Revs McClelland and McKay was not uniformly successful. A measure of this is that in 1849 at least twenty-five of the sixty-one vested schools (where the board's regulations as to religious instruction applied and which were not affected by the 1839–40 compromise) were under Presbyterian management.[47] Ten of these were within a ten mile radius of Larne (where there were no Orange lodges in 1835), and five more within an equal distance of Ballymoney. There was even one in Ahoghill, the centre of the 1833–34 agitation. These were silent witnesses against the hysteria of 1834.

Any religion that affirms a radical discontinuity between the perfection of God and the inherent sinfulness of man necessarily has to have something very definite to say about the possibilities of human redemption. To deny that man can know anything of such redemption except by the grace of God means that divine revelation is necessarily from God without human agency. The sanctity of the Bible—the Word of God, not a book about God—is as central as is man's incapacity to know anything of God through his own intellectual reasonings. So long as such a religion focuses on the sinful condition of the believer and upon God, its principal impact is that of inward discipline. But it enters different ground when it concentrates attention on those who are not of its own faith. The absolute enemy relationship toward unbelievers endows the perception of human unrighteousness with an altogether different implication. It is now something "we" have and unbelievers do not have. Far from being a source of inner self-awareness, it becomes a "spiritual possession" and its absence a mark of spiritual inferiority.[48]

However we judge Henry Cooke, he certainly paved the way for identifying the righteousness of Protestantism with all manner of supposedly superior achievements of Protestants in economic, social and political life. At the great meeting at Hillsborough in 1834 in opposition to "Godless education", to which vast contingents of Orangemen came, Dr Cooke proclaimed the "banns of marriage" between the Anglican and Presbyterian Churches. The meeting brought together opposition to the national education scheme, pan-Protestant popular organization, and indeed every other kind of opposition to the Whigs' overtures to O'Connell. Shortly thereafter followed the dismissal of Lord Melbourne's government and the return of Peel for the short-lived Conservative government of 1834–35. Fighting the 1835 election on "Defence of the Church", the metropolitan questions and Irish questions were closely interlocked. In later years the Hillsborough meeting was credited with having felled the Whigs.[49] Because the Anglican establishment accorded him a status comparable to its own dignitaries, Dr Cooke was in a position to bring about a Conservative political union between Presbyterians and Anglicans in Belfast. In 1842, at the time of the first elections for the Belfast Corporation, a coherent Conservative alliance, independent at least in a local sense of patronage and landlord control, took up the "Protestant" rallying cry of Dr Cooke as the standard bearer of Anti-Repeal.[50] Pan-Protestantism, which originally expressed a controlling strategy in the countryside, was being refashioned and shed of its purely "Anglican" character.

4. Onset of Rural Crisis in Pre-Famine Ulster

It has often been stated that the industrial development of the North generally, and Belfast in particular, contrasted with the agricultural backwardness of the rest of Ireland. And in this contrast—the uneven development of capitalism—some writers find the central basis of the later confrontation of nationalism and unionism.[1] This chapter is concerned not so much with North-South contrasts as with intra-regional contrasts within Ulster. The central problem is not about northern unionism confronting southern nationalism, but rather about Protestant unionism confronting Catholic nationalism within the North. Now it may be that the second contrast is somehow a reflection of the North-South contrast, but if that is so then it would need to be shown how and why the northern Catholics aligned themselves with the South. Whatever is the case, at least some effort must be made to sketch out how Catholic and Protestant experiences within the North related to each other.

In a rather tentative way, I will outline something of the intra-regional contrasts. To do this I will look at the crisis pressures that were building up in the North of Ireland before the Great Famine, looking at different kinds of pressures and different districts. The starting point is the collapse of the wartime boom about 1815–17. The removal of tariff barriers between Britain and Ireland in 1825, the improvement in transport facilities and the increasing mobility of labour brought the relationship between the two islands closer to the paradigm model of a free market system.[2] At this stage my focus will be principally on areas outside Belfast, which I will treat more thoroughly later on. None the less the influence of Belfast upon the surrounding countryside is of paramount importance. And in this period, when transport costs were very much higher in relation to commodity values than they were to become later, and when human mobility was very much less, the effects of Belfast on the surrounding countryside varied considerably with distance.

The Ulster frontier does not of itself demarcate a sudden break point between North and South. One of the reasons why I have taken the whole nine-county area to study is to emphasise that within it are to be found many regions which are just like the South. Thus the visible differences between south Armagh and Louth, or between south Cavan and Meath might be slight. Within the larger Ulster region we can also see a mixture of ways in which class and religion may be correlated. The landlord class throughout Ireland was Protestant and the relative social differences between Catholic and Protestant become wider, the fewer Protestants there were in an area. Protestant ascendancy meant very different things in different regions. Take for example County Sligo. Its population was 90 per cent Catholic in 1861. Yet even making some allowance for Catholic Conservative votes in 1880, the electorate was between 30–40 per cent Protestant.[3] Such a state of affairs is strong *prima facie* evidence of economic inequality. The plantation of Sligo was carried out on the Cromwellian principle and did not have the mass character of the plantation of Antrim or Down. So, whereas the social relationships in Sligo may be characterized by "Protestant employers and Catholic labour", that description will not by any stretch of the imagination fit most areas of County Antrim. In this chapter I will not so much look at cases of economic subordination of "Catholics" to "Protestants", as at contrasts between areas with different sectarian balances.

If there are any safe generalizations to be made about the economic differences between Protestants and Catholics in the early period of the settlement, the safest is that Protestants tended to occupy lands which were at that time considered to be well situated. That meant high quality lands in a period when quality was judged without the later possibilities offered by drainage or crop rotation. It also meant that they were near to the north-east coast. At the time of the plantation it was easier to travel any distance by water than by land. Thus the very high Protestant densities in the hinterlands of Belfast and Coleraine and the high Protestant density (compared with areas on either side) in the Foyle valley. Conversely, there is the very high Catholic density of population in the Sperrin Mountains, the northern Glens of Antrim, the marshlands round Lough Neagh, and the Mournes and the Fews in south Down and Armagh. These original relationships between locations of incoming Protestants and prime commercial opportunities were specific to an earlier phase of economic history. The coming of more advanced methods of transport and the commercial opportunities provided by the linen industry meant that earlier locational advantages would not necessarily retain the same salience.

Belfast was the centre from which commercial stimuli rippled outwards. The rise of Belfast from a small town to a big city has its roots in the pre-famine era. Through 1801 to 1841 it doubled its population every twenty years. Initially engaged in linen and the export of provisions, it became in the late 18th century the centre of the Irish cotton industry.[4] Cotton spinning, the first large-scale mechanized trade in Ireland, was found at various ports along the east coast, as it depended on the import of its raw materials, and a coastal location or access by water (e.g. to Glenavy after the opening of Lough Neagh to sea traffic) was a major advantage. The weaving of cotton, conducted on a putting-out basis, paid considerably higher wages and was lighter work than linen weaving. Thus around 1820, cotton weaving had displaced linen from the Lagan valley and from the coasts about Belfast Lough.[5] It will be clear from the map of rural religious distributions that the hinterland of Belfast to a distance of about 15 or 20 miles is overwhelmingly Protestant. And it is a reasonable conjecture that in its early stages of expansion it drew much of its population from these districts. It was only rather later that the more distant migrants into the city began to include a much higher proportion of Catholics. The shorter the migration distance, the more easily could it arise from less traumatic causes, and be preceded in the first instance by some contact with the town through education, trade or apprenticeship of a family member. But once the rural crisis began in 1817–19 and intensified in the 1830s the relatively local sources of new population were swamped by long-distance sources.

In the early years of the 19th century there was a considerable expansion of trade union activity amongst the cotton spinners and other trades in Belfast. But the violent end of the handloom weavers' strike in 1814 and the defeat of the spinners' strike in 1825 weakened union organization.[6] The decline of the cotton industry, though slow and protracted, had different effects on different areas. In 1829 the first experiment in Ireland with mechanized linen weaving started a general movement away from cotton. The cotton trade was reduced to a system of outwork for Glasgow weavers who found the (by that time) lower wages in Ulster adequate compensation for the inconvenience of the extra transport costs. The cotton weaving wages fell dramatically from their 1815 peak to their lowest levels ever in 1833.[7] Furthermore, in the transition from cotton to linen, adult male labour was displaced by female and child labour. The recent migrancy and high levels of underemployment among much of the Belfast working population made working-class organization difficult. The cotton manufacturer, Alex Moncrieffe, thought that "trade unions are not likely to exist to any extent in Belfast, for this reason: there is so much political (sectarian) difference between the men, that they cannot permanently co-operate together". But as he went on to say, "if there be not a demand and the stocks of goods be heavy, [wages] can be reduced to almost any extent".[8] It was not until after the Famine and a very much increased scale of emigration and seasonal migrations that enduring trade unions appear in the 1850s.

The 1830s were years of fairly general underemployment. The turn to mechanized linen yarn production, with Belfast as its centre, involved a thorough reorganization of the linen trade beyond Belfast also. The bleach greens on the various rivers of Ulster had previously been the centres for the purchase of brown linen from domestic weavers and small manufacturers. But now the yarn manufacturers displaced them. The geographical concentration of the industry about the yarn mills left many old weaving-bleaching areas in decline.[9] Mechanized yarn spinning during the 1830s simply devalued the labour of the female family members—the principal spinning labour force. Some carried on the domestic system and sold the now reduced value cloth in more distant markets. Others still grew flax for sale and bought yarn from spinning manufacturers. But the spinning manufacturers began to import flax and, in the period up to 1833, the price of flax fell, while that of wheat rose. In many areas, even in Armagh, any landowner with enough land turned to wheat.[10] So the demand for agricultural labour fell, while the value of the spinning labour was devalued by the machine product. At that time cotton weaving wages also fell to their lowest levels for the pre-famine period. Flax cultivation revived thereafter to 1837 when its price rose owing to the failure of continental flax crops and competitive demand from Dundee spinners. But by then it was becoming divorced from weaving. In 1810, the domestic industry had covered most of Ulster.[11] The 1840 map shows the proportions of male population in rural parishes engaged in producing "clothing" as distinct from "food"—a crude index of the scale of rural weaving at that time—and it is clear that the "weaver belt" was drastically reduced. While it was still providing employment in a contracting area, it had also left behind a trail of difficulty. Up to 1815, rental values had been generally increasing for a very long time. A rising population, the growth of the linen industry and the effects of wartime demand had sustained expectations of perpetually rising rentable values. Leases had acquired a value proportionate to the gap between the rent fixed in the lease and the rentable value of land at a later time. In the post-1817 period all this changed as agricultural values fell.[12] The linen industry's gradual retreat from the countryside exacerbated this and left behind many holdings which had been economically viable only while it lasted. There was a large belt of territory in southern Ulster which had been cut into ribbons of holdings during the linen era and where now the holdings could barely provide the means of subsistence, let alone rent.

So far I have looked at the forces radiating out from Belfast. Now we must turn around and look at economic pressures coming from the more remote and mountainous districts. The first of these concerns the reclamation tenantry. Up to 1815 the area under cultivation had been gradually extended for over a century. And in the period of high agricultural prices, much land of bog, mountain and waste quality had been reclaimed. A great deal of this land was of decidedly marginal quality. Its yields tended to be strongly affected by bad weather and after a few years of use its fertility might be rapidly exhausted.[13] It had usually been let, to begin with, at a very low rent in tacit recognition that the tenant was converting it from "raw earth" into a holding. But then reclamation tenants generally experienced massive rent increases after the fall of their first leases. Landlord valuation of holdings generally excluded buildings and obvious tenant outworks, thereby giving substance to the notion of dual ownership (i.e. the tenants' equity in the buildings, etc.). But when the same practice was applied to mountain tenants, all too often the landlords' valuation engrossed items which were direct products of tenant labour in the recent past.[14] So raising the rent, after leases fell in the 1820s, magnified the marginality of such lands and that in turn was reflected in the post-1817 devaluation of agri-prices. William Greig's report on the Gosford estate in mid-Armagh dwells at length on the impact of the bad season of 1816 and the subsequent crop price falls on mountain tenants.[15] Some agents (e.g. those of the Earl of Caledon and Colonel Wm Verner) considered that reclaiming wild mountain land in the northern climate "will never pay in tillage . . . except at war time prices". Lord Caledon, who was clearly one of the best landlords, instead of simply renting out tracts of mountain to intending tenants, actually built houses for 15–20 acre farms in the Donegal mountains but decided later that it was not a successful scheme.[16] Others with less scruple may have contrived to make reclamation tenancy a "success" at least by getting a financial return out of it.

A second crisis pressure that was new after 1817 was the more effective disruption of one of the few forms of commercial activity, which was viable in areas remote from agricultural markets. Illegal distillation provided a local market for grains and the production of a high value bulk commodity which (no doubt assisted by its illegality) amply covered the costs of its transport to areas of consumption. Its disruption sharply reduced the stimulus to commerce, rendering distance from markets for agricultural produce a consideration of no mean

4. Rural weavers, 1841

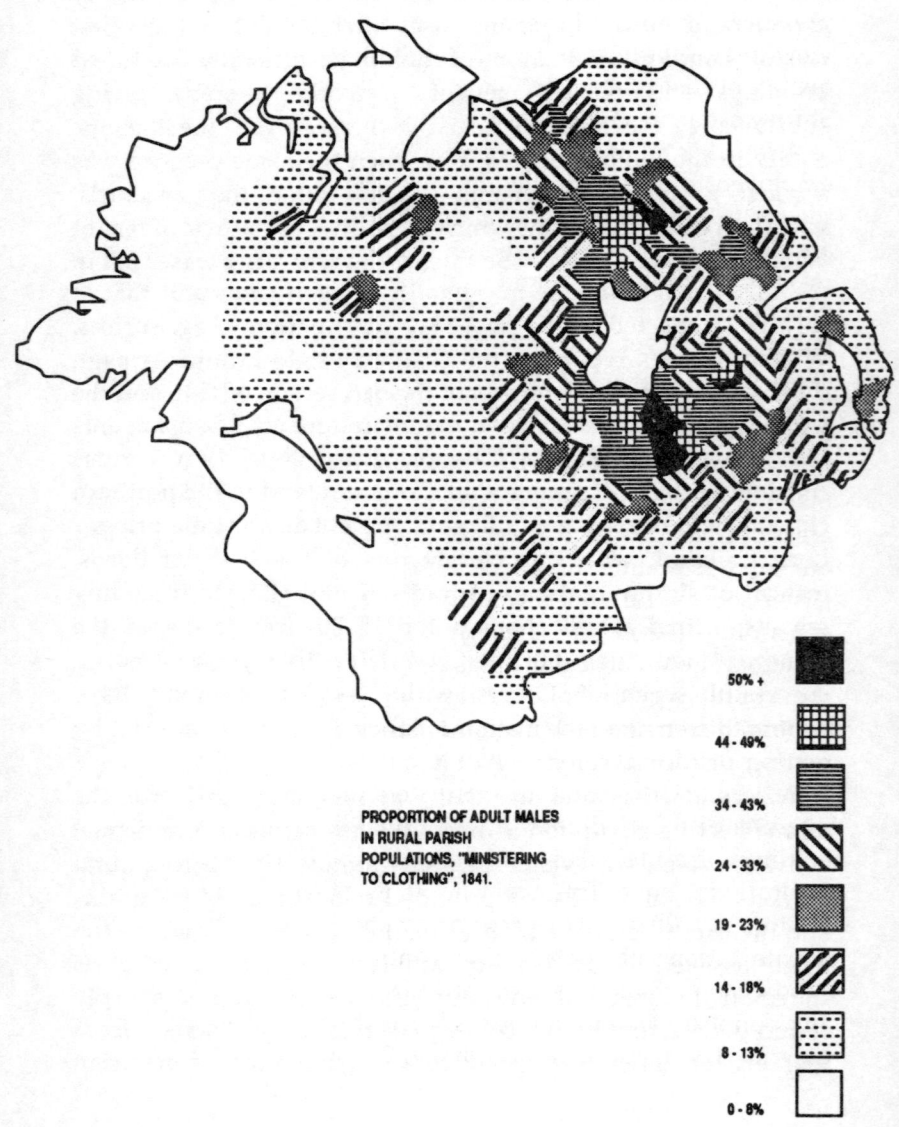

PROPORTION OF ADULT MALES IN RURAL PARISH POPULATIONS, "MINISTERING TO CLOTHING", 1841.

50% +
44 - 49%
34 - 43%
24 - 33%
19 - 23%
14 - 18%
8 - 13%
0 - 8%

significance. This affected particularly the mountainous areas of Donegal such as the Innishowen Peninsula.[17]

A third type of crisis pressure was directly linked to the rising population—the pressure on turf fuel supply. One of the attractions of reclamation tenancy was that the process of bog reclamation provided fuel. In many of the more densely settled areas, the available supplies of bog were coming under heavy pressure. Significantly, some landlords and agents took the view that subdivision could be prevented by "limiting the quality of fuel", an action which, in one spectacular case on the Shirley estate in south Monaghan, provoked a major crisis.[18]

A fourth kind of crisis pressure arose out of one of the means employed to deal with the other pressures mentioned. During the early 19th century, seasonal migration for English, Scottish and Leinster harvesting became an increasingly important means of enduring on land that was fast becoming unable to generate the means of subsistence and rent.[19] But when bad harvests were general and demand for agricultural labour fell, areas which depended on migrancy were doubly hit. Both the local and the distant means of subsistence were pressurized simultaneously.

Taken together, these four elements are a large part of the material history of some of the remoter and more mountainous areas of Ulster. As such they provide us with a starting point for our understanding of a specifically Catholic experience of Ulster society. I do not mean that these conditions affected the generality or even the "majority" of Catholic experience, but only that these particular kinds of experience were sharpest in some of the very Catholic districts.

Both the retreat of the linen industry and the pressures on the remoter districts pointed in the same direction. As smallholdings were less and less able to generate subsistence and rent, the interests of the landlords moved towards the consolidation of holdings. Besides these interests there appeared two new institutional ones. The abolition of the 40 shilling freeholder electors in 1829 simply removed any political concern about the maximization of potentially controllable voters through subdivision of holdings. Dependent smallholders no longer had any political value to landlords.[20] The introduction of the Poor Law in 1838 made landlords liable for payment of the whole poor rate on smallholdings valued below £4 per annum and formally placed the responsibility for looking after the destitute on the newly established poor law unions.[21] Both the desire to minimize liability for the rate, and the desire to reduce the likely absolute burden of the poor rate pointed to the removal of marginal tenants. In particular, an effort would be made to displace non-viable ex-weavers to consolidate holdings for larger tenant farmers.

So far we have dealt with a series of rural crisis pressures. Areas where proximity to sources of machine spun yarn enabled weaving to survive can be partly excluded. The "weaver belt" formed a ring around Lough Neagh, extended in the Lagan valley towards Belfast, and along the Lower Bann towards Coleraine. But there were also agricultural districts which had already begun to adapt to the era of falling agricultural prices. These were generally areas in close proximity to larger market towns which were affected by commercial stimuli in a qualitatively different way from their more isolated counterparts. Holywood was so close to Belfast that farmers did very well out of the bad seasons preceding 1819. There was no scope for mere subsistence when the costs of the means of livelihood were high. Fuel, for example, was imported coal, and had to be paid for in cash. More than 40 per cent of the houses were first or second class. Weaving was only a part-time occupation (in a high-wage cotton district at that), which says something about the availability of relatively lucrative sources of local employment. Mention is made of the summer tourist trade, but proximity to Belfast facilitated entry into urban crafts and trades generally.[22] It is very probable that 18th-century Presbyterian emigration had helped to prevent subdivision of holdings. In some of the more densely Presbyterian areas around the hinterlands of Belfast, Larne, Coleraine and Portrush, larger size probably made them more able to absorb modern agricultural techniques. Thus Scotch ploughs and crop rotation showed considerable advance through large areas of County Antrim in the early 19th century.

Taken altogether, the probability is that Presbyterian districts close to market outlets (particularly ports) experienced fewer traumas during the switch to more capitalized farming than more inland areas. If we take those districts which fill much of the geographical space between the 1840 weaver belt and the north-east coast, we arrive at a definition of inner Ulster—a predominantly but by no means exclusively Protestant area—which experienced the shock of the Famine with considerably reduced severity.

Much has been written about the role of the Ulster custom or tenant right in the economic history of Ulster. It is often invoked to explain its greater prosperity compared with the other three provinces. By itself the custom did nothing for the prosperity of a district, as we shall see when we look at the parts of Donegal where the tenant right prices were proportionately highest. What is clear, however, is that it could have had a benign effect, and did so in many places and at many times. During the period after the 1817–19 collapse of agri-prices it began to acquire new meanings, which varied from place to place. We shall look at it here besides the various crisis pressures in different situations.

In the aftermath of the Williamite wars, much of the Scottish immigration was induced by the shortage of tenants and the prospects of lands at low rents with long leases. Notwithstanding that rents were generally raised at lease-ends, an unexpired lease had a value. And though the origins of the practice of selling the goodwill of a tenancy by the outgoing to the incoming tenant are unclear, it bore some relationship to the sale of unexpired leases.[23] What is utterly plain is that, as one landlord complained as late as 1880, in these circumstances the whole weight of local sympathy was always with the outgoer and never with the incomer.[24] The implicit sanctions to enforce payment of tenant right to the outgoing tenant were very real. The payment implied some informal but none the less substantial notion of dual ownership between landlord and tenant. The system had various advantages. First, a departing tenant had the means to pay a migrant passage, to settle any arrears to landlords and debts to anyone else. Second, in so far as there was any relationship between the improvements carried out by the tenant and the ultimate value of his realized tenant right, these improvements were loosely recognized as a species of tenant property. Improvements also raised the rentable capacity of the holding possibly by more than was recognized in the tenant right value, so it was to the landlord's

5. Quality of rural housing

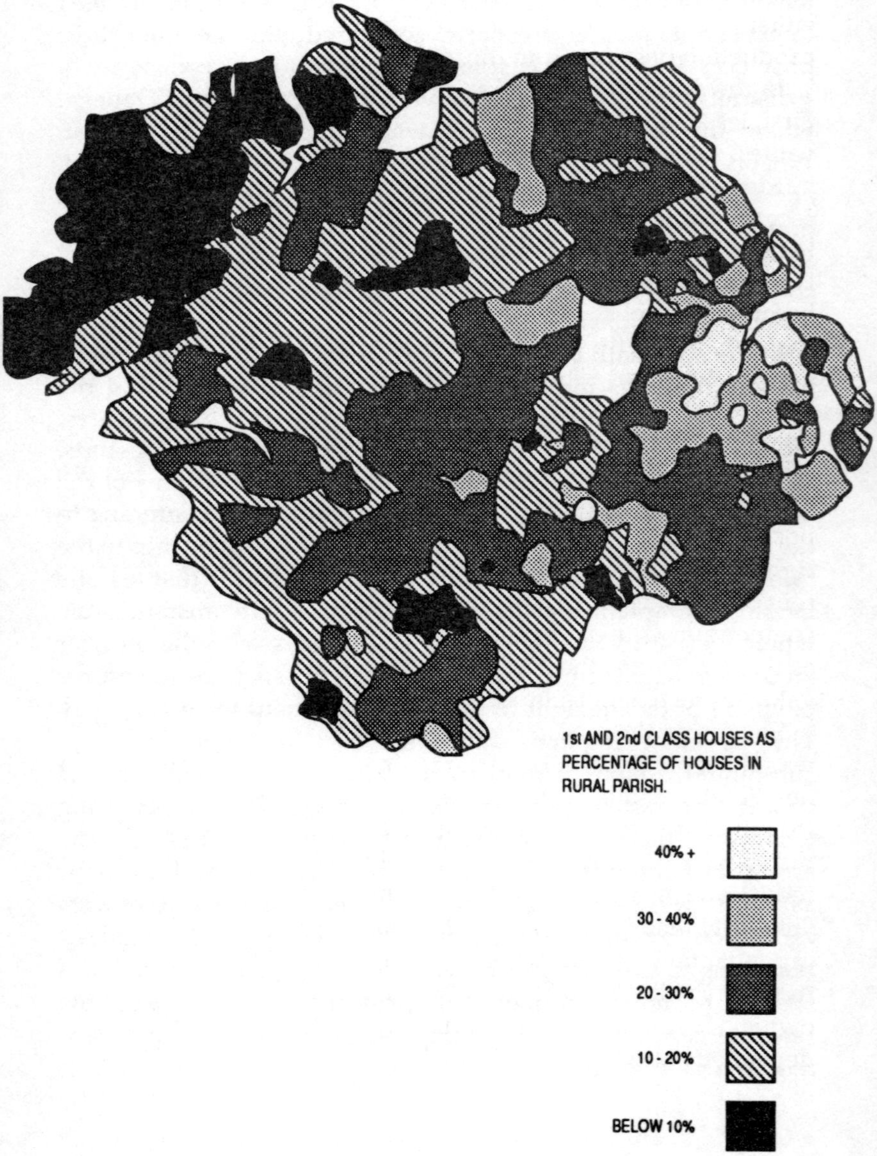

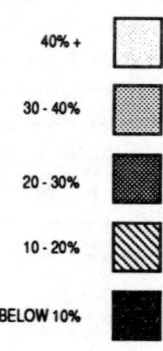

1st AND 2nd CLASS HOUSES AS PERCENTAGE OF HOUSES IN RURAL PARISH.

40% +
30 - 40%
20 - 30%
10 - 20%
BELOW 10%

advantage not to undermine the security which encouraged them in the first place. And so long as agricultural values or, more precisely, the values of holdings were increasing, there was space for increase in both rents and tenant right values. This might be the case whether the tenant actually undertook major improvements or merely kept up a holding in working condition. In the latter case, his motive could be an increase in either the pressure of demand for holdings or the value of production possible from those holdings.

In the post-1817 situation, however, several things changed. First, leases were no longer a security against future rising agri-values. All too often they might become excessively burdensome commitments in periods of falling prices. But secondly, under the new crisis pressures, the landlords' and the tenants' preferences for land use could sharply diverge. When landlords wanted to consolidate holdings, tenant right could become a big obstacle. And it was in these circumstances that the tenant right system experienced considerable strain. Obviously as leases became rarer tenant right payments ceased to be even notionally related to the purchase of interests in unexpired leases. But the link to the notion of dual property is clearly expressed in the formula that £1 addition to the rent reduces the tenant right by £20.[25] Logically and in fact it was possible for the rent of land to be at such a level that the tenant right sank to zero. In the circumstances of falling values, the rent and the tenant right values would be placed in obvious competition with each other. And if the rent did not fall as fast as the agri-prices, the greater part of the fall would occur in the value of the tenant right.

So long as the landlord depended upon a substantial farmer tenant keeping a farm in good repair, not to exhaust it or leave it derelict, he also had an interest in not squeezing him too hard for rent. If his own credit rating as a borrower depended upon the regularity of payment of rent by his tenants, a judicious reduction for a larger farmer at times of falling prices might yield dividends in the shape of regular payment and continued capitalization of the farm. In sum, it was in his interest to recognize, albeit implicitly, the status of the tenant as joint owner, if only because the maintenance of the "joint property" depended on mutual trust: the landlord recognized the difficulty of securing replacement tenants with comparable capital.[26]

From the landlord's point of view, the problem with tenant right payments was that they reflected the valuation put upon holdings by those who bid for them. If we are thinking of large farms, then it is likely that bidding is guided by fairly cautious criteria. But the smaller the farm, the more capricious might be the considerations influencing the bidding. In a period when accommodation close to a weaving centre was much sought after, such an accommodation, even at a high rent, might still attract a proportionally vast tenant right payment. The smaller the holding the more elastic might the possible payments per acre become, given that a smallholder was not looking for many acres. Even so, if the reason for the high tenant right payment was that the holding was to be used for weaving, that was still not to the disadvantage of the landlord. The problem was that tenant right was still paid on holdings where the prospect of paying the rent and securing subsistence were making the medium term (as distinct from the short term) very doubtful. This was especially true in areas which relied upon migrant labour for income and had adequate fuel supplies. Any landlord attempt to abolish tenant right by simply raising the rents would be counterproductive because land shortage would induce many prospective tenants to find the money to bid for tenant right and, once in possession, hang on in the hope of being bailed out by another like themselves if they fell into arrears. In some smallholding districts, local usurers advanced tenant right sums at colossal interest rates, reflecting the sheer desperation of people to secure holdings. All existing tenants and all creditors had an interest in tenant right values being held up, if necessary by hugely inflated valuations of smallholdings. The whole local credit system depended on it. So it could carry on although, taking anything more than the short term, it was not viable and although the tenants would often be in rent arrears. The only prospect of ultimately securing higher rents paid more punctually was the enlargement of holdings and the reduction of the volume of subsistence sought per acre. That meant the establishment of larger farms which would permit their tenant families to utilize labour time fully in productive agriculture. But the difficulty there was that no such person was likely to take on a cluster of smaller farms, possibly in need of considerable adaptation, provide stock, and pay the tenant right that might be offered by a cluster of smallholders. The only avenue open was to find a way of easing a large holder into possession of a big farm, made up of lots of small amalgamated ones, so that he did not have to reckon with the tenant right values to the land as smallholdings.

That, however, generated other difficulties. If tenant right was not secure on an estate—if the basic principle of the tenant's right to sell his interest was undermined—it would attack the necessary trust between landlords and tenants. And not only would it create insecurity amongst other tenants, but it would also undermine their security in dealing with merchants and traders, and reduce their propensity to undertake improvements of an investment character.[26]

The solutions that the northern landlords arrived at in regard to this problem generally involved: (a) imposing a limit of £5 or £10 per acre for tenant right; and (b) offering adjoining farmers the option of purchasing a vacated holding to enlarge.[27] This solution involved the *de facto* expropriation of part of the outgoing tenant's free market tenant right value and the sharing of the "proceeds" between the surviving enlarged tenant and the landlord. It would obviously work only if the adjoining tenant was in a position to make use of the advantage thereby offered. But in so far as this strategy was successful, not only was it an attack on the principle of free sale, but it also had profound political and social implications. In place of a generalized solidarity of tenants and traders to maintain tenant right, it created a bond of dependence between the landlord and the tenant who hoped to be offered an adjoining farm on some future occasion. And it rendered his credit worthiness dependent on his standing with his landlord. This was the real risk posed by tenant right limitation and adjoiner preference. It was a line of least resistance to attack tenant right in general. A species of informal tenant property that depended upon certain very real tenant sanctions might in this way come to depend instead upon the favour of individual landlords, who could chip away at the custom in the knowledge that some of their existing tenants might hope to gain from their action in future.

The importance of this particular transformation of tenant right was the tenant's equity in his holding which might make him become dependent on landlord power.

In the next sections I shall look at experiences of particular districts, starting with two where the common description of the settlement—"Protestants on the low land and Catholics on the mountains"—was much in evidence.

The western centre of the Ulster Presbyterian settlement was the valley land along the Foyle and its tributaries, the Finn, the Mourne and the Derg Rivers. In one of William Carleton's stories he puts this description of the "Black Pig" (the Black pig's dyke)[28] into the mouth of a Catholic hill farmer:

"The prespitarian church that stretches from Enniskillen to Derry, an' back again from Derry to Enniskillen". The farmer digging his potato ridges looks down at the fertile valley below and exclaims to his son. "Why thin, sure I know well I oughtn't to curse yez, anyway, you black set! An' yit, the Lord forgive me my sins, I'm almost tempted to give yez a volley, an' that from my heart out! Look at thim, Jimmy agra—only look at the black thieves! How warm an' wealthy they sit there in our ould possessions, an' here we must toil till our fingers are worn to the stumps, upon this thieving bent. The curse of Cromwell on it! You might as well ax the devil for a blessin' as expect anything like a dacent crop out of it! . . . Well, God send the time soon, when the right will take place Jimmy agrah!"

Ardstraw parish in west Tyrone is a large area "diversified with hill and dale", at the centre of which sits Newtownstewart on the Mourne River. In 1814 it was very much a linen district.[29] Plenty of bog fuel abounded for weavers and for bleaching establishments. Children, although generally apprenticed to the linen trade after they had learned to read and write at school, often preferred emigration as they looked upon trade as a "degradation". In the Newtownstewart area there were some substantial farmers and some demand for six-monthly hire of 11 or 12-year-old children as farm labourers. But in some of the surrounding mountain parishes, from which beggars came in "scarce years", "the population in that part of the North exceeds the means of subsistence, and seems to be the chief cause of the frequency of emigration".

The parish was a decidedly Protestant one. Sixty-eight per cent of families were Protestant, Dissenters outnumbering Anglicans 3 to 1. The people spoke "English only". And the yeomanry "who contribute so much to the security and good order of the parish . . . could, on any emergency, be assembled by beat of a drum at a moment's warning". "We have no carders, threshers or ribbandmen." The only "objectionable characters" are the illegal whiskey distillers who occasionally lift corn prices beyond the reach of the poorer classes. (This last suggestion, if true, speaks volumes about the localization of markets for agricultural products as distinct from linen and yarn in the period.)

By 1840 this area was hit very hard by the mechanization of spinning. Although Mulholland and Herdman set up a spinning factory in Strabane in the early 1840s, employing about 600 people, it is reported that once there was "scarcely such a thing as a small farmer without a loom", and many of these used to employ labourers. Now the domestic system was more or less dead.[30] A linen bleacher who knew the River Derg valley said that consolidation was impossible from the tenacity with which smallholders kept their farms. The linen industry had facilitated multiple subdivision and, despite its disappearance, the subdivision didn't stop. This continued not only to share land between children, but also to pay debts. The loan fund interest rate in Newtownstewart was running at 12 per cent.

What methods of adaptation were being found? Some of the larger farmers in the lowland areas were carrying out drainage works which led to a temporary increase in demand for labour, but their use of horses for ploughing offset the effect. Tenant right values, although falling generally, varied with the size of the farm, larger numbers of years' purchase being paid for the smaller farms. "The landlords hereabouts have put their heads together to try to decide how many years purchase to allow."[31] In some cases they resorted to straightforward compensation to carry out consolidation by ejectment. The effort to create bigger holdings by tenant right limitation was not getting very far yet.

An incident drawn from the Killygorden estate on the River Finn in Donegal provides a clue as to how the policy of consolidating tenancies and linking tenant right prices was affecting the balance of Protestant and Catholic farmers in the district. An old Protestant farmer in arrears of rent complained that he was being ejected because he could not get an acceptable (to the landlord) buyer of tenant right. "Many Romans would have wished to buy my place, for it was a large one. [But the landlord] does not let two families live on the same farm."[32] The agent explained that the estate policy was that each religion sold to its own kind "to prevent a collision or bad feeling".[33] There are two separate but interrelated issues here. The practice of enforcing sales by each tenant to his own kind was becoming quite common in the western areas of Ulster. For example, in the mountainous Badoney parish on the north-west border of Ardstraw, different townlands in the various valleys were often exclusively of one religion, and it was one landlord's policy that they should stay that way.[34] The same practice was employed in Drumhone parish, an area of southern Donegal coastal land with a higher proportion of Protestants than its surrounding parishes.[35] This concept of "Protestant" and "Catholic" land was one way in which displacement effects could be prevented. And if it was accepted it was a way of keeping a balance of tranquillity between the religious groups, even though it made very sure that everyone was conscious of the importance of religious differences. One suspects that this practice was actually much more widespread than the Devon Commission evidence suggests, and that it was an unwritten law between tenants themselves. One of William Carleton's stories, "Vesey Vengeance", is based on the animosities created by the successful purchase of a Catholic farm by a Protestant tenant.[36]

There is, however, another aspect to the Killygorden example. In this case the barrier to Catholic purchase had also prevented a maximization of tenant right payment leading to subdivision. At the time when the linen industry was at its height the landlords might not have minded about subdivision. And in those circumstances people from the surrounding mountains (far more Catholic than the lowland parishes) would not have found this obstacle raised against them. But the changing priorities of the landlords was actually going to put an end to the displacement effect in another way.

In the classic settlement displacement crisis, the natives' lower subsistence level is used as a lever against the settlers' higher level. In the case of the tenant farming society, the native offers a higher rent than the settler, who emigrates. The situation in the consolidating period was that the landlord, rather than seeking the highest rent offer (and certainly not the highest tenant right offer) was looking for a tenant who had adequate capital to run the farm and be able to pay a rent out of long-term income. In short, the desired tenant was not the person prepared to undergo the greatest self-exploitation through intensified labour in order to secure a lowland farm, so much as the holder of sufficient capital who was prepared to embark on a farming venture at a certain rent after first paying a limited tenant right. The raising of the necessary capital, to begin with, tended to lift expectations whether of Protestant or Catholic, regardless. The most sought after tenants were now those with a considerable capital, amongst whom minimal standards of tolerated subsistence on a mountain ridge would be a thing of the past or alien to their experience altogether. The division of territory embodied in the notions of "Protestant" and "Catholic" farms was a restriction on free market mechanisms, but it would scarcely have been tolerated, let alone imposed by landlords, if its economic impact upon their rent rolls had been significantly adverse. (To return to the theme of Chapter 1: the *Newsletter* 1883 editorial on Sligo.) It was a socially and politically possible strategy just because its economic impact was marginal. After the Famine had forced a much "freer" movement of labour between Britain and Ireland, higher levels of migration and emigration reduced not only the poverty of the mountain parishes, but their populations and their impact upon the lowlands about them. Irish under-employment then spread its effects more widely.

Even if the peace of the parish depended upon yeomanry in 1814, and if the landlords of the area encouraged Orangeism, none the less they had adapted to the new order of the Whigs' 1830s reforms. The gap between public utterance and the private behaviour of landlords in matters of a sectarian character could be very wide. One priest praised Lord Abercorn as an excellent landlord because he displayed "not a particle of religious feeling" in his conduct. "That is what does all the harm here."[37] Be that as it may, the Lord's brother, Lord Claud Hamilton, permitted himself to be chaired around the town of

Dungannon after his public enrolment into the Orange Order in 1834.[38] As it can be fairly certainly presumed that the priest would not have praised Lord Abercorn in this way if he had given him any resistance on the question of school sites, what is suggested here is that even landlords with definite Orange connections might quite easily come to local good understanding and accommodation with Catholic priests. It is a reasonable suspicion that the policy of each religion selling only to its own kind was yet another part of a growing fabric of accommodation between differentiated subsocieties.

Another Catholic mountainous area with much more Protestant lowlands about it is the Sperrin chain stretching through the middle of Counties Londonderry and Tyrone. County Derry is the only one for which we have details of the distribution of farm size by parishes before the Famine.[39] I have broken the county up into four groups of parishes. Group A is the lowland parishes along the Bann and on the north-west shore of Lough Neagh. It is religiously heterogeneous, much cut up into small farms (less than 10 acre farms 58–71 per cent) and with considerable variation in the amount of weaving (15–37 per cent). Group B is the mountain parishes (plus Killelagh) between 60 and 90 per cent Catholic; farms of less than 10 acres account for 40 to 45 per cent of the total, and by 1841 weaving was accounting for less than 7 per cent of the adult male employment. Fourth-class housing made up 35–44 per cent of the 1841 total. Group C is the environs of Coleraine, 80–90 per cent Protestant, 25 per cent in weaving, and between 20 and 40 per cent in small farms. In these districts there was an influx of harvest labour in 1835. Fourth-class housing made up 20–24 per cent of the 1841 total. Group D is a miscellaneous group, whose indices are intermediate in all respects except that they have fewer small farms than the other districts (25 per cent or below). My focus here is on areas where smaller farms are still very prevalent.

In 1840 rural weavers' small farms were both prevalent along the east of the county below the 500 ft contour line. None the less the very Catholic mountain parishes of Dungiven and Ballynascreen had few weavers and about half their farms were below 10 acres. Dungiven was the subject of a rather lengthy report in 1814 which has, for reasons which will become obvious, been employed to demonstrate the ethnic character of the national conflict in Ireland. The parish is mostly mountain, falling away in the north-west down the Roe River valley to Dungiven town. In 1814, on account of the bog fuel supply, much of the mountain was more thickly inhabited than the plain. Emigration to America was "never so prevalent", but the report also stresses "the readiness of young men to set out for Scotland and England, in search of that employment which their native mountains cannot afford to a superabundant population". In the mountains subdivision has created divisions of arable land to 3–4 acre holdings. "The inhabitants of the parish are divided into two races of men, as totally distinct as if they belonged to different countries and regions. . . . The Scotch are remarkable for their comfortable houses and appearance, regular conduct, prudence and perseverance in business, and their being almost entirely manufacturers." Whereas the Irish are "more negligent of their habitations . . . total indisposition to manufacture", enjoying the extravagance of fairs, wakes and merry-making. The Scotch would hand the farm to one son and put the other to trade, but the Irish have "the notion of the equal and unalienable right of all children to the inheritance of the father's property. . . . It is a singular fact that there is not perhaps in any part of the South, a more truly primitive race, than that which is found in the mountains of Dungiven, surrounded on all sides by the Scotch and English settlers."[40]

What tendencies were either reinforcing or attenuating these differences? In some of the mountain townlands "which lie within the reach of constant observation . . . neat houses, enclosed fields, and greater attention to the appearance of decency begin to distinguish the present inhabitants from their predecessors: even the linen manufacture has crept into a few native families". There are also some hints of reinforcing tendencies. The practice of cattle-driving from the mountains to Carlisle is described as "a species of gambling", which in the last few years brought a considerable influx of wealth into several mountain districts. In the lowlands the Scotch plough was coming into use, but in the mountains where reclamation was proceeding, the old plough was more manageable on steep, stony and unequal surfaces. The writer describes with evident respect the great learning of some of the mountain people. And as an obvious carry-over from the hedge-schools of the penal era, there were private schools in every townland which were kept by the native Irish "who having pursued their taste for literature, can afterwards find no other employments for their talents and acquirements".[41] The preservation of oral tradition was conducted by seanchus, gatherings for recitals at which any disagreements over correct versions were settled by vote. Unfortunately we don't have information on the scale of seasonal migration from Dungiven in the 1830s, but it seems reasonable to suppose that here in the mountains reclamation and migrant working were offsetting the subdivision of existing natural resources.

In the lowlands towards the Bann and Lough Neagh in this early period, weaving and spinning were very prevalent, together with much subdivision and rundale—the system of joint tenancy. In 1819 the overwhelmingly Catholic parish of Killelagh beneath Carntogher Mountain had turf in abundance and a very fast expanding population engaged in weaving and spinning.[42] And rundale seems to have been less widespread away from the mountains. In Tamlaght the Scotch plough and clover/turnips were gaining ground; but even in this 75 per cent Protestant parish, there was some rundale.[43] The ethnic differences were noticed in Maghera (in much the same terms as Dungiven), but with certain variations. The Irish were increasingly using the English language and engaging in the linen trade. The peasantry were described as political and "litigious", and mention is made of the fact that in 1798 Maghera was in a state of insurrection (pre-empted only by the defeat of the rebels at Antrim). There were many hedge-schools in "wretched huts".[44] Trade with Belfast seems to have been rapidly expanding in the period.

By the 1840s, linen weaving had retreated toward the immediate edges of the Bann and the parishes adjoining Lough Neagh. Thus it was still a considerable presence in Tamlaght, receding in Maghera, and more or less dead in Killelagh. The Drapers' Company was attempting to reverse the linen-generated subdivision and to abolish rundale, sending some smaller tenants to work reclamation tenancies on what had been grazing lands. With ten years' rent as compensation, they set them to build houses and clear and drain new farms.⁴⁵ This process was still very much in operation on the eve of the Famine. The district as a whole was clearly stretched badly. About three-quarters of the tenants in some townlands in the mountainous part of Lissan parish (Co. Tyrone) were dependent on the Cookstown loan fund. The low interest rates of the loan fund (about 6½% – 4½%) were only the first line of credit. The numbers who were dependent on meal mongers and usurers (with 35 per cent interest rates) are not stated. Larger farmers in the lowlands could borrow from banks at about 5 per cent.⁴⁶

The drapers' efforts to create larger farms involved the use of the mountains to create space in the low country. It was one way to resolve the difficulty from the standpoint of estate management. The Drapers' Company agent said that they did not employ any religious criteria in deciding who to send up the mountains, but in so far as the clearance of rundale holdings involved predominantly Catholic tenants, it is reasonable to presume that they were particularly affected. The agent declared that he would not allow a known Ribbonman on the estate and would put out any he knew to be such.⁴⁷

The areas where subdivision was most rife in 19th-century Ulster were generally remoter areas where the opportunities for commercial farming were either weak or had been overpowered in an earlier phase by the linen industry. For without the prospects of commercial farming the incentives to individual families to avoid subdivision were substantially undermined. But there were other commercial stimuli which had also facilitated subdivision and then left it behind. In the Innishowen Peninsula of north Donegal, a remote area even in later years, the economy in 1814–19 depended on illegal distillation. It propelled the work of reclamation for fuel consumption and for increased crop acreage. It kept up the price of corn, provided employment for corn mills, and the product was smuggled to the Hebrides and across the Foyle. By the testimony of an Anglican clergyman, it was superior to legal brands.⁴⁸ This Gaelic area preserved its isolation and developed a market linkage simultaneously. The suppression of the illegal distillation and the collapse of agri-prices delivered a double blow. The area now had to function through migrant labour income or much more bulky trade with distant markets through Derry. Reclamation under the new circumstances was much less a paying proposition, and the lands left to reclaim were probably more marginal. This story in varying degrees was applicable to other remoter parts of Donegal such as the west coast. From those areas, there was fairly considerable seasonal harvest migration by the 1840s. The lands had become very subdivided indeed, and people claimed that landlords revalued the lands to impossible rent levels after they had been reclaimed. Lord George Hill attempted to connect the area by road, but subdivision had reduced holdings to the point where they barely produced subsistence, and so commerce was hardly possible.[49]

It was in precisely those areas, some of the poorest and economically most backward in Ireland, that tenant right was highest. Twenty years' purchase seems to have been a norm, and anything up to 50 years' purchase could be paid for a patch of sea coast (for seaweed and fishing).[50] How were these sums acquired? For the most part probably by migrant earnings; but they were sustained by a system of usury and meal mongering with effective interest rates in the region of 300 per cent. The vast valuations of tenant right were a self-sustaining speculation in which most people from the area had an interest at some level. It would last so long as there was enough incoming cash to keep the bids high and to enable those who left for whatever reason to sell up and pay off their debts. It was also a direct challenge to any landlord ideas about consolidation. For people determined to stay on their own land in an area which they knew, the holding of a piece of land was an absolute. The outside world was an alien world.

In large areas of County Monaghan, the subdivision process had been accelerated by the domestic linen trade. Here tenant right values were also sustained for a long time at levels reflecting the earlier opportunities provided by linen. But here the speculative bubble burst even before the Famine. Donegal had fishing, dulce and peat fuel; but in many parts of the county, unlike the mountain districts just mentioned, the bog was running out. In 1842 the very high prices being paid for tenant right suddenly collapsed. In Tedavnet and Monaghan parishes where tenant right was recognized, it was stated that many would sell if they could find a purchaser. But their arrears were so high that at tenant right levels obtaining at that time they wouldn't have enough to emigrate.[51] In the few areas where farms were at all sizeable, such as Castleblaney in the very Presbyterian Muckno parish, the adjoiner purchase and tenant right limitation strategies were used to promote gradual consolidation.[52] But in the southern Farney barony where mass seasonal migration to Leinster harvests was occurring in 1835,[53] the limits of reclamation had been largely reached. The farms, subdivided for children and to pay debts, were too small to lie fallow. There were few cattle and therefore no manure. The land was being fast exhausted. On the Shirley estate an attempt was made to impose a bog-rent, described by the parish priest as a thing unheard of in Ireland until the 1830s.[54] Shirley also caused great irritation by attempting to impose estate schools, by employing a moral agent who went about distributing religious tracts, and attempting to enforce the purchase of lime from his estate kiln.

Information about the scale of seasonal migration is rather difficult to quantify. The answers in the appendix to the 1835 Poor Law Inquiry in Ireland show very considerable variations between the different estimates given for some parishes.[55] The estimates given by the parish priests tend to be highest and often suggest precise inquiry and the suspicion that their parishioners were more generally concerned by it than others. To take an example from the area where the migration was very heavy, Rev. D. O'Rafferty, P.P. said that of the 6,978 people in Forkhill (south Armagh), 1,161 were involved. The very Catholic southern fringe of Ulster, south Armagh, south Monaghan and south-east Cavan appear to have been very heavily dependent on seasonal harvest work indeed. From Creggan parish (Crossmaglen) it was reported that many who used to go did not go anymore on account of prejudices against them in England and low rates of return in the South of Ireland. When they went they often left wives with some provisions and heavily dependent on usury, the debts being settled after their return. In some cases the migration was systematized and people would be "written for". Many of the migrants were married small farmers.

It was areas like this where the determination to keep smallholdings was greatest. When there was an adequate bog supply and still some reclamation possibilities (as in south Armagh), the strategy for endurance had a definite character that marked it out as an experience alien to much of inner Ulster and most of Great Britain. To get an idea of just how unusual this kind of lifestyle of seasonal migration was, Chambers and Mingay state that down to the middle of the 19th century "English farm labour was normally mobile only over fairly short distances."[56] Ribbonism revived in this period before the Famine, no longer as a purely pan-Catholic fraternity against Orangeism, but rather as a means of organizing a migrant labour/small farm society. Its vital experiences were the struggle to hold on to land in Ireland against landlords, and the alienness with which they were regarded by indigenous peoples of areas they moved to in search of work, not just in the North but in areas of Scotland and England. They were on the receiving end of the Protestant nativism so unambiguously expressed by the Select Committee on Emigration of 1827: No scheme for facilitating emigration has any advantage that does not "primarily apply to Ireland".[57] Otherwise the Irish population "unless some other outlet be opened to them, must shortly fill up every vacuum created in England or in Scotland and reduce the labouring classes to a uniform state of degradation and misery". The landlords did not want them in Ireland, nor did Anglo-Saxons want them in Britain, and that was the first political lesson to be clearly impressed upon them.

So far I have concentrated on the areas of Ulster that experienced the economic crisis pressures in the most severe forms. Taking the province of Ulster as a whole, only a minority lived in such districts, but those districts included an overwhelmingly Catholic population. So far then, we have concentrated on the asymmetrical, rather than the conflictual, relationships between Catholic and Protestant experience. We have seen signs of truce over Protestant and Catholic land. There were some places and occasions when this broke, showing what possibilities there were for sectarian aggravation over land questions. The experience of County Cavan in the 1830s was rather unusual. The great bulk of its landlord class were "Liberal Protestants" or Whigs. Alone among the Ulster counties it had no areas with Protestant majorities. Reflecting the limited destiny of the Protestant population in the county, it is reasonable to reckon that in the Whig era the landlords sought to preserve order by accommodation with local Catholic leadership and acceptance of the Whig programme. But there were enough Protestants in the county to make this strategy a choice. It was also possible for firebrands to promote confrontation.

The linen industry had come and gone, leaving vast areas carved up into micro-holdings with little means of income. Sizeable Protestant minorities were surrounded by overwhelmingly Catholic districts. In the period of O'Connell's mobilization, the growth of a climate of confrontation and the potential for intimidating violence and exclusive dealing tended overwhelmingly to affect the Protestant minorities rather than the Catholic mass. Lord Farnham's much publicized setting up of a colony on his estate in Cavan for converts of the "Second Reformation" no doubt contributed to the general elevation of tensions,[58] and sowed the seeds of a project to solve simultaneously the problem of consolidation and the pressure on the Protestant population—displacement of Catholic microholders to make way for consolidated Protestant farms.

On the estate of Sir George Hodson near Bailieborough this was done in about 1829–31.[59] John C. Beresford who promoted the Protestant Colonization Society was rebuked by the Grand Lodge of the Orange Order for expounding views "inconsistent with the principles of Orangeism"; and at the foundation of the Cavan Conservatives in 1834, the Rev. Marcus Beresford called for action to stop the displacement of Protestants by popish tenants.[60] In 1837 he ejected five tenant families in Larah parish, followed by a further seven after shots had been fired at himself. Anglicans were then settled in their stead.[61] In 1842, on the Bishop of Kilmore's land in Killinkere parish, some families were displaced after a murder and replaced by Protestants.[62] This district around Bailieborough is the only area of Ulster where this kind of thing was done in the 1830s, and even here on a very small scale. It was also an area where local magistrates dispersed an Orange procession in 1834 with a military charge. In later years landlords and agents declared that today (1844) it "is a matter of serious consequence to enlarge farms".[63] At that time landlords who tried to remove tenants were said to be denounced from the altar. Yet emigration was beginning before the Famine. "In former years, the Roman Catholic population were not disposed to wander, but a great many of their friends and relations have gone, and good accounts have come over from them: and now they are emigrating very rapidly indeed, particularly females, about (Virginia)."[64]

Beresford's antics were a renewal of strategies for extending settlement colonization; and Whig landlords in the southern fringe of Ulster must have had some idea what the consequences of that would have been. The determination of people to stay on their land reflected the fact that it was all they had. The decline of the linen industry made the landlords keen to consolidate; but Beresford and others were, from the point of view of those on the receiving end of consolidation, going to make the principles of political economy look like nothing more than a modern face of an enemy of longer standing.

What happened in County Cavan was, as far as I know, unique. Otherwise it seems as though the pattern of farm holdings was being governed by the kind of truce we saw earlier in the Newtonstewart area. But this kind of territorial stability did not hold in the weaving districts. By the 1840s the main types of weaving systems were:[65] (a) smallholders working irregularly on their own account for the market, still partly engaged in working their own holdings and doing agricultural labour for larger farmers. These, who had once been a "norm", were now concentrated about Ballymena, and to a lesser extent at Coleraine and Ballymoney; (b) the largest group were cottier weavers working for manufacturers who accounted for most of those in County Derry (i.e. those in the south-eastern parishes we dealt with earlier), and some in the north-central areas of County Down (e.g. Banbridge and Dromore); (c) landholders working for manufacturers, concentrated in north Armagh and north-west Down where some still worked the old system production of the highest quality cloth. Not surprisingly it was in this last sort of area where the proportion of "clothing" to "agricultural" workers in rural areas was highest.

In north Armagh and north-west Down, the centre of the 1840 weaver belt below Lough Neagh, efforts made at consolidation of holdings were fairly limited and many landlords permitted the free sale of tenant right (Colonel Blacker), even if some required that adjoining tenants be given the first right of refusal (Lord Lurgan).[66] In the district along the Bann, bleach greens and a few spinning mills (at Gilford and Banbridge) were situated in areas where weaving was dominant. The turf in these areas was largely exhausted, as it had been in Seagoe parish by 1820, and the districts depended on coal imported up the Bann.[67] Tenant right values rose and fell with the fortunes of the linen trade. Away from accessibility of coal, they depended upon the proximity of bog or other fuel supply (e.g. Tartaharhan, west Armagh), or on distances weavers might need to travel to yarn manufactories (an 8 mile journey cost a day's travel).

The weaving districts were affected by the political crisis of the 1830s. South-east Tyrone still had a lot of smallholder weavers who probably had to travel to manufactories for yarn and disposal of finished cloth. Killyman and Clonfeakle were on the edge of Protestant majority territory and experienced sectarian contestation during the 1830s, the low point in the linen trade. Here political and economic pressures to emigrate or, conversely, to band together were strongly interrelated. The Rev. Mortimer O'Sullivan, rector of Killyman, described an occasion in the early 1830s when one night the Catholic population carried lighted turfs from house to house as the occasion when Protestant alarm was kindled.[68] In 1835 he reckoned five-sixths of the adult male Protestant population were in the Orange Order. What did Orangeism do for them? It gave Protestants courage to stay rather than emigrate. In Killyman Protestant emigration had stopped altogether. He was careful to talk of the things Orangemen fear as "persuasion of the people" rather than facts; these fears were not of individual Catholics, but arose rather from the belief that there was a conspiracy in Ireland to exterminate Protestants which included nine-tenths of humble rural Catholics. Was it the local wing of that conspiracy that they feared? Not as much as the belief that if a general rising of Catholics occurred, the locals would be compelled to take up arms also. If there was a separation of Ireland from England, the Orange Society would be the means of preventing a massacre. "It is better that there should be a battle than a massacre." And why did he fear such an apocalyptic consequence of repeal of the Union? "Discontent, when power is connected with it, will naturally encourage daring projects and expectations."

In what sense did this fear correspond to reality? If one seriously believes there is even a possibility of such an event as a general massacre, it doesn't matter what the chances are, so long as they are significant. This is a clear case of people judging "them" by the most threatening things that any of "them" seem to be doing. Catholic society, becoming self-assertive (carrying around these lighted turfs) for the first time during O'Connell's mobilizations, did not easily reveal its collective thoughts. Because any sectarian occurrence can easily seem representative of "them", it follows that those who fear this occurrence are at the mercy of those of their own kind who frighten the "others", unless there exist mechanisms of communication through which fears can be allayed. In the early 1830s, when landlords were busy mobilizing Orangeism against O'Connell and the Whigs, there were areas where there was no such mutual mechanism.

I stress this last point because it is necessary to rehabilitate in part at least a supposedly discarded thesis, i.e. that Orange leaders manipulated the Protestant masses by playing on their "bigotry". The part I quarrel with is the word "bigotry", but there is no doubt that leaders could and did stir things up. This is what happened in nearby Dungannon in 1832. An Orange meeting was held, as part of the anti-Whig reaction, in the Court House and presided over by two magistrates. Resolutions were passed against national education, and reform: and after several affirming the need to "encourage Protestant tenants . . . defend Protestant landholders . . . preserve a Protestant population", they declared that they saw "no reason why Protestant colonization should not be attempted on lands that are reclaimed" (and by implication already inhabited perhaps?), as well as unreclaimed land.[69]

A declaration of this kind from the local ruling figures could not possibly have failed to alarm Catholics. It should not surprise us that local sectarian relations in this area in the 1830s were very bad. This was an area where the old patterns of settlement society were more disrupted than most by the weaving industry and the old cultural differential of "settler" and "native" was eaten away. In these areas smallholdings might be readily exposed to competitive tenant right bids. And in the linen crisis of the early 1830s, when political contestation was rising, the question of who held the land might be resolved by issues of strength. But the only outward sign of a Protestant colonization policy in 1844 was on the Powerscourt estate at Benburb. The agent operated a policy that Protestants must sell to Protestants, but Catholics may sell to Catholics.[70] In effect, the landlords' contribution to holding the line was not so great in deed as in word, but then as we have seen in the evidence of Mortimer O'Sullivan, the word spoken by the right person in the right place is a deed when people are frightened enough.

So far I have looked at some areas which experienced the crisis pressures of pre-famine Ulster most severely. I have looked at the Catholic west, south, and mountain centre. I have also looked at the Protestant edge of the 1841 weaver zone south of Lough Neagh. Most of the rest of the story of rural political agitation through to the 1880s will concentrate more upon areas of inner Ulster where those pressures were generally less. As we shall see, the tendency in those areas was for the major adaptation to capitalized farming to have gone some distance before the Famine. This is only a general rule: and in Ballintoy, a Protestant area of north Antrim, the Devon Commission was told that long ago the inhabitants had been given perpetuity leases, which was why it was alleged to be so run down. But the second part of the explanation, that many of the inhabitants were fishermen, seems more plausible,[71] as does the fact that in 1835 there was evidence of growing seasonal harvest migration to Scotland. Although there were areas not far to the south of Ballintoy where in summer seasons there was a labour shortage (Macosquin and Aghadowey),[72] it seems quite possible that that parish was engaged in similar kinds of adaptation as the western and southern areas.

Taking inner Ulster as a whole, what stand out are: first, in some districts the continued presence of weaving on a large scale; second, districts where large-scale farms went together with a clearer separation between cottier labourers (part-time weavers) and farmers; and third, there were some areas where the exhaustion of bog supplies meant a sharp increase in fuel costs making marginal existence impossible, so the spur behind subdivision was reduced. Wherever the structure of farm holdings already included some sizeable units, consolidation by adjoiner purchase and tenant right limitation was a viable proposition.

An example of an area where the linen and cotton industries had flourished in 1816, but had departed more or less by 1840 leaving fairly substantial farm holdings, is the Glenavy, Tullyrusk, Crumlin area of south Antrim.[73] In 1816, despite the presence of a cotton manufactory at Glenavy, a linen spinning mill at Crumlin, a "spinning-wheel in every house" and a "loom in every third house", the average farm size was around 20–30 acres and some were as big as 200 acres. Land use was two parts tillage to five parts grazing and meadow, and clover was in regular use. Yet in 1835 the farmers of the three parishes used to employ migrant labour from County Tyrone in harvest seasons.[74] Weaving had become marginalized (except in Glenavy) and was a secondary occupation for agricultural labourers (or vice versa). The vital difference between areas of this kind (which incidentally had sizeable Catholic populations) and some of the southern, now decayed, weaving areas, was that weaving had never "displaced" farming. As its decay in this area was gradual, there was no catastrophic collapse of employment opportunities which continued to be provided in varying proportions by agricultural labour and weaving. To the extent that some weavers had been held as cottiers rather than establishing themselves as small farmers, having for example no *de facto* rights to bog fuel or tenant right, and being under the control of farmers, they could be removed. Where this kind of arrangement operated, larger farmers and landlords had a common interest in ensuring that cottiers were "controlled". And the cost of the decline of the weaving industry could be more easily imposed on them than it could be in areas where landlords confronted a general solidarity of small marginal holders fairly uniformly in crisis. Class differentiation between farmers and labourer/weavers had proceeded further in the inner North than elsewhere.

To get round the difficulties tenant right put in the way of consolidating landlords, they had to be able to break the general solidarity with the outgoing tenants. That meant giving some tenants a hope of gaining by another's departure, creating an "estate solidarity" in contradiction to the solidarity of tenants generally to defend tenant right values. County Fermanagh and parts of adjoining Monaghan and south-east Tyrone had considerable numbers of resident gentry. Fermanagh, a primarily stock farming county turning to crop rotation for dairying, had never had much of a linen industry, and labourers, who were scarce, tended to be employees of resident gentry. The county cess was very high, reflecting a large-scale road building programme. The main objection the landlords in this area had to tenant right was not that it promoted subdivision, but that it detracted from the capital of incoming tenants necessary to provide livestock for the farms.[75] Various efforts were made to devise arbitration procedures involving tenants on the estate in the process, the general tenor of which was to allow a certain number of years' purchase for mere possession, and to arbitrate for "unexhausted" (i.e. recent) improvements. Some landlords such as the Earl of Caledon actually purchased the tenant right themselves and added the interest on it to the rent.[76]

In areas where tenant right was falling and was not exposed to super-high bids—as it was in weaving districts and the mountain subsistence areas—these kinds of procedures could work quite easily. In the early 1840s, the fall in agri-prices began to lower tenant right values generally. Once they fell low enough, reflecting the low levels of valuation of tenant equity in holdings, it often paid landlords simply to buy the right out themselves as compensation for removing tenants. This exposed the basic difficulty in the concept of tenant right. As a species of dual ownership, but one which fluctuated according to the difference between the current market value of the land and the going rent, it would always do much more of the falling than would the rents which were fixed for very long periods. It was a volatile property, representing the very variable upper slice of valuation over the rent. When it fell to low levels, it was quite easy to substitute for it "compensation for recent improvements", which might even turn out to the financial advantage of an outgoer. This kind of thing seems to have occurred not only in County Fermanagh, but even in the far outer edges of the northern weaver belt. Thus in Ballymoney by 1844, the tenant right levels had fallen to around two years' purchase, which landlords were quite prepared to pay as a compensation payment to secure consolidation.[77] What this meant was that the consolidation process was being oiled by the tenant right system. It was providing the means of liquidating arrears, debts and paying emigration money.

All the same the process did not proceed easily. Whenever and for whatever reasons the tenants could get high tenant right payments, the landlords were tempted to interfere. In east Down, some of the best agricultural land in Ireland, fairly intensive efforts were being made in the 1840s to limit the size of tenant right payments and enforce adjoiner purchase.[78] An earlier attempt near Banbridge to evict without recognizing tenant right had led to agrarian outrages which had been sufficient to deter landlords from trying it generally.[79] In the Killinchy area, a similar effort had deprived the remaining tenants in the district of access to the usual sources of credit, thereby stimulating usury and arresting agricultural improvements.[80] Here more than anywhere, perhaps, where landlords were attempting to promote crop rotation and wheat cultivation, their efforts to consolidate had to be carefully balanced against discouragement of improvement. It was not so much a question of stopping potential subdividers and micro-holders, although the removal of such people where they existed was intended as one of ensuring that whoever got the holding was not denuded of a large part of their capital on entry.

Finally, we come to a situation where the tenants seemed to have the upper hand. In the Sixmilewater valley (Donegore and Nilteen Grange) large areas of land, including plenty of reclaimable mountain, had been leased at fairly low rents in perpetuity on payment of large fines. Here reclamation was going on but with a difference. The lands leased in perpetuity were not going to face a rent increase after they came to maturity.[81] The proximity of Ballymena market provided a ready outlet for produce in a growing linen district; but the absence of a local supply of bog made the district inhospitable to labourers. Weaving was fairly marginal (15–17 per cent in 1841) in the area itself, even though its much greater presence near by (35 per cent in Connor and Ballycor) created a ready market. Donegore was a predominantly Presbyterian parish with an Anglican minority amounting to about 20 per cent. Its population was described as "bigoted" in their attitudes toward other religions, but particularly toward Anglicanism.[82] The parish had provided much of the force for the rebels at the Battle of Antrim in 1798 and the encampment on Donegore hill was part of the legend of the area. Efforts to agitate the district in 1833 against national schools may have worked as there was no national school there in 1838.[83] That area, heartland of the United Irishmen, was probably very little affected by the sectarian aggravation of the 1830s. It did not share in some of the economic crisis pressures that were affecting areas to the south and west of Ulster; it is probable that its politics connected with that of other areas through the education question. The next question will be about how its experience of the Famine linked it to the south and west.

5. The Famine in Ulster

The Great Irish Famine of 1845–50 was precipitated by successive failures of the potato crop. That failure which was first noticed in late 1845, and which was repeated in 1846, 1848 and, to a lesser extent, in 1849, worked a virtual revolution in all aspects of Irish society. Estimates of about a million deaths through starvation and disease, plus a million lost through emigration, are in the right order of magnitude, if nowhere near precise.[1] Today it is a very powerful memory and yet somehow it leaves an unanswered question. If it was so important to most of Ireland, why is it not much mentioned as part of the history of the North? Did it not happen in Ulster? In this chapter I will not try to describe the Famine in Ulster as a whole; my purpose is to show that there are very good reasons why it may have been remembered differently, even before we start to make any allowance for later interpretations of its significance in Unionist or Nationalist myth.[2]

This massive trauma had some effects which were more or less universal. Besides leaving many without food, or the means to feed livestock, or pay rent or taxes, it reduced demand for agricultural employment, reduced the rental income that landlords might spend on local employment-generating works, and increased local taxes (county and barony cess and poor law rates) on those who were not themselves already destitute. In short, it had a multiplier effect which generalized the impact of the crisis. But, especially after mid-1847, the crisis afflicted different areas in different ways. And, a fact to which we will attach considerable importance: the potato failure did not lead to very high food prices generally except in the latter half of 1846, and most acutely in the first half of 1847 (see diagram of oat prices in Belfast). As far as the inner North was concerned, 1847 was "the famine year".³ In other areas, the later stages were quite as bad as 1847. The death rates for each Ulster county rose and fell, and it is clear from the diagram that Monaghan and Cavan experienced a renewal of Famine pressures in 1849, when the death rates elsewhere in Ulster were declining. The main difference between inner Ulster and most of the rest of the island had to do with the continued existence of sources of employment which—rather than being undermined by the Famine—were intensified. Rural textile work on the one hand, and the expansion of Belfast on the other, gave the Famine experience a different tempo. In many parts of Ireland it left people with literally no source of income whatever. Everywhere many people died of starvation and disease; but the political messages conveyed by the experience were not made "uniform" by the enormous death toll, nor, conversely, were they divergent just because proportionately "fewer" died in Ulster than elsewhere.

Having said little about Belfast in the last chapter, I shall start with an outline of some of the effects of the Famine on the city. In effect the city was an area where an unwitting "Keynesian" solution to the distress was adopted. During the Famine years there was large-scale construction and infrastructural work done. The resident magistrate William Tracy said of the works done between 1845 and 1852 that "they wanted to make Belfast a great city before its time; and they condensed into some seven years taxation that should have been spread over three times that period".⁴ The government-sponsored public works more or less dried up in 1847, but the deficit-financed work of the Belfast Corporation proceeded apace; poverty-stricken people coming from the countryside in search of work often found it. The 1842 Conservative town council elected under the Municipal Corporations Act did not take office until 1844, when it won its dispute with the old police commissioners.⁵ In 1842 the new toll-free bridge over the Lagan had been erected at the expense of the grand juries of Antrim and Down, and the harbour commissioners were arranging the removal of the coal quarries to the Down bank to clear space for other shipping on the Antrim side. The town council, on taking office, set about clearing a large number of small and narrow streets to create the new and spacious Victoria and Corporation Streets. They also set about removing much of the market from Smithfield down to Maysfield on the Lagan riverbank. The whole process was designed to facilitate the import of coal and its distribution to mills on the sloping western and northern edges of the town; to expand the shipping facilities generally; and to create space for the erection of offices and warehouses on the new streets.[6] The timely financial embarrassment of the Donegall family removed large tracts of the city from its control in 1844.

The expansion of employment, coming at the time of the Famine, had ambiguous effects upon working-class organisation. We know fairly little of the history of such organisation, but some of its trials are recounted in the short-lived *Labour's Advocate* of April/May 1847. Of that otherwise very bleak period it said: "One ray of consolation, however, lights up the gloomy picture: the mechanical branches of industry are generally in a healthy state, and employment is tolerably abundant."[7] It describes how able-bodied beggars, "an influx from other counties", are appearing at the soup kitchen, while the indigenous unemployed labourers are most unwilling to resort to the soup kitchen or to be "in any other way recipients of private charity". There was evidence that established labour forces were having difficulty preserving even a semblance of workplace organisation. For example, the ratio of apprentices to journeymen amongst the shipwrights had reached 1 to 3. There was enormous demand for bakers, and the "most inferior workmen will be put up with . . . If we [the operative bakers] leave one situation on account of excessive labour we will be no better off in another." Similar complaints about dilution were made by printers.[8]

Working-class organisation, already weakened before the Famine, showed no ability to capitalize on the industrial upswing. In 1847, when the 10-Hours Act (for women and children) was before parliament, the Liberal MP for Belfast, David Ross, stated in parliament: "So far as the important town which I represent is concerned, this Bill is neither wanted nor asked for—not a single petition has emanated from its factory workers praying for a reduction of the hours of labour; on the contrary, several against the Bill lie on the table of the House." Ross originally attempted to move an amendment excluding

Ireland from its provisions, and no sign of protest was made. The *Advocate* reported that hints were given that if the workers did petition for the Bill, there would be consequences.[9] Precisely why the amendment was not pressed in unclear. The mill owners are said to have wanted it.[10] But seeing that the town council was at that time pressing for the Borough Bill and that Lord Shaftesbury had a hand in its committee stages, the explanation that seems most likely is that the town council didn't want to prejudice the passage of the Bill and found ways of getting at the mill owners who had put the Liberal MP, David Ross, up to it.[11] In short, the inclusion of Ireland (and therefore, what is more meaningful, of Belfast, which was one of the few places where it would have meant anything) within the 1847 Factory Act was determined by metropolitan forces rather than by Belfast working-class organisation. When the *Advocate* folded up shortly afterwards it lamented: "Had we commenced our labours in Glasgow, Manchester or Leeds ... our fate would have been very different."[12] Belfast's experience of the Famine later included the outbreak first of fever and then, in 1849, cholera, which killed about 2,000 people. Protests about the state of sewerage and health were to figure prominently in later local politics, but essentially within a municipal context.

We cannot here give more than an outline of the working out of the Famine in different districts. But there are some general points which do none the less emerge quite forcibly. Landlords were never popular in Ireland and the Famine did nothing to enhance their reputation as a whole. They are often remembered for the performance of their worst representatives. But one of the most striking things about the North is that in later years even radical land reformers avoided the kind of incendiary language about landlords, which was frequently used elsewhere. They sensed the need to support criticism of landlords with argument, whereas there were parts of Ireland where it could be taken for granted that landlords were a harmful species. So it is interesting that the northern landlords survived the Famine with their moral credibility much less damaged. Some people today believe that northern Protestant deference to landlords could be stretched to ridiculous lengths and that sectarianism must have blinded them to the realities of the Famine. The implication is that northern Protestants have

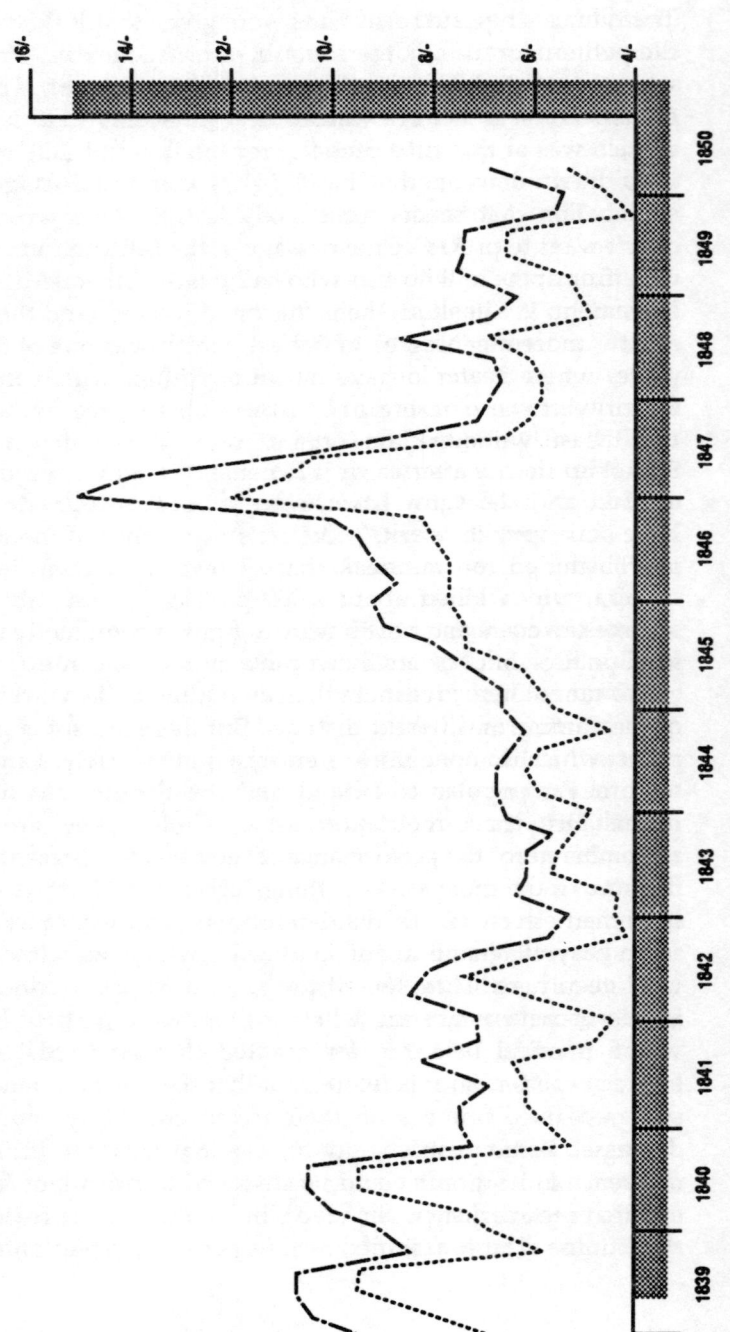

6. Oat prices at Belfast markets

"forgotten" the Famine. But at the time it did not uniformly undermine the authority and "legitimacy" of landlords everywhere, and under some conditions, it could even strengthen them. The North contained many such areas. The post-1847 divergence of experiences between parts of the North and elsewhere was sufficiently sharp to enable crude contrasts to be drawn between the "Protestant" North and the "Popish" South. These contrasts emanated not only from expected quarters such as Rev. Dr Drew, but also, in a less moralistic way, from people who became leaders of the agrarian protest movement. We shall see later on that the Famine did to some extent undermine some "unionist" strands of politics for a while, but its greater long-term result was probably to reinforce the growing sense of sectional identity of "Ulster".

In the early stages of the Famine,[13] during the term of office of Sir Robert Peel, measures were taken to import large quantities of food and the Corn Laws were repealed. Simultaneously, large-scale public works were started to ensure that Irish purchasing power was sustained. Local relief committees were set up to provide lists of applicants for places on public works schemes, to administer the sale of the imported Indian corn and small-scale works of local utility (farm work, stone-breaking, etc.), and to organize a relief fund collection locally to which government grants would be added proportional to the amount collected. Relief operations worked much more effectively in the first Famine year than they were to do later on. But from August 1846 it became clear that the potato harvest had failed again. The new Whig government discontinued the government-financed food imports, and Ireland began to experience the combined effects of the total harvest disaster of 1846 at home, and a generally bad European harvest. Food prices began to rise very steeply, reducing the efficacy of public works wages as a means of preventing starvation.

In September 1846 the Labour Rate Act offered government loan finance for baronial works and required the baronial ratepayers to select works of sufficient scale to employ all the distressed of the district. Although it was anticipated that the removal of the grant element of the government finance (a feature of the earlier public works provision) would reduce the attractions of the scheme, the desperate situation and the provision of an explicit objective—to employ all the destitute—more than counterbalanced this, and baronial sessions were characterized by scenes of mass pressure and intimidation of ratepayers to approve any proposal that might bring employment. Despite the delays in approving schemes caused by the enormity of demands on the tightly stretched administrative manpower of the Board of Works and by concern about the probable cost of these operations, their scale grew inexorably.[14]

Notwithstanding the inutility of much of the public works, or the opportunities they provided for often arbitrary determination of who was in need and who was not (or, to be more precise, who would or who would not starve without the wages provided), they provided about the only source of currency income in large parts of the country at the time, and therefore the only means of purchasing food. Their greatest weakness as a means of preventing starvation lay in the level of food prices which reached astronomic heights before the landing of American cargoes in spring 1847.

In January 1847 the government did a complete policy about-turn. It decided to try to end the public works and instead provide free food. In 1846 one of the alleged effects of the public works was to discourage agricultural labour, particularly in the sowing season, and it was hoped that this year that effect could be avoided. So the relief committees were called into operation to provide soup kitchens in preparation for the transfer of all relief responsibilities on to the new Poor Law. The significance of this last measure was that, having extended the powers of Poor Law unions to grant outdoor relief (from June 1847 onwards), the whole weight of local distress was placed upon local resources.[15]

The very high price levels of 1846–47 caused a massive speculative demand for food in 1847. The outflow of gold associated with these purchases abroad caused the Bank of England to attempt to reduce the currency circulation of notes. To achieve this the interest rates were raised very steeply from January 1847 through to their peak in October 1847. This led in August to some spectacular collapses in the corn trade. The falling prices and rising interest rates caught speculators in a fix, and these collapses later spread to other sectors of the economy.¹⁶ For Ireland the significance of the crisis was twofold. First, imported food prices fell back to "normal" levels. But second, Treasury pressure to cut down public spending and lending in Ireland intensified. And from the time of the setting up of the new Poor Law in summer 1847, the Poor Law unions were left to carry the costs of the overwhelming part of the burden of destitution out of current revenue from local taxation without recourse to further government borrowing.

In this way, as a result of the mid-1847 changes, the global crisis of the Famine turned more and more into a series of local crises for each Poor Law union. Everything would now hinge on the relative size of the taxable base of each compared with the demand on its resources posed by the extent of local destitution. An obvious consequence of this was that if the Poor Law rates escalated, many who might previously have been ratepayers would give up their holdings and become paupers. And the chances of this happening would grow as the scale of destitution grew. To set this snowball effect in motion, however, two additional malignancies entered the picture. Landlords were liable for the whole poor rate of all holdings valued at £4 or below. So the higher the poor rate rose, the stronger became the incentive to evict smallholders. And the rule which required that no one on relief should be a holder of more than a quarter of an acre meant that temporary destitution forced smallholders to give up their holdings altogether. Although this rule was eventually rescinded in May 1848, the quarter-acre rule was imposed during one of the most intense phases of destitution.¹⁷

The central importance of the period of high food prices in the weaving districts from late 1846 to mid-1847 is quite clear. In Castledawson (Magherafelt parish) on the edge of the south-east Derry weaving district, it was reported in January that the area had no shortage of food, "but it is at such a price as to make it totally impossible for a poor man to support his family with the wages he receives". There were 5,000 men on public works in the barony (a very large one, incidentally—Loughinsholin with approximately 70,000 inhabitants), and the district was inundated with "wandering poor, who came from the mountains or other districts less favoured by a resident gentry". On account of the weaving, George Dawson declared in an otherwise desperate report, "if provisions were cheaper, we might look forward with some hope".[18] His area was fairly average for the North, but another weaving area was not. Tartaharan parish, in north-west Armagh, was one of the twelve Ulster parishes (excluding west Donegal) where more than half the housing in the 1841 census had been fourth class. Its population of weavers "were sitting up three nights a week in order by any means to procure food for their families . . . This has been and is now the only means of employment."[19] Many cases of death from actual starvation of able-bodied men had occurred, not to mention the mortality rate amongst infants, the aged and infirm.

At this time the misery in the countryside was a source of speculation in the towns, and Belfast in particular. "Haberdashers' apprentices, pork-curers, muslin manufacturers, and even pawnbrokers . . . every creature who could beg or borrow from £50 upwards" was engaged in the speculation on food prices. "By the time the meal or flour purchased in Belfast arrives in remote country districts (the poorer the better for the usurious petty dealer) the price is often doubled."[20] The price falls in May took much of the pressures off wage-dependent districts. The year 1847 was the one year when the harvest, including the potato crop, was good. Shortage of potatoes was relative and due to limited planting that year. In Castledawson, the Lancashire and Carlisle manufacturers—who were laying off workers at home—were sending over yarn to be woven at half-price. In November 1846 there were two manufacturing agents: a year later there were five and the competition between them had "doubled" the price of a web.[21] The distress had largely lifted in this area.

Throughout the Famine not only did weaving intensify, but spinning and embroidery were widely diffused throughout inner Ulster. The number of women engaged in weaving rose significantly. In March 1847 it was reported of Ballymena Union that the distress amongst the cottiers was very great, where "nearly all are weavers".[22] Their earnings at between five shillings and six shillings a week suggest what was happening. A 60 yard web took about a week to weave in the ordinary course of events, and in Tartaharan in February 1847, a weaver got between 2s. 6d. and 4s. 6d. for such work.[23] In 1847 the

THE FAMINE IN ULSTER 113

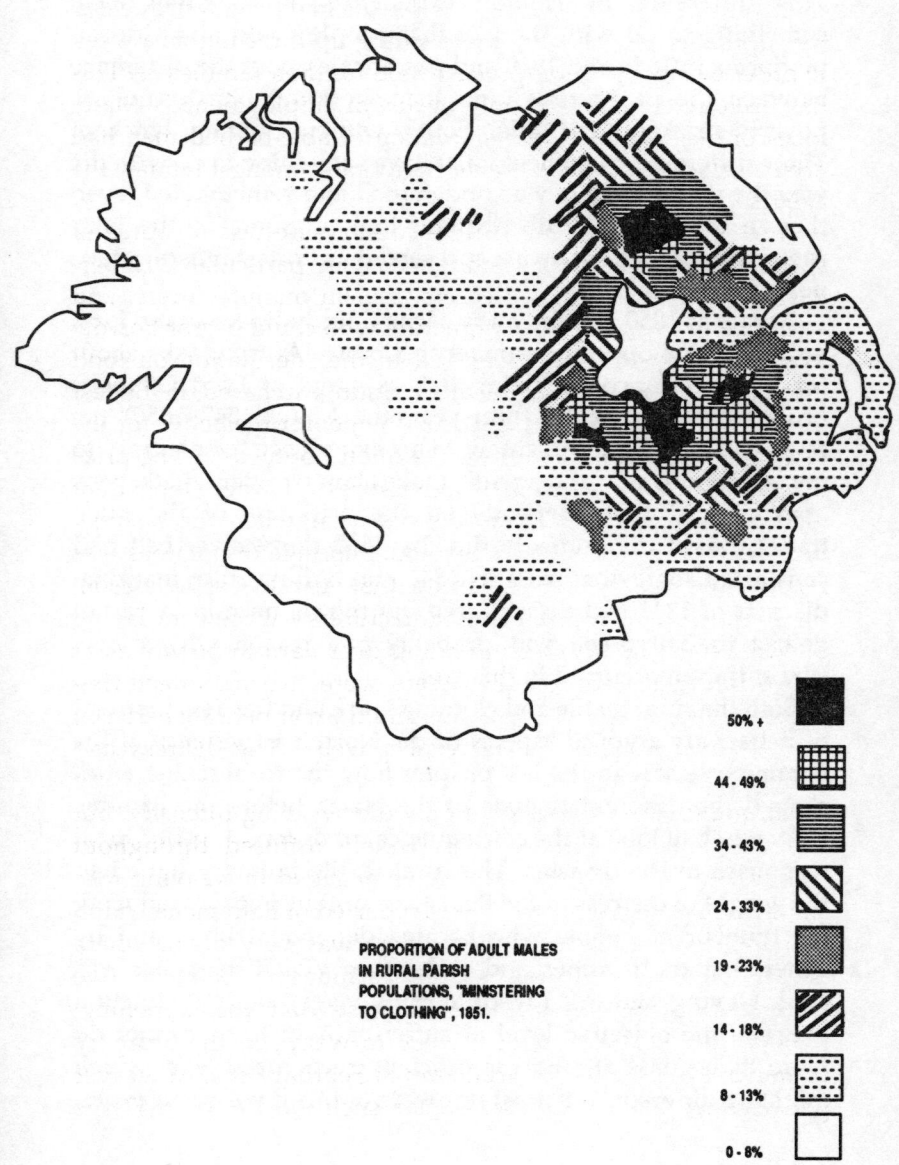

7. Rural weavers, 1851

PROPORTION OF ADULT MALES IN RURAL PARISH POPULATIONS, "MINISTERING TO CLOTHING", 1851.

50% +
44 - 49%
34 - 43%
24 - 33%
19 - 23%
14 - 18%
8 - 13%
0 - 8%

cottier-weavers could stay alive by super-intensification of their work. The crisis pressures at their worst therefore took the form, not of searching about in vain for something to eat, or lying down to conserve energy and food, or die in their cabins, but instead to go through an appallingly arduous work regime. This difference in Famine experience must surely have something to do with the fact that people could stand up on platforms in 1848 and 1849 and pontificate about the difference between the prosperous (and hard-working) North and the poverty-stricken (and idle) South without getting lynched. These different experiences must have something to do with the way the whole trauma was understood and remembered, even though it does not fully explain how in some of the later rhetoric the experience was represented as Protestantism versus popery.

As late as 1850, the secretary of the County Down grand jury, writing to his opposite number in County Antrim, asks about Mr George Hancock's claim that, as agent of Lord O'Neill's property during the last three years (i.e. March 1847–1850), the rents had been paid punctually. This experience "so contrary to my experience as a land agent", makes him wonder whether the "payment of rents depends on the briskness of the linen trade",[24] as it undoubtedly did. By 1850 the weaver belt had contracted somewhat from its 1841 area. All its outer marginal districts of 1841 had disappeared but the connection by rail of Belfast to Ballymena was probably one reason why a new concentration occurred in this area.

Both the rural textile and clothing work and the development of Belfast are atypical aspects of the North's experience of the Famine. We saw in the last chapter how the rural textile work shaped the different regions of the North before the Famine. Now we shall look at the consequences of different institutional responses to the disaster. The rural textile industry lightened the weight of distress in the Poor Law system, both by reducing the number of people who became dependent on it and by generating the incomes and rents from which the relief was paid. Having said this I want to draw a very sharp distinction between the objective level of suffering, which we cannot do more than guess at, and the officially recognized level which might be different. We must be aware of this if we are to avoid, without having done the investigative work to demonstrate the point, saying that people were "well off" in the North, a theme of later rhetoric. As I have not studied the operation of the monstrously inhumane poor relief system in the detail it deserves, I confine my remarks to this. The scale of "official" distress was, in part at least, a measure of the strength of pressures to get distress recognized as such; but it also measured negatively the success of those who put up barriers to prevent its recognition. I say this because I am going to use official measures of distress and am aware that it is not safe to say that certain unions' populations were tolerably well off because these unions did not operate outdoor relief. All that is shown in these cases is that the pressure to provide outdoor relief was more than matched by local forces opposed to doing so. So whatever the degree of objective distress, areas that did experience massive officially recognized distress were on the verge of an experience that was going to have a profound political effect. When it happened, local landlords were discredited; then the population found itself dependent upon direct agencies of the British government; and then it faced a major trauma when British policy abruptly changed in 1847.

Mass pressures were mobilized to get public works schemes going after the passage of the Labour Rate Act in September 1846. The outcome of baronial sessions did not always have a close relationship to the scale of distress. Captain Oldershaw reported in March 1847 that in Omagh East barony a "strong party from Omagh opposed the wishes of the community" at the presentment session. None the less he saw outright starvation in Dromore parish (one of the twelve non-Donegal parishes in Ulster, where more than half the 1841 houses had been fourth class). "One cannot travel any distance without living skeletons staggering from debility caused by hunger and inanition."[25] While at Dungannon presentments, Lieutenant Columb said that some landlords "exhibited bad feeling in making great opposition to the employment of other than their own tenants" on drainage works.[26] This rather suggested a source of influence available to a landlord who was in the process of carrying out significant works, and gives some idea of the possible importance of the Marquis of Downshire's circular of December 1846, calling on ratepayers (of the baronial cess) to attend the meetings authorised by the Lord Lieutenant, as only ratepayers were entitled to vote. It ends with a significant warning that "compulsory" works for which all ratepayers, including landlords, would be liable might induce landlords not to undertake private works of their own.[27]

In fact the importance of public works within Ulster was very uneven, taking the province as a whole. By April 1847, when efforts were being made to phase them out, the eastern area had almost none: most of the centre had works employing less that 2 per cent of the 1841 population, and it was in a ring starting with Upper Fews (south-west Armagh) and around through most of Monaghan and Fermanagh, all of Cavan and all the transmontane Donegal that these projects employed large proportions of the population.

The resort to massive-scale public works—where landlords failed to get works going themselves—was not only a symptom of mass distress, it was also a symptom of the collapse of landlords' social functions, if not of their authority. The government became the agency of relief in a direct and immediate sense, and dependence upon public works for life support became greatest. In that way the eventual shut-down of the works put into stark relief the decision of the British government to let a starving people depend on their own resources. The landlords, whose incapacity had made the government intervention so necessary, were doubly incapable of picking up the pieces when the government decided to cut its responsibilities. Many landlords had tacitly or openly accepted the "write-off" of large sections of their tenantry. Lieutenant Milward in western Donegal reported that landlords were refusing to give seeds as it would only temporarily stave off crisis. The tenants would need the produce to feed themselves, so it was better to force them to give up their lands now. This rather obstructed Milward's efforts to make arrangements for boys to replace people who went off to cultivate their smallholdings during the sowing season.[28] A month later, Mr Townsend reported—at a time when plans to cut the works were afoot—that there was a common notion about that the government, the Board of Works and its officers were keeping back public works to save expense to the rates and "drive people out of the country".[29] The few local gentry there and he

8. Reduction in population by Baronies, 1841-51

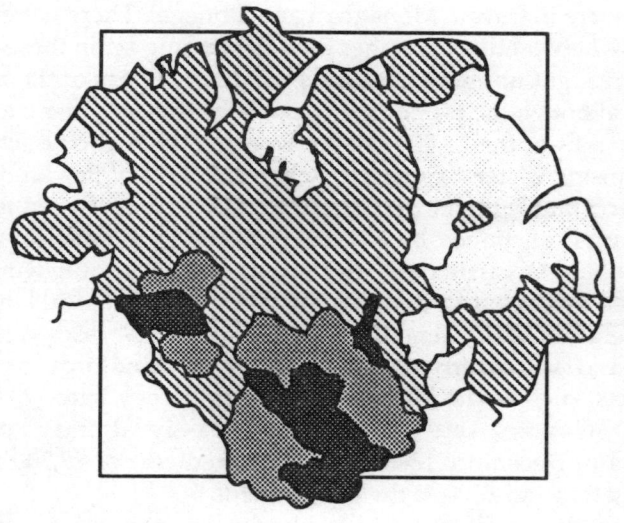

1851 POPULATION AS % OF 1841

OVER 90%

OVER 80 - 89%

OVER 70 - 79%

OVER 55 - 69%

himself feared the consequences of ending public works. And in fact when the general order to stop all relief works at the end of June went around, the three far western Poor Law unions of Donegal were exempted from the stoppage.

The public works schemes in March 1847 were employing 729,000 people of whom 86,500 were in Ulster. All but 26,000 of these were in Cavan, Monaghan and Donegal. There were some areas where landlords, rather than depending upon these kinds of works, got up more obviously productive ones of their own. Thus, although the proportion of public works in Ulster was low, 35 per cent of the 21,000 people working on drainage schemes were inside Ulster.[30] Generally schemes works of this kind were only acceptable under the Labour Rate Act when the request for them was sanctioned by all the landlords in the district where they would be carried out, and whose property value would be affected by the works done, so the requirement of local landlord co-operation was essential. In some exceptional cases works of this kind were carried out privately by landlords of large districts, such as the Marquis of Bath in Farney barony. There, 15,000 labourers were employed on a massive drainage project started in December 1846 at an estimated cost of £8,700 to the proprietors and £500 to the government.[31]

Once the landlords lost authority in one sphere it was challenged in another. Wherever large-scale public works took place, local relief committees tended to be involved in both the selection process and the defence of the project against attempts to pare down its workforce. This threw up opportunities for local groups to build up influence in direct conflict with British power. Captain William O'Neill, an Inspecting Officer in Donegal in April 1847, alleged that the parish priests of Gweedore, Templecarn and Arranmore Island forced labourers to contribute to them out of their earnings.[32]

The areas most affected were the most subdivided and those most dependent on migrant labour before the Famine. The bad harvest of 1846 had not only done enormous local injury, but had cut off sources of migrant harvesting labour (even if the public works had also discouraged would-be migrants from going). When the mass exodus in 1847 brought 300,000 Irish men and women to Liverpool in five months, the passage of a tough Removal Act[33] in May of that year discouraged migrants

9. Population employed on public works (road building), April 1847

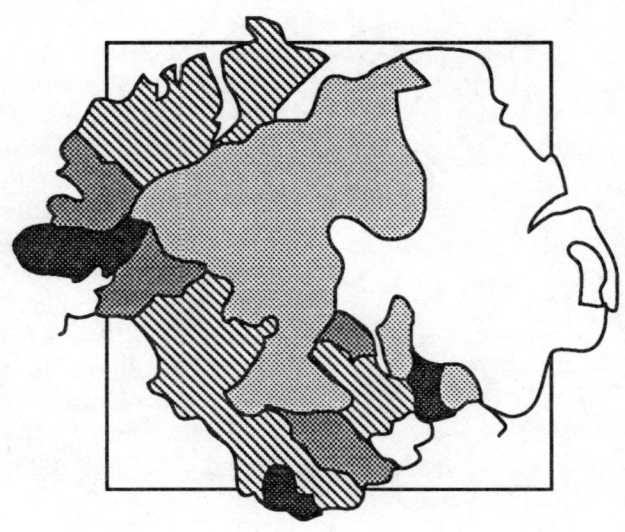

10. Poor Law Union boundaries

from landing, while at the same time farmers in Ireland had much less than normal need for seasonal labour. It was also in such areas that the requirements of local self-sufficiency imposed by the new Poor Law were to be most absurd and heartless. Emigration from those districts to America took on flood proportions. Remittances that began to flow back helped those who remained. And as William Kirk, the Liberal MP for Newry, was to remind a select committee in 1852, "what you trample on in Ireland will sting you in America".[34]

In areas where the distress was not very great in the first place, the landlords' chances of responding constructively were very much greater than in harder hit areas. In those cases the resident landlord, or one with an active and resident agent, had some freedom of action. If a landlord was not financially embarrassed by heavy mortgages, and if his estate covered a large part of a Poor Law union or barony—or if he could secure the co-operation of a sufficiently large group of landlords in his area—he could start private works of improvement or productive baronial works which would keep down the general liability of the union (and himself) for poor relief. Obviously an isolated resident landlord would not have the same incentive to do this as the inactivity of other landlords would still leave their tenants as a cost on the Poor Law. Furthermore, freedom from financial embarrassment would enable a landlord to pay compensation to tenants who emigrated. In areas of the inner North where larger holdings were already in considerable numbers and tenant right not altogether devalued, the early effect of the Famine was greatly to accelerate the process of adjoiner purchase. As tenant right values fell sharply in all areas, or even disappeared, they ceased to act as a brake to consolidation. In some rare cases such as that of Tristram Kennedy, agent to the Marquis of Bath, agents enforced the sale of tenant right in order to oblige the tenants engrossing the vacated tenancies to pay some of the compensation to the outgoers necessary to enable them to emigrate.[35] Even in east Down, tenant right collapsed by 1848 and 1849. Colonel Forde (Seaforde, near Downpatrick) said that in those years "there was no tenant right at all except a mere trifle to get a man away".[36] At the beginning of the Famine, the existence of tenant right enabled better circumstanced farmers to consolidate and the outgoers to receive sums adequate in some cases to permit emigration. Increasingly, in the later years of the Famine, the costs of consolidation by compensated emigration had to be borne by the landlords, if at all.

The difference between regional responses to the crisis at its most intense show up important contrasts. After two successive potato crop failures, farmers' capital was severely depleted in 1847, assuming they had anything left at all. As 1847 was to be a very good season the overall Famine experience depended upon the capacity of different regions to make use of this period. Farmers' scepticism as to the possibility of another potato crop failure led to many middle- and large-size farmers planting grain, using family labour supplemented by horses. Many middle and smaller farmers sold up and emigrated, while some who were very hard pressed failed to plant their lands and stayed wherever possible on the relief works. In Cavan, for example, many with four or five acres stayed on public works; whereas around Ballymena it was very unusual to find anyone with more than two acres on relief works. And along the coast from Belfast to Cushendall, labourers were planting potatoes from last year's saved seeds and there were almost no beggers about.[37] But it was clearly at times like this that landlord provision of seed could make a definite difference as to what happened. Some proprietors around Dungannon did so, but the Board of Works engineer feared their "example would not be followed".[38]

The Famine encouraged landlords, where they could, to lower or abate rents and provide seeds to smaller tenants whose capital had been eroded by bad harvests in previous seasons. Or to be more precise, the incentives were there in cases where the landlords had not decided to let people go where fate disposed. As their rents depended on their tenants' survival as tenants, it was in their interests to see that such people were not pushed to the wall. A bit of help at a timely moment might make the difference whether they struggled on or gave up. The picture of evil landlords intent on squeezing the last farthing out of their starving tenants is only an approximation to the truth in districts where the scale of distress was so overwhelming that it was outside the power of landlords to take any sort of active part in seeking a remedy, and where they thought only of their short- and medium-term rent collection. One of the best indicators of the way those with lighter loads were able to act constructively, while those who could not sank deeper, is provided by the Soup Kitchen Act.

At the beginning of the Famine, the relief committees were offered government grants on the basis of 20 shillings, or £1 per £1 collected. This procedure was not altogether abandoned when the big changes came in 1847. In January 1847, when the Temporary Relief (Soup Kitchen) Act was passed, the government offered a choice of methods to fund the operation. Either moneys collected locally would be eligible for grants at £1 per £1 collected; or unions could borrow the whole sum from the government and pay it back later. This choice created an obvious collective interest for the inhabitants of a Poor Law electoral division in proceeding by the first method if it was possible. One report mentions (for an unnamed flax-growing district) that local committees were particularly keen to avoid the second method as it would entail a rate collection on the smaller and more distressed landholders.[39] But local collection meant two things. It meant first that the inhabitants of the district could raise the sum required to cover the costs of very varying levels of local distress; and secondly, that a way could be found to ensure that as the advantage would ultimately be a collective one, so too should the cost be collective. No individual had an interest in making a voluntary subscription unless others did likewise. The electoral divisions which used this method were concentrated in the middle areas of Ulster—in other words, areas where public distribution of free food was an inescapable necessity, but where the demands imposed by it were relatively manageable from immediate resources—and by 31 December 1847, 40 per cent of the total grants in aid of subscriptions were due to Ulster Poor Law unions, particularly large sums being due to Dungannon, Downpatrick, Cookstown, Clogher, Banbridge, Ballycastle and Monaghan.[40]

The importance of the use of this method of collection is that it illustrates not only the relatively manageable scale of the local problem, even in 1847, but also the presence of local leadership groups capable of making this system work—often clergy, landlords, etc. And in so far as landlords had a hand in making the system work it was one more way in which they could contribute towards the solution of the crisis in a positive way. There are some particularly notable examples of electoral divisions where subscriptions were raised to attract the grant, despite the fact that the rest of the union went for outright borrowing. These included Florencecourt (the Earl of Enniskillen), Castlecoole (the Earl of Erne), Brookeborough and Colebrooke (Sir A. B. Brooke), and it is unlikely that the landlords of these divisions did not have a prominent part to play in organizing the subscriptions.[41] In another place it might be done in a quite different way. Crossmaglen, for example, collected significant sums and this was done by direct cooperation between the clergy.[42]

In some areas the formation of relief committees to work the Soup Kitchen Act was stalled in the hope of forcing the government to continue with public works. In western Donegal this was done successfully. In Cavan a meeting of angry ratepayers, mostly Catholic but under the leadership of an Orangeman, protested against it as a prelude to a system of permanent outdoor relief.[43] A report from Monaghan union in October gives us a fairly clear idea of the meaning of these crises in social terms. The scale of relief under the Soup Kitchen Act was found to vary with the degree of subdivision of an electoral division. To begin with, resistance to the voluntary subscription scheme was based on the supposition that the alternative source of finance—the government loans—would not ultimately be collected, so they would end up better off borrowing all the money. In this area it was also highly unlikely that the means to take up significant collections were available. But once the fiscal screw began to tighten and concerted efforts were made to collect the rate, "the farmer and the labourer are no longer identical and they are breaking into separate classes", as the terms "ratepayer" and "pauper" were acquiring a more definite meaning. "It is evident that the apparent interests of these two classes are no longer identical." It breaks through "the bond of secrecy, hitherto the bane of Ireland". "And farmers are now prepared to take in neighbouring smallholdings."[44]

The reporter from Monaghan was expecting more change than actually happened. The bond between labourers and small farmers was manifested in the breaking of the quarter-acre rule in May 1848. But the report is very significant because it shows

THE FAMINE IN ULSTER 125

11. Maximum dependence upon the soup kitchens established under the 1847 Temporary Relief Act

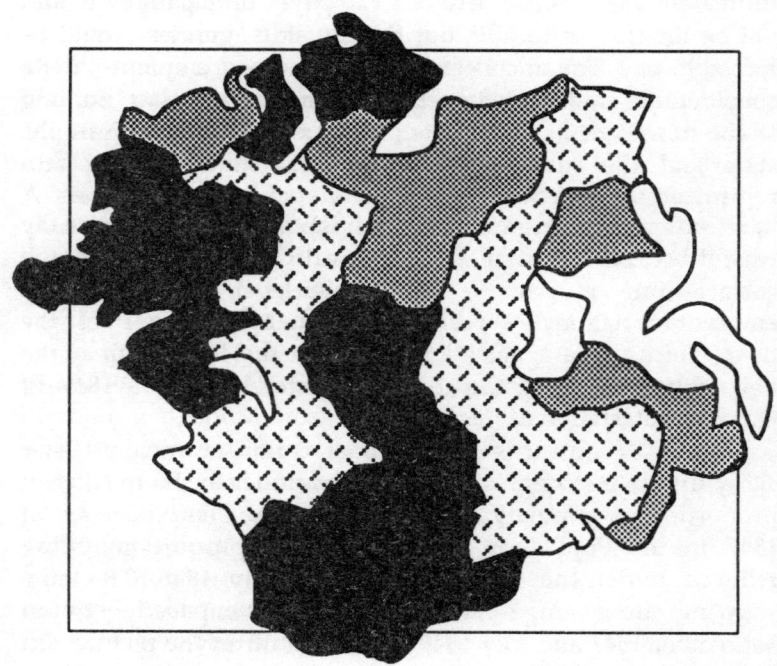

THOSE RELIEVED UNDER THE 1847 ACT AS % OF 1841 POPULATION BY POOR LAW UNION.

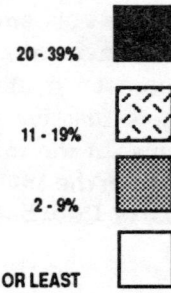

20 - 39%

11 - 19%

2 - 9%

1 OR LEAST

how resistance to the government's plans by local bodies meant refusing to accept the principle that localities should be responsible for dealing with the disaster. This response was incipiently nationalist. It kept people of a locality together against the government; they remained determined that ultimately the conflict between ratepayer and pauper would not be fought out locally, but that outside agencies would be forced to pay. The uncollected poor rates were a symptom of a considerable contrast between inner and outer Ulster. So long as the new Poor Law operated, its "success" showed how the state and the ruling groups had maintained control and routinized the difference between "ratepayers" and paupers. A new class reality became more than the material fact it already was; it became a recognized social reality. This difference will surface time and again, for at one level it expresses an embryonic nationalist reality—the interdependence of the people of an area against something alien. The growth of the new ribbonism along the southern Ulster frontier in 1849–52 was a manifestation of this.

From 1847 onwards the regional contrasts within Ulster show up quite strongly. Two of the maps show the maximum proportions of population relieved under the Temporary Act of 1847 in the Poor Law unions, and the proportions being relieved under the new Poor Law in July 1848. The map showing the average rate in the pound imposed between September 1847 and July 1848 tends to confirm the picture. On any measure used, the contrast between Cavan and, say, mid-Antrim is of quality, not quantity. Attention should also be paid to the maps by baronies which show the pattern of farm holdings. In 1847 there were already districts where the proportions of 30 acre farms had risen to very significant levels. And in those areas the failure of the potato crop in 1848 (but not other crops) made the bigger farms able to expand at the expense of smaller ones. The second map shows the percentages of small farms in 1855 as against 1847. This map should be treated with some caution as it shows two areas where massive percentage reductions occurred in the small farms. In the mid-Antrim area, the proportion of such small farms in the 1847 base figure was fairly low, but in the southern area of Cavan and south Monaghan, the 1847 base figure is

12. Proportion of 1841 population being relieved by the Poor Law, July 1848

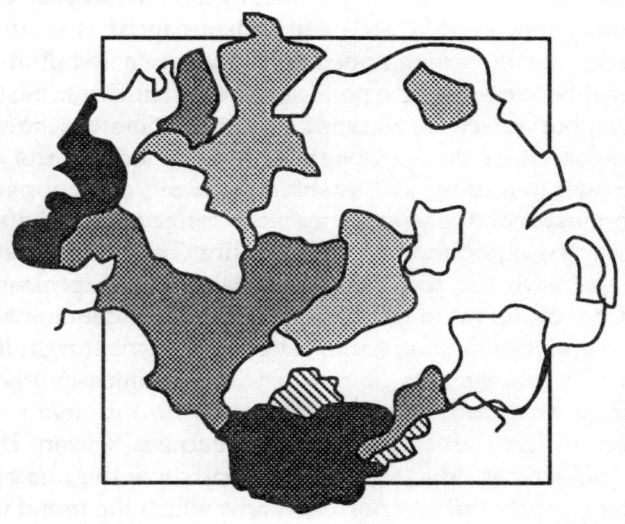

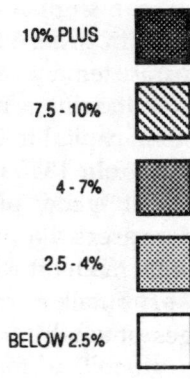

10% PLUS

7.5 - 10%

4 - 7%

2.5 - 4%

BELOW 2.5%

large and the massive percentage reduction is large in absolute terms. It was in those areas that the 1848/49 death rates remained high and rose, when they were falling elsewhere.

The failure of the potato harvest in 1848 had rather different consequences from previous years. After the success of the 1847 crop which many had not planted, small farmers in Ulster liquidated much of their remaining capital to prepare themselves for the much hoped for bonanza in 1848.[45] But by October it became clear the potato crop was ruined. Wheat was defective, but otherwise all crops except the potato were good. Flax was excellent. At the Doagh cattle show in 1848 the cattle were greater in number and quality than in any previous year.[46] But we must wonder who the cattle belonged to. If the small tenant capital liquidation to buy seed involved the sale of his cattle, we reach the conclusion that larger farmers probably bought them up at a bargain price. When the inevitable renewed emigration occurred in October, the tenant right levels were down to near zero, if not extinct. Landlords' resources were hard stretched to pay compensation, and many such tenants must have left empty handed or became paupers. Public works of almost any description had stopped, not just emergency works but any normal works which the grand juries carried out. The Antrim grand jury, from summer 1848 to the end of the Famine, was unable to carry out any works on account of the stoppage of Board of Works loans.[47] Even in County Antrim, where the poor rates were low and landlords gave some abatement of rent to tenants who were not then in arrears, small farmers now often had to leave their holdings with minimal capital to emigrate.

At the 12 July 1848 Orange meeting in Garvagh, Dr James McKnight, the leader of the northern tenant right movement, delivered a speech about agrarian questions. The banner round the platform, "Tenant Right and No Surrender", was certainly novel.[48] As the price of food fell the pressure of the crisis ceased to be felt so much by "consumers" of food. Now the fall was creating difficulties for farmers attempting to meet their obligations for rent, rates, cess and arrears. Their tenant right was more or less destroyed, and even landlord compensation to secure quitting was drying up. McKnight articulated the anxiety of small farmers to stay on the land and larger farmers

13. Poor rate collected by Poor Law Union (pence on £ valuation), October 1847-September 1848

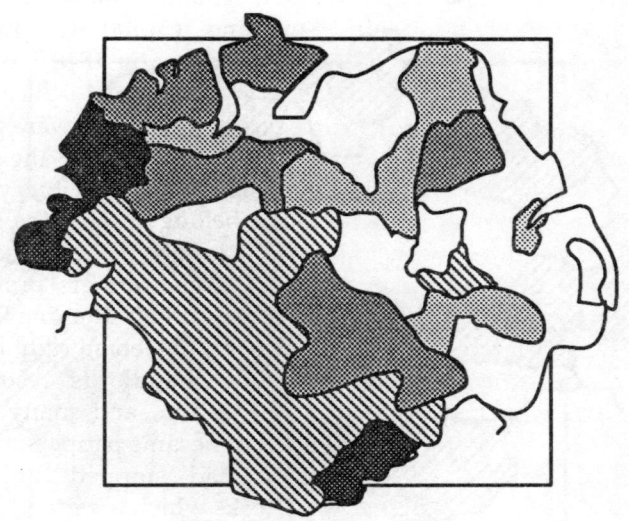

40 PENCE PLUS

30 - 39 PENCE

20 - 29 PENCE

16 - 19 PENCE

BELOW 16 PENCE

14. Percentage of farms over 30 acres in 1847

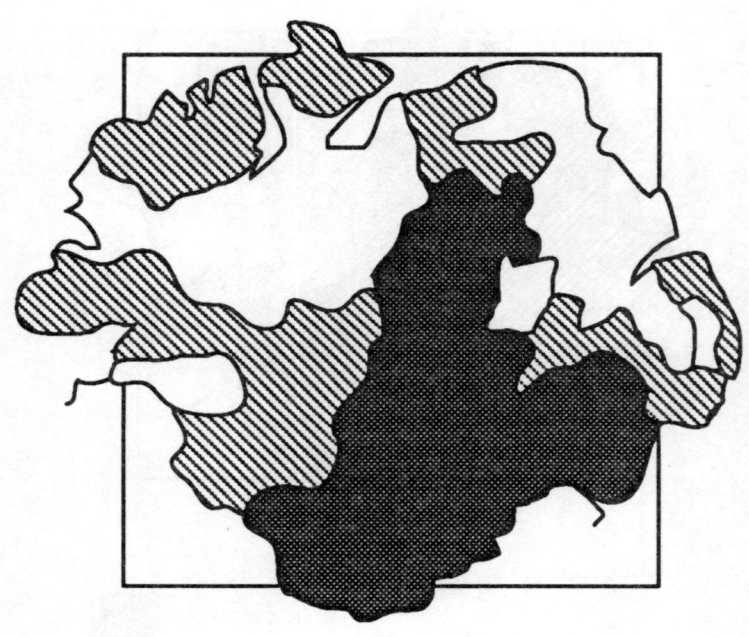

15 Percentage reduction in numbers of 1-5 acre farms between 1847 and 1855

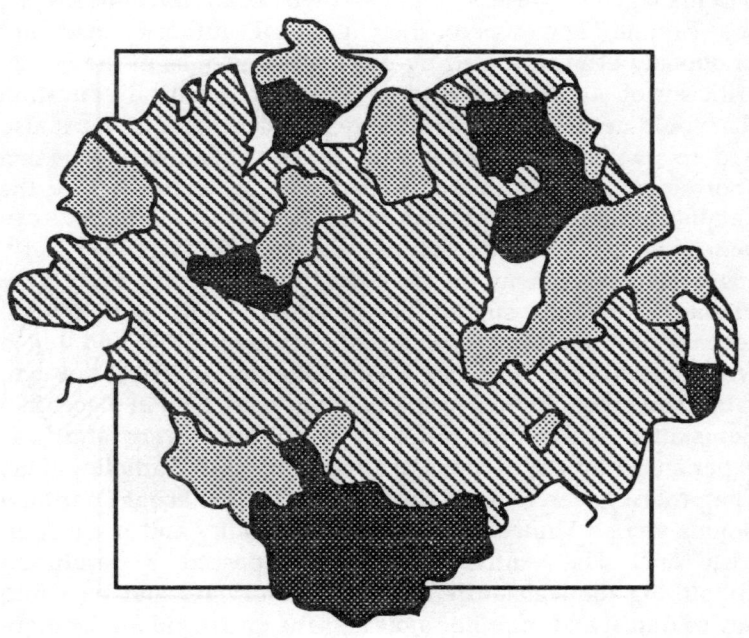

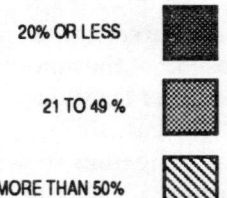

20% OR LESS

21 TO 49 %

MORE THAN 50%

to secure the independence of their capital. In the circumstances of 1848, tenant right could not recover without rent reductions. And without rent reductions many could not hold on.

James McKnight asserted that the tenant's claim on the land took priority over the landlord's. In a society where landlords had managed to preserve many of their social functions during the Famine, and where their political authority had not previously been uprooted by pan-Catholicism as in the South, criticism of landlords had to be a work of political education that could not lean upon any long-established traditions. It also had to overcome the now very potent asymmetry between "northern" and "southern" experiences, a reality before the Famine, but now strongly reinforced. Just how real this was can be seen by the northern reaction to rate in aid. In late 1848/early 1849 the government decided that the bankrupt Poor Law unions in Ireland should be subsidized not from general revenue, but rather by those Poor Law unions in Ireland which were still solvent. The rate-in-aid scheme, as it was known, caused an outcry in the North. Meetings were held in places like Enniskillen where the suffering had been severe and was experienced by populations of Protestants and Catholics alike. The protest generally took the line that the bankrupt Poor Law unions were a United Kingdom responsibility and not just an Irish one. The Antrim grand jury passed a resolution "imploring the legislature not to press forward and pass into law so unjust and impolitic a measure as rate in aid on the more industrious districts of Ireland to relieve the distressed portions of the South and West, the amount of which we feel confident would be quite inadequate to meet their wants . . ." The grand jury favoured tighter fiscal union of the United Kingdom, and opposed not the amount they were asked to pay but "the unjust principle of taxation".[49] The Newry Poor Law guardians denied that "the industrious population of this province are under any moral obligation to which any fault of ours has in any way contributed", and "Ulster has no relations with Connaught which are not equally shared by any other divisions of the British Empire."[50]

At Larne, Rev. William Glendy, a Unitarian minister who had sponsored the national education system from the beginning, and who stood out as an opponent of anti-Catholicism, said: "It is true that we are comfortable in the

North, but who have we to thank for that? We have only ourselves to thank and our own industry, for even the poorest man would work to the last rather than go to the workhouse, until he was driven to it by necessity." This statement may have been easier to make in a place like Larne which suffered very little from the Famine, but there is a lack of imagination about what possibilities were actually open to people in a place like Bailieborough. His co-speaker, Rev. Molyneaux, pushed the point a little further. "I believe that, for the purpose of passing this rate the government has greatly exaggerated the condition of the country. The alternative was put to them: would they pay the rate or let the people starve? I answer, if we must adopt the alternative, pay the rate certainly: but I do not believe we are called upon to adopt one or the other alternative. Let the government enquire into the carrying on of the bankrupt Unions—let every workhouse in the South and West be converted into a self-supporting institution—let the paupers be set to till the uncultivated land and the moral consequences would be that the people would be taught to be industrious and self-reliant."[51]

At one level the protest was a demand to tax London as well as Newry to deal with the "Southern and Western" distress, a proposition that is hard to quarrel with. But much of the protest was doing more than that. Mr Molyneaux was sincere about not wanting people in the South to starve, but he showed something less than empathy with them. Once the real differences of experience were hidden, then there was an open season on moralistic explanations of the different regional experiences. That was one step from contrasts between Protestant industry and popish idleness, which became more popular eventually. Then it would be little wonder that northern catholics, including those who had themselves experienced the northern Famine, found themselves uncomfortable with some of the themes of Ulster sectionalism.

One of James McKnight's first lessons in the catechism of Ulster tenant right is the answer to the question, "What is Rate in Aid?" "A rate levied off the peaceable and industrious portion of the community (who have paid all their own local taxes) to pay for the support of those whom the grasping squireen and the rack renting absentee of the South and the

West have beggared."[52] McKnight never let his readers imagine that the Famine in the South was a result of the moral weakness of the people. And that was an important part of the political education he had to do in his day.

The Famine did not in any automatic way lead to the reassertion of Irish nationalism, let alone separation. Nor can those who subsequently refused to draw nationalist conclusions from it be accused of "bigotry". The proper place to look at that accusation is not during the Famine itself but at the later stages when Irish nationalism itself began to talk about the Famine experience. I will show in the next chapter what problems were involved in drawing nationalist conclusions from the Famine experience while it lasted. Inner Ulster was the area where landlords' capacity both to retain local control and to exercise the traditionally positive aspects of the landlord's function were greatest. In an area where the class differentiation of labourer and farmer was already beginning to be noticeable before the Famine, keeping the new Poor Law system in operation, providing works for labourers, giving emigration compensation, and keeping the rates within relatively manageable proportions, enabled the landlords to preside over the crystallization of these class differentiations. They by no means came out of the Famine politically unscathed, but they were far from being isolated politically, socially redundant or bereft of institutional control as many of their more embarrassed counterparts were to be in the rest of the island. Paradoxically, it was their relative marginality in an increasingly industrial society that enabled them to survive with many of their levers of influence intact.

In many of the more southerly districts, where the strains imposed by the new Poor Law were simply unmanageable, the effect of being on the sharp end of the British government's decisions to economize (i.e. end the relief works in 1847 and create local financial self-sufficiency) was to strengthen resistance to English power on a pan-class basis. And when the government feared to end public works (as in western Donegal) or had to bale the Poor Law unions out (as in Bailieborough), this embryonically nationalist political pressure worked.

6. Ulster Politics in 1848

In 1843 Ulster politics looked straightforward. The Conservatives dominated political life. In Belfast they had managed to bring Anglican and Presbyterian together, despite being an essentially Anglican party of landlords and their retainers in the countryside. The Whigs had been embarrassed by O'Connell's breach with them and by his Repeal campaign. They were not only carrying some of the unpopularity felt by Protestants against the Melbourne administration; they were also aware that they could no longer be sure of Catholics in the North following them either. The Catholics in the North were still in a very weak position within institutional politics. During 1843 Repeal meetings came no further into Ulster than Newry and Carrickmacross.[1]

Then in quick succession the fixed points crumbled. When the disruption in the Church of Scotland occurred in 1843, Ulster Presbyterian sympathy went with the Free Church against the establishment and the Tories, undermining the relationship Dr Cooke had tried to build up between Presbyterians and Anglicans.[2] Then O'Connell called off the monster Repeal meeting at Clontarf, when confronted by Peel's ban, and found himself under attack from the Young Ireland group within the Repeal organization.[3] After this Peel abandoned his previously hostile attitude towards the Catholic Church and set about actively accommodating the hierarchy. This, and the abolition of the Corn Laws, provoked the Tory secession from the Conservative Party. The whole of the Ulster Conservatives went with the Bentinck-Disraeli secession under Lord Derby. It might have been expected that the Whigs in Ireland would have profited from this disruption of the two major blocs, but their period of office during the Famine cost them support from Protestant Liberal and Catholic alike.

And so it happened that there was a space opening up which the existing political forces were ill equipped to fill. Repeal, at least as it had been understood until 1843, seemed dead. The Famine was generating despair with the Whigs' policies. In 1848, the year of the continental revolutionary upsurge, Chartism stirred in England and a breakaway group from the Young Irelanders threatened a revolution in Ireland. The Whig government, fearing Chartism in England, saw fit to magnify the threat of the rebellion in Ireland. And in a move that was a reversal of its policy during the 1830s, it briefly flirted with the Orange Order as a force of defence against the rebellion. At the same time its land policy was becoming more and more clearly identified with the landlord interest and objectionable to tenants. When the threatened emergency occurred in 1848, it was something of a fiasco and farce. But the thoughts and feelings uttered in the middle of it are all the more instructive for that reason, because they give some idea of the forces that would appear during the democratization of northern politics.

In this chapter I shall go through each of the various political currents in turn. First, I will look at the consequences of the collapse of O'Connell's challenge to Peel. This was the prelude to a new situation in which all British governments would attempt to accommodate the Catholic hierarchy. Second, I will go on to look at what happened to the idea of Repeal after O'Connell's policy was discredited, and in particular what meaning it was given in the North in 1848. Third, I shall look at what happened to the Orange Order which, having been dissolved in 1836 to avoid being banned, reappeared in 1848 with government connivance. It was becoming more and more difficult for its landlord leaders to lead it on their own terms. Fourth, I will look at how the Scottish Church disruption undermined Dr Cooke's authority within the Presbyterian Church. I will describe how in 1848 various Presbyterian ministers started to take an active part in tenant politics. Finally, I will explain why the northern Whigs were not in a position to capitalize upon the break-up of the Conservatives and the repealers. This will lay the ground for the story of the Tenant League, which was the first modern democratic movement in Ulster, and is the subject of Chapter 7.

During the later part of the 1830s O'Connell's alliance with the Whigs created difficulties for his movement. As with any nationalist movement of an enduring rather than a revolutionary kind, the strategy was one of building up a communal infrastructure. That meant opening up spaces for the new national middle class in the professions. And it meant promoting an educational system that gave the nation cohesion and drew its classes into closer interdependence. This required a kind of diplomacy between the Nationalists' leaders and the government of the state from which they ultimately wanted to become independent. The Nationalists got the space to develop some autonomy and the state got a native leadership which actually had a very strong interest in preserving the new status quo. However, the nationalist leadership very rarely opposed radical social classes if they came into confrontation with the state. If they thought they were losing control over the people, they would nearly always change direction and lead them against the state instead.

Despite considerable achievements O'Connell's alliance with the Whigs was being overtaken by a major rural crisis. Irish landlords made increasingly effective attacks on the Mulgrave administration. "Property has its duties as well as its rights."[4] Thomas Drummond's famous reply to the Tipperary landlords, who called for coercion to put down agrarian disturbance, was as far as any Whig government would go against the interests of landed property. The Whig reforms were not enough to sustain the momentum of his movement. Indeed once they were achieved the movement tended to demobilize. The turn to Repeal was therefore an effort to refurbish the fundamental strength of the movement—its mass pan-Catholic base—without which it had no bargaining power within the existing framework. The timing was probably influenced by the increasingly explicit opposition of Archbishop MacHale to accommodation with the Whigs, and the realization that the days of their ministry were numbered in any case.[5] So he judged that the probable return of Tories to power necessitated a renewed show of strength, if for no other reason than to discourage them from attempting to reverse the Whig reforms.

O'Connell's visit to Belfast in 1841 was part of this turn. The original plan had been that he be escorted to Belfast (i.e.

through the solidly Protestant district beyond Banbridge) by a great mass of Repeal supporters.[6] The concept of "moral force" which underlay his strategy was to assemble vast numbers to demonstrate the scale of support and to leave the English government to draw its own conclusions about the consequences of resisting it. In the context of the North the central issue, as far as both O'Connell and his pan-Protestant opponents were concerned, was whether such a Repeal demonstration could take place at all. And by calling off the mass procession and avoiding a major battle, he conceded without a struggle. But throughout the next two years mass meetings were held all over the other provinces as a build-up to the great Clontarf meeting of 1843.

O'Connell's career is notable for his success in effectively undermining the institutional supports of Protestant ascendancy and for his failure to make any impact upon the material basis of Irish underdevelopment. Desmond Bowen has described how the agrarian agitation against rents in the early 1830s was deflected into the anti-tithe war.[7] While the tithe was economically of much less significance than the rent, its claim to legitimacy was far more galling because it was a direct contribution to the Anglican Church. Rents were merely the property claim of land ownership. The anti-tithe agitation shows up quite clearly the basis of O'Connell's political practice. Defeating the tithe undermined the position of the Anglican clergy by mobilizing a "pan-Catholic" opposition. But the tithe was also a politically soft target, because the Whigs were not required to capitulate on the issue of the "rights of property" in general. O'Connell's strategy was to attack institutions which expressed Protestant ascendancy and whose very existence was an offence to the Catholic population. This not only secured a fairly high success rate, but its long-term effect was that English governments learned how meeting "pan-Catholic" wishes would preserve good relationships with Catholic and nationalist leaders, hence the possibility of eventually institutionalizing accommodation between government and Catholic leadership bodies. In the confrontation with Peel over Repeal, however, the stakes were raised much higher. Peel had returned to office in 1841 and, to begin with, did very little to indicate how he planned to deal with the crisis. But shortly before the proposed Clontarf meeting, the government banned it and assembled a show of military strength. For reasons which are not altogether clear, O'Connell called the meeting off.[8] But whatever the reasons, the effect was to break his unchallenged ascendancy over Irish political life. Peel as the leader of the Tory Party had been expected to resist O'Connell. But sections of the Tory Party—including most of its northern supporters—now hoped for a reversal of the Whig reforms. In this they were to be disappointed, for Peel now set about the task of creating accommodative arrangements with the Roman Catholic hierarchy as the body with the most demonstrable authority in Ireland. Before 1843 he had firmly rejected requests for an increased grant to the Maynooth seminary. But he reversed his earlier position and in 1845 increased the annual grant and placed it on a permanent basis,[9] drawing howls of execration from pan-Protestantism in the North. He further proposed to establish a system of university education on the lines of the mixed national education system to break down the monopoly of Irish university education in the Anglican Trinity College, Dublin. The fall of Peel in 1846 left the Whigs the task of attempting to secure the hierarchy's approval of the system, an effort in which they eventually failed. But the overall tendency in these years was for English governments of all shades to recognize the representative role of the Irish hierarchy, by-passing O'Connell and his followers.

In effect it became the bi-partisan policy of British governments to treat the hierarchy as the leadership of the Catholic Irish people. It was a case of trying to satisfy them and reduce their independence at the same time. Thus the Whigs' efforts to secure its acceptance of the Queen's colleges were combined with overtures to secure the direct state endowment of the Irish Church, to formalize diplomatic relationships with the Vatican, and to instruct government departments on the proper modes of address for Catholic clergy.[10] As Don Akenson says, "By 1850, the hierarchy seems to have had every reason for being in a state of collective paranoia."[11]

The internal divisions within the hierarchy were still very real, but all the bishops opposed any educational institutions that might undermine the integrity of the Catholic faith. In doing so they were in effect taking up a conventionally nationalistic stance; the notion that there was some connection between the weakening of Catholicism and the strengthening of the legitimacy of British rule never died. A lot of the time it remained well buried but it often broke out, as later parts of this story will show. At the risk of some rather drastic simplification, I intend to argue that the basis of much of the internal tension between Catholic leaders must have had to do with the different impact of growing commercialization and political reforms in different areas of the country. Thus in relation to the attitudes of the bishops toward the national education system there is a striking contrast between Archbishop John MacHale of Tuam (i.e. Connaught) and Archbishop Crolly of Armagh (Ulster), supported by Bishop Denvir of Down and Connor (Belfast).[12.] Whatever influence each individual personality may have had, it is patently obvious that the Whig reforms did not touch these areas in similar ways. In Connaught marginal subsistence holdings were something of a norm. The Protestant ascendancy in this area was a relatively insubstantial presence. Endowed Protestant schools were few; the resident landlords fewer than elsewhere; and the limited influence of commerce on daily life was reflected in the continual dominance of the Irish language. The national education system looked like an institution of Anglicization (even if not proselytization). Whig reforms generally had a several-fold implication. They promoted adaptation to the world of commerce; they refurbished the instruments of British power; and they undermined formal and institutional Anglican ascendancy. The strengthening of the arm of the state meant increasing the capacity to control agrarian disorder. The contrasting significance of these same developments for much of the North was total. First, there were the unique implications of the law and order reforms for Catholics; secondly, in a much more thoroughly commercialized society with a full infrastructure of endowed schools, the national education scheme was the best approximation that could be devised for a Catholic system. And northern clergy could not afford to be particular because education would be sought by Catholics whether or not it was provided through acceptable channels.

If the demise of O'Connell's leadership after 1843 led to an ever more routine relationship between British governments and the hierarchy at one end, it also led to a new kind of criticism from another. Although O'Connell had quarrelled with his one-time northern Protestant supporter, William Sharman Crawford, over the question of federalism and lost much of the little Protestant support he had in the course of it,[13] there was a section of the Repeal movement organized around the *Nation* journal whose fundamental conception of nationalism was at odds with his own. The *Nation* group was a small body of intellectuals including some Protestants. After 1843 it became the focus for various strands of discontent with O'Connell's leadership. It was particularly opposed to the alliances between O'Connell and the Whigs and the reduction of the Repeal movement to the role of Irish Catholic Whig office-seekers. It was very conscious of the pervasive influence of utilitarianism and *laissez-faire* economics which it saw as both economically detrimental to Ireland's development and subversive of social morale. After an attempt to revive interest in the fast declining Irish language as literature, it concentrated its efforts on building up a literary movement in opposition to the near monopoly of the established order. The spirit of the movement is summed up in a letter of Thomas Davis to Dr Madden:

"The machinery at present working for Repeal could never in circumstances like the present achieve it: but circumstances must change. Within ten or fifteen years England must be in peril. Assuming this much I argue thus. Modern Anglicanism—i.e. Utilitarianism, the creed of Russell and Peel, as well as of the Radicals—this thing, call it Englishism or Yankeeism, which measures prosperity by exchange values, measures duty by gain, and limits desires to clothes, food, and respectability: This damned thing has come to Ireland under the Whigs: and is equally the favourite of the Peel Tories. It is believed in the political assemblies of our cities, preached from our pulpits (always Utilitarian or persecuting), it is the Apostolic creed of the Professions and threatens to corrupt the lower classes who are still faithful and romantic. To use every literary and political engine against this seems to me to be the duty of every Irish patriot who can foresee consequences. Believe me, this is a greater though not so obvious a danger as Papal supremacy. So much worse do I think it, that sooner than suffer the iron gates of that filthy dungeon to close on us, I would submit to the certainty of Papal supremacy. Knowing that the latter should end in some twenty years—leaving the people mad it might be, but not sensual and mean

. . . You seem to underrate our resources . . . the Protestants of the lower orders are neutral: the land question and repeated disappointments from England have alienated them from their old views. Most of the educated Protestants now profess an ardent nationality and say that if some pledge against Catholic Ascendancy could be given them, they too would be Repealers."[14]

This approach was real romanticism. Davis was hoping somehow to stop the tide of capitalist culture. In fact every nationalist movement's task was to detach the modern materialist culture from the culture of their national enemies and to make it their own. O'Connell, perhaps unwittingly, but certainly Cardinal Cullen later, were only too well aware of what Davis speaks of as utilitarianism. It was for them rather a question of removing its anti-Catholic implications, and otherwise coming to terms with it. The passage about the romantic lower orders places Davis rather close to Dr MacHale who wanted to resist Anglicization altogether.[15] But what made Davis's position so important was that he went against the unwritten assumption that what was really Irish was actually Catholic. He was attempting to go back, in this respect, to Tone. And it was in fact the effort to revive the legacy of 1798, the notion of a non-sectarian nationalism, for which Young Ireland was to be noted. Young Ireland had a small but not insignificant body of Protestant support in the North.

The crisis that precipitated the departure of Young Ireland from the O'Connellite movement was O'Connell's renewed partisanship for the Whigs. He opposed the Queen's colleges when Peel proposed them. But notwithstanding their dislike of utilitarianism the Young Irelanders supported them. They looked upon these non-sectarian institutions as possible seed beds for a national intelligentsia.[16] Then the O'Connellites failed to support William Smith O'Brien's opposition to the 1846 Coercion Bill. O'Brien, MP for Limerick and a Protestant landlord, became the adoptive leader of the Young Ireland Party, and his attacks on the Whigs grew bolder as the Famine intensified.[17]

To attack the O'Connellite movement for its Catholicity and for its pro-Whig position did not indicate that Young Ireland was appealing to any recognizable constituency. In the absence of any sign that Catholics and Protestants could come together or that there was any sign of Protestants supporting Repeal, it was not clear where this led to. To attack the accommodation with the Whigs seemed like a commitment to revolution because it was not clear who else an Irish party could ally with. So it was as though there were some disembodied ideas going about looking for an incarnation. What was made of these ideas in Belfast?

Charles Gavan Duffy, one of the leading lights of both Young Ireland and the later Tenant League, claimed quite accurately that when the Young Ireland deputation visited Belfast in 1847 they received a considerably more friendly welcome than O'Connell had done in 1841.[18] That fact requires some elucidation. During the Famine, the opposition amongst northern Protestants to government policies became very strong, especially after the introduction of the new Poor Law in 1847. Nationalisms are rarely very explicit about precisely how they propose to deal with problems that an alien administration has failed to deal with. But the assumption is always made that a government whose first responsibility is its own people cannot do as badly as one whose first responsibility is elsewhere. It is in the absence of other considerations a tolerably good argument, and in the context of Whig famine policy it was perhaps an increasingly powerful one. The visit of the Young Irelanders to Belfast helps to elucidate the problems of a non-sectarian Irish nationalism in the 19th century.

In mid-1846 the *Newsletter* observed that the Belfast repealers had announced a public dinner for William Smith O'Brien, but that the local Repeal newspaper, the *Vindicator*, carried no news of the announcement. And hinting at its subsequent thoughts on the subject declared that "Mr. O'Brien's presence might be endured here, as he is, after all, more silly and harmless than malignant or knavish . . . but another visit from Mr. O'Connell would be an altogether more serious affair."[19] And two weeks later, referring to the increasingly sharp attacks of the Young Irelanders on the harmfulness of O'Connell's "moral force" Repeal strategy, it declared: "Physical force exerted, as the Young Irelanders would exert it, would be speedily prostrated, but the vicious influence of such men as O'Connell, his sons and satellites, will long be felt in the future destinies of Ireland should the Whigs continue much longer in power."[20]

In September the *Newsletter* gleefully reported the proceedings of a meeting of the Belfast repealers which passed an unqualified vote of confidence in O'Connell and, by implication, of censure on O'Brien. "It must be admitted that a meeting of five hundred people, even though consisting of the 'great unwashed', attracted by such an occasion, represents properly the political feelings of the Roman Catholics of Belfast." One speaker is reported as having said, "Yes! men of Ireland, he has the whole of you but a few rotten Repealers in the North. Mr. O'Connell could not go astray for he had it from the Holy Father himself, the Head of the Church, that it was impossible for him to go astray." Or, as the *Newsletter* put it, when the speaker argued that "Repeal was an essentially Romanist movement, there was not one to contradict him, but on the contrary half a thousand voices were raised in plausive cheers."[21] It suited the *Newsletter*'s purpose very well that the Belfast repealers should be O'Connellites and "essentially Romanist", for the intrinsic attraction of the Young Ireland movement was its opposition to that very tendency in the movement. But it should also be clear that there were very good reasons why the repealers in Belfast were so disposed. Nowhere more than in the North were the achievements of O'Connell so tangibly felt by Catholics: being locally powerless, the scope of their activity was to affirm solidarity with the wider "pan-Catholic" movement in Ireland as a whole. Nowhere more than in Belfast did Young Ireland look like a dangerous schism in a movement whose strength was its unity. It only looked otherwise to those who thought that Young Ireland might secure Protestant support for Repeal. But to throw over a tried strategy for an experiment of this kind was a decided gamble.

The *Newsletter*'s comment on the relative ease with which Young Ireland could be prostrated would not have been lost on them either.

The Drennan clubs, as the Belfast Young Irelanders were known, were fairly small. The relationship between these clubs and the old repealers in Belfast was far from cordial. In November 1847 a Young Ireland deputation came to speak in the Belfast Music Hall. The *Newsletter* gave a lengthened account of the successful efforts of the repealers to turn the meeting into chaos.[22] Successful that is, until the county constabulary cleared them from the hall with fixed bayonets. At this point Francis Meagher, later to become a general in the Union Army in the US Civil War and elected governor of Montana State, began a speech. He started by appealing to the Volunteer tradition of the 1770–80s, echoing the standard themes that the Act of Union had taken away Ireland's power to tax for her own purposes, stressing the possible developmental advantages of an Irish government and the end of the present outflow of resources consequent on absenteeism. These were all themes which aroused considerable sympathy in a period when taxation was rising on an increasingly squeezed society, while the outflow of food to pay rent continued and people starved. But then he moved on to areas specifically directed at a Protestant audience:

"Is what we advocate tainted with sectarianism? Is it distempered with Whiggery? Does it predict the downfall of Protestantism? Does it threaten the rights of property? [All charges against the O'Connellites.] I know that many of you are the enemies of Repeal. I know full well that in the north Repeal has been identified with Popery, whilst the Union has been identified with Protestantism. . . . Your fathers did not say so. On the 1st July 1779, the Volunteer Companies of Belfast held a different opinion . . . that there have been circumstances connected with the Repeal movement which justify in great measure your hostility to Repeal, I candidly admit. Until very lately the movement has worn the features of the Catholic movement of 1827 . . . Besides it seems to me that a predominance in the movement was conceded to the Catholic priests, which the Protestant portion of the community could not recognize, and which I maintain it would be an abdication of their civil liberty for Protestants to tolerate . . . The meetings of 1843 failed to promote Repeal. There was no mind at work within these gigantic masses. There was faith—trust—heroism. But that which outlives the tumult of a meeting—that which survives, though the aim may shrivel and the heart grow cold—a free intelligent opinion, was wanting."

So far his speech was a vindication of Protestant opposition to Repeal of the past and a contrast between old Repeal and the spirit of the Young Ireland movement. What now does he argue in favour of Repeal as such?

"You cite Belfast and because Belfast has prospered, the Union must be maintained. Is that your argument? I do not deny that whilst Belfast has been industrious, other places have been inert. The indolence of the country dates from the passing of the Union and the fact is indisputable that whilst the Union has grown old, the country has grown decrepid . . . The Act of Union, you say, is the great charter of Irish Protestantism. Has that charter been held inviolate? . . . The Castle has slipped from your hands. The sleek Catholic slave [*groans and uproar from the audience*] The sleek Catholic slave, I say, is a greater favourite in that quarter nowadays than an Alderman of Skinner's alley. The Orange flag is designated by a Conservative minister the symbol of vagabondism: your processions are prohibited: and when you declaim against the spread of Popery and pray for the repeal of the Emancipation Act, they knock ten mitres off the established Church into the Kingdom come and vote £26,000 a year to Maynooth. I say that there is a spirit growing up amongst the young Catholics of Ireland which will not bend to any clerical authority beyond the sanctuary. Catholic Ascendancy! It is a ghost that frightens you—and whilst you stand trembling before it the Union, which is no ghost, is playing the thief behind your back."[23]

Assuming for a moment that his audience looked at the Union from a wider standpoint than the immediate experience of Belfast and its hinterland, Meagher was telling them that they were right to oppose the old Catholic Repeal, but that the new Repeal movement of Young Ireland was non-sectarian.

There was a difficulty with this line of presentation which Meagher may not have anticipated, and which may account for the fury of the Old Repeal mob whose ringleaders the constabulary had just removed. The *Newsletter* was delighted at the conflict between the repealers. "When Repeal is divided against itself it will not long stand."[24] After praising the honesty and integrity of Young Ireland, rubbing in the fact that the Catholic repealers of Belfast regard Young Ireland as an enemy of an "essentially Romanist" movement, and observing that Young Ireland's open strategy would render it easy to put down (unlike the "vicious" influence of O'Connell), the *Newsletter* was in effect saying, "Thank you, Young Ireland, for showing up what the Belfast Repeal movement is all about; but when the chips are down, Repeal means them, not you."

What answer would it have been possible to give to this argument? Only one answer would have taken care of it. At that time the O'Connell Repeal movement was moribund and therefore there was a possibility of starting something new that was free of the old clash between Protestantism and popish Repeal. Then the Protestant repealers would not find themselves having to take sides between their own people and the O'Connellites. So paradoxically, the big argument in favour of coming out and supporting Repeal at that time was that the "Old" repealers were defunct and there was actually no chance whatever of securing Repeal unless the British government wanted to just give it. This was probably not what Meagher had in mind, but it is none the less the reason why he got such a large and reasonably friendly Protestant audience. Two manifestations of support for the repeal of the Union in early 1848 demonstrate this point. In April 1848 a rather inconclusive meeting was held in Belfast which doesn't seem to have excited the magistrates despite one speaker advocating the sale of cows to purchase arms.[25] The magistrates clearly did not regard it as serious, and as long as the old repealers were as hostile to it then as they had been, the Confederates were probably a knot of no consequence. The 1848 events in France encouraged the most militant of the Young Irelanders, John Mitchell, editor of the *United Irishman*, to push the issue to the point of rebellion, although few went with him. The British government passed legislation, ostensibly to deal with Irish rebellion, but actually framed for use in England against Chartists.²⁶ So despite the preparations in Ireland the 1848 Rebellion as a rebellion was not fundamentally serious. In fact it was for this very reason that the other manifestation of Protestant support for Repeal was interesting.

The Protestant Repeal Association, which filled the Music Hall, opened with the reading of a letter from William Sharman Crawford, the one time MP for Dundalk, who had parted company with O'Connell over the question of federalism.²⁷ He was landlord of Crawfordsburn, near Holywood, and had been a Radical MP for Rochdale. He was about to become a figure of central importance during the period of the Tenant League.

"I consider that no beneficial result could arise from a Repeal of the Union unless carried by the joint approval of Protestants and Catholics . . . I apprehend that a Repeal of the Union, if carried by Catholic power against the general opinion of the Protestant community, would either have (the effect of an assertion of Catholic power over Protestant interests) or else produce a continued and aggravated struggle between Catholic and Protestant, and create an extent of evil which would counteract every benefit that might otherwise be anticipated from the locality of legislation. But if Protestants came forward to join their Catholic countrymen in demanding a Repeal of the Union, the objection I have stated at once vanishes."

He then proceeded to welcome the association and to argue in favour of Repeal, but "would resist every attempt to carry it by violent or seditious means, of any description". The meeting was clearly large and mention is made of the enrolment in batches of 62, 140, 86 and 96 members. How did the meeting deal with the fear of Catholic ascendancy? D. R. Ireland, a barrister, declared:

"The real danger to Protestant toleration consisted in the tardy concessions of privileges and rights to Ireland, not as a matter of justice to the great body of the people, but as something taken by force from the Protestants and handed to the people, until when England should be driven to her own shores, the Protestants of Ireland would be left to an overbearing and exasperated multitude who have been taught to look on them as their enemies".²⁸

The message is very much the same as the Tone of 1791. If Protestants do not take the risk of joining together with Catholics now, then they will be condemned to fear them later.

"Let the administration proceed to play upon the terrors of the Protestants, the hopes of the Catholics, and balancing the one party by the other, plunder and laugh at, and defy both."[29]

There was a substantial body of Protestant opinion favourable to the repeal of the Union in 1847–48. The Orange Order expelled a number of members for joining the Protestant Repeal Association.[30] And when Smith O'Brien was sentenced to death after the brief and very localized insurrection, the signatures on the petitions for clemency that circulated in the North included many who had earlier signed the loyalty pledge. Several Orange masters signed and even petitioned as representatives of their lodges.[31] The overlap between the clemency petition and the loyalty pledge in Ballymena was very considerable indeed.[32] But Mr Ireland's speech had made clear the paradoxical basis for this support for Repeal; and it explains why those who did not actually support Repeal showed such a very broad tolerance of those who did.

In 1840 the whole question of Repeal was of "us" and "them". It had this significance whether Protestant critics of the Union liked it or not. The experiences of the inner North before and during the Famine also fuelled the growing contrast between the development of "North" and "South". Protestants who saw the malignancy of the Union included those who (a) repudiated a purely sectional Belfast-centred understanding of the economic impact of the Union; (b) understood how divisive sectarian politics in Ireland enabled Britain to treat her as a lesser responsibility than metropolitan Britain; and (c) were aware of the long-term risks attached to the Union being under perpetual attack from pan-Catholic quarters. Perhaps disillusion with English rule was sharply exacerbated by the Whigs' famine policy, but the sympathy aroused for Young Ireland was in direct proportion to the impossibility of achieving it. It was precisely because the Confederation did not have the machinery of pan-Catholic power behind it that Protestant Repeal could declare its sentiments without fear. But Repeal could never become realistic politics under these circumstances. It would have needed an overwhelming Protestant expression in its favour, a quiescence of "pan-Catholic" agitation in the same direction, and a preparedness of English power to meet such a demand. Such conditions were manifestly unrealizable. Given the actual level of Ulster "unionism", as manifested at the 1848 loyalty meetings, and the absence of any intention on the part of English power to grant Repeal, no move towards Repeal could even have become serious without the reappearance of the physical power of O'Connell's movements behind it. That was what William Sharman Crawford was expressly opposed to. It was also the very situation that D. R. Ireland wanted to avert by calling for Repeal now rather than later. The whole episode showed that, even if there was a substantial minority of Protestants who were favourable to Repeal as an abstract idea, even these would disappear if ever Catholic mass action for Repeal was reactivated. It would also become more dangerous for them to announce the fact in those circumstances. It was precisely because Repeal was impossible in 1848 that so many Protestants felt able to support it.

The Orange Order dissolved itself in 1836 to pre-empt demands that it be legislated against.[33] In the 1834–36 period it achieved an importance in UK affairs that it never had before or has had since. Apart from the high level of aristocratic support and patronage accorded to it in Ireland, its grand master, Ernest, Duke of Cumberland, was regarded in ultra-reactionary circles as a possible successor to the throne. Orangeism in Britain had established itself within the army, and after the Lichfield House treaty between O'Connell and the Whigs, the putting down of Orangeism became a common concern for more than straightforward Irish reasons. A select committee established to its own satisfaction the danger posed by Orangeism in the army,[34] and Irish conservatism took a decision in favour of tactical retreat. The metropolitan forces of reaction lost much of their audacity and Duke Ernest left for Europe to become King of Hanover in 1837. There he distinguished himself among European reactionary rulers by abrogating the new constitution of that state, provoking an insurrection that took the combined forces of neighbouring German monarchies and principalities to put down.[35] Severed from its connection with English reaction and disavowed by the greater part of the Irish landlord class, Orangeism was cut down to its essentials, a popular organization of Ulster Protestantism. It is in this role that we must now consider it.

The dissolution of the Order was not achieved without opposition from its membership. Despite its obvious use as a political tool, it was a great deal more than that, and embodied a strategy for endurance such as we described in Killyman parish. Organizations which have this kind of significance, however manipulable they may be, or appear to be, do not just disappear or fade when the calculations of their manipulators dictate that they are expendable. But a question arises as to what kind of direction they are likely to take when left to their own devices. One of the themes which comes over consistently through the 1835 inquiry is that elite membership tends to discipline and temper the conduct of the mass: that without the gentry connection, Orangeism would be simply a less manageable entity.[36] This claim implies two things: first, that Orangeism has substantial popular roots; and second, that it is not capable of independent activity of anything other than a threatening kind. After 1836 the truth or falsity of the second point was to be tested.

As a body for deterring Catholics from making trouble, its control was territorial. It depended upon the Order showing that it was the dominant force in a district and that Catholic or Ribbon mobilizations would not be tolerated. The degree to which Orangeism guaranteed anything like "tranquillity" depended upon whether its activities were, or could be, controlled by local landlords or anyone else; the ease with which deterrence practices could become routine or be ritualised; and the degree to which Catholics accepted the *de facto* supremacy of Orange organization in an area. It is probable that in areas where there was a clear understanding about whether land was "Protestant" or "Catholic", some kind of accommodation was much easier than in instances where demarcation lines were not so clear.

But anything which disturbed demarcation lines tended to give rise to conflict. For example, as democratization proceeded, places which seemed "Protestant" often ceased to be so, because the new institutional framework changed the implications of local numbers. This happened in Monaghan where in 1826 a Catholic Emancipation election contest occurred. The Orange sub-sheriff of Monaghan, Sam Gray, committed murder in broad daylight in front of a large number of witnesses and several efforts to convict him stumbled on a variety of legal technicalities.[37] The same kind of disturbance was threatened whenever there was uncertainty about sectarian control over space, as often happened in growing towns.

The dissolution of the Order in 1836 and the determined efforts of the Drummond administration to put down Orange processions led to a mass exodus of magistrates, landlords, peers and Anglican clergy. In some districts the less calculative landlords, who regarded their obligations to the Order as more than expedient, stayed with it. Thus in County Armagh Colonel Blacker, who was deprived of his magistracy in 1833, remained as Deputy Grand Master of the county lodge which took on the duties of the grand lodge after the latter's dissolution.[38] Other lodges remained federated in restricted localities, such as the small numbers in north Antrim and north-east Derry. The sentiments pronounced by the lodges reveal something of the sense of betrayal. Thus a residual grand lodge in November 1838 representing largely areas outside Ulster said:

"The quiescent endurance of persecution has become intolerable and has already produced the alarming evil of a stationary if not diminishing Protestant population. The tide of Protestant emigration bids fair to reduce our yeomanry to a truly despicable minority, while the wealthier amongst us find in absenteeism that safety which Romish violence and Conservative timidity deny them at home."[39]

And from a later report a description is given of how, in the early 1840s (during the Repeal agitation) in County Derry, Ribbonmen patrolled nightly "even coming into the villages unchecked by the police and dealing out threats and insults to the Protestants, and proceeding to deeds of violence. In one of these villages in 1844, the old members of the Orange Lodge assembled for self-defence and the step was followed by the immediate cessation of Ribbon demonstrations."[40] In the final analysis, the relationship between Orangeism and ribbonism was one of incipient local rivalry, and where one was clearly in control, the effective intimidation of the other was taken for granted. That was the meaning of tranquillity.

In 1845, by the account of Lord Enniskillen, the Orange Order was reorganized in County Fermanagh and some adjacent areas to meet the threat of the Molly Maguires,[41] an agrarian organization about which little is known. But while the early reorganization was a small-scale affair, the events of 1848 permitted a full-scale reorganization. It is clear that an agent of the Castle made arrangements with the Orange Order to provide it with weapons. Dr McKnight later wrote of the affair which he knew of from the Derry Orangemen:

"The leaders [of the Orange Order] wanted to humbug the Castle authorities by taking advantage of their supposed necessities, and the Castle authorities coquetted with these leaders, while both these classes of gentry combined their efforts in humbugging the Orange masses, who are usually, in all similar transactions, treated as the merest tools, to be used according to the expediencies of the current hour. The Orange landlords wanted to disengage the Orange multitude from the tenant right movement by turning their attention to the shooting of Papists and Repealers, who to do them justice, were behaving in so outrageous a manner as to work out this landlord policy right admirably. The Whig government have no love for tenant right, nor for any other measure of really national value, and the Orange landlords and the Whig government were consequently drawn together by a common sympathy."[42]

On 25 May 1848 a large Tenant Right gathering had been held at Dungannon representing a very wide political spectrum, and had declared in favour of the "authoritative determination and limitation of rents" and "continued occupancy legally ensured to all tenants who paid them". The 12 July 1848 parade was on the scale of the early 1830s. At Garvagh 20,000 Orangemen listened to a speech by Dr McKnight and passed resolutions condemning the Bill brought forward by Sir William Somerville. "No measure founded on principles similar to those contained in that Bill can ever be accepted by the Protestant tenantry of Ulster."[43] They affirmed the position of the May meeting at Dungannon. But in most places the occasion was marked by the return of the respectable to the Order. The *Newsletter* said of the Dungannon celebrations: "The Dungannon Lodge was particularly conspicuous for its high respectability and its splendid appearance." It mentioned a list of JPs taking part and members of the Knox family (the proprietors of Dungannon) and other local notables.[44]

In fact, the reintegration of the Orange Order was difficult for more reasons than just tenant right, serious though that had become. What happened at Lisburn tells why. On the 12 July parade, the Watson Lodge, "consisting as it did exclusively of persons of the highest class of society", led the procession. At the end of the day it dined in the Hertford Arms. "A large number of the most influential gentry, lay and clerical, have expressed a wish to be admitted to this Lodge", reported the *Newsletter*.[45] Efforts to repatronize the Order were well under way. On 29 July a Loyal demonstration was held in Lisburn to discuss the defence of the town.[46] The agent and other functionaries of the Hertford estate, together with representatives of the linen and damask manufacturing interests, were present. Various speeches from the hall mentioned the "insults that were heaped upon Protestant brethren of the North by the traitor Peel". One had a warning for the Whigs:

"To the landlords I would say, if you do not adopt a very contrary course to that adopted this session of Parliament, when Sir William Somerville, by your aid, endeavoured to rob the tenantry of Ulster of their indisputable rights, I for one will not bail them that they may not turn on you in support of what I believe is their just and equitable rights."

But then the real trouble started. A resolution was moved that they, as Protestants, "do respectfully invite the Orangemen of the town to take that leading part in its defence to which they are entitled". Obviously the arms distribution had not reached Lisburn, which was hardly surprising as Lisburn would not have been vulnerable even to much bigger rebellions than this one turned out to be. It was complained that the government had "withheld arms from the Orange yeomanry". Then it was complained that the new Lord Hertford, unlike his father, was not an Orangeman. But it was left to one of the Richardson manufacturing family to declare that he would rather place his confidence in the Orangemen than in the government. The meeting was getting a little out of hand and the seneschal was having difficulty refusing the resolution, which would have given a very high profile to the Orange lodges in the town, which had probably been without much supervision by the elite for many years. Into the breach stepped Rev. H. Hodson, a leading Anglican cleric and a long-time grand lodge chaplain. He was soon in full flight:

". . . the restraints which our fathers saw fit and felt necessary to impose upon men, who could not be trusted or left to full exercise of liberty without danger, were removed in 1829—after this a grant was given from the public treasury to endow Jesuitism and Popery—after this our Protestant operatives were not only removed, but Popish ones established in their stead. . . . In the present perilous times the only bond of connexion between the two countries is formed by the Protestants of Ulster . . . If we want arms, we ask for them as Protestants—as Protestants of Ulster—as men entitled to every confidence . . ."[47]

The embarrassing issue of linking the elite of Lisburn to an explicit demand on the government to arm the Orangemen had been side-stepped. The issue of the Somerville Bill had been put off the centre of the agenda. But even in a manufacturing town in the middle of the weaver belt, warning shots had been fired about the land question, and some signs of self-assertion had been made by Orangemen. In fact a year later the government found pretext to restore the Orangemen to official disfavour and the elite left as rapidly as they had rejoined.

The government patronage of the Orange Order was fairly well disguised, but it became a source of embarrassment to the Whigs. On 12 July 1849 a major collision occurred between Orangemen and Ribbonmen at Dolly's Brae in south Down. In the shoot-out several Catholics were killed, and in the aftermath three magistrates dismissed from the commission of the peace. The opportunity was then taken to reimpose the Party Processions Act and restore the policy of official discouragement.[48] Within a short period, most of the landlord luminaries who had rejoined the Order in 1848 disappeared from the grand lodge.[49] Several lodges in Armagh dissolved themselves in disgust. One in Portadown which did so declared itself no longer obliged to defend the Crown and that "if stern necessity compel us to re-embody, it will be for the purpose of self-defence and mutual assistance to each other, and not for the support of any government whatever".[50] The gentry that stayed with the Orange Order were now generally smaller landlords around the southern areas of Ulster, together with the large landholders of County Fermanagh.[51] But in early 1850 the disillusion in the ranks of the Order ran high. Some began to draw independent political conclusions from these events. One of the first manifestations of this was at the County Down meeting to call for the reimposition of agricultural protection.

Dr Cooke was able to lead Ulster Presbyterianism into an alliance with the Anglican landed interests so long as opposition to national education was seen as a religious issue. The settling of the compromise in 1840, which allowed non-vested schools to operate a policy of merely giving children of different denominations the right to leave the schoolroom during hours of religious instruction, took the political steam out of that issue. In the same year the synod, purified of non-subscribers, reunited with the Secession Presbyterians in the General Assembly of the Presbyterian Church in Ireland.[52]

In 1843 two issues arose which put Peel very decidedly on the wrong side of Presbyterian interests. The question of the validity of Presbyterian marriages was followed speedily by the crisis in the Church of Scotland over the patronage question. The secession of the evangelical ministers under the leadership of Dr Chalmers to form the Free Church of Scotland created a very profound evangelical distaste for Peel, which was widely echoed in the General Assembly in Ireland. Cooke's opposition to the Whigs could be represented as a religious question; his continued support for Peel after 1843 could not. Until the major break in the Conservatives in 1845 over the Maynooth grant and repeal of the Corn Laws, Dr Cooke's continued support for conservatism was increasingly unpopular.[53] In 1843 at the General Assembly, Dr John Brown of Aghadowey moved a resolution recommending the adoption of measures for securing the more adequate representation of the principles and interests of Presbyterians in the legislature.[54] Cooke opposed the resolution which struck at the basis of his alliance with the Anglican ascendancy. And on losing the issue he withdrew from the assembly until 1847.

The 1843 resolution was only the beginning of what was to become an increasingly evident tendency of Presbyterian ministers to support Liberals for peculiarly Presbyterian purposes. Dr Brown, for example, was in later years to take a prominent part in helping the campaigns of Samuel McCurdy Greer in County Derry. Unlike the earlier Whigs who saw themselves as leaders for the Catholics in the North, these Liberals became less and less embarrassed about opposing Catholic claims. Unlike the earlier Whigs many had taken Cooke's position against visitorial rights for Catholic priests at national schools.

To have created a religiously plural society, denominational differences would have had to be freed from any wider political or social meaning. Only then could the clergy have been only clergy, rather than figures of wider political and social importance. But the essence of the settlement colonial legacy in Ireland was the fear of Catholic self-organization. And one of the tests of whether the Protestant society could ever get past this fear was whether it could accept that Catholics had good reason to fear Protestant-run educational institutions. The penal era had been all about rupturing Catholicity amongst the educated, and the Second Reformation was planning more of the same. The national education scheme, as originally conceived, was designed to get round this problem of Catholic distrust, but the Presbyterian reaction to it showed that the Catholic suspicion was not altogether misplaced. So long as the Whigs were committed to the system, as it was originally conceived, Catholic suspicion of the northern Whigs was neither general nor justifiable. The Whigs had taken risks to promote national education at a time when mobs were attacking national schools. But when the modified national system settled down in the 1840s, this new Presbyterian Liberal support for the system had a rather different implication. Just how different can be inferred from what happened over the Whigs' efforts to secure the hierarchy's support for the Queen's colleges in 1848.

Lord Clarendon circulated the proposed statutes to the hierarchy for their comments and criticisms, assuring them that

Catholic clergy would have visitorial status and that "in the council, professorships and other posts of such Colleges, the Catholic religion will be fully and appropriately represented".[55] One statute provided that a student's failure to attend the place of worship prescribed by his parent or guardian would be sanctioned by the threat of expulsion. The *Banner of Ulster* described this as a provision that a Roman Catholic youth "may be expelled . . . for attending a Protestant place of worship"—not, one might think, a very frequent occurrence—but the *Banner*'s response indicated that an institution run according to its principles should keenly encourage such things. "If the Government are determined to play into the hands of the Papists in this manner, we say, perish the Queen's Colleges. Let them be shunned by all true Protestants, let them be handed over at once to Dr. Murray and to the Pope."[56] Fortunately for the *Banner* and for Presbyterian educational interests generally, they did not have to live with this anathema. The colleges were condemned by the hierarchy and two years later the *Banner* suggested that Presbyterians should now "take possession" of the Queen's colleges "so as to obtain a practical establishment within their walls".[57] This, at least as far as the Belfast college was concerned, was what actually happened. And in later years, when Presbyterians were defending the principle of "united secular and separate religious education", this slogan was not always an even-handed statement of principle. It was a shield for this "practical establishment" of Presbyterians. The more the Catholic Church attempted to secure an explicitly denominational system of education, the more support for "united secular education" began to be a flag of convenience for a general defence of Presbyterian educational interests.

Many Presbyterians, as they became more involved in politics in this period, were not linked to either Conservative or to Whig traditions. It took the Famine to turn many of them into spokesmen for tenant interests. An example of how such things happened occurred at the Loyalty meeting in Comber in 1848. Comber was much more of an agricultural service town than Lisburn. Unlike Lisburn, which had Presbyterian country on one side and Anglican on the other, Comber was surrounded by a solidly Presbyterian farming district and was more or less free of Orangeism. At the May 1848 Loyalty meeting, John

Andrews, J.P., agent to the Marquis of Londonderry, and other estate personnel took the platform.[58] Presbyterian ministers raised the tenant right question with sufficient effect to drive the estate management away from the meeting altogether. The Rev. John Rogers said that the Loyalty meetings had been used to make the government believe "that the people think this is a land flowing with milk and honey". Rev. Mr Gamble, who started by declaring that he was an anti-Repeal and an anti-rebel man whose motto was "No Surrender", went on to say: "While the Presbyterian clergy are loyal, we should prevent the people from being robbed out of the place." Another, who was later to be involved deeply in conflict with Lord Londonderry, declared: "If the country were invaded by enemies from abroad—or if Ulster were invaded by the other three provinces—every man in the Province would do his duty." While this might have been true about Comber, it shows already how deeply ingrained the habit had become of treating Ulster as Protestant Ulster. Rev. Mr Killen rounded out the various sentiments:

"Our loyalty arises from being a Bible-taught people and from an experimental knowledge of the benefits derived from the Union. . . . Most of us would acknowledge that Ulster had prospered since the Union. Belfast which has now as great an emporium of commerce as Liverpool, was at that time fifty years ago, little better than a fishing village. If then the Union was bad for Ireland, would it not have been bad for Ulster? But Ulster has improved and this shows that the evils of the country are of a moral kind, and that it is the inculcation of right moral principles only that will cure them."

The sense of moral difference between North and South is also illustrated in the *Banner of Ulster*'s diagnosis of the 1848 crisis. There were many, it said, who expected that the passage of the Catholic Emancipation Act would create an era of tranquillity and stability, but it declared that those who entertained such views "did not understand aright the spirit and character of Popery, for ever since that enactment, Ireland has been a theatre of interminable excitement". O'Connell "was the tool of Romish ecclesiastics", but he awoke a spirit throughout Ireland "too turbulent for the agitator himself". The

Famine "has weakened the power of the priest, and added to the natural recklessness of the national character". "Evangelical Protestantism has often come forth purified from the furnace of trial; but it would seem that Popery pines away and dies when it has to pass through the same ordeal." Its verdict on the impending rebellion was that the priests were now powerless to stop it and were "awaiting, in a position of neutrality, the issue of the pending struggle".[59] It asks whether in the light of all this any purpose is served by "concession to Popery".

Even though this interpretation does not see the Confederacy rising as some super subtle manifestation of "Romanism", it offers only one kind of alternative explanation. When Catholic political agitation is not under the control of priests, it is naturally reckless. Once again the sum and total of Irish Catholic politics is reduced to essentially moral faults. What hope does the *Banner* editor hold out for Ireland in that case? In Nenagh in 1849, the congregation of the Roman Catholic church barricaded the entry against an unpopular nominee to the office of parish priest over the head of the local curate. The curate begged the people to desist and submit to the bishop's appointment. The *Banner* commented: "His reverence will of course be obeyed and ecclesiastical despotism will be triumphant, so that by this time the Roman Catholic laity may be thoroughly convinced that pure Presbyterianism is their only refuge, if they wish to enjoy so much as the name of spiritual enfranchisement."[60] In other words, there seem to be three paths for the population of the South: priestly control; indulging the natural recklessness of the national character; or conversion to Presbyterianism. Any kind of understanding of the land beyond inner Ulster seemed remote and there was very little sign of empathy with Catholic Ireland about the time of the beginning of the Tenant League.

We need now to consider the position of the Belfast Whigs in 1848. The return of the Whigs to office in 1846 had linked the Belfast Whigs to the government which presided over the Irish Famine and threw Ireland on to her own resources when they were approaching exhaustion. When Sir William Somerville introduced his Land Tenure Bill in 1848, causing protests of massive proportions to well up in Ulster, the local Whigs were obliged to intervene to keep any rural credibility they had. But the style of their intervention placed them in virtual opposition to much of the popular ground swell. I shall now put aside the various sources of specifically Catholic and Presbyterian reservations about the Whigs and consider instead how they compared with other kinds of Liberals elsewhere in this period. There was a tendency for manufacturing and mercantile classes to take the leadership of popular democratic moves against pre-capitalist landowners. In Barrington Moore's[61] writing this is the paradigm move towards democracy. When, by contrast, the landowners remain in control politically and manage to co-opt sections of the rising capitalist class, this is in the long run the path towards Fascism.

In many ways the relationship worked out between the Conservatives of Belfast and the surrounding landowners was fairly close to Moore's model of the proto-Fascist alliance. And its success also shows up the other side of Barrington Moore's thesis: the inability of the Liberal capitalists to take the initiative meant that they grew old and cautious, and lost the ability to bring the masses into politics. Then the landholder-capitalist alliance was able eventually to absorb much of the populace into a reactionary alliance. The Whigs did lose their opportunity in 1848–52. But the new "Liberals" who outflanked them were unable to establish themselves either. In the end we shall see that the real problem for democratization in the North of Ireland was that so long as no political group was able to develop creative and empathetic relationships with other forces in Catholic Ireland, there was never any chance of the landowner bloc losing the political initiative in the North.

The Conservative leadership in Belfast, in the early phase of their rule, managed to reconcile their developmental objectives with their alliance with the landlords. Wide diffusion of the benefits of the developmental works and pan-Protestant political strategy enabled them to hold the lead until the mid-1850s. The county grand juries of Antrim and Down were predominantly controlled by the major landholders. Generally the county members of parliament were drawn from their numbers and, in the early life of the Belfast Corporation, that body was dependent in some measure on their approval for the passage of its private acts of parliament. There is ample evidence that the corporation was concerned to conciliate the old landed interests of the town. The purchase of Mays fields from Sir Stephen May (of the Donegall family) to accommodate new market facilities rescued the latter from mild financial embarrassment, though the utility of the purchase was questioned with some justification later on.[62] Until 1850, the corporation made no attempt to secure the removal of the county cess from Belfast ratepayers, although the roads inside Belfast were repaired by the council out of the local taxes. Also the grand jury of Antrim maintained turnpikes on the entries into the city whose proceeds reduced the rate of the county cess on landowners.[63] The landlords ensured that the greater part of the infrastructural costs of commerce between the borough and the county were borne by Belfast and by those taking merchandise in and out of the cities.

The grand jury was also very hard-nosed in its dealings with railroad developments. Railroads tended to compete for traffic with turnpike surface roads. In 1838, when the Ulster Railway was building Belfast–Lisburn, and in 1847, when the Northern Counties railway company was building Belfast–Ballymena, the grand jury exercised a close vigilance to make sure that these works did not "damage" the county roads.[64] It was only in the 1850s when the general utility of railroads appears to have become beyond dispute that the Antrim grand jury started removing turnpikes. In the early days it looks as though the first priority in their minds was the saving of county taxation expenditure on transport infrastructure.

So long as the corporation was content neither to raise protests about the position of the grand juries, nor to attempt to align itself politically with any of its rural opponents, there was no reason why the Conservative alliance at an elite level need have run into difficulties. In the 1850s the opposed pressures of the grand jury for the maintenance of the county cess and the popular pressures for a reduction in urban rates never came into head-on collision. The costs incurred by the massive deficit-financed development scheme only began to create conflicts about the rates structure or who was going to pay for the works after the most difficult questions with the Antrim grand jury had been sorted out. When this happened in the late 1850s and early 1860s, it turned out that the Whig leaders and the Conservatives had the same economic interests which drew them together and meant that the popular protest of the late 1860s was outside the control of either.

The Whigs' first opportunity to capitalize on tensions in the Conservative alliance had come not so much from within the framework of the city as in the countryside beyond. In the process of democratization, Liberal manufacturers often broke down landlord monopolies over representation, agrarian tariff barriers, pre-capitalist restrictions on trade and commerce, and the mobility of labour. The Whigs in Belfast were keen electoral reformers in the early 1830s and strongly supported free trade. In the early 1830s they were opponents of the insecurity of tenant holdings at landlords' will, and supporters of grand jury reform. They included prominently in their number linen bleachers and manufacturers, and retained a considerable popular following in Belfast. Despite their embarrassment at the time of O'Connell's visit to promote Repeal in 1841, and their total exclusion from the corporation in 1842, they had been strong enough to be able to enforce a compromise on the borough representation in parliament from 1842 to 1852. Their own internal conflicts and the Tories' manipulation of the municipal electoral register ensured their continued exclusion from the corporation, but parliamentary committees' investigations into the conduct of Westminster elections strengthened their hand somewhat in such contests, and obliged the Conservatives to be rather more accommodating.

The partial tariff abolition of 1842 by Peel took something of the urgency out of the free trade question as far as manufacturing interests were concerned. This made the incorporation of Conservative mill owners in Belfast fairly easy and blunted the cutting edge of Whig support for free trade. In Ireland the abolition of the Corn Laws in 1846 was practically speaking a dead letter given Famine conditions in 1847. It was only in 1848 that falling agricultural prices began to be added to the themes of rural concern. In 1849 and 1850, low agricultural prices were, given current rent levels and other charges, beginning to put a squeeze on farmers. When in 1850 landlords attempted to mobilize a general agrarian demand for the revival of protection, they had difficulty securing the assistance of Belfast Conservative manufacturing and mercantile spokesmen, who were clearly embarrassed. Their embarrassment would have been far greater if the Whig manufacturing interest had been prepared to link its opposition to protection with strong support for the demand for rent reduction. In fact the Whigs did not feel safe using the free trade question as a popular rallying cry, because they did not feel safe with popular movements demanding rent reduction. So the popular movement of 1848–52 fell into the hands of some of the political miscellany whose origins we have seen in this chapter.

7. 1848–1852: The League of North and South—the Tenant League

"The men of Ulster are proverbially averse to agitation. Large masses of an excited and discontented population can easily be congregated in the other provinces of Ireland. Their sufferings and wrongs are a fertile theme, by which the honest or interested patriot can readily awaken a maddening enthusiasm amongst a generous, but suffering people. Change—change of any kind—is to those acceptable; but not so with the men of Ulster."

So spoke the Rev. John Doran, parish priest of Loughbrickland, before a largely Protestant audience of Lurgan tenant farmers assembled to agitate against Sir William Somerville's Irish Land Bill.[1] The organizers of the meeting had hoped that John Hancock, Lord Lurgan's agent, would come. He was a prominent Whig who was regarded as one of the most important supporters of the tenant right custom, but he had declined stating that the subject had been made the occasion of "expressing revolutionary opinions, immediately destructive of the fair rights of the landlords, and ultimately ruinous of the permanent interests of the tenants". The northern Whigs were generally opposed to the Sommerville Bill. It recognized improvements as being entitlement to compensation only if they had been made within the last twenty-one years. It thereby struck directly at Ulster tenant right. Hancock himself observed that the benefit arising from the custom was in proportion "to the degree to which the management of the estate approaches legal certainty and precision" and he favoured putting the custom on a legal basis.[2] But the "revolutionary opinions" with which Mr Hancock took issue were not about whether to recognize the custom. One of the resolutions was: "This meeting is further of the opinion, that an authoritative provision should be introduced for the limitation of rents . . . as in the absence of this provision, all tenant right legislation would be useless and would still leave the tenantry in the power of their landlords."[3]

The *Northern Whig* commented that "to attempt authoritatively to limit rents would be as clearly in opposition to principle, as to attempt to prevent a merchant from getting what he could for a hogshead of sugar, or a farmer what he could for a quarter of wheat . . . anyone who countenances it thereby proves himself, practically, whatever may be his professions, an enemy to the just claims of the farmer".[4]

Throughout the rest of the story many political and clerical figures will appear, declaring themselves in favour of tenant right. In fact to say anything directly against tenant right in Ulster after 1848 (and perhaps earlier) would have been like advocating wife-beating. To understand Ulster politics in this period, it becomes necessary to learn to decode the various kinds of tenant right concepts being advocated. We have noticed earlier that tenant right values and rent levels are competing claims on the value of the land and that, especially when credit tightens, the conflict between the two claims is sharpened. In 1848 market values of tenant right had in most areas been wiped out altogether. Market values of tenant right would only recover as tenants accumulated capital (now heavily depleted), prices rose, or rents fell. This is why the issue of mandatory rent reductions had come to the fore, because without such reductions tenant right was dead. And this was the "revolutionary opinion" that the Lurgan meeting had endorsed.

In 1848 landlords were busy displacing smaller tenants. The worst of the Famine had passed in the inner North. Food prices were falling back to normal levels, but with crop failures continuing, that spelt another kind of difficulty for farmers. The very low values of tenant right also made displacement a much easier option for a landlord, because it expressed a general lack of confidence amongst the farming community. There simply were no well-capitalised people eager to take over a vacated farm. And a neighbour, offered the opportunity to take in more land without tenant right payment, would be glad of the opportunity. The problem of displaced tenants did not just stop with the question of compensating them. Displaced tenants, without the means to emigrate, might increase the Poor Law burden and therefore the rates which surviving tenants were obliged to pay in addition to their rents and county cess.

When the tenant right levels sank so low, many landlords who gave even small sums to persuade a tenant to quit were actually paying more than the current tenant right values of the holdings. So the questions of tenant right and compensation for disturbance were becoming in every way confused. There were many who admitted the need for some kind of legislative action, even though they did not support mandatory rent reductions. If tenant right values were very low, what compensation would be required from a landlord when a tenant had to quit without any tenant right payment? Should obstacles be put up to regulate how landlords did this?

Shortly before the Lurgan meeting, the Antrim and Down Tenant Right Association had held a meeting in Belfast at which the Rev. Dr Henry Montgomery was the main speaker.[5] While the meeting opposed Sir William Somerville's Bill, its resolutions "disclaim all right, on the part of the tenants, to absolute fixity of tenure, or to interfere unreasonably with the landlord's letting of his land" and accepted the good intentions of the government proposal. As to the details of their scheme: they sought to preserve the right of free sale of tenant right by an outgoer to an incomer who satisfied a landlord as to his solvency. They also sought provision that where a landlord dispossessed a tenant either by demand of an "exorbitant rent" or otherwise, he be compensated in two ways: (a) full compensation for all improvements which "permanently increase the value of the property" whether made by the tenant, purchased or inherited; (b) a sum equivalent to five or six years of "beneficial interest which he would have had in the property from which he has been removed, had he been allowed to hold it as a fair rent". Fair rents were to be determined and all compensation disagreements settled either by a jury or by arbitrators chosen mutually by the parties. If necessary, there would also be an umpire either of their own choosing, or else a government appointee.⁶

There are several points to be made about these proposals. First, the notion of fair rent does not enter their scheme until after a tenant is dispossessed. In other words, no limitation is applied to the rent a landlord may ask of a sitting tenant. Second, in a circumstance of falling prices the meaning of both parts of the compensation procedure hang critically upon the arbitration process. One of the objectionable features of the Somerville Bill was that it extinguished all claims for improvements which were over twenty-one years old, and in this proposal the problem is superficially overcome by talking of permanent improvements which have been purchased or inherited. But actually this simply displaced the problem. If a tenant had purchased tenant right that went back in a line of succession from the first tenants who created the holding, precisely what permanent improvement had he not "inherited or purchased"? The compensation procedures laid down here look fairly real, but they state the problem rather than solve it. We can probably get no further with our understanding of this scheme without looking at the thinking behind it.

Montgomery stated that he was only persuaded to take part in the discussion of the land laws "by some moderate, just minded, and most intelligent farmers, who felt, with myself, that extreme views, on both sides, were essentially injuring a good cause". It was necessary to show to the legislature that such people had no desire to "trench in the smallest degree upon the just rights and real interests of their landlords". He had no sympathy with those who wanted to pull down the aristocracy. "It is good for men to have something to look up to—the graduations of social rank are a social benefit." After comparing favourably the landlords' economic behaviour with that of corn dealers and other classes, and praising the Londonderrys and Crawfords (Capt. Crawford, one of the most widely respected landlords of the North, was in the chair), he proceeded to outline the need for legislation:

"Nothing but an honest law of Tenant Right can prevent a wholesale system of clearances from producing incalculable miseries. As to the landlords I think they will act wisely, both for themselves and for their country, by replacing a crowd of pauper cottiers with a reasonable number of respectable tenant farmers and well paid labourers; but as in times past they derived large incomes from the exorbitant rent paid by these holders of two or three acres, they should be compelled by law to prevent these from becoming a burden upon others, whom, for selfish objects, they allowed to accumulate upon their own estates . . . In Co. Down, there are 13,700 families holding less than five acres of land, each. Now if these farms were condensed into holdings of twenty acres, each, about 10,000 families or 50,000 individuals, might be cast upon the poor rates or compelled to emigrate. . . . The farmers are only beginning to feel the pressure of the new law, but if landlords shall be allowed to eject small tenants, without adequate compensation, the existing workhouse will soon be overstocked, hundreds of new ones must be erected, and the poor rates will become, in many places, if not in all, an intolerable burthen."[7]

If, however, most landlords in the North were "good landlords", why precisely did he fear such an eventuality? The proposed Encumbered Estates Bill was designed to facilitate the sale of estates of embarrassed proprietors, perhaps in divided lots. Montgomery feared that these smaller lots might be purchased by "low money grabbers and usurers". He didn't deny "that some small proprietors are just, considerate and humane men". He knew many who were, "but as a general rule, they are high renters, and keen sticklers for their rights". The law he proposed was to "draw their fangs, and to render them not merely harmless, but even useful".

Montgomery's scenario included large-scale displacement of smaller tenants. What he wanted to do was to make sure that these people had the wherewithal to emigrate and not become a burden on the Poor Law. As the standard bearer of the old Whigs, his design was to construct an alliance between the more substantial farmers and the big (preferably Whig) landlords. The law was only needed to keep the *nouveaux riches* upstarts in their place, to prevent the Poor Law from being deluged by small tenants evicted by the "low money grabbers".

Apart from the difficulty of trying to counter the rising tide of tenant demands for compulsory rent reductions, politically there was another difficulty. This was the shortage of Whig landlords and the rather poor correlation between the "goodness" and Whiggish sympathies of landlords in general. Thus when the demand for rent reductions took off, Colonel William Blacker, the Orange leader in County Armagh, summoned his tenants, asked them to name their proposed reduction, and promptly accepted their proposal.[8] The same could not be said for the Peelite Marquis of Londonderry, whom the *Northern Whig* was rather actively courting.

About this time the Marquis, whose free trade convictions probably owed something to his coal-mining interests in Britain, held a dinner for his tenantry. He boasted that he didn't give into the popular cry for rent reductions "when all landlords around him were called on for reduction and yielded to the cry".[9] The cry, however, from his farmers had never reached him. The estate had never applied for any government money under the various relief schemes. Tenant right had always been respected on his estate and the rents were generally low. He spoke of the tenant right issue as "a sort of second Repeal question . . . improperly used by persons of dangerous character, who cloaked their nefarious designs, under the cry of the tenant right agitation".[10] The Whigs' affection for this particular landlord was to become very costly indeed. And at this stage it should be noted that though his father was a Presbyterian, he had become a member of the Established Church. A year or so later this conversion was to acquire a potent significance.

Montgomery led a delegation to London to see Sir William Somerville, with whom he had a long interview. "It is due to the Right Honourable Baronet to state that he kindly invited the Doctor to communicate with him, at any time and to any extent which he might desire."[11] The big resource that the northern Whigs had at this stage was their access to the government. They were also concerned to do what they could to repair locally its very damaged credibility. So who were the agitators who were alarming the Whigs? John Rea, a prominent member of the Drennan club was heckling and accusing Montgomery and the Whigs of attempting to undermine tenant right. Montgomery replied, "We have nothing to do with what the *Whig* or the *Standard* says, or with the amount of falsehood which Dr. McKnight may write in the *Standard*, for neither the statements in it, nor the individual, could receive from me further notice."[12]

Dr James McKnight, editor of the *Londonderry Standard* for most of his adult life, was shortly to begin a four-year spell as editor of the official Presbyterian paper, the *Banner of Ulster*. An orthodox Presbyterian, his primary preoccupation in life was to secure tenant property on an independent basis. He was largely responsible for getting Ulster tenants to become articulate in defending their rights. His particular skill was to start off from where Ulster Protestant tenants were, and lead them to an understanding of the wider realities, including, especially, some grasp of the differences between their own relative good fortune and the sufferings of other parts of the island. So although the basis of his position was as "sectional" as possible—his theory of tenant right was derived from the origins of the Ulster Plantation—his actual position was about the most serious corrosive applied to sectional narrowness in the 19th century. He shared much of the sectional feeling of Ulster Protestants, but lost few occasions to attempt to draw his listeners and readers to an awareness of wider Irish realities. And his most audacious effort to link the northern tenant right agitation with the Irish Tenant League brought down the wrath of Tory and Whig establishments alike upon him.[13]

McKnight's first task was to get tenants to think about their rights. In a society born of settlement colonization, what passed for political thought was often a preoccupation with the enemy all about them. It was not a political culture that encouraged a clear perception of class realities. When interdependence between Protestants broke down, as in the displacement crisis of the late 18th century, it was all too readily seen in terms of betrayal of the people by landlord selfishness. On the face of it, McKnight's assertion that the original grants to the undertakers of the plantation gave them only limited rights and bestowed on them trustee status appeared to do the same thing with a vengeance.[14] He demonstrated that the undertakers' leases required them to encourage Protestant settlement, and specifically limited the rents they could charge to secure that effect. The tenants, he argued, had done all the improvements on the land from the conversion of the raw earth upwards. The tenants' interest in the land which they had turned into cultivated farms from barren wastes was protected by the plantation contracts which restricted the landlords' rents. And the tenant right was a product of the difference between the legally restricted landlord interest denominated by the plantation rent, and the current value of the farms. In its most simple form, this doctrine could be expressed by saying that the landlord's interest in a holding was restricted to the value of the "raw earth".

David Millar is quite correct in saying that the contrast between southern tenants' claims and northern tenants' claims was based upon antithetical myths of origin.[15] In the southern case, lands had been "taken" by the Crown; in the northern case, they had been "given" by the Crown. So the demand for "land-to-the-tenants" was based in one case on the principle of reversing a confiscation, and in the other on restoring a thing once given. But differences of this kind are not necessarily politically fundamental in the long run. If this plantation-rights thesis was one step to getting Protestant tenants to understand their rights, it does not follow that it constrained their subsequent politics. Indeed McKnight was very explicit as to the "morally" ambivalent character of the original rights.

"Exclusiveness and intolerance were amongst the dominant vices of the age in which the Plantation settlement was effected, and all parties at that era were more or less tainted with these infirmities whenever they had their adversaries in their power, while the unhappy civil wars, by which Ireland had been previously desolated, made one-sidedness to be a political necessity of the first Plantation arrangements. The Liberal legislation of subsequent ages has, by the establishment of civil and religious equality before the law, entitled all tenants, resident within the Plantation boundaries, to the equal enjoyment of Plantation rights and immunities without regard to differences of race or religion."[16]

The affirmation of the peculiar origins of northern tenants' original rights is only a problem when the different conceptions of the origins of rights conflict, and one denies the other. The test of this question was how the landlords' failure to honour that part of their undertakings—which required them not to take on Irish tenants—was handled. McKnight makes it utterly clear that the Catholic tenants in the North are now beneficiaries of the plantation rights also. And the priest who addressed the Lurgan meeting felt quite able to say this to a gathering full of Lurgan Protestant farmers.

"I don't say that the landlords kept all their agreements, for one of the conditions imposed on them was, that they should not let any of their lands to the 'natives'. But the landlords in order to get rack rents from these said 'natives' gave them some of their lands, and but for this, though it was not over and above honest in the landlords, according to the conditions to which they had agreed, I would not be here this day as an Ulsterman. [*Loud cheers*] ... Now, you are the descendants of these colonists, and your rights are as ancient and as legal, if you had only the courage to maintain them, as are the rights of your landlords [*loud cheers*] and I deem it madness on the part of the Government to provoke the discussion of this question, by an actual aggression upon your acknowledged rights."[17]

McKnight's thesis was not a way of affirming differences between "North" and "South". It was necessary to understand the differences in order to accept them and to move past them. It was a case of getting Protestant tenants to think of their rights. By contrast, southern Catholic tenants, for whom landlordism and confiscation were one, did this uncritically. Protestant tenants were not used to thinking critically about landlordism, whatever they may have felt about it. Perhaps the knowledge that they too were in some way beneficiaries of the displacement of the natives had stopped them. So how then did McKnight teach about landlordism?

"The philosophy of rent as being the clear profit remaining after all the costs of production, and the interest of the farmer's capital have been deducted, ought to be kept habitually in view."[18] In short, the tenants' claims on the product of the land are always anterior to those of the landlord. In an article on the contraction of the monetary circulation in Ireland, he pointed out how it indicated a massive reduction in the value of national property.[19] "The social system hitherto maintained is falling asunder by its own weight ... the potato failure was not the efficient cause of this national calamity, as the potato failure merely brought to light, by a destructive process no doubt, the horrible nature of that feudal relationship in society, which has ground down the bulk of the population to the lowest possible description of food, in order that the productive wealth of the soil might go into the pockets of the landed gentry. Absentee landlordism sweeps away between six and seven million a year, a profit revenue of four to five million is absorbed by Imperial taxation, while every source of public employment is a source of aristocratic jobbing or party corruption."[20]

He proceeds to argue that the system of primogeniture and entail almost necessarily involves pressures to rack-rent. Estates cannot be alienated or subdivided, so younger branches of aristocratic families have to be provided for through mortgages and encumbrances. "The pursuit of honest industry would be equivalent to that which feudal legislation had denominated a 'corruption of blood', and hence the army, the navy, the colonies, the Church, and every other department of public jobbery, must be kept open for the maintenance of titled pauperism, created by the laws of progenitory succession." So long as aristocratic pauperism multiplies and the aristocracy has control not merely of the House of Lords but a large part of the Commons also, it constitutes a malignant system.[21]

He then goes on to look at the question of free trade. In 1848, for the first time Irish agriculture was beginning to feel its full impact. He does not mince his words about the need to live with free trade prices of food. So what is involved in the demand for renewed "protection"?

"Agricultural protection is protection of rack rents, and to the other class immunities of the favoured oligarchy, and what the tenant farmers of Ireland have now to do is to demand the extension of free trade, in all its comprehensive application, to the tenures and to the occupation of the soil itself. So long as the land monopoly shall remain in force, the establishment of free trade, in relation to the produce of the land, can only have the effect of ruinously depressing the producers as a class . . . fragmentary free trade is wholesale injustice towards all interests which have within their own circle, to contend against an exclusive monopoly."[22] This was the challenge that Liberals had to take up if they were to lead popular forces against landlordism. Because land ownership was actually monopolised, tenant property had to be given a defence against it. The demand for rent reductions became part of the defence of free trade.

It may very well be argued that McKnight is here failing to grasp the fact that so long as the level of underemployment remains high, whoever has property will be able to secure a rack-rent from it. He himself says when discussing the free market rent levels, "Popular competition is manifestly no criterion, as man's necessities, rather than their own judgments, are in this case almost always the contracting agents."[23] Hence the standard counter-argument of 19th-century landlordism, that if you give a tenant fixity of tenure at an authoritatively limited rent with the right of free sale of his interest, you create the possibility of that individual subletting his land or selling his interest to someone else who will.[24] But such an observation misses the vital political point. Any measures such as McKnight (and indeed the Tenant League) were demanding would have spread the basis of secure rural property far more widely than hitherto. Perhaps a few million secure landholders would have been as selfish as a few thousand landlords had been. But at least the selfishness would have spread its advantages and disadvantages more evenly; and the arrogance of monopolistic power would have been broken. The tenant right question was very much at the heart of politics, as well as economics. And even so, even in the worst scenario in 1848-50, it is not very probable that secured tenancies would have permitted tenants to start turning again to "middlemanship". What is likely is that fewer would have found it impossible to stay on their holdings instead of "being left without their capital itself, and driven either into the union workhouse at home, or into migratory banishment at the other extremity of the globe, if they are happy enough to have saved from their ruined fortunes a sufficiency to defray the charges of their own transportation".[25] The rural patterns of land usage under a regime of effectively secured tenants might have had its disagreeable characteristics, but it manifestly would not have involved the optimization of land use strategies dictated by landlord interests.

McKnight challenged the fundamental principles of Whiggery in relation to the land question. Where the Whigs merely wanted to regulate the transition to larger farms, McKnight sought first and foremost to establish the farmers' independent status. All legalization of tenant right, he declared, is "delusive" without fixed tenure, that is, secured occupancy, so long as a fair rent is paid. And fair rents must be limited by an independent tribunal. Without such rights tenants must also be slaves in political matters, so long as their property depends upon landlord favour. The objective of the legislature ought to be "the creation of as numerous a class of men as possible, who shall have an indestructible interest in the soil of the country".[26] While they disagreed on how it should be achieved, McKnight and William Sharman Crawford agreed about the importance of protecting smallholders from consolidating landowners. Crawford, then Radical MP for Rochdale, has already figured in our story. He had attempted on many occasions to secure a legal basis for the tenant right custom. At the beginning of the 1848 land crisis, when Whigs generally worried about "Agitation" and "cloaked nefarious designs", Sharman Crawford wrote to the Lurgan Tenant Right Association, describing the opposition that would be encountered by any acceptable Tenant Right Bill.

"There are three sections of enemies. First, the Irish landlord interest, which include the Government, who appear to me to be under the thraldom of that power. Second, the English landlord interest. Third, the free trade economic section, on whose behalf Mr. Trelawny on this occasion takes the lead."[27]

Of the free trade section, he said that all their arguments had one feature—the consolidation principle ought to be sustained as the only means of regenerating Ireland. Crawford said he trusted the day would never come when the smallholders of Ulster would be displaced.

In January 1850 the High Sheriff of County Down issued a summons to a County meeting to call for the restoration of protectionism. With much of the County Down aristocracy on the platform, it might have been supposed that the amassed audience, like that at Hillsborough in 1834, would be so much support for pre-arranged sentiments.[28] But some Downpatrick Orangemen and the principal leaders of the local Catholics had organized an opposition, and the body of the hall was filled with a determined set of supporters of altogether different opinions. The first part of the proceedings illustrated clearly enough the tensions in Ulster conservatism. A letter from S. K.

Mulholland, the mill owner, was read out. It said that he "might" have come but that it was probable that most present would not have agreed with his views (the landlords, that is) as "to the extent at which free trade becomes a desirable principle". At the present time he thought it was doing injury. What he advocated was a partial free trade with those who were prepared to free trade with the UK. In other words, he would use a smaller tariff on agricultural imports as a bargaining counter against those who operated protective tariffs against UK manufacturers. That can hardly have been much comfort to the County Down squirearchy. The Director of the Belfast Bank, and Treasurer of the Belfast Corporation, John Thompson, was one of the few non-landowning luminaries who could be induced to appear, and he too only managed to give utterance to similar lukewarm protectionist sentiments. That was as far as they got with the scheduled programme. In the uproar that followed, William Sharman Crawford came forward to move an amendment.

Crawford showed that the only gainers from protection would be the landlords, and he spoke of the evil of raising the price of food in the face of a starving people. He spoke of the rising linen exports over the previous two years, and asked what higher food prices would do for those employed in this and any other kind of employment. But his argument, far from being a sectionalist appeal, was just the reverse. He concluded with a reading of the report on the condition of the Union of Kilrush, Co. Clare, one of the bankrupt unions which had attracted so much agitated feeling during the rate-in-aid controversy. "Now, gentlemen", he said, "every farthing, every single penny that you could add to the price of food increases the destruction of human life; and if through the increase of price it would become impossible to provide food, and death takes place, then you are responsible before God for the destruction of human life. . . . Therefore, it becomes more especially just and necessary that the rent of all lands let at the former higher scale of prices should be reduced in conformity with the fall in the rates of produce—and that the tenants' rights of property in all improvements created by his money and labour should be established by law, and the values secured to him, according to the custom of the country, known under the name of 'tenant right'."²⁹ Faced with a display of overwhelming support for Crawford, the sheriff agreed rather reluctantly to take a show of hands vote, and the amendment was passed by an overwhelming majority.

Following this unprecedented popular victory, a meeting was held the following week at Saintfield to call for a reduction of rents. Here Dr McKnight took the opportunity to transcend characteristically sectionalist sentiments, and he used as his text the words of the "late lamented" Thomas Drummond:

"Property 'meaning landed property' has its duties as well as its rights. In the first place the creations of tenant industry are, in point of proprietory sacredness, far beyond all rights which territorial landlordism can ever acquire: and this just because they are 'absolute' rights according to Judge Blackstone. In the second place, the 'duties' of landlordism being of a public character, common sense tells us that one of the first of its obligations must be to protect the property that is confessedly superior in point of right to its own; and if it shall either neglect this duty or shall do the very contrary of this duty, then it palpably nullifies the whole end of its own institution. In the one case it becomes useless for all the legitimate purposes of its own social being; and on the other hypothesis, it assumes a positively mischievous character, and lays the State under a direct necessity of putting forth its own corrective authority. The necessity becomes absolutely imperative, when the powers of the landlord institute are employed for the destruction of tenant property, either by direct agency, or by the absorption of tenant property into its own separate possessions, while the extermination of the people is an ulterior offence, which admits of no palliation whatever."³⁰

Taking care to admit the possibility of landlordism having a positive social function, he delivers a very decided statement as to the circumstances in which it ceased to have one. Then he generalizes the implication of the campaign. He says that the tenant farmers of Ireland are fighting the battle of English merchants and manufacturers and that of the working and industrious classes generally, in opposition to a powerful party in England, "so that you have some claims on the score of gratitude". But then he says that where John Bull is concerned he wouldn't rely on gratitude alone but rather rely on another argument "that John Bull understands very well—I mean his self interest". The financial and political reformers in England also want to fell feudalism. "We want emancipation from the feudalism of our landlord system." Mentioning also Dr Beggs of the Free Church of Scotland and his campaign against the "barbarous laws of entail and primogeniture, together with the entire system of purely feudal economy", he concludes an overall picture which places the Irish tenant struggle in the wider framework of UK politics.[31]

In the story of the United Irishmen we can forget about what they may or may not have felt about the largely Catholic population in the rest of the island. As a piece of republican romance it is only satisfactory because the gap is filled with conjectures. At all events such matters were not uppermost in the minds of the United Irishmen themselves. But when it comes to other periods it is all too easily assumed that, because sectionalism seemed so strong overall, that it was all pervasive. In the 1840s it was no longer possible for northern Protestants to forget about the "South". The Tenant League had to deal with North-South differences directly, though the political problems associated with them were then clearly very real. It is therefore important to know how positive signs were in 1850. A mass tenant movement, facing a fair amount of opposition from the Whig elite as well as the Conservative landlords, had begun to challenge landed hegemony in the North. In less than twelve months after the catastrophe at Dolly's Brae, Orangemen and Catholics helped Sharman Crawford to run Lord Downshire off his platform. The sectionalism expressed during the rate-in-aid agitation cannot have been a totally overriding issue when Crawford could make the starvation of the people of Kilrush his clinching theme in an argument against protection. And obviously Protestant distaste for Thomas Drummond who put the Orange Order down cannot be anywhere near universal if McKnight can describe him as the "late lamented", and proceed to use his text to deliver an onslaught on landlordism. Let us start with McKnight's editorial efforts to make local questions the vehicle of wider lessons. Following the Downpatrick meeting he wrote this.

"Daniel O'Connell's begging box (the Catholic Rent and Repeal Rents) used to be a subject of prime ridicule, and we ourselves, too, have often wickedly sneered at it; but then all contributions in this quarter had the outward show of voluntaryism. The great Parliamentary begging-box which Downshire's chivalry, and its nobility, had gathered in Downpatrick to establish, had not even this shabby element of decency."[32]

And in connection with the Antrim grand jury's collection of county cess in Belfast, the turnpike tolls on Belfast road exits while the borough payed for the upkeep of its own streets, he calculated that Belfast was overtaxed to the tune of £6,000 a year, which "is the amount of the 'rate-in-aid' which the people of Belfast have hitherto been paying for the benefit of the squirearchy of Antrim, and what the distinction is, in point of principle, between this assessment and the supplementary poor rate for the South, about which so much agitation was lately raised, we confess our utter inability to discover."[33]

He takes it for granted that his readers have sectional sentiments with regard to the "South", implicates himself to avoid preaching at his reader, and then confronts them with a message that forces them to see themselves in what they are sneering at or dismissing. How does he deal with the most difficult theme of all, the sense amongst Protestants that Catholicism is somehow something they have a duty to discountenance and discourage, rather than just the faith of other people they happen to live with? On the first day of Dr McKnight's editorship the *Banner of Ulster* ran this editorial on the subject of the Church Education Society, the Anglican body set up in opposition to the national education system to promote "Bible"-oriented education.[34]

"Dr. Drew . . . began with a fearful description of Popery, and we have no disposition to quarrel with his account of its character, except that we doubt whether it is correct to allege that Popery is the 'sole cause of all the poverty, wretchedness and insubordination and crime which affect this unhappy country'. We apprehend that there are other causes in operation besides Popery, though it too has its pernicious influence; while as to 'poverty' and 'crime', we greatly suspect that bad landlordism has operated as a faithful and most efficient ally of Popery in this work of national disorganization.³⁵

The Rev. Mr. St. George laid it down as a fundamental principle, that if any class of individuals should refuse a Scriptural education, then, to give them any education whatever is 'worse than useless' . . . in other words, if he cannot do all the good he might wish, he will do no good at all . . . the mere statement of this Gothic sentiment is enough for its exposure.

The plain principle of National Education is this—that if any class of individuals shall unhappily object to the reception of the Protestant version of the Scriptures—then no functionary of the Board shall be at liberty to compel them to receive the aforesaid version of the Scriptures.

In this event we should not, in the nineteenth century, find ministers virtually maintaining, that, a right of 'preaching the gospel' means a right of forcing the Gospel upon reluctant sinners, under the terror of any human penalty whatsoever, much less under the penalty of being cast out of the precincts of educated humanity . . .

In the movements of the Church Education Society there is not one particle of Protestant principle really concerned . . . the whole is an ill-disguised attempt on the part of the Established Church, to regain its own old monopoly over the educational institutions of this country."

He then goes on to notice Dr Drew's charge that ministers who put schools under the national system are "dry-nurses to Popery" because they send Roman Catholic children to the chapel the "moment the Bible is introduced". Even if true, he says, it would be "less objectionable than teaching children to adore walking sticks" as his own church did when connected with the Kildare Place Society. He concludes:

"Our principles, as Presbyterians, are fundamentally opposed to all forms of secular coercion in matters of religion, and Dr. Drew would do well to inquire whether it was not the counter policy pursued by his own Church, which has made Irish Popery the proverbially inveterate evil that it is, and this, too, from the very quality of the means usually employed for its extirpation."

McKnight's "constituency" was orthodox Presbyterian tenant farmers. Catholicism was widely understood to be an abasement of Christianity. For better or worse, this much was taken as a "fact". The problem was to strip this religious sentiment of its various secular and worldly corollaries, so that people of different denominations could coexist with each other, treating these differences as things they recognized and accepted about each other. In the editorial attack on Anglican educational monopolism, we see two aspects of this. First, the "southern" experiences cannot be reduced to "Popery". Bad landlordism is an "efficient ally in the work of National disorganization". Second, the attempts to break Catholicism by coercive means have much to do with the strength and hostility of Catholicism to things Protestant. McKnight does not pretend to like Irish Catholicism, but shows some grip upon how persecution has made it what it has become.

But even so, very few Protestants understood how important it was not to engage in Protestant triumphalism if they wished to avoid a degeneration into anti-Catholicism. Where they might see a defence of their faith, a Catholic would always be confronted with an offence to his own. In April 1850, a Dr Achilli, one-time member of the papal civil service who had renounced his offices, had become a Protestant and had been imprisoned by the Inquisition and subsequently toured Europe as an emissary of anti-papal forces, came to Belfast.[36] He spoke at a meeting presided over by Dr Cooke. Cooke's introductory remarks included the following:

"Without civil liberty, a man is nothing—without religious liberty, a Christian is nothing. The man whose civil liberties are enslaved is somewhat less than a man, and the man whose conscience is trammelled and fettered by another is something less than a Christian . . . The sun of heaven suffers an eclipse, but it is soon gone, and so I trust it will be with Rome . . . I have beside me a representative of that religious liberty . . . His is liberty from the yoke of bondage which the Jews voluntarily imposed on themselves in going about to establish their own righteousness, and in not submitting themselves to the righteousness of God, which is by faith, and his is liberty, also, from that same power which was enchained Rome, and made her what she is . . . it was the spirit of Protestantism which went to visit him in the dark cells of the Inquisition."

Dr Achilli's speech concerned the necessity of sending Bibles to Rome:

"Bibles have been introduced into and circulated through Rome which the priests have not been able to burn. . . . At present Pius IX has got back to Rome; he has found the Bible there; we shall see whether Pius IX and the Bible can remain together in the same place. It is now difficult to exclude the Bible from Rome and if it is not excluded it will exclude the Pope. . . . the people of Rome have penetrated the true spirit of Popery, which is not a religious but a political system."

Whatever the meaning of these sentiments might have been in Rome, they meant something quite different in Belfast. The whole ethos of the meeting was a celebration of the superiority of Protestantism over "Popery", and the eventual collapse of the latter. Not surprisingly some local Catholics took offence at this proceeding, and Dr Dorrian, brother of the future Roman Catholic Bishop of Down and Connor, came to the meeting to make some objections. An argument ensued about whether the Bible was or was not available in Rome. Dr Dorrian produced a version of the Bible printed in Venice with the benediction of the Archbishop of Florence in 1778. The benediction concluded by noticing that the explanatory notes extracted from the Holy Fathers "precluded every possible danger of abuse". Great play was made of the fact that he said it was printed in Rome, whereas in fact it "came from Rome", and the whole tenor of the discussion was that of a point-scoring match. Dr Cooke pressed Dr Dorrian on the subject of whether the Inquisition existed. The latter replied, "With regard to that institution, I do not know whether it exists; but if it does, we have an Inquisition of the same sort in this country." And after a few further altercations, Dr Cooke came back: "You say you do not know whether there is an Inquisition at Rome, because you were never there. Do you doubt the existence of the Pope because you have never been in Rome and have never kissed his toe?"[37]

The *Banner* (Dr McKnight incidentally was in London on a tenant deputation at the time) denounced the local Catholic paper, the *Vindicator*, for declaring Achilli a "notorious imposter" and an "unclean vowbreaker" (a reference to the fact that he had got married in circumstances which were not properly elucidated), and concluded by "congratulating our Protestant readers of all denominations, upon the good feeling that has been generated by Dr. Achilli's visit to Belfast. Romanism has received a heavy blow and a great discouragement, and a strong additional evidence has been furnished of the substantial unity of Protestantism, as well as of the unassailable foundation upon which it rests."[38]

Justly might Dr Dorrian complain: "You never heard of our Catholic Bishop, Dr. Denvir, bringing to Belfast any of the Oxford or other divines, who have seceded from the Church of England, in order to exhibit them in the churches, to the insult and mockery of the religion of those who differ from us."[39] Dr Cooke may have had the advantage over Dr Dorrian on the facts about the Inquisition, but the whole manner of his response—and even the *Banner* editorial on the meeting—was to do exactly as Dr Dorrian said had been done. It was indeed a mockery and insult to Catholics in Belfast. Precisely what "good feeling" the *Banner* alluded to is hard to imagine, unless it was purely that arising from having delivered "Romanism" a "heavy blow" and illustrating that under such circumstances "the substantial unity of Protestantism" became manifest.

Only six weeks later a great provincial tenant right meeting was held in Belfast, which expressed political demands at one with those of southern tenant organizations. It was to be the prelude to the establishment of the Irish Tenant League, commonly known as the League of North and South. The *Banner* declared that the meeting showed "that in Ulster the days of sectarian and factious division are ended and consequently every tyranny built upon that division may now begin to set its house in order, if it expects long to have any house to be put into a condition of arrangement".[40] The meeting was the greatest, it said, in point of national importance to be held in Belfast since the Volunteers; it had the patriotic objective of "elevating the masses of the Irish people, without distinction, to the realized dignity of British citizens". It may be surprising that these sentiments could sit alongside the ones uttered about the Achilli visit. It may of course be said that Wolfe Tone's sentiments about the Pope were not very flattering either. He was not above joking about Catholics sprinkling their mistresses with holy water, much as Cooke jested about kissing the Pope's toe. And Arthur O'Connor of the *United Irishman* was then spending the last years of his life writing fanatical attacks upon Jesuitry, Daniel O'Connell and popery.[41] The essential difference was that in 1798 it was possible for those United Irishmen to do such things and still behave as though the success of their rising would have loosened the links between the Catholic and the priest, and the priest and the Pope. In 1850 this was simply unrealistic. Protestants who applauded Dr Cooke mocked the "Romanists" of Belfast together in chorus. Either they knew the extent of the offence or they continued in the illusion that the "ordinary" Catholic could be separated from popery, which in the words of Achilli was "not a religious but a political system". It is a reflection of the very real subordination of Catholics in the North that such illusions could still be held by people who saw themselves putting an end to sectarian division. We shall see how, in the process of making the Tenant League a reality, McKnight had to bring Protestants of the North with him beyond this kind of sneering at "Romanism".

The League of North and South has been described by Dr John Whyte as a southern League with some northern allies.[42] By early 1852 it would sadly have been hard to quarrel with this description. But when it first took off, it was a lot more than that. In the first part of this chapter I looked at the growth of the northern movement and demonstrated how it developed not as an extension of Whig politics into rural areas, but rather in spite of the Whigs. In the second part I showed how Dr McKnight approached sectional ideologies and sought to break through them. The sense of superiority over "Romanism" remained a blind spot, which he could sometimes draw his readers through and at other times got trapped in himself. The northern and southern leaders of the League had a common perception of the relationship between their objectives and UK politics. Both had the profoundest distrust for the Whig and Tory blocs and neither reposed any faith in English generosity. As Dr McKnight put it, "The reforming and anti-reforming parties in

England itself are so nearly balanced, that a single cohort of forty or fifty Irish members, acting together in an unbroken fraternity, could at almost any vital crisis determine the fate of any British administration and could in fact virtually give law to it in reference to the Tenant Right question."[43] The strategy was therefore national in the 1791 sense of the word, although not nationalist in the 1840 sense. Every other question was to be excluded from the council of the Tenant League except fixity of tenure at fair rents.

The first meeting of the League was held in Ballybay, Co. Monaghan, in October 1850. This was a highly significant place to start. It was the headquarters of Sam Grey, the Orange leader who had opposed Jack Lawless's campaign for Repeal in Ulster. The possibility of local co-operation had become clear in January when J. J. Hughes and the Rev. David Bell, the local Presbyterian minister, had successfully defeated a landlord protectionist gathering as Sharman Crawford had done in Downpatrick.[44] But in this part of the world where relationships between Orangemen and Catholics had been full of antagonism, considerable delicacy was required to launch a venture of co-operation for any purpose. Gavan Duffy and Frederick Lucas agreed with Rev. David Bell that they would stay at the York Hotel which was kept by Sam Grey's family as "a sign and seal of the union". But before they arrived in Ballybay they were met by J. J. Hughes, who indicated that the Catholics would be insulted if they did so.[45] Lucas, who was an English convert to Catholicism, agreed to go elsewhere. But Duffy, a Monaghan Catholic by birth, went to the York. "Next day I found the amiable Mr. Hughes had whispered about that I preferred the society of bitter Orangemen to my own relations in my native country; and on the other hand a distrust of Lucas was sown in the minds of the Northerners." The suspicions did not break up the gathering. The next night many Catholics from Farney dined in the York Hotel.[46] But the conclusion of Mr Godkin that "all the old animosities of the people were forgotten, buried in oblivion" was not an accurate representation of a state of affairs in which putting those animosities on one side required tact and forbearance.[47] The meeting was an important step.

One of the biggest difficulties that faced the League in the

North was that any suggestion that it was somehow linked up with Irish rebellions would damn it. At that time people were often thought of in terms of the things that made their areas notorious. Forkhill, for example, was linked with the 1791 outrage and anything violent in that district seemed to be an echo of it. The League had to be able to speak to tenant farmers throughout Ireland. The Protestants of inner Ulster were probably less comfortable with the "redshanks" of Killeavy and Forkhill than with any other group.[48] From 1850 through to 1852, agrarian outrages became increasingly regular occurrences, particularly in the southern Ulster frontier districts. We have noticed how in the Forkhill and Crossmaglen area the reclamation-migration strategy was operated with particular vigour before the Famine. In these areas in the aftermath of the Famine, efforts to displace and consolidate were resisted by murders of agents and landlords.[49] The Ribbon society had been strengthened in these areas by the spread of public works, drainage projects and railway construction works. The operations of the society were concerned with regulating who got work on these projects, and the organization of the migrancy to British cities and Belfast. They had prevented evictions by making it impossible to let lands from which people had been evicted. Emigration from these areas was much less than others about them.[50] In 1851/52, stipendiary magistrates were sent into the districts and a parliamentary select committee inquired into the agrarian outrages in these areas.[51] In fact agrarian outrages of lesser proportions spread further north, certainly into south Down and possibly further yet. Lord Londonderry actually attempted to have the county proclaimed.[52] The spread of agrarian violence was made a weapon with which to beat the Tenant League.

How did the League react? In early 1850 the *Banner* spoke of those who were "by means of agrarian outrages . . . endeavouring to prevent tenant right meetings", and strongly urged tenant right associations to exert themselves to discover the perpetrators. But it added significantly: "Where oppression exists in a community, it will inevitably drive some individuals into despair of constitutional redress; and if it had not this effect, the enemies of reform would triumphantly quote the argument that 'well enough' ought to be 'let alone'."[53]

This was certainly bold reasoning in a society where every manifestation of disorder was habitually linked by demagogues with projects of "Popish extermination of Protestantism". But in early 1852, when these agrarian outrages were occurring with some frequency and the south Down, south Armagh and Monaghan outrages were the subject of parliamentary inquiry, a meeting was held in Belfast in support of Sherman Crawford at which both Crawford and McKnight took the issue by the horns.[54]

Crawford: "When I go to the Legislature, if any proposition be made for the purpose of suppressing agrarian crimes in those districts where agrarian crimes have been perpetrated, I shall feel it my bounden duty to support every such proposition which I shall conceive likely to effect the purpose.

But gentlemen, my opinion is that all the misfortunes of Ireland, all the miseries and crimes that are unfortunately perpetrated on our soil, are traceable originally to one point—the want of security for property in the soil."

McKnight: "I believe property has its duties as well as its rights—and while I would denounce the murders committed by Ribbonmen, or by whatever other name the parties may be called, I believe I am not bound to conceal the murders committed by the thing that calls itself property. Human nature, whether in Ireland or England or America is the same and an authority I am bound to respect—that is the Word of Almighty God—declares that 'oppression will make even a wise man mad'. If it will do so with a wise man, what will it not do with a half-informed Irish peasant, who sees his hearth desolated by extermination, his family thrown out of their homes in winter's inclemencies, and himself left as a vagrant without a hope save the workhouse or a home save the grave?"

There can be little doubt that by 1852 the level of agrarian outrages was being used to sever the northerners from the League. Both of these statements are about empathy with people of whom their audiences probably knew little and maybe feared a lot. They were about as direct as possible an answer to the earlier quoted perambulations of Dr Drew on popery as the sole cause of crime in Ireland; and, in this case, very important because the speakers took risks to explain the behaviour of the reclamation tenants. In fact one of the big drawbacks of the Whig approach to tenant issues had been that talk of regulating the consolidation process in a tenant right district had very little to do with the experience of most Irish tenants. Generally Ulster sectionalist agrarians displayed little concern with mountain and reclamation tenants who tended to be Catholics. Many of these had experienced of truly massive rent increases on farms they had themselves hewed out of the sides of mountains. Paradoxically Dr McKnight's thesis about the Plantation and the restriction of landlords' interest to the "raw earth" struck a vital chord with the reclamation tenancy. In the tenant right catechism McKnight included a section on them. Significantly, in the light of the subsequent contest with the Marquis of Londonderry, the example was drawn from the latter's estate at Ballylawn, Co. Donegal.[55]

In late 1849 the tenantry of the Kilmood estate, a solidly Protestant district on the inland side of Strangford Lough, petitioned the Marquis for a rent reduction which he refused.[56] In the public anger that followed, two Presbyterian ministers, Revs William Dobbin and John Rutherford, took a prominent part. Rutherford in particular gave utterance to Dr McKnight's "raw earth" thesis.[57] Lord Castlereagh, the Marquis's son and MP for County Down, had declared that Sir Wm Somerville's new Bill of 1850 would destroy tenant right, for which intervention he probably lost his father's parliamentary seat. He now asked parliamentary questions about Rutherford's speech.[58] But his father went further and sent letters to Lord Clarendon, asking him to bring the tenant right speeches under the notice of the General Assembly with the hint that the government was not pleased. As the *Banner* declared, "The plain meaning of this application is that the Government should by means of the Regium Donum (the government stipends to Presbyterian ministers) exercise a coercive authority over the free agency of the Presbyterian clergy ..." [59] The *Newsletter* now gleefully exploited the embarrassment of the Whigs. "At all events for the sake of religion and the independence of the Church, such assailants as Lord Londonderry ought to be made to understand that the Royal endowment is not purchased by the Presbyterian clergy as the price of their fealty to pompous feudalism; and by the spineless acquiescence in every caprice and crochet of weak-minded and mistaken, though often well meaning Marquises."[60] It was even happier to see the *Whig*, now very much in a corner, supporting the Tory, Lord Downshire, against his tenants also.[61]

The intervention of Lord Londonderry had fairly far-reaching implications. In mid-1850 four out of five of the northern synods of the Presbyterian Church had declared either unanimously or nearly so for tenant right,[62] though none mentioned rent reductions. The Londonderry intervention put the opposition on to rather weaker ground than it might otherwise have occupied. In the Belfast synod, where most resistance was encountered, the proponents argued in terms of the danger of oppression driving people to adopt an injurious and criminal course of procedure (Julius McCullough, Newtownards) or people staying away from church because of the deterioration of their clothing (Rev. Johnston, Tullylish).[63] They faced two kinds of opposition: first, there were those who objected to bringing political or secular issues into a Church court; and second, Dr Cooke stated that if tenant right stood free of other issues, there would be no problem. But in the actual circumstances two of their number stood accused in high places of having advocated "perfect Communist interpretations". He would himself have had no objection to the resolution were he not "thereby identifying myself with the parties who had been injuring the cause". This was exceedingly weak ground to choose, for it made him appear to be somewhat on the side of Lord Londonderry. And the ground looked even weaker when the assembled synod appealed to him to rewrite the resolution and include a repudiation of "Communist doctrines". He declined the offer.

When the issue came to the General Assembly, Dr Alex Goudy of Strabane moved the petition, and did so in a manner which clearly posed it as a vote of confidence in the ministers who had taken part in the tenant right movement, and a repudiation of Lord Londonderry's efforts at interference in Presbyterian affairs. He made lengthy references to the Marquis's remarks about how his ancestors had been Presbyterians, though he himself was an Anglican. "He thought perhaps that that announcement would bespeak him the ready hearing of the titled among whom he was standing—on the principle no doubt that Presbyterianism, which was not suited to a gentleman, was still less suited for a noble Lord."[64] The vote was nearly unanimous. Even Dr Cooke appealed to the Assembly to let it pass. What is so significant about this meeting is the role of Alex Goudy who specifically defended the Presbyterian ministers in the tenant right movement, for Goudy himself was one of those who was most strongly opposed to political co-operation between Presbyterian ministers and Roman Catholic priests. His biographers record this opinion on the subject. "What I conscientiously object to is a common platform on which Presbyterian ministers and Romish priests shall stand together in discussing before miscellaneous audiences a question which touches on all sides great principles and which has manifold and marked religious bearings. I may be deemed a bigot, and wanting in common sense, but I protest against this on the ground of principle and expediency."[65]

It is quite obvious that the Londonderry intervention served to remove a number of reservations various ministers had about taking an active role in the tenant right movement. It also helped to push the Whigs altogether off the popular stage in County Down and to pave the way for a more explicit understanding between big property Tory and Whig against tenant radicalism.

In the later part of 1850 the Tenant League began to hold a series of meetings addressed by delegations all over the country, and some of the northern members including Dr McKnight, Rev. John Rogers (Comber), and Rev. David Bell (Ballybay) went on deputations to southern League meetings. At a meeting in Kilkenny, Dr McKnight explained how the vital part of the League's programme—fixity of tenure and fair rents—included the custom of Ulster, and sought to confirm its main element legislatively throughout Ireland. But, as an example of the dangers that lay in store, Dr John Rogers got somewhat carried away in his efforts to show that "Presbyterian Ulster is not Orange". He contrasted the intolerance, Toryism, etc. of Orangeism with the opposite qualities in Presbyterianism. "No one therefore, but an ignorant and apostate Presbyterian could be an Orangeman. [*Tremendous cheering*] No, I will tell you who the Orangemen of the North are—landlords and agents in the one extreme—bailiffs and the rag-tag and bobtail of society in the other, which landlordism and Church of Englandism may be able to buy up for Orange purposes. . . . I have read that two sparrows are sold for a farthing, and two hundred of the gentry which Ulster landlords purchase up for the aforesaid purpose would not be equal in value to two sparrows."[66] The speech was, to say the very least, an injudicious performance. He rather forgot the 20,000 at Garvagh who supported McKnight on 12 July 1848 and the role of the Orangemen who supported Sharman Crawford at Downpatrick against the protectionists. It was also a godsend to the *Newsletter*. But it was perhaps an inadvertently damaging speech from the point of view of the long-term future of the League. If, after all, a northern Presbyterian minister said these things about Orangeism, who were his Catholic audience in Kilkenny to contradict him? Back in the North, when he appeared at a meeting at the Newtownards market house organized to present a submissive address to the Marquis of Londonderry, his presence was a liability to the Presbyterian ministers who were attempting to show that the address was a put-up job.[67] "What is the price of sparrows?" and "Two hundred Orangemen for a sparrow" greeted his efforts to wade in on the popular side. His apology was given gracefully, but the damage done to the adhesion of Orangemen (of whom there were few in Newtownards) to the popular cause can only be guessed.

In November the *Banner* announced that the foundation meetings of the League for Antrim and Down would be postponed in order to concentrate its energies on the Limerick by-election.[68] Privately McKnight wrote to Gavan Duffy describing the League candidate's address as "a furious Repeal manifesto". "So far as outward appearances go, the League is in this case formally and openly identified with Repeal, as well as with several other matters contained in Ryan's address. Now in the North, any impression of this kind would destroy us, and you will consequently see the need of getting the League out of this predicament."[69] John Rogers and David Bell now had to find ways to deal with this new difficulty.

John O'Connell, son of Daniel O'Connell and leader of the

old Repeal Party, had charged John Rogers with "denouncing Repeal", whereas what he had actually done was to indicate that he himself did not support it.[70] "It was the least intention on my part to offer them [old repealers] the least possible offence or to say that they should not adhere to and carry out their principles by every means in their power." The *Newsletter* thundered, "Is it to be endured that the North shall be degraded, through such a mission as that of Messrs. Bell and Rogers under the stigma of an implied alliance with Popery and Repeal?"[71] That brings us to the other matters which it was David Bell's task to deal with at Limerick.

"Why should I object to Catholics, whose religion has been stigmatized and reprobated by Lord John Russell, repelling the insult and banding together in sustainment of civil and religious liberty . . ."[72] The issue to which he was referring was Lord John Russell's response to the re-establishment of the Roman Catholic hierarchy in England, announced in October by Cardinal Wiseman.

The consequences of re-establishing the English hierarchy for anyone other than the English Roman Catholics was not altogether obvious. Lord John Russell's famous letter to the Bishop of Durham declared his agreement with the latter's characterization of "the late aggression of the Pope upon our Protestantism" as "insolent and insidious".[73] Any reader of my text so far who feels that I have bent over somewhat to distinguish finer shades of difference between opponents and enemies of Roman Catholicism in Ireland, especially if he or she be of English origin, would be well advised to reflect on the fact that this letter promoted an outburst of English anti-Catholicism directed against Irish immigrants, the Catholic Church in general, and "Romanizing" tendencies in English Anglicanism. The Whigs who had blotted their copy-book with Irish Catholics by their use of Orangeism in 1848, now put together what amounted to a new penal law. The Ecclesiastical Titles Act made it illegal for any Roman Catholic prelate to assume title to any diocese which was also an Anglican diocese. In so far as it had any practical significance it was to prevent any attempts being made to recover charitable bequests made in times past to the Church of England by legal arguments to the effect that the "Bishop of London" for example, meant the

Roman Catholic as distinct from the Anglican bishop of the diocese. But a wave of anti-Catholic intolerance whipped up by the Whigs was a new departure, and lent the whole affair the aspect of a nativist British Protestant outburst in a society with a much recently augmented population of Irish Catholic immigrants.

The *Banner* was now faced with the challenge of sorting out the relationship between religious and political questions. And here it received powerful moral support from the Free Church of Scotland. The following are some of its editorial comments:
"It is not with penal acts of Parliament or with the secular arms provided by any merely state partisanship that Popery, or any other form of religious error, can ever be successfully overcome . . . we must never forget that universal toleration is a fundamental element in the religion which we profess. . . . Political faction under the name of religion invariably destroys the real interests of the latter. . . . If error is making progress in any direction, the notoriety of this fact is no argument on behalf of indolent complaint—it is an imperative call to activity in all the departments of missionary evangelism.

In our own case it is of vital importance that the true principles of the Presbyterian Church should be plainly and prominently declared at the present crisis, in order that, under a vague idea of opposing Popery, men may not be led into the propagation of doctrines as thoroughly opposed to the Bible as any that Popery itself has ever advanced."
"As Presbyterians we have no more religious sympathy with the sovereign 'headship' over the Established Church, usually called her Majesty's 'supremacy in all causes ecclesiastical' than we have with a parallel demand on the part of the Bishop of Rome. Both supremacies are in direct contradiction to the law of the New Testament and to the whole spirit of apostolic Christianity."[74]

As Dr McKnight fended off theological attack he became increasingly forthright about the need for northerners to co-operate with the southerners. At the founding meeting of the northern Tenant League in Newtownards in December, he spoke thus:

"We in the North are too apt to regard our Southern friends as wild, ungovernable, theoretic enthusiasts, who are carried away by the impulses of their own poetic imaginings rather than guided by the deduction of calm reasoning. An anti-national policy has hitherto kept North and South from making each other's acquaintance so familiarly as both communities ought to have done, and hence we entertain mutual impressions often as different from the reality as fiction is from fact. Had I not associated intimately with the men of the South, I too might have suspected that their temperament was not quite characterized by that intellectual sobriety upon which we Northerners pride ourselves, though without all the good reason that is sometimes assumed in our favour. Hence I might have been predisposed to receive as probable truth the allegation that contact with the men of the 'sunny' South had heightened the complexion of our joint tenant-right demands".[75]

Then he went through the recent history of the tenant movement in the North, demonstrating the basic continuity of the Tenant League's demands with those made at earlier times by local bodies. And on the crisis created by the "Papal Aggression" agitation:

"But while it might be deemed too much to say that the breaking up of the Irish Tenant League was a primary element in the calculations of statesmanship, I have no doubt of its having been reckoned upon as a secondary consequence; and of this fact we are all aware, that sectarian dissentions, encouraged by Ministers of State, have actually been employed by landlords and by politicians in the hope of working out the League's destruction by the hands of its own members. I freely confess that in matters of purely religious character I am not indifferent; and I would not give much for that man's moral integrity who would compromise the smallest religious obligation for any merely secular object; but then on the other hand, I have no language sufficiently strong to convey my reprobation and contempt for that policy which under the hypocrisy of theological profession, degrades Christianity into an engine of State intrigue.... It is for the people of Ireland, then, by one indignant effort to abolish for ever all these trading hypocrisies whose object is the perpetuation of Irish serfdom; and we must moreover teach our statesmen that the science of government in this country must henceforth consist of something else than playing playing off one class against another for the sake of trampling upon the whole people in a body."[76]

In February 1851 the Bill was finally published and, contrary to some expectations, its provisions were to embrace the whole of the UK including Ireland. The *Banner* wrote: "[The] measure is, if possible, more contemptible than anything which even we ourselves had imagined beforehand, and our readers know that, from the very first we have laboured to save them in this respect, from the disappointment incident to overcharged expectation . . . There is just enough to fret and to irritate the Papal bishops, and to present them before their own people as victims of Protestant jealousy, while there is an utter want of all legal or other power to work out a single issue of practical benefit to the community itself."[77]

Any hopes that had been entertained heretofore of sustaining the Tenant League as a body with a single objective to which all others were subordinated were now compromised. Now it may well be argued that to present the issue in this way is to credit the "Papal Aggression" agitation with too much. After all, most of the southern leaders were either repealers or Young Irelanders, and that fact alone implied that the tension between Repeal and pro-Union positions would have to be contained within the League. But if that is argued, it is well to remember that Sharman Crawford himself favoured Repeal in the abstract, and the fact that he was to be the candidate in County Down in 1852 and that he got two-thirds of the vote in Newtownards rather undermines the notion that Unionist credentials had to be strong. What was required was the clear paramountcy of the Tenant League's programme over all other questions. The circumstances created by the Ecclesiastical Titles Bill made this highly improbable.

In the year or so preceding the crisis, the Roman Catholic hierarchy in Ireland had undergone significant modification. Dr Paul Cullen who had been in Rome for the preceding decade was appointed to the Archbishopric of Armagh over the heads of all local nominees and, replacing Dr Crolly, his appointment swung the balance of divided opinion on the education question. The Synod of Thurles in 1850 condemned the Queen's colleges and came down firmly in favour of an explicitly denominational system of education.[78] Committed first and foremost to resolving the internal disputes within the hierarchy and deeply suspicious of the intentions of any English government as regards the interests of the Roman Catholic Church, he was also anxious to stop the disintegrative effects of post-1848 political developments in Ireland.[79] The "Papal Aggression" crisis, restoring in an almost paradigm manner the imperatives to pan-Catholic political strategy, now catapulted the hierarchy into a dominant political position. The relatively secular strategy of the Tenant League would have to come to terms with these new realities.

The Belfast *Vindicator*, the local Catholic paper, for example, was far from carried away by a fit of "pan-Catholic" sentiment. It almost apologised for having to ask that opposition to the Titles Bill become a policy of the League. In an editorial which observed that the basis of previous Catholic support for the Whigs was now broken, it said: "There is no use in attempting to deny that the religious element must have the principal place at the hustings this many a day." The main object of the newly formed Catholic Defence Association would be "to keep from office all who will not endeavour to repeal the obnoxious measure and stand in defence of civil liberty". But, it said: "Religious liberty is of precious little service to the helpless farmer who trembles at the door of the agent begging leave to use a little of his own—beseeching a brother worm for 'leave to toil'." While it appreciated the difficulty it would cause the League, it strongly urged it to make a declaration in favour of religious liberty, for otherwise "The League will be thrown in the shade, and religious grievances will swallow at one fell gulp, all the other grievances for the time being."[80]

In August 1851 a Roman Catholic Aggregate meeting was held in Dublin and the *Banner* commented: "It is quite clear that the altered spirit of legislation indicated in the late enactment is that which most alarms the supporters of the Roman Catholic System, and that the disappointment of their hopes from the

Liberalism of Protestants is the grand secret of the present excitement." But it also noticed how Dr Cullen's definition of religious equality included the establishment of an explicitly denominational Roman Catholic university.[81]

The future of the League now hung vitally on the person of William Sharman Crawford. He was the obvious leader of the northern movement, and having opposed the Ecclesiastical Titles Bill from start to finish, his credibility in the South was unassailable. In the wave of feeling generated by the crisis any settlement of the Tenant League's final programme was going to depend upon him. It is important to grasp just how central he was. In the North the great bulk of the urban Whigs had stayed aloof from the tenant cause so far. Of established political figures he was the only one who had not. As Whiggery collapsed, he was the refuge of those who sought a Liberal political leadership. Second, as far as the tenants were concerned, he was the only person in a position to strike any kind of acceptable compromise between what the League sought and what it was practicable to press for in parliament. Third, for those secular elements in the southern League, Crawford's opposition to the Titles Bill was the greatest single proof that the League was capable of defending religious liberty more effectively than any purely "pan Catholic" movement might do.

In May 1851, at a tenant right demonstration in Belfast attended by a considerably larger proportion of urban merchants and professionals than usual, a letter from Sharman Crawford was read out which indicated a difference of opinion with the League as to the mode of achieving their objectives. He considered that the basis of claim for the advantages of tenant right must be industrial improvement. In other words, any Bill put forward must have as its fundamental premise the notion of compensation for improvement rather than an abstract fixity of tenure.[82] Dr McKnight defended the view that the compromises Crawford sought to achieve were motivated by honest practicality. "Mr. Crawford never put his own Bill forward as a measure of finality. None of his Bills had come up to his own ideas of perfectability, because he believed that the House of Commons was not prepared to agree to such a measure."[83] Although some of the speakers at the meeting commented on the absence of certain classes of people who ought to have been there, it was none the less significant that the importance of "home consumption" and the dangers of emigration were getting through to the mercantile community. Thus William Mullan, referring to the *Whig* and others, said that he had no doubt that "that portion of the press which was most hostile to the interests of the tenant farmers would, ere long, be found advocating just and popular rights, and striving to obtain for them an equitable law regulating the relations between them and their landlords".[84]

In August Sharman Crawford called a conference with the League leadership in Dublin at which a final version of the League's Land Bill was worked out.[85] Afterwards, however, at a public meeting chaired by Mr Crawford, several prominent southern politicians delivered speeches to the effect that they would only support Mr Crawford's Bill on condition that the advocates of tenant right co-operated with them in opposition to the Ecclesiastical Titles Bill. They were quickly put down by southern members of the League, but the antics of Mr Sadleir, MP for Carlow, were noticed by the *Newsletter* and interpreted as a case of Presbyterians of Ulster having agreed to support "the Pope, if the Pope will save the League".[86] During the previous months Sadleir and his colleague William Keogh, ostensible supporters of the Tenant League, had made their presences very widely felt in another capacity. As parliamentary leaders of the Catholic Defence Association they fuelled a growing tendency in southern politics for the politico-religious controversy to supersede all other issues.[87]

In the North the *Vindicator* confessed itself surprised at the vigour of opposition to Catholic claims for a denominational university.

"Catholicism is the national faith in Ireland—the faith of suffering, the faith hourly assailed, the faith whose perverts are honoured, rewarded and caressed. Every man, not within its sacred pale, has his hand raised against it . . . Would the Queen's Colleges in Ireland answer all the educational wants of the Catholic people of Ireland? Could any educational institution founded under the authority of a Parliament composed as the present British one is . . . tended by ministers—we do not allude to the present bigoted cabinet—who must of necessity be almost wholly

Protestant . . . be relied upon as capable of soundly and honestly rearing the Catholic mind and strenuously abstaining from efforts to proselytise it?. . . We believe that these condemned institutions would never have been so determinedly maintained . . . if they did not all imagine that a Government education might corrupt a voluntary faith, and its principles be undermined by contact with establishments founded by purely Protestant hands . . . If a Catholic loses his faith he loses his all . . ."

The *Banner*, after observing that there could be no objection to the establishment of such an institution so long as it was at denominational expense, proceeded to point out that the argument that had been given in its favour was not one of mere utility but was bound up with anathematization of all mixed education as "dangerous to faith and morals". It too would oppose claims for endowment of the Catholic university and strenuously opposed the principle of purely denominational education. After the collapse of the League, education questions were to become proxy for the incipient national question. But this process had already begun before 1852.[89]

Beginning with the Catholic hierarchy's much clearer commitment to denominational education, progressing through the hiatus over the Titles Bill, and coming to Presbyterian alarm over the minority Conservative government's treatment of the vote on Regium Donum, both Catholic and Presbyterian became very concerned with the parliamentary support of their denominational concerns. In June the Tory government allowed the annual vote on Regium Donum to pass with a much reduced majority as compared with previous years.[90] The emphasis in the *Banner* shifted visibly: "Wherever a Presbyterian candidate is in the field, all secondary matters of policy, free trade and tenant right being universally fundamental, ought at once to be sunk, and that candidate should be supported by every Presbyterian who is not prepared to vote for the degradation of his own church."[91]

The fall of the Whigs from office in February 1852 and the defeat of the Sharman Crawford Bill in April had changed the situation in the North in several other respects. The Whigs had experienced a severe loss of credibility during the period when the Tenant League was making the running in the North, and though they had not been friendly to Sharman Crawford in the preceding years, the imposition of the 1851 compromise Bill as the official policy of the League permitted them to realign themselves with the tenant cause. Lord Castlereagh, Colonel Rawdon and R. J. Tennent all supported the April 1852 vote on the Crawford Bill, and the former at least became on that account an acceptable partner for Sharman Crawford in County Down.[92] His enforced retirement was not unconnected with his father's opposition to that measure. The drift toward "Presbyterianism and Tenant Right" allowed the northern Whigs to edge back toward the popular cause by taking up the Presbyterian cause. Needless to say this did not impress Catholics. R. J. Tennent, Liberal MP for Belfast, had only voted against the Ecclesiastical Titles Bill on the third reading (after it had been successfully amended by a Tory motion), and the *Vindicator* also remembered how the Rate-in-Aid Act which Tennent had opposed was "regarded as a Protestant grievance. It was warmly opposed as a means of compelling Protestant Ulster to grant a subsidy to the Popish South." Tennent they now opposed. They also quoted some remarks of Mr Grimshaw, the Belfast Whig leader, about not being prepared to "leave the education of children to any particular church".[93] So while they warmly supported Sharman Crawford, Catholic support could no longer be counted upon by any candidate just because he declared himself an opponent of Toryism.

We must now consider the general significance of the defeat of the Tenant League in Ulster. This was the first occasion since the Union on which landlord power was seriously threatened by a class-based movement rather than challenged by pan-Catholicism. What happened in 1852 was qualitatively different from the Monaghan of the Catholic emancipation campaign in 1826, or the various contested borough elections in earlier times. Many landlords who had previously considered themselves Whigs or Peelites were now allying themselves with the Tories[94] against a mixed bag of popular candidates, some of whom were "Presbyterian tenant righters" and others, most notably Sharman Crawford, representatives of the Tenant League. In every case except Newry, the popular candidates were defeated. In Newry a "Presbyterian tenant right" candidate was returned by largely Catholic votes.

Much complaint was made after the election about the participation of priests, and the *Vindicator* quite reasonably pointed out that the priests had generally been a mainstay of the popular cause.[95] At this stage the important general point is that where pan-Catholic political practice was well established, the situation in 1852 made it all the more compelling. It was as though the Titles Bill, and the battles already fought over Emancipation, had broken the power of the landlords and had carried the land question with them. As long as the "popular" cause is loosely understood, the *Vindicator's* point that the priests were the "natural guardians of their flocks" and that they supported the popular cause when others let it down cannot be denied. What is significant here is the moral the *Banner* drew from this, so different in every way from the earlier comments about popery:

"So long as the aristocracy of this country shall be permitted to carry out the despotism which they have been in the habit of exercising over the electoral people, there neither is nor can be any effectual help for the counter evil necessarily generated by it, the highly unnatural and dangerous growth of an ecclesiastic-secular power of the Roman Catholic priests. It is the unconstitutional dominion of landlordism which puts power into the priests' hands, and it is worse than futile to lament over the consequent mischief, so long as men choose to protect the abuse in which that mischief notoriously has its primary origin. We care not how badly the Southern priests may be proved to have acted; it is impossible for them to have outdone the proceedings which we are prepared to substantiate against Northern landlordism."[96]

The *Banner* was profoundly worried by the tendency manifest in this election for clerical leadership to assume an increasing significance. But this editorial comment is a clear recognition of the sources of pan-Catholic political practices. It echoes Tone's saying about how oppression binds the papist to the priest and how removing the oppression will untie the bond. Without even the usual hints of moralizing, this editorial recognizes the part supporters of landlordism play, and in what way northern Protestants can do something about the problem practically. Where non-Catholics do not oppose landlordism, it is unreasonable to turn about and condemn Catholics for following clerical leadership, all the more so when the landlord status quo makes anti-catholicism its primary political slogan.

The Catholic *Vindicator* also with some justification claimed that Protestant voters were significantly affected by "religious bigotry", a charge backed up by the *"Nation"*[97]. Ulster constituencies, which at this stage all had Protestant majorities in their electorates, failed to return any popular candidates. In County Down, Sharman Crawford got 3,135 votes against 4,124 and 4,663 for Ker and Hill respectively. But in the Newtownards area Crawford polled 1,120 votes compared to 673 each for the two Tories.[98] The *Vindicator* praised the people of that district and did not include them in its general contempt for the "men of Down". But although Sharman Crawford's own estate and that of Lord Dufferin who both declared a "Free vote" for their tenants were situated in this district, it is still worthy of notice that it was the most overwhelmingly Protestant of all four polling districts in County Down. The *Banner*'s comment, that wherever there was a semblance of fair play, Protestant voters supported Crawford, is quite accurate.[99] Although detailed figures do not exist for County Derry, I have a strong suspicion that the same general point could be made for this constituency also. Samuel Greer got 1,518 to 1,909 and 2,098 for Jones and Bateson respectively.[100]

The *Banner*'s comments on the general question of why the North did not successfully support the League and popular candidates can be summarized under several headings. First, the landlord power in the South was unsupported by the savage machinery established in the North, so that landlord coercion was elsewhere deprived of much of the terror it held locally. Second, initial efforts at "constitutional insurrection of the democratic masses for their own class emancipation" are seldom successful and they need to be persevered in. Third, and perhaps most vitally as a specifically local factor, "the Tenant voter [in Ulster] is his landlord's slave in exact proportion to the amount of unlegalized tenant right which he possesses".[101] Fourth, the *Banner* did not deny the influence of "No Popery"; indeed, in the case of County Tyrone, it could find no other explanation of the scale of the landlords' victory.

The difficulty of dealing with the question is that these four apparently separate issues are not in fact easily separable in theory, let alone measurable as "independent" factors in the result. If we accept the general proposition that the scale of support for the popular candidates was considerably greater than the final voting figures suggested—a conclusion strongly implied by what happened in Newtownards—the question is to look at the coercive power of the landlords as a whole. They cannot be individually isolated because they constitute a system of control which was being attacked for the first time.

When McKnight spoke of a "constitutional insurrection of the democratic masses for their own class emancipation" he was not engaging in mere rhetoric. That is precisely what was involved, for the power structure was under attack explicitly because it was based upon monopolistic property ownership. It was not under siege from any kind of force comparable to the pan-Catholic pressures which had so effectively destroyed the landlords' capacity to control elsewhere in the country. And the very nature of the opposition was constrained by its objectives to play by a set of rules which the landlords decided to totally disregard. Overt force and intimidation were used on a grand scale. Indeed after the election Sharman Crawford, who said as much, was threatened with legal action by the Tory leaders. At a banquet held in his honour he repeated the charges before a far wider group of people than those who had supported him at the election.[102] It is significant that large numbers of leading Belfast Whigs were quite prepared to stand behind him on this issue.

The Famine had not successfully undermined the northern landlords' social functions. They had managed to "work" the Poor Law system, and had in varying degrees been able to ameliorate aspects of the Famine experience. They still had a powerful local legitimacy and therefore a body of retainers. The opposition they might have faced was divided; the local Whigs, far from attacking landlordism, actually lent it moral authority in the face of opponents like Dr McKnight. And even McKnight himself never gave utterance to revolutionary expositions against landlords as a socially illegitimate class. He was careful in all his attacks upon them to demand the stripping of their monopolistic prerogatives, not their outright expropriation.

McKnight was attempting to start something new; not to play upon an established tradition. Paradoxically it was the very dominance of industry in the North which rendered the landed status quo so formidable. The capacity of landlords to retain their positive social functions during the Famine was a direct consequence of the prevalence of rural non-agricultural occupations, which both increased the local tax base and reduced the weight of dependence on the Poor Law. The dominance of industry was also expressed in the relative conservatism of the urban Whigs whose property base was sufficiently stable to make them unwilling to participate in even partial attacks on landlord property, such as McKnight was promoting. And in so far as industry implied the existence of classes whose fortunes were not intimately tied to the land, such as weavers or mill workers, not to mention the bodies of direct estate employees, the sharpness of the collision between tenants and landlords was blunted. It is here too that we should return to the thesis about rural prosperity. The sections of the rural society who had votes (£12 poor law valuation or upwards) were in many cases people who had absorbed other people's holdings during the Famine at times when tenant right values had sunk disastrously or disappeared. These people were certainly squeezed by the price falls in 1849 and 1850; but as prices rose and their operations again became more viable, they began to see definite assets in the shape of reviving tenant right values on their now enlarged farms. In short, the dependent status of their property on landlord favour became again a reality.

Given the balance of risks, the absence of pre-existing practices of anti-landlord activity and the novelty of the objectives, the absence of a tradition of such efforts is surely a vital element in the whole. The areas where the most effective resistance to landlord control were to be built up over the long run were precisely those places where the effort was sustained over a long period. Thus the Newtownards-Comber area, for example, in the 1880s (the only election for which we have close detailed results is 1884) was voting about 75 per cent Liberal.[103] It was these areas where the conflict between Presbyterian ministers and Lord Londonderry had first created an immediate and very definite source of local irritation. But the best argument in defence of this position is the political history of County Derry. Here Samuel McCurdy Greer first achieved great local popularity in 1850–52 by his successful legal opposition to efforts by the grand jury to put the cost of rebuilding Downhill Castle on the county cess, after it had been burned down by a probably malicious fire. During the 1852 election, a Presbyterian minister was arrested and imprisoned for making a speech on his behalf in disobedience of a magisterial order not to hold a meeting.[104] After McKnight's return to Derry city to take up again the editorship of the *Derry Standard*, the tradition was persevered in more thoroughly here than in any other Ulster county. East Derry became a very powerful Protestant Liberal stronghold, and Greer continued to fight the county elections here when Liberals in other counties gave up. In 1859 the owner of the aforementioned Downhill Castle, Sir Harvey Bruce, stood as one of the Tory candidates, and Greer won. The Grand Orange Lodge confirmed the expulsion of at least forty Derry Orangemen for supporting him.[105] After this tradition of opposition had been established, the agent of one estate started the practice of refusing bog-tickets to Greer supporters.[106] From the time of the first secret ballot election in 1874 to the extension of the franchise to labourers in 1885, no Tory ever sat for County Derry.[107]

How then are we to understand the role of "No Popery"? Lord Claud Hamilton, the brother of the Marquis of Abercorn, managed to secure 1,000 plus votes each for himself and the other Tory in the Strabane district of County Tyrone against a mere 148 for his tenant right opponent, whipping up a very vicious "No Popery" agitation.[108] The balance of probabilities is that nearly all Protestants and a significant number of Catholics must have voted for the Tories under the kind of duress that was locally applied.

There are those who imply that there was actually no need for land legislation, or rather that Ireland did not need the enactment of the Tenant League's programme. Post-Famine Ireland experienced a period of prosperity which made it clear that such movements were only expressions of an acute period of distress.[109] As an economic judgment there is perhaps much to be said for this, but it misses what was so important about the politics of 1852. It was the effort to cast off reasons for fear and sycophancy towards a class, some of whose members behaved very properly towards their tenants, but who none the less reserved the right not to.

The failure of 1852 postponed effective rural bourgeois self-organization in the North for the best part of twenty years. In the North the opposition that still had any space to exist at all freely was the remnant of the Belfast Whigs who had played no part in 1852. So the conflict between McKnight's position and the Belfast Whigs was to be fought out all over again in the 1870s.

David Millar has pointed out that the basis of much of southern nationalism was a demand to "stay in our own land", a protest against emigration.[110] We shall see this is a recurrent theme in northern Catholic support for nationalism. But it is as well to remember that McKnight's campaign of 1848–52 was concerned with that issue also. The difference of approach here was not between Catholic and Protestant, but between McKnight and the Whigs. McKnight's campaign was an effort to transcend the particularities of local experience of inner Ulster, to detach religious from political questions, and affirm a unity of democratic purpose throughout the island. Whiggish utterances on tenant questions rarely mention the emigration issue as a wound. The *Northern Whig* behaved in a sycophantic manner towards Lord Dufferin in the 1860s when he was preaching emigration as the cure of Ireland's rural problems.[111] As time went on, protest against emigration became a distinguishing preoccupation of Catholic political life, North and South, while it gradually ceased to be a Protestant preoccupation.

8. The Decline of the Old Whigs

Even before the defeat of the Tenant League in the North in 1852, we saw how denominational questions were preventing the partners of the League from keeping the land question free of other issues. In the South the election focused round the opposition to the Titles Bill. And in the North the first attempt at democratic challenge to landlord power failed. There was a common view amongst contemporaries, such as Charles Gavan Duffy[1] and A. M. Sullivan,[2] that political life in Ireland atrophied for about fifteen years afterwards. And in 1868 the *Banner of Ulster* could declare "When men cease to struggle, they cease to hope, and when hope dies out, it is no wonder that apathy seems to reign."[3] Belfast experienced rapid industrial development during the years up to 1867 and its influence on the region about it grew by degrees. I have already drawn attention to the paradox that in countless ways proximity to Belfast enabled the landlords to survive the Famine with their social credit intact. Hence their ability to beat down the challenges from 1848 to 1852. In the post-1852 period politics was more or less confined to Belfast, so its peculiarities began to percolate through the politics of the region as a whole.

The public works undertaken by the Belfast Corporation promoted export development fairly ruthlessly. They were undertaken by a clique that organized its political base round pan-Protestantism. When it first got into difficulties it seemed as though the moment had come for the old Whig elite, and their mainly Catholic following, to insist upon a reconstruction of the corporation. Instead the greater part of the Whigs was drawn into a compromise arrangement with the Conservatives. Their support for the developmental drive outweighed their dislike of the politics of the corporation. The ways of the Whigs and the Catholics, already strained by the period of Whig government and the Titles Bill, parted further. The Belfast Whigs had shown their distaste for agrarian radicalism before 1852. The Chancery suit completes the story of their shift to economic conservatism.

The other theme of this chapter relates to the link between Presbyterianism and the Whigs. From the 1850s the Queen's colleges and the model schools became a key Presbyterian vested interest within the nominally non-sectarian education system. Throughout the 1850s a series of developments sharpened the tension between Presbyterians and Catholics particularly, they being the two main parties involved in the national education structure. The Belfast Whigs became more and more linked with Presbyterian education interests. The revival of 1859 sheds some light on the difficulties the two denominations were having merely existing as two separate types of denomination. The revival has to be looked at as a development internal to Protestant faith first, and only second as a development affecting the relationship between Protestants and Catholics. But the effects were there none the less. The revival sharpened the edge of religious antagonism, because it was a manifestation of the breakdown of the old structure. In its place it substituted a zealotry that affected all who came in contact with it. It is a perfect example of how purely subjective conflicts could erupt which were in the end about nothing except a refusal of each to accept the other. The only way to stay free was to treat the other people's culture as their culture.

The two themes together will tend to emphasise the way that Belfast was growing apart. The crisis in Belfast's political life during the Chancery suit cast a shadow over corporation affairs between 1855 and 1864, and eventually drew Whig and Tory leaderships together in an alliance based upon the interests of large property. It doubly alienated the Belfast Catholics. First, the economic basis of the compromise was opposed to the interests of the mass of the Catholic population. Second, the form of the compromise allowed an only very slightly chastened Conservative group to re-establish itself. The Whigs did not actually betray any formal obligation to the Catholic leadership by failing to press forward the reform of the corporation. But the Catholic disappointment with Whig paternalism was very real. Belfast was also the place where co-operation between Presbyterians and Catholics within the national system was most residual. Where once the old Whig's had taken a strong stand for the original national education scheme, the new Belfast Presbyterian liberalism did not rest its claim to sustain "non-sectarian" education on any ground that Catholics might recognize. Taken overall, Belfast's liberalism was socially and economically conservative, and tending increasingly to become a mouthpiece for specifically Presbyterian educational and institutional interests. Not only did its expressions of rural concerns tend to stress "Presbyterianism" rather than the land question, but its overall outlook was more and more underpinned by the experience of Belfast. Where James McKnight had attempted to overcome sectionalism between North and South, the new Belfast liberalism affirmed it. The understanding of differences which would have been necessary to preserve a sense of the unity of the island gradually evaporated. Inner Ulster began to feel more and more like the surroundings of Belfast.

Before the Famine Ireland was becoming a reserve supply of labour for the metropolitan British economy. But it had not so far been associated with anything like the development of "perfectly mobile" labour supply. The difference between typically Irish and typically British standards of proletarian subsistence was very marked. Increasingly, after the Famine, the growing extent of emigration and the greater ease of passage led to an upward pressure on wage levels, now more strongly influenced by market forces in Britain.[4] Ireland's underdevelopment became gradually less and less a function of its low wage levels relative to the metropolis; it became more like a peripheral region of the metropolitan country and less and less like a colony.[5] The position of the North within this matrix was altogether ambiguous. So long as low wage levels prevailed, they drew into the North productive activity that was withdrawing from parts of Britain. Thus the cotton trade, especially embroidery and sewed muslin, which had been established before the Famine, was widely diffused across the North in 1851, employing for the most part female labour.[6] But the economic revival in 1851–52 applied a strong upward pressure on wage levels in the North. As the demand for harvest labour increased and the labour-intensive flax cultivation revived, the supply of weaving labour began to become highly seasonal.[7]

Power loom weaving had not advanced far in Ulster before 1850, and one of the effects of rising labour costs was to accelerate its development in the North[8] in all areas of the weaving trade except the fine linen productions which continued to be produced in significant quantity by the old domestic system and sold directly to bleachers. One of the main stimuli to economic development of Belfast was therefore the extension of power loom weaving, one which was to be given added force in the early 1860s by the American Civil War, which led to a major disruption of cotton supply and the temporary replacement of cotton by linen products in many markets.[9]

Before 1845 most of the machinery for linen spinning and weaving was imported from Britain. But the growing volume of investment in the linen trade and the iron shipbuilding industry led to the expansion of a native engineering industry from the mid-1850s onwards,[10] a development no doubt assisted by the extension of the railway system. The iron shipbuilding industry was the subject of a *Banner* editorial in 1855[11] which began, "a new trade often arises of great importance and becomes the staple of a district in an almost arbitrary manner". It then proceeded to talk of the advantages of the Clyde, the Tyne and the Mersey "in cheapness of fuel for iron and machine works" over this port, "although that may be met partly by the greater number of building sites". The prospects it held out for the development were not particularly great. "Without activity and earnest struggle, it is evident that a new stable trade cannot be formed in any country; and yet without its formation, we must expect emigration to continue and even to increase." The preoccupation with emigration is most significant, because this is one of the themes which begins to disappear from the Belfast-centred press and indeed from its public discussion over the decade, once the accelerated industrial development of Belfast comes to be celebrated as the fundamental economic reality of the North.

The development works on the harbour during the Famine and afterwards, the reclamation of slob land, the deepening of the channel of the lough, and the rationalization of traffic through the port (the separation of coal from other cargoes) contributed to Belfast's ability to capitalize upon cheap marine bulk transport of coal and iron from the Clyde and the north of England in the second half of the 19th century.[12] Harland and Wolff, the principal iron shipbuilders, employed a mere 120 men in 1855, 500 in 1860, and 2,400 in 1870.[13] In later years it was to become one of the key industries of the North.

The pattern of development within Belfast was diversified. In the old town, the clearing and widening of Victoria and Corporation streets, the removal of both street markets, and much of the custom of the old Smithfield market to Mays Fields on the Lagan bank, shifted the commercial centre of gravity in a south-easterly direction. This is shown by the black arrow on the adjoining map.[14] The gainers were the mercantile-warehouse proprietors of the new streets, and the losers were those displaced to make way for them. The inhabitants of the old more north-westerly centre also lost out. But the works on the harbour and port area streamlined import-export trades, and eventually provided the shipbuilding sites.

In the more western and northern areas of the city beyond its 1850 boundary, the mills for spinning and weaving and the foundries were clustered along the various streams that flowed down from the mountains; and the roads leading out of the town in their directions became the focus for expanding working-class residents. From 1850 through the whole of our period the expansion of the proletarian west and north-west districts was proceeding apace, and we shall look at specific effects in the next chapter on sectarian violence.

Although it is a generalization of only approximate character, the Conservative "developmental" alliance tended to be built upon the interests of the merchants in wholesaling, elements associated with the old Donegall landed interests, and the legal profession. The shipping interests were divided politically, and the Whigs generally were associated with the longer established parts of the linen trade. The division was expressed loosely in the exclusively Tory character of the

Belfast Bank directorate[15] and the much less sharply politically aligned Northern Bank directorate.[16]

Increasingly as the landlord class came to recognize the interdependence of its own prosperity and the industrialization of Belfast, the political tensions between urban and rural elites evaporated. I have already mentioned how the county grand juries were ceasing to be concerned about the effects of railways on turnpike tolls on county roads.[17] And though it was far from his intention merely to kill the possibility of a protectionist revival, Sharman Crawford's 1850 victory at Downpatrick effectively put paid to protectionism as an issue locally. It is significant that at the banquet to vindicate his charges of electoral malpractice against the County Down Tories, his service to free trade was recognized by many who had been rather reluctant to promote the collateral cause he had then been advocating—rent reduction.[18]

How then did the urban and rural Tory elites relate to each other in the early 1850s? In January 1851, at a time when the tensions between the Belfast Corporation and the County Antrim grand jury were beginning to crystallize over the grand jury's opposition to the 1850 Borough Bill, the Ulster Protestant Association assembled at the Music Hall to denounce "Papal Aggression".[19] On the platform, besides some prominent landlords, Anglican clergy and leaders of Orangeism in surrounding areas, were a sample of the Belfast Conservative leadership: at least three solicitors, two wholesale merchants—one of whom was an elder in Dr Cooke's church—and a linen manufacturer. The occasion was taken to "remind" English Protestants of the situation of Protestants in Ireland, and to capitalize upon the sympathy that might be expected from an England itself in the throes of a "No Popery" agitation. The gap between the anti-papal spirit in England and the government's previous efforts to conciliate the Catholic hierarchy in Ireland was seized upon to demand the recall of the "traitor Clarendon". Mr John Bates, the town clerk and solicitor to the corporation, was warmly applauded for his contribution, which included: "If Protestants moved in this matter, they moved in order to preserve their own liberty, the liberties of Protestants of various denominations, and the liberties of Roman Catholic brethren in Ireland, and all over the world. It is of importance that our Roman Catholic brethren should understand this, that Protestants were moved to resist the aggressions of the Pope, in order to secure their own self-preservation."[20]

When opposing some recent symptom of "Popery" these men could present an outwardly united facade, while privately grinding their teeth at each other about pounds, shillings and pence. But the opposition to Catholic political expression, rhetorically justified by the need to defend the liberties of Catholics against the "tyranny" of their own clerical leaders, was not a form of defence for which Catholics would be grateful to John Bates when his day of reckoning came. The governance of the town was largely in the hands of a few committees of the corporation, most of whose work was conducted in secret.[21] The system could be sustained so long as the corporation as a body was a well-controlled entity. John Bates organized local ward committees which, together with the rate collectors, ensured that the collection of rates (whose prompt payment was a condition of municipal franchise) from political opponents might be delayed and a suitably purged voting register produced.[22] Occasionally individuals who displayed too obvious a lack of "Protestantism", such as John Clarke who took a collection for a Roman Catholic chapel, would be deprived of their seats at the renomination stage.[23]

The corporation, so far as can be gathered, was not for the most part financially corrupt. There were several cases of merchants who supplied it with goods at retail prices in excess of likely prices that would have been quoted by tender. And the evidence of corrupt intent here was the precaution it took to disguise the origins of the articles purchased.[24] The greatest area of questionable expenditure was the scale of legal fees charged by John Bates for his various services to the corporation. But the secrecy of the corporation's affairs did have one very important implication. The moment the suggestion was made that its practices were less than financially scrupulous, all its operations came under general attack, and its "Protestantism" ensured that both Protestant Liberals and Catholics demanded its thorough reconstruction before consenting to its release from financial embarrassment. When the edifice crumbled it was Bates who was made the scapegoat. As James Bristow, Director of the Northern Bank, put it, "I should say that if there was anything wrong, it was Mr. Bates who did it."[25]

The corporation had already secured borrowing powers up to £200,000 under various Acts of Parliament since 1845, before it attempted to promote the Act of 1850 which was intended to permit a further £100,000 borrowing.[26] The Bill, however, also contained provisions to free Belfast of a large part of the county cess, a move which had not been cleared with the grand jury. It therefore mobilized opposition simultaneously from the Antrim grand jury,[27] various members of the corporation itself and the Belfast Whigs, worried by the growing size of the borough debt. The corporation was now in a position of some difficulty. It held a substantial amount of property and calculated that if it held on to it, it would be likely to be able to sell it for substantially larger sums in future than if it attempted to sell it off at that time.[28] So it decided instead to continue borrowing (illegally) by issuing unsecured debt to new borrowers. Some of these loans were secured: the corporation paid off parts of the secured £200,000 by transferring them on to the lists of legal borrowings. By November 1854 the total unsecured was £47,800. In addition to this, the corporation's treasurer, John Thompson, Director of the Belfast Bank, allowed the overdraft to rise to £36,000.[29] The whole operation was facilitated by the publication of a "property account"[30] which, though it contained no actual falsehoods, led many to believe that the corporation's finances were in good order.

In the period between the defeat of the 1850 Bill and the 1853 borough extension, the corporation and the Antrim grand jury entered into negotiations backed up by the latter body's determination that if the corporation tried to escape the county cess again, they would seek "a separation between the county of Antrim and the Borough of Belfast embracing criminal jurisdiction as well as all fiscal arrangements".[31] The extension of the boundary in 1853 appears to have involved fairly lengthy negotiations. There was some opposition from people to be included in the extended borough area.[32] On the plus side, they were to be relieved of the turnpike which previously stood between them and the borough; the roads and bridges element of the cess was to be removed from the inner borough; and the outer borough which continued to pay the cess would receive a "refund" of £1,500 a year from the grand jury for road works by the corporation. Some of the outer boundary opposition was conciliated by specific exemptions. Thus Ewart's and Carlisle's mills were to be free of the police rates for watching and lighting because they were far enough up Crumlin Road to be beyond residential areas.[33] Other larger property owners were conciliated by the 1853 Act's provision to reduce the highest level of differential rating on property valued £80 and upwards (4s. 6d. maximum) to the level applied to property valued between £20 – £80 (3s. 0d. maximum), and a further assurance that the actual rate would stay well below that level.[34] This specifically affected six or seven mill owners. The trouble was that the agreement provided that the rates could not be collected until the lighting and watching had been serviced on newly included areas. Hence in order to extend the rate base, more expenditure had to be incurred.[35]

In June 1855 John Rea, the one-time leader of the Drennan club, took an action in Chancery to prove various charges of over-borrowing, misapplication of funds, etc. and secured injunctions which held the "special respondents" (parties to the over-borrowing) personally liable for a total of £273,000 misapplied or illegally raised since 1845.[36] Over the next eight years, from 1855 to 1864, the Chancery suit, as it became known, hung over the affairs of the corporation. At the November 1855 municipal elections, the municipal control system broke down and six Liberals or oppositionists were elected, including John Rea himself, and Bernard Hughes, a Catholic baking proprietor.[37] With the flood gates open, all manner of pent-up anger against the corporation was unleashed.

In essence the problem that confronted the corporation was to secure some kind of indemnity against the misdemeanours it was charged with under the Chancery decrees. It had been saddled with personal responsibility for nearly the whole of Belfast's corporate debt. And that in itself guaranteed that it would be obliged to meet only part of the whole cost. The question therefore was what price its various opponents intended to exact from it. It is not altogether clear precisely what Rea's own objectives were. In the various parliamentary hearings on the subject of Belfast's affairs, he mercilessly pursued certain themes time and again, blocking various efforts at compromise, and exasperating nearly all others concerned with the affair.[38] But in the early stages, it is clear that he wanted a full-scale purge of the corporation (a minimum of half the corporation seats to be filled by Liberals), and extensive actual financial damages not merely against John Bates but against the special respondents as individuals.[39] Backing Rea to begin with were the prominent leadership of the Belfast Catholic population, including Bernard Hughes and Bishop Denvir. For the Catholics, the Chancery suit was a defeat for the corporation, and the odiousness of its pan-Protestantism made them particularly keen to ensure that the old apparatus could not be reconstructed. The only prominent Whig who supported their position was John F. Ferguson, D.L., J.P., of the family of bleachers, whose father J. S. Ferguson had presided at the dinner to celebrate the commencement of the Northern Banking Company's business. The Ferguson family were among the leading Whig dynasties in Belfast. Ferguson's view in 1858 was that the special respondents should pay all the legal costs of the Chancery suit, the (aborted) Indemnity Bills, and the costs of the opposition (about £8,000); he also thought Rea should get £5,000, as he had been of "service to the town".[40] But both he and Dr Denvir were quite clear that these costs apart, the unsecured creditors' debts should be honoured and the whole made a cost on the rates. In that respect, it is likely that Rea ultimately disagreed with them.

The actual working out of a compromise, however, found the majority of the Whigs elsewhere. To start with the opposite extreme, William Mullan, a prominent merchant, had property in Victoria Street—the new street cleared and widened by the corporation—and now mainly occupied by large mercantile wholesale and retail houses. Mullan, who had appeared at the 1851 tenant right conference in Belfast which began the process of reaching a compromise Land Bill, was a brother-in-law of Robert Lindsay who was later to become the Tory leader of the corporation. And though Mullan was a Whig elected to the corporation in 1856, he was one of the first to align himself with the Conservatives on the generality of municipal questions. After the defeat of the first effort to secure the passage of an Indemnity Bill in 1857, Mullan proposed in October to make another attempt, and in so doing contributed to the breakdown of an attempted compromise measure that was being worked out between William Dunville, a distiller, and James McNamara, a wealthy Catholic, James Lemon, a Conservative shipowner, and James Bristow, Director of the Northern Bank.[41] The treaty was however unworkable, as Dunville and McNamara had settled for seventeen Liberals on the council, whereas Rea was holding out for twenty.[42] Between Rea and Mullan the treaty broke down.

We must now look at what the Dunville, McNamara, Lemon and Bristow treaty was intent upon achieving. It is quite clear that the events of 1857 convinced many of the leading elements in the city that the Chancery suit posed real dangers to the continued stability of the town. Any settlement which could wrap it up was keenly sought after, and the importance of the intervention of James Bristow in the treaty, a man who had little direct political concern, was that he was the leading figure in the relatively Whiggish and Liberal Northern Bank. The involvement of the Northern Bank was indirectly a means of securing the solidarity of property to ensure a settlement. Bristow's earlier quoted comment to the effect that anything that was done wrong was Bates's fault, expressed the line that was now to be pursued by the exponents of compromise. The election of John Rea to the town council in November 1855 had totally changed the nature of the meetings. His denunciations of the council spared nobody and attracted large crowds to the "galleries".[43] There is little doubt that some of the Whig leaders were profoundly worried at the forces which the one-time leader of the Drennan club was mobilizing. In the elections of April 1857, some kind of arrangement was entered into with the Conservatives to facilitate the election of Thomas McClure, a leading Whig merchant, to one of the seats at Westminster. But in the event the anti-compromise party led by John F. Ferguson put up two Liberals to oppose both McClure and the Tories. At the nomination meeting rival sectarian mobs appeared and the town police used a lot of force to remove the Catholic supporters of the Ferguson Liberals. The Tories reneged on whatever agreement they had made with McClure, and the three Liberals were at the bottom of the poll.[44] The first effort to secure an Indemnity Act failed in June and was the occasion for several nights of lighted tar-barrels. The major sectarian rioting of which we will speak at greater length in the next chapter began in July and reached a hideous climax in September in a confrontation over street preaching, in which the Rev. Hugh Hanna first appeared in the public eye.

During the brief Conservative administration of 1858–59, a Royal Commission investigated Belfast's affairs and substantially vindicated the Dunville/McNamara/Bristow/Lemon treaty.[45] The legal counsel employed by the corporation set about demonstrating the utility of the works that had been carried out. They managed to effectively demolish each of the various opposition groups and individual critics of the corporation, except the Ferguson and Denvir group. They undermined this group by demonstrating that Rea's activities were creating a blanket of insecurity over Belfast and arresting developmental progress. So they left Ferguson and Denvir's proposal that Rea should get £5,000 to speak for itself. The strategy was to demonstrate that most of the opponents were motivated by narrow personal motives, or by a desire to restore things irretrievably outmoded, and to concentrate on the developmental benefits of the corporation's activities. This guaranteed that the new city merchant elite, most of the shipping interest, and a large part of the manufacturing interest (engaged in export) could be brought to bear against a variety of oppositions, some of whose objectives were mutually contradictory.

The first example is provided by an exponent of the old system of street markets which had been done away with by the corporation, but which had been made economically redundant by the extension of the railway system. Richard Waring, a provision merchant elected to the council in 1855, stated that the removal of these street markets ruined many small shopkeepers.[46] The concentration of the pork market in Mays Field North was associated with the concentration of the trade in the hands of about twelve merchants. But the difficulty with his own proposal became clear when he complained about tolls displacing pig markets from the towns. With the spread of railways "every railway station [is] a sort of market". In short, though he had not seen it, the spread of the railroad system and the activities of large pork merchants in the country districts had undermined the very basis of the street market which he wanted to restore.

As to the other opposition groups, the most important was the "outer boundary" group, who objected to being saddled with payment of rates to service the corporation debt, of which only a minute proportion had been spent in their district.[47] They argued that the improvement works had moved the commercial centre of gravity of the city in a south-easterly direction towards the new Corporation-Victoria Street area; that the movement of the coal quay to the Down side of the river had added two pence a ton to the cost of coal deliveries to the mills in the west side of the town; and that the movement of most of the markets from Smithfield to Mays Fields had also contributed to falling property values in their direction. The group's position was supported in sentiment by a few representatives of those who had been displaced at the time of the widening of Victoria and Corporation streets, and had generally moved in a westerly direction. As one of these men, an architect, put it, "it destroyed me and many other families as well as me".[48]

James Cameron's evidence illustrates the difficulty of the "outer boundary" case. He, despite the disadvantages of his area as compared with the south-centre, had bought land in the far north-west of the city near the court house about 1844 for £200 an acre, and sold some at £800 an acre. He remarked critically on the coal transport costs, and was asked: "Are you considering what is a benefit to yourself, and to a few other persons, or are you taking the great space of the whole borough into account, and the entire mercantile community of Belfast; which are you considering, them or yourself?"[49]

Another person, a linen spinner and power loom weaver, Montague Mulligan, also complained about the extra coal costs. Mr Macdonogh ran rings round him.

MACDONAGH: "Be kind enough to tell me are you much concerned with the export trade, Mr. Mulligan?"
MULLIGAN: "No, we are altogether concerned in the home trade."
MACDONAGH: "Where is the market for your commodities; where do you sell?"
MULLIGAN: "To different [Belfast] merchants and in the surrounding [areas]."
MACDONAGH: "They work the goods . . . into fine linen?"
MULLIGAN: "We manufacture ourselves."

MACDONAGH: "They export?"
MULLIGAN: "I suppose they do."
Then Macdonogh took the opportunity to run him through a humiliating cross-examination about the importance of the shipping interest for his own prosperity.[50]

Towards the end the shipping interest, Tory and Whig, was brought in in force to vindicate the development works. James Barnett and Thomas Sinclair, two of the biggest Whig shipping owners, approved the settlement.[51] Although Barnett was slightly critical of the Dunville-McNamara treaty, he said it was "most unjust to repudiate it", and blamed Rea for its repudiation rather than Mullan. Significantly, one Liberal who later became mayor of Belfast, Edward Coey, stated that he wished the corporation had got further into debt and had done more improvement.[52]

After the Royal Commission, the Tories vacated enough of the council seats for the Liberals to acquire half the total corporation membership. The plan was in this way to do a voluntary sharing of power, and to create a municipal body that would be more likely to be able to get an Indemnity Bill through parliament. In 1861 Sir Edward Coey became Liberal Lord Mayor. Significantly, in 1861-62, two of William Sharman Crawford's sons, who had opposed the 1857 and 1858 Indemnity Bills, were elected to the boards of the Belfast and Northern banks.[53] Without any further explanation of the matter, the Belfast Bank's official history describes what followed the death of Thomas G. Batt in 1861 as follows. Arthur Sharman Crawford "was chosen in what appeared to be indecent haste" as his successor.[54] With the Liberals in power at Westminster it was imperative that the ultimate compromise be endorsed by a representative cross-section of property and not by any group which could be suspected of Tory partisanship. John Rea later charged the two banks with applying a "screw" to their customers to ensure support for the indemnity.[55]

What emerged very clearly from the 1858 inquiry was how the development works had laid the basis of a new property status quo. Whig and Tory leaders were in favour of what had been done, even if all of the Whigs and some of the Tories disapproved of the corporation's political methods. The Tories were for the greater part merchants, lawyers, and other professional men with some elements of the old Donegall land owning interest attached. They had secured the adhesion of significant sections of the linen trade (such as Ewart and Carlisle whose mills lay beyond the area liable to the police rates). If anything the Whigs were men of larger property. They had a larger proportion of the linen trade, especially the longer established sections who began in bleaching. The shipping interest, represented in both camps, strongly endorsed the developmental works as a positive gain to Belfast. Most of the Belfast elite could unite to blame Bates for what was done improperly and to regard Rea as an obstacle to a satisfactory solution. And now the potential rates burden to cover the debt was gradually building up as the unsecured debt went unserviced. So the big preoccupation for the larger property owners was whether, when it was placed upon the rates, the rates would continue to be charged on a differential basis.[56] They also felt that the punitive terms Rea—backed to some degree by Ferguson and Bishop Denvir—was seeking should be resisted. So the gap between themselves on the one hand, and Ferguson and the leadership of the Catholic population on the other, widened. As Rea was succeeding in keeping up popular feeling about the Chancery suit, the men of property were keener and keener to resolve it without involving the mob of the town.

In the 1860s Protestant Liberals constituted roughly a quarter of the Protestant municipal electorate.[57] Even if the electoral system had been cleaned up, they could only have secured a dominant position in alliance with Ferguson's supporters. So unless they were prepared both to set aside the unification of the rating system—which they wanted but which was very unpopular with Ferguson's supporters—and to extract retribution from the old leaders, they could make little use of the seats on the council which the Tories had vacated. So they tried, notwithstanding the opposition of Ferguson and Rea, to mend their fences with the Tories and move towards an Indemnity Bill. They were content with a token "deprotestantisation" of the corporation, involving the continual absence of some of the more notorious firebrands such as F. H. Lewis. This would last so long as the Chancery suit hung *in terrorem* over the old special respondents. But once it was decided to settle the indemnity, and to charge the debts to the rates, they shared as owners of large property a common interest with their Tory opposite numbers. The differential rating system had been partly undermined by the 1853 Borough Extension Act which abolished the top rate on property valued over £80. But the major element of local taxation, the police rate, continued to be charged at a differential rate. Property valued at £20 or more was liable to double the rate applied to property valued under £20. By 1861, it was reckoned that nearly the whole of the council favoured the abolition of the differential and hoped to include its abolition in the ultimate Indemnity Bill.[58] Of all the causes Rea hung on to with total consistency, it was his opposition to this move. And as he lost allies in 1861-64, his denunciation of Whig and Tory big property alliances grew louder.

Much of the Whigs' lack of enthusiasm for the local council, which subsequent writers have tended to ascribe to lack of political motivation or a sense that this body was "not respectable",[59] probably has far more to do with the fact that on this fundamental issue the leadership of the Whigs and the Tories were united. By 1864, J. F. Ferguson and the Catholic leadership were viewing the settlement of the indemnity as a sell-out by the Whigs. True, the differential rating system was not abolished openly. As we shall see later, it was undermined by the subterfuge of moving most of the rate burden from the police rate (which was differentially rated) to the borough rate (which was not). But the abdication of the Whigs from the council and the absence of any serious measures of reform of its administration created Catholic resentment. The Catholic *Ulster Observer* said of John F. Ferguson:

"At the time that others abandoned from selfish motives, the ranks to which they had pledged allegiance, and from the dread of pecuniary loss forsook the struggling poor, who had so often fought their battles, Mr. Ferguson, uninfluenced by bad example, remained faithful to them".[60]

As the Belfast Whigs became more and more economically and socially conservative and lost the impetus to lead any sort of popular political forces in the city, liberalism became the alliance between the Presbyterian merchant and manufacturing elite and the Presbyterian educational interests (notably Queen's College, Belfast). The major concerns of this alliance were shaped by the Catholic hierarchy's demands for the denominationalization of the national education system and the government's response to it. The growth of voluntaryism amongst English non-conformists—which expressed itself in parliament as adverse votes cast on money voted to denominational bodies—began to create anxiety about the status of Regium Donum. So the increasingly "Presbyterian" tone of Liberals in Belfast also expressed defensiveness.

In early 1859 the government had announced that it planned to set up an intermediate educational system in Ireland on the same principles as the national primary system. The move was warmly welcomed by northern Presbyterians and by some middle-class Catholics (e.g. in Newry).[61] Towards the end of 1859 the Catholic hierarchy issued its strongest denunciation so far of the "Mixed" system of education. The timing of this broadside was influenced mainly by the government's plans, but a secondary consideration was the Great Revival that had swept through the North that year.[62]

It is clear enough that educational questions were already the major axis round which sectarian relationships revolved, whether for better, when local clergy worked the national system in a way that spread goodwill rather than heartburn, or more usually for the worse. The firmer the institutional structure, and the clearer each Church was about where it stood, the more able each denomination was to give the other space to be themselves. This was obviously much easier in the countryside where each communion had related to the others in ways that had become stabilized over a long period of time. In fact a big part of the educational aggravation in Belfast had to do with the precariousness of any such relationships. But the increasing mobility of people, and the greater the presence of the state as a body with meaning for people, the more the role of the Church decayed. The Great Revival is partly about this undermining of the structures of the Presbyterian Church. Its place in the community was being shaken by modernity and the revival enthusiasm sought to replace the structure that was decayed. While this was its primary aspect, no such transformation could take place without affecting the relationship between Presbyterians and the people they shared the space with. When structure was replaced by enthusiasm, it was much more difficult for them and the Catholics merely to live side by side accepting the fact of their differences. The differences now became rivalrous. And so it happened that an event reflecting the internal decay of structure within one denomination spread out and corroded the structure of interdenominational coexistence. The rivalry escalated so that denominational differences became more and more absolute. And in becoming absolute, these differences became national differences.

We begin by looking at the inner Ulster countryside after 1852. I showed earlier how Catholics' capacity to capitalize on the Whig reforms in the North depended upon clerical leadership to bargain or negotiate with landlords and magistrates. Access to school sites, and avoidance of Catholic collisions with the institutions of local control, depended upon the success with which priests could simultaneously relate to their own flocks and to the local ruling elites. The 1852 election had impressed upon all opponents of landlord power in the North the very high costs that had to be borne in a challenge that was defeated. And at the same time the relatively benign economic climate tended to reinforce the dependent status of tenant property on landlord favour. Tenant right values recovered quite quickly after 1852, the frequency of evictions fell away sharply, and for a few years the demand for flax remained high.[63] Emigration, no longer in flood proportions, now settled to the level of a steady drain. And in so far as the new status quo was stabilized, landlords had little cause to disturb the tranquillity by actions that undermined the informal security of tenant property. In 1855 the *Banner* protested that farmers didn't seem interested in the legalization of the tenant right custom, and signifying a major departure from its position of four years previously, regretted that the security of tenant right in Ulster should be connected with the overall problem of landlord-tenant legislation for Ireland as a whole.[64]

Under these circumstances abstract concern with legalizing tenant right was not a strong enough incentive to oppose landlord power. It was for this reason that popular challenges tended to integrate everything that could be used to oppose landlordism. County Derry was the one northern county in which the challenge of 1852 was continually repeated. Even in this county, and even in 1852, the parish priest of Magherafelt had supported the Conservatives and it would be no surprise if others did likewise at subsequent elections.[65] Samuel McCurdy Greer, supported by Dr McKnight and Rev. Dr John Brown of Aghadowey, was successful only in a by-election in 1857 when his opponent was Sir H. H. Bruce. Bruce owned Downhill Castle which had been burned down in 1851, and Greer had managed to stop the grand jury from placing the rebuilding costs on the county rates. This particular grievance—the attempted imposition of Sir Harvey Bruce as Conservative candidate—was adequate to secure Greer an extra 500–700 votes over his usual score.[66]

Neither the Catholics nor the Presbyterians in the North outside Belfast were in any position to be able to dispense with landlord favour in the matter of sites for national schools or churches. The Catholics were perhaps in a particularly weak position. In 1861 there were still very substantial numbers of Catholic children in Church education,[67] and other endowed schools, and though it may not have been universally an object of grievance to Catholics in general, it was certainly a source of concern to the clergy. In some areas mixed national schools might continue to function (or even endowed schools provided by landlords) frequented promiscuously by children of different denominations. But to render an arrangement of this kind workable, a very high degree of trust was required between ministers of different denominations and, where they were concerned, landlords. Only very gradually as each denomination built up its structure of *de facto* denominational schools would the necessity for this kind of accommodation disappear. But in general local efforts at accommodation implicitly involved repudiation of religio-educational controversy. Part of the cause of Greer's defeat in 1859 was related to the tensions between his various supporters over that question.

Although it is obviously rather too broad a generalization, the depoliticization of daily life in the countryside meant both the restoration of landlord hegemony and routine elite accommodation. National politics seemed far away. There were some positive sides to this. The detachment of the Orange Order from the coat-tails of local squirearchy allowed it in some areas to become a network of fraternal clubs, less and less related to practical anti-Catholicism. Throughout the 1850s, large numbers were expelled from the Order by the Grand Lodge for "marrying Papists", "introducing Papists into Lodge meetings", "giving offerings to Popish priests, etc." not to mention the forty County Derry Orangemen expelled for voting for Greer.[68] Sadly, but inevitably, much that passed for peace and tranquillity in this society involved precisely the capacity to insulate local realities from wider national ones. The full meaning of this became apparent only in the 1860s when national tremors began again to reverberate through hitherto insulated localities.

The revival of 1859 began in the environs of Ballymena, the centre of the Presbyterian handloom weaving district, which had been connected by rail to Belfast during the later years of the Famine. It started in Connor, spread to Ahoghill and thence along the "entire line of country from Toome to Rasharkin".[69] In its early stages it was carried by "converts" from one meeting to another. At these meetings individuals fell prostrate and were surrounded by others who prayed for them or sang psalms.[70] The first manifestations left the local clergy and indeed most other people decidedly confused as to what was happening.[71] The revival started entirely without the assistance of clerical leadership.[72] It spread thereafter throughout much of the more Presbyterian area of the North, and though its forms varied according to the differences between the districts it came to, it was not in any sense a particular class or occupational group experience. It appeared in weaving districts,[73] urban linen mill districts,[74] farming districts,[75] smaller rural towns,[76] and in Harland's shipbuilding yard.[77] This fact is more central than the observation that amongst particular groups (such as mill workers) it took particular forms.

Some observers, struck very much by the more outlandish manifestations of the revival, have viewed it as a popularization or enthusiastic outburst in contrast to the intellectualized nature of orthodox Presbyterianism.[78] There is certainly some truth in this, but emphasis upon it misses the rather more universal nature of the revival experience as a religious experience. The churches' role as popular instruments of social control—in the case of the Presbyterian churches, the kirk sessions—was being undermined by the delocalization of community relationships. A popular instrument of this kind can function to the extent that social relationships approximate to a state of general interdependence, rather than a set of relationships of superiority and subordination. It can do so to the extent that the community actually controls access to social resources. But the class stratification of the society, the growing presence of other civil institutions (such as Poor Law guardians, constabulary, etc.), and the increasing possibilities of human mobility tend to undermine the character of such a social control mechanism.[79] In common with many areas of Britain in this period, religious authorities are to be found complaining of the effects of railways or the spread of public houses on popular "morality".

The revival did at least three things. It intensified concern with religious observance and the fundamentals of Calvinistic faith amongst sections of the population who may have become distant from Church structures, even if the effect may have been somewhat temporary. It also gave rise to "enthusiastic" religious expressions which were a new departure from existing Presbyterian practice. And it generated a new dimension in the separateness between Presbyterians and Catholics. In so far as it changed Presbyterian-Catholic relations, it widened a sense of the spiritual superiority of Protestantism over Catholicism (Protestant perception) and a fear of fundamental determination to eradicate Catholicism (Catholic perception). The response of the majority of orthodox Presbyterian ministers to the revival was ambivalent. They saw an enormously increased awareness of the sense of sin, a reimposition of social discipline (less drunkenness, less frivolity, less combativeness), and an increased attention to religious observance.[80] But they were troubled by the physical manifestations which many were honest enough to admit they could not understand and certainly did not go out of their way to promote.[81] Indeed several, including Dr Henry Cooke, offered very strong warnings about letting the revival become the work of this or that particular person.[82] Can we summarize what was happening?

The sense of man's inherent sinfulness stands at the centre of Calvinistic theology. The only redemption is by grace through faith in Jesus Christ alone. The meaning of this doctrine is far from self evident, and a precondition for any understanding of it is the thorough sense of one's own sinfulness and the stripping away of pride in "one's own" achievements or virtues. It manifestly contradicts the day-to-day operating assumptions of humanity—that people's works and virtues are somehow "their own". It is obvious that any system of belief such as this offers no certain guarantees of salvation—it is not faith as such, but grace through faith which redeems. It recognizes no human as having power or authority to convey assurance. Confronted by a collective human experience of a deep sense of sinfulness and a fear of damnation, however it may be produced, there is nothing that any human agent can formally do or say to assuage this. We cannot penetrate the minds of those who underwent these experiences, but some who went through them described the sensation as a deep and depressing sense of guilt which was the cause of the physical debilitation, followed by a variously manifested sense of that guilt being lifted.[83] Whether subconsciously the knowledge that others had been released in this way, or whether the communion of others in prayer about one, or whatever the source of release, it none the less carried people through an experience of the sense of sin and the release from it. It matters not at all for the meaning of this experience generally, that in many cases it was employed as a means of excitement or a source of charlatanism.

Beyond the physical manifestations, it is quite clear that far more people were affected by the revival than by its more remarkable outward signs. The decline of the place of the Church in the life of the community was reversed by a movement of mass enthusiasm. Obviously the new kind of Church centrality was different. In the past it was a natural thing to be taken for granted; now it was something to be asserted against the rival attractions made visible by railroads. The new kind of ministry would be defensive, and therefore more aggressive, about the world it was part of. And it is clear why the supposedly more intellectual ministry declined. If the revival's common denominator was the impression of the sense of sinfulness and the necessity of saving grace;[84] and if there can be no human agency involved in conveying the sense of forgiveness and grace, it follows that all manner of human means were brought to bear to deal with this contradiction, which is inherent in this theology. The problem that confronted the orthodox Presbyterian clergy was that they recognized the power of impression of sinfulness, whether in its physical or other manifestations. But from their position, the theologically consistent among them denied both their power to induce such a condition and their capacity to bring people to a sense of grace.[85] Their only legitimate intervention was preaching the Word, the means of faith, through which grace might be given. But in practice they were confronted with a popular manifestation of religious feeling which threw up its own leadership; and some of the ministers were less concerned than others about avoiding the encouragement of physical feeling states or giving the impression that they had any kind of power to convey grace. The Rev. Hugh Hanna, for example, whose earlier exploits in vindicating "Protestantism" in combat we will come to in the next chapter, preached a sermon on the text:

"Then was brought unto Him one possessed with a devil blind and dumb and He healed him, insomuch that the blind and dumb both spake and saw." He then addressed them "at great length on the necessity of coming to Jesus to get His Holy Spirit that they should be made both to see and hear for the benefit of their immortal souls and be healed by Him."[86]

Very few sermons I have come across in the revival reports of the *Banner of Ulster* contain such explicit suggestions about the need to "cast out devils". Once the revival affected the Crumlin Road mill district, it spread through factories and residential districts, and the *Banner* reported extensively about its incidence in these districts.

Some of the women mill workers, many of whom had not been at the revival meetings, exhibited the symptoms of debilitation at work, and were put under medical supervision; most recovered after a few hours "but retain a deep conviction of the urgent necessity of saving grace. Others have been enabled to rejoice in the presence of a revealed Saviour." Those who had reached this state showed "ardent affection" for those who were currently impressed in this state or who they wanted to become so. "It is somewhat singular that although they worship in various congregations, the majority, when in the calmer state of spiritual fervour, expressed an earnest desire to be visited by a particular minister (Rev. Hugh Hanna) who has since been most assiduous in his attentions to them."[87] It is clear that Hanna was acquiring something of an individual charisma and the distinction between a preacher of the Word as the source of faith, and a preacher as an agency through which grace might be found was, to say the least, being somewhat blurred. In this sense then the vital and unbridgeable contradiction between God and man, the unknowability of the former, was being broken down and divine grace rendered more tangible.

Gibbon and Millar are quite correct to speak of this kind of experience as a breaking down of the intellectualist character of Presbyterianism, making it accessible as an experience with definite and identifiable characteristics.[88] It was certainly very much opposed to the matter of factness and self-restraining nature of orthodox Presbyterianism. But we should hesitate to identify the revival as a whole with such things. Furthermore it seems to me to be a mistake to treat, as Gibbon does, the enthusiastic and physical manifestations of the revival as though they themselves prepared the ground for a breach between the proletarian Presbyterianism and the hitherto "dominant" Liberal currents (breaking down the spirit of 1798) of Presbyterianism.[89] There were Unitarians who were socially very conservative and Revivalists who were land radicals, such as the Rev. Professor Richard Smyth. Gibbon's thesis claims far too much, and incidentally is insulting to the mental capacities of those involved. There is no evidence at all that such dramatic changes of political persuasion followed the revival experience. Even if it was supposed that Hanna himself made use of these opportunities for political ends, he was very much in a minority within the Presbyterian ministry at that time. It was precisely amongst the sections of the population who were outside the sphere of regular Church connexion that the revival took the most decidedly "physical" form.[90] Hanna was perhaps quicker on the uptake in responding to situations where the Church had ceased for the moment to be relevant, whether he saw an opportunity to "kick the Pope" or to comfort people smitten with physical symptoms during the revival. Later on we will have cause to discuss Hanna's role as an initiator of various political developments, but unlike his 1857 defence of the right of street preaching and his later political interventions where he equated Protestantism with anti-Catholicism, that is not what the revival was "about" in the first instance. It does not follow from the fact that Hanna was so deeply involved in something that it was necessarily an emanation from the gutter of anti-Catholicism, however understandable such a suspicion might be. Taken as a whole the revival meant far more than one might infer from attention to these physical manifestations. That it did not, for example, simply take on the character of a mass disruption of day-to-dayness is amply testified by the (temporarily) increased church attendance,[91] the cessation of drunkenness, abstention from many species of popular entertainment,[92] the absence of Orange parades on 12 July,[93] and the proliferation of prayer meetings.[94] And it is perhaps significant that in its centre, about Ballymena, the production of handloom cloth appears to have remained quite steady and the market to have been unaffected by the revival.[95] In short, it tightened the bonds of collective self-restraint in a society where the Church was increasingly becoming unable to impose such discipline by its own efforts. An interesting feature of the revival is the way in which popular activity took over the clerical function. It should not be any surprise, nor should it be held to belittle the religious character of the revival, that within a few years much of its effects were invisible or had disappeared. Structures that were once taken for granted cannot be restored by enthusiasm alone. But the attention to the Word—Bible study and prayer meetings, etc.—involved a very definite intensification of the religious experience. And the danger with looking at the revival as a primarily crypto-political event becomes clear at this point.

Let us now turn to the question of the relationships with Catholics. Although I candidly doubt whether many Roman Catholics were converted to Protestantism as a result of the revival, I am prepared to hazard a guess that more were converted by this experience than by every effort at overt proselytization conducted before or since.[96] Until this time, attacks on "Romanism" had been precisely that—taunting Catholics, but having almost nothing to do with preaching about Christ. The 1834 campaign against the national education system made the restrictions on the use of the Bible in schools an explicitly political question, a stick with which to beat Catholicism; and at the Achilli meeting in Belfast in 1850, the question of access to the Bible in Rome was made an overt weapon for a triumphal display of Protestantism over "Romanism". The attention to the Bible during the revival experience was sometimes a primarily religious question internal to the life of believers. The revival was first and foremost a religious experience of believers, and it did not always have the secondary implication of being a challenge to "Romanism". But occurring in the actual situation in which it did occur, it necessarily brought into play all the various politico-religious concerns for the "destruction of Romanism" that had hitherto functioned purely politically with little more than a religious fig-leaf to cover them. Precisely because it was not its initial intention to do so, the revival was a far more real proselytizing threat to Catholicism than any of its more overtly political predecessors, which simply insulted Catholic self-respect.

From the start of the revival the *Banner of Ulster* was in the habit of claiming that it was securing converts amongst "Unitarians, Romanists and other errorists".[97] There were some spectacular examples of crisis created by successful conversions, such as the Costello case in Carrickfergus which led to Costello's mother and a Presbyterian minister filing charges of assault against each other. The case created a lot of local interest, and in a packed court house the following exchange occurred:[98]

MR SEEDS: "Well, now, did you burn a Bible?"
MRS COSTELLO: "A Bible is a thing I never saw with my son."
[*sensation in the court*]
MR SEEDS: "And you are the lady who so admirably educates your family, and yet never saw a Bible in the house with your sons!"
MR O'ROURKE: "She doesn't want any of your Protestant Bibles".

Exchanges of this kind only served to bring out the face of the revival which Catholics were made aware of as soon as it began to touch them, its secondary intention to undermine Catholicism. Mention is made of "Romish mobs" attacking missionaries who went to visit converts and others afflicted in predominantly Catholic districts.[99] And it is clear that the introduction of the revival into the mills drew attention to religious differences. In some mills with Catholic overseers and managers, strong efforts were taken to discourage the revival entering the mills.[100] "One little boy was seen pointing out a passage of Scripture to two female workers, when the manager took the Bible from him, locked it up, and in the evening discharged all three", claimed the *Banner*, whereas in other mills, the revival was positively encouraged.[101] The way in which the revival could not escape the trammels of sectarian controversy was shown by the *Downshire Protestant*, an ultra-Orange Anglican paper. So long as they saw the revival as a religious manifestation they had some of that denomination's reservations about it. But their minds were changed: "Romish priests pronounce the revival to be a device of the devil. This is a strong argument in its favour."[102]

It is small wonder that in 1859 the revival experience taken as a whole was regarded as another effort to undermine Catholicism, for in so far as it affected Catholics, that is what it was. The fact that this was only an incidental part of the revival experience for those most intimately concerned with it, does not materially change this religio-political implication. The revival took place in a context where any religious manifestation had a meaning derived from the relationships between denominational subsocieties. In terms of our earlier remarks about the nature of local accommodation between elites and clerical leaders, it put the framework of accommodation under some considerable strain.

An example of how this happened is provided by a newspaper controversy in Ballymena that arose out of the revival. The parish priest, Rev. John Lynch, wrote a letter to the *Ballymena Observer* which contained the following remarks about the revival: "Catholics have not had, and have not now, anything to do with the matter. If it be found beneficial to the Presbyterian community, we shall rejoice. For ourselves we believe that religion, and religious truth must rest on surer foundations, and be recommended by arguments more intelligible and more reliable than those furnished by such manifestations."[103]

The Presbyterian minister, Rev. S. M. Dill, replied, thanking him for the interest expressed in the spiritual welfare of Presbyterians:

"Now I think I cannot better reciprocate your good will towards us than by earnestly praying that both you and all the members of your communion may be brought to share (as some have already) in the blessed results of this gracious visitation . . . I have been informed by the most trustworthy witnesses of several persons who have been led by it to abandon the tenets of Romanism and to embrace 'the truth as it is in Jesus'."[104]

He then broadens the issue by challenging Lynch on the question of "unwritten word of God or tradition". The correspondence continued and eventually Dill came up with this:

I have never concealed my hatred of the fundamental and fatal errors of Romanism—a hatred all the more deep because of my feelings of good will towards those who have been involved in those errors."[105]

The controversy then bent off into the question of whether or not Peter was ever in Rome,[106] and the scriptural basis of "Revivals".[107]

This controversy exposed all the raw nerves of difference between Presbyterian and Catholic theology in a manner which was all the more notable for the absence of personal bitterness or animosity between the two writers. But if these two men had got on reasonably well before, this controversy was hardly calculated to make that any easier subsequently. In fact local accommodative relationships were put under direct pressure by the revival around Ballymena. A revival meeting was to have been held on Fair Hill at Craigbilly—a past and future scene of pugilistic encounters. Rev. John Lynch applied to a magistrate to prevent the meeting on the grounds that it would lead to a breach of the peace.[108] Lynch was a "loyal" priest—he had been at the Ballymena Loyalty meeting in 1848[109]—and though the *Ballymena Observer* corrected the innuendo that the grounds of the supposed breach of the peace was incitement, Lynch himself had raised against the meeting—it gently reprimanded him for not having made the application against the leaders of any such incitement rather than against the meeting itself.[110] The revival put pressure upon denominational coexistence especially in the Presbyterian heartlands of inner Ulster. They became more vulnerable thereafter to infection by sectarian rivalries, including those which originated from a distance.

The Evangelical Alliance which met in Belfast in 1859 was concerned with two subjects primarily, the Ulster revival and the hierarchy's pastoral letter. The pastoral affirmed the necessity of separation in the educational sphere and made explicit demands that the government finance a wholly denominational Catholic system. Included in the demands were the chartering and endowment of the Catholic university in Dublin, the dividing up of the national schools between the various denominations, and the total and unrestricted oversight of all such Catholic educational institutions by the clergy.[111] The Anglican Bishop of Down and Connor, talking of the principles of toleration, said: "I felt that they [the Roman Catholic hierarchy] claim not toleration, which I certainly would have extended to them, but that these resolutions, or Pastoral Address, passed without the safe limits of just toleration and assumed the character of ascendancy ... I feel satisfied that if anyone who guides and governs this great country be inclined, from any cause or from any circumstance, to favour any one ecclesiastical body may be—to the injury of others, he will lose the support of that great Liberal party to which it is my pride and honour to belong."[112]

This speech expressed a sentiment which Presbyterians, whose educational institutions, unlike those of the Anglicans, were within the framework of the national and Queen's college systems, felt very keenly. It also represented the beginning of a general alignment of Protestants of all denominations, open anti-Catholics and Liberals alike, against the claims of the Catholic hierarchy. From the standpoint of the Catholics, this Protestant unity at an elite level was at one with the mass spirit of the revival which the Alliance also celebrated so earnestly. Thus the Rev. Charles Searer, a Belfast Anglican minister, described the relatively undenominational character of the revival: "It is not the union of indifferentism or Popery, but of earnest Christians; those who, agreeing in holding the Son only, the Spirit only, and the Word only, have an intelligent and Scriptural bond of brotherly union." And the overall unity of the Alliance was described by the Moderator of the General Assembly as follows: "United on the basis of a broad evangelicalism . . . [the Alliance] has already done good service to the Reformation cause, by manifesting that the boasted unity of Rome—a unity secured by the repression of mental liberty, by anathema, and espionage and torture—is but an idle dream as compared with the substantial harmony of thought and feeling which reigns throughout the happy and free domain of Protestantism."[113]

Any attempt to preserve the national education system as a genuine co-operative venture could only work so long as there was no question of it being a proselytizing agency. Clergy had to accept that a Catholic was a Catholic by birth, and likewise a Presbyterian was a Presbyterian by birth. If this could not be assumed no trust was possible. There were no doubt some Catholic priests in the North who were prepared to operate this arrangement so long as they considered it in the light of local circumstances, where they felt trust. Many Catholics went to schools which didn't even have national educational safeguards (such as those on the Draper's estate about Moneymore).[114] The problems posed by the revival for local relationships of trust were severalfold.

Reawakening Protestant religious fervour and concern for the teaching of the Bible, it created pressures at local levels for Protestant ministers to reaffirm the principles of Bible education and to pay renewed attention to the prospects of converting Catholics. The whole movement occurred at a point in time when the Catholic hierarchy made explicit the claims for denominalization of education. This was opposed by both those Presbyterians who looked upon the national system as a satisfactory mode of compromise, as well as by those who had never concealed their wish to weaken "Romanism". Those Presbyterians who now sought to defend the national system were confronted with a difficulty. There was all the difference between keeping a trusting relationship with local Catholic clergy and pontificating on behalf of the "united system" in company with those who merely wanted to oppose Catholic claims. It mattered vitally therefore whose political company they kept. The only practical argument in favour of "united education" that would have carried any weight with Catholic and Presbyterian alike was its success within their own experience. That was the very thing the revival tended to undo. If the defence of national education became mixed up with revivalist trumpeting about defeating "Romanism", then it was no longer anything more than an ideological shield for Presbyterian interests.

In Belfast the intervention of Hanna had put the mainline Presbyterian clergy on the defensive. As a sign of what was to come, the Crumlin Road mills' experience of the revival illustrated the growing distance between nominal Presbyterians and the established structure of the Church. Second, there had been "confrontation" situations arising out of the revival which had brought into play opposition between Protestants and Catholics as "supporters" or "opponents" of the revival. And third, the national system in Belfast more closely approximated to a *de facto* denominational system than in most places. So not only was there very little of the practical substance of clerical accommodation to lean upon in defence of national education, but also to cherish that which there was, ministers who favoured national education would have to have explicitly opposed the "conversionist" and "confrontationist" tendencies in their own Church, if they hoped to secure Catholic support. Instead the 'conversionist' tendency in the revival, far from being repudiated, continued to linger amongst the forces which supported "united education". Though many of the old style Whigs opposed the revival as a fraud—and the *Northern Whig* itself attacked its proselytizing manifestations[115]—the decline of the Old Whigs was to leave Belfast liberalism in rather different hands. A new kind of liberalism arose which distinguished between "enlightened" Catholics and papists. The defence of "united education" in opposition to the hierarchy and papists was made to stand upon a supposed common interest of "enlightened" Catholics and Protestant "Liberals". This concept of the "enlightened" Catholic in fact served to obscure the reality of the northern Catholic experience and to allow these

Liberals to take up a position barely less anti-Catholic than those of the Conservatives.

The *Banner of Ulster's* advice to the new Palmerston administration on taking office illustrates how far this tendency had gone.

"We are not of course, to be understood as meaning that Romanists, merely because they are such, should not, in any way be patronized by the new Administration, for we must strongly deprecate all such narrow and foolish sentiments, but we contend that only those members of the Church of Rome should be encouraged by the State who are known to be men of independent character and of Liberal sympathies. We protest against Ultraism in all its forms; and we desire to see as the rulers of this country neither the abetters of Ribbonism nor the organizers of Orange Lodges."[116]

Such "Liberalism's" test of "enlightenment" in Catholics was whether they were prepared to oppose the hierarchy on the education question. In the light of what we have seen of the impact of the revival, and the common front of opposition to Catholic clerical claims from Protestant Liberals and "No Popery" men alike, this was a very tall order indeed. We shall see later that even Catholics who did not share the hierarchy's enthusiasm for denominational education were very loath to allow themselves to be paraded as "intelligent Catholics" as the *Northern Whig* was later to describe them. The education question allowed religious subjectivities with all their national undertows free vent.

The linkage that developed between Belfast liberalism and the unself-critical defence of "united education" was to be one of its biggest liabilities. Its social and economic conservatism expressed the interests of big property of Belfast in a manner not easily distinguishable from that of its Conservative counterpart. And when this was taken together with the reluctance of the Whig leaders in Belfast to punish their Tory counterparts for their doings on the corporation, the gap between the Catholics and the Whigs grew wider. After the riots of 1864, the *Observer* wrote: "Even the Protestant Liberals in Belfast are, with, of course, many praiseworthy exceptions, liberal only in a degree. They too are leavened with the old Spirit of Ascendancy. They are disposed to be kind to Catholics, so long as Catholics are dependent—they would shield them, at the hazard of their lives, from Orange fury—they would patronize and protect them to the end of time. But the moment a Catholic asserts his equality . . . that moment he is treated as an ingrate or an enemy. Should he aspire to honours, he is regarded as insolent; should he amass wealth, he is looked upon with jealousy and suspicion."[117]

9. Violence and the Law

By the 1850s it seemed possible that relationships between Protestants and Catholics in the North of Ireland could be normalised. Now that the scale of migrancy was so great and the Irish and British labour markets were being unified, employers had no reason whatever to care about the sectarian colour of their labour forces. The law no longer recognized the different religions as having different civic statuses. Throughout much of the North the Drummond system of law and order was more or less intact, despite the interlude in 1848 when the government had looked to the Orangemen for support against Young Ireland. So why were sectarian confrontations able to regenerate themselves from the late 1850s and in the 1860s? At all levels of Protestant society there were contributions to the revival of vigilantism—Orange deterrence of Catholics—once weaknesses appeared in the Drummond system. In the 1860s, plebeian opposition to the spread of Catholic institutions in inner Ulster, fear of Fenianism in mid-Ulster, and Conservative mobilization of Orangemen to oppose Catholic electoral challenge in Monaghan all came together to restore deterrence relationships.

In Belfast the system of law and order had been less affected by the Drummond reforms than elsewhere. A large part of this chapter explores law and order in Belfast before 1868. In the last chapter I looked at how the Belfast Whigs went into decline and lost the ability to lead their Catholic followers in the 1850s. Their class interests overrode their earlier interest in overthrowing the pan-Protestant corporation. And in the field of educational policy the Presbyterian and Catholic interests began to collide. In this chapter I want to look at how their commitment to normal law fared. I shall argue that in the end this was the single most important distinguishing feature of the northern Liberals. This was what kept them at a distance from pan-Protestant notions of deterring Catholics. When Catholic clergy became less able than they once had been to prevent Catholics from responding to Orangeism, adhesion to the idea of normal law became the hallmark of committed liberalism. However, this made the anchorage of liberalism dependent on the actions of stipendiary magistrates and the constabulary. What will become clear is that once violence became more reciprocal or less one sided, people were in danger of finding their identity determined by those whose violence they feared most. Once this point was reached and other dimensions of difference reinforced, we can speak of national conflict pure and simple.

The major riots in Belfast in 1857, 1864 and 1872—and most of the lesser ones—either began in or were centred upon west Belfast, as shown in the map. Most of the district shown on the map was built between 1845 and 1870, and the grey area is that built up by about 1868. This western sector of the city contained mills and foundries. By the end of the riots of 1872, it was fairly strongly segregated. The Catholic district started with the old trading and market district about Smithfield and Millfield, and then took in a space bounded in the east by Durham Street, its northern boundary running along the lower end of the streets connecting the Shankill Road and Falls Road, and its southern boundary along Albert Street, down from there in a south-westerly direction. The 1872 riots removed the Protestant presence from the Leeson Street district which had previously constituted part of the circle around the Catholic area, and thereby left it with an "open" end. The 1872 riots also saw the displacement of Catholics from the newer parts of the Shankill and from the old mixed districts on the north side of Peter's Hill.

In 1850 there was fairly little development to the west of Durham Street and Townsend Street, and the first embryonic residentially segregated districts appeared in the Pound (Catholic) to the north of Albert Street, and the district from there southwards commonly described as Sandy Row (Protestant), but including the area up to Albert Street which was north of the railway track, the boundary of Sandy Row proper. The extension of these districts settled large numbers of recent immigrants from the countryside during and after the Famine. The mills employed women as the greater part of their labour force, and though men filled the posts of overseers, loom-tenters, mechanics, etc., male employment was more diversified—foundry work, construction work, porters and railwaymen, shoemakers, and bakers, to mention the numerically dominant trades,[1] and most of the retail trade, such as grocery or spirit dealers. In this way the women mill workers were wives, daughters and mothers of many involved in other areas of economic activity, and any crisis which touched the mills had a universal bearing on the districts.

In the borough as a whole in 1871, out of a total of 31 per cent of the occupied male labour force, Catholics made up about 40 per cent of the general and factory labourers—the two residual census categories—and in a selection of skilled trades averaged around 20–25 per cent.[2] It is probably a tolerable assumption that, for the period we are dealing with before the growth of shipbuilding as a major industry, the occupational differentiation between Sandy Row and the Pound was not great. The riots commission reports described them as similar, but reckoned that labourers were more numerous in the Pound.[3] Various writers dealing with a somewhat later period have spoken of the existence of two sectarian classes of Orange/Protestant shipyard workers and Ribbon/Catholic navvies.[4] We are bound to admit to a suspicion as to whether this judgment gives a true picture of the lack of occupational differentiation of Catholic and Protestant labour as a whole. Indeed it will be part of our argument that the terms "ship carpenter" and "navvy" are employed to describe large gatherings of Protestant and Catholic workers arrayed for combat, sometimes with little regard to their actual occupations. Thus, for example, the parish priest of Downpatrick in 1866 wrote in some anxiety to the magistrates of that town about the impending descent of 5,000 ship carpenters at a time when, on the widest definition of the terms, there were barely two-thirds of that number in the whole of Belfast;[5] and after carrying reports of the combative activities of "ship carpenters" during the 1872 riots, the Catholic newspaper, the *Examiner*, wrote in 1873 that after careful investigation they had found that the ship carpenters were not involved at all![6] The reason for invoking the intervention of these two "sectarian classes" has to do with the fact that the shipyard and the navvy construction gangs expressed in their most polar forms the differences that did exist.

The shipyards which grew rapidly in the 1860s were large employers of skilled craft labour. In the early stages some were drawn over from the Clyde, and here more than in most trades workplace organizations were in a position to regulate entry. In 1864 it transpired that the Catholics in Harland's were mostly painters, and that McLaine's yard contained no Catholics at all.[7] Of all the separately listed trades in the 1871 census the general category "shipwrights" (which probably included many workers in smaller wooden shipbuilding) contained merely 9½ per cent Catholics, a ratio so low as to be bettered only by the small employer, the Gas Works, at 4½ per cent Catholics.[8] Living for the most part (before the coming of the tramways) in the north-east (Dock ward) area of the town or on the Down side of the river,[9] the shipyard workers lived at some distance from the scenes of the earlier riots.

The navvy gangs and ribbonism were tied together in the popular mind. The southern frontier areas of Ulster had functioned by migrant labour and reclamation/smallholding. In 1852 Ribbonmen had been resisting consolidation of holdings and securing rent reductions by agrarian violence. As a tightly organized system it had been strengthened by the public works, railroad construction work and some of the harbour works during the Famine. Stipendiary magistrates described how the Ribbon system provided passes for members migrating to distant places to work.[10] After the great "No Popery" riots at Stockport in 1852, the Belfast *Vindicator* commented, "instead of teaching Irish residents in England the inutility of combination [these riots] will press upon them its essential necessity".[11] Ribbonism—as a form of the collective rather than individual migrant experience—was an expression of determined strength. Sam Tracy, the resident magistrate, said that the priests had it "nearly snuffed out" in 1857.[12] Indeed in the context of Belfast the term "Ribbonman" meant different things in the minds of different people. Thus landlords of houses in Stanley Street (the northern edge of Sandy Row, more or less on the border) received anonymous notices to remove "Ribbonmen" from their houses shortly before the riots of 1857.[13] And George S. Hill, one-time sub-inspector of the constabulary, told of people being beaten up for refusing to join the Ribbon society. He described its primary object as the "extermination of heretics",[14] and how it had spread locally with the building of the Ulster Canal. Obviously its presence in a district tended to undermine clerical discipline. But in an area like south Armagh which was basically Catholic territory, ribbonism was in conflict not with Orangeism but with landlords who it successfully prevented from consolidating holdings.[15] In Belfast a priest might be able to discountenance violence with the argument, "Keep the peace and let the law take care of the Orangemen"; but in south Armagh it was far more difficult because violence was successfully used for a quite different purpose.[16] The point to be made is that whereas in the general context of the North clerical accommodation with the magistracy and constabulary made good common sense, it did so only when the law could be brought to bear against a sectarian opponent and the Catholics themselves gave the law no opposition.

In situations of sectarian violence or potential for it, one of the triggers for alarm is the appearance of unknown quantities, unknown in the sense that they are external to the immediately affected localities. Such people, if they really are external, have little to lose by confrontation, and the risks they bring with them are multiplied. To describe a combative body as "ship carpenters" or "navvies" was to draw attention simultaneously to the most pronounced form of sectarian occupational differentiation in the city and to the risks that such freebooters presented away from their home patch. The mere appearance of navvy gangs was a frequent cause of alarm. Thus in 1868 William Johnston of Ballykilbeg uttered a warning to the navvies on the Downpatrick and Newcastle railway to "behave themselves in a Protestant district". He expected that the peaceable Catholics of the district would disown "disturbers of the peace".[17]

Let us now turn our attention to the law in west Belfast in this period. The Police Committee of the Corporation was in charge of the selection of members of the town police force. In 1857 it transpired that of 160 members, about seven were Catholics.[18] Apart from some of the sillier explanations given for this (such as that Protestants tended to be taller; and there was a minimum height qualification),[19] the more plausible one was that the police tended to be sons of local farmers "who are generally Protestants in this neighbourhood".[20] The latter statement was generally true, but not only were the particular parishes from which large numbers of the force came, ones with significant Catholic minorities (adjoining Lough Neagh, near Glenavy),[21] it also turned out that most of the force had been labourers, not farmers. It was effectively established that members of the town force from these areas attended an Orange parade on 12 July that year.[22] Some of them lived in the Sandy Row district and were decidedly reluctant to take any action against or take lists of names of those engaged in Orange processions or disorders.[23] Various Protestant Liberals considered them a partisan force and argued that this had been shown up in the way they treated rival mobs during the 1857 election.[24] In the light of what follows it is well to notice that Thomas Lindsay, the Chief Constable of the local police, considered that Orange processions were calculated to offend Catholics,[25] and not only was he not an Orangeman himself, but he clearly had difficulties keeping Mr Hyde, the Conservative Cromac ward secretary, away from the office. He admits it is "very likely" he complained about Hyde having too much to do with appointments.[26]

The police attitudes toward Orange manifestations seem to have ranged between regarding them as a nuisance that needed curbing on account of irritation to Catholics, and regarding them as a legitimate activity by their own neighbours. But though the higher officers tended toward the first position, the behaviour of the councillors who were their employers legitimized the second. As regards the Catholics, the main local presence in the Pound area was Hugh Heany, one of the few Catholics in the force. In years prior to the 1857 riots, two members of the force had been convicted of assault,[27] another of shouting "To hell with the Pope" when drunk in the police station,[28] and a Catholic member of the Irish Constabulary declared that two or three years ago (i.e. about 1854) he had seen the local police going down Cullingtree Road (in the

Pound) "beating all before them".[29] This may not add up to what the editor of the (Catholic) *Ulsterman* claimed: "I may mention with regard to these policemen that it is a common occurrence for them to beat Catholics".[30] However the riot commission reports of the pre-July 1857 period show tacit police tolerance of Orange activity, combined with a determination to keep Catholics in their own area and to move against anything that looked like Catholic self-organization (hence their ejection of Catholics from the 1857 election nomination meeting).

The second arm of the law was the Irish Constabulary stationed in Belfast, augmented during disturbances and eventually supplemented by the military. In Ballymacarrett (Down side of the river) these were the only police presence. In general, however, wherever the town police operated, this body rather than the constabulary had the "duty of appraising where it was necessary to act ".[31] In other words, how the constabulary was deployed was determined by the town police definition of a situation rather than its own. The magistracy included a cross-section of Belfast's elite, presided over by the resident magistrates—William Tracy in 1857, and Messrs Orme and O'Donnell in 1864. Only in 1865 was the town police force abolished and the Irish Constabulary made directly responsible for policing the city.

In the years preceding 1857, efforts had been made to exclude Catholics from work in the mills below Boyne Bridge (in Sandy Row proper). The effort appears to have been orchestrated from outside rather than inside the mills, and in some cases it is quite clear that it lacked even implicit employers' sanction. The manager of Grimshaw's mill in Sandy Row was himself a Catholic,[32] but the mill of John Hinds was commonly known as the "Orange Cage",[33] and here managerial opposition to expulsionist tendencies was weaker or non-existent. On 12 July a Catholic funeral from a house in the district was treated to mild irritation from young boys but nothing worse.[34] Catholics who lived in the area said they had not been disturbed or annoyed by neighbours,[35] and a significant number worked in local mills. In the early phases of the rioting in 1857 it is evident that the scale of practical anti-Catholic activity within Sandy Row proper (as distinct from its northern extension facing the

Pound) was low. As a general rule it is safe to say that the expulsionist pressures in this district did not set in until the late stages when tensions generated north of the railway track had been generalized by the street preaching crisis in late August/early September.

The focal point of the earlier troubles was the boundary between the two districts on Albert Crescent. Durham Street itself had "once" been part of Sandy Row, and just off Durham Street stood the Christ Church. Rev. Dr Thomas Drew had been in charge of the working-class Anglican Protestant congregation of the district from 1833. From the time when the elite began to distance itself from the Orange Order, Drew's activities received a declining amount of local patronage. From 1852 he had been in the habit of publicizing sermons on the errors of the Church of Rome to which Catholics were "invited",[36] and he became involved in a controversy about how many Catholics had been converted to Protestantism in Connaught during the Famine.[37] In 1854 he established the Christ Church Protestant Association, which attracted membership of some of the remaining smaller Orange gentry in the countryside (W. J. Gwynn of Antrim, and his son-in-law William Johnston of Ballykilbeg), and the formal adhesion of Richard Davidson, one of the MPs for Belfast.[38] Its political objectives included the repeal of the 1829 Catholic Emancipation Act and the enforcement of all the existing anti-papal laws.[39] As the area to its immediate north and west became increasingly Catholic districts, the Christ Church became a symbol of the Protestant presence on Durham Street. Any Orange procession to it would involve making a presence felt within close proximity to a Catholic district.

One of the growing class of Belfast Catholic businessmen was William Watson, a house owner in the newly expanding areas of west Belfast. In 1855 he had completed about 75 houses on the north side of Albert Crescent and in the side streets from here into the Pound. On the Crescent itself he had hoped to secure "respectable tenants", and for about a year they remained unoccupied. Eventually he secured them, and seventeen of the twenty were Protestants. He was pleased by this as he reckoned that with Protestants on the Pound side of Albert Crescent it would help to prevent the periodic riots in

16. West Belfast, 1864-72, naming streets and ward boundaries mentioned in text

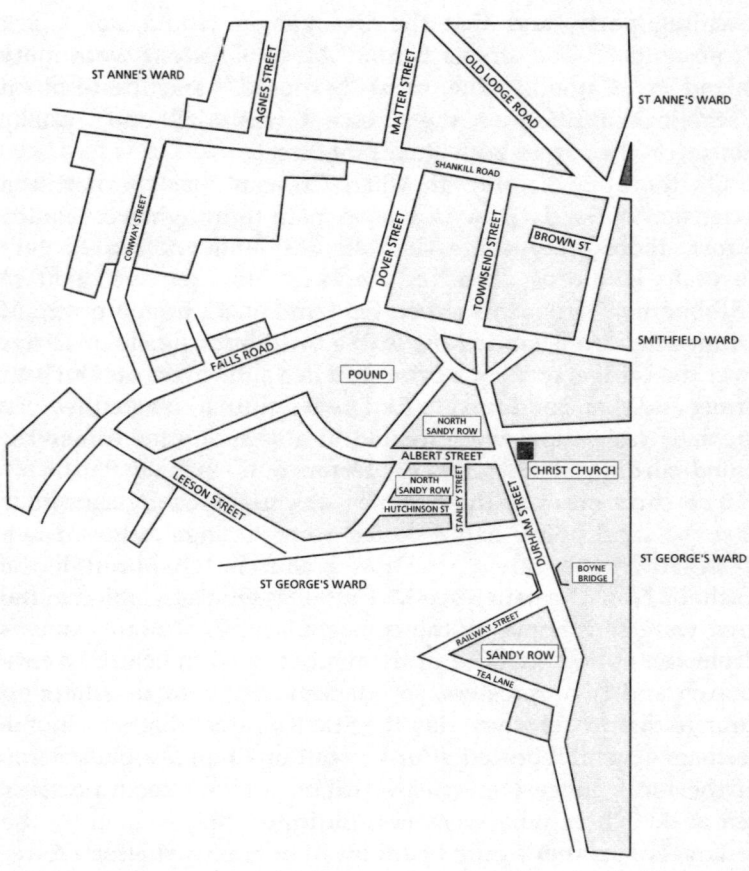

that border street. His testimony as to the reasons why he thought so is of some value, not because he was a Catholic but because he invested £9,000 on the strength of the opinion. "I was under the impression that the Catholics were never the assailing party, and that the Orangemen would not attack Protestants."[40] The streets behind Albert Crescent were more mixed or Catholic. The most "exposed" and best-known Catholic institution on the Crescent was McIlhone's public house, on the corner with Quadrant Street.

On the opposite side of Albert Crescent was the northern extension of Sandy Row in whose main thoroughfare, Stanley Street, there were some Catholic residents. Before 12 July several landlords received notices to remove certain "Ribbonmen" from this street. On Sunday, 12 July, a group of Orangemen from Sandy Row walked without banners or sashes over the bridge, making a brief stop in a side-street off Durham Street and then continued to Dr Drew's church, where they put on their sashes and were treated to a sermon of a somewhat blood-curdling character on the terrors of the papacy.[41]

The early onset of the troubles was triggered by a rumour that the local police had escorted some Orange lodges down from Townsend Street to Drew's church (i.e. through the Catholic New Durham Street).[42] Catholics who assembled in the area were sent home by the constabulary. That night various Protestants were attacked in the district to the north of Drew's church and two ministers, so attacked, fled into an adjoining Orange district. The next day the Stanley Street district was the scene of several repeated efforts to put up Orange arches: some of the local police were clearly dilatory about securing their removal. Others who were not, indicated that frequently the removal of an arch would be followed by repeated efforts to re-erect them. It is worth noticing that some Protestant residents helped the police to remove the arches.[43] The issue so far then can be reduced in its essentials to this. It appeared that a more than usually determined effort was being made to celebrate the "Twelfth", and that the effort was being conducted at the very edge of the Orange district. The local police were regarded—not altogether accurately—as aiding and abetting this effort. A knot of Catholics responded to this by attacking various Protestants seen in the district, through which the police were supposed to have escorted the Orangemen. But at this stage the levels of involvement in aggravation were very low. We are still at this stage speaking of the work of quite small groups, and certainly not of "representative" bodies.

On the evening of Monday, 13th, rival chanting mobs appeared at McIlhone's corner. The town police kept the Pound people back. As Chief Constable Green put it, the "people still had some fear".[44] Various clashes took place that night and in successive nights in the more mixed district along the south side of the Falls Road beyond the central area of the Pound (Peel, Lemon and Mary streets). On Tuesday, as the mills were emptying, returning mill girls crossing the north Sandy Row and Pound districts were harassed by local residents. And in the evening, when another mob assembly occurred at McIlhone's corner, some town police who were attempting to put Catholics back in their houses were attacked and had to take refuge in a house. It was on this occasion that the town police found that they could no longer go into the Pound district.[45] There is some conflict of evidence as to precisely who started the wreckings in the upper Falls district on that Tuesday night (Lemon and Mary streets), but the constabulary arrived and, after shots had been fired at them, did a house search of Catholic Peel Street.[46] On that night the first full-scale attack was made by about fifty people on Albert Crescent (Watson's houses), and a mob of about twelve to eighteen people started putting Catholics out of Stanley Street.[47] It is claimed that from about this time, a sniper began shooting from an empty house in the north Sandy Row into the Albert Crescent district, particularly in the direction of McIlhone's pub, and that this sniping continued for most of the week.[48]

So far as can be gathered at this stage, the local police regarded Albert Crescent as the street where the "border" began. Assemblies of Protestants opposite McIlhone's corner seem to have been "tolerated". But the strategies of different mobs were very different. The Catholics considered that the town police were in effect legitimizing triumphal displays in north Sandy Row, turning a blind eye to what was going on inside it, and concentrating their efforts on keeping the Pound controlled.

The collision with the town police brought the constabulary to their district and as a result of the disturbances in the lower Falls mixed district, searching began. In short, the Catholics were in collision with the law.

The Protestant mobs' activities were different. They exploited the collisions between the Catholics and the law to inflict damage on the southern edge of the Pound, and then disappeared back into their own districts. The size of Protestant mob involvement grew during the week as the Catholics got the upper hand in the upper Falls district. It doesn't appear that any legal opposition was put up to the displacement of Catholics from Stanley Street, nor does it appear that the sniper's concealed hideout was searched for. This notwithstanding, there were searches carried out by the constabulary and magistrates in Cullingtree Road in the middle of the Pound.

After a day of firing across the wasteland between the two districts on Friday, two boys were shot by a sniper from Stanley Street on Saturday, 18 July, and an argument occurred between the town police and the Pound inhabitants at McIlhone's corner.[49] The police chased them up the street and were then repulsed. After they departed a very large mob of about four or five hundred people appeared and attacked the Watson houses. A small group of constabulary stood by, its head constable angry at not being sent forward to do something about the attack,[50] and when the cavalry arrived, the attacking mob dispersed. The constabulary was then sent in with the cavalry to put the Pound people indoors. On Sunday the military saturated the area, and at Mass Mr Watson was criticized by the Catholics for not having provided weapons. He taxed his powers of persuasion to ensure that they did not go and attack Stanley Street.[51] He made a treaty with the magistrates whereby he agreed to quieten the Pound district and left them to go and quieten down Sandy Row.

The basic relationships between the law and the sectarian working-class communities can be summarized as follows. The town police had mixed feelings about the illegality of Orange processions and displays. In strictly Protestant districts like Sandy Row proper where some of them lived, they did not see the harm in such activities. In areas near the "borders" they were regarded as a nuisance and efforts were made to curb them. But they did not press these efforts beyond the point where they felt confident they could rely upon their local legitimacy in Protestant districts to do so. Orange celebration was therefore a "nuisance" but not, as it is to the Catholics, a demonstration of hostile intent. When the rumours spread that the police had actually abetted these demonstrations—whose sinister form is suggested by preparations evidently being made in Stanley Street—Catholic reprisals against strictly innocent parties, like the two non-controversialist preachers attacked in the Barrack Street district, whipped up some Protestant and police anger. These actions were viewed by the law as "representative" of Catholics as a whole and their behaviour towards Catholics reflected this. In the past tranquillity had consisted of Catholics keeping quiet and the police preventing Protestants from engaging in heavily provocative forms of display. But when tranquillity was broken by provocative actions, these were regarded only as irritation, while Catholic reprisals were regarded as threats and brought down the full weight of the law. Then as the conflict between the law and the Catholics intensified, the Protestant expulsionists exploited the spaces so created, and with the devastating consequences demonstrated on Saturday, the 18th. The mob attack on the southern edge of the Pound was not checked by the law, which arrived on the scene only in time to prevent the possibility of Catholic reprisals.

Normal law can only appear to operate in situations of this kind so long as the threatened cycle of aggression is bottled up and not allowed to unleash itself. So long as Catholics ignored the signs given off by some Orangemen that Orangeism was a means of demonstrating superiority over Catholics, it was possible to keep up the charade that it was merely a "tradition". By no means everyone who supported Orangeism—not, for example, the 12 July attenders at Drew's church—can have approved of expulsionism. Some regarded Orange displays as a mere holiday, others as celebrations of great deeds of past history, and perhaps only a few as a reminder to the Catholics about who is "on top" in an area. So long as the Catholics knew the likely consequences of interfering with these displays, they acquiesced in them as an annual event to which it was better not to pay any attention. The priests were able to discountenance any kind of response. And so the different motives of the marchers could remain uncertain. But the moment anything happened that actually broke the routine of tranquillity, it quickly multiplied. When the local police at the 1857 election made it their job to remove Catholics from the hall during the nomination proceedings, leaving it to the largely Orange supporters of the Conservative candidates, it was difficult not to be provoked. And it took only a few Catholics to act, to bring out the worst in the Protestant counter-action. An exchange between the Orange legal counsel and the editor of the *Ulsterman* at the riots inquiry sums up the point very well. Referring to the period before the *Ulsterman* started publication, Purcell asks dryly:

"At that time, your unfortunate co-religionists were not enlightened as to the state of oppression and bondage they were placed in this country?"

John McLaughlin, the editor, replied: "Perhaps not as efficiently".[52]

This meant that only when the Catholics began to respond to aggravation with aggravation did it become clear how dangerous and nasty things actually were.

When it became impossible to contain Catholic reaction as a whole—for that is what was necessary to ensure tranquillity—any manifestation of hostilities quickly acquired a representative character. That is to say, a reprisal could be delivered to any member of the other side defined only by shared religion with the party that committed the aggression. In such circumstances the difference between aggression, reprisal and self-defence was speedily dissolved, both objectively and subjectively. No single act was an isolated act, and the presumption of normal criminal law—that all criminal acts have a definable beginning and end—was inoperable. Or, to be more precise, it could only be operated by ignoring realities.

The rioting of July 1857 started a breakdown of existing methods of control, of whose full implications many Protestants had been unaware. The anger against things Orange, anti-Catholic etc. now found a target. Since the early 1850s the (Anglican) Belfast Parochial Mission had been operating open-air preaching on Sundays. The body itself was very far from being an anti-Catholic organization, containing on its board, for example, John F. Ferguson and Adam Duffin. On 12 July 1857 the preaching was done as usual by Presbyterian ministers. But after the rioting of the week that followed, the Anglicans cancelled their service for 19 July. The temperature had been raised by the suggestion that it would be given by Rev. William McIlwaine who was in the practice of delivering lectures on "Popery". The magistrates also asked them to call it off on 26 July and 2 August when large crowds assembled. They eventually started on 9 August and carried on until 23 August when, after a slight disturbance, the Bishop thought it better to call it off. On 29 August the *Northern Whig* carried a report that Dr Drew was to preach the next day, and though the report was fake, a really riotous assembly gathered.[54]

The Anglicans having called off street preaching on account of anticipated violence, Rev. Hugh Hanna decided that he would oppose this "surrender" of the right to preach the Gospel in the face of anticipated violence. The issue had become a confrontation between the "right to preach the Gospel" and the insult to Catholics involved in "allowing Protestant firebrands to preach". Hanna moved the proposed site of his preaching a few blocs further northwards from the regular site at the Customs House, to just outside the harbour yard. Whether he prepared them or not, there lay hidden within the yard some fifty "ship carpenters", armed with heavy wooden objects and, suffice it to say, that when a party of stone-throwing opposition arrived to disrupt the meeting, these people appeared and a battle ensued.[55] The question of whether the "Gospel" could or should be preached in Belfast was to be decided by force.

In the aftermath of this collision the scale of expulsionism in west Belfast escalated. Catholic anger at the proceedings of 18 July and the subsequent shooting of a mill girl in early August crystallized in the formation of a Gun club,[56] and the incapacity of erstwhile Catholic leaders to keep control became clear as McLaughlin acquired the lead over the opposition to street preaching. Expulsionism now spread to Sandy Row proper, and attacks were made by larger mobs on mill girls crossing the Boyne bridge to work.[57] On the night of 10 September, a bugler woke up the inhabitants of Sandy Row with a warning that the "rebels were coming down the Blackstaff", and calling on everyone with a weapon to get up and be prepared.[58]

It is clear that up to this stage there were few on either side who took part in expulsionist violence. But that did not mean that few were affected, or that everyone was affected in the same way. We must now look at the coercive effect of expulsionist violence upon those who were not part of it. In 1857, but decreasingly in later riots, there was an important distinction between Catholic and Protestant expulsionism. In general, expulsionist gangs in Protestant districts went for any Catholic at all, or families in which one partner was a Catholic. By contrast, the Protestants who were expelled from Catholic areas tended to be those upon whom Catholics could not rely to support them in their collisions with the law (e.g. people who wouldn't let rioters flee through their houses).[59] It was therefore possible for Protestants to "assimilate" to Catholic society by taking the side of the Catholics against the town police and later the cavalry. This is not to say that in streets (such as Lemon and Mary streets) where conflict occurred as to who the street "belonged" to, or in the Barrack Street area where Protestants were attacked at the early stages of the riots, that they were only attacked because they "supported" the Protestant side. What is being said is that there were some situations where not all Protestants were likely targets for eviction from Catholic districts.

The evidence given by expellees from Protestant districts indicates that neighbours were almost invariably opposed to expulsions which targeted all identifiable Catholics. We can start with George McMullan who refused to put out a lodger, Biddy Burke, a Catholic millworker, though a mob threatened to bring his house down. He went to the police to tell them, and it seems that Biddy Burke eventually left because, despite George McMullen's protection, there was no way she could feel safe.[60] In Combermere Street there were three families with at least one Catholic member. When a mob appeared in the street, a Protestant neighbour told the mob that there were no Catholics in the street. The mob summoned out a second time by the bugler returned later, two hundred strong. A couple of town police stood by the doorway of one of the families and told the mob that they respected the Grants, and that if anyone got leave to live there, they would see it was the Grants. But all three families left. One stayed with a Protestant neighbour, who was threatened, so they moved on.⁶¹ Often Protestant neighbours, in friendship, would warn Catholics of risks and impending threats. A case is recounted of one Protestant who got his house wrecked for refusing to join a mob,⁶² and another of a man who came and repaired a wrecked Catholic house for nothing.⁶³

It takes few people to start an expulsionist crisis in this situation, and any disapproval their efforts meet from their neighbours (e.g. the Protestants in Stanley Street who helped the police to get down the arches) loses its effect once their "own" expulsionists can point to the work of the ones on the other side. The mobs expand as their reprisal or defensive functions become more plausible. To make a Catholic feel safe enough to want to stay in a Protestant area, it is not enough that some Protestant should stand up for their right to do so—as George McMullan and a few morally heroic individuals did. It does not make it safe to stay just because one knows that most of the neighbours don't want you to have to go. You have to feel secure and that is not possible when expulsionist mobs can choose their own time to attack. It takes few such people to make it quite unsafe for Catholics to remain, so long as the police cannot put them out of action. Having failed to stamp out the cancer when it was small (and, it must be added, when it did not look very threatening except to a Catholic targeted by it), the police who wanted to stand up for the Grants found themselves facing a mob that could not be criminalized. Practically speaking, the good will and even moral heroism of some Protestants could not add up to a security for Catholics against the malignancy abounding. Even less could it do so once some Catholics became involved in aggression and these expulsionists could present themselves as "defenders".

All this needs to be said to emphasise how much truth there is in the traditional charge that preachers of bigotry have an important role in the conflict. If the only educated man in the district preaches that ribbonism is merely the military wing of a popish conspiracy orchestrated by priests—and there are many people about who through fear, malice or bad experience believe this—it takes considerable courage to contradict him. It is one thing to joke about these malignant influences, in order to keep some distance from them, but a wholly different matter to confront them. It seems that in 1857 people who did such things were not so intimidated as they subsequently became. Or putting the point in another way, the redeeming figures who probably appear in all such circumstances were actually recorded in 1857.

And what was the Catholic conclusion from such experiences? The good will of their Protestant neighbours, real though it was, could not enable them to live in a Protestant area. The objective reality was that the law could not protect them from expulsionist violence, so they sought security amongst their own people. And those who were on the receiving end of attacks in the Catholic ghettos experienced Protestant society only in its most malignant form—the force used against them by expulsionist mobs and absence of security provided by the force of the law. The power of expulsionist forces grew dramatically between the July and September riots. The anti-Catholic public ethos of the society and the continuity of these irritations meant that when the established Catholic leaders did lose control, the forces that took over were full of hurt, vengeance, and certainly not thinking straight. They were locked into rivalry with the supposed right of a man to preach about the evils of popery on a public platform.

But the challenge of McLaughlin and the stone-throwing assailants of Hanna was more than just an attack on Hanna. It was a blind rivalry with him. Hanna was showing that he could say who could preach in the streets, when and where. So would they. It was a very volatile assertion of "rights" by people in a rage—a rage against everything that defined Catholic alienation from the society. But once McLaughlin got into rivalry with Hanna, he became a threat like Hanna. If McLaughlin could shut Hanna up, who would he shut up next? The awkwardness of these questions shows in Rev. James Speers' thoughts on street preaching. He was a non-controversial Presbyterian preacher who stopped street preaching when the trouble began. To begin with he thought the cessation was a temporary expedient; later he sadly reckoned otherwise.

"I do but consider it just to say, that while Roman Catholics attended the open air sermons, they did so with order and attention, and I do not think they would have interrupted the sermons, if they had been left to themselves."[64]

Speers' view of the situation had at this stage become focused on McLaughlin. The Catholic mob's action in attacking Hanna's "preaching" obscured very real differences of opinion amongst Protestants. For example, Rev. Speers almost certainly felt differently about Hanna's action than, say, Thomas Ward, the master of the lodge which went to the Drew church on 12 July 1857. "Catholics are always the promoters of every disturbance, and they are against Protestants of every denomination", said Ward.[65]

Speers recognized in a way that Ward certainly did not, that Catholics were irritated. His own action showed consideration for their feeling as far as he understood them. But once Catholic anger broke both Speers and Ward felt threatened by it. McLaughlin's action had made Speers think more as Hanna had pretended to think and it corroded the differences between Speers and Ward. Rivalry erases differences. The identity of each of us in this society is shaped by the quarter from which anger and violence feels most threatening to us. And so because Protestant society knew about only one kind of peace—where Catholics kept quiet and were not led by people like McLaughlin—despite the perorations of Hanna and the perambulations of Ward, there was in the end a Protestant consensus. So long as Catholics were not led and were quiet, there would be no trouble. The idea that they could be "led" so easily found expression in many ways. Capt. Thomas Verner, for example, said, "John Rea is the source of all the disgrace for destroying Roman Catholic confidence in the police."[66] The reasons why men like Rea and McLaughlin were propelled into leadership positions by the Catholics was unintelligible to those who understood nothing of the provocation of being always on the receiving end of the law.

But those who had some understanding of what the Catholics had to endure would hardly go to the point of supporting Catholic reprisal. Even as virulent an anti-papist as Hugh Hanna was acknowledged by sections of respectable and Liberal public opinion as having a right to preach, however much they disliked his actual exercise of that right. If they had to chose between Hanna and McLaughlin, they would choose Hanna. In future Hanna and his successors would exert themselves to create situations where people had to make such choices.

In 1857 there were still some gaps in the picture of polarization. Precisely because the Catholics did not go far into reprisalism, there were a significant number of Liberal Protestants who endorsed most of the things the Catholics had to say about the police. Some had seen how their Catholic supporters had been treated by the town police at the election. In subsequent riots the differences between Catholic and Protestant violence were increasingly erased, and instead of supporting Catholics as victims, more and more Protestants found themselves facing choices between their "devil" and "ours", as Rev. Speers did over Hanna and McLaughlin. In 1864 the line taken by the Liberal leaders shifted markedly. Thus William Mullan, mentioned earlier as a Whig ally of the Conservatives, declared that the town police enjoyed the confidence of property owners, but were "misrepresented",[67] whereas the leader of the mainline pro-compromise Whigs, William Dunville, thought it was a "disadvantage" that they were exclusive because some "consider" them unsatisfactory.[68] He added that he would like politics taken out of local affairs. But in contrast, Bernard Hughes, the Catholic baker, stated that in riots the town police strategy was to push the Catholics back into their own areas and let the Protestants move in behind them.[69] In the last chapter we saw how the Whigs and the Catholics parted company over the Chancery suit and the education questions. Here we see how the different experiences of fear and violence shape identity most deeply.

Between 1857 and 1864 Belfast experienced a very considerable expansion. The cotton famine, beginning in 1861, destroyed the livelihood of a mass of weavers and embroiderers in north Down (of whom we shall hear more in connection with Orangeism in Lisburn in 1863), and applied a massive stimulus to the construction of linen factories. In August 1864 a memorial was erected to Daniel O'Connell in Dublin. The *Ulster Observer*, the new Catholic newspaper in the North, declared, on the occasion of many Belfast Catholics going to the opening ceremony:

"Nowhere have the results of his labours been so conspicuously revealed as in Ulster. Not a day passes over us that we do not behold—even in the influences engaged in undoing his work—the evidence of the good that he accomplished. They who still have to do battle with intolerance which no longer dares openly to assert its usurptions can form some idea of the monster which he had to confront and which he did not fail to subdue."[70]

The *Newsletter* fulminated about this excursion, and thought it outrageous that it should be permitted when Orange processions were illegal. On the return of the excursionists an effigy of Daniel O'Connell was hung over the railway bridge by Protestants and set on fire; it was subsequently carried by a mock funeral procession to the Friars Bush (Stranmillis Road) Catholic cemetery, which was much abused when the caretaker refused them entrance.[71] The Liberal papers, the *Whig* and the *Banner of Ulster*, were outright in their condemnation of the *Newsletter*'s remarks and the mock funeral of O'Connell, and equally strong in defending the rights of the Catholics to go to the Dublin celebration.[72] In the early stages of the developing riots, Protestants attacked the Pound and town policemen arrested Catholics who were engaged in fighting back.[73] Only after a few days did the augmented constabulary move in and begin a policy of "impartial" arrests. Later in the week, a surprise attack was launched on the Bankmore penitentiary, and attacks were started on Catholic mill workers on Boyne bridge. So obviously were the Protestant attacks unprovoked that even the *Banner of Ulster* was moved to remark that one might expect Catholic retaliation.[74]

The retaliation when it came was fairly horrific. A group of "navvies" appeared at St Malachy's chapel volunteering to defend it, but were sent away by the priests. They went to Brown Street national school during school hours and set about wrecking it with the children inside, and were only stopped by workers from the nearby Soho foundry.[75] Thereafter they were pursued about the town, having a pitched battle in Albert Crescent, and driven into the Pound by the constabulary who thought they were about to attack the Christ church. That night St Malachy's chapel was besieged, the attackers only departing when Captain Verner arrived. The intervention of the navvies provoked a very definite parting of the ways between the Liberal and Catholic press. The *Observer* declared in the light of the earlier phases of the riots that there was a conspiracy to exterminate Catholics.[76] It pointed to the connivance of the town police in the effigy business, and the arrests of Catholics after the first Protestant attack on the Pound. When challenged by the *Whig* and *Banner* for "inflaming", it stated, "we could not and cannot admit that the [Brown Street attack] was unprovoked".[77] The *Banner* described the attack as "the most cowardly and disgraceful" episode to date.[78]

The day after the Brown Street attack, the constabulary attempted to help mill girls cross Boyne bridge, and faced a larger than usual crowd which the town police did little to help them move. The constabulary then fired on the crowd and John McConnell was killed.[79] He had evidently saved the life of a Catholic in Durham Street on the previous night and was widely reckoned to be a mere bystander;[80] and Sandy Row, morally supported by the town police and a solicitor of whom we will hear more later, Charles H. Ward, began to adopt a very hostile attitude toward the constabulary. The same day a body of "ship carpenters" marched through the centre of the town toward the Shankill Road looking for "navvies", and in the course of their activities raiding gun shops on route. The Liberal press was less worried about this obviously irregular proceeding than it had been about previous episodes, and the *Whig* praised them for not wrecking houses as some other parties had done.[81] The earlier consensus between the Liberal and Catholic press was breaking down. And as in 1857, the Catholic elites' leadership grip broke. At a meeting in the Catholic Institute, William T. McCoy, later to be a prominent supporter of the Fenian amnesty movement, successfully moved a resolution against the opposition of the barrister Daniel O'Rorke, affirming the need for self-defence measures, notwithstanding the very pointed public circular issued by Bishop Dorrian opposing any such measure and any "self-appointed" leaders.[82]

The following day, backed up by the military, the magistrates began a massive arms search of Sandy Row and the Pound. Special constables had been sworn in the day before with an eye on preventing the spread of rioting across further districts of the city.[83] It is quite clear that by this stage in the riots supporters were going around country districts collecting weapons. Lisburn, which was very much an Orange town (see Chapter 12) was acting as a service depot for Sandy Row.[84] While the searches were going on, some "ship carpenters" eventually came across a gang of navvies working on the docks. It appears that shortly before the major encounter, some of those who had been involved in the rioting had come to the docks to persuade those working (who hadn't been involved) to join in. While they were there a small body of ship carpenters arrived whom the latter repelled. There then followed a massive attack in which the whole body of navvies was driven into the water and forced to swim for their lives. Respectable people watched the proceedings and cheered.[85] The spirit of vengeance against the navvies is well illustrated by a comment tucked into a report (not an editorial) in the *Whig* shortly preceding the attack. The best way to punish them, it said, would be to send them out of the city starving the way they were when they came.

"In the disturbed parts of the town, the riots are mainly caused by the influx of strangers, who at home could not obtain employment, and coming to Belfast, where there is work for all who are willing, took up their habitation, unfortunately amongst us."[86]

It went on to point out that all people charged with offences were either non-resident or residents of less than five years standing. "Newspapers from Dublin, Cork and Galway should know" that it is from the "South and West" that the "vast majority of these scoundrels come". The *Whig* reporter echoed precisely the sentiments of John Thompson, the Belfast bank director:

"I think our Roman Catholic working population would act peaceably and quietly if we had not the inundation of these southern gentlemen."

And R. J. McGeagh, a Tory councillor, on the subject of the effigy of O'Connell said:

"If they [the Catholics] had not known there were a number of navvies in the town, they wouldn't have resented the matter." . . . and furthermore, "The ship carpenters never came out that they did not clear the streets and there was quietness immediately afterwards."

Strongly though they had denounced the Protestant outrages which started the riots, Protestant Liberal reactions to the navvies' intervention brought them closer to the position of the Conservatives. The unguarded welcome to the ship carpenters and the ambivalence about their subsequent activities matched that of the *Observer* about the navvies. They were beginning to be caught in a nasty dilemma: if Protestant outrages could provoke such threatening Catholic reprisals, which in turn exacerbated Protestant counter-attacks (e.g. the confrontation on Boyne bridge with the constabulary), precisely how would order be ultimately restored? Was it possible they might eventually find that the only means of restoring "order" was to rely upon the physical power of those who provoked "disorder" in the first instance? In 1864 they were saved from the embarrassment by the constabulary and military—and not obliged to place too much weight on the ship carpenters, let alone the generality of Protestant mobs. But what might happen if the activities of the navvies in 1864 became something of a norm in subsequent disorders? What if clerical discipline generally broke down and, above all, what if the constabulary and military could not be relied upon as ultimate restoring agencies?

The *Observer* likewise was embarrassed. Its editor A. J. McKenna was a very different man from John McLaughlin of the old *Ulsterman*. Before the riots he had expressed the hope that Orangeism was dying away and had always counselled Catholics to pay no heed to it. He was a man who was keen on secular co-operation for secular ends. With much greater reluctance than McLaughlin, we suspect, he reached pessimistic conclusions about what he described as an Orange conspiracy bent upon extermination. And in future years he was able to appreciate signs that things might yet be changing for the better. But 1864 had clearly shown how self-defence could override all else, once the riots had got to the point where aggression, reprisal and self-defence became indistinguishable.

The presence of the constabulary and military enabled some of the city elite to take an initiative to bring back some kind of peace. Three concerns faced them immediately. As William Mullan stated, "If not put an end to, the next move would be to attack banks and warehouses." The three concerns were residential expulsion, employment intimidation and, most novel, collection of money with thinly disguised threats to purchase arms. Indeed, the collectors had even been seen on the residential Malone Road.[90] The most important figure at these meetings was the Rev. John MacNaughton, a Free Church of Scotland minister who had come to Belfast in 1849, a very hard-nosed Liberal who had a gift for arguing Liberal and egalitarian points in a manner that suggested he had no sympathy for the people for whose liberty or equality he was contending. In the period when Belfast liberalism was no longer being led by old Whigs but being taken over by a Presbyterian professional and mercantile intelligentsia, MacNaughton was one of its prime movers.

The 1864 rioting had led to massive wrecking convulsing most of west Belfast, including the Shankill. One of the immediate antecedents of the Brown Street attack had been the Protestant destruction of Mary Street in the upper Falls, which had been "Catholicized" in 1857.[91] In later phases, the lower Shankill/Old Lodge district experienced massive Catholic displacement and in the upper Falls and Pound districts Protestant displacement. The *Banner* described Millfield and Brown Square, two of the longest established Catholic and Protestant exclusive districts as "entered on a career of extermination".[92] It mentioned that mills had stopped and feared that owners will "either have to employ Protestants or Catholics. If this state of things were tolerated we should soon have the Indian system of caste established among us",[93] it added with surprised disgust. Looking at the peace meetings it declared (seeing Hanna, Kisby the *Newsletter* editor, and A. J. McKenna present): "We find the names of zealous partisans who have done their best to uphold a factious party spirit in the town" and a "presumptuous self glorification . . . that is exceedingly offensive."[94]

The peace committee set to work to establish precisely who was being expelled from where and to negotiate to restore expelled employees. In the middle stood Liberals for whom the whole experience of the riots was a rebellion against everything civil. MacNaughton, echoing the *Banner*'s fears of a caste system, said of exclusive dealing that it "must be put down at all hazards and all costs",[95] and in a sermon spoke of the riots as illustrating the terrible nature of "sin as exhibited in unrestrained human passion".[96] MacNaughton's initiative became possible because the state force had managed to impose a stand-off, and he was in the position to act as a mediator between sectarian factions. But to secure compliance with his efforts to reverse expulsions, he found himself co-operating with some strange partners. True, the Chamber of Commerce through the mouth of John Hinds (owner of the Orange Cage) indicated that mill owners were keen to get their workers back.[97] And McKenna, representing the Catholics, was obviously concerned because most of the expelled workers were Catholics. But what were Hugh Hanna and Kisby of the *Newsletter* doing there? They are later supposed to have explained to a secret Orange meeting that their presence was tactically required on account of McKenna's presence:[98] it turned out that they wanted to limit the prosecution of Protestants for riot and were prepared to trade a restoration of Catholics to their workplaces for an agreement that Catholics would not give evidence against them.

During and after the 1864 riots, large numbers of workers were forced to leave their workplaces. Intimidation spread rapidly. For example, J. F. Ferguson put out a notice offering a reward to anyone who gave information as to who had attempted to intimidate his workers at the Ballysillan bleachworks.[99] The contractor who was doing the dock works was reported to have dismissed all his men and got a six-month contract extension.[100] Painters leaving Harland's shipyard was noticed by other workers.[101] In Murphy's mill, Sandy Row, a Protestant strike demanded the removal of Catholic millworkers.[102] And on the Ulster railway various Catholic employees were sent away, as it turned out, temporarily and for their own safety.[103] The peace committees had some success in first sorting out the facts of what had happened, and second, in securing the return of Catholic employees.

At Murphy's mill, Hugh Hanna and a future town councillor ally, John Rogers, were sent to sort out the strike on the grounds that they had influence with the strikers.[104] The ultimate upshot of the proceedings was that most of the Catholic millworkers were taken back, except those who gave evidence to the Riots Commission. Murphy stated to the Riots Commission: "We have means of knowing, which you cannot have, that it [taking back the ones who gave evidence to the Commission] would have the effect of producing disturbance in our establishment."[105] Hanna also sorted out the Ulster Railway, where he said that all the Catholics had been taken back except one who was unpopular with his own kind and who was supposed to have pointed out some Protestants to a Catholic mob.[106] MacNaughton and others, supported by Harland himself, prevailed upon the shipyard workers not to put out the painters, and it appears that some kind of understanding arose whereby the Catholic workers would not give information to the magistrates about the activities of other workers.[107] They also secured the reversal of the dismissal of the navvies and the restoration of the original contract timescale.[108] McKenna thanked Hanna for his part in these proceedings.[109]

It will be noticed that the evolving rule here was to let Catholics back so long as they are quiet, i.e. not involved in the judicial inquiries after the riots. In September there was a Protestant strike in Harland's shipyard on account of arrests being made, for which they blamed Catholic workers. The strike delegation was received by the Mayor, although both resident magistrates refused to meet it.[110] MacNaughton declared at a peace meeting that one of the RMs had told him that no Catholic on Queen's Island had given information leading to arrests, and when a delegation appeared he said he would meet them to explain. The solicitor, C. H. Ward, whom we noticed on the occasion of the death of John McConnell, however, announced that no one from the meeting could have any influence with them "for the plain reason that the compact was broken".[111]

In fact, in the later stages of these meetings it became clearer what had brought Hanna, Kisby, C. H. Ward and others along. Hanna said that it wasn't acceptable that there were only twenty Roman Catholics compared to sixty Protestants in jail, and pronounced the doctrine that there should have been "something like an equality of arrests",[112] a position I suspect he would not have taken if the proportions had been reversed. He referred to the case of a man he knew who fired on a mob which attacked his house and was now in jail. Mr Tierney thought some of the arrests were going a bit far and would provoke more riots; and C. H. Ward declared that the authorities "want further riots" because "O'Hagan is in power in the Castle" (a reference to the Catholic Solicitor General in the Liberal administration).¹¹³ It is certainly clear what Tierney's complaint was about. The Soho foundry worker who went out to fight off the navvies attacking Brown Street school and a Presbyterian meeting-house, and was arrested when the constabulary arrived, spoke a language similar to that of the Catholics in the Pound whom the town police arrested for defending their district against an unprovoked attack. "I have done your duty and saved this church from being wrecked, and now you come up and take me for doing your duty", he said.¹¹⁴ But the fact is that given the assumptions on which the law had operated in the past, this was a more common experience for Catholics. Protestants were only put in a similar position by the navvy reprisals and the intervention of the constabulary with its policy of "impartial arrests". It only became possible to see the full malignancy of sectarian violence when the repression of it approached the condition of even-handed bluntness, for it was only then that the inadequacy of the assumption that all formal breaches of the law were individual and single acts became manifest to everyone. In a very obvious sense, the human response to this situation was to vindicate the defensive character of one's own rioters and to argue that the law was blind to the overall situation in which "defensive" and "reprisalist" actions took place. But the law necessarily had to be so, if it was to be the law at all. The alternatives were either to build it upon assumptions of dominance and subordination, or to let it get enmeshed in a quite arbitrary effort to measure the provocations that led to each offence.

In Belfast, at the end of 1864, the Castle put pressure on the corporation to promote a Police Bill abolishing the town police force and adopting a large-scale permanent constabulary presence. The annoyance at their abolition is itself instructive. The *Banner*, for example, thought it unfair to saddle them with the blame for the riots, which it thought they were unable to contain alone. It supported the retention of the town police, but with a stronger arrangement for imposing ultimate force at the first signs of its necessity.¹¹⁵ The ultra-Protestant meetings held to denounce the "betrayal"—though outwardly saying the same thing—were actually an attack on the constabulary itself.¹¹⁶ The party character of the McConnell funeral in 1864 was only the first of a series of anti-constabulary manifestations. In late August Major Esmond reported to the Inspector General how he had overruled the local magistrates' opposition to mass arms searches by telling them he had "positive instruction to proceed to search forthwith".[117]

Throughout early 1865 the constabulary had considerable difficulty patrolling Protestant districts. Renewed riots were anticipated and they had difficulty with the reluctance of the town police (before their disbandment) to help put processions down. In February, Sub-Inspector Harvey reported that the working classes of both sects were doing their utmost to secure firearms.[118] Illustrative of the texture of relations in Sandy Row was the case in which Jane Wallace prosecuted Constable Patrick Fallon for waving a sword over her head and calling her an Orange b——. The constable in question, together with one other, said they were in the process of arresting another woman for calling them "Black Popish Peelers".[119] In the period from 1865 onwards, plebeian Protestant opposition to the constabulary took the form of increasingly bold attempts to hold Orange processions, though as we shall see this was generally done outside Belfast, which was fairly effectively sealed against such exercises. In 1864 the Belfast District of the Orange Order was separated from County Antrim and became a County Grand Lodge in its own right. The City Hall Conservatives, who controlled it, began by supporting the no-processions policy of the Grand Lodge of Ireland, but within the Fourth District opposition began to develop under the leadership of C. H. Ward.[120]

High-speed extension of residential districts and consequent risks of disputes about boundaries of sectarian sub-districts made west Belfast very vulnerable to political crises and riots. So long as tranquillity was preserved by clerical restraint upon Catholics, Liberal Protestants opposed Orangeism as irritating and provocative. They even endorsed Catholic criticisms of the town police. But when Catholics responded physically, then Protestant Liberals began to part company with them. Distinctions between aggression, reprisal and self-defence became increasingly subjective as sectarian identities became a question of whose violence one feared most. But bureaucratically administered force prevented the situation from coming full circle as had happened in Armagh in 1784–96.

Liberals who deplored pan-Protestant plebeian violence did not find themselves depending on pan-Protestantism to defend society against Catholic anger it had itself provoked into existence. Despite some lurches, like the Whigs' praising the ship carpenters' antics, Rev. John MacNaughton's initiative preserved the Liberal commitment to the rule of law. There were still possibilities of preserving Belfast from the "Indian caste system" that the *Banner of Ulster* had been so alarmed by. Formal equality before the law still meant something.

Formal equality was a two-edged condition. Because Catholics were not a coveted labour supply ripe for super-exploitation, there were no strong class differences in Protestant attitudes towards them. They were neither desired as compliant workers by employers, nor did other workers have reason to fear them as cheap labour. Because equal pay for equal work had been clearly established, Protestant society was not likely to be divided along class lines about where Catholics belonged. There was a possible consensus about the Catholics' place, of the kind we saw emerging towards the end of the riots of 1864. So long as they "behaved themselves" and knew their place, so long as they were not "led" (as in 1857) or stirred up by "outsiders" from the "south and west" (as in 1864), they would be tolerated. If they became a threat they could anticipate that sections of all classes of Protestants would cheer when "ship carpenters" drove "troublemaking navvies" into the Lagan. Formal equality contained a promise, but it also contained this threat. It spelled the end of upper strata Protestant Liberal paternalism of the old Whigs.

> "Every 12th July there would be bloodshed through the length and breadth of Ulster were it not for the forbearance of the Catholic population under the influence of their clergy..."[121]

So spoke the *Northern Whig* in March 1869. The benefits of the Whig law and order reforms could only be effectively secured by Catholics when clerical discipline over the people was combined with good relationships between the clergy and magistracy, and in particular the government appointed RMs. We must now explore the operation of law and order outside Belfast.

Orangeism was at a very low ebb in the 1850s. The reimposition of the Party Processions Act reduced it to a shadow of its former self. But during the latter half of the 1860s Orangeism revived. In County Monaghan in 1865 it was brought into action to oppose a Liberal candidate supported by the Catholic clergy. This had devastating effects upon the nature of local power relations. In the latter half of 1865, the rise of the Fenian conspiracy promoted Orange re-organization in the east Tyrone and south-east Derry areas beneath the Sperrin Mountains. And in some of the faster expanding mill towns plebeian Protestant organization revived and concentrated its attacks upon Catholic religious and teaching institutions, which were being set up at this time. Finally, in 1867, some Anglican clergy encouraged Orangeism as part of the "Church Defence" reaction to Disestablishment. All those developments posed threats to patterns of local accommodation. Some of these developments will be looked at in Chapter 12 and what will be selected here is intended for illustrative purposes.

In the Monaghan election of 1865, several Presbyterian ministers nominated a local Liberal landlord, Lord Cremorne. The Catholics had been intending to nominate A. J. McKenna, editor of the *Ulster Observer*, but he withdrew in favour of Cremorne. The county as a whole had a three-quarters Roman Catholic population, but its electorate was probably around half Catholic. In an open voting situation, with very considerable distances to the few polling stations, and plentiful opportunities for the employment of landlord sanctions, the result of such an election would hinge on the effective organization of both sides. In the Carrickmacross district of south Monaghan, the weight of Catholic numbers was so overwhelming that with effective clerical backing the Cremorne candidacy could not be stopped. But in some of the other polling districts, particularly Monaghan town and Castleblaney, Conservative magistrates organized bodies of armed Orangemen to the polls.[122] The Ballybay Orangemen, for example, came to Castleblaney by train, were escorted through the streets to and fro by lancers, and back at the station they opened fire on some of the opposition, killing a man.[123] It is not our purpose here to attempt to assess how much violence and coercion was employed by each camp. But the effect of this very bitter election is shown in the legal aftermath. R. C. Leslie French, D.L., J.P., Master of the Ballybay market house, shortly afterwards refused the parish priest the use of the market house to entertain the Bishop who was coming to consecrate a new church. "I think it my duty", said French, "to discountenance in every way any appearance of sympathy with the clergy of the Romish Church in Ireland"[124] because of their involvement in politics. This same individual presided in his capacity as magistrate over several cases arising out of the election including one in which a boy from Ballybay, who brought three charged pistols with him because he "thought it necessary to bring them", gave evidence against someone else accused of firing at him![125] Even if French had been the most scrupulously judicious of magistrates, it would not have been easy for any Catholic to have much faith in a justice administered by him. Many of the Monaghan magistrates were in equally compromised positions. Three Protestants who were in Ballybay station and had been shooting were acquitted of murder. Not a single Protestant was convicted of anything, though various Catholics were made amenable for minor offences.[126] As the *Observer* remarked, "Is there any wonder that there should be Fenians in [Monaghan]."[127]

The Maddens, two prominent members of the Conservative elite, had a very definite understanding of what politics was about. At an 1868 church defence meeting, Capt. William Madden declared that "the meeting should give a wide berth to that class of Protestants who said they belonged to no party". And John Madden declared that all concessions given to Roman Catholics were merely levers to enable them to demand others.[128] The rector of Aghamullen parish who had an Orange flag removed from the steeple of his church in July 1868 found himself with a drastically reduced congregation.[129] Such was the fate of Protestants of "no party".

On 12 July 1868 a small body of Orangemen entered Monaghan town with fifes, drums and banners, and on arriving in the Diamond where the market was in progress, they were attacked—in one account with bludgeons; in another account they lost a flag and sustained a damaged drum. They retreated to Baird's public house where they barricaded themselves in and fired on their assailants outside.[130] One man was killed.

Again the details of the battle are less important than its legal aftermath. William Madden collected a subscription for the defence of Baird, who was found not guilty of murder, and later others were found not guilty of shooting with intent to do bodily harm.[131] Then a Catholic was put on trial for another murder, and the legal counsel, Isaac Butt and Denis Heron, decided to challenge the jury panel. The sub-sheriff, whose task it was to draw up the jury panel, had been reappointed in 1865 and was an Orangeman. There were 1,207 jurors on the books, of whom 33 per cent were Catholics; on the panel selected from the books there were 250 of whom 20 per cent were Catholics. But the manner in which the panel operated ensured that only the first 70 names had any likelihood of being jurors. These contained five Catholics, one an innkeeper, who would usually be set aside on that account. The Catholics constituted less than 10 per cent of the possible jurors. The legality of the panel was tried and quashed by a special jury of two who headed the panel list.[132]

This unprecedented development occurred at a propitious moment as the Gladstone government was in power in England. The High Sheriff did not dismiss the sub-sheriff or change the panel and the Chief Secretary for Ireland wrote regretting this.[133] Subsequently after the sheriff made public remarks challenging the credibility of one of the two special triers, the Chief Secretary dismissed him.[134]

Whatever allowances might understandably have been made by Protestant juries for Protestants who used weapons in "self defence", if any such circumstances could be pleaded, the straightforward reality of this situation was that the Conservative landlords had enlisted the Orangemen to help them fight the Monaghan priests and Catholic people. The pressures put on "Protestants of no party" or non-Orange rectors give some idea just how polarized Monaghan was. It is easy to see how Denis Heron in his legal attack on William Mitchell, the Orange sub-sheriff could say: "Men whose every feeling was poisoned with prejudice and with hatred of their fellow men, and who lived as foreigners in a land which they should love as their native land, were unfit for such positions."

Monaghan County was the most extreme example of elite resort to overt pan-Protestantism, bending the legal system to the point required to overawe a three-quarters majority opposition population. In most of the Ulster counties the public boards' employment was restricted overwhelmingly to Protestants; but in a county with this sort of population, to have only six Catholics out of 192 county officials, was altogether different from doing the same thing in, say, Antrim.[135] In this county Catholic self-organization had explicitly challeged the Conservative hold, which had reacted by reaffirming a form of pan-Protestant solidarity that had echoes of the pre-Drummond era.

Nowhere in Ireland were there fewer Fenians than in Ulster. Fenianism was a revolutionary separatist organization strongly influenced by the experience of the Famine and the political collapse of Ireland after 1852. Many Irish immigrants to the United States had fought in the US Civil War, and its termination provided any Irish insurrectionary movement with a potentially large body of militarily trained men. It was militantly opposed to participation in the Westminster system and to the clerical accommodation with English power. Its slogan, "No priests in politics",[136] was reciprocated by clerical anathema and the famous remark of Dr Moriarty, Bishop of Kerry, that "hell was not hot enough for Fenians".[137] Despite the fairly diminutive scale of northern Fenianism where its presence would have been a very serious threat to clerical accommodation indeed, it none the less created something of a panic in parts of the North from late 1865 onwards.

Orange meetings in Cookstown and Moneymore expressed alarm, the latter saying the setting up of an Irish Republic would involve "the massacre of every loyalist in the Kingdom".[137] Practically speaking the most striking fact about the Fenians was that in large areas of the South the law found it expedient to let them parade openly, which gave grist to the mill of those who sought to defy the Party Procession's Act in the North. The law responded to the revival of Orange demonstrations in the south-east Derry and east Tyrone districts in a very ambiguous way. Unlike the Monaghan case just outlined, the Conservative elites did not actually promote such manifestations, but they were more than indolent about stopping them.

In Dungannon on 12 July 1865, a drumming party was compelled after a scuffle to leave their musical instruments behind before leaving the town. Later that afternoon, 2,000 people armed with bludgeons, guns and hay forks entered the town making mayhem and wrecking Catholic houses. When the law arrived it rounded up eighteen people, but it was too late to stop massive damage.[139] On 7 August another armed Protestant group came into the town and the Catholics speedily set about defending themselves. When the Protestants withdrew, there were some Catholics still on the streets, and Mr Brooke, the agent to the Earl of Ranfurley, had eighteen Catholics charged on the grounds that on 12 July only Protestants had been charged. And in this way an "equality" of punishment was achieved.[140] In July 1865 the local Orange District Master, Mr Evans, and the Hon. Stewart Knox, MP for the borough, Deputy Grand Master of the Orange Order and scion of the Ranfurley family, had attempted to stop the Protestant attacks in the town to no avail. We can only suppose that the efforts to secure "equality of punishment" were not unconnected with a fear of total loss of elite control over plebeian pan-Protestantism.

Thereafter the provocative character of all drumming parties in the area was interpreted in the light of the 1865 experience. Catholics were keen to have them stopped and were convinced that the local magistrates were less than serious about their efforts to put them down.[141] The reality was that privately the Hon. Stewart Knox wrote to the Castle, suggesting that the RMs keep all elements whether processing or otherwise out of the town on 12 July 1866.[142] At the inquiry into the Dungannon judicial arrangements, it emerged that the local elite and the leading Catholics agreed about the need to put these drumming parties down.[143]

What actually happened in east Tyrone in this period was an elite failure to repress such activities. The road out of Dungannon towards the mountains in a north-westerly direction passes through the mill village of Donoughmore up to Pomeroy. Before 12 July 1866 the parish priest received word that Pomeroy chapel would be wrecked, and on the day an armed body of Orangemen passed through the village firing shots. The chapel bell rang and armed Catholics poured into the village. When the military and police arrived from Dungannon the Catholics dispersed only when assured that the chapel would be untouched. On 17 September the police were brought out to stop Orangemen entering Donoughmore, which they failed to do. Catholics came out and attacked them. For both incidents Catholics were charged, and the only Protestant charged was one who attacked the police in the course of securing entry of Donoughmore.[144] At the March 1867 assizes, the defence counsel started by attempting to show that an article in the *Tyrone Constitution* entitled "The Assizes v. Fenianism" was prejudicial to the outcome. Justice Keogh read the article and declared that the writer purported to remind the judge of the facts of the case, described the article as having murderous intent and showing no conception of the administration of justice. But he allowed the trial to proceed. Having handed down sentences of six months' hard labour on the Pomeroy offenders, the court moved to the Donoughmore case, during which the single Protestant defendant pleaded guilty with "extenuating circumstance" to assaulting Sub-Constable O'Neill. In the course of this case, O'Neill mentioned that he had told the magistrates the names of several Protestants on the Donoughmore march who were summoned to the petty sessions. Mr Lyle (whose steward had led the Pomeroy march) interjected to say that the Protestant parties were strangers from another part of the county and identification of them had failed. Justice Keogh was appalled. In passing sentence of one month's hard labour on the Catholic offenders he stated:

> "I have now to pass sentence on these men, but I do so perfectly convinced that the aggressors in this case—the really guilty party—are not before me."

And he proceeded to give the Catholic offenders the following advice.

> "You by leaving your homes played their game; for had you stayed indoors and let them play their party airs, you would not now be standing in this dock. Therefore learn wisdom for the future. Keep within your houses, but watch their movements doggedly, silently and departminedly and when they break the laws of the land

appeal to the laws of your country and I tell you that you will find them able to protect you."¹⁴⁵

The *Observer*'s comment on this advice, which contained in effect the whole basis upon which clerical accommodation with the law functioned, was that

"It is not human nature to obey it. . . . More patience than what is human, courage of a more than heroic order, confidence in the authorities of an extravagant order, perfect security in defiance of warning, experience and actual danger."¹⁴⁶

The outward appearances did not altogether reflect the inner realities. Mr Lyle had actually pressed for the prosecution of the Orange parties and his interjection at the court had shielded others who were opposed to prosecution.¹⁴⁷ The legal basis of their decision not to prosecute was probably that a procession in itself was not an offence whatever the irritation intended. In short, the blindness of the law to the intent behind the symbol made it incapable of grasping the totality of the circumstances. When confronted with a charge of breaking the Party Processions Act, they were reluctant to convict. In fact, at the Sixmilecross petty sessions in August 1867, a trial of cases under the Party Processions Act led to acquittals on the ground that a supposed procession was really two separate bodies. The first body carried a flag but, it was held, had no connection with the music played by the second body!¹⁴⁸

At the Dungannon Inquiry of 1871, the parish priest, Rev. F. Devlin of Donoughmore, while crediting the magistrates with a desire to put down drumming parties, estimated his influence over the Catholics to be about equal to that of the magistrates over the Orangemen. If true, then clerical accommodation with the law was in deep trouble.¹⁴⁹

Occasionally when the constabulary and stipendiary magistrates were on hand in force, even this might be of no avail. In 1867 Capt. Plunkett, R.M., failed to persuade the Orangemen to furl their banners before processing through Stewartstown. He arrested three men who were carrying banners and lodged them together with their flags in the barracks. About 350 processionists then threatened to attack the barracks. After negotiations with Mr Hunt Chambre, brother-in-law of William Johnston of Ballykilbeg, local flour miller and leader of the Orangemen, the arrested Orangemen and the banners were released. As Capt. Plunkett said in his report to the Castle, he had no means of securing the necessary reinforcements![150] The necessity of stopping Orange processions in Stewartstown, a heavily Protestant locality, was perhaps less urgent than elsewhere. And in 1868, despite letters from Catholic inhabitants they were permitted to go ahead. The RM reported that the local magistrates had argued there was no danger of a breach of the peace "because the Catholic party are so insignificant numerically and consequently wouldn't dare to interfere".[151]

The theme that echoes through the official papers on Orange processions in this period is the pressure that the accommodative arrangement with Catholic clergy was placed under. In effect these arrangements remained strongest in areas where Catholics were weak numerically, and most jeopardised as distinct from undermined, where there was an uncertainty about local strengths. The parish priest of Bellaghy, east Derry, complaining of magisterial refusal to remove an Orange arch over the road to the chapel, stated: "The Catholics will no longer be controlled by priests nor prevented from asserting their rights."[152] And Hugh McClean, P.P. Rasharkin, who co-operated with the magistrates to secure the conviction of some Protestants who let off guns in defiance near Catholic houses in Cushybracken, wrote the next year (1867) of his fear of reprisals against the Catholics whose evidence had been the basis of the convictions.[153]

The most outstanding case of total breakdown of control occurred in the mill town of Banbridge in 1868.[154] In early June the Rev. John O'Brien, P.P. Banbridge, organized a mission planned for a fortnight, at which three Fathers of the Order of Charity and priests of surrounding parishes participated. Shortly after it started drumming parties began to pay it attention, which the local constabulary found themselves unable to disperse. On the night of 4 June, Head Constable Mervyn went to a nearby magistrate, Mr Waugh, for help, and was sent by him to a more distant one, Mr Ferguson. The delay allowed the drumming party time to collect large numbers of recruits and to stone the chapel and adjoining school house (the constabulary confined their activities to preventing entry to the chapel grounds). When Rev. O'Brien went to the petty sessions clerk he was pelted on the way with stones. The next day Mr Eglington, R.M., with constabulary reinforcements, arrived in Banbridge.

On 6 June the drumming party did the rounds of the mills at Gilford and Lawrencetown before entering Banbridge, a thousand strong. The constabulary cordoned off the road to the chapel and the mob threw stones and fired shots. The RM wanted to disperse the mob but Mr Ferguson counselled delay. They were forced back to defend the chapel, and the mob then went through the town stoning the police barracks and Catholic houses. For the time being that was the end of the disorder.

But about 12 July the Anglican church in Banbridge was supporting an Orange flag. As Rev. O'Brien wrote to the Castle, it was

"a small thing in itself, but it shows that those who have position and influence in the town, and that at least one—I mean the rector—who might have been expected to act the part of peace makers, are willing to countenance and as it were give a sort of religious sanction to the present, if not the last proceedings of the Orange party in Banbridge."[155]

In fairness to the Orange Order, its hand in the proceedings of June was not proven in the sense that it was not orchestrating them. But confronted with the irregular Orange auxiliaries attacking his church, it was idle to suppose that Rev. O'Brien would pay much significance to that distinction which had little practical bearing on his problem—his church was being wrecked and local influences were doing little to protect it.

In August the petty sessions were hearing charges of riot and assault against thirty-four people.[156] Just as Rev. O'Brien was beginning his evidence, a drumming party arrived and made so much noise it was impossible to proceed. The crown prosecutor Mr Magee wanted military assistance to be called for, but two of the magistrates, Mr Waugh (who had refused to do his duty with the constabulary on the night of the attack on the mission) and Lord A. E. Hill Trevor (an Orange Deputy Grand Master), refused to make such a call. So the court was treated to a proposal from the defence counsel that a deputation of the prisoners go out to attempt to stop the drumming! In the absence of military assistance, it was the only possible option. It later transpired that the drumming party had been organized by two men who hired a yard in which the drums were housed along with a lot of liquor. But the original source of information was not prepared to repeat his charge in court (although he himself rented out the yard); nor was anyone else prepared to implicate the organizers. Most of the defendants were bound over to the Downpatrick assizes where they were eventually convicted. But the *Whig*'s comment on the proceedings at the Court House speaks for itself:

"When such is the manner in which the magistrates are treated, it may be judged what must be the position of the Roman Catholics. These drumming parties are the cause of many riots. They ought to be put under the Party Processions Act, if they be not, what they surely must often be, direct offences at Common Law."[157]

So far we have indicated that the local elites' attitude toward these manifestations was decidedly ambivalent. In the Banbridge case, for example, the role of Mr Waugh in effect legitimated the drumming parties. And even Mr Ferguson showed a hesitation about putting them down the way Mr Eglington, the RM, would like to have done. But in each example the important point is that the ambivalence clearly owes its origin to some perception on the part of the elites of the need to treat Orangeism with kid gloves. They had an inhibiting sense that keeping satisfactory relations with Orangeism had something to do with the stability of local order. Even where the elite did not outrightly collide with the Catholic clergy (as they did in Monaghan), pan-Protestant exploitation of the space between the letter and spirit of the law put local accommodation with the Catholic clergy under stress. When it is said that the source of pan-Protestant solidarity is the fear of Catholics organized by and for themselves, we must not lose sight of one of the strongest reasons (or provocations) for just such Catholic organization. Pan-Protestant activism was concerned to keep Catholics down. These drumming parties frequently managed to exploit their own twilight legality to provoke Catholics into confrontation with the law.

Whereas before 1867 these manifestations we have described were less than general experiences, the "Church Defence" campaign of 1867–68 rapidly brought Conservative leadership closer to popular Orangeism. Part of this was a Conservative desire to wrest the control of Orangeism from William Johnston of Ballykilbeg who aimed explicitly at overthrowing the Party Processions Act. None the less in the "Church Defence" campaign the elites either loosened their grip or shifted towards actual encouragement of Orange demonstration. The concluding instance of this comes from County Fermanagh where elite control over the Orange Order and Protestant society generally was much stronger than elsewhere. In October 1866, at a time when local agitation against Fenianism in east Tyrone was very high, the Fermanagh gentry held a meeting of a most temperate character to show support for the new minority Conservative government's anti-Fenian measures.[158] The Earl of Erne addressed the meeting reassuringly demonstrating how low the risks of Fenianism were. He had asked the local constabulary several questions. Did their patrols meet parties of men at night? Did they see the houses of the peasantry lighted more frequently than usual? Were there many more dance meetings (i.e. opportunities for plotting) going on than usual? To all these questions the answer was "No". It is interesting how the questions concentrated on "outwardness" and show how little was actually known about what the Catholic peasantry thought or did—but none the less there were no "outward" symptoms of anything suggesting Catholic self-organization. The speeches delivered all talked of the objectives of the Fenians as "plunder", and mentioned the opposition of the clergy to Fenianism. There was not a word of "No Popery" at the meeting, and a Catholic JP, Edward Maguire, was glad to be present to reaffirm the opposition of the clergy to Fenians and to quell rumours.

Around 12 July 1867 the resident magistrate reported no signs of excitement in Enniskillen, and that the Twelfth appeared to be less widely celebrated each year.[159] But in July 1868 the impending doom of the Established Church brought about a change in the disposition of the Orange gentry. A Church demonstration in Enniskillen saw the local landlords leading into the town bodies of their tenantry.[160] The spirit of the meeting was leavened with "No Popery" from start to finish. The thesis that Roman Catholic discontent was "perpetual", that they were used by mischievous politicians, that self-preservation was the first law of nature, were coupled with attacks on the Wesleyan Methodists—the main Protestant minority in County Fermanagh—for looking at the Church question "from a narrow-minded point of view as a mere Church question in fact", and failing to see it as an "empire" question. One particularly virulent speaker said he had recently been in Beragh (in the Sperrins) and had seen the "Fenians". "I would say this—there is not one present would dirty their hands with them. [*Cheers*] One would hardly hunt his dogs at them." [*Applause*] The general tenor of the meeting showed that "pan-Protestantism" was being orchestrated by the elite, despite their capacity to keep a grip on it at the time of the actual Fenian emergency.

Throughout 1867 and 1868 efforts made to keep popular pan-Protestantism under control were decidedly slackened. Orange flags fluttered from church tops, adding the Anglican churches' defiance to that of more plebeian forces. And though the popular momentum was there without having to be given much elite encouragement, there can be little doubt that by exposing the elites' sense of ultimate dependence upon pan-Protestantism, the two moved together in step. The striking and brief exception to this in County Down (see Chapter 10) will prove the rule.

The whole fabric of order was perched on a knife edge. Pan-Protestantism properly understood is not merely a possible unity in the event of another 1641, or even a general Protestant opposition to O'Connell as in 1840. It is a way of life, a preoccupation with the Catholics "in the midst". Catholic society contained unknowns. Protestant vigilance which this society could never criminalize was a strategy of perpetually ensuring Catholic compliance "externally" because there could be no real security about what Catholics felt at all. Vigilance claims free scope to define what a "Catholic threat" is, because any form of Catholic self-assertion can be seen as one, whether it be substantial—like an electoral challenge in Monaghan, or totally symbolic—like a religious mission in Banbridge.

Within Ulster the balance of force—physical, magisterial and judicial—generally ensured that Catholics did not provoke contest. Even when provoked by vigilantes, the whole thrust of clerical leadership was to avoid retaliation and the start of spiralling disorders in which Catholics could expect to come out worse. In places like south Armagh violence was a weapon of agrarian struggle to prevent eviction from marginal holdings. But in inner Ulster, where the possible reasons for violence were quite different, the cost of being the aggressing party in local sectarian conflict was far too high to embrace lightly. At the same time the vigilant Protestants never believed that the Catholics were any different in south Armagh than in, say, Banbridge, so they distrusted this clerical accommodation as just a super subtle form of popish conspiracy. The more uncertain the landlords and other local powers were about the compliance of the Catholics, the greater was the temptation to them to tolerate the activities of vigilantes. And the more anxious they were to keep an influence over the vigilantes, the more reluctant they were to risk confrontation with them.

10. Belfast 1868—Expectations of Democracy

In December 1865 the Belfast Corporation elected Alderman William Mullan to be the mayor of the borough for 1866. Despite the unanimity of the votes cast in favour of this Whig ally of the Conservatives, some of the more "Protestant" members of the council absented themselves from the meeting.[1] At a demonstration in the Corn Exchange,[2] C. H. Ward denounced the thirty years of Whig misrule in Ireland, and declared that whatever patronage the Conservatives had should be given to "Protestants". David Ruddell, an upholsterer, said: "We should have a council of sound Conservatives from the Mayor down to the lowest officers, and not let a Radical among them."

Three years later Ward and Ruddell were part of the rising tide of democratization that led to the election of William Johnston and Thomas McClure as MPs for Belfast. Besides, and sometimes instead of, talking about "Protestants", they were speaking about the "working classes" and "Reform". This chapter analyses the changes that led up to the 1868 election, showing how the democratizing and hopeful aspects were mixed up with more menacing aspects of plebeian pan-Protestantism.

The gathering at the Corn Exchange was certainly not party to the complex manoeuvring of Alderman Robert Lindsay, Mullan's brother-in-law and architect of the restoration of Tory rule. In early 1864 Chief Secretary Cardwell had given an arbitration award that the whole £84,000 with interest, for which the special respondents had been liable, could be put on the rates. But the differential rating system previously in force was to remain.³ Despite Catholic opposition, the council managed to get the Indemnity Bill through the Liberal House of Commons with only verbal promises of reform of the structure of the corporation.⁴ Lindsay brought into the council the Police Bill, which had been virtually dictated to him from the Castle, and braved the anger of those who regarded it as betrayal.⁵ His overall objectives were altogether far from transparent. In 1865 the parliamentary passage of separation of Belfast from County Antrim was achieved in the face of some opposition from the county grand jury.⁶ The separation for fiscal and police purposes enabled the corporation to begin the process of evading the rating provisions of the 1864 Indemnity Act. The police rate had been the bone of contention because it bore the greatest weight of taxation and was levied on a differential basis. It took some while for people to realize what was happening, but the increase in the uniform borough rate and the decrease in the police rate had the twofold effect of shifting the tax burden off the higher value property in the borough and of decreasing the size of the harbour board electorate who, under the 1847 Act, were composed of those who paid £4 or more of police rate.⁷ The harbour commissioners were becoming an increasingly independent body of big property owners. Lindsay's objective was to secure the indemnity by the line of least resistance, with the smallest possible number of collateral reform undertakings, and to sort out the taxation question by devious side-steps. As much of this required parliamentary approval, it was expedient to avoid giving too obvious an indication of the revived Protestant character of the corporation. His Whig brother-in-law was an ideal choice for mayor. The Liberals had won the 1865 general election, and getting Bills through Westminster would be easier if the council proposals seemed to have cross-party backing in Belfast.

However the strategy of "Protestantism" at home and "non-partisanship" for more distant audiences was going to run into difficulties. In June 1866 Lord John Russell's Liberal government was unexpectedly felled during the efforts to secure a Franchise and Parliamentary Reform Bill, and replaced by a minority Tory administration under Lord Derby and Benjamin Disraeli. The senior member of parliament for Belfast,

Sir Hugh Cairns, was elevated to the House of Lords to become the Lord Chancellor in October, and a by-election was necessary to fill his place. A meeting was held in the Ulster Hall to select the Conservative candidate Charles Lanyon, architect and earlier Mayor of Belfast.[8] He was proposed by F. H. Lewis, a one-time special respondent of pan-Protestant zeal, who had been absent at the election of Mullan to the mayor's office. Robert Lindsay seconded the proposal.

"Who had put down the wearing of an emblem in Ulster and tolerated a display of party emblems in the metropolis? Who had endeavoured to sap the present system of National Education by giving to the convent schools the training of school masters and school mistresses?"

In a year's time this rather convenient means of hitting the Liberals would become rather less handy, when it transpired that the minority Tory government aggravated both the above "offences". But in the later half of the meeting the *Newsletter* editor Kisby was interrupted by shouts of "Whig Mayor . . . You sold the Party . . . You are a deceiver." The interrupters, like the earlier protesters in the Corn Exchange and opponents of the Police Bill were a miscellaneous collection of pan-Protestants, mostly small merchants, artisans and shopkeepers. But inauspicious though the start of this attack upon the corporation Tories was, it was the seed of bigger things. A few days later they went on a deputation to Lanyon to ask him where he stood on the differential rating question, the proposed new loan the council sought for a sewerage system, and significantly—in the light of the importance of the issue in Britain at that time—the reform question.[9]

Such people were unlikely allies of Liberals and Catholics; nor were they the kind of people one would have expected to display much interest in metropolitan questions except in their bearing upon "pan-Protestantism". C. H. Ward and the printer Tom Henry, secretary of the 4th Orange District Lodge, were associated with the more extreme sections of the Order in opposition to the constabulary and the efforts to implement the Party Processions Act. William Trimble, a shoe manufacturer, and John Moffatt, a chandler, both had premises in Ann Street and had been strong "Protestant Conservatives". But in the November municipal elections Moffatt was included in an Independent ticket in Smithfield ward along with John Rea and a few Liberals.[10] The Conservatives saw the danger to themselves and did a deal whereby the Liberal George Horner, proprietor of the Falls foundry—a man unlikely to be an opponent of uniform rating—was included on the Conservative ticket. So far trouble could be contained. Whigs on the council were acceptable, but opponents of the uniform rate were not.

In early 1867, the town council prepared a new Borough Bill to incorporate Ballymacarrett and Ballynafeigh (the Down side of the river) into the borough for taxation purposes. It was at this point that the owners of small house property became alarmed. The Bill attacked the differential rating system directly, providing for a "consolidated borough rate" to be raised on a uniform scale and not subject to any limit. On property valued below £8 per annum, it was to be recovered from the landlord.[11] The Property Protection Association brought together the dissident Conservatives recently alienated from the corporation by its lack of "Protestantism", John Rea, the Liberal solicitor John Dinnen, and a prominent Catholic publican Hugh McLorninan, who set to work to collect a petition from owners and occupiers of low value property against the Bill. The council uncharacteristically agreed to receive the deputation, but the proposed Bill was supported by most of the corporation, including nearly all its remaining Liberal members. The deputation told the crowd gathered outside that it had been "most scurvily treated".[12]

The novelty in the proceedings was not so much the unity of various kinds of ratepayers of different political persuasions, but the method chosen to fight the issue. The owners of small house property might very well have been able to pass the increased taxation on to their tenants, but they chose to raise this possibility as a means of rallying their tenants behind them, and taking up the highly topical question of franchise reform. When the Town Bill was to be put before the Commons committee, they organized a huge demonstration with banners bearing "No Borough Bill", "No increase in taxation", "Oppress not the working man", "Peace and Harmony among all classes", and "Reform at Home". The deputation that set off for

London was cheered by enormous crowds at the Custom House, and the apprentices' band of the Lagan foundry played as the boat departed.[13] At Westminster the Bill was thrown out and the deputation returned in triumph. David Ruddell declared: "I hope we will all unite for the benefit of the town and bring the working classes into the movement."[14]

It is an interesting question how it came to pass that such a potentially powerful group as small house property owners should have been outside the framework of the major political blocs. There was certainly something rather audacious about their leadership of a working-class reform movement. For example, when the water commissioners required that all houses should have piped water, the *Whig* reported that though the average cost of installation was about 15s. 0d., typically the rent rises imposed to cover it were between 3d. and 6d. on an estimated average rent of two shillings.[15] The ownership of property in this period of very fast urban expansion was clearly a very sound speculative investment. For example, in December 1868 fifteen recently erected dwellings in Ballymacarrett were yielding a gross rent of £117 a year, which after subtraction of a fee farm ground rent of £30 left a profit rent of £87. The auction of this lot started at £300 and ended at £500. Making no allowance for anticipated annual pre-tax increases in the capital value of the houses, this is an annual return of about 15 per cent.[16] The extension of such residential construction during the 1860s boom provided an outlet for investment for middle-size holders of capital, some of whom like Samuel Tierney became large-scale rentiers.[17] The interest group thus formed provided the leadership of a new political tendency in Belfast drawing widespread popular support in opposition to the big warehouse and manufacturing Whig and Tory leaderships.

In June they organized a reform meeting which was attended by about three thousand people.[18] Tom Henry, district secretary of No. 4 Orange Lodge, was elected chairman, and called upon the working men of Belfast to consider their position:

"Sink minor differences and rise above the mists of prejudice. By encouragement of party animosity some of your enemies have prospered . . . but let them divide you no more. Show the government that you are as anxious to receive the franchise as they are willing to bestow it."

A. J. McKenna, the editor of the *Observer*, spoke and was warmly received by the very mixed audience. Various speakers dwelt on the demand for parity of reform with England, the need for working men to be independent and secure their rights. And most significantly, when the town hall functionary C. N. Davis attempted to argue against extending reform to Ireland, he got nowhere.

"They must not forget the South of Ireland. They might as well attempt to mix light with darkness as mix the Protestant body with its opponents: there was such a division between the two races they could never be brought together."

The argument was rejected with derisive laughter.

After the meeting the deputation that went to see Charles Lanyon questioned him about his efforts to secure Ireland's exclusion from the provisions of the Reform Act. The deputation got an unfavourable response, but the very fact that A. J. McKenna, Tom Henry, David Ruddell and John Dinnen went on it with a mandate from such a large meeting indicates a considerable change in the texture of Belfast's politics.[19]

For the time being all the various strands of this new opposition seemed to be working together, but there were big differences not very deeply buried between some of the ultra-Protestants of early 1866 and others. C. H. Ward, for example, was notably absent from the reform demonstrations and took an equivocal position when efforts were later made to expel Tom Henry from the Orange Order for his part in them.[20] Then, at the municipal elections in 1867, there were some very demagogical confrontations at the Conservative selection meetings. In St Anne's ward, for example, the town hall nominees standing for re-election included a one-time Liberal T. B. Johnston, and a Catholic merchant John Hamill.[21] Tom Henry moved the nominations of John Moffatt and an outright Liberal, John Dysart. The discussion centred around C. N. Davis's and Tom Henry's denunciation of each other for proposing "Papists" and "Radicals". This kind of effort to "out-Protestantize" opponents was interwoven with assertions of other objectives such as "the working classes and the owners of property in the various wards are not represented on the Town Council, while the millowners and large merchants are". The

Observer noted the conflicting tones of much of the "Independent" rhetoric, commenting that in some wards the question of whether a candidate was a "Conservative" or not seemed to be all that mattered, and were particularly annoyed with John Rea's rather unprincipled efforts to exploit this tension.[22]

Alongside these developments in borough politics, trade unions began to become more active. The industrial and residential expansion of Belfast during the cotton famine had been overshadowed by the riots of 1864. At the riots commission Bernard Hughes had stated that there was a widespread practice of exclusivism in many skilled trades, and Orange lodges in nearly all of them.[23] The *Observer* mentioned on one occasion that power loom minding was more or less closed,[24] but we saw that in the aftermath of 1864 the tendency was to restore workers to employment and for exclusivism to be attenuated. William Kirkpatrick told the riot commissioners that he knew of "at least" twelve trades without Orange lodges, and that printing in which he was engaged "hadn't got one".[25] Peter Hoey, president of the Trades Association, also contradicted Hughes's suggestion.[26] In the period we are dealing with there is evidence of large-scale workplace organization and successful strikes for wage increases.[27]

Most of the leaders of the "Reform" movement were small traders or house property owners. There is not much evidence of organized working-class involvement in 1868, except as auxiliaries of other currents. Let us look, for example, at co-operatives in the North. In 1864 some of the larger employers in Comber attempted to promote a co-operative retail store which folded within a year.[28] The *Whig* bemoaned their absence in Ireland and indeed the general absence of working-class "self improvement".

"In Ireland members of building societies are not of the working class proper. The feeling which has prompted English workmen to combine for the purpose of becoming their own landlords, their own purveyors, their own employers, has never developed amongst us. Sectarian and political controversies have left the Irish people little time to discuss social problems."[29]

Birkenhead also has Orange lodges and sectarian troubles, but it also has co-operatives. Why could not Belfast follow its example, asked the *Whig*?

In 1867 the revival of the cotton industry punctured the artificial boom in the linen industry, and short time began in many of the mills.[30] In November after a successful bakers' strike and a bad harvest, the bakers raised the price of bread, and a protest meeting was called, attended by about six thousand people and presided over by Sam Tierney.[31] The men who proposed him were Daniel Pettigrew, a millwright who was to take an important place in the Working Men's Institute, and William Henry Hand, who in 1872 was chairman of the Flaxdressers' committee during the strike of that year. As far as can be made out, the other speakers were two mechanics, a bricklayer and a blacksmith. Tierney's speech drew attention to Belfast's dependence on the linen trade: "If it fails all goes with it." And he made a plea for co-ops to "provide the people with bread, butcher's meat, and articles of clothing at a cheap rate". The meeting set up a central committee to plan a campaign to boycott the bread sellers and to organize collective purchasing in each locality. In the initial flurry of enthusiasm afterwards, some leading employers encouraged the formation of the "Belfast Working Men's Co-operative Ltd" by factory operatives in the Crumlin Road and Oldpark area.[32] The effort to draw lessons from Belfast's dependence on the linen trade, now that it was at a low point, was particularly taken up by mechanics who were especially badly hit by layoffs.[33] But within a year or so, no further mention is made of these co-operatives; nor do they at any point appear to have affected the content of political discussion. The strong probability is that the co-operatives became mill-stores. For example, in January 1868 there was a co-operative connected with Brookfield spinning mill.[34] In February 1868 Robert H. Reade, director of the York Street flax mill, addressed a meeting to set one up in York Street, and emphasised the importance of avoiding dependence on small traders.[35]

We shall see that there was a current which attempted to give political meaning to such manifestations of working-class organization. William Kirkpatrick, the printer already mentioned who worked on the *Northern Whig*, was to become prominent in the Working Men's Institute. He delivered lectures on the history of the co-operative movement, and told of its origins in Rochdale in 1844.[36] He is one figure who stands out as a kind of model labour-aristocrat Gladstonian Liberal. A typical speech in favour of the Liberal candidate, Thomas McClure, gives an idea of the tone he was trying to set:

"The working classes are entitled to be provided with all that is qualified to promote their social comforts and facilitate their onward progress in the march of improvement. They require in this town baths and wash houses, people's parks and public libraries and public reading rooms—places where they can have access to all the undefiled fountains of intelligence, which can so easily be provided, if proper means are taken to divert the current of the masses of the people. All these wants cannot be met under the present municipal system".[37]

But though Kirkpatrick and a few others appear to have played an important part in helping to give a secular working-class colour to the 1868 election, the edge of their message was rather blunted by a much more diffuse sense of generalized opposition to the City Hall. We shall find that by 1872, the Working Men's Institute which he helped to set up had become a very marginal part of Belfast's public life.

Altogether more typical of working-class direct involvement in 1868 was Isaac Hall, a prominent figure in the Carpenter and Joiners Society in Belfast.[38] At a meeting which he chaired in 1863 to deal with a dispute over the employment of unskilled non-society men by McLaughlin and Harvey, he said:

"Our members . . . could not agree to work along with these inefficient incapable men brought in from country districts."

and

"A trades union instead of being a reproach, should be the proper means of raising the tradesmen in the social scale."

Other speakers incidentally mentioned the importance of co-operatives. There is not the world of difference between these sentiments and those propounded by Kirkpatrick. What perhaps is different is that the carpenters, unlike the printers, were not by any means in such a well-organized position. It is far more likely that Orange solidarities did enter into the protection of some of its workplace boundaries. Isaac Hall, at all events, participated in 1868 as one of the leaders of Independent Orangeism and remained to be one of its more consistent supporters against efforts to reabsorb it into Conservatism. At this stage the suggestion we want to make is that typically Gladstonian labour aristocratic sentiments—efforts to "uplift" the working man—were fairly plastic and could readily be absorbed by other political currents, such as Independent Orangeism. Subsequent developments will show that workplace experience had a fairly limited influence on political alignments: as working-class organization developed, it tended to distance itself from "politics".

By the end of 1867 there was a hitherto unprecedented degree of popular organization amongst Belfast working men, led by a highly amorphous leadership of elements excluded from the Conservative and Whig establishments. The unifying theme was the demand that people should "awaken" to their interests and take an active part in public affairs and efforts to shape their own livelihood. Ultra-Protestants, disillusioned Conservatives, more radical Liberals and Catholics were sprinkled in a promiscuous motley of opponents of the City Hall. In order, I will look at the Belfast Catholics, second, the Presbyterian establishment, and finally the dissident elements of the Orange Order.

It took some very considerable time before Catholics in many districts had any direct influence upon local politics. In the course of the 1870s the Belfast Catholics' political experience was to become increasingly "focal" for northern Catholicity as a whole. What is necessary here is to show how social differentiation amongst Belfast Catholics, far from leading to political disunity, had the opposite effect.

Greatly alarmed by the scale of Fenian agitation in the 1860s, Cardinal Cullen decided in 1864 to make a direct intervention in politics with the formation of the National Association.[39] This explicitly clerical body had three basic objectives. It sought to disestablish and disendow the Church of Ireland, to secure freedom of (i.e. denominational) education from primary to university level, and reform of the land tenure laws. Dr Dorrian, the Belfast Bishop, was an active member of this body, which was a clerical effort to give renewed cohesion to Irish Catholic political forces.⁴⁰ The foundation of the association is significant not so much for what it achieved practically, as for the welcome it received from John Bright, the leader of the radical section of the Liberal Party in England, at a time when the importance of the Radicals was growing. Bright remained tactfully silent on the subject of denominational education, but suggested an alliance based upon "Free Land, Free Churches", and support for reform of the franchise and representation. And during the latter part of the long era of Whig dominance, the Roman Catholic hierarchy began to make some progress to secure a settlement of the position of the Roman Catholic university. In short, the ground was laid for a renewed alignment of Catholic clerical political forces in Ireland with English liberalism. Locally in Belfast, despite earlier disintegrative tendencies, it was possible to organize the Liberal candidacy of Lord John Hay in 1865 with support embracing old Whigs, Presbyterian Liberals and Catholics.

It is interesting to notice how this local political accommodation was achieved. Lord John Hay visited Dr Dorrian and spent a few hours talking to him. He declared in answer to the inevitable charge of "secret deal" that they hadn't even discussed politics! It is quite conceivable that that was true. For the most part the public aspect of his campaign was organized by Presbyterian interests. A meeting which the *Banner of Ulster* described as a "Presbyterian" meeting, notwithstanding the presence of most of the local Catholic leadership, was attended by Presbyterian clergy from all over the province.⁴² A. J. McKenna's feelings about the occasion only became clear later when he mentioned, after the 1867 municipal election in Smithfield in which co-operation between Protestant and Catholic Liberals broke down, that no Catholic had been permitted to second the nomination of Hay.⁴³ In a situation where Belfast liberalism was becoming increasingly linked to "Presbyterian" interests, it was considered adequate to pay respects to the bishop and let him, so to speak, approve the candidate without too close an inspection being made of his political position. Tact if nothing else might have disposed everyone to silence on the education question. But it will be no surprise that this procedure was at best acquiesced in by the more politically minded of Catholic laymen. What we need to consider is precisely what kinds of forces held the internal solidarity of Belfast Catholics together and prevented these tensions from being aired openly.

The Catholic middle class was small and in a great measure its existence depended upon the service of its own community. In 1864 it was estimated that Catholics paid 9 per cent of the local taxation, occupied 13 per cent of the houses rated £8 or upwards, and composed 13 per cent of the municipal and 16 per cent of the parliamentary electorate.[44] At this time they were probably about 33 per cent of the population. Their political leverage was therefore fairly small and, such as it was, confined to their 25 per cent of the municipal electorate in Smithfield ward.[45] There were some large Catholic merchants and manufacturers. Besides Bernard Hughes, the bakery owner, there was William Ross, a flax spinner on the Falls Road, the Keegans who were large merchants, and John Hamill, another merchant originally elected to the corporation as a Catholic Liberal in the 1850s, but later adopted by the Conservatives and regarded as a "renegade". The Catholic professional elite included Daniel O'Rorke the barrister, and several doctors, notably Harkin, Murney and Cuming. A. J. McKenna, the editor of the *Observer* might be added to the list, but with some qualification.

The interdependence between Catholics was perhaps best expressed in Bernard Hughes's remark about Catholic opposition to the Indemnity Bill of 1864. The only Catholics, he said, in favour of it were "those out of the church, such as Freemasons and those holding government appointments".[46] Very few Catholics availed themselves of the opportunity to go to Queen's College, Belfast, which the hierarchy had condemned. In 1865 only 22 of its 405 students were Catholic.[47] The wealthier Catholics, far from being rejected, were treated as an asset to the Catholic community. Clerical collectors for chapels and schools from surrounding countryside and small towns, for example, had to secure Dr Dorrian's permission before doing the rounds of Belfast.[48] The relative economic paucity of Catholic communities outside Belfast made the urban middle class a very important source of voluntary subscriptions. Inside the borough there is evidence of "organic work" type strategies such as that manifested in the foundation of the "Belfast Economic Building and Investment Society" set up in 1864 with James Cuming, M.D., as president, Bernard Hughes, treasurer and Peter Keegan, William Ross and Richard Waring (a Protestant Liberal) as trustees.[49] By and large the formation of an educational, institutional and religious infrastructure depended upon co-operation between the Catholic middle class and clergy. The 1864 riots had re-enforced Catholic solidarity in the western section of the city. The national education system, although supposedly non-denominational, was more denominationalized in Belfast than elsewhere on account of the relatively high density of schools of all denominations. The heightening of religious subjectivity during the revival emphasised that Catholicism was something "different".

There were two kinds of tendencies which might have weakened Catholic solidarity. The first had to do with Catholics entering "Protestant" educational institutions and loosening their links with co-religionists. This might also happen through trade unions and other associations. It is very noticeable that even after the 1864 riots, the patterns of religious residential segregation were fairly quickly blurred at the edges,[50] and the growth of working-class organizations created a basis for trans-sectarian solidarities. Furthermore, the abstract appeal of better endowed secondary schools (Protestant) and the lack of any but "mixed" opportunities for higher education might have weakened Catholic communal solidarity. Some secular currents in Belfast's political and institutional life might have begun to draw in Catholics, and in the process loosen their ties to their own community. Many of the Catholic Liberals were Liberals in politics who happened also to be Catholics, and were less than enthusiastic about the hierarchy's efforts to promote exclusive education.

We shall see, for example, that after A. J. McKenna's loss of clerical sanction for his newspapers, he lost much enthusiasm for denominational education and other explicitly clerical causes.

The second tendency that might have weakened Catholics' solidarity would have been Catholics repudiating clerical leadership and forming self-defence associations of a Ribbon variety or engaging in Fenianism. We have seen how during the riots of 1864, a meeting in the Catholic Institute decided on self-protection measures and declared the law unable to protect them. In practice in the North the distinction between "Ribbon" and "Fenian" organization might be imperceptible. We have seen how in east Tyrone, Orangemen regarded "Fenianism" as just another name for the programme of exterminating every Loyalist in the country. We can go to Carrickfergus for a further example. The *Carrickfergus Freeman* described Fenianism as follows:

"There is a kind of mania for a Republic among a certain portion of the lowest class of Roman Catholic Irishmen, which seems to be hereditary."[51]

After a fight between a Protestant ship carpenter and a drunken Catholic, the latter was charged with Fenianism on account of some verbal exchange that occurred during the fight. The case was dismissed. So much for Fenianism in Carrickfergus.[52] But as far as the North was concerned, "the chief result of the conspiracy and of the Government action against it in Belfast has been to make a slight addition to the somewhat limited vocabulary of party expressions".[53] That was not of course the whole story. In Newtownards some members of a Freemasons' lodge were expelled for promoting Fenianism[54] and two national schoolmasters, Alex Darragh (Ballycastle) and John Magee (Dromore), were arrested for supporting it.[55] In 1867 significant numbers of arrests were made in the Catholic area of Belfast. The *Whig* described the "arrest of nine people and the seizure of a large quantity of ammunition and a lead bullet manufactory in Hamill Street as certainly the most important that have yet been made in Belfast in connection with Fenianism".[56] Later on twenty rifles and 2,000 percussion caps were found in Pound Street. Most of those arrested were labourers, but the leaders were supposed to be a foreman moulder and a power loom tenter.[57] In fact, Fenianism in the North came to very little. With a few isolated exceptions it did not amount to a new secular political tradition, and certainly not a challenge to clerical leadership. That would come only after the November 1867 executions of the "Manchester Martyrs". But this challenge did not so much disrupt Catholic solidarity as set up a clerical v. anti-clerical tension within the Catholic community. The demand for amnesty for the Fenian prisoners may have weakened clerical leadership but it also widened the social distance between Catholics and Protestants in the North.

One of the most important factors promoting Catholic solidarity was the very distrust Protestants had of Catholics. Most of the time Protestants did not recognise any real differences existing amongst Catholics. But on the rare occasions when they did, their interest could have a disturbing influence on Catholics themselves.

Pan-Protestantism—the fear, distrust or hatred of Catholicism—could always see a solidarity within the Catholic community under clerical domination, regardless of the outward signs. Cardinal Cullen certainly lent them a lot of help in this, but that much-abused cleric can scarcely be blamed for the staying power of pan-Protestantism however narrow his sentiments may have been. In the pan-Protestant conspiracy theory, the Catholic clergy could not win. If they failed to suppress insurrection, that showed they secretly supported it. If they did manage to suppress it, that showed the Catholics were priest ridden and that the priests' failure to suppress rebellion on all occasions meant that they had tacitly supported it. Thus the idea that Fenianism, despite clerical denunciation, was just another manifestation of popish conspiracy was also easily sustained. This speech was delivered by one of Johnston's supporters in 1868:

"Some people had endeavoured to impress them with the idea that things had entirely changed with the last number of years in Ireland; but I deny that things have changed. Look at the Fenian organization for instance. If matters were changed could it occupy the position it did? The priests, it was said, were entirely opposed to it, but let them try that statement by the rules of logic. They all knew that the Roman Catholics of Ireland obeyed their priests in everything. The priests know everything they do or say. They had been told that the Fenian organization had been denounced by the priests: and why if they were so obedient in everything, were they so disobedient in this?

Either the people of the Church of Rome had showed disobedience to the priests or else the priests were not in earnest. The great evil they had to deal with hitherto was the unqualified obedience of the people to the priests. In his opinion it would be a bright day for Ireland when the priests would not have so much power over the people; but he could not believe that with every fact against it, that in every other matter the people were obedient and on this matter at open and direct opposition."[58]

It is important to notice the basic premise of the argument. Priests are absolutely dominant regardless of any evidence to the contrary. Therefore any evidence to the contrary is a deception. So what was actually meant by the "bright day when the priests would not have so much power over the people"? Pan-Protestants did welcome a breakdown in clerical power so long as it also seemed to weaken "Irish" solidarity. Fenianism did not do this, but middle-class Catholics trying to behave like members of the middle class did.

In 1865 Bishop Dorrian was involved in a dispute with the lay trustees of the Catholic Institute, over which he sought to impose direct control, including the supervision of the books and newspapers provided within it. The lay trustees refused to give ground. After several months of quite bitter argument the Bishop threatened to withhold the sacraments from those who would not bow to his demands.[59] In the end the trustees signed over the deeds to him. Whether or not they would have done so under other circumstances is an open question. But the dispute drew the attention of other parties whose interest in the welfare of Catholicism was, to say the least, questionable. The *Carrickfergus Freeman* which expressed pan-Protestant sentiments with relatively little varnish had this to say:

"The firm stand taken by the laity against the tyranny and usurpation of their Bishop prove that we were mistaken . . . and that the Roman Catholics are not such serfs or poltroons lying under the feet of their clergy as we supposed."[60]

A. J. McKenna of the *Observer* was profoundly embarrassed by the whole affair. He was almost certainly opposed to the Bishop's actions. But in the circumstances, seeing what "allies" the laity were collecting, he could hardly afford to say so. In fact, during the period rumours were widely circulated that he was writing anonymously against the Bishop in the *Newsletter*, a charge that hurt deeply and which he was only given the chance to refute when the rival *Ulster Examiner* printed the innuendo three years later.[61] The *Newsletter*'s intervention at the time caused a very definite closing of ranks, expressed by McKenna in November:

"We hardly need say that Catholics can settle their own affairs, without any interference on the part of their enemies. They require no instruction from the ignorant, no assistance from the hypocritical . . . That subject will be settled by Catholics themselves, who are not accustomed to make scandals, or to perpetuate them, and whose unbroken unity is the best guarantee of their continued concord. . . .

The only effect which the comments of our Orange contemporary could have on the Catholics of Belfast would be to make them adopt exactly the opposite course of that which it had the presumption to recommend. . . .

The feeling of apprehension entertained by the Trojans of the gift of the Greeks, was no more natural than is Catholic alarm at Tory approval and Orange advocacy."[62]

For a statement of the ultimate sources of pan-Catholic solidarity in the North, this cannot be bettered. It implies a great deal about the nature of sectionalism in the North. There was all the difference in the world between Catholic anti-clericalism, such as Fenians might display, and weakening the general solidarity of Catholic society as such. The imperatives to internal solidarity were far too strong to permit the growth of an anti-clericalism that weakened the boundary of the Catholic community unless some "neutral space" existed where a new relationship could be built up with Protestants who were doing the same thing.

Belfast liberalism was not a "neutral" ground on which people from both communities could meet and break down barriers between them. It had always been a "Protestant" space, but in the earlier time when the Whigs' relationships to the Catholics had been paternalistic this was not a problem. Once Catholics began to become organised and to define issues—especially education issues—in their way, the "Protestantism" of the Liberals became more defensive and the Protestant-Catholic tension became more explicit.

Rev. John McNaughton, mentioned earlier, was the pioneer of a new tendency inside the Presbyterian Church to make support for "united secular and separate religious instruction", rather than merely a practical co-operation in the national educational system, a matter of actual Church policy. In effect what he sought to do was to secure the Church's approval of a particular arrangement for social and political reasons, and to make it a political force for the defence of the system. The Anglican Church, although bending somewhat after 1866, had preserved a separate system in the Church Education Society, a series of endowed secondary schools and Trinity College, Dublin. The Catholic Church was seeking the explicit denominationalization of the national system. Between "Popery and Prelacy", MacNaughton sought to rally friends of non-denominational education to defend a status quo in the national system, the Queen's college and the Model Schools (for teacher training).

Besides this, he also wanted to see a disendowment and disestablishment of the "Prelatic" establishment and the setting of all religious bodies on a voluntary basis. Although not a declared voluntaryist—one who repudiated state support for Churches on principle—he none the less sought to secure a voluntary arrangement in Ireland for essentially political and social reasons. Through his activities we shall see the meaning acquired by the term "religious equality", which was initially the rallying cry of Presbyterians, but later became the flag for pan-Protestant opposition to Catholic clerical claims generally.

In 1864, at the Belfast presbytery, MacNaughton presented resolutions warning of the dangers of permitting convent schools to become acceptable alternatives to Model Schools as teacher training colleges.[63] The educational question began to assume greater urgency when agitation began for a charter for the Catholic university (April 1865). The *Banner* argued that if granted, Roman Catholic students would withdraw from the Queen's colleges.[64] Initially there seemed little chance of the charter being granted, but then the Presbyterian general assembly voted to approve an application from its own Magee College in Derry to apply for affiliate status to the Queen's University. The issue suddenly changed. The proponents of the Roman Catholic university shelved their demand for a charter and seemed to be negotiating instead for affiliate status on the same basis that Magee was asking for.⁶⁵ The issue that suddenly appeared was: how did the Presbyterians regard the prospect of affiliation not merely of Magee College, but also of the Roman Catholic university, to Queen's? And a special meeting of the general assembly was held in February 1866 to discuss the question.

As this meeting was greeted by both the *Northern Whig* and the *Banner of Ulster* as a "Liberal victory"⁶⁶—an affirmation of the principle of united national education—it is important to understand what that Liberal victory involved. MacNaughton opened the debate by arguing that the Presbyterian Church was committed to the system of united secular education as a matter of principle; that the gradual denominationalization of the national education system through the introduction of the principle of sectarian representation on the Board was dangerous; that the Magee College application would be employed as a "wedge" to secure changes in the Queen's University senate constitution which (in the process of affiliating Magee and the Roman Catholic university) would permit the denominational principle to creep in there too.⁶⁷ Therefore he wanted the Magee application withdrawn, in order not to use Presbyterian influence to assist Ultramontanism. Dr Dill, who led the opposition of the first instance, objected to the view that the Presbyterian commitment to the national education system was one of principle. He considered it a mistake to say that they should not use their political influence in this way, because they had none anyway. The only issue to attend to at the moment was to oppose denominational representation on the proposed senate of Queen's.

In fact, the issue of support "on principle" or for expedient considerations for the national education system turned into a side-show. The central question that dominated the debate was whether to proceed with the Magee application and accept the consequences for the Catholic university also, or to call on the Magee trustees to withdraw their application. It would be a more proper conclusion to draw from this debate to say that it demonstrated that the standard of "non-sectarian education" was a rallying cry for the Presbyterian educational interests. It was a position in which concepts of formal equality of educational rights could be used to resist the claims of Catholic denominationalism. But formal equality very definitely denied Catholic clerical conceptions of "equality". Much was said of the need to defend the rights of the Catholic laity to education that was not dominated by clerics. The argument ran that if Roman Catholic colleges were affiliated it would reduce the incentive to go to the Queen's colleges "and mix with their brethren of other denominations". At the moment Catholics went to these colleges "in the face of priestly denunciations". The view that "the spirit of all our modern legislation was that Government should not recognize Churches as such, but should deal simply with every man as a citizen of the state" was made the premise of the following. The Roman Catholic university was "an institution which was to regulate the Roman Catholic youth of the country in such a manner that it would not be possible for the superstitions which they advocate to be touched by the enlightenment of the present age". Put simply, "non-sectarianism" meant keeping "Popery" out of higher education.

This is not to say that there were no bona fide arguments for defending the non-denominational principle. MacNaughton's view that what happened to the Queen's colleges might affect national education generally brought forth an impassioned plea from Rev. William Johnston to the effect that once denominationalism was tolerated, the force of landlordism and Anglican clerical proselytism in the North would be brought to bear to crush (Presbyterian) national schools. And others brought out the importance of the national system for small minorities of any denomination in an area where they had to rely on mixed schools (i.e. Presbyterians in southern Ulster and beyond). All of these various considerations were brought to bear against the Magee application for, so to speak, "selling the pass". The reality of this session was that behind this defence of the status quo was assembled a host of elements who had very different conceptions of Catholic rights in the educational sphere. It was scarcely necessary for any overt proselytizers to declare their hand. Advocates of formal equality said on this occasion all that any opponent of Catholic claims needed to say.

The consensus was "not an inch" to Catholic denominational claims in higher education.

If it were to become possible for lay Catholics to accept non-sectarian education in the North, "non-sectarianism" should not have been such a happy partner with anti-Catholicism. When such "non-sectarianism" was linked so closely to hostility to Catholicism, no Catholic opponent of clerical obscurantism was ever going to declare himself as such. There was a small minority in the Presbyterian assembly who, while they supported non-sectarian education, had some empathetic grasp of how the issue looked to Catholics. They understood the dangers of alliance with anti-Catholics. And they grasped quite clearly that the prospect of Catholic university affiliation to Queen's rather than the granting of a separate charter, might be a viable solution to a very real difficulty. Most of the time there did not seem to be much chance of compromise in dealing with ultramontane educational demands, but here were the promoters of the Catholic university doing something unusual and something which promised a possible route to a compromise. MacNaughton's approach effectively blocked the possibility of compromise from the Presbyterian end. Admittedly Rev. Richard Smyth, as a professor in Magee College, had a vested interest, but his speech sums up the knots in which the advocates of "united non-sectarian education" had tied themselves.

The Rev. Henry Henderson, one of the more rabid no popery men, had declared that if the change in the constitution of Queen's were carried out, it would become a Roman Catholic university. Smyth asked:

"Let this Assembly take care how it endorses that view . . . if this thing be done, and the university given over to the ultramontanists, are you prepared to follow your position to its logical issue and break forever with the Queen's Colleges?"

Dr. Cooke shouted 'I am.'

"Then I go with Dr. Cooke for I want to test the impartiality and sincerity of our opponents on this question. But I warn you that if you follow the view put forward by these ardent defenders of the status quo, it will land you in embarrassment and perhaps disgrace. No one has yet attempted to show what is wrong with the Government proposal. The students who will be admissible for degrees under the new charter can get them now in London University (by external examination) at additional expense. And what I want to know is whether what is right in London can be wrong in Dublin? What right have you to banish our students to London for degrees? Will you tell young Irishmen of education that if they wish to be admitted to the right of literary citizenship they much go to England and there they will find a door open which is shut against them here? Nor does this comport with the professions of extreme liberality that have found vent on the other side. 'Liberty of conscience', say these its latest expounders, does not include an Irish University degree. They can afford to be generous, comprehensive and liberal in England, but Ireland would not be Ireland if it did not retain some remnant of intolerance. But I now push the battle into the enemy's camp, and I tell our opponents that they are the worst friends of United Education, for when a great crisis does arise, as some day it shall when United Education will be in real danger, these noisy brethren will be regarded as consistently discontented, hard to please, and their influence will be lost. Concede what is right without reference to wedges and resist where you should offer resistance."[68]

Thus spoke the future Liberal MP for County Derry. His voice in the assembly was supplemented by a few others who spoke of the need to meet Catholic claims, and the fortunate fact that on this occasion they were presented in a meetable form.

Denominationalization did threaten serious difficulties in two areas of primary education. First, it would have faced small minorities with a choice between someone else's denominational education and none at all. In much of south and south-west Ulster Presbyterians might have found themselves in this situation. Second, it might become easier for landlords to refuse to give ground for schools of particular denominations, and it would have increased the grip of Anglican proselytism. These were both real dangers; and it was on this basis that Rev. William Johnston expressed such alarm about precedents. But the substantial animus behind this "Liberal" victory was the desire to prevent the growth of Catholic-controlled institutions of higher education. It cannot be supposed that the small minority who accepted the need to meet these demands felt particularly keen on the idea. But they realized that Protestant resistance could be counterproductive or even dangerous.

It would be a severe exaggeration to imply that this affiliation scheme, applied in 1866, would have disposed of the education question as "proxy" for the national question. In fact there are very strong grounds for thinking that the Catholic proposal to follow the Magee precedent was only tactical. But there is no way of knowing what might have followed if they had been successful in persuing this tactic. An open hand from Presbyterianism then might have changed the way Catholics pursued educational questions. Someone had to change and here was a possible starting point. Instead Protestants carried on the farce of "defending the rights of the Catholic laity" (or "intelligent Catholics" as they were often described) against clerical despotism. In a society where religion was becoming, or had become, a proxy for national affiliation, and where the corrosion of Catholicism was all too often associated with weakening Irish nationality, Protestant opposition to Catholic clericalism was simply not even-handed "anti-clericalism". Any serious pluralism in religious affairs had to take cognisance of the fact that Catholic clerics were in a high degree representative figures of the Catholic society, and the necessity of working out a compact with them.

The Liberal government fell after it had passed the Supplemental Charter, but before carrying through any reconstruction of the senate.[69] It was therefore left to the senate to decide to accept the charter and to invite applications from interested bodies to affiliate. But a legal battle was to ensue over whether the senate had the power to do this without the charter also having been approved by the convocation of graduates.[70] At a convocation meeting, the vice-chancellor was hissed and groaned when he mentioned the charter. The debate that followed was of such a character that forty-five Roman Catholic graduates walked out.[71] And the presidents of the colleges refused to co-operate with the senate in giving it effect until its legality was tested.[72]

In early 1867 a meeting in Belfast of "Friends of United Education" drew this comment from the *Observer*:
"There were Whigs, who would be insulted or pretend to be insulted, if you called them bigots, who stood on a common platform with men who glory in their bigotry, and who espouse the 'mixed system' of education simply because they believe it inimical to Catholic interests."[73]
The substantive issue at this meeting was the question of convents as teacher training establishments. Rev. J. S. Porter, a Unitarian, said that teachers would emerge "with strong prejudices having never seen a Protestant child or teacher".[74] The *Observer* found the meeting discreditable to Belfast Protestants and offensive to Irish Catholics.[75] The legal opposition to the implementation of the supplemental charter was one of the factors which moved the Conservative government towards the idea of an actual charter for the Catholic university.[76]

Dr McKnight's *Derry Standard*, which had supported Professor Smyth's earlier solution to the university difficulty, now observed that the Roman Catholic university charter was intended as a ramp to defend the Anglican monopoly in Trinity College. "Even for the interests of the Catholic University the competition of its students at the hands of a national body of examiners would be infinitely preferable to the Charter scheme as a permanent arrangement."[77] The *Banner of Ulster*, which had taken the "Liberal" view in February 1866, now declared that Tories would do anything for political support, but failed to appreciate the role of its own position in prompting the new initiative. The argument from precedent was again employed. If Roman Catholic university students need their faith protected, how much more would the hierarchy push the case where schoolchildren were concerned? Hence the university scheme would have to be viewed as a "complete triumph of denominationalism in Ireland".[78]

The United Education Leaguers' reaction to the new scheme, following the Radical MP, Fawcett of Brighton, was that the only way to resist the charter was to "open" Trinity College, meaning to remove explicit tests on those seeking its degrees.[79] Making Trinity a formally "non-sectarian" university like Queen's would remove the "precedent" for a Catholic university. The embarrassment of this group was well illustrated when some Anglican supremacists appeared at the meeting to oppose the idea of "opening" Trinity. They moved a resolution opposing the Roman Catholic university charter "as opposed to the Word of God".[80] MacNaughton opposed this resolution by making out that the proposition refused the teaching of sciences etc. to Roman Catholics. Confusion prevailed. "You forget your own speech", they replied, and one jester, alluding to the magistrates' court fine for party exclamations in public, heckled him "forty shillings and costs!".

The *Derry Standard*, in a strong attack on the "Queen's College monopolists" who dominated the meeting, said the talk of "opening" Trinity simply missed the point which was that the Roman Catholic college must be able to affiliate to something. It praised one speaker who pointed out that somehow a supplemental charter was necessary, whether to Queen's or to the National University of Ireland (i.e. Trinity).[81] But with the spirit of such meetings united by opposition to Roman Catholic claims alone, A. J. McKenna commented that "it is strange and painful to see staunch Liberals going hand-in-hand with extreme Tories in this crusade against freedom and equality."[82]

The Conservative government continued to look into the possibilities of a separate charter. After Gladstone's resolutions on Disestablishment in 1868 the government briefly toyed with the idea of endowing the Roman Catholic Church as well. Both measures were designed to secure the position of the Anglican Church and Trinity College. But the negotiations for the charter ran into difficulties over questions of college endowment and the extent of clerical control over the institution.[83] The proposal for "concurrent endowment" of the Church was rejected by the hierarchy in favour of the alternative overall solution proposed by Gladstone—disestablishment and disendowment of all Churches in Ireland.[84]

Liberal support for "United Education", according to the MacNaughton line, had got itself into an impossible position from which Gladstone's resolutions rescued it. In the face of Catholic demands for some kind of recognized institutions of Catholic higher education, these Liberals had committed themselves to total opposition in the name of "religious equality", and they had created the embarrassment that in future Conservatives (interested principally in defending the Anglican monopoly of Trinity College) might simply conciliate Catholic claims over their heads. The minority position of Professor Smyth and James McKnight, who saw the need to conciliate Catholic claims, was the only conceivable basis for a wider understanding between Protestant and Catholic Liberals.

We turn now to the response of Presbyterian Liberals to Gladstone's proposals. Presbyterian response to this question reflected more diversity of considerations than any other. The insecurity of Regium Donum has already been mentioned. Subject to annual vote in parliament, it was increasingly attacked by an unholy alliance of Anglican supremacists and English voluntaryists. During the moderatorship of Dr John Rogers of Comber, great efforts were made to secure an increase in the grant. Rodgers, whose good relations with southern Catholics went back to the days of the Tenant League, was consistently supported by a large number of southern MPs.[85] But by 1867, with increasing discussion of the future of religious establishments, a question mark began to hang over Regium Donum following Lord John Russell's resolution to inquire into church revenues.[86] The speech of the Ulster Whig leader, Lord Dufferin, in September 1867 threw up the problem in the way in which it increasingly came to be discussed. Practically speaking the choice was between the Disraeli-Derby policy of "levelling up" (endowing Roman Catholicism) or the Gladstone policy of "levelling down" (disestablishing Anglicanism and terminating all religious endowments).[87] This did not prevent the Conservatives in the North from attempting a rearguard action to defend the status quo, beginning with the Hillsborough church defence meeting in October 1867.[88]

Before the issue had crystallized in March 1868, the *Banner* dealt with the disestablishment question in the abstract.[89] First, it worried about the precedent of disendowment as an attack on property rights generally. Second, it considered that Catholics might then want their religion established on the ground that the majority religion is usually so established. But third, it took up the question posed by MacNaughton that "religious equality" was a barrier to Catholic endowment. "The great ram of Romanism would soon smash up the fragile craft of 'religious equality', and we don't care to commit the interests of Protestantism to so hazardous an adventure." But they were in an impossible position. The Church defenders were silently accepting Roman Catholic endowment as a rampart for Anglican property, they said. And so long as the place of Regium Donum in the various schemes remained uncertain, the *Banner* did not know which way to turn. On 31 March it said that it approved of establishment in principle, but disliked this one.[90] If Anglicanism reformed it might have been looked upon favourably. But "we cannot ally ourselves with Romanism against any Protestant church, nor can we afford to the Establishment the aid that under other circumstances we would like to render".

Later (25 April) they retreated yet further into pan-Protestantism with an attack on the Lord Lieutenant for addressing Cardinal Cullen as "Catholic Archbishop of Dublin" in contravention of the Ecclesiastical Titles Act. The Cardinal's honoured place at the Castle banquet was a sin against the law and "compromised the Protestantism of the country".[91] It reacted furiously against the Ulster MPs who voted the wrong way on the supplementaries to the Gladstone resolutions, which recognized Regium Donum as a vested interest to be considered alongside other Church endowments.[92] The *Derry Standard* did not suffer from the same indecisiveness. It approved Gladstone's proposals and said it wished that Presbyterians would start waking up to the reality that they would have to do without Regium Donum quite soon and stop making agitated visits to ministers on its behalf.[93]

At the June 1868 Presbyterian General Assembly[94] the issue was debated in the form of a choice between two sets of resolutions. Dr Dill's resolutions affirmed the principle of Regium Donum and protested against the threat posed to it, while affirming the principle of an ecclesiastical establishment (the duty of the state to support truth against error). Dr Kirkpatrick's resolutions affirmed the principle of Presbyterian connection with the state and its past acceptance of support. It then declared that the endowment of error (Roman Catholicism) was wrong and, rather than this, preferred a full and impartial disendowment of all Churches. As in 1866 the common ground between the rival factions was that endowment of Catholicism was wrong. But there was a difference here between the use of "religious equality" to justify a serious anti-ascendancy principle and its use in the education controversy where it acted as a support for the status quo. It was here that the MacNaughton line led to objective agreement with Catholic claims.

In the debate, the line pursued by Dr Dill and Dr Cooke was that what was required was to reaffirm a principle (i.e. the claim to Regium Donum) and not, as Kirkpatrick did, to renounce that right and thereby take a side in a political controversy. Alex Gray then made the political points which they had declined to make, and which were the essence of the "No Surrender" position. He attacked the idea that giving up endowments was a way of checking popish endowment; he suggested some of the other side were not even opposed to popery and actually supported Gladstone. He said he was just as opposed to prelacy as they were, but would never consent "to blot out any form of Protestantism to make room for Popery". He concluded by pointing to the practical necessity of Regium Donum for ministers in areas with sparse and poor congregations (in the South and West).

MacNaughton then moved in to say that there was no difference of principle at stake. It was a question of what to do in this particular emergency situation. "It is vain to hope that [ministers and legislatures] will look upon the matter as a question between truth and error, without taking into account the numbers of those from whom these demands proceed." In other words, you must face the fact of the Roman Catholic majority in Ireland—a fact which limits the outcome to either levelling "up" or "down". And lest his support for disestablishment and disendowment be taken as support for Catholic claims: "As long as the grass grows and the water runs and the Pope remains in his place, and the Man of Sin is not destroyed and there is money in the British Exchequer, Rome will find some way of making demands on it." Several others indicated support for the Kirkpatrick resolutions on much the same basis—absolute opposition to the endowment of popery. There were rather few who actually endorsed the disestablishment proposal for reasons of equity or justice. Rev. Robinson of Broughshane openly stated that he sympathized with Catholics finding the establishment a grievance, and Professor Wallace said: "I maintain that an Established Church not supported by the sentiments of the country is an oppression." But such outright statements of the justice of Catholic claims were few.

The implications of the debate were profoundly murky. Dr Killen who, like MacNaughton, based his support for disestablishment on the ground of intransigent opposition to prelacy (which he wanted to disestablish and disendow) and popery (which he wanted to deprive of the prelatic precedent for endowing), asked the assembly to compare the Edinburgh meeting in favour of Catholic emancipation with the Oxford meeting against it. None of the former but plenty of the latter had since changed to Romanism. He was making an effort to point out that there is no connection between the solidity of someone's Protestant faith and their attitudes toward equality of rights for Catholics, but he presented the issue in a very backhanded way.

The final confusion was introduced by Professor Smyth, who so disliked arguments about "precedents" and "wedges". What, he asked, would happen if the Established Church were disestablished but not disendowed? Would the proponents of the Kirkpatrick resolutions then be pleased if the Presbyterians were shorn of their endowments, as the Kirkpatrick resolutions suggested? Although a supporter of disestablishment, Professor Smyth effectively endorsed the Cooke/Dill line that a political statement was inexpedient, and that it was required only to affirm the principle of Regium Donum now in order that it be considered in any settlement of the question as a vested interest.

In sum, the upshot of the meeting was clear as mud. Taking the Belfast ministers alone, there was a cast-iron relationship between the way they voted on Dill v. Kirkpatrick and the way they voted in the 1868 general elections.[95] Everyone who voted for Kirkpatrick voted for the Liberal, Thomas McClure (either alone or with Johnston), and of those who voted for Dill, none cast a vote for McClure. But aside from Belfast there was a whole range of unresolved issues. On the Dill side were (a) those who supported the status quo; (b) those who thought it improper to do more than affirm the theological basis of

Regium Donum acceptance; and (c) those who feared the consequences of the surrender of the right to Regium Donum in the event of an adverse settlement (Professor Smyth's warning), whether they actually supported "religious equality" in principle or not. On the Kirkpatrick side there were (a) those who wanted to erect "religious equality" as a barrier to Romish endowment; and (b) those who supported religious equality on principle. Significantly, given the use made of the country minister argument, the presbyteries which voted most heavily for Kirkpatrick were Connaught and Dublin; while those most strongly opposed were Carrick, Derry, Comber, Magherafelt, Armagh, Limavady, Omagh, and Route (where Presbyterianism was quite strong enough to hold its own). Only Bailieborough and Ballybay—of the areas where the "country ministers' argument" was strongest—voted solidly for Dill.[96] It is also worth mentioning in passing that Derry and Route were two of the strongest areas of political liberalism of the advanced kind. In short, the result was a confusion which scarcely touched the issue with the urgency that was required. As the *Derry Standard* put it: "Levelling down is the only possible policy unless there be perpetual rule by coercion acts."[97]

The *Banner* only moved in behind the MacNaughton line when the place of Regium Donum as a legitimate vested interest (in relation to the Gladstone proposals) was recognized and when the Conservative government scheme for Roman Catholic endowment was made public. In July it declared that voting for the Tories meant supporting the present establishment "in its position of galling Ascendancy—for endowment of the Church of Rome and for the destruction of the National Education system".[98] Only in September, however, did they begin to talk of the establishment as an insult to Catholics and a hindrance to Protestantism.[99] And in November, any Presbyterian who voted Tory was described as saying that "the Free Church of Scotland made a mistake in forsaking the Erastian Establishment".[100]

The conception of "religious equality" which MacNaughton had been propagating from 1868 onwards in the Presbyterian Church was a step away from the old Protestant supremacism. But its popularity grew because it became a defensive slogan for the protection of the Presbyterian Church and its educational interests. It created a space in which those who believed in religious equality on principle, and those who saw it as a "barrier to Romanism", could coexist. In fact it blurred the distinction between the two so that a "rationalist" egalitarianism and "No Popery" could coexist. But whereas on educational questions that was the sum of its effect, at the crucial conjuncture in 1868 it was doing something rather more. It was calling on Presbyterians to offer a concession to secure "equality". The force of the argument for the concession grew as the credibility of a status quo position collapsed, and the only practicable alternatives became levelling "up" or "down". When William Johnston, the Independent Orange candidate whose total opposition to "endowment of Popery" no one questioned, indicated that if he had to choose he preferred Gladstone's solutions ("It's just an auction", he said), he was taking up the MacNaughton line under circumstances which maximised the possible basis of its support.[101] Here was someone saying that he would prefer the status quo, but as that was not a viable proposition any more, he would prefer the levelling "down" as the means of arriving at religious equality. The twists and turns of the *Banner*'s position on the question show that this was indeed the basis upon which many ended up supporting the Johnston/McClure ticket in 1868.

MacNaughton had successfully confused abstract secular liberalism with political anti-Catholicism. In one way it was a positive achievement to secure significant Presbyterian support for disestablishment of the Anglican Church. At an important stage in Irish history some took the same side as the Catholics in opposition to this minority-backed state Church. But so long as "religious equality" and "united education" were also implicit sticks with which to beat Catholicism, the prospect of them providing a platform for an authentic non-sectarian northern liberalism was nil. In 1868 Gladstone's disestablishment proposal brought Presbyterian and Catholic concepts of religious equality together in a unique and unrepeatable unity.

So far we have shown that Belfast in 1866–68 began to experience an upsurge of popular activity associated with ratepayer self-assertion, working-class self-improvement, and other secular causes. The Catholics were rather on the sidelines, somewhat alienated from the tenor of much of public life, including Belfast liberalism. The Presbyterian Liberals' efforts to define a political programme floundered until the issue was clarified as a choice between "levelling up" or "levelling down". So how was this diverse array of opponents to Toryism focused? And what of the huge unknown quantity—the expansion of the franchise from around 3,000 to 11,000? Belfast Toryism was certainly embarrassed by the Conservative government's offer of a charter to the Roman Catholic university and of endowment to the Catholic Church. It was certainly embarrassed by the enfranchisement of a mass of new voters, nearly every one of whom was adversely affected by its manipulation of the rating system. But the focus of all these various strands of opposition was to come from a quarter they least expected as little as two years previously.

We now turn to the story of a figure who will dominate the rest of this chapter and most of the next, the landlord of a small estate at Ballykilbeg outside Downpatrick, William Johnston. The *Ulster Examiner* commented after reading a passage from Johnston's novel, *Nightshade*, that the Ribbon society "is a gorgon making his nights sleepless and burdening his daily life with needless and unnecessary cares".[102] This is perhaps the most charitable thing they had to say about the book, which includes a passage in which a priest gives absolution in advance to an intending murderer. Johnston had written *Nightshade* in 1857 at a time when he was one of the most far-flung eccentrics in Ulster politics.

His diaries for 1847 reveal a decidedly fundamentalist view of the world. In the worst year of the Famine in Downpatrick district, he speaks of the work of the relief committee and the potato failure. Something of a political change is indicated by the 6 June entry:

"I have long had an idea in my head that I was to do something for the cause of God, I mean against our rulers, till today when God forcibly impressed my mind 'Thinkest thou that I could not destroy these men.' Yes, O Lord. I see the folly and vanity of my thoughts; Thou hast permitted these things to be for Thine own good purpose; let me henceforth labour and pray for my own loved, Erin."[103]

And somewhat earlier his diary contains extracts from a letter of a clergyman on the sufferings of the Famine.

"I do trust the poor benighted people will now learn who are their real friends, and that the gentry will do their very utmost to improve the present momentous crisis, toward giving them the true panacea for their woes, even that blessed word, which is 'for the healing of nations'."[104]

Johnston's early adult life was concerned with promoting ultra-Protestantism in politics. He shared with many the hope that the European revolutions and the Famine would weaken popery. At the end of 1847, "Evidences not a few have there been, that Popery's death struggle has commenced in the hearts of the people of Ireland."[105] The Ribbonmen mentioned above were a real concern. In December 1847 a nearby farmer had been sworn to leave his farm by eleven or twelve armed men: "This looks pretty bad so near home."[106] And in March 1848, "There is certainly something determined by the rebel party in this country: some day set on to begin the revolt."[107] The diaries for the 1849 Dolly's Brae incident are unfortunately missing, but the existence of ribbonism as a real force is clear.

Nightshade contains a crude but very tight conception of a popish intention to exterminate Protestants in which the Ribbon society figures as a tool of the priesthood. Seen from this angle, his politics are a simple expression of a need to check any kind of political or financial encouragement of popery. Johnston participated in the protest meeting got up against the Diplomatic Relations (Rome) Bill of 1848,[108] and after the official about turn on Orangeism in 1849–50 he became one of the stalwarts of the new residualized Orange Order. Of the May 1850 meeting of the Grand Lodge in Derry, "Some people were insane enough to believe that the Grand Lodge had come to Derry for the purpose of dissolving. Dare a Protestant breathe the word surrender in sacred Derry?"[109]

Johnston continued to keep his relations with the local Orange lodges, entertaining them to dinner and attending their meetings through the years when other landlords tended to distance themselves.[110] He looked with deep distrust on the more important local landlords such as the Kers who had influence in the county and more or less controlled Downpatrick. The test of their Protestantism was for him their determination to stop the Maynooth grant: as he said to them of Lord Aberdeen, "I hope you don't call such Free Trade, popery men Conservatives."¹¹¹ He actively promoted the Downshire Protestant Association (the local wing of his father-in-law Dr Drew's Christ Church Protestant Association). And in 1854, when a county meeting was being held to deplore the Trillick outrage (the derailment of an Orange excursion train in which Lord Enniskillen was seriously injured), he made it his business to ensure that the resolutions were "Protestantised". "It was nearly spoiled by [?] interfering to emasculate the resolutions, by leaving out any allusion to the Church of Rome", but he "got one in" showing "from documentary evidence that Rome approved of heretic murder".[112]

Notwithstanding his zeal against popery he did not hate Catholics. In later years the *Examiner* commented very favourably on how he treated his Roman Catholic tenants at Ballykilbeg,[113] and his diary entry records the death of a Catholic "the decentest, loyalest, honestest Roman Catholic in these here parts. . . . He never joined the Repealers for, he said, 'I swore to be true to King George, Sir, and you wouldn't have an old yeoman break his oath.'"[114] The contrast between his attitude towards "Popery" and toward his Roman Catholic neighbours in Downpatrick was very real, and later on a great deal of practical liberality found expression between these two poles of his personality.

Until the mid-1860s, however, Johnston was regarded as a fringe crank who lacked political sense. He threatened to stand in Downpatrick in 1857, but withdrew from the poll (at which he received one vote) after Ker had been absent from a vote on the Maynooth grant without a pair. The paucity of his vote was made up for by the populace who "cheered and drew me round the town".[115]

His interest in Belfast politics began about 1860. Then aged 31, his diaries suggest an association with some of its more fringe elements. A meeting of the Society for the Propagation of the Gospel in Foreign Parts, he describes as a "glorious row in Belfast last night".[116] The Lord Bishop Dr Knox found himself confronted by an audience "composed principally of working men", angry that he had refused the Rev. Mr Potter permission to preach in the parish church on the recent 12 July.[117] The audience groaned and hissed and spoke about "pitching out the Puseyite", "No Popish bishop here", etc. C. H. Ward who led the mob moved a resolution to displace the Bishop from the chair. The meeting ended in a take-over after the Bishop and nearly all the clergy left. Ward became Johnston's main link with Belfast before 1868.

Johnston's own sentiments in the early 1860s can best be described as impatient with the established Tories. In the course of an attack on Conservatives at a Belfast Orange meeting in 1861,[118] he said:

"It is time that we should tell men that loyalty is due on the part of the governing party to the governed as much as on the part of the governed to the governing. . . .

Popery is something more than a religious system: it is a political system also. It is a religio-political system for the enslavement of the body and soul of man and it cannot be met by any mere religious system or by any mere political system. It must be opposed by such a combination as the Orange Society based upon religion and carrying our religion into the politics of the day."

For all his later ambivalence, he never actually departed from this position which he expounded in 1861. Johnston had not been representing any coherent set of interests, for example, the class of small landlords. We hear very little on the subject of agricultural protectionism in Johnston's diaries after the early 1850s; and certainly not a word of this when he moves into the limelight in the mid- to late 1860s. Nor does his concern for Protestantism seem to have meant economic exclusivism. His tenants included large numbers of Roman Catholics, and if there was ever any basis for attacking his treatment of them, it would surely have been made. The Society for the Relief of Distressed Protestants in Newry (1850) disappears without further mention in his diary.[119] His concern is solely with stopping the drift toward government accommodation with Catholicism and its discouragement of Orangeism. This in fact is the secret of his success in 1868. He was the perfect embodiment of a set of "Protestant" principles, almost a framework person around which a plethora of other questions could cluster.

When Belfast was broken away from County Antrim and formed into a separate Grand Lodge in 1864, his position as the renowned "no compromise" man made him a very suitable figurehead for the anti-Conservative elements. By 1866 he had been made District Master of No. 4.[120] With the Conservative minority government in power at Westminster, the local Tory leadership appears to have been aware of Johnston's disruptive potential. Thus in 1866, when he held an Orange meeting at Ballykilbeg, Lord A. E. Hill Trevor wrote him a letter opposing the meeting.[121] In Downpatrick the magistrates met to discuss what Johnston described as the "cursed lie of O'Kane's [the Roman Catholic priest], that the brethren were coming from Belfast to fire at the big cross [on his church]". A district inspector served him with a letter from the Lord Lieutenant forbidding the meeting, to which he replied, "No Surrender."[122]

The Conservative government that came to power in 1866 was a minority government, as indeed had been every such administration from 1845. Its priority was the passage of its own Electoral Reform Bill. Much of its Irish policy was a continuity from the previous Liberal administration and it showed no tendency whatever to support the claims of Ulster Toryism. It included, for example, Michael Morris, a Catholic, as Solicitor-General for Ireland, and made very plain its intention to continue the Party Processions Act. Ulster conservatism could discountenance party processions and simultaneously criticize the law so long as the Whigs were in power. But their position was altogether more difficult when the Conservatives were in power at Westminster. William Johnston became a serious problem for them.

Most moderate Conservatives, nearly all Liberals, and Ulster Catholics almost without exception favoured the Party Processions Act. The threatening potential of such manifestations was only too clear as we saw in the last chapter. Charles Lanyon, M.P., promised Johnston he would attempt to get it repealed,[123] but the Conservative leadership and Lord Enniskillen, the Grand Master, were adamant in their opposition to breaches of it.[124] In July 1867, against the opposition of the Belfast Grand Lodge leadership, Johnston (now District Master of No. 4 Belfast) organized a massive demonstration in Bangor.[125] Trainloads poured in from every part of Belfast and County Down; and choosing an area in which there were very few Catholics indeed to offend, he himself led a large march from Newtownards into Bangor, where he declared from the platform:

"The advocates of Reform have gained it by great outdoor demonstrations—the concessions to the Papacy have been gained by great demonstrations and here we can show 50,000 men in Bangor determined to gain our rights by loyal and peaceable means.

It is utterly insufferable and not to be borne that it is illegal for Protestants on the 12 July to display an Orange flag or Protestant drum, while it is perfectly legal for Roman Catholics to march through the streets of Dublin."[126]

This defiance could not be ignored. The government decided to prosecute and the County Down Grand Jury prepared an address supporting the putting down of all processions.[127] In September Johnston wrote to the Castle:

"I am grateful for the honour done me, by including me in the number singled out for prosecution. And I am sure the course adopted by the government will do more to advance Orangeism than anything I can have done in the last ten years."[128]

The same day he issued an election address for an anticipated by-election in Belfast, which ensured that Samuel Getty, M.P., was virtually ordered not to resign for the present.

From this point onwards a certain ambivalence crept into some Whig and Liberal statements about the Party Processions Act. The *Banner of Ulster*, for example, which supported the Act, had none the less missed no opportunity to point out to Orangemen how cynically Toryism treated them. "We cannot but admire the bold and spirited manner in which [Mr Johnston] gives expression to his views."[129] And Lord Dufferin, the Whig leader who was one of the magistrates who had signed the County Down Grand Jury address against processions, observed in a public speech the disparity between the treatment of Orangemen in the North and Fenian demonstrations in the South.[130] The line taken in the *Northern Whig* shifted as it stressed how it favoured an even-handed application of the Party Processions Act. It even began to suggest that it was only the partiality of its application that Orangemen were protesting against.[131]

The Conservative landlords attempted to cover their tracks somewhat by organizing a mass meeting at Hillsborough to declare support for the Established Church, a meeting to which Orangemen were mustered but which eschewed all mention of the Party Processions Act.[132] And thereafter church defence meetings (without the attendant processions) were employed as a means of assembling the faithful without actual breach of the Party Processions Act, and to distance themselves from the Conservative government's conciliation of the Catholic hierarchy. In the meantime Colonel Forde attempted in February 1868 to get Johnston to sign an admission that he had "broken the law" which could be employed to persuade Lord Mayo, the Chief Secretary, to call off the Bangor prosecutions.[133] Johnston however insisted on pleading "not guilty", and in March he was sentenced to imprisonment. While the *Banner* said that the prosecution would raise Johnston to the dignity of martyrdom,[134] McKenna's paper, the *Northern Star*, praised the County Down Grand Jury for its action against processions.[135]

The difference of approach between the *Banner* and the *Star* reflected very fundamental disagreements about the meaning of Orange parades.[136] For the *Star* Johnston was seen as the "fanatic of Ballykilbeg" who was stirring up the flames of pan-Protestant violence. His actions were part of a piece with the contents of the last chapter. The *Banner*'s view was that party processions were irritating (rather than threatening):

"They very unnecessarily remind the Catholics that they are a conquered race. Out of consideration for feelings of Roman Catholics, Protestants might abstain. The demonstrations have not united in the bonds of national concord the Roman Catholic population. It is alleged that such an end cannot be attained—that loyalty to a Protestant state from such a quarter is impossible. But would it not be well to try what the absence of provocation would effect?"[137]

The ambiguity of Protestant Liberals towards Johnston was not altogether a cynical exploitation of the Tory embarrassment at prosecuting an Orangeman. The Fenian Rising of March 1867 had come no closer than Louth,[138] but after the execution of the Manchester Martyrs a wave of popular feeling spread over in Ireland far greater than anything which had been displayed in the way of support for Fenianism itself. Mock funeral processions drew enormous crowds and the Catholic clergy, the greater part of which had opposed Fenianism, were drawn strongly into the wave of revulsion against the "judicial murders".[139] Efforts were made to apply the Party Processions Act against some of the sympathy demonstrations, but the prosecutions were generally unsuccessful.[140] In contrast to these, Johnston's march from Newtownards to Bangor was not even an encouragement or sympathy for "rebellion" and it looked quite innocuous. Also, because of its location it had very little prospect of promoting a sectarian collision. So long as Orange processions were seen as displays of loyal sentiment which happened incidentally to irritate Catholics, they could hardly be regarded as "more" illegal than expressions of sympathy with Fenian prisoners. If, on the other hand, the well-ordered Orange procession in County Down was regarded as a ram to legitimize the kinds of activities we saw in the last chapter, Johnston was quite a different kind of problem.

His imprisonment in March sparked the intervention of a new political force in Belfast. We have noticed already how some of the pan-Protestants of 1865–66 became heavily involved in the agitation for reform and against the City Hall, and how Tom Henry was expelled from the Orange Order for his part in it. It was at this point that those who had not joined forces with "Papists and Radicals" intervened. The inaugural meeting of the Protestant Working Men's Association in March 1868 expressed little of the generalized class consciousness of the reform meetings. Its focus was strictly upon the "betrayal of Protestantism" by the upper-class Conservatives and support for the "martyred" William Johnston.[141] "We believe that Mr. William Johnston has been deserted and betrayed by the aristocracy of Ulster on the grounds of his thorough identification with the Protestant working classes of this province." The themes of the working class having great power if only they thought "about themselves as we ought" echoed the sentiments of the reform meeting. But the content was different. The *Newsletter*, the County Down Grand Jury, the Ulster Conservatives generally and the "monster meetings in honour of rebels and murders" were denounced. And one speaker announced that Johnston would be released the next day (wrongly, as it turned out).

The *Star* saw in this last announcement proof that the people who met in the Ulster Hall were the "real masters of Ireland" and said: "the one solitary incident that was calculated to show that at last there was such a thing as firm and impartial Government for Ireland has suddenly vanished like a shadow".[142]

Dr McKnight's *Derry Standard* noticed the resolution displayed in all the speeches that working men should think for themselves, and though less than enthusiastic about the sentiments expressed, suggested that the Protestant Working Men's Association should take up the land question.[143] In fact, at this stage the association was very much a single-issue body concerned exclusively with the right of procession, and its future would hang upon its pronouncements on other issues.

Dr McKnight's suggestion was followed rather quickly from several quarters. Dr Drew, Johnston's father-in-law, made a rather cryptic utterance about how he hadn't understood the land question until he himself argued with his landlord,[144] Colonel Forde; and the *Northern Star* indicated that it would gladly sink all other issues for this one.[145] Shortly thereafter followed the resolutions of the Orangemen of Ballymoney, Dervock and Rasharkin pledging their support for Johnston:

"resolved that whereas civil liberty as established by William III has been taken from the people of Ireland by the Priests and Landlords—in the one case by the terrors of the Church and in the other by the progress of eviction, as witnessed at every county election—we will stand firmly together and endeavour to public odium any party—either Priest or Landlord—who interferes with this right.

... that we pledge ourselves to use every legal means to procure for the Tenant Farmers of Ireland fixity of tenure".[146]

The next stages followed with Johnston's release from prison. Commenting on the conflict between the Conservatives' "levelling up" and Gladstone's "levelling down" policy, he said the whole thing was "just an auction" but that he preferred Gladstone's policy which was far more Protestant than the endowment of Catholicism. It was one step from here to the ambiguous remark in his September address about wanting "no undue Ascendancy".[147]

All the signs were that Johnston was linking land reform and some kind of support for disestablishment to his demand for repeal of the Party Processions Act. Was this to be treated as a question of equal rights or was it after all a question of licensed supremacism? In June the Protestant Working Men's Association through William McCormick, a glass manufacturer and one of Johnston's more "secular" lieutenants, denounced the impending visit of a Murphyite orator to Belfast in terms which left no doubt that the association did not want to encourage sectarian confrontation.[148] This was noticed by the *Northern Star* with approval, and it began to suggest a possible meaning to Johnston's publicly stated view that he sought an equality of marching rights. For Catholics and Liberals watching in the wings, the real question now was whether the Johnston supporters would come to an arrangement with Toryism, or whether he would collide with them and perhaps under such circumstances become a "lesser of evils" for Liberals.

The signs remained ambiguous. In June, at the Grand Lodge of Ireland, Johnston's explanation of his conduct was well received and efforts made to secure his censure failed.[149] This actually marked the beginning of a new development whose significance was not clear at the time. The long-established smaller Orange gentry, who had remained with the Order at a time when this was scarcely a path to magisterial or other honours, were concerned above all else to preserve the unity of the body. They had the strongest distrust of some of the Belfast Conservative leaders who had held aloof and were now keen to put Johnston down. To subordinate the Order to mainline Conservative policy at this juncture was emphatically not what they had in mind. And for all the embarrassment Johnston had caused, no one doubted his sincerity. Some kind of arrangement was arrived at whereby the July celebrations would bring together protest about the Party Processions Act and the threat to the Established Church. Even if Johnston remained in opposition to Belfast conservatism, he remained closely linked with the committed Orange gentry and, at a crucial stage later on, would accept their mediation between his supporters and the Belfast Tories.

The *Northern Star* was never at all credulous about Johnston. It admired his candour, honesty and straightforwardness, and never pretended to see a "Liberal" in him.[150] It simply liked his distance from Toryism and his support for some causes which Catholics also supported. But the *Northern Whig* professed to see signs of a different kind, and therefore the appearance of Johnston and his supporters together with church defenders at Lisburn in July caused it some difficulties:

"The Orangemen could only be induced to attend in any considerable numbers by the promise that the meeting should make a protest about the Party Processions Act . . . we are confident that were it proposed to the Orangemen who have any pretence to judgement and independence for them to make their choice between the repeal of the Party Processions Act and the continuance of the Irish Established Church, they would at once prefer the repeal of what they consider a one-sided law to an institution they nominally support, but for which many of them have begun to care very little . . . . It is the church surmounted by an Orange flag that they care for and not the church standing by itself."

and

"The working classes have, at least, nothing to gain by Orangeism; but the landlords and the clergymen, in contending for ascendancy, are fighting for themselves. When the inevitable disestablishment shall have been accomplished, it is possible, it is even probable, that the Orange democracy may, like the working classes of Great Britain, put away the childish things which have hitherto amused them, become proud of being freemen, and, standing upon the common ground of equality, like the more intelligent representatives of the Trades Unions who recently conferred with Mr. Gladstone, be proud of their 'order', as working men, and endeavour to maintain the dignity of labour. When the State Church falls many prejudices and errors which it supports may fall along with it, though the principles of the Revolution of 1688 as they were understood by that great Liberal statesman and Sovereign, William of Orange, need not be abandoned".[151]

The *Whig*'s optimism about the future direction of Orangeism was either naive, cynical or else an effort to smother difficult realities with diplomatic soft soap. The line that Johnston and his supporters were "potential Liberals" comes over clearly in the *Whig* editor Thomas MacKnight's speech at a Liberal meeting in October:

"For these men the principles professed by Liberals might prove too oppressive for the present, but if they were sympathized with they might gradually accustom themselves to contemplate them. . . ."[152]

The fact that some members of the Protestant Working Men's Association talked a language every bit as hysterical as that of the church defenders—for example, its secretary Robert Maxwell, the printer, declared that "nothing would satisfy them [Roman Catholic hierarchy] except the extermination of every Protestant in Ireland"[153]—was largely ignored by the *Whig* which concentrated instead on speeches of William McCormick and William Johnston himself.

In May, Johnston met the Liberal agent John Dysart, who "explained" the views of the Liberal Party;[154] and in September he met Thomas MacKnight and William Dunville, who offered financial aid to support his election.[155] This private arrangement only came out later at the election petition, but the public overtures were made by Rev. John MacNaughton who indicated that, besides the Liberal candidate McClure, he would support Johnston because of his position on disendowment.[156] Meetings of the reformers[157] and the Ratepayers Property Protection Association declared for Johnston and McClure as both were opponents of the town council and both promised to seek the reduction of the municipal franchise.[158] C. H. Ward's remark about how the Tories served "bankers, managers and gentlemen in the Corporation", together with Johnston's position on the land question helped to cement secular popular protest to his cause.[159] And it appears that Johnston gave some indication in the Pound that he favoured leniency with the Fenian prisoners.[160]

On the other hand, when the Tories decided to put up the relatively liberal Conservative John Mulholland, linen manufacturer and High Sheriff of County Down (who had presented the grand jury address on party processions) as a partner with Charles Lanyon, a number of middle-class Conservatives who had hoped to see an alliance between Lanyon and Johnston now decided to change sides.[161] Mulholland was clearly opposed to the Party Processions Act and would probably have supported concurrent endowment if it had remained Conservative policy. Lanyon had made no parliamentary protests against the policy, but did declare against it in 1868. At an October meeting for Johnston, John Clarke, a druggist, suggested the name of the association be changed because many of the middle classes "including some millowners" supported Johnston.[162] Robert Hamilton said that no one regretted the absence of the wealthier classes from Johnston's supporters more than he.[163] It was about this time that Robert Kelly, the solicitor, appeared prominently on Johnston's campaign, and it was through Clarke and Kelly that the Liberals' campaign contribution was channelled.[164]

By the time the election came round the Conservatives were hemmed in on all sides. Catholics voted for McClure and for Johnston in significant numbers, the clerical *Examiner* even permitting itself to believe that Johnston would support denominational education "if he could see the way to its introduction".[165] Large numbers of Presbyterians on the Church question did likewise. Municipal reformers voted the same combination for taxation and franchise reasons also. Large numbers of Protestant workers, alienated from conservatism but scarcely enamoured of liberalism in any shape or form, voted for Johnston alone. And many who wanted to vote against concurrent endowment voted for Lanyon and Johnston. Only the small group of Conservative upholders of the City Hall voted for Lanyon and Mulholland. In the confusion, Johnston won easily and McClure secured second place. Official conservatism had been defeated in Belfast by an Independent Orangeman and a Liberal.

Throughout the Ulster countryside bonfires and celebrations were held mostly for Johnston but in some areas, notably Ballymoney, Dervock and Stranocum, for McClure also.[166] There was no doubt that something new had started, although as we shall see it was hard to be sure what. In Newry a Liberal won with the solid Catholic vote supported by about thirty-five Protestant votes.[167] In Derry about a third of the Presbyterian vote plus the whole Catholic vote secured a Liberal victory.[168] And in Carrickfergus another Independent Orangeman won.

In the local elections to the council that came shortly afterwards, the alliance of the general election was repeated. Robert Kelly and John Clarke were elected as Johnstonian Independents in Dock ward, while Liberals won in Smithfield ward. To crown everything, Johnston and his allies defeated the town hall Conservatives inside the Orange Order, making a "clean sweep" of the Belfast Grand Orange Lodge.[169] The *Examiner* saw the victory as proof of a determination to cast aside bigotry and said the election had softened sectarian rancour to an unprecedented degree.[170] Even the more cautious *Northern Star* described it as "the first time this century that Protestants and Catholics had united in Ulster".[171] Johnston himself declared

"My Roman Catholic fellow countrymen have not misunderstood me. My conduct was not an insult or a scorn to them. It was a defence of the Protestants of Ireland."[172]

Analysis of the Election result[173]

In view of the claims made for the achievements of this election, we will subject the votes of a few districts to closer inspection. The easiest of the wards to deal with is George's, which included a wedge of the south-centre of the old borough of a prosperous commercial character, together with the newly enfranchised areas of west Belfast that had been scenes of riot in earlier times.

There were five voting combinations that were overwhelmingly displayed and we will ignore the others. First, Lanyon/Mulholland, the "straight" Conservative vote; second, Lanyon/Johnston, a combination cast in greater numbers after Mulholland withdrew from the poll, but also a conscious first-choice vote of opponents of "concurrent endowment" and in a sense a "pan-Protestant" unity vote; third, Johnston only, in opposition to the City Hall and to the Liberals; fourth, Johnston and McClure. This combination is by far the most ambiguous, embracing all the possible sources of support for the "Independent" position and the cases of those who, supporting either Johnston or McClure, organized "swaps" of second-preference votes with supporters of the other candidate in a similar position to themselves. It was alleged that many Roman Catholics and Orangemen, so to speak, linked in pairs and voted for each other's candidates. Finally, McClure only votes were cast by Catholics and Protestant Liberals who either did not want to vote for Johnston or could not find a pair.

The following Table embraces 73 per cent of the whole of George's ward. It is not quite representative because areas of the commercial district have been missed more frequently than other districts. As a result the total proportions are shown in Table One.

TABLE ONE

	L/M	J/L	J	J/McC	McC	Others
	%	%	%	%	%	%
Our sample	12	26	17	22.5	20.5	2.5
Residue outside sample	19	24	7	27	21	2
Whole ward (actual)	14	25.5	14	24	21	2
Catholic area (282)	2.5	3	2.5	25.5	64	3
Leeson Street (94)*	13	20	13	20	31	3
Protestants north of Boyne Bridge (276)	9	36.5	22.5	26.5	2.5	3
Sandy Row (452)	9.5	40	32	16.5	1.5	–
Commercial area (232)	29.5	15.5	1.5	26.5	22	5
Southern residential	[8]	[9]	[3]	[11]	[7]	–
	(actual numbers)					

*Mixed area

The most striking observation to make is that votes for Johnston only were almost entirely confined to Protestant working-class districts. The point can be amplified by extracting the wholly proletarian area of north-west Sandy

Row, around Railway Street, where that vote is 43.5 per cent of the total. The strongest observable occupational class correlation of voting is also in Sandy Row. "Labourers" vote overwhelmingly for Johnston only (64 per cent) while "grocers" voted invariably for a Conservative combination. In no other district can such a sharp contrast be found. Actual votes for McClure only are restricted to the Catholic area and the commercial central area. They are almost unknown in Protestant working-class areas. Votes for the official Conservative combination are few outside the commercial central district. The overall contrast between the Catholic and Protestant working-class areas shows up in the approximately 90 per cent support for McClure and Johnston in the two areas respectively.

The problem is to deal with the Johnston and McClure joint votes. In the mixed Leeson Street area these are noticeably lower than in the two sectarian areas it adjoins, suggesting that simple proximity of Protestant and Catholic voters did not lead to pronounced tendencies to swap votes.

Altogether more probable is the influence of separate local reasons for voting for each other's candidates. Thus it was in the Pound that Johnston is supposed to have stated that he was in some way favourable to the Fenian prisoners. And the somewhat higher vote of the area north of Boyne bridge for Johnston and McClure than in Sandy Row is probably not unconnected with the presence in Hutchinson Street of an Orange lodge master who actively supported McClure.

TABLE TWO

L/M %	J/L %	J %	J/McC %	McC %	Others %
7.5	26	28	25	12	1
or after subtracting the likely Catholics					
8	29	31	24	7	1

The pattern in the Shankill district is harder to assess on account of the presence of a very approximately estimated 10 per cent Catholic minority. But it suggests much the same overall distribution. Taking the south side (in Smithfield ward) (see Table Two).

We know that the Johnston campaign was particularly well organized in this area and it shows up in the rather higher percentage for Johnston only. But the influences affecting voting do not seem to match any particular occupation. Rather, in particular streets there are signs of a local influence. Thus there are a few of the newer streets where nearly all the votes go the same way (e.g. New Street, 16 out of 21 for Johnston only; and Sixth Street, 10 out of 16 for Johnston and McClure). The area I have found so far with the highest percentage of paired Johnston-McClure votes is the relatively mixed district on the north side of the lower Shankill/Old Lodge Road, where they were 31 per cent of the total. In this district there were a considerable number of construction workers (carpenters and bricklayers), and though they don't show any very visibly different voting patterns from those around them, it is possible that their presence in the area affected the character of the whole. In general, however, it is very difficult to find any occupational group, whether mechanics or ship carpenters (in the Dock ward area), who display any outstanding voting patterns. The only general exception to this is that Johnston only votes are cast by working-class and particularly by labourers rather than artisan voters.

In the commercial central area, the voting patterns followed those of 1865. All votes for Lanyon, whether linked to Johnston or to Mulholland, were also cast for Conservatives in 1865. There were no votes cast for Johnston alone. All votes cast for McClure alone in 1868 were cast for Hay, the Liberal, in 1865. The 1868 voters for Johnston-McClure were drawn equally from 1865 Conservatives and Liberals. The 1865 Liberals voting for Johnston-McClure in 1868 were scattered over many streets; but the 1865 Conservatives who voted for Johnston-McClure were concentrated in the Ann Street area where John Moffatt, the chandler who started as a pan-Protestant opponent of the City Hall in 1866 and became a "Reformer" thereafter, had his premises. In other words, where some Liberals regarded Johnston as a "half Liberal", the Tories who changed sides were people who had experiences of conflict with the City Hall. Very approximately 20 per cent of 1865 Conservatives and 40 per cent of 1865 Liberals voted for Johnston and McClure, as did nearly all those who split their votes in 1865 to vote for the Liberal as well as the Presbyterian Conservative.

The votes of the bank directors and committees tell most clearly what had happened. The banks had come together with the men of big property of both parties to secure the indemnity and the equalization of the rating. But before they arrived at this united position, in the days before the Chancery suit, the Belfast Bank had been Conservative, while the Northern had been more Whiggish and the Ulster Bank almost entirely so. What shows up here is the extent to which "pre-Chancery suit" differences were resurrected between Tories on the one hand and old Whigs and Presbyterian Liberals on the other. The Belfast Bank voted solidly Tory (except for William Mullan, Robert Lindsay's brother-in-law, and Mayor of 1866). The Ulster Bank was solidly opposed to the City Hall, and the Northern Bank was split down the middle. Not a single vote was cast by any of these dignitaries for Johnston only.

Otherwise sharp correlations are shown by the clergy. The Anglican clergy all voted Conservative. The Presbyterian clergy split in the same way they did over the Kirkpatrick-Dill resolutions at the 1868 general assembly. The Kirkpatrick supporters (who were in favour of disendowment and disestablishment in order to avoid endowing error/popery etc.) all voted for McClure, sometimes only and sometimes paired with Johnston. The Dill supporters of affirming the status quo of 1868 all voted for Lanyon with either Mulholland or Johnston. The only exception was the Rev. Alex Gray who voted for Johnston only.

The year 1868 gave rise to a very unusual convergence of support for the anti-City Hall candidates. It is only necessary, however, to point to one source of the union to show the future difficulty. For whatever the reason, the Liberal McClure secured more votes on the south Shankill than did the Tory Charles Lanyon. Could that ever happen again? Or was it just an accidental by-product of the different relationship each man had to the unquestionable leader in the field, William Johnston?

11. Belfast 1869–1874—Democracy and Disillusion

During the years from 1869 to 1874, the Gladstone government carried through a series of major reforms in Ireland, disestablishing the Anglican Church and beginning the process of securing tenants on their holdings. The introduction of the secret ballot was particularly important in Ulster where landlord power was still a potent force. The government's concern with Irish questions weakened after the unsuccessful effort to resolve the Irish university question in 1873. Having come to power at a time when sympathy for the Fenian prisoners was fast becoming an overriding issue in Catholic Ireland, and having itself declared that the Fenian rebellion stirred the conscience of England in relation to Ireland, the government was faced from the beginning with the problem of amnesty. Its treatment of that question affected its capacity to deal with other issues. In the North, the rising profile of the education question in late 1871, the Fenian amnesty question, and the crisis precipitated by Judge Keogh's judgment on the Galway election petition led to sharp polarization of sectarian differences. The Home Rule movement's beginning elsewhere in the island was echoed in the North in 1872.

There were some tendencies working against polarization. Outside Belfast, tenant farmers organized in response to weaknesses in the working of the 1870 Land Act. And there were places where local popular organizations grew up in some of the smaller towns. For a while this happened in Belfast, and in this chapter I concentrate mainly on Belfast and the early political career of Johnston of Ballykilbeg as its MP and Orange leader. The next chapter will deal with experiences of districts outside Belfast, and in particular the significance of the land question, and early signs of democratization in some of the smaller towns.

My major theme here will be how the hopes kindled in Belfast by the election of 1868 rose and fell and were virtually destroyed by the 1872 riots. By 1873 the Conservatives had restored their control over Protestant politics. Internal tensions within the Catholic community—manifest in the separate existence of A. J. McKenna's *Northern Star* and the clerical *Ulster Examiner*—were also contained. By 1873 the hopes that democratization would transform Belfast for the better were broken. Its tranquillity then depended upon elite accommodation between the Conservatives and the Catholic clergy.

The Liberals and the Johnston Independent supporters, who held the initiative in 1868, lost it altogether by 1873. Liberalism remained a small section of the Protestant community with occasional Catholic backing. Independent Orangeism remained a significant force in its own right until around 1871, but it was thereafter integrated into the Conservative bloc. Ultra-Protestant sectarians within the Orange Order broke the Johnstonites' control of it by the end of 1871. The Protestant Working Men's Association, diminished by the ballot controversy, was bound very much to the person of Johnston himself. He had given them leadership in asserting themselves independently. When Johnston himself became one of the Conservative candidates in 1874, along with a moderate Conservative shipowner James Corry, they went with him. The realignment is not altogether surprising. With the rise of Home Rule in Ireland, and in the North from about 1872, any repeat of the alliance of 1868 seemed increasingly unlikely; so the price of political survival for any Protestant group was to mend its fences with the Conservatives. At the municipal level, many of the Independents were absorbed into the Conservative alliance, while others who were not either became *de facto* Liberals or sank into political oblivion.

There were at the time those who wondered whether Johnston might remain Independent or even become a Liberal. He very quickly abandoned any special sympathy for

Anglicanism, and his language often sounded like Rev. John MacNaughton's. He used ideas like "religious equality" and "non-sectarian" education just as Presbyterian Liberals tended to do. It would not have done Liberals much good in their relations with Catholics to have had Johnston join them, but in the process of trying to woo him and the Independent Orangemen they may have done themselves all the damage they could do already with the Catholics. However it would certainly have done them some good from the point of view of getting Protestant support. So where then did the essential points of difference between Johnston and the hard core of Protestant Liberals lie?

There was a section of Conservatives of pre-1866 vintage who sought municipal reform, favoured land reform and grand jury reform, people who favoured "levelling down" as a means of securing "religious equality" in 1868, and thereafter supported the defence of the national education system. For these people voting Conservative before 1868 was summed up by a remark in the old *Banner of Ulster:*

"To be sure no sensible Protestant feared Papal Aggression, but then Papal insolence was difficult to be endured, and the result was that lukewarm liberals, and those who wanted to palliate their desertion, made Papal Aggression a pretext for siding with Toryism."[1]

Certainly there were many who supported Johnston in 1868 on this kind of basis and who might have stayed with him politically if he had stayed Independent. But would they have gone with him if he had become a Liberal? Why in fact did the Liberals not attract this kind of support in spite of Rev. John MacNaughton's way of linking liberalism with opposition to ultramontanism? The key difference takes us back again to Orangeism and attitudes towards the law.

MacNaughton never supported Orangeism. He actively opposed any introduction of politico-religious elements into economic or legal realms. He worked to restore the credibility of the law after the riots of 1864. He was a strong supporter of normal law, and anything that tended to complicate its exercise by introducing elements of feud or its usurpation, he firmly opposed. MacNaughton had a conventionally Liberal idea of how peace was kept in the very unconventional setting of

Belfast.² Johnston, however much he wished to preserve good relations with Catholics, was the hero of an organization which considered that it had a legitimate task in deterring Catholics. All hopes of Johnston becoming a Liberal depended either on Johnston cutting his political roots, or of Liberals abandoning their concept of law which, as we saw, some were tempted to do during the riots of 1864. No doubt Johnston and the Independents who followed him in the Orange Order wanted to discipline Orangeism and to make it capable of relating directly to Catholics; but when collisions occurred they were locked into Protestant combatants' perceptions of what happened.³ They supported restorative action by Orangemen, and shared their perception of aggression, self-defence, reprisal etc.

Liberals did sometimes stoop to elitist sneers at the vulgarity of sectarianism, but the substance of their legalism, as MacNaughton showed in 1864, went far deeper than that. It was a perception that any legitimacy accorded to popular sectarian organization was actually dangerous. If Johnston had been able to somehow remove the sting from popular sectarianism, the issue between liberalism and Independent Orangeism might have been blurred. But ultimately liberalism was not so much a faith that Catholics might be brought to support the Union, as a reckoning that the framework of bourgeois society itself could not be sustained without an authority strong enough to be impartial. As the Liberal councillor, William Dobbin, put it after the 1872 riots: "If life becomes insecure, and property becomes insecure, I would be willing to submit to any amount of despotism necessary to provide such securities."⁴

The Protestant Working Men's Association, who kept a separate existence after the realignment of Johnston's supporters with the Conservatives in 1874, had some tendencies towards alliance with the Liberals. But the riots of 1872 may, paradoxically, have been what forced them to accept Conservative leadership again. They wanted to represent the working classes within the Protestant alliance.⁵ Under the impact of the rising force of Home Rule, and aware of their weakness numerically, their opting for the Conservative alliance was a question of keeping Johnston in a position to secure election in 1874. For these people's independent position to be taken seriously, especially by Catholics, they had to show that their Orangeism was disciplined and capable of thinking about secular issues. All hopes for Orange discipline and for the idea of equal marching rights were destroyed by the riots. And because they did not abandon Orangeism, their only possibility was to accept that Orangeism should now be subjected to stronger elite control. Orangeism was not an abstract determination to preserve the Union and even less a commitment to normal law; it was an institution for deterring Catholics. Johnston attempted to "civilize" this process, but after 1872 few Catholics or indeed non-Orangemen were very impressed. After the riots of 1872, the Conservative leadership and the Belfast Catholic leadership came to an effective understanding whereby each operated to curb any kind of procession or display within the city boundary. Conservatism acted as a constraining influence upon its Orange following, now without an independent leadership. The Catholic leadership came to view the Conservatives as a "straightforward" opponent with whom they could deal.[6] Liberals still sought their votes but offered them little that they could not secure from the Conservatives. The riots of 1872 seemed to convince everyone that no species of law or justice could actually prevent such occurrences.[7] On this occasion the issue was not a question of the partiality of the police or judicial system. The riots were no longer seen as symptomatic of a particular set of arrangements but rather as endemic to the structure of Belfast. The moral drawn was that only tight elite control would stop recurrences. It suited the purpose of both Conservative and Catholic elites to sustain each other in mutual opposition and occasional mutual admiration.[8]

The hope that Johnston's election would inaugurate a new era in Ulster politics had depended on his ability to transform the relationship between the Orange Order and those outside it, particularly the Catholics. It was hoped that he could provide some other way of preserving peace than the one that depended upon stipendiary magistrates and constabulary holding the line to prevent sectarian clashes. Could he bring about the kind of change in Orangeism that would enable people to feel confident about it controlling itself and conducting peaceable relationships with Catholics? Could Johnston create a situation where the law could be the law and not continually confronting Orangeism as a source of threat and disturbance? If he could do this then not only would centralized British state mediation between Protestants and Catholics become less necessary, but it would also be possible for Catholics and Protestants to relate directly to each other without having to resort to elite accommodation between landlords, clergy and magistrates etc. If this could happen then it might be possible for popular co-operation to grow amongst workers and farmers of different denominations. In short, the questions about marching and related issues actually touched upon everything. Had Johnston an alternative concept of equal relationships to the traditional one upheld by Whigs and Liberals?

Merely to state the problem is to show that it would have been far beyond the power of any one individual to achieve it. In some rural areas and a few towns it was achieved, although generally in the mill towns it was not. The central point here is that after some considerable success in Belfast in 1870 and 1871—and not before a nearly disastrous 12 July 1869—the riots of 1872 blew these hopes to the winds. But to say that still does not take care of the question of what Johnston did when it was clear that the transformation he may have hoped for was impossible. It is tempting to say that he needed money too badly to avoid an alliance with the Conservatives; but even if this were true, we cannot ignore the problems he would have faced as an Orangeman if he had tried to do differently. At no point in Johnston's career can his position be viewed independently of his relationship to the Orange Order. He always had an eye on two constituencies, "the people" and the Orange Order, and only briefly was there ever a suggestion that he would permit his popularity with the people to take him into direct conflict with Orangeism. That one highly significant occasion was when efforts were being made to undermine his position inside the Order because of his support for the secret ballot. The Catholic and Liberal press watched with some admiration when he declared that he represented the whole of Belfast and not just the Order;[9] but over the space of the later months of 1871 and early 1872, he retreated on this question. Quite why he did so is uncertain, but in doing so he preserved the one continuous theme of his life. He briefly resigned after the Grand Lodge passed a resolution in 1871 critical of the ballot;[10] but during the later part of the year it became evident that, with clerical support, Home Rule was a growing force. It is likely that after he had made the pronouncement that Home Rule meant "Rome rule" in mid-1871,[11] he had recognized that there was no chance of winning Belfast again with Catholic and Orange support if he was both opposed to Home Rule and also weakened inside the Orange Order. In December he appeared to have accepted that he had lost and he subsequently retreated on the ballot question as part of a process of making an alliance with the Belfast Conservatives.[12]

The ballot controversy was an early example of a perverse and new kind of politics that became systemic as institutional democratization occurred. Even many of Johnston's supporters during the ballot controversy criticized him for supporting the secret ballot, and took the line that the issue was being used by unprincipled opponents to hit him in an underhand way.[13] That such a defence could be given for his position in this situation shows how exceedingly unpopular the Ballot Act was within the Orange Order, even amongst Johnstonites. The main objection raised to a secret ballot was that it would remove all barriers to priestly political dictation to Catholic voters. The open ballot allowed landlords to counter the priests' influence. But with the ballot, it was supposed that the confession box would be the only and unchecked influence on Catholic votes. And yet one of Johnston's own committee men, Thomas Ward, a flax buyer, had found it difficult to get work after the 1868 election because of the way he had voted.[14] This same man now opposed the ballot. Why?

There are two parts to the answer. The first is that the issue was fought out entirely within the Orange Order, and the Order had by that time been purged of people who had voted for McClure in 1868.[15] But the second and far more important point was the developing approach or system of pan-Protestant politics, which insisted upon viewing every question in terms of whether it would strengthen or weaken Catholic nationalism in the rest of the island. It was once caricatured by the Liberal Ballymoney *Free Press*:

"They would actually try to make us believe we should ask nothing that Romanists want. They would like to allow us to ask for neither food nor raiment, because the Pope and Cardinal Cullen wanted them."[16]

The focus of this approach was always upon Protestants close to the "battle front" whether they were landlords in Connemara or isolated pockets of Protestants in the border areas of Ulster. This perverse development of democratization undermined the spirit of democracy itself. Everything became more and more an obsession with keeping control of territory against the rising tide of popery. And one of Johnston's own claims to popular esteem had to do with the way he mobilized people in the inner Ulster core area over the question of the defence of "Derry's Walls", a combative and popular version of this concern with the "frontier". In 1870 during the height of the conflict over marching rights in that city he said in Lisburn:

"The man who wouldn't defend Derry in her danger, who would not resolve to maintain those proud celebrations at any risk or at any cost was a coward and a traitor to the Protestant cause."[17]

Just how popular advocacy of such issues could be was seen in 1872, when Thomas Mooney, secretary of the Apprentice Boys, came to Belfast after a successful legal prosecution against the commander of the military force in Derry sent there to prevent processions. He was greeted at the station by a crowd of about twenty thousand, including most of the shipyard workers who left work for the occasion.[18] Johnston's popularity for his activities in Derry, and his loss of support over the ballot question, suggest something about his popular base back in 1868. He was the martial figure respected for his assertion of Protestant power and strength by direct action.

The consistent theme then that runs through all William Johnston's political life is concern for the unity and strength of the Orange Order. We saw earlier how he regarded it as a politico-religious institution necessary to combat Catholicism which he also considered politico-religious. His speeches stress the reliability, dependability and sincerity of honest artisans and tenant farmers, often contrasted with the absence of these qualities in landlords, clergy and capitalists. He supported "popular" causes such as land tenure legislation and Factory Acts because he felt that this would promote the interdependence of the different classes of Protestant. He saw these Acts as legislative checks to class egoism.

For Catholicism as such he had a total enmity, but unlike many others we shall mention, he took utterly seriously Christian precepts of good neighbourliness. It is necessary to fix this starting point in order to make any sense of the occasionally confusing aspects of his attitudes toward processions. One of his clerical supporters, whom the *Star* once credited with attempting to bring common sense into an otherwise rather hysterical meeting,[19] summed up what I take to be something like Johnston's feelings on the relationship between religion and marches. Rev. Mr Frackleton said at Ballykilbeg in 1866: "Can we forget our history? Were the Israelites to forget theirs? To please the Philistines and the Amalekites, were the monuments erected to commemorate their battles and deliverances to be overthrown? Was the land of their possession to be given back to them or divided between them, because they were the original possessors? Although they were only usurpers themselves, as Jeptha told them, were they to obtain from the great abundance provided for the priests and Levites a share of their tithes and revenues, to support their idolatry in opposition to the tabernacle of the Lord? Were the banners of the tribes not to be carried in procession—no horns blown by the priests and Levites, because the Philistines might take offence at it? The Israel of God thought not thus."[20]

This analogy between the Protestants in Ireland and the tribes of Israel in the land of the Philistines and Amalekites implies that the object of Orange public ritual is internal to Protestant society. It is not done on account of the Catholics the Protestants share the land with. This point of view was clearly at odds with the reasons for marching which we saw in Chapter 9. But it was in keeping with Johnston's often repeated statement that the man who shouted "To hell with the Pope" was no Orangeman, and with his public condemnation of Protestants who attacked Catholic processions, such as those at Poyntzpass and Drumalee in 1868. And regardless of what the Israelites were supposed to do about Philistine party processions, he made it very clear that Protestants should not claim rights for themselves they were not prepared to concede to others. The model he drew upon was the coexistence of Orange and Green organizations in Canada, and even in

1872–73 when he was returning to the Conservative fold the *Newsletter* observed of one of his speeches, which it otherwise found very agreeable, that it disagreed with him on the "equality of rights".[21]

Now on the face of it this might not seem very important, but in the light of what we have seen of pan-Protestant activism, Johnston's position on this subject was very important. If after all Catholics' marching rights were to be respected also, it followed that neither these nor their Protestant counterparts could have a meaning of "control" if both could promiscuously parade over the same ground. Either marches were purely commemorative and served to maintain a solidarity entirely internal to their participants, or letting both sorts of marches happen on the same ground meant accepting that the ground was both Orange and Green.

The difficulty with either conception was that Johnston saw Orangeism and Catholicism as total oppositions and therefore such equality of rights could only make for an unstable equilibrium. But it would have required both sides to exercise discipline over those who might otherwise have engaged in provocation. And that, in so far as it was achieved, would have been a very real step forward. We shall see that in 1870 and 1871 there was a general consensus that Belfast Orangeism was self-disciplined and that some such change had indeed come about.[22] The tragedy of Johnston, and the much bigger tragedy of the society as a whole, was that when for the first time party processions became legal and Catholics organized the celebrations of 15 August 1872, such discipline and restraint was too weak to give practical effect to the doctrine of equal marching rights. It was the full-scale rioting of 1872 which reduced Johnston's conception of such rights to a question of mere sentiment and ensured that, within Belfast at least, pre-1868 assumptions about the meaning of Orangeism recovered with full force amongst the Catholic population.

To understand what Johnston was hoping for, we need to look at how he regarded the British government in Ireland and its accommodation with the Catholic hierarchy. This is what he said after the election of O'Donovan Rossa, the Fenian prisoner, as MP for Tipperary:

"We see, on the one hand, the statesmen of England treating us with contempt and every consideration, on the other hand, paid to the demands that come through Cardinal Cullen from the Court of Rome. [*Groans*] We see arrayed in many a procession, and assembling in many a meeting, those who boldly and fearlessly proclaimed their twofold hostility to England and the priestcraft, and we see men endeavouring to establish a Fenian Republic in Ireland—[*Hisses*]—under a mistaken sense or misguided feeling of nationality. But, for my part, I must say that, little sympathy as I have, and as you have, with the Fenians, between them and Cardinal Cullen and the Ultramontanes, I could have no hesitation in choosing the honest Fenian, who hates the Ultramontane domination—as at least an open and avowed foe that we can meet as such and know what he is, and as such is much preferable to the Jesuitical hypocrisy of those who one day profess to be Fenians to frighten England, and at another day be exceedingly loyal to keep down the Fenian confederacy. I hold it is no part of the duty of Orangemen to fire a shot or draw a sword between the English Government and the Fenians. [*Enthusiastic cheers*] The Government of England have got into a difficulty. [Hear, hear!] They calculated, to a certain extent, upon the loyal feeling in Ireland; they have imagined that the Orangemen and Protestants were like a spaniel, the more you kick it the more it will like you. [*Laughter and cheers*] I think it is high time that we should tell the Government and the English people that, if there is to be a fight, or an attempt to set up a Fenian Republic, the Orangemen will stand aside, and will protect themselves, maintain their Protestant religion, and protect their homes and hearths, and let the English Government and the Fenians fight it out between them."[23]

What he liked about the Fenians was that they had the same twofold enemy as the Orangemen. Although he exaggerated the distance of Fenianism from the Catholic clergy in this period (the time of the amnesty movement), he was pleased that they were giving both the British government and the Catholic hierarchy a problem. He seems to have had a vision of an Ireland no longer run by a centralized British administration responsive to hierarchy pressure, but one where Orangemen and Fenians might somehow relate to each other directly and be responsible together for the peace of the island. But he seems to have had some fantasy about Fenian anti-clericalism linking up with his own hostility to popery. None of this touched the immediate difficulties he faced. To translate the idea of equal marching rights into anything meaningful, it would have to be done in much more ordinary and therefore difficult situations.

In the aftermath of the 1868 election in Derry, when Liberal meetings inside the walled city (attended by Catholic workers) had been broken up by Orangemen, the Liberal Working Men's Defence Association was set up to "assist the constituted authorities" to suppress all party (Orange) processions inside the walls.[24] Johnston's reaction to this was to describe it as an effort at papal ascendancy and to taunt the Roman Catholic bishop with responsibility in advance for any failure on his part to stop his people from joining the attack.[25] A major crisis threatened on this issue; but when in December 1869 the Apprentice Boys held their demonstration and entered the cathedral, the resident magistrates overruled the local magistrates and allowed the Catholic demonstrators to walk round the inside of the walls. On emerging from the cathedral, Johnston spoke approvingly of the RMs' conduct.[26] In so saying he upheld the concept of equal marching rights. But in August 1870 the Apprentice Boys took precautions to prevent the resident magistrates from doing the same as they did in 1869, and Johnston who was present does not appear to have prevailed upon the Apprentice Boys with the doctrine of equal procession rights. Instead, the probability of a collision was assumed and the resident magistrates kept the Catholics out.[27] Major rioting followed.

Why were there no negotiations to ensure equal marching rights before the collision of 1870? Johnston took the line that they had to oppose the combined menace of the English government and the Catholics, who together were trying to put down the celebrations. Whenever he saw clerical accommodation with English power he saw a threat of papal ascendancy and he stopped thinking about equal rights. At least Fenians could be relied upon not to co-operate with the constabulary and the stipendiary magistrates, and to steal an advantage over Orangemen by that means. For Johnston, the joy in the election of O'Donovan Rossa was precisely that it upset the hierarchy.

His conception of peace in Ireland contained a wholly irresolvable contradiction: a desire for good neighbourliness between "open and avowed foes" who might even co-operate politically for the common good of the country (as over the land question). But they had first to find some way to jointly renounce English mediation between each other. They were hardly able to do this when they were confronting each other to make sure that the British magistrates did what each thought the British magistrates ought to do to the other!

All of this can be summarized simply. The important thing about mending distrustful sectarian relationships was to create new relationships. If some kind of better understanding came out of this then one result, which everyone in a locality would have understood, would have been equal marching rights. Johnston's fantasies about Fenians are then much less important than, for example, his denunciations of the Orangemen who ambushed Catholic processions. But when it came to applying the brakes to the kind of vitriolic mischief Hugh Hanna was leading Orangemen into, Johnston was out of his depth.

It was Johnston who in 1871 described "Home Rule" as "Rome Rule". Thereafter there was less and less in Johnston's utterances to distance him from orthodox Orangemen. Increasingly he came to talk about "Popery" as an undifferentiated mass subject embracing all Catholics within it, and to see English politics as divided between the Tories who were generally "pro-Protestant" and Liberals who were "pro-Catholic". In 1874 he spoke of McClure, with whom he won the 1868 election, as the candidate "of Cardinal Cullen".[28]

We will now trace through the fortunes of the various elements who appeared after the 1868 election as "Independents". Some of these went into *de facto* alliance with the Liberals, and sank with them in 1873–74. Some remained within the Orange Order and were absorbed into the reconstituted Conservative bloc after 1872. In 1869 there was a real ambivalence as to what "Independence" meant. After Hanna and Henderson had attacked Johnston over the ballot, the Independents were about 20–25 per cent of the Belfast Orange Order. But because of their mainly working-class composition their strength in the municipal electorate was low.[29]

Johnston had been elected Grand Master of Belfast just before his election as MP for Belfast. The municipal election results suggested that the "1868" parliamentary alliance could be reproduced more generally. In Smithfield, William Ross, the Catholic mill owner, was elected in alliance with George Horner, the foundry owner, which was an unambiguous Liberal victory; and in Dock ward, two of Johnston's middle-class lieutenants, John Clarke the druggist and Robert Kelly the solicitor were elected.[30] One of Kelly's first actions in the corporation was to move that the municipal advertisements be put in the *Star* and the *Examiner* "so that all parties might have an opportunity of seeing them"—a small but significant signal of good will to the Catholics.[31]

Meanwhile inside the grand lodge a dispute over the election led to a re-ballot under the supervision of Stewart Blacker.[32] On this occasion the Johnstonites made a clean sweep of all the offices, but certain precedents were laid down. The Johnstonites had attacked efforts at clerical dictation, and one of their grievances was the ease with which clergy could appear at the grand lodge as deputy grand chaplains.[33] Although Blacker appears to have disqualified some for lack of proper election, he set a precedent that they could vote when properly connected. Not only that, but a Grand Lodge of Ireland resolution required the grand secretaries to collect names of all members who had voted for pro-disestablishment candidates (i.e. McClure) with a possible view to expelling them. This was not acted upon immediately;[34] but after the trial of the election petition against McClure revealed the hidden financial transaction between the Johnstonites and the Liberals, action was taken.[35] At one stage Tom Henry reckoned about 130 Orangemen were under threat of expulsion, although I have no way of cross-checking the numbers actually expelled.[36] But the main point was that what with these precedents, and the later sanction against anyone who worked for the "Radical" press (i.e. the *Northern Whig* printers), rules were laid down which meant that the Independent Orangemen were fighting inside the Order with one hand tied behind their back.[37] Over the course of the next few years each side worked actively to create "new" districts, often by subdividing those they controlled, so as to increase their voting strength in the grand lodge.[38]

During 1869 the whole edifice of "Independence" looked very threatened. In municipal affairs, the failure of the corporation to come to any agreement with Dr Dorrian over the arrangements for the Catholic cemetery left a lot of bitterness against not merely Independents, but Liberals also.[39] In July of that year, although the Orange processions (outside Belfast) passed over peacefully, they were followed by efforts of a drumming party to burn down the new chapel at Ardoyne,[40] and later successful efforts to destroy the new Catholic national school on Conway Street[41] (around the border of sectarian districts). Though the Orange Order took pains to assert that no member had been involved, not surprisingly this failed to impress the Catholic press. In the later part of the year Johnston's challenge to "defend Derry's walls" suggested to Catholics that the independence of Orangeism might not add up to anything worthy of celebration.

In fact, the Independents were being squeezed on several fronts, and in view of the importance they attached to Orangeism, the assault within the grand lodge was the most serious. Ultra-sectarians around the Rev. Hugh Hanna had begun to isolate the Protestant Working Men's Association in the Orange Order. In 1869 the Anglican clergy and sections of the landlord class continued to promote a mobilization against the disestablishment of the Anglican Church. Efforts were made to employ the Order to provide the audiences. It was at this time that some of the ministers of the Presbyterian Church in Belfast, associated with the anti-disestablishment campaign, joined the Order.[42] And the origins of this group need to be briefly told.

Inside the Presbyterian Church Rev. Hugh Hanna was a consistent advocate of the view that Presbyterian claims should be pressed forward, while all concessions to Roman Catholic claims should be opposed. He formed one of a small party which often contrived to exploit the differences between the more Liberal elements who disagreed over whether to "level up" (endow Catholicism) or "level down" (disestablish Anglicanism). Significantly in the period 1868–70, he was a keen advocate of the new Presbyterian congregations of Sandy Row and Agnes Street.[43] The circumstances surrounding the setting up of these congregations were an indication of the distance between the established Presbyterian clergy in Belfast and the mass of Presbyterian migrants into the city, unconnected with any church. Two young town missionaries, Hans Woods and Samuel McComb, had been charged with the task of visiting such people and reconnecting them to existing congregations. What they actually did was to get up support for the formation of congregations of their own. That these two men, together with Hugh Hanna, were the first Presbyterian ministers in Belfast to join the Orange Order is clearly no accident. The October 1869 meeting of the Belfast presbytery showed that some of the existing ministers (especially several Liberals) regarded the new congregations as a dangerous precedent.[44] If, when there were empty pews in nearby churches, new congregations could be got up on this basis, the door was open to a form of insidious backdoor politicization.

At this stage the influence of Hanna and his friends in the general assembly was fairly minimal. When, for example, various people in the Belfast presbytery praised Dr T. Y. Killen's resolutions in favour of disestablishment and disendowment of all Churches because they were so rigorous in their "opposition to Popery", Henry Henderson was moved to complain that he had done more to arrest the progress of popery than ever Dr Killen had done.[45] The group at this stage concentrated instead on linking up with the Anglican Church defenders in a rearguard action of defiance against Gladstone's policy, uniting on a common ground of straightforward "No Popery" without much reference to any intelligible conception of Christianity.

The "Church Defence" campaign was an obvious loser. The more realistic elements amongst Conservative Presbyterians realized that the problem now was to come to terms with the fact of disestablishment and disendowment. At the special meeting of the assembly in January 1870, men such as John Lyttle and J. P. Corry joined together with the Liberals to put forward a scheme for commutation of Regium Donum in the interests of the Church.[46] Although the Hanna group, led on this occasion by the new Tory boss, Adam MacCrory, attempted to get up a counter movement, it failed miserably. For the first time, in fact, they became an isolated minority in Church affairs.

At the Diocesan Synod of the Anglican Church, the Bishop's announcement that he proposed to have a conference with Gladstone to obtain modification of the Bill was greeted with cries of "Never" and "No Surrender".[47] The Bishop was forced to back down and resolutions were passed which declared that disestablishment was a breach of the Act of Union. Dr Drew, with the backing of various Orange dignitaries, declared: "If this bill is passed, it is inevitable that there should be vote by ballot; there would be an extinguishing of the right of primogeniture; then there would be repeal of the Union; and the North would be arrayed against the South." Anglican clergy and landlords reacted to disestablishment by mobilizing Orangeism. The practice of putting flags on churches, which began in 1867, spread throughout the frontier areas of Ulster in 1869.

There was not so much enthusiasm for the Anglican Church in Belfast. An effort to get up such a meeting in 1869 without Johnston had to be abandoned. To the humiliation of the organisers the audience was treated by Johnston to a speech in which he spoke of possibly benign effects of disestablishment.[48] But Belfast was not Ulster. As Lord Enniskillen said: "It may not affect Belfast, but it will affect the South and West."[49]

Hanna and his friends promoted the Church issue as a crisis question in opposition to Johnston. In doing this they began to shift the balance of forces in the Belfast Grand Lodge by drawing in more clergy as deputy chaplains. As an example of Hanna's activities in this period we can look at the Cookstown church defenders meeting, where he claimed that Church tithes would henceforth be applied "to nurse feed Cardinal Cullen's idiots and the hungry clodpoles who are sent to Maynooth to be translated into popish priests".[50]

It is significant that he could complain of the absence of Presbyterian clergy at the meeting, but when he asked Presbyterians to hold up their hands, about one quarter of the audience did so. At this meeting, where the chairman started by regretting that there was no longer a monarch like George III, who had refused to sign the Catholic Emancipation Act, Hanna was engaged in an exercise to supplant Presbyterian religion by the adherence of Presbyterians to gutter "No Popery". But while this kind of activity had some success in the countryside it was not so immediately effective as a means of defeating Johnston in Belfast.

In the municipal elections in November 1869, the Independents led by C. H. Ward attempted to repeat their successes of 1868. Ward described the contests as a "family affair".[51] "The only object each party had in view was the welfare of this common town and the honour and credit of Protestant Belfast." Having earlier that year been instrumental in getting Johnston to the Belfast church defence meeting (while abusing the Protestant Working Men's Association to the point where they stayed away), Hanna now denounced certain members of the association for supporting the Independents in the municipal election.[52] The affair caused immense bitterness in the Belfast Grand Lodge. The Independents accused the town hall party of efforts at "clerical dictation" and of attempting to "destroy the independence of the honest artisans of Belfast" by implementing the Grand Lodge of Ireland's resolution against membership of people in the employment of the Radical press.[53]

In fact, the "Independents" of 1869 were on a declining path so long as they could not secure Liberal and Catholic votes for their candidates. C. H. Ward's statement that the election was a "family affair" between Protestants was heartily reciprocated by the Catholic press which was disenchanted by the treatment of the Catholic cemetery question.[54] The church defence mobilization had worked a considerable injury upon the "Independents" by making Orangeism appear as the tail for a plainly supremacist reaction. Johnston's mildly anti-supremacist utterances were less important to those outside the Order than the fact that he lent his credibility to the campaign at all. True, the Belfast meeting in May was a fairly inoffensive affair of which the *Star* reported that it was "peaceful and good humoured" and that Catholics and Radicals could mingle in the crowd and joke and even express their opinions "with the most perfect impunity".[55] But the combined effect of the purge of McClure voters, and the loss of specific identity amongst those who remained, strengthened the hand of Hanna and others who were out to break the grip of the Protestant Working Men's Association on Orangeism altogether.

Johnston's public image changed very much during 1870 when he took an active part in attempting to amend the Land

Act, supported the ballot, participated in the foundation of the Working Men's Institute, and took up the question of lowering the municipal franchise in earnest. But while Johnston's general popularity and that of the Independents in the borough as a whole rose, the ballot question began to work its mischief inside the Order. Very early on the precedent had been set that enabled dissident Orangemen to be expelled, and as time went by the definition of dissidence was tightened. Eventually Johnston found himself with fewer and fewer of his allies of 1868. For example, in Carrickfergus Marriot Dalway, M.P., had supported the Liberals in the County Antrim by-election in 1869, and despite Johnston's and Ward's efforts to defend him inside the grand lodge, that body decided to expel him.[56] The shape of things to come was indicated by the grand lodge meeting in June. There were murmurings made about the ballot, and the Earl of Enniskillen pointedly excluded the "humbler brethren from Belfast" from the dinner afterwards.[57]

In June, Isaac Hall, the Independent Orange carpenter, held a meeting to secure popular non-sectarian support for the repeal of the Party Processions Act. The Catholic *Examiner* said of him, "he is thoroughly honest and sincere . . . but he seems lamentably deficient occasionally in the exercise of common sense", having an "awfully extravagant idea of the power and influence of Orangeism".[58] The *Examiner* claimed that the few Roman Catholics present were unrepresentative, while Thomas Ward said inside the Belfast Grand Lodge that he would like to have had Hall expelled for associating with papists.[59]

The general improvement in relations between the Orange Order and the Catholic community in the period was recognized by both Catholic papers. Thus the *Examiner* spoke of "the very creditable feelings of tolerance and forbearance which for some time past have distinguished the 'brethren' of Belfast in their relations with their Catholic fellow citizens";[60] and the *Star* said of 12 July 1870: "Desirous to be just even though we may be severe, we willingly admit that the conduct of the Belfast Orange contingent was better than it was wont to be; they were exceptionally sober and kept within the usual limits of traditional offence."[61]

The opportunity for renewing closer co-operation across sectarian lines arrived providentially in the shape of heavy rain in November and flooding. C. H. Ward and the Poor Law guardians did a study of the flooded districts and, concluding that the council could easily remedy the causes, they made the issue part of their municipal election campaign.[62] The campaign issues included dealing with the drainage system, lower municipal taxation, and the abolition of the mayor's salary. In Smithfield both Liberals would have won but for the intervention of John Rea. In George's, Anne's, and Cromac "Independents" won. Significantly, in Dock ward one of the "Independent" candidates of the previous year's election, to whom Hugh Hanna had objected, was William Harvey the building contractor. This year he appeared as a Conservative candidate. Already in 1870 there were signs of the eventual alliance of 1872.[63]

The victory was followed by a vote to abolish the mayor's salary in which the Dock ward "Independent" victors of 1868, Clarke and Kelly, voted for retention, while all the newly elected members without exception voted for abolition.[64] And when the new Town Council Bill was before the council in December—to borrow to form sewers, new streets, and reclaim harbour slob land—the pattern of alliances broke up completely.[65] Much of the Independent opposition took on a demagogical anti-taxation colour while the Liberals generally supported the measures. The atmosphere in the council chamber was full of debate and dispute, but nothing that could be called a coherent framework or programme was emerging from it.

Although the Independents succeeded in the municipal election and established some credibility in the town, inside the Order Hanna's campaign against Johnston succeeded. Johnston was deposed from the grand mastership in December 1870,[66] and the factional splits were clearly indicated by two rival meetings. Rev. Hugh Hanna held a meeting in the Ulster Hall to celebrate the loss of temporal power of the Pope, attended by only a small section of Johnston's supporters;[67] while the Johnstonites themselves held a meeting for "working men only" to reassert the principles of 1868.[68] As William McCormick propounded, it was the "right of labour to be represented as well as capital". Some of the resolutions protested about the procedure used to outvote Johnston from the grand mastership, and one speaker declared that a lot of masters and deputy masters of lodges got elected as Johnstonites and then turned, presumably—although he doesn't say it—on account of the ballot. The *Examiner* contrasted the audiences of the two meetings: of the latter "all were working men with nothing of the appearance of the rabble (at the 'clerical spouters' meeting)"; and "they may be taken as indicating changes, however slightly, which will in the end add to the peace, welfare and prosperity of the country generally and give the finishing stroke to the schemers and stumpers who are labouring to resuscitate militant Protestantism".[69]

Although Johnston was temporarily reinstated as Grand Master because the votes of the newly created District No. 7 were disallowed, he was in effect already beaten.[70] In June came the Grand Lodge of Ireland's resolution condemning vote by ballot. Wherever he went at Orange meetings he was heckled about the ballot.[71] And on 12 July 1871 the Belfast lodges were offered a very obvious choice of venues.[72] At Comber, William McCormick denounced "archtraitors smuggled into the Orange Institution to back up Johnston"; while at Lisburn, the Rev. H. Henderson said that anyone who didn't like the Grand Lodge of Ireland resolution on the ballot "should walk out of it". Perhaps most significant of all, Rev. Hugh Hanna at Doagh came out in the open and attacked Johnston's doctrine of equal marching rights: "I would not be an advocate for Orange processions by consenting to processions of Fenians", after which he delivered a harangue on the ballot and the confessional.

In December Johnston was finally ousted as Grand Master of Belfast, and the old City Hall faction which he had displaced in 1868 was resecured in office.[73] At the Grand Lodge of Ireland meeting, he accused Hanna of anonymously libelling him—a charge Hanna said he would "neither deny nor admit". For some reason they were induced to shake hands.[74] The *Examiner* wondered what consequences this would now have for the Independents' future.[75] The 1871 election in Dock ward where Robert Kelly was allied to Joe Biggar—shortly to become the leader of the Home Rule Party in Belfast—was almost a last effort to hold the general Independent alliance together. The issue that united them was support for municipal franchise extension.[76] With Johnston's defeat inside the Order by the City Hall faction, C. H. Ward began the process of working out a deal with the Tories.

For 1872, we have more information about the Independents than any other period as they published a newspaper, *The Belfast Times*. From the beginning of the year that paper was preoccupied with Home Rule and with the possibility of an alliance being made between Johnston and the Conservatives.[77] The Orange and Protestant Working Men's Association in February spoke of the "stupid and disastrous policy of 1868", and regretted that the Conservatives opposed Kelly in the municipal elections of 1871 and "let in" Biggar.[78] C. H. Ward wrote a letter to the *Newsletter* disassociating himself from a Catholic who proposed to run in alliance with him in the Poor Law elections.[79]

How much support did the Orange and Protestant Working Men's Association have, and upon what basis? At one of its early meetings in February 1872, twenty lodges were represented by one or more of their officers.[80] On 12 July 1872 about twenty-five to thirty Belfast lodges went to Bangor where the speakers were the Orange and Protestant Working Men's Association leaders (without Johnston). At a rough guess then about 25-30 per cent of the Belfast lodges supported the Independents in early 1872, compared to around 35-40 per cent in July 1871 before the Home Rule tempo rose.[81] Of these, most were drawn from Districts 6 and 8 which included the Queen's Island. The tenor of the meetings suggests opposition to the ballot, but respect for Johnston's honesty, and some relief that he had voted for the destructive amendment to the Bill. The meetings are more obviously concerned with his (and John Rea's) efforts to defend the Apprentice Boys' marching rights, and with franchise reduction in Belfast. Although this is a period when the nine hours movement was afoot in the shipyards and foundries, the issue does not seem to have carried over into the Orange and Protestant Working Men's Association proceedings.[82] With the support of roughly a quarter of the lodges, they were attempting to negotiate an alliance with the Conservatives. They were in a position of weakness, illustrated by the St George's by-election in late July when C. H. Ward's candidate secured 58 votes against 220 for the Conservatives in the first municipal election under the Ballot Act.[86]

In May and June there was a massive strike in the linen industry by flax dressers which led to a total shut-down. Johnston's offer to mediate was accepted by the men, but refused by the employers.[83] Meanwhile Hanna, at a meeting in Lisburn, opened a lecture on "Liberty upon the Continent of Europe" by alluding to the "misunderstanding which had taken place between the mill owners and their employees, and while hoping that the latter would get remunerative wages and apply them profitably, he also hoped that the owners who had large capital invested in new establishments, and who as a matter of right and justice were entitled to large profits, would be once more able to open their palaces of industry, in which so many received a remunerative employment".[84] He then asserted that the papacy was ever detrimental to the interests of mankind, that Romanism was eventually an "ignorant system", and that its principles had not and could not change; the Lord Chancellor of Ireland wanted a Roman Catholic Queen, and, after describing at length the total absence of liberty for Protestants under the rule of the Pope, he said: "I tell you [the Catholics] what we will do: we will accord you in this country all that the Pope himself accorded to Protestants in the country over which he ruled." These were the words of the man who had done most to undermine the position of the Johnstonites in the Orange Order, on the eve of riots which were occasioned by attacks upon a Catholic procession in August. Rev. Hugh Hanna swore informations to prevent the Home Rulers' assembly on Carlisle Circus outside his church, and assembled several thousand people there to obstruct the Catholic assembly at that point.[85]

This next section looks at the Belfast Catholic community from 1869 to 1872. Starting with the tension between the relatively anti-clerical *Northern Star* of A. J. McKenna, and the clerically approved *Ulster Examiner*, I will look at its identification with wider political currents in Ireland.[86] To speak of McKenna as anti-clerical is admittedly a little confusing. It would be more accurate to say that his clerical supporters tended to be the priests of Monaghan and south Down,[87] and that within Belfast the emphasis of his writings and political activity was more on the Fenian amnesty issue and less upon educational questions—whereas the reverse was the case with the *Ulster Examiner*. McKenna died in 1872 and his paper did not long survive his death. Before his death, however, the convergence of approach between both papers indicates something of the enforced solidarity that is associated with the coming into its own of an explicit nationalism.

Thomas MacKnight, the editor of the *Whig*, said of the executions of the Fenian prisoners in November 1867, that they were considered just by the Ulster Liberals as well as by the Conservatives.[88] This statement needs some qualification because it makes the assumption that the Liberals referred to were Protestants. It was, in fact, an issue that generally counterposed Catholic and Protestant subjectivities in a very striking way and did not touch the question of support for or opposition to the Fenian conspiracy as such.

Although writing about ribbonism, Father Denis Rushe's writing might just as well apply to the Fenians who were not numerous in his native Monaghan. These are some of his feelings as he wrote them in 1895.

"Good Irishmen often wonder how, in spite of their better judgment, they feel a sort of sympathy with the conspirators and murders of former times, how we feel sad at the overthrow of a conspiracy, or rejoice at the successful escape of a criminal. This feeling is explained by, first, the old saying that 'blood is thicker than water', and all these misguided Ribbonmen were of our own race and religion; second, the object for which they struggled was to relieve the suffering of our downtrodden fellow-countrymen; and third, their enemies were ours and our country's enemies. The principal lesson taught by the foregoing pages to the young men and old men of our country is, that it is perfectly useless, not to say wicked and dangerous, to entrust themselves into a secret oath-bound society. All such have failed in the past, bringing suffering to the noblest hearts, and sorrow to the fondest. Thank God, experience, coupled with education, has made the great national organisation of the last thirteen years the most successful in any country of recent times. The doctrine of passive resistance has been brought to great perfection. Societies not oath-bound have kept their secrets better than any of the old oath-bound secret organisations.

We have passed through a great social revolution without almost feeling it, with the least bloodshed or suffering that ever marked a great change. Our national hopes are now stronger and better founded, and our prospects are brighter than they have been for centuries. Still, let us look back on those who had the same end in view, yet, through ignorance or passion, adopted wrong means, with a sigh for those who suffered, and a prayer for those who died."[89]

McKenna's view of Fenianism was not so very different from this as he spelled it out in February 1868. Separation is impossible given England's power. "When she is unable to hold her own in the imperial arena, when she is shorn of her strength and pauperized in her resources, then indeed, the dream of separation may be realized."[90] But for the time being there was a need to unite the people of the North for the regeneration of "our common country".

He had observed that the execution of the Manchester Fenians would turn them to martyrs. ". . . an act of revenge leaving a deep and lasting exasperation against the law".[91] It was now to the question of amnesty for the Fenian prisoners that he was to turn. Although little is said openly about the subject in the 1868 election campaign, Johnston gave certain unverifiable pledges in Catholic areas of Belfast to support the Fenians' claims. I have found no definite statement of what he did say, but he did initially support G. H. Moore's resolution in their favour and later withdrew to a position which he described as "strict neutrality" on the amnesty question.[92] There was some understanding which probably accounts for the rather large number of combined Johnston/McClure votes in the Pound district of Belfast (an area that otherwise voted solidly Liberal). Johnston's "support" for Fenianism, as he later declared more openly, was based on their "honest if mistaken" patriotism, their opposition to ultramontanism etc., and as we saw in the circumstance of O'Donovan Rossa's election in Tipperary, their capacity to embarrass the Liberal government.

The first Belfast amnesty meeting in January 1869 was chaired by McKenna and notable for the absence of clergy or associates of the *Examiner*. Welcoming the election of the Liberals, he made it clear that the treatment accorded to the Fenian prisoners, who Gladstone himself admitted brought the grievances of Ireland out into the open, was to be the test of the spirit in which all other issues were received.[93] "They may have been mistaken, they may have been deceived, but they never were fit associates for the convicted rascality of Britain." He believed now in the promises of concession from England "because they are founded on a secure basis—that of a wholesome fear". "We ask for no mercy—for every person will agree with me that, if they were set free tomorrow, there would still be a lasting stain on the name of England." Town Councillor William Ross, the Catholic mill owner, was present, and Bernard Hughes sent a sympathetic letter. The presence of the wealthy Catholics showed how far the issue ran in the Catholic community generally, but at this stage the clerical *Examiner* was a little embarrassed by the amnesty meetings. True, it spoke of the prisoners as confined for "an error of judgment".[94] The editor was glad all those lifted under habeas corpus suspension were freed and said that the amnesty should be without conditions, for otherwise it would be looked upon as a dishonourable thing to accept. But he was glad the tone of the amnesty meetings was "moderate" and thought that if the demands were met, it would be "productive of a more satisfactory union between Great Britain and Ireland".[95]

But the granting of the partial amnesty in February called forth criticism from both papers. The *Star* said that "while anyone of our countrymen is in prison for a political offence, it would be a mockery to attempt to pacify the nation by remedial measures, instigated by that offence".[96] And the *Examiner* took the line that the distinction between leaders and followers was unacceptable, as on Gladstone's own admission the Fenians woke the English conscience in relation to Ireland. It also took a swipe at the *Whig*, "a periodical which is an advocate of revolution in any place except Ireland, thinks the decision of the Government the very acme of wisdom". Guarding its tail it said, "We have no more advocated Fenianism than the *Whig*, but we think we have a juster appreciation of the causes of it."[97]

The question of the fate of the Fenian prisoners, though a matter of apparently symbolic importance and with little relevance to Ulster where Fenianism had made few inroads, was unquestionably a very important indicator and/or cause of subsequent Catholic alienation from English governments and northern Protestant society which almost unanimously opposed the amnesty demands. That it should have done so is scarcely a surprise. That Johnston did support them, and felt able to do so, even after some backing away, would be remarkable were it not for the way he contrasted Fenianism and ultramontanism, and used his support for Fenians as part of his anti-Catholicism. The simple fact was that understanding of Fenianism, or to be more precise violent Catholic self-organization, depended upon having some grasp of a complete "Catholic experience" of life. In the North this arose most strongly from the experience of the society's' general capacity for violence which we discussed elsewhere. To see how divisive this issue was to be, we can look at the way the *Star* commented on the advice Johnston gave to the Belfast Orangemen, not to interfere with an amnesty procession to Hannahstown in October 1869.

In August Johnston had refused an offer from Isaac Butt to chair an amnesty meeting, but stated that he was still "prepared to maintain the position of strict neutrality in the matter of the political prisoners".[98] In October he says in his letter to C. H. Ward that "misguided and honest as I believe many of them to have been, still I hold the punishment was not unjustly administered". He then went on to say that anyone who attempted to interfere with the amnesty meeting would in effect weaken that case for repeal of the Party Processions Act. "Take care not to play the game of delusive politicians who use and then abuse us".[99]

This very creditable advice to avoid disorder was taken by the *Star* in a quite different sense. "If his words have meaning, this is a declaration of opinion that the political prisoners were justly punished and still are justly retained in a degrading confinement."[100] The possibility of believing the people were justly confined but that an act of mercy was both expedient and likely to have benign effect was not entertained by the *Star*. That was somewhat closer to the proper interpretation of Johnston's opinion, itself far out of line with the feelings of the mass of his Protestant supporters. If the reader is inclined to doubt the depth of sectarian division of feeling on this matter, then the October amnesty meeting furnishes proof of it from another angle.[101] William John McCoy complained of the absence of Roman Catholic dignitaries (except McKenna), but in response to a shout of "To hell with McClure" he replied, "There are worse than he—men of our own flesh and blood—men of our creed." When one speaker said, "this may be called a Fenian meeting", he was greeted with a cacophony of "Yes" and "No" in proportions which it is not possible to discern from the reports available. As time went by the amnesty question began to draw Catholics as a whole together.

At the end of October, the *Star* observed that the bishops and the wealthy, who did a lot to put Fenianism down, didn't hesitate to join in the amnesty demand. Gladstone had made a mistake. "He has taken the best and surest means to recruit to its ranks and give it a strength, solidity and universality such as it has never before acquired."[102] In November, at the time when land meetings were being held over large areas of the country, the meeting in Cavan had banners "Ireland for the Irish", "God save Ireland", etc. National tunes were played, and though the *Whig* report doesn't mention it, the *Star* later claimed that at nine-tenths of the tenant right meetings "the amnesty cry was raised and awoke a response which not even the question of the hour elicited".[103] The Cavan meeting may have been one of the remaining one-tenth, but as the Belturbet section returned home, they were ambushed by armed men at Drumalee after they had refused to surrender their banners. One man was killed. Johnston later felt moved to mention this attack on a procession "wearing green emblems and with green banners", and "indignantly disclaim[ed] that such an attack could have been made by anyone worthy of the name of Orangeman".[104] In fact, as we shall see, it was precisely the fear of tenant right agitation becoming complicated by the amnesty question that made some Protestant political leaders withdraw from tenant right meetings when they were most needed.

But though the amnesty question provoked mass Catholic self-organization in the frontier districts of Ulster, the real shock was to be delivered in the Tipperary election, which served notice on both the English government and the Catholic clergy of its potential uncontrollability. Denis Heron, the barrister who defended the Fenians and who, together with Isaac Butt, had secured the overthrow of the Monaghan jury panel, was beaten by the imprisoned O'Donovan Rossa. The *Star*, following the logic of its earlier position, denied that the protest was mistaken. It was expressed in "a way that cannot be misunderstood".[105] The *Examiner*, however, described it as a "grave political blunder . . . a purposeless and idle victory has been somehow achieved over the chosen candidate of the priests and people of Tipperary; a great moral triumph has been gratuitously accorded to the Tories".[106] Heron was an "exemplary Catholic", in favour of fixity of tenure, freedom of (denominational) education, and full and unconditional pardon.

The glee displayed by the Tory press did rather vindicate the *Examiner's* perception of the issue. For a brief period all manner of ultra-Protestants relished this repudiation of the priests and the English Liberal government. Johnston's speech which we quoted earlier on this subject gives some indication of the Protestant-Conservative reaction to the O'Donovan Rossa victory, although in his case the enthusiasm for Fenians was less disingenuous than some others. These reactions did rather cool down the *Star's* enthusiasm and vindicate the *Examiner's* conservatism. When John Martin, the 1848 veteran, was put up for Longford (probably without his consent as he was out of the country) the *Star* opposed the nomination on the ground that opposition to the candidate of the clergy would give glee to Toryism.[107]

When John Bright refused to support the amnesty demand, the *Star* declared: "the best minister of the government has proved that no English ministry can be regarded by the Irish people with any other feelings than those of fear or suspicion",[108] and a week later that the Irish people had lost confidence in the best ministry since the Union, which was "merely as good as a purely English ministry can be expected to be". When Kickham, another prisoner (despite his own repudiation of his candidacy), came within four votes of defeating Heron in the March 1870 election at Tipperary, the *Star* said: "the moral is that failure to meet popular feeling on issues most excited makes conciliation [by the Land Bill] nearly impossible".[109]

The amnesty question affected the North with great force. Nowhere was the pressure for internal political unity amongst Catholics greater. Overt Fenian sympathy tended to remain low key; instead, internal solidarity was gradually arrived at. By degrees the question ceased to be a cause of division between the clerical *Examiner* and McKenna. At the same time it underlined the distance of Catholics from the Liberals. Thus when the new Coercion Bill became law in March 1870, both Catholic papers greeted it with total hostility, and the *Examiner* contradicted the tenor of all its previous and some future editorials on the subject by calling for the Repeal of the Union.[110] Indeed, in November 1870 it said, when discussing the (largely Protestant) repeal movement, that the time was not ripe for repeal. The Roman Catholic bishops had not called for it; they had concentrated instead on the Church, land and education questions, not because they were the most important, but "only the most attainable measures for the country", and they said that raising the Home Rule question at the moment would get in the way of settlement of the education question.[111] In point of fact it was also getting in the way of the other clerical priority which was to mobilize sympathy for the Pope, following the loss of his temporal domains.

In December 1870 the government granted an amnesty conditional on exile for the majority of the prisoners still in custody. It was only at this point that the difference of emphasis between the *Star* and the *Examiner* reasserted itself. The '*Star*' said:

"A year ago and Irishmen would in the excess of their gratitude have forgotten that we are a Nation ... Amnesty then would have been a boon. Now it is a right wrung from England's necessity."[112]

Though he forgets his own remarks of a year before (quoted above), he still has a point that it took the Tipperary elections and the Franco-Prussian War to give the sections of the English government who favoured amnesty and understood the expediency of it the leverage to secure its passage against opposition from within itself.

The *Examiner*, by contrast, while regretting the banishment condition, was generally glad of the outcome and believed the step to be one toward complete amnesty. It recognized that any imperial government would be concerned to tranquillize Ireland and concurred "in the prevailing opinion, that the gross indiscretion of ardent but short-sighted friends of the prisoners powerfully led to the protraction of their confinement". But above all it seemed glad the issue was out of the way. It took the opportunity to advocate an organic work response to the present situation.[113] "Let us, in a word, get a hold of the country, root ourselves into it, instead of feeling as if we were a camp of squatters—get a hold of its soil, its industrial resources, its public administration, its legislation, its government—'Ireland for the Irish'. We desire no less: what Fenian could demand more? The goal is the same, but our road to it is different. They fruitlessly storm and shell where we sap and mine."

The Fenian prisoner question played an important part in undermining the conciliatory efforts of Gladstone's work in Ireland. It affected northern Catholic feeling and promoted an undercurrent of reservation about liberalism which reinforced all other sources of alienation. Not only that, but its effect upon the interplay between the clerical and anti-clerical in the North was vital. We have seen how the *Star* retreated from its position of delight over O'Donovan Rossa's election when it saw how much grist it gave to Tory mills. Here we have the 1865 conflict over the Catholic Institute replayed. Toryism, and tragically certain species of liberalism, delighted in anything which disrupted Catholic clerical control. For example, when John Martin was elected for Meath in January 1871, the *Whig* was pleased. Martin was a Young Irelander, it said, rather than a Fenian, but he had defeated the candidate of the priests who was put up in protest at Gladstone's failure to support the temporal power of the Pope.[114] A surer means of consolidating Catholic clerical solidarity than editorials like this would be hard to devise! Probably similar conditions account for such matters as northern Catholics' sympathy for the Pope. At a November 1870 meeting of Belfast Catholics, Dr Harkin pointed out that the suppression of the Fenians was mainly the work of the Pope (the encyclical against Fenianism).[115] But one wouldn't think this to hear the tenor of the "Protestant" meeting got up by Hugh Hanna and Henry Henderson to celebrate the loss of temporal power of the Pope. With local utterances of this kind abounding, any Catholic would feel they were betraying their heritage not to support the papal cause even if they hardly found his role in suppressing Fenianism agreeable. Thus though the *Examiner* doesn't say it, the *Whig* reports that McKenna was at the sympathy meeting.[116]

The Fenian amnesty question stopped absorbing so much attention in early 1871. It was one issue that divided people denominationally. Later in 1871 the education question reappeared in a form that did much the same thing. The *Star*, after the foundation of the *Examiner* and its own definitive break toward independence, was not in the habit of talking at length about the education question. The turn here came in late 1871 after the education pastoral and the mobilization of all strands of Protestant opinion behind the National Education League. Up to December 1871 there was a tendency to see this body as narrow and rather lacking in understanding of the basis of Catholic demands for denominational education. In that month, however, William Johnston spoke at a meeting of the league in Cookstown at which he and other local dignitaries appeared wearing Orange sashes. This, said the *Examiner*, threw off the non-sectarian disguise of the league. "The Orange sashes and paraphernalia of the Cookstown education meeting will carry this question beyond the domain of non-sectarianism, exposing as it does the real feeling which animates the Presbyterian and Unitarian ministers on the subject."[117] And the *Star* in an only slightly lighter vein described the "solemn farce which coupled education with politics, and made both subservient to the grand lodge, illustrated by the scarf and the badge".[118]

The move towards supporting the principle of national education which John MacNaughton had started within Presbyterianism in the 1860s, was catching on. Besides Johnston and the Orange Order, even the Church Education Society moved toward this position. It had previously put a number of its schools under the board for financial reasons. It too now lined itself up as a supporter of "non-sectarian education".[119] So great was the seeming conversion of hitherto denominational Protestants to "non-sectarianism" that James McKnight became alarmed at the prospect of national education becoming the "pet" of Irish Toryism.[120] Alex Johns, J.P., a moderate Conservative from Carrickfergus, warned against letting the issue become a "Protestant question" and permitting its meetings to be infected with talk of "Romish errors".[121]

Faced with a need to contain Fenian separatism, and confronted with the gap between denominational aspirations and Liberal education policy, the Catholic hierarchy had begun to align educational denominationalism with Home Rule.[122] With general Protestant opposition to Catholic educational claims, all that was required to harden the linkage between Catholicity and a revived nationalism was some great symbolic question which expressed the alien character of Catholicism to the British constitution.

The first meeting of the Home Rule Association in Belfast in April 1872 was not well attended.[123] Its theme expressed by John Duddy was the relationship between Home Rule, the stimulation of trade, and the stopping of "that hitherto incurable cancer", emigration. "If the loss of four million of our population in seventy years of English rule does not awaken them to a sense of the prostrate condition of their country, I know of no argument capable of doing so."

But the second meeting two months later is a different story. In the intervening period, Justice Keogh had delivered judgment declaring the election of Captain Nolan, MP for Galway, invalid. In the course of the judgment he had made some profoundly offensive remarks about priestly intimidation and altar denunciations, etc.

The rights and wrongs of the issue were quickly put aside. The *Observer* (McKenna's old paper) later in the year made mention of the Portacarron Award, a ruling requiring the reinstatement of evicted tenants by Captain Nolan, whose implementation had been somewhat delayed.[124] It commented that Captain Nolan's "contrition" for evicting his tenants "appeared almost simultaneously with a declaration of his intention to become a candidate for County Galway, when an act of generosity on his part might be supposed to be of some political virtue". The *Observer* obviously didn't think much of Captain Nolan, but that didn't matter in the heat of the previous four months. The Belfast Home Rule meeting passed a resolution condemning Judge Keogh; and Isaac Nelson, a lone

Presbyterian minister in favour of Home Rule, declared that Keogh "had done more to bind the hearts of the Roman Catholic people of Galway to their spiritual counsellors than has been done by any single act of any single party for the last half century".[125] Keogh's report to the House of Commons put the government in the embarrassing position of having to prosecute criminal charges against Galway priests, something the priests themselves asked for, in order to give them an opportunity to clear themselves. But the issue had vast implications in Belfast.

In late July a Belfast Catholic meeting to oppose Keogh was very widely supported.[126] Notwithstanding the letters of apology from some Catholic leaders, whose letters made protest about the language of Keogh's denunciations, the *Examiner* attacked such Catholic notables as JPs for their absence. A resolution condemning J. C. O'Donnell, the Catholic RM of Belfast, for his support for Keogh's judgment was passed. Meanwhile, grand juries in the North passed resolutions supporting the judgment with remarkable unanimity. For example, even Lord Waveney, the Liberal candidate for Antrim in 1869, concurred in the Antrim Grand Jury resolution.[127] The tension spread right up into the upper reaches of society. The one large Catholic landowner of County Down, J. J. Whyte, felt moved to publicly disassociate himself from the County Down resolution, saying he disapproved of Keogh's language in delivering the judgment.[128]

In short, the issue raised was not the guilt or otherwise of Galway priests, but the insult delivered by Keogh to Catholicity. His effigy was burned in the Pound district of Belfast and in many largely Catholic small towns.[129]

It is perhaps not without significance that all this occurred shortly before the Lady Day processions of 1872. The Keogh affair added yet one more layer of alienation of Catholic northerners from the society in which they lived, which enthusiastically supported Keogh's judgment ("language" and all). The meetings that took place that day arrayed the amnesty question, the Galway judgment, denominational education and Home Rule as combined issues. To complete the circle we remember Edward Maguire, the Catholic JP, who had attended the Enniskillen anti-Fenian meeting of 1866, along with the gamut of Orange and Protestant gentry of that county. On 15 August 1872, he chaired a meeting in Swanlinbar, Co. Cavan, for denominational education, Home Rule and the release of the remaining Fenian prisoners.[130]

The full force of the Fenian prisoners question is demonstrated by the clash between this very widespread Catholic support for amnesty and the *Whig*'s comment on the subject in October 1872, pointing out that the only remaining prisoners were those implicated in the Manchester and Clerkenwell incidents, and soldiers who sought to induce others to desert:

"Yet the government have not been thanked for their clemency: and we have it openly maintained, that soldiers who have enlisted in the service of their Sovereign are to be treacherous with impunity, though at any former time, and by any other Government in the world, they would have been tried by court martial and summarily shot."

The more it is known that the government cannot "the more is the demand for their release continued, in order that the great principle may be established, that treason and sedition on the part of Irish soldiers are only to be regarded as pardonable and even justifiable offences".[131]

In the end every one of these issues—amnesty, denominational education, the Galway petition and Home Rule—served as layers of specifically Catholic feeling, emphasising their distance from Protestant society.

Against the background of the preceding sections it will hardly need to be explained that there was a very strong tendency to keep "politics" as far away as possible from workplace organization. There was some tendency in 1868–71 to link emerging working-class organisations with vaguely democratic ideas; but even before the riots of 1872, there was a tendency during the mill strike of 1872 to keep "political" issues away for fear of their divisive qualities.

The period from 1868 to 1874 was one of large-scale expansion of shipbuilding and relative stagnation in the linen industry. Harland & Wolff's employment rose from 900 to 2,400 between 1865 and 1870, and the first admiralty orders were received in 1867.[132] Of the 2,400, 200 were mechanics from London and Liverpool, employed fitting engines.[133] Although in

1871 the chamber of commerce still pointed to the dependence of all branches of trade on the fortunes of linen, that era was beginning to end. The sheer numbers of organizable members of trades were growing.

One of the bright hopes of 1868 had been the Working Men's Institute. That body failed to secure Dr Dorrian's approval. In a polite reply to the prospectus, he indicated the difficulties surrounding "non-sectarian" discussion of apparently non-political and non-religious subjects.[134] But his polite discouragement did not prevent Catholic participation. A. J. McKenna spoke at the institute on several occasions, and there was if anything a rush to patronize it.[135] It was involved in preparations for Belfast's participation in the Workingmen's International Exhibition in London of 1870, and secured the involvement of some of the "Independents" such as Tom Henry, David Ruddell and William McCormick.[136] Some of the material reasons for involvement are suggested by a compositor who said that success at the exhibition would enable Belfast workers who went to other towns to get higher wages.[137] In May 1870, for the first time in Belfast's history, a procession of trades marched through the city on the occasion of the laying of the foundation stone of the institute.

The trades represented included all the large skilled manual occupations and all those in particular which had been represented at the trades delegates meeting of 1865.[138] Taking the larger trades as represented in the census (over 500 persons), Catholic percentages in all cases fell between 20–29 per cent, except in the case of ship carpenters (9½ per cent) and tailors (38 per cent) and butchers. The engineers and mechanics at 25 and 29 per cent Catholic contrasted with general and factory labourers at 39–42 per cent Catholic. The contrast probably gives a fairly good idea of the degree of Catholic inequality.[139] The presence of Catholic and Protestant bands and the absence of anything that could be conceived as a "party" banner, with the exception of the Union Jack on the ship carpenters' float, conveys the spirit of the occasion.

The width of possible political meanings attached to the demonstration is suggested by comparing the speeches of William Kirkpatrick, the "Liberal" working men's leader of 1868, and William Johnston.

"... this is the first time, I believe, in our history that such a procession as has been witnessed today, and animated with such purposes, has passed through the thoroughfares of Belfast: and the happy forgetfulness of all sectarian and party differences which has characterized our demonstration; the unanimity and brotherhood which animates this assembly, must, I have no doubt, bring us forward to the front rank of the intelligent working men of the U.K. [*Cheers*] It has proved to ourselves and we trust that it will prove to all those interested in concord and progress of the artisans of this town, how trifling, after all, are the differences among them and how easy it is to band them together on any question which appeals to their true welfare and manhood." [*Applause*]

(William Kirkpatrick)

and

"... I am proud today that the working classes of Belfast have set an example to the British Empire—each of you earnestly holding his own belief in religion and in politics and prepared to yield to no man at the proper time, in manfully asserting your beliefs and acting upon them— have united here today around the flag of 'The United Working Classes of Belfast' [Hear, hear! *Cheers*] determined to show that there are times and circumstances when religious differences and party creeds must be forgotten, and when it is the highest privilege of the citizen of a free state to unite with his fellow citizens in endeavouring to promote the common good and common welfare of all." [*Cheers*]

(William Johnston, MP for Belfast)[141]

The contrast is between Kirkpatrick's sense of the triviality of sectarian differences and Johnston's suggestion that a hopefully long interlude in sectarian tension makes such demonstrations possible. The two men were not saying the same thing. I suspect most Protestant workers present were closer to Johnston than to Kirkpatrick.

The next year the town council, dominated now by a much more assorted collection of Liberals, Independents and very loosely connected Conservatives, reversed its decision to open two public parks—one at Ormeau and the other at Falls.¹⁴² A working men's demonstration for the opening of Ormeau Park was shortly followed by a deputation to the town council to secure the reversal of the decision not to go ahead with Falls Park.¹⁴³ The deputation was successful. The *Observer* commented afterwards on the demeanour of the artisans' self-assertion as ratepayers and the praiseworthy courage of the town council for undoing a wrong act.¹⁴⁴

But toward the end of 1871 the Working Men's Institute was in difficulty. Efforts were made to put Temperance advocates on to the board of trustees.¹⁴⁵ Daniel Pettigrew, the millwright, was having difficulty sustaining enough interest of working men to prevent the drift. A small indication of the changing times was that a flour mill operatives' meeting in January 1872 to organize a campaign for shorter hours was held in the Orange Order's newly constituted Burial Society rooms in Agnes Street.¹⁴⁶ And, as the Working Men's Institute was taken over by Temperance advocates, the *Examiner* found that it had been turned "into a conventicle for psalm singing and for lecturing on the terrible errors and evils which find embodiment in the Church of Rome", a reference to a lecture on religion in Spain.¹⁴⁷ No wonder, it said, that Catholics "view with suspicion the several efforts made to bring them into contact with their Protestant townsmen, when it is borne in mind how difficult it is to share in such association without receiving insult or being compelled to listen to sentiments at once an outrage on their understanding and libel on their principles". The Working Men's Institute was one currently attempting to create secular consciousness in opposition to religious solidarities. Lacking an adequate basis of support it was ground between sectarian millstones on the eve of the flaxdressers' strike.

The flaxdressers were in the habit of deputising one of their number each day to read the newspapers out loud in the flaxdressing rooms.¹⁴⁸ They were by no means a politically inarticulate body. When their strike began, William Henry Hand, who was active in the bread strike meeting of 1867, took the chair and declared, "political and religious matters must succumb to the common welfare".¹⁴⁹ Most of the mill owners refused the 4s. 0d. increase, and in June closed their mills down altogether and started a lockout of the whole mill workforce.[150] Most of the trades in Belfast met and promised financial assistance as the flaxdressers' funds could last only a couple of weeks, and the unemployment of the bulk of the women in industry affected everyone.[151] Johnston's offer to mediate between the 2s. 0d. employers' offer and the 4s. 0d. demand was welcomed by the workers and refused by management—itself an important indication of how Johnston was regarded at that time.[152] By 8 June, there were 25,000 out of work. The strike started a wave through other towns. In Derry, mechanics in shirt factories, painters, tailors and horse-shoers came out. In Bessbrook in south Armagh, the model town was described as being in an uproar and cries of "Home Rule" were heard at meetings.[153] In Belfast efforts by the clergy and Poor Law guardians to mediate came to nothing.[154] The amalgamated trades societies attempted to keep up support for the strike, but in the end at the recommendation of this body, the flaxdressers gave in and accepted the 2s. 0d. increase.[155] Many unemployed millworkers appealed to the dressers to go back as the lockout was affecting a far wider body than the strikers themselves.[156]

The unity of working-class organization was clearly shown during the strike. The support lent by other trades was substantial. On a question of a trade union character there was no intervention of sectarian divisiveness at the time. There was rather an awareness that any political or extraneous question would be dangerous to working-class unity, as indeed seems very likely in the light of earlier indications we have seen of polarization in the society as a whole. Straightforward common sense dictated using whatever levers were available. No one, for example, suggested that accepting Johnston's arbitration offer was "political" or "religious". In the climate of Belfast where sectarian subjectivity was being rapidly charged by the Keogh affair, workers knew the dangers of letting the "genie" find any crack to escape from its bottle.

The strike had the interesting side effect of showing up the marginality of the Working Men's Institute, now expelled from the Temperance Hall. At a meeting in the Oddfellows Hall, the old leaders of the institute were discussing how to recover control when Mr Connolly and Robert Ritchie who took a prominent part in the strike came in.[157] Connolly told the

Working Men's Institute leaders that if they had been properly organized it wouldn't have been possible to treat them the way they were treated. "You don't appeal to the public as representatives of the working people and tradesmen of Belfast", and he suggested they ignore the Temperance Hall and get up another one. The clash between the newly charged enthusiasm and the somewhat dispirited older group was all too clear.

In 1872 the Party Processions Act was finally allowed to lapse. While the Orange processions would now be legal, there was strong pressure within Catholic areas to hold marches also on Lady Day. This happened in the same year that the Home Rule Association became organised in Belfast; and the Home Rule organisers appear to have been strongly involved in organising the demonstrations, even if it was strictly speaking a celebration of a religious day observance.

The marches were obstructed or resisted in many parts of the province. Many of them were linked to quite explicit political aspirations including Home Rule and Fenian amnesty. On this occasion in Belfast the law, from the start of the outbreak, was under the control of stipendiaries and the constabulary. The gestation period in which Protestant "activism" was permitted a fairly free space in 1857 and 1864 was missing on this occasion. To be more precise, Rev. Hugh Hanna's intervention involved a new technique. The riots themselves were a relatively straightforward trial of rival strengths which left the forces of the state unable to reassert themselves. In a more final way than on previous occasions, the conclusion was drawn that popular self-expression itself was intrinsically dangerous.

The demonstration had planned to form at Carlisle Circus, but after Hanna swore informations and a crowd of five to ten thousand Protestants gathered to "defend" his church, the police were obliged to keep the two bodies separate. The march went down past Brown Street on to Divis and up the Falls Road; at the bottom of Dover Street it was attacked by stone throwers but made its way to Hannahstown.[158] After the meeting, which called for Home Rule and the release of the remaining Fenian prisoners, a large section of the march cut down trees to make pointed staves and placed themselves at the front of the march. On the return journey, police were at the collision point of the morning march out. As they passed by, the armed body waved their weapons in defiance at the opposing crowd from whom they were separated by the police. Although there was some collision that night and some wrecking on the Shankill, the police seemed to have it bottled up. Hugh Hanna appeared on the Shankill to thank the people for "protecting his church" that morning. The next day was quiet until the evening.

The sequence of events over the next week was one long catalogue of attacks on "border" districts in both directions, with unlimited expulsions. Significantly on this first night of renewed rioting a battle was fought for what the *Observer* described as "the disputed territory" of Leeson Street in the upper Falls.[159] The Catholics won this battle. Later on in the week a major wave of expulsionism displaced Catholics out of the Shankill and Old Lodge districts, and Protestants out of the Falls-Leeson Street district, thereby creating a sharp boundary across west Belfast, with the Catholic area then having an open end into the countryside along the Falls Road. The riots on this occasion spread to districts, previously unaffected, to the Nile-Trafalgar Street district of Dock ward, a residence of ship carpenters; to Ballymacarrett; even to the town centre about Rosemary Street. Established frameworks of authority broke down altogether. Hanna's demagogical offer to restore tranquillity to the Shankill if the military withdrew, which was naturally refused, looked profoundly ridiculous in the light of the difficulty the military was having preventing collisions in places where past precedent gave no grounds for anticipating them.

The sheer incapacity to stop expulsions was noted by the *Observer* in Donegall Pass, where it said that Catholics had been given notice to quit to the annoyance of the Protestants of the district, but that any attempt to interfere would be "positively dangerous". "They are therefore obliged to remain passive spectators . . ."[160] On the Shankill, Mr Samuel Criglington, an Orange leader in charge of the Burial Society, called a meeting to denounce the wreckings in the neighbourhood, but it doesn't appear as if they were able to put much of a restraint on them before most possible expellees were removed.[161] At the end of the riots Criglington participated in an effort of millworkers from both sides to secure free passage to return to mills in opposing districts.

Let us for a moment take a brief snapshot history of two streets. McTier Street on the Shankill in 1868 had voted 8 Conservative or Lanyon/Johnston; 9 Johnston only; 5 Johnston/McClure; and 5 for McClure only. One of the Liberal voters was a Catholic shoemaker, John Britton. It was a street with a high population turnover, with a fairly miscellaneous set of occupations—three grocers, a mechanic and a tenter, otherwise some shoemakers, carpenters, carters, bakers and travellers.[162] On 19 August a mob appeared in the street looking for "Papishes" to put out.[163] "No papishes would get living at that side of town; and there were plenty of houses for them on the Falls Road" (this was some days after the Catholics won the battle for Leeson Street). It appears that at least three of the mob lived in the street, but the great mass were outsiders. For one of the three, John Britton had taken measurements to make a pair of shoes only a week before the riots. But what appears to have happened is that these people only led the mobs that came on intimidatory excursions. When they returned to actually put people out, the local members were not amongst their numbers. One woman who was a Protestant married to a Catholic (who was away at the time) said of a mob leader who told her not to fret so long as he was away: "Although [his] language was friendly his heart was not so." The general impression that comes over is (a) very few people from the street were prepared to join the mob; (b) those that didn't could not do anything practical to protect people, except help them to get away without too much damage to their possessions; and (c) the few that did join the mobs claimed to have used their influence to protect persons known to them; the more likely reality was that they actually identified such people as targets for mob violence.

Leeson Street was mixed in 1868 and voted 13 Conservative or Lanyon/Johnston; 2 Johnston; 6 McClure; 2 Johnston/ McClure and one other. One of the Lanyon/Johnston voters was Robert Lunn, a shoemaker.[164] He was visited on 20 August by four or five men who informed him: "The authorities of the Pound district" required him "to leave that night at six o'clock."[165] He said he wouldn't go and would shoot anyone who tried to put him out, to which one replied, asking if he would like to be shot now. The group went down and warned every other Protestant remaining in the street. Either before or after, all the Protestants in the street left except one. Occupations are difficult to pin down. The only other definitely identified expellee was a millworker.

On this occasion expulsionism was carried out with no possibility of intervention by the authorities for the most part. It was clearly organized on a fairly grand scale. Once it got under way each group of expulsionists justified its activities in terms of the need for houses for people displaced by their opposite numbers. What occurred on this occasion was war in all but name. It is scarcely surprising that the Catholic papers were enraged by the claims that no enrolled Orangemen had taken part. And despite the efforts to claim as much by Johnston on his return from Canada, the embarrassment of Orangeism was very real. The *Examiner* declared that under Home Rule

"the low Orange ruffians who arrogate to themselves the right to guard the town would receive a lesson that for ever would teach them to respect the law and leave unmolested peaceable, loyal, and law abiding citizens".[166]

and

"No system of police can protect the Catholics of Ulster from periodic outrage" or from economic exclusivism. It "can't be touched by legislation".[167]

And the *Observer* which had hitherto been rather better disposed toward Orangeism wrote:

"Henceforth whatever may have been our opinions heretofore, we have no hope, politically or socially, or from the broadest point of view as a Christian, for the man who remains an Orangeman. We must regard him not only as a partisan irreconcilable and without reason, but a monster."[168]

Let us rehearse again the essentials of this war. A Catholic procession in Belfast, outside the confines of their district, was a novelty. A demonstration for Home Rule and the Fenian prisoners was a very emphatic political statement. The editorials written on it argued "proof that a strong National feeling exists in Belfast", and "the illusion is blown to the winds. Ulster is not Protestant Ulster as much as it is Catholic Ulster."[169] The Catholics' demonstration was conceived in the same terms as all previous Orange demonstrations had been, i.e. to demonstrate the dominance over Ulster. The occasion therefore involved setting a precedent. Hanna's intervention at Carlisle Circus showed—albeit in a token manner—that Protestants could interfere with the Catholic capacity to do this kind of thing. And the Catholic response to attacks upon themselves was uncharacteristic: large numbers of them prepared for a fight. Clerical accommodation with the law was on this occasion a dead letter. The Catholics were not behaving as they had done in the past. A substantial minority of Catholics, whose actions could not be stopped by other Catholics, were demanding rights which had been the property of a similar activist minority of Protestants, the rights to triumphal display and reprisal if any attack was made upon them. In the circumstances of 1872 the distinctions between aggression, reprisal and self-defence were dissolved with greater thoroughness and speed than heretofore because the violence became circular much more rapidly. The enforced spectatorial role of those who disapproved of what was happening, which we saw in 1857, was here reinforced far more thoroughly. The combatants on both sides were determined to teach each other a final lesson.

The effort to create a state of affairs where the equality of marching rights was respected had clearly and unambiguously failed. So long as Catholics did not in fact march, it was possible to be uncertain about how far Protestant marches were ceremonial and how far deterring actions to keep down Catholic self-organization. When Catholics did march, there were enough Protestants, who regarded this as something to be put down, to start cyclical violence. In these circumstances it became both more necessary and more difficult for Orangeism to control its own extremists, or anyone else who could start something the Orange Order could be blamed for. No such disciplining or restraining machinery existed. The Johnston supporters were not the dominant force in Orangeism and were in no position to impose the kind of discipline required. It is very probable that many were drawn into the conflict once it started. The claim that Orangemen were not involved seemed contemptible to the Catholics. By making such a blanket claim to blamelessness, the Order made every actual case of an

Orangeman who had participated a proof of their dishonesty and provoked wreckless countercharges. The denunciations of ship carpenter involvement were, for example, later conceded by the *Examiner* to be unfounded.[170]

The significance of Criglington's meeting on the Shankill was that it took things to reach crisis proportions before he felt able to attempt to use Orange machinery to put it down. That shows how much space for expulsionism existed. Because the society contained assumptions about collective enmity and dominance engraved in the way it organised itself, it was always in unstable equilibrium. The conditions for equilibrium were defined entirely without regard for any bourgeois or democratic principle of justice or equity. The riots had proved that Catholic efforts to hold nationalist demonstrations would not be tolerated; and as they had shown that if the Johnstonian doctrine of equal marching rights could not be implemented in Belfast, then the only way of ensuring tranquillity was to prevent all marches, as under these circumstances permitting Orange marches only was no longer practicable. Catholics would not tolerate an inequality of rights; Protestants would not tolerate Catholic rights. Therefore all marches would be put down. The new Conservative Mayor, James Alex Henderson, and the Catholic Bishop Dorrian were happy to agree on this point, which was a cornerstone of the good relationship that developed between them.

With this agreement the last remaining reasons for Catholics to support Liberals weakened. Witnessing the bitter conflict between the *Examiner* and the *Whig* on the Keogh judgment, the education question, the amnesty issue, and the riots, the *Newsletter* declared:

"We are Irish Protestants, as the *Examiner* people are Irish Catholics; and though fighting on parallel lines, the fight is for our country and our kinsmen—a battle with which the *Whig* cannot be expected to sympathize."[171]

And the *Examiner*, referring to Johnston's now famed alliance with the Conservatives, stated:

"Much as we dislike him, we would prefer to have him as our misrepresentative in St. Stephens rather than be instrumental in returning the nominee of a party that professes friendship and stabs in the dark."[172]

On the Derry by-election the *Examiner* wrote that Tories were bigoted but bigoted from principle. "Principle should be respected even in a persecutor." They had "far more principle and religious conviction than their Liberal opponents". Liberals were allied to the Republican and Radical Party "determined and unflinching opponents of all religion and the professed or covert advocates of communistic principles".[173]

At the municipal elections in November 1872, the first under secret ballot, some curious things occurred.[174] In Smithfield the Conservatives put up only one candidate and left the battle between some Catholic Liberals (Hughes and Ross with one Protestant ally) and Independents, including David Ruddell allied to John Rea. The Liberals won easily. In Dock the alliance between the Conservatives and Independents was sewn up and provided an easy victory. In George's the "Protestant" section of the Independents allied with the Conservatives and defeated the Liberals allied to Trimble and Moffatt. In St Anne's, an effort by Independents to fight the Conservatives failed disastrously. Alderman Savage, the Mayor, spoke of the St Anne's election as "rolling back the tide of Democracy", of defeating a "contemptible faction" who wanted to slur his conduct as mayor. He thanked the Catholics who had voted for him.[175] It looks rather as though the Conservatives were absorbing some of the more "Protestant" Independents at one end, but also getting some Catholic support at the other! The *Examiner* congratulated James Alex Henderson, proprietor of the *Newsletter*, on his elevation as mayor at the next council meeting.[176] In his capacity as mayor he was to prohibit all processions inside the city boundary during his two years of office.[177]

What was happening was that the *Examiner*—increasingly concerned with educational questions—was intent upon breaking the Presbyterian liberalism which supported national education. It was simultaneously intent on removing the volatile and unstable elements of Belfast's "independent" politics. The possibility that a respectable conservatism might be able to subdue both, and perhaps even revive the old plan for a charter to the Catholic university, was worth taking when all else failed. They need not really have worried about Gladstone's Irish Universities Bill. It was opposed at both ends by the hierarchy for attempting to sustain the mixed system,[178] and by Presbyterians because they wanted more advantages for Queen's. Indeed, the unanimity of the presbytery was shown by the composition of the committee that proposed the resolutions[179] against the Bill: Dr Watts (a thorough Liberal), Drs Knox and T. Y. Killen (whose liberalism bore a MacNaughton stamp), and Henderson and Hanna (anti-Catholic supremacists).

The formation of the Ulster Catholic Association in June was intended to "weld" Catholics together to "prevent a recurrence" of 1872. Having found that processions caused breaches of the peace, they wanted to prevent them altogether "by such a unanimity of Catholics as would prevent any cause for a disturbance of the peace".[180] As to organization, "the working men had the power, but they required officers to direct that power, and they were contained in the middle and upper classes". Catholics should not be "dragged at the tail of an insignificant party . . . a miserable clique of Presbyterians". And as to the future, Rev. M. H. Cahill, editor of the *Examiner*, declared:

"The difference in many important points bearing on Catholic questions between Mr. McClure and Lord Claud Hamilton is not very great and hence, unless we get substantial consideration . . . we are prepared to support the rankest Tory."

On 15 August James Alex Henderson repaid the compliment by thanking Dr Dorrian for the peace of Belfast.[181] At the municipal elections of 1873, the Conservatives were well prepared.[182] In all the contested seats, they won, except in one where a moderate Independent, N. A. Campbell, took the precaution of distancing himself from the "extreme Liberal party". Significantly the *Examiner* accused Protestant Liberals of betraying the Catholic Liberal candidate in Smithfield, Peter Macauley. Ignoring the presence of Bernard Hughes and William Ross, it untruthfully declared: "Up to the present Catholics have no representation as a body at the Council board."[183] The *Examiner*'s fury with Protestant Liberals in this period knew few bounds. So it omitted any word on the disgraceful eviction of the Conservative Catholic John Hamill by his own party. It only reversed its hostility to the Liberals in

January just before the 1874 election, possibly because two out of five of McClure's nominators on the occasion were Catholics.[184] Perhaps they merely intended to scare Presbyterian Liberals into a bit of obeisance. But it made little odds, for McClure's position was then hopeless.

The final element of the story is the Tories' completion of their reorganization. The nomination of James Corry—who had voted for McClure and Mulholland in 1868—was a very definite overture to doubtful Protestant Liberals. Having absorbed Johnston whose independent power base was now largely eroded and having regained the leash over pan-Protestant ultraism, now without an independent political leadership, it set about wooing "moderate" Conservatives and Liberals. At the meeting to nominate Corry, Rev. Alex Grey got up to ask some questions.[185] "Does Mr. Corry support the Act of Settlement passed to secure Protestant Ascendancy in these lands?" and, amongst others, "Did he assist or oppose the formation of the congregations [Orange] of Sandy Row and Agnes Street?" Corry was not actually present, and so a messenger went off to look for him. When he appeared he said he had opposed the congregations as "irregularly got up", and satisfied Grey with a few fairly airy statements.

Some days later an opposition meeting was got up against Corry's nomination by Rev. Hugh Hanna and John Rogers, one of the more ultra-Protestant figures on the council.[186] Hanna criticized his friend Alex Grey for not putting his questions "in such a manner that Mr. Corry would have been driven into a corner". Strangely, he offered no explanation of why he had not done so himself!

In 1874 conservatism had contrived a skilful balancing act. It had managed to contain independent Orangeism, woo the remaining Liberals to its moderate conservatism, put a leash on militant Protestantism, and convince the clerical Catholic leadership that it was preferable to any other kind of local leading group.

The subordination of Orangeism, and the total suppression of marching inside the city, provided the best pragmatic solution to the problem of public order at the time. It would look like normal order so long as the Conservative elite both wished to and was able to keep pan-Protestant activism under control. That depended upon the bishop also being able to impose similar control over Catholics. The key difference between this and 1867 was that the central state—by legalising the processions—effectively left the local balancing of power in the hands of the local (mostly Conservative) magistrates. So long as this happened, Hanna would not be able to drive local leaders "into a corner". It was a brittle arrangement held together by the haunting memory of 1872, of which Hanna was one of its most frightening elements.

After the local elections of 1874 confirmed the demise of the Liberals and Independents, and the relative comfort of Henderson's new order, the non-political *Morning News* wrote this epitaph on Belfast liberalism. Asking itself if there was a Liberal Party in Belfast, it said:

"We have a recollection of people who differed very widely and earnestly as to some things combining or apparently combining for others on which they seemed to be agreed. And we have a recollection, which is not required to extend far back, of those people apparently ceasing to agree upon anything. Did their partial union constitute the 'Liberal party' of Belfast? . . . We doubt whether the said partial union ever constituted a real Liberal party. Strictly speaking the phrase 'Liberal party' is a self contradiction. Partyism and liberalism are antagonistic ideas.

We have no recollection of any genuinely Liberal teaching in any party organ of professed Liberalism in this town. We have seen bitter sectarianism—venomous anti-Irish prejudice—intense hate of the people—grovelling toadying of the aristocracy—miserable, unmanly and outrageous personal abuse all chaotically mixed up in, and mischievously belched forth by organs which were supposed to represent that Irish myth, the Belfast Liberal party.

There is no thing or shadow of a thing to prevent the existence in Belfast of an independent organization for local purposes, which would probably be called the Liberal party. . . . Such a party as we refer to would be merely one for local purposes for managing Belfast affairs.

What has Mr. Gladstone's pamphlet [on Vaticanism] to do with the police rate? What have Archbishop Manning's ideas to do with town improvement? What has Cardinal Cullen to do with the water rate? What has the Pope's infallibility to do with regulating the streets? Must the streets be paved and the side paths flagged according to the Vatican decrees? Is it absolutely necessary that any reformation of the Blackstaff should be carried out on strictly Protestant principles?

It was necessary to sweep the streets of Belfast in a Catholic manner and have the besoms made on Protestant principles: and as these the absolutely necessary things could not be reconciled by the two illiberal papers, the Liberal party has been disintegrated into sewage."[187]

12. The Region Beyond Belfast

Sam McElroy, editor of the *Ballymoney Free Press*, auctioneer, and secretary of the Route Tenants' Defence Association, commented on the Belfast municipal elections of 1873: "it is evident that the Home Rule question is working irreparable mischief among the Liberals of Ulster". They were dividing on religious lines and the Protestant Liberals "converging more and more toward Conservatism".[1] For him in Ballymoney it was still possible to view Home Rule as "a" question rather than "the" question, and this chapter is about how far the sectarian polarity of Belfast's politics was becoming a regional norm.

During the 1870s either independent Orange or else Liberal opposition groups challenged Conservative and landlord dominance in a number of the smaller towns of inner Ulster. In parts of Ulster, especially the mountainous areas, Catholics began to take up Home Rule during the 1870s. Owing to the restricted municipal franchises, it did not affect the composition of municipal bodies. During the 1870s the subjects of political controversy in small towns were often very parochial, and the bigger events happening in the island as a whole touched some towns only slightly.

It took some time before Ulster shared with other parts of Ireland the continuous drain of population that set in after the Famine. Until the mid-1860s, the old weaver belt population held up, in rather marked contrast to other regions. And although this was partly a consequence of urban growth, it also reflected the continued presence of rural weaving and textile activity. Between 1862 and 1872, however, the cotton famine

(1861–66) destroyed what remained of the cotton weaving industry. Then the break in the flax boom in the late 1860s undermined the demand for agricultural labour and the viability of smallholder farming.[2] In Maghera, for example, emigration in 1872 was at the worst level since 1847.[3] The overall population fall between 1852 and 1872 was over 20 per cent in parts of south-west Ulster, most occurring after 1864. In these years the Irish language began to disappear even from its 1850s fastness.

Generally speaking, in most districts the number of farms over fifteen acres rose until 1862, and then remained more or less stationary until 1872, although with rises or falls in some areas. The pattern for farms between one and fifteen acres was variable before 1862. In County Monaghan there is a fall in all baronies; in County Tyrone a rise in all baronies; in Counties Derry and Antrim, a mix. But in nearly every district there is a substantial fall in small farms from 1862 to 72.[4] Consolidation of holdings was clearly a general tendency during this decade. But though the consolidation was proceeding fairly rapidly, it was not associated with a general collapse of tenant right values.[5] Rather, the reverse was the case, and it seems likely that tenant right had once again acquired something of a facilitating role in the consolidation process. Landlords had generally attempted to take control over the tenant right sales in order to facilitate adjoiner purchase and reduce it to a regulated compensation for displacement.

Gladstone's major practical step to pacify Ireland was to be the Land Act of 1870. Insecure tenure meant different things to different people. For some more marginal farmers it meant anything that made it easier to hold on. For many farmers the problem was to secure themselves against expropriation of often substantial capital investments in their farms. For urban traders it was a question of securing the credit extended to farmers and stopping the local population from emigrating. The most conservative concepts of land reform were not so much about rent control as about creating legal security in a property that virtually existed. Its more radical variants involved rent controls and were concerned with ways of slowing down emigration. From 1869 onwards, when it was clear that land reform was going to happen, there were three issues drawing people in rural areas towards political meetings and organisation. There was the land question, which involved reopening many of the unfinished controversies of 1848-52. There were the Fenian prisoners and the church defence meetings, both of which were occasions for party displays.

In the areas beyond Belfast in the late 1860s, the church defence campaign and the revival of Orange marches were closely linked. Here the tension between the independent current of Johnstonian Orangeism and the church defence campaign which we saw in Belfast was minimal. Elsewhere, 1869 was a major year for processions, while in 1870 the impending collision in August in Derry ensured a much higher degree of contestation on 12 July everywhere. In many districts Catholics assembled with arms to prevent the Orange parades.[6] After the Derry collision in August a series of largely spontaneous outbreaks of rioting occurred at the time of the Prussian victory over France.[7] The temper of collisions over processions died down somewhat thereafter, except in the faster expanding manufacturing towns. Lisburn, Lurgan and Portadown became the scenes of the worst disturbances.[8] In 1872 the Catholic Lady Day processions in those districts were effectively stopped by direct action. Elsewhere there was some evidence of the beginning of a recognition of the notion of equal marching rights. This notion was more readily put into practice in rural areas, where territorial demarcation was clearer and local controlling agencies stronger than it was in the manufacturing towns, which revealed many of the characteristics of west Belfast of 1872. In short, the sectarian antagonism which enforced identities upon people was exacerbated by the process of urbanization. Indeed urbanization effectively crystallized them as opposing national identities. Portadown and Lurgan (and to a lesser extent Lisburn) will show up the process without much of the varnish that softens it in Belfast.

On 12 July 1869 sections of Protestant clergy, for the most part Anglican, attempted to raise a reaction against the disestablishment proposals. Rev. H. Henderson (Presbyterian) declared to the assembled company at Saintfield that they "could chase the Fenians from Donegal to Cape Clear", and that

17. Populations of Baronies, 1872, as percentages of 1851 population

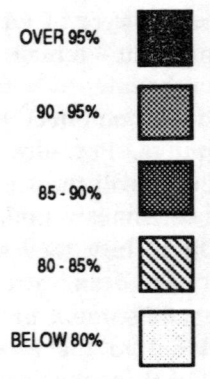

OVER 95%

90 - 95%

85 - 90%

80 - 85%

BELOW 80%

the policy of the present government is "driving the people of Ulster into civil war".⁹ Rev. Mr Flanagan at Seagoe is reported to have spoken of the likelihood of Repeal of the Union and declared, "they will fight hand to hand and sweep every Fenian rebel and every infringer of their rights out of the country".¹⁰ The new rector of Ballyward, Rev. Mr Eager, had Orange flags placed on his church, near the notorious Dolly's Brae, to a volley of celebratory gun shots.¹¹

It was a dangerous year, for in many areas Catholics assembled armed to resist the Orangemen's processions. At Muff Glen, where armed Orangemen had attempted to march in 1868 and had been separated from armed Catholics of Innishowen Peninsula, a repeat performance was thwarted by the military.¹² At Desertmartin, where Orangemen put up and guarded an arch each year (which led to a shoot-out in 1868), the resident magistrate advised the priest to tell his people not to try removing the arch as it was well defended by cannons brought from Derry.¹³ At Keady the chapel bell rang to call together armed Catholics, but collision was prevented by the resident magistrate refusing the Orangemen entry to the town.¹⁴ At Newtownhamilton Parker Synott, J.P., led the Orangemen into the town, but the resident magistrates reckoned that he was there to keep them under control and he did his best to get them out of town sober and early.¹⁵ Colonel Barton, J.P., an Orange leader in County Fermanagh, was attacked by Protestants while he removed the Orange arch from the church gate at Pettigo.¹⁶ The placing of flags on churches was clearly seen by all as an act of defiance, as was Orange entry into predominantly Catholic areas. That year, despite the efforts of landlords like Synott and Barton, the aggravation was being given a great deal of elite encouragement, and the Catholic clerical capacity to curb Catholic responses was being stretched. Next year it would snap in many places.

The crisis precipitated by Anglican disestablishment and the Fenian amnesty question had a material effect upon the land question. Nationalist processions of sympathy for the Fenian prisoners were few and far between in the North at this stage, although they became more frequent over the 1871–73 period. A St Patrick's Day procession at Poyntzpass had been fired upon by people who, in the words of William Johnston, "showed themselves worse foes of Protestantism and worse enemies of Orangeism than Roman Catholics who went out that day to walk".[17] The start of the land agitations showed up a clear clash of priorities, for virtually any assembly in public for any purpose at all during that period was obliged to say something about Fenian prisoners. In November two tenant right meetings were held in southern Ulster. At Scotstown, Co. Monaghan, a meeting of largely Catholic character with several clerical speakers set the tone: tenant right in Monaghan was a myth. The resolution on security of tenure was "nothing more than wishing that the people should be allowed to live on the soil which God had made for their use". At Cavan, town banners with inscriptions "Ireland for the Irish", "Fixity of Tenure" etc. were accompanied by bands playing national tunes. The same themes were echoed: tenant right does not exist, and speakers talked of "banishment". The Belturbet contingent returning home refused to give up their banners to some armed men who accosted them. They were fired upon and a man was killed.[18]

The same theme, that tenant right did not really exist, was repeated at another meeting at Magherafelt; but here a Union Jack flew from the roof of the meeting house where the session was held.[19] Mr Glover accused the Derry companies of "hating" towns and obstructing their development. In Omagh the town commissioners passed a resolution for tenant right: "the farmers' interests are our interests in a pecuniary point of view, apart from any other consideration".

The Ballymoney gathering was a large one, presided over by Thomas McElderry, chairman of the town commissioners and lessee of the markets.[20] He started by repudiating any sympathy with Fenianism and read a letter from Thomas MacKnight, editor of the *Northern Whig*, who hoped that "moderate and temperate resolutions would be adopted and deprecating the advocacy of such extreme and impracticable theories as that of fixity of tenure". James McKnight's speech on the occasion was about as clear a rebuff as could politely be given by one section of liberalism to another. Repeating the themes he had been expounding since 1848: tenant right is "a virtual perpetuity or 'fixity of tenure'". Unsecured tenant right is "the grand instrument of political bondage . . . There is thus in the very forefront of our social economy an irreconcilable antagonism between free representative institutions and feudal territorialism." And most important of all, "It is deceiving the Government to pretend that any merely fractional compromise will affect the object in view." As the *Examiner* observed, praising James McKnight: "The speech of the able and distinguished editor is a true exposé of the custom so much misunderstood called Ulster tenant right . . . The Ballymoney meeting had the merit of enabling the agricultural classes of Ulster to distinguish between their true and false friends."[21] It destroyed the "pretensions of the *Whig*. Between McKnight and MacKnight there was "no similarity of opinion".

The *Examiner* was right about that. Thomas MacKnight was first and foremost a party Liberal of English extraction. His approach to the question echoed that of the Belfast Whigs of 1848–52, who had appropriated the mantle of liberalism after the election disaster of 1852. He sought an alliance of Whig landlords and respectable (large) tenant farmers. He eulogized the Whig Lord Dufferin, who before 1867 had achieved great public notice for his argument that emigration was the cure to Ireland's land problems. In his famous speech covering many aspects of Irish affairs to the Social Sciences Association in 1867 Lord Dufferin said:

"With regard to the various schemes for the introduction into Ireland of compulsory leases at rents fixed by Parliament, I do not propose to trouble you. They are advocated, I have no doubt, with the most benevolent intentions, but I differ so completely with their authors not only as to the first principles of political economy, but as to the very meaning of the terms right and wrong, justice and injustice, liberty and tyranny, that we have no common ground for discussion between us."[22]

MacKnight was concerned to build up a Liberal Party in Ulster certainly, but his first priorities were those of the government faced with the Fenian amnesty agitation and worried about the passage through parliament of an acceptable land measure as a work of pacification. He had no serious interest in tenant farmers' organization for its own sake. The cautious approach to land issues adopted by the Whigs quickly created a situation in which Liberals were outflanked by the Independents or Conservatives.

After the 1870 Land Act was passed, it became apparent that it was failing in several crucial respects to do what it was hoped it would do. William Johnston had attempted to move a strengthening amendment in 1870 and was alone amongst the Ulster MPs in doing so.[23] Because the Whigs did not press the cause of the tenant farmers any more effectively than did Independent Orangemen and "moderate" Conservatives, they risked losing command of the one issue which deeply concerned the mass of the middle class in Ulster, the tenant farmers.

In the Antrim by-election in August 1869, the landlord of Ballymena, Sir Shafto Adair, had stood for the Liberals. Any such challenge—the first of its kind since 1852—involved risks under open ballot. The *Examiner* which suggested the setting up of an indemnity fund for victimized voters observed:

"The difference between the candidates is not of that overpowering character which should warm them into enthusiasm or cause them to run the slightest risk of eviction to secure the return of Sir Shafto Adair."[24]

The *Northern Star*, the more pro-Liberal of the Catholic papers, generally supported Adair.[25] But the *Whig* merely encouraged the tenants on the Hertford estate (Lisburn, south Antrim) to vote for Adair and "see if Walter Stannus dare evict them".[26] Adair's campaign certainly came nowhere near "fixity of tenure". He advocated mild changes in the grand jury system, the repeal of the Party Processions Act, and commented on the need to make tenant right which was presently a favour into a legal right.[27] Much praise was lavished on various good landlords who respected the custom.[28] What was the point of risking the wrath of a landlord purely to make him legally bound to give what he already allowed by "favour"? This was what much of the "moderate" tenant right politics tended to be about. As in 1848–52 it proposed that the practices of existing good landlords be made legally binding. By implication, all that was wrong was the fact that holdings were presently by "favour". While this was indeed the issue for many larger farmers, there was no suggestion that land legislation had anything to do with preventing emigration or with reducing

18. Irish speakers by Baronies, 1851

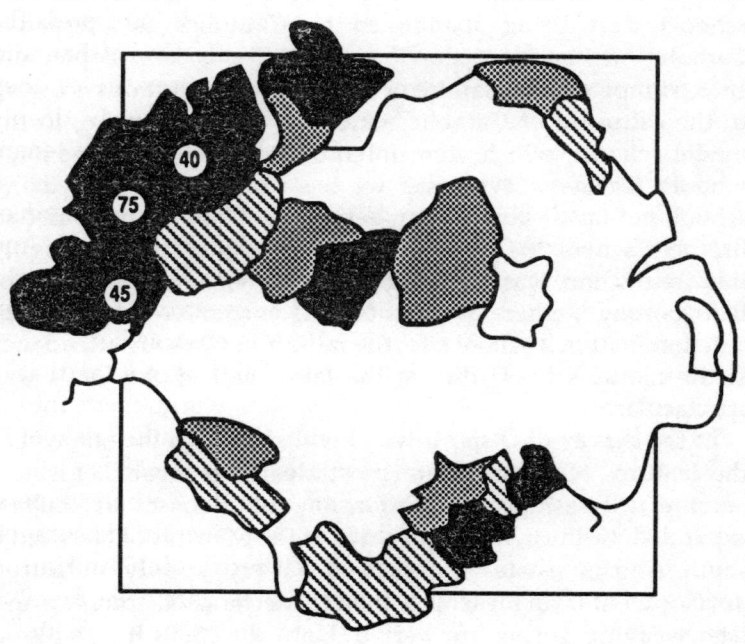

23% PLUS

10 - 20%

5 - 10%

rents. If this was the substance of Liberal land politics, then there was very little to prevent Conservatives adopting it also.

In the background, during the 1860s a silent but very important change was coming over the education system. One of the key pillars of the "non-sectarian" national education system was crumbling, as our diagram shows. The model schools were being abandoned by Catholics as alternative Catholic institutions opened up. The *Examiner* in September 1868 trumpeted: "the failure of the Godless institutions is owing to the diffusion of Catholic education". And referring to the model schools, which were intended to provide the national schools' teachers, "Wherever we see a model or proselytizing school, not far distant we can behold the Convent or Christian Brothers' school."[29] Our diagram shows up just how thoroughly this innovation was working.[30] Everywhere in Ulster except Bailieborough, where obstruction was encountered looking for a denominational school site, the fall-off in Catholic attendance at the model schools during the latter half of the 1860s was spectacular.

In the survey of Ulster towns I will start with the one where the features of Belfast were most clearly replicated. Lisburn became increasingly an extension of Belfast, as Belfast expanded. Lisburn, the major town of the Marquis of Hertford's south Antrim estate, experienced a very speedy industrial development from bleaching, then to mechanized spinning and later weaving during our period. Until the 1860s it was also a centre for handloom cotton work for Glasgow manufacturers. The Richardson families were the backbone of the manufacturing interest, and divisions between them are of some importance for the development of Lisburn's political life. It was one of those which proposed the embarrassing resolution about leaving the defence of the town to the Orangemen in 1848.

In 1853 J. J. Richardson opposed the nominee of the Hertford interest as a Peelite and a popular opponent of the landlord party. He was supported by a number of prominent Orangemen, including Redmond Jefferson, an ironmonger, and George Thompson.[31] Both of these were expelled from the Order after Richardson's victory.[32] In 1857 another, Jonathan Richardson of Lambeg, a deputy grand master of the Order,

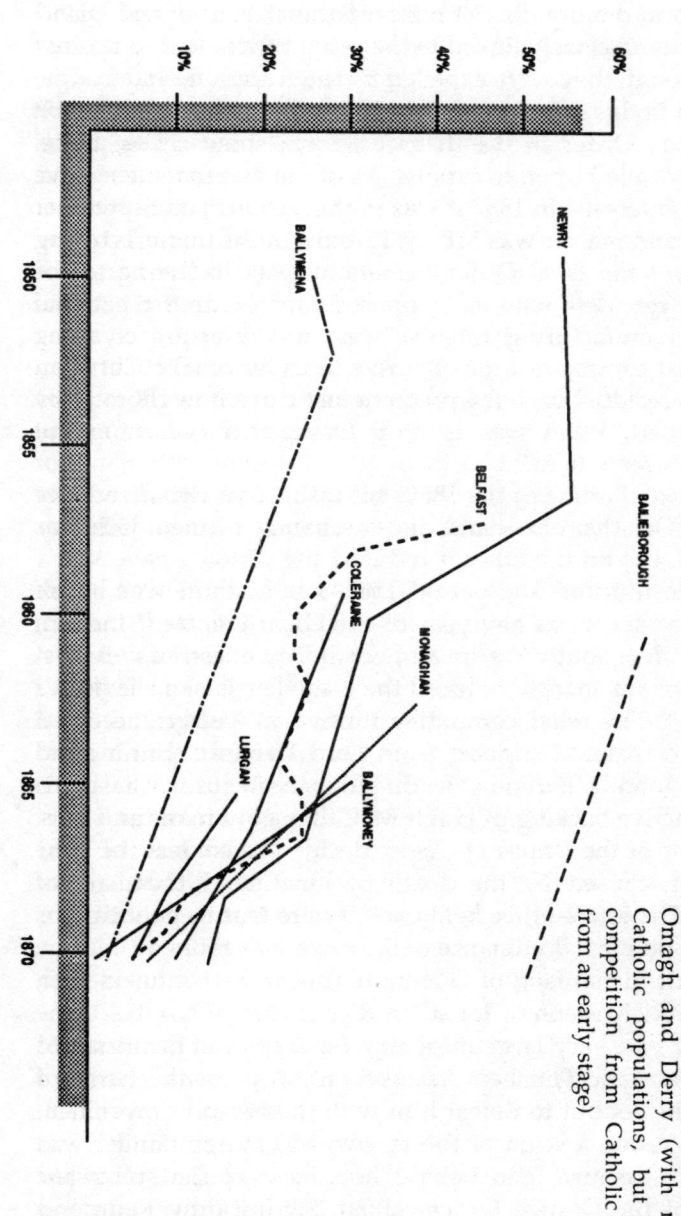

19. Catholic pupils at Model Schools up to 1870

(Other schools never had more than 10% of Catholic pupils. These included the Models at Newtownards and Carrickfergus (with very low local Catholic populations); also those at Enniskillen, Newtownstewart, Omagh and Derry (with much larger Catholic populations, but exposed to competition from Catholic institutions from an early stage)

was put up as the "Independent" against the Hertford interest, and the local deputy district master Samuel Young, and David Graham—both closely linked to the estate office—voted against him. Although they were expelled by the Antrim Grand Lodge, the Grand Lodge of Ireland refused to sanction the expulsions.[33] The Orange Order in the district was in some chaos, being alternately called upon to expel allies of the manufacturing and the estate interests. In 1857 it was in the curious position that a deputy grand master was MP for Lisburn in the manufacturing interest, yet the local Order leadership was in the hands of the estate retainers who had opposed him. Neither the estate nor the manufacturing interest was in a position to exert undisputed control. Yet the objective basis for conflict between them was residual once the protectionist current in UK politics had declined. What was to stop Orangeism becoming the cement between them?

The cotton famine of the 1860s hit Lisburn in two directions at once. On the one hand its mechanized linen industry expanded, but on the other it reduced the cotton weavers to a state of destitution. The period 1862–3 in Lisburn was by all accounts as severe as any year of the Great Famine.[34] Indeed, across much of south Antrim and north Down, cotton weavers' unemployment sharply reduced the wage levels of agricultural labourers.[35] The relief committee formed in Lisburn received little or no material support from Lord Hertford, but a great deal from John D. Barbour, the thread manufacturer.[36] Barbour, with the active backing of Hugh McCall, pawnbroker and one-time editor of the *Banner of Ulster*, decided to contest the 1863 by-election caused by the death of Jonathan Richardson of Lambeg. The estate office held back, aware that its capacity for unilateral political dominance of the town was broken.

Jonathan Richardson of Glenmore (not to be confused with either J. J. Richardson or Jonathan Richardson of Lambeg) was proprietor of a very large bleaching business and chairman of the Bleachers and Finishers Association.[37] A personal enemy of Barbour, he set out to defeat him with the weapons available. Edward Verner, a scion of the renowned Orange family, was brought to Lisburn, and behind him most of the splintered sections of the Orange Order rallied. Significantly Redmond Jefferson and George Thompson, expelled in 1853 for supporting J. J. Richardson, campaigned for Verner and were readmitted to the Order that year.[38] The 1863 election was probably one of the most corrupt ever fought in the North of Ireland, involving bribery, violence and even "temporary" kidnapping of potential voters.[39] Barbour won the election which was annulled, and Verner won the subsequent election. On the second occasion, the Barbour organization collapsed and Vernerites brought into the town large numbers of country Orangemen to intimidate potential opponents.[40]

There was a big price to be paid for victory acquired in this way. The usually apolitical Poor Law guardians were "Vernerized",[41] as were the town commissioners,[42] and even the session committee of the First Presbyterian Church.[43] Lisburn became a kind of Orange base. During the 1864 riots in Belfast it supplied weapons and human resources to Sandy Row, and served as the site for Orange meetings excluded from Belfast thereafter. The licence awarded to Orange rowdiness is illustrated by a case before Lisburn magistrates, involving the ringleader of an attack upon the house of Rev. Fr Kelly, parish priest, during the election. The bench said that for each of the assaults he was guilty of, he could get two months; but they would "make great allowance for the excitement of the day", and gave him one month's hard labour.[44] The magistrates included W. T. Stannus, the estate agent, William Gregg, Senechal, and John S. Charley, a manufacturer.

In 1868 all the town commissioners were "Vernerites". Redmond Jefferson was chairman, and they included four tanners and leather merchants—an interesting reflection on the kinds of agricultural interests to which the town was linked—a damask manufacturer, a grocer, a plumber, and a bailiff from the estate.[45] Orangeism provided the cement which held together a bloc previously wrought asunder by rival landed and manufacturing elites. And it paid dividends in terms of control over the estate as Lisburn ceased to be a centre of disaffection. In the Antrim County by-election of 1869, Sir Shafto Adair got less than 2 per cent of the vote in the Lisburn polling district, compared to his county average of 30.7 per cent.[46] At least writing off Lisburn politically helped to keep the Hertford interest's half-share of County Antrim.

The arrangements in Lisburn imposed a considerable strain on the discipline of the Order. Lisburn had been one of the towns affected by the Franco-Prussian War enthusiasm in September 1870.[47] Tar barrels had been lighted and drumming parties had been out parading the streets. Some gentlemen were "chaired" around the bonfire. Dean Stannus was visited, but he counselled them to give no offence and go home. In 1871 the parish priest expressed fears for the convent school, and an acting constable reported information that some lodges intended to wreck the chapel on 12 July.[48] The magistrates, presumably aware of the risk, asked for 200 police. The Lady Day demonstrations of 1872 saw one of the most threatening symptoms of loss of control. A body of Catholics returning from Belfast were attacked, and later that evening attacks were made upon Catholic houses.[49] Rev. Pounden and Samuel Young, leading Orangemen, were praised for their efforts to curb the attacks, but found they had little influence. Pounden was told by the mob to "Go to hell".

In 1872, after a dispute over the title to the estate, Sir Richard Wallace became lord of the soil and W. T. Stannus was dismissed from the agency following a period in which he and Claud Capron, Wallace's nephew and agent, had been attempting to maintain competing jurisdiction. Wallace's arrival in 1873 was a signal for a clean-up. Capron soon appeared on the town commissioners. Jefferson and Thompson remained, as did Lucas Waring, a Vernerite, now solicitor to the estate, but Rev. Pounden was added. When he arrived, Wallace was introduced to "all parties", including Hugh McCall and Father Kelly, in the town, having first met the commissioners.[50] And at his election as MP for Lisburn, two non-partisans of 1863, together with Jefferson and another Vernerite, were the nominators.[51] By 1877 the town commissioners even included John D. Barbour and two of his 1863 supporters, alongside two non-partisans of 1863, and four Vernerites.[52]

The town commissioners were elected from a more restrictive franchise than the parliamentary one, and by 1877 it is clear that they were relatively depoliticized or, to be more precise, they were drawn from different factions. The constabulary was in charge of patrolling the town, and municipal efforts at improving sanitation after 1874 were given a glowing testimony.[53]

The experience of Lisburn demonstrates how far the opposition between landed and manufacturing interests could be accommodated once the town no longer had any value as a base from which to articulate farmer opposition to landlords. Much of the urban anti-landlord forces could be accommodated within the framework of Orangeism and posed no threat whatever to the control of County Antrim. Orangeism was employed in the first instance to permit Richardson of Glenmore, Chairman of the Bleachers and Finishers Association, to secure the services of Lisburn's MP without that individual being an exponent of other potentially more threatening middle-class democratic interests. But once brought into action, it proved very dangerous and difficult to control. In the end the new Liberal-Conservative landlord presided over the partial depoliticization of the town's affairs.

Securing "Protestant" control of the town governing bodies did not necessarily require a physical mobilization as is shown by the case of Armagh. Before 1863 the municipal authority had a Catholic majority, possibly a follow-on from the citizens committee which took control of the market arrangements from the defunct corporation in the 1830s.[54] Achieved apparently by a secret canvas in 1863, T. G. Peel, the coroner of whom we shall hear a lot more later on, organized what the *Observer* described as an "Orange" list for the commissioners' elections, although for an "Orange" list it contained a lot of rather Catholic names. The whole twenty-one member list was successful,[55] and fourteen years later nine of them were still commissioners.[56] In 1877 there was one identifiable Liberal on the body, though there may have been more. Armagh was a declining town[57] and not, generally speaking, the scene of overt sectarian disturbance.

Lurgan and Portadown were two of the very worst places for sectarian disturbance during this period. There was a strong and (at most) very loosely controlled plebeian current of anti-Catholicism. In Lurgan, the landlord Lord Lurgan and his agent John Hancock were active Whigs of the old school and firm opponents of pan-Protestantism. The Duke of Manchester's position in Portadown was more doubtful and the temper of the town that much worse. In Lurgan, Hancock and the constabulary kept something resembling control. On two occasions in Portadown, the influential people of the town were on the sidelines during direct conflict between the constabulary and the Orangemen, and afterwards adopted a position more critical of the law than of the Orange drumming parties.

Both towns were still centres of handloom weaving of cambrics and damask, and contained substantial machine manufacture of linen also. The surrounding countryside was majority Protestant, but not in the same degree as Lisburn. Furthermore, the Protestants being Anglican, liberalism was weak. The Shankill district of Lurgan and the Tunnel of Portadown were the Catholic quarters. In both towns there was a massive imbalance in female/male proportions in the population in 1861, but especially marked in the case of the Portadown Catholics,[58] and suggestive of a large dependence of Catholic males on migrant labour. In 1877 Dr Stewart said that one cause of disease in Portadown was labourers travelling to England and Scotland "who go to these countries for employment and who when they are attacked by sickness, come home to be nursed".[59] There were other things said about the sanitary conditions. In Portadown the cattle fair was held in the open streets and innkeepers opposed removing it. When the town commissioners on one occasion discussed breaches of the nuisance bye-laws they found that two of their number were prime culprits. One of these took the opportunity to declare that he would defy them and do nothing about the provision of ashpits or anything else.[60] As in Newtownards, most of the commissioners were shareholders in the gas company.[61]

In Lurgan, where Hancock was on the commissioners (and chairman in 1873), co-operation between that body and Lord Lurgan was good, and the town seems to have been well managed. On the Lurgan commissioners, Hancock apart, there are no traceable Liberals, but six traceable Conservatives, two of whom, a yarn merchant and a cambric manufacturer, supported Verner in 1880.[62] In Portadown liberalism was generally weak despite the prominent linen manufacturer Thomas Shillington (Junior). In the absence of an interventionist paternalist landlord, Father Hughes experienced difficulties setting up Catholic schools.[63] Independent politics was contained within conservatism. Arthur Thornton, the chairman in 1870, chaired a tenant right meeting that year and supported Verner in 1880 when he was attempting to secure election as an "Independent Orange" candidate in favour of land reform.

The church defence campaign of 1869 generated considerable activity in County Armagh. On 1 July 1869 in Portadown,[64] and 12 July in Lurgan,[65] a drumming party from Seagoe succeeded in creating major confrontations. In Portadown they marched with flags and drums about the Roman Catholic chapel, and then lit bonfires in the street. A local magistrate, Thomas Shillington (Senior), disagreed with the constabulary sub-inspector Nunan as to what to do about these, and he left the scene as the constabulary attempted to put one of the fires out. In the conflict that followed the sub-inspector read the Riot Act and ordered his men to fire. The crowd shouted that the shots were blanks, and renewed their assault on the police. On the second volley a railway porter, Thomas Watson, was killed. Later an Orangeman was stabbed in the Killicomaine area where Watson lived. Two Catholics were charged with the stabbing and let out on bail. The landlord of the district, under pressure from angered Protestants, gave all the Catholics in the area notice to quit.[66] The funeral of Watson, who was reckoned to have been a bystander, drew a crowd of 10,000, mostly farmers, and included large numbers with sashes. In the course of the subsequent inquest Sub-Inspector Nunan was charged with manslaughter, and Thomas Shillington exonerated by the local coroners' jury.[67] The incident precipitated a local Protestant solidarity in opposition to the constabulary that was to become a regular feature of Portadown.

On 12 July the drumming party headed for the convent in Lurgan where a large Catholic crowd was gathered. A stone was thrown at the party, whereupon all hell was let loose. Hancock arrived on the scene with some police and separated the parties, but while his attention was engaged there, part of the drumming party rushed to a Catholic weaving district, Faloon's Row, and managed to do considerable damage before Hancock arrived and apprehended a few of the attackers who were cheered as they were taken off to the barracks.[68]

In Lurgan magisterial action depended largely upon one man who managed to bring the weight of the law down on the "activists" themselves. During the Franco-Prussian excitement of September 1870, a mob of "Prussians" smashed the windows of prosperous Catholics, while the constabulary prevented their entry into the Shankill. In November the Lurgan magistrates decided to forbid all drumming parties in the town,[69] but that decision was easier to take than to impose successfully. On 1 July 1871 the police, charged with keeping drumming parties out, were beaten back by a stone throwing crowd.[70] An "Orange circular" (which may have been a forgery in so far as T. G. Peel took action to prevent its summons being heeded) declared:

"We are sorry to inform you that we partly failed in the attempt, but we succeeded in dispersing the police and had we been supported by the brethren, we would without difficulty have been successful.

We are assailed on all sides by Roman Catholics, Radical Magistrates, Popish police and other...

Come to Lurgan and assist us in retrieving our honour and liberty as all true brethren should do..."[71]

On 12 July a much larger police presence imposed a re-routing of a very much bigger and peaceful procession.

It seems as though leaders of the Orange Order made efforts to impose some disciplines but that these efforts were usually ineffective. On the occasion of the Lady Day celebrations of 1872, the local Orange officers issued a placard warning Orangemen against any interferences on pain of expulsion.[72] In fact, the Catholic processionists took the train to Scarva but were unable to leave the station and were sent home on the train by the magistrates on account of a Protestant counter-demonstration at the station entrance. When they returned to Lurgan, Hancock, with the help of some leading Catholic inhabitants, had difficulty persuading them to furl their banners before escorting them home. The whole Lady Day programme for Gilford, Lawrencetown, Banbridge, Scarva and Loughbrickland district was largely subverted by actual or threatened counter-demonstrations.[73] During the time of the riots in Belfast, a procession of Methodist schoolchildren was fired upon from a house in Lurgan. The house was wrecked, its owner (a Catholic) arrested, and a subscription raised for his prosecution.[74]

Having read Ulster newspapers for the forty years after the Famine at some length, I am left with an impression that whenever the name Portadown came before my eyes it was nearly always bad news. Rather than attempt to describe it further, I shall leave its local journal to describe the goings on in the town itself. Pressures which were contained in various ways elsewhere seem to have found unbridled expression in Portadown in the 1870s.

What follows below is the story of efforts by Orange drumming parties to assert their right to drum in the Tunnel, their opposition to the constabulary, and the way the rest of the citizenry of Portadown was drawn into the slip-stream of their confrontations.[75] The *Portadown and Lurgan News*'s basic ideas are summed up in its comments on the clerical Catholic *Examiner*'s motto "Pro Aris et Tous"("For our altars and firesides"):

> "In other words for superstition and mud cabins, and bogs, when all the civilized world was for true religion, and good drainage and ventilation."[76]

On 23 July 1873 there was an Orange meeting at Armagh to welcome a delegation of Canadian Orangemen, to which a contingent from Portadown travelled by rail. On their way to the station in the morning the Orangemen "beat all the way", and when they returned they marched through the town "beating and playing". After they broke up[76]

> "It chanced that the route of three lodges lay through the Tunnel, and in this direction they at once proceeded, playing and beating, and having their flags unfurled."
>
> Having gone some distance "it was beginning to be hoped that the inhabitants of this unenviably notorious locality would manifest for once a forbearance peculiarly foreign to their training and inculcations".
>
> Then came the attack on "peaceable men whose only crime was that they were Protestants and loyal subjects".
>
> Because the attackers were invisible and refused to come out, "the crowd assaulted the windows and doors of the houses with all they could find on the road".

While the lodges went onward, the following of "two or three hundred" went back through the Tunnel. It isn't explained why they followed the three lodges on their way home. But the police who were following the procession were also hit by missiles thrown at the following. When the case came up for trial the paper commented:

"We want to point out, however, that in both instances (this and another at Derryadd) the Roman Catholics left their work, and mustered together on a day which was no holiday of theirs, and want only interfered with bodies of Protestants going to their homes by the public road."[77]

They expected the magistrates to make a distinction between the rioters and "rioters, who when thus attacked, retaliated". Further trouble ensued on 5 November in Portadown. On this occasion the constables with the sanction of a resident magistrate not surprisingly blocked the entrance of the Tunnel. The *News* commented:

"Anything that has occurred since then [1862] worth the name of a riot has been caused solely by the interference of Resident Magistrates and Constabulary Officers with that liberty which the public have long looked upon as their sacred right."[78]

Orange anniversaries were peaceable in 1860, 1861 and 1862 "when a single orderly kept the Barrack"; there had never previously been trouble on 5 November. This year there was only trouble because Sub-Inspector Warre (who had been hit by a brick on 23 July in the Tunnel) swore informations before Mr McSheehy, Resident Magistrate. There was a large body of extra police present on the occasion. And what would have happened if there hadn't been? "The Orange Lodges would have passed into the town by the usual and direct route—the Tunnel."

There was in fact an outcry about the resident magistrates and the constabulary interference, and an "Indignation" meeting was got up in the Town Hall.[79] At least seven of the town commissioners were present, including the Liberal Thomas Shillington (Junior). Resolutions were passed expressing annoyance at the disruption of the markets as a result of the cordon across the Tunnel. "The constituted authorities have little interest in the commercial prosperity of the town." Complaints were made about the treatment of market customers, and about the absence of local magistrates who should have been called upon. The meeting got a bit out of hand. Mr J. H. Mulligan said: "This is a Protestant town and it is well known that it is a Protestant town to most people of Ireland, and therefore I object entirely to reports which have been given . . . as if the riots were being continually got up between the Roman Catholics and Protestants and that it required periodically an armed force of H.M. troops and constabulary to come here and keep these savages from worrying each other."[80]

After this speech, Mr Paul, the chairman of the town commissioners, felt it necessary to avoid the "insinuation" in some speeches that there was objection to the constabulary in the town as such. But if he was in doubt about this, the *Portadown and Lurgan News*[81] was not:

"The contest between the people and the police on (5th November) was not of a party character. It was a simple struggle for freedom."

The main difference between Portadown and, say, Lurgan (or anywhere else we shall look at) is that when efforts were made to enforce this right to march through Catholic areas, the subsequent conflict lined the Portadown middle class up on the side of the pan-Protestant drumming parties and against the forces of the law. Presumably only some of the people at the meeting in the Town Hall favoured these "sacred rights". It is more than likely that some, like Shillington, went to try to cool the proceedings down. But the general tenor of the meeting was a protest about the state authority's interference with the routine of the market, by implication accepting the "sacred right" of the drumming party. The law which had attempted to curb the drumming party was seen as the cause of trouble in the town centre. In effect the initiative in Portadown, the defining of issues and so on, had been taken by the drumming parties. If they created disturbances they expected the result to be a reinforcing of pan-Protestant unity. Once the "sacred right" to beat drums in the Tunnel was accepted, then logically all Catholic physical opposition to marches, however provocative, became "aggression". The law, so understood, could have become an instrument for ensuring Catholic subordination.

Although it must be a guess, I sense that in many towns affected with the same kinds of risks—working-class districts without stable sectarian boundaries or accepted patterns of coexistence—the traders and prominent people were keen to keep down such dangers. A resident landlord such as John Hancock or, in Lisburn, Sir Richard Wallace, who would bring in the constabulary and act with it, could do a lot to prevent outbreaks. This is what Portadown lacked.

It seems the influence of elites is more often restraining than provoking. It took only a few to start trouble, but many to prevent it. In Chapter 9 I looked at what happened in Banbridge in 1868. Afterwards the local merchants—spurred on by the damage done to the market custom and the extra cost of the constabulary—resolved to keep down such disorders.[82] By the list of names it seems that this 75 per cent Protestant town included two Catholics on its town commissioners, elected by a strongly Protestant electorate.

When a town took such action, however, it did not stop firebrands from attempting to stir it. For example, there is the address of T. G. Peel to Orangemen on 12 July 1873 at their meeting in Banbridge: "Should they not feel proud that only for them the Papists would at present be in possession of the entire country. The Fenian society was not yet extinct in Ireland and it behoved Orangemen to oppose strenuously the progress of Home Rule and Fenianism. It was only the other day that a weapon which had been used by some of these outlaws after having been drilled had been discovered near Lurgan. . . . There might be similar instruments in the immediate vicinity of Banbridge and could they rest quietly in the face of such a state of affairs. He implored them to guard well their dwellings, so that they might keep those Romanists in the state which they deserved—the hewers of wood and the drawers of water."[83]

With these kinds of sentiments in the air the possibility of disturbances was ever present. An effort to make an agreement on equal marching rights broke down in Lurgan in 1874 at the first attempt. But popular initiative rather than magisterial action brought it to life in the small mill town of Gilford. During a mill strike, the 15 August 1874 was celebrated by a Home Rule demonstration.[84] On arriving at Gilford the Home Rulers offered to furl their banners and remove their sashes before entering. They removed the sashes and then, accompanied by the Gilford Protestant flute band, headed with a banner, "Workers Combined", they marched together through the town with the approval and greeting of the local Orange leaders. This was a town where two years previously Orangemen had determined not to let the Home Rulers enter. Tentatively I suggest that it took some generally appreciated imperative—such as the need for solidarity in a strike—to enable local Orange leaders to impress upon their followers and more wayward activist fellow travellers the need to respect "equal marching rights".

What Lurgan, Portadown and Lisburn share in common is high speed urban growth and industrialization in the decade before 1870. For the magistrates to take a firm line with Orange militancy, as John Hancock had done in Lurgan, was not sufficient to curb it. His own limited achievement, despite his courage and determination, shows that this was not enough. Orangeism had a momentum of its own. Its leadership was often unable to curb activist provocation, and the absence of stable territorial demarcation made any effort to sort out "equal" marching rights by treaty between leaders very difficult indeed. However much larger sections of the Protestant population might have "disagreed" with activist excesses, once the sacredness of the right to march was accepted, it logically entailed that in any confrontation Catholics would be seen as the "aggressors". Sympathy for the Catholics who were being "irritated" depended upon the Catholics failing to respond, and that left them in a no-win situation. If they failed to respond, that showed that the marches were not really provocative; if they did respond, it showed they were out of control and perhaps the Protestant march that provoked them had been justified.

For me this situation is in itself enough to account for the growth of Home Rule manifestations in the North after 1872. They were expressions of strength, confronting the Orange assertion of control with a direct rivalry. Catholics were employing the weapon of marching, which had been the means of controlling them, to repudiate that control and assert their equality. It was the obvious way to do it; they had learned from the Orangemen's desire to march that marching was important. And so the conviction became "squared". The fact that Home Rule might have made little or no economic sense in industrial Ulster was fundamentally irrelevant. The Orangemen were against it and that was a very strong argument in its favour.

The weakness of working-class solidarity in the North of Ireland is often lamented. The proper measure of what is involved here is the rare example of Gilford 1874. It was difficult enough even for tenant farmers, who at least had the advantage of a more or less stable demarcation of territory between each other, to achieve this. In urban working-class society any unity generated in the workplace had to be very strong indeed in a situation where there was a threat of dispute about the control of residential space.

Towns with an essentially agricultural servicing function were likely to contain bourgeois elements with a definite interest in confronting territorial power; and less likely to contain plebeian groups whose uncontrollability characterized the faster growing manufacturing towns.

Like Lisburn, Newtownards was very badly hit by the cotton famine in the early 1860s; but although weaving was still practised on some scale in the early 1870s, the town was generally declining and mechanized manufacture was not absorbing the unemployment created by the run-down of hand weaving.[85] It was put under the Town Improvement Act in 1865, but not without efforts by small house property owners to exclude sewerage and drainage powers, whose inclusion was supported by Mr Boal, a leading Orangeman and Poor Law guardian.[86]

The landlord of the town, the Marquis of Londonderry, was popular. He provided ground for the market set up in 1873 and the leases of sites for industrial use were "for ever". But there was a general malaise about the place. The brewery went into liquidation in 1874, and little new manufacturing had developed there.[87] Its low level made it vulnerable to sewerage percolation into drinking wells when Strangford Lough rose.[88] The small house property lobby had managed to circumvent the sanitary requirements of ashpits or privies, and about a quarter of the 2,000 houses had no means of nuisance disposal.[89] Many of the small houses had no back entrances and no effort was made to ensure their provision, as the end apartments were often weaving shops and it would have required removing a loom set and lowering the houses' letting values.[90] Despite the obvious need for a high pressure water supply, the population could not be induced to extend the commissioners' power to provide it. Condemned public wells were reopened.[91] Most of the commissioners were shareholders in the gas company, and about the only health regulations which were imposed were those of inspection of slaughterhouses (there were no butchers, cattle dealers or any other interested parties on the commissioners!). The town commissioners did not exactly seem a highly motivated body concerned with municipal improvement. So why should Newtownards have been a centre of liberalism?

In 1874, four of its commissioners worked for James Sharman Crawford as Liberal candidate for County Down: a baker, a painter and decorator, a draper, and an auctioneer. Only one, a publican who was an Orange leader in the Ards district, worked for the Conservatives.[92] There were several dimensions to this. First, the district surrounding Newtownards was a farming district with a strong Liberal tradition (i.e. 1852).[93] We shall see that in later years the hinterland taken as a whole was about 75–80 per cent Liberal.[94] It was an area where there were still survivors of 1798;[95] a district in which three Freemasons were expelled for supporting Fenianism in 1865;[96] a district in which a largely Protestant band (with a few Catholic members) played at a Catholic church bazaar and was known by some Protestants, who made an attempt to attack it, as a "Fenian" band.[97] Second, the farming district had a strong interest in land legislation. In March 1870 a tenant right meeting held in the town was attended by the commissioners' chairman and the local branch manager of the Ulster Bank. The chairman of the meeting, Rev. Joseph Bradshaw, was keen to depoliticize the meeting and started by attacking "agitation" and "political adventurism".[98] Third, the town was in conflict with the grand jury as it wanted to be separated from the county. In fact, in 1877 it looks as though the town's cess payments (after deducting the county at large gaol and infirmary expenses) were less than the grand jury's expenditure on drainage and streets in the town.[99] The complaint was therefore about the expenditures of the county at large.

It is no surprise then that a town and hinterland so described should support a candidate in favour of securing tenant right and grand jury reform. Orangeism in this district was fairly minimal; but so too was the Catholic population at 12 per cent in the town (1861), and considerably less in the surrounding countryside. Catholicism in Newtownards was growing throughout the period, but it was very much a new and loosely established presence. It may not be accidental that in 1876 the Marquis of Londonderry built a new Catholic chapel in the town shortly before the 1878 election, when a major effort was put into securing Catholic votes for the Conservatives. The Catholics in the district were subjected to a certain amount of annoyance by public bodies such as the Poor Law guardians. In 1871 the priest was offered times to celebrate Mass at the workhouse which he could not make use of, and the Catholic paupers were obliged to go in workhouse apparel through the streets to the chapel, attracting ridicule *en route*.[100] The outward liberalism of Newtownards should be treated, when it is compared with Portadown, say, not as an achievement but as a mercy. Newtownards had assets which enabled it to avoid the virus of Portadown, but it would be a mistake to imagine that its people were much more sympathetic to Catholics. Here, for example, is how the local pro-Crawford journal spoke of Home Rule—the *Chronicle* said Home Rule meant separation.[101]

"That any such preposterous demand could be granted is one of the miserable delusions to which the Irish race have been prone . . . and from which it has so often suffered 'in mind, body and estate'. They are engendered by priestcraft and overweening self conceit and entertained by ignorance, credulity and superstition; and no assurance of their wickedness and folly, no lesson, however severe as the consequence of such blind and crass fatuity has ever sufficed to banish their periodic recurrence out of the historical annals of our island."

The local 1798 tradition notwithstanding, the battle with Lord Londonderry of 1848–52 forgotten ("Disputes between owner and occupier are unheard of"), the *Chronicle*'s support for Crawford was "pragmatic".

At several stages I will have cause to comment on the absurdity—from an economic point of view—of Catholic workers supporting Home Rule. The point is that, in a national conflict, no one's first thoughts are about what is economically rational. Instead they find the way to rival most effectively with their opponent. The same point can now be made about the *Newtownards Chronicle*'s rejection of Home Rule's developmentalist promises.

Despite its complaint about how Newtownards, with its excellent railway links, fertile soil, etc. hadn't developed more manufacturing, the *Chronicle* was utterly hostile to Home Rule. If any town in the inner North suffered from "malaise" for which such things appeared as panaceas, Newtownards was one of them. Without giving any credit to the developmentalist claims of "Home Rule", the *Chronicle* could see nothing in it except negatives: "Assaults, stealthy at first, at last open and daring, would be made on every Protestant Institution"[102]—a tyranny of ultramontanism, protectionist and constraint.

We now turn to Carrickfergus for an example which owes a great deal to local peculiarities. Carrick was one of the very few areas where the status of freeman continued to have any substantial reality in the 19th century.[103] The town was a parliamentary borough and freemen had the vote as well as the capacity, subject to the mayor's veto, of adding to their number. As a result, virtual adult male suffrage existed. Up to 1868, the elections were usually occasions for bribery and treating on a grand scale, and the interests of Lord Downshire and the remnants of the Donegall family prevailed. Marriot Dalway, a small resident local landlord engaged in salt mining, was part of a line of a family which had taken the "Independent" side in political contests from the 1770s, but until 1868 he showed no signs of any but Conservative political interest.[104] There was, however, some annoyance in the town at the way Lord Downshire had negotiated his interest in the Woodburn stream with the Belfast water commissioners in violation of the so-called Linden treaty, whereby he agreed to supply the town with water "for ever".[105] The town was actually declining. Its harbour lacked a breakwater which rendered it fairly useless and was too far from a rail track for it to remain competitive in trade with Belfast.[106] In 1868 Marriot Dalway stood as an Independent Orangeman—a sort of miniature version of William Johnston—and in an election which saw land agents being physically removed from the polling stations, he won easily.[107]

His position thereafter was somewhat peculiar. He voted with Johnston against disestablishment, but in August 1869 he supported the Liberal candidate Adair in the County Antrim election, for which he was expelled from the Orange Order. The Carrick District then broke away altogether and declared him Grand Master.[108] He voted for the 1870 Land Act and the Ballot Act. He took up temperance reform and the women's suffrage question, and became in all but name a Liberal. His most prominent local supporters were a shipowner, a shipbuilder, a large merchant and a group of farmers.[109]

To begin with, he was regarded as a local arbitrator of conflicts. In the 1870 municipal elections the Conservatives and the Independents both put up lists, and though the former won, Dalway and a few others were on both lists.[110] In 1872 he was accepted as an arbitrator by Alexander Taylor, the flax spinner, as well as the workers during the flaxdressers' strike.[111] Though significantly, the apprentice ratio was so high that Taylor's was able to continue in operation with apprentice flaxdressers,[112] and the agreement reached was simply to follow the Belfast outcome. Efforts were made in 1873 to reinvigorate the official Orange Order, and Rev. Henry Henderson delivered a speech which Rev. Warick, who led the five remaining "official" lodges, described as "such as has not been heard before in Carrickfergus".

"Although Protestantism abounds in your neighbourhood and Popery, thank God, has but very, very small bounds in this district, yet Romanism just now is making gigantic efforts to attain supremacy in this country . . .

Away with you Protestants out of the country! That is what they want to do, what Dan O'Connell said, to sweep us into the sea with cabbage stalks."[113]

He went on to attack the concept of religious equality and suggested that Jesuits who were in difficulties in Europe might soon be coming to Ireland.

There were indeed fairly few Catholics in Carrickfergus, and no one seems to have paid much attention to Henderson. Although in 1874 C. H. Ward and Robert Kelly tried to get up support for a Tory, they didn't have much luck.[114] In 1874 a pact was made between the Conservatives and Independents to split the council 50/50 in order to sort out a peculiar local difficulty.[115]

The only revenue Carrick had was rent from lands. It had no power to charge rates.[116] Part of the commons was in a dubious status, and the plan was for Dalway to sort out the rights of the corporation and the interests of the farmers who had been using them. Briefly, although his decisions were later found to be entirely scrupulous, the word was put about that he had shown favour to his friends.[117] During his time the affairs of the corporation were not effectively resolved. And in 1880 a local merchant, Thomas Greer, was put up as a Conservative with the backing of Taylor, the flax spinner, on a programme of harbour improvement and the creation of a connection branch railway. Dalway was defeated but remained chairman of the town commissioners for a number of years.[118] It would be hard to point to a district of the North where the salience of "national questions" was lower than in Carrickfergus.

Ballymena's landlord, Sir Shafto Adair, had been the Liberal candidate for Antrim in 1869. Here, unlike Lurgan, there was a real possibility of a landlord-led liberalism taking some popular roots. Most Protestants were Presbyterians and there were few Catholics. Ballymena was very much an agricultural market town surrounded by a district containing generally large farms. Here perhaps as much as anywhere the Whigs' notion of a political alliance of good (Liberal) landlords and substantial farmers based upon legally securing the status quo had some foundation. But there was another side to it. Ballymena was also the centre of the hand linen weaving district of mid-Antrim and east Derry. Many of the agricultural labourers were part weavers. Class differentiation of weaver-labourers and farmers was a reality. And though for the most part the former would not be voters until 1885, it is as well to see where they stood. Another landlord in the district, John Young of Galgorm, was a classic Conservative paternalistic who contained in his person many of the positive arguments in favour of landlords. However liberalism might develop before the labourers were enfranchised, the political significance of men like Young grew as the franchise approximated to the universal. He occupied a position in society which was very much one of arbiter.

Quite frequently cases involving disputes between farmers and labourers came before the magistrates, and Young's approach to such cases can be gauged from a remark he made to the Bessborough Commission.[119] "There is no greater tyrant than the tenant farmer when he becomes a landlord himself."

He argued the case for landlord veto on incoming tenants "without giving any reason" on the grounds that there were "all sorts of reasons . . . cannot be publicly given". When he raised his rents in 1874 only two people objected. They were, on his description, "advanced politicians on the tenant right question, and largish holders, independent men in fact". A landlord who was seen to use his powers to exclude unwanted strangers or unpopular people from his estate, but who rarely used it and did not otherwise interfere with free sale, might very well be very popular. It was amongst the larger farmers whose tenant right capital was often very large that the demand for unrestricted free sale by auction, total security of that right to ensure standing with creditors, was most pressing. For these people strictly commercial dealings needed to be enshrined within a framework approaching legal exactness. When potential bidders for their farms were having to offer very substantial sums of money, the £1 on rent = £20 of tenant right formula operated with much less elasticity than on smallholdings where the lump sums involved were smaller. It was obviously these people too who would be most likely to be substantial employers of year-round or six-month labour, and most prone to find themselves in courts over questions of contract. Thus in a non-crisis situation (where general demands for rent reductions were not pressing) it was precisely these "independent men" who would be most likely "land reformers", supported by urban creditors and tradesmen and such ancillary figures as auctioneers who got a percentage on the total proceeds of tenant right sales. Over smaller farmers, labourers or weavers, a paternalistic landlord sovereignty in spirit was possible.

In 1873 the Associated Weavers of Antrim and Derry sought to hold a meeting in the Linen Hall at Ballymena.[120] Adair refused them the use of this, but offered the Town Hall instead. The Ahoghill central committee cancelled the meeting, but about a thousand from Portglenone and County Derry arrived anyway to find the constabulary guarding the Linen Hall. The situation was potentially rather menacing and they agreed to go to the people's park on condition that "a number of gentlemen connected with the linen trade should accompany them and hear their grievances". John Patrick, whose family was in the business, together with John Young, attempted to get together deputations of weavers and merchants to meet and to get the rest of the weavers away. But their numbers, swelled by report of what was going on, rose to 3,000. There were not enough of the merchants present for those that were there to be sure they spoke for the whole body. John Young chaired the meeting which disputed the question of how long the webs should be (between 56 and 58 yards), and eventually secured agreement that the weavers' demand for 56 yards be met, obliging the manufacturers present to accept the weavers' demand, with the caveat that they had no binding authority to agree.[121] This put the onus on the merchants to break the agreement. However, when they met the Belfast merchants it transpired that the latter had passed a resolution not to accept less than 60 yard webs.[122] The manufacturers were then obliged to offer extra payment for the four extra yards to square the difference between the Ballymena agreement and the Belfast merchants' demand. In fact, the webs had been gradually lengthened from 52 yards in 1855 to 65 at its peak,[123] and the real rates of return from weaving were being harder and harder pressed by power loom competition. The weavers' gain was probably not very enduring, but Young had secured considerable popularity and preserved "order". At least three of the leading linen merchants in Ballymena were Liberals (Edward Currell, James Patrick and Robert Chesney), and it cannot be supposed that in a conflict of this kind the arbitrating role of a Conservative landlord did anything but good for Conservative political capital.

Coleraine, like Carrickfergus, was a parliamentary borough. It elected a Liberal MP, Daniel Taylor, in 1874 on a basis which was rather typical of liberalism. The town contained a 22 per cent Catholic minority on the east bank and a 38 per cent Catholic minority in the Kilowen suburb on the west bank of the Bann. Its commissioners' occupations reveal a very extensive dependence upon agricultural trades:[124] they included a seed merchant, a grain merchant, a provisions merchant, a leather merchant, four woollen drapers, a saw mill owner and an auctioneer. Orangeism was somewhat plebeian and unruly. There was a practice of putting up an arch next to the chapel in Kilowen which was justified by the claim that "they should have known the Commons was another Sandy Row". The chapel was "brought to the arch", not the arch to the chapel.[125] But Orangeism had a slightly independent tinge, probably because it was made up of Anglicans in a Presbyterian dominated town. In 1868 a Coleraine working men's Protestant defence association was formed and three of its leading members were on the council in 1877.[126] Significantly, one of these, an auctioneer, was ousted in that year. And in 1879 a representative Catholic (so described by the *Examiner*), also an auctioneer, was elected on Protestant votes.[127] In 1874 a local Orange landlord, J. L. Beers, threatened to stand against Sir H. H. Bruce on a platform of land and grand jury reform every bit as advanced as any Liberal,[128] but for some reason he withdrew and Daniel Taylor stood as a Liberal.

Taylor in 1874 expressed himself in favour of no further amendment of the 1870 Land Act (a characteristic position of Conservatives at that time), and made significant concessions on denominational education (something which virtually no other Liberal or Conservative did even in the border areas).[129] His main appeal was based upon developmentalism. He, like his opponent Sir H. H. Bruce, was a director of the Derry Central Rail Company which some hoped would break[130] the monopoly of the high tariff Northern Counties Railway Company on traffic from Coleraine.[131] He seems to have had the backing of the Irish Society,[132] and his major proposal was development work on Coleraine harbour which was threatened by competition from Portrush. In fact, during his period as MP the harbour works got into serious difficulties. Heavily burdened with loan expenditure for dredging, the scale of harbour dues required to service the debt would have driven the shipping to Portrush. Unable to borrow any further because the security was so bad, they were stuck with uncompleted works and were attempting in 1877 to secure a Treasury loan of £60,000.[133] Not a particularly strong figure on the land question, unpopular with the "non-sectarian" education lobby after his support for the Irish Universities and Intermediate Education Acts, and having secured little in the way of practical benefits on the harbour development, Taylor was defeated by Sir H. H. Bruce in 1880 with a programme which was generally vacuous, but which mentioned "retrenchment".

The most characteristically "Liberal" districts were generally those where larger farms were the norm, where Presbyterianism was strong, and where towns were both dependent in an exclusive way upon agriculture and their development compromised by insecure urban leaseholding. In these situations both the dominant rural and urban interests had a powerful and compelling reason to seek a sound legal basis for middle-class property rights which was independent of the onset of any crisis pressures (e.g. for general rent reductions). Where such interests could be linked up with Presbyterian traditions of opposition to Anglican landlord supremacy, all the necessary ingredients were present. The classic case is Ballymoney,[134] which had no manufacturing base at all, and some of the County Londonderry towns (not Coleraine or Derry itself) where urban construction had to proceed on the security of the tenant right custom alone, because the London companies refused very long leases for such development.[135] In these areas, especially where weaving was altogether absent, the agricultural and urban working classes were small and in no position to assert themselves, even through the medium of Orangeism. Where Catholics were few, local significance of pan-Protestantism was marginal. It is noteworthy that in Ballymoney, like Coleraine, a "representative Catholic" was elected on Protestant votes.

Because these districts had a permanent non-crisis interest in securing bourgeois property and in political organization, they were also areas where party liberalism might become strongest. Much of the "Liberalism" we have looked at in, say, Newtownards and Carrickfergus had a decidedly parochial colour. Ballymoney's cosmopolitanism was reflected in its town meeting in support of Gladstone's attack on Turkish atrocities in Bulgaria.[136] But northern liberalism, whether of the Ballymoney or the Carrickfergus variety, rarely had to come to grips with how it related to the politics of the island as a whole. As we shall see in the next chapter, Ballymoney Liberals were not unaware of the difficulty. But what shaped North-South relations did not depend on what happened in Ballymoney. It depended on the frontier districts where the tendency toward "nationalization" of religious divisions was expressed in local politics.

Newry was a strongly Catholic town, but until democratization of the franchise, local control remained fairly balanced. As compared with Derry a much lower proportion of the Protestants were Liberals, so the Liberal identity of Newry depended on a small group of about 30–50 Protestants, without whose support the Catholics could not win the parliamentary seat. In fact this meant that a Protestant Liberal was usually elected by an overwhelmingly Catholic vote. This generated considerable pressures and resentments amongst Catholics against clerical accommodation which eventually broke loose in 1879 (see Chapter 13). The larger part on the Down side of the river was 68 per cent Roman Catholic and the remaining Armagh side 60 per cent Roman Catholic. Although the parliamentary electorate contained a slight Protestant majority, the municipal electorate contained a substantial Protestant majority. The leading Tory was a land agent and the leading (Catholic) Liberal a woollen draper.[137]

In this town the Catholics "ruled the streets" to a much greater extent than in most other places we have noticed. In July 1869 some decorations were put up and drumming occurred in Protestant districts. The next day a stone throwing attack was made on the Orange Hall where a dinner was in progress.[138] The constabulary arrived in time to break it up, but not before shots had been fired on the crowd from the hall. A Fenian amnesty demonstration was held in Newry in October 1869. Some Protestants had beaten up a few Catholics shortly before the demonstration which was held on a Sunday, and Protestants going to church had "Bibles taken and trampled by mobs wearing green hat bands".[139] The further we move away from the clear Protestant majority districts, the more dangerous collisions arising out of Orange manifestations became, for the very simple reason that each was able to give as good as they got. In such situations there was not much room for a paternalistic alliance between influential Protestant Liberals and a Catholic minority.

East of Newry, between Slieve Croob and the Mourne Mountains was the notorious district about Dolly's Brae, which was the subject of lengthy reports to the Castle from Mr Butler, R.M., in 1870 and 1871. The rector of Ballyward, in spite of opposition from some of his congregation and the local

Presbyterian minister, continued to decorate his church with Orange flags.[140] The Orange Lodges in these districts calculated on police protection and marched through "Catholic townlands where the Orangemen had not passed since 1849". The hoisting of the flags and the departure for Rathfriland were, in the words of the RM, a challenge to the Roman Catholics "to come down from the mountains to attack Ballyward church". Hundreds of Protestant farmers and their labourers marched with drums and colours.[141] Increasingly, the Orange marching that mushroomed in the late 1860s and early 1870s met armed Catholic responses. They gathered in July 1870 in overwhelming numbers, often armed, and forced the constabulary to find ways of preventing collisions. In 1870, for example, such gatherings occurred at Keady,[142] Swanlinbar,[143] Ballybofey,[144] Muffglen,[145] Manorcunningham,[146] and even in Bellaghy[147] and Downpatrick.[148]

By this stage then, Newry had become more and more an area "beyond dispute" in the Catholics' favour. The local preponderance of Catholics was sufficiently represented in the elite of Catholic merchants to ensure that there were some Catholic JPs. But it was scarcely a town inside the framework of the northern "prosperity belt". Part of the town which was once "respectable" had been carved up into tenements.[149] The council had assumed nearly all the powers of the grand jury in 1871 (a separate company controlled the harbour and the canal to Portadown) but its borrowing powers were exhausted.[150]

How would Newry relate to the agricultural areas adjoining it? On both sides the land was largely mountainous or hilly. The small, nearly totally Catholic village of Camlough a few miles west had a tenant right association supported by Rev. Charles Quinn of Lower Killeavy parish. At the Bessborough Commission, Father Quinn dwelt on the problems of reclamation tenants.[151] He was emphatically not a Nationalist. He actively supported the Liberal candidacy of J. N. Richardson, proprietor of the Bessbrook spinning factory in 1880, and thought that if land was sold to the tenants "you would have no such men as Parnell, nor any of those land agitators".[152] His liberalism could not consist of merely putting legal sanctions on the Ulster custom. One of his colleagues,

Patrick O'Callaghan, explained the centrality of the reclamation tenantry in the area. Lord Gosford, he said, "may be a good landlord to some—about Markethill and on the good land—but on the waste land and the mountainy land he is a bad one".[153]

Liberalism in these districts was closer to Peter Gibbon's model of a transitional presence than it was in the inner North.[154] Here there was something artificial about an arrangement where 300 Catholics and 30 Protestants voted together to support a Protestant Liberal. Clerical accommodation with Whig elites was under pressure precisely because Catholics were in a position to assert themselves. The Fenian amnesty question provided the occasion for doing so in the first instance. But the tensions sharpened during the 1878 County Down by-election and Parnell's first visit to the North in 1879.[155] In 1880 Protestant Liberal support more or less vanished in Newry town. Liberalism was sustained in parts of south Armagh for a while by Father Quinn's alliance with Richardson of Bessbrook and given a new breath of life by Gladstone's handling of the 1880–81 land crisis.

The mountain districts were as a general rule areas of unquestioned Catholic dominance. For many northern Catholics, politics and their own identity was shaped by their conflict and rivalry with Orangeism. This is one reason why Home Rule cannot be seen except in these terms for people locked into such a situation. But the mountainous areas were mostly free of Orangeism, or at all events had no cause to be preoccupied with it. Home Rule in these areas was not about conflict with Orangemen, but rather about the asymmetry of experience of the Catholic highlander. Their experience as reclamation tenants was distinctive, and even if their numbers were not great, they imparted something to the Home Rule movement equivalent to what was imparted by the shipyard worker to Unionism. For them, Home Rule made economic sense as well as carrying a strong emotional resonance.

In early 1873 there was widespread Home Rule organization growing in the districts of Pomeroy, Carrickmore and Cappagh in County Tyrone.[156] These were areas where reclamation tenancy had been something of the norm for a very long time. The meetings were mostly presided over and addressed by laymen, and the tone of the speeches was far more blatantly anti-English than was usual at the more clerical and ritualized 15 August 1873 meetings. The meetings in Pomeroy and Carrickmore were strikingly "secular" and notable for the expression of a thoroughgoing nationalism.

There was none of the often ambivalent praise for Gladstone. And there was much very strong criticism of the Land Act. Terence O'Neill, classics teacher, Carrickmore:

[To Protestants:] "Let them not for one moment imagine this splendid demonstration is intended to give them the slightest offence, nor is it a display of strength either—it is a Home Rule demonstration pure and simple—and we cordially invite them to join us in a formation of a Home Rule Association."

He speaks of artificial famines, a reference to grain exports in 1845–50:

"Such a result the unscrupulous robber England can bring about at any time while she commands the Irish markets and enters into league with the landlords, most of whom are of her own kith and kin, doctrine and practice."[157]

Although he spoke of the country flourishing during the Irish parliament, he did not pretend it was other than corrupt. He did not seem to be enamoured with the "constitutional" myths about that body.

"If under such a corrupt Parliament our country was flourishing to such a degree, how much more flourishing would it be if England, even now at the eleventh hour could be coaxed, or if she cannot be coaxed, if she can be coerced, to allow us to manage our own affairs."

He spoke of the legacy of Orr, McCracken and Wolfe Tone in conjunction with Meagher and MacManus and the Young Ireland tradition. But the grand theme of his speech was the need to arrest the tide of emigration. This theme was central to every speech. For example, John Quinn of Cappagh, on the experience of emigration, said:

"Millions of your race and mine oppressed at home, and leaving Ireland because they cannot support their existence here, must mix up with all the squalidness and wretchedness and sin that poverty is but all too often subject to in foreign cities. And in England itself, the country which is to blame for all this sad state of things, they have not only to mix with the lowest, but to bear their scoffs and taunts." Home Rule was needed to reverse the English encouraged emigration. "And the land which misrule and landlord tyranny have laid out a pasture for cattle would be converted into a happy home for the bravest race in existence."[158]

The programme of the House Rule association was "Home Rule, Fixity of Tenure and Fair Rents". The association spread fairly rapidly through the mountains. In Greencastle, Lower Badoney parish, it received the support of the parish curate, and once again the declared objective was "to preserve the Irish race from extinction in their native land".[159]

The *Examiner* generalized the message. In other areas perhaps there was some considerable rural prosperity, it said. But "Gradually our island is becoming a stock farm to give food for the people of England. Some few of our countrymen may be better off now than they were twenty or thirty years ago, but this is no proof whatever of national achievement."[160] It was rather a "prosperity that is one day destined to extinguish us as a nation".

For another aspect of northern Home Rule, we must look at Derry where it posed its first electoral challenge within Ulster in 1872. Derry's position was in some ways like Newry's. On the west side of the river where the greatest part of the town was situated, there was a 58 per cent Catholic majority. But unlike Newry, much of its farming hinterland was Protestant. Its corporation, which was elected from an exceedingly narrow franchise, was largely Conservative. Of its politically identifiable councillors, twelve were Conservatives, three were Liberals, and one, Thomas O'Hanlon, a merchant, was the only councillor elected in the North to be prominently aligned with Parnell during the early stages of the Land War.[161] In the parliamentary electorate of about 1,300 (compared to the municipal 680) the Catholics were about 40 per cent.

Presbyterian liberalism was much stronger in Derry than in Newry. Apart from their greater proportion in the population, the linkages to the rural population around were stronger; and their interest in Magee College reduced their enthusiasm for the "National Education League". A not inconsiderable factor was the presence of the *Derry Standard* and its editor James McKnight. In 1868 Derry elected Richard Dowse, a Liberal MP, with the solid backing of the Catholics plus 38 per cent of the Presbyterian voters.[162] Derry had the misfortune to be the symbol of the triumph of 1689-91, and we mentioned earlier how William Johnston made the defence of its celebrations a major part of his political activity. In fact, in August 1870 the confrontation of that period saw the more or less complete takeover of the leaderships of local Catholic and Protestant demonstrations by outside agitators. John O'Donnell of the Liberal Working Men's Defence Association (the Catholic working men's organization of the Bogside), left the stage to A. J. McKenna of the *Northern Star*, and Catholics poured into the Bogside from Muff and beyond in Innishowen.[163] The Orangemen, with Johnston at their head, were joined by those of Coleraine.[164] We will miss the details of the conflicts that ensued. The corporation and the Castle authorities in 1870-71 attempted to put the Apprentice Boys processions down, but in early 1872 were defeated by John Rea's legal action against Colonel Hillyer.[165] Out of this emerged the first explicit treaty of equal marching rights. The Catholics paraded inside the walls on 15 August 1872 without opposition.[166] Faced in other words by threats of perpetual disorder, and not without preceding trials of strength, the doctrine of equal marching rights was applied explicitly.

Derry was then, however, to be the testing spot of another kind of conflict. In 1872 Dowse was elevated to the Bench and a by-election was to follow. The government candidate, the first Catholic Liberal candidate to stand in an Ulster election, Richard Palles, was the Attorney General in charge of conducting the prosecutions of the Galway priests arising out of the Keogh judgment on the election petition.[167] Besides the Galway election and the education question, the conflict between Father O'Keeffe and Cardinal Cullen was coming out into the open. The Apprentice Boys "supported" O'Keeffe, seeing the issue as "whether the law of the Queen or those of the Pope will be supreme in this country".[168] The election saw the first intervention of a Home Rule candidate, Joseph Biggar, the chairman of the association in Belfast.

Of the dispute between the local Conservative candidate, Bartholomew McCorkell, and the nominee of the Abercorn interest, C. E. Lewis, we need say very little except that a substantial body of the city merchants backed McCorkell who eventually withdrew.[169] Lewis was something of a novelty in that he was an English Presbyterian and a firm supporter of national education. His very appearance indicated how far conservatism was moving in the direction of appropriating the MacNaughton "Liberal" policies, a move which generally speaking tended to undermine urban Presbyterian liberalism, and to draw into sharp relief the clash of religious oppositions on that theme. What is important here is the way the Biggar campaign was launched against Palles, who was supported by Dr Kelly, the Roman Catholic Bishop of Derry.

The *Ulster Examiner* fulminated about how Catholics would not "give aid to the Priest-hunting policy of Castle lawyers".[170] The theme of "priest hunting" echoing the penal era was made a Home Rule chanting cry and the embarrassment of the government, which had been asked by the clergy of Galway to prosecute in order to allow them to vindicate themselves of Keogh's charges, was exploited to the full. All the subjective anger about the Keogh judgment was turned against Palles with a vengeance. An attempt to hold a meeting for Palles in Hogg's shirt factory was broken up by Home Rulers, who took over the platform before it was due to begin.[171] And during Palles' speech he was greeted with "Priest Hunter", "Judge Keogh", "Political Prisoners", "Coercion Bill", etc. It is significant that the very last issues of A. J. McKenna's old paper, the *Ulster Observer*, show visible disquiet with the fervour being worked up, and take a rather neutral position between Palles and Biggar after praising the former as "none more worthy of support".[172] The *Examiner*, which opposed the Bishop, and John O'Donnell of the Liberal Working Men's Defence Association, which supported Palles, made great play of Biggar's declaration in favour of denominational education,[173] while Palles remained silent on the subject. What else then was there to the campaign beyond playing upon "priest hunting" and appeals to Catholic subjectivity?

John Ferguson's lecture at the first meeting of the Home Rulers is very revealing as, unlike the sentiments of Tyrone mountain meetings, it is explicitly opposed to separatism: "all our interests point to union with England . . . But a large number of Irishmen require some reason for entering into union upon any terms with that nation which has been such a terrible destroyer in the past and is today proud and insulting in its demeanour towards us."[174]

His reasons were that geographical and commercial interests pointed to unity and that the "people", who were now in power in England, were willing to concede self-government. If there was separation, then a prohibition duty might be put on the export of coal, iron and machinery, and that would make it impossible for Ireland to become a manufacturing nation. "In fact the trade of Belfast would be as completely destroyed by such a course as was the old woollen trade." If separation were the only alternative to the Union, then he would favour it "as twenty years like the past will have exterminated our race."[175]

The significance of this intervention cannot be underrated. It amounts in effect to a recognition that some form of commercial union with Britain is vital and reduces the role of the proposed Irish parliament to a much less than economically protectionist body. Separation, which, it is recognized, would ruin Belfast's commerce, is only a last resort if the alternative is the Union. Without paying too much attention to the details, what was going on here was an effort to surmount all the really awkward problems of economic nationalism. Ferguson's efforts were bent towards making some economic sense out of an aspiration that had arisen from quite different causes.

The novelty of the intervention in Derry was that this expression of pan-Catholic solidarity was being turned against liberalism, rather than Toryism, and against one of the most authentically liberal wings of liberalism at that. The *Standard* was thrust into the position of having to face the simultaneous possibility of Catholic defections to Home Rule and Presbyterian defections to Conservative supporters of "non-sectarian education". The education difficulty was dealt with by a letter writer, who observed that nothing could be more damaging to national education than its becoming "a pet of Irish Toryism", which only supported it because it was distasteful to Roman Catholics.[176] Toryism is "contempt of all consistency except the consistency of hate and bigotry". This extremely powerful attack on Toryism and its associated leader editorial obviously disturbed some Liberal Presbyterians. Richard Smyth said that he had every intention of voting Liberal, but would not do so if he was required to subscribe to the view that all Presbyterian Conservatives were "shams" or "hypocrites".[177] But the *Standard*'s real alarm was the tactics of the Home Rulers. These it compared with the Tories' tactics in 1868, the only difference being that the Tory leaders of 1868 kept clear of direct association with their mobs, while the Home Rule leaders took no such precautions.[178] And, appealing explicitly to middle-class bourgeois standards of order and clerical accommodation simultaneously:

"It is time for the public of all classes to take some united action for putting an end to this anti-Christian movement in Derry which . . . must not be allowed to assume the attitude of an organised terrorism."[179]

The *Standard* was being consistent in this approach. It had remained much more consistently anti pan-Protestant than others in the past, and its liberalism was far more than just a polite name for opposition to ultramontanism. Indeed over the Galway judgment it observed a relative silence "partly from motives of denominational delicacy".[180] It confined its remarks now to support for Isaac Butt's position (the matter of complaint was Keogh's language): no lawyer would judge the election other than a nullity; the Roman Catholic Bishop of Galway showed such actions were violations of Roman Catholic Church law; the evidence against the priests was provided by Roman Catholics; the government had no choice but to prosecute; new evidence may be forthcoming at the trial which will exonerate the priests. But above all else McKnight was the firmest and most consistent northern Protestant supporter of fixity of tenure, and every bit an ally on the secular question of "rooting people in the soil".

The *Standard*'s description of the Home Rule movement was misrule (not Rome rule), and its keenness to preserve a popular accommodation is reflected in its implicit stress on Christian unity in opposition to the sneering at religion in some of the Home Rule speeches which bore "an ominous likeness to the revolting eloquence occasionally spouted at Fenian assemblies seven or eight years ago".[181] The election left the *Standard* very bitter. Compared to 1868, the Liberal vote fell by 183, and the Tory vote rose by 97. The Home Rulers got 89 votes. The obvious conclusion to draw would be that the 97 extra Tories were 1868 Presbyterian Liberals and the 89 votes for Home Rule were 1868 Catholic Liberals.[182] The *Standard* suggested—on what authority is uncertain—that some Catholics had voted Tory for tactical reasons to defeat the Liberals.[183] The suggestion might seem far fetched but for the fact that Lord Claud Hamilton ostentatiously praised the Home Rulers (who had bust up two Liberal meetings) for their "highly peaceable and constitutional" carriage of the campaign.[184] The *Examiner*, whose hatred for the "Whigs" had reached the point of hysteria, published several editorials on this election in succession. In one it accused the Presbyterian Liberals of not voting for Palles because "he was a Papist", but in another it snapped: "Those who voted for Mr. Palles must be regarded as being entirely English in their views and sentiments." The Liberal and Tory voters had voted for "English domination in Ireland".[185] But the following week they described the Derry election as "one of the brightest victories ever gained by the patriotic people of Ireland".[186] The only consistency in these two approaches is hatred of the Liberals. The unspoken alliance of enemies "fighting in parallel lines" to keep down liberalism came to Derry before anywhere else.

The great barometer of northern politics was Cookstown. Just about everything that happened in northern political life had an echo here. In June 1869 Gunning's weaving factory was closed to provide an attendance at a church defence meeting.[187] In February 1870 a tenant right meeting was held here. In December 1871 it was the place where Orangemen with sashes appeared for the first time at a "National Education League" meeting. Pan-Protestant organization was exceedingly powerful and militant, but there was sufficient clerical accommodation between Presbyterian and Catholic clergy to facilitate political co-operation on the land question. In the first secret ballot election in a rural constituency in 1873, an Independent Orange candidate nearly won the County Tyrone seat, which he then won in the 1874 general election.

From 1866 Cookstown and Dungannon had been centres of Orange revival. During the period of the church defence campaign, massive Orange demonstrations had taken place in this lowland district of east Tyrone. Killyman and Clonfeakle parishes, which I singled out as Orange weaving districts in the pre-famine period, were directly south of them. At the 1870 tenant right meeting, the proceedings were dominated by Presbyterian and Catholic clergy, but a spinning manufacturer and various other large businessmen were also present. The Catholic priests present were representative not just of the lowland parishes but of mountainous parishes such as Termon, Pomeroy and Carrickmore. The message of Rev. Bernard Murphy, Catholic curate of Carrickmore, contrasted rather with that of the Home Rule meeting in his parish in 1873. On this occasion he explained his presence thus:

"When they became ministers of the Gospel they did not renounce their allegiance to their Sovereign—they did not relinquish the right of citizenship—but they still continued citizens of the British Empire and it is in this capacity that I appear today."[188]

His message on the land question, though the language was tempered, was about the evil of emigration, and he spoke about the reclamation tenantry on the mountain estate of Sir John Stewart. Massive rent increases on reclaimed land were not something restricted to the South and West of Ireland. The issue in Carrickmore was clear enough.

Rev. Knox Leslie, Presbyterian minister of Cookstown, felt it necessary to answer charges that had apparently been made about association for political purposes with Catholics in his opening speech, mentioning that his sentiments were similar to those of Johnston of Ballykilbeg:

"If I were asked to advocate party politics here on the ascendancy of one class over another class, I would not have identified myself with this meeting. . . . Those gentlemen who object to our associating with other religionists would not for the life of them associate with them in the egg market or the pork market." [*Laughter*][189]

The resolutions included a call for a tribunal to limit rents, and for Bright's scheme of peasant proprietorship.

It is significant that there were no Orangemen taking a high profile role in the proceedings. It was likely that they were the people Rev. Leslie was referring to, as objecting to association with Catholics. The development of Orangeism toward land agitation took a peculiar path. William J. Devlin, its driving force, was a flax merchant who had made his fortune during the flax boom in the mid-1860s.[190] In the 1870s he was associated with the Liberal MPs Dickson, Whitworth and Taylor in the promotion of railways.[191] He was a friend of Stewart Knox, MP for Dungannon, and Sir John Stewart, the landlord of Carrickmore estate amongst other places, both prominent Orangemen. In 1872 Devlin was elected chairman of the town commissioners of Cookstown. Of his local influence, the *Belfast Times* claimed, "one word from him and neither an Act of Parliament, constabulary or their own strength could have enabled [a Catholic procession] to have carried a green banner through Cookstown Street".[192] The changes in Cookstown politics during the 1870s were closely connected with his career. On 2 August some Orangemen collided with a Nationalist procession and the clergy, including Very Rev. Canon McCrystal of Cookstown (Roman Catholic) and Revs Knox Leslie and H. B. Wilson and others, organized a truce and a dropping of charges.[193] They also secured an agreement that on 15 August, when both parties intended holding meetings, neither would enter the town. The proceedings of the Orange meeting are significant for what they show of the gradual adoption of the doctrine of equal marching rights.[194]

Devlin described the meeting as a "defence meeting to enter their protest against any demonstration that might take the form of Fenianism, disguised or undisguised", and he deplored the occurrences of 2 August.

Rev. H. B. Wilson:

"Protestantism is a religion of peace . . . the events and talk of the past week made him sorrowful to think that fellow men of different religious persuasions might have met today in deadly conflict . . . He hoped they would show themselves good and loyal men, by leaving the town as they came, giving offence to no one. In regard to their Roman Catholic friends, he was not going to say whether they were right or wrong to observe these days. All he could say was that from his intercourse with the Roman Catholic pastor of this town (Canon McCrystal) no man could go further than he had done to preserve the peace."

W. D. Aston, district secretary of Cookstown Orangemen and lessee of the town markets

"had a great deal of respect for the majority of his Roman Catholic townsmen, yet he wished to say that this meeting was to proclaim that Cookstown was and is the town of Protestants: that they had no idea of giving it up to the orgies of any Fenian or Ribbon party".

This was an area which had been very jumpy about Fenianism in the mid-1860s. The town had a marginal Protestant majority. Basically, the Orangemen were not accepting the doctrine of equal rights without the intervention of effective clerical accommodation, and some were accepting it rather reluctantly. The point was that the land question would provide the incentive to make it work.

In fact, the tone of Orangeism in this district remained very militant even after the beginning of political co-operation. The district between Stewartstown (Protestant) and Coalisland (Catholic) was particularly bad. Devlin and others give us some idea of the spirit of Orangeism in 1873, shortly after an attack on a procession of Protestant Sunday school children at Coalisland.

"There are some people so illiberal and thin skinned who consider that we have no right to go about disturbing the peace of the country; but I say we have and we will continue to do so in future as our fathers did in the past."

(William J. Devlin)[195]

"The only excuse that can be given [for not becoming an Orangeman] is a certain moral cowardice which prevails in the minds of many men, and a desire for popularity among the members of a certain religion. They know that once in the Orange ranks they must stand shoulder to shoulder together and fight the battle with the main body; and some like to see a Roman Catholic priest nod his head to them and bid 'good morrow'."

(Rev. H. W. Young, Rector of Stewartstown)[196]

Just how difficult sorting out the rights and wrongs of sectarian march clashes might be is illustrated by the comment of the "neutral" *Ulster Weekly News* on the conflict on St Patrick's Day in Magherafelt in 1873.[197] Although there was no illegality the march was said to be "opposed to the feelings of a large majority of the inhabitants of Magherafelt (45 per cent Roman Catholic), and the case of Derry is not parallel":

"The people of Derry have entered into a formal agreement as regards the respective demonstrations of the two parties, but it appears that no such understanding exists in Magherafelt. On the contrary it is said that it is forty years since a Roman Catholic procession passed through the town, the event being signalized by the death of a man. Thus an infraction of a long established rule may be cited as leading to the untoward occurrence of St. Patrick's Day; but on the other hand it is argued that certain other precincts are invaded on the 12th July and that if one party has a right to demonstrate on forbidden ground, so has the other."

This was the crunch. "Long-established rules" were actually a product of a previous balance of forces which reflected local dominance rather than any conception of justice or equality of rights. Quite small groups of people could in effect keep these patterns alive by creating collisions which ensured that new precedents were not accepted. Unless the society was to be traumatized by major fights and battles before such rights were accepted in the interests of general tranquillity, some other very powerful stimulus was needed, like that of the strike in Gilford in 1874. Despite the tensions in east Tyrone, the land question provided something of a solution, although it wasn't till 1880–81 that it became more than an approximation.

Devlin's role as chairman of the commissioners and later of the Poor Law guardians all fitted a style. "Anything he took up, he carried with a high hand."[198] He had an extensive sewerage works done in the town at considerable expense, and even tried to get up a proposal for a water works. When the ratepayers opposed him at a meeting he attempted to leave it "in the hands of the mob of the town", unsuccessfully, as the ratepayers stuck to their ground. His approach to the land question was similar. In 1873 one of the MPs for Tyrone died and the Orange Lodges of Killyman held a meeting which refused to accept the nomination of a scion of the Belmore family which had held the seat for decades.[199] They decided instead to support J. Ellison McCartney, a small landlord, who also farmed as a tenant. The weakness of the Land Act—its failure to prevent rent raising, the assertion of legal validity of the state rules, and the ruling that at the end of leases tenants had no tenant right interest remaining—were by this time apparent. Devlin and other more militant Orangemen, such as Hunt Chambre, now got up McCartney's candidature as an Independent Orangeman supporter of tenant right.

Although McCartney's campaign was decidedly "Protestant", his address was to the "Protestant county" and he mentioned his opposition to Home Rule and denominational education, most of the Catholics and Presbyterians of the 1870 meeting joined in his campaign. They must have been somewhat alarmed at the tenor of some of McCartney's statements. He said, for example, that if Stewart Knox or Sir John Stewart had been candidates—both Conservative Orangemen and the latter the landlord of Carrickmore—he would not have stood.[200] In fact, his views on the land question were indistinct (as was to become clear in 1880-81), and some doubt might have been entertained as to exactly why some people were supporting him. In the first county election under secret ballot he only just failed to win.[201]

In the 1874 general election, at which both Conservative candidates made concessionary noises about tenant right and Lord Claud Hamilton indicated that he had supported the 1870 Act, the overt distinctions between the different candidates' statements were not very great. And it transpired that a rumour had been put about that Lord Claud had voted against Presbyterian interests on the Burial Bill.[202] In fact, it was Lord Claud's nephew, of the same name who was MP for Derry before 1868 and now represented Kings Lynn, who had cast the hostile vote. But that didn't matter. McCartney had an overwhelming victory and the House of Abercorn was defeated in County Tyrone which it had controlled beyond living memory.[203]

The McCartney victory in itself was a dubious achievement in that all manner of rather murky currents were admixed with a general opposition to landlord rule. In fact Devlin, who was the central figure in the Orange aspect of the campaign, suddenly disappeared in 1877, having been raised to the status of a local dignitary and made a JP.[204] He was discovered to have left behind a trail of bad debts, and his disappearance caused considerable loss to many farmers and traders. But for all the murky quality of his political career, it had one vital and lasting result. Catholic and Orange tenant farmers had managed to co-operate for political purposes in spite of the very considerable local uncertainty about popular sectarian *de facto* strengths. In 1880–81 this would be manifest again without the more ambivalent trimmings.

In a way the Devlin era in Cookstown expressed in that setting what Johnston expressed in Belfast. In neighbouring County Fermanagh, where landlord control of the Orange Order was very thoroughgoing, ultra-sectarian manifestations also appeared in this period. Thus at the time of the great crisis in Derry in August 1870, a meeting outside Enniskillen was critical of the absent gentry who "would subscribe to a chapel but would not show their faces here",[205] and the Franco-Prussian War manifestations saw a virtually unprecedented outbreak of street violence in the town.[206] But even in the west in this early period liberalism had some clear expressions. T. A. Dickson, coalmine owner and railway promoter, whose developmentalist interests opened up Coalisland during the period of very high coal prices in 1873, stood as a Liberal in Dungannon in 1874.[207] Like Taylor in Coleraine in many respects, he took a less than hard line on "non-sectarian" education, necessitated in this case by the higher proportion of Catholic voters in Dungannon. Unlike Taylor, however, he was to take a very active part in the land agitation. His victory in 1874 the Tory *Tyrone Constitution* could only explain "by the assiduity with which the mischievous theory of necessary conflict between the upper and middle classes has been instilled into the minds of a very partially enlightened people".[208] As a testimony to the non-parochial character of Dickson's campaign, such hostile witness could hardly be bettered.

13. The Land War and the Climax of Liberalism—the Land League

This chapter is about the impact of the rural crisis in the late 1870s and early 1880s. It will demonstrate the "limits" of Ulster liberalism, showing what it became at its strongest point. The ultimate test of liberalism in all its various phases was its capacity to directly oppose pan-Protestantism. At various points liberalism had created successful electoral coalitions that defeated conservatism; but to undermine pan-Protestantism it was necessary for more to happen than this. Pan-Protestantism was a way of looking at the society and seeing everywhere threatening Catholic power. It was a way of confronting these threats, which tended to make them a reality; it was a trap Protestants could find themselves in once polarization had been created by confrontation. To break the pan-Protestant process was to take pre-emptive action that prevented the polarization from occurring and opened up different horizons, instead of enforcing sectarian choices. At the beginning of the Land War in Ulster the pan-Protestant strategy began to be put into operation against the Land League. It looked as though it was going to be successfully carried through. But then liberalism became involved in agitation and put pan-Protestantism "off the streets".

The story of the Land League in the North is, from this angle, a story of virtual co-operation—in spite of latent differences on the national question—in which a kind of territorial division occurred. Land League meetings tended to occur in "Catholic" space and Liberal meetings in "Protestant" space. But that remark should immediately be qualified. What the Liberal agitation did was actually to legitimize land agitation in general. And some of the Land League meetings were held in areas where, had pan-Protestantism been effectively mobilized, they would not have been possible. Not only that, but the Land League made very considerable inroads on Protestant support in areas (such as County Fermanagh) where no previous tradition of tenant right liberalism had been established. The achievement of liberalism therefore was to prevent the definition of the land agitation in terms of "pan-Catholicism" versus "pan-Protestantism". It is important to stress that all of this was without prejudice to the question of what would or would not happen when the question of nationality was posed explicitly. Anyone viewing this period looking for signs of "Protestant nationalists" may find them in more than "usual" numbers, but to look at it primarily in these terms is to miss what is really important about it.

Ulster Toryism was rooted in the territorial power of landed property, the institutions of local government—principally the grand juries and their urban ally, the Belfast Corporation—and in its capacity to mobilize pan-Protestant agitation. To match this Ulster liberalism needed a strategy of change. It needed to capitalize upon its membership of a wider British Liberal alliance and hence its membership of a party of government; and also it needed to build a popular organizational activity as well. In 1880–81, for the first time, it acquired a new base and made sense of its alliance with and membership of metropolitan liberalism. In many Presbyterian districts it entrenched itself as by far the strongest party. The Land War was also the occasion when northern Catholics were able to take part in a movement in Ireland as a whole. Pan-Catholicism—the sense of power that came from Catholic Ireland as a whole—had been a sentiment. We have indicated that northern support for Home Rule was first and foremost an expression of alienation from northern Protestant society. Parnell and the Land League provided it with a practical opportunity to do something in concert with pan-Catholicism in all of Ireland.

The co-operation between northern liberalism and the Land League masked very important underlying divergencies.

Ultimately those divergencies were exposed when Parnell came into direct conflict with Gladstone. The question that would then be posed would be "Who was the author of the great achievements of the period?" Was it the Land League and Parnell whose agitation had "wrenched" the concessions from "England", or was it Gladstone who had passed a Land Act which laid the axe to the pretensions of territorialism in Ireland and drew the sting from potentially revolutionary forces in the south and west? Such a question drew a line between Parnellite nationalism and Northern liberalism. While this was a big step for Parnell in the North, it had its limits. Northern liberalism would, for the time being at least, include a large number of northern Catholics.

The conflict within liberalism over the land question had crystallized at an early stage. At a tenant right conference in Belfast in March 1870, after the publication of the Bill, some of the representatives showed real disappointment that the measure did not clearly define the Ulster custom, let alone extend it southwards.[1] Dr McKnight observed that, at this stage, the Bill only laid down general principles and that the actual machinery would only be introduced at the second reading stage. The government seemed mystified as to what the Ulster custom was, and it was the duty of that gathering to tell them. His own fear was that the Bill would give legal force not only to the custom but to all the various infringements that had been made under the heading of "usages". But it was, he said, the best Bill so far, going beyond Sharman Crawford's which only referred to compensation for improvements. Thomas MacKnight, by contrast, did not discuss the Bill at any length but talked instead of presenting Gladstone with a spinning wheel, much to the irritation of some of the delegates present. When the question of a delegation to go to London was discussed, Professor Rogers—the same who had been active in the Tenant League twenty years before—said "he was satisfied that when Dr. McKnight went to London everything would be all right"; and in a blunt reference to Thomas MacKnight, "it is not every man who conducts a newspaper who understands this question".

The delegation that Dr McKnight led was most impressed by Gladstone who "displayed an amount of local knowledge not a little remarkable", but was ultimately disappointed.² The *Northern Star* commented on the attitude of the *Whig*, which counselled against efforts that might embarrass the government.

"We are certainly amused with the arguments persistently put forward by some pretentious advocates of the tenants' cause against any 'demonstrations' calculated to embarrass the government. In fact, the gentlemen who advance these arguments appear to think the first consideration should be the government and the last, those principally concerned—the tenant farmers. . . . [they] regard it as important only in so far as it tends to keep the Whigs in and the Tories out of office."³

In fact, William Johnston, M.P., against the opposition of the Ulster Liberal leadership, introduced an amendment to define the custom, and at a conference in Ballymoney in April the sense of betrayal with everyone except Johnston was very strongly expressed.⁴ Professor Rogers attributed what he called the misleading of Gladstone to the influence of certain "Liberal journals". So heavy were the proceedings with these kinds of sentiments that Dr McKnight, who admitted his own disappointment, felt moved not only to praise Gladstone but also to thank Thomas McClure, the Liberal MP for Belfast, for his part in the negotiations on the Bill. But the *Star* noticed that the resolutions seemed to "shirk the ground adopted at the conference".⁵ Ten years later at the Bessborough Commission, Sam McElroy said that Dr McKnight had framed three resolutions which had not been put because "some people thought these resolutions too strong and feared to embarrass the government".⁶ The first of these covered the ominous possibilities inherent in reference to "customs and usages" which would turn out to involve legalization of every infringement of the custom of any standing. The second covered the dangers of legal expenses swallowing up substantial parts of any award made; and the third warned that the Act contained no effective safeguard against rent raising. In order to bring the Act to bear, it was necessary first to give up one's holding as the Act only dealt with compensation for those displaced.

The full meaning of the Act did not become clear until it was given substantive content by early cases in the courts. And a great deal depended upon the way each individual county chairman dealt with such cases.[7] Some particularly spectacular decisions given on appeals lent the Act altogether unexpected implications. The most notorious was Judge Barry's decision in *McKeown v Beauclerc* which stated that at the expiry of a lease, a tenant had no claim under the custom.[8] This proposition was in direct conflict with pre-1870 realities and did much to actually weaken the custom. One consequence of the way the Act was drawn up, providing separate procedures for claims where the Ulster custom prevailed and where it did not, was that a series of locally disturbing precedents (such as McKeown, above) generated a host of peculiarly "Ulster" grievances against the Act. In this way specifically sectional Ulster grievances might be taken up by those seeking the support of tenant farmers which had little bearing on the wider land question in the island as a whole. This weakened the land question as a way of promoting political co-operation as a whole.

Liberals enjoyed greater credibility on land questions after 1870 mainly because a Liberal government led by Gladstone would be more likely to do something about them, regardless of the particular proclivities of individual MPs. Often assessments of the credibility of individual candidates would have led to a different outlook. For example, Daniel Taylor, the Liberal MP for Coleraine, expressed himself in 1874 in favour of no further change in the land laws; but the Independent Orangeman and good landlord, J. L. Beers, who very nearly stood against him, wanted to amend it to bring it into line with the custom, a somewhat Johnstonian position implying closer proximity to the Ballymoney programme than Taylor's.[9]

From the early 1870s some of the tenant organizations, most notably the Route Tenants Defence Association (Ballymoney), began to move towards an altogether more thoroughgoing critique. The Route was an area in which large farming was something of a norm, and the generality of landlords in the district recognized the right to sell tenant right by public auction.[10] This was the classic area where the stimulus to engage in tenant politics was independent of any crisis pressure and a question first and foremost of securing large-scale tenant investment. What was significant about the Route association was that it was one of those which most clearly grasped the national bearings of the land question. They favoured the introduction of fixity of tenure throughout Ireland, and saw the necessity for a National Tenant League to secure it.[11] "Our country has been rent in twain long enough... as Ulstermen we claim nothing that we wish withheld from the men of the South." And they linked their demands to those for local government reform: "a local parliament in each county" to replace the grand juries.[12] The Ballymoney programme was an expression of awareness of the needs of liberalism in Ireland as a whole, and an explicit repudiation of sectionalism.

So the question we must now consider is precisely what potential the land question held for any kind of "national" unity. The Route organization was instrumental in setting up a National Tenant Right conference in Belfast in January 1874, to which a large number of southern tenant farmer organizations sent representatives.[13] Almost total harmony marked the proceedings. The resolutions demanded throughout Ireland: the legal establishment of a fairly assessed rent, free sale, and right of continuous occupancy so long as the rent was paid. Further resolutions called for government loans to facilitate tenant purchase of holdings and deplored the continuing emigration. There was only one occasion when serious disagreement appeared and that related to the question of whether Gladstone or the Fenians were responsible for the passage of the 1870 Land Act. Mr Thomas Robertson of Athy, in a paper on "Yeomen and Peasant Proprietorship" stated:

"The Land Act of 1870, which never would have been obtained from his sense of justice, was obtained from John Bull's fears of that Fenian vengeance which his conscience told him he had done so much to evoke."

Rev. Archibald Robinson countered that Gladstone had promoted the Church and Land Acts

"not merely because of the Fenian agitation that was in this country and the outbursts that occurred in England, but because the man, as an honest and conscientious man, was convinced that injustice had been done to Ireland in the past".

But even if these actions were "the emanation of Fenianism", "Was it wise policy to fling that in the face of their legislators, who had done all that they could do for them, and were willing to do more good for them in future?" And another northerner, Mr Eagleson of Ballyclare, asked pointedly:

"Was Mr. Gladstone, did anyone imagine, so utterly incapable of estimating public opinion as to think that the passage of the Irish Land Act could, in the slightest degree, conciliate the Fenians? Surely not."[14]

We can see that even at this stage, whatever the agreement on actual policy between northern and southern farmer organizations, the assumptions underlying political practice were beginning to be delineated "nationally". The northern Liberal enthusiasm for Gladstone was not merely for his person, but rather for the view that Ireland's secular needs could be met by a wider liberal alliance within the British constitutional system. The reason why the issue was personalized was that liberalism under Gladstone was the first vehicle for this kind of action that had presented itself. "Metropolitan" political activity was now a possible way forward for popular politics. By contrast, the southern tendency was to view any advance secured for Ireland as a product of moral or physical force being applied to a basically unsympathetic English system. The ultimate dividing point then was the underlying assumption about the relationship of popular forces to the English power system, and that dividing point was manifest even between people whose secular purposes were virtually identical. The question will recur again in different forms hereafter.

In the 1874 election in the North—the first general election under secret ballot—the Liberal successes in the counties were considerable. The Home Rulers won in Cavan. But in Derry and Down, scenes of earlier contests, Liberals were successful, and in Antrim and Donegal they were narrowly defeated. McCartney won in County Tyrone.[15] It is unlikely that the *Examiner*, which had been unsparing in its criticism of the Liberals until January 1874, would have been in any position to undermine Catholic support for Liberals in the counties (as distinct from Belfast) as the urgency of a Land Act amendment clearly preceded other questions. It would be some years yet before the strength of the *Examiner*'s anti-Liberal position would be tested in the counties. Yet the aftermath of the election showed up only too clearly that the kinds of tensions we have just seen at the Belfast conference would be amplified from other causes.

In England the Conservatives' election victory owed a great deal to the convergence of Anglican and Catholic support for denominational education. The *Examiner* remarked that if Irish conservatism could shed itself of Orangeism it might secure Irish Catholic support for the same reasons.[16] The tendency of the education question to act as a proxy for the national question in Belfast we have noted already; but Gladstone's defeat on the Irish Universities Bill in 1873 had apparently confirmed him in his belief that the Irish Catholic hierarchy's demands were unmeetable. And in his pamphlet on Vaticanism, issued at the end of 1874, he said that after his efforts to solve the university question had been thwarted by the Roman Catholic hierarchy, "The debt to Ireland had been paid", the Church and Land Acts being the major preceding instalments.[17]

He repeated words used in his earlier pamphlet on ritualism:
1. That Rome has substituted for the proud boast of *semper eadem* a policy of violence and change in faith.
2. That she has refurbished and paraded anew every rusty tool that she was fondly thought to have disused.
3. That no one can now become her convert without renouncing his moral and mental freedom, and placing his civil loyalty and duty at the mercy of another.
4. That she has equally repudiated modern thought and ancient history.

The great change he saw in the Vatican Council of 1870: "The death warrant of that [Catholic] constitutional party has been signed, and sealed, and promulgated in form."[18]

It is not commonly appreciated just how far Gladstone's new line on Vaticanism—echoing so much of Conservative anti-Catholicism—tended to draw the line between British and Irish along the lines of denomination. In all he said, he said little that Rev. Dr John MacNaughton might not have said in Belfast. Already this kind of liberalism had forfeited most Catholic support it had had. Now Gladstone gave official support to the more anti-Catholic strand in Protestant liberalism. To avoid tearing Ulster liberalism apart meant curtailing enthusiasm for Gladstone's "Vaticanism". In fact very few did curtail it. The publication caused an uproar. The *Derry Standard* said that every genuine Liberal would concur in Gladstone's sentiments.

"It is well that Ultramontanism, as the enemy of all enlightened progress, whether religious or secular, should have no chance whatsoever of re-establishing in the British Isles the 'reign of chaos and old night' by playing off one section against another, thus accomplishing their common subjugation, through their own instrumentality."[19]

The *Ballymoney Free Press* commented on the fact that after all Gladstone had done

"the best recommendation which a candidate for parliamentary honours in the South of Ireland can have is that he opposes Mr. Gladstone. Never in the history of our country has such ingratitude been exhibited. . . ."[20]

And the *Belfast Morning News* on its wider political implications for future alliances, said:

"If he at one time sought to make political use of the Irish Roman Catholics, he has now evidently abandoned the wish or the hope. The University Bill, in fact, severed whatever alliance there was between him and the Catholic Hierarchy in Ireland."[21]

The *Northern Whig*, on the aspect of dual allegiance as it applied to Ireland, stated:

"It is very true that a portion of the Catholic clergy have gone in for the Home Rule movement and that even two or three Catholic Bishops may have allowed their clergy to use violent and even seditious language on the platform and in the Press; but those bishops, if such there are, are exception, and we know that his Eminence the Cardinal has never countenanced this reckless movement, constitutional as it may yet be represented, whatever it threatens to become. Considering the freedom which the Irish Catholic Church enjoys in Ireland, and considering the great sacrifices England has made to carry out a policy of reconciliation and equality, we may, perhaps, think that the Irish Catholic clergy do not always give all the assistance to the Government they might do."[22]

The *Examiner's* position was one of unmitigated hostility: "A persecution of our faith means, at the very least, a war of races, and we fear not for the result. We defy Mr. Gladstone and all his 'No Popery' followers to do their worst. We shall not tamely submit to persecution, and challenge him or any other statesman just to try the experiment. The army is filled with Catholic Irishmen, England is filled with Catholic Irishmen.

Gladstone has fallen: the once vaunted friend of Ireland has thrown off the mask and by doing so has ruined his own prospects for ever. Mr. Gladstone has terminated a seemingly glorious career by a most ignoble and disgraceful end."[23]

Gladstone's pamphlet had wide ramifications. Professor Fawcett, who had opposed the Irish Universities Bill, declared himself in favour of Gladstone's continuing leadership of the English Liberals.[24] The assumption that Liberal governments would in future seek to conciliate the hierarchy became uncertain. Locally in the North "non-sectarian" opponents of denominational education could seal their ears to Catholic complaints. It was particularly significant to find the *Derry Standard*, which had always taken the minority Liberal position in favour of a university reform on the lines of the 1873 Act, now aligned with this species of "Liberals".

So what would be left of northern liberalism under such circumstances? The boundaries between Protestant liberalism and conservatism could only be built to Liberal advantage around the land question, but even here there were doubts. The *Ballymoney Free Press*, for example, had said during Johnston's realignment with the Conservatives in 1873, that if he had formed an Independent party determined to "maintain Protestantism and popular rights", they would be for him.[25] And referring to C. E. Lewis, the Presbyterian Conservative MP for Derry who was making great mileage out of his opposition to denominational education "anywhere", it said that it hoped he would not convert other Ulster Conservatives, because if he did, "no Liberal candidate would have the slightest chance against any one of them".[26]

With liberalism in such disarray, with even land radicals disagreeing about whether it was Gladstone or the Fenians who were responsible for the Land Act, and with the gulf between liberalism and Catholics growing so wide, what was to stop the northern Catholics from completing the destruction of liberalism by mass defection to the Conservatives? At least in England Conservatives were sponsoring a Catholic-Anglican alliance for denominational education. Just how close this was to happening can be seen in the County Down by-election of 1878 caused by the death of the Liberal MP, James Sharman Crawford.

During 1875 and 1876, the clash between the cautious policy of northern liberalism and the Home Rulers on the land question was brought into the open by differences over various land measures tabled in parliament. Crawford put forward a measure which practically speaking would have applied only to Ulster, and which contained a provision that the Route association regarded as highly dangerous, permitting tenants to accept leases which explicitly repudiated tenant right claims.[27] Not only that, but Isaac Butt, the leader of the Home Rule Party, proposed a Bill designed to extend tenant right, inclusive of fixity of tenure at fair rents with the right of free sale over the island as a whole, and to remedy the defects in the 1870 Act outlined at the 1874 conference. Of the northern Liberals, only Rev. Professor Richard Smyth, MP for Derry, supported Butt's measure which was keenly urged by the Route Tenants Association.[28] The gap between northern and southern agrarian representatives was becoming clearer, as the northerners showed visible reluctance to support the southern efforts to secure fixity of tenure. At a Home Rule meeting in Ballyshannon in November 1874, demands were raised for fixity of tenure, "Tenant Right in its strongest form", and release of the political prisoners.[29] With the hopes that the Conservatives might bend on denominational education, the *Ulster Examiner* called on Catholics to vote Conservative in the Donegal by-election of 1876.[30] In all probability substantial numbers did so and the Conservatives won.

This was the first of a series of warnings that previous threats by Catholics and Home Rulers to vote Conservative to damage the Liberals might be actualized.

The *Ballymoney Free Press* commented:
"There is a close bond between the Protestant landlords and the Protestant farmers of Ulster, and if the sectarian is to over-ride the social, the feuds among Protestants can easily be healed."[31]
But at this stage such utterances were little more than expressions of irritation. Commenting on a "Conservative Tenant Right" meeting in Ballyclare, they noted that it made a great ado about preserving the Union between England and Ireland. "Does anybody believe this Union is in the slightest danger?"[32]

The character of the question, however, changed toward the end of 1877, at a time when Isaac Butt's leadership of the Home Rule Party was under threat. The *Free Press* remarked that the Ulster Home Rule Association was "utterly reckless as to how Tenant Right may fare in the general interest", that they proposed to buy out landlords knowing that their proposals hadn't the "slightest chance" of being carried out. "They would teach the people to believe that they cannot get any substantial measure of justice until an Irish Parliament sits in Dublin."[33]

In fact, as we shall see, there was some truth in this observation, but the cause of the northern Home Rulers' alienation from northern liberalism ran deep, and the failures of the Ulster Liberal MPs to support the Butt Bill had intensified it. In this respect the *Derry Journal* commented in early 1878 that it was glad to see other northern tenant right organizations following the Ballymoney lead and demanding the extension of the Ulster custom to the other provinces.

"The electors of southern constituencies returned to Parliament representatives who did battle at a critical moment for the Ulster farmers, and Ulstermen would be guilty of ingratitude or perhaps something worse, if they neglected to stretch out a helping hand to their former friends."[34]

Professor Smyth was alone amongst the northern Liberal MPs in seeing the danger, and when a revised version of the Crawford Bill had been put forward, he publicly thanked Butt for his support of it and attempted to encourage northern tenant right associations to take up the southern cause.[35] In July 1878 Charles Parnell and thirty-five Home Rule MPs failed to support an Ulster Tenant Right Bill,[36] indicating just how far the absence of symmetry of northern and southern conditions was expressing itself politically. Shortly before this eruption of disunity at the national level, the County Down by-election had revealed it within the North.

The Liberal candidate for County Down, W. D. Andrews, was a member of the family who had been agents for the Marquis of Londonderry in times past. The Conservative was Lord Castlereagh, the Marquis's son. The Conservatives capitalized upon the confusion between tenant representatives in parliament. Lord A. E. Hill Trevor, Conservative MP for County Down, moved a Leasehold Tenant Right Bill, which simply affirmed that wherever tenant right existed amongst tenants at will, it would be presumed to exist for leaseholders also, unless explicitly surrendered in the lease.[37] Professor Smyth now had charge of Crawford's Bill, whose principal differences were that leases could only include surrender of tenant right for "valuable consideration", and that the provisions of the Bill should extend to leaseholders in the South of Ireland "where usages analogous to the Ulster custom prevail".[38] It was claimed that southern tenants, who could previously receive compensation only when ejected, would be able to sell their interest under this Bill. To begin with, the campaign showed no very remarkable signs. At Downpatrick four priests appeared on the Liberal platform.[40] But at Saintfield Hans McMordie, a solicitor and campaign manager for Andrews—and a strong supporter of the National Education League—brought up the conflict of 1868 between Colonel Forde and Dr Drew, "an amiable, kindly man, who was disposed to live at peace with his neighbour, but he could not get a house to cover his head in Seaforde".[41] The *Ulster Weekly News,* usually careful to avoid dragging religious issues into politics, but enraged by some remarks of a Londonderry estate bailiff on religion, remarked that the Londonderry family were "renegade Presbyterians".[42]

The *Examiner* entered the campaign by observing that the Crawford-Smyth Bill, which purported to extend its provisions to areas "where usage analogous to the Ulster custom prevail", was practically useless as such usages did not exist outside the province.[43] This wasn't true, but it hardly mattered once

Liberals started playing up Presbyterian issues. "If they imagine that they can benefit themselves without benefiting their neighbours they are much mistaken." And stressing the failure of northern Liberals to support the Butt Bill:
"Every measure of land reform which we have got has been procured without the help of Ulster, so that the best friends of the Ulster farmers are those who live outside the province."[44]

The hyperbole apart, the general theme that came across was: that the northern Liberals were a nuisance; in practice, most Conservative landlords conceded all that the tenants asked; and as far as Catholics were concerned, they should stay neutral in the election contest.

Then came the surprise. A week later the Ulster Home Government Association declared its support for Lord Castlereagh;[45] and Rev. M. H. Cahill, editor of the *Examiner*, wrote a lengthy signed letter[46] in which he stated that Andrews would represent "Ulster Whiggery and Presbyterian bigotry". He was a graduate of "the Godless Queen's University and will support it through thick and thin".

"I feel convinced that the Whig and Radical party are now in fierce antagonism to religion and constituted authority, and that it is the duty of every Catholic, of every man not imbued with Communist notions, to oppose them."

The Whigs were against them on Butt's Land Bill and, as compared with the rest of Ireland,

"Ulster, especially the Plantation portion, has but very little to complain of. The Ulster Conservative landlords are the best in Ireland and their acts are proof of this assertion."

Perhaps remembering Lord Londonderry's construction of the Catholic church in Newtownards a few years previously:
"The Catholic clergymen throughout Ulster and Ireland must acknowledge that in procuring sites for schools and churches and parochial houses the Conservative landowners were immeasurably better in their dealings toward them than the land-jobbing Whigs.

In your own interests you must teach the bigoted Presbyterians of the province that you have severed connection with them for ever unless they adopt your views and advance your claims. Their principles are rotten, their advocates are rotten, and their whole system is utterly and completely rotten."

And in the editorial he wrote:

"Mr. Andrews cannot and will not represent your views on the land question. If you vote for him you sever the ties between North and South and as shrewd practical men, you must know this cannot be to your advantage. Abstain from voting unless you see your way to support good landlordism against Whig land-jobbing and its abettors."

In fact, the issues involved in the election were legion. The questions that concerned Cahill most deeply were the impending Intermediate Education and the Irish Universities Bills, both of which were Conservative efforts to meet denominational demands.[47] The hostility toward the Whigs was given added thrust by the Parnellites' effective displacement of Butt from the leadership of the Home Rule Party. While Butt had attempted to co-operate with the northern Liberals, his failure to secure significant results, either in terms of northern support or in terms of larger legislative achievement, had caused growing impatience within the Home Rule Party.[48]

The *Ballymoney Free Press,* also impatient with the Liberal leadership for failing to support Butt's Bill, conceded much of Cahill's argument against the Whigs. It was only "by inference", it said, that Lord Castlereagh could be condemned as a candidate less worthy than Mr Andrews. And Castlereagh's inferiority "existed more in his political associations than his professions".[69] He won the seat previously held by the Liberals with a majority of 1,375 votes.

It wasn't only party Liberals who condemned the Catholic-induced Conservative victory. The *Weekly News* remonstrated as much as the *Whig.* And to emphasize the importance attached to the result by denominational education and Home Rule supporters the *Examiner* compared the results to O'Connell's victory for Catholic Emancipation:

"A victory the most glorious on record since the historic election of Clare has been achieved by the noble Catholic electors of patriotic Down . . . [who did not] for selfish purposes, sever their fortunes from that of their suffering brethren, the tenant farmers of the other three provinces."[50]

There can be no doubt whatever that the election was decided by Catholic votes. The Conservative vote increased by over a thousand and it is not unlikely, given the "national education" aspect of the Liberal campaign, that the switch of Catholic votes to the Conservatives was rather greater than this, in so far as Protestant votes may have transferred in the opposite direction. We can be reasonably sure that the Catholic vote, which was concentrated in the southern part of the county, went less strongly Conservative in the lowland farming districts about Downpatrick than in the more south-westerly districts about the Mourne Mountains and toward Newry.[51]

In some senses the Conservative victory here replicated the "overture" in Belfast in 1873. Catholic impatience with Liberals manifested itself in support for a supposed "lesser of evils". There were obvious differences. In 1873 one of the attractions of Belfast conservatism was that it applied a firm leash on Orangeism. In this case the main attraction—the claim that Castlereagh gave anything like a pledge to support or to be neutral on Home Rule was absurd—was the possibility that the Conservatives would meet denominational claims. It might also be added that just before the election, three Fenian prisoners were released.[52] But there is none the less a general unifying theme in the two cases. In both, the Catholics were keen to "punish" the "Whigs", for Liberals were acceptable only to the extent of their agreement with southern forces on the land question, but were unacceptable because of their enthusiasm for the maintenance of "non-sectarian" education. Clearing Liberals to one side in the context of growing national polarity had the "advantage" of defining national blocs more clearly, and it suited Conservative purposes to do this also. In a sense, therefore, the Liberals' role in the situation was one of arresting that national polarization. This could not in fact be done unless potential Protestant and Catholic Liberals saw good reason to do it. And the County Down election served as a warning.

In August 1878 the Belfast presbytery attacked the Intermediate Education Bill which was a major innovation in that there had previously been no state support for any education between primary and university levels.[53] It provided for schools to receive payment by results, and prizes or exhibitions to be received by students. But candidates presenting themselves for examinations were not required to state where or how they received their education. In other words, any secondary school, including denominational ones, could gain by the system. The convergence between MacNaughton's "religious equality" and "non-sectarian" education positions and Toryism now became evident. J. P. Corry and C. E. Lewis, Presbyterian Conservative MPs for Belfast and Derry, opposed the proposal of a Conservative government, while T. A. Dickson and Daniel Taylor, Liberal MPs for Dungannon and Coleraine, supported it. The Belfast presbytery, hitherto the voice of Presbyterian professional and educational interests which had dominated liberalism from the 1860s, now suggested that Corry and Lewis better represented Presbyterianism than did Dickson.[54]

T. A. Dickson replied to the charge of opposing the principles of national education:

"Do our Presbyterian ministers direct parents to send their children to Catholic schools, being protected by the conscience clause, or do they not rather gather the children into their own purely denominational schools under their own management connected with the National Board?"[55]

And the *Ballymoney Free Press* approvingly reported Dickson's suggestion that the basis of Presbyterian opposition was that the Bill couldn't be good or it wouldn't have been supported by the Catholic MPs. The *Weekly News* said of the Bill, that if it was denominational education,

"What a pity we didn't know it earlier" because it was a good measure.

We have a strong opinion that there is no ecclesiastical organization which would not desire to have denominational teaching imposed on the country if only it were possible for each sect to have an advantage over all the others."[56]

Dickson's action repudiated the claim the Presbyterian educational lobby had made on Liberal representation. The reversal of roles of the Ulster Liberals and Conservatives over the Conservatives' measure improved the Liberals' standing with Catholics. The more untoward effect was that in boroughs where the education question was of more importance in comparison with the land question, a further Presbyterian deflection towards the "non-sectarian" position of Conservatives like Corry and Lewis occurred. The *Ballymoney Free Press*, in early 1879, was moved to remark, after commenting favourably on the Intermediate Education and Irish Universities Bills, that the Conservative government was "ahead" of Irish Conservatives who deeply opposed the measures;[57] and they might have added "ahead" of the Belfast presbytery also. Liberalism had unhooked itself from the Presbyterian election lobby.

We saw how in the famine period, tenant right values sank to very low levels, and in 1848–49 were largely extinguished. In such circumstances the demand for rent reductions became a common denominator of northern and southern agrarian protest. And we also saw how the peculiar Ulster aspects of the land question became most marked in periods of relative prosperity. Large farmer concern for securing investment was independent of crisis pressures, and had become possible organizationally with the changing political situation after 1868. It was precisely that kind of pressure that dominated the councils of northern liberalism. The agricultural crisis of the late 1870s was therefore going to resurrect some of the tensions between what we might think of as the "investment securing" liberalism and more radical demands for rent reductions. The harvest of 1877 had been bad as the 1878 harvest was to prove good.[58] In September it was reported that large-scale American grain imports were keeping down prices, and that farmers would get no better returns than in the bad year of 1877 when prices were high.[59] Shopkeepers were having difficulty collecting their country accounts because farmers were reluctant to sell in a low market. In April 1879 the Dublin Central Tenants Defence Association put out its call for rent reductions.[60]

The implication for Ulster was drawn by the *Ballymoney Free Press* in June 1879. It reckoned that prices would never again regain their former levels and that all agricultural values, fee simple and tenant right would decline.[61] The inability of the established tenant right organizations to respond to the new situation was demonstrated by a virtually spontaneous meeting at Toome in favour of rent reductions. One resolution called for a tribunal to fix rents before the process of ejection began; another of the need to legislatively confirm tenant right and extend it to the whole island. But the significant points were rent reductions now, and a general fixing of rents by tribunals. No existing tenant right organization was involved in setting up the meeting.[62] The *Examiner*, with one eye on the growing agitation in the South and the beginning of Michael Davitt's New Departure agitation in Mayo, said the demand for tenant right must give way to "peasant proprietary", and on the Ulster tenant right advocates: "Now a real crisis has come, they are utterly silent."[63] The *Free Press* admitted that Ulster had been slow in moving on the land question, and indicated that a meeting was being organized at Ballymoney to focus on peasant proprietorship and rent reductions.[64] But at this stage the initiative came from elsewhere.

In October, on the eve of the foundation of the Land League, Parnell, leader of the militant wing of the Home Rule Party, came to the North. His meeting in Belfast was supported by Dr Quinn, John Duddy and other members of the Home Rule movement.[65] There was present a very large group of priests from Belfast and the surrounding countryside. Two of the four priests who had supported Andrews at Downpatrick in 1878 were there, so the clerical attendance does not appear to have been "selective". Father Michael Cahill's speech in favour of Home Rule was interrupted by Fenian sentiments in favour of the use of the "rifle" and exclamations for an Irish republic. Cahill was in favour of the constitutional method, but Parnell, who followed him, blurred the issue in a way in which speakers at clerically attended gatherings in Belfast had not done before. Disclaiming any intention to define exactly what measure of self-government "we shall be disposed to accept when the time comes for obtaining it", he thought that Ireland and England "might live together in amity connected only by the link of the crown". But such questions were not for the present. "In other words I think the Repealer, the Federalist and the Separatist should work together so far as they can in common, upon a common platform." He then turned to the impending crisis (waterlogged turf and failed crops) in the west of Ireland during the coming winter. And he pointed to the moral that in the west where the agitation had begun, rent reductions had been secured. His speech concluded with an appeal for all-class action to achieve a thorough land reform, the nature of which could be inferred from the resolution in favour of peasant

proprietary as the "only final and practical solution of the land question". Dr Quinn, proposing it, said:
"Talk to me no more of Tenant Right, of fixity of tenure, compensation, etc. The whole thing [landlordism] is rotten from its very roots and the tree is rapidly falling of its own decay."⁶⁶
The stakes in the land agitation were being substantially raised.

The clerical leaders' presence indicated that there was widespread support for Parnell in the North. He had made a name for himself as the author of the "obstructionist" tactics at Westminster and was now leader of that section of the Home Rule Party which was preparing to adopt the agrarian radicalism of Michael Davitt in Mayo.⁶⁷ But the conduct of the meeting allowed the Home Rule leaders of Belfast to assume a considerably more central place in the Catholic political life of the town than they had done hitherto. In addition to raising the agrarian demand from "fixity of tenure" to "present proprietorship", sentiments were expressed of a decidedly anti-constitutional kind, such as those of John Duddy in support of Parnell's obstructionism.

"I don't think any good can be obtained for Ireland by appealing to the reason or sympathies of Englishmen. As well might we in the North appeal to the reason and sympathies of Orangemen. Any effort in that direction in my opinion would be a mere waste of national energy. The English and Scottish people together with the Irish Orangemen are so blinded by their old religious and ascendancy prejudices that they are incapable of reasoning on this subject and consequently unable to sympathize with our efforts in the cause of freedom. The English people are much wiser and less generous than the Irish in this respect. They never trust to the reason or the sympathies of a conquered or subject people; they govern principally by coercion and brute force. We who are struggling to gain our lost rights should imitate them and appeal only to their fears and necessities."⁶⁸

Duddy was "covered" by Parnell's stress on the need for united action between all kinds of nationalists. But at Newry the next day, Dr Quinn pressed the point home somewhat harder.[69] Proposing a resolution that the electors of Newry would vote for no candidate who "will not vote for a parliamentary enquiry into the nature and extent of the demand of the Irish people for the restoration of the Irish parliament", he said that they wouldn't let themselves be dragged at the tail of any party. "We must be true to ourselves, even though the priests told us we should put in a Whig instead of a Home Ruler." Significantly Father O'Neill of Rostrevor protested against anyone coming to Newry to divide the priests and the people "who were at one in the cause of Ireland". But the report does not give any indication of Parnell adding his voice on the subject.[70]

The Parnell visit had an important sequel. At Ballymoney a meeting was being organized to discuss rent reductions and peasant proprietorships.[71] This in itself was a significant shift in focus, brought about not only by attention to local distress but by the growing momentum of land agitation elsewhere in Ireland. The *Examiner*, on receiving the text of the resolutions, declared that they were "lengthy and irresolute" but that it was glad to see that the promoters "condescended to include the rest of Ireland in their programme", a statement revealing total ignorance of the role of the Route association over the past ten years, and illustrative of the high costs for liberalism of not having made the "Ballymoney programme" Liberal policy much earlier. The *Examiner* also declared that the question of self-government needed to be settled and "the tenant righters if they be sincere in their professions will join us in that". They urged some Catholics to attend to raise this issue.[72]

The *Free Press*'s response was understandably bitter.[73] "The policy of Mr. Parnell and the policy of the farmers of the Route are wide as poles asunder. [They] are tenant righters not revolutionists." Various charges of "recent" interest in the South and of Presbyterian exclusivism were also rebutted. It happened that only a week previously the *Examiner* had complimented Ballymoney on electing a Catholic to its Board of Commissioners by the votes of an overwhelmingly Protestant electorate.[74] In the subsequent correspondence the *Free Press* was wrongly accused by John Duddy of saying, "We permitted a Catholic to be elected as a town commissioner."[75] The vituperation of the *Examiner* against the Presbyterian Whig exclusiveness and against the failure of northern Liberals to support the Butt Bill was not without justification. Unfortunately, if the more Whiggish elements and "non-sectarian education" enthusiasts were regarded as the Liberals, much of what the *Examiner* said was true. Until T. A. Dickson's open repudiation of the Belfast presbytery, men such as Hans McMordie and Edward Gardner—the organizers of Andrews' campaign in County Down—had sustained the link between Presbyterian educational interests and northern liberalism.[76]

But even the advanced Liberals, whom the *Examiner* falsely accused of ignoring the South, none the less behaved as though it was Gladstone rather than the Fenians who had secured the Land Act of 1870. What the *Examiner* was in effect working towards was the view that the central axis of Irish politics was Britain versus the National movement. Northern liberalism was for it a distracting side show.

The "recklessness" of the Ulster Home Government Association with regard to the land question had a lot to do with the fact that they took their lead from the forces outside the province. Fixity of tenure until 1878 and peasant proprietorship in 1879 were the demands being articulated elsewhere in Ireland, and the latter particularly as a result of the onset of major crisis in the West. The coming of Parnell to Belfast on the eve of the Land League's foundation was an occasion to link northern Catholics with forces elsewhere in the island. We noticed how the *Examiner* in County Down in 1878 played heavily upon the theme of retaining the bonds with the other provinces. It was the old lesson of pan-Catholicism which we have seen repeatedly enforced by experience of life in the North. It may have been perverse to compare the election of a County Down Tory on Catholic votes with the election of Daniel O'Connell in 1828-29, but the perversity was an expression of the fact that the only political power Catholics had in the inner North was negative, i.e. the ability to thwart one or other of the established blocs. The coming of Parnell brought participation in national politics back into the realms of possibility. The suggested disruption of the Ballymoney meeting, however odious its manner, was part of a resurrection of confidence. That it should have been directed at one body of potentially real allies on main questions was perhaps regrettable, but it expressed far more than just bad temper or bad etiquette. The northern Liberals had, taken *en bloc*, shared very little concern for the island as a whole, and the Ballymoney group's sentiments seemed so far to be only sentiments. Ballymoney may have justly taken some pride in having elected Daniel Dempsey to its commissioners, but what were the results of that? A small example will make the point. In November a circular was sent round by a group of southern MPs requesting the municipal Boards to adopt a memorial calling on the government to establish public works for relief of unemployment.[77] Dempsey was its main advocate in Ballymoney. The issues discussed were whether it was needed in Ballymoney and the possibility of the benefits flowing to the landlord rather than the ratepayer. A plea was entered for the smaller farmers, but one speaker said, "Let the landlord plant his own mountain and reclaim his own bog." The vote to sign was four to four, and the chairman declined to vote so the matter dropped. The point was that whether or not it was needed in Ballymoney, some such works might very well have relieved distress elsewhere, as indeed resolutions at the Ballymoney tenant right conference a few months later were to recognize. The sharper class differentiation of a district of this kind meant that some commissioners paid more heed to the concerns of the ratepayers rather than to any conception of general interests: a small thing in itself, but indicative of the asymmetry between the social structure of the Route and the areas on whose behalf the plea was entered. As it was, in December 1879 the *Free Press* remarked: "While agricultural depression intensified the land agitation in the South, it seems to have had the opposite effect in the North." Apart from the Toome meeting, there had been "absolute silence" which they "cannot explain".[78] Was it possible that the gap between "southern" and "northern" experience was so wide that once again, as in times past, northern ideologues would say as the Presbyterian *Witness* did, "We cannot help thinking that it is Popery and the ignorance which Popery always has as its close companion, which is at the bottom of the lawlessness of Connaught and Munster."[79]

The most notable feature of the land agitation at this time was indeed its unevenness. In December Michael Davitt was arrested for sedition and the Tory government set out on a path of coercion. Under these circumstances the *Examiner* called on Catholics to vote for the successful Liberal candidate in Donegal, a change noted by the *Free Press* with approval.[80] But as far as agitation was concerned, the North remained unaffected until late December 1879.

We must now unfold the story of the Land League in the North. The dominant strategy of the League in the South was to call for a reduction of rent to Griffith's valuation and to resist payment of rent to the last possible moment.[81] In the North, Griffith's valuation had been carried out during the flax boom, and as a result the actual rent levels were much closer to that valuation than they were elsewhere.[82] A reduction to Griffith's valuation rent might therefore be a fairly mild demand. But the effectiveness of rent resisting strategies, for example, boycotting the sale of seized goods depended on the absence of landlord retainers, and therefore in large parts of the North it was likely to be of dubious efficacy. The other dimension of the campaign was opposition to coercion. But the objects of coercion were the western separatists and militant Parnellites, so that in the North powerful expressions of sympathy for these would be likely to be confined to particular areas. In fact, for the most part, northern participation in the League would involve participation in declaratory meetings; organization to ensure that no one took up farms of ejected tenants; and only in limited districts actual rent strikes. It will also become apparent that there was a very high degree of "blurring" of objectives and sentiments dictated by the political character of districts where meetings were held. As we shall see from the tenor of League meetings, a major objective was to ensure that meetings were held in the North at all, and to this end the content of the meetings was often subordinated. In the early stages the Land League as such did not appear. Events at three meetings suggest different types of local responses to the onset of crisis in late 1879/early 1880.

At Camlough in south Armagh in December 1879, Father Quinn presided over a large gathering calling for rent reduction and "either fixity of tenure or peasant proprietorship".[83] We have already seen that Father Quinn was a Gladstonian and an opponent of Parnell, and without making the latter point obvious, he stressed the former. However, Thomas O'Hanlon, a town commissioner from Derry who had been at the Parnell meeting in Newry, was standing in for Joe Biggar, M.P., who was unable to come. Another resolution pledged that no one would take a farm from which a tenant had been ejected. In April Father Quinn organized south Armagh Catholic support for the Liberals. It would be difficult to say that the Camlough meeting was either "Liberal" or "League". It was obviously both. Such ambiguity would later be replicated in other places.

At Portadown an attempt to hold a tenant right meeting was broken up by a Loyalist mob, notwithstanding that the resolutions were very "moderate" and in no way suggestive of links with the Land League.[84] This was the first indication of pan-Protestant efforts to define the land agitation as a symptom of "pan-Catholicism", but coming from Portadown it was fairly predictable.

Again we focus on Ballymoney where for the first time Ulster tenant right organizations met since the beginning of the agitation in the South.[85] The meeting was attended by leaders of the Ulster Liberals. The resolutions showed some shifts from earlier positions. The gradual establishment of peasant proprietorship was described as being fraught with "unspeakable advantages" to the country and the state. Landlords were "appealed to" to lower rents. And town commissioners were called upon to avail themselves of all facilities for the execution of public works in order to deal with labourer unemployment—the very thing the Ballymoney commissioners had failed to do in November. The standard theme of supporting tenant right for all Ireland was expressed. On this occasion it took the form of support for a Bill introduced on behalf of the Munster Tenant Farmers Association, one of the more moderate of southern groups later to be swept up in the League agitation. It was the speeches, however, that reflected the changing climate. Thomas MacKnight, for example, spoke of the benefit of peasant proprietorship and said a "proper tribunal to settle upon the reduction, as well as the raising of rents, would have to be conceded". If even Thomas MacKnight could concede such propositions, the speech of the future leader, T. A. Dickson, took up the typically southern themes of opposition to emigration and support for peasant proprietorship with some vigour, and he pressed the point that merchants and traders had a vital interest in standing by the farmers in the "coming struggle" for the settlement of the land. "Set your faces against every scheme for emigration, your businesses depend upon a well populated country. We have a common platform", he said, "upon which Ulster and Munster can meet and join in a united effort." Even here an Orange drumming party was got up, "the first time such a thing was done in Ballymoney". The leaders of the Order apologised afterwards.[86] Ballymoney was not Portadown, but some indication was being given of a possible response to northern participation in the current agitation.

The March–April 1880 general election saw Irish issues thrust into the forefront. Disraeli's policy of coercion of the Land League was broadened out into an attack upon Gladstone's supposed sympathies with Home Rule, the "policy of decomposition".[87] The presence of Fenian separatists as organizers of the campaign in the West lent credibility to the charge that the land agitation was a disguise for separatism. In the election campaign in Ireland, Parnellites successfully challenged moderate Home Rulers, Whigs and others over large areas of the South and West. In the aftermath Parnell himself became the elected leader of the Home Rule Party, ending the interregnum that followed the overthrow of Isaac Butt.[88]

In the North the charge that Gladstone was favourable to Home Rule was potentially damaging with Protestant voters. But so far the Land League itself had not made its presence felt within Ulster, as indeed it had not yet done throughout much of Munster and Leinster. Catholic support for the Liberals was secured by the Conservatives' Coercion Act, but the character of liberalism had undergone a change. Everywhere in the counties candidates of all parties indicated support for all manner of reforms in the land laws. Liberals were generally identified with support for fair rents, free sale, and permanence of possession, admixed with general approval of "Peasant Proprietorship".[89] Conservatives almost without exception spoke of amending the 1870 Act in the interests of tenants.[90] The loss of the Liberal seats in all the boroughs except Dungannon was compensated by successes in the counties. Donegal,

Monaghan and Derry returned two Liberals each; Armagh and Tyrone one each. Once again the Tories just held Antrim, and Major John Sharman Crawford lost in County Down by twenty votes. McCartney in County Tyrone made a pact with the Conservatives and was, on this occasion, elected for the most part as a pan-Protestant candidate. The overall results showed a slight strengthening of liberalism in the outer areas of Ulster and a slight weakening in the inner areas as compared with 1874.[91] But at all events, liberalism was now an unambiguously rural phenomenon. T. A. Dickson's initiative in repudiating the close dependence upon Presbyterian educational interests and leading liberalism towards the programme of the Leinster and Munster larger farmer organizations freed northern liberalism from the erstwhile constraints imposed by its Belfast leadership. At the eleventh hour, James McKnight's conception of liberalism had become its dominant voice four years after his death and just as it was about to face a major test of its capacity for independent organization. The irritating drums outside the Ballymoney meeting in January and the disruption of the meeting in Portadown in March were signals of what might happen when the Land League itself attempted to move into Ulster.

The Gladstone administration, installed in May, put through the Compensation for Disturbances Bill which rendered eviction for non-payment of rent a "disturbance", enabling a tenant to secure compensation under the 1870 Act.[92] It was a limited measure to apply only to scheduled "distressed districts". But the House of Lords, deluged for the occasion by Irish landlords, threw the Bill out. As A. M. Sullivan wrote, up to that moment compromise was possible and moderation stood a chance. "Now revolution was inevitable."[93]

The Lords' action followed shortly after 12 July. The celebrations passed off without incident, except in Dungannon where shots, fired at a carload of Orangemen passing through a Catholic district near the town, killed the horse drawing the car.[94] Dungannon was the one borough that had remained Liberal, and although T. A. Dickson was deposed by an election petition, his son James was elected in his stead. Speakers at the Twelfth celebrations had called "shame" on Dungannon for turning to "absolute Radicalism".[95] The town was now marked out as a major flashpoint for what was to follow, and in August a Nationalist procession in the town was fired upon and two Catholics killed.[96] In Antrim, the Compensation Bill was denounced;[97] and at Holywood the government was condemned for allowing the Coercion Act to lapse.[98] As far as Orangeism was concerned, the land question was subordinate to Home Rule and putting down rebellion. But in the middle of 1880 the issue lacked much urgency.

On 30 August, at the foundation of the Donacloney Orange Hall, the Rev. R. R. Kane, rector of Tullylish, speaking about the happenings in the West, advocated the establishment of a Protestant Individual Life Protection Society. The speech caused an uproar and, as it was subsequently claimed he was misrepresented, we can only say that it was widely understood to be a proposal that murder in the West be met with reprisal elsewhere.[99] A friendly source reports his retort to his critics thus:

"Are the Protestants of the South and West to be shot down like rotten sheep? Has the Irish Chief Secretary told us that he apprehends a serious increase in the number of private assassinations? Did Mr. Parnell bring from America large sums for bread, in the proportions £5 for bread and £15 for lead? Did Mr. Biggar say that force, even such force as was used in the case of Lord Leitrim [who was assassinated] was justifiable and that there were other Hartmans in Ireland? The sum of what I said was that the game of lead was a game that two could play at if driven to it and this I repeat."[100]

A. M. Sullivan said of the language employed at some of the Land League meetings:

"A few speakers here and there used language [on the subject of resisting clearances by violent means] which in its levity or palliation, was scandalously culpable. Even some of the more responsible leaders, on one or two occasions, angered by the exaggerations and falsehoods then being widely employed to get up a cry against outrages, retorted in a style much too cynical. But the brutal incitements to assassination ejaculated at some of the western meetings, and which invariably went the rounds of the English press, were proved at the Dublin

State trials to have been the utterances of a man whom the League people used every exertion to keep from their platforms."[101]

Although Kane's outburst was largely repudiated by Conservative leaders at the time, the murder of Lord Mountmorres in late September changed the situation. Demands for coercion now rose to a high pitch.[102] And when Captain Boycott, the Earl of Erne's agent in County Mayo, found he could not get his crops harvested—the origin of the term "boycotting"—the Orange Order organized a body of Monaghan farm labourers to go to his aid.[103] With the crisis rising, the *Coleraine Chronicle* observed that the landlords were quite unaware of the need for anything but coercion and that their opposition to such mild measures as Butt's Land Bill in the past now faced them with something far more serious. "Moderate tenant righters deplore the extent to which the agitation has gone", but "Instead of demanding a reform of landlordism, the demand in the South of Ireland and even in parts of Ulster is for the abolition of landlordism."[104]

In mid-October the *Ballymoney Free Press* praised the Roman Catholic Archbishop of Dublin for his denunciation of outrages and his call for comprehensive land reform;[105] but ominously it was noted the constitutional (Conservative) associations were getting up meetings to protest against "lawlessness in the South and West"[106] at the same moment as Land League meetings were being organized in the North. The meeting at Carndonagh, Co. Donegal, in the middle of Catholic Innishowen, was scarcely likely to run into opposition, but the ground was being prepared.[107] A sympathy meeting was held for Rev. R. R. Kane at Donacloney, and the *Free Press* observed that "various evidences are now being given that the Orangemen are less opposed to the just claims of the farmers than to the manner in which these claims are being advocated, especially in the south of Ireland".[108] They observed that Kane had declared:

"So far as we are concerned they may root the tenant as firmly to the soil as it is in the power of legislative wisdom to do. Not one of us would raise our voice against a general revision of rents. . . . Not one of us would raise our finger against the power of raising rent on the incoming tenant so as to depreciate the Tenant Right of the outgoing tenant being taken from the landlord who is capable of thus putting into his own pocket the fruit of an industrious tenant's hard work and intelligent outlay."[109]

The last rather awkward sentence needs to be read carefully, as it was obviously uttered in a flight of oratory, and the "against . . . being taken" sufficiently separated to make its meaning opaque. The *Free Press* observed that his views were in line with Ulster tenant right except on the question of free sale; but if my reading is correct, they were ostensibly in line on this also. They regretted the fact that Kane had not used his influence to secure Conservative amendment of the Land Act earlier on. Though the *Free Press* was clearly rather pleased to find an Orange meeting taking up the tenants' demands, what was actually going on?

Kane was not explicitly taking up the land question. His "support" for the tenant position was simply a way of demonstrating that he didn't regard it as the real issue. In short, the decks were being cleared to maximize support (including that of Protestant tenant farmers) for opposition to the Land League. Any doubt on this score should be dispelled by T. G. Peel's letter to the meeting which constituted a reworking of McKnight's plantation thesis into an instrument of war, or to be more precise, a "contract" landlords would have to honour to secure popular support in such a war.

"It was a condition made with the early landlords of this country that they should encourage English and Scottish tenants, but they violated that condition and let their lands at high rents to any and every man who would pay those rents. They sowed a wind and now they reap the whirlwind. . . . The Protestant people of Ireland have been sat upon. They have been discouraged and ill treated by many of the men who now look to them for aid . . . Till they reform themselves—till they come to the front—till they solicit our aid, I would do no more than arm and be ready."[110]

In late October the Land League moved into the North and held a meeting at Dungannon, while Colonel Knox called an Orange meeting near by. At this point the *Free Press* reaction shows how dangerously close even "advanced liberalism" was to taking cover behind Orangeism.

The sole cause of the agitation "is not the unsatisfactory nature of land tenure. We apprehend that the time is coming when all persons who believe in and are prepared to support the Union between Great Britain and Ireland must take this fact into consideration. . . . The universal expropriation of landlords would be too rude a wrench to Irish society . . . we are inclined to think that the duty of opposing it cannot be much longer postponed by those who want the land difficulty solved without the entire abolition of any class. . . . It is amazing to find an audience composed to a large extent of farmers, at Dungannon listening to language [of Joe Biggar] the coarseness of which could hardly be excelled in far-famed Billingsgate. . . . The land agitation has gone far enough. It is threatening to do the cause of the farmers more harm than good. To this conclusion we have been driven by the reckless speeches of prominent Land Leaguers. Much as we dislike Toryism, we would prefer it to connivance at revolution. The end and the means should be alike just and proper."[111]

Although the same day they quoted an editorial from the *Coleraine Chronicle* on how the Tory Party was pulling down the flag of landlordism and raising the flag of Protestantism, in an editorial which argued rather that the land question should be taken on its merits,[112] none the less the tendency at this time to see the crisis becoming a conflict between Unionism and Nationalism was rising.

By mid-November the League's meetings were no longer confined to the Catholic edges of the province such as Buncrana, Ballyshannon and Belleek. Besides the Dungannon meeting, others were held at Enniskillen and Derry.[113] Parnell at Enniskillen declared that the meeting at Belleek had opened the land campaign in the Protestant North.[114] "Catholics and Protestants might both unite in the doctrine of the Land League that the land belongs to the people." In south Armagh the tenants of estates at Jonesborough, Deburren and Killeavy made demands for rent reductions to Griffith's valuation and refused to pay any more than that when the demands were refused by landlords.[115]

In view of the contrast between the tone of the *Free Press* in early November and the subsequent intervention of the Liberals in the agitation, it cannot be stressed too strongly that their reaction in the first instance was a near paradigm example of the way Liberals could be drawn into the polarizing vortex of the pan-Protestant "process". The Portadown Orange break-up of the tenant farmers' meeting in March, Rev. R. R. Kane's stress on the need for Protestant solidarity throughout the island to "protect" Protestant landlords in the South and West, and the getting up of meetings to protest about "lawlessness", all threatened to provoke collision with the Land League. The holding of the counter-demonstration at Dungannon during the Land League meeting there might very well have led to a serious collision. Sooner or later, if things had gone on in this way, there would almost certainly have been one. The *Free Press*, by accepting that the Orangemen followers of Kane were not opposed to land reforms, were sliding into a position in which it would indeed have been obliged to choose Orangeism in preference to the Land League, for the agitation was developing into a bi-polar confrontation. There can be no doubt that had a collision occurred on this kind of basis, considerable numbers of Protestants, especially in the outer areas of the province, would have supported the League, although the question of numbers raises some difficulties. Once such a collision process had begun, Kane's "land reforming" Orangeism would likely as not have taken over the leadership of pan-Protestantism and absorbed most other Protestant supporters of land reform. At the same time the Land League could have been driven more rapidly towards separatism. Certainly, whatever happened, liberalism would have been ground to pieces. In fact, the decision to conduct state trials against the Land League leaders in November would have aligned liberalism entirely with anti-Land League positions, if its local wing had not then attempted to show that it was more than just a passive body of supporters of the government.

To give some kind of idea of the way the issue was shaping, a Catholic meeting was held in Belfast to protest against the prosecution of Parnell and his associates.[116] Rev. M. H. Cahill who presided took the line that the government as a whole was not in earnest about the prosecutions, but it intended rather to allow the defendants the opportunity to vindicate the League. He also suggested that if the government didn't do what was right, John Bright, whom he praised highly, would "break it up". The Bishop, Dr Dorrian, sent £5 for the defence fund and said the government might have done better to have "begun by removing the cause of our wretchedness and discontent". One priest stated:

"If it had not been for the obedience engendered in the Irish people by the teachings of the Catholic Church, all the might of England never could have stayed the power of Ireland . . . her priests who have been England's best soldiers."

Therefore he argued for an improvement in Ireland's condition by treating Ireland justly rather than coercively, as by implication there were limits to what clerical control could do in the way of reserving respect for the Constitution. Such sentiments coexisted uneasily with Dr Quinn's wholehearted nationalist defence of Parnell, which made no such friendly assumptions about the English government as those made by the clerical speakers.

A Land League meeting at Mayobridge in south Down on the western slopes of the Mourne Mountains also passed resolutions regretting that the Liberals should have prosecuted the "friends of the farmers".[117] And Joe Biggar engaged in a lengthy attack on W. E. Forster, the Chief Secretary, and Hugh Law, Solicitor General and Liberal MP for County Derry, although he did exempt Bright and Chamberlain from the general attack on the Whigs. The meeting otherwise passed resolutions not to take up holdings vacated by ejected tenants, and though it was not framed as a resolution, Tim Healy, M.P., suggested they pay only Griffith's valuation as rent.

In short, the tenor of some Land League gatherings in the North allowed space for favourable judgments on the intentions of the government. But such space was not very wide and would not for example have been wide enough to include the *Northern Whig*'s old favourite, Lord Dufferin, who continued in 1880 to advocate emigration as the only remedy for Irish distress.[118] Some of this space could be accounted for only by the constraints imposed upon the tenor of Land League proceedings in the North. Thus some Orangemen who were at the Mayobridge meeting came away with the impression that all the meeting desired was good land laws and good landlords, not an impression it would have been possible to receive at some League meetings elsewhere.[119] At all events it was at this point that T. A. Dickson took the Liberals into direct involvement in the agitation.

At Monaghan, on 21 November, a massive meeting was organized by Dickson, the two Liberal MPs Givan and Findlater, William Ancketell (a Liberal landlord) and Canon Smollen, P.P. Clones.[120] Henry Overend, a Carrickmacross Orangeman, opened the meeting by proposing a resolution that tenant right did not provide protection against eviction or unjust rents, and Canon Smollen went through the situation in Monaghan where tenant right had virtually ceased to exist. The objectives of the meeting were indicated by T. A. Dickson in a speech which clearly demonstrated that it was a new departure for Ulster liberalism.

"When in March we canvassed you for support, we advocated fixity of tenure at fair rents and free sale with the creation of tenant proprietary. . . . But we were regarded as visionaries [one suspects this is a reference to the more Whiggish Liberals]. But what is our position today? We don't recede nor take one step backwards. The force of circumstances has driven public opinion up to our platform and today we see the farmers' three F's and a tenant proprietary . . . recognized by leading statesmen as the true and only solution of the Irish land question . . .

The coming Land Bill will meet with tremendous opposition. The men whose only remedy for Ireland's miseries is coercion and Peace Preservation Acts, failing in their dastardly attempts to frighten the Executive into suspending the liberties of the people will, in the Houses of Commons and Lords . . . endeavour to fritter away the Bill and by cunning amendments, to render its clauses ambiguous and negating. Then will be the time for Irish members, North and South, to stand by the government and resist insidious compromises and thereby prevent the disastrous mistakes and blunders of the Land Act of 1870 from again being repeated."[121]

Meetings were vital to keep up the pressure. The Liberal leadership's discouragement of "embarrassing demonstrations" in 1870 was here turned on its head. The tacit link with the Land League was implied in Findlater's speech when he said

"a scheme somewhat on the lines of our Fixity of Tenure Bill, with such improvements as the more advanced views of land reformers might commend, would ultimately satisfy all parties."[122]

And in defence of agitation, John Givan, M.P., said:

"If anyone tells me that agitation is based on lawlessness I will throw back the falsehood in his face, and tell him that agitation in its legitimate form has been caused by unjust laws—and in its aggravated development I can trace it to the gilded chamber of the feudal lords—and to the treatment the Disturbance Bill received at their hands."[123]

Liberalism, so constructed and brought out into the open, not only provided a practical means of participating in the agitation, but also a clear understanding of the purpose of doing so. Here was an effort to promote tenant participation in the definition and achievement of land reform, instead of sitting back and watching while the Land League and Dr Kane battled it out between themselves.

In Cookstown the same group organized another meeting which was composed almost entirely of Protestants and Orangemen and where much the same message was put across.[124] On this occasion the chairman was an Orangeman and, what was most significant, J. Ellison MaCartney, the Orange MP elected in 1874 and 1880 as a tenant right representative, failed to appear. His letter of apology indicated opposition to the call for a rent reduction, and mention of his name on several occasions was met with jeers and groans. John Givan, M.P., explicitly attacked Macartney before an audience composed of his one-time supporters. In short, the difference between those who were prepared not only to indicate verbal support for tenant farmers but actually to attend "pan Protestant" anti-agitation meetings, and those who actually joined in the practical campaign on their behalf, was now being exposed. Liberalism was defining itself as those in the latter camp, a definition considerably more meaningful than any previously given to it. The Cookstown meeting was followed over the next few months by others of much the same character in Dungannon, Moneymore and Kilrea.

If the Liberals had asserted their presence effectively, we should now look at the general tenor of meetings in the North, for it will become evident that after their intervention, the differences between the sentiments uttered at different kinds of meetings become exceedingly blurred. The first point to make is that many of the Land League meetings were strongly charged with the same sentiments as the Liberal meetings in respect of strengthening the hand of the more progressive members of the government. Thus the Ballynascreen-Draperstown branch of the League concluded its first meeting with cheers for Bright, Gladstone and Dr Dorrian, Roman Catholic Bishop of Down and Connor.[125] The same was true of the meeting at Glenfarne, presided over by the Anglican rector on the south Fermanagh border, where it was stated that most of the Magheraboy Orange lodges were for the League.[126] Even at the December Land League meeting in Ballycastle, presided over by the Presbyterian minister of Cushendun—who said he didn't agree with all the principles of the League—John Pinkerton, one of its most notable Protestant recruits, said he didn't want to condemn the landlords as a class, but sought to strengthen Gladstone's hand in putting through a Tenant Purchase Bill.[127] Joe Biggar refrained on this occasion from attacking Hugh Law and spoke of the League's policy as government financed tenant purchase of holdings. Later that month another Land League meeting at nearby, solidly Catholic, Loughguile was addressed by Pinkerton and Biggar. On this occasion Biggar attacked Hugh Law—perhaps because the League did not need to shelter under the wing of a Presbyterian minister in an undisputably Catholic area—but in no other respect did the tenor of either speaker's speeches change.[128] The potential union of sentiments was also expressed by the meeting held at Toome, which was largely a tenant right association gathering of mainline Liberals, but was also addressed by the chairman of the Magherafelt Land League.[129]

In general then, the sentiments uttered at Land League and tenant right Liberal meetings were not wide apart on the question of strengthening the hand of the Gladstone/Bright section of the cabinet. Only at some Land League meetings was the occasion taken to explicitly condemn the government prosecutions of the League. Where they did tend to differ, although even here the difference was only a tendency, was over the question of whether to back up demands for rent reductions with refusal to pay the amount of the reduction demanded. Thus the Dungiven branch of the Land League demanded a revoking of the recent increase in rent by the Skinners Company, refusing to pay any rent until it was revoked.[130] Clear cases of refusal to pay any more than Griffith's valuation we saw in the south Armagh mountain district. Demands for rent reductions in the order of 40 and 50 per cent were made on two estates in the Derryadd area of Montiaghs parish on the shore of Lough Neagh,[131] and a clear case of rent strike occurred at one estate in Portglenone.[132] More generally, however, Land League meetings in the North tended to pass resolutions declaring that no one would take land from which a tenant had been ejected. They did not actually settle on terms for a rent strike.

The most striking case of a Land League meeting which echoed the spirit of western agrarian revolution was that of Maghera.[133] Here Isaac Nelson, the Belfast Presbyterian minister who had been elected Parnellite MP for Mayo, declared that "no man could be a friend of Ireland without being an enemy of English rulers", and John Duddy of the Belfast Home Rule Association spoke of "people who talked of fixity of tenure and that kind of nonsense". Duddy stated that the "rent for land is an unjust and immoral tax on the produce of labour and on this ground alone it must be abolished". Joe Biggar seconded a resolution which condemned Hugh Law for his part in the prosecution of the Land League leaders. The Orangemen who attended the meeting at Mayobridge had reported that all the meeting wanted was good land laws and good landlords; and indeed the chairman had stressed the standard theme of the right to live in our own land. No one attending this meeting at Maghera could have reached similar conclusions. Overall, most of the northern Land League meetings bore a closer resemblance to the Mayobridge than the Maghera pattern.

In fact, the split between that which was explicitly Land League or Liberal was only to become evident during the January 1881 parliamentary session when the government decided to put through a coercion measure, before the Land Bill.[134] In mid-December at Waterford, Parnell delivered a speech which made his ultimate intentions plain:

"We declare it is the duty of every Irishman to free his country if he can. We will work by constitutional means so long as it suits our purpose. Our present path is within the lines of the Constitution. England has given the Constitution for her purpose; we will use it for ours, and if I ever call, or if anybody over whom I have any influence ever calls upon the people of Ireland to go beyond the lines of the Constitution, we shall do so openly and above board, not by any subterfuge."[135]

The bearing of this speech in Waterford was clearly to curb any non-constitutional action, but to do so by recourse to the argument that it was inopportune. Seen from the standpoint of pro-Union forces it was a statement that constitutional nationalism had a reserve force that might be employed even if it wasn't being so employed currently. Up to that time it was fairly easy to think of the Land League as "separate" from Home Rule and related to it only in a somewhat accidental manner.

Let us now try to give an overall assessment of the effect of the crisis in late 1880/early 1881. The Land League had managed to hold meetings in areas of the North such areas as Enniskillen and Dungarvan, where "Nationalist" gatherings, had they been held, would probably have been resisted. It had managed to draw a significant Protestant support, particularly in areas like County Fermanagh where there was no Liberal tenant right tradition. It had organized most of the predominantly Catholic areas of the North, being notably successful in the mountainous districts such as the Mournes (Mayobridge-Castlewellan), the Antrim Glens (Ballycastle-Loughguile), the Sperrins (Dungiven, Draperstown), Innishowen or south Armagh. There were rent strikes in south Armagh in support of rent levels pegged to Griffith's valuation; these strikes later spread somewhat further into the Ulster core area. Although the League had generally adopted a rather tempered tone in most of the North, it did not always do so. And the example of Maghera shows that even on such occasions it did not forfeit Protestant attendance. What is more, in some districts where there was an established tenant right tradition of Liberalism, it secured considerable backing in early 1881. Sam McElroy described how in the Route:

"People said 'These Tenant Right associations are quite too moderate in their demands; if we abide by the policy of these associations we will not get all we want and the best thing for us to do is to throw in our lot with the association that demands more than the Tenant Right associations and then we will probably get all we want.' And what proof did they give? It was this—they said that the Irish Land League had achieved more in twelve months than the Tenant Right associations had done in eleven years". (Hear, hear, responded his Ballyclare audience.) "And in a short time there was a sort of uprising against the Tenant Right associations and a repudiation of their policy."[136]

This is a fairly powerful testimony as to the effect of the Ballycastle-Loughguile meetings which were the nearest ones to McElroy's home town. It does not necessarily appear to have become a general rule. In the east Tyrone, south-east Derry district where T. A. Dickson's meetings were mostly held—areas which had once been scenes of powerful sectarian agitation—the effects of the crisis seem to have been to radicalize Liberalism and draw into it much of the previously rather nebulous "independentism" of the 1870s. Thus at Kilrea, resolutions were passed against outrages and expressing confidence in Hugh Law, but at the same time another resolution pledged them to vote for candidates in favour of the abolition of the House of Lords, if that body sought to obstruct the passage of the Land Act.[137]

The effects of the crisis on the Orange Order were somewhat contradictory. In Cookstown, Moneymore and Kilrea, the popular element of Orangeism seems to have linked up with Liberalism. In some districts landlords joined the Order in the hope of mobilizing it against the Land League. It is possibly in this light that we should view the resolutions of the Monaghan County Grand Lodge which passed rather nebulous tenant right motions.[138] In north Down, where a meeting presided over by a prominent Conservative clergyman called for rent reductions on the Castlereagh-Downshire estates, resolutions condemned the Land League and called for Conservative-

Liberal co-operation to settle the land question. The two Down MPs, Lords A. E. Hill Trevor and Castlereagh—who had joined the Orange Order that month—indicated they would support the coming Land Bill.[139] Conservative-Orange meetings tended to be concerned with opposition to "lawlessness" and were taking up an "advanced position on the land question" partly to strengthen their real animus—a call for coercion. Liberal meetings, like the one in Ballyclare, which the chairman described as "no heterogeneous mass of Home Rulers and Republicans", often said nothing about coercion or outrages, but demanded "occupying proprietary" with fixity, free sale and fair rents as an interim measure.[140]

Perhaps the clearest indication of the difference between the Land League and the Liberals is provided by the events in Coleraine. A rumour was put about that the Land League was to hold a meeting and an Orange circular summoned the brethren to come and demonstrate against it.[141] Shortly afterwards another circular was put out stating that it wasn't the Land League but the Coleraine Tenants Defence Association that was holding the meeting, and "whereas the Orangemen have never been opposed to any just settlement of the question affecting the rights of the tenant-farmers, we therefore propose to withdraw any opposition".[142] The resolutions of the meeting included one against "agrarian outrage", but it otherwise followed the usual pattern. The tacit alliance between the League and the Liberals to secure the three F's and peasant proprietorship expressed itself in this case as a division of territory. Coleraine would not have been a hospitable venue for a Land League meeting.

The Land Bill was published in April, and in September a by-election occurred in County Tyrone.[143] T. A. Dickson was the Liberal candidate; Colonel Knox who had organized Orange meetings against "lawlessness" and the League, but who had on such occasions given verbal support for the three F's and recently indicated support for the Land Act, was the Conservative; and the Home Rulers put up Harold Rylett, a Presbyterian minister. Parnell's response to the Land Act had not been one of unequivocal acceptance. The Coercion Bill passed before the Land Act had kept the temperature high in the south and west, and his position was reserved until the Act had been "tested" in practice.[144] He was in fact engaged in a careful balancing act, knowing full well that much of the larger farmer class in the east would be quite content with the Act, while at the same time the agrarian revolutionary current in the west would not. And his ultimate purpose was to hold the movement built around the land agitation as the base for a Nationalist Party that would necessarily contain discordant elements.[145] The Catholic hierarchy had approved the Land Act, so the position he was adopting stood him in opposition of sorts to the forces upon whom Gladstone hoped to rest his new-found legitimacy—larger and more eastern farmers and the clergy.[146]

The Tyrone by-election was a test of strength between the Parnellites and Gladstone. But it was also a test of strength of liberalism against the Tories. The main weapon of the Home Rulers was opposition to coercion, but here they were at a slight disadvantage in so far as Dickson had opposed that measure;[147] and Canon Byrne, P.P. Cookstown, took a strong line for Dickson.[148] In 1880 the Liberal candidate got all the Catholic vote and about 33 per cent of the Protestant vote (7 per cent of the Protestant vote was probably split Liberal and Macartney votes).[149] In 1881, the Liberal got 50 per cent of the Catholic vote and about 44 per cent of the Protestant vote; while the Home Ruler got 50 per cent of the Catholic vote. The real victors in this election were clearly the Liberals, not just because they won the seat, but because the victory did not depend upon Home Rule votes.[150] The proportion of Protestant Liberal votes in this area—once a scene of bitter sectarian relationships—was proof of a very real change politically.

I have no definite evidence to sustain the supposition, but it seems very likely that, as the constituency included the first area to organize for Home Rule (the Carrickmore/Pomeroy area of the Sperrin mountains), the Catholic vote was likely to have divided on a high land/lowland basis between Home Rule and the Liberals. If this were the case, it would then show that liberalism had managed to assert itself as a serious presence expressive of the solidarity of Catholic and Protestant lowland tenant farmers. And the achievement would be all the more notable in so far as this was an area where there had been a real prospect of sectarian collision at the point where the Land League "entered" Ulster. Paul Bew has demonstrated how the Land League was actually a very loose umbrella under which established tenant farmers and agrarian radicals could operate despite very real differences of objectives. The point can be extended to the North. In the North the League managed to attract some Protestant support, nearly all of which was pragmatic and non-transferable to nationalist objectives. It also secured, as it did elsewhere, the large-scale adhesion of Catholic large and middle-sized tenant farmers, and the participation of many of the clergy who were still essentially accommodationists favourable to liberalism, wherever that was a viable prospect. All of these groups might just as readily have appeared at Land League or Liberal meetings. Exceptions can prove rules and there was at least one place where the Land League linked together Fenianism and agrarian radicalism. There was very little agrarian outrage in the North during the Land League period,[151] but significantly the one area where neo-Fenianism and agrarianism did link up was in Crossmaglen in February and March 1881, shortly after the Coercion Act.[152] An American Fenian, Patrick Burns, arrived in Crossmaglen and hung an American flag from his residence on market day, and set about gathering together the local Ribbon and Fenian organizations under one umbrella, the Patriotic Brotherhood. Among their intended activities was the murder of an exceedingly unpopular local landlord, Mr Bond McGeough,[153] and a land agent, Mr Brooke. The conspirators put on trial in 1883 were mostly farmers, but included one schoolmaster.

The Crossmaglen case was not typical. The *Newsletter* remarked that such a trial in the North was an "abominable novelty".[154] But the Land League period did make nationalism in the North a real presence. The size of the Catholic vote for the Home Rule candidate in County Tyrone was without a standard of comparison, but none the less 50 per cent of the Catholic vote for that option was a substantial achievement. Nationalism up to that time had been for the most part a series of negatives. It was strength in opposition to Orangeism; it was alienation from Protestant hostility to denominational claims; but it was also an expression of opposition to the emigration drain. It was this last which expressed the positive and immediate secular concerns, and informed the basis of the Sperrin Mountain Home Rule Organization as far back as 1873. It was this, John Duddy had declared at the first Belfast Home Rule meeting in 1872, which was the primary and unanswerable argument for Home Rule. And it was this that Parnell's movement took hold of. Those who had most cause to distrust orthodox tenant right organizations were those mountain reclamation tenants who typically faced rent increases in the order of 100 per cent or more after they had brought their wastelands into cultivation, whose livelihoods depended on balancing migrant labour with ekeing out an existence on poor quality land exposed to magnified risks in damp and cold weather. These people were for the most part outside the framework of common material experience with lowland tenant farmer Liberalism, and their counterparts in the south and west were the very people Parnell had brought into a national movement.

It is an obvious truism that politics is all about the defence and promotion of interests. People do not by and large support causes in which they are wholly disinterested parties. But the uncertainties and fluid aspects of politics have to do with how people conceive their interests. The hideous genius of northern society was, and is, that because mere day-to-day security was not taken for granted, security was perpetually a crucial "interest". Any symptom of Catholic self-organization raised at least some Protestant fears about that question. At the same time, the process whereby Catholics were controlled was so overarching that many Protestants were unaware of any participation in it.

The more subtle of these mechanisms of control were inscribed in pre-1880 liberalism. Liberalism's stand against denominational education—given the clash of subjective conceptions of equality of educational opportunity—was the intellectual equivalent of an Orange arch. Certainly there were very odious features of "denominationalism", but it was an expression of an experience of Irish Catholicism that required empathetic grasp. It could not be brushed aside without forgetting the penal era. When "non-sectarian" education was linked to a land programme that had all the hallmarks of lowland Ulster sectionalism—and a tendency to look upon the south and west as morally deficient—the arch ceased to be worth walking under. The historical lesson the Catholic experience within the North had taught was that advances came from forces outside the province. When all the narrowness and unpleasantness of the *Examiner*'s language is ignored they had a point. Without Dickson's intervention, even the experience of the Land League might have reinforced the lesson which the *Examiner* had learned and was preaching. But the Liberal intervention did not just mean expressing sentiments. It meant undertaking practical activity which made real the community of purpose with the League and showed that it would not allow the issue to be shunted aside by pan-Protestant efforts to provoke and then repress the incipient nationalism of the League. It rejected those converts to "land reform" whose principal interest was putting down Catholic self-organization. And quite certainly if in 1880-81, the Ulster Liberals had "watched" the struggle between the Land League and the Tories, that would have been the end of liberalism. T. A. Dickson's achievement was to help liberalism become something empathetic with Protestant and Catholic experience and interest. It was, to use Tone's word, a work of compact.

14. Militant Pan-Protestantism and Conservatism—the Formation of Unionism

There has been a tendency in writing about the Ulster Unionists to regard the Convention of 1892 as a kind of finishing touch to the creation of an all-class Protestant alliance. The convention was indeed a display of Protestant unity in opposition to Home Rule, embracing all sections and classes; and in so far as industrial capital was strongly represented in the organizational leadership, some writers have regarded it as the manifestation of Belfast capitalist hegemony over Ulster unionism.[1] At one level this thesis is quite accurate but it does not focus on what is politically peculiar about the North of Ireland. Wherever capitalism had come to maturity in the late 19th century, it was invariably the capitalist classes who were part of the politically dominant elites. But what made these mature capitalist societies different from each other were the kinds of alliances and compromises these economically dominant classes had to make. The relatively unproblematic fact that capitalists were pre-eminent in Belfast politics in the 1880s is therefore not so interesting as the fact that they had to share this power with a most unusual race of demagogues who were not to be found in most other societies. Furthermore, the landed classes came back into their own politically in these years as arbiters and martial leaders because of (rather than despite) their loss of economic centrality. These are the things that tell us about the kind of society the North of Ireland had become.

This chapter is about the forces thrown up by the polarization of national conflict. The most promising means of approaching this issue is to concentrate on the manifest disarray of 1883–86. Through this we will gain an idea of the forces that threatened the existing leaderships of Ulster conservatism and liberalism. The new styles of leadership and rhetoric developed in this period give an indication of just how vulnerable to plebeian demagoguery unionism then became, and in one sense remained thereafter.

The most important feature of the period 1883–86 is the rising profile of organized nationalism in Ireland. The Irish National League founded by Parnell in October 1882 began to make efforts to organize in Ulster after the Monaghan by-election victory of Tim Healy in July 1883.[2] The "Invasion of Ulster", as it became known, was met by a counter-demonstration movement, which meant confrontations between massed bodies of Nationalists and Orange-Conservatives. The idea of the Orange counter-demonstration was to prevent the Nationalist action by threatening a collision, or by making sure that both the demonstration and the counter-demonstration were banned. This strategy contained big risks of collision not only with Nationalists but also with state authority. Anyone setting out to head such an action had to be prepared to disregard the state's claim to be the guardian of order. Not surprisingly a lot of respectable Conservatives backed away from this role.

Some Conservative landlord-magistrates took the lead in this action. Their presence as magistrates at the head of counter-demonstrations gave participants some immunity from any legal consequences. They also acted as a kind of restraint upon these actions. So although the government disliked their actions, it hesitated to take action against them. These leaders by their action stretched to the limit the contradiction between the rule of law and the pan-Protestant conception of order. Paradoxically, it was their loss of economic paramountcy after the 1881 Land Act that enabled them now to become leaders of the Protestant people. They could be arbiter figures between farmers and labourers, or indeed between any contending class elements. In urban areas, by contrast, Conservative capitalist leaders were less well placed to assume such leadership roles and, as we shall see, orthodox conservatism was effectively challenged in Belfast and Portadown-Lurgan by demagogic leaders of plebeian pan-Protestantism.

These demagogues equated commitment to pan-Protestant action with altruism—and all politics of economic or class interest as a kind of egoism or class selfishness. They were not committed to the politics of any class. They concentrated attention upon the disputed frontier areas of Ulster, making the defence of these citadels a test of loyalty. They were unconcerned with the politics of the main British parties in this period because they distrusted both parties and behaved as though England needed kicking in the right place to make sure it upheld loyalty against rebellion. In fact, imposing any kind of effective control over the forces these people conjured up involved the Conservative leaders in developing alliances and links with unionism in mainland Britain from 1886–87 onwards. This was difficult and nearly impossible in the period around 1883–86, when it was uncertain whether in fact any such alliance could be depended upon.[3] The uncertainty ended in 1886–87 with the realignment of British politics, in which the British Conservatives and anti-Gladstonian Liberals regrouped as Unionists. The solidarity of a new party arrangement, premised explicitly upon defence of the Union between Britain and Ireland, and copper-bottomed by the overwhelming majority of that party in the House of Lords, provided a clear-cut strategy for defence of the Union. Once that happened Unionist leaders in Ulster could maintain that the main priority was to maximize electoral support for a united Ulster unionism. The antics of pan-Protestant demagogues then became both unnecessary and possibly counterproductive from the point of view of keeping the alliance with British unionism. So it was then easier to curb them.

Simultaneously, nationalism lost its momentum with the internal divisions over the Parnell divorce case. In short, the optimal strategy for defence of the Union was then to apply restraint to pan-Protestant activism. This does not mean that the forces unleashed in 1883–86 were wholly "tamed". It does mean that in 1892, at the time of the second Home Rule crisis, there was a coherent strategy for defending the Union in which only ritual expressions of defiance were necessary. That partially restored the initiative to the respectable bourgeois who had lost it in 1883–86.

The reason why I focus upon this period is to highlight the chaos that remained incipient in unionism. From 1883 the Orange-Conservative mobilization tended to undermine the orthodox Conservative and Liberal leadership. The marginalization of Ulster liberalism was not just a consequence of Gladstone's conversion to Home Rule in early 1886. By 1884 Ulster liberalism was strongest in Presbyterian rural areas with a tradition of independent secular organization, and so far untouched by territorial confrontation. But all Liberals, along with the orthodox Conservatives, found themselves powerless in the face of territorial confrontation. In the final analysis dependence upon the rule of law meant relying upon the state to assert itself, which was all these groups could then do. So they left others to organize many of those who were to be electorally enfranchised for the first time by the 1884 Reform Act in the rival demonstrations. This politics required qualities of martial leadership over plebeian muscle. There was a kind of brinkmanship about it. In order to be able to exercise any restraint over massed (potential or actual) mobs it was necessary to be respected by them, and the way to earn this respect was to lead them into tense situations. Whether knowingly or otherwise, it meant that those competing for leadership were engaged in a very dangerous competition to excel at confronting both British power and the Nationalists.

We begin by looking at the character of Belfast Protestant "independent" political activity from 1874 to the eve of the "Invasion of Ulster" in July 1883. In 1874 the Orange and Protestant Working Men's Association (OPWMA) had been incorporated into the Belfast Conservative alliance on the basis of "equal representation of labour and capital".[4] So long as William Johnston remained MP for Belfast, the OPWMA kept a sense of direction.

Shortly after the 1874 election, the downturn in demand for linen, and the effects of the post-1873 coal price increase, put economic pressure on the northern linen industry.[5] The introduction of the Conservatives' 1874 Factory Bill came at a time when linen manufacturers were keen to secure the reversal of the wage gains of 1872.[6] While virtually every northern MP,

Liberal and Conservative, opposed the extension of its provisions to Ireland, William Johnston supported the extension.[7] The local press divided in its reactions to the strike which was mounted to resist the wage cuts. The mainline Liberal[8] and Conservative[9] press opposed both the Factory Act and the strike with some vigour, and it was left to the independent[10] press and the *Examiner*[11] to show any kind of sympathy for the strikers. It was noticed that some of the privately owned mills did not attempt to impose the reduction while the generality of joint stock companies did so, and the demand was raised for a reduction in directors' salaries.[12] Significantly, when the strike ended after the intervention of the British Association, meeting at that time in Belfast, the women employees ended up facing the full reduction proposed by the employers, whereas the flax dressers and roughers took only half the proposed reduction.[13] During the strike women millworkers organized meetings, probably the first occasion when women adopted a high public profile in 19th-century Belfast.[14] As in 1872, the strike created a powerful solidarity around the immediate issue, but employers were well able to present themselves in the public mind as "providers of earnings".[15] The effort to counter this claim with the attack on joint stock directors' salaries was significant both for the implicit class basis of the thinking behind it, and for the tacit acceptance of the employers' claims that company profits had indeed been badly squeezed.

Working-class self-organization in this period meant a periodic reassertion of trade union solidarity during wage conflicts, but its political effects were exceedingly limited. Confronted with the total opposition of established liberalism and Toryism, the only local political direction in which they might have looked was towards William Johnston. Probably that was what most Protestant workers did; but Catholic millworkers would have noticed that Joe Biggar, Home Rule MP for Cavan and once leader of the Belfast Home Rule Association, was the other Ulsterman to support the Factory Act extension.[16] Both Johnston and Biggar were announcing a style of politics in which the task of public representatives would be to articulate anything that served to cement their respective sectarian constituencies, but in neither case were they likely to face any responsibility for consequences of the positions they took up. So the secular questions which they adopted ceased to have any significant bearing upon political affiliations which were now defined in sectarian terms.

To see what was happening to independent political self-organization we need to look at what became of the independent Orange current in conservatism. During the mayoralty of James A. Henderson in 1873 and 1874, the clerical Catholic leadership recognized thankfully the ability of reconstituted conservatism to keep processions out of the town.[17] This policy frayed round the edges in 1875 and onwards; and during 1876 and 1877, Catholic leadership was unable to prevent Catholic processions. These were generally restricted by a military presence to specifically defined Catholic areas and obliged to follow the straight route up from Smithfield through the Falls Road and out to Hannahstown.[18] Even on this route they were not entirely free from attack. Efforts by the magistrates to curb Orange processions tended to be directed at unscheduled or non-traditional displays. Two events in 1878 give a snapshot picture of the position of Independents in the period.

The Mayor in 1878 was Sir John Preston, one of the old Conservative leaders who had always disliked processions and had opposed Johnston in 1868. In that year William Johnston—now virtually bankrupt—resigned as MP to become an Inspector of Fisheries, and the Conservative organization secured the selection of William Ewart, the mill owner, to be second member besides the shipowner, Mr J. P. Corry. Johnston himself lent the succession his blessing. But his old colleagues, William McCormick and C. H. Ward at the head of the Orange and Protestant Working Men's Association, charged that the arrangement violated the "treaty of 1874" and put up Dr Seeds, a prominent lawyer.[19] What substantive issues were involved? McCormick was still campaigning to secure equalization of the municipal and parliamentary franchise,[20] but of that very little was heard during the campaign. Much was said of the "equal rights" of labour and capital to be represented, but almost no substantive issue was touched upon. Various papers commented that between the two candidates there was no clear issue of policy at all. The *Whig* took the view that Seeds might be preferred on the grounds that he was backed by McCormick, of whom they still approved;[21] while the *Examiner* took the opposite view, that Seeds might have been worthy of support had he not been backed by McCormick.[22] Stripped of any obvious policy choice, the issue was between established conservatism and "popular" Orangeism, with all the ambivalence that entailed. McCormick himself had always been one of the more genuinely independent of the Independents, as his intervention at the time of the proposed Murphyite visit in 1868 had shown. He attempted to give substance to the notion of "equality of rights". But the intrinsic credibility of such small house property owners as a vanguard of popular causes was limited, and after 1872 any link at all with Orangeism was deeply suspect in Catholic eyes. Those who chose to do so could see the Independents merely as the force upon which official conservatism had put an effective leash in 1873–74. The *Examiner's* comment, although not unmixed with a hidden sympathy for the Conservative government, none the less expresses Catholic suspicion of the contemporary meaning of independence:

"[Mr. Ewart's] return for Belfast sounds the political death-knell of that unintelligent thraldom with which we were threatened. It is degrading enough to have the borough of Belfast at the mercy of such men as Corry and Ewart, and Savage and Preston, but it would do immeasurably worse to have it at the mercy of such men as McDade and Bingham, Charlie Ward and McCormick. It is preferable to be persecuted gently rather than to be pelted with brickbats."[23]

The Independent Orange faction "translated into ordinary language means the fighting element of the body". The trouble with this judgment was that it contained just enough truth to be plausible. In practice, the distinction between conservatism and Independent Orangeism, when the issue was judged solely by reference to the question of processions, was between limitation and opposition to limitation. The *Examiner's* judgment could be justified by the assumption that this was the only matter at stake and that all processions led to riots.

In the aftermath of Ewart's victory, Sir John Preston responded to disorder in Belfast during the July and August celebrations by proclaiming a ban on all marches in the city,[24] the policy for which James Alex Henderson had been famed since 1873–74. The *Examiner*, which had canvassed the proposal, strongly supported the move.[25] But as chance would have it, the first procession to be affected by the ban was the shipyard workers' annual excursion to Ballymena. Even the Independent *Morning News* considered the ban a mistake.[26] It sympathized with the mayor's intentions, but thought his duty lay in stopping attacks on processions rather than processions themselves. The Orange and Protestant Working Men's Association held a protest meeting in the Victoria Hall.[27] Many of those who had supported Seeds earlier that year attended; but the meeting did not confine itself to the abstract Liberal sentiments of the *Morning News*.

The mayor had "allowed himself to be made a cat's paw for the Ultramontane section of the town", said Mr Irvine.[28] Comparison between the 12 July and 15 August processions in the town showed the "Papists" had neither people of "a respectable appearance to form a procession" nor the "money", so they wanted the ban to avoid having to match the spectacle of the Orange parades. He was followed by William McDade, one of those singled out by the *Examiner* as an objectionable advocate of the Seeds candidacy. "The other day", he complained, "five young lads of a Protestant band, who under circumstances of great provocation, broke a "solitary pane of glass in Ballymacarrett, were made amenable to justice and returned for trial to the County Down Assizes to stand a state trial. Would the Protestant inhabitants of Belfast stand idly by while this was being done?" Referring to an alleged promise, made at the time of the introduction of the police force into the town, that two-thirds would be Protestant, he said that in two police barracks, 7 of 29 and 4 of 25 were Protestants. If members of the town council did not see that justice was done to Protestants, they should be turned out.[29]

Uncertainty about what the OPWMA stood for can be illustrated by the career of one of its secondary organizers, William John Ferris. His distinctive name enables one to trace his political antecedents through scattered newspaper reports of a decade. Charged with membership of a wrecking mob on the Shankill in riots in 1872 (it is probable from his next appearance that he was found not guilty),[30] he was a speaker at a mill strike meeting in 1874.[31] What were the real feelings of the meeting on the subject of "equal marching rights"? C. H. Ward's speech on the theme of equal marching rights was interrupted with shouts about "Papishes".[32] Faced with defiance from the OPWMA and the shipyard workers, and tacitly opposed by a large section of the elite who felt that the proclamation was either unenforceable or injudicious, the mayor withdrew it.[33]

The Orange and Protestant Working Men's Association might not be a dominant power in Belfast, but it would not be lightly defied. In 1880–81 McCormick spoke out against the Conservative anti-Land League meetings and in favour of the three F's.[34] But his influence inside the Orange Order had declined. C. H. Ward was elected as a Conservative to the city council and died in 1883.[35] The new leaders of the "popular" section of the Order were E. S. W. Cobain, the borough cashier, who had hitherto been a pliable tool of the Conservative leadership and, in much more forthright opposition to conservatism, Rev. Dr R. R. Kane. We will return to their role in the crisis following the "Invasion" of Ulster, but their speeches at Lambeg on 12 July 1883 give an idea of how far the language of popular "independent" Orangeism was diverging from the spirit of the old Protestant Working Men's Association under McCormick. The themes of Protestant interdependence in opposition to class-selfishness came through strongly. Dr. Kane:

"There was selfishness in the Protestant camp—too much of an eager disposition to drive as good a bargain for a class as circumstances would allow, and at the same time to let the country and the Protestant religion take care of themselves."[36]

Or, as Cobain said of the Land Act:

[it] "would never have been passed if the majority of Irish landlords had not been Protestants ... a Land Act which in its most generous provisions had but copied that law of proscription which had ever been recognized by that noble house from which the Chairman [Lord Arthur Hill, M.P.] sprang."[37]

Whatever "independent" forms emerge in 1885, it is well to keep their immediate antecedents in mind.

The Land League had established a definite relationship between northern Catholics and Irish nationalism. The County Tyrone by-election may have been a defeat for Parnell at one level, but securing half the Catholic vote for his party against the most effective spokesman of northern liberalism was an achievement. What then was the significance of the fact that half the Protestants and half the Catholics in County Tyrone had voted for Dickson and had not been polarized with sectarian blocs?

In 1880 land reform had been presented as something to be extracted from English power under the implicit threat of Nationalist revolution; but because northern liberalism did not shelter behind those who sought to repress the Land League, and because it showed that it could distance itself from pan-Protestantism, it also postponed the development of outright sectarian conflict for territory. Much of northern Catholic alienation had arisen from the response of pan-Protestantism to any efforts at Catholic self-organization. Yet here were Catholics and Protestants co-operating, sometimes as Liberals and sometimes as the Land League, for common class objectives. Gone were the days when Protestant Liberals declined to organize land meetings in the North for fear of appearing to encourage "disorder" and tacitly assisting Fenianism; gone were the days when Catholics organizing such land meetings themselves in the outer frontier were ambushed by armed men on their return journey. Such a response had been threatened in 1880, but the actual outcome was a tacit co-operation of "Nationalist" and "Liberal" agitations for a common objective. This solidarity of the rural bourgeois classes occurred at precisely the moment when sectarian national identities might have polarized and prevented it from happening.

The solid core of liberalism were Protestant tenant farmers and small town middle classes. Nationalism was now a reality that had to be lived with, but there were two ways of doing this. The first was for Orange confrontation with the Land and National Leagues in those areas of Ulster susceptible to Protestant "control". The second was to uphold the closest possible approximation to the rule of law. That meant leaving the law to be the law. In the frontier areas, Dickson had opposed coercion and still secured about half the Protestant vote; and those, like Canon Byrne of Cookstown, who grasped the practical needs of coexistence in the North, sought to do likewise. But faced with the Nationalist "invasion" and the Orange counter-demonstrations, the Liberals had no means of actually breaking the pattern of confrontation. Liberals were reduced to the role of spectators when the law was challenged. Often the challenges occurred in insidious rather than direct and spectacular ways. For example, Clonoe (Coalisland), a heavily Catholic parish on the south-west corner of Lough Neagh, was an area where the Land League strategy and tactics had some visible and lasting effect.[38] In terms of famine experience it was part of inner Ulster. Weaving had been dominant in the 1840–50 period. It was thereafter a small farm district experiencing decline as weaving disappeared. It was a Catholic enclave and its local experiences were much affected by the territorial agitation in east Tyrone in the late 1860s and early 1870s, of which nearby Coalisland was frequently a centre. But its situation scarcely permitted it to link up with rising Nationalist organization surrounded by Protestant majority parishes.

After the suppression of the Land League, the practice of boycotting to stop evictions succeeding continued in some districts where the League had established a presence in 1880–81. The Crimes Act was fashioned to afford protection to its victims. In 1883 a Mr Hamilton purchased a holding from which the previous tenant had been evicted, and five extra police were quartered in a hut near by to protect his family. When his wife went to Mass, accompanied by a police escort, it is reported that "nearly half" the congregation walked out in protest. Why, asked the *Newsletter*, should the Protestants of the parish be obliged to pay the extra police rates levied on the parish, when the boycotting was entirely the work of their Catholic neighbours?[39] Once able to effectively organize for this purpose, by whom would such communal Catholic power be limited: by the intervention of the state or by pan-Protestant efforts to thwart such self-organizing power? It was issues of this kind that would become the real substance of political life from henceforth, rather than any clash of ostensible party programmes.

The Monaghan by-election of 1883 brought these incipient questions to a head. The Nationalist candidate Tim Healy was associated with some of the advantageous clauses attached to the Land Act of 1881. In a three-cornered contest for a previously held Liberal seat, the Liberal vote collapsed.[40] Healy won and the vast bulk of the Protestant vote went to the Conservatives. The success persuaded the Nationalists that they were now strong enough to demonstrate their popular hold in the province of Ulster generally, and the method was to be the time-honoured procedure of holding public meetings and demonstrations.

Many of the Liberals of the frontier districts looked on with great apprehension as Nationalist meetings were announced in areas where Orange counter-demonstrations would be a near certainty.[41] They hoped and implored the government to ban all such demonstrations. When pan-Protestantism and the Land League had threatened to collide, they found a way to change the issue by intervening themselves. Now there was none.

If liberalism at this stage depended upon the state to sustain the credibility of its position, conservatism was now faced with the question which it had long managed to subdue: it would have to resolve its relationship with Orangeism. If it chose to ignore the "Invasion" or merely call for the suppression of Nationalist demonstrations in disputed areas of the North, while at the same time repudiating the strategy of counter-demonstrations, its distance from liberalism would have been substantially reduced. But this was never in fact a serious possibility. The counter-demonstration movement would have occurred anyway. The question for conservatism was whether to join it and lead it, or permit the state to put it down, or simply try to ignore it.

Derry was once again to be thrust into something of an unwanted prominence. At the Apprentice Boys' demonstration on 12 August 1883, speakers declared that the money used by Tim Healy to canvass Monaghan came from the same source as that "which furnished the motive for the Phoenix Park murders", and Rev. Dr Kane declared that "at first sight" he could not think of any method of preventing "the dismemberment of the empire, except a great and gallant response to the well-known formula of 'Ready, Present, Fire'", a sentiment greeted with "laughter and cheers".[42] He had, he said, little faith in the members of parliament and wanted to see them more frequently on public platforms. The sentiments were echoed at a meeting in Clones, Co. Monaghan. The Monaghan election had shown that Ireland was divided into two camps, "the loyal and the disloyal".[43] The failure of the gentry to take an active part in the election was deplored. "The flag of disloyalty had been planted in Ulster through the apathy, carelessness and selfishness of Loyalists", a veiled reference to Protestants who had voted for Healy, the Liberals, or who had not voted at all. The theme that Gladstone's method of ruling Ireland was hopelessly inefficacious was dwelt upon at length. Parnell was "too much" for Gladstone. Gladstone had been reduced to seeking the diplomatic aid of the Vatican. The witness upon whose evidence the Phoenix Park murders had been convicted had been assassinated during the flight from Ireland. All the speeches pointed in much the same direction. Colonel Barton declared at Irvinestown that the government should recognize and accept the services of the Orangemen.[44] The theme of "Protestantism versus Popery" found unconditional expression. It would be hard to make out, after what we saw of the Famine, that Monaghan shared in the general "prosperity" of Ulster, but none the less the connection with England "has been the chief cause of prosperity".[45] And why was Ulster "thriving and prosperous, although her land was poorer quality than that at Cork? The secret is that Ulster is Protestant. Protestantism is synonymous with prosperity just as Romanism has always been accompanied by material poverty."

In November, Charles Dawson, the Lord Mayor of Dublin, was to deliver a lecture on the franchise question in the Corporation Hall in Derry.[46] "The Loyalists in the city and neighbourhood determined to make a counter-demonstration as a protest against the invasion of the city by a propagandist of the National League." The corporation had previously given permission for the use of the hall. But on the day they debated the issue again and were in the process of rescinding the earlier decision when a body of Orangemen took over the hall by direct action. There were significant numbers of the established Conservative leadership at the head of the take-over, including Lord Ernest Hamilton and Colonel Waring. Lord Ernest indicated that he was present as a representative of the Abercorn family. Loyalists considered that Dawson's lecture on the franchise question was a subterfuge to enable him to pronounce Nationalist sentiments from Derry. The Conservative affiliates of this demonstration were following the example of Lord Rossmore who had put himself at the head of the Orange counter-demonstration at Roslea. The oratorical themes followed the usual preoccupations of pan-Protestantism. Franchise extension would be perfectly acceptable in County Down, said Colonel Waring, but the real issue was the south and west, "where it would only have the effect of swelling the ranks of those who would go to the hustings driven there by their priests." "Too long had they allowed disloyalty and sedition to stalk in their midst without protest", declared Rev. Richard Babington and, directing a lesson on the meaning of Protestant interdependence to the members of the Derry Corporation who had allowed the Nationalists to book the City Hall, "With some of them it was a matter of pounds, shillings and pence, and the screw of their Donegal customers for their little wares was the influence brought to bear and which made them become sympathetic with sedition and disloyalty."[47] Failure to support direct action, or to resist the power of organized nationalism, was being branded as egoistic and selfish behaviour. Altruism was the property of the advocates of Loyalist interdependence.

One of those present at the meeting was the leading Conservative, Sir William Miller, a doctor who had been an alderman in Derry for many years. The next day a thousand Catholic women stitchers left work at Tillie and Henderson's shirt factory in protest at the refusal of the firm to appoint a new factory doctor in place of Sir William.[48] One hundred and fifty Protestant women refused to join the protest. The power of territorial conflict to overcome any theoretical solidarity of the workplace could hardly have been more clearly displayed. The Nationalists announced an indignation meeting at the quays to protest about the take-over of the Corporation Hall, but the mayor and the resident magistrate banned it and placed the military in readiness to stop it.[49] Once upon a time the Catholic clerical leadership in Derry had strongly supported the Liberals. In these circumstances it is hardly surprising to find that the territorial disturbances were polarizing the society and that by 1885 the Catholic clergy were aligned with nationalism.[50] Dominance of streets and public places had become the political question of moment.

Only at the end of November did the government start banning the rival meetings when another collision threatened at Garrison, south Fermanagh.[51] By then the stakes for the leadership of popular conservatism were clearly laid. Preparedness to take the leadership of territorialist forces was the *sine qua non* of Conservative-Orange leadership. The threat from the Castle to suspend Colonel Waring from the magistracy for his part in the Derry action served only to enhance his credibility with Orangeism.[52] Throughout 1884 and 1885, figures like Colonel Waring and Lord Arthur Hill were propelled into positions of political leadership. But their ability to keep that leadership was hard pressed. The forces now being mobilized were not easily controlled in urban areas, however effectively they might have been in rural areas.

At the end of May 1884, a group of Constitutionalists—as the Conservatives were renaming themselves—met in Belfast to plan a counter-demonstration to the impending Nationalist meeting in Newry. Lord Arthur Hill, M.P., Grand Master, and Colonel Waring, Deputy Grand Master, took a prominent part in the proceedings.[53] The Lord Lieutenant banned both demonstrations and the news was greeted as an Orange victory.[54] A few days later, however, the victory rebounded somewhat, when a follow-up statement indicated that a point would be made in future of banning specifically counter-demonstrations.[55] The pan-Protestant strategy had been to threaten counter-demonstrations, and after the switch of policy at the end of 1883, when the government took to preventing confrontations by "impartial" bans, it became relatively easy to thereby secure costless victories. Newry Orangemen now intended to defy the ban, after the Nationalists had successfully held a meeting of their own, and were only dissuaded from doing so by Lord Arthur Hill.[56]

It happened that the corporation and the harbour commissioners had invited Earl Spencer, the Lord Lieutenant, to visit Belfast in mid-June, and Belfast conservatism was now faced with the embarrassment of a loyalist meeting in the Constitutional Club to discuss the possibility of holding a mass protest meeting on the day of Lord Spencer's visit. Dr Kane argued that a meeting must be held during the visit.[57] If Orangemen didn't show they had been grossly insulted they would be labelled throughout the country as "mere windbags". The point was not easy to refute without attacking the counter-demonstration strategy in general, but its implications were very awkward. It was one thing to employ pan-Protestant counter-demonstration to confront nationalism, but the consequences of using it—however symbolically—against the state were altogether incalculable. And if the precedent was successfully set, the capacity of orthodox Conservative leaders to retain any hold over the forces set in motion would be substantially undermined.

Neither Edward Harland, the shipbuilder, nor William Ewart, M.P., the mill owner, had identified themselves with "counter-demonstration", and so their leverage at the meeting was not very great. Harland argued that such a protest would give a "handle to the opposite party. Let us remember that the Lord Lieutenant was representative of the Queen. It would be playing into the hands of our revolutionary opponents if we held a counter-demonstration during the visit." Voices of protest were raised disputing the proposition that the Lord Lieutenant represented the Queen. "Was the Lord Lieutenant not like a famous man who was in authority called Lundy?" asked one, to a chorus of loud cheers. The pressure to hold a meeting was irresistible, so the Conservative leaders fell back on an attempt to move it to a period outside the duration of the visit or to get the whole question left to a committee, presumably to achieve the same result. As Kane and the other clerics attempted to get a definite date, one Conservative staller hit upon the idea that the meeting was "too much a Belfast affair". "Let them consult Lord Arthur Hill", suggested some speakers. William Ewart, M.P., who considered the suggestion to hold the meeting the day before the visit an "improvement", eagerly clutched at the Hill solution. But if they reckoned to escape the difficulty altogether, Cobain warned them that they had better have a meeting or else there might be a "spontaneous" one. The orthodox Conservatives, supported by Hugh Hanna, took refuge in the reported opinion of Lord Arthur Hill. A demonstration was scheduled for the day before the Lord Lieutenant's visit. Kane might be defeated, but only by appealing to the influence of rival clerics and tribune figures like Hugh Hanna.

The temper outside the confines of the Constitutional Club gave some indication of the determination to launch a "spontaneous" meeting. The next day Dr Kane together with Revs Cotter and McComb held a massive meeting at Agnes Street in the Shankill.[58] McComb, one of Hanna's protégés of 1869, regretted the town council and harbour commissioners' invitation to the Lord Lieutenant, and Dr Kane issued a warning to MPs to associate themselves with the protest. On subsequent days he spoke of various parties to the Lord Lieutenant's invitation as having "elected to defy" the Orangemen.[59] When the great meeting was held in the Botanic Gardens, so powerful was Kane's attack upon much of the Conservative leadership, that Rev. Hugh Hanna voiced his alarm at Kane's sizeable ambitions, which were about equal to his own:[60]

"I think I should be made the commander-in-chief of the loyal forces in Ulster. . . . I am cherishing it in this very high hope, that you have made up your minds that this is the post I am to occupy."

When conservatism had to suffer Hanna's ambitions in order to thwart Kane's, it was indeed in some difficulty. We can but wonder what went through the minds of mild aristocrats such as Edward MacNaghten, MP for County Antrim, as he sat upon the platform while Kane taunted his class for their likely attendance at the Lord Lieutenant's banquet the next day. Others more used to this kind of occasion might take it in their stride. Lord Arthur Hill was presented with an album in honour of his part in establishing the Ulster Constitutional Club. The embarrassment of a counter-demonstration on the day of the visit had been avoided, but a clear indication had been given as to what kind of popular elements there were to be harnessed and the price Conservative respectability could be expected to pay for its continued leadership.

Kane's performance as the most unequivocal exponent of plebeian pan-Protestantism eventually bore fruit. At the end of 1884 he displaced Cobain from the Grand Mastership of Belfast,[61] thereby giving a kickstart to Cobain's new career as a spokesman for east Belfast shipbuilding and engineering workers. Cobain's claim to be independent of city hall control was very questionable. He had opposed Johnston in 1868,[62] played a prominent part in attempting to undermine him within the Orange Order in 1870–71,[63] and was still employed as the borough cashier at the time of his eviction from the Grand Mastership and his appearance as a candidate in East Belfast. He had taken an active part in the counter-demonstration movement, but remained just within the parameters of the acceptable relationship of conservatism to Orangeism.[64] He was displaced by a man who had missed few opportunities to attack established conservatism in 1880–81 and 1883. Kane described Irish Protestants and their parliamentary representatives as a "body without a head".[65] When the Franchise and Seat Redistribution Bills proposals were announced, Cobain was invited to stand in the Conservative interest in East Belfast.[66] "We trust", said his Orange working-class supporters, "you will support the "amendment to the Employers Liability Act in the sense desired by the parliamentary committee of the T.U.C." He replied that he would consider himself "in a special sense the representative of the working class".

Cobain's conversion to the McCormick school of Independent Orangeism was rather sudden. It was a necessary expedient to secure a new base after his eviction by Kane from the Grand Mastership. Functionally his candidacy served to channel secular working-class demands within the framework of the pan-Protestant mobilization. When the town council gave the contract for plastering the city hall to a Scottish firm, Cobain attended the protest meeting organized by the Trades Council.[67] The meeting declared its support for the franchise extension, which the Conservatives had opposed. A month later Cobain was echoing the same sentiment.[68] At the beginning of 1885, Harland and Wolff had locked out 400 riveters and many others were laid off in consequence.[69] In March, Cobain presided at a meeting to distribute funds for the relief of the unemployed shipyard workers and appealed for charity on their behalf.[70] But he only shifted his rhetorical position and declared himself the candidate "exclusively of the working classes" after the Conservatives nominated J. P. Corry, the sitting Belfast MP, to contest East Belfast against him.[71]

Dr Kane had tried to oppose Cobain's nomination and had refused to endorse him until after Corry's nomination.[72] His intention had been to enforce joint selection procedures involving the Orange Order and the Conservatives.[73] So the Corry nomination made it difficult for Kane to avoid endorsing Cobain. Kane considered that Orangemen had been treated with "scant courtesy", but at this stage confined himself to reminding the Conservatives that the Grand Lodge had claimed at least two seats in Belfast.[74] Now resolutions in support of Cobain from the Ballyhackamore Lodge contrasted the consideration they had always received from the County Down Conservatives with that of their Belfast counterparts.[75] By accident, Cobain's candidacy was becoming part of a drive for Orange representation, regardless of Dr Kane's dislike of the man or the causes he had lately espoused.

In South Belfast, the Conservatives and their erstwhile opponent William McCormick together agreed on the candidacy of Dr Seeds, the Orange and Protestant Working Men's Association candidate of 1878 and 1880.[76] Such a combination nominating a Conservative candidate should have sewn the issue up; but Kane now began to mobilize the Orangemen for William Johnston of Ballykilbeg,[77] thereby attacking two enemies—orthodox conservatism and the secular independent followers of McCormick—with one blow. Speaking a language of violent anti-Catholicism, with barely a hint of his earlier politics, Johnston now represented a straightforward militant pan-Protestantism. The Constitutional Club selection meeting for South Belfast none the less nominated Dr Seeds.[78] A few weeks later Johnston's speeches on loyalist platforms secured his dismissal from the Inspectorate of Fisheries, a pale version of his "martyrdom" in 1868, but quite handy for lashing the established Conservative MPs who failed to protest about the dismissal.

Cobain suddenly discovered that "the men who had been the bone sinew of the country had never had but one man in parliament to directly represent them—William Johnston of

Ballykilbeg".[79] And linking his own cause to that of the man he had once been paid to subvert, "Was it unfair that the Orange body should have two or was it unfair that the working class should have two seats?" Shortly afterwards, the town council passed a resolution giving Cobain the choice of remaining borough cashier or candidate for East Belfast,[80] and he too became a "martyr". Gradually the causes of Cobain and Johnston became linked in opposition to the "shameless piece of effrontery" of the Constitutionalists.

Even though Cobain attached secular working-class issues to his campaign—something that was scarcely true of Johnston on this occasion—it is quite clear that the primary focus of both was to prove that they were more authentic representatives of pan-Protestant militancy than their Conservative opponents. Cobain sought an interview with Lord Arthur Hill and agreed to a test ballot.[81] Johnston and Kane did likewise in order to show that they would accept Lord Arthur's intervention, although Seeds would not.[82] Cobain even went so far as to invoke Lord Enniskillen's support for his own campaign, although Enniskillen's subsequent statement dispelled this claim and could have been read as support for Corry.[83] Working-class supporters of the Conservative candidates had no difficulty demonstrating the dubious credentials of their Orange opponents as spokesmen of secular working-class interests.[84] But ultimately it is very doubtful—especially in the case of Johnston—whether that was what the election contests were about.

Similar observations can be made about other urban constituencies. In North Armagh (including Lurgan and Portadown areas) the handloom weaving industry was still a substantial presence. Producing cambrics and damasks for the finest end of the cloth market, the position of the weavers had been gradually declining but was by no means "terminal". The Conservatives supported John Monroe, the Solicitor-General in the Conservative administration that took office in mid-1885; but the Orangemen put up Major Saunderson, a recent convert to Orangeism and one-time Whig MP for County Cavan.[85] The objection to Monroe pronounced by Rev. Thomas Ellis, Grand Chaplain, was that:

"As attacks were more frequently made by the National Party on the Orangemen of Portadown and Lurgan than on those in mid-Armagh" (to which he proposed to consign Monroe) "it was considered that Major Saunderson rather than the Solicitor-General should represent North Armagh, inasmuch as the one would be able to defend the Orangemen on the floor of the House of Commons when the other might be called upon, in his official capacity, to prosecute them in a Court of Justice."[86]

A more candid confession of the anticipated trials between the Orangemen and the law could scarcely have been pronounced. In a draft reply to this, written by the chairman of the Constitutional Association, Orangemen were described as "brute force" men, and stated that no attacks were ever made by the National Party on the Orangemen of Portadown and Lurgan "except when they deserved it and could not be defended by any man with sincerity".[87] In a constituency where sections of the local landed society were associated with Orangeism, the Conservatives thought of trying to persuade Sir William Verner to step in as an alternative to the candidate of the militant lodges; but Verner's agent indicated that as an Orangeman he could scarcely do this.[88] Later on it seems they thought of attempting to import Lord Arthur Hill to arbitrate, but as in East Belfast, the very distance of the pan-Protestant candidate from orthodox conservatism allowed him to shape his "secular" programme to maximize plebeian appeal.

"Fair trade"—a demagogic medley of tariff protection promises, usually articulated to suit particular localities—was part of Lord Randolph Churchill's efforts to widen the popular element of his brand of democratic and plebeian conservatism. In the depression of the mid-1880s, it was a useful stick with which to beat Liberals in constituencies where declining older industries were concentrated. The Cambric Weavers' Trade Union which claimed to represent the majority of the North Armagh constituency[89] was not very impressed with the first utterances of Saunderson, who praised them but did not offer to support protective legislation, and even attacked "fair trade".[90] But in September he admitted that the weavers he had met "had completely won his sympathy—they could always calculate on him doing anything he could to help them".[91] He advised them to put their case before the Commission on Trade, and said that he favoured a tax on manufactured but not food imports. A Liberal could have given no such commitment, nor probably would a ministerial Conservative have done so either. Saunderson's distance from the majority parties—initially a function of his militant pan-Protestantism—allowed him greater scope to articulate popular causes in an *ad hoc* way. His "support" was better than nothing, and the weavers endorsed him.[92] As a matter of historical record, "fair trade" came to nothing, if for no other reason than that the later alliances of Conservatives with Liberal Unionists altogether precluded it as part of the Unionist programme; but it provided a demagogical opportunity for some of the primarily pan-Protestant and only loosely Conservative candidates to minimize the obstacles to a plebeian pan-Protestant unity.

Taken overall, the Conservative-Orange candidates had little difficulty integrating secular issues into their programmes. We have mentioned earlier how the incipient class conflict between farmers and labourers might become politically salient. After the franchise extension of 1884, labourers were armed with the vote. In areas distant from territorial confrontation, a paternalist Conservative magistrate such as Edward MacNaghten might capitalize on this. It was to labourers as much as to anyone else that the charge that liberalism was a form of class selfishness was directed. Explicit statements of labourers' feelings are few and far between, but during the Land War the Orangemen of Coleraine district held a meeting to denounce the Land League. One of the resolutions stated that

"in the event of any legislation for improving the condition of the inhabitants of Ireland [they hope] the grievances of the labouring classes and cottier occupiers will not be overlooked".[93]

Evidence of the tense relationships between labourers and farmers runs through the Bessborough Commission reports of 1880, and in one case a claim was made that labourers reported the conversations of farmers they worked for to estate bailiffs at Orange Lodge meetings.[94] Conservative speakers in 1884–85 frequently harped upon how little the Liberals had done for the working classes. William Ellison McCartney, the Conservative in South Antrim (Lisburn), listed all the various Conservative measures of protective character and particularly the recent Dwellings of the Working Classes Act of the 1885 Conservative administration. He described "fair trade" as legislation to secure "the well being of our working classes".[95] The pan-Protestant Orange-Conservative alliance was not ultimately dealing in simple questions of class interest. The greater part of its rhetoric was designed explicitly to stigmatize the types of politics that made class questions central.

The eradication of liberalism in 1885 from parliamentary representation, even in areas of inner Ulster which had recently been Liberal strongholds, depended initially upon the enfranchisement of the new electorate and the tactical decisions of the Nationalists to vote Conservative to remove Liberals. The new franchise and seat distribution did not come into effect until the December 1885 general election. In the early 1880s the Liberals retained their strength in areas of inner Ulster relatively unaffected by the "Invasion". In 1883 they won a council seat in St George's ward in Belfast, a reflection of good organization by Liberals in what had previously been a generally Conservative ward.[96] In May 1885 they won a parliamentary seat in County Antrim for the first time ever.[97] The *Newsletter* blamed both on the apathy of Conservative voters from Belfast. But the contest which shows up most clearly what was happening was the November 1884 by-election in County Down for which we have a breakdown of votes by polling districts.[98] The Conservatives won the seat, and it was claimed by both the *Newsletter* and the *Morning News* (now Nationalist) that the Catholic voters had abstained. That was a reasonable supposition in so far as Parnell was opposing the Liberals' coercion policy and had sent out instructions to this effect. But the *Northern Whig* set out to show that the Catholics voted Conservative. It divided the constituency into three parts. In one with 5,100 electors, of which 2,014 were Catholic, the Conservatives won by 1,032 votes. In another of 4,549, with only 162 Catholics, the Liberals won by 1,003 votes. In the last with 2,790 electors of which 315 were Catholics, the Conservatives won by 300 votes. The *Whig* drew the conclusion not only that Catholics had largely voted for Conservatives, but that the "great mass of the Down Presbyterian yeomanry were Liberal to the core". It can be shown that neither the *Whig*'s nor

20. County Down by-election, May 1884. Electorate in each polling district; Catholic percentage in electorate; Percentage turnout and Liberal vote

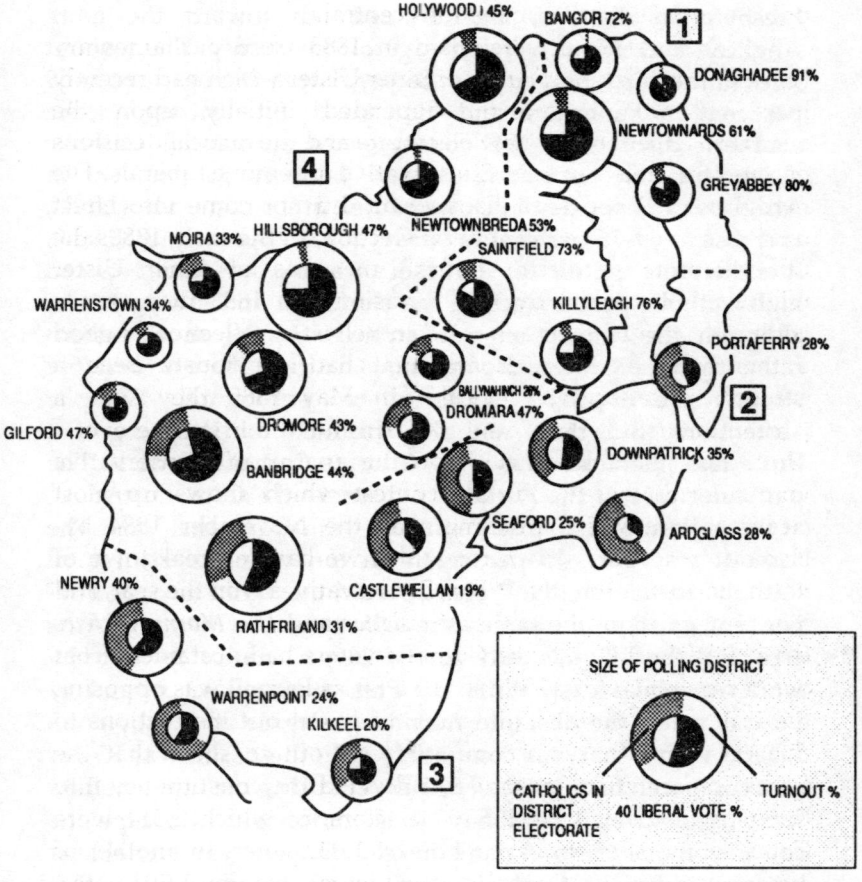

AREA 1   SOLIDLY PROTESTANT (AND MOSTLY PRESBYTERIAN), AGRICULTURAL RATHER THAN MANUFACTURING,
         LIBERALS 61 - 91%

AREA 2   ABOUT 50% CATHOLIC ELECTORATE, LOWLAND PROSPEROUS AGRICULTURE AND FISHING,
         PROBABLE CATHOLIC ABSTENTION.

AREA 3   ABOUT 50% CATHOLIC ELECTORATE, HILL COUNTRY AGRICULTURE,
         PROBABLE CATHOLIC VOTE FOR THE CONSERVATIVES.

AREA 4   LIMITED CATHOLIC ELECTORATE, PROBABLY ABSTAINING, THE CONSERVATIVE VOTE RISES AS THE PROPORTION OF
         ANGLICANS RISES AND DISTRICTS BECOME MORE INDUSTRIAL IN THE NORTH - WEST.

the *Newsletter*'s analysis was generally valid for the county as a whole.

We start by looking at the areas where there were virtually no Catholics. Across the whole of North Down the Liberal vote varied from 91 per cent in Donaghadee to 34 per cent in Waringstown. In these solidly Protestant electoral districts, the Liberal vote was highest in the most rural and most Presbyterian districts, and thinned out toward the more Anglican and urban western edge of the county. The turnout rates in the north ranged from 86 per cent in Donaghadee to 68 per cent in Banbridge and Holywood. By contrast, in the southern districts of the county, with substantial Catholic electorates, the turnout rates were between 36 per cent in Ardglass to 53 per cent in Downpatrick in the eastern lowlands, and rose to 60–75 per cent in Newry, Warrenpoint and Kilkeel. It is therefore quite clear that there was a connection between high Catholic percentages in the electorate and low turnouts, although the connection was stronger in the south-eastern rather than the western mountainous district. There is therefore strong presumptive evidence of substantial Catholic abstentions. But there are also grounds for believing that Protestant liberalism was weak in more Catholic districts. The particular case of the Portaferry district—the Catholic enclave at the bottom of the Ards Peninsula—illustrates the point. The turnout was only 45 per cent. On the supposition of total Catholic abstention, the Protestant turnout would have been 87 per cent, or about the same as it actually was in the north Ards area. But the Liberals only scored 28 per cent of the vote by whoever it was cast. With 119 Presbyterian electors and 42 Liberal votes, the absolute maximum degree of Presbyterian Liberal voting that was compatible with this result was 35 per cent compared to a figure of 82 per cent using the same method for neighbouring Greyabbey. It is impossible to escape the conclusion that Presbyterian Liberal voting was very variable as between different localities. But as to the suggestion that Catholics provided a large part of the Conservative vote, the only area where that can be proved beyond doubt is Warrenpoint. My suspicion is that just as Newry, Warrenpoint, Kilkeel and Castlewellan were the areas where Home Rule organization developed first, where it is alleged that Catholics voted Conservative in 1878, and where the Land League established a footing in 1880, so too it was in these areas that some Catholics voted tactically for the Conservatives in 1884. The paradox is that in so far as Newry was the scene of territorial agitation in the early 1884 period, "Conservatism" was strengthened on two fronts. First, it accelerated pan-Protestant consolidation amongst Protestant voters; and second, it was the area where Nationalist organization was sufficiently well advanced to permit some clandestine tactical Catholic "Conservative" voting to be carried out.

A far more suggestive conclusion to be drawn from these poll figures is that Protestant Conservative voting rises with the proximity of a district to scenes of sectarian territorial disturbance. Take for example Rathfriland and Castlewellan, the mid-point between which was the notorious Dolly's Brae. They contained 538 and 180 Presbyterian electors respectively.[99] Even allowing that all the 148 and 40 Liberal votes were cast by Presbyterians, Presbyterian Liberal voting could not have exceeded 27 and 22 per cent respectively. The overall conclusion to be drawn seems to be twofold. First, the development of a tradition of Liberal voting required political effort over long periods. Starting with 1848-52, we have seen this in the Ards-Castlereagh district. Second, in so far as liberalism was a statement about the basis of order and the necessity for the rule of law, it could not survive as a major presence in an environment of territorial confrontation. No doubt its presence was one significant factor in keeping an area free. The more generalized and nationalized the conflict became, the more difficult it would have been to sustain liberalism.

The election of 1885 demonstrated that even before Gladstone's turn to Home Rule, liberalism was a minority presence amongst the enlarged electorate. Several constituencies enable us to get a bearing on this. North Down covered a sizeable part of the Liberal district we have just looked at. Its population was about 12 per cent Catholic,[100] and in 1886 the Nationalist vote was equal to 13 per cent of the total 1885 turnout.[101] Even on the assumption that in 1885 those Catholic votes went Conservative, Protestant Conservatives exceeded Protestant Liberals by 6 to 5. In East Antrim, using the same assumption, Protestant Conservatives exceeded Protestant Liberals 4 to 3. In the area of North Antrim, where John Pinkerton of the Land League stood and collected 26 per cent of the vote (the Catholic percentage of the population was also 26), Conservatives outnumbered Liberals 3 to 2; and in South Derry, with a 49 per cent Catholic population, the Nationalists got 53 per cent while the Conservative to Liberal ratio was 5 to 4.

It can therefore be said with certainty that at this stage the Liberals were everywhere a minority amongst the Protestant electorate even if a minority of substantial proportions; and in every area where a Nationalist stood in 1885 or 1886, the candidate's vote was within a few percentage points of the proportion of Catholics in the population. There can therefore be little doubt that by 1885–86, the greater part of the Catholic population was clearly within the Nationalist camp. Thus stood political alignments at the time of the first Home Rule crisis. The unmistakable drift of Protestant political expressions was away from conventional politics, whether Liberal or Conservative, towards a conservatism in which plebeian militancy had a growing place, especially in the urban context. The plebeian militancy became ever more important as the national conflict became more and more the central fact of political life.

Of all the aspects of northern experience which tended to reaffirm sectarian identity, the strongest was that of direct sectarian confrontation itself. Sectarian violence, or more often just the threat of it, had a coercive effect upon the identity of those who lived in fear of it. More than anything else it forced people to recognise their own sectarian identity, however much they might repudiate it in other ways.

Kane's persistent theme was that Loyalists should not let themselves be regarded as "windbags". His political strategy was to make the British government and the Nationalists know that Loyalists could be reckless if their vital interests were at stake. He would defy the British government and make it reckon on the costs of offending the only "friends" of the British Empire in Ireland. He was not unsuccessful. We know that Randolph Churchill, a master of political recklessness himself, was afraid of Kane.[102] This kind of strategy made some sense, if British governments seemed to be preoccupied with conciliating

Nationalists, and if it could be assumed that, when confronted with Loyalist defiance, they would do what was necessary to conciliate it. But to put things in this way credits the practitioners of this strategy with a strategic sense they may not have had, and it certainly ignores the danger that leaders competing for leadership would outbid each other in the recklessness of their defiance. How could this be prevented from getting out of hand? In order to impose some restraint, it had to be possible to show how reckless actions were having counterproductive effects upon the overall strategy of preserving the Union, but that could only be done by a leadership which had a credible strategy itself.

The political climate that Kane and others were creating was thoroughly unbourgeois. It set the rule of law at nought. In many ways what it was doing was not new. Orangeism had always asserted the need and the right to patrol Catholic areas. But so long as the balance of forces in the society was so uneven, the full implications of this had not come to light. When Drummond's law and order system was still in place, the Catholic clergy prevented Catholics from responding, and that meant that the stipendiary magistrates could suppress Orange marching fairly easily. And even when that did not happen, the unequal position of the sectarian communities could be reflected in a limited exercise of Orange marching rights kept in bounds by landlord magistrates.

The alternatives to Drummondism were Johnstonian equal marching rights and elite accommodation worked out by James Alex Henderson in Belfast. In practice, we have seen that equal rights either presupposed a stable sense of how the sectarian communities coexisted in an area, or it occurred as a way of making a treaty after confrontations. The smaller the area covered by such a treaty, the easier to make it stick. The commoner way, after the demise of Drummondism and the repeal of the Party Processions Act in 1872, was Hendersonian elite accommodation. This involved a treaty between the elites reflecting the balance of forces, which they could impose upon or sell to their followers. Elite leaders could avoid openly confrontational stances although in fact the forces on the ground might be quite volatile, hence the *Examiner*'s remark about preferring to be persecuted gently rather than pelted with brickbats.

What Kane did was to bring all the volatile dangers inherent in such a deterrence relationship to the surface. What had been happening was that the reality of the deterrence relationship could be concealed somewhat while the Catholics were actually deterred. As Catholic strength grew, so did the dangers of confrontation. In 1883-86 it seemed that the Catholics were becoming much more assertive and that they were being wooed by both British parties. At the same time, in the North they were directly confronting the methods of control that had been used to keep them in their place heretofore. Drummondism could not be restored; Johnstonian equal rights was a non-starter given the clearly rivalrous intent of the marches; and Hendersonian elite accommodation was impossible because neither the Conservative elite in Belfast nor the Catholic clergy were in any position to make or impose treaties, given the instability of the overall political situation. In point of fact this period of 1883-86 illustrates how any stability that would ever return to this deterrence relationship depended critically upon the external allies of both northern communities. The North of Ireland had become a contested nationality district and the relations between the communities could no longer be separated from the relationship each had to the wider nations to which they belonged.

In the period of tension from 1883 to 1887, those like Lord Arthur Hill, Lord Crichton and Colonel Waring were trying to find ways of defending the Unionist position, preserving their own influence and sometimes preventing the tempo of confrontation from rising. The inevitability of pan-Protestant opposition to the "Invasion" was part of their calculations. Later literature which emphasizes the role of the landlords as a restraining and disciplining leadership over Orangeism must be substantially right, even though the landlords had very strong interests of their own in filling this role.[103] The tribune role of such landlord-magistrates depended on their ability to contain tensions between the pan-Protestant conception of order and the rule of law. Thus the strategy of calling counter-demonstrations in the hope of getting all demonstrations banned usually ended without having to actually defy the law.

And leadership given by magistrates at the front of counter-demonstrations meant that pan-Protestant mobilization could always represent itself as an "auxiliary" of order. A magistrate leading an Orange parade or a counter-demonstration did indeed lend it a legitimacy which the state could not then deny without confronting the landlords' magisterial position (as the Liberals did with Lord Rossmore, but not for example with Lord Crichton who led the main body of the Rosslea counter-demonstrators). In short, such people provided a bridge between the legality of the state and local assumptions of Protestant dominance. And with the rising profile of Nationalist organization, governments could ill afford to repudiate such "bridging" roles, however much they disliked the implications of tolerating them.

The problem for these landlords was that they were operating in a context where it was as yet unclear how the major parameters would evolve. Not least of their difficulties was the uncertainty of the Conservative Party's intentions in Ireland. A. B. Cooke's edition of Sir Stafford Northcote's diary during his visit to Ulster in 1883 makes the point that such a visit by a prominent Conservative was fairly unprecedented.[104] The diary reveals a continuing anxiety as to how far he should allow himself to be associated with Orangeism. Coming at the time when the "Invasion" was getting under way, he received conflicting opinions as to whether he should lay the foundation stone of Clifton Street Orange Hall. Lord Arthur Hill "strongly urged" him to do so, but in the end he decided against it. "I was most anxious to avoid giving an Orange character to my visit. It has, however, been impossible to keep clear of that character. Orangemen have crowded round me everywhere. Their bands and scarves have been conspicuous in all the meetings." However, this did not stop him from uttering the words "No Surrender" in Derry, or privately approving of Lord Crichton's leadership of the Orange counter-demonstration at Rosslea.[105]

If this identification was somewhat cautious and did not altogether accord with Lord Arthur Hill's hopes, the Conservatives' subsequent failure to oppose the Franchise and Seat Redistribution Bills accentuated the sense of distance. In February 1885 Lord Crichton introduced a deputation to Sir Stafford at the House of Commons which had come to protest about the Redistribution Bill. Mr Weir, a stone cutter and longstanding Orangeman, described himself as representing the working classes of Belfast "who are a great factor in the maintenance of law and order in the North". And Kane stated that he couldn't believe "that you have committed yourself to the bill as it is, for in that case they could not but conclude that their interests, the existence never once crossed your mind when deliberating . . ."[106] Cooke ascribes the rise of Saunderson in the Ulster Conservative leadership to the disappointment over the Conservatives' handling of the Redistribution Bill.[107]

This was one of a number of factors which disposed various leaders to press for the establishment of a separate Ulster Unionist Party. But we can see that so long as the linkage between British conservatism and the Unionists was uncertain, then the leadership of unionism would tend to fall to those who were able to balance between Kane on the one hand, and conventional Conservatives like Corry on the other. The more uncertain the link, the more reckless we would expect the Unionist leadership to have been in its efforts to reconcile technical observance of the law with sponsorship of Loyalist direct action. We have only to remind ourselves of how Rev. Thomas Ellis justified displacing Solicitor-General Monroe in favour of Saunderson as candidate for North Armagh, to see that pan-Protestant strategy was in potential conflict with the formal law that a Conservative administration would be bound to uphold. The leadership of pan-Protestantism could not be bound by Conservative legalism.

So long as the Conservative Party sought to retain any kind of accommodative arrangement with the Catholic hierarchy or the Nationalist leadership, there were definite limits to its relations with Orangeism. After the fall of the Liberal government in mid-1885, the new Conservative government depended upon tacit tolerance by the Nationalists.[108] Lord Caernarvon sought to conciliate the hierarchy's demands on the university question and the government even discussed various kinds of Home Rule-type arrangements for Ireland. Parnell's instruction to Irishmen, to vote for the Conservatives in December 1885 wherever there was no Nationalist candidate, was designed to ensure a balance between the two parties nationally which he could then exploit. It was a blessing to the

Conservatives who wanted to do nothing to jeopardize such a windfall gain; but it also temporarily cemented the distinction between Ulster Conservatives and the British Conservatives.

In Belfast, both Cobain and Johnston attempted to introduce Lord Arthur Hill as an arbitrator between themselves and Conservative candidates. The seeming paradox of "working men's" candidates seeking the approval of a landlord to fight against Conservatives is really no paradox at all, once it is clear that the issue at stake was how ready any candidates were to organise direct action against the law if necessary. They wanted the endorsement of the leader of the counter-demonstration movement.[109]

Before 1883 conservatism had been absorbing both bourgeois supporters of "religious equality" and proletarian currents based upon "Disraelian" social reformism. Conservatism under James A. Henderson in 1873–74 was able both to contain Orangeism as a subordinate element and secure good relations with the Belfast Catholic leadership. The rise of nationalism as a formidable presence broke this tight rope. The attempt in South Belfast to finally marry the McCormick Independents and established Conservatives by the latter's acceptance of Dr Seeds was decisively brushed aside by William Johnston of Ballykilbeg on a platform of virulent anti-Catholicism. The Johnston of 1868 would scarcely have uttered during an election campaign the words he used in 1885:

"Rome was an imitation of the Christian religion raised by Satan to turn the bodies and souls of man... there was no book Rome hated so much as the open Bible. A Roman Catholic publication had stated that the Roman Catholics, if they got the power, might burn or hang the Protestants, but they would never tolerate them.... Alcohol and Rome the Anti-Christ were the two curses of Christendom."[110]

In West Belfast, where the eventual majority over the Nationalists was a bare 37 votes, internal schism was avoided and an Orange Conservative, James Haslett, supported without argument.[111] But the one seat that was won by a non-Orange Conservative, William Ewart, shows that even here the pan-Protestant plebeian current had to be actively courted. Ewart's speeches might be fairly "clean", but that can scarcely be said of his major campaign worker, the Rev. Hugh Hanna.[112] Ewart's opponent, Alexander Bowman, secretary of the Trades Council, articulated the demands of authentic working-class organization. Any incidental similarity between Bowman's campaign and that of Cobain arose from Cobain's demagogical casting about for ancillary issues with which to attack the "Liberal-Conservative" shipowner Corry. Bowman's meetings were broken up by thuggery.[113] In a constituency with an 18 per cent Catholic population—where he received Nationalist support—he got 25 per cent of the vote. It is probably a fair guess that he secured about 10 per cent of the Protestant vote.

After the Gladstone conversion to Home Rule, we find Hugh Hanna warning that the Nationalists had prepared a "new code" under which property and positions of influence would be taken over from Protestants when Home Rule became a reality. A newspaper boy would become Marquis of Donegall, or a riveter would become proprietor of the shipyard.[114] The visit of Lord Randolph Churchill to Belfast in February threw the balance further against voices of restraint. Cooke and Vincent have observed that he did not actually call for armed resistance to Home Rule, but the lines quoted by Andy Boyd were a quite unprecedented intervention from an important English politician:

"Now may be the time to show whether all those ceremonies and forms which are practised in your Orange Lodges are really living symbols or idle and meaningless shibboleths."[115]

In the context of 1884, this would have amounted to a straightforward endorsement of Kane against the Conservatives. Now it shifted the centre of political gravity of conservatism toward some kind of direct action. With Saunderson as leader and William Johnston preparing for armed Orange mobilization, it meant disintegration of unified leadership and of restraint. The riots of 1886 were qualitatively worse than all previous Belfast riots.[116] They were primarily between Loyalists and the police. The Home Rule Bill was defeated shortly after the Mayor, Sir Edward Harland, had telegraphed the Castle for police reinforcements to deal with rioting already in progress. A rumour spread that the chief secretary, Morley, had brought in "Papish policemen to shoot down the Loyal Protestants of Belfast". In the expectation that the Home Rule Bill would pass, it was not an impossible conjecture that police would be sent to deal with disturbances that might follow. But after a collision between Loyalists and the police, demagogues competed with each other in their denunciations of Gladstone and Morley and sowed the conviction that the police now had a secret order to coerce Loyalists. Despite the defeat of the Bill, the rumour was alive and well until after the July general election, when Morley was replaced in the Castle by the new Conservative chief secretary, Michael Hicks-Beach.

As late as August, Inspector-General Reed went to Belfast and was astonished to find that most of the magistrates were fully convinced that the police had been sent to impose Home Rule. He explained to them that this was not so, and that if the officers sent to Belfast had suspected Morley of having some secret plan, they would have resigned. Once the magistrates were convinced themselves, they had Reed's statement published and began to become more energetic in their support for efforts to put down the Loyalist confrontation with the police. A few days later, after the Catholics had been noticed leaving the shipyards, Reed secured massive military reinforcements and faced down Kane's threat to hold a protest meeting against the building of a constabulary barracks near Sandy Row. Until it was clear that the rumour about the secret coercion plan was untrue, the magistrates did not feel able to exert themselves to put down the Loyalist lawlessness.

To keep control over the movement—which was now unionism—meant having a strategy for preserving the Union. But how easily that could be reconciled with conservatism depended upon whether conservatism supported the Union with sufficient vigour to deprive any more plebeian currents in unionism of any pretext for taking the initiative themselves.

15. Conclusions

The North of Ireland was becoming during the 19th century an ethnic frontier between the British and Irish nations. As the settlement colonial structure decayed, the two communities became opposed national peoples in conflict for the same land. In such places bourgeois order fails to take root. As the modern state and its judicial system came to be ever more central to the order and routine of every nation, so their ethnic frontiers, where the judicial system could bring no such order, stood out as more and more exceptional. Normally democratization tended to put all citizens of a modern society on a plane of formal equality. The judicial system gradually became the foundation of the bourgeois society as the old social structure decayed.

In ethnic frontier societies, by contrast, democratization meant that the ethnic antagonism became increasingly difficult to restrain; and criminalization of non-state violence became less and less possible. Eventually deterrence relationships force people to be different, because their identities are shaped by the different directions from which the threat of force comes towards them. This is an objective basis for difference between people which goes far beyond any mere opinion. It is something that metropolitans often cannot understand, unless they themselves have experienced fascism in the metropolis.[1] People who live in a metropolitan society experience the law criminalizing offenders (which is to say isolating them from sympathy) and rendering them powerless to rival with society. That creates the sense that all citizens relate to the law in an objective manner. Only when (or if) the system of public order has eradicated sources of identity, which have to do with who we are afraid of, can other differences become important. Thus, for example, Marxism is one of many philosophies which are parasites upon bourgeois order, because class could only become the fundamental reality when all other more fear-based differences have lost the urgency they once had.

In the development of an ethnic frontier one sort of difference between it and the metropolis disappears while another grows. We have seen how the flawed system of order and justice stands out more and more as the thing which marks the frontier apart. On the other hand, the growing freedom of movement of labour, as well as capital, means that the socio-economic structure of the frontier becomes more and more like the metropolis itself. There was far less difference left between Ulster and northern England in 1880 than there had been in 1840. Just as the differences between the different areas within Ulster were shrinking, freer movement ensured that wage levels within Ulster and across the water began to come closer and closer together. And as Catholic society built up its own middle class, it began to replicate more and more of the features of Protestant society. In this respect the spread of commerce and capitalism indeed tended to erase socio-economic differences which had once been fundamental.

So how did the erasing of socio-economic difference affect the growing uncontrollability of ethnic antagonism, and the more and more unbourgeois character of the law? As the Protestant and Catholic worked for the same wage levels, when in the same job, the typical settlement colonial structure decayed. Protestant employers had no special interest in employing Catholics, and therefore Protestant employees did not have to think of the entry of Catholics as a prelude to their own displacement by employers. The absence of a quantum wage gap meant that relationships between Catholic and Protestant were no longer adversely determined by economic forces. In fact, they could co-operate with Catholic workers in workplace solidarity, as we saw they did on numerous occasions (e.g. the mill strikes of 1872 and 1874). These relationships were then shaped by wider political forces in the society as a whole, and the influence of the residential environment might be stronger than any trade union solidarity in a workplace. Hence if relationships became adverse, as for example in 1864 or even more so in 1886, employers had limited interest in standing against the expulsion of Catholic workers. This meant there was a tendency towards a cross-class consensus within Protestant society, as in 1864, when Conservatives of all classes united behind the view that Catholics were acceptable so long as they "knew their place". The economic determinants of ethnic antagonism had disappeared, but the antagonism had a life of its own, which ensured that it would express itself again.

After the 1870s the Protestant dominance in the skilled working-class occupations in Belfast became more and more pronounced. Thus discrimination was a possibility because the Catholics were sufficiently equal that neither free market forces nor (to personalize them) employers' interests were anywhere near strong enough to counter the very real force that constricted the Catholic space in west Belfast.[2] Nor could the equality express itself as solidarity so that Catholics could feel secure living in Protestant space. The relative equalization never dissolved distrust and fear. The inequalities that remained were ever more grievous because they were increasingly those imposed by outright force in periodic outbreaks of workplace and residential expulsion. The greater the equalizing tendencies of economic life, the more visible was the intent displayed in preserving the differences that remained. Taking a long view, antagonistic intent became more manifest as substantial inequality declined. This is why it should not surprise us to find antagonism sometimes escalating in societies as they come out of the settlement colonial phase into the condition of an ethnic frontier.[3]

Ulster society's growing difference from the UK mainland throughout our period was expressed in another way. Once upon a time Protestant cultural values had been norms throughout the UK. But as the modern state became the centre of authority, the role of the Churches declined. When the cultural values of Church-centred living were losing their importance in the metropolis altogether, these same values were being transformed into the (British) national ideology on the frontier. The revival of 1859 was an enthusiastic effort to restore the old cultural values which were being undermined by human mobility. As such it was like similar things in other

Protestant societies. But we also saw its specific by-products, its impact upon Catholic-Protestant relationships, whether in the Costello case, the public correspondence of the clergy in Ballymena, or the opportunity it gave to the Rev. Hugh Hanna who pioneered the degeneration of Protestantism from a branch of the Christian faith into a political weapon of war. It was only as a weapon of war that it could be interchangeable with a national ideology. At that point it was more concerned about the relative situations of Protestant and Catholic than about the relationship between the believer and God.

It does not really help us to pay too much attention to the continuity of Protestant religious expression in Ulster, unless we probe the changes in meaning that can be hidden behind a continuity of words. Consider how very "normal" the typical anti-Catholicism of Protestants in the North of Ireland looked to 19th-century British mainlanders. Remember how Orangeism was part of the great Conservative reaction of 1834–35; how the 1850–52 outcry about No Popery led to the Stockport riots; or how in this same period in the USA the Know Nothing Party took over state legislatures and passed anti-papal legislation, while in Boston WASPs burned down convents. Finally, Gladstone in his writing about Vaticanism said nothing less than was usually said in Belfast by Rev. John MacNaughton. But the North of Ireland became more and more unlike the rest of the UK as "religious" identity became linked with deterrence relationships. John MacNaughton and his ideas would indeed have fitted very well in Scotland where he in fact came from; but in most towns in the mainland the traditional upholders of the law would probably have been able to take a much more vigorous stance to deal with Hugh Hanna, R. R. Kane, E. S. W. Cobain or William Johnston (1885 vintage). It was the pervasiveness of the deterrence relationship which marked the North of Ireland apart. It was this which placed it on the edge of the bourgeois world.

What we are seeing in the North of Ireland in this period is a one-time settlement colonial structure which had decayed. What was left of the colonial economic distortion was the emigration drain. What we have seen here is that it is the relative equalising of the communities which drew them into a more reciprocal conflict. So long as the Protestant superiority over Catholics approximated to the settler colonial relationship, there might be much oppression, but there was much less chaos. Chaos comes with the possibilities for reciprocal antagonism. The first sign of the reciprocity is the corrosion of authority. The weaker authority becomes, the less and less is it authority. Consider some of the Whigs we met in this story. John Hancock of Lurgan in the 1830s knew he was the law and he walked out in front of mobs and ordered them to do as he said. Sometimes they did. John MacNaughton, decades later in 1864, also knew he upheld the law, but he was negotiating with people who were, to put it mildly, on the fringes of the mobs. And the controlling power in the background was the military and the massed constabulary. By 1872, William Dobbin simply prayed for a despotism to put an end to lawlessness. The solution on this occasion was to remove the fiction of unified authority and for James Alex Henderson and Bishop Dorrian to more or less negotiate a treaty of stable deterrence. Finally in 1886, the Liberal magistrates along with all the other magistrates felt powerless to restrain anything until the rumour about Morley's secret orders to the constabulary had been squashed. The more reciprocal mob actions became—and of course to most participants it was the differences between mobs, not the similarities that stood out—the more structure decayed. Hancock knew that he could leave the priests to keep Catholics quiet, and that the Orangemen were the problem he had to cope with. By 1872, they were no longer separate problems. Peace, when it was restored, was not about some higher authority asserting itself, but about a deterrence treaty. Equalization in the middle of a deterrence relationship leads not to resolution and reconciliation but to more reciprocal and less controllable conflict. And that is what national conflict is. In national conflict there is in the end no agreement about contexts. No peace can be imposed by criminalizing disturbers because no one can be isolated in this way. In fact, democratization goes hand in hand with martial leadership.

In the last chapter I looked at how the national conflict finally threw up an all-class Unionist political movement in the North of Ireland which was no longer truly Conservative. It was being led by people who became more and more reckless in asserting their "Loyalty" to the British Empire. They distinguished themselves not by the social class interests they represented, but by the lengths to which they were prepared to go, both in waging conflict for territorial control with the Nationalists, and in defying any British government that tried to conciliate Nationalists. This fundamentally anti-bourgeois style was typical of ethnic frontiers. In much the same way the pan-German inhabitants of Bohemia defied the central government of the Austrian empire in order to force it to side with the German citizens against the dominated Slav peoples (the Czechs). There were defiance actions against the Badeni decrees (1897–1901) on the use of the Czech language in Bohemia, like those against the Irish Home Rule Bills. In both cases the central governments found that the German and British people of the imperial core area were not prepared to let their kith and kin in Bohemia or Ulster be abandoned to the rule of the hitherto dominated Czech and Irish nations. Bohemia, like Ireland, had a 20–25 per cent imperial national minority, which was also a local majority in a compact area. These ethnic frontier areas were the places where the ethnic nationality of the imperial nations was defined. Colonel Saunderson, MP for Portadown and Lurgan, was to Ulster what George Ritter Von Schoenerer, deputy for Eger, was to Germanic Bohemia.

There have been a lot of difficulties in the way of recognizing the Ulster Protestants as British. The only difference between the North of Ireland and most other national conflicts was that the settler-native division ran between peoples of different religions rather than of different language groups. But such a peculiarity alters only the details, not the essential ground rules of national conflict. Similar things happened in the land of the South Slavs, where the military frontier of Austro-Hungarian Croatia contained Serb settlers. Serbs (Orthodox), Croats (Catholics) and Bosnian Moslems shared the same language, but were of separate nations.[4]

In Chapters 1–3 I looked at how, during the 19th century, the idea of nation and nationality shifted from being a geographical statement of belonging to a place to becoming an ethnic sense of belonging to a people or community. The mechanism depended upon conflicts about education systems once education began to become widespread.[5] When the community in question was built around language, the shift in the definition of nation was usually fairly objective. If the Irish had spoken Irish, then it would have been much clearer that an English speaker in Ireland was British. The 19th-century community around which Irishness was formed was Catholic. Irish Nationalists never resolved the ambiguity about where Protestants fitted in because it was never in their interests to call them British and admit the case for drawing an ethnic border through the geographical entity which they hoped to inherit in one piece. Nor was it in the interests of Gladstonian Liberals to allow a confusion about ethnic boundaries to interfere with long-established institutionalized boundaries of provinces and counties. And as it was not in the interests of intransigent imperialists to admit that the Irish had a claim to rule any part of the island, they—for opposite reasons—had no cause to accept any equivalence in the status of Protestant and Catholic in Ireland. It would only have been in the interests of Ulster Protestants to make this point about themselves, if they had first had to concede that the Catholics were not British but Irish in a different sense from their own.

One of the things that we have seen happening in this book has been occasional efforts to restore the old-fashioned 18th-century meaning of the word "Irish". By not using the word "British" to describe themselves ethnically, many Protestants were showing some hope that geographic Ireland would again become something all its inhabitants could cherish together, in spite of the difficulty of expressing this politically. That was the attraction of Repeal in 1848; and even perhaps of William Johnston's fantasy island where Orangemen and Fenians would together have kicked the Ultramontanes into the sea. It had been possible in 1846–48 to indulge the wish that the old nation would recover precisely because the ethnic realities seemed to be slackening. To see the same thing in 1869 was rather far fetched; but then so was Johnston's understanding of what the Fenians meant by "No priests in politics". At various stages, I have shown Protestants, who were unionists with a small "u", thinking and acting as though the entity of Ireland might still exist as more than just a geographic fact. One of the tragic features of the national conflict as it intensified was that this old 18th-century sense of Ireland—a place that exists without any political sense of nationality—gradually decayed.

There have been some recent efforts to construct a view of a second nation in Ireland, which are based upon the supposed effects of the uneven development of capitalism in Ireland, North and South.[6] It is argued that the southern agricultural economy and the northern industrial economy would have produced opposed political directions and eventually opposed nations. In the most positive interpretations of the Protestant nation, such as that developed by the British and Irish Communist Organization (BICO), unionism is presented as a liberal reaction to ultramontanism. The 1798 Rebellion is used to show that the Protestants were no longer settlers, because they no longer behaved like settlers. And pre-1791 United Irish ideas are shown to have continued amongst the northern Whigs. O'Connell, and more especially Cardinal Cullen, can be employed to justify just about every tendency amongst northern Protestants towards Ulster unionism. In this picture the settlement origin of northern Protestant society, and above all, the Protestant-Catholic relationship within the North which is a product of it, disappears.

The justification for such an interpretation, in so far as there is one, is that hitherto the view of northern Protestants as settlers and colonists has been crude and ideological. These new interpretations quite rightly protest at the black and white picture of the North that nationalist interpretation often presents. But by making the settlement origins almost disappear, they in their turn become ideological. We have seen far too much evidence that Protestants felt and behaved in the insecure manner of settlers to allow this fact to be other than central. Indeed, our only chance of explaining their behaviour, and removing the moral stigma that attaches to settlement origins, is to accept this and look at its consequences. The moment the originality of the settlement relationship is lost sight of, the way is cleared for using history as a weapon of justification. All that happens in this two nations version is that the usual justificatory purpose is turned around to serve unionism rather than nationalism.

There is another school of thought which, while stressing the importance of uneven development, argues that the BICO approach does not attend to the reality of class. The best work of this school, Henry Patterson's *Class Conflict and Sectarianism*, is concerned with the leadership role acquired by the industrial capitalist class of Belfast.[7] He shows how the dominant ideology stressed the essentially moral interpretation of the difference between the industrial North and the South. This approach does much to show how ideological some of the constructions upon uneven development have actually been, and it therefore helps to underline the moralistic blindspots of unionism. He shows that the working-class Protestant organizations never developed an analysis that would have enabled them to stand independently of the capitalist leadership.[8] But his work is curiously silent about just how much freedom of political movement a better understanding would have given them. He only suggests that if socialists had understood the realities of uneven development properly they would have accepted the reality that the Southern nation was also a nation. That would have increased their space for independent action; but the most it would have done would have been to enable socialists to advocate partition as a compromise before conflict between sectarian blocs made it come about by other means.

For me Patterson's work, while it puts the claims of the uneven development thesis in a much better perspective, only serves to highlight its central difficulty. There was no serious possibility of a movement surviving that cut across sectarian lines, once the O'Connellite pattern of Southern nationalism had been set. But there was very little that was accidental about O'Connellism. O'Connell's movement was an all too typical nationalist movement. It made the colonial mark of stigma (Catholicism) into the badge of nationality. (For evidence of this, see the 1852 *Vindicator* editorial on Catholicity and Irishness in Chapter 7.) Uneven development, far from being the cause of the growth of separate nations, was a development whose significance was shaped by the appearance of two nations. It would be closer to the mark to suggest that when a national conflict has developed, the spokespersons of each bloc tend to be those whose material interests are best served by the settlement of the national conflict in their bloc's favour, but they carry the other classes of their national community with them. In other words, the economistic logic attached to any national cause is always the best available in the circumstances. But however good the economistic logic, few people ever change camps on account of it.

To illustrate this, turn back to Chapter 12 and look at the way in which Home Rule was explained to the linen industry-dependent proletarians of Derry city. While they clamoured for separation, the speaker had to explain to them why tariff barriers between Britain and Ireland might not be very good for Derry shirt manufacturing. So they would be wise to support Home Rule, which he implied would be as close as they could get to separation without running the risk of creating tariff walls. In fact, Home Rule speakers in other places made tariffs a selling point of Home Rule. But such inconsistency hardly mattered. When they wanted to get their own back on Orangemen or to show their dislike of Whigs for the prosecution of the priests of Galway, Home Rule made very good sense indeed.

If one looks for an exposition of Home Rule that makes sense of the total circumstances of the speaker and his environment, a more appropriate figure is Terence O'Neill from Carrickmore. Tariff protection probably would have been a positive move in a land of small farms, reclamation and migrant labour. His homeland was being decimated by emigration, and some kind of protectionism, plus expropriation of landlords, would have made separation something like the remedy he proposed. It does not matter that it might have created chaos for Catholics in the industrial economy. Likewise, we can look at the *Newtownards Chronicle* invective against the developmental claims for Home Rule. These claims deserved more serious treatment from a town decaying, as Newtownards then was, than the *Chronicle* gave them. Even more absurd was the Unionist suggestion that Monaghan was somehow part of the industrious North in 1883. The uneven development thesis cannot explain much without first invoking the reality of ethnic division, and the settlement relationship which is its substance.

A two-nation thesis, derived primarily from the uneven development of capitalism in Ireland, rationalizes much which many people at the time were wise enough to know was tragic. The space people had, in which to be rational and not to be endlessly preoccupied with "them", shrank as the two societies became more balanced and equal. So much was this the case that it was difficult, especially for Protestant Liberals, not to regret some of the often very disagreeable symptoms of equalization. Reading 19th-century Protestant newspapers, Cardinal Cullen seems to have become a phobia for some and an obsession for others. But the situation in the North was waiting for a Cardinal Cullen; and if he had not existed he would have been invented. The Catholic society, having been held down, had every reason to distrust Protestants and British power. It is true this distrust helped keep alive the behaviour in both Protestants and the British which they distrusted, but that does not alter the point. It rather reinforces the point that in an ethnic frontier, as forces become balanced, distrust becomes circular and self-reinforcing. Any hint of an assumption of superiority, any hint of Protestant efforts to keep control over Catholics, even a suggestion that equality for Catholics would be *given* by upright Protestants, could infuriate Catholics. Only so long as Catholics really were in a position of extreme weakness were Liberal Protestants (including United Irishmen) able to define the way forward, and to expect that in future Catholics would trust their leadership. But the moment the Catholics had any power, this space shrank. We have seen here how much Catholic power in the North was enhanced by the rise of pan-Catholicism in the rest of the island; and the *Observer* editorial of August 1864 (see Chapter 9) on the importance of O'Connell for the North says it all.

For the Catholics the period I have written about was a slow process of gaining confidence. Answering back presumptions of superiority, or asserting the right to define the terms of debate, was sometimes done very crudely. The *Examiner* editorials on the County Down by-election of 1878, I found pretty repulsive—until I read the *Whig*'s editorials about non-sectarian education and "enlightened" Catholics which provoked them. For Protestants, this period was one in which politics became gradually more and more restricting as the spaces to behave liberally towards Catholics shrank. When you have got used to being thanked for your generosity of spirit towards those who have been dependent upon your help, it can be a rude surprise to be rebuked for not accepting a quite new concept of how issues look. For example, the Protestant repealers of 1848 were, to say the least, not welcomed by the Belfast (Catholic) repealers.

The episode in 1879 (see Chapter 13), where the *Examiner* one week praised Ballymoney for electing a Catholic to its municipal commissioners, was an example. The following week it published an ignorant editorial about Ballymoney and the land question which showed how little the *Examiner* knew about Ballymoney. But quickly the argument generated some substance. It turned into a harangue about the *Ballymoney Free Press* adopting a supposedly patronizing attitude towards the Catholic who had been allowed on to the council. When Catholics were much weaker politically, the patronizing language would not even have attracted a moment's attention. As the two communities became more alike, the boundaries between them hardened and the dangers of tension between them affected ever more people. It is not a sign of degeneracy that fewer and fewer Protestant Liberals supported Catholic perceptions of each successive riot in Belfast. What happened was that Catholics rivalled more and more thoroughly with Protestants in each riot. That meant that the riots became more and more lethal, and that the two sorts of rioters became more and more alike. Eventually, when their differences expressed themselves as opposed national differences, they had become total rivals.

After Gladstone had gone for Home Rule, the abstention rates at the 1886 general election were enormous in all the Protestant majority constituencies where there was no chance of a Nationalist winning. To get the proper measure of this story we need to see how destructive this experience was for everyone who lived through it. Between the 1830s and the first Home Rule crisis, sectarian division was never a problem from which people could stand at a distance. It became increasingly a trap in which people found themselves, whether they liked it or not. They were forever facing choices they might rather not have had to make, like O'Connell v. Cooke in 1840, Hanna v. McLaughlin in 1857, the "shipcarpenters" or the "navvies" in 1864, whether Fenians or Gladstone were the real authors of the 1870 Land Act, and so on. In the end none of these choices was "rational". Everything benign seemed to be ground to dust and the most vile influences were often able to set the terms of debate, or to be more precise, of conflict. Many of the most redeeming things that happened seemed to be ineffective, or effective only in limited spaces and times. When polarization forces us to look pessimistically at the worst thing coming from "their" side, that which is redeeming often disappears from our attention. And indeed history is put together as a string of incidents which explain and rationalize the endless circles of hostility. Some of the anti-heroes I have tried to reinsert into the story were ineffective, judged from the point of view of any partisan story of conflict. Only sometimes did they manage to open up spaces, so unpleasant choices retreated somewhat.

In the 1780s, Protestants had considerable political space. The United Irishmen may or may not have been separatists, but amongst their leaders were Protestants who were actively concerned about the expulsion of Catholics out of the areas round the south shores of Lough Neagh. They earned the respect and following of many Catholics on that account. Wolfe Tone's writings describe the historical time-bomb. To Protestants, he says you do not experience what it is to be a Catholic. If you take their part now, we may be Irishmen together; but if not then England will play upon the fears of Protestants and the hopes of Catholics, and plunder and laugh at both. To which it may be added, that once Catholics had become a cohesive force and Protestants could only become part of Irishness as isolated individuals, Britain no longer needed to try very hard, if at all, to divide them. The last time this unpleasant truth could be recognized was when O'Connell's Repeal agitation seemed to be laid low and the space created for Francis Meagher and Young Ireland to redefine Irishness in 1846–48. Thereafter, the lines of national division have been clearly set, even if sometimes buried somewhat. And to bring out what is constructive and redeeming has been a question of building relationships across the sectarian division. Tone's words about compact are always coming back, because there is never any secure foundation upon which to build a trans-sectarian alliance, except what can be built in actual situations by Catholics and Protestants creating relationships with each other. This is what making peace in the middle of a national conflict entails.

Breaking the force of sectarian choices could rarely be done on a grand scale, as it was in the Land War. It was more often a question of finding an opportunity to reinsert sanity in the middle of chaos, as Rev. John MacNaughton did with the peace committees in 1864. Then there were the local opportunities, such as those taken by Canon McCrystal and Rev. H. B. Wilson in Cookstown, or by the Orange district master of Gilford and his counterpart in the Home Rule Association, who made 1874 a year to remember in that village. And for me at least the most important was George McMullan of Railway Street, Sandy Row. He had no resource to turn the tide except his own conviction as he stood in his doorway facing a mob. There were probably many like him who never were remembered; so in remembering him, I am thinking of all like him.

NOTES

Chapter One.
Introduction: The Settlement Legacy (pages 1–22)

1. Thomas Macknight, *Ulster as it is, or twenty-eight years experience as an Irish editor*, two volumes (London 1896); Ernest W. Hamilton, *The Soul of Ulster* (London 1917).
2. David W. Miller, *Queen's Rebels: Ulster Loyalism in Historical Perspective* (Dublin and New York 1978).
3. A. T. Q. Stewart, *The Narrow Ground: Aspects of Ulster 1609–1969* (London 1977).
4. Peter Gibbon, *The Origins of Ulster Unionism* (Manchester 1975).
5. Gibbon, op. cit. 22–43, esp. 33–4.
6. Frank Wright, "Protestant Ideology and Politics in Ulster", *European Journal of Sociology*, No. 14, 1973, 213–80.
7. Rene Girard, *Violence and the Sacred* (Baltimore and London 1981) 12–25.
8. Frank Wright, *Northern Ireland: a Comparative Analysis* (Dublin and Totowa, NJ 1987) Chapters 1, 2 and 6.
9. Frank Wright, "Reconciling the Histories of Protestant and Catholic in Northern Ireland", 68–83, in Alan D. Falconer (ed.) *Reconciling Memories* (Dublin 1987).
10. For example, an unnamed old Belfast Loyalist quoted by Sarah Nelson in *Ulster's Uncertain Defenders*: "I seen it before, before ever Ireland was divided, and in the twenties, and each time after that; and Ireland will never be at peace, or us and them stop fighting, till the end of the world."
11. Girard, op. cit. 15–16; Frank Wright, "Communal Deterrence and National Identity in 19th Century Ulster", in John Darby, A. C. Hepburn and N. Dodge (eds) *Political Violence in Comparative Perspective* (Belfast 1990?).
12. *Report from the Select Committee on Outrages (Ireland)*, H.C. 1852 (438) XIV, paras 94 and 959 (referred to hereafter as *Outrages 1852*).
13–14. *Belfast Newsletter*, 9 Feb., 22 Aug. 1883.
15. Wright, *Comparative Analysis*, Chapter 3.
16–17. Wright, op. cit. 34–5, 41–2, 76, esp. 119.
18. W. Macafee and V. Morgan, "Population in Ulster 1660–1760", Chapter IV, esp. 58, in Peter Roebuck (ed.) *Plantation to Partition. Essays in Ulster History in Honour of J. L. McCracken* (Belfast 1981); L. M. Cullen, *An Economic History of Ireland since 1660* (London 1976) 20, 28–9.
19. Cullen, ibid.; Macafee and Morgan, op. cit. 47, 49, 57; W. H. Crawford, "The influence of the landlord in 18th century Ulster", Chapter 14, esp. 194, in L. M. Cullen and T. C. Smout, *Comparative Aspects of Scottish and Irish Economic and Social History, 1600–1900* (Edinburgh 1978).
20. J. C. Beckett, *The Making of Modern Ireland 1603–1923* (London 1966) 46–7; Crawford, ibid.
21–23. Beckett, op. cit. 64–81, 118–21, 149–51.
24. R. J. Dickson, *Ulster Emigration to Colonial America, 1718–1775* (Belfast 1966) 4, 13n, 21, 35; W. H. Crawford and B. Trainor, *Aspects of Irish Social History 1750–1800* (PRONI, Belfast 1970) 88.

25. P. Roebuck, "Rent Movement, Proprietorial Incomes and Agricultural Development, 1730–1830", Chapter VI, in Roebuck (ed.) op. cit.
26. Dickson, op. cit. 69, 150, 182–3.
27. First Report of the Commissioners Appointed to Inquire into the Municipal Corporations in Ireland, H.C. 1835, M.C. General Report, 9–40.
28. H.C. 1835, Appendix (Part 3) 1128.
29. H.C. 1835, General Report, 19–20.
30. H.C. 1835, Appendix (Part 2) 986.
31. Maureen Wall, "Catholics in Economic Life", Chapter III, in L. M. Cullen (ed.) The Formation of the Irish Economy (Cork 1969) esp. 42–3.
32. This point is presented as though it was an accepted fact, although he offers no illustration of it by T. Wolfe Tone in his "Argument on Behalf of the Catholics of Ireland", see Chapter 2.
33. L. A. Clarkson, "Household and Family Structure in Armagh City, 1770", in Local Population Studies, No. 20 (1978).
34. Wall, op. cit. 40; Beckett, op. cit. 214; Edith Mary Johnston, Ireland in the 18th Century (Dublin 1973) 42–3.
35. For example, Andrew Boyd, Holy War in Belfast (Tralee 1969) 2; and Liam de Paor, Divided Ulster (Harmondsworth 1970) 44–57.
36. W. Shaw Mason, A Statistical Account or Parochial Survey of Ireland, Vol. 2 (Dublin 1816) sections on parishes in Glenavy, Tullyrusk and Camlin; and Vol. 3 (Dublin 1819) section on Killelagh parish.
37. William Gregg, General Report on the Gosford Estate in County Armagh in 1821, with an introduction by F. M. L. Thomson and D. Tierney (PRONI, Belfast) 76.
38. Johnston, op. cit. 36–7.
39. Tone, op. cit.; see Chapter 2 for extended treatment.
40. Wright, "Protestant Ideology".

Chapter Two.
The Decay of the Colonial Settlement Structure (pages 23–46)

1. Richard R. Madden, The United Irishmen. Their Lives and Times, three vols (Dublin 1844) Vol. 3, 41.
2. Beckett, Modern Ireland, 277.
3. Richard R. Madden, Antrim and Down in '98 (Glasgow 1845) 14.
4–5. Beckett, Modern Ireland, 232, 247, 250–74.
6. Crawford in Cullen and Smout, 198; Cullen, Ec. Hist., 57, 58, 67 and 83.
7. Crawford and Trainor, 36; Dickson, Ulster Emigration, 69, 75; F. J. Biggar, The Land War in Ulster (Dublin 1910).
8. Dickson, op. cit. 60–81.
9. Beckett, Mod. Ireland, 215–19.
10. Banner of Ulster, 12 October 1852.
11. Crawford and Trainor, 167.
12. William Blacker, Third Report of the Select Committee on Agricultural Distress, H.C. 1836, VIII, Part II.
13. W. H. Crawford, Domestic Industry in Ireland. The Experience of the Linen Industry (Dublin 1972) 5.
14. Gibbon, Ulster Unionism, 26–7.
15. David W. Miller, "The Armagh Troubles, 1784–95", Chapter 4 in Samuel Clarke and James S. Donnelly, Jr., Irish Peasants. Violence and Political Unrest 1780–1914 (Madison and Manchester 1983).
16. Madden, Antrim and Down, 102 and 229.

17. Committee of Inquiry into the Irish Linen Trade, H.C. 1835, V, 7; also Devon 1835, evidence of John Hancock.
18. Madden, op. cit. 46.
19–20. Gibbon, op. cit. 25, 35.
21. Donald H. Akenson and W. H. Crawford, James Orr, Bard of Ballycarry (PRONI, Belfast 1977).
22. L. A. Clarkson, "The Economy of Armagh City, 1770", in Irish Economic and Social History, V, 1978.
23. J. Borne, An Impartial Account of the Late Disturbances in the County of Armagh, from 1784 to 1791.
24. Conrad Gill, The Rise of the Irish Linen Industry (Oxford 1925) 342.
25. Gregg, Gosford Estate, 76.
26. Samuel Leighton, Freemasonry in Northern Ireland (Belfast 1938) 25–7.
27. Rev. M. W. Dewar, Rev. John Brown, Rev. S. E. Long, Orangeism—a new historical appreciation (Belfast 1967).
28. See Chapter 1; and on the special situation in Carrickfergus, see the Report on Municipal Corporations, H.C. 1835, Part One, 761–2.
29. Weekly Northern Whig, 14 August 1869.
30. Beckett, Modern Ireland, 250–6; Madden, United Irishmen, Vol. I, 22, and Vol. II, 14.
31. Madden, United Irishmen, Vol. I, 181.
32–34. Madden, United Irishmen, Vol. II, 22, 57–84; Madden, Antrim and Down, 94-5; Madden, United Irishmen, Vol. I, 148–50.
35. Beckett, Modern Ireland, 258.
36. Madden, United Irishmen, Vol. II, 99.
37. Leighton, op. cit. 25–7.
38. Madden, Antrim and Down, 9, 13, 14.
39. McComb's Guide to Belfast (Belfast 1861) 14.
40. Thomas Pakenham, The Year of Liberty (London 1872).
41. Madden, Antrim and Down, 240.
42. McComb's Guide, 12.
43. C. L. Falkiner, Studies in Irish History and Biography (London 1902).
44. Theobald Wolfe Tone, "An Argument on Behalf of the Catholics of Ireland, (1791)" in The Life of T. W. Tone, edited by himself and his son (Washington 1826) 358.
45. Tone, op. cit. 353, 355, 365.

Chapter Three.
Ulster, O'Connell and the Whigs (pages 47–69)

1–2. Beckett, Mod. Ire., 270–1, 286, 303.
3. Wright, Comparative Analysis, Chapter 1.
4. Ernest Gellner, Thought and Change (London 1964).
5. Madden, United Irishmen, Vol. II; Memoir of W. J. Macneven, (B) 28.
6–7. James McKnight, Repealer Repulsed (Belfast 1841) 103, 120.
8. Donald H. Akenson, The Irish Education Experiment (London and Toronto 1970); Galen Broeker, Rural Disorder and Police Reform in Ireland 1812–36 (London and Toronto 1970); Desmond Bowen, The Protestant Crusade in Ireland 1800–1870 (Dublin and Montreal 1978); Angus Macintyre, The Liberator. Daniel O'Connell and the Irish Party 1830–1847 (London 1965).
9. Macintyre, op. cit. 262–3.
10. Broeker, op. cit. 35–8.

NOTES 527

11. Mason, op. cit. Vol. III, parishes of Ardclinis and Layd.
12. Broeker, op. cit. 84.
13. *Report from the Select Committee Appointed to Inquire into the Nature, Character, Extent, and Tendency of the Orange Lodges, Associations or Societies in Ireland*, H.C. 1835, XV (377) and H.C. 1835, XVI (476) (hereafter referred to as *Orangeism 1835*, Vol. I and Vol. III respectively) evidence of Patrick McConnell, Vol. III, paras 6363–78.
14–16. *Orangeism 1835*, evidence of the Earl of Gosforth, Vol. I, 234, and of W. J. Hancock, Vol. III, 110–20; *Orangeism 1835*, evidence of Randall Kernan, Vol. III, 70–98, esp. 70; *Orangeism 1835*, contained in the evidence of the Earl of Gosford, Vol. I, 249.
17. *Orangeism 1835*, contained in the evidence of Patrick McConnell, Vol. III, 18–19, quoted opinion of Col. Blacker on Whig laws.
18. R. Barry O'Brien, *Thomas Drummond, Life and Letters* (London 1889).
19–20. *Municipal Corporations 1835*, Appendix, Part II, 951, 966, 984, 986, 992.
21. *Report from H.M. Commissioners of Inquiry into the State of the Law and Practice in Respect to the Occupation of Land in Ireland*, H.C. 1845.
22–23. *Municipal Corporations 1835*, Appendix, Part II, 914; Part III, 1086.
24. *Orangeism 1835*, evidence of Capt. David Duff, Vol. III, 127–8.
25–26. *Municipal Corporations 1835*, Appendix, Part III, 1029–36, 1140–50.
27. Madden, *United Irishmen*, Vol. II, 188–90.
28. Akenson, op. cit. 77–8, 89–90, 102, 121.
29. Bowen, op. cit. 94–6; Homes, *Henry Cooke*, 54.
30. See No. 36, Chapter 1.
31. Wright, *Comparative Analysis*, Chaps 1 and 2.
32. Akenson, op. cit. 150.
33. Boyd, A., *Holy War*, 5–9; De Paor, L., *Divided Ulster*, 57–8.
34. R. Finlay Holmes, *Henry Cooke* (Belfast, Dublin and Ottawa 1981).
35. Holmes, op. cit. 24, 48, 52.
36. Edwin Darley Hill, *The Northern Banking Company Limited. An Historical Sketch 1824–1924* (Belfast 1925) 32–3.
37. Holmes, op. cit. 50, 70.
38–42. Akenson, op. cit. 150, 175–6, 160, 166, 92–7, 109, 187.
43–45. Holmes, op. cit. 101, 115, 99.
46. W. D. Latimer, *History of the Irish Presbyterians* (Belfast 1902) 450–9.
47. *16th Report of the Commissioners of National Education in Ireland for the year ending 31st March 1949*.
49. Wright, *Protestant Ideology*.
49. MacKnight, *Ulster as it is*, Vol. I.
50. Ian Budge and Cornelius O'Leary, *Belfast: Approach to Crisis. A Study of Belfast Politics, 1613–1970* (London and Basingstoke 1973) 53.
51. *Devon 1845*, evidence of Rev. Samuel Young, P. P. Aghagallon, at Antrim.
52. *Devon 1845*, evidence of Rev. Henry McLoughlin, P. P. Loughguile, and George Macartney at Coleraine.
53. McKnight, *Repealer Repulsed*, 59.

Chapter Four.
Onset of Rural Crisis in Pre-Famine Ulster (pages 70–103)

1. Gibbon, *Ulster Unionism*, 19, 20; Belinda Probert, *Beyond Orange and Green: The Political Economy of the Northern Ireland Crisis* (London 1978) 16.

2. Cullen, *Economic History of Ireland*, Chap. 5, esp. 127.
3. *Belfast Newsletter*, 22 August 1883.
4. Cullen, op. cit. 102, 106, 122.
5. Gill, *Irish Linen Industry*, 239–41.
6. *Report from the Select Committee on Handloom Weavers*, H.C. 1834, X, paras 5677–90, Philip Halliwell; *Report from the Select Committee on Combinations of Workingmen*, H.C. 1837/8, paras 2937–44, James Campbell.
7. Crawford, *Domestic Industry in Ireland*, 41.
8. *Select Committee on Handloom Weavers*, H.C. 1835, XIII, Alex Moncrieff, 106, 120–1.
9. Cullen, op. cit. 120; Gill, op. cit. 321–2.
10. *The Third Report of the Select Committee on Agricultural Distress*, H.C. 1836, VIII, Part 2, evidence of William Blacker.
11. The map for 1810 is in Crawford, *Domestic Industry*, 5; figures are from *Census 1841 and 1851*.
12. W. H. Crawford, "Landlord-Tenant Relations in Ulster, 1609–1820", in *Irish Economic and Social History*, Vol. II, 1975.
13. William Gregg, *Gosford Estate*, 99, 109–18, 129, 137.
14. *Report of H.M. Commissioners of Inquiry into the Working of the Irish Land Act of 1870*, H.C. 1881, XVIII and XIX (C 2779-I and -II) (cited as *Bessborough 1881*) evidence of Patrick O'Callaghan.
15. Gregg, op. cit.
16. *Devon 1845*, evidence of H. L. Prentice and Capt. Henry Crossle at Caledon.
17. W. S. Mason, op. cit. Vol. II, survey of Culaduff parish.
18. *Devon 1845*, evidence of John Sheil and Fitzherbert Filgate at Castleblaney, and the whole section of evidence taken at Carrickmacross, esp. Rev. Daniel Boylan, P. P. Magheraclone.
19.–21. R. D. C. Black, *Economic Thought and the Irish Question 1817–1870* (Cambridge 1960) 8, 106, 209, 20, 127.
22. W. S. Mason, op. cit. Vol. III, survey of Holywood parish.
23. W. H. Crawford, "Landlord-Tenant Relations in Ulster, 1609–1820".
24–25 *Bessborough 1881*, evidence of Andre M. Ker, agent to Lord Dartrey, summary report.
26. *First Report of the Select Committee Inquiring into the State of Ireland*, H.C. 1825, VIII, 147, Hugh Wallace.
27. *Devon 1835*, e.g. J. W. Maxwell, J. P., a Downpatrick landlord, at Belfast.
28. William Carleton, *Traits and Stories of the Irish Peasantry* (London 1854).
29. W. S. Mason, op. cit. Vol. I, survey of Ardstraw parish; all material in the following pages on 1814 is from this source.
30–35. *Devon 1845*, evidence of Edward Sproule at Castlederg, and John Humphreys, agent to the Marquis of Abercorn at Strabane; James Sinclair, a landlord near Strabane, John Cairns at Strabane, John Cochran, agent to Alexander Stewart; evidence regarding Badoney parish from Pat McAnulty and John Montgomery Reid at Omagh; T. J. Atkinson, J. P., agent to Col. George Knox, at Ballyshannon.
36. William Carleton, op. cit.
37. *Devon 1845*, Rev. William Brown, P. P. at Strabane.
38. *Banner of Ulster*, 31 October 1867.
39. J. E. Portlock, *Report of the Geology of the County of Londonderry* (Dublin 1843).
40. W. S. Mason, op. cit. Vol. I, Survey of Dungiven parish.
41. ibid.

42–44. W. S. Mason, Vol. III, survey of Killelagh parish, survey of Tamlaght parish, survey of Maghera parish.
45–46 *Devon 1845*, evidence of Rowley Miller, Hugh Hagan, Alex Patterson and Samuel Glasgow.
47. *Devon 1845*, charge of religious criteria, see Hugh Hagan and Rowley Miller reply.
48. W. S. Mason, Vol. II, survey of Culaduff parish.
49–54. *Devon 1845*, Lord George Hill at Dublin; James Donleavy at Donegal; John O'Donnell of Inniskele parish at Donegal; Peter Coyle, Patrick Corfield, John Wallace, Edward Golding, J.P., agent to Lord Blaney, Rev. James Mulligan, P. P. Carrickmacross, Peter Hoey and Edward McCabe at Carrickmacross; Rev. Daniel Boylan, P. P. Magheraclone and Rev. William Thompson, Carrickmacross.
55. *First Report of H.M. Commissioner of Inquiry into the Condition of the Poorer Classes in Ireland*, H.C. 1835.
56. J. D. Chambers and G. E. Mingay, *The Agricultural Revolution 1750–1880* (London 1966).
57. *Report from the Select Committee on Emigration from the United Kingdom*, H.C. 1827, V, Third Report, 41.
58. D. Bowen, *The Protestant Crusade*, 94.
59. *Devon 1845*, evidence of William O'Reilly, J. P., at Dundalk, and Sir G. Hodson's reply.
60. *Orangeism 1835*, para. 3186, and R. M. Sibbett, *Orangeism in Ireland and Throughout the Empire* (London 1938) Vol. 2, 125.
61–63. *Devon 1845*, evidence of Peter Smith at Cavan; Rev. Marcus Beresford, Charles Riley at Virginia; Rev. Robert Sargent, agent to Marquis of Headfort.
64. ibid.
65. *Assistant Commissioner's Reports on Handloom Weavers in Ireland*, H.C. 1840, XXIII, Richard Muggeridge.
66–67. *Devon 1845*, evidence of William Blacker and John Hancock at Lurgan; John McCartan at Lurgan.
68–69 *Orangeism 1835*, Vol. I, paras 609–14 and 2694–834; and Vol. III, 104–12.
70–71. *Devon 1845*, evidence of Capt. G. Cranfield, agent to Lord Powerscourt; Alex Miller at Coleraine.
72. *First Report of H.M. Commission of Inquiry into the Condition of the Poorer Classes in Ireland*, H.C. 1835.
73. W. S. Mason, Vol. II, survey of Glenavy, Camlin and Tullyrusk parishes.
74. *First Report of H.M. Commission of Inquiry into the Condition of the Poorer Classes in Ireland*, H.C. 1835.
75. *Devon 1845*, Richard Mayne, J. P., on the contrast between Fermanagh and Monaghan, William Patterson, John Hamilton, J.P., and Capt. Edward Archdall.
76. Arbitration procedure and Lord Caledon's purchase.
77–81. *Devon 1845*, evidence of James Thompson at Coleraine; Rev. Fletcher Blakely at Belfast; John Lindsay at Banbridge; M. W. Lowry and G. Orr at Belfast; William Beck and Arthur Molyneux at Antrim.
82. *Ordnance Survey Memoir for the Parish of Donegore, 1835* (PRONI).
83. ibid.

Chapter Five.
The Famine in Ulster (pages 104–134)

1. Beckett, *Making of Modern Ireland*, 343–5.
2. Alan D. Falconer, *Reconciling Memories*.
3. James Brown, "Reminiscences—Donoughmore, Co. Tyrone", in *The Great Famine*; PRONI, education facsimiles.
4. *Report of the Commissioners Appointed to Inquire into the State of the Municipal Affairs of the Borough of Belfast in Ireland*, H. C. 1859 (sees. 1) XII (2470) (hereafter cited as *Belfast 1858*) evidence of William S. Tracy, R. M., para 4338.
5. Budge and O'Leary, *Belfast*, 54.
6. *McComb's Guide*, 17-21; see also Chapter 8.
7–10. *Labour's Advocate*, 3, 10 and 24 April 1847.
11. *Belfast 1858*, Robert S. Lepper, paras 1165–73.
12. *Labour's Advocate*, 8 May 1847.
13. R. D. C. Black, op. cit. 113–14.
14. Cecil Woodham–Smith, *The Great Hunger* (London 1962) 106–8.
15. ibid. 165–9.
16. *Second Report from the Select Committee on Commercial Distress* (584) H.C. 1848, evidence of James Bristow.
17. Black, op. cit. 10; T. P. O'Neill, "The Organization and Administration of Relief, 1845–52", in R. D. Edwards and T. D. Williams, *The Great Famine: Studies in Irish History, 1845–52* (Dublin 1956).
18. Rt Hon. George Dawson to Thomas F. Fremantle, 17 January 1847, ed. fac. No. 6, *The Great Famine* (PRONI).
19. *Transactions of Central Relief Committee of the Society of Friends during the Famine in Ireland, 1846 and 1847*.
20. *Labour's Advocate*, 3 April 1847.
21. George Dawson to Sir T. F. Fremantle, 14 November 1847, ed. fac. No. 14, *The Great Famine* (PRONI).
22. *The Measures Adopted for the Relief of the Distress in Ireland, Uncorrected Correspondence—Board of Works Series, Feb—Aug. 1847*, Part 3, Capt. Maxwell, March 1847, 69.
23. *Transactions of the Central Relief Committee of the Society of Friends during the Famine in Ireland, 1846 and 1847*.
24. R. Gordon to J. Coates, 28 March 1850, *Antrim Grand Jury papers*, PRONI, CII (102) No. 8.
25. *The Measures Adopted for the Relief of the Distress in Ireland, Feb.–Aug. 1847*, Part 3, Capt. Oldershaw, March 1847, 95.
26. ibid. Lieutenant Colomb, March 1847, 96.
27–28. Notice to tenants and ratepayers of Lord Downshire's Upper Iveagh estate, 30 December 1846 (PRONI); also *The Measurers Adopted for the Relief of the Distress in Ireland*.
29. ibid. 101, Mr Townsend, engineer's report from Donegal.
30. ibid. 288, Return showing the daily average number of persons employed on public works in Ireland, for week ending 13 March 1847.
31. ibid. 166, Report (E) Drainage, under Mr Labouchere's letter, in Farney Barony, Co. Monaghan.
32. ibid. 258, Capt. William O'Neill, April 1847; see also Mr Townsend.
33. Woodham–Smith, op. cit. 266–75.
34. *Outrages 1852*, William Kirk, paras 4527–31; also *Supplementary Appendix to the Seventh Report of the Relief Commissioners 1847*, on remittances through Rathmelton Post Office, 13.

35. *Londonderry Standard*, 4 February 1874.
36. Bessborough 1881, Col. Forde, para. 7085.
37. *The Measurers Adopted for the Relief of the Distress in Ireland*, uncorrected correspondence.
38. ibid. Dungannon, Lieutenant Colomb, 27 March.
39. Reports of the Relief Commissioners for Distress (Ireland), Third Report (836) June 1847, Appendix B, 18.
40. Report of the Relief Commissioners for Distress (Ireland), Second Report (819) May 1847, Appendix D, 22.
41. Supplementary Appendix to the Seventh Report, 62, Lisnaskea Union, and more strikingly page 49.
42. *Outrages 1852*, Rev. M. Lennon, paras 3448–57.
43. *The Measures Adopted for the Relief of the Distress in Ireland*, uncorrected correspondence.
44. Supplementary Appendix to the Seventh Report, 13–14.
45. *The Irish Agriculturalist*, 9 June and 8 September 1848, and after the extent of the disaster, 13 October 1848.
46. ibid. 8 September 1848.
47. Grand Jury of the County of Antrim, Resolutions Book, Ant C & P, CII, No. 2, entries for summer 1848, Lent 1849, summer 1849, Lent 1850, and on the non-availability of loan finance.
48. *Banner of Ulster*, 31 December 1850.
49. Grand Jury of the County of Antrim, Resolutions Book, Lent 1849.
50. Resolution of the Newry Board of Guardians, 24 February 1849.
51. *Banner of Ulster*, 13 March 1849.
52. *A Catechism of Tenant Right*, by James McKnight (Belfast 1850) para. 13.

Chapter Six.
Ulster Politics in 1848 (pages 135–164)

1. S. J. Connolly, "Catholicism in Ulster, 1800–1850", Chapter X, in Peter Roebuck (ed.) *Plantation to Partition. Essays in Ulster History in Honour of J. L. McCracken* (Belfast 1981).
2. Finlay Holmes, *Henry Cooke*, 156.
3. Beckett, *Modern Ireland*, 327–35.
4. J. F. McLennan, *Memoir of Thomas Drummond* (Edinburgh 1867).
5. Akenson, *Irish Education Experiment*, 206–8; Beckett, op. cit. 323.
6. McKnight, *Repealer Repulsed*, 25.
7. Bowen, *Protestant Crusade*, 156–77.
8. Macintyre, *The Liberator*, 271; Beckett, op. cit. 323.
9. Bowen, op. cit. 198–9.
10. *Banner of Ulster*, 11 and 18 August 1848.
11–12. Akenson, op. cit. 253, 209.
13. B. A. Kennedy, "William Sharman Crawford, 1780–1861" (D.Litt. thesis, Queen's University, Belfast 1953).
14. Sir Charles Gavan Duffy, *Young Ireland, 1840–45* (London 1880).
15. The differences between MacHale and Davis might seem to be as sharp as possible. It was the non-sectarianism of the Queen's Colleges that Davis liked and MacHale so strongly opposed. The point of similarity is that both saw their own scenario as a way of keeping utilitarian culture at a distance.
16. Beckett, op. cit. 332–3.
17. Woodham-Smith, op. cit. 64–5.
18. Charles Gavan Duffy, *The League of the North and South* (London 1886).

19. *Belfast Newsletter*, 9 June 1846.
20. ibid. 24 June 1846.
21. ibid. 18, 22 September 1846.
22. ibid. 16 November 1847.
23. ibid.
24. ibid. 19 November 1847.
25. *Northern Whig*, 11 April 1848.
26. Elie Halevy, *Victorian Years*, 243; A. M. Sullivan, *New Ireland* (London 1877) 84–93.
27. *Northern Whig*, 11 May 1848.
28. ibid.
29. Wolfe Tone, "Argument on Behalf of the Catholics".
30. *Report of the meetings of the Grand Lodge of Ireland*, 1849 and 1850. The Grand Lodge held two half yearly meetings, whose shorter minutes were published. The records of expulsions and suspensions are very clearly laid out for the years 1853–70. The specific offences before and after those dates are not always clear. In 1853, ten were expelled from Co. Antrim for supporting "Radical" candidates. By far the largest block of clear "political" expulsions was the 40 expelled for supporting Sam McCurdy Greer in Co. Derry in 1857.
31. In the papers relating to Orangeism in the State Paper Office in Dublin is a collection of petitions for clemency for William Smith O'Brien. Amongst these is one from 14 masters, representing 396 members of Orange Lodges of the Fivemiletown district, signed by Robert Hall, district master, who also reminds of their earlier declaration of loyalty. Also *Belfast Newsletter*, 20 October, the Orangemen of Dublin petitition the Lord-Lt for William Smith O'Brien.
32. Comparing the Ballymena declaration of loyalty and the petition for Smith O'Brien, I found at least seven names on both, including John O'Neill, M.D., Randalstown, and James Boyle, manager of the Ulster Bank in Ballymoney.
33. Dewar, Long and Brown, *Orangeism*, 131.
34. ibid. 127–30.
35. J. A. R. Marnott and C. G. Robertson, *The Evolution of Prussia* (London 1915) 302.
36. *Orangeism 1835*, e.g. Hugh R. Baker, paras 2877–3201, explaining how Cavan County Orangeism was so lawless on account of the "prejudice" of the gentry against it and its leadership falling into other hands.
37. *Outrages 1852*, Maxwell Hamilton, paras 1777–1862, 1924.
38. Dewar, Long and Brown, op. cit. 132.
39. Report of the meetings of the Grand Lodge of Ireland, 1838, May 1849.
40. Report of Grand Lodge, May 1851, contains this item as part of an address to the Protestants of Great Britain.
41. *Belfast Riots 1857*, Lord Enniskillen, paras 8488–95.
42. *Banner of Ulster*, 4 December 1849.
43. ibid. 12 December 1850.
44. *Belfast Newsletter*, 14 July 1848.
45. ibid.
46. *Banner of Ulster*, 1 August 1848.
47. ibid.
48. Dewar *et al.*, op. cit. 136–7.
49. Report of the meetings of the Grand Lodge of Ireland, e.g. compare attendance for 1848 and first half yearly meeting of 1849 with 1853 and 1854.

50. Belfast Newsletter, 10 May 1850, Lodge 948, Portadown.
51. Information from Grand Lodge Reports: cross-checking the Grand Lodge membership against the *Return of Owners of Land in Ireland for 1873*, H.C. 1873 [C-1492], the very large owners are the Earl of Enniskillen, 29,600 acres, Capt. Mervyn Archdall, 27,400 acres, both of Fermanagh. Next tier are Lord A. E. Hill Trevor (Antrim), Sir Wm Verner (Tyrone), Wm Humphreys (Cavan), Parker Synott (Armagh), Capt. Madden (Monaghan), who were all in the 4,000–5,500 acre range. All except Hill are in the south-west and central Ulster area.
52. Finlay Holmes, *Henry Cooke*, 128.
53. Holmes, op. cit. 156.
54. Rev. J. H. Mullin, *Aghadowey. Parish History* (Belfast 1970) 174–5.
55. *Banner of Ulster*, 18 August 1848.
56. ibid. 11 August 1848.
57. ibid. 17 September 1850.
58. *Belfast Newsletter*, 26 May 1848.
59. *Banner of Ulster*, 28 July 1848.
60 ibid. 12 October 1849.
61. Barrington Moore, Jun., *Social Origins of Dictatorship and Democracy* (Harmondsworth 1977).
62. *Belfast 1858*, the Commissioners Report (10–11) comes to the conclusion that the purchase was "not improvident" and was "for the benefit of the borough", but the verdict was not well received by all.
63. Grand Jury for the County of Antrim, Resolution Book, Lent 1850, thanks Sir E. W. MacNaughten, MP for Co. Antrim, for his defence of the interests of the county in opposing the 1850 Belfast Town Councils Bill in parliament. A subcommittee was formed to resist proposals to release owners and occupiers of houses in the borough from the cess.
64. Grand Jury for the County of Antrim, Resolution Book.

Chapter Seven.
1848–1852: The League of North and South—the Tenant League (pages 165–207)

1. *Northern Whig*, 28 March 1848.
2. ibid. 18 March 1848.
3. ibid. 1 April 1848.
4. ibid.
5. ibid. 4 March 1848.
6. ibid.
7. ibid.
8 *Belfast Newsletter*, 19 February 1848.
9. *Northern Whig*, 21 March 1848.
10. ibid.
11. ibid. 28 March 1848.
12. ibid. 4 March 1848
13. *Weekly Northern Whig*, 15 February 1873, Rev. W. G. Boyd at Route Tenants Defence Association.
14. *Ulster Weekly News*, 24 January 1874, Paper prepared for the National Tenant Right Conference in Belfast, "Ulster Tenant Right Custom. Its origin, essence, and legalised development", by Dr James McKnight.
15. David Miller, *Queen's Rebels*, 76–8.
16. McKnight, *Ulster Tenant Right Custom*. This work cited in Note 14 is the last statement of Dr McKnight's position made before his death in 1876.

17. *Northern Whig*, 28 March 1848.
18. *Banner of Ulster*, 12 October 1849.
19. ibid.
20. ibid.
21. ibid 13 November 1849.
22. ibid.
23. ibid.
24. Marquis of Dufferin, *Irish Emigration and the Tenure of Land in Ireland* (London 1869).
25. *Banner of Ulster*, 13 November 1849.
26. James McKnight, *Catechism of Tenant Right* (Belfast 1850) paras 3 and 10.
27. *Northern Whig*, 28 March 1848.
28. *Banner of Ulster*, 11 January 1850.
29. ibid.
30. ibid. 18 January 1850.
31. ibid.
32. ibid. 11 January 1850.
33. ibid. 18 December 1849.
34. ibid. 4 September 1849.
35. ibid.
36. ibid. 30 April 1850.
37. ibid.
38. ibid.
39. ibid.
40. ibid. 14 June 1850.
41. Arthur O'Connor's views were the subject of the following comment from Dr Madden: "The wary old soldier and skilful tactician generally introduces into these denunciations . . . [of the Christian religion] . . . a furious tirade against Popish frauds and Romish miracles. The innocent reader, of very strong anti-catholic opinions, might therefore imagine the general was only manifesting his zeal against 'the errors of Popery' and not seriously impugning the vital tenets of Christianity." Madden, *United Irishmen*, Vol. III, 175–7.
42. J. H. Whyte, *The Tenant League and Irish Politics in the 1850s*, Irish History, series No. 4, Dublin Historical Association (1963) 8.
43. *Banner of Ulster*, 31 December 1850.
44. ibid. 11 January 1850.
45. Charles Gavan Duffy, *The League of North and South*.
46. ibid.
47. ibid.
48. For a reference illustrating this point, see one of McKnight's earlier works, *Repealer Repulsed*, 26, on the subject of the mob that was supposed to be coming with Daniel O'Connell to Belfast in 1840.
49. *Outrages 1852*, Capt. Warburton, paras 10–28 and Capt. George Fitzmaurice, paras 273–303.
50. ibid. Capt Fitzmaurice, paras 540–59.
51. ibid. Capt Fitzmaurice, paras 563–4; *Banner of Ulster*, 22 June 1852.
52. *Banner of Ulster*, 17 September 1850.
53. ibid. 22 February 1850.
54. ibid. 30 January 1852.
55. *Cathechism of Tenant Right*, paras 14 and 16.
56. *Banner of Ulster*, 18 January 1850.
57. ibid. 22 February 1850.

58. ibid.
59. ibid. 8 March 1850.
60. *Belfast Newsletter*, 26 February 1850.
61. ibid. 1 March 1850.
62. J. H. Whyte, *The Independent Irish Party 1850–59* (Oxford 1958) 8.
63. *Banner of Ulster*, 17 May 1850.
64. ibid. 5 July 1850.
65. T. Croskery and T. Witherow, *Life of A. P. Goudy*.
66. *Banner of Ulster*, 1 October 1850.
67. ibid. 12 November 1850.
68. ibid. 26 November 1850.
69. Duffy, op. cit.
70. *Belfast Newsletter*, 10 December 1850.
71. ibid.
72. ibid.
73. E. R. Norman, *Anti-Catholicism in Victorian England*, Chapter 8, including letter of Lord John Russell to the Bishop of Durham, 4 November 1850.
74. *Banner of Ulster*, 12, 26 November 1850.
75. ibid. 31 December 1850.
76. ibid.
77. ibid. 11 February 1851.
78. Akenson, *Irish Education Experiment*, 255–7.
79. Peadar MacSuibhne, *Paul Cullen and his Contemporaries* (Naas 1961).
80. *Weekly Vindicator*, 16 August 1851.
81. *Banner of Ulster*, 22 August 1851.
82. ibid. 2 May 1851.
83. ibid.
84. ibid.
85. ibid. 26 August 1851.
86. *Belfast Newsletter*, 25 August 1851.
87. Whyte, *Irish Party*, 25–30.
88. *Weekly Vindicator*, 4 October 1851.
89. *Banner of Ulster*, 18 October 1851.
90. ibid. 15 June 1852.
91. ibid.
92. ibid. 6 April and 17 August 1852.
93. *Weekly Vindicator*, 10 July 1852.
94. *Banner of Ulster*, 30 July 1852.
95. *Weekly Vindicator*, 31 July 1852.
96. *Banner of Ulster*, 6 August 1852.
97. *Weekly Vindicator*, 24 July and 7 August 1852.
98. *Banner of Ulster*, 27 July 1852.
99. ibid. 3 August 1852.
100. ibid. 27 July 1852.
101. ibid. 3 August 1852.
102. ibid. 31 August 1852.
103. See Chapter 14 figure for details.
104. *Ballymoney Free Press*, 2 December 1880.
105. Reports of the meetings of the Grand Lodge of Ireland, 1858/9.
106. *Londonderry Standard*, 7 February 1874.
107. See Chapters 12 and 13 below.
108. *Banner of Ulster*, 30 July 1852.

536 TWO LANDS ON ONE SOIL

109. The hardest hitting statement of the revisionist view of landlord-tenant relations that I know is W. E. Vaughan, "Landlord and Tenant Relations in Ireland between the Famine and the Land War, 1850–78", in L. M. Cullen and T. C. Smout, *Scottish and Irish Economic and Social History 1600–1900*, Chapter 14, 216–25. He rightly attacks the idea that the landlords were for ever evicting and rack renting; but as a tenant I would very much have liked not to be under endless "threats" of eviction "served to secure some other end by threatening removal", 219.
110. David Miller, *Queen's Rebels*, 76.
111. Dufferin, *Irish Emigration*.

Chapter Eight.
The Decline of the Old Whigs (pages 208–240)

1. Charles Gavan Duffy, *The League of the North and South*.
2. A. M. Sullivan, *New Ireland* (London 1882) 156–77.
3. *Banner of Ulster*, 17 September 1868.
4. *Agricultural Labourers' (Ireland) Wages. Poor Law Inspectors' Reports*, H.C. 1870 [C 35] XIV. Dr Alex Knox speaks of the "very great increase over the last twenty years" in east Ulster, especially near Belfast and around harvest time.
5. See my *Northern Ireland: A Comparative Analysis*, Chapter 3; also see Jim Smyth, "Dependent Interdependence. Ireland and British Imperialism", 34–55, in *Thames Papers in Social Analysis*, series No. 1, N. Ireland.
6. *Banner of Ulster*, 23 May 1851.
7. *Report of the Linen Merchants Association, 1852*.
8. Max Goldstrom, Chapter 8, "The Industrialization of the North-East", in L. M. Cullen (ed.) *Formation of the Irish Economy*.
9. ibid. 105.
10. W. E. Coe, *The engineering industry in the North of Ireland*.
11. *Banner of Ulster*, 2 August 1855.
12. Coe, op. cit. 167–8.
13. Report of the Belfast Chamber of Commerce, quoted in *Ulster Examiner*, 18 February 1871.\
14. *Report of the Commissioners Appointed to Inquire into the State of the Municipal Affairs of the Borough of Belfast, in Ireland with Appendices and Minutes of Evidence*, H.C. 1859, [2470] XII [hereafter referred to as *Belfast 1858*]. The definition of the area benefiting as described in James Cameron's evidence was not disputed at the inquiry, though there was much dispute about the relative gains and disadvantages to particular areas, paras 3559–74.
15. Noel Simpson, *The Belfast Bank* checked against the *1868 Election Poll Book*.
16. E. D. Hill, *Northern Banking Company*, ditto Note 15.
17. Antrim Grand Jury, Resolutions Book, Lent 1852, a resolution extolling the benefits of railways, following the lead of Lord Enniskillen.
18. *Banner of Ulster*, 31 August 1852. Report of banquet in honour of Wm Sharman Crawford.
19. ibid. 3 January 1851.
20. ibid.
21. *Belfast 1858*, e.g. William Ewart examined paras 1824–60.

22. At the inquiry on the 1864 Belfast Improvement Bill, Wm Ewart agreed with John Rea that (para. 3347) Mr Bates "developed the franchise on his own side" and agreed that (para. 3961) the failure to collect the borough rate looked "suspicious", as the much bigger police rate was properly collected.
23. *Belfast 1858*, allegation of John Rea, not denied, para. 3173.
24. ibid. allegation of John Rea, not denied, paras 1950–64.
25. ibid. James Bristow, para. 7224.
26. ibid. John Clarke, opposition to the 1850 Bill, para. 3134.
27. Grand Jury for the County of Antrim, Resolution Book, Lent 1850, summer 1850. Grand Jury refuses a request from Bates to meet, discuss or provide further information to same.
28. *Belfast 1858*, Robert Lindsay, paras 1351–2, 1366, 1372 and 1390.
29. ibid. John Thomson, para. 8577.
30. ibid. John Suffern, paras 6464–98.
31. Grand Jury for the County of Antrim, Resolution Book, summer 1850, Lent 1853.
32. Incl. John Charters, James Cameron and others.
33. *Belfast Improvement Bill Inquiry 1864*, paras 2799–907; also *Belfast 1858*, paras 3820–3.
34. *Belfast 1858*, e.g. John Charters, para. 3888.
35. This is the inverse of the point in Note 33 above.
36. *Belfast 1858*, John Rea, para. 10774.
37. ibid. Bernard Hughes, paras 10157–62.
38. At *Belfast Improvement Bill Inquiry 1864*, William Ewart, when asked by Rea why he did not call a town meeting (paras 1745–50), received the following reply: "I knew that a town meeting would be turned into a bear garden by you." His feelings about Rea were widely shared.
39. See Note 36 above.
40. *Belfast 1858*, John F. Ferguson, paras 10080–2 and 10129.
41. ibid. William Dunville, paras 9681–2.
42. ibid. William Dunville, paras 9733–41.
43. *Belfast Riots 1858*, William Hamilton, paras 6688–94 and Belfast Improvement Bill Inquiry, Charles Lanyon, para. 865.
44. ibid. paras 925–49.
45. *Belfast 1858*, Report, 5–20.
46. ibid. Richard Waring, paras 5229–81.
47. ibid. James Cameron, para. 3477.
48. ibid. Hugh McLorinan, para. 6303.
49. ibid. para. 3620.
50. ibid. Montague Mulligan, paras 4174–7.
51. ibid. James Barnett, para. 9383, and Thomas Sinclair, paras 9576–95.
52. ibid. Edward Coey, para. 8064.
53. E. D. Hill, *The Northern Banking Company*, 132.
54. N. Simpson, *The Belfast Bank*, 82.
55. *Belfast Improvement Bill Inquiry*, Rea to Ewart, paras 2448–60; and to Lanyon, paras 969–1027.
56. *Belfast Improvement Bill Inquiry*, para. 3615. It transpires that in 1861 the whole of the town council membership including the large number of recently selected Liberals, and excluding very few of the whole forty, favoured the increase in the rate on low value property from 1/6 to 3/-.

57. This figure is arrived at from two sources. On 10 October 1862 the *Newsletter* published an analysis of the parliamentary electorate, showing 1,988 Conservatives and 1,082 Liberals. The *1865 Riots Report* has an estimate of 547 Catholics out of a parliamentary electorate of 3,420, from which a very rough estimate of 500 to 600 Protestant Liberals is in order, out of a Protestant electorate of 2,500–3,000.
58. See Note 56.
59. e.g. *Belfast Improvement Bill Inquiry*, Sir Charles Lanyon, para. 865 or Thomas Macknight, *Ulster as it is*.
60. *Ulster Observer*, 29 November 1862.
61. E. R. Norman, *The Catholic Church and Ireland in the Age of Rebellion* (London 1965) 53–68.
62. ibid. 31–3.
63. Vaughan's judgment that from about the early 1850s to the late 1870s there was a "significant re-distribution of the relative shares of total agricultural income received by landlords and tenants is indisputable and is evident from the feel of the popular press at the time". What Vaughan does not seem to think important are the social and political consequences of the insecurity of this material bounty. Vaughan 216, in Cullen and Smout, op. cit.
64. *Banner of Ulster*, 18 August 1855.
65. ibid. 6 August 1852.
66. *Ballymoney Free Press*, 2 December 1880.
67. From *1861 Census of Population, Part IV, Religious Professions, Education, and Occupations of the People*, 616. Out of Catholic children attending primary schools in Ulster, 5% were in Church education or parochial and 3% in endowed, making 8% in Anglican or other Protestant denominational establishments, compared to only 2% in Christian Brothers. All the rest were in National Schools.
68. From minutes of the half yearly meetings of the Grand Lodge of Ireland: the "offence" of "marrying papists" was either commoner or more frequently made the cause of expulsion in some areas rather than others. Taking 1853–70, 123 were expelled of whom 27 were from Antrim and Down before the formation of the Belfast Grand Lodge in 1864, and another 9 were from Belfast afterwards. Derry, Monaghan, Tyrone and Armagh lost 8 or 9 each. Fermanagh and Cavan lost 1 or none. Antrim lost 21 and Down 28 between 1864–70 which strongly suggests this "offence" was commoner amongst Presbyterians from the Presbyterian heartlands. In 1854 there was a spate of interesting ecumenical offences in County Antrim, mostly around Ballymena, including "introducing Papists to Lodges, attending Mass, conversion to Popery, making offerings to Popish priests ..."
69. *Ballymena Observer*, 21 May 1859.
70. ibid. 18 June 1859.
71. *Banner of Ulster*, 2 June 1859.
72. *Ballymena Observer*, 28 May and *Banner of Ulster* 16 July 1859.
73. *Ballymena Observer*, 21 May and 9 July 1859, Hanna at Cullybackey.
74. *Banner of Ulster*, 14 June 1859, at Glasgow's mill at Cookstown.
75. ibid. 14 June 1859, amongst companies of turf cutters at Ballyclare; and at harvest work at Faughanvale, *Banner of Ulster*, 27 August 1859.
76. *Banner of Ulster*, 16 June 1859, at Coleraine, where the *Chronicle* shut for the day for lack of staff.
77. *Banner of Ulster*, 27 September 1859.

78. Gibbon, *Ulster Unionism*, 57–8.
79. This problem is illustrated graphically by the "teetotallers' riot" in Belfast in June 1852 (*Belfast Newsletter*, 9 June 1852). After a rail excursion to Ballymena the TTs were met by a crowd of spectators on arrival back in Belfast and a riot mysteriously started between the police and the spectators—railways, drink, and the police all rolled into one!
80. *Banner of Ulster*, 13 September 1859, Address of Rev. Wm Breakey.
81. *Ballymena Observer*, 25 June, and *Banner of Ulster*, 13 September 1859.
82. *Banner of Ulster*, 14 June 1859.
83. *Ballymena Observer*, 2 July 1859.
84. *Banner of Ulster*, 20 September 1859.
85. See Rev. Breakey above, Note 80.
86. *Downshire Protestant*, 10 June 1859.
87. *Banner of Ulster*, 4, 9 June 1859.
88. Gibbon, op. cit. 63–4; David Miller, *Queen's Rebels*, 85.
89. Gibbon, ibid. 51.
90. *Banner of Ulster*, 14 June 1859.
91. ibid. 21 June 1859, and *Ballymena Observer*, 18 June 1859.
92. *Banner of Ulster*, 2 June 1859.
93. *Ballymena Observer*, 2, 16 July, *Banner of Ulster*, 14 July 1859.
94. *Banner of Ulster*, 27 August 1859.
95. ibid.
96. ibid. 4, 28 June 1859, claims about conversions.
97. ibid. 2 June 1859.
98. ibid. 25 August 1859.
99. ibid. 14 June 1859.
100. ibid. 9 June 1859.
101. ibid. 9, 14 June 1859.
102. *Downshire Protestant*, 10 June 1859.
103. *Ballymena Observer*, 28 May 1859.
104. ibid. 4 June 1859.
105. ibid. 18 June 1859.
106. ibid.
107. ibid. 25 June 1859.
108. ibid. 2 July 1859.
109. *Belfast Newsletter*, 28 April 1852.
110. *Ballymena Observer*, 9 July 1859.
111. E. R. Norman, op. cit. 53–68.
112. *Banner of Ulster*, 24 September 1859.
113. ibid. 22, 24 September 1859.
114. See evidence of Rowley Miller at *Devon 1845*, witness No. 146, paras 163–5; and the *Census of 1861* (see Note 67) Catholics in non-National, non-Catholic schools in Co. Derry were 14% of all Catholic pupils.
115. *Banner of Ulster*, 27 August, attack on the *Whig* for its defence of Mrs Costello in the case above, Note 98.
116. ibid. 14 June 1859.
117. *Ulster Observer*, 6 December 1864.

Chapter Nine.
Violence and the Law (pages 241–283)
1. These observations are somewhat impressionistic as they are based upon the *Belfast Street Directory*, which only gives one name and occupation per house. None the less considerable differences show up,

most notably the fact that, whereas there are ship carpenters listed in the Dock ward (i.e. North), there was hardly a single such entry for Sandy Row or the Shankill. West Belfast was without ship carpenters in 1868.
2. From *Census of Ireland for the year 1871, Occupations of the people, Appendix L—Occupations of Males by Ages, Religious Professions and Education, in the Borough of Belfast.*
3. *Report of the Commissioners of Inquiry into the Origin and Character of the Riots in Belfast in July and September, 1857,* H.C. 1857–8 [2309] XXVI, (cited hereafter as *Belfast Riots 1857*) 1–2.
4. Thomas Macknight, *Ulster as it is.*
5. State Paper Office, Dublin, registered and official papers relating to Orangeism, consisting of official correspondence concerning July anniversaries and related matters (cited hereafter as SPO), SPO 1866, 13001, 6 July 1866, Rev. Patrick O'Kane to Chief Secretary.
6. *Weekly Examiner,* 7 June 1873.
7. *Ulster Observer,* 20 September 1864, Rev. John MacNaughton's report to the peace committee.
8. As Note 2 for *Census.*
9. As Note 1 for the *Street Directory.*
10. *Outrages 1852,* Capt. Warburton, paras 125–6, 200–202; Capt. George Fitzmaurice, paras 765–8.
11. *Weekly Vindicator,* 10 July 1852.
12. *Belfast Riots 1857,* William Tracy, RM, para. 444.
13. ibid. John Smyth, house owner of Durham Street who received a threatening letter telling him to evict one of his tenants who it described as a Ribbon Master, paras 5925–29. The house was left alone in July but wrecked in September, see John Smith, paras 6014–15.
14. *Belfast Riots 1857,* George S. Hill, paras 7293–4.
15. *Outrages 1852.* This comment should be qualified in so far as Catholic clergy tended to explain ribbonism more in terms of opposing Orangeism than opposing landlords. The reason is that they (correctly) judged that there would be a more understanding attitude taken towards people provoked by Orangeism than towards people waging class war. For example, Rev. J. McMeel, P.P. Castleblaney, paras 3175–83. After giving this explanation of ribbonism in terms of opposition to Orangeism, he is unable to state whether at that moment there were any Orange societies in his parish.
16. *Outrages 1852,* Capt. Fitzmaurice (para. 567) vouches that Rev. Michael Lennon, P.P. Upper Creggan (Crossmaglen), did his utmost to put down ribbonism, but at the same time his lack of success is self-evident; and Rev. Lennon is later interrogated by the committee on account of the more sympathetic behaviour of his curates towards agrarian outrage (paras 5517–44, James O'Callaghan).
17. *Weekly Northern Whig,* 10 July 1868.
18. *Belfast Riots 1857,* Report, 4.
19. *Belfast Riots 1864,* Isaac Murphy, paras 3555–6.
20. *Belfast Riots 1857,* Capt. Thomas Verner, paras 10407–12.
21. *Belfast Riots 1864* contains in Appendix B, 359, Table A, a return respecting the Belfast borough police. This shows the birthplaces of the members of the 160 town policemen and their previous occupation as well as religion: 116 are listed as labourers, compared to 6 farmers; 40 came from the block of parishes with substantial catholic minorities of

over 20%, and out of these 24 came from Glenavy which was 45% Catholic; only one of the Catholics in the force came from this area, instead of, say, about 12–16. These facts render Capt. Verner's explanation unsatisfactory.

22. *Belfast Riots 1857*, Report, 4.
23. ibid.
24. *Belfast Riots 1857*, James Barnett, paras 10169–88.
25. ibid. Thomas Lindsay, para. 1083.
26. ibid. Thomas Lindsay, paras 4067–70.
27. ibid. McMaster, paras 5367–9; John McLaughlin, para, 4772.
28. ibid. Lindsay, paras 4073–5.
29. ibid. McGiveny, para. 10599.
30. ibid. McLaughlin, para. 4771.
31. ibid. Bindon, paras 1654–5.
32. ibid. Heaney, paras 2872–82.
33. ibid. Cardwell, paras 6968–70.
34. ibid. Rev. Martin, paras 3064/77/83 and 3115.
35. ibid. Ellen Grant, para. 6325; Ellen Crawford, paras 3528–9; John Smith, paras 6073–40.
36. *The Annals of the Christ Church. 1831–58* by Rev. Abraham Dawson, M.A. presented to Rev. Thomas Drew, D.D., Rector (PRONI, T 1075/11) entry for August 1852.
37. *Annals*, June 1853.
38. *Annals*, 23 May 1854.
39. *Annals* objectives: No. 7, enforcement of the existing laws for the protection of Protestantism; No. 12, repeal of the 1829 Catholic Emancipation Act.
40. *Belfast Riots 1857*, Watson, paras 5618–19.
41. ibid. Bindon, paras 1340–50.
42. ibid. McLaughlin, paras 4717, 4867–9.
43. ibid. Carolan, paras 3925–33, 3969, 3676–87; Cardwell, paras 6954–61, 6979–90; Faulkner, para. 7374; Heaney, paras 6816–26.
44. ibid. Green, paras 1985–8; Heaney, para. 2938.
45. ibid. Lindsay, paras 1066–8; Tracy, paras 94, 227–8.
46. ibid. The most striking clash of evidence is between Town Constable James Spence, paras 9273–402, and a young catholic, James McKenna, paras 5939–6000. In the town policeman's version of events Catholics attacked their side's houses. The question of whether or not there was a green arch in Mary Street became a matter of some importance to the rival legal council, if not to the commissioners, 223, para. 10527; also Bindon, paras 1642–51; and Lindsay, 807–15.
47. ibid. Ellen Crawford, paras 3470–522; Bindon, paras 1701–6; Tracy, paras 263–4.
48. ibid. Carolan, para. 3998; Green, paras 2442–8; Tracy, para. 236; Lindsay, paras 1027–8.
49. ibid. Kelly, paras 3672, 3713–60; Tracy, paras 242–3; Jones, paras 4200–13.
50. ibid. McGiveny, paras 10576–632.
51. ibid. Watson, para. 5579.
52. ibid. McLaughlin, para. 4825.
53. ibid Rev. McIlwaine, para. 2595.
54. ibid. Rev. McIlwaine, para. 2601.
55. ibid. Lindsay, para. 1175; Verner, para. 10400; McLaughlin, paras 4791–802.

56. ibid. Watson, para. 5632; Carolan, paras 4012–14; Bindon, paras 1797–805; McLaughlin, para. 4805.
57. ibid. Cummings, paras 5463–87; McCabe, paras 5182–91; McDowall, paras 5370–94.
58. ibid. Ellen Grant, paras 6251–340.
59. ibid. Sarah Charlewood, para. 9568; John Allen, paras 9016–25.
60. ibid. Biddy Burke, paras 5488–521.
61. ibid. Grant, paras 6251–340.
62. ibid. Mary Anne Donohue on John Russell, paras 3374–82.
63. ibid. Betty Donohue on David Rankin, paras 3342–3.
64. ibid. Ward, para. 8869.
65. ibid. Rev. Speers, paras 8279, 8295.
66. ibid. Thomas Verner, para. 10454.
67. *Report of the Commissioners of Inquiry, 1864, Respecting the Magisterial and Police Jurisdiction Arrangements and Establishment of the Borough of Belfast*, H.C. 1865, XXVIII [3466] (hereafter cited as *Belfast Riots 1864*); William Mullan, paras 10124–7.
68. *Belfast Riots 1864*, Dunville, paras 10487–8.
69. ibid. Hughes, paras 2420–4 and 2432.
70. *Ulster Observer*, 30 July 1864.
71. ibid. 13 August 1864.
72. *Banner of Ulster*, 6 August, and *Weekly Northern Whig*, 20 August 1864.
73. *Ulster Observer*, 13 August, and *Weekly Northern Whig*, 20 August 1864.
74. *Banner of Ulster*, 16 August 1864.
75. ibid. 16 August, and *Weekly Northern Whig*, 20 August 1864.
76. *Ulster Observer*, 16 August 1864.
77. ibid. 18 August 1864.
78. *Banner of Ulster*, 16, 18 August 1864.
79. ibid. 18 August 1864.
80. ibid. 20 August 1864.
81. *Weekly Northern Whig*, 20 August, and *Ulster Observer*, 18 August 1864.
82. *Banner of Ulster*, 18 August, and *Weekly Northern Whig*, 20 August 1864.
83. *Weekly Northern Whig*, 20 August 1864.
84. ibid.
85. *Ulster Observer*, 20 August, and *Banner of Ulster*, 18 August 1864.
86. *Weekly Northern Whig*, 20 August 1864.
87. *Belfast Riots 1864*, R. T. McGeagh, paras 8465–8.
88. ibid. John Thompson, para. 6347.
89. *Ulster Observer*, 2 July 1862 and 14 July 1864.
90. *Weekly Northern Whig*, 20 August 1864.
91. *Ulster Observer*, 16 August 1864.
92. *Banner of Ulster*, 20 August 1864.
93. ibid. 20, 23 August 1864.
94. ibid. 20 August 1864.
95. *Weekly Northern Whig*, 27 August 1864.
96. ibid.
97. *Ulster Observer*, 20 August 1864.
98. ibid. 17 September 1864.
99. *Banner of Ulster*, 23 August 1864.
100. ibid.
101. *Ulster Observer*, 20 August, and *Banner of Ulster*, 23 August 1864.
102. *Banner of Ulster*, 23 August 1864.
103. ibid. 25 August 1864.
104. *Weekly Northern Whig* and *Banner of Ulster*, 27 August 1864.

105. *Belfast Riots 1864*, Murphy, 83.
106. *Banner of Ulster*, 25 August 1864.
107. *Ulster Observer*, 17, 20 September 1864.
108. *Banner of Ulster*, 25 August 1864.
109. *Weekly Northern Whig*, 27 August 1864.
110. *Ulster Observer*, 20 September, and *Weekly Northern Whig*, 17, 24 September 1864.
111. *Ulster Observer*, 20 September 1864.
112. ibid.
113. ibid.
114. *Weekly Northern Whig*, 20 August 1864.
115. *Banner of Ulster*, 3 June 1865.
116. ibid. 15 June 1865.
117. SPO, OP 1864, No. 34, Major Esmonde to Insp. Gen., 31 August 1864.
118. SPO, 1865, 2012 and 2148, Sub Inspector Harvey to Insp. Gen., 27 February 1865.
119. SPO, 1865, s792.
120. *Reports of the Grand Lodge of Ireland 1864/5*.
121. *Weekly Northern Whig*, 13 March 1869.
122. *Ulster Observer*, 20 July 1865.
123. ibid. 20 July 1865.
124. ibid. 29 July 1865.
125. *Banner of Ulster*, 29 July 1865.
126. *Ulster Observer*, 10 March 1866.
127. ibid. 10 March 1866.
128. *Northern Star*, 6 June 1868.
129. *Weekly Northern Whig*, 11 July 1868.
130. *Northern Star*, 16 July, and *Omagh News and Tyrone Advertizer*, 25 July 1868.
131. *Northern Star*, 6 August 1868.
132. ibid. 9 March 1869.
133. *Ulster Examiner*, 3 July 1869.
134. *Weekly Northern Whig*, 7 August 1869.
135. *Northern Star* 5, 23, 30 January, and *Ulster Examiner*, 20 March 1869.
136. A. M. Sullivan, *New Ireland*, 237–8.
137. E. R. Norman, op. cit. Chapter 3, esp. 117.
138. SPO 1866, 11730.
139. *Dungannon Commission of Inquiry*, H.C. 1871, XX, General Report.
140. ibid.
141. *Dungannon Commission of Inquiry*, evidence of Dr David Mooney and John Hayden.
142. SPO 1866, 13295, Hon. Stewart Knox, M.P. to Chief Sec.
143. *Dungannon Commission of Inquiry*, evidence of Hon. S. Knox and Rev. F. Devlin, P.P.
144. *Ulster Observer*, 19 March 1867.
145. *Weekly Northern Whig*, 23 March 1867.
146. *Ulster Observer*, 21 March 1867.
147. *Weekly Northern Whig*, 25 March 1867, *Report of the Government Inquiry into the County Tyrone Magistracy*.
148. SPO 1867, 14795, Cecil Moore to Larcom.
149. *Dungannon Commission of Inquiry*, Father F. Devlin.
150. SPO 1867, 13343, Capt. Plunkett, RM to Larcom.
151. SPO 1868, 8994, Ryan, RM to Larcom.

152. SPO 1868, 8477, Rev. Michael Conway, P.P., petition to Lord Lt.
153. SPO 1867, 11775, Rev. Hugh McLean, P.P. to RM
154. SPO 1868, 12663, Magee to Solicitor General.
155. SPO 1868, 8738, Rev. John O'Brien, P.P. Banbridge, to Larcom, 3 July 1868.
156. SPO 1868, 12663, Magee to Solicitor General.
157. *Northern Whig*, 7 August 1868.
158. *Omagh News and Tyrone Advertizer*, 22 December 1866.
159. SPO, 1867, 12316, Capt. Butler, RM to Larcom, 15 July 1867.
160. *Omagh News and Tyrone Advertizer*, 25 July 1868.

Chapter Ten.
Belfast 1868—Expectations of Democracy (pages 284–332)

1. *Banner of Ulster*, 2 December 1865, notably F. H. Lewis is missing.
2. ibid.
3. ibid. 18 February 1864.
4. ibid. 25 June, 19 November 1864, and *Ulster Observer*, 19 July 1864; report of the council meeting at which the proposal to create a collector-general of taxes, in accordance with undertakings given to secure the Indemnity Bill, was rejected by vote of the councillors.
5. *Banner of Ulster*, 8 December 1864; *Weekly Northern Whig*, 17 June 1865.
6. Antrim Grand Jury, Resolutions Book, spring and summer 1865.
7. *Ulster Observer*, 21 February 1867, the police rate fell from 3/8d to 2/- between 1865 and 1867.
8. *Weekly Northern Whig*, 20 October 1866.
9. ibid. 27 October 1866.
10. ibid. 1 December 1866.
11. *Ulster Observer*, 19 February 1867, letter from Samuel Tierney.
12. *Weekly Northern Whig*, 2 March 1867.
13. ibid. 18 May 1867.
14. ibid. 25th May 1867.
15. ibid. 6 July 1867.
16. ibid. 7 December 1867.
17. ibid. 26 October 1872, sale of Samuel Tierney's estate.
18. ibid. 22 June 1867.
19. ibid.
20. *Reports of the Grand Lodge of Ireland, December 1867*, half yearly meeting, debate on the appeal of Tom Henry against his expulsion from the Order by the Belfast CGL for "taking part in public meetings and otherwise with Radicals, Papists and Rebels".
21. *Weekly Northern Whig*, 9, 16 November 1867.
22. *Ulster Observer*, 21, 26 November 1867.
23. *Belfast Riots 1864*, Bernard Hughes, para. 2475.
24. *Ulster Observer*, 6 December 1864.
25. *Belfast Riots 1864*, William Kirkpatrick, paras 12211–12.
26. ibid. Peter Hoey, statement, 342.
27. In 1866 there were strikes by, for example, carpenters and joiners, railway pointsmen, stonecutters, quay labourers, bakers and bricklayers. It was stated that it was the bricklayers who usually took the lead in general wage pushes.
28. *Weekly Northern Whig*, 24 May 1864, 14 January 1865 (for liquidation proceedings).

29. ibid. 12 August 1865.
30. ibid. 24 August 1867
31. ibid. 30 November 1867.
32. ibid.
33. ibid. 14 December 1867.
34. ibid. 4 January 1868.
35. ibid. 29 February 1868.
36. ibid. 7 December 1867.
37. ibid. 7 November 1868.
38. ibid. 14 November 1863.
39. E. R. Norman, *The Catholic Church and Ireland in the Age of Rebellion 1859–73* (London 1965) Chapter 4, 135–89.
40. Norman, 151 & 14, 29.
41. *Ulster Observer*, 4 July, and *Banner of Ulster*, 13 July 1865.
42. *Banner of Ulster*, 13 July 1865.
43. *Ulster Observer*, 26 November 1867.
44. *Banner of Ulster*, 26 March 1864; *Belfast Riots 1864*, John Thompson, paras 6288–9, and Appendix, Table E, 363.
45. *Belfast Riots 1864*, Appendix, Table E, 364.
46. *Banner of Ulster*, 12 May 1864.
47. E. R. Norman, 198, James Cuming, MD had been to QCB.
48. *Ulster Examiner*, 22 February 1870.
49. *Ulster Observer*, 30 July 1864.
50. *Belfast Street Directory 1868*, for south Shankill and Old Lodge districts.
51. *Carrickfergus Freeman*, 30 September 1865.
52. ibid.
53. *Weekly Northern Whig*, 23 September 1865.
54. Leighton, *Freemansonry in Northern Ireland*, three members of the Lodge of Friendship, No. 447, Newtownards, 22 October 1865.
55. *Weekly Northern Whig*, 11 November 1865, Alex Darragh (Ballycastle) and John Magee (Dromore).
56. ibid. 5 January 1867.
57. ibid. 16 March 1867.
58. ibid. 9 May 1868.
59. E. R. Norman, 210; and rather uninformative reports of the liquidation; *Ulster Observer*, 18 November and 5 December 1865.
60. *Carrickfergus Freeman*, 11 November 1865.
61. *Northern Star*, 23 March 1869.
62. *Ulster Observer*, 11 November 1865.
63. *Banner of Ulster*, 3 March, 5, 7 April 1864.
64. ibid. 8 April 1865.
65. Norman, op. cit. 198/9.
66. *Weekly Northern Whig*, February 1866, and *Banner of Ulster*, 10 February 1866.
67. *Weekly Northern Whig*, 10 February 1866.
68. ibid.
69. Norman, op. cit. 229–31.
70. ibid. 234–9.
71. *Ulster Observer*, 16 October 1866.
72. *Banner of Ulster*, 18 October 1866.
73. *Ulster Observer*, 17 January 1867.
74. *Banner of Ulster*, 17 January 1867.
75. *Ulster Observer*, 19 January 1867.
76. Norman, op. cit. 245.

77. *Londonderry Standard*, 18 September 1867.
78. *Banner of Ulster*, 1 October 1867.
79. ibid. 31 March 1868.
80. ibid.
81. *Londonderry Standard*, 1 April 1868.
82. *Northern Star*, 31 March 1868.
83. Norman, op. cit. 256–81.
84. ibid. Chapter 7, 282–352.
85. *Ulster Observer*, 9 July 1863, a eulogy of Rogers on the occasion of his installation as moderator.
86. Norman, op. cit. 297.
87. *Weekly Northern Whig*, 21 September 1867.
88. ibid. 2 November 1867.
89. *Banner of Ulster*, 11 February 1868.
90. ibid. 31 March 1868.
91. ibid. 25 April 1868.
92. ibid. 12 May 1868.
93. *Londonderry Standard*, 6 June 1868.
94. *Weekly Northern Whig*, 6 June 1868 (full report taken from here).
95. *1868 Belfast Election Poll Book*.
96. In the following Presbyteries, there was one vote for Kirkpatrick and all others for Dill. Ballybay 7; Bailieborough 4; Omagh 5; Dungannon 3.
97. *Londonderry Standard*, 18 July 1868.
98. *Banner of Ulster*, 25 July 1868.
99. ibid. 24 September 1868.
100. ibid. 14 November 1868.
101. *Weekly Northern Whig*, 9 May 1868.
102. *Ulster Examiner*, 14 September 1869.
103. *The Diaries of William Johnston*, 6 June 1847.
104. ibid. 12 February 1847, extract from a letter of Rev. J. D. Hill.
105. ibid. 31 December 1847.
106. ibid. 17 December 1847.
107. ibid. 28 March 1848.
108. ibid. 2 March 1848.
109. ibid. 14 May 1850.
110. e.g. 1 July 1850 (dinner for the lodge); 5 June 1851, a confirmation class; 5 January 1852, a lodge meeting "a pleasant fraternal evening".
111. ibid. 5 August 1851.
112. ibid. 10 November 1854.
113. *Weekly Examiner*, 12 October 1872.
114. *The Diaries of William Johnston*, 28 March 1851.
115. ibid. 11 January 1857.
116. ibid. 13 November 1860.
117. *Weekly Northern Whig*, 17 November 1860.
118. *Belfast Newsletter*, 15 May 1861.
119. *The Diaries of William Johnston*, 22 September 1850.
120. ibid. 24 April 1866.
121. ibid. 6 July 1866.
122. ibid. 7, 10 July 1866.
123. ibid. 24 March 1867.
124. *Ulster Observer*, 15 August 1867; see also the debate at the Grand Lodge of Ireland in June 1868, held in Lord Enniskillen's absence, where Johnston's breach of the ban in July 1867 is discussed.
125. *Weekly Northern Whig*, 20 July 1867.

126. ibid.
127. *Londonderry Sentinel*, on how Lord Dufferin helped to get up the address but then opposed the "partial" imposition of the PPA against Northern Orangeism because Fenians got away with marching elsewhere; see also Note 130 below.
128. SPO, 1867, 15885, William Johnston to Chief Sec.
129. *Banner of Ulster*, 5 September 1867.
130. *Weekly Northern Whig*, 21 September 1867.
131. ibid. 2 May 1868.
132. *Banner of Ulster*, 31 October 1867.
133. *The Diaries of William Johnston*, 10 February 1868.
134. *Banner of Ulster*, 3 March 1868.
135. *Northern Star*, 3 March 1868.
136. *Ulster Observer*, 13 July and 17 August 1867.
137. *Banner of Ulster*, 5 March 1868.
138. A. M. Sullivan, *New Ireland*, 276.
139. E. R. Norman, 120–34.
140. A. M. Sullivan, 294–5.
141. *Weekly Northern Whig*, 7 March 1868.
142. *Northern Star*, 5 March 1868.
143. *Standard*, 7 March 1868.
144. *Weekly Northern Whig*, 19 September 1868, see the letter from Dr Drew to Isaac Butt. Here he spells out how his change of view on the land question is the result of personal experience. See also *Orangeism, its History and Progress*, Independent Orange Order, 33.
145. *Northern Star*, 14 March 1868.
146. *Londonderry Standard*, 21 March 1868.
147. *Banner of Ulster*, 12 September 1868; see also *Belfast Election*, 21 and 28 October 1868.
148. *Weekly Northern Whig*, 30 May 1868. The impression made by PWMA's repudiatation of Flynn, the Murphite preacher, can be seen by contrasting the *Ulster Examiner* of 14 May 1868 with the same paper two months later. See also the *Northern Star*, 25 June 1868.
149. *Report of the half yearly meeting of the Grand Lodge of Ireland*, June 1868.
150. *Northern Star*, 20 October 1868.
151. *Weekly Northern Whig*, 11 July 1868.
152. *Belfast Newsletter*, 16 October 1868.
153. *Weekly Northern Whig*, 18 July 1868.
154. *The Diaries of William Johnston*, 14 May 1868.
155. ibid. 14 September 1868.
156. *Belfast Newsletter*, 2 October 1868.
157. *Weekly Northern Whig*, 7 November 1868.
158. ibid. 31 October 1868.
159. *Belfast Newsletter*, 5 November 1868.
160. What Johnston said about the Fenian prisoners is uncertain. What is certain is that whatever he did say was not heard loud and clear. If it had been it is inconceivable that the Conservative organ, the *Belfast Election*, would have let it pass without mentioning it. It is also very improbable that the two Catholic papers would have delayed stating the fact until after the poll. But that is what is alleged to have happened. See *Northern Star*, 2 November 1869; *Ulster Examiner*, 10 August 1869.
161. *Belfast Election*, 7 November 1868.

548 TWO LANDS ON ONE SOIL

162. *Weekly Northern Whig*, 17 October 1868.
163. ibid.
164. ibid. 30 January 1869, Report of proceedings of *Belfast Election* Petition, evidence of John Clarke.
165. *Ulster Examiner*, 15 September 1868.
166. *Londonderry Standard*, 23, 28 November 1868.
167. *Weekly Northern Whig*, 1 May 1869. Presbyterians in Newry divided 30 Liberals to 194 Conservatives in 1868.
168. ibid. Presbyterians in L'derry divided 177 Liberals to 284 Conservatives in 1868.
169. *The Diaries of William Johnston*, 30 December 1868, record a "clean sweep" and satisfaction with Stewart Blacker who presided over the election. Johnston had already been elected Grand Master in November.
170. *Ulster Examiner*, 21 November 1868.
171. *Northern Star*, 21 November 1868.
172. *Ulster Examiner*, 21 November 1868.
173. The material for this electoral survey is drawn from the printed *1868* and *1865 Poll Books*, together with the *1868 Street Directory*. Also used were the bank histories (Hill and Simpson), the Reports of the General Assembly and the Report of the *Election* petition in *Weekly Northern Whig*, 30 January 1869.

Chapter Eleven.
Belfast 1869–1874—Democracy and Disillusion (pages 333–382)

1. *Banner of Ulster*, 15 June 1865.
2. See Chapter 9, MacNaughton at the peace meetings after the 1864 riots.
3. *Newsletter*, 28 September 1872.
4. *Weekly Northern Whig*, 7 September 1872
5. ibid. 14 January 1871.
6. *Weekly Examiner* and *Ulster Observer*, 7 June 1873.
7. See Note 4 above and *Weekly Examiner*, 24 August 1872.
8. e.g. *Weekly Examiner*, 7 December 1872, 16 November 1872, 23 August 1873. *Newsletter*, 1 October 1872 and especially *Newsletter*, 9 April 1883, obituary of James Alex Henderson, Mayor of Belfast in 1873, quoting from the (nationalist) *Morning News*.
9. *Ulster Observer*, 24 May 1870; *Weekly Examiner*, 4 February 1871.
10. *Weekly Northern Whig*, 17 June 1871.
11. ibid. 23 June 1871.
12. ibid. 9 December 1871.
13. *Belfast Times*, 26 January 1872.
14. *Weekly Northern Whig*, 28 May 1870.
15. Derived from the *1868 Election Poll Book* and the *Report of the Grand Lodge of Belfast 1876–7*; also from the records of Orange Protestant Working Men's Association in 1872 (see *Belfast Times*).
16. *Ballymoney Free Press*, 26 June 1873.
17. *Weekly Northern Whig*, 20 August 1870.
18. *Belfast Times*, 12 July 1872.
19. *Northern Star*, 7 January 1869.
20. *Downpatrick Recorder*, 14 July 1866.
21. *Newsletter*, 28 September 1877.
22. *Northern Star* and *Ulster Observer*, 14 July 1870; *Weekly Observer* and *Northern Advertiser*, 3 June 1871.

23. Weekly Northern Whig, 11 December 1869.
24. ibid. 4 September 1869.
25. ibid. 11 September and 13 November 1869.
26. ibid. 25 December 1869.
27. ibid. 20 August 1870.
28. Newsletter, 4 February 1874.
29. This estimate is constructed using the record membership of the Belfast Grand Lodge and the associated private lodges available for 1876–7, comparing these with the lists of lodges attending the "Johnstonite", 12 July 1872, when there was a choice of venues available. It is cross-checked against the officers of lodges present at OPWMA meetings as reported in the Belfast Times.
30. Weekly Northern Whig, 28 November 1868.
31. Northern Star, 2 January 1869.
32. The Diaries of William Johnston, 9, 30 December. It is clear that Johnston had very great trust in Stewart Blacker, despite his having moved "severe" resolutions against him over the Bangor march (see 4 December 1867).
33. Weekly Northern Whig, 31 October 1868 (the chaplains controversy) and 9 January (the reballot).
34. ibid. 30 January 1869, report of the Amalgamated Districts, where it is decided that exercise of the franchise should not be interfered with.
35. Newsletter, 19, 25, 27 February; 4, 9, 11, 12 March; reports of lodges calling for action to be taken against McClure voters and recipients of Radical money.
36. Weekly Northern Whig, 13 February 1869.
37. ibid. 1 January 1870.
38. ibid. 6 August 1870. The method used to fight the battle inside the Order was to create new districts with the right to have their officers as voting members of the Belfast Grand Lodge. The report here is of E.S.W. DeCobain's efforts to set up District 7 as part of the anti-Johnston forces, by peeling some lodges off District 2. When these No. 7 votes were used to defeat Johnston in December 1870, they were disqualified on appeal to the GLI (see Weekly Northern Whig, 4 February 1871). The Johnstonites tried to get up a rival No. 8 District based on Queen's Island (see Weekly Northern Whig, 8 April 1871).
39. Ulster Examiner, 9 August 1869.
40. The following communications to the Castle concern the threat to burn down the new chapel in Ardoyne, the mob gathering in response to the rumour in order to defend it and the priest assuring the people of the Pound that the authorities would protect it, SPO 1869, 10491, O'Donnell, RM 10 July; SPO 1869, 10275, Inspector Bailey to Insp. Gen., 13 July; SPO 1869, 10244, Orme, RM 13 July; and SPO 1869, 10823. 41 SPO 1869, 10444, 15 July, Inspector Bailey on how Conway Street National School was wrecked.
42. Besides Hugh Hanna, there was Hans Woods and Samuel McComb, also Henry Henderson, from reports of the Grand Lodge of Ireland where they are listed as Deputy Grand Chaplains for Belfast.
43. Weekly Northern Whig, 9 October 1869.
44. ibid.
45. ibid. 17 April 1869.
46. ibid. 29 January 1870.
47. ibid. 3 April 1869.

48. ibid. 20 March 1869.
49. ibid. 3 April 1869.
50. *Northern Star*, 5 June 1869.
51. *Weekly Northern Whig*, 27 November 1869.
52. ibid. 4 December 1869 and 1 January 1870.
53. ibid. 1 January 1870.
54. *Ulster Examiner*, 23 November 1869.
55. *Northern Star*, 25 May 1869.
56. *Weekly Northern Whig*, 11 December 1869.
57. ibid. 4 June 1870.
58. ibid. 25 June 1870, and *Ulster Examiner*, 23 June 1870.
59. *Weekly Northern Whig*, 2 July 1870.
60. *Ulster Examiner*, 4 June 1870.
61. *Northern Star* and *Ulster Observer*, 14 July 1870.
62. *Northern Star* and *Ulster Observer*, 5 November 1870.
63. *Daily Examiner*, 24 November 1870; *Northern Star* and *Ulster Observer*, 24, 26 November 1870.
64. *Weekly Northern Whig*, 3 December 1870.
65. *Northern Star* and *Ulster Observer*, 13 December 1870.
66. ibid. 15 December 1870.
67. *Weekly Northern Whig*, 10 December 1870.
68. ibid. 14 January 1871.
69. *Weekly Examiner*, 14 January 1871.
70. *Weekly Northern Whig*, 4 February 1871.
71. ibid. 17 June 1871.
72. ibid. 15 July 1871.
73. ibid. 9 December 1871.
74. ibid.
75. *Weekly Examiner*, 16 December 1871.
76. *Weekly Observer* and *Northern Advertiser*, 25 November 1871.
77. *Belfast Times*, 1 January 1872.
78. ibid. 1 March 1872.
79. *Weekly Observer* and *Northern Advertiser*, 23 March 1872.
80. *Belfast Times*, 23 February 1872.
81. *Weekly Northern Whig*, 15 July 1871.
82. *Belfast Times*, 25 March 1872.
83. *Weekly Examiner* and *Weekly Northern Whig*, 18 May 1872.
84. *Belfast Times*, 24 May 1872.
85. *Weekly Northern Whig*, 17 August 1872.
86. *Belfast Times*, 6 August 1872.
87. *Northern Star*, 20 March 1869, St Patrick's Day meeting of clergy from Monaghan, south Armagh and south Down indicating their confidence in McKenna at the time of his worst conflict with the *Examiner*.
88. Thomas Macknight, *Ulster as it is*.
89. Rev. Denis Rushe, *Historic Sketches of Monaghan* (Dublin 1895).
90. *Northern Star*, 6 February 1868.
91. *Ulster Observer*, 19 November and 7 December 1867.
92. See Note 160, Chapter 10.
93. *Northern Star*, 16, 23 January 1869.
94. *Ulster Examiner*, 18 February 1869.
95. ibid.
96. *Northern Star*, 23 February 1869.
97. *Ulster Examiner*, 25 February 1869.
98. *Weekly Northern Whig*, 7 August 1869.

99. *Northern Star*, 2 October 1869.
100. ibid.
101. ibid. 5 October 1869.
102. ibid. 23 October 1869.
103. ibid. 25 January 1870.
104. ibid. 4 November 1869 and *Weekly Northern Whig*, 13 November 1869.
105. ibid. 27 November 1869.
106. *Ulster Examiner*, 27 November 1869.
107. *Northern Star*, 4 January 1870.
108. ibid. 15, 25 January 1870.
109. ibid. 1 March 1870.
110. *Ulster Examiner*, 31 March 1870.
111. ibid. 5 November 1870.
112. *Northern Star* and *Ulster Observer*, 20 December 1870.
113. *Daily Examiner*, 15 December 1870.
114. *Weekly Northern Whig*, 14 January 1877.
115. *Daily Examiner*, 18 November 1870.
116. *Weekly Northern Whig*, 19 November 1870.
117. *Weekly Examiner*, 9 December 1871.
118. *Weekly Observer* and *Northern Advertiser*, 9 December 1871.
119. *Belfast Times*, 31 January 1872.
120. *Londonderry Standard*, 2 November 1872.
121. *Belfast Times*, 24 January 1872.
122. E. R. Norman, op. cit. 416–30.
123. *Daily Examiner*, 17 April 1872, Rev. M. H. Cahill, editor of the *Examiner*, was present but very few of the Catholic elite. The main figures were Joe Biggar and Rev. Isaac Nelson.
124. *Weekly Observer* and *Northern Advertiser*, 9 November 1872.
125. ibid. 22 June 1872.
126. *Weekly Examiner*, 27 July 1872.
127. Antrim County Grand Jury, Resolutions Book, summer 1872, a unanimous resolution supporting Justice Keogh.
128. *Weekly Examiner*, 27 July 1872.
129. ibid. 29 June 1872.
130. *Weekly Northern Whig*, 17 August 1872.
131. ibid. 26 October 1872.
132. *Banner of Ulster*, 21 May 1867.
133. *Weekly Examiner*, 18 February 1871, Report of Belfast Chamber of Commerce.
134. *Ulster Examiner*, 19 September 1868.
135. *Northern Star*, 10 July 1868.
136. *Weekly Northern Whig*, 25 September 1869.
137. ibid. 13 November 1869.
138. Trade delegates meeting, *Northern Whig*, March 1865.
139. *Census of Ireland for the year 1871, Province of Ulster, Occupations of the people, Appendix L Occupations of Males by Ages, Religious Professions and Education in the Borough of Belfast*, 146/7.
140. *Weekly Northern Whig*, 21 May 1870.
141. ibid.
142. *Weekly Observer* and *Northern Advertiser*, 22 April 1871.
143. *Weekly Northern Whig*, 22 April 1871.
144. *Weekly Observer* and *Northern Advertiser*, 29 April 1871.
145. *Weekly Northern Whig*, 11 November 1871.

146. *Belfast Times*, 4 January 1872.
147. *Weekly Examiner*, 18 May 1872.
148. ibid. 25 September 1871.
149. *Belfast Times*, 29 May 1872.
150. *Weekly Observer* and *Northern Advertiser*, 8 June 1872.
151. ibid.
152. *Weekly Examiner*, 18 May 1872.
153. *Belfast Times*, 30 May 1872; *Weekly Northern Whig*, 30 May 1872.
154. *Belfast Times*, 14 June 1872.
155. *Weekly Observer* and *Northern Advertiser*, 22 June 1872.
156. ibid.
157. *Belfast Times*, 8 July 1872.
158. *Weekly Observer* and *Northern Advertiser* and *Weekly Northern Whig*, 17 August 1872.
159. *Weekly Observer* and *Northern Advertiser*, 24 August 1872.
160. ibid.
161. *Weekly Examiner*, 24 August 1872.
162. McTier Street, from *1868 Poll Book* and *Street Directory*. Shoe making was at that time being mechanised, see *Weekly Examiner*, 25 September 1872.
163. *Weekly Northern Whig*, 14 September 1872.
164. Leeson Street, as for Note 162.
165. *Weekly Northern Whig*, 21 September 1872.
166. *Weekly Examiner*, 24 August 1872.
167. ibid. 28 September 1872.
168. *Weekly Observer* and *Northern Advertiser*, 31 August 1872.
169. ibid. 17, 24 August 1872.
170. See Chapter 9 for previous mention of this.
171. *Newsletter*, 1 October 1872.
172. *Weekly Examiner*, 12 October 1872.
173. ibid. 16 November 1872; for further details see Chapter 12.
174. *Weekly Northern Whig*, 23 November 1872.
175. *Weekly Examiner*, 30 November 1872.
176. ibid. 7 December 1872.
177. *Newsletter*, 9 April 1883, Henderson's obituary and extract from the *Morning News*.
178. *Weekly Northern Whig*, 8 March 1873.
179. ibid.
180. *Ulster Weekly News*, *Weekly Examiner* and *Ulster Observer*, 7 June 1873.
181. *Weekly Examiner* and *Ulster Observer*, 23 August 1873.
182. *Weekly Northern Whig*, 29 November 1873.
183. *Weekly Examiner* and *Ulster Observer*, 29 November 1873.
184. *Weekly Northern Whig*, *Weekly Examiner* and *Ulster Observer*, 31 January 1874.
185. *Newsletter*, 24 January 1874.
186. *Weekly Northern Whig*, 31 January 1874.
187. *Ulster Weekly News*, 5 December 1874.

Chapter Twelve.
The Region Beyond Belfast (pages 383–431)

1. *Ballymoney Free Press*, 4 December 1873.
2. *Agricultural Statistics, Ireland*, The Flax acreage in Ulster (in thousands of acres) rose from 85 (1850); 160 (1853) peak; 88 (1855) trough; 143

(1861); 207 (1863); 278 (1864) peak; 192 (1868); 115 (1872). In some counties the fall from 1864 to 1872 was very steep: Antrim 35 to 10; Armagh 32 to 7è.
3. *Weekly Examiner*, 22 June 1872, emigration from Maghera was then at its highest since 1847.
4. *Agricultural Statistics, Ireland*, 1852, 1862, 1872.
5. *Bessborough 1881*, Samuel McElroy, paras 4480–2.
6. For example, SPO 1869, 10222, 13 July, from Hamilton, RM in Portglenone, mentions the threat of RCs firing on Orangemen, because they claim that Orangemen are in the habit of firing after dark. He speaks of "a reckless and indiscriminate use of firearms, so incessant as to resemble volley firing".
7. *Weekly Northern Whig*, 10 September 1870.
8. *Local Government and Taxation of Towns Inquiry Commission (Ireland)*, H.C. 1877, [C-1696] Part 1 and [C-1787] Part 3, hereafter referred to as *Towns Inquiry 1877*. Part 1 284, Lisburn, para. 2. It is here stated that Lisburn has increased from 9,000 to about 11,000 between the 1871 Census and the 1877 Inquiry. See also on population changes, *Census of Ireland 1871*, H.C. 1874, LXXIV, Part 1, Increase 1861–71, Lurgan 37%; Lisburn 18%; Portadown 22%; Banbridge 39%; but the relationship is far from straightforward. Ballymena 41% was relatively free of sectarian trouble.
9. *Weekly Northern Whig*, 17 July 1869.
10. *Ulster Examiner*, 3 August 1869.
11. SPO 1869, 10312.
12. *Weekly Northern Whig*, 17 July 1869.
13. SPO 1869, 10199, report from Sub Insp. Burke; and SPO 1869, 9693, enclosed petition from Rev. O'Loughlin, P.P. Desertmartin[?], to Lord-Lt about the Desertmartin arch.
14. SPO 1869, 10220, Beckett, RM.
15. SPO 1869, 10099, Cronin, RM.
16. SPO 1869, 10290, Butler, RM.
17. *Weekly Northern Whig*, 17 July 1869.
18. *Northern Star*, 4 November 1869.
19. *Weekly Northern Whig*, 6 November 1869.
20. ibid. 27 November 1869.
21. *Ulster Examiner*, 27, 30, November 1869.
22. *Weekly Northern Whig*, 21 September 1867.
23. See Chapter 13 for more on the Johnston amendment to the 1870 Land Bill.
24. *Ulster Examiner*, 10 August 1869.
25. *Northern Star*, 7 August 1869.
26. *Weekly Northern Whig*, 14 August 1869.
27. ibid.
28. ibid.
29. *Ulster Examiner*, 5 September 1868.
30. *Weekly Examiner*, 15 July 1871.
31. See *Belfast* and *Ulster Street Directory 1868* for occupations of people in this account of Lisburn.
32. *Reports of the half yearly meetings of the Grand Lodge of Ireland, November 1853*. More expulsions arising from this election also at May 1854 and November 1854 meetings.
33. ibid. May 1857 meeting.
34. *Banner of Ulster*, 19 January 1864.

35. *Weekly Northern Whig*, 16 May 1863.
36. *Ulster Observer*, 14 July 1863.
37. *Weekly Northern Whig*, 30 April 1864, Richardson presides over a meeting of the Association of Bleachers, Finishers and Linen Merchants of Ireland, concerned to oppose the extensions of the Factory Acts to include lapping rooms and warehouses. *Weekly Northern Whig*, 16 September 1865, the association passes a resolution expressing thanks for "valuable service" of Verner, Cairns and Getty.
38. *Report of Grand Lodge 1864*.
39. On this election, see two publications produced shortly after the 21 February election that was overturned: John Rea, *List of Voters* at the Lisburn election held on 21 February 1863, with a few observations thereon; and Alex McCann, *Lisburn Election, 1863*.
40. *Banner of Ulster*, 20 February 1864.
41. *Weekly Northern Whig*, 2 April 1864.
42. Cross-reference *Lisburn Poll Book 1863* and TCs from *Belfast* and *Ulster 1868 Directory*.
43. *Weekly Northern Whig*, 27 February 1864.
44. *Banner of Ulster*, 29 July 1865.
45. See Note 42.
46. *Northern Star*, 21 August 1869; *Weekly Northern Whig*, 28 August 1869.
47. *Weekly Northern Whig*, 10 September 1870.
48. SPO 1871, 13209, report of magistrates meeting, encloses letter of Rev. Kelly, P.P. to magistrates.
49. *Weekly Observer* and *Northern Advertiser*, 24 August 1872.
50. *Weekly Northern Whig*, 5 April 1873.
51. ibid. 22 February 1873.
52. *Towns Inquiry 1877*, Part 1, Appendix 41, 530.
53. ibid. Part 1, Lisburn, 288, paras 169–71 and 196–220, also paras 85–6.
54. *Municipal Corporations 1835, Appendix to the First Report of the Commissioners*, Part I, 678.
55. *Ulster Observer*, 9 July 1863.
56. *Towns Inquiry 1877*, Part 1, Armagh, Appendix No. 38, 530.
57. *Census of Ireland 1871*, H.C. 1874, LXXIV, Armagh population falls from 9,468 to 8,946 between 1861 and 1871.
58. From the *Census of Population 1861*. There was a large imbalance of males to females in Lurgan (0.84:1) and Portadown (0.88:1); and in Portadown it was very different between Protestants (0.92:1) and Catholics (0.81:1).
59. *Town Inquiry 1877*, Part 3, Portadown, 67, para. 250, Dr William Stewart.
60. *Portadown and Lurgan News* and *Armagh Advertiser*, 12 July 1873.
61. *Towns Inquiry 1877*, Part 3, Portadown, 67, para. 258, John Eccles, Petty Sessions Clerk.
62. ibid., Part 1, 531, Appendix No. 43, cross-checked against political meetings in Lurgan in the 1870s.
63. ibid., Part 3, 350, Appendix No. 1, cross-checked against political meetings in Portadown in the 1870s. *Ulster Examiner*, 22 February 1870, Father Hughes's problem was that he had got the sites for the schools but would lose them if the buildings were not erected by a deadline. "Should the ground be lost it is needless to say that no amount of money would suffice to repurchase it . . . [it was] . . . vital to the existence of catholicity in Portadown."

64. *Weekly Northern Whig*, 10 July 1869 and *Ulster Examiner*, 3 July 1869.
65. *Weekly Northern Whig*, 17 July 1869.
66. ibid. 10 July and *Ulster Examiner*, 8 July 1869.
67. *Ulster Examiner*, 14 September 1869.
68. *Weekly Northern Whig*, 17 July 1869, and *Ulster Examiner*, 3 August 1869.
69. *Weekly Northern Whig*, 10 September and 19 November 1870.
70. ibid. 15 July 1871.
71. SPO 1871, 12694.
72. *Weekly Examiner*, 10 August 1872.
73. *Weekly Examiner* and *Ulster Observer*, 17 August 1872 and *Weekly Northern Whig*, 17 August 1872.
74. *Weekly Northern Whig*, 24 August 1872.
75. *Portadown and Lurgan News*, 12 July 1873.
76. ibid. 26 July 1873.
77. ibid. 16 August 1873.
78. ibid. 8 November 1873.
79. ibid. 15 November 1873.
80. ibid.
81. ibid. 22 November 1873.
82. *Weekly Northern Whig*, 7 August 1869, and *Weekly Examiner*, 2 November 1872.
83. *Weekly Examiner* and *Ulster Observer*, 19 July 1873.
84. *Ulster Weekly News*, 24 August 1874.
85. *Newtownards Chronicle*, 21 March 1874.
86. *Banner of Ulster*, 15 February 1865.
87. *Newtownards Chronicle*, 21, 28 March 1874.
88. *Towns Inquiry 1877*, Part 1, Newtownards, 276, paras 439–45, and 279, para. 506.
89. ibid. Newtownards, 273, paras. 307–14.
90. ibid. Newtownards, 275, para. 401.
91. ibid. Newtownards, 272, paras 279–92.
92. ibid. Newtownards, Appendix 39, 530.
93. Refer to Chapter 7.
94. Refer to Chapter 14 including diagram of 1884 election results.
95. *Northern Star*, 21 June 1870.
96. Leighton, *Freemasonry in Northern Ireland*.
97. *Northern Star*, 26 April 1870.
98. *Weekly Northern Whig*, 12 March 1870.
99. *Towns Inquiry 1877*, Part 1, Newtownards, paras 106–108, 257–59, 508.
100. *Weekly Observer* and *Northern Advertiser*, 3 June 1871.
101. *Newtownards Chronicle*, 28 March 1874.
102. ibid. 28 February and 13 June 1874.
103. *Municipal Corporations 1835*, Appendix, Part 1, paras 743–87.
104. *Carrickfergus Freeman*, 3 September 1865.
105. ibid. 15 July 1865.
106. *Towns Inquiry 1877*, Part 1, Carrickfergus, 242, para. 141.
107. *Londonderry Standard*, 25 November 1868.
108. *Weekly Northern Whig*, 8 January 1870.
109. *Towns Inquiry 1877*, Part 1, Appendix 36, 530, cross-checked against political meetings during 1870s.
110. *Weekly Northern Whig*, 26 November 1870.
111. *Weekly Observer* and *Northern Advertiser*, 22 June 1872.
112. ibid.
113. *Newsletter*, 7 April 1873.

114. *Ulster Weekly News*, 7 February 1874.
115. *Weekly Northern Whig*, 22 November 1873.
116. *Towns Inquiry 1877*, Part 1, Carrickfergus, 238, para. 15.
117. ibid. Carrickfergus, 238, paras 39–42; 244, para. 175; paras 191–200; paras 237–44.
118. *Newsletter*, 19 January and 2 February 1883.
119. *Bessborough 1881*, John Young, paras 5858–6040; see also *Ballymoney Free Press*, 19 July 1879, a petty sessions case brought by a farmer to evict a cottier tenant from his weekly tenancy.
120. *Newsletter*, 17 March 1873.
121. ibid.
122. *Ulster Weekly News*, 22 March 1873.
123. *Weekly Northern Whig*, 29 March 1873.
124. *Towns Inquiry 1877*, Part 3, Appendix 9, 360, and the *Belfast* and *Ulster Street Directory*.
125. *Weekly Northern Whig*, 11 July 1868.
126. ibid. 20 June 1868.
127. *Weekly Examiner* and *Ulster Observer*, 25 October 1879.
128. *Ballymoney Free Press*, 29 January 1874.
129. ibid.
130. ibid. 4 March 1880, meeting of the shareholders of the Derry Central Railway includes an extensive discussion about how the timetabling of the trains was adversely affecting Coleraine.
131. ibid. 10 July 1873, meeting of the Northern Counties Railway; also *Newsletter*, 21 January 1874, Lord Waveney thanks the directors as a shareholder for the high profit, but asks as a consumer for a lower tariff; *Ballymoney Free Press*, 15 June 1876, report of the Cookstown and Magherafelt Company. The three Liberal MPs for Dungannon (Dickson), Taylor (Coleraine) and Whitworth (Newry) are all directors.
132. *Ballymoney Free Press*, C. E. Lewis supported, but D. Taylor opposed, Rev. Professor Richard Smyth's resolution for a Select Committee to inquire into the Londonderry companies.
133. *Towns Inquiry 1877*, Part 3, Coleraine, 156/7.
134. *Weekly Northern Whig*, Route TDA, Speech of Rev. J. B. Armour.
135. ibid. 12 March 1870, tenant right conference at Belfast, speech of John Harbinson of Cookstown.
136. *Ballymoney Free Press*, 14 September 1876.
137. *Weekly Observer*, 4 February 1871.
138. *Weekly Northern Whig*, 17 July 1869.
139. ibid. 12 February 1870.
140. SPO 1870, 13737, Butler, RM 8 July; SPO 1870, 13786, Butler, RM 10 July; SPO 1870, 14290, Butler, RM 15 July; SPO 1870, 13566, Rev. Mr Hughes, P.P. Drumgooland, to Chief Secretary.
141. SPO 1871, 12622, French, RM 2, 5 July.
142. *Weekly Northern Whig*, 15 July 1870; and SPO 1871, 13141.
143. *Weekly Northern Whig*, 15 July 1870.
144. ibid.
145. ibid.
146. ibid.
147. SPO 1870, 14141, Percy, RM.
148. *Weekly Northern Whig*, 15 July 1870.
149. *Towns Inquiry 1877*, Part 3, Newry, 199, para. 348.
150. ibid. Newry, 193, para. 74.
151. *Bessborough 1881*, Rev. Charles Quin, paras 5649–797.

152. ibid. Rev. Charles Quin, para. 5779.
153. ibid. Patrick O'Callaghan, para. 5825.
154. Gibbon, *Ulster Unionism*, 107/8.
155. See Chapter 13.
156. *Weekly Examiner* and *Ulster Observer*, 1 February, Cappagh; 29 March, Carrickmore; 26 April, Pomeroy, 1873.
157. ibid. 29 March 1873.
158. ibid.
159. ibid. 20 September 1873.
160. ibid. 18 October 1873.
161. *Towns Inquiry 1877*, Part 3, Appendix 8, 358, the list of councillors checked against political meetings during the 1870s.
162. *Weekly Northern Whig*, 1 May 1869.
163. *Northern Star* and *Ulster Observer*, 28 July, McKenna's challenge to William Johnston; also *Weekly Northern Whig*, 20 August 1870.
164. *Weekly Northern Whig*, 27 August 1870.
165. *Belfast Times*, 10 February 1872.
166. *Weekly Northern Whig*, 17 August 1872.
167. Thomas Macknight, *Ulster as it is*.
168. *Weekly Northern Whig*, 26 October 1872.
169. *Towns Inquiry 1877*, as Note 161. Of the listed members of the Corporation of 1877, 5 were supporters of McCorkell and 4 of Lewis. 15 were not clearly identifiable with either party.
170. *Weekly Examiner*, 2 November 1872.
171. *Londonderry Standard*, 6 November 1872.
172. *Weekly Observer* and *Northern Advertizer*, 9 November 1872.
173. *Weekly Examiner*, 16 November 1872.
174. ibid. 2 November 1872.
175. ibid.
176. *Londonderry Standard*, 2 November 1872.
177. ibid. 6 November 1872.
178. ibid. 9 November 1872.
179. ibid.
180. ibid.
181. ibid. 16 November 1872.
182. *Weekly Northern Whig*, 30 November 1872.
183. *Londonderry Standard*, 27 November 1872.
184. ibid.
185. *Weekly Examiner*, 30 November 1872.
186. ibid. 7 December 1872.
187. *Northern Star*, 5 June 1869.
188. *Weekly Northern Whig*, 12 February 1870.
189. ibid.
190. *Ballymoney Free Press*, 1 February 1877.
191. ibid. 15 June 1876.
192. *Belfast Times*, 1 August 1872.
193. *Weekly Northern Whig*, 17 August 1872.
194. ibid.
195. ibid. 19 July 1873.
196. ibid.
197. *Ulster Weekly News*, 22 March 1873.
198. *Towns Inquiry 1877*, Part 3, Cookstown, 185/6, para. 139, John Harbinson.

558 TWO LANDS ON ONE SOIL

199. *Ulster Weekly News*, 22 March 1873.
200. *Weekly Northern Whig*, 29 March 1873.
201. *Weekly Examiner* and *Ulster Observer*, 12 April 1873. It is stated that 25% of the constituency electorate is Catholic and that Catholic abstentions were responsible for MacCartney not winning.
202. *Tyrone Constitution*, 6, 13 February 1874.
203. *Londonderry Standard*, 14 February 1874.
204. *Ballymoney Free Press*, 1 February 1877.
205. *Weekly Northern Whig*, 20 August 1870.
206. ibid. 10 September 1870.
207. *Tyrone Constitution*, 23 January 1874, on the formation of the Tyrone Coal Mining Company.
208. ibid. 13 February 1874.

Chapter Thirteen.
The Land War and the Climax of Liberalism—the Land League (pages 432–475)

1. *Weekly Northern Whig*, 12 March 1870.
2. *Londonderry Standard*, 18 March 1870.
3. *Northern Star*, 14 August 1870.
4. *Weekly Northern Whig*, 20 April 1870.
5. *Northern Star*, 21 April 1870.
6. *Bessborough 1881*, Samuel McElroy, paras 4411–13.
7. ibid. Mark Synnot, para. 7259.
8. ibid. Samuel McElroy, paras 4494–5.
9. See Notes 128, 129, Chapter 12.
10. *Bessborough 1881*, Samuel McElroy, paras 4443–6.
11. *Weekly Northern Whig*, 15 February 1873.
12. ibid.
13. *Ulster Weekly News*, 24 January 1874.
14. ibid.
15. *Ulster Weekly News* and *Weekly Northern Whig*, 14, 21 February 1874.
16. *Examiner*, 23 February 1874.
17. E. R. Norman, *Anti-Catholicism in Victorian England*, 316–18.
18. ibid. 217.
19. *Londonderry Standard*, 11 November 1874.
20. *Ballymoney Free Press*, 19 November 1874.
21. *Ulster Weekly News*, 14 November 1874.
22. *Weekly Northern Whig*, 28 November 1874.
23. *Weekly Examiner* and *Ulster Observer*, 14 November 1870.
24. ibid. 28 November 1874.
25. *Ballymoney Free Press*, 12 June 1873.
26. ibid. 6 November 1873.
27. ibid. 16 March 1876.
28. *Weekly Examiner* and *Ulster Observer*, 11 May 1878.
29. ibid. 28 November 1874.
30. *Ballymoney Free Press*, 24 August 1876.
31. ibid.
32. ibid. 8 February 1877.
33. ibid. 20 December 1877.
34. Quoted in *Ballymoney Free Press*, 3 January 1878.
35. ibid. 21 December 1876. Smyth also put his name to the Butt Bill of 1876.

36. *The Nation*, 23 July 1878.
37. *Ballymoney Free Press*, 9 May 1878.
38. ibid.
39. *Ulster Weekly News*, 11 May 1878, letter of a "Tenant at will".
40. ibid.
41. ibid.
42. ibid.
43. *Weekly Examiner* and *Ulster Observer*, 11 May 1878.
44. ibid.
45. *Ballymoney Free Press*, 16 May 1878.
46. *Weekly Observer* and *Ulster Examiner*, 18 May 1878.
47. Cahill may have had hopes of becoming the Assistant Commissioner of Intermediate Education.
48. A. M. Sullivan, *New Ireland*, 395–429; *Weekly Examiner* and *Ulster Examiner*, 18 May 1878.
49. *Ballymoney Free Press*, 23 May 1878.
50. *Weekly Examiner* and *Ulster Observer*, 25 May 1878.
51. *Weekly Examiner* and *Ulster Observer*, 3 April 1880, meeting at Castlewellan.
52. *Ulster Weekly News*, 11 May 1878.
53. *Ballymoney Free Press*, 15 August 1878.
54. ibid.
55. ibid.
56. *Ulster Weekly News*, 17 August 1878.
57. *Ballymoney Free Press*, 30 January 1879.
58. ibid. 13 September 1877 and 22 August 1878.
59. ibid. 26 September 1878.
60. ibid. 24 April 1879.
61. ibid. 19 June 1879.
62. ibid. 14 August 1879.
63. *Weekly Examiner* and *Ulster Observer*, 27 September 1879.
64. *Ballymoney Free Press*, 2 October 1879.
65. *Weekly Examiner* and *Ulster Observer*, 18 October 1878.
66. ibid.
67. Paul Bew, *Land and the National Question in Ireland 1858–82*, (Dublin 1978) 69, for the setting up of the Land League on 21 October 1879.
68. *Weekly Examiner* and *Ulster Observer*, 18 October 1879.
69. ibid.
70. ibid.
71. *Ballymoney Free Press*, 2 October 1879.
72. *Weekly Examiner* and *Ulster Observer*, 1 November 1879.
73. *Ballymoney Free Press*, 30 October 1879.
74. *Weekly Examiner* and *Ulster Observer*, 25 October 1879.
75. ibid. 8 November 1879.
76. ibid. 4 October 1879.
77. *Ballymoney Free Press*, 6 November 1879.
78. ibid. 6 December 1879.
79. *The Witness*, 20 December 1879.
80. *Weekly Examiner* and *Ulster Observer*, 13 December 1879; *Ballymoney Free Press*, 24 December 1879.
81. Paul Bew, op. cit. 115–29.
82. *Bessborough 1881*, Charles U. Townshend, paras 1580–97.
83. *Weekly Examiner* and *Ulster Examiner*, 20 December 1879.
84. *Ballymoney Free Press*, 4 March 1880.

85. ibid. 29 January 1880.
86. ibid.
87. A. M. Sullivan, op. cit. 446–7.
88. ibid. 448.
89. e.g. address of Hugh Law and John S. Crawford, *Weekly Examiner* and *Ulster Observer*, 20 March 1880.
90. e.g. address of James Chaine and Sir Richard Wallace, *Weekly Examiner* and *Ulster Observer*, 20 March 1880.
91. 1874/1880, Liberal gains: Donegal and Monaghan two each, Tyrone and Armagh one each. Liberal losses: Down, Coleraine, Newry. Liberal gains of 1874 held in 1880: County Derry both seats and Dungannon. In addition, Derry city and Belfast had been lost by 1874, and Carrickfergus, though never overtly Liberal, was recovered by the Conservatives in 1880.
92. Bew, op. cit. 119–21.
93. Sullivan, op. cit. 450.
94. *Ballymoney Free Press*, 15 July 1880.
95. ibid.
96. *Witness*, 20 August 1880.
97. *Ballymoney Free Press*, 15 July 1880.
98. ibid.
99. Richard Braithwaite and Lindsay Crawford, *Orangeism. Its History and Progress. A Plea for First Principles* (Belfast 1904) 39.
100. ibid. 40.
101. A. M. Sullivan, op. cit. 452.
102. Braithwaite and Crawford, op. cit. 40; *Ballymoney Free Press*, 7 October 1880.
103. Braithwaite and Crawford, op. cit. 41. Paul Bew, op. cit. 133.
104. *Coleraine Chronicle*, 5 October 1880.
105. *Ballymoney Free Press*, 14 October 1880.
106. ibid.
107. *Weekly Examiner* and *Ulster Observer*, 16 October 1880.
108. *Ballymoney Free Press*, 21 October 1880.
109. ibid.
110. ibid.
111. ibid. 4 November 1880.
112. ibid.
113. ibid. 18 November 1880.
114. ibid.
115. ibid.
116. *Weekly Examiner* and *Ulster Observer*, 20 November 1880.
117. ibid. 27 November 1880.
118. ibid. 4 December 1880, Dufferin to Royal Agricultural Commissioners.
119. *Ballymoney Free Press*, 9 December 1880.
120. *Weekly Examiner* and *Ulster Observer*, 27 November 1880.
121. ibid.
122. ibid.
123. ibid.
124. ibid. 4 December 1880.
125. ibid. 27 November 1880.
126. ibid. 4 December 1880.
127. *Ballymoney Free Press*, 2 December 1880.
128. ibid. 30 December 1880.
129. ibid.

130. ibid. 2 December 1880.
131. *Weekly Examiner* and *Ulster Observer*, 27 November 1880.
132. *Ballymoney Free Press*, 30 December 1880.
133. ibid. 9 December 1880 and *Weekly Examiner* and *Ulster Observer*, 11 December 1880.
134. Sullivan, op. cit. 455–6.
135. *Ballymoney Free Press*, 16 December 1880.
136. ibid. 27 January 1881.
137. ibid. 30 January 1881.
138. ibid. 16 December 1880.
139. ibid. 16, 30 December 1880.
140. ibid. 27 January 1880.
141. ibid. 30 December 1880.
142. ibid. 13 January 1881.
143. ibid. 15 September 1881.
144. For this period, see Paul Bew, op. cit. Chapters 7 and 8, 145–90.
145. Bew, op. cit. 154–5, observes how the struggle against the Coercion Act united the Irish Party in parliament and raised its position in relation to the Land League.
146. *Ballymoney Free Press*, 5 May 1881, praises the Bishops' statement on the Bill.
147. ibid. 15 September 1881.
148. ibid.
149. *Weekly Examiner* and *Ulster Observer*, 17 April 1880, estimates the RCs as "nearly a quarter" of the constituency. The 7% is based on the assumption that the difference between Macartney and Hamilton votes was a result of Liberal-Macartney split votes.
150. It is here assumed that all Conservative votes were Protestant and that all Home Rule votes were Catholic.
151. E. Rumpf and A. C. Hepburn, *Nationalism and Socialism in Twentieth Century Ireland* (Liverpool 1977) map of Agrarian Outrages, 1880–82, per thousand of population by counties.
152. *Newsletter*, 22 March 1883.
153. *Bessborough 1881*, Rev. Charles Quin, P.P., paras 5756–8, on Bond McGeough.
154. *Newsletter*, 22 March 1883.

Chapter Fourteen.
Militant Pan-Protestantism and Conservatism—the Formation of Unionism.
(pages 476–509)

1. Peter Gibbon, *Origins of Ulster Unionism*, 138, and Henry Patterson, *Class Conflict and Sectarianism*, 22–3. Both emphasise the way in which the part played by the Orange Lodges and minor gentry had diminished between 1885/6 and 1892/3.
2. Thomas Macknight, *Ulster as it is*, Vol. II, 36.
3. A. B. Cooke and John Vincent, *The Governing Passion: cabinet government and party politics in Britain 1885–6* (London 1974).
4. See Chapter 11.
5. *Weekly Northern Whig*, 11 July 1874, and *Belfast Newsletter*, 3 January 1874.

6. *Ulster Observer* and *Weekly Examiner*, 18 July 1874.
7. *Ballymoney Free Press*, 16 July 1874, and *Ulster Weekly News*, 18 July 1874.
8. *Londonderry Standard*, 27 June 1874, and *Weekly Northern Whig*, 11 July 1874.
9. *Belfast Weekly News*, 11 July 1874.
10. *Ulster Weekly News*, 25 July and 8 August 1874.
11. *Weekly Examiner* and *Ulster Observer*, 18 July 1874.
12. ibid. 1 August 1874 and *Ulster Weekly News*, 8 August 1874.
13. *Weekly Northern Whig*, 29 August 1874.
14. *Ulster Weekly News*, 25 July 1874.
15. Obviously employers tended to use this argument to their political advantage, but an index of how effective it was is provided by a statement from the Belfast House Painters Society. It says that their members would use their influence on behalf of Ewart and Corry on account of them being such large employers of labour (*Belfast Weekly News*, 27 March 1880).
16. *Ulster Weekly News*, 18 July 1874.
17. *Weekly Examiner* and *Ulster Observer*, 4 October 1879.
18. *Ballymoney Free Press*, 17, 24 August 1876 and 16 August 1877.
19. ibid. 28 March 1878.
20. ibid. 12 July 1877.
21. *Weekly Northern Whig*, 30 March 1878.
22. *Weekly Examiner* and *Ulster Observer*, 30 March 1878.
23. ibid. 6 April 1878.
24. *Ulster Weekly News*, 20 July and 17 August 1878.
25. *Weekly Examiner* and *Ulster Observer*, 20 July 1878, and for the accusation that the story in the *Examiner* was untrue, see *Ulster Weekly News*, 20 July 1878.
26. *Ulster Weekly News*, 17 August 1878.
27. ibid. 24 August 1878.
28. ibid.
29. ibid.
30. *Weekly Examiner*, 12 October 1872. Here Ferris is charged with being a member of a mob that wrecked a Shankill Road pub. He was identified because he lived only two doors away and the publican knew him. He was granted bail, and I have not come across the rest of the case.
31. *Weekly Examiner* and *Ulster Observer*. Here Ferris appears as a speaker at a mill strike meeting.
32. *Ulster Weekly News*, 24 August 1878.
33. ibid. 31 August 1878.
34. *Ballymoney Free Press*, 6 January 1881.
35. *Belfast Newsletter*, 14 March 1883.
36. ibid. 13 July 1883.
37. ibid.
38. ibid. 25 January 1883.
39. ibid.
40. Thomas Macknight, *Ulster as it is*.
41. ibid.
42. *Belfast Newsletter*, 14 August 1883.
43. ibid. 15 August 1883.
44. ibid.
45. ibid.

46.	ibid. 2 November 1883.
47.	ibid.
48.	ibid. 5 November 1883.
49.	ibid.
50.	e.g. in a communication address to Sir Charles Dilke Bt, M.P. by Sir John Lambert, KCB and Sir Francis Sandford, KCB relative to "the alterations made after local enquiry into the provisional schemes for division of the counties of Armagh, Donegal, Londonderry, Tyrone and Dublin and the Borough of Dublin" there are mentioned five County Tyrone priests who appeared to present the nationalist case, including Rev. Mr McCartan, P.P. Donoughmore, who presided over a nationalist county meeting. Rev. Dean Byrne also appears, the same who supported Dickson in 1881. And Very Rev. Dr Logue of Raphoe was represented for the nationalists by Mr O'Dougherty, solicitor.
51.	*Belfast Newsletter*, 14 November 1883.
52.	ibid. 5 May 1884.
53.	ibid. 29, 30 May 1884.
54.	ibid. 31 May 1884.
55.	ibid. 4 June 1884.
56.	ibid. 7 June 1884.
57.	ibid. 12 June 1884.
58.	ibid. 13 June 1884.
59.	ibid. 16 June 1884.
60.	ibid. 17 June 1884.
61.	ibid. 20 January 1885, McCormick's attack upon Kane for wanting to be a Birmingham caucus "in his veritable self".
62.	*Belfast Election Poll Book 1868*. Cobain did not even cast a Lanyon/Johnston split vote. He voted for Lanyon and Mulholland, a vote otherwise cast by the well to do and those on the city hall payroll.
63.	*Weekly Northern Whig*. In the Grand Lodge election of 1870, Cobain appears as the District Master of No. 7, casting the votes of the district against Johnston. This was the district which had been formed by a subdivision of District No. 2, under the mastership of the borough rate collector C. N. Davis. The manipulative intention was sufficiently blatant that the votes of District 7 were disallowed by the GLI. Cobain was deeply involved in the 1868–71 anti-Johnston campaign with the Lodge.
64.	e.g. clash between Cobain and Kane at Sandy Row, *Belfast Newsletter*, 16 June 1884.
65.	ibid. 14 August 1883.
66.	ibid. 21 January 1885.
67.	ibid. 25 January 1885.
68.	ibid. 2 March 1885.
69.	ibid. 23 January 1885.
70.	ibid. 10 March 1885.
71.	ibid. 12 February, 6, 30 March 1885.
72.	ibid. 24 January and 5 May 1885, Kane demanding South and West Belfast seats for Orangemen, but not making clear what he wanted to happen in East Belfast.
73.	ibid. 12 February 1885.
74.	ibid. 6 April 1885, letter from Kane.
75.	ibid. 4 April 1885.

76. ibid. 6 April 1885, editorial for Seeds.
77. ibid. 15 April 1885.
78. ibid. 6 May 1885.
79. ibid. 30 May 1885.
80. ibid. 1 July 1885.
81. ibid. 21 October 1885.
82. ibid. 28 October 1885.
83. ibid. 29 October 1885.
84. ibid. 31 October 1885. John McCormick of the OPWMA on Johnston and the Factory Acts; 6 June, S. Kerr on the suddenness of Cobain's conversion during the dispute over the plastering contract.
85. Patrick Buckland, *Irish Unionism 1885–1923* (PRONI, HMSO 1973) 110–20.
86. Buckland, op. cit. 115.
87. ibid. 117/18.
88. ibid. 120.
89. *Belfast Newsletter*, 7 August 1885.
90. ibid. 18 August 1885.
91. ibid. 3 September 1885.
92. ibid. 22 August and 3 September 1885.
93. *Ballymoney Free Press*, 30 December 1880.
94. *Bessborough 1881*, Dr Gawin Orr, para. 35005.
95. *Belfast Newsletter*, 16 October 1885.
96. ibid. 19 March 1883.
97. ibid. 23 May 1885.
98. *Northern Whig*, 5 December 1884.
99. ibid.
100. *Return of Religious denominations of peoples in the various parliamentary constituencies in Ulster*, H.C. 1884–5 (325) LXII, 339.
101. Brian M. Walker, *Parliamentary Election Results in Ireland 1801–1921* (Dublin 1978).
102. R. F. Foster, "Lord Randolph Churchill and the prelude to the Orange Card", 269, in F. S. L. Lyons and A. J. Hawkins, *Ireland Under the Union* (Oxford 1980).
103. R. McNeill, *Ulster Stands for Union* (London 1922).
104. A. B. Cooke, "A Conservative Party leader in Ulster: Sir Stafford Northcote's diary of a visit to the province in October 1883", *Proceedings of the Royal Irish Academy*, Vol. 75, Section C, No. 4, 61.
105. ibid. 83, Note 121.
106. *Belfast Newsletter*, 19 February 1885.
107. Cooke, op. cit. 65.
108. A. B. Cooke and John Vincent, *The Government Passion: cabinet government and party politics in Britain 1885–86* (London 1974).
109. *Belfast Newsletter*, 10 July 1885.
110. ibid. 23 October 1885.
111. ibid. 27 November 1885.
112. ibid. 20 June 1885.
113. ibid. 14 November 1885.
114. ibid. 19 January 1886.
115. Andrew Boyd, *Holy War in Belfast*, 123, and see also Foster (Note 102) and Cooke and Vincent (Note 108).
116. Boyd, *Holy War*, Chapter 8 and 9.

Chapter Fifteen.
Conclusions (pages 510–523)

1. Frank Wright, *Northern Ireland. A comparative analysis*, Chapters 1 and 6.
2. A. C. Hepburn and B. Collins, "Industrial Society: the Structure of Belfast 1901", Chapter XIII in Peter Roebuck (ed.) *Plantation to Partition*, 221.
3. Wright, op. cit. 112–25.
4. Fred Singleton, *A Short History of the Yugoslav Peoples* (Cambridge 1985).
5. Ernest Gellner, *Thought and Change*, Chapter 5; and Wright, op. cit. Chapter 1.
6. The British and Irish Communist Organisation. *The Economics of Partition* (Belfast 1972); Peter Gibbon, *Origins of Ulster Unionism*.
7. Henry Patterson, *Class Conflict and Sectarianism*.
8. Patterson, op. cit. 144–50.

INDEX

Abercorn, Marquis of, 87–8, 206, 422, 430
Abercorn family, 489
Aberdeen, Lord, 316–17
Achilli, Dr, 182–3, 184, 185, 233
Act of Union, 18, 24, 27, 47, 50–51, 145, 146, 349, 443
Adair, Sir Shafto, 390, 395, 409, 411, 412
Advocate, 107
Aghadowey, Co. Antrim, 99, 156, 226
Aghamullen, Co. Monaghan, 272
agriculture. *see also* land question
  after Famine, 384
  intra-regional contrasts, 70–103
  pre-Famine, 70–103
Ahoghill, 68, 227, 412
Akenson, Don, 139
America
  emigration to, 28, 96, 121
  grain imports, 449
  Presbyterian emigration, 13–14
  sectarianism, 513
American Civil War, 211, 274
American War of Independence, 27, 28, 39
Ancketell, William, 465
Andrews, John, 158–9
Andrews, W.D., 444, 445–7, 450, 453
Anglicanism, 15, 39, 58, 95, 170, 194, 293, 335, 398
  ascendancy, 51, 52
  "Church Defence", 347, 348–9, 350, 385, 387, 399, 425–6
  distribution of, 32, 103
  and education, 51, 139, 140, 180–82, 236, 301, 303, 305
  Hillsborough meeting, 69
  and Orange Order, 31, 271, 414
  relations with Presbyterians, 135, 156–7, 234, 415
  street preaching, 254–5
  tithes, 51, 138
  Trinity College monopoly, 307–9

  veto over English policy, 13
Antrim, County, 23, 26, 32, 54, 72, 90, 105, 114, 269, 274, 351, 397, 459
  agricultural modernization, 78
  Belfast separates from, 285, 318–19
  cotton famine, 394
  election, 1869, 390, 395, 409–10
  election, 1874, 438
  election, 1880, 458
  grand jury, 161–62, 180, 213, 215–16, 366
  Great Famine, 126, 128, 132
  Liberal vote, 498, 501–2
  linen industry, 411
  number of farms, 384
  Orange Order, 152
  Tenant League, 192
  United Irishmen, 29–30, 31
Antrim and Down Tenant Right Association, 167–9
Antrim town, 103
Apprentice Boys, 340, 344, 354, 421, 487
Ards, Co. Down, 500, 501
Ardstraw, Co. Tyrone, 84–5, 86
"Argument on Behalf of the Catholics of Ireland" (Tone), 27, 43–6, 475, 521
Armagh, County, 31, 71, 72, 74, 283
  agrarian outrages, 188
  church defence, 399
  election, 1880, 458
  election, 1885, 495–6
  Great Famine, 112, 116
  Land League, 462, 468, 469
  Orange Order, 29–30, 41, 152, 156
  regional variations, 31–4
  rent reductions, 170
  Ribbonism, 245
  seasonal migration, 93, 94
  sectarianism, 23, 25–6, 30, 34–8, 42–3, 46
  tenant right movement, 455–6

weavers, 96–7
Armagh town, 15, 32–3, 34, 269, 313, 401
  disturbances, 1780s, 17
  politics in, 397
  arms, 264, 395
  for Catholics, 17, 33, 35, 37–8, 297
  searches, 262, 269
Arranmore Island, Co. Donegal, 118
Ascendancy. *see* elite
Associated Weavers of Antrim and Derry, 412
Aston, W.D., 428
Aughnacloy, Co. Tyrone, 38

Babington, Rev. Richard, 489
Badoney, Co. Tyrone, 86, 420
Bailieborough, Co. Cavan, 95–6, 133, 134, 313, 391
Ballintoy, Co. Antrim, 99
Ballot Act, 339, 410
Ballybay, Co. Monaghan, 186, 191, 271, 272, 313
Ballybofey, Co. Donegal, 417
Ballycastle, Co. Antrim, 123, 297, 467, 469, 470
Ballyclare, Co. Antrim, 31, 43, 438, 443, 470, 471
Ballycor, Co. Antrim, 102
Ballykilbeg, Co. Down, 21, 245, 248, 277, 281, 317, 341
Ballylawn, Co. Donegal, 189
Ballymacarrett, Belfast, 247, 287, 288, 483
Ballymena, Co. Antrim, 39, 44, 96, 102, 114, 149, 513
  Adair election, 390
  excursion banned, 483
  Great Famine, 122
  Great Revival, 227, 232, 234–6
  Loyalty meeting, 235
  politics of, 411–13
Ballymena Observer, 234–6
Ballymena Union, 112
Ballymoney, Co. Antrim, 68, 96, 323, 327, 339, 415, 521
  rent reduction meeting, 452, 453–4
  tenant right meetings, 456–7, 458
  tenant right movement, 101–2, 388–9, 435, 436–7
Ballymoney Free Press, 339–40, 383, 440, 441, 443, 446, 448, 449
  land agitation, 454, 455, 460–62, 463
  tenant right movement, 449, 450, 452
Ballynafeigh, Belfast, 287
Ballynahinch, battle of, 42
Ballynascreen, Co. Derry, 88, 467
Ballyshannon, Co. Donegal, 442, 462
Ballysillan bleachworks, 266
Ballyward, Co. Down, 387, 416–17
Banbridge, Co. Down, 96, 97, 123, 138, 282, 283, 400, 500
  Orange Order, 278–80, 404
Bangor, Co. Down, 39, 319–20, 321, 322
Bank of England, 110
Bann river, 78, 88, 90, 97
Banner of Ulster, 171, 183–4, 189, 208, 211, 225, 239, 270, 294, 394
  Belfast riots, 261, 262, 268
  Catholic emancipation, 159–60
  Catholic university, 200
  clerical leadership, 202–3
  disestablishment, 309–10, 313
  Ecclesiastical Titles Bill, 194, 196, 197–8
  education, 158, 180–81, 301, 302, 307
  Great Revival, 230, 233, 234
  Johnston, 321
  Party Processions Act, 320
  population displacement, 265
  Tenant League, 187, 192, 203–4
Barbour, John D., 394–5, 396
Barnett, James, 221
Barry, Judge, 436
Barton, Colonel, 387, 488
Bates, John, 213–14, 217, 218, 222
Bateson, Thomas, 203
Bath, Marquis of, 118, 121
Batt, Thomas G., 221
Beers, J.L., 414, 436
Beggs, Dr, 179

Belfast, 28, 40, 159, 423, 438, 448, 458. *see also* Belfast Corporation
Achilli meeting, 182–3
Catholic politics, 293–300, 355–67
Conservative control, 135
Convention, 1892, 476
demagogues, 478
democratization, 284–332
election, 1868, 326–32
  analysis of, 328–32
  fate of Independents, 345–7
flooding, 351–2
franchise reform, 315
Great Famine, 105–7, 112, 114
Great Revival, 227, 230, 236–7, 238
Home Rule movement, 450–51, 474
Independent Orangeism, 479–85
industrial development, 19, 70, 208, 211–12
influence of, 70–71, 72–4, 78, 90, 208–10, 383, 391
Johnston in politics, 21, 317–19, 333–47
labour force, 247–8, 290–93, 368–9, 371–2
leadership class, 518
marches banned, 1878, 482–3
migration to, 187
municipal improvements, 105–6, 162, 208–9, 219–21
O'Connell visit, 50–51, 137–8
"outer boundary" group, 219–21
Parnell meeting, 463–4
Parnell visit, 418, 450–52, 453
peace committee, 264–8
polarization, 260
politics, 1869–74, 333–82
population displacement, 256–8, 265, 373–5, 377
Reform agitation, 287–90
riots, 242, 521
  1857, 218–19, 245, 247–52, 254
  1864, 6, 260–64, 395
  1872, 22, 336–7, 338, 342, 355, 367, 372–6, 483–4
  1886, 508–9
sectarianism, 241–5, 256–8

segregation, 242–3
separation from Antrim, 285, 318–19
taxation, 180
tenant right movement, 198
Whig dominance, 64–5, 204, 207
Whigs v. Conservatives, 160–64
Young Ireland movement, 143–8
Belfast Bank, 177, 213, 215, 221, 332
Belfast Chamber of Commerce, 266
Belfast Charitable Society, 65
Belfast Corporation, 39, 64, 69, 105, 177, 241, 284, 322, 433, 447
  activities of, 161–2
  Borough Bill, 213
  Catholic cemetery, 347, 350
  Catholics in, 295
  Chancery suit, 209, 216–19, 222–3, 260
  and marching rights, 377–8
  mayor's salary, 352
  municipal elections, 346, 350, 352, 353–4, 379–80, 381, 383
  secret ballot, 378
  Police Committee, 245–7
  public parks, 369–70
  rates controversy, 284–7
  reform sought, 208–10, 214–16
  Royal Commission on, 1858, 219–21
  Spencer protest, 490–92
Belfast Economic Building and Investment Society, 296
Belfast harbour commissioners, 285
Belfast Home Rule Association, 468
Belfast Lough, 72
Belfast Morning News, 440
Belfast Parochial Mission, 254–5
Belfast presbytery, 447, 453
Belfast Times, The, 354, 427
Belfast Trades Council, 493, 508
Belfast Working Men's Co-operative Ltd, 291
Bell, Rev. David, 186, 191, 192, 193
Bell, Saunders, 54
Bellaghy, Co. Derry, 278, 417
Belleek, Co. Fermanagh, 462
Belmore family, 429

Belturbet, Co. Cavan, 14–15, 58, 360
Benburb, Co. Tyrone, 99
Bentinck, Lord George, 135
Beragh, Co. Tyrone, 282
Beresford, Sir John, 59
Beresford, John C., 95, 96
Beresford, Rev. Marcus, 95
Bessborough Commission, 411, 417, 435, 497
Bessbrook, Co. Armagh, 371, 417, 418
Bew, Paul, 473
Biggar, Joseph, 456, 459
  election candidate, 421, 422
  and Factory Act, 480–81
  Home Rule leader, 353, 354
  and Land League, 462, 464, 467
Bingham, 482
Blacker, Stewart, 346
Blacker, Colonel William, 55, 97, 152, 170
Blackstone, Judge, 178
Blackwatertown, Co. Armagh, 34–5
Bleachers and Finishers Association, 394, 397
Boal, Mr, 406
Board of Works, 110, 116, 122, 128
bog reclamation, 77
Bohemia, 10, 515
Borough Bill, 1851, 107, 213, 287–8
borough corporations, 14, 38, 39, 58, 60–61
Borough Extension Act, 1853, 223
Bowen, Desmond, 138
Bowman, Alexander, 508
Boycott, Captain, 460
boycotting, 460, 486–7
Boyd, Andy, 508
Bradshaw, Rev. Joseph, 407
Bright, John, 294, 361, 426, 464, 467
Bristow, James, 214, 218, 219
Britain. *see also* seasonal migration
  Catholic hierarchy re-established, 193–4
  emigration to, 210
  employment in, 89
  free trade with, 70, 163–4, 174–5, 213, 519

  landlords depend on, 27
  plantations, 12–13
  responses to Great Famine, 109–11, 123–4, 126, 132–4
  and tenant right movement, 178–9
  war with France, 40
British and Irish Communist Organization (BICO), 517
British Association, 480
Britton, John, 374
Brooke, Mr, 275, 473
Brooke, Sir A.B., 124
Brookeborough, Co. Fermanagh, 124
Brookfield spinning mills, 291
Broughshane, Co. Antrim, 311
Brown, Rev. Dr John, 156, 157, 226
Bruce, Sir Harvey, 206, 226, 414
Bulgaria, 415
Buncrana, Co. Donegal, 462
Burial Bill, 430
Burke, Biddy, 256
Burns, Patrick, 473
Butler, Mr, 416
Butt, Isaac, 273, 359, 361, 424, 446, 460
  and Crawford bill, 443
  Land Bill, 442, 445, 453
  loses leadership, 457
Byrne, Canon, 472, 486
Byrne (publican), 32–3, 34, 35–6

Caernarvon, Lord, 506
Cahill, Fr Michael, 450
Cahill, Rev. M.H., 379, 445–6, 463–4
Cairns, Sir Hugh, 286
Caledon, Earl of, 75, 101
Cambric Weavers' Trade Unions, 496
Cameron, James, 220
Camlough, Co. Armagh, 417, 455–6
Campbell, N.A., 379
Canada, 341
Cappagh, Co. Tyrone, 418, 419–20
Capron, Claud, 396
Cardwell, Chief Secretary, 284–5
Carleton, William, 84, 86
Carlisle's mill, Belfast, 216, 222

Carndonagh, Co. Donegal, 460
Carntogher Mountain, 90
Carpenter and Joiners Society, 292
Carrickfergus, Co. Antrim, 39, 59, 297, 313, 351, 365, 413
  election, 1868, 328
  Great Revival, 233
  politics of, 409–11, 415
Carrickfergus Freeman, 297, 299
Carrickmacross, Co. Monaghan, 135, 271, 465
Carrickmore, Co. Tyrone, 418–19, 426, 427, 430, 472, 519
Castleblaney, Co. Monaghan, 5, 93, 271
Castlecoole, Co. Fermanagh, 124
Castledawson, Co. Derry, 111, 112
Castlereagh, Co. Down, 501
Castlereagh, Lord, 39, 189, 201, 447, 470, 471
  Down by-election, 444–6
Castlewellan, Co. Down, 469, 500–501
Catholic Defence Association, 197, 199
Catholic emancipation, 32, 47, 159–60, 202, 312, 446
  election, Monaghan, 152, 201
  Liberal support, 51, 54
Catholic Emancipation Act, 1793, 58, 248, 349
Catholic hierarchy, 321
  and 1881 Land Act, 473
  British advances to, 135, 136, 139–40, 506
  and education, 62–3, 197–8, 224, 294, 439, 440
  pastoral letter, 236–8
  and Fenianism, 342–3, 344
  and Home Rule, 362
  and liberals, 440–41
  "Papal Agression" crisis, 195–7
  re-established in England, 193–4
  university question, 157–8, 379
Catholic Institute, 262, 297, 299–300
Catholic Relief Act, 1793, 40–41, 47
Catholics, 13, 43–6, 58, 138, 157, 334. *see also* Defenders; expulsionism; marching rights; sectarianism
  and Belfast politics, 217, 223, 293–300, 355–67
  Derry, 420–25
  distribution of, 32, 71–2, 84–8, 397, 398, 407–8, 413, 416–18
  dual allegiance, 439–41
  education question, 49–50, 61–9, 301–9
  equality, 17–20, 35, 63, 341–2, 520
  growing assertion, 97–8, 135–6, 296–9, 504, 520–21
  and Home Rule movement, 383
  and Independent Orangeism, 350, 351–2
  labour force for settlers, 11–13
  and Land League, 453–4, 472–5
  migration to Belfast, 72–3
  and nationalism, 142, 518–19
  oppose protectionism, 176–7, 179
  Orange co-operation, 429–31
  and Presbyterian Revival, 228, 232–40
  and Presbyterians, 26–7, 40, 241
  Protestant attitudes to, 2–3, 182–4
  relations with Conservatives, 337, 442–3, 444–7
  relations with Liberals, 161, 201, 209–10, 225, 239–40, 455–8
  seen as immoral, 159–60
  and tenant right movement, 433
  and United Irishmen, 42–4
cattle-driving, 89
Cavan, County, 54–5, 58, 71, 495
  amnesty movement, 360
  Great Famine, 105, 116, 118, 122, 124, 126, 128
  Home Rule movement, 438
  seasonal migration, 93
  tenant right movement, 94–6, 388
Cavan Conservatives, 95
Chalmers, Dr Thomas, 66, 156
Chamberlain, Joseph, 464
Chambers, J. D., 94
Chambre, Hunt, 277–8, 430
Chancery suit, Belfast, 209, 216–19, 222–3, 260, 284–5, 332

Charlemont, Lord, 34, 35
Charley, John S., 395
Chartism, 136, 148
Chesney, Robert, 413
Christ Church Protestant
    Association, 248, 317
Christian Brothers, 391
"Church Defence", 271, 280–82,
    309, 321
    and Orange Order, 425–6
    outside Belfast, 385, 387, 399
Church Education Society, 180–81,
    301, 364
Church of Ireland. *see* Anglicanism
Church of Scotland, 64, 135, 136,
    156–7
Churchill, Lord Randolph, 496, 502,
    508
Clare, Lord, 41, 47, 49–50
Clarendon, Lord, 157–8, 189, 213
Clarke, John, 214, 327, 328, 346, 352
clerical leadership, 19–20, 48, 52,
    202–3, 270, 334, 363, 381, 503
    fails to prevent processions, 481
    Home Rule movement, 450
    importance of, 55–6, 225
    under strain, 245, 253–4, 269, 278,
        296–9, 387, 418
    supports nationalism, 490
Clogher, Co. Tyrone, 123
Clones, Co. Monaghan, 465, 488
Clonfeakle, Co. Tyrone, 97, 426
Clonoe, Co. Tyrone, 486
co-operatives, 290–91, 292–3
coal industry, 106
Coalisland, Co. Tyrone, 428, 431,
    486
Cobain, E.S.W., 7–8, 484, 491–2,
    493–5, 507, 508, 513
Coercion Act, 362, 457, 459, 473
Coercion Bills, 143, 471
Coey, Edward, 221
Colebrooke, Co. Fermanagh, 124
Coleraine, Co. Derry, 39, 72, 78, 88,
    96, 421
    development, 415
    Land League, 471
    markets protest, 59–60
    politics of, 413–14, 431, 436, 448
Coleraine Chronicle, 460, 462
Coleraine Tenants Defence
    Association, 471
Columb, Lieutenant, 115
Comber, Co. Down, 191, 205, 309,
    313, 353
    co-operative, 290
    Loyalty meeting, 157–8
combinations, 54, 244
Communism, 190
Compensation for Disturbances
    Bill, 1880, 458
Confederation, 147, 149–50, 160
Connaught, 313, 454
Connolly, Mr, 371–2
Connor, Co. Antrim, 102, 227
Conservatives, 22, 53, 59, 67, 69,
    285–6, 383, 470–71. *see also*
    Tories
    attitude to Catholics, 226, 239,
        337, 512
    Ballymena, 411–13
    Belfast politics, 217–18, 269,
        284–90, 285–90, 334, 352,
        369–70, 378–9
    and OPWMA, 479–84
    reorganization, 380–81
    Whig opposition, 160–64
    and Belfast riots, 263, 374, 377–8
    Carrickfergus, 409–11
    Catholic opposition, 457–8
    Catholic support, 226, 337, 408,
        442–7, 498–502
    Down by-election, 444–7
    "Church Defence" campaign,
        280–82, 348
    and class issues, 497–8
    coercion, 455, 457
    Coleraine, 414
    and constabulary, 246
    Cookstown, 430–31
    declining power, 135–6
    dependent on nationalists, 506–9
    Derry, 420–25, 488–90
    education question, 307–8, 439,
        441, 442
    and Home Rule, 477–8

Conservatives *continued*
  influence on Orange Order, 273–7, 293, 380–81, 447, 477, 487–93, 504–5, 513
  Johnston opposition to, 318–21
  and labour organization, 293
  and Land League, 460–62, 462, 472, 475
  Lurgan, 398
  Newtownards, 407
  opposed to Whig reforms, 19, 52
  Party Processions Act agitation, 319–25
  Portadown, 398–9
  protectionism, 176–9
  and tenant right movement, 390, 391, 470–71
  unionism, 50–51, 476–509, 479, 514–15
constabulary, 18–19, 51, 56, 228, 242, 245, 286, 514
  arms searches, Belfast, 262–3
  Belfast riots, 250–54, 261–2, 508–9
  and Belfast riots, 264, 268–9
  boycott protection, 486
  and Catholics, 259–60
  Catholics in, 483
  and drumming parties, 399–400
  and expulsionism, 256–7
  Lisburn, 396
  Lurgan, 398
  and Orange Order, 276, 277–8, 278–9, 337
  Police Committee, Belfast, 245–7
  police rate, 223
  Portadown, 398, 400–403
Constabulary Bill, 1836, 55
Constitutional Association, 496
Constitutional Club, 9, 491, 492, 494
Constitutionalists, 490, 495
Convention, 1892, 476
Convention Act, 40
Cooke, A.B., 505, 506, 508
Cooke, Dr Henry, 182–3, 213, 228, 521
  and Anglicanism, 65–9, 135, 156–7
  Regium Donum, 311, 312
  sectarianism, 51, 63, 184, 185
  and tenant right, 190, 191
  university question, 304–5
Cookstown, Co. Tyrone, 123, 274, 349, 364, 472, 486
  Land League, 470
  politics of, 425–8
  tenant right meeting, 466
Copeland, Alderman, 59
Corn Laws, 109, 135, 156, 163
Corry, J.P., 334, 348, 381, 448–9, 481–2, 494, 506, 508
Costello, Mrs, 233, 513
Cotter, Rev., 492
cotton industry, 72–3, 78, 210–11, 260, 291
  decline, 383–4, 394
county cess, 28
Covenanters, 42
Craigbilly, Co. Antrim, 235
Crawford, Arthur Sharman, 221
Crawford, Captain, 168
Crawford, James Sharman, 407, 442
Crawford, Rev. J.D., 7
Crawford, Major John Sharman, 458
Crawford, Dr William, 192
Crawford, William Sharman, 141, 148, 150, 176, 179, 186, 221
  on agrarian outrages, 188
  favours Repeal, 196
  and free trade, 213
  Land Bills, 198–201, 434, 443, 444–5
  on protectionism, 176–7
  Tenant League election, 203, 204
Crawfordsburn, Co. Down, 148
Creggan, Co. Armagh, 32, 93
Cremorne, Lord, 271
Crichton, Lord, 504, 505–6
Criglington, Samuel, 373–4, 377
Crimes Act, 486
Croatia, 515
Crolly, Dr, Archbishop of Armagh, 140, 197
Cromwellian plantation, 12, 13, 71
Crookstown loan fund, 91
Crossmaglen, Co. Armagh, 32, 54, 93, 124, 187, 473
Crumlin, Co. Antrim, 100

Cullen, Cardinal Paul, 142, 198, 298, 343, 345, 349, 382, 517, 520
  appointed to Armagh, 197
  in Dublin Castle, 310
  and Fr O'Keeffe, 421
  National Association, 293
cultural nationalism, 35, 48–9, 141–2, 512–13, 516
Cumberland, Ernest Duke of, 150
Cuming, Dr James, 295, 296
Currell, Edward, 413
Cushendall, Co. Antrim, 122
Cushendun, Co. Antrim, 467
Cushybracken, Co. Antrim, 278

Dalway, Marriot, 351, 409–10, 411
Darragh, Alex, 297
Davidson, Richard, 248
Davis, C.N., 289
Davis, Thomas, 141–2
Davitt, Michael, 450, 451, 454–5
Dawson, Charles, 488–9
Dawson, George, 111–12
Deburren, Co. Armagh, 462
Defenders, 34–5, 36–7, 38, 41, 54
  clashes with Volunteers, 35–6, 37
  and United Irishmen, 42
democratization, 21, 52–3, 56–60, 340, 510–11
  Belfast, 163, 284–332, 334
Dempsey, Daniel, 454
Denvir, Dr, Bishop of Down and Connor, 140, 184, 217, 219, 222
Derby, Lord, 135, 285, 309
Derg river, 84, 85
Derriaghy, Co. Antrim, 32
Derry, County, 96, 157, 227, 415, 464
  election, 1874, 438
  farm size, 88–90
  Great Famine, 111
  Land League, 470
  Liberal stronghold, 206
  number of farms, 384
  Orange Order, 152, 153, 271, 274, 278
  Tenant League election, 203
  tenant right movement, 226
Derry Central Rail Company, 414

Derry city, 92, 316, 387, 430, 448, 456
  administration of, 60–61
  crisis, 1870, 431
  Defence of Walls, 340, 344, 347
  development, 388, 415
  election, 1868, 327–8
  election, 1872, 378
  election, 1880, 458
  freeman status, 14
  Home Rule movement, 519
  Land League meeting, 462
  linen industry, 411
  marching rights, 421, 429
  Orange counter-demonstration, 488–90
  politics of, 420–25, 441, 442, 448
  riots, 1870, 385
  strike, 1872, 371
  synod, 1834, 66
Derry Corporation, 488–9
Derry Journal, 443
Derry presbytery, 313
Derry Standard, 206, 307, 308, 310, 313, 323, 421, 423–5, 440, 441
Derryadd, Co. Armagh, 468
Dervock, Co. Antrim, 323, 327
Desertmartin, Co. Derry, 387
deterrence relationship, 2–8, 8–12, 513–14
developmentalism, 414
Devlin, Rev. F., 277
Devlin, William J., 427, 428, 429–31
Devon Commission, 86, 99
Dickey, James, 42
Dickson, James, 458
Dickson, T.A., 427, 448, 453, 471–2, 485
  Coalisland development, 431
  tenant right movement, 456–7, 458, 465–6, 470, 475
Dill, Rev. S.M., 235, 302, 310, 311, 312–13, 332
Dinnen, John, 287, 289
Diplomatic Relations (Rome) Bill, 1848, 316
disestablishment, 271, 280–82, 293, 308, 309–13, 321, 323–5, 333, 347, 348. *see also* "Church Defence"

Disraeli, Benjamin, 135, 285, 309, 457, 507
distillation, illegal, 75, 77, 85, 91–2
Doagh, Co. Antrim, 128, 353
Dobbin, William, 189, 336, 514
Dolly's Brae, Co. Down, 155, 179, 316, 387, 416–17, 501
Donacloney, Co. Down, 459, 460
Donaghadee, Co. Down, 500
Donegal, County, 112, 455
  election, 1874, 438
  election, 1880, 457–8
  Great Famine, 116, 118, 124, 134
  illegal distillation, 77, 91–2
  Land League, 460
  tenant right, 79, 85–6, 92–3
Donegall, Marquis of, 65
Donegall family, 106, 162, 212, 222, 409
Donegore, Co. Antrim, 102–3
Donoughmore, Co. Tyrone, 275–6, 277
Doran, Rev. John, 165
Dorrian, Dr, 183, 184
Dorrian, Dr, Bishop of Down and Connor, 262, 295, 347, 464, 467, 514
  Catholic cemetery, 347
  Catholic Institution controversy, 299–300
  marching rights, 377, 379
  National Association, 293–4
Down, County, 71, 72, 156, 177, 213, 282, 287, 355, 489, 494
  agrarian outrages, 187, 188
  cotton famine, 260, 394
  election, 1874, 438
  election, 1878, 418, 442, 444–7, 450, 453, 520
  election, 1880, 458
  election, 1884, 498–501
  grand jury, 105, 114, 161–2, 326, 366
  Land League, 470–71
  liberalism in, 407–8
  Party Processions Act agitation, 319, 320, 322
  sectarian clashes, 155

Tenant League, 192, 203
tenant right movement, 102, 121, 169, 191, 196, 201
United Irishmen, 23, 29–30, 39
weavers, 96–7, 114
Down and Connor, Anglican Bishop of, 236
Downhill Castle, 206, 226
Downpatrick, Co. Down, 121, 176, 186, 192, 243, 279, 417, 444, 447, 450, 500
  Crawford victory, 213
  Great Famine, 123, 315
  Johnston in, 316, 317
  sectarianism, 319
Downpatrick and Newcastle railway, 245
Downshire, Lord, 115–16, 179, 180, 190, 409, 470
Downshire Protestant, 234
Downshire Protestant Association, 317
Dowse, Richard, 421
Drapers' Company, 90–91, 237
Draperstown, Co. Derry, 467, 469
Drennan clubs, 145, 170, 216, 218
Drew, Rev. Dr Thomas, 20, 180, 188–9, 248, 250, 255, 317, 323, 349, 444
Dromore, Co. Tyrone, 96, 115, 297
Drumalee, Co. Cavan, 341, 360
Drumbee, battle of, 35
Drumhone, Co. Donegal, 86
drumming parties, 275–80, 416, 417
  Ballymoney, 457, 458
  Lurgan, 399–400
Drummond, Thomas, 56, 137, 152, 178, 179, 241, 503, 504
Dublin, Archbishop of, 460
Dublin Castle administration, 41, 47, 56, 267–8, 278, 285, 310, 320, 416, 509
  patronage of Catholics, 52
Dublin Central Tenants Defence Association, 449
Dublin presbytery, 313
Duddy, John, 365, 450, 451, 452, 468, 474

Dufferin, Lord, 203, 207, 309, 320, 389, 464
Duffin, Adam, 254
Duffy, Charles Gavan, 143, 186, 192, 208
Dundee, 74
Dungannon, Co. Tyrone, 88, 276, 427, 431, 448, 457
  Great Famine, 115, 122, 123
  Land League meeting, 461–2
  Liberal influence, 458–9
  Orangeism, 275, 425–6
  sectarianism, 98
  tenant right meetings, 153–4, 467
Dungannon Inquiry, 1871, 277
Dungarvan, Co. Tyrone, 469
Dungiven, Co. Derry, 88–90, 469
Dunville, William, 217–18, 219, 221, 260, 326
Durham, Bishop of, 193
Dwellings of the Working Classes Act, 498
Dysart, John, 289, 326

Eager, Rev. Mr, 387
Eagleson, Mr, 438
Ecclesiastical Titles Act, 193–4, 196–201, 202, 208, 310
economic revival, 210–11
education, 17, 90, 137, 356, 364, 421, 441, 515. *see also* national education system; university question
  and Belfast politics, 378–9
  and Catholic hierarchy, 139–40, 224
  of Catholics, 19, 21, 226, 296
  and culture, 49–50
  denominalization question, 224, 236–9, 366, 367, 391, 414, 423, 430, 439, 442, 446–9, 474–5, 520
  liberal reforms, 48, 51
  National Association, 293–4
  non-sectarianism in, 301–9
  Presbyterian, 209, 241
Eglinton, Mr, 279, 280
electoral reform. *see* franchise reform

Electoral Reform Bill, 319
elite, 22, 247, 404. *see also* landlords
  and Catholic clergy, 334
  Catholic support for, 418
  community of interests, Belfast, 221–3, 239–40
  and education, 224
  and Great Revival, 236–7
  leadership class, 517–18
  and marching rights, 503–5
  and militant Orangeism, 34–5, 55, 151, 154–6, 271–7, 337, 380–81
  resurgence of, 476, 477–8
  urban-rural tensions, 213–14
Ellis, Rev. Thomas, 495–6, 506
emigration, 73, 84, 96, 134, 187, 211, 225, 241, 384, 464, 513
  to America, 28, 89
  to Britain, 87, 89, 194, 210
  Great Famine, 87, 121–2, 128
  opposition to, 199, 207, 365, 419–20, 426, 456–7
  Presbyterian, 13–14
  Select Committee on, 94
Employers Liability Act, 493
employment. *see* labour force
Encumbered Estates Bill, 169
engineering industry, 211
Enniskillen, Co. Fermanagh, 55, 281, 349, 431
  anti-Fenian meeting, 366–7
  Great Famine, 132
  Land League meeting, 462, 469
  landlord control of, 58–9
Enniskillen, Earl of, 58–9, 124, 153, 317, 319, 351, 495
equalization, 17–20, 35, 63, 341–2, 520
Erne, Earl of, 124, 281, 460
Esmond, Major, 269
Evangelical Alliance, 236–7
evangelical revival, 61, 63–5
Evans, Mr, 275
evictions, 95, 169, 187, 225, 365, 449. *see also* expulsionism
  boycotting, 486–7
  disturbance payments, 458
  Great Famine, 111

Ewart, William, 481, 482, 491, 507–8
Ewart's mill, Belfast, 216, 222
Examiner, 414
expulsionism, 23, 247–8, 253, 255–8, 265–6, 373–5, 377, 512, 521
  residential areas, 256–8

Factory Acts, 106–7, 340, 479–80
fair trade, 496–7, 498
Fallon, Constable Patrick, 269
Falls Park, Belfast, 370
Farney barony, Co. Monaghan, 93, 118, 186
Farnham, Lord, 95
Fascism, 161
Fawcett, Professor, 307, 441
federalism, 141, 148
Fenian amnesty movement, 262, 333, 343, 356–64, 366, 375, 389, 418, 447
  Catholic support, 5, 297–8, 367
  effects of, 297–8, 363–4
  marches, 372, 416
  outside Belfast, 385, 387–8
  partial amnesty granted, 362–3
Fenianism, 241, 262, 271–2, 281–2, 320, 326, 356–7, 404, 450, 516, 521
  Catholic response to, 293–4, 296–8
  Cookstown, 427–8
  and Freemasons, 407
  Johnston on, 342–5
  and Land Act, 437–8, 442, 453
  and land agitation, 457, 473
  and Liberals, 485
  Manchester Martyrs, 297, 321–2, 357
  Orange response to, 274
  rising, 1867, 321
Ferguson, John, 422–3
Ferguson, John F., 217, 218, 219, 222, 223, 254, 266
Ferguson, J.S., 64, 217
Ferguson, Mr, 278, 279, 280
Ferguson, Sir Richard, 60
Ferguson, Sir Robert, 61

Fermanagh, County, 32, 282, 387, 431
  Great Famine, 116
  Land League, 433, 469
  landlord control, 58–9
  Orange Order, 153, 156, 281
  tenant right, 101–2
Ferris, William John, 483
feudalism, 179
Fews, the, Co. Armagh, 116
Fews Mountains, 72
Findlater, William, 465, 466
Finn river, 84, 85
fishing industry, 99
Fitzwilliam, Lord, 40–41
Flanagan, Rev. Mr, 387
flax cultivation, 74
Flaxdressers' committee, 291
flaxdressers' strike, 355, 370–72, 410
"Fleets", 33
Fletcher, Judge, 55
Florencecourt, Co. Fermanagh, 124
food prices, 104–5, 110–11, 112, 174, 291
  and protectionism, 176–8
Forde, Colonel, 121, 321, 323, 444
Forkhill, Co. Armagh, 32, 36, 37, 93, 187
Forster, W.E., 464
Foyle valley, 72, 84
France, 27, 40
  and rising, 1848, 147
  and United Irishmen, 41–42
Franchise Bill, 285, 493, 505
franchise reform, 39, 47, 163, 287–8, 411
  40-shilling freeholders, 77
  expansion, 315
  secret ballot, 206, 333, 338–9, 378, 430, 438
Franco-Prussian War, 362, 385, 396, 399–400, 431
Free Church of Scotland, 156, 179, 194, 265, 313
free trade, 70, 163–4, 174–5, 213, 519
Freemasons, 30, 38, 39, 41, 59, 295, 297, 407

French, R.C. Leslie, 272
Friends of United Education, 307
fuel, 77, 78, 97, 99–100, 102

Galgorm, Co. Antrim, 411
Galway, County
  election controversy, 333, 365–6, 367, 421–2, 424, 519
Gamble, Rev. Mr, 159
Gardner, Edward, 453
Garrison, Co. Fermanagh, 490
Garvagh, Co. Derry, 128, 153, 192
Getty, Samuel, 320
Gibbon, Peter, 2, 29–30, 31, 231, 418
Gilford, Co. Down, 97, 279, 400, 404–5, 429, 522
Givan, John, 465, 466
Gladstone, W.E., 273, 308–9, 325, 415, 436, 455, 458, 467, 473, 488
  and amnesty movement, 358, 360, 363
  disestablishment, 310, 311, 313, 314, 323, 348–9
  Home Rule movement, 457, 479, 501, 508, 509, 521
  Land Act, 1870, 384–5, 434–5, 437–8, 442, 453
  land crisis, 418
  and Parnell, 434, 488
  reforms, 333
  university question, 378–9
  on Vaticanism, 382, 439–41, 513
Glasgow, 73
Glenavy, Co. Antrim, 42, 72, 100, 246
Glenavy, County Antrim, 32
Glendy, Rev. William, 132–3
Glenfarne, Co. Fermanagh, 467
Glover, Mr, 388
Godkin, Mr, 186
Golding, Edward, 5
Gosford, Lord, 418
Gosford estates, Co. Armagh, 35, 75
Goudy, Dr Alex, 190–91
Graham, David, 394
grand juries, 31, 35, 105, 114, 321, 326, 390

Belfast, 161–2
county cess, 28
Newry, 417
Newtownards conflict, 407
reform sought, 163, 213, 285
relief works, 128
support Keogh judgment, 366
Tory strongholds, 433
Grant family, 256, 257
Grattan, Henry, 48
Gray, Rev. Alex, 311, 332, 380
Gray, Sam, 152, 186
Great Famine, 21, 73, 79, 91, 96, 99, 103, 104–34, 160, 163, 166, 187, 208, 227, 394
  effects of, 10–11, 87, 136, 158
  food speculation, 110–11, 112
  Johnston on, 315, 316
  and landlords, 204, 205, 208
  long-term effects of, 104–5, 134, 449
  McKnight on, 173–4
  migration to Belfast, 243
  population drain, 383
  proselytism, 248
  regional differences, 122–6, 128
  relief food, 109–11
  relief works, 115–18, 212
  Whig policy, 136, 143, 158
Great Revival, 224–5, 227–32
  effect on Catholics, 232–40
Green, Chief Constable, 251
Greencastle, Co. Down, 420
Greer, Samuel McCurdy, 157, 203, 206, 226, 227
Greer, Thomas, 411
Gregg, William, 395
Greig, William, 75
Greyabbey, Co. Down, 500
Grieg, William, 35
Griffith's valuation, 455, 462, 464, 468, 469
Grimshaw, Mr, 201
Grimshaw's mill, Belfast, 247
Gunning's weaving factory, Cookstown, 425
Gweedore, Co. Donegal, 118
Gwynn, W.J., 248

Hall, Isaac, 292, 293, 351
Hamill, John, 289, 295, 379
Hamilton, Lord Claud, 87, 206, 379, 425, 430
Hamilton, Lord Ernest, 489
Hamilton, Mr, 486
Hamilton, Robert, 327
Hancock, George, 114
Hancock, John, 54, 56, 165–6, 397–8, 399, 400, 403–5, 514
Hand, William Henry, 291, 370
Hanna, Rev. Hugh, 20, 22, 63, 219, 265, 266, 345, 352, 381, 492, 513, 521
   Great Revival, 230, 231–2, 238
   on marching rights, 353
   on nationalism, 370
   obstructs Belfast march, 372–3
   opposes Corry nomination, 380
   on papacy, 355, 363–4
   street preaching, 255, 258–60
   supports Presbyterian claims, 347–50
   worker intimidation, 266–7
Hannahstown, Co. Antrim, 359
Harkin, Dr, 295, 363
Harland, Sir Edward, 267, 491, 508
Harland and Wolff, 212, 367, 493
Harland's shipyard, 227, 244, 266, 267
Harvey, Sub-Inspector, 269
Harvey, William, 352
Haslett, James, 507
Hay, Lord John, 294, 331
Healy, Tim, 464, 477, 487–8
Heany, Hugh, 246
Hearts of Steel, 28
hedge-schools, 62, 90
Henderson, Rev. Henry, 304–5, 345, 348, 353, 363–4, 410
   and disestablishment, 385, 387
Henderson, James Alex, 377, 378–9, 381, 481, 483, 503, 504, 507, 514
Henry, Tom, 286, 288, 289, 322, 346, 368
Heron, Denis, 273, 361
Hertford, Marquis of, 154, 391, 394, 395

Hertford estate, 390
Hicks-Beach, Michael, 509
Hill, Lord Arthur, 203, 484, 490, 492, 495–6, 504–5, 507
Hill, Lord Edward, 491
Hill, Lord George, 92
Hill, Sir George, 60–61
Hill, George S., 245
Hillsborough, Co. Down, 67, 69, 176, 309, 321
Hillyer, Colonel, 421
Hinds, John, 247, 266
Hodson, Sir George, 95
Hodson, Rev. H., 155
Hoey, Peter, 290
Hogg's shirt factory, Derry, 422
Holmes, Rev. R. Finlay, 63, 64
Holywood, Co. Down, 78, 148, 459, 500
Home Rule Association, 365–6, 372, 522
Home Rule Bills, 1, 20, 508–9, 515
Home Rule movement, 354, 371, 375, 408–9, 430, 438, 447, 519
   assembly barred, Belfast, 355
   Biggar candidate, 421, 422
   Catholic support for, 408, 433
   Derry, 422–5
   Down, 500–501
   effects of, 333, 334, 336
   first crisis, 502
   Gilford marches, 404–5
   and Gladstone, 457, 479, 501, 508, 509, 521
   Johnston on, 339
   and Land League, 450, 469–70, 473–4
   Liberal divisions, 383
   marches, 372
   opposition to, 477–509
   riots, 508–9
   "Rome Rule", 345
   second crisis, 1892, 478–9
   spread of, 418–20
   support for Conservatives, 506–7
   and tenant right, 442–4
   Tyrone by-election, 1881, 471–2

INDEX 579

Home Rule Party, 353, 442, 443–4, 446, 451, 457
Hope, Jeremy, 30
Horner, George, 287, 346
housing, 78, 242–3
Hughes, Bernard, 216, 217, 260, 290, 295–6, 358, 378, 379
Hughes, Father, 398
Hughes, J.J., 186
Hyde, Mr, 246

illegal distillation, 75, 77, 85, 91–2
Indemnity Act, 1864, 285, 295
Indemnity Bills, 217, 218, 221, 222–3, 285
Independent Orangeism, 328, 345–54, 369–70, 381, 481–4, 507. *see also* Johnston, William
  Co. Tyrone, 425
  Cobain, 493–4
  and Conservatives, 293, 334–6, 378, 379–80
  optimism, 21–2
  outside Belfast, 383, 394, 399, 409–10, 430, 436
  and tenant right movement, 390
  and Tories, 354
industrial development, 205, 414, 517
Inishowen Peninsula, Co. Donegal, 387, 421, 469
Insurrection Act, 1796, 41
intermediate education, 224
Intermediate Education Bill, 414, 446, 447–9
"Invasion of Ulster", 7, 22, 477, 479, 484, 498, 504
Ireland, D.R., 148, 149, 150
Irish Constabulary, 246, 247
Irish language, 35, 36, 48–9, 90, 140, 141, 384, 515–16
Irish National League, 477
Irish Society, 59, 60
Irish Universities Bill, 378–9, 414, 439, 440, 441, 446, 449
Irish Volunteers, 17–18, 27–9, 30, 41, 50, 64, 145, 184
  battle of Drumbee, 35

Catholics in, 32, 33, 34
  clashes with Defenders, 35–6, 37
  relations with landlords, 28–9
  and sectarianism, 34
  and United Irishmen, 39–40
Irvine, Mr, 483
Irvinestown, Co. Fermanagh, 488

Jackson, Mr, 36
Jacobitism, 15, 28, 42, 44
Jefferson, Redmond, 392, 394–5, 396
Johns, Alex, 365
Johnston, Rev., 190
Johnston, T.B., 289
Johnston, Rev. William, 303, 305
Johnston, William (of Ballykilbeg), 20, 21, 245, 248, 277, 298, 357, 409, 426, 431, 493
  and 1870 Land Act, 390
  and 1872 riots, 375, 376
  and amnesty movement, 359–60
  attitude to Catholics, 314, 340–41, 345
  career as MP, 333–47
  career of, 315–28
  and Conservatives, 338, 377, 441, 507
  defence of Derry, 421
  and denominational education, 364
  deposed from grand mastership, 352–3
  election campaign, 284, 326–32, 374
  and Factory Act, 479–81
  and flaxdressers' strike, 371
  and marching rights, 387–8, 503, 504
  and Orange Order, 281, 316–17, 318
  pan-Protestantism, 494–5, 507, 508, 513, 516
  Party Processions Act agitation, 319–25
  resigns as MP, 481
  tenant right movement, 435
  Working Men's Institute, 368–9

joint stock directors, 480
Jones, Capt. Theobald, 203
Jonesborough, Co. Armagh, 32, 462

Kane, Rev. R.R., 20, 484, 491, 492, 506, 508, 509, 513
  and Cobain, 494, 495
  Grand Master, Belfast, 493
  and land agitation, 463, 466
  political strategy, 502–4
  sectarianism, 459–61, 487–8
Keady, Co. Armagh, 387, 417
Keegan, Peter, 296
Keegan family, 295
Kelly, Dr, Bishop of Derry, 422
Kelly, Rev. Fr, 395, 396
Kelly, Robert, 327, 328, 346, 352, 353, 354, 410
Kennedy, Tristram, 121
Keogh, Judge, 276–7, 333, 365–6, 371, 421, 422, 424
Keogh, William, 199
Ker family, 316
Ker, David Stewart, 203, 317
Kernan, Randall, 55
Kickham, Charles, 361
Kildare Place Society, 62, 181
Kilkeel, Co. Down, 500–501
Killeavy, Co. Armagh, 187, 417, 462
Killelagh, Co. Derry, 88, 90
Killen, Dr T.Y., 159, 312, 348, 379
Killinchy, Co. Down, 102
Killinkere, Co. Cavan, 95
Killygorden estate, Co. Donegal, 85–6
Killyman, Co. Tyrone, 97, 151, 426, 429
Kilmood estate, 189
Kilmore, Bishop of, 95
Kilrea, Co. Derry, 467, 470
Kilrush, Co. Clare, 177, 179
Kirk, William, 121
Kirkpatrick, Dr, 310, 311, 312–13
Kirkpatrick, William, 290–91, 368–9
Kisby (newspaper editor), 265, 266, 267, 286
Knox, Colonel, 461, 471
Knox, Dr, 317–18, 379
Knox, Stewart, 275, 427, 430
Knox family, 58, 154

labour force, 73–4, 210–11, 241, 511–12, 518
  agricultural, 87
  Belfast, 106–7, 243–5
  effects of Famine, 105
  exclusivism, 290
  expulsionism, 247–8, 253, 255, 265–6, 512
  and franchise reform, 287–9
  and Independent Orangeism, 21–2
  intimidation, 266
  nine hours movement, 354
  organization of, 290–3, 508
  and politics, 367–71, 493–5, 496–8
  and sectarianism, 11, 480–81
  shipyard lockout, 1885, 493–4
  weakness of, 405–6
  women in, 480
  women workers, 73–4
Labour Rate Act, 1846, 109–10, 115, 118
Lady Day processions, 366, 372, 385, 396, 400
Lagan river, 72, 78, 105
Lambeg, Co. Antrim, 392, 394, 484
Land Act, 1870, 384–5, 410, 414, 419, 434, 437–8, 442, 453, 521
  amendments sought, 333, 350–51, 390, 429–30, 438, 457, 461, 465
  effects of, 435–6
Land Act, 1881, 471–2, 477, 484, 487
Land Bills, 217, 362, 469, 471
  Butt Bill, 442, 445, 453, 460
  Crawford Bill, 443, 444–5
  Somerville Bill, 153–5, 160, 165–6, 167, 168
Land League, 432–75, 450, 453, 455–75, 501, 502
  effects on nationalism, 485–6
  and Orange Order, 497
  relations with Liberals, 433–4, 462, 464–9, 472–5
  suppressed, 486
  Tyrone by-election, 471–3

INDEX 581

land question, 28. *see also* landlords; tenant right movement
  agrarian outrages, 102, 244, 283, 473
  and Tenant League, 187–9
  peasant proprietary, 450, 452, 453, 456–7
  rent reductions, 213, 449–52, 455–6, 468
    Londonderry estate controversy, 189–91
  tenure, 293, 323–4, 326, 333, 340, 424, 442, 453
Land Tenure Bill, 1848, 160
Land War, 21, 420, 432–75, 454–5, 497, 522
  Co. Tyrone, 429–30
  and Orange Order, 427–8
landlords, 8–9, 13, 75, 208, 383. *see also* reclamation tenantry; tenant right movement
  charges for lease renewals, 28
  consolidation of estates, 77–8, 82–4, 94–6, 100–103, 121–2, 166–9, 176, 187
  dependent on Britain, 27
  effects of Great Famine, 107, 109, 121–3, 134
  lack of opposition to, 225–7
  and Land League, 460–62
  local control by, 58–9
  McKnight on, 172–4
  and Orange Order, 54–5, 132, 431, 504–5
  provision of schools, 305
  public works, 454
  relations with tenants, 10–11, 75
  relief works, 116, 118, 121–2
  rent reductions sought, 166, 169–70, 176, 177–8
  role of, 411–12
  sectarianism of, 87–8
  and tenant right, 384
  and Volunteers, 28–9
  and Whigs, 137–8
Lanyon, Charles, 286, 289, 319, 327
  election, 1868, 328–32, 374
Larah, Co. Cavan, 95

Larne, Co. Antrim, 59, 68, 78, 132–3
Law, Hugh, 464, 467, 470
law and order, 61, 241–83, 510–11. *see also* marching rights
  in Belfast, 270
  Catholic definitions, 21
  and Catholic organization, 37–8
  effects of 1798 rebellion, 53–4
  liberal reforms, 48, 51
  outside Belfast, 271–83
  sectarian administration of, 54–6
  and sectarianism, 4–8, 247–54, 337–8
  Whig reforms, 140
Lawrencetown, Co. Down, 279, 400
Lawless, Jack, 186
League of North and South. *see* Tenant League
Leasehold Tenant Right Bill, 444
Leinster
  Land League, 457, 458
  seasonal migration to, 77, 93
Leitrim, Lord, 459
Lemon, James, 218, 219
Leslie, Rev. Knox, 426, 427
Lewis, C.E., 422, 441, 448, 449
Lewis, F.H., 222, 286
Liberal Working Men's Defence Association, 344, 421, 422
Liberals, 3–4, 161, 205–6, 285, 294, 319, 479. *see also* disestablishment; Gladstone, W.E.; Whigs
  and 1864 riots, 261–4
  and 1872 riots, 374, 377–8
  alliance with Catholics, 294–5
  and amnesty movement, 358, 362–3
  Armagh, 397
  attitude to Catholics, 238–9, 260, 269–70, 439–41
  Ballymena, 411–13
  Belfast politics, 210, 216, 218, 222–3, 286, 352, 357, 369–70
    decline, 334, 381–2
    lose Catholic support, 379–80, 444–7, 498–502
    reforms, 286–90

Liberals *continued*
  Carrickfergus, 409–10
  Catholic support for, 209–10, 378–80, 455–8
  and class issues, 496–8
  coercion, 469, 498
  Coleraine, 413–14
  and constabulary, 246
  Derry, 420–25
  distribution of, 415, 416–18
  education question, 306–7, 307–9, 446, 447–9
  and evangelical revival, 64–5
  and Factory Bill, 480
  and Home Rule movement, 383
  and Independent Orangeism, 345, 350
  Johnston election, 326–8
  and Land League, 433–4, 462, 464–9, 472–5
  landlords, 94–5
  law and order, 242
  Lurgan, 398
  and nationalism, 485–6, 487–8
  Newtownards, 406–9
  opposed to sectarianism, 21
  and Orangeism, 8, 269–70, 271–2, 344, 351
  and Party Processions Act, 320
  Portadown, 398
  and Presbyterians, 59, 156–8, 209–10, 223–4, 231, 265, 415
  and Repeal movement, 51
  and tenant right movement, 388–90, 432–75, 442, 452–4, 485–6
  Unionists, 478
  and United Irishmen, 41
Lichfield House Treaty, 150
Limavady, Co. Derry, 313
Limerick by-election, 1850, 192, 193
Linden treaty, 409
Lindsay, Robert, 217, 284–5, 286, 332
Lindsay, Thomas, 246
linen industry, 17, 38, 58, 72, 78, 95–6, 177, 260, 291, 355, 394, 398, 519. *see also* weavers

Armagh, 32
Ballymena, 411–13
Belfast, 222
  Catholics in, 33–4
  crisis, 1830s, 99
  cultural influence of, 35, 48
  decline, 100, 210–11, 367–8
  economic influence of, 29, 72–4
  mechanization, 85
  protest meeting, Ballymena, 412–13
  recession, 479–80
Lisburn, Co. Antrim, 30, 158, 340, 353, 403, 497
  arms for Belfast riots, 262
  election, 1863, 394–5
  marching rights, 405
  Orange Order, 154–5, 260
  politics of, 391–7
  riots, 385
Lissan, Co. Tyrone, 91
London University, 305
Londonderry. *see* Derry
Londonderry, Marquis of, 159, 168, 170, 187, 192, 206, 406, 408, 444, 445
  refuses rent reductions, 189–91
Londonderry Standard, 170
Londonderry yeomanry, 60
Longford, County, 361
Loughbrickland, Co. Down, 165, 400
Loughguile, Co. Antrim, 467, 469, 470
Loughinsholin barony, Co. Derry, 111
Louth, County, 71, 321
Loyalists. *see* unionism
Loyalty meetings, 159–60
Lucas, Frederick, 186
Lunn, Robert, 374–5
Lurgan, Co. Armagh, 54, 403, 411, 495–6, 514, 515
  demagogues, 478
  marching rights, 404, 405
  riots, 385, 399–400
  sectarianism in, 397–400
  tenant right meeting, 165–6, 173

Lurgan, Lord, 54, 97, 165, 397, 398
Lurgan Tenant Right association, 176
Lyle, Mr, 276, 277
Lynch, Rev. John, 234–6
Lyttle, John, 348

Macauley, Peter, 379
McCall, Hugh, 394, 396
McCann, Thomas, 15
McCartney, J. Ellison, 429–30, 438, 458, 466
McCartney, William Ellison, 497–8
McClean, Rev. Hugh, 278
McClelland, Rev., 68
McClure, Thomas, 218, 292, 339, 345, 346, 350, 357, 360, 379, 380
  election campaign, 284, 312, 314, 326–32, 374
  Land Bill, 435
McComb, Rev. Samuel, 348, 492
McConnell, John, 262, 267
McCorkell, Bartholomew, 422
McCormick, William, 324, 326, 352, 353, 368, 481–2, 484, 493, 494, 507
McCoy, William John, 360
McCoy, William T., 262
McCracken, Henry Joy, 42, 419
MacCrory, Adam, 348
McCrystal, Very Rev. Canon, 427, 523
McCullough, Julius, 190
McDade, William, 482, 483
Macdonogh, Mr, 220–21
McElderry, Thomas, 388
McElroy, Sam, 383, 435, 470
McGeagh, R.J., 263
McGeough, Bond, 473
MacHale, Dr John, Archbishop of Tuam, 137, 140, 142
McIlwaine, Rev. William, 255
McKay, Rev., 68
McKenna, A.J., 265, 266, 294, 295, 421, 422
  amnesty movement, 358, 360, 362
  and clerical support, 296
  and Dr Dorrian, 299–300
  editor *Northern Star*, 321, 334, 355–6
  editor *Ulster Observer*, 264, 271
  and Fenianism, 357–8, 364
  on reform, 289
  on university question, 308
  Working Men's Institute, 368
McKeown v Beauclerc, 436
McKnight, Dr James, 153, 183, 206, 207, 210, 226, 421
  on agrarian outrages, 188
  concept of liberalism, 458
  on Crawford bill, 198–9
  deputation to Gladstone, 434–5
  on education, 364–5
  on landlords, 189, 204–5
  on north-south cooperation, 194–6
  plantation thesis, 461
  on rent reductions, 178–9
  on sectarianism, 179–82
  and Tenant League, 185–6, 191–2
  on tenant right movement, 128, 132–4, 170–76, 323, 388–9, 424
  on university question, 307, 309
MacKnight, Thomas, 325, 356, 388–9, 434, 456
McLaine's yard, 244
McLaughlin, 254, 255, 258–60, 264, 521
McLaughlin and Harvey, 292
McLorninan, Hugh, 287
MacManus, 419
McMordie, Hans, 444, 453
McMullan, George, 22, 256, 257, 523
MacNaghten, Edward, 492, 497
McNamara, James, 217–18, 219, 221
MacNaughton, Rev. John, 265–7, 270, 364, 379, 422, 439, 513, 514
  and disestablishment, 310–13
  and education, 301–4, 308, 310, 448
  and Orangeism, 335–6
  peace committees, 522
  supports Johnston, 326
Macneven, William, 49–50
Macosquin, Co. Antrim, 99
McSheehy, Mr, 402
Madden, John, 272

584 INDEX

Madden, Richard R., 42, 141
Madden, Captain William, 272, 273
Magee, John, 297
Magee, Mr, 279
Magee College, Derry, 301–4, 306, 420
Maghera, Co. Derry, 90, 384, 468, 469
Magheraboy, Co. Fermanagh, 467
Magherafelt, Co. Derry, 111, 226, 313, 388, 428–9
Magherafelt Land League, 467
magistrates, 51, 242, 244, 245, 247, 514
   arms searches, 262–3
   Belfast riots, 252, 255
   and drumming parties, 399–400
   leadership roles, 18–19, 477–8
   and marching rights, 344, 381, 396, 405, 503–5
   and Orange Order, 54–5, 271–2, 276–8, 278–80, 337, 395, 402–3
Maguire, Edward, 281, 366–7
Manchester, Duke of, 397
Manchester Martyrs, 297, 321–2, 357
Manning, Archbishop, 382
Manorcunningham, Co. Donegal, 417
marching rights, 5, 274, 276–80, 321, 353, 354, 381, 417, 503–5
   Belfast, 378, 483–4
   Derry, 340, 344, 421
   Johnston's views, 340–41, 344
   Magherafelt, 428–9
   outside Belfast, 385, 387, 396, 404–5
   riots, 1872, 372–7
Markethill, Co. Armagh, 32, 418
markets, 58, 59
Martin, John, 361, 363
Marxism, 511
Maxwell, Robert, 326
May, Sir Stephen, 162
Maynooth College, 139, 156, 316–17, 349
Mayo, County, 450, 451, 460, 468
Mayo, Lord, 321

Mayobridge, Co. Down, 464, 465, 468, 469
Meagher, Francis, 145–7, 419, 521
meal mongers, 91, 92
Meath, County, 71, 363
Melbourne, Lord, 69, 135
Mervyn, Head Constable, 278
Methodists, 282, 400
middle class
   Catholic, 62, 295–6, 511
   creation of, 29
   evangelical revival, 64
   lack of role for, 56, 58
   nationalism, 137
   Presbyterians, 38
   Volunteers, 28
military, 41, 276, 387, 514
   Belfast riots, 262, 264, 373
mill workers, 243, 255, 261, 262
   Great Revival, 227, 230–31, 234
Millar, David, 1–3, 30, 172, 207, 231
Miller, Sir William, 489
Milward, Lieutenant, 116
Mingay, G.E., 94
Mitchell, John, 147
Mitchell, William, 273
model schools, 301, 391
Moffatt, John, 286, 287, 289, 331, 378
Molly Maguires, 153
Molyneaux, Rev., 133
Monaghan, County, 101, 201, 280, 282, 355, 356, 519
   agrarian outrages, 188
   election, 1826, 47, 58
   election, 1880, 458
   election murder, 152
   Great Famine, 105, 116, 118, 123, 124, 126, 128
   Healy victory, 1883, 477, 487–8
   jury panel, 361
   land subdivision, 77, 92–3
   number of farms, 384
   Orange Order, 271–3, 274, 460, 470
   tenant right movement, 92–3, 388, 465–6
Monaghan parish, 92–3
Monaghan town, 271, 272–3
Moncrieffe, Alex, 73

moneylenders, 91, 92, 102
Moneymore, Co. Derry, 237, 467, 470
Monroe, John, 495–6, 506
Montgomery, Dr Henry, 63, 64, 167–9, 170–71
Montiaghs, Co. Armagh, 468
Mooney, Thomas, 340
Moore, Barrington, 161
Moore, G.H., 357
Moriarty, Dr, Bishop of Kerry, 274
Morley, John, 508–9, 514
Morning News, 381–2, 483, 498
Morris, Michael, 319
Mountmorres, Lord, 460
Mourne Mountains, 72
Mourne river, 84
Muckno, Co. Monaghan, 93
Muff, Co. Derry, 387, 417, 421
Mulgrave, Constantine Henry Phipps, 6th Earl of (later Marquis of Normanby), 137
Mulholland, John, 326–7, 381
  election, 1868, 328–32
Mullan, William, 199, 217, 260, 264, 332
  Belfast mayor, 284–5, 286
Mullholland and Herdman, 85
Mulligan, J.H., 402–3
Mulligan, Montague, 220–21
Municipal Corporations Act, 1840, 51–2, 58, 105
municipal elections, 379–80, 381, 383
Munro, Henry, 30
Munster, 454, 457
  Land League, 457, 458
Munster Tenant Farmers Association, 456
Murney, Dr, 295
Murphy (miller), 266–7
Murphy, Rev. Bernard, 426
Murphy's mill, Belfast, 266

Nation, 141, 203
National Association, 293–4
National Education League, 364, 420, 425, 444

national education system, 103, 132, 236–8, 335, 391
  aims of, 65–6
  and Catholics, 19, 51, 140, 157, 226
  Church Education Society, 180–81
  controversy, 61–9
  denominalization sought, 224, 301–9
  McKnight on, 180–81
  non-sectarianism, 364
  and Presbyterians, 156
National League, 485, 488
National Party, 496
National Tenant Right conference, 1874, 437
nationalism, 23, 53, 137, 207, 376, 417, 453, 464, 472, 518. *see also* Fenianism; Young Ireland movement
  and Catholicism, 140, 365
  and Conservatives, 506–9
  effects of Great Famine, 126, 134
  effects of Land League, 462, 469–70, 473–4, 485–6
  election, 1884, 498, 500–502
  Fenian amnesty movement, 360
  Fenianism, 387–8
  frontier districts, 415
  growing strength, 477–9, 487–90
  and Liberals, 8, 485–6
  nationhood, 48–9
  procession fired on, 459
  Sligo by-election win, 8–9
  Tenant League, 186
  and unionism, 515
navvy gangs, 243–5, 261–2, 262–4, 267, 268, 270, 521
Nelson, Isaac, 365–6, 468
Nenagh, Co. Tipperary, 160
New Departure, 450
Newry, Co. Down, 121, 135, 224, 318, 420, 447, 500–501
  demonstration banned, 490
  election, 1868, 327
  Great Famine, 132, 133
  Parnell meeting, 456
  politics of, 416–18

Newry, Co. Down *continued*
  tenancies, 58
  tenant right movement, 201–2, 451–2
Newsletter, 154, 189, 261, 265, 266, 286, 342, 354, 377, 378, 473, 498, 500
  boycotting, 486
  denounced, 322
  Dorrian affair, 299–300
  on *Examiner*, 377
  Repeal movement, 143–5, 147
  on Sligo Protestants, 8–9, 10
  on Tenant League, 192, 193, 199
Newton Hamilton, 43
Newtown Act, 1747, 14
Newtownards, Co. Down, 39, 190, 196, 320, 322, 398, 445
  centre of liberalism, 406–9
  Fenianism, 297
  Liberal vote, 205
  Orange Order, 192
  politics of, 415
  Tenant League, 195, 203, 204
Newtownards Chronicle, 408–9, 519
Newtownhamilton, Co. Armagh, 387
Newtownstewart, Co. Tyrone, 84, 85
Nightshade (Johnston), 315, 316
Nilteen Grange, 102
Nolan, Captain, 365
Northcote, Sir Stafford, 505–6
Northern Bank, 213, 214, 218, 221, 332
Northern Banking Company, 64, 217
Northern Counties Railway Company, 162, 414
Northern Star, 321, 325, 328, 334, 346, 350–51, 390, 421
  on land question, 323
  rivalry with *Examiner*, 355–63
  on sectarianism, 324
  tenant right movement, 435
Northern Whig, 170, 190, 207, 239, 255, 288, 346, 364, 464, 481–2, 520
  amnesty movement, 367
  analysis of Down election, 1884, 498

  Belfast riots, 263
  clerical leadership, 270, 363
  co-operatives, 290–91
  conflict with *Examiner*, 377
  drumming parties, 280
  on dual allegiance, 440–41
  Fenianism, 297, 356, 358
  Great Revival, 238
  Party Processions Act, 320, 325–6
  tenant right movement, 166, 199, 388–9, 390, 435
  Ulster riots, 261, 262
  on university question, 302
Nunan, Sub-Inspector, 399

Oak Boys, 28, 34
O'Brien, Rev. John, 278–9
O'Brien, William Smith, 143–4, 149
O'Callaghan, Fr Patrick, 418
O'Connell, Daniel, 20, 21, 47–8, 53, 95, 98, 150, 159, 180, 185, 192, 282, 453, 518, 520, 521
  Belfast visit, 163
  breakdown of Whig alliance, 137–9
  Catholic emancipation, 446
  discontent with, 141–4, 147
  mock funeral, 260–61, 263, 268
  Repeal movement, 49, 52, 135, 136, 137–9
  sectarianism, 50
  Whig support, 69, 142–3
O'Connell, John, 192–3
O'Connor, Arthur, 185
O'Donnell, J.C., 366
O'Donnell, John, 421, 422
O'Donnell (RM), 247
O'Donovan Rossa, Jeremiah, 342–3, 344, 357, 361, 363
O'Hagan, Thomas 267–8
O'Hanlon, Thomas, 420, 456
O'Keeffe, Father, 421
Oldershaw, Captain, 115
Omagh, Co. Tyrone, 115, 313, 388
O'Neill, Father, 452
O'Neill, Lord, 114
O'Neill, Sub-Constable, 276
O'Neill, Terence, 419, 519
O'Neill, Captain William, 118

INDEX 587

O'Rafferty, Rev. D., 93
Orange and Protestant Working
    Men's Association, 354–5,
    479–84, 494
Orange Order, 2, 22, 23, 38, 52, 68,
    94, 95, 158, 170, 239, 248, 418,
    439. *see also* drumming parties;
    Independent Orangeism;
    marching rights; Party
    Processions Act
  Armagh, 41, 42, 397
  ballot question, 351, 353
  Belfast, 269, 286, 318–19
  Belfast riots, 250–54, 266, 372–7
  Burial Society, 370, 373
  Carrickfergus, 410
  Catholic co-operation, 429–31
  "Church Defence" campaign,
    280–82, 321, 348–9, 425–6
  Coleraine, 413–14
  Conservative control of, 273–7,
    293, 380–81, 447, 487–93,
    504–5, 513
  Cookstown, 425–8
  counter-demonstrations, 477,
    488–93, 504–5
  as defence force, 38, 53–6, 136,
    154–5, 241, 273–7
  density of lodges, 59
  Derry, 421
  dissolved, 1836, 150–53
  and education, 364
  exclusivism, 290
  expulsions from, 206, 227, 346,
    350, 351, 392, 394–5, 410
  Fermanagh, 59
  flags on churches, 349, 387, 417
  government patronage, 155–6
  and Great Revival, 232
  growth of, 29–30
  influence of, 97–9
  and Johnston, 316–17, 318, 328,
    333–47
  and Land League, 460–62, 463–5,
    467, 469–71, 497
  and land question, 427–8, 429–30,
    457, 458–9
  and landlords, 87–8
  and liberalism, 7–8
  Lisburn, 260, 392, 394–7
  Newry, 416–17
  Newtownards, 406, 407
  opposition to Home Rule, 479
  opposition to protectionism,
    176–7, 179
  opposition to Union, 24
  and Party Processions Act, 320–26
  patrolmen, 18
  police links, 246–7, 252–4
  Portadown, 398
  Presbyterians in, 347–50
  processions curbed, 261, 481
  provocation by, 275–80
  and Reform movement, 289
  and Repeal movement, 149
  response to Fenianism, 297
  response to nationalism, 495–8
  revival, 1860s, 271–4, 385, 387
  roots of, 30–31
  select committee enquiry, 55
  and Tenant League, 186
  and tenant right movement, 128,
    132, 153–6, 191–2, 461, 466–7
  territorial control, 151–3
  and Volunteers, 27
  and workers' organizations,
    292–3
Order of Charity, 278
Orme (RM), 247
Ormeau Park, Belfast, 370
O'Rorke, Daniel, 262, 295
O'Rourke, Mr, 233
Orr, William, 419
O'Sullivan, Rev. Mortimer, 97, 99
outdoor relief, 110, 115, 124
Overend, Henry, 465

Palles, Richard, 421, 422, 425
Palmerston, Lord, 239
pan-Catholicism, 520
  development of, 18–20
  emancipation drive, 54
  land agitation seen as, 456
  opposes liberalism, 423–4
  strengthened by reforms, 48
  and Young Ireland, 149–50

pan-Protestantism, 11, 415
  defines land agitation as pan-Catholicism, 456
  distrust of Catholics, 298–9, 339–40
  liberal opposition to, 432
  moves from Anglicanism, 69
  opposition to Home Rule, 477–9
  patronage system, 59–60
"Papal Aggression", 195–7, 213–14, 335
parks, 370
parliament, Irish, 12, 27, 39
  abolished, 47
  reform sought, 32, 39–40
Parnell, Charles Stewart, 417, 420, 446, 455, 459, 474, 498, 506
  and 1881 Land Act, 471–2
  divorce case, 478
  and Gladstone, 434, 488
  and Land League, 433, 485
  leads Home Rule Party, 457
  National League, 477
  prosecution of, 463–4
  and tenant right movement, 443–4
  visits north, 418, 450–52, 453, 456, 462
  Waterford speech, 469
partition, 518
Party Processions Act, 280, 286, 372
  agitation against, 281, 319–25, 327, 351, 359, 390
  defiance of, 274, 277
  reimposed, 155–6, 271
  repeal of, 503
Patrick, John, 412–13
Patriotic Brotherhood, 473
Patterson, Henry, 517–18
Paul, Mr, 403
Peel, Sir Robert, 20, 21, 69, 109, 135, 138–9, 154, 163
Peel, T.G., 397, 400, 404, 461
Peep O'Day Boys, 34–7, 38
penal laws, 2, 11, 13–15, 21, 31, 33, 44, 61, 157, 193, 422
  control system, 17–18, 24–5
  effects on Catholics, 15, 17
  and Presbyterians, 38–9
Pettigo, Co. Donegal, 387
Pettigrew, Daniel, 291, 370
Phoenix Park murders, 487–8
Pinkerton, John, 467, 502
Pitt, William, 40, 47
Pius IX, Pope, 183
Plunkett, Captain, 277, 278
Poland, 10
polarization, 477–509, 521–2
  Land League, 463–4
  tendencies against, 333–4
  two nations, 519–23
police. see constabulary
Police Bill, 268, 285, 286
Pomeroy, Co. Tyrone, 275, 276, 418–19, 426, 472
Ponsonby family, 14
Poor Law, 204, 205, 228, 395, 429
  1838, 77–8
  1847, 111, 121
  displaced tenants, 167, 169
  elections, 354
  and Great Famine, 110, 111, 114–15, 118, 123, 124, 126, 134
  rate-in-aid scheme, 132–3, 177, 179, 201
  treatment of Catholics, 408
Poor Law Inquiry, 1835, 93
population displacement, 187
Portacarron Award, 365
Portadown, Co. Armagh, 54, 156, 385, 408, 495–6, 515
  demagogues, 478
  marching rights, 405
  riots, 399
  sectarianism in, 397–404
  tenant right meeting disrupted, 456, 457, 458, 463
Portadown and Lurgan News, 401–3
Portaferry, Co. Down, 500
Porter, Rev. J.S., 307
Portglenone, Co. Antrim, 68, 412, 468
Portrush, Co. Antrim, 78, 414
Potter, Rev. Mr, 317
Pounden, Rev., 396
Powerscourt estate, Benburb, 99

Poyntzpass, Co. Armagh, 341, 387
preaching. *see* street preaching
Presbyterians, 78, 135, 170. *see also*
    United Irishmen
  and Anglicans, 102–3, 135, 156–7,
    234, 415
  Armagh, 32
  attitude to Catholics, 191, 194, 241
  attitude to Whigs, 161
  and Catholics, 1, 26–7, 40, 294
  Coleraine, 414
  Derry, 420–25
  disabilities of, 38–9
  and disestablishment, 309–14
  Down, 500–501
  education question, 180–81,
    301–9, 364, 378–9, 447–9
  emigration, 13–14
  evangelical revival, 61, 63–5
  exclusion, 13
  Great Revival, 224–5, 227–32
  land occupation, 84–5
  and Liberals, 59, 156–8, 209–10,
    223–4, 265, 415, 444–7
  McKnight on tenant right, 171–6
  opposition to Tories, 135, 136
  and Orange Order, 347–50
  religious equality, 313–14
  and tenant right movement,
    157–60, 189–91, 199, 200–201,
    201–2, 206
  university question, 157–8
Preston, Sir John, 481, 482–3
priests. *see* clerical leadership
primogeniture, 174
Property Protection Association,
  287
proselytism, 237
protectionism, 156, 163–4, 176–8,
  213, 318
Protestant Colonization Society, 95
Protestant Individual Life
  Protection Society, 459
Protestant Repeal Association,
  148–9
Protestant Working Men's
  Association, 322–3, 324, 326,
  327, 334, 336–7, 347, 350, 484

Protestants. *see also* elite; Orange
    Order; sectarianism
  ascendancy, 71
  distrust of Catholics, 2–3, 36–8,
    45–6, 182–4, 298–9
  and Land League, 459–60, 472–3
  land occupation, 71–2, 84–8
  and Liberals, 19–20, 269–70, 416
  opposition to Home Rule, 476
  opposition to Union, 148–50
  pan-Protestantism, 282–3
  as settlers, 517–19
  Ulster-British differences, 50,
    514–16
  Ulster defined as, 159–60
  Wexford atrocities, 43
public works, 105–6, 109, 187
  Great Famine, 115–18, 122, 124,
    128, 134
Purcell (barrister), 254

quarter-acre rule, 111, 124
Queen's College, Belfast, 295
Queen's colleges, 139, 142, 157, 199,
  209, 236, 301, 303
  condemned by Synod, 197
Queen's University, Belfast, 301–2,
  304, 306, 307, 308, 379
Quinn, Rev. Charles, 417–18, 455–6
Quinn, Dr, 450–52, 464
Quinn, John, 419–20

Radicals, 294, 307, 378
railways, 162, 213, 219, 228, 245,
  317, 414
Ranfurley, Earl of, 275
Rasharkin, Co. Antrim, 227, 278,
  323
Ratepayers Property Protection
  Association, 326
rates, 78
Rathfriland, Co. Down, 417, 501
Rawdon, Colonel, 201
Rea, John, 259, 287, 290, 352, 378,
  421
  Chancery suit, 216–23
  and tenant right movement, 170
Reade, Robert H., 291

590 INDEX

reclamation tenantry, 74–5, 89–90, 92, 94, 187, 417, 418, 426, 474
  and agrarian outrages, 187–9
Redistribution Bill, 505–6
Reed, Inspector-General, 509
Reform Act, 58, 61, 289
Reform question, 284, 285, 286, 322, 326, 335
  Belfast, 287–90
Regium Donum, 189, 200, 309, 310–13, 348
relief works, 454, 456
religious orders, 33
Remonstrants, 63, 65
Removal Act, 1847, 118, 121
Repeal movement, 49, 52, 136, 152, 186, 516, 521
  Belfast meeting, 50–51, 137–9, 163
  conflicts within, 135, 141–4, 147
  fear of, 97–8
  and Tenant League, 192–6, 196
  in Ulster, 148–50
Ribbonism, 91, 94, 239, 250, 257, 356, 428, 473
  after Great Famine, 126, 187
  Dolly's Brae, 155, 179, 316
  and Johnston, 315, 316
  and navvy gangs, 244–5
  and Orangeism, 56, 151, 152–3
  self-defence, 296, 297
  and Tenant League, 188
Richardson, J.J., 392, 394, 395
Richardson, J.N., 417, 418
Richardson, Jonathan (Glenmore), 394–5, 397
Richardson, Jonathan (Lambeg), 392, 394
Richardson families, 154–5, 391
riots commissions, 247, 254, 266–7, 290
Ritchie, Robert, 371
Robertson, Thomas, 437
Robinson, Rev. Archibald, 311–12, 437
Rogers, Rev. John, 159, 191–2, 193, 266, 309, 380, 434, 435
Roman Catholic Aggregate meeting, 197–8

Ross, David, 106–7
Ross, William, 295, 296, 346, 358, 378, 379
Rosslea, Co. Fermanagh, 489, 505
Rossmore, Lord, 489, 505
Rostrevor, Co. Down, 452
Route, the, 59, 313, 454
Route Tenants Defence Association, 383, 436–7, 442, 452, 470
Rowan, Archibald Rowan, 24
Ruddell, David, 284, 288, 289, 368, 378
rundale, 90
Rushe, Fr Denis, 356–7
Russell, Lord John, 193, 285, 309
Rutherford, Rev. John, 189
Ryan, Michael, 192
Rylett, Harold, 471

Sadleir, Mr, 199
St George, Rev. Mr, 181
Saintfield, Co. Down, 178, 385–6, 444
Saunderson, Colonel, 495–7, 506, 508, 515
Savage, Alderman, 378, 482
Scarva, Co. Down, 400
Scotland, 89, 513
  evangelicalism, 63–4
  immigration from, 79
  seasonal migration, 94, 99, 398
Scotstown, Co. Monaghan, 388
Scullabogue, Co. Wexford, 43, 51
Seaforde, Co. Down, 121
Seagoe, Co. Armagh, 97, 387, 399
seanchus, 90
Searer, Rev. Charles, 236–7
seasonal migration, 73, 77, 87, 89, 99, 210, 398
  Britain, 398
  effects of Great Famine, 118, 121
  extent of, 93–4
Seat Redistribution Bill, 493
Secession Presbyterians, 63–4, 156
Second Reformation, 19, 49, 61–2, 95, 157
sectarianism, 1–3, 19–20, 61, 347,

502–6, 511–12, 518, 521–2. *see also* expulsionism; marching rights
Belfast, 483–4
Belfast riots, 242, 514, 521
  1857, 218–19, 245, 247–52, 254
  1864, 260–64, 395
  1872, 22, 336–7, 338, 342, 355, 367, 372–6, 483–4
  1886, 508–9
Derry riots, 1870, 344
and education, 224, 226, 296
effects of, 4–8, 56, 58
Fenian amnesty movement, 360
Fermanagh, 431
and Great Famine, 132–4
inflamed, 98–9
jury selection, 273
and labour force, 480–81
and land question, 485–6, 522
of landlords, 87–8
Liberal fear of, 336
outside Belfast, 383–431, 397–405
polarization, 23
renewal of, 1850s, 241–5
before 1830s, 17
Tenant League, 184–5, 194–6, 199–204, 206
trades unions, 371
Seeds, Dr, 233, 481–2, 494, 495, 507
Select Committee on Emigration, 1827, 94
Select Committee on Outrages, 1852, 5
separatism, 24, 274, 423, 450, 519, 521
and land agitation, 457
and Land League, 463
settlement legacy, 1–3, 8–12
decay of structure, 23–46, 511–14
displacement, 86–7, 95–6, 98–9
economic factors, 9–11
effects on democratization, 53
fear and distrust, 11–12, 20–21, 157
frontier areas, 485, 510–11
polarization, 24–7
Protestants as colonists, 517–19

and tenant right, 171–3
Shaftesbury, Lord, 107
Shillington, Thomas (Jnr), 398, 402, 403
Shillington, Thomas (Snr), 399
ship carpenters, 243–5, 262, 263–4, 270, 377, 521
shipbuilding industry, 211–12, 221, 222, 243–5, 367–8
lockout, 1885, 493–4
Shirley estate, 77, 93
Sinclair, Thomas, 221
Sixmilecross, Co. Tyrone, 277
Sixmilewater valley, 102–3
Skinners Company, 468
Sligo, County, 8–9, 71
Smollen, Canon, 465
Smyth, Rev. Professor Richard, 231, 304, 307, 309, 312, 313, 424, 442, 443
Social Sciences Association, 389
Society for the Propagation of the Gospel in Foreign Parts, 317–18
Society for the Relief of Distressed Protestants, 318
Somerville, Sir William, 170
Land Bill of, 153, 154, 155, 160, 165, 167, 168, 189
Soup Kitchen Act, 1847, 123–6
soup kitchens, 110
Speers, Rev. James, 258, 259, 260
Spencer, Earl, 490–91
Sperrin Mountain Home Rule Organization, 474
Sperrin Mountains, 72, 88
Stannus, Walter T., 390, 395, 396
Stewart, A.T.Q., 1–3
Stewart, Dr, 398
Stewart, Sir John, 426, 427, 430
Stewartstown, Co. Tyrone, 277–8, 428
Stockport riots, 244
Strabane, Co. Tyrone, 85, 190
Stranocum, Co. Antrim, 327
street preaching, 248, 254–5, 513
influence of, 257–8
rivalry, 258–60

strikes, 511
  Factory Act, 480
  flaxdressers, 355, 370–72, 410
  mill strike, 1872, 367
  weavers and spinners, 73
Stuarts, 13
Sullivan, A.M., 208, 458, 459–60
Swanlinbar, Co. Cavan, 367, 417
Synod of Ulster, 64, 65
Synott, Parker, 387

Tamlaght, 90
Tartaharan, Co. Armagh, 97, 112
taxation, 104, 145, 174, 205
  Belfast, 287–8
  police rate, 223, 285
Taylor, Alexander, 410, 411
Taylor, Daniel, 413, 414, 427, 431, 436, 448
Tedavnet, Co. Monaghan, 92–3
temperance movement, 370, 410
Templecarn, Co. Donegal, 118
Templepatrick United Irishmen, 30
Temporary Relief (Soup Kitchen) Act, 1847, 123–6
Ten-Hours Act, 1847, 106–7
Tenant League, 21, 136, 143, 148, 160, 165–207, 171, 309, 434
  country-wide meetings, 191–2
  Crawford's Land Bills, 198–201
  establishment of, 185–6
  north-south cooperation, 179–82
  reaction to outrages, 187–8
  and Repeal movement, 192–6, 196
  sectarian problems, 194–6, 199–201, 199–204, 206
  significance of Ulster defeat, 201–7
tenant right movement, 225, 384, 388–90, 392, 399, 412, 417–18, 426, 430. *see also* rent reductions
  and amnesty movement, 360, 388
  Belfast meetings, 184–5, 434, 437
  and consolidation, 101–3
  Cookstown, 425
  description of, 79–84
  displacements, 166–9
  Down by-election, 1878, 444–7
  effects of Great Famine, 121–2, 128, 132–3, 133–4, 449
  examples of, 84–8
  and free trade, 174–5
  and Home Rule movement, 442–4
  and Liberals, 442
  Londonderry estate controversy, 189–91
  McKnight on, 170–76
  Newtownards meeting, 407
  and Orange Order, 128, 132, 153–6, 191–2, 461, 466–7
  and Presbyterians, 157–60, 189–91, 199, 201
  problems of subdivision, 89–93
  religious discrimination, 84–8, 95–6, 98–9
Tennent, Emerson, 51
Tennent, R.J., 201
Termon, Co. Tyrone, 426
Test Act, 39
Thompson, George, 392, 394–5, 396
Thompson, John, 177, 215, 263
Thornton, Arthur, 398–9
Thurles, Synod of, 197
Tierney, Samuel, 267, 288, 291
Tillie and Henderson's shirt factory, 489
Tipperary, County
  O'Donovan Rossa win, 357, 360–61, 362
tithes, 14, 39, 138
Tone, Theobald Wolfe, 43–6, 60, 142, 149, 184–5, 202, 419
  compact with Catholics, 18, 27, 45–6, 475, 521
Toome, Co. Antrim, 227, 449–50, 454, 467
Tories, 433. *see also* Conservatives
  banking interests, 212–13
  Belfast politics, 208–9, 221–3, 239–40, 284–5, 288
  by-election, 1868, 326–32
  and Catholic endowment plan, 314–15
  Catholic support for, 379–80
  distribution of, 416
  education question, 364–5

and Independent Orangeism, 354
and O'Donovan Rossa election,
   361, 363
opposition to reforms, 139
and Presbyterians, 200
and tenant right movement, 191,
   201–7
tourist trade, 78
town commissioners
  Ballymoney, 452, 454, 521
  Banbridge, 404
  Lisburn, 396–7
  Lurgan, 398
  Newtownards, 406–7
Town Council Bill, 352
Town Improvement Act, 406
Townsend, Mr, 116
Townshend, Lord Lieutenant, 28
Tracy, William, 105, 247
Trade, Commission on, 497
Trades Association, 290
Trades Union Congress (TUC), 493
trades unions, 73, 292, 296, 325,
   367–8, 480–81, 496–7, 511–12
  Belfast procession, 1870, 368–9
  and sectarianism, 371
transport, 71, 72, 162
Trelawny, Mr, 176
Trevor, Lord A.E. Hill, 279, 319,
   444, 471
Trillick derailment, 317
Trimble, William, 286–7, 378
Trinitarian Shorter Catechism, 65
Trinity College, Dublin, 139, 301
  Anglican monopoly, 307–9
Tullylish, Co. Down, 190, 459
Tullyrusk, Co. Antrim, 100
turf supply, 77, 97, 99–100, 102
Tyrone, County, 100, 101, 422, 486
  election, 1874, 425, 438
  election, 1880, 458
  election, 1881, 471–3, 485
  farm size, 88–90
  Home Rule movement, 418–20
  Land League, 470
  number of farms, 384
  Orangeism, 271, 274, 275–7, 297
  sectarianism, 429

Tenant League election, 204
weavers, 97
Tyrone Constitution, 276, 431

Ulster Bank, 332, 407
Ulster Canal, 245
Ulster Catholic Association, 379
Ulster Constitutional Club, 492
Ulster custom. *see* tenant right
Ulster Examiner, 300, 346, 351, 366,
   475, 482, 503–4, 521
  anti-liberal, 438–9, 442
  conflict with *Northern Whig*, 377–8
  Down by-election, 1878, 444–6
  education, 378–9, 391, 442
  Factory Act strike, 480
  on Gladstone, 441
  Home Rule movement, 420, 422
  Independent Orangeism, 353
  on Johnston, 315, 317, 327, 328
  march bans, 483
  motto of, 401
  riots, 243–4, 375
  rivalry with *Northern Star*, 334,
     355–63
  support for Tories, 379–80
  tenant right movement, 389, 450,
     452–3, 455
  Working Men's Institute, 370
Ulster Home Government
  Association, 445, 453
Ulster Home Rule Association,
   443
Ulster Observer, 271, 272, 289, 290,
   295, 299, 365, 397, 520
  education, 307
  on Ferguson, 223
  last issues, 422
  on Liberals, 239–40
  on O'Connell, 260–61
  on public parks, 370
  riots, 261–2, 264, 277, 373, 375
  on university question, 307
Ulster Plantation, 171, 189
Ulster Protestant Association, 213
Ulster Railway, 162, 267
Ulster Tenant Right Bill, 444
Ulster Unionist Party, 506

Ulster Weekly News, 428, 444, 446, 448
Ulsterman, 247, 254, 264
ultramontanism, 302, 304, 343, 357, 359, 440, 483, 516
unionism, 23, 50–51, 456, 487–8, 514–16
  confused leadership, 479
  development of, 476–509
  and Land League, 462
  sense of siege, 1–3
  and Tenant League, 196
Unitarians, 231, 364
United Education League, 307–9
United Irishman, 147, 185
United Irishmen, 1, 2, 21, 23–6, 49–50, 51, 63, 64, 520, 521
  attitude of Catholics to, 42–4
  attitude to Catholics, 179, 184–5
  reasons for growth, 29–30
  rebellion, 1798, 18, 41–2, 47, 59, 90, 103
    effects of, 53–4
    epicentres of, 30–31
  roots of, 39–40
  and Volunteers, 27
university question, 197–200, 236, 294, 333, 378–9, 439
  affiliation proposal, 301–5
  Peel's proposals, 139, 142, 157–8
  and Presbyterians, 224
urbanization, 385
utilitarianism, 141–2

Vatican, 139, 195–7, 213–14, 335, 355, 363–4, 382, 439–41, 513
Verner, Edward, 394–5, 396, 398–9
Verner, Captain Thomas, 259, 261
Verner, Colonel William, 75
Verner, Sir William, 496
Vincent, J.R., 508
Vindicator, 143, 184, 197, 201, 244, 518
  on Catholic university, 199–200
  on clerical leadership, 202, 203

Wall, Maureen, 15
Wallace, Jane, 269
Wallace, Professor, 312
Wallace, Sir Richard, 396, 403–4
Warburton, Captain B., 5
Ward, Charles H., 289, 317–18, 350, 351, 481–2
  and amnesty movement, 359
  drainage issue, 352
  on marching rights, 286, 484
  and riots, 262, 267–8
  and Tories, 284, 326, 354–5, 410
Ward, Thomas, 259, 339, 351
Warick, Rev., 410
Waring, Colonel, 489, 490, 504
Waring, Lucas, 396
Waring, Richard, 219, 296
Waringstown, Co. Down, 500
Warre, Sub-Inspector, 402
Warrenpoint, Co. Down, 500–501
Waterford, 469
Watson, Thomas, 399
Watson, William, 248, 250, 251, 252
Watts, Dr, 379
Waugh, Mr, 278, 279, 280
Waveney, Lord, 366
weavers, 29–30, 31, 54, 102, 398, 411, 426, 486, 495
  disturbances, 33–4
  effects of Great Famine, 111–12, 114
  labour organization, 73
  meeting, Ballymena, 412–13
  tenant right, 82
  "weaver belt", 78, 90–91, 96–8, 383–4
Weir, Mr, 506
Wentworth, Thomas, 13
Westminster Confession of Faith, 63
Wexford, County, 43, 51
Whigs, 53, 55, 59, 69, 149, 411, 514. *see also* Liberals
  attitude to Catholics, 193–4, 225, 239–40, 260
  Belfast politics, 64–5, 208–9, 215, 221–3, 239–40, 241, 265, 284, 288
  Belfast riots, 270
  Catholic support for, 418

and Chancery suit, 217–19
decline of influence, 19, 56, 58, 208–40, 241, 284
education reform, 62–3, 157
and Great Revival, 238–9
and labour organization, 293
as landlords, 94–5, 96
liberalizing changes, 19, 47–8, 51–2, 87
linen industry, 212
links with Presbyterians, 156–8, 209–10
Lurgan, 397–8
O'Connell alliance, 69, 137–9, 142–3
and Orangeism, 98, 155–6
and Party Processions Act, 320
rising influence, 135–6
and tenant right movement, 154, 165, 169–70, 174–5, 189–91, 198, 200–201, 204–5, 207
and United Irishmen, 39–40
Whitworth, William, 427
Whyte, Dr John, 185
Whyte, J.J., 366

William III, king, 11, 12, 325
Williamite plantation, 12, 79
Wilson, Rev. H.B., 427–8, 523
Wiseman, Cardinal, 193
Witness, 454
women's suffrage, 410
Woods, Hans, 348
working classes. *see* labour force
Working Men's Institute, 291, 292, 351, 368, 370, 371–2
Workingmen's International Exhibition, 1870, 368

yeomanry, 18, 24, 30, 41, 60, 85, 87, 152
Orangemen as, 38, 53–6, 154–5
terrorism, 42
votes of, 59
York Street flax mill, 291
Young, Rev. H.W., 428
Young, John, 411–12, 413
Young, Samuel, 394, 396
Young Ireland movement, 135, 136, 141–7, 196, 241, 363, 419, 521
rebellion, 1848, 147–8, 149